THE NEW CORPORATE FINANCE

Where Theory Meets Practice

The McGraw-Hill/IRWIN Series in Finance, Insurance and Real Estate

Stephen A. Ross
Franco Modigliani Professor of Finance and Economics
Sloan School of Management
Massachusetts Institute of Technology
Consulting Editor

THE NEW CORPORATE FINANCE
Where Theory Meets Practice

EDITED BY
Donald H. Chew, Jr.
Stern Stewart & Co.

Third Edition

McGraw-Hill
Irwin

Boston   Burr Ridge, IL   Dubuque, IA   Madison, WI   New York   San Francisco   St. Louis
Bangkok   Bogotá   Caracas   Lisbon   London   Madrid
Mexico City   Milan   New Delhi   Seoul   Singapore   Sydney   Taipei   Toronto

McGraw-Hill Higher Education 𝕏
A Division of The **McGraw-Hill** Companies

THE NEW CORPORATE FINANCE: WHERE THEORY MEETS PRACTICE

Published by McGraw-Hill/Irwin, an imprint of The McGraw-Hill Companies, Inc.
1221 Avenue of the Americas, New York, NY, 10020. Copyright © 2001, 1999, 1993,
by The McGraw-Hill Companies, Inc. All rights reserved. No part of this publication may be
reproduced or distributed in any form or by any means, or stored in a data base or retrieval
system, without the prior written consent of The McGraw-Hill Companies, Inc., including,
but not limited to, in any network or other electronic storage or transmission, or broadcast for
distance learning. Some ancillaries, including electronic and print components, may not be
available to customers outside the United States.

This book is printed on acid-free paper.

3 4 5 6 7 8 9 0 DOC/DOC 0 9 8 7 6 5 4 3 2

ISBN   007233973X

Publisher: *John Biernat*
Sponsoring editor: *John Biernat*
Editorial assistant: *Brian Moore*
Marketing manager: *Rhonda Seelinger*
Project manager: *Kimberly D. Hooker*
Production supervisor: *Gina Hangos*
Coordinator freelance design: *Mary Christianson*
New media project manager: *Ann Rogula*
Cover designer: *Adam Rooke*
Cover photograph courtesy of Wonderfile
Compositor: *Concepts Unlimited* ®
Printer: *R. R. Donnelley & Sons Company*

Library of Congress Cataloging-in-Publication Data

The new corporate finance : where theory meets practice / edited by
    Donald H. Chew, Jr.—3rd ed.
        p.   cm.
    ISBN: 0-07-233973-X
    (The McGraw-Hill/Irwin series in finance, insurance, and real estate)
    Includes bibliographical references and index.
        1. Corporations—Finance.   I. Chew, Donald H.   II. Title.
HG4011.N44 2001
    658.15 dc—21   00-106022

www.mhhe.com

To my wife, Susan Emerson

TABLE OF CONTENTS

FOREWORD

by Stephen A. Ross
Franco Modigliani Professor of
Finance and Economics
Sloan School of Management and
Economics Department MIT

If anyone doubts that there is a new corporate finance, then this exciting collection of readings drawn from the *Journal of Applied Corporate Finance* should resolve the issue. To a great extent, Modigliani and Miller defined the modern theory of corporate finance as being the study of the valuation of corporate claims. Since then, however, there has been another revolution in corporate finance that also must be represented in any modern treatment of the subject. Alongside of valuation, the study of agency theory and the market for corporate control develops the intimate connection between corporate finance and the very theory of the firm itself.

The foundation of corporate finance—and, indeed, of all of finance—lies in the capital markets, and that is where this book begins. Readings on market efficiency are interspersed with sound analysis of how markets and trading work in practice. The second focus of corporate finance, though, lies in the rather different set of markets where management is retained to run firms which they don't necessarily own. The study of management acting as agents of control for others, i.e., their stockholders, is called agency theory, and the attendant study of the market for corporate control comprises the second major research theme of modern corporate finance. This volume treats agency theory and incentives with care, and places them squarely in the context of the market. This is an accomplishment not only of the authors of the individual articles themselves, but also of the insightful choices and groupings made by the editor. The introductory section ends with a lively roundtable that brings out the major issues and differences that still exist between practitioners and academics on these issues.

The reader is now well equipped to tackle the next section of readings on the relation between finance and corporate strategy. Of particular interest here is the inclusion of topics such as organizational structure and compensation. This section ends with a roundtable discussion that showcases the goal of maximizing shareholder value. Roundtable discussions follow major sections and they are a wonderful feature of this book of readings; not merely do they summarize what has preceded them, they illuminate what is truly important and controversial.

Next we come to the more traditional purview of corporate finance with a section of readings that brings the reader up to date on financial structure and the Modigliani-Miller theories, followed by a section on debt and capital structure alternatives that present the option and asymmetric information approaches along with empirical analyses of traditional issues. What is the role of leverage and debt in general and what of the old puzzles with dividends and taxes? What are we to make of the growth of project finance, convertibles, and other kinds of "hybrid" financing? How does the form of financing affect managers' project selection? This section is followed by a very timely section of readings on risk management that nicely embeds this topic in the theories of valuation and agency. The final section of the volume returns to the theme of agency theory and the market for corporate control, with some seminal articles on the tradeoff between internal control mechanisms and external, market driven controls such as mergers and hostile as well as friendly takeovers. The last roundtable discusses the role of the board of directors.

Throughout the entire work, there is a seamless blending of theory, empirical findings, and case study that combine to give the reader a nearly hands-on sense of the subject. This is a carefully constructed collection of articles that is a tribute to the editor as well as to the contributing authors.

INTRODUCTION:
FINANCIAL INNOVATION IN THE 1980s AND 1990s
by Donald H. Chew, Jr., Stern Stewart & Co.

T he past 40 years have witnessed remarkable changes in the theory and practice of corporate finance. Beginning with the work of Franco Modigliani and Merton Miller in the late 1950s, the evolution of the "modern" theory of corporate finance into its present shape has both anticipated and responded to a wave of innovations in corporate practice. The 1960s saw the first takeovers of public corporations by other companies during the era of leveraged conglomerates—a movement that was largely reversed in the 1980s. The 1970s gave rise not only to original-issue "junk bonds," but to stock options and a host of other exchange-traded "derivatives" such as futures on foreign exchange, interest rates, and commodity prices.

It was during the 1980s, however, that the rate of financial innovation accelerated most dramatically. Building on the success of the futures markets established in the '70s, the '80s spawned an astonishing variety of new "risk management" securities: (1) currency, interest rate, and commodity swaps; (2) exchange-traded options on foreign currencies, interest rates, and commodity prices; (3) futures on stock market indexes, as well as other new futures contracts on an expanding range of currencies, interest rates, and commodity prices; and (4) "hybrid" debt securities combining standard debt issues with forward- or option-like features. At the same time, a burgeoning junk bond market, besides furnishing capital for promising growth companies too small to obtain investment-grade credit ratings, was also making possible an unprecedented wave of leveraged acquisitions, large stock buybacks, divestitures, spin-offs, and multi-billion dollar LBOs—all of which were yoked together under the name of "corporate restructuring."

As the pace of innovation quickened, moreover, the relationship between theory and practice became more dynamic. On the one hand, theoretical advances helped stimulate the process of innovation. Indeed, the 1980s can be viewed as a decade in which Wall Street first adopted and then pushed to their limits principles of financial economics that most practicing businessmen once dismissed as hopelessly arcane. But if theory has affected practice, the flood of new corporate securities, risk management practices, and organizational structures has also influenced development of the theory. The experimentation throughout the '80s with corporate securities and structures has provided financial economists with a vast laboratory in which to observe and test the workings of our capital markets. And, as should become clear from the articles in this book, such experimentation has helped finance scholars to extend and, in some cases, to revise their thinking—which in turn has greatly influenced corporate practice in the 1990s.

THE CONSEQUENCES OF CORPORATE RESTRUCTURING

Before tracing the progression of academic thought that contributed to the new developments in corporate finance, let's briefly examine the economic *consequences* of financial innovation. What has really been accomplished by all this change? And to begin with the most controversial, let's consider the case of corporate restructuring.

In the popular mind, of course, the verdict on leveraged restructuring has already been pronounced. As a result of the cluster of bankruptcies starting in 1989, the popular outrage over the S&L debacle, and the depressed economic climate of the early 1990s, Wall Street was subjected to a backlash of public opinion, political scrutiny, and "reregulation" reminiscent of the 1930s. On the one hand, corporate restructuring brought about a pronounced trend toward smaller, less diversified, more efficient—and in many cases private—corporations. But, in the process of streamlining corporate America, the leveraged restructuring movement also enriched a new breed of capitalists known as "corporate raiders" while imposing painful changes upon some corporate managers, employees, and local communities. It was predictably these latter effects that the mass media and politicians seized upon. Those few media accounts of LBOs and leveraged takeovers that managed to expand their focus beyond the "morality play" of private greed and misery almost invariably reached the same conclusion: Leveraged restructurings and other forms of "financial engineering" were destroying the competitive future of American industry by forcing shortsighted cutbacks in employment, R&D, and capital investment.

From financial economists, however, we have received a very different assessment of the *public* consequences of corporate restructuring. A large body of academic research suggested that the leveraged restructuring movement created enormous increases in stockholder value—and thus, presumably, major improvements in corporate efficiency. On the basis of this research, Harvard professor Michael Jensen offered $650 billion as a conservative estimate of the stockholder gains over the period 1976 to 1990 arising from mergers, takeovers, divestitures, spin-offs, and LBOs. These numbers represented only the gains to the "sellers" in such transactions, not to the "buyers" (a group which includes those raiders whose allegedly vast profits became a favorite media target during the '80s). Nor did this estimate include the value of efficiency improvements by companies pressured by the *threat* of takeover into reforming without a visible transaction.

As Jensen also reported, a growing body of work on LBOs and other leveraged recapitalizations documented significant improvements in corporate operating efficiency—improvements that would appear to justify much of the stock price increases accompanying these transactions. Moreover, there has been no evidence in such companies of major cutbacks, on average, in employment, maintenance expenditures, or R & D. Indeed, at the height of leveraged restructuring activity in the '80s, the U.S. economy was near the midpoint of a 92-month expansion that saw record-high percentages of people employed, as well as steady increases in corporate capital spending and R & D. (And, after a brief and relatively mild recession in the early 1990s, the U.S. economy has continued to expand at a remarkable rate.)

Of course, many of the highly leveraged transactions (HLTs) executed in 1986 and thereafter got into trouble (in large part, Jensen argues, because of a gross misalignment of incentives between dealmakers and investors that led to systematic overpayments). And thus part of the stockholders gains from HLTs came at the expense of the bondholders and lenders that financed the deals. But Jensen placed a likely upper bound of $50 billion on total losses to bondholders, banks, and other creditors from leveraged transactions. The extraordinary recovery of the junk bond market, together with the relaxation by bank regulators of the HLT constraints

a few years after they were put in place, suggest that actual losses turned out to be far less than this estimate.

Such losses, it's also important to recognize, were dwarfed not only by the stockholder gains from restructuring, but also by losses on commercial real estate loans. Such loans were by far the largest troubled asset category for S&Ls (junk bonds hardly showed up in the statistical analysis!), not to mention many commercial banks. And if pushed to speculate, I would argue that such real estate losses, along with the regulatory reaction and "credit crunch" they prompted, were the primary contributors to the recession of the early 1990s.

Some macro data released by the Commerce Department in the early '90s were also sharply inconsistent with the popular claim that the restructuring of the '80s weakened the international competitiveness of the U.S. manufacturing sector. According to U.S. Bureau of Labor Statistics, the productivity of U.S. manufacturing increased dramatically between 1982 and 1990, while the real unit costs of labor declined sharply. Partly reflecting such productivity gains as well as the depreciation of the dollar, the export of U.S. goods and services increased by 75% in real terms during the six-year period 1985-1991. Such continuing export growth was all the more impressive, given the depressed condition of most of the world's developed economies at the time.

THE 1990s: INNOVATION AND THE "CREDIT CRUNCH"

In the first years of the 1990s, leveraged restructuring all but disappeared, and there were few signs of a well-functioning corporate control market. The only "hostile" deal of note in the early '90s was AT&T's acquisition of NCR, a transaction that suggested a return to the diversifying acquisitions of the '60s and '70s—the very activity that provided many opportunities for corporate raiders in the first place. And, as if to reinforce that lesson of the '80s, AT&T's market value predictably dropped by some 15% during the month after the deal was first announced. (For corporate finance theorists, it was also edifying to watch AT&T's management volunteer to raise the purchase price when granted the ability to use "pooling" rather than "purchase" accounting.)

But if the scale of leveraged restructuring was greatly diminished, financial innovation continued on the other major front established in the '80s: corporate risk management. The corporate use of futures, swaps, and options, while rising steadily throughout the '80s, has accelerated in the 1990s. Rather ironically, the regulatory crackdown on one form of financial innovation—LBOs and other HLTs—ended up providing the impetus for another by contributing greatly to the severity of the "credit crunch." And, as I will suggest below, the early '90s saw a flurry of new securities—notably, both derivatives and "hybrid" debt instruments incorporating derivatives—designed to help smaller, riskier companies raise capital in spite of the restrictive credit conditions.

The primary reason for the strength of corporate interest in risk management in the early '90s was thus somewhat different from what it was a decade earlier. The rise and expansion of new kinds of futures, swaps, and options during the late '70s and early '80s was primarily a capital market response to the sharp increases in the volatility of exchange rates, interest rates, and commodity prices. Besides offering investors and corporations a low-cost means of hedging against such price volatility, these new markets also provided financially sophisticated corporations with opportunities for financing "arbitrages." For example, combining zero-coupon, yen-denominated debt issues with yen-dollar currency swaps reportedly enabled some large, well-known corporations to reduce their all-in funding costs below that of the U.S. Treasury. And creating "synthetic" fixed-rate debt by coupling floating-rate issues with interest rate swaps reportedly reduced the cost to riskier borrowers of conventional fixed-rate funding (although the extent of the cost savings from this strategy has been greatly exaggerated).

When coupled with increased price volatility, the high level of interest rates in the early 1980s also contributed to another innovation in corporate risk management: the proliferation of new kinds of corporate "hybrid" debt issues. Hybrids are so called because they effectively combine a conventional straight fixed-rate debt issue with a forward- or option-like feature. One familiar example is convertible debt, which amounts to lower-coupon debt combined with an option (technically, a warrant) on the firm's equity. What was distinctive about the hybrid debt instruments of the '80s is that their payoffs, instead of being tied to the issuing company's stock price, were linked to a growing variety of *general* economic variables. In 1980, for example, Sunshine Mining issued bonds whose principal repayment was tied to future silver prices. And subsequent corporate hybrids introduced in the '80s indexed principal or interest payments to exchange rates,

interest rates, stock market indices, and the prices of commodities such as oil, gold, copper, and natural gas. Such securities were designed to enable somewhat riskier companies—typically those with significant exposures to commodity prices—to reduce their interest payments to manageable levels by giving bondholders, in effect, an equity-like participation in corporate profits.

The 1990s have also proved, as one *New York Times* article put it, "A Hot Time for Hybrids." Unlike the '80s, however, the stimulus for hybrids in the early '90s was not the *level* of interest rates (which are quite low by recent standards), but rather the pronounced widening of credit *spreads* that then existed for all but blue-chip borrowers. Such spreads reflected not only a natural market "correction" in response to recent bank and bondholder losses, but also the effect of the severe regulatory constraints imposed on all non-investment-grade debt beginning in 1989.

As Charles Smithson and I have argued (see "*The Uses of Hybrid Debt in Managing Corporate Risk*" in this book), many companies in the early '90s were using hybrid debt to lower their risk profiles, and thus their current interest payments. By lowering interest payments and stabilizing the expected level of (after-interest) operating cash flow, such innovative instruments allowed issuers to avoid the disproportionately higher funding costs then being imposed on corporate borrowers. In this sense, financial innovation in the form of new hybrid debt securities played a role much like that of junk bonds in the early '80s: They allowed riskier companies to raise capital on economic terms, thus helping them weather the restrictive financing climate of the early '90s.

Such securities innovation also provides yet another illustration of Merton Miller's conception of regulatory change as "the grain of sand in the oyster" that irritates the financial system into invention. The continuing proliferation of new forms of hybrid debt in the '90s demonstrates once again the ingenuity of our capital markets in circumventing regulatory obstacles to economic growth.

THE BEGINNINGS OF MODERN THEORY

With this allusion to Professor Miller, let's turn from this survey of changes in corporate financial practices to a brief account of the development of the theory.

The modern theory of *corporate* finance begins with the well-known "irrelevance" propositions formulated by Franco Modigliani and Merton Miller in the late

1950s and early 1960s. Given the dramatic recapitalizations of the '80s, typically accompanied by large increases in stockholder value, it may seem odd to begin with the notion that corporate financial policies "do not matter." The M & M propositions are the natural starting point because they represent the first attempt to apply rigorous economic logic to corporate *financial* decision-making in the aggregate. In so doing, Miller and Modigliani began the transformation of the study of corporate finance from what then amounted to an apprenticeship system transmitting folklore between generations—in effect, the traditional Harvard Business School case-study approach—into a more systematic and scientific discipline. The Nobel Prizes awarded first to Modigliani in 1985 and then to Miller in 1990 (and, still more recently, to Robert Merton and Myron Scholes) are only the most visible acknowledgments of the aspirations of corporate finance to the internal consistency and predictive power of a "hard" science.

But what do the M & M "irrelevance" propositions really say about financial decision-making? Paradoxically, the M & M capital structure propositions appear to say that a company's financial policy—whether it chooses to fund its operations with debt or equity, and what kinds of securities it chooses to issue—have no material effect on the value of its shares. And the twin companion to this M & M capital structure proposition seems to say that the firm's dividend policy—the fraction of earnings it chooses to pay out to stockholders rather than retain—also has no effect on market value. That value, according to M & M, is determined solely by corporate investment and operating decisions, by those "real" decisions that produce the firm's operating cash flows. (More precisely, the value of the firm was formulated as the discounted present value of "future cash flows from the firm's present assets and future growth opportunities," net of "the additional investment necessary to initiate and sustain those flows.")

Corporate capital structure and dividend decisions were accordingly viewed as nothing more than ways of dividing up the operating cash flows produced by the business and repackaging them for distribution to investors. And, as long as such "merely financial" decisions are assumed not to affect the "real" decisions in any systematic way—for example, provided management behaves the same whether its debt-to-equity ratio is 30 percent or 300 percent—then such financial decisions "do not matter."

But, as Miller himself said in his 1989 reassessment of *"The Modigliani-Miller Propositions After Thirty Years"* (also in this book),

the view that capital structure is literally irrelevant or that "nothing matters" in corporate finance, though still sometimes attributed to us, is far from what we ever actually said about the real-world applications of our theoretical propositions.

The M & M propositions were intended to hold only under a deliberately restrictive set of conditions, the most important of which are as follows: (1) there are no significant differences in the tax treatment accorded different securities; (2) reliable information about the firm's earnings prospects is freely available to investors (and, by implication, what management knows about the future is not significantly different from what investors know); and (3) corporate investment decisions, as mentioned above, are not influenced by financing (or dividend) choices.

What, then, do the M & M propositions have to say to corporate practitioners, to those financial executives who get paid a lot of money to make decisions that purportedly "do not matter"? There are really two distinct messages: a negative one and a positive one.

The negative one is captured in Stewart Myers's formulation that "there is no magic in leverage." Investment bankers who market debt instruments to their clients are fond of showing them the wonderful effect of increasing leverage on pro forma earnings per share. The message of Miller and Modigliani is that this effect is an illusion. It is true that if companies issue debt and use the proceeds to retire their shares, then EPS will go up as long as the return on invested capital simply exceeds the after-tax corporate borrowing rate—which, of course, is hardly an acceptable standard of profitability. What such analysis fails to mention is that, as companies take on more financial leverage, the risk of the equity rises commensurately. And as the risk of the equity increases, stockholders increase their required rate of return, the P/E of the firm goes down, and the net effect is a wash.

One of the accomplishments of LBOs and other leveraged recaps was to reveal the fundamental futility of "managing earnings" by manipulating accounting techniques. The leveraged restructuring movement thus held out another important lesson for corporate managers: Until the hostile takeover movement came to an abrupt halt around the middle of 1989, public companies that continued to make uneconomic investment and financing decisions guided by the old accounting yardsticks were creating opportunities for aggressive investors piercing the veil of accounting statements to discover underlying cash flow. To corporate raiders and other investors in private (or highly leveraged) companies, EPS was clearly irrelevant! All that mattered to them was the expected ability of the business to generate adequate cash flow to service the debt and leave themselves with a large enough return on their equity investment to justify the large financial risk.

In short, the discounted cash flow valuation framework stemming from the Chicago school principle of "market efficiency"—and tirelessly advocated by my colleague Joel Stern over the past 20 years—was being put to use daily during the restructuring of the '80s. Unfortunately, it was not the majority of professional corporate executives who came to understand that "earnings per share don't count," but rather the corporate raiders who were supplanting them.

Now let's turn to the positive side of the argument. The positive import of the M & M propositions, and thus their main message to corporate practitioners, can be seen by turning the propositions "upside down"—as Clifford Smith likes to say—and standing them on their heads. That is, if changes in corporate financial or dividend policy cause significant changes in stock values, they are likely to do so only for the following reasons: (1) they affect taxes paid by issuers or investors; (2) they provide a credible "signal" to investors of management's confidence (or lack thereof) in the firm's future earnings; or (3) they affect the probability that management will operate as efficiently as possible, undertaking only profitable investments and returning "excess" capital to investors.

Beyond the Irrelevance Propositions: Tax and Signalling Effects

The academic process of relaxing each of these conditions was begun by Miller and Modigliani almost 30 years ago. In the so-called tax-adjusted M & M proposition presented in a 1963 paper, they argued that the benefits of substituting tax-deductible interest payments for non-deductible (and thus potentially twice-taxed) dividend payments could push the optimal capital structure toward 100% debt—provided, of course, the offsetting costs of high leverage are not too great.

In the early 1960s, of course, the world did not conform to this vision, and M & M were inclined to

dismiss their model, in Miller's words, as "simply another inconsequential paradox arising from an economist's frictionless dreamworld." Facing the reality of corporate debt-equity ratios in the early 1960s that were not much higher than they were in the low-tax 1920s, Miller recalls,

we seemed to face an unhappy dilemma: either corporate managers did not know (or perhaps care) that they were paying too much in taxes; or something major was being left out of the model. Either they were wrong or we were.... [Our thinking] suggested that the high bond ratings in which the management took so much pride may actually have been a sign of their incompetence; that the managers were leaving too much of their stockholders' money on the table in the form of unnecessary corporate income tax payments.

In sum, many finance specialists, myself included, remained unconvinced that the high-leverage route to corporate tax savings was either technically unfeasible or prohibitively expensive in terms of expected bankruptcy or agency costs.

In the 1980s, this kind of tax "arbitrage" between debt and equity likely played some role in every leveraged acquisition or recapitalization accomplished by Wall Street. Debt-equity ratios in LBOs, and in some public recaps, achieved levels that Miller described as "far beyond anything we ever dared use in our classroom illustrations of the tax advantage." Of the rise of junk bonds, Miller says simply, "The only puzzle is why it took so long."

But tax savings alone, as Miller noted in his Nobel Prize speech, could not account for the "size of the observed LBO premiums." And Miller himself qualified the tax-adjusted M & M proposition in his 1976 Presidential Address to the American Finance Association. Entitled "Debt and Taxes," the paper argued that the tax savings of corporate debt financing were exaggerated by the failure to account for any *increase* in taxes paid by the holders of corporate debt. To the extent such holders are taxable (although many clearly are not), some of the savings from converting equity into debt will be offset by the increase in taxes paid by the new debtholders.

Some financial economists have attempted to take finance theory beyond capital structure irrelevance by exploring the possibility that corporate financial decisions provide "signals" to investors about the firm's earnings prospects. To the extent management knows more about the firm's prospects than outside investors, corporate choices among financing alternatives—and the very attempt to raise outside capital—could communicate "insider" information about the company's future. To take the most obvious case, large block sales of stock by insiders are almost always accompanied by significant decreases in share values.

But while signalling theories help explain why the market typically reacts negatively to announcements of equity offerings, and positively to major exchange offers to retire equity with new debt, they have not furnished a convincing explanation of how (value-maximizing) corporations in the aggregate choose their capital structures. As Miller himself concluded in his 1986 paper on "The Informational Content of Dividends," none of the signalling models has provided—nor is one likely to provide—a signalling "equilibrium" in which one dividend or financial policy is clearly superior to another. That is, even though signalling theories offer a plausible explanation of how investors interpret *changes* in corporate leverage and payout ratios, they nevertheless fail to address the questions of *optimal* capital structure and dividend policy.

Further Beyond the Irrelevance Proposition: The Rise of Agency Cost Theory

Perhaps the most significant departure from the M & M irrelevance propositions—one with more definite import for financial policy—can be traced to a 1976 paper written by Michael Jensen and William Meckling called "Theory of the Firm: Managerial Behavior, Agency Costs, and Capital Structure." What the theory of "agency costs" accomplished was to call attention to the potential loss in value of public corporations caused by the divergence of interest between management and shareholders. Most finance scholars, including Jensen and Meckling, began by arguing that the agency costs of separating ownership from control could not be too great for several reasons: product market competition (including challenges from foreign competitors) as well as a market for executive labor should both serve to limit the natural tendency of management to pursue its own interest at the expense of shareholders; and management incentive plans are presumably designed to reduce this conflict of interest. If all of these fail to join managerial and stockholder interests, then a vigorously operating takeover market—in academic parlance, the "market for corporate control"— should prevent self-serving managers from entrench-

ing themselves. But the size and consistency of the stockholders gains from the leveraged restructurings of the '80s suggested otherwise.

The relevance of "agency cost" theory to developments in the 1980s was set forth in Jensen's 1986 paper, "The Agency Costs of Free Cash Flow: Corporate Finance and Takeovers," published in the *American Economic Review.* Jensen's "free cash flow" theory said, in short, that leveraged acquisitions, stock repurchases, and management buyouts of public companies were adding value to corporations by squeezing capital out of organizations that had few profitable growth opportunities. Subjecting companies in mature industries to the "discipline" of high leverage was also intensifying the search for operating efficiencies.

Before the wave of hostile takeovers and LBOs in the 1980s, corporate managements in mature industries could continue their customary practice of reinvesting excess capital ("free cash flow") in their core businesses even while the expected returns to capital at the margin were falling lower and lower. Or, if things got bad enough, they would choose to diversify into unrelated businesses through acquisition. (For example, oil companies facing a massive "free cash flow problem" in the early '80s responded initially by choosing both strategies, thus inviting the attention of Boone Pickens.) The massive substitution of debt for equity in the '80s provided a systematic solution to this free cash flow problem by converting discretionary dividend payments into contractual, and considerably more demanding, payments of interest and principal. As Miller himself rephrased Jensen's argument, "By accepting such heavy debt-service burdens, the managers made a binding commitment to themselves and to the other residual equity holders against yielding to the temptations to pour the firm's good money down investment ratholes."

The Re-Emergence of Active Investors. Besides returning excess capital to investors and curbing uneconomic reinvestment, the replacement of equity by debt also allowed for the concentration of equity ownership among large investors. In "*The Modern Industrial Revolution, Exit, and the Failure of Internal Control Systems*" (which begins the last section of this book), Jensen argues that such concentration facilitated the rise—or, more precisely, the "re-emergence"—of "active investors" in the U.S., a group that includes "Warren Buffett, Carl Icahn, Sir James Goldsmith, and the principals of KKR and Forstmann Little." Active investors, as

Jensen defines them, are those holding large blocks of a company's stock (sometimes its debt as well) who "actually monitor management, sit on boards, are sometimes involved in dismissing management, are often intimately involved in the strategic direction of the company." On occasion (witness Warren Buffett's recent assumption of the chairmanship of Salomon Brothers), they even manage.

Active investors are by no means a new phenomenon. In the Japanese and German economies, Jensen maintains, large-block stockholders, notably commercial banks, have long been the most effective force binding management's interests to those of its stockholders. And, prior to the enactment of Glass Steagall and other legislative acts of the 1930s and '40s, investment and commercial bankers like J.P. Morgan played a similar role in the U.S., sitting on boards of directors, monitoring management, and sometimes enforcing changes in management.

But, over the 50-year period between 1930 and the beginning of the '80s, the rift between corporate ownership and control continued to grow. Between 1937 and 1990, according to Jensen and Kevin Murphy, the percentage equity ownership of the CEOs of the largest U.S. companies fell 10-fold, from roughly 3 percent to less than .03 percent today. Corporations also became much larger over this period, but only by a factor of 3 or 4 times (in real dollars), thus implying a 66% reduction in the real dollar investment of corporate CEOs in their own companies' stocks.

And, as for the sharp growth in the size of U.S. companies since the '30s, part of it was undoubtedly justified by scale economies in some businesses. But perhaps the largest contributor to such corporate growth was the trend toward corporate conglomeration initiated during the late 1960s—a development that, although initially welcomed by stockholders, ended up contributing significantly to the negative real returns to stockholders over the decade of the 1970s.

For Jensen, the rise of the LBO held out an economic solution to "massive inefficiencies" arising from the corporate conglomerate movement—which in turn was a predictable consequence of the growing separation of ownership and control. Indeed, Jensen views "LBO associations" such as KKR and Forstmann Little as "new organizational forms" that compete directly with the headquarters of large public corporations, especially conglomerates. They are said to accomplish with professional staffs that number in the 30s or 40s what many hundreds of headquarters employees are supposed to do in public conglomerates. "In effect," Jensen argues, "the LBO association substitutes incentives provided by compensation and ownership for the direct monitoring and centralized decision-making in the typical corporate bureaucracy." In the average Fortune 1000 firm, Jensen reports, the CEO's total compensation changes by $3 for every $1000 change in shareholder value. By comparison, the average CEO in an LBO firm experiences a change of $64 per $1000. And the partners of the LBO firm itself (the KKRs of this world), which is the proper equivalent of a conglomerate CEO, earn close to $200 per $1000 change in value. Given such dramatic concentrations of ownership and improvements in the pay-to-performance correlation, it is not surprising that researchers reported major operating improvements in firms that have gone private.

THE PRIVATIZATION OF BANKRUPTCY

In equally provocative fashion, Jensen also argued that the highly leveraged transactions of the '80s, though clearly more likely to get into financial trouble, created far stronger incentives to reorganize troubled companies outside of court. Such a shift in incentives was leading, at least in the first part of the '80s, to a Japanese-like "privatization of bankruptcy" in which active investors (like the main banks in Japanese *keiretsu*) were using low-cost means (typically involving exchange offers) of avoiding our costly and chronically inefficient Chapter 11 process. This "privatization" movement, however, came to an abrupt halt in 1989 as a result of regulatory interference with the junk bond and credit markets, a change in the tax code, and a misguided bankruptcy court ruling.

As Jensen also acknowledges, however, our private capital markets were by no means blameless in provoking this regulatory overreaction. A gross misalignment of incentives (which Jensen calls a "contracting failure") between dealmakers and suppliers of capital in LBOs and other HLTs led to a concentration of overpriced deals in the latter years of the 1980s. But capital market adjustments to this problem—including larger equity commitments, lower up-front fees, and more conservative deal prices—were already well underway when the set of regulatory initiatives launched in 1989 overrode them, thereby adding significantly to HLT defaults and bankruptcies.

Workout veteran David Schulte (adviser to Revco and partner with Sam Zell in putting together the Zell-Chilmark Fund), confirms Jensen's argument in the following assessment of current trends in reorganization:

I've always hated bankruptcy. The problem I have with Chapter 11 is that it takes a business problem and turns it . . . into a legal case. I don't know what a guy who wears a black robe has to offer that the parties in interest can't do privately themselves... If we could devise a simple way for exchange offers to work outside of Chapter 11 . . . investors would be well served and we'd all be a lot better off. In short, I'd like to have a non-bankruptcy bankruptcy. It's virtually impossible to do an out-of-court deal right now. All in all, 1990 was a very bad year for exchange offers.

Part of the difficulties in reorganizing troubled companies outside of court could be traced to the dispersion of claims among creditors. In the last half of the '80s, the problem of systematic overpayments was greatly compounded by the sale of the debt to public junk bondholders (whom, it now appears, could be induced to reorganize their claims only through the agency of Milken and Drexel) and commercial banks' practice of "participating" or "assigning" rather than holding their loans. All this ensured that if companies did get into trouble, then private reorganizations would be very difficult.

And when troubled companies, unable to reach an out-of-court consensus, then filed for protection under Chapter 11, some of the problems would only be exacerbated. The unanimity provisions of the Trust Indenture Act, the grant of "exclusivity" to management (and routine extensions thereof), and failures to enforce strict priority of claims all serve only to intensify fighting among creditors. In so doing, they also remove any incentive for interested parties to provide unbiased information about the underlying value of the firm, thus making creditor consensus all the more difficult to reach.

Noted bankruptcy lawyer Leonard Rosen summed up the current situation as follows:

I always thought that the purpose of a workout was first to create the biggest possible pot, and then to fight about the division of the pot afterwards. That was the spirit in which workouts used to be done in the old days . . .
What worries me [today] . . . is that, if creditor fights about the division of the pot start at the

beginning of the process, then nobody's probably paying attention to more fundamental questions like: Have we got the right management running the business? And are they making the right strategic and operating decisions? . . . We're starting the fights so early, spending so much energy on the intercreditor struggle, and creating such divisiveness in the process that we're making it much less likely that companies will be restructured quickly and economically.

Jensen and other economists argued that much of the intensity of intercreditor conflicts built into our current Chapter 11 process could be eliminated simply by auctioning the control of bankrupt companies to the highest bidder at the outset of the Chapter 11 process. Such a process, which is already well-developed in countries like Germany, would effectively separate the valuation of the assets from destructive squabbles over how that value is to be divided among claimholders. Such an auction process would also help preserve the operating value of such companies by shielding the day-to-day management of Chapter 11 companies from such potentially destructive conflicts.

Insulating operations from claimholder conflicts is, of course, what Chapter 11 is supposed to accomplish. And the process actually appears to have worked quite well in some cases. For example, Allied and Federated Stores re-emerged from bankruptcy after incurring legal and administrative costs of at most 3% of total asset value; and operations remained fundamentally profitable (indeed, stores like Bloomingdale's were reporting record operating earnings throughout their stay in Chapter 11). Such well-managed reorganizations, however, should not be allowed to obscure the sheer waste of investor value in cases like Eastern Airlines and Revco. It is the latter cases that expose the fundamental flaws in the current system.

In sum, the movement toward a "privatization of bankruptcy" described by Jensen was derailed (although a new movement toward "pre-packaged" bankruptcy represents a promising hybrid between a private workout and formal bankruptcy). And thus the "costs of financial distress" today appear considerably higher than economists like Jensen once predicted. But the verdict is not yet in. Financial economists are now mining a rich new lode of data to determine if bankruptcy costs are indeed as large as critics of restructuring have made them out to be. And such findings will not only contribute to the ongoing debate about optimal corporate capital structure—they will also likely affect future developments in corporate practice.

BACK TO THE CORPORATE "FREE CASH FLOW" PROBLEM (WITH A DIGRESSION ON THE ROLE OF THE MEDIA)

We are told almost daily by the financial press that corporate America suffers from an underinvestment problem—from a failure to invest in new technologies, modern plant and equipment, and the education of its workforce. All this may well be true (especially in cases where management bonuses are determined largely by near-term EPS). Moreover, as Michael Jacobs argued convincingly in his widely-cited book, *Short-Term America*, shareholders of U.S. companies may rationally demand higher and quicker payoffs because they have virtually no power to influence corporate policy.

What we are almost never told by the press, however, is that much of corporate America has also long had a chronic "overinvestment" problem. The case of RJR-Nabisco documented in *Barbarians at the Gate* is undoubtedly one of the most flagrant (remember Ross Johnson's insisting to John Greeniaus that he find a way to spend the "excess" profits of his tobacco division rather than raise stockholder expectations by revealing its true profit potential). But the fact that Johnson was held up by *Fortune* as a model corporate leader only a month before the LBO suggests that major inefficiencies in cash-rich companies may be not only widespread, but very difficult to detect by outsiders. And the large stockholder gains from the corporate control transactions of the '80s are suggestive evidence of the systematic waste of shareholder capital by companies dedicated to growth at all cost.

Why is it important that such growth be checked? At the end of the 1970s, when the Dow was trading around 900 and the outlook for corporate America was far from bright, Lester Thurow complained in his apocalyptic bestseller *The Zero-Sum Society* that "mixed" economies like ours—those in which government was always intervening to "correct" free-market solutions that were politically unacceptable—had one very serious (and to Thurow irremediable) problem. Such economies couldn't bring about the large-scale "disinvestment" in declining industries, with the resulting decline in employment and real wages, necessary to release growth capital for emerging industry.

When I heard Thurow repeat this point in a speech at MIT in the mid-'80s, I raised my hand and objected that the then burgeoning leveraged restructuring movement was a free-market solution to precisely that disinvestment problem. The widespread substitution of temporary debt capital for more permanent equity—in leveraged takeovers, leveraged buyouts, and leveraged buybacks—was forcing excess capital out of companies in mature industries like oil and gas, tobacco, forest products, publishing, broadcasting, tires, food processing, and commodity chemicals.

It is no coincidence, moreover, that while billions of dollars of capital were being squeezed out of our largest companies and returned to stockholders, the venture capital industry was booming. Funding for the U.S. venture capital industry achieved its peak in 1987, close to the time when the volume of leveraged restructurings was reaching its own high point. At the same time, the small and medium-sized U.S. companies that prospered throughout the '80s were contributing to record employment and capital spending.

After the '80s, of course, the economy went into recession. Widespread failures in the S&L industry, combined with a number of highly-publicized cases of troubled leveraged transactions, led to a significant re-regulation of our financial markets. With the eclipse of the new issue market for junk bonds, the application of HLT rules to commercial bank lending, and new restrictions on insurance companies, funding for large highly-leveraged transactions all but disappeared and there were few signs of a well-functioning corporate control market.

In one sense, the financial press was right in attributing the depressed conditions in our debt and takeover markets to too many unsound transactions. Such transactions, as Jensen argued, were overpriced by their promoters and, as a consequence, overleveraged. What seems equally clear, however, is that intense political pressures to curb the corporate control market greatly compounded the existing problems, creating a capital shortage for non-investment-grade companies, and thereby contributing significantly to the recession.

The media, as suggested earlier, played no small role in inflaming popular opinion and bringing political forces to bear on private economic activity. Even with the current prosperity and record job growth in the U.S., populist attacks on Wall Street financiers and concentrations of financial power continue to be the order of the day for most mass-market publications. Even business publications such as *The Wall Street Journal* (at least the front-page stories) and *Forbes* resort increasingly to the techniques of muckraking sensationalism while avoiding all but the most simplistic economic analysis.

Perhaps the nadir of this kind of journalism was a piece by Susan Faludi on KKR's LBO of Safeway Stores that, ironically, won a Pulitzer Prize for "explanatory" journalism. The irony stems from the fact that, from an economist's perspective, the Safeway LBO has turned out to be one of the most unambiguously successful of the leveraged transactions of the '80s. Although now considerably smaller, the company has become extraordinarily profitable, capital spending (largely on store renovation) has increased significantly, and employee morale has improved in large part because the increased profitability has restored the basis for future growth. And while journalists are doubtless continuing their obsession with a handful of unfortunate individuals displaced by such changes, financial economists from the Harvard Business School are now at work anatomizing the transformation of Safeway into a remarkably efficient competitor.

There are a number of reasons why the quality of business journalism in this country continues to be poor. Although the business establishment undoubtedly furnishes the media with a major portion of its advertising revenues, it is probably unnecessary to go much beyond the incentives of the press to appeal to the mass markets, to the "man on the street," to arrive at the heart of the problem. As American movie producers and popular novelists have long understood, the American public is most responsive to stories that pit simple goodness against unmistakable evil. In this modern-day "morality play," the principal requirement is that heroes and villains be clearly distinguished from one another, and that all ambiguity be suppressed. The more heinous the villain, the greater the pleasure taken in his defeat (another essential requirement of popular American film) by the forces of good.

In economic life, however, all successful actions come at a cost, all change that increases social wealth comes at the expense of some groups and individuals. In this world where choices are rarely between good and evil, but only between the lesser of two evils (for all change causes pain to some), it is often the most callous-seeming actions that produce the greatest benefits for the economy at large. Those benefits, and their beneficiaries, cannot be detected—much less subjected to measurement—by the unaided eye of the journalist.

To return to our earlier argument, the primary accomplishment of the leveraged restructuring movement has been to stimulate general economic growth by forcing resources (people and capital) out of mature or shrinking industries and into vital ones. In the typical newspaper account, we learn much about the personal plights of employees who lose their jobs. But what the average journalist fails to acknowledge is that not all employment and corporate investment is "good for the economy," and that overall growth depends importantly on the ability to transfer people and capital from where they are not needed to where they are. Such mobility of resources, in the long run, is likely to add not only to stockholder wealth, but to increase total employment and corporate spending. And by each of these indicators of general economic performance, the 1980s—and now the 1990s—have been very productive indeed. (The fact that wage rates have fallen in some industries, so often deplored by market critics, is in fact a sign that the control market is doing its job in making our industry more competitive internationally.)

In the typical journalistic account of a highly leveraged transaction, we also generally learn very little about why the acquirer (or "raider") can afford to pay large premiums over current value to buy out the existing stockholders. Such premiums are invariably attributed to market undervaluation, which in turn is ascribed to the shortsightedness of investors. Rarely is there an account of the corporate inefficiencies and expected operating changes that typically make the payment of such premiums possible (though *Barbarians at the Gate* surely provides the first). And never have I seen a story that attempts to trace the subsequent path of stockholder capital liberated by restructurings and then describe the productive activities and new employment that capital eventually makes possible.

Private distress makes good copy, as always, but social benefits are difficult to detect with the journalist's tools. Here the statistical methods and abstract "truths" of the economist must serve.

I. MAN AND MARKETS

Most financial economists believe that the primary aim of corporate management is (or, at least, should be) to maximize shareholder value (or, more precisely, "the value of the firm"). To the extent management is intent on maximizing shareholder value, all its operating as well as financing decisions are grounded in some theory of (1) human behavior and (2) market pricing. How senior management chooses to evaluate and reward its managers and employees depends fundamentally on a theory of human motivation. And how management decides to use the assets at its disposal, what yardsticks it uses to evaluate performance, and what it chooses to tell investors are all shaped by its understanding of how the stock market works.

In "The Nature of Man," Michael Jensen and William Meckling, the pioneers of agency cost theory, provide a foundation for the other articles in this book by presenting a "model" of human behavior they call "REMM"—short for "Resourceful, Evaluative, Maximizing Model." The authors define REMM in large part by showing how it addresses the failings of other models commonly used in the social sciences. In contrast to the "Economic" model, REMM is not a simple, single-minded money-maximizer—but nor is she or he a "perfect agent" for accomplishing the goals of her organization, whether it operates in the public or the private sector. And, because the interests of corporate managers and employees can conflict sharply with those of shareholders, one of the major challenges in managing large corporations is to improve the alignment of those interests.

Critics of this view of human nature have objected to the tendency of economists to identify "rationality" with self-interest. Some people also object to what they take to be the "cynicism" of Jensen-Meckling agency theory and its prescribed use of financial incentives to motivate corporate executives to increase shareholder value. But, as Jensen and Meckling suggest, the pursuit of self-interest "in no way rules out or devalues altruistic behavior." And, as they also go on to say, the fact that people often devote their time and resources to others by no means makes them "perfect agents" for the organizations that employ them. Costly conflicts of interest abound in business and political organi-

zations; and, for this reason, the management of "agency costs" is an important social undertaking. Reflecting on his 20 years of teaching agency theory, Jensen remarks,

I find that students and business people are excited by the central proposition of agency theory. And the proposition that excites them is not that people are self-interested, or that conflicts abound. The central proposition of agency theory is that rational self-interested people involved in cooperative endeavors always have incentives to reduce or control conflicts of interest so as to reduce the losses resulting from them.

And Jensen's argument plays a prominent role throughout this book, particularly in the sections on Corporate Strategy and Structure, Capital Structure and Payout Policy, and Corporate Restructuring and Governance.

From human behavior, the focus of this first chapter then shifts to the behavior of financial markets. It was not until the late 1960s that the stock market began to be taken seriously by economists as a proper subject for scholarly research. But, since Eugene Fama introduced the notion of an "efficient" stock market to the finance literature in 1965, the growth of academic research on stock market behavior has been prodigious. Over the same 30 years, moreover, the rise of the "modern theory" of finance has had profound effects on corporate practice. Today's financial decision-making—everything from the setting of corporate goals and compensation plans to risk management and securities design—bears the imprint of past research.

In "The Theory of Stock Market Efficiency: Accomplishments and Limitations," the University of Rochester's Ray Ball provides a first-hand account of how stock market research has evolved over the past 30 years. The account is "first-hand" because Professor Ball was one of the pioneers in efficient markets research. While working at the University of Chicago in the mid-'60s, Ball and colleague Philip Brown produced what is now regarded as the first scientific study of the market's reaction to the release of financial statements.

For all its accomplishments, however, efficient markets theory has had its setbacks. As described in the article, a large body of empirical studies in the

1970s provided "remarkably consistent evidence of the stock market's ability to process information in a rational, in some cases ingenious, fashion." But, after a 15-year period in which one triumph of modern financial theory succeeded another—the Miller-Modigliani irrelevance propositions, the Sharpe-Lintner Capital Asset Pricing Model (CAPM), and the Black-Scholes option pricing model—evidence began to surface of "anomalies" that appeared to contradict the theory of efficient markets. For example, the prices of both individual firms and the market as a whole were reported to "overreact" in certain circumstances; and variables such as low market-to-book ratios and low P/E ratios, as well as a pronounced "small firm effect," appeared to provide opportunities for investors to earn higher rates of return than those predicted by the CAPM.

But, as Ball argues in the second half of his article, such anomalies may stem less from flaws in stock market pricing than from the limitations of the model of market efficiency itself and from defects in the design of researchers' tests (particularly their mechanical application of the CAPM). "Whether," as Ball concludes, "the existence of such anomalous findings indicates a fatal flaw in the theory—or, more likely, the value of incorporating greater realism—only time and more research will tell."

In "Market Myths," Bennett Stewart summarizes a good deal of academic evidence attesting to the rationality and sophistication of financial markets. Much of the behavior of Corporate America, Stewart argues, is dictated by unthinking adherence to what he calls the "Accounting Model of Value"—at its most simplistic, the notion that the market establishes a company's value by capitalizing its current earnings at a "standard" industry-wide multiple. In place of the Accounting Model, Stewart proposes adoption of the "Economic Model of Value" as the basis for corporate decision-making. The Economic Model estimates a company's worth as the sum of all future expected operating cash flows, net of required new investment and discounted at a cost of capital that reflects risk and investors' alternative investment opportunities. It is essentially this model, Stewart claims, that the most sophisticated, influential investors (the "lead steers") use in pricing corporate securities.

After a long exposition of the follies of accounting-based as opposed to value-based management, Stewart goes on to challenge a number of other popular beliefs about the market—namely, that

dividends are an important fundamental variable in the pricing of stocks, and that the market responds mechanically to accounting earnings while ignoring changes in operating cash flow.

Another perennial criticism of U.S. financial markets is that they encourage short-sighted behavior. As the popular argument has it, analysts' obsession with quarterly earnings leads to value-destroying cutbacks in productive long-term investment. But, in "R&D and Capital Markets," Baruch Lev's ambitious survey of the growing body of research on R&D provides clear testimony to the stock market's willingness to take the "long view." Besides documenting the rising "R&D intensity" of U.S. companies (which far exceeds that of any other industrialized nation), the studies are remarkably consistent in showing that investors place a high value on corporate R&D. That is, although U.S. accounting rules require that R&D expenditures be fully expensed in financial reports, investors effectively "capitalize" such expenditures in setting stock prices.

But if investors are generally able to work around U.S. accounting and the related problem of inadequate disclosure, there is also evidence of undervaluation among some R&D-intensive U.S. companies. And Professor Lev suggests that expanded disclosure of a company's R&D capability as well as adjustments of conventional GAAP accounting (in particular, capitalizing instead of expensing R&D) could help market analysts correct such a problem.

In the "Stern Stewart Roundtable on Relationship Investing and Shareholder Communication," Joel Stern and Bennett Stewart discuss the opportunities and challenges held out by the shareholder activism of the 1990s with a group of corporate CFOs, representatives of institutional investors, investor relations specialists, and academic accountants. Why academic accountants? The new activism by institutional investors is in part a response to an "information gap" between management and investors about corporate prospects. This information disadvantage of investors—which almost certainly causes the share values of some companies to be lower (and others' higher) than they should be—is made worse by the failure of accounting statements to reflect long-run corporate profitability. Some panelists accordingly argue that more realistic accounting conventions could stimulate relationship investing by providing a "new language" for companies to use in communicating their long-term prospects to investors. (A vigorous dissenter from this line is the University of Rochester's Jerold Zimmerman, who argues that accounting information was never intended to help outside investors value companies—nor can it be expected to do so, given the liabilities now facing Big Six accounting firms.)

Other panelists—including former New York State Controller Edward Regan—discuss the promise held out by nonfinancial corporate performance measures. And still others, particularly the corporate investor relations specialists, discuss new trends in shareholder communication that concentrate on appealing directly to the "buy side"—that is, on achieving direct contact and continuous dialogue with institutional shareholders. But better information is, of course, only part of the story. Besides better channels of information, institutional investors are also seeking more of a voice in major corporate decisions. Exemplifying this trend, the LENS Fund's Nell Minow describes the recent attempts of institutional investors to bring about change at some large U.S. companies.

DHC

THE NATURE OF MAN*

by Michael C. Jensen,
Harvard Business School, and
William H. Meckling,
University of Rochester

U nderstanding human behavior is fundamental to understanding how organizations function, whether they be profit-making firms in the private sector, non-profit enterprises, or government agencies intended to serve the "public interest." Much policy disagreement among managers, scientists, policy makers, and citizens derives from substantial, though usually implicit, differences in the way we think about human nature—about the strengths, frailties, intelligence, ignorance, honesty, selfishness, generosity, and altruism of individuals.

The usefulness of any model of human nature depends on its ability to explain a wide range of social phenomena; the test of such a model is the degree to which it is consistent with observed human behavior. A model that explains behavior only in one small geographical area, or only for a short period in history, or only for people engaged in certain pursuits is not very useful. For this reason we must use a limited number of general traits to characterize human behavior. Greater detail limits the explanatory ability of a model because individual people differ so greatly. We want a set of characteristics that captures the essence of human nature, but no more.

While this may sound abstract and complex, it is neither. Each of us has in mind and uses models of human nature every day. We all understand, for example, that people are willing to make trade-offs among things that they want. Our spouses, partners, children, friends, business associates, or perfect strangers can be induced to make substitutions of all kinds. We offer to go out to dinner Saturday night instead of the concert tonight. We offer to substitute a bicycle for a stereo as a birthday gift. We allow an employee to go home early today if the time is made up next week.

If our model specified that individuals were never willing to substitute some amount of a good for some amounts of other goods, it would quickly run aground on inconsistent evidence. It could not explain much of the human behavior we observe. While it may sound silly to characterize individuals as unwilling to make substitutions, that view of human behavior is not far from models that are widely accepted and used by many social scientists (for example, Maslow's hierarchy of human needs and sociologists' models portraying individuals as cultural role players or social victims).

We investigate five alternative models of human behavior that are used frequently enough (though usually implicitly) in the social science literature and in public discussion to merit attention. For convenience we label the models as follows:

1. **The Resourceful, Evaluative, Maximizing Model (or REMM)**
2. **The Economic (or Money-Maximizing) Model**
3. **The Sociological (or Social Victim) Model**
4. **The Psychological (or Hierarchy of Needs) Model**
5. **The Political (or Perfect Agent) Model.**

*We use the word "man" here in its use as a non-gender-specific reference to human beings. We have attempted to make the language less gender-specific because the models being discussed describe the behavior of both sexes. We have been unable to find a genderless term for use in the title which has the same desired impact.

The first draft of this paper was written in the early 1970s. Since then it has been used annually in our course on Coordination and Control at both Rochester and Harvard. We are indebted to our students for much help in honing these ideas over the years. An earlier version of some of the ideas in this paper appeared in

William H. Meckling, "Values and the Choice of the Model of the Individual in the Social Sciences," *Schweizerische Zeitschrift fur Volkswirtshaft und Statistik Revue Suisse d'Economie Politique et de Statistique* (December 1976).

This research has been supported by the Managerial Economics Research Center, University of Rochester, and the Division of Research, Harvard Business School. We are grateful for the advice and comments of many people, including Chris Argyris, George Baker, Fischer Black, Donald Chew, Perry Fagan, Donna Feinberg, Amy Hart, Karin Monsler, Kevin Murphy, Natalie Jensen, Steve-Anna Stephens, Richard Tedlow, Robin Tish, Karen Wruck, and Abraham Zaleznik.

These alternative models are pure types characterized in terms of only the barest essentials. We are sensitive to the dangers of creating straw men and concede that our characterization of these models fails to represent the complexity of the views of scientists in each of these fields. In particular, these models do not describe what all individual economists, sociologists, or psychologists use as their models of human behavior. Nevertheless, we believe that enough use is made of such admittedly reductive models throughout the social sciences, and by people in general, to warrant our treatment of them in these pages.

RESOURCEFUL, EVALUATIVE, MAXIMIZING MODEL: REMM

The first model is REMM: the Resourceful, Evaluative, Maximizing Model. While the term is new, the concept is not. REMM is the product of over 200 years of research and debate in economics, the other social sciences, and philosophy. As a result, REMM is now defined in very precise terms, but we offer here only a bare-bones summary of the concept. Many specifics can be added to enrich its descriptive content without sacrificing the basic foundation provided here.

Postulate I. Every individual cares; he or she is an evaluator.

(a) The individual cares about almost everything: knowledge, independence, the plight of others, the environment, honor, interpersonal relationships, status, peer approval, group norms, culture, wealth, rules of conduct, the weather, music, art, and so on.

(b) REMM is always willing to make trade-offs and substitutions. Each individual is always willing to give up some sufficiently small amount of any particular good (oranges, water, air, housing, honesty, or safety) for some sufficiently large quantity of other goods. Furthermore, valuation is relative in the sense that the value of a unit of any particular good decreases as the individual enjoys more of it relative to other goods.

(c) Individual preferences are transitive—that is, if A is preferred to B, and B is preferred to C, then A is preferred to C.

Postulate II. Each individual's wants are unlimited.

(a) If we designate those things that REMM values positively as "goods," then he or she prefers more goods to less. Goods can be anything from art objects to ethical norms.

(b) REMM cannot be satiated. He or she always wants more of some things, be they material goods such as art, sculpture, castles, and pyramids; or intangible goods such as solitude, companionship, honesty, respect, love, fame, and immortality.

Postulate III. Each individual is a maximizer.

He or she acts so as to enjoy the highest level of value possible. Individuals are always constrained in satisfying their wants. Wealth, time, and the laws of nature are all important constraints that affect the opportunities available to any individual. Individuals are also constrained by the limits of their own knowledge about various goods and opportunities; and their choices of goods or courses of action will reflect the costs of acquiring the knowledge or information necessary to evaluate those choices.[1]

The notion of an opportunity set provides the limit on the level of value attainable by any individual. The opportunity set is usually regarded as something that is given and external to the individual. Economists tend to represent it as a wealth or income constraint and a set of prices at which the individual can buy goods. But the notion of an individual's opportunity set can be generalized to include the set of activities he or she can perform during a 24-hour day—or in a lifetime.

Postulate IV. The individual is resourceful.

Individuals are creative. They are able to conceive of changes in their environment, foresee the consequences thereof, and respond by creating new opportunities.

Although an individual's opportunity set is limited at any instant in time by his or her knowledge and the state of the world, that limitation is not immutable. Human beings are not only capable of learning about new opportunities, they also engage in resourceful, creative activities that expand their opportunities in various ways.

The kind of highly mechanical behavior posited by economists—that is, assigning probabilities and

---

1. When one takes into account information costs, much behavior that appears to be suboptimal "satisficing" can be explained as attempts to maximize subject to such costs. Unfortunately, "satisficing" (a much misused term originated by Herbert

A. Simon in "A Behavioral Model of Rational Choice," *Quarterly Journal of Economics*, Vol. 69 (1955)) does not suggest this interpretation.

expected values to various actions and choosing the action with the highest expected value—is formally consistent with the evaluating, maximizing model defined in Postulates I through III. But such behavior falls short of the human capabilities posited by REMM; it says nothing about the individual's ingenuity and creativity.

REMMs AT WORK

One way of capturing the notion of resourcefulness is to think about the effects of newly imposed constraints on human behavior. These constraints might be new operating policies in a corporation or new laws imposed by governments. No matter how much experience we have with the response of people to changes in their environment, we tend to overestimate the impact of a new law or policy intended to constrain human behavior. Moreover, the constraint or law will almost always generate behavior which was never imagined by its sponsors. Why? Because of the sponsors' failure to recognize the creativity of REMMs.

REMMs' response to a new constraint is to begin searching for substitutes for what is now constrained, a search that is not restricted to existing alternatives. REMMs will invent alternatives that did not previously exist.

An excellent illustration of how humans function as REMMs is the popular response to the 1974 federal imposition of a 55-mile-per-hour speed limit in all states under penalty of loss of federal transportation and highway moneys. The primary reason offered for this law was the conservation of gasoline and diesel fuel (for simplicity, we ignore the benefits associated with the smaller number of accidents that occur at slower speeds).[2]

The major cost associated with slower driving is lost time. At a maximum speed of 55 mph instead of 70 mph, trips take longer. Those who argue that lost time is not important must recognize that an hour of time consumed is just as irreplaceable as—and generally more valuable than—the gallon of gasoline consumed. On these grounds, the law created inefficiencies, and the behavior of drivers is consistent with that conclusion.[3]

Let's calculate the dollar benefits of fuel saved by the 55 mph speed limit and the value of these savings per additional hour of driving time. These dollar savings can then be compared to the value of the driver's time. Suppose driving at 55 mph instead of 70 saves 10% on gasoline consumption, so that, for example, if gasoline mileage is 14 mpg at 70 mph, it will be 15.4 mpg at 55 mph. To travel 70 miles at 55 mph will take 1.273 hours instead of one hour at 70 mph. The gasoline consumed is 4.545 gallons at 55 mph instead of 5 gallons at 70 mph. This means that for every additional hour of travel time required by the slower speed, a driver saves 1.665 gallons of gasoline = (5.0 – 4.545) divided by (1.273 – 1.0).

At a price of $1.20 per gallon for gasoline, the driver saves $2.00 per hour of additional travel time—a sum significantly less than the minimum wage. If there are two occupants in the car, they each save $1.00 per hour; and the rate sinks to 66¢ per hour per person if there are three occupants. Therefore, the law requires that drivers and their passengers spend time in an activity that earns them about $2.00 per hour or less, depending on the particular car, the driver's habits, and the number of passengers.

Judging from the widespread difficulties state authorities have had in enforcing the law, drivers understand the value of their time quite well. People responded in REMM-like fashion to this newly imposed constraint in a number of ways. One was to reduce their automobile, bus, and truck travel, and, in some cases, to shift to travel by other means such as airplanes and trains. Another response was to defy the law by driving at speeds exceeding the 55 mph maximum. Violating the speed limit, of course, exposes offenders to potential costs in the form of fines, higher insurance rates, and possible loss of driver's licenses. This, in turn, provides incentives for REMMs to search out ways to reduce such costs.

The result has been an entire new industry, and the rapid growth of an already existing one. Citizen's Band radios (CBs), which had been used primarily by truckers, suddenly became widely used by passenger car drivers and almost all truckers. There were about 800,000 FCC CB radio licenses outstanding throughout the period 1966-

---

2. The original temporary law was made permanent in 1975 with safety being cited as a primary reason.

3. Moreover, in 1987 the law was changed to allow states the option of raising the speed limit to 65 mph on interstate highways outside highly populated areas, and later extended to certain non-interstate highways.

> **No matter how much experience we have with the response of people to changes in their environment, we tend to overestimate the impact of a new law or policy intended to constrain human behavior. It will almost always generate behavior which was never imagined by its sponsors.**

1973. By the end of 1977, there were 12.25 million licensed CBs in use.[4] These two-way radios with relatively short ranges (less than 15 miles) allowed drivers to inform each other about the location of police cars, radar traps, unmarked cars, and so on. They significantly reduced the likelihood of arrest for speeding. REMMs by the millions were willing to pay from $50 to $300 for radios in order to save time and avoid speeding tickets.

CB radios have been largely replaced by radar detectors that warn drivers of the presence of police radar. These devices have become so common that police have taken countermeasures, such as investing in more expensive and sophisticated radar units that are less susceptible to detection. Manufacturers of radar detectors retaliated by manufacturing increasingly sophisticated units.

The message is clear: people who drive value their time at more than $2 per hour. When the 55 mph maximum speed limit was imposed, few would have predicted the ensuing chain of events. One seemingly modest constraint on REMMs has created a new electronic industry designed to avoid the constraint. And such behavior shows itself again and again in a variety of contexts—for example, in

- taxpayers' continuous search for, and discovery of, "loopholes" in income tax laws;
- the development of so-called clubs with private liquor stock in areas where serving liquor at public bars is prohibited;
- the ability of General Dynamics' CEO George Anders and his management team, when put under a lucrative incentive compensation plan tied to shareholder value, to quadruple the market value of the company even as the defense industry was facing sharp cutbacks; and
- the growth in the number of hotel courtesy cars and gypsy cabs in cities where taxi-cab licensing results in monopoly fares.

These examples are typical of behavior consistent with the REMM model, but not, as we shall see, with other models that prevail in the social sciences. The failure of the other models is important because the individual stands in relation to organizations as the atom is to mass. From small groups to entire societies, organizations are composed of individuals. If we are to have a science of such organizations, it will have to be founded on building blocks that capture as simply as possible the most important traits of humans. Although clearly not a complete description of human behavior, REMM is the model of human behavior that best meets this criterion.[5]

REMM MEANS THERE ARE NO "NEEDS"

REMM implies that there is no such thing as a need, a proposition that arouses considerable resistance. The fallacy of the notion of needs follows from the proposition that the individual is always willing to make trade-offs. That proposition means individuals are always willing to substitute—that is, *they are always willing to give up a sufficiently small amount of any good for a sufficiently large amount of other goods.*[6] Failure to take account of substitution is one of the most frequent mistakes in the analysis of human behavior.

George Bernard Shaw, the famous playwright and social thinker, reportedly once claimed that while on an ocean voyage he met a celebrated actress on deck and asked her whether she would be willing to sleep with him for a million dollars. She was agreeable. He followed with a counterproposal: "What about ten dollars?" "What do you think I am?," she responded indignantly. He replied, "We've already established that—now we're just haggling over price."

Like it or not, individuals are willing to sacrifice a little of almost anything we care to name, even reputation or morality, for a sufficiently large quantity of other desired things, and these things do not have to be money or even material goods. Moreover, the fact that all individuals make trade-offs (or substitute in virtually every dimension imaginable) means that there are no such things as human "needs" in the sense that word is often used. There are only human wants, desires, or, in the economist's language, demands. If something is more costly, less will be wanted, desired, demanded than if it were cheaper.

---

4. Obtained in private communication with the Federal Communications Commission.

5. REMM is not meant to describe the behavior of any particular individual. To do so requires more complete specification of the preferences, values, emotions, and talents of each person. Moreover, individuals respond very differently to factors such as stress, tension, and fear, and, in so doing, often violate the predictions of the REMM model. For purposes of organizational and public policy, many of these violations of REMM "cancel out" in the aggregate across large

groups of people and over time—but by no means all. For a discussion of a Pain Avoidance Model (PAM) that complements REMM by accommodating systematically non-rational behavior, see Michael C. Jensen, "Economics, Organizations, and Non-Rational Behavior," forthcoming *Economic Inquiry* (1995).

6. The word need has meaning only when used in the conditional sense. For example: An individual needs X cubic liters of air per hour in order to live. This statement, or others like it, do not imply, however, that individuals are willing to pay an infinite price for that air.

Using the word need as an imperative is semantic trickery. The media and press are filled with talk about housing needs, education needs, food needs, energy needs, and so on. Politicians and others who use that language understand that the word need carries emotional impact. It implies a requirement at any cost; if the need is not met, some unspecified disaster will take place. Such assertions have a far different impact if restated to reflect the facts. The proposition that "people want more housing if they can get it cheaply enough" does not ring out from the podium or over the airwaves with the same emotional appeal as "people *need* more housing."

If individuals are required to specify what they mean by need, the emotional specter of the unexamined catastrophe that lies behind the need simply becomes another cost. Needs would be exposed for what they are—desires or wants—and discussion would focus on alternatives, substitutes, and costs in a productive manner.

ECONOMISTS, POLITICIANS, AND BUREAUCRATS AS REMMs

National Planning and Needs

While economists generally profess fidelity to REMM, their loyalty is neither universal nor constant. Their economic models of human behavior often fall short of REMM—such as, for example, when they characterize the individual as a pure money-income maximizer. Moreover, in matters of public policy, there is a systematic relationship between the policies espoused and the degree of infidelity to REMM. One of the better-known members of the economics profession and a recipient of the Nobel Prize, Professor Wassily Leontieff, was featured as a proponent of "national economic planning" in a *New York Times* advertisement that said:

No reliable mechanism in the modern economy relates needs to available manpower, plant and material... The most striking fact about the way we organize our economic life is that we leave so much to chance. We give little thought to the direction in which we would like to go. (March 16, 1975)

Notice that the emotional content and force of the statement is considerably strengthened by the authors' use of the word "needs" rather than "desires" or "wants."

But let's examine this statement more closely. If by "needs" the authors mean *individual* preferences, wants, or desires, the first sentence is simply false. There *is* a mechanism that relates such needs or wants to "manpower, plant, and materials" and it is central to the study of economics: namely, the price system. What the authors are saying is that no one organization or group of individuals *directs* (not plans) production in such a way that what is actually produced is what the advertisement's authors would define as needs. When they go on to say, "We give little thought to the direction we would like to go," the antecedent of we is meant to be "we the general public." But, of course, we as individuals (and REMMs) give a great deal of thought to where we want to study and work, how much we will save, where we will invest our savings, what we will buy, what we will produce, and so on.

Professor Leontieff's reputation rests largely on his work on input-output models. It is not surprising that he is a planning buff, for input-output models generally ignore most of the adjustment processes (that is, price changes and substitutions) that serve to balance supply and demand in a market economy. His input-output models specify fixed relations between inputs like labor, materials, and capital—and outputs like tons of steel. More or less steel can be produced only by adding or subtracting inputs in fixed proportions. There are no resourceful, evaluative maximizers in Leontieff's models. Like ants in an ant colony, his individuals possess productive capacities but very limited adaptability. In a society of such dolts, planning (or, more accurately, directing) appears unavoidable. In the words of another Nobel Prize winner, Professor Friedrich von Hayek, the real planning issue is not *whether* individuals should plan their affairs, but rather *who* should plan their affairs.[7]

The implication of input-output models, then, is that people are incapable of planning and thus require the direction and leadership of "planners." This import has not escaped the notice of bureaucrats, politicians, and managers, who themselves

---

7. See Friedrich von Hayek, "The Use of Knowledge in Society," *American Economic Review*, Vol. 35, No. 4 (September, 1945); and "'Planning' Our Way to Serfdom," *Reason* (March, 1977).

> The implication of input-output models is that people are incapable of planning and thus require the direction and leadership of "planners." This import has not escaped the notice of bureaucrats and politicians, who themselves behave as REMMs when they recognize the value of models and theories that imply an increased demand for their services.

behave as REMMs when they recognize the value of models and theories that imply an increased demand for their services. By their very framing of the issue, Leontieff and politicians assume the answer to Hayek's question: planning does not exist unless the government does it.

For example, politicians are likely to see the value of an energy industry input-output model which, given projections of future energy "needs" (no prices and no substitutions here), tells how many nuclear energy plants must be built, how many strip mines should be opened, and how many new coal cars must be produced in order to become independent of foreign oil sources. The model suggests that, without extensive government intervention, the country cannot achieve energy independence. Such intervention, of course, implies an increase in politicians' power.

It is worth noting that the "we" in the Leontieff-endorsed planning statement is a common but generally unrecognized debating trick. It is standard practice in the political arena to label one's own preferences as the "people's preferences" or as the "public's preferences," and to label the policies one supports as "in the public interest." But organizations or groups of individuals cannot have preferences; only individuals can have preferences. One could supply content to terms like the people's preferences or the public interest by making them synonymous with other concepts—for example, with what a majority would support or what every voter would approve in a referendum. But the typical user would then find the terms far less persuasive, therefore less attractive, and, in the case of a complete consensus, never relevant.

Self-Interest and the Demand for Disequilibrium

Bureaucrats and politicians, like many economists, are also predisposed to embrace the concept of market "failure" or "disequilibrium" with the same enthusiasiasm they have shown for input-output models, and for the same reasons. If something is in disequilibrium, government action is required to bring about equilibrium.

Generally, economists tend to identify equilibrium with stable prices and quantities: a market is in

equilibrium when there are no forces causing changes in the price or the quantity exchanged. Yet it is reasonable to argue that all markets are always in equilibrium, and all forces must always be in balance at all times—just as there is an equilibrium rate of heat transfer when heat is applied to one end of a steel bar. This is simply another way of saying that sophisticated, rational individuals always adapt to their opportunity set, where the opportunity set is defined to take account of the cost of adapting. That is, all voluntary exchanges will take place that will make both parties better off (taking all costs into account).

The view that markets are always in equilibrium does not depend on the stability of prices; prices and quantities can change dramatically. Their rate of change, however, is controlled by individual behavior—a balance is struck between the cost of change and the benefits. For example, if the dollar price of a good is prevented by law from changing, the opposing forces are balanced by the introduction of other costs such as queues and waiting time, or by the introduction of other goods as a consideration in the exchange.[8]

Although it is a tautology, the view that markets are always in equilibrium has important advantages. It focuses attention on interesting adjustment phenomena, on information and search costs and how they affect behavior, and on qualitative characteristics of the exchanges that arise to balance the opposing forces. If markets are always in equilibrium, the task of the scientist is to explain how the equilibrium is brought about.

In contrast, the word disequilibrium has strong emotional content. It denotes something unnatural, unsightly, and undesirable that requires "corrective action." A market—whether for labor, energy, sugar, health care, or derivative securities—described as being "in disequilibrium" is generally regarded as bad, and we are immediately led to think of the desirability of some form of government intervention (e.g., price controls, embargoes, subsidies, or output restrictions) to eliminate the assumed problem.

One popular pursuit of bureaucrats—making projections of supply and demand—is the outgrowth of their preoccupation with disequilibrium. Such projections usually consist of estimates of numbers of physicists, doctors, mining engineers,

---

8. For example, it is common practice in rent controlled areas for new tenants to make higher-than-market-price payments to old tenants and/or landlords for furniture or minor improvements they have no use for to get the right to rent the apartment for a below-market rate.

barrels of oil, or tons of steel "required and/or available" at some future date, again without reference to prices. Not surprisingly, the projections invariably imply a disequilibrium (a shortage or surplus) that requires government action.

But if these supply and demand projections are interpreted as forecasts of the quantities *and* prices that will prevail in a future economy in equilibrium, they lose all interest for policy makers. None of the usual policy implications follow—no subsidies, taxes, or constraints on individual behavior are called for, nor can any governmental enterprise be justified. Yet the practice of making projections goes on because politicians and bureaucrats, as REMMs, find them useful tools for expanding the role of government and the market for their services.

THE ECONOMIC MODEL
OF HUMAN BEHAVIOR

The economic model is a reductive version of REMM. This individual is an evaluator and maximizer who has only one want: money income. He or she is a short-run *money maximizer* who does not care for others, art, morality, love, respect, or honesty. In its simplest form, the economic model characterizes people as unwilling to trade current money income for future money income, no matter what rate of return they could earn.

The economic model is, of course, not very interesting as a model of human behavior. People do not behave this way. In most cases, use of this model reflects economists' desire for simplicity in modeling; the exclusive pursuit of wealth or money income is easier to model than the complexity of the actual preferences of individuals. As a consequence, however, noneconomists often use this model as a foil to discredit economics, that is, to argue that economics is of limited use because economists focus only on a single characteristic of behavior—and one of the least attractive at that, the selfish desire for money.

THE SOCIOLOGICAL MODEL
OF HUMAN BEHAVIOR

In the sociological model, individuals are viewed as the product of their cultural environment. Humans are not evaluators any more than ants, bees, or termites are evaluators. They are conventional and conformist, and their behavior is determined by the taboos, customs, mores, and traditions of the society in which they were born and raised. In this model, individuals are also often viewed as *social victims*, a concept that has gained widespread acceptance in many quarters.

By contrast, REMM is an evaluator. The REMM model recognizes that customs and mores serve as important constraints on human behavior, and that individuals who violate them incur costs in many forms. But REMMs compare the consequences of alternative courses of action, including those that involve the flouting of social norms, and consciously choose actions that lead to their preferred outcome. Moreover, if the costs or benefits of alternative courses of action change, REMMs change their behavior. In the sociological model individuals do not.

To be sure, social practices, customs, and mores play an important role in determining the attitudes and actions of individuals at any point in time. They represent a major force for teaching, learning, disciplining, and rewarding members of a group, organization, or society. But if the group or organization is to prosper—and, indeed, if the society itself is to survive—these cultural practices or values must adapt to approximate optimal behavior given the costs and benefits implied by the opportunity set faced by individuals in the society.

Changes in knowledge, technology, or the environment change the opportunity set. Therefore, a scientist who uses REMM to model behavior would predict that changes in knowledge, technology, and the environment that alter the costs or benefits of actions of large numbers of people will result in changes over time in social customs and mores. In contrast, the sociological model leaves social scientists with no explanation of changes in social customs, mores, taboos, and traditions.

For example, social scientists who use the sociological model would look to changes in morals and social attitudes to explain the increase in sexuality and the simultaneous decline in birth rates over the past several decades. By contrast, a social scientist using REMM to explain the same phenomena would place greater emphasis on advances in birth control techniques. Why? One major cost of sexual intercourse is the cost associated with bearing and rearing a child. By making it possible for those who do not want children to avoid conception more effectively, better birth control techniques substantially reduce the cost of sexual intercourse.

In addition, extramarital sex and cohabitation of unmarried couples are more acceptable now than

Social practices, customs, and mores represent a major force for teaching, learning, disciplining, and rewarding members of a group, organization, or society. But if the group or organization is to prosper—and, indeed, if the society itself is to survive— these cultural practices or values must adapt so as to approximate optimal behavior given the costs and benefits implied by the opportunity set.

prior to the introduction of effective birth control techniques. In this sense, the culture has adapted to the changes in optimal behavior implied by changes in the costs of sexual activity. At the same time, however, one can also predict that increases in the costs of sexual activity through the appearance of new untreatable sexually transmitted diseases will cause a resurgence of puritan ethics and a renewed emphasis on the family. This is consistent with the changes occurring as a result of the AIDS epidemic.

But the cultural changes required by the new birth control technology go well beyond the family and changes in sexual mores. By allowing women more control over the timing of childbirth, the new technology increases their labor market choices substantially. The lag in cultural and institutional practices in reflecting this newly optimal behavior is both inefficient and a major catalyst for the feminist movement. But the changes required to adjust to optimal behavior under the new cost conditions are unavoidable. Inefficient practices such as discrimination against women in hiring provide profit opportunities for those REMMs with the vision to perceive and act upon the gap between current and optimal practices.[9]

There is a crucial distinction, then, between the REMM model's recognition that cultural factors are *reflected* in human behavior and the sociological model's assertion that cultural factors *determine* human behavior. If behavior is completely determined by acculturation, as the sociological model suggests, then choice, purpose, and conscious adaptation are meaningless. Indeed, if humans are endowed with little originality, have no ability to evaluate, and simply imitate what they see and do what they are told, it is not clear how *any* social change could take place.

The REMM model, in contrast, explains the evolution of customs and mores as the reflection in habits, unquestioned beliefs, and religion of behavior patterns that reflect optimal responses to the costs and benefits of various actions. When the underlying costs and benefits of various actions change, individuals are faced with a conflict between new, optimal forms of behavior and culturally accepted but inefficient forms. In this situation there

will be social conflict. And if the new behavior patterns are indeed optimal, the population will— through experience, education and death—gradually accommodate the new behavior in the culture.

For example, consider the clash of economic reality with cultural values that lies behind the fairly recent decision by IBM's top management to abandon its longstanding (and socially revered) policy of lifetime employment. Beginning with the post-War prosperity of the 1950s and lasting well into the restructuring wave of the 1980s, the concept of lifetime employment by large U.S. corporations became a social expectation—an "implicit contract"—and top executives who resorted to layoffs just to maintain profitability (that is, unless threatened by bankruptcy or extinction) were harshly criticized by the media if not ostracized by their communities.

Although vigorous social criticism of layoffs persisted throughout the restructurings of the '80s, corporate America has been forced by increasing global competition to recognize that lifetime employment ends up debilitating rather than strengthening companies. Because the expectation of long-term job security became so engrained in the culture, it has been much more difficult for companies to adjust their practices. In the meantime, Japanese and European companies—traditionally far more committed to lifetime employment than their U.S. counterparts—are also being forced to rethink the policy while confronting their own problems of chronic industrial overcapacity and the resulting inefficiencies.[10]

Because of its ability to explain such remarkable shifts in cultural values, REMM also provides the foundation for thinking about how to change corporate culture. The shared beliefs, attitudes, customs, and values of people within an organization can be a critical determinant of success or failure. And although an organization's culture constitutes a barrier to valuable innovation at any given moment, culture can be molded through conscious, coordinated effort over time. The values and attitudes of people within an organization will respond over time to view positively those actions which are rewarded in the organization and negatively those

---

9. In particular, employment or wage discrimination against women implies profit opportunities for new firms that can therefore hire superior women at market rates. Such profits can be shared with the employees through profit sharing or partnership structures.

10. For an account of the role of corporate restructuring in addressing both the U.S. and worldwide problem of industrial overcapacity, see Michael C. Jensen, "The Modern Industrial Revolution, Exit, and the Failure of Internal Control Systems," *Journal of Finance*, Vol. 48 No. 3 (July, 1993), pp. 831-880.

actions which are punished. It will also respond to selection policies designed to bring into the company people with values and attitudes consistent with the desired culture.

The sociological model, then, has serious shortcomings as the basis for a body of theory about social behavior. With its near-exclusive focus on cultural continuity, it cannot account for the enormous diversity of human behavior at any given time. Nor can it explain dramatic changes in behavior such as those brought about by improved birth control and other technological advances. The model also ignores the process of conscious deliberation by individuals and organizations when contemplating different courses of action.

Given its limitations, why is the sociological model so popular?

The popularity of the sociological model can be traced to the relationship between models of human behavior and policy positions, as well as the human tendency to deny personal causal responsibility. If people's behavior is largely determined by factors beyond their control, they are victims and therefore cannot be held responsible for their actions or the states of their lives.

The appeal of such a theory to those who find themselves in trouble or wanting in any way is obvious; and the extent to which this theory is played out everyday in the media, courtrooms, families, and organizations is discussed at length by Charles Sykes in *A Nation of Victims* (St. Martin's Press, 1992). Several all-too-common examples from the book (p. 3): an employee fired for repeatedly late arrival sues his employer, arguing that he is a victim of "chronic lateness syndrome"; an FBI agent is reinstated after being fired for embezzling funds to repay his gambling debts because the court rules that gambling with the money of others is a "handicap" and hence protected under federal law.

Under the social victim model, if an individual steals, it is only because society has made him or her a thief, not because he or she has chosen that activity. And the solution is not to punish the individual for such actions because no thief chooses to be a thief. In this model, raising the costs of thievery can have no effect on the amount of thievery. The solution is to educate and rehabilitate.

Although education and rehabilitation programs can help to change people, they alone are unlikely to reduce criminal behavior significantly. As these programs become more widespread, and as they

are accompanied by a reduction in the penalties and other "costs" of criminal behavior, we should not be surprised to find that REMMs more frequently choose to be criminals.

For the same reason, it is not surprising from the viewpoint of REMM that Singapore has no drug problem. Arrivals to the country must sign a statement recognizing that they have been informed that possession or sale of drugs is punishable by death. And the population is well aware of these policies; as illustrated by the recent caning of an American for vandalism, punishment for infractions of Singapore law is carried out swiftly and publicly.

Educating people about the effects of their choices does, of course, affect behavior; and it takes time for cultural attitudes to change. A complete programmatic attack on crime would include the use of both formal punishments and rewards as well as education and consensus building among the population. Properly carried out, such education and consensus building can tap social rejection and approval as additional (and decentralized) sources of punishments and rewards to reinforce sanctions against criminal or other undesirable behavior.

As another illustration of the workings of the sociological model, consider the current debate over the causes of homelessness. The very use of the term "homeless" suggests no choice on the part of street people (who are therefore victims of the system); it also carries little or none of the social disapprobation of "vagrant," a now unfashionable label. This change in language and attitudes reduces the decentralized sources of social or cultural punishment for being a street person—again, something the REMM model predicts would result in an increase in this socially undesirable behavior. New York City now spends in excess of a half billion dollars a year on subsidies for the homeless, and the problem shows no signs of going away, even with the improvement in the economy. (And the "de-institutionalizing" of the mentally ill, a common explanation, by no means accounts for the vast increase in the numbers of street people.)

The sociological model suggests that if an individual's income and wealth are small, it is entirely due to cultural factors, environmental adversity, or bad luck—not to conscious effort, the choice of leisure over work, the choice of a particular type of work, or the failure to invest in learning. Therefore, "justice" requires that we confiscate the wealth of the more fortunate to recompense the unfortunate.

Politicians, bureaucrats, and special interest groups understand that public policy choices are affected by the concept that individuals are responsible for their own fates.

Of course, the higher the recompense, the more attractive it is to be poor, and REMMs will respond by taking more leisure, by choosing occupations in which employment is more unstable, and by investing less in learning. The REMM model predicts that if we make the payoff high enough, we can attract an arbitrarily large number of people to become poor or unemployed—or at least to meet the established criteria for those programs. This describes important aspects of our welfare and unemployment systems.

Politicians, bureaucrats, and special interest groups understand that public policy choices are affected by the concept that individuals are responsible for their own fates. Strong popular support for the principle that individuals ought to be rewarded or punished in accordance with their own behavior means that measures that aim to redistribute wealth, or rehabilitate criminals rather than punish them, would encounter strong opposition. But resourceful politicians and others who want to put such measures into effect can neutralize public opposition by persuading people that everything we do is forced on us by our cultural environment—we are social victims, and thus neither our behavior nor our status is a product of deliberate choice. By undermining the link between choice and consequences, they can overcome the resistance that stems from beliefs that individuals are responsible for their own behavior.

In addition, individuals constantly face a conflict when attempting to help others who are experiencing difficulty, especially those related through family or other ties. The conflict is between the desire to ease or eliminate the difficulties of others through gifts or charity, and the reluctance to distort the incentives of people to take charge of their own lives—say, by investing in education and making other efforts to improve their condition. All parents face such trade-offs when deciding how much help to give their children, and the choices are not easy. The short-term pain associated with denying help to a loved one is very difficult to bear. But casual observation together with evidence of the futility of various social programs seem to indicate that people systematically underestimate the counterproductive long-run effects on individuals of actions that we take to shield them from the consequences of their own choices.[11]

The Sociological Model and Marxism

A discussion of the sociological model would be incomplete without touching upon the use of that concept by Marxists, socialists, and other groups around the world. Marxist politicians understand that the sociological model is the foundation for the centralization of power. Marxism has received wide support in Europe. It has also had substantial support among the Catholic clergy and American academics. Recent evidence on the widespread failure of Russian, Eastern European, and other economies dominated by Marxist thought has revealed the shortcomings of this view and diminished, but not eliminated, support for it. Ironically, as many formerly socialist Eastern European and Asian countries are moving toward capitalism, the U.S. is moving toward more socialistic regulatory and political policies.

Socialism is supported by a philosophy that idolizes the state. The urge to subordinate the individual to the organization has ancient roots going back at least to Plato. In portraying his ideal state, Plato says:

...[T]here is common property of wives, of children, and of all chattels. And everything possible has been done to eradicate from our life everywhere and in every way all that is private and individual. So far as it can be done, even those things which nature herself has made private and individual have somehow become the common property of all. Our very eyes and ears and hands seem to see, to hear, and to act, as if they belonged not to individuals but to the community. All men are molded to be unanimous to the utmost degree in bestowing praise and blame, and they even rejoice and grieve about the same things, and at the same time...Nor should the mind of anybody be habituated to letting him do anything at all on his own initiative, neither out of zeal, nor even playfully...But in war and in the midst of peace—to his leader he shall direct his eye, and follow him faithfully. And even in the smallest matters he should stand under leadership. For example, he should get up, or move, or wash, or take his means... only if he has been told to do so...In a word, he should teach his soul, by long habit, never to dream of acting independently, and to become utterly incapable of it.[12]

---

11. The "tough love" movement and twelve-step programs such as AA for treating substance dependence are designed to provide help while insisting that individuals maintain their personal responsibility for their fate.

12. Plato, *Laws*, 739c, ff and 942a, f, as cited by Karl Popper in *The Open Society and Its Enemies* (2nd ed.) (Princeton, New Jersey: Princeton University Press, 1950), p. 102.

Plato's ideal state is an example of the most extreme anti-individualist position, one which makes the organization itself the ultimate end. The state is treated as a living organism; it is the overriding value. Individual purpose is not only unimportant, it is an evil that must be stamped out.

Plato's views are not very different from those of most Marxists. The role of the individual poses a dilemma for Marxists. Avowed Marxist states around the world such as the former USSR, China, and Cuba display an attitude with respect to individual citizens that is close to Plato's utopia. Party doctrine denounces individualistic motivation and invokes the common good. In intellectual discourse, Marxist theorists press for an organizational or social class approach to the study of society. In Marxist theory, the worker and the capitalist play out their roles regardless of the costs and benefits of their actions. Capitalists are what they are and do what they do because they are capitalists, and so too for workers. In the Marxist model, individuals do not evaluate, choose, or maximize; they behave according to the sociological model.

The sociological model is devoid of prescriptive content, yet it is commonly used for normative purposes. If humans are not evaluators (they only play the roles given to them by the culture), it is meaningless to talk about making people better off. While Marxists reject the Western economic tradition of considering the individual as the basic unit of analysis, they also express great concern for the plight of the less fortunate, and make much of concepts such as class conflict and exploitation.

Thus, these concerns for the welfare of people (primarily the workers or underclass) exhibit an obvious and fatal inconsistency. To repeat, unless we attribute preferences to the individual, language that describes differences in an individual's well-being makes no sense. Notions like equality and justice are popular among those who employ the sociological model of humanity, but such ethical norms are not internally meaningful because they imply that individuals care about their condition—that is, that they are evaluators, they experience envy, and they choose.

Furthermore, if the state is all that matters, as Marxist doctrine maintains, concern for the plight of the individual is irrelevant at best and can be inimical to the general good. Concepts such as exploitation and conflict can be used in a group context to refer to more than one individual, but such language has meaning only in terms of individuals. Organizations cannot be exploited any more than machines or rocks can be exploited. Only individuals can be exploited, can suffer, can make war; only individuals can be objects of compassion. Organizations are purely conceptual artifacts, even when they are assigned the legal status of individuals. In the end, we can do things *to* and *for* individuals only.

THE PSYCHOLOGICAL MODEL OF HUMAN BEHAVIOR

The psychological model is a step up the evolutionary ladder from the sociological model. Like REMM, humans in this model are resourceful, they care, they have wants and drives. But the individual's wants are viewed essentially as absolutes that are largely independent of one another. Therefore, substitutions or trade-offs are not part of individual human behavior. In effect, the individual is said to have "needs" in the sense of that word which we have already rejected.

Perhaps the best-known formulation of what we call the psychological model was provided by A. H. Maslow. "Human needs," wrote Maslow in 1943, "arrange themselves in hierarchies of prepotency. That is to say, the appearance of one need usually rests on the prior satisfaction of another more prepotent need."[13] Maslow's needs, in order of their "prepotency" from high to low, are physiological (food, water), safety, love, and self-actualization.

In contrast to REMM, in Maslow's *hierarchy of needs* model the individual is unwilling to give up any food for any amount of safety until his or her food needs are satisfied. Only after the food needs are completely satisfied will he or she be concerned about safety. What Maslow and his followers have done is to confuse two entirely different issues: how an individual allocates resources among alternative goods at a given level of wealth, and how that allocation pattern varies as an individual's wealth rises.

Maslow himself, in the latter part of his famous article, qualifies his early statements that deny substitution. He argues that he did not mean that literally

---

13. A.H. Maslow, "A Theory of Human Motivation," *Psychological Review*, Vol. 50, (January, 1943), p. 370.

While Marxists reject the Western economic tradition of considering the individual as the basic unit of analysis, they also express great concern for the plight of the less fortunate. But, unless we attribute preferences to the individual, language that describes differences in an individual's well-being makes no sense.

100% of a person's food need had to be satisfied in order for him or her to begin to satisfy the safety needs, and so on.[14] Although most of Maslow's followers have ignored his qualifications, these latter statements show him moving toward the notion of substitution and the income elasticity of demand, a relationship known to economists for many years and incorporated in REMM.[15]

Moreover, ample evidence of human behavior contradicts Maslow's hierarchy of needs model. We see astronauts, skiers, and car racers accepting less safety in return for wealth, fame, and just plain thrills. Poets, artists, and gurus go without material comforts to devote their time to contemplation and art, and, to us, these pursuits sound closer to self-actualization than physiological goods.

The psychological model, like the sociological model, is not satisfactory for describing the behavior of individuals in the study of social phenomena. Yet there is some content in Maslow's model. His ordering of wants probably corresponds to how most people would allocate a $1,000 increment of wealth on expenditures at increasing levels of wealth. Wealthier people tend to spend less of their additional wealth on goods satisfying physiological wants, and more on each of the categories of goods higher in Maslow's hierarchy.[16] Nevertheless, inconsistent with Maslow's model, individuals at any level of wealth are willing to sacrifice some amounts of any good for sufficiently large amounts of all other goods.

Thus, while Maslow's ordering of categories of human wants tends to describe how expenditures increase with increased wealth, it is neither a hierarchy nor does it describe needs. It is difficult to infer much else about social behavior from the hierarchy of needs model that is not trivial or false. The psychological model predicts that if the cost of any good rises, the individual will reduce outlays on whatever is the highest-ranking good he or she currently buys, a behavioral reaction clearly contradicted by actual consumer behavior. When the price of one good rises relative to other goods, consumers react by reducing purchases of the good whose price has risen, not the purchases of goods that are highest on Maslow's list.

Once substitution is ruled out, the individual's attempt to maximize by reconciling wants with means is largely ignored, and attention focuses instead on the study of individual wants (or classes of wants). Examples from the field of organizational behavior (OB) are numerous. One general problem (an extremely important one) is how to get employees to be more productive. The general answer is to reward them by satisfying their needs.

The OB literature does not generally recognize that the employer's problem is one of designing an overall employment package that takes into account the potential for trade-offs. Instead, each good that the employer can provide the employee is considered in isolation. Job enrichment and the quality of the working environment are examples. More of each is always taken to be better than less, and not only is the optimality criterion seldom applied to determine the correct level of job enrichment or quality of the environment, optimality itself is rarely discussed.

The prevalence of Maslow's model in the behavioral science field is, we believe, a major reason for the failure of the field to develop a unified body of theory. Theory erected on the basis of individuals who are driven by wants, but who cannot or will not make substitutions, will necessarily consist of a series of independent propositions relating particular drives to actions and will never be able to capture the complexity of human behavior.

THE POLITICAL MODEL OF HUMAN BEHAVIOR

While resourceful and, in a certain sense, evaluators and maximizers, individuals under the political model are assumed to evaluate and maximize in terms of other individuals' preferences rather than their own. Unlike REMM, the individual

---

14. "So far, our theoretical discussion may have given the impression that these five sets of needs are somehow in a step-wise, all-or-none relationship to each other... This... might give the false impression that a need must be satisfied 100 per cent before the next need emerges. In actual fact, most members of our society who are normal, are partially satisfied in all their basic needs and partially unsatisfied in all their basic needs at the same time. A more realistic description of the hierarchy would be in terms of decreasing percentages of satisfaction as we go up the hierarchy of prepotency...

As for the concept of emergence of a new need after satisfaction of the prepotent need, this emergence is not a sudden, salutatory phenomenon but rather a gradual emergence by slow degrees from nothingness." Maslow (1943, pp. 388-89).

15. The income elasticity of demand describes how an individual's consumption of a good changes with a given change in income. It is the percentage change in the quantity of a good demanded by an individual divided by the percentage change in the individual's income (holding all prices and quantities of other goods constant).

16. Economists call such goods "necessities" and "luxury" goods. They are defined by their income- or wealth-elasticity of demand.

is a *perfect agent* seeking to maximize "the public good" rather than his or her own welfare.

It is important to distinguish between altruism (that is, a willingness to sacrifice some of one's own goods, time, or welfare for the benefit of others) and the political model. Altruists do not behave according to the political model. Since they have their own preferences, they cannot be perfect agents. A perfect agent is a person that will maximize with respect to the preferences of the principal while, if necessary, denying his or her own. Perfect agents would be equally satisfied working to save the whales, feed the poor, make computers, or care for the musical interests of the rich through the local symphony orchestra at the bidding of their employers. Altruist that she is, Mother Teresa's devotion to caring for the poor of Calcutta does not make her a perfect agent. It is highly doubtful that she would agree to (or effectively) represent the interests of someone who wished to save the whales or make computers. Like all REMMs, she has her own preferences and will exercise her choice over whom or what cause she devotes her time to helping.

The logic in which the political model figures so prominently is simple, though it will not withstand careful scrutiny. Whenever individuals acting on their own behalf will not bring about the "desired" outcome, government must take a hand. If consumers might be misled by deceptive advertising, have government regulate advertising. If sellers might market products that are harmful to consumers, have government regulate consumer product safety. If consumers might not understand the terms of lending contracts, have government regulate the language that can be used in such contracts.

The fatal flaw in the above propositions is their assumption that when politicians intervene, they act to accomplish the desired result—that is, they act in the public interest. Those who argue for such government intervention simply assume that politicians can and will behave in accord with the desires of the electorate.

This political or perfect agent model lies at the heart of virtually all campaigns that purport to solve

problems by creating a governmental agency or appointing a political body. Worried about too many dangerous drugs or injuries in coal mines? Establish an FDA to regulate drug testing and grant approval for the marketing of new drugs. To reduce injuries in coal mines, pass a mine safety law with the Department of Mines to administer it. Unfortunately, the results of such programs do not lend support to the political model. After the 1962 amendments regulating the efficacy of new drugs, the number of new drugs approved in the U.S. fell by half.[17] Moreover, between 1966 and 1970, more than 2,000 small nonunion coal mines closed down with no measurable reduction of injury or death rates in coal mines.[18]

These results occur—and are indeed predictable—because the people who enact and administer the laws are REMMs. The bureaucrats in the FDA, for instance, face high costs if they err and allow a drug that has injurious side effects (such as Thalidomide) to be marketed. On the other hand, the people who suffer and die because FDA procedures have kept a new drug bottled up in the testing laboratories for several years (or perhaps never let it on the market) usually don't even know that they have been harmed. Patients now able to get efficacious drug treatments in Europe that are not available in the U.S. are becoming aware of the consequences of FDA regulations, but their number is small. Political action by AIDS patients and their advocates has persuaded the FDA to relax restrictions limiting access to promising AIDS treatments before they have satisfied all normal FDA regulations for public use.

The mine safety law that closed down many nonunion mines was passed after active lobbying by both the United Mine Workers Union and the Bituminous Coal Operators Association (which represents the mining firms unionized by the United Mine Workers). Both of these groups faced competition from small mines that were generally staffed by nonunion labor. The costs imposed on these mines by the law were so onerous that many of them were driven out of business.

Allegiance to the political model has been a major deterrent to the development of a body of

---

17. See Sam Peltzman, *Regulation of Pharmaceutical Innovation* (American Enterprise Institute, 1974), pp. 15-16. See also William M. Wardell, Mohammed Hassar, Sadanand N. Anavekar, and Louis Lasagna, "The Rate of Development in New Drugs in the United States, 1963 through 1975," *Clinical Pharmacology and Therapeutics*, Vol. 24, No. 2 (August 1978). For a review of the literature on the effectiveness of the FDA drug regulation procedures, see Ronald W. Hansen, "The Relationship Between Regulation and R&D in the Pharmaceutical Industry: A

Review of Literature and Public Policy Proposals," *The Effectiveness of Medicines in Containing Health Care Costs: Impact of Innovation, Regulation and Quality* (National Pharmaceutical Council, 1982).

18. See David R. Henderson, "Coal Mine Safety Legislation: Safety or Monopoly?," Graduate School of Management, University of Rochester (November 1977).

> **Legislators have an interest in enlarging the role of the state and, as REMMs, they engage in continuous marketing of programs to achieve that end. If crises do not exist they create them, or at least the illusion of crises.**

theory that could explain with reasonable accuracy how the political system operates. Social scientists, especially political scientists, have been aware of the anxiety politicians exhibit to be reelected, and they have usually tacitly assumed that this induces them to behave in accord with the wishes of the majority. But this model of the legislative process is incapable of explaining what actually occurs.

We know that legislators consistently vote for measures that cannot possibly be in the interest of a majority of their constituents.[19] Except Wisconsin (and even there it is doubtful), there surely is no state in the Union where a majority benefits from government sponsorship of a cartel among milk producers. Other examples are tariffs on TV sets, oil import quotas, "voluntary" quotas on foreign automobiles, and punitive tariffs on flat-panel computer screens, to name just a few.

Elected officials who are REMMs sense that they have the opportunity to become entrepreneurs. They have access at relatively low cost to mass advertising via television, radio, newspapers, and magazines. Resourceful politicians also ally themselves with organized groups that get media attention and encourage the organization of new groups. Indeed, now that the general nature of the process and the payoff to such organizations have been perceived, popular fronts have proliferated, each vying for publicity, even to the point of using violence to demonstrate their sincerity.

Individually and collectively, legislators have an interest in enlarging the role of the state and, as REMMs, they engage in continuous marketing of programs to achieve that end. If crises do not exist, they create them, or at least the illusion of crises. Then, they rescue their constituents from disaster with legislation that sacrifices the general welfare to benefit special interests.

The Current Health Care Debate. For example, in recent years members of the Clinton Administration and associated special interest groups have campaigned to create the public impression of a health care crisis and mobilize support for legislation to "reform" the U.S. health care system. The proposed changes would result in massive new regulations and centralization of the system. In so doing, it would transfer substantial control over an additional 14% of the U.S. gross national product to the government, with obvious implications for the power base of the bureaucracy.

Almost as clear, unfortunately, is the import of these changes for the efficiency and quality of U.S. health care. The proposed changes would result in a centralization and cartelization of the health industry in the hands of government and newly proposed private bodies. This is exactly the wrong way to go with this industry. Because the specific knowledge of each case lies in the hands of the doctor and the patient, decision-making in the health care industry, to be effective, must be decentralized and thus kept in the hands of doctor and patient. The proposed centralized process for deciding on patient treatment and care will inevitably result in large declines in the quality of health care. Even ignoring the effects of the centralization, the Administration's original plan to take $150 billion of annual costs (and therefore real resources) out of the system while adding as many as 37 million people to it would reduce the quality and timeliness of future care; it would also create shortages and lead to rationing.

There is a U.S. health care *cost* problem, to be sure; but it does not stem from too little regulation and too few subsidies. Rather, it comes from our third-party insurance system that effectively removes responsibility for the costs from the most important decision-maker—that is, the patient. The key to solving this problem is to impose the financial consequences of their medical decisions on patients through greater use of co-pay insurance with larger deductibles that place first-dollar costs on patients while protecting them against catastrophic illness.

The Political Model in the Private Sector

The political (or perfect agent) model is also widely used by managers of private organizations in managing their employees. Corporate managers often wish to believe that people are perfect agents with no preferences of their own. If there is a problem in part of the organization with a manager who is making the wrong decisions, the problems must come from having a "bad" person in the job. The solution is then to fire the manager and replace him or her with a new person. Tell that person (who is assumed to be a perfect agent) what you want done, and then wait for it to happen.

---

19. See James M. Buchanan and Gordon Tullock, *The Calculus of Consent* (Ann Arbor, Michigan: University of Michigan Press 1965).

In contrast, managers using the REMM model would predict that if the manager has the proper talent and training, it is the organizational structure and incentives that are at the root of the problem. The solution would then be not to fire the manager, but to reform the organizational policies.

Problems in organizations often arise because managers are rewarded for doing things that harm the organization—for example, empire building or maximizing market share at the expense of shareholder value. In compensating managers according to negotiated budgets, many companies effectively induce line managers to negotiate budget targets that are well below the level that would maximize the value of the organization. The managers do this, of course, to ensure they can easily meet the target.

In a related problem, large public corporations also regularly retain and tend to waste large amounts of free cash flow—that is, cash flow in excess of that required to fund all profitable projects of the firm. Spending the cash on acquisitions or other unprofitable projects (undertaken with the aid of unrealistically high forecasts of future profitability) gives management a bigger company to run, thereby increasing their power and prestige in the community. Because managerial pay tends to be positively related to the size of the company, these actions generally increase their compensation as well. In addition, keeping the cash in the firm gives them a cushion for spending during tough times, whether it is economic or not. Retaining the excess cash also makes it easier to avoid closing plants, laying off employees, cutting charitable contributions, and making the other hard choices associated with freeing up underutilized resources. Yet it is important for managers to make these difficult choices so that the resources can be put to higher-valued uses in the rest of society.[20]

IN CLOSING

We argue that the explanatory power of REMM, the resourceful, evaluative, maximizing model of human behavior, dominates that of all the other models summarized here. To be sure, each of the other models captures an important aspect of behavior, while failing in other respects. REMM incorporates the best of each of these models.

From the economic model, REMM takes the assumption that people are resourceful, self-interested maximizers, but rejects the notion that they are interested only in money income or wealth.

From the psychological model, REMM takes the assumption that the income elasticity of demand for various goods has certain regularities the world over. Nevertheless, in taking on this modified notion of a hierarchy of needs, it does not violate the principle of substitution by assuming people have "needs."

From the sociological model, REMM takes the assumption that "society" imposes costs on people for violating social norms, which in turn affect behavior; but it also assumes that individuals will depart from such norms if the benefits are sufficiently great. Indeed, this is how social change takes place.

From the political model, REMM takes the assumption that people have the capacity for altruism. They care about others and take their interests into account while maximizing their own welfare. REMM rejects, however, the notion that people are perfect agents.

In using REMM, detail must be added (as we have done implicitly in the examples above) to tailor the model to serve as a decision guide in specific circumstances. We must specify more about people's tastes and preferences that are relevant to the issue at hand—for example, by making explicit assumptions that people have a positive rate of discount for future as opposed to present goods and that they value leisure as well as intangibles such as honor, companionship, and self-realization. Finally, combining these assumptions with knowledge of the opportunity set from which people are choosing in any situation (that is, the rates at which people can trade off or substitute among various goods) leads to a powerfully predictive model.

REMM is the basic building block that has led to the development of a more or less unified body of theory in the social sciences. For example, some economists, like recent Nobel laureate Gary Becker, have applied REMM in fields previously reserved to sociologists such as discrimination, crime, marriage,

---

20. See the following articles by Michael C. Jensen, "The Agency Costs of Free Cash Flow: Corporate Finance and Takeovers," *American Economic Review*, Vol. 76, No. 2 (May 1986); "Takeovers: Their Causes and Consequences," *Journal of Economic Perspectives*, Vol. 2, No. 1 (Winter 1988), pp. 21-48; "Eclipse of the Public Corporation," *Harvard Business Review*, Vol. 89, No. 5 (September-October 1989), pp. 61-74; and Larry Lang, Annette Poulsen, René Stulz, "Asset Sales, Firm Performance, and the Agency Costs of Managerial Discretion," *Journal of Financial Economics* (1994) and the references therein.

and the family.[21] Political scientists in company with economists have also employed utility-maximizing models of political behavior to explain voter behavior and the behavior of regulators and bureaucrats.[22] Still others are using REMM to explain organizational problems inside firms.[23]

For all its diversity, this growing body of research has one common message: Whether they are politicians, managers, academics, professionals, philanthropists, or factory workers, individuals are resourceful, evaluative maximizers. They respond creatively to the opportunities the environment presents to them, and they work to loosen constraints that prevent them from doing what they wish to do. They care about not only money, but almost everything—respect, honor, power, love, and the welfare of others. The challenge for our society, and for all organizations in it, is to establish rules of the game and educational procedures that tap and direct the creative energy of REMMs in ways that increase the effective use of our scarce resources.

REMMs are everywhere.

21. See Gary Becker, "A Theory of Marriage: Part 1," *Journal of Political Economy*, Vol. 82 (July/August, 1973); and "Crime and Punishment: An Economic Approach," *Journal of Political Economy*, Vol. 76 (March/April, 1968)

22. For discussions of political choice, see Anthony Downs, *An Economic Theory of Democracy* (New York: Harper & Row, 1957); and James M. Buchanan and Gordon Tullock, *The Calculus of Consent* (Ann Arbor, Michigan: University of Michigan Press, 1965). For an analysis of bureaucracies, see William A. Niskanan, Jr., *Bureaucracy and Representative Government* (Aldine-Atherton, Inc., 1971).

23. For discussions of organizational problems, see Armen Alchian and Harold Demsetz, "Production, Information Costs, and Economic Organization," *American Economic Review*, Vol. LXII, No. 5 (1972), pp. 77-79; Kenneth J. Arrow, "Control in Large Organizations," *Essays in the Theory of Risk-Bearing* (Markham Publishing Co., 1971); Michael C. Jensen and William H. Meckling, "Theory of the Firm: Managerial Behavior, Agency Costs and Ownership Structure," *Journal of Financial Economics*, Vol. 4, No. 4 (October 1976); Michael C. Jensen and William H. Meckling, "Specific and General Knowledge and Organizational Structure," in *Contract Economics*, Lars Werm and Hans Wijkander, eds. (Blackwell, Oxford, 1992; Oliver E. Williamson, *Corporate Control and Business Behavior* (Prentice-Hall, 1970); and Paul Milgrom and John Roberts, *Economics, Organization, and Management* (Prentice Hall, 1992).

THE THEORY OF STOCK MARKET EFFICIENCY: ACCOMPLISHMENTS AND LIMITATIONS

by Ray Ball,
University of Rochester*

T hirty years have passed since Eugene Fama introduced the idea of an "efficient" stock market to the financial economics literature, and it continues to stimulate both insight and controversy. Put simply, the idea is that investors compete so fiercely in using public information that they bid away its value for earning additional returns. In so doing, they quickly incorporate all publicly available information into prices.

Harvard economist Benjamin Friedman has dismissed the idea as a "credo"—a statement of faith, not scientific research.[1] Warren Buffett, whose legendary investment performance and philosophy have caused some soul-searching among efficient markets theorists, has described the stock market as "a slough of fear and greed untethered to corporate realities."[2] In my view, the concept of efficient stock markets is one of the most important ideas in economics.

In the theory of stock market efficiency, public information that has not been fully reflected in stock prices is like gold lying in the streets; reports of either are treated with equal skepticism. Take the case of a company reporting a $3 increase in annual EPS when the consensus forecast at the beginning of that year was a $2 increase. How should such information, which is essentially "free" for investors to acquire the moment it is placed in the public domain, affect the company's stock price?

In an efficient market, the expected part of the earnings increase ($2 of the $3, in this case) should already be reflected in the price, and investors should trade on the new information (the extra $1, or the earnings "surprise") until all the gains from so doing are competed away. The stock price adjustment to the information should be rapid (if not "instantaneous"), and the new price should make the stock a "fair game"—one which promises new investors a normal rate of return.

In the mid-1960s, while working together at the University of Chicago, Phil Brown and I set out to test these propositions by exploring how the stock market actually responds to announcements of annual earnings. We examined some 2300 annual earnings reports by about 300 New York Stock Exchange companies over the nine-year period 1956-1964. After classifying each of the 2300 reports as containing either "good news" or "bad news" based on past earnings, we calculated the stock returns to an investor holding each of the two groups of companies from one year before to six months after the announcement.

What we found provided stronger support for the theory than practitioners in finance and accounting—not to mention most of our academic colleagues—had expected. The results of our study,[3] which are summarized graphically in Figure 1, suggested that the market had already anticipated roughly 80% of the "surprise" component in annual earnings by the time the earnings were announced. There was some further upward "drift" following the announcements of earnings increases and small downward movements following decreases. But, over the entire six-month period after the announce-

---

*This article draws heavily on my earlier article, "On the Development, Accomplishments and Limitations of the Theory of Stock Market Efficiency," *Managerial Finance* 20 (1994, issue no. 2/3), pp. 3-48. Permission from the editor and publisher is gratefully acknowledged.

1. Cited in R. Thaler, ed., *Advances in Behavioral Finance* (New York: Russell Sage Foundation, 1993), p. 213.

2. *The New York Times*, February 18, 1995, p. 35.

3. R. Ball and P. Brown, "An Empirical Evaluation of Accounting Income Numbers," *Journal of Accounting Research* 6 (1968), pp. 159-178.

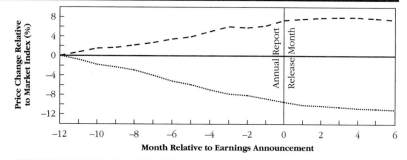

FIGURE 1
STOCK PRICE CHANGES IN
RELATION TO ANNUAL
EARNINGS
ANNOUNCEMENTS*

- - EPS Increases
— Market Index
······ EPS Decreases

*Stock prices rise during the year before firms announce EPS increases as information flows into the market. Prices also fall in advance of EPS decreases. There is some price reaction at the time of the announcement. The graph shows price movements for the average firm. Firms with larger EPS changes tend to experience larger price movements. Source: Ball and Brown (1968).

ments, investor returns from holding each of the two groups of firms (those with unexpected EPS increases and those with decreases) would have been close to zero. Thus, prices had incorporated the information released in annual earnings reports in a way that virtually eliminated future opportunities to profit from that news. (And, since publication of our study in 1968, these results have been replicated by many other studies of different time periods in 15 different countries.)

The impact of the simple idea of market efficiency has been extensive and enduring. Stimulated in large part by a new research design known as the "event study" (introduced in a 1969 study by Fama, Fisher, Jensen, and Roll that I discuss later), a large body of empirical research in the 1970s provided consistent evidence of the stock market's ability to process information in a rational, in some cases ingenious, fashion. This research so transformed our view of stock markets that contemporary observers cannot begin to appreciate the general suspicion of and ignorance about stock markets that prevailed 30 years ago.

At the same time it was expanding our knowledge of how the stock market processes information, the early work on market efficiency helped to establish a receptive climate for three other major developments in financial theory: the Miller-Modigliani theories of corporate financial policy; the Sharpe-Lintner Capital Asset Pricing Model (CAPM); and the Black-Scholes option pricing model. Each of these theoretical developments has in turn affected financial practice in important ways. The CAPM, for example, is widely used today both by institutional investors (in establishing their asset allocation and performance measurement criteria) and industrial corporations (in setting their investment rate-of-return targets). The Black-Scholes model is one of the most popular, if not the dominant, procedure for valuing stock options, as well as many other derivatives and so-called "contingent claims." And widespread practices such as indexing, performance measurement, and asset securitization are all unthinkable without the idea of well-functioning security markets.

Our current understanding of how information is incorporated into stock prices has also influenced corporate disclosure policy. For example, it is now common for corporations to release between two and six different earnings numbers (for example, those including and excluding earnings from businesses that were sold during the period, both before and after the effects of accounting method changes). Whereas the pre-efficiency mentality of accountants (and the SEC) was to distrust investors' judgment and thus to choose *the* earnings number for them, the dominant corporate practice today, with the blessing of the SEC, is to present and then leave it to users to digest the full range of information.

In short, the theoretical developments of the '60s and '70s have helped transform the practice of finance. And, in addition to these theoretical and practical achievements, the early empirical testing of market efficiency coincided with the more general emergence of interest in and respect for free markets that began in the 1970s, first among economists and then later among politicians. Indeed, the market efficiency literature has helped pave the way for what has proved to be a worldwide "liberalization" of financial and other markets.

Despite its insights and accomplishments, however, the theory of efficient markets has obvious limitations. For example, it treats information as a commodity that means the same thing to all investors. It also assumes—with potentially serious consequences, in my view—that information is *costlessly* incorporated into prices. In reality, of course, investors interpret events differently; they face considerable uncertainty about why others are trading; and, especially in the case of smaller firms, they face high costs (as a percentage of firm value) in acquiring and processing information. Given these limitations, it is not surprising that researchers soon began to accumulate evidence that appeared to contradict the theory. Whether the existence of such "anomalous" findings indicates a fatal flaw in the theory—or, more likely, the value of incorporating greater realism—only time and more research will tell.

My aim in this article is to provide an admittedly somewhat personal perspective on the accomplishments and limitations of the theory, and to offer a few suggestions about how the theory might be modified to explain some of the contradictory evidence. Briefly put, my view is this: the theory of efficient markets was an audacious and welcome change from the comparative ignorance about stock market behavior that preceded it; and despite its now-obvious theoretical and empirical flaws, it has profoundly influenced both the theory and practice of finance.

THE IDEA THAT MARKETS ARE "EFFICIENT"

When Phil Brown and I started the research for our 1968 paper, academics in finance and economics conducted little or no research on stock prices, and we were strongly discouraged by highly skeptical colleagues. The prevailing view among academic economists, even at the University of Chicago, was that the stock market was not a proper subject of serious study. While part of the skepticism about our research stemmed from economists' reservations about the way accountants calculate earnings, much more could be traced to a deep suspicion of stock markets. Indeed, the notion of modelling the stock market *in rational economic terms* was academic heresy at the time.

What little research had been conducted on stock prices up to this point had been performed for the most part by statisticians. The scant empirical literature that preceded the efficient market hypothesis modelled price behavior in statistical, not economic, terms. Successive daily stock price changes seemed for the most part "independent"; that is, they displayed no discernible trends or patterns that could be exploited by investors. Prices on any given day appeared likely to go up or down with roughly equal probability. Lacking an economic explanation for this result, researchers described it in statistical language as the "random walk hypothesis."

Moreover, it was a statistician at the University of Chicago, Harry Roberts, who first saw the potential import for economics of the "random walk" literature. In an important paper published in 1959, Roberts mused, "Perhaps the traditional academic suspicion about the stock market as an object of scholarly research will be overcome." And, as he went on to say,

...there is a plausible rationale [for the random walk model]. If the stock market behaved like a mechanically imperfect roulette wheel, people would notice the imperfections and, by acting on them, remove them. This rationale is appealing, if for no other reason than its value as counterweight to the popular view of stock market "irrationality," but it is obviously incomplete.[4]

Among financial economists and other students of the stock market, statistical dependence in returns came to be viewed as valuable information just sitting there in the public domain, that is, as so much gold in the streets. Any predictable trends in prices over time would mean that knowledge of past returns (which is essentially costless to acquire) could be used to predict future returns. In short, dependence across time was viewed as inconsistent with rational behavior in competitive markets and thus as evidence of what later became known as "market inefficiency."[5]

The first use of the term "efficient market" appeared in a 1965 paper by Eugene Fama, who defined it as:

---

4. H.V. Roberts, "Stock Market 'Patterns' and Financial Analysis: Methodological Suggestions," *Journal of Finance* 14 (1959), p. 7.

5. For a review of the random walk literature and precedents, see E.F. Fama, "Efficient Capital Markets: A Review of Theory and Empirical Work," *Journal of Finance* 25 (1970), 383-417.

a market where there are large numbers of rational, profit-maximizers actively competing, with each trying to predict future market values of individual securities, and where important current information is almost freely available to all participants...

"In an efficient market," Fama argued,

on the average, competition will cause the full effects of new information on intrinsic values to be reflected "instantaneously" in actual prices.[6]

The economics underlying this model are very simple. Publicly-available information by definition is accessible to all investors at zero cost. While earnings reports, for example, are costly for firms to produce, once made public they are nearly costless to obtain (though not necessarily costless to interpret, as I discuss later). And since revenue and cost are equated in competitive equilibrium, the implication of stock market efficiency is that if the cost of reproducing public information is zero, then so are the expected gains. Security prices should therefore adjust to information as soon as (if not before) it becomes publicly available. Ideas don't come much simpler in economics.

ACCOMPLISHMENTS OF THE THEORY OF STOCK MARKET EFFICIENCY

It is difficult to trace the influence of ideas because their effects range from the direct and concrete (such as the effects on financial practice I noted earlier) to the more subtle and abstract (for example, their influence on how we think about issues, and on the concepts and language we use). To gain some appreciation of how thoroughly the research on market efficiency has changed our thinking about stock markets, imagine the mindset of an observer of stock markets prior to the research that began in the late '60s. Ordinarily we view the market's reaction to information through the lens of chronological time. Reading the daily financial press, for example, we observe the market's response at a single point in time to what is often a bewildering variety of events and circumstances affecting compa-

nies' values. There are announcements of earnings and dividend, new promotional campaigns, labor disputes, staff retrenchments, new debt and equity issues, management changes, proxy contests, asset write-offs, bond rating changes, and changes in interest rates, money supply figures, and GDP data. Thus, what we see with the unaided eye are price reactions to many events at once, without seeing the underlying pattern for any one of them.

In 1969, however, a study of the stock market reaction to stock splits by Eugena Fama, Lawrence Fisher, Michael Jensen, and Richard Roll (hereafter "FFJR") introduced the concept of "event time," which may well have been the single most important breakthrough in our understanding of how stock prices respond to new information.[7] In attempting to isolate the market's reaction to stock splits (by eliminating the surrounding "noise" of other events), FFJR took many instances of the same event occurring in many different companies at different times, and "standardized" them all in terms of a single "event" date (designated in the literature as "t=0"). In so doing, they were able to provide an "event-time" view of the market's reaction of the kind presented in Figure 2.

What does Figure 2 tell us? Conventional wisdom held then, as it does today, that stock splits are good news for investors (and, although why stock splits should be good news has long been something of a puzzle to economists, FFJR reported a plausible reason in their 1969 study: namely, 72% of the splitting firms in their research sample announced dividend increases above the NYSE average in the year *after* the split). What the conventional wisdom may not have predicted, however, but what emerges in Figure 2, is the speed with which investors restore the market to its equilibrium or "fair game" condition after the announcement (as revealed by the immediate flattening of the line after t=0).

Thus, where we had previously seen only the chaos of daily stock price movements, FFJR's research design enabled us to see order. And the large empirical literature on market efficiency that came after FFJR both refined their "event study" technique and accumulated impressive evidence—unimaginable before the late '60s—that stock prices respond in apparently ingenious ways to information.[8] One

---

6. E.F. Fama, "Random Walks in Stock Market Prices," *Financial Analysts Journal*, September-October (1965), p.4.

7. E.F. Fama, L. Fisher, M.C. Jensen and R. Roll, "The Adjustment of Stock Prices to New Information," *International Economic Review* 10 (1969), 1-21.

8. For surveys with detailed analysis of individual studies and their findings, see Fama (1970), cited earlier; E.F. Fama, "Efficient Capital Markets: II," *Journal of Finance* 46 (1991), 1575-1617; and S.F. LeRoy, "Efficient Capital Markets and Martingales," *Journal of Economic Literature* 27 (1989), 1583-1621.

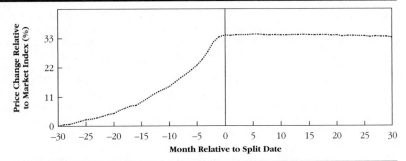

FIGURE 2
STOCK PRICE CHANGES
IN RELATION TO
STOCK SPLITS*

*Stock prices rise during the 30 months before stock splits. Because all the information in the split is public knowledge bt the time it occurs, the stock price reaction to the split is complete by "month 0." The graph shows price movements for the average firm. Firms with larger splits tend to experience larger price movements. Source: FFJR (1969).

surprising and illuminating example: announcements of new public stock offerings are associated with an immediate 3% average stock price reduction. The prevailing explanation of this negative market response is as follows: Investors recognize that managers, as representatives of existing shareholders, are more likely to issue new stock (rather than debt) when they think the company is overvalued; hence announcements of new stock offerings are interpreted, at least in the average case, as conveying managers' private assessment of the firm's prospects relative to its current valuation.[9] Another example worth noting (in part for its touch of the bizarre): unexpected CEO deaths are associated with price *decreases* in the case of professional managers, as we might expect in an economy where most companies are well run. But, in the case of those CEOs who are also the founders, death notices are accompanied by price *increases*, with the implication that many founders tend to hang on to their companies too long.[10]

There was one other notable factor contributing to the remarkable successes of efficient markets theory in the late 1960s and early 1970s. At that time, the stock market was one of the few areas in which a large amount of data could be used to test a simple competitive economic theory. And the data were unusually plentiful. The University of Chicago's

Center for Research in Securities Prices (CRSP), which was established (with exceptional foresight) by James H. Lorie in 1960, provided comprehensive data on the universe of all NYSE stocks going back to 1926. Such a rich source of data—which, rare for the time, came in machine-readable form and were essentially error-free—was a luxury almost unheard-of among economists.

Influencing the Climate for Other Financial Economic Theories

Together, then, the new theory and evidence on market efficiency demonstrated to economists for the first time that share price behavior could be viewed as a rational economic phenomenon. And this development in turn helped set the stage for other breakthroughs.

Two other broad areas of financial-economic enquiry were launched around the same time as efficient market theory. First were the "dividend" and "capital structure" irrelevance propositions formulated by Merton Miller and Franco Modigliani (first at Carnegie Mellon, later at the University of Chicago) and presented in papers published in 1958 and 1961.[11] Soon after came the capital asset pricing model (CAPM), which was developed separately by William Sharpe (at Stanford in a 1964 paper) and

---

9. For a nice summary of how the market responds to new securities issues, see C.W. Smith, "Raising Capital: Theory and Evidence," *Midland Corporate Finance Journal*, Vol. 4 No. 1 (Spring 1986), 6-22. This article was based in turn on "Investment Banking and the Capital Acquisition Process," *Journal of Financial Economics*, Vol. 15 (1986), pp. 3-29.

10. W.B. Johnson, R.P. Magee, N.J. Nagarajan, and H.A. Newman, "An Analysis of the Stock Price Reaction to Sudden Executive Deaths," *Journal of Accounting and Economics* 7 (1985), 151-174.

11. F. Modigliani and M.H. Miller, "The Cost of Capital, Corporation Finance, and The Theory of Investment," *American Economic Review* 48 (1958), 261-297; and M.H. Miller and F. Modigliani, "Dividend Policy, Growth and the Valuation of Shares," *Journal of Business* 34 (1961), 411-433.

Whether the existence of such "anomalous" findings indicates a fatal flaw in the theory—or, more likely, the value of incorporating greater realism—only time and more research will tell.

John Lintner (at Harvard in 1965).[12] The consistent evidence of market efficiency offered strong support for these concepts that shared similar assumptions about the working of financial markets. Indeed, without the impressive body of empirical research on efficiency as background, it is not clear that the equilibrium-based reasoning of the Sharpe-Lintner CAPM (and later the Black-Scholes option pricing model, introduced in 1973) would have been so well and so quickly received.[13] Development of the CAPM (as I discuss later) was particularly important for subsequent research on market efficiency because it provided researchers with a method of estimating investors' "expected" returns—the returns passive investors would otherwise have earned in the absence of the information being tested.

A considerable body of knowledge on corporate capital structure has also been built on the work of Miller and Modigliani. The arbitrage-based arguments M&M used to buttress their "irrelevance propositions" were a novelty in corporate finance. They were developed over approximately the same period that Roberts and Fama were formulating their ideas on efficiency, and they relied in part on the same basic reasoning of competitive economic theory underlying market efficiency. Among other practical contributions, M&M's then revolutionary thinking on capital structure appears to have supplied an important part of the logic for the leveraged restructurings of the 1980s.[14] As in the case of the CAPM, finance scholars were more receptive to the M&M propositions in large part because of their consistency with the closely-related area of efficient markets.

Summing Up

Encouraged, then, by its initial accomplishments and reinforced by other theoretical developments like the CAPM, research on market efficiency spread rapidly across the globe, with results that provided remarkably consistent support for the theory. This research had an enduring impact on our view of stock markets, of financial markets generally, and perhaps of markets of all kinds. Because this

evidence tended to contradict prior assumptions, which were based on prejudice and casual observation rather than on systematic research, academic attention was quickly drawn to it. In a surprisingly short time, academic attitudes toward stock markets had shifted from one extreme to the other, from suspicion to almost reverence.

LIMITATIONS IN THE THEORY OF EFFICIENT MARKETS

It was not long, however, before researchers began to report evidence that appeared to contradict the theory. But, as I argue below, finance scholars should not have been completely surprised by such evidence. The theory of efficient markets has not influenced theory and practice because it is free of defects. Its influence has been due to the insights it provides, not those it fails to provide. The cup remains half full, even though it is half empty.

I now discuss a number of limitations of the theory that I have divided into three overlapping categories: (1) the theory's failure to explain certain aspects of share price behavior, referred to in the literature as "anomalies"; (2) defects in efficiency as a model of markets; and (3) problems in testing the efficiency model.

Empirical Anomalies: Problems in Fitting the Theory to the Data

No theory can explain all the data with which it is confronted, especially when the data are as abundant as stock prices. There is now a large body of anomalous evidence that at least appears to contradict market efficiency. The list of such "anomalies" includes:

■ **Price Overreactions.** There is evidence that the prices of individual stocks overreact to information and then undergo "corrections." The resulting negative correlations in prices appear to create profit opportunities for "contrarian" trading strategies.[15]

■ **Excess Volatility.** Robert Shiller, among others, has argued that the stock market in general overreacts to

12. W.F. Sharpe, "Capital Asset Prices: A Theory of Market Equilibrium under Conditions of Risk," *Journal of Finance* 19 (1964), 425-442; and J. Lintner, "The Valuation of Risk Assets and the Selection of Risky Investments in Stock Portfolios and Capital Budgets," *Review of Economics and Statistics* 47 (1965), 13-37.

13. Teachers and researchers made frequent reference to the Sharpe-Lintner model well before it was formally tested (by Black, Jensen, and Scholes in 1972 and Fama and MacBeth in 1973), relying in part on the strong evidence of market efficiency and on the perceived overlapping of the two ideas.

14. See M.H. Miller, "The Modigliani-Miller Propositions Thirty Years After," *Journal of Applied Corporate Finance*, Vol. 2 No. 1, (Spring 1989).

15. W.F.M. De Bondt, and R.H. Thaler, "Does the Stock Market Overreact?, *Journal of Finance*, (1985), 793-805; and W.F.M. De Bondt and R.H. Thaler," "Further Evidence on Investor Overreaction and Stock Market Seasonality," *Journal of Finance* 42, 1987, 557-581.

events because of investors' pursuit of fads and other herd-like behavior. In support of his argument, he presents evidence suggesting that the volatility of stock prices is much too large to be explained by the volatility of dividends.[16]

■ **Price Underreactions to Earnings.** In seeming contradiction of the the tendency of prices to overreact to information in general, research indicates that prices *underreact* to quarterly earnings reports, thus lending support for "earnings momentum" strategies.[17]

■ **The Failure of CAPM to Explain Returns.** The Capital Asset Pricing Model, as mentioned, has provided the primary means for measuring investors' expected returns; indeed, it was the workhorse for calculating discount rates for an entire generation of practitioners as well as researchers. But evidence that high-beta stocks do not earn higher returns than low-beta stocks has led some to pronounce the horse dead.[18] (But recent research suggests that announcements of the death of beta may be premature.)[19]

■ **The Explanatory Power of Non-CAPM Factors.** Stocks with (1) small capitalization, (2) low market-to-book ratios, (3) high-dividend yields, and (4) low P/E ratios tend to outperform their expected returns (as estimated by the CAPM), thus providing justification for yield-tilted, small-cap, and other popular investment strategies.

■ **Seasonal Patterns.** Researchers have provided evidence of seasonal patterns of hourly, daily, monthly, and quarterly duration. Particularly puzzling is the "weekend effect": the tendency of stock returns to be negative over the period from Friday's close to Monday's opening. Such seasonals could lend support to technical analysts' claims to outperform market averages.

As I argue below, however, it is difficult to tell whether such anomalies should be attributed to defects in markets themselves, to flaws in "market efficiency" as a way of thinking about competitive markets, or to problems with the research itself.

Defects in "Efficiency" as a Model of Stock Markets

Failure to Incorporate Information Acquisition and Processing Costs. One of the most important explanations of these anomalies is likely to be the neglected role of information costs. Information costs are neither new to economists nor inconsistent with competitive markets. Nevertheless, the costs of acquiring and processing information have received scant attention in the theory and empirical research on stock market efficiency.

The first "event studies" such as the FFJR study of stock splits and the Ball-Brown study of annual earnings reports investigated relatively simple cases in which information is widely disseminated in the financial press and on the wire services to analysts and other investors. The cost to individual investors of acquiring such public information (as opposed to the cost of producing that same information prior to disclosure) was assumed to be negligible. The information was also assumed to be simple to use, with negligible processing (or interpretation) costs.

But what about those academic research designs that simulate trading strategies that in fact have substantial information acquisition and processing costs? In such cases, the abnormal returns reported by the research could be significantly overstated. Consider the following:

1. If 1,000 professors of finance worldwide annually incur costs of $50,000 each (including salary, computer costs, and overhead) in searching for anomalies, the expected return from their discovery of pricing errors in the market could be as much as 5% per year (or $50 million) on a $1 billion portfolio. And, if they have been searching for 20 years, the expected return from producing such *private* information could be many times larger.

2. But, if the expected returns from such strategies are this large, why have some researchers published their anomalous evidence? Why have they not instead used that information for private gain?

3. More generally, what are the expected gains from producing and trading on private information?

4. What is the meaning of gains from a trading rule that is simulated using *historical* data together with *modern* computing and statistical techniques? (Does this differ from, say, the simulated gains from owning a helicopter gunship during the Middle Ages?)

16. R.J. Shiller, "Do Stock Prices Move Too Much to Be Justified by Subsequent Changes in Dividends?," *American Economic Review* 71, (1981a), 421-436.

17. V.L. Bernard and J. Thomas, "Evidence That Stock Prices Do Not Fully Reflect the Implications of Current Earnings for Future Earnings," *Journal of Accounting and Economics* 13 (1990), 305-340.

18. For a survey, see M. Reinganum, "The Collapse of the Efficient Market Hypothesis: A Look at the Empirical Anomalies of the 1980s," *Selected Readings in Investment Management* (Institutional Investor, 1988).

19. For a defense of beta, see S.P. Kothari and J. Shanken in this issue.

5. If an analyst forecasts the earnings of 25 stocks each quarter at an annual cost of $200,000 (including salary and overhead), then the average cost of a forecast is $2,000. This is one ten-thousandth of 1% of the market value of a $2 billion firm. It is one tenth of 1% of the market value of $2 million of stock in the firm held by clients. If we further assume that the gains from forecasting are approximately equal to the costs, can we reliably detect such a low number in stock rates of return?

We have no well-developed answers to such questions. To date, and for obvious reasons, researchers have tended to ignore information costs and have relied on cases of publicly-disclosed information (whose cost we somewhat arbitrarily define as zero) in testing market efficiency.

The direction of the bias from ignoring information costs is consistent with the anomalies evidence. For example, information costs are a likely candidate for explaining the small-firm effect, the tendency of small-cap stocks to produce higher returns. Such firms tend to have small analyst followings, presumably because the cost of acquiring and processing information is large relative to the amounts invested in them. Investors may rationally require higher returns (than those predicted by the CAPM) to compensate for their higher information costs (as a percentage of value).

But little more can be said without knowing more about the size of such information processing and acquisition costs, and how such costs are likely to affect actual (pre-cost) expected returns. Moreover, there can be significant differences *among* investors in the information they possess, in the extent of their efforts to seek information, and in their ability to process it. Although the CAPM is silent on this issue, it would be logical to expect more sophisticated, better-informed, and more active investors to earn higher returns. The question, however, is: How much higher? For example, what is the predicted rate of return in a competitive market for an investor like Warren Buffett who sits on the corporate board, is a close friend of the CEO, and has a voice in major corporate decisions? Much of Buffett's success may be attributed to his ability to reduce the information (and "agency") costs that confront ordinary passive investors. Lower information costs could in turn be viewed as reducing

Buffett's perceived risks and required rates of return, thus making stocks more valuable to him than to ordinary investors.

Heterogeneous Information and Beliefs. This brings us to another, closely related deficiency of efficient markets theory—one which stems from its "mechanical" characterization of investors as homogeneous, wholly objective, information-processing machines. Investor sentiment and confidence play no role, and publicly available information is assumed to have the same implications for all. In reality, of course, individual investors can differ greatly in their beliefs, and a single piece of information—say, IBM's latest earnings report—may be interpreted quite differently by different investors.

The assumption of homogeneous investors was understandable at the time the theory was developed. For one thing, it allowed researchers to demonstrate to highly skeptical readers that stock prices do respond to information, and in rational ways. But there were other grounds for using such a clearly unrealistic assumption. As the great Austrian economist F. A. Hayek argued in his 1945 classic, "The Use of Knowledge in Society,"[20] market prices incorporate information that is not—and perhaps cannot—be fully known by any individual. For this reason, markets are likely to be more rational in viewing information than the individual investors who comprise them. Indeed, that is the beauty of markets.

But this does not mean markets are infallible. (To paraphrase Churchill on democracy, it's not that markets are perfect in allocating resources; it's just that all other systems are so much worse.) For all their virtues, markets cannot fully overcome the inevitable limits of individual knowledge—limits that, under certain circumstances, can have pronounced effects on market behavior.

To see how such limits might affect markets, consider that the trading decisions of individual investors are based not only on the individual's information about a given stock or commodity, but also on that individual's beliefs about the information on which *other investors* base their trading. And because an investor possessing a piece of information or holding a belief about the future cannot know with certainty the extent to which that information or belief is shared by others, he does not know the

20. *American Economic Review* 35 (1945), 519-30.

extent to which the information is already reflected in prices.

One plausible way of interpreting episodes of high turnover and rapid price changes, such as the stock market crash of 1987, is that investors' costs of becoming quickly informed about the motives for others' trades can become extraordinarily high. Under such conditions of extreme uncertainty, the "mechanistic" model of efficiency, with its assumptions of zero information costs and homogeneous investors, clearly breaks down. In such cases, investors' required rates of return can be seen as rising sharply in response to the sudden surge in price volatility, and the general uncertainty is resolved only gradually over time (in part through the commentary of market analysts and others whose economic role efficient markets theory has largely ignored).

A central question for finance theory, then, is whether events such as the crash of '87 are unambiguous evidence of market irrationality. Are we forced to conclude, along with Keynes (and the new "behaviorialist" school of thought in finance), that the market is a game of musical chairs in which "animal spirits" regularly prevail over reason? Or can such episodes plausibly be described by Hayekian models in which *rational* individuals with different information confront extreme uncertainty?

Expanding efficient markets theory to accommodate information costs and differences among investors may help us decide this issue. For, in addition to the basic uncertainty that attends all business activity, differences among investors' information and beliefs are an added source of uncertainty and hence information costs; and, in cases where such costs are high, investors may expect to earn significantly higher returns.

A Brief Digression on the Role of Security Analysts. As mentioned above, efficient markets theory has virtually nothing to say about the economic role of security analysts and public commentary. The theory's silence on security analysts has even led many academics to view them as redundant.

What do stock analysts do? Besides talking to management on a regular basis, they pay close attention to economic events affecting the companies they follow, and to the accompanying market reactions. They also talk to large investors about their reasons for buying or selling and so attempt to gauge "investor sentiment." In so doing, analysts can be viewed as reducing investor uncertainty about the information and trading motives of *other* investors.

For example, analysts' earnings forecasts function as estimates of the information about near-term profitability that has already been built into current prices. The existence of such forecasts enables investors to compare their own private forecasts against what amounts to a public consensus. And by reducing one source of investors' uncertainty—namely, about why others are trading—securities analysts reduce information costs and raise the market value of publicly traded companies. Media commentary on markets can be viewed as playing a similar role.

Failure to Consider Transactions Costs. Besides assuming zero information costs and homogeneous investors, early versions of efficient markets theory also assumed that the markets themselves are costless to operate. But if stock markets are large-scale, high-turnover institutions whose primary purpose is to minimize the transactions costs associated with helping firms raise capital, they have not succeeded in *eliminating* such costs.

Having said this, it is not clear what role transactions costs play in setting stock prices. In a paper published in 1978, Michael Jensen argued that an efficient market can only be expected to adjust prices within limits defined by the cost of trading.[21] According to this view, for example, if transactions costs are 1%, an abnormal return to a trading strategy of up to 1% would be considered within the bounds of efficiency. It could not be exploited for profit *net of costs.*

This view makes sense to traders, but it has several shortcomings from a broader economic perspective. First, there must exist some level of transactions costs at which we are unwilling to call a market "efficient." If transactions costs were extremely large, there would be few opportunities to profit from price errors, net of costs. Nevertheless, it makes little sense to describe a market with extremely large costs of trading and thus extremely large price errors as "efficient."

Second, although transactions costs of x% may be consistent with price *errors* of ±x%, they are not consistent with price *biases* of that size. Since most

---

21. M.C. Jensen, "Some Anomalous Evidence Regarding Market Efficiency," *Journal of Financial Economics* 6 (1978), p. 96.

"event studies" and related efficiency tests study average returns, the pricing errors due to transactions costs should net to zero over a broad sample of trades; and thus transactions costs are not obviously relevant to interpreting the results of the studies.

Third, because transactions costs vary across investors, defining efficiency in terms of transactions costs can produce as many definitions as there are investors. Whose transactions costs are to be used in judging *the market* to be efficient? A possible solution might be to define efficiency in terms of the lowest-cost trader. But, because some specialists and institutional investors face transactions costs as low as one tenth of one percent, this approach can degenerate into ignoring transactions costs entirely. Thus, the role of transactions costs in the theory of market efficiency remains largely unresolved.

Market Microstructure Effects. A closely-related issue is the effect of the actual market mechanism on transacted prices, known in the literature as market "microstructure" effects. Researchers typically assume that trades could be executed at the closing prices recorded in data files such as CRSP's. These price estimates, however, have a margin of error that is as large as their quoted spreads, which run about 3% for the average NYSE-AMEX stock (and average close to 6% for NYSE-AMEX stocks with prices less than $5). To compound the problem, investors cannot always execute at quoted spreads because of illiquidity.

Such market microstructure effects can be quite large relative to the size of the short-term abnormal returns reported by many event studies. Consider the "turn of the year" or "January" effect—the widely-recognized tendency of stocks (particularly low-price stocks) to produce large returns in the first trading days of the calendar year. A 1989 study by Donald Keim demonstrates that this effect can be explained largely by a pronounced (if unexplained) tendency of stocks to trade near the bid at the end of the year and then move toward the ask at the beginning.[22]

Similar microstructure effects may well also be exaggerating the size of the short-term price reversals, the seasonal patterns in daily or weekly returns,

and even the abnormal longer-term returns reported in the anomalies literature. Such effects are especially likely to influence the findings of research on low-price stocks. In 1985, for example, Werner DeBondt and Richard Thaler published a study reporting very large gains from a contrarian strategy of buying stocks immediately after large percentage declines and holding them for five years.[23] In a study published this past year, however, two of my Rochester colleagues and I discovered that DeBondt and Thaler's results were distorted by some very large percentage gains on some very low-priced stocks. One stock earned 3500% after trading at $1/16 (which is half of $1/8, the minimum increment in which NYSE stocks are typically quoted). We also found that adjustments of $1/8 in the prices of their "loser" stocks would have reduced the five-year returns of this contrarian strategy by 2500 basis points.[24]

Like transactions costs, microstructure or trading-mechanism effects present the researcher with a dilemma. Trading mechanisms certainly are not costless to operate, and thus the prices at which trades are transacted are likely to be affected in systematic ways by institutional arrangements. This seems particularly likely for small-capitalization and low-price stocks, and for stocks and stock exchanges with low turnover. But, unlike transactions costs, it seems unreasonable to interpret price behavior caused by the trading mechanism as evidence of market inefficiency, because recorded prices are not those at which the simulated trading strategies could have been executed at the close of trading.

Yet taking this view to its limit leads here, as in the case of transactions costs, to the perverse outcome that the probability of a market's being judged efficient increases with the size of bid/ask spreads. Thus, as with transactions costs, the precise role of market microstructure effects in the *theory* of market efficiency is not apparent.

Problems in Testing "Efficiency" as a Model of Stock Markets

As noted earlier, investors' ability to exploit public information for gain can be tested only by

22. D.B. Keim, "Trading Patterns, Bid-Ask Spreads and Estimated Security Returns: The Case of Common Stocks at Calendar Turning Points," *Journal of Financial Economics* 25 (1989), 75-98.

23. DeBondt and Thaler (1985), cited earlier.

24. As a more general indication of skewed returns, we found that although the median returns of "winner" and "loser" stocks differed by only 5%, the average

returns differed by 57%. See R. Ball, S.P. Kothari and J. Shanken, "Problems in Measuring Portfolio Performance: An Application to Contrarian Investment Strategies," *Journal of Financial Economics* 38 (1995), pp. 79-107.

comparing the returns earned when trading on public information against the returns otherwise expected from passive investing. In many empirical tests of market efficiency, the Capital Asset Pricing Model has been used to estimate such expected returns. But, as also mentioned, the CAPM has come under attack from empirical studies showing at best weak correlations between actual stock market returns and those predicted by the CAPM. And because tests of market efficiency are thus "joint tests" of *both* the CAPM's success in measuring expectations and the market's ability to incorporate new information in prices, flaws in the CAPM raise doubts about the reliability of the existing empirical research—both the work that appears to contradict market efficiency as well as that which supports it.

Changes in Riskless Rates and Risk Premiums. The CAPM states that a stock's expected return is equal to the riskless rate (in practice, the interest rates on Treasury notes or bonds) plus a risk premium obtained by multiplying the stock's beta times the market equity risk premium (the amount a stock of average risk is expected to earn above the riskless rate). Expressed as an equation:

$$E(R) = Rf + B (Rm - Rf).$$

Unfortunately, the model is completely silent on a number of important issues of practical as well as theoretical import. For example, what riskless rates, market risk premiums, and individual betas would be consistent with an efficient market? And how are such measures expected to change over time, if at all? (Most empirical tests of market efficiency simply assume that riskless rates, market risk premiums, or betas are constant.)

The second question is potentially troubling because the more we allow both interest rates and the market risk premium to vary over time, the less ability we have to answer a question such as: Are stock prices in general too volatile? In 1981, for example, Robert Shiller published a study concluding that the historical variance of stock prices over the 108-year period from 1871 to 1979 was much too large to be justified by the variance of corporate dividends.[25] Using the CAPM, however, it's impossible to say whether Shiller is right. Because of its assumption of constant riskless rates and market risk

premiums, the CAPM provides no means of judging the "correct" amount of variance in the market index. Shiller's test, for example, assumes in the tradition of the CAPM that the market-wide expected return is constant in *nominal* terms over the entire sample period 1871-1979 in order to place bounds on the price variance allowable in an efficient market. Under this assumption, the probability of rejecting market efficiency seems almost 100%![26]

But consider what happens when we relax this assumption. Consider the S&P 500 as the value of a claim on a perpetuity of expected earnings produced by the 500 companies comprising the index. If the real riskless rate is assumed to be zero (close to its historical average), then an increase in the risk premium from 6% to 8% will reduce the value of the S&P 500 by 25%. Do we see too few or too many such percentage declines in the S&P 500? It seems quite plausible that market risk premiums could change dramatically in response to sudden changes in investors' perceptions of political risk and economic uncertainty. But the answer to this question depends on how frequently the risk premium can be expected to change by as much as 2%. (And, although the CAPM is silent on this issue, researchers are now attempting to find ways to address it.)

Trends in Real Rates and Market Risk Premiums. Moreover, there is nothing in the CAPM that would rule out serial correlation in changes in either the riskless rate or the market risk premium.[27] In fact, the investment opportunity set facing companies and investors seems likely to exhibit positive serial correlation—that is, a tendency for increases to be followed by further increases—due to bursts of invention, among other factors. A gradual aging of the population seems likely to induce positive dependence in interest rates (as a growing number of retirees seeks to live off income from investment and a shrinking workforce operates those investments).

In contrast, the market risk premium seems particularly likely to have elements of *negative* dependence. Consider, for example, how risk premiums would change if the level of general economic uncertainty perceived by investors varies over time, but tends eventually to return to "normal" levels. Increases in perceived risk will cause the

25. Shiller (1981), cited earlier.

26. This is a case of using an excessive and misplaced faith in the CAPM to undermine what appears, in my view at least, to be a more reasonable belief in the rationality of market pricing.

27. For some informal evidence of a sharp decline in market risk premiums over the past 20 years, see J.R. Woolridge, "Do Stock Prices Reflect Fundamental Values?," (in this issue).

index to fall (even given the same *level* of expected corporate profits) in order to give investors a temporarily higher expected return over the period of increased uncertainty. And, if the uncertainties that trigger sharp price declines are resolved over time, the index then tends to rise.[28]

Working along with such cycles in economic uncertainty and investor confidence, changes in the *supply* of risky assets (due to the creation of new assets and the obsolescence of old) by corporations would reinforce this pattern of negative serial correlation in investors' required returns and market risk premiums. For example, suppose expectations of increased political and economic stability are associated with rising stock prices and P/E ratios (as has happened since the recent U.S. House and Senate elections) in response to declines in both interest rates and the general market risk premium. For U.S. corporations, this means a reduction in their cost of capital; and, in response to the lower cost of capital, they can be expected to expand the supply of new risky investments over the next few years. As the aggregate supply of risky assets increases, investors' required rates of return will tend to rise back toward normal levels over time, causing prices and P/E ratios to fall.

Given the above assumptions, then (all of which seem fairly plausible), an efficient market would be expected to exhibit serial dependence in both real interest rates and market risk premiums. The point of these conjectures is to illustrate that the cyclical patterns (or "mean reversion") in stock returns are not necessarily evidence of the market irrationality asserted by Shiller and the so-called behavioralists. Such negative dependence is equally consistent with rational responses by (1) investors to changes in general political and economic conditions and (2) corporations to the resulting changes in investor demand (as reflected in interest rates and risk premiums) for stocks.[29]

Changes in Betas. Finally, consider the relation between beta and market efficiency. Finance theory says nothing about how betas vary both among companies and over time. It thus offers no guidance as to what betas and what patterns of changes in observed betas are consistent with efficiency.

The current theory fails to account, for example, for the fact that betas can be expected to change in fairly predictable ways in response to changes in stock price levels. To illustrate, if we assume that a company has a given level of overall risk (a fixed "asset beta"), the beta of the company's stock (its equity beta) will rise along with increases in its degree of financial leverage (or debt-to-equity ratio). When expressed in market value terms, moreover, a company's debt-to-equity ratio will increase not only when it issues more debt, but also when its stock price falls. Loosely speaking, this means that *when a company's stock price drops sharply, investors' perception of the stock's risk and hence its required return actually increases.* Conversely, *when the stock price rises significantly, its perceived risk and required return fall.*

Such systematic changes in betas in response to large stock price changes could account for a number of the "anomalies" noted earlier. For example, the longer-term "mean reversion" of stock returns—the tendency of high stock returns to be followed by low ones, and vice versa—discovered by Gene Fama and Ken French could be explained largely by systematic shifts in beta after price changes, as could the ability of low P/E and low market-to-book stocks to outperform market averages.[30]

Seasonal Patterns in Betas. To take another example, betas could well exhibit seasonals. There is no reason in principle why securities' relative risks, or even aggregate risk, cannot vary with, say, the day-of-the-week. Consider a firm that routinely makes its major announcements—earnings, dividends, investments, acquisitions—on Thursdays,

28. This point has been made by E.F. Fama, *Foundations of Finance* (Basic Books, New York), p. 149; K.C. Chan, "On the Contrarian Investment Strategy," *Journal of Business* 61 (1988), 147-163; E.F. Fama and K.R. French, "Permanent and Temporary Components of Stock Prices," *Journal of Political Economy* 96 (1988), 246-273; and R. Ball and S.P. Kothari, "Nonstationary Expected Returns: Implications for Serial Correlation in Returns, Apparent Price Reversals and Tests of Market Efficiency," *Journal of Financial Economics* 25 (1989), 51-74.

29. The *supply* of risky investment assets produced by corporate investment decisions is typically assumed by the CAPM to be fixed and thus unaffected by changes in prices and other financial variables. But, without any "supply-side" theory about how corporations respond to changes in real rates and risk premiums, it is difficult to see how we could be surprised by *any* observed sequence of market returns or use the sequence to judge any market to be efficient or inefficient. This is a deficiency not only of the CAPM, but of all major models in modern finance

theory including the DCF present value model, the option pricing model, and efficient market theory itself. Each of these financial models is concerned exclusively with investor demand for (and hence the price of) a certain asset in relation to other assets with given prices. Indeed, I would argue that *the failure to consider the supply of investments is perhaps the greatest deficiency in modern financial economic theory.*

30. Ball and Kothari (1989) provide evidence that endogenous risk variation explains much of the serial correlation observed in Fama and French (1988). A related issue is the evidence of apparent price reversals in De Bondt and Thaler (1985, 1987). Both Chan (1988) and Ball and Kothari (1989) report that the equity betas of the most extreme "losing" stocks can be expected to increase because of the extreme increase in their market debt-equity ratios. Conversely, the extreme "winning" stocks are likely to have equity beta decreases due to extreme leverage reductions.

perhaps because it schedules board meetings on that day. Thursday returns then will exhibit higher variance and, possibly, covariance. To the extent this is so, what appear to be seasonal patterns of superior returns may turn out to be normal ones when adjusted for the associated temporary increases in risk.

IS "BEHAVIORAL" FINANCE THE ANSWER?

Given such limitations in the concept of market efficiency and the existing empirical tests of the theory, a group of finance scholars known as behavioralists has suggested that it is time to abandon the premise of collectively rational investors on which the theory rests. Behavioralists argue that stock price "corrections" and cycles reflect systematic biases in how investors use information. Investors are said to place too much weight on current information, focusing myopically on short-term earnings, for example, while ignoring companies' long-run propects. And stock prices accordingly are viewed as highly unreliable guides to corporate resource allocation and other important decisions. But, is behavioral finance the answer to the limitations of efficient markets theory?

I don't think so. First of all, the profit opportunities created by such alleged investor myopia seem grossly inconsistent with competitive markets. They are much too large to be credible, thus casting doubt on the research methods. Moreover, the failure of the vast majority of professional money managers (including contrarians as well as earnings momentum types) to outperform market averages with any degree of consistency should reinforce our skepticism about such claims.

Second, behavioral finance has anomalies of its own. The extensive evidence of post-earnings-announcement drift cited earlier means that investors place *too little weight*, not too much, on recent earnings information. Showing that a theory has anomalies is one thing; replacing it with an anomaly-free theory is another.

Finally, behavioralists have also criticized the objectivity and openness of the research process over the 1960s and '70s, arguing that the process was slow to accept dissenting views. Benjamin Friedman, for example, comments:

It is no coincidence that the research [in support of efficient markets theory]...has emerged almost entirely from the nation's business schools. From the perspective of the private-interest orientation of these institutions, this identification is both understandable and appropriate.[31]

While Friedman is correct that the idea of efficiency arose in business schools, his further implication that the schools' "private-interest orientation" influenced the research findings represents not just a distortion, but in fact a complete inversion of the incentives of both researchers and teachers. In my experience, businessmen and MBA students have been more receptive to the message that there is gold in the streets than to the lesson that fiercely competitive financial markets eliminate the easy opportunities for gain.

Many critics of the literature on market efficiency have suggested that it took too long to recognize anomalies. Consider this recent statement by Richard Thaler in his introduction to a collection of behavioralist studies in finance:

The financial world as described in Eugene Fama's 1970 efficient markets survey was one that had no urgent need for people. Markets were efficient, prices were unpredictable, and financial economists did not know how to spell the word "anomaly."[32]

This statement, perhaps precisely because it is made from the secure vantage of hindsight, is strongly at odds with my own view of how the research evolved. In our 1968 paper cited at the beginning, Phil Brown and I mentioned anomalous evidence of post-earnings-announcement "drift" in prices. Since this was the second "event study" ever conducted (in the first, FFJR found no signs of anomalies) and was published just three years after the first time the words "efficient market" appeared in print, it seems that the efficient markets literature was not slow in introducing anomalous evidence.

Moreover, the word "anomaly" was introduced to the financial economics literature in a paper I published in 1978 that surveyed a number of puzzling findings related to earnings and dividends.[33] While that survey encountered some resistance and

---

31. In Thaler (1993, p.213).
32. Thaler (1993).

took two years to get published, other anomalies were uncovered in the meantime. Recognizing the pattern, Michael Jensen quickly put together an issue of the *Journal of Financial Economics* devoted entirely to studies of anomalies that was published in the same year.

Overall, then, critics of the literature's responsiveness to anomalous results seem to have overstated their case. In retrospect, I am surprised by how *quickly* the literature embraced the idea of anomalies in the late '70s. We had much more difficulty convincing people that markets were efficient a decade earlier.

CONCLUDING OBSERVATIONS

Are stock markets efficient? Yes and no. On the one hand, the research provides insights into stock price behavior that were previously unimaginable. On the other hand, as research has come to show, the theory of efficient markets is, like all theories, an imperfect and limited way of viewing stock markets. The issue will be impossible to solve conclusively while there are so many binding limitations to the asset pricing models that underlie empirical tests of market efficiency.

Our models of asset pricing began with the CAPM and thus have an accumulated history of only 30 years. With such a limited tradition in asset pricing, we could hardly expect to have a strong basis for concluding that security prices do (or do not) immediately restore equilibrium in response to new information, particularly in the presence of extreme uncertainty. Bearing such constraints in mind, I believe that much of the evidence on stock price behavior does not and cannot reliably address

the *factual* issue of "efficiency" at this point in time. Our models of price equilibrium and our data are not yet up to the task.

This is not to say that empirical research cannot be informative under these circumstances. We have learned a great deal from the "anomaly chasing" of the last decade, and there are enough puzzles and clues to work on for some time. Nevertheless, I do not believe that we can reliably learn much about whether (or to what extent) markets are efficient from these results.

Do we have a better theory? I think not. But, as researchers comb through the evidence and seek more realistic ways of modelling stock price behavior, we are bound to improve the theory over time.

Have we learned much from the theory of stock market efficiency? I think so. And I think this is a better question. The economic theory of competitive markets now seems unlikely to be dislodged from its central role in stock market research, for several reasons. First, stock markets must rank highly among markets on *a priori* likelihood of being competitive: there are no entry barriers; there are many buyers and sellers, who by and large appear to be greedy and enterprising people; and transaction costs are relatively low. Second, as outlined above, the inevitability of binding limitations in both our models of efficiency and in the available data provides a credible alternative explanation for the range of anomalies that have been documented over the last decade. Third, I personally went through the transformation from the pre-EMH view of securities markets, and I am still impressed by how well prices respond to information, *relative to what we expected thirty years ago.*

33. R. Ball, "Anomalies in Relationships Between Securities' Yields and Yield-Surrogates," *Journal of Financial Economics* 6, (1978), 103-126. I borrowed the word "anomaly" from Thomas Kuhn's famous book, *The Structure of Scientific Revolutions* (University of Chicago Press, 1970), which introduced the term to the philosophy of science and scientific method. Kuhn's book, I might note, was published in the same year as Fama's review of the EMH literature, and only eight years before the word appeared in the financial economics literature.

MARKET MYTHS

by G. Bennett Stewart III,
Stern Stewart & Co.

I t is easy to forget why senior management's most important job is to create value. Of course, a higher value increases the wealth of the company's shareholders who, after all, are the owners of the enterprise. But, of greater import, society at large benefits. The quest for value drives scarce resources to their most productive uses and their most efficient users. The more effectively resources are deployed, the more robust will be economic growth and the rate of improvement in our standard of living. Adam Smith's invisible hand is at work when investors' private gain is a public virtue. And, although there are exceptions to this rule, most of the time there is a happy harmony between creating market value and enhancing the quality of life.

The pursuit of value often is made more difficult by a failure to understand how share prices are really set in the stock market. I regularly encounter senior executives and board members who believe stock prices are determined by some vague combination of earnings, growth, return, book value, cash flow dividends, and the demand for their shares. (In one particularly memorable meeting, I was harangued for several hours by an elderly gentleman who claimed that mysterious forces—the so-called gnomes of Wall Street—controlled the market. His "voodoo valuation" framework will not be formally rebutted in this book.)

Confusion over what it is that investors really want can make it difficult for management to reach sensible decisions regarding business strategy, acquisitions and divestitures, accounting methods, financial structure, dividend policy, investor relations, and, most important of all (let's be honest), bonus plans. With the competition for capital growing ever more hostile and global, the cost of ignorance is escalating. It is high time management learns the answer to the question: What is the engine that drives share prices?

P/E multiples adjust to changes in the "quality" of a company's earnings, and this makes EPS a very unreliable measure of value.

IN SEARCH OF VALUE: THE ACCOUNTING MODEL VERSUS THE ECONOMIC MODEL

Right away there are two competing answers. The traditional "accounting model" of valuation contends that Wall Street sets share prices by capitalizing a company's earnings-per-share (EPS) at an appropriate price/earnings multiple (P/E). If, for example, a company typically sells at ten times earnings, and EPS is now $1.00, the accounting model would predict a $10 share price. But, should earnings fall to $0.80 per share, then—however temporary the downturn—the company's shares are expected to fall to $8.

The appeal of this accounting model is its simplicity and apparent precision. Its shortcoming is an utter lack of realism; the accounting model assumes, in effect, that P/E multiples never change. But P/E multiples change all the time—in the wake of acquisitions and divestitures, changes in financial structure and accounting policies, and new investment opportunities. P/E multiples, in short, adjust to changes in the "quality" of a company's earnings. And this makes EPS a very unreliable measure of value.

A competing explanation—the "economic model" of value to which I subscribe—holds that share prices are determined by smart investors who care about just two things: the cash to be generated over the life of a business, and the risk of the cash receipts. More precisely, the economic model states that a company's intrinsic market value is determined by discounting its expected future "Free Cash Flow" (FCF) back to a present value at a rate that reflects its "cost of capital."

The cost of capital is the rate of return required to compensate investors for bearing risk. It is a rate determined in practice by adding a premium for risk to the yield prevailing on relatively risk-free government bonds.

FCF is the cash flow generated by a company's operations that is free, or net, of the new capital invested for growth. To compute it, imagine that all of a company's cash operating receipts are deposited in a cigar box, and that all of its cash operating outlays are taken out, regardless of whether the outlays are recorded by the accountants as expenses on the income statement or as expenditures on the balance sheet. What's left over in the cigar box is FCF.

Which is the more desirable, then, positive or negative FCF? While you may be tempted to say a positive FCF will maximize a company's value, the correct answer actually is: It depends. It depends on the expected rate of return on the new investments a company is making. A profitable company investing lots of capital to expand (such as Federal Express) has a negative FCF, while an unprofitable company shrinking its assets to pay creditors (like Western Union) generates positive FCF. Which company is worth more? In this case (and many others like it), the company with the negative FCF creates greater value.

People say to me, "Bennett, you are a great believer in cash flow. Why is it that your incentive compensation plans do not reward management for generating more Free Cash Flow, if that is what determines value?"

"Ah," I say, "because it is Free Cash Flow *over the entire life of the business* that matters. FCF in any one year is a nearly meaningless measure of performance and value. A positive or negative FCF cannot be judged to be good or bad without examining the quality of FCF—that is, the rate of return earned on the investments."

But now I am getting ahead of myself. There will be plenty of time later to expound on the finer points of the economic model. For now, let's return to the fundamental debate: Is it earnings or cash flow that truly drives stock prices?

Because most companies' earnings and cash flow move together most of the time, it can be difficult to say for sure whether stock prices truly result from capitalizing earnings or discounting cash flow. To sort out this potentially misleading correlation, academic researchers have studied how share prices react to events that cause a company's earnings and its cash flow to depart from one another.

The Accounting Model versus the Economic Model—Some Evidence

The accounting model relies upon two distinct financial statements—an income statement and balance sheet—whereas the economic model uses only one: sources and uses of cash. Because earnings are emphasized in the accounting model, whether a cash outlay is expensed on the income statement or is capitalized on the balance sheet makes a great deal of difference. In the economic model, where cash outlays are recorded makes no difference at all—unless it affects taxes. This conflict is highlighted when a company is permitted to choose between alternative accounting methods.

LIFO vs. FIFO. Switching from FIFO (First In, First Out) to LIFO (Last In, First Out) inventory

Companies switching to LIFO experienced on average a 5 percent
increase in share price on the date the intended change was first
announced. A second study revealed that the share price gain was in direct
proportion to the present value saved by making the switch.

costing in times of rising prices decreases a company's reported earnings because the most recently acquired and, hence, most costly inventory is expensed first. But, in so doing, it saves taxes, leaving more cash to accumulate in the cigar box.

Now we have an important question: Does the market focus on the decline in earnings or the increase in cash? Following the empirical tradition of the "Chicago school," let's find out what investors actually do to stock prices instead of asking them what they might do.

Professor Shyam Sunder demonstrated that companies switching to LIFO experienced on average a 5 percent increase in share price on the date the intended change was first announced. An analysis performed by a second group of researchers revealed that the share price gain was in direct proportion to the present value of the taxes to be saved by making the switch. Taken together, these studies provide powerful evidence that share prices are dictated by cash generation, not book earnings.

These findings also prove that a company adopting LIFO will sell for a higher multiple of its earnings than if it used FIFO. The higher multiple is consistent with the higher quality of LIFO earnings; inventory holding gains are purged from income, and there are the tax savings besides.

And if, as this research suggests, a company's share price depends upon the "quality" as well as the quantity of its earnings, then the accounting model of value collapses. It collapses because a company's P/E multiple is not a primary *cause* of its stock price, as the model seems to suggest, but a consequence of it. The accounting model cannot answer the question: What determines a company's stock price in the first place?

In the LIFO-FIFO example, earnings go down while cash goes up. Let us now examine a second accounting choice, one where earnings go down but there is no change in cash.

The Amortization of Goodwill. When the purchase method is used to account for an acquisition, any premium paid over the estimated fair value of the seller's assets is assigned to goodwill and amortized against earnings over a period not to exceed forty years. Because it is a non-cash, non-tax-deductible expense, the amortization of goodwill per se is of no consequence in the economic model of valuation. In the accounting framework, by contrast, it matters because it reduces reported earnings.

With pooling-of-interests accounting, by contrast, buyers merely add the book value of the sellers'

assets to their own book value. No goodwill is recorded or amortized, and this usually makes the acquirer's subsequent reported earnings and return on equity look much better than if purchase accounting had been employed.

Now, if the amortization of goodwill were the only difference between pooling and purchase, I might consider a preference for pooling accounting to be harmless. But, many times sellers will take only cash, or buyers are unwilling to issue equity, thereby ruling out pooling transactions. Avoiding a sensible transaction merely because it must be recorded under purchase rules is the height of folly.

Sad to say, it was apparently just this foolish thinking that prevented the disposition of some of Beatrice's last remaining properties. The press has reported on more than one occasion that interested suitors balked at purchasing Beatrice units because of a concern over how the market would react to the enormous goodwill they would be forced to record. H. J. Heinz, for one, canned a bid in part over just such a concern with goodwill.

Now, if Don Kelly, Beatrice's CEO at that time, was asking too high a price—one that the potential buyers could not justify by the likely future generation of cash—then that would have been a good reason for them to step back. But if, as the press suggested, the potential buyers walked away from value-adding acquisitions merely because it would have required the recognition and amortization of goodwill, then they let the accounting tail wag their business dog (and I can only shake my head in wonder).

As these cases suggest, it is important to know whether investors are fooled by the cosmetic differences between purchase and pooling, or if instead they penetrate accounting fictions to focus on real economic value. To find out which answer is correct, let us once again trust our eyes and not our ears. Let's look over the shoulders of researchers who have carefully studied the shares prices of acquiring companies.

Hai Hong, Gershon Mandelker and Robert Kaplan, while associated with Carnegie-Mellon's business school, examined the share prices of a large sample of American companies making acquisitions during the 1960s. They divided all the acquirors into two camps: those electing purchase and those using pooling. Over the interval covered by their study, it was much easier to qualify an acquisition for pooling than it is now. Most acquisitions could be recorded using either purchase or pooling, with the choice largely up to management.

Like any capital expenditure that is expected to create an enduring value, Merck's R&D should be capitalized onto the balance sheet and then amortized against earnings over the period of projected payoff from its successful R&D efforts.

Thus, if it were true that investors were concerned with the recognition and amortization of goodwill, the stock prices of purchase acquirors should have underperformed the pooling acquirors. And yet, no significant difference in stock returns could be detected.

This evidence supports the view that accounting entries that do not affect cash do not affect value. It also proves that what matters in an acquisition is only how much cash (and cash-equivalent value) is paid out to consummate the transaction relative to how much cash is likely to flow in afterwards, and not how the transaction is recorded by accountants.

The studies I have cited (along with many other tests of share price behavior too numerous to review here) offer persuasive evidence that share prices are determined by expected cash generation and not by reported earnings. A company's earnings explain its share price only to the extent that earnings reflect cash. Otherwise, earnings are misleading and should be abandoned as the basis for making decisions (and, as I shall argue later, for determining bonuses).

Just Say No

Just how damaging an addiction to earnings can be is illustrated by the case of RJR, the tobacco giant. As reported in a recent *Wall Street Journal* article, RJR puffed up its sales and earnings for several years prior to its LBO by "loading" cigarette inventories on its distributors. Dealers were encouraged to purchase billions of surplus cigarettes just before semi-annual price increases were put into effect. (Company officials estimated that there were a staggering 18 billion excess cigarettes on dealers' shelves as of January 1, 1989.) As a result, RJR was able to report higher sales and earnings. But, in so doing, management forfeited future sales at higher prices, accelerated the payment of excise taxes and turned off smokers with cigarettes that had turned stale.

Within months of the LBO, RJR announced it would discontinue this harmful practice cold turkey, slashing cigarette shipments 29% in the third quarter and 17% in the fourth quarter of 1989 compared to year earlier levels. Though the accounting symptoms look bad (reported profits will be reduced by about $170 million in each quarter), the vital signs of corporate health are restored right away.

"This is a very positive development for the company as far as cash flow is concerned," noted Kurt von der Hayden, RJR's CFO. "I view it as a very positive contribution to our debt service."

Because RJR offered extended payment terms to induce its dealers to load inventories, cash flow would not be hurt by the shipment drop. But excise taxes will be postponed, production and distribution can become more efficient and fresher cigarettes may help to stem a further loss of market share to Phillip Morris.

A former senior RJR officer said that management had been aware of the problem, but couldn't withdraw from the practice because they feared the impact on earnings would have outraged Wall Street. James W. Johnston, the head of the RJR Tobacco Company, stated, "Here is probably the clearest, most positive statement of what we can accomplish by being private for a while."

For shame! What about the evidence that the stock market really responds to the generation of cash and not to illusory accounting profits? As my colleague Joel Stern puts it, "Run your public company as if it were privately held, and you will be making the right decision for your public stockholders." And maybe you won't be vulnerable to its being taken private at twice the current stock price (RJR traded for $55 a share before being taken private for $110 a share).

Kick the earnings habit. Join the Cash Flow generation.

MORE TROUBLES WITH EARNINGS

Is R&D an Expenditure or Expense?

Another problem with earnings as a measure of value is the improper accounting for research and development. Accountants are required to expense R&D outlays as if their potential contribution to value is always exhausted in the period incurred. But common sense says otherwise.

Why would Merck, the spectacularly successful pharmaceutical company, spend more than 10 percent of its sales each year on R&D if it did not expect a substantial return to follow? In fact Merck is looking for a long-term payoff from such spending, and so are its investors. The company's shares sell for a multiple of over 20 times reported earnings and nearly 10 times accounting book value. Merck's earnings and book value apparently understate the company's value by a wide margin. Expensing R&D is one of the reasons why.

While the payoff from any one of its projects is unpredictable, Merck's overall R&D spending is almost certain to bear fruit. Like any capital expenditure that is expected to create an enduring value, Merck's R&D should be capitalized onto the balance sheet and then amortized against earnings over the period of projected payoff from its successful R&D efforts. Such accounting would lead Merck to report both a higher book value and higher current earnings, thereby making the company's actual P/E and price-to-book multiples more understandable.

The accountants' cavalier dismissal of R&D is what accounts in part for the sky-high share price multiples enjoyed by the many small, rapidly growing high-tech Silicon Valley and Route 128 firms. As in Merck's case their stock prices capitalize an expected future payoff from their R&D while their earnings are charged with an immediate expense. It is especially ironic to note that, following the acquisitions of R&D-intensive companies, the accountants will agree to record as goodwill for the buyer the R&D they had previously expensed for the seller. Thus, according to the accountants, R&D can be an asset if acquired but not if it is home-grown. (Again, I shake my head in wonder.)

What possible justification could there be for writing off R&D as an immediate expense when it is so obviously capitalized in stock market values? My answer is that the accountants are in bed with the bankers.

Accountants Take Downers, Too

To protect their loans, bankers prefer to lend against assets that retain value even if the borrower must be liquidated. Such "tangible" assets include receivables, inventories, and property, plant and equipment—assets that have a use to others. But because an insolvent company is unlikely to recover much value from its prior R&D investments (if it did, why is it going bankrupt?), lenders are reluctant to lend against it. Their accounting pals accommodate their desire for concreteness by expensing "intangibles" like R&D.

Accountants, to be sure, do not accept my contention that they are the unwitting slaves of the bankers. They explain their overzealous pen strokes as an adherence to the "principle of conservatism," a slogan that in practice means, "when in doubt, debit." You may have more appreciation for the poor accountants' cynical bent if I told you they are much more likely to be sued for overstating earnings than for understating them. So perhaps their conservatism is more pragmatic than principled.

The key question remains: Are the investors who set share prices knee-jerk conservatives or hard-headed realists when it comes to R&D? Do they consider R&D a cost to be expensed or an expenditure to be capitalized?

Stock prices provide the answer that economic realism prevails (the academic evidence to support this is reviewed later in this article). R&D outlays should be capitalized and amortized over their projected lives—not because they always do create value, but because they are expected to.

Full Cost versus Successful Efforts

One objection that might be raised to capitalizing R&D is that it may leave assets on a company's books that no longer have any value. What if the R&D fails to pay off? Should not at least the unsuccessful R&D outlays be expensed? I say no. Full-cost accounting is the only proper way to assess a company's rate of return.

The issue of successful efforts versus full cost accounting is best illustrated by oil companies. With successful efforts accounting, an oil company capitalizes only the costs associated with actually finding oil; all drilling expenditures that fail to discover economic quantities of oil are immediately expensed against earnings. While such a policy reduces earnings early on, it causes a permanent reduction in assets that eventually leads to the overstatement of future rates of return.

With full-cost accounting, by contrast, an oil company capitalizes all drilling outlays onto its balance sheet and then amortizes them over the lives of the successful wells. If you believe (as I do) that part of the cost associated with finding oil is that unsuccessful wells have to be drilled (if not, why are they drilled in the first place?), then full-cost accounting must be employed to properly measure an oil company's capital investment and thus its true rate of return.

The misuse of successful efforts accounting is not limited just to oil companies, though. Any company that writes off an unsuccessful investment will subsequently overstate the rate of return its investors have realized. Such an overstatement may tempt management to overinvest in businesses that really are not as profitable as they seem to be on paper.

Citibank illustrates the point. In 1987, Citibank took a $3 billion charge to earnings to establish a reserve for the eventual charge-off of LDC loans. Now Citibank sleeps better, for in the years after the charge-off, loan losses are charged against the reserve, never to touch earnings. And, with $3 billion of equity erased with an accounting stroke of the pen, Citibank's accounting return on equity has rebounded quite smartly. Management may wonder why, though, with such an improved return, the bank still sells for such a lowly multiple. One reason is that while Citibank has employed successful efforts accounting, the market uses full cost to judge rates of return.

To overcome such distortions, the economic model of accounting for value would reverse unusual write-offs by taking the charges off the income statement and adding them back to the balance sheet. This way a company's rate of return will rise only if there is a genuine improvement in the generation of cash from operations after the write-off.

Abraham Briloff, an accounting professor at NYU, is one who has fallen into the trap of advocating successful efforts accounting. For example, in a book entitled *Unaccountable Accounting*, he chastised United Technologies for not writing down the goodwill associated with its acquisition of Mostek, a semiconductor company. He argued that, in light of the severe operating problems that materialized at Mostek in the years after the acquisition, the goodwill on UT's books clearly overstated Mostek's value to UT's stockholders, and should be written off just as if it were an unsuccessful drilling expenditure.

I am afraid that Briloff labors under the mistaken belief that a company's balance sheet somehow attempts to represent its market value. He and, it seems, the entire accounting profession apparently have forgotten one of the first principles of economics: sunk costs are irrelevant.

Burn the Books

As any first year economics student knows, the cash already invested in a project is an irrecoverable sunk cost that is irrelevant to computing value. Market values are determined not by the cash that has gone into the acquisition of assets, but by the cash flow that can subsequently be gotten out of them. Therefore, a company's book value simply cannot be a measure of its market value (as Briloff seems to assume).

Rather, a company's balance sheet can at best be a measure of "capital"—that is, the amount of cash deposited by (debt as well as equity) investors in the company. Whether such "capital" translates into "value" depends upon management's success in earning a high enough discounted cash flow rate of return on that capital. This is the question that, although critical to the economic model of value, no balance sheet can answer. This judgment is best left to the stock market.

The Deferred Tax Chameleon

The inadequacy of conventional accounting statements is further exposed by the question: Is the deferred tax reserve appearing on a company's balance sheet debt or equity? Clearly the accountants cannot decide; that's why they stick it in the no man's land between debt and equity. My answer to the question is uncomfortably close to the accountants' hedged position. I too say, "It depends."

Pity the pessimistic lenders, for they must consider the deferred tax reserve to be a debt-like liability. Bankers realize that if a company's condition deteriorates, it probably will not be able to replace the assets that give rise to the deferral of taxes. Moreover, should the assets be sold to secure debt repayment, the company may be obligated to pay a recapture of the past deferred tax benefit. In either event, the deferred tax reserve is quite rightly considered by creditors to be a quasi-liability that uses up a company's capacity to borrow money.

But if you divorce yourself from the downright depressing company of lenders and take up with the more genial society of shareholders, you will discover that the entire character of the deferred tax reserve changes right before your eyes. For as long as a company remains a viable going concern—an assumption taken for granted in the stock market valuation of most companies—the assets that give rise to the deferral of taxes will continue to be replenished. Because the shareholders in a going concern do not expect the company's deferred tax reserve ever to be repaid, it is properly considered to be the equivalent of common equity and thus a meaningless accounting segregation from net worth.

Furthermore, if the deferred tax reserve is properly considered to be a part of shareholders' equity, then to be consistent the year-to-year change in the reserve ought to be added back to reported profits. That way taxes are taken as an expense only when paid, not when provided for by the accountants.

An analogy can be drawn to the Individual Retirement Accounts (IRAS) many people opened some years back. If you are accounting for yours property, you must consider only part of the funds in your account to be true equity. An accountant would insist that you set aside a deferred tax reserve because eventually you will have to pay taxes when you withdraw the funds from the account. Do you expect to earn a return from that part of your account that is the deferred tax reserve, or do you consider that to be a free loan from the government?

> *Accountants... can prepare financial statements either for creditors or for stockholders... but they simply cannot do both at once. It should be clear by now that the lenders won this debate: The accountants take the position that a company is more dead than alive.*

Of course, you expect to earn a return on the entire balance in your account. Nonetheless, I have heard otherwise level-headed corporate executives suggest that their corporate deferred tax reserve ought to be considered a free advance from the government. But, just as you do, corporations should expect to earn a return on all cash invested, no matter what the accountants may call it.

Steal This Book

Permit me one final accounting irony. No doubt the cash you parted with to buy this book has been expensed by your company's accountants. I wish they had had the charity (if not the wisdom) to capitalize it. They insult me by assuming that, when you put this book down for the last time, you will forget everything you've read.

Where They Ought to Be

The accountants, then, are stuck between a rock and a hard place. They can prepare financial statements either for creditors or for stockholders-that is, either for judging a company's debt capacity or its stock market value. But they simply cannot do both at once. It should be clear by now that the lenders won this debate: The accountants take the position that a company is more dead than alive.

Managers must stop making business decisions with financial statements that assume their company is one day away from bankruptcy. To make realistic judgments of performance and value, accounting statements must be recast from the liquidating perspective of a lender to the going concern perspective of shareholders. The balance sheet must be reinterpreted as the cash invested in a "capital" account, and not as the value of "assets." To do this, all of the investments a company makes in R&D along with bookkeeping provisions that squirrel away cash from operations (for deferred tax reserve, warranty reserve, bad debt reserve, inventory obsolescence reserve, deferred income reserve, etc.) must be taken out of earnings and put back into equity capital (a topic discussed in numbing detail in a later chapter).

EARNINGS PER SHARE DO NOT COUNT

Although EPS suffers from the same shortcomings as earnings, it is such a popular measure of corporate performance that it warrants further attention.

Consider an acquisition in which a company selling for a high P/E multiple buys a firm selling for a low P/E ratio by exchanging shares. Because fewer of the high P/E shares are needed to retire all the outstanding low P/E shares, the buyer's EPS will always increase. Many think that is good news for the buyer's shareholders. And, yet, it will happen even if the combination produces no synergies.

To see how really silly is a preoccupation with EPS, reverse the transaction so that now the low P/E firm buys the high-multiple company through a share exchange. This time the buyer's EPS must always decrease; a greater number of low-multiple shares will have to be issued to retire all the high-multiple ones. Many think such EPS dilution signals bad news for the buying company's shareholders, and advise that it be avoided at all cost.

But regardless of which company buys or which sells, the merged company will be the same, with the same assets, prospects, risks, earnings and value. Can the transaction really be desirable if consummated in one direction but not in the other? Of course not. Yet, that is what accounting EPS suggests.

Let's take an example. Assuming that two companies each currently earn $1.00 a share and have 1,000 shares outstanding, and that one firm sells for 20 times earnings while the other sells at 10 times its earnings, the facts are as shown in Exhibit 1.

EXHIBIT 1

	Hi	Lo	Hi Buys Lo	Lo Buys Hi
No. shares	1,000	1,000	1,500*	3,000**
Total earnings	$1,000	$1,000	$2,000	$2,000
Total value	$20,000	$10,000	$30,000	$30,000
Price p/share	$20.00	$10.00	$20.00	$10.00
EPS	$1.00	$1.00	$1.33	$0.66
P-E Ratio	20	10	15	15

*   *Hi* must issue 500 shares at $20 to retire all 1,000 of Lo's $10 shares.
** *Lo* must issue 2000 shares at $10 to retire all 1,000 of Hi's $20 shares.

To make it simple, assume that there are no synergies and that the buyers pay precisely market price for the seller's shares. With fair value paid for value acquired, these transactions have all the excitement of kissing your sister. A proponent of the economic model would expect the acquiror's stock price to sit still.

Yet, when Hi buys Lo, EPS increases to $1.33 and when Lo buys Hi, EPS falls to $0.66. Preoccupied

> *Managers must stop making business decisions with financial statements that assume their company is one day away from bankruptcy. To make realistic judgments of performance and value, accounting statements must be recast from the liquidating perspective of a lender to the going concern perspective of shareholders.*

with EPS, accounting enthusiasts may see a good deal and a bad deal when in fact the two transactions are both the same: Lo-Hi is just Hi-Lo with a two-for-one stock split.

EPS does not matter because, in the wake of an acquisition, a company's P/E multiple will change to reflect a deterioration or improvement in the overall quality of its earnings. In our example, observe that no matter which firm buys and which sells, the combined company will have a P/E multiple of 15 (the consolidated value of $30,000 divided by the consolidated earnings of $2,000). Hi's 20 P/E must fall, and Lo's 10 P/E must rise.

Hi must give up part of its P/E multiple to acquire relatively more current earnings from Lo, and Lo must surrender part of its current earnings to purchase Hi's more promising future growth prospects and a higher multiple. P/E counters EPS, rendering it a meaningless measure of an acquisition's merits.

In the economic model, what does matter is the exchange of value, and not the exchange of earnings so popular with accounting enthusiasts. If a buyer receives from a seller a value greater than it gives, this difference (which I call *Net Value Added*) will accrue to the benefit of the buyer's shareholders (in many cases the benefit will show up as an increase in the value of the buyer's shares immediately after the deal is announced).

Now if this seems a simple and sensible way to judge an acquisition's merits, please note that it has nothing to do with EPS. If a prospective acquisition promises to generate a positive Net Value Added for the buyer, but the accountants inform us that EPS will be diluted, then I conclude that the acquiror will sell for a higher P/E multiple, that's all. Once again, a company's P/E multiple is not the cause of its stock price, but a consequence of it. Let's take an example.

I once advised a large telecommunications company on an acquisition in which EPS dilution was a potential stumbling block. Our client was thinking about buying a company engaged in a rapidly growing and potentially highly-profitable business—one that appeared to have an excellent strategic fit with its own capabilities and business plan. I was enthusiastic about the transaction because I saw a prospect for the value created through the combination to be shared by both the buyer and the seller (the candidate was a unit of another company).

The chairman, too, was enthusiastic until he saw how much the deal would dilute EPS. He pointed out

that the P/E multiple they would have to pay was much higher than their own, so that the acquisition would lead to a substantial dilution in EPS.

I remarked that the target had far brighter growth prospects than they did so that, when the new business was added to their more mature operations, he could expect his company to command a higher P/E multiple. He said: "You mean it's like adding high-octane gas to low-octane gas; our octane rating will increase."

"Right," I said. "The candidate has super-charged earnings, and when you add them to your under-powered earnings, your pro forma earnings power will take off. Your multiple will climb, and that will counter the dilution in EPS."

"Then we are in big trouble," he said. "My compensation plan is tied to EPS. We are rewarding just the quantity of earnings. But you're telling me that the quality of our earnings matters, too. So what should we do?"

"Well, you could change your incentive compensation plan," I said, "and then make the acquisition."

Which is what they did. And on the date of the announcement of the transaction, the seller's stock price increased, our client's price increased, and a key competitor's stock price plunged. Now that is what I call a successful acquisition. The seller wins. The buyer wins. And the competition gets clobbered.

I warn you, however, that my definition of a successful acquisition is different from that of many investment bankers. For them, successful acquisitions are all those that happen.

That's No Reason to Spin Off

A spin-off is a pro rata distribution of the shares of a subsidiary unit to the shareholders of the parent. It is simply the reverse of a stock-for-stock acquisition, and is subject to the same accounting quirks. This time, though, instead of acquiring a lower-multiple company to boost EPS, the accounting enthusiast will recommend spinning one off to boost the parent company's P/E multiple.

Referring again to the example presented above, suppose Hi did acquire Lo to form Hi-Lo, a company that sells for a P/E multiple of 15, an even blend of Hi's 20 multiple and Lo's 10 multiple. Now why not spin off Lo to leave behind a company that sells for Hi's P/E of 20? Is this really advisable? I don't think so, but for a definitive answer you will have to ask an investment banker whose finger is on the pulse of the market.

Several years after acquiring it, Reynolds' management decided to spin off Sea Land to its shareholders and was quite pleased to note that, as a result, Reynold's P/E multiple jumped from 7.5 to 9.5. But that increase in multiple just reversed the decline suffered when Reynolds first acquired Sea Land, no doubt to increase EPS.

Seriously, though, the increase in P/E cannot by itself benefit Hi-Lo's shareholders. They are still stuck with their pro rata share of the low-multiple business after it is spun off. The spin-off merely takes Lo's earnings from Hi-Lo into a separate company where they are capitalized at Lo's multiple of 10. Thus, the increase in multiple that attaches to Hi's earnings is offset by the diminished multiple the market places on Lo's share of the consolidated profits. No matter how the accounting pie is sliced, it's still the same pie.

Just such a spinoff was used to "undo" R.J. Reynolds' acquisition of Sea Land, a containerized shipping operation whose P/E multiple was even lower than that of Reynolds. Several years after acquiring it, Reynolds' management decided to spin off Sea Land to its shareholders and was quite pleased to note that as a result Reynold's P/E multiple jumped from 7.5 to 9.5. But that increase in multiple just reversed the decline suffered when Reynolds first acquired Sea Land, no doubt to increase EPS.

So what we have described here is an investment banker's fantasy—an infinite deal generator: Have Hi multiple acquire Lo multiple in an exchange of shares to improve Hi's EPS (never mind, please, the collapse in P/E), and then, after a respectable period lapses, spin off shares in Lo to improve the multiple (never mind what happens to EPS); and then have Hi reacquire Lo to improve Hi's EPS . . . and, well, you get the idea (and the investment bankers get the fees).

Now please don't get the idea that I oppose spin-offs. As a matter of fact, I believe that spin-offs have been one of the most neglected tools of corporate finance. But the merits of a spin-off and other financial restructurings simply cannot be judged by the accounting model of value.

THE PROBLEM WITH EARNINGS GROWTH

Earnings growth also is a misleading indicator of performance. While it is true that companies that sell for the highest stock price multiples are rapidly growing, rapid growth is no guarantee of a high multiple.

To see why, consider a situation in which two companies, X and Y, have the same earnings, and are expected to grow at the same rate. At this point, we would be forced to conclude that both companies would sell for the same share price and P/E multiple because, as far as we can tell, they are identical.

Suppose now that X must invest more capital than Y to sustain its growth. In this case Y will command a higher share price and P/E multiple because it earns a higher rate of return on the new capital it invests. X merely spends its way to the growth that Y achieves through a more efficient use of capital.

This example illustrates that earnings growth for any company is determined by multiplying a measure of the *quality* of its investments—the rate of return—by a measure of the *quantity* of investment—the investment rate:

Growth = Rate of Return × Investment Rate

The rate of return is measured in relevant cash flow terms before financing costs. The investment rate equals new capital investment (both for working capital and for fixed assets) divided by earnings. The investment rate is the ratio of a company's uses-of-funds for operations to its sources-of-funds from operations—one which indicates the fraction or multiple of current earnings that are plowed back into the business.

To make the example more concrete, suppose X and Y are growing earnings at 10 percent, but X must invest all of its earnings to grow at that rate whereas Y needs to invest only 80 percent of its earnings to keep pace. Y would warrant a higher value because it earns a 12.5 percent rate of return on capital, while X returns just 10 percent.

From this information, you may be tempted to conclude that X is worth less than Y simply because it would not be able to pay a dividend while Y could. However, even though X reinvests all of its earnings, it still could pay a dividend simply by raising new debt or equity. In fact, X could grow at the same rate as Y, pay the same dividends as Y, and even have the same capital structure as Y (if it periodically raises equity), but still be worth significantly less.

Financial cosmetics are widely available to gloss over a company's true performance. Rate of return is the only measure that allows Y to be reliably distinguished from X.

Growth Gone Haywire: The Case of W.T. Grant

I had an opportunity, while completing the Chase Manhattan Bank's credit training program in 1976, to analyze W.T. Grant's financial performance over the period leading up to the eventual liquidation of the company in 1975. Grant's management decided in the late 1960s to embark on an aggressive growth strategy to shift their stores from depressed inner-city locations to more attractive suburban ones.

Company X could grow at the same rate as Y, pay the same dividends as Y, and even have the same capital structure as Y (if it periodically raises equity), but still be worth significantly less.

Besides the brick and mortar investment, this strategy also entailed a large initial outlay for the new stores' inventory. To build volume, store managers were compensated to generate more sales.

Not surprisingly, credit approval became quite lax. This plan led to impressive sales and reported earnings gains for a time; but, with the pile-up of receivables and inventories, it also resulted in a cash flow problem. In fact, with poor and declining rates of return on capital, Grant's Free Cash Flow was negative for each year from 1968 to 1975. And, despite this need for new capital, dividends were maintained at 30 percent of earnings and not a penny of new equity was raised. Growth was financed with new debt, commercial paper, and leases. By 1974 the grim reaper was at the company's door.

W. T. Grant's management apparently forgot one important principle: growth without a commitment to careful capital management—earning an acceptable rate of return—is a sure formula for disaster. Their bankers forgot something, too. Risky expansions should be financed with equity, not with debt.

In sum, rapid growth can be a misleading indicator of added value because it can be generated simply by pouring capital into a business. Earning an acceptable rate of return is essential to creating value. Growth adds to value only when it is accompanied by an adequate rate of return. If returns are low, growth actually reduces value. (Just ask Saatchi and Saatchi.)

THE ROLE OF LEAD STEERS

How can it be true, as I claim, that the cash generated over the life of a business (adjusted for risk) is what determines share prices when most investors seem to be preoccupied with such traditional accounting measures as earnings, EPS, and earnings growth? The answer is that prices in the stock market, like all other prices, are set "at the margin" by the smartest money in the game, leaving the majority of investors as mere price-takers. The concept of marginal pricing—one of the most difficult in all economics to grasp—can be illustrated by the metaphor of the "lead steers" made popular by Joel Stern. He says, "If you want to know where a herd of cattle is heading, you need not interview every steer in the herd, just the lead steer."

The stock market works in very much the same way. While millions of people invest in the stock market, a relative handful of prominent investors

account for the great majority of trades. For example, about 55 percent of the volume on the NYSE consists of block trades of 40,000 shares or more, and over two-thirds of all volume is attributable to trades of 5,000 shares or more. The importance of small, unsophisticated investors has been exaggerated in the press and, I am afraid, in the minds of many senior executives.

The price of oil is set in just this way, too. When I pull my car into a gas station, I may feel in some way responsible for determining the price of oil. But, no, I am just a price-taker. Be it cash or credit, the price is posted, and I can take or leave it. I realize now that the price of oil is set by professional oil traders who compete with each other to get the price right before the other traders do.

But even this characterization is not really accurate. For the astute traders I just tipped my hat to must in turn bow to the economic forces of supply and demand. They cannot make oil depart from the price that will clear the market—the one that will leave no excess supply or unsatisfied demand. You see, even the lead steers do not really lead. They too must follow the will of economic forces.

My point is this: Let's not confuse the process by which prices are set in the market with the economic forces that truly set market prices.

A Lead Steer Up Close

Getting a "lead steer" to reveal his true investment strategy is about as easy as getting a magician to disclose the secret to his tricks. Both prefer that you enjoy their performance without figuring out how it is done. As one particularly astute investor (who wishes to remain anonymous) put it to me: "Why should I popularize my approach—that's my edge."

But there are some who will draw the curtain back for a tantalizing peek at their magic. What they reveal goes far beyond a myopic preoccupation with next quarter's EPS. Consider, as but one example, O. Mason Hawkins, president of Southeastern Asset Management, Inc. (SAM), an investment management firm located in Memphis, Tennessee. Since hanging out a shingle in 1975, Hawkins has never had a down year, and only once has he underperformed the S&P 500—and this with a billion dollars under active management. According to CDA Investment Technologies (a firm which evaluates portfolio management), SAM was the fifth best money manager for the five years ending June 30, 1988, with an annualized return of 19.7 percent versus 14.4 percent for the market.

> "We'd rather get with a guy who pays himself $100,000 a year and can make millions on his stock than someone... who's making a million dollars a year and has a couple hundred shares of his stock... We are looking for a partner rather than an adversary in the executive office."
> —0. Mason Hawkins—

Here is some straight bull from Mr. Hawkins:

Our investment philosophy is based on the approach of trying to buy stocks at a significant discount from what we appraise their private market value to be. There are several ways to do that.

The first method is to determine what the free cash flow is and can be in the coming business cycle under normalized conditions. Then we buy the company at a very reasonable multiple of that free cash flow.

Another way is liquidating value; we simply add up all the assets on the balance sheet, subtracting all the liabilities, and adjust for things like understated inventories or real estate, overfunded or underfunded pensions, overdepreciated plant and equipment and trademark, franchises and brand names. We come up with a net value for what the company could be liquidated for on the courthouse steps, if it came to that, and buy the company at a significant discount.

We also take sales in the marketplace, arm's-length transactions between competent businessmen, and compare what they will pay for businesses versus the market value of the company we are looking at.

We talk with management, we talk with suppliers, we talk with competitors. However we reach most of our conclusions by looking at the numbers and analyzing them.

Next comes the qualitative things, because we don't want to own stocks just because they are cheap... We are interested in companies whose insiders, management members and board members, have a vested interest in the company and who are adding to that position. We are looking for a partner rather than an adversary in the executive office.
—The Daily News, *April 29, 1986*

We're trying to avoid a situation like Phillips Petroleum, where management was virtually willing to destroy the company in order to maintain their positions.
—Pensions and Investment Age, *February 17, 1986*

We'd rather get with a guy who pays himself $100,000 a year and can make millions on his stock than someone... who's making a million dollars a year and has a couple hundred shares of his stock.
—Investor's Daily, *November 1, 1985*

Mason practices what he preaches. He sold sixty percent of his firm to employees and then invested the proceeds in a mutual fund that they manage. Hawkins admits, though, that having his own mother-in-law's money in the fund is his greatest motivation to perform well.

Mason Hawkins' record and philosophy is typical of the "lead steer" investors who truly set stock prices: they think like businessmen, not like accountants. Perhaps surprisingly, many of the lead steers have no formal association or identity with Wall Street, preferring the anonymity and perspective that is gained by distancing themselves from "the Street." You can't find them. They find you.

DIVIDENDS DO NOT MATTER

At this point I will make a bold statement. Not only do earnings and earnings growth not matter; dividends do not matter either.

In the economic model, paying dividends is an admission of failure—management's failure—to find enough attractive investment opportunities to use all available cash. Companies are valued for what they do, not for what they do not do. By paying dividends, management has less money available to fund growth. The value of profitable investment opportunities forgone is subtracted from share price.

If management chooses to raise debt or equity to replace the dividend, then current shareholders' interests are diluted by introducing new claims on future cash flow. Such a policy makes a company incur transactions costs for unnecessary financings, and forces investors to pay taxes on dividends that might otherwise be deferred as capital gains. So why pay dividends?

What if a company has exhausted its investment opportunities? Then it certainly would be better to pay dividends rather than to make unrewarding investments. In most cases, however, it would be even better to use the funds to buy back stock. Then only the investors who choose to sell will be taxed; and they will be taxed only on the gain realized after the basis in their shares is applied against the proceeds from the sale. Although the tax rate on capital gains is now the same as it is for dividends, so long as the tax basis in the shares is not zero investors will pay a lower tax on a capital gain. The Tax Reform Act of 1986 did not make dividends attractive, only less unattractive than before.

Moreover, if paying any dividends at all is thought to be advisable, then borrowing to pay them

Depending upon where a company's cash flow is in relation to its investment needs, it makes sense either to pay no dividends at all or to pay them all at once. The middle of the road is the most reckless place to drive a company's dividend policy.

all at once is probably even better. One benefit is the corporate income taxes saved when debt replaces equity, and yet no additional tax burden is placed on investors. Shareholders will just pay in advance the discounted present value of the taxes they otherwise would have paid over time. Moreover, it will probably reassure investors to know that the tendency of cash-rich companies to overinvest in their undeserving basic businesses and to make overpriced acquisitions will be reined in by the obligation to service debt first. And, it may also bring about the transfer of a more significant equity stake into the hands of key managers and employees, thereby heightening their incentives to add value.

But I am getting ahead of the story at hand. I will discuss the benefits of such financial restructurings in greater detail later on in this book. For now, let me summarize the discussion thus far by saying that, depending upon where a company's cash flow is in relation to its investment needs, it makes sense either to pay no dividends at all or to pay them all at once. The middle of the road is the most reckless place to drive a company's dividend policy.

But the corporate perspective certainly is not all that matters on this question. What about investors? Do they want dividends?

Granted some may need cash for consumption, and thus may require a dividend. But they can create their own dividend by selling or borrowing against some of their shares or, better yet, by adding income-yielding bonds and preferred stocks to a non-dividend paying common stock portfolio. Investors who need cash do not need to get it from every component of their portfolio.

Even so, the payment of dividends actually taking place is out of all proportion to the consumption needs of investors. Most get reinvested back into the market, but only after the brokers' turnstile has been ticked. Besides, if a cash yield is so desirable, why have deep discount bonds, which pay no cash return at all, become so popular? Much like a non-dividend paying common stock, the return on such bonds is entirely in the form of expected price appreciation.

Does paying a dividend make a stock less risky to own? Some argue that a bird in the hand (a dividend) is worth two in the bush (capital gains). But the retort is not that dividends not paid will show up as capital gains for sure, but that dividends that are paid are capital gains lost for sure. Stock prices fall by the amount of any dividends paid, never to be recouped. Paying certain dividends out of uncertain

earnings cannot make earnings, or common shares any less risky. It only makes the residual capital gain that much riskier.

It is true that some investors will not buy the shares of companies that do not pay at least a nominal dividend. Will the share prices of companies that pay no dividends be penalized by not appealing to this group? Absolutely not. Once again, share prices are not set by a polling technique in which all investors have a vote on value. Prices in the stock market are set at the margin. So long as there are a sufficient number of investors with sufficient wealth who are not seeking dividends, companies that pay few or no dividends have no cause for concern. They will sell for their fair value.

How can the view that I am articulating for investors—namely, that "dividends do not matter"—be reconciled with the fact that dividend announcements often have a pronounced effect on stock prices? Managements and boards of directors apparently have conditioned investors to associate dividend increases with a healthy outlook and dividend cuts with impending catastrophe. For example, in 1983, Bethlehem Steel halved the dividend and the stock price collapsed. At the same time management disclosed their intention to close basic steelmaking at the Lackawanna mill, a decision that would trigger the payment of one billion dollars in unfunded vested pension benefits.

Bethlehem's stock price would have collapsed no matter what had happened to the dividend. But, in light of the company's need for cash, cutting the dividend made sense. And thus, there is just a correlation, but not a true causal relationship, between dividend announcements and share prices. Radical changes in dividend policy simply tend to coincide with the release of other important news to the market.

The Evidence on Dividends

Finally, and most decisively, let us once again turn to definitive academic research to answer the question.

The most important empirical study on dividends appeared in the prestigious *Journal of Financial Economics* in 1974. Although it has been updated and retested on several occasions, the fundamental findings have withstood the test of time. The study, performed by Professors Fischer Black and Myron Scholes, tested whether the total returns achieved during the period 1936 to 1966 from 25 carefully-constructed portfolios depended upon the dividend yield or dividend payout

> *A high real rate interest is the market's way of attracting more savings with the one hand and discouraging less rewarding capital projects... For management to ignore this obvious market signal is to misallocate capital, to destroy wealth and welfare, and to attract raiders like bees to honey.*

ratios of the underlying stocks. Their analysis revealed that the return to investors was explained by the level of risk, and was not at all affected by how the return was divided between dividends and capital gains. They found that within a given risk category, some stocks paid no dividends, some paid modest dividends, and some paid a lot of dividends, but all experienced the same overall rate of return over time.

Black and Scholes concluded that investors will do best by assuming that dividends do not matter and by ignoring both payout and yield in choosing their stocks (that is, they should worry about risk, diversification, taxes and value, but not dividends per se). Their advice to corporate managers is no less important than it is to investors: Do not formulate dividend policy in an attempt to influence shareholders' returns. Instead, set dividend policy in the context of the company's own investment needs and financing options, and then carefully explain it to investors.

THE MYTH OF MARKET MYOPIA

It is easy to imagine that the pressure put on money managers to perform each quarter will force them to ignore the long-term payoffs from farsighted business decisions and instead focus only on near term results. Here is the popular view of a myopic stock market, as articulated by Donald N. Frey, the former CEO of Bell & Howell:

> *When the typical institutional portfolio in the U.S. has an annual turnover rate of 50% and some smaller ones have turnover rates of more than 200%, it is no surprise that American business is hobbled compared with foreign ... Playing the market the way our money managers do ignores two critical factors: the time required to bring a product from development to market, and the time required to redirect resources from a maturing business to a new one... The pressure for short-term results puts unnecessary hurdles in the way of sound management. Investors' expectations for simultaneously high dividends on stocks, high interest rates on bonds, and rapid growth in the price of securities force managers to forgo many of their most promising ventures. Ultimately, these pressures rob consumers of future products, workers of future jobs, and investors of future profits.*

Frey is joined in this view by Andrew C. Sigler, chairman and CFO of Champion International Corporation, a large paper products company:

> *The only pressure I have on me is short-term pressure. I announce that we're going to spend half a billion dollars at Courtland, Alabama, with a hell of a payout from redoing a mill and my stock goes down two points. So I finally caved in and announced I'm going to buy back some stock, which makes no sense. If the economy is supposedly run by corporations and corporations are supposed to invest and be competitive, buying back your own stock, if you have alternatives, makes no sense. But you can't fight it. The share price today is refined constantly by that proverbial young man looking at a CRT screen. There's an assigned P-E ratio based on what I did last quarter and what I'll do next quarter.*

Now, in one sense, Frey and Sigler are right. Because rates of interest have been quite high this past decade, especially in real terms, distant payoffs are more heavily discounted by investors. Projects must pay off more quickly and handsomely in order to pass muster. That is just a fact of life with which all projects must contend.

After all, the amount of capital available for companies to invest is limited. It is constrained in the aggregate to an amount equal to just what individuals throughout the world choose to save. High real interest rates are the result of too many promising projects chasing too little savings. A high rate of interest is the market's way of attracting more savings with the one hand and discouraging less rewarding capital projects with the other in order to strike a balance between the available supply of and demand for capital.

For management to ignore this obvious market signal is to misallocate capital, to destroy wealth and welfare, and to attract raiders like bees to honey. Frey and Sigler seem not to understand that capital budgeting is the process of deciding which projects ought not to be funded so that other, even more promising ones can be.

But their allegations go farther still. They claim our economic system is fundamentally flawed because of the tendency of investors—mainly professional money managers—to be unduly shortsighted. If it were true that stock prices failed to reflect the true value of insightful investment decisions, then regulations preventing hostile corporate takeovers (a fate, I might add, that eventually befell Bell & Howell) might be in order.

Unfortunately—at least for those who believe in greater market regulation—their claims are refuted by both logic and observations of share prices.

> If all the market cared about was near-term earnings, wouldn't all companies sell for the same P/E ratio? But it is precisely those companies whose prospects for long-run growth and profitability are brightest that sell for the highest P/E multiples; and this is a strong sign of market sophistication.

Economic logic says that a company's stock price should depend upon the cash expected to be generated over the entire life of the business—otherwise there are large profit opportunities for long-term investors. The simple fact that stocks trade at multiples of current earnings is *prima facie* evidence of the stock market's extended time horizon. For, with a stock selling at a multiple of, say, just 10 times earnings, it would have to be held for ten years for the earnings to recoup just the principal paid, and held indefinitely for an appropriate return on investment to be earned.

Moreover, differences in P/E ratios indicate that the market responds to the relative prospects for profitable growth. If all the market cared about was near-term earnings, wouldn't all companies sell for the same P/E ratio? But it is precisely those companies whose prospects for long-run growth and profitability are brightest that sell for the highest P/E multiples; and this is a strong sign of market sophistication.

The CEOs also go astray when they accuse institutional investors of impatience. The long-term nature of pension and life insurance liabilities suggests that most of the large institutional investors accused of a short-term mentality actually would be better off investing in risky stocks that promise a higher long-term payoff than more conservative investments are apt to provide.

And, apparently, the institutions do just that. A study undertaken by the SEC's economics staff shows that institutional investors own a far larger percentage of the shares of R&D-intensive companies than of more mature, blue-chip stocks. Far from indicating shortsightedness, this ownership pattern reveals patience and, indeed, a positive appetite for long-run payoffs.

But even if it is true that money managers are evaluated each quarter—and no doubt many are—it still does not logically follow that share price movements each quarter are dictated by that quarter's results. In fact, because share prices are forward looking, share price movements quarter-to-quarter must be determined by the change in outlook extending beyond that quarter into the indefinite future. For, if share price movements did respond myopically to quarterly results, a simple trading rule would exist: just buy "depressed" stocks (those where the most recent earnings understate the long-term outlook) and sell short overpriced ones (where current earnings overstate long-term value), and you will outperform the market over time. But such a simple investment rule does not work.

Most fundamentally, does the frenetic trading activity that Frey in particular disparages arise from a short-term horizon on the part of American investors? And does trading activity motivated by a quick payoff depress the value of companies investing for the long term? Not at all.

For every buyer there must be a seller, and for every seller a buyer. If both buyers and sellers are equally shortsighted, trading per se would have no effect on value. For if the seller is selling because of an unwarranted concern over a near-term earnings problem, is the buyer buying because of an unjustified enthusiasm about near-term earnings prospects? Trading volume simply does not affect the level of stock prices (a theme to which I will return shortly).

The real reason why the market rises or falls is simply that the lead steers decide that intrinsic value has changed. When this happens, trading volume may surge as investors adjust their portfolios to accommodate a new market value. It may seem as if the trading volume is what causes a change in value when, in fact, it is the trading volume that results from a change in value. Beware of correlation masquerading as a cause.

I believe that the increase in trading volume this past decade is best explained as a consequence of the deregulation of brokerage commissions in May 1976 and the automation of the brokerage industry, both of which have made the U.S. the low-cost producer of trades worldwide. Lower trading costs mean more trades, and more trades mean that even more information is being digested by market participants and actively impounded into stock market values. In my view, the growing demands placed on management to invest capital wisely actually are the result of an increasingly efficient and sophisticated capital market. They are not, as the CEOs assert, some new-found institutional focus on the short term at the expense of the long term. But, again, do not take my word for it. Nor the words of Frey or Sigler, for that matter. Let's consult the academic experts who have no axe to grind.

The Evidence on Market Myopia

Definitive evidence proving the market's farsightedness comes from research performed by John McConnell of Purdue University and Chris Muscarella of Southern Methodist University. They examined share price reactions to announcements of capital spending plans (like Mr. Sigler's Courtland new machines), including research and development outlays. Because of the lag between making an investment and realizing its payoff, the immediate effect of an increase in a company's capital spending would be to reduce both its earnings and cash flow—a result Mr. Sigler is convinced leads inevitably to a markdown in a company's stock price.

Indeed, if the market were dominated by the callow, computer-driven automatons familiar to Mr. Sigler, then share prices would be expected to decline with almost any planned capital spending increase no matter how significant might be the long-term payoff. If, however, the projects to be undertaken are generally sound—ones in which discounted cash flows over the lives of the investments offer promising returns—and if the market is dominated by astute, forward-looking lead steers, then share prices should rise despite any negative near-term accounting consequences. The converse would be true for an announced decrease in capital spending.

McConnell and Muscarella's evaluation of 547 capital spending announcements made by 285 different companies over the period 1975 to 1981 reveals a statistically significant share price appreciation for companies announcing an increase in capital spending, and a decrease in share price for firms announcing reductions.

Their findings do not imply that every single capital spending increase was greeted favorably (Sigler's Courtland project, for example, was not), only that most were. When in early 1984 Federal Express announced Zapmail, a service designed to preempt fax machines, the company's stock fell in price nearly $10 a share, from the mid-$40s to the mid-$30s. Several years later, the project was called off in the wake of a widespread proliferation of fax machines, and Federal's stock price rose by nearly $8 a share. Investors heaved a sigh of relief to learn that no more money would be poured into a black hole. The point, though, is that Federal Express's share price fell initially not because the market was unable to visualize the long-run payoff from the Zapmail project, but because it saw the consequences so clearly.

Will Sigler's Courtland project suffer a similar fate? Only time will tell. For now, he is free to rail against the stock market and to protest that spending half a billion dollars to redo a paper mill is the world's best use for that scarce capital (despite the fact that his stock price fell when the project was first announced and rose when, by repurchasing shares, he freed up funds for other companies to invest). Essentially,

then, we have one man's opinion arrayed against the collective wisdom of market investors who, in moving stock prices, are putting their money where their mouth is.

The R & D Issue. Returning to the research of McConnell and Muscarella, let me mention that they also discovered that share prices reacted no differently to announcements of stepped-up research and development that was to be immediately expensed against earnings than they did in cases of new capital expenditures to be added to the balance sheet. Here is the proof that R&D is a capital expenditure, not an expense, and should be capitalized onto a company's books just like any other capital expenditure that is intended to create an enduring value.

They also found that 111 capital spending announcements made by 72 public utilities over the same time period had, as expected, no discernible impact on share price. The explanation here is that regulators constrain public utilities to charging prices intended to provide only a zero net present value for new capital projects.

The McConnell/Muscarella study provides impressive evidence that, far from being myopic, the market:

■ factors into stock prices a realistic estimate of the long-run payoff from management's current investment decisions;

■ is able to distinguish value-adding from value-neutral opportunities; and

■ does not care whether the accountants expense or capitalize value-building outlays.

The burden of proof lies on those who think otherwise.

SUPPLY AND DEMAND

Mr. Frey's aforementioned concern about excessive trading volume is particularly confusing to me because I have met with many CEOs who are concerned that their stock price is depressed because of insufficient trading activity, a view to which I also cannot subscribe.

Both misconceptions hinge on the belief that share prices are set by a relationship between supply and demand, and that management accordingly can (and should) market its common stock in much the same fashion as any other consumer product. After all, if the number of common shares outstanding is fixed, would not advertising in concert with frequent analysts' presentations spark demand for the shares and thereby raise their price through a surge in volume?

Don Carter, Chairman and Chief Executive officer of The Carter Organization, the world's largest proxy solicitation and corporate governance firm, is (quite predictably) a proponent of the supply/demand model of stock price behavior. "Every company," he asserts,

has a shareholder family and that family consists of many components: mom and pop shareholders, institutional shareholders, management holdings, and speculative holdings. We identify those holders and generate two-way communication by mail or visit to learn why they own their stock. Their answer will help us in our search for new investors with similar motives. Our job is to make sure that those who are in the stock stay in it, and those who are not come in and join the party. When you have more buyers than sellers, the stock price will rise—period. It's still supply and demand that determines stock price.

Bell South has in the past adopted this "Madison Avenue" approach to Wall Street. For some time, hardly a week would pass without a full-page advertisement appearing in the *Wall Street Journal* scouting the company's investment appeal. After the reader was informed of a little-known fact—namely, that rapid growth in population in the southeastern part of the United States is expected to continue—Bell South would let us know that they were preeminently positioned to benefit from this trend. We were then advised to call our broker and purchase their shares.

To repeat our opening question: Will such a campaign increase share price? It will not, because it simply is not true that the supply of a company's shares is fixed. Instead, supply is perfectly flexible by virtue of options and short-selling. The lead steers can combine call options on Bell South stock with less risky T-bills to create a position equivalent to owning Bell South stock, but without owning Bell South stock directly. Or, they could sell Bell South shares short—that is, sell shares they do not own. When this happens, the total number of shares owned by all investors will exceed the number of shares that have been issued by the company, with the difference being accounted for by the short sales. Would you be surprised to learn that Bell South has one of the largest short positions of any stock on the Big Board?

Another, though admittedly less precise, approach to recreating the unique investment opportunity that Bell South claims it represents would be for investors to purchase certain proportions of the shares of other regional telephone companies, such as Bell Atlantic, along with, say, Wal-mart, or Food Lion—retailers who, like Bell South, are benefiting from the burgeoning growth of the Southeast.

Through these and other actions, sophisticated investors can create an artificial supply of a company's shares or close proxies for those shares in order to offset any surge in demand a PR campaign might generate. And the evidence on this issue reveals that efforts to promote a company's appeal to investors lead to an increase in trading volume, but not in stock price, thereby benefiting brokers (and maybe Don Carter), but not shareholders.

An elegant indictment of trading volume comes from Warren Buffett, the highly-regarded Chairman of Berkshire Hathaway:

One of the ironies of the stock market is the emphasis on activity. Brokers, using terms such as "marketability" and "liquidity," sing the praises of companies with high share turnover. . . But investors should understand that what is good for the croupier is not good for the customer. A hyperactive market is the pickpocket of enterprise.

Flexibility in the demand for a company's shares also makes trading volume an unimportant determinant of value. Investors for the most part are not interested in buying shares of stock in only a single company. To diversify risk, investors hold a portfolio of stocks. The attributes that an investor wants a portfolio to exhibit—in terms of income, risk, potential for capital appreciation, exposure to the business cycle, etc.—can be obtained by selecting shares from among a wide variety of easily substitutable companies. When shares are purchased to play a role in a portfolio, the shares of stocks in individual companies will be priced much like undifferentiated commodities; advertising will serve to raise only volume, not price.

The Evidence on Supply and Demand

Fortunately, this important issue has also been the subject of expert academic research. A test conducted by Professor Myron Scholes as part of his doctoral dissertation at the University of Chicago provides strong evidence that share prices are determined by intrinsic values and not by an interaction between supply and demand.

His ingenious study examined secondary offerings where already-issued shares of a company's common stock are sold by investors who own them. Because no new shares are sold, a secondary offering by itself should not affect the intrinsic cash-flow value of a company. And yet, a supply-demand enthusiast would predict that, given a downward sloping demand schedule, additional shares could be sold only at a discount from market price. The greater the number of shares unleashed on the market, presumably the greater would be the discount required to induce investors to take up the shares. Another implication of the supply-demand view is that the price decline would likely be temporary. After the surplus supply of shares is absorbed into the market, a more normal share value should return.

Secondary offerings thus provide a very clear test of whether intrinsic value or supply and demand best explains how individual company's share prices are set.

Professor Scholes did find that secondary offerings reduced share price (an average of two percent measured against the market), but the price decline was unrelated to the size of the offering. It is reasonable to assume that secondary issues are timed by sellers to occur when they believe the shares are overvalued. Scholes concluded, therefore, that the price decline was caused by the adverse connotation associated with the decision to sell, and not the temporary "overhang" of supply.

He obtained further support for this interpretation by dividing the sellers into various groups. The largest price decline was associated with sales by management (as when Charles Schwab sold large blocks of Bank of America stock shortly before a more devastating decline in share price), the next largest by venture capitalists and by others close to the company, and little, if any, price decline was detected following large block sales by third-party institutions. Scholes' study showed that the quality of information rather than the quantity of shares traded is what determines the depth of the price discount.

Scholes traced the price decline several months after the offering and found that it persisted, though not in every case, as some shares recovered in value and others fell further. But, as a statistical statement, the price decline apparently was in response to some likely fundamental decline in the company's prospective economic performance.

Scholes' research offers convincing and reassuring evidence that stock prices are set by the lead steers' appraisal of intrinsic values (that is, the prospect for cash generation and risk), not supply and demand.

Lest the case be overstated, I add that supply and demand do play a role in determining share values, but only in the aggregate. The intersection of the aggregate demand for capital relative to its worldwide supply determines the underlying level of real interest rates and hence, indirectly, the value of all stock markets. But it is only in setting the value of the market as a whole, and not for any single company, that supply and demand operate.

There are two important implications of Scholes' research. First, the objective of investor relations should be to revise expectations, rather than to stimulate demand. To increase share price, management must convince the right investors—the "lead steers"—to pay more, not simply convince more investors in the herd to buy. It is unfortunate that most of what passes for investor relations is "retail" as opposed to "wholesale" in orientation, aims to inform the herd and not the lead steers, and stimulates volume instead of price.

Second, the price decline associated with raising new equity capital can be mitigated through a clear program of financial communication and by raising equity through a pre-announced sequence of small issues (ideally a 415 shelf registration). Investment bankers' protestations about the "market overhang" from a shelf registration should be discounted as an obvious attempt to use the discredited supply-demand argument to their own benefit.

IN CONCLUSION

Earnings, earnings per share, and earnings growth are misleading measures of corporate performance. Earnings are diminished by bookkeeping entries having nothing to do with recurring cash flow, and are charged with such value-building capital outlays as research and development, all in an attempt to placate lenders' desire to assess liquidation value. EPS at best measures only the quantity of earnings, but the quality of earnings reflected in the P/E multiple matters, too. Rapid earnings growth can be manufactured by pouring capital into substandard projects; earning an adequate rate of return is far more important than growing rapidly.

While many investors are fooled by accounting shenanigans, the investors who matter are not. Stock prices are not set through a polling technique where all investors have an equal vote. They are set rather by a select group of "lead steers" who look through misleading accounting results to arrive at true values. The rest of the herd, though blissfully ignorant of why the price is right, is well protected by the informed judgments of the "lead steers."

While it is fashionable to think so, the market is not myopic. The investors who set stock prices take into account the likely payoff from a capital project, no matter how distant, but discount it for the additional investment, risk, and time involved in getting there. On those occasions when a company's stock price responds unfavorably to a new capital project, it probably is not because the market is unable to visualize the eventual payoff. The real reason is that the market predicts that the long-run return will be inadequate; and its judgment will prove to be right more often than not. The record shows conclusively that betting against the market is simply not rewarding.

The best research on the subject shows that paying dividends does not enhance the total return received by investors over time. But paying dividends may deprive worthwhile projects of capital, or may force the company and investors to incur unnecessary transactions costs. And because boards of directors usually are loathe to cut the dividend except in the most dire circumstances, dividends become an additional and unnecessary fixed cost of running the business. Returning excess cash through periodic share repurchases, or a large, one-time, special dividend (with future dividends suspended to support the repayment of debt) is likely to be more rewarding than paying out a stream of dividends over time.

Stimulating investors' demand for shares will increase share volume, but not share price, benefiting brokers, but not shareholders. Lead steers head off a stampeding herd of investors by selling shares short or buying puts, providing an artificial supply of shares to siphon off any temporary surge in demand. To increase share price through more effective financial communication, management needs to convince the right investors that the company is worth more, not just persuade more investors to buy the stock.

The sophisticated investors, or "lead steers," who set stock prices, care about the generation of cash and the risks taken over the entire life of the business. This is the economic model of corporate value creation.

Despite the impressive evidence assembled in the academic community in support of an economic model of value, many companies still forsake truly economic decisions in deference to an earnings totem. How many senior managers of publicly traded companies, for example, relish the thought of switching to LIFO to save taxes, gladly ignore goodwill amortization when an acquisition is contemplated, and care not a whit about the hit to earnings suffered when capital spending is increased? Not many, I suspect. They have been hypnotized by the cant of the popular press, sell-side security analysts, and many investment bankers and accountants into believing the myth that the market wants earnings, and wants it now. To make matters much worse, their incentive compensation often is tied to near-term earnings and earnings-related measures, so that they cannot afford to let their common sense be their guide.

What is the answer? Senior managers and boards of directors must be educated about how the stock market really works, and their compensation schemes must change accordingly.

R&D AND CAPITAL MARKETS

by Baruch Lev,
*New York University**

E conomic growth and the consequent welfare improvement of nations and individuals are driven mainly by *techno-logical change*, as manifested by the introduction of new products and services, the development of more efficient systems of production, and improvements in the organization and management of commerce and industry. Research and development is the major driver of technological change—hence the central role of R&D in economic growth and welfare improvement. The impact of R&D and technological change on economic growth has long been recognized by proponents of free market economies such as Adam Smith, Marshall, Keynes, and Solow. Even two of the most ardent critics of capitalist societies, Marx and Engels, argued in the Communist Manifesto that capitalism depends for its very existence on the constant introduction of new products and processes.

This sequence of effects—from R&D to technological change to increases in productivity and growth—holds not only for nations, but for individual companies and business units as well. A large and growing number of empirical studies have confirmed a significantly positive association between national, industry, and corporate R&D expenditures, on the one hand, and economic growth, productivity gains, and increases in corporate earnings and market values.[1]

The growth of R&D expenditures over the last two or three decades, together with the continuous substitution of knowledge (intangible) capital for physical (tangible) capital in firms' production functions, has elevated the importance of R&D in the performance of business enterprises. The ability to evaluate the risk and eventual payoffs from corporate R&D is therefore of considerable importance to capital market practitioners and researchers. The evaluation of R&D activities is seriously impeded, however, by antiquated accounting rules and insufficient disclosure by corporations. Despite the obvious benefits of R&D, which generally stretch over extended periods of time, this investment is immediately expensed (written off) in corporate financial reports, leaving no trace of R&D capital on firms' balance sheets and causing material distortions of reported profitability.[2] Immediate expensing is practiced not only for internally generated R&D, but also in the growing number of acquisitions involving large amounts of "R&D-in-process," further distorting reported performance.[3]

The fact that only scant information on R&D and other innovative activities is publicly disclosed by firms compounds the information problems of investors when evaluating high-tech companies. Investors are generally told little about the nature of firms' research activities, such as the share of total R&D devoted to basic research, new product development, or efforts to increase the efficiency of production processes (known as "process R&D"). Nor is information typically furnished about the expected benefits and duration of products under development. Even the total R&D expense reported in corporate income statements often misrepresents the extent of activities aimed at producing innovations, particularly for small companies that do not formally classify such activities as R&D.

Given the importance of corporate research activities to capital market practitioners and researchers, and the inadequacy of public information on R&D, I provide in this essay:

■ salient statistics about recent trends in corporate R&D;
■ a brief summary of international disclosure regulations;
■ a survey of the major empirical findings concerning R&D and its benefits, particularly as reflected in capital markets; and
■ some guidelines for investors and analysts engaged in the valuation of R&D-intensive enterprises.

*I am grateful to Mark Hirschey, Frank Lichtenberg, Min Wu and Anne Wyatt for their assistance and suggestions.
1. See, for example, Griliches 1995, Hall 1993a, Lev and Sougiannis 1996, Coe and Helpman 1995.

2. The most obvious effect of this accounting practice is to reduce current earnings for companies with high R&D growth. But, as discussed later in this paper, a more subtle distortion is the tendency to *inflate* popular return-on-investment measures like ROE and ROA.
3. Deng and Lev (1998).

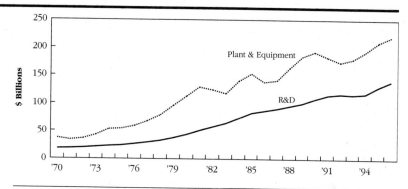

FIGURE 1
ANNUAL EXPENDITURES
OF MANUFACTURING
FIRMS ON NEW PLANT
AND EQUIPMENT AND ON
R&D

Sources: Economic Report of the President, 1997 for investment in new plant and equipment, and National Science Foundation/
SRS for R&D.

RECENT TRENDS IN R&D

Total annual R&D expenditures in the U.S. increased from $26 billion in 1970 to $206 billion in 1997, representing an average yearly growth rate of 8.0%, while investment in plant and equipment over the corresponding period increased annually by 6.8%, on average.[4] By comparison, the aggregate growth rate of R&D in the European Union countries during 1991-1996 was about half the U.S. rate. Of the $206 billion devoted to R&D in the the U.S. in 1997, $151 billion (or 73.3% of the total) was industry R&D, while the rest was sponsored by the federal government ($16.5 billion, or 8.0%), universities ($27 billion, 13.1%), and other institutions (5.6%).

Some perspective on the relative magnitude of industry R&D is provided by Figure 1, which portrays the relationship over the last 25 years between total annual expenditures of U.S. manufacturing firms on new plant and equipment (tangible investment) and their expenditures on R&D. While investment in plant and equipment has been very volatile, exhibiting sensitivity to economic conditions (particularly the recessions of the early 1980s and 1990s, which led to *decreases* in plant and equipment investment), expenditures on R&D have increased smoothly due to the constantly expanding opportunities in emerging technologies, such as biotech, computers, and telecommunications.

Besides increasing steadily in absolute terms, corporate investment in R&D has also increased relative to the scale of firms' operations. Figure 2 presents the annual average "R&D intensity" (that is, R&D as a percentage of revenues) of Compustat companies that report R&D (upper curve) and of all Compustat companies (lower curve). As shown in the upper line of Figure 2, for the former group, R&D expenditures as a percentage of revenues more than doubled from 1.9%, on average, in 1978 to 4.0% percent in 1997.[5] And the R&D intensities of high-tech, science-based companies have been substantially higher than the overall averages shown in Figure 2. For example, in 1996 the average R&D intensities of electronics, drugs, software, and biotech companies were, respectively, 6.1%, 12.0%, 17.8%, and 41.0%.[6]

Structural changes that occurred in the U.S. economy during the 1980s and early 1990s helped to increase the relative role of R&D in publicly traded companies. The increased focus of manufacturing firms on core operations accomplished by restructurings and spinoffs had the economy-wide effect of moving capital out of low-R&D sectors, such as chemicals, metals, and machinery, and into the high-tech sectors of pharmaceuticals, biotech, software and electronics.[7] The R&D intensity of the public-company sector increased further because the firms that went private through LBOs or were

---

4. The statistical data in this section are derived from the Economic Report of the President, 1997; the National Science Foundation/SRS; and the OEDC publication : Main Science and Technology Indicators, 1998.

5. The increase of R&D intensity is not due to increases in R&D input prices, rather to enhanced R&D activities of corporations (see Scherer, 1992, p. 1428)
   6. Computed from Compustat, for SIC codes: 3600-3699, 2834, 2836, and 7372.
   7. Hall (1993a).

R&D expenditures as a percentage of revenues more than doubled from 1.9%, on average, in 1978 to 4.0% percent in 1997. And the R&D intensities of high-tech, science-based companies have been substantially higher than the overall averages.

FIGURE 2
AVERAGE R&D INTENSITY (R&D OVER REVENUES) OF FIRMS HAVING R&D AND ALL FIRMS

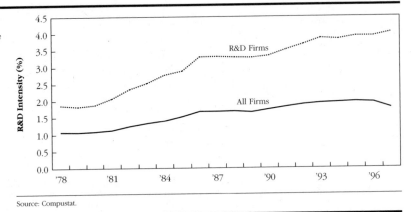

Source: Compustat.

acquired by foreign companies during the 1980s tended to be low in R&D (such as food companies and retailers). At the same time, the majority of the new entrants to capital markets in the 1980s and 1990s were high-tech firms traded on the NASDAQ.

Disclosure Regulations

Disclosure requirements in corporate financial reports for *internally generated* R&D vary across countries.[8] The main differences concern the income statement and balance sheet treatment of R&D. Public companies in the U.S. are required to expense all R&D outlays as incurred.[9] German companies also generally expense all R&D outlays, to conform to tax regulations. But most other developed countries allow—and, under certain circumstances, require—the capitalization (i.e., recognition as an asset) and subsequent amortization of certain R&D outlays, particularly identifiable product costs. For example, in the U.K., Canada, France, Australia, the Netherlands, Israel, and Sweden, public companies may capitalize the costs of development (but generally not basic research) when the projects under development are clearly defined and the expenditures separately identifiable. Japanese companies may capitalize R&D, but have to amortize it within five years. The amortization of the R&D capital is determined by the expected useful life of the projects.

Most countries require disclosure in the financial reports of the amounts of R&D expensed or capitalized, typically in footnotes. Moreover, in September 1998, the International Accounting Standards Committee (IASC) issued Standard No. 38 on Intangible Assets, which calls for the capitalization of R&D costs for projects that meet certain criteria. Most important are that the projects (1) be clearly identified (i.e., costs and expected revenues are clearly separable from general corporate R&D), (2) have passed a technological feasibility test, and (3) be shown capable of recovering the capitalized costs.

In recent years, an increasing number of firms have been *purchasing* "R&D-in-process" (i.e., still incomplete projects and processes), generally through a corporate acquisition. Here, too, U.S. reporting standards are less flexible than those of most other countries. In the U.S., the purchasing companies are required to write off immediately the entire value of the acquired R&D-in-process. In contrast, the U.K., Canada, Australia, and New Zealand, as well as countries that have adopted the international standard, allow the capitalization of acquired R&D, which then must be amortized over its expected useful life.

As should be evident from this brief international survey, the required public disclosure of R&D activities by U.S. companies—essentially a single line item in the income statement—is wholly inad-

---

8. Information on international R&D disclosure regulations was obtained from Coopers & Lybrand (1993).

9. The only major exception in the U.S. to the immediate expensing of R&D are software development costs (FASB Statement No. 86) which have to be capitalized when a product passes successfully a technological feasibility test. Pre-feasibility development costs are expensed as incurred.

equate for the purpose of financial and security analysis. Reported profitability is seriously distorted; sometimes understated, often overstated. And the absence of R&D capital from financial reports denies investors the ability to assess the firm's return on innovative activities.

THE EMPIRICAL RECORD

Systematic economic research on the relationship between R&D and the attributes of firms and the markets in which they operate was initially motivated by Joseph Schumpeter's (1942) hypothesis that large and monopolistic companies have significant advantages in conducting research and developing products, mainly due to their sustained profitability and access to relatively inexpensive capital. Extensive empirical research, however, failed to substantiate a reliable association between either input or output measures of R&D and individual company or market attributes, such as size or the extent of competition in the product market.[10] In fact, the success of many small software, electronics, biotech, and pharmaceutical companies in conducting R&D and marketing products within highly competitive environments clearly runs counter to Schumpeter's hypothesis.

Research on R&D and Productivity

From examining industrial organization and market structure issues, mainstream economic analysis of R&D largely shifted in the 1970s to investigating the social and private returns to investment in R&D. This empirical work, which started with extensive historical case studies and proceeded to large-sample cross-sectional analyses of the impact of R&D on productivity and growth, was aimed mainly at assessing the consequences of R&D investment and addressing public concerns such as the

role of R&D in the protracted productivity slowdown in the U.S. in the 1970s and early 1980s.[11]

This research effort yielded several important findings:[12]

- R&D expenditures contribute significantly to the productivity (value added) and output of firms, and the estimated rates of return on R&D investment are quite high—as much as 20-30% annually—although varying widely across industries and over time.[13] Indeed, the estimated returns to R&D are more than double the returns to tangible capital, reflecting the higher productivity as well as riskiness of R&D capital relative to physical assets.

- The contribution of *basic* research—research aimed at developing new science and technology—to corporate productivity and growth is substantially larger than the contribution of other types of R&D, such as product development and process R&D. In fact, the estimated contribution differential is about 3-to-1 in favor of basic research[14]—a finding that is particularly intriguing, given the widespread belief that firms have been recently curtailing expenditures on basic research and the skepticism expressed by many financial analysts and institutional investors about basic research.[15] Basic research is, of course, more risky than applied R&D, but it is inconceivable that risk differentials account for a 3-to-1 productivity superiority of basic research.

- The contribution of privately financed corporate R&D to productivity growth is larger than that of corporate R&D that is financed by the government (granted primarily to government contractors). The fact that most contracts with the government are based on "cost plus" terms may partly explain this finding. Nevertheless, the contribution to the technological infrastructure of industry of government-funded research conducted by government agencies and in federal laboratories (such as, for example, the National Institutes of Health) as well as university research is very significant.[16]

10. For surveys of this research, see Cohen and Levine (1989) and Scherer (1992).

11. See, for example, Lichtenberg and Siegel (1991).

12. For a discussion of these findings and the methodological issues involved in analyzing the cost-benefit relationship of R&D, see Griliches (1995).

13. See Hall (1993a); and for estimates of returns on tangible capital, see Poterba (1997). Documenting a positive contribution of R&D to productivity and growth is hardly surprising; why else would managers invest so heavily in R&D? Yet, this finding stands in stark contrast to a major assertion underlying the Financial Accounting Standards Board's (FASB) requirement for the immediate expensing of R&D in financial reports: "A direct relationship between research and development costs and specific future revenue generally has not been demonstrated, even with the benefit of hindsight." (FASB, 1974, p. 14).

14. See Griliches (1995). Related findings concern the importance of university research to industrial innovation (e.g., Mansfield 1991, Acs et al. 1994).

15. First-hand evidence of adverse analyst attitudes toward basic research can be found in an article by Richard Mahoney, former chairman and CEO of the Monsanto Company, describing how Monsanto developed over an extended period its biotechnology capacity, while analyst "naysayers offered a constant drumbeat of advice: reduce R&D, sell off any asset that wasn't nailed down and use the cash proceeds to buy back shares." (*The New York Times*, May 31, 1998).

16. See Mansfield (1991). Striking examples of major contributions of government R&D to industry are the Internet, funded originally by the Department of Defense as a bomb-resistant communications network, and later developed by the National Science Foundation, and the Human Genome Project, initiated by the National Institutes of Health, now leading to revolutionary advances in biomedicine.

■ The gap between the private and social benefits of R&D is wide. R&D "spillovers"—that is, benefits to one firm (industry or nation) from another firm's (industry or nation's) R&D or pool of knowledge—are substantial. Consequently, the "social" rate of return on R&D is considerably higher than the return to individual firms.[17] This finding generated extensive analysis of the adequacy of corporate incentives to conduct R&D, and the optimal design of arrangements for appropriating R&D benefits (e.g., patents, trademarks).

Because of the scarcity and other shortcomings of information *published* by individual companies, the research findings outlined above were based primarily on survey data and industry aggregates. In fact, none of the examined variables and attributes—return on R&D capital, basic vs. applied research, company vs. government sponsored R&D, and private vs. social benefits of R&D—can be directly estimated for individual companies from information publicly disclosed to investors. Thus, one of the most promising uses of the above findings is to suggest the kinds of information and data that investors should seek from R&D-intensive companies and that companies should consider disclosing to investors.

Research on R&D and Capital Markets

The research effort surveyed above related R&D inputs (intensity, capital) to firms' productivity, sales, or profit growth in an attempt to estimate the return on corporate investments in innovation-producing activities. But this approach encounters various problems. Perhaps most obvious, the time lag between the investment in R&D and the realization of benefits is generally unknown and often long (particularly for basic research), increasing the uncertainty about the estimated regression parameters. Furthermore, biases and distortions in reported profits (such as those arising from "opportunistic" decisions by managers to cut back or expand

R&D to "smooth" reported income) may cloud the intrinsic relationship between the cost of R&D and its benefits.

Such measurement difficulties have prompted a search for alternative and more reliable indicators of R&D *output* than conventional profitability measures. Two measures have received considerable attention—patents and capital market values—and they are discussed in the following review of the growing number of studies examining the relation between R&D and market values.[18]

Investors' Recognition of R&D Value. Despite widespread allegations of stock market "short termism" throughout the 1980s and early '90s, the research indicates persuasively that capital markets consider investments in R&D as a significant value-increasing activity. Thus, for example, a number of "event studies" register a significantly positive investor reaction to corporate announcements of new R&D initiatives, particularly of firms belonging to high-tech sectors and operating on the cutting edge of technology.[19] Moreover, when information is available, investors distinguish among different stages of the R&D process, such as program initiation and commercialization, rewarding in particular mature R&D projects that are close to commercialization.[20] Furthermore, econometric studies that relate corporate market values or market-to-book ratios to R&D intensities consistently yield positive and statistically significant association estimates.[21] Further probing into such associations suggests that firm size affects the valuation of R&D in the sense that investors value a dollar R&D spent by large firms more highly than R&D of small firms, perhaps due to better information available on large firms.[22] The evidence thus indicates unequivocally that the stock market views R&D expenditures as enhancing the value of firms, on average, and that investors also demonstrate some ability to differentiate the value of R&D across industries, firm sizes, and stage of R&D maturity.[23,24]

Estimating R&D Capital (Cost Basis). While R&D capital is the major asset of most high-tech and

---

17. (Griliches 1995)

18. The research using patent counts and citations as R&D output measures is voluminous, and is summarized in Griliches (1989) and Hall et al. (1998).

19. See, for example, Chan et al. 1992. It was widely believed in the 1980s and early 1990s that, prodded by investors' "obsession" with quarterly earnings, U.S. managers routinely sacrificed the long-term profitable growth of their firms by curtailing investments, such as R&D, with long payoffs but immediate hits to earnings. The evidence of investors' positive reaction to R&D increases, despite the negative effect of such increases on near-term earnings (due to the immediate expensing of R&D), largely dispels the allegation of investor myopia, at least with respect to R&D.

20. (Pinches et al. 1996)

21. (Ben-Zion 1978, Hirschey and Weygandt 1985, Bublitz and Ettredge 1989)

22. (Chauvin and Hirschey 1993)

23. Hall (1993a, 1993b) reports an intriguing finding that investors' valuation of R&D decreased substantially during the mid-to-late 1980s. This decrease, however, was found to be most evident in the electronics sector and has been largely reversed in the 1990s.

24. While investors as a group reward R&D expenditures, a recent study (Bushee 1998) found that institutions engaged in momentum trading (i.e., short-term oriented investors) tend to have large holdings in firms that "manage" earnings by cutting R&D to reverse earnings declines.

science-based companies, its value is nowhere to be found in financial reports. Obviously, the absence of a major asset from the book value (equity) or total assets of firms reduces the reliability and usefulness of conventional return-on-investment measures like ROE and ROA for performance evaluation. The assessment of companies' effectiveness in using investor capital requires that estimates of their investment in R&D be considered.

Economists often estimate the value of firms' R&D capital by assuming a uniform 10-15% annual amortization rate, which implies an amortization period, or average economic life, for R&D investment that ranges from roughly six to ten years. The assumed amortization rate is then used to "build up" a firm's R&D capital in cost terms. For example, based on a straight-line 15% annual amortization assumption, a firm's R&D capital at the end of a given year would be equal to 85% of its R&D expenditure in that year, plus 70% of R&D in the prior year, plus 55% of R&D expenditure in the year before that, and so on until a fully amortized R&D layer is reached.[25]

Since the pattern of R&D benefits varies across firms and industries, an industry- or firm-specific amortization rate is likely to do a better job of reflecting economic reality than a universal 10-15% rate. In a study published in 1996, Theodore Sougiannis and I estimated industry-specific R&D amortization rates using a (simultaneous equations) model that relates companies' operating profits to their tangible assets, advertising expenditures (proxying for brands), and the time series of their annual R&D expenditures extending back ten years.[26] The derived R&D lag structure allowed us to estimate the contribution to current profits of R&D expenditures made ten years ago, nine years ago, and so forth, ending with the contribution of current year's R&D to current profits. For example, in applying our model to pharmaceutical companies, our findings suggest that a dollar spent on R&D today increases future profits by $2.63, on average, and that the average life of R&D projects is 9 to 10 years.

The pattern of lagged contributions to future profits by R&D spending in turn allowed us to estimate firm-specific R&D capital for about 1,500 companies spanning a large variety of industries. In the case of Merck, for example, we found that an appropriate R&D-adjusted balance sheet would contain R&D capital with a value of some $3 billion at the end of 1991. This would represent a 60% addition to Merck's equity capital base.[27]

To examine the potential relevance of our estimates of R&D capital for investors, we used the estimates to calculate *capitalization-adjusted* earnings and book values and then ran a series of regressions to estimate the strength of the correlation of such *capitalization-adjusted* measures with stock prices and returns. Our regression analysis confirmed that the adjustments of both reported earnings and book values for the immediate expensing of R&D yield performance measures that are more strongly associated with market values than reported earnings and book values.

Firm-specific estimates of R&D capital, based either on a uniform (15%) amortization schedule or on industry-specific rates, could prove useful in the kind of corporate performance evaluation that relies heavily on financial ratio analysis.

Estimating R&D Capital (Market Values). Given the magnitude of corporate expenditures on R&D (over $150 billion in 1997) and ever-increasing demand for technology, one would expect *markets* for R&D to develop. Of course, markets for patent rights and the licensing of R&D have long been in operation. But recent years have witnessed a relatively new development—a large number of corporate acquisitions in the software, pharmaceutical, biotech, and electronics industries in which *R&D-in-process* was by far the major asset acquired. This became evident due to an accounting requirement ("purchase accounting" for acquisitions) that acquiring companies estimate separately the fair market value of the acquired assets, including R&D-in-process. In a recent study of such acquisitions, Zhen Deng and I found that the fair market values of acquired R&D (yet-to-be-completed R&D projects) amounted, on average, to 75% of the acquisition price.[28] Such acquisitions, numbering in the hundreds per year, are primarily trades in R&D and technology.

25. Sometimes a geometrically decaying R&D capital is assumed.
26. Lev and Sougiannis (1996). The rationale for estimating industry- rather than firm-specific amortization rates in our study was similar to that underlying the use of industry- rather than firm-specific beta values in cost of capital estimation. That is, the loss of specificity involved in an industry estimate is likely to be compensated for by reduction of noise in the industry data.

27. For a detailed example of the computation of firm-specific R&D capital for Merck & Co., see the appendix of the Lev and Sougiannis paper.
28. Deng and Lev (1998)

> *In applying our model to pharmaceutical companies, our findings suggest that a dollar spent on R&D today increases future profits by $2.63, on average, and that the average life of R&D projects is 9-10 years.*

The fair market values assigned by management to acquired R&D-in-process are generally based on the present value of estimated cash flows from projects under development.[29] Our study finds that those fair values are closely associated with stock prices of acquiring firms, which in turn lends some credibility to management estimates. Moreover, a recent study of Australian companies reported that revaluations of intangibles (a procedure allowed in Australia but not in the U.S.) are significantly associated with stock prices, suggesting once more that investors pay attention to managers' assessments of market values of R&D.[30]

In addition to acquisitions where R&D is the prime asset acquired, another manifestation of developing markets for R&D are the "targeted stocks" issued in recent years by high-tech companies such as Alza and Genzyme. In those still small number of cases, the value of the security is derived from a specific R&D program or pool of patents transferred by the patent company to the new entity, thus representing a further step in the progressive securitization of intangibles.[31] In time, the prices observed in such markets will provide "comparables" or multiples for the purpose of intangibles' and enterprise valuations.

Nonfinancial Indicators of R&D Value. In search of reliable measures of R&D *output*, economists have experimented with various nonfinancial indicators, such as the number of patents registered by a company (patent counts), patent renewal and fee data, number of innovations, and citations of patents.[32] Patent counts and the number of innovations emerging from a company's R&D program have been found to be associated with both the level of corporate investment in R&D and with firms' market values. It is clear, however, that those R&D output measures are rather noisy due to the "skewness" of their value distributions—that is, the tendency of a few patents or innovations to generate substantial returns, while most turn out to be virtually worthless.[33] Citations (references) of a firm's patents included in subsequent patent applications ("for-

ward citations") offer a more reliable measure of R&D value than the absolute number of patents, since such citations are an objective indicator of the impact of a firm's research activities on the subsequent development of science and technology.[34]

Various studies have shown that patent citations capture important aspects of R&D value. For example, Trajtenberg (1990) reports a positive association between citation counts and consumer welfare measures for CAT scanners; Shane (1993), in examining 11 semiconductor companies, finds that patent counts weighted by citations contribute to the explanation of cross-sectional differences in Tobin's q measures (market value over replacement cost of assets); and Hall et al. (1998) report that citation-weighted patent counts are associated with firms' market values (after controlling for the firms' R&D capital).[35]

In a direct test of the usefulness of patent citations to investors, Deng et al. (1999) and Hirschey et al. (1998) examine the ability of various measures derived from patent citations to *predict* subsequent stock returns and market-to-book (M/B) values in various R&D-intensive industries. The following three measures were all found to be significantly associated with future market-to-book values and stock returns of up to three years: (1) the number of patents granted to the firm in a given year; (2) the intensity of citations of a firm's patents in subsequent patents; and (3) a "science linkage" measure that reflects the number of citations in a firm's patents ("backward citations") of scientific papers and conferences (in contrast with citations of previous patents). The science linkage indicator is of special interest since it reflects the extent to which the firm engages in science-related or basic research as opposed to product development or process improvement. Furthermore, the predictive power of the science linkage measure with respect to stock performance is consistent with previously mentioned research that finds the contribution of basic research to firm productivity substantially larger than that of applied research aimed at product development.

---

29. See, for example, IBM's description in its 1995 annual report of the way it estimated Lotus' value of R&D-in-process ($1.84 billion).

30. Barth and Clinch (1998)

31. See Solt (1993) on R&D targeted securities and Beatty et al. (1995) on other R&D financing arrangements.

32. For a survey of this research, see Griliches (1989).

33. See, for example, Patel and Pavitt (1995).

34. The compilation of citations of previous patents or scientific studies in patent applications is of considerable importance and is checked carefully by patent examiners since patent citations assist in delineating the "claims," or property right boundaries, of the invention. Indeed, patent citations are used as evidence in patent infringement lawsuits. See Lanjouw and Schankerman (1997).

35. In two other studies, Austin (1993) reports that patents identifiable with end products tend to be more valued by investors than the average patent, and Megna and Klock (1993) find that patents of rival firms have a negative effect on a company's q-ratio.

As noted earlier, information about the nature of a company's R&D activities is generally not available in its financial statements. But, as the research just summarized suggests, non-financial indicators of R&D output such as number of patents, innovations, and trademarks—and in particular measures based on patent citations—offer a promising set of measures for firm valuation and security analysis.[36]

Firms' Capitalization of R&D. Software development costs are the major exception in the U.S. to the uniform expensing of R&D. FASB Statement No. 86 (enacted in 1985) requires companies to capitalize software development costs incurred after a project under development has reached technological feasibility (as generally evidenced by a working model or pilot).[37] The cumulative capitalized development cost (net of amortization) is presented as an asset on the balance sheet, while the periodic capitalized amount is subtracted from quarterly or annual development costs, which are then expensed in the income statement.

The amount of subjective judgment involved in the determination of technological feasibility of projects and the amortization of the capitalized asset led certain analysts and investment advisors to view software capitalization skeptically as detrimental to the quality of financial information. For example, the Association for Investment Management Research states: "We are not enamored of recording self-developed intangible assets unless their values are readily apparent; it usually is next to impossible to determine in any sensible or codifiable manner exactly which costs provide future benefit and which do not."[38]

But some recent empirical research suggests that the capitalization of intangibles may in fact provide useful information to investors. When David Aboody and I examined capitalization data disclosed during 1986-1995 by 168 software companies, we found that:

■ annually capitalized software development costs (i.e., the part of the total development cost that is not expensed) are positively and significantly associated with stock returns;

■ the value of the software asset that is reported on the balance sheet is reliably associated with stock prices; and

■ software capitalization data improve the prediction of future earnings.[39]

Particularly intriguing, moreover, was our finding that software companies that consistently expensed all their development costs (about a third of the examined sample) experienced positive abnormal return *drifts* that persisted for at least three years after the cost expensing, while firms that capitalized development costs did not. This evidence is consistent with some undervaluation of the shares of fully expensing firms, attributable perhaps to the lack of timely information about the progress and success of their software development programs (information that could be partly disclosed by the capitalization process).[40]

The evidence thus suggests that despite the subjectivity involved in the capitalization of software development costs, this procedure provides useful information to investors. The extent to which this conclusion can be generalized to other types of R&D (e.g., drug development) awaits further research. Nevertheless, it is worth noting that a recent simulation study clearly demonstrates the superiority of intangibles' capitalization over expensing in providing meaningful earnings data to investors. The simulation model measures the performance of pharmaceutical companies under immediate expensing of R&D and alternatively under capitalization, and compares the performance measures with economic returns and values (based on future cash flows). The results show that capitalization-based performance measures explain twice the variation in value as expensing-based measures.[41]

R&D and the Deteriorating Usefulness of Financial Information. It is widely acknowledged that the accounting measurement and reporting system has failed to keep up with recent sweeping changes

---

36. Stephan (1998) reports that the number of scientific publications of scientists associated with biotech startups is positively correlated with the IPO prices of these companies.

37. FASB Statement No. 86 applies to software developed for *sale*. In March 1998, the Accounting Standards Executive Committee of the AICPA (AcSEC) issued a statement of position (SOP 98-1) which applies the main criteria of FASB Statement No. 86 to software developed for *internal use*.

38. (AIMR 1993, p. 50)

39. Aboody and Lev (1998). This predictive ability of capitalized values is consistent with the FASB's capitalization criterion—the establishment of technological feasibility. Projects achieving technological feasibility are more likely to

generate higher earnings in the near future than earlier-stage projects, hence the association between the amounts capitalized and subsequent earnings.

40. The subsequent return drifts associated with full expensing software companies is consistent with a similar finding in Lev and Sougiannis (1996, section 6), indicating that the shares of firms intensive in R&D (which is fully expensed in the U.S.) are associated with subsequent positive returns, after controlling for various risk factors. Relatedly, Chan et al. (1998) report that poorly performing firms that continue to invest substantially in R&D are also characterized by subsequent positive abnormal returns, which is consistent with undervaluation.

41. Healy et al. (1998)

The extent of the association between earnings and stock returns has continuously decreased over the past 20 years.

FIGURE 3
THE ASSOCIATION
BETWEEN ANNUAL
EARNINGS AND STOCK
RETURNS

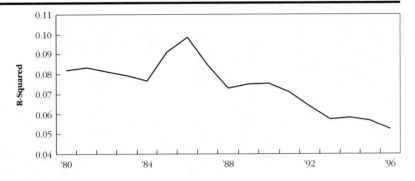

Source: Lev and Zarowin (1998, Table 1). The data are R-squared measures (3-year moving averages) from yearly regressions of annual returns on levels and changes of annual earnings.

in the economy. Such changes have been driven by the continuous restructuring of firms' operations and the extensive deregulation of important economic sectors (such as telecommunications), as well as by the innovation-producing activities of companies that are the focus of this paper. Various public committees that have examined the usefulness of financial information to investors report widespread concerns of financial statement users with both the timeliness and relevance of information conveyed by corporate reports.[42] The popularity of business performance measures like EVA, which makes potentially large adjustments to reported earnings, also attests to the dissatisfaction of users, both internal and external to the firm, with the product of the accounting measurement system.

In a recent study, Paul Zarowin and I examined changes in the usefulness of financial information by analyzing the association over the last 20 years between stock prices and returns, on the one hand, and key financial variables such as earnings, cash flows, and book values.[43] This research comes to the following conclusions:

■ the extent of the association between stock returns (prices) and financial variables has continuously decreased over the examined period, as portrayed in Figure 3 for earnings and stock returns;

■ the major culprit responsible for the deteriorating usefulness of financial information is *business change*, since the costs and benefits associated with change are mismatched in the computation of earnings;[44] and

■ R&D, a major driver of change, is directly associated with the decreasing usefulness of earnings.

More specifically, our study finds that firms that increased their R&D intensity over the 1977-1997 period experienced an above-average *decrease* in the association between earnings and stock returns, while firms whose R&D intensity declined experienced an *increase* in the strength of their returns-earnings association.[45]

The capital market consequences of informationally deficient financial reports have yet to be fully established, but some recent studies suggest they could be significant. For example, Boone and Raman (1998) report that unexpected changes in R&D are associated with a widening of the bid-ask spreads of stocks (an expected market-maker reaction to an increase in information asymmetry), leading to increased investors' transaction costs and decreased stock liquidity. Barth et al. (1998) document an increased level of analysts' efforts and possible mispricing of securities associated with high levels of R&D intensity. Aboody and Lev (1998) find

---

42. See, for example, AICPA (1993).
43. Lev and Zarowin (1998).
44. The costs associated with change (e.g., restructuring charges, R&D expenditures) are recognized immediately in the financial reports, while the benefits are reflected in future periods. Such a mismatching of costs and benefits adversely affects the informativeness of earnings and book values.

45. A mini-research industry has recently developed around the examination of temporal changes in the usefulness of financial information. Essentially all studies document a decrease in the returns-earnings association. On the other hand, Collins et al. (1997) report that the decrease in the returns-earnings association was compensated for by an increase in the stock price-book value association. Chang (1997) corroborates the Lev and Zarowin (1998) findings of a temporal decrease in the informativeness of both earnings and book values.

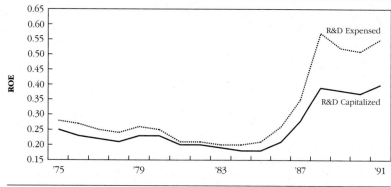

FIGURE 4
MERCK & CO.: RETURN ON
EQUITY (ROE) BASED ON
EXPENSING AND
CAPITALIZATION OF R&D

Source: Lev and Sougiannis (1996, Appendix).

that officers of R&D-intensive firms gain from insider trading significantly more than their counterparts in firms not engaged in R&D. And Lev and Sougiannis (1996), Aboody and Lev (1998), Chan et al. (1998), and Lev et al. (1999) all report evidence consistent with mispricing (generally undervaluation) of the shares of R&D-intensive companies. Finally, there is also evidence that some firms "manage" their reported earnings—say, by cutting R&D in response to shortfalls in operating earnings—which further compounds the information problems confronting investors in high-tech companies.[46]

In sum, the preliminary evidence suggests that the information and reporting deficiencies related to R&D activities have various adverse capital market consequences, which in turn may reduce firms' value by increasing monitoring costs and the cost of capital.[47]

OPERATING INSTRUCTIONS

What inferences can capital market practitioners draw from the empirical research on corporate R&D? I will classify such inferences, or "operating instructions," into two themes: (1) those that can be applied to the on-going performance evaluation of firms and (2) those useful for special purpose assignments, such as valuations for IPO pricing and corporate control transactions such as acquisitions and divestitures.

Performance Evaluation

Financial statements of R&D-intensive companies fail to provide adequate information for the assessment of profitability, growth, and enterprise risk. Contrary to widespread beliefs, the immediate expensing of intangible investments—including expenditures on brand maintenance and human resources as well as R&D—is not even necessarily a conservative practice. In fact, for firms with relatively low growth rates of intangibles—that is, the typical mature company—the immediate expensing of intangibles leads to a substantial *overstatement* of reported profitability.[48] In such cases, the effect of excluding intangible capital from the denominator of profitability ratios like ROE and ROA far outweighs the increased earnings under capitalization.[49] For example, as shown in Figure 4, the reported ROE (with immediate expensing of R&D) of Merck & Co.

---

46. See, for example, Baber et al. (1991).

47. In a similar vein, Bronwyn Hall (1993a, p. 290) comments: "asymmetric information between firms and investors implies that, to fund [R&D] projects about which they do not have full information, investors will demand a 'lemons' premium in the form of a higher rate of return." Obviously, in assessing the desirability of increased disclosure about firms' R&D activities, the competitive harm to firms from such disclosure and its effect on incentives to engage in R&D should be considered.

48. The exact relationship between ROE (ROA) under expensing and capitalization of intangibles is as follows: When the firm's growth rate of intangible investment is higher than its return on equity (which is typical of young firms and

industries), ROE (ROA) under expensing will be lower than under capitalization. But ROE and ROA under expensing will be higher for firms whose growth rate of intangibles is lower than their return on equity. For details, see Lev et al. (1999).

49. Under intangibles' expensing, earnings are charged with the periodic R&D expenditure, while under capitalization the amortization of the R&D capital (asset) is subtracted from earnings. For firms with a low growth rate of R&D, the difference between R&D expenditure and amortization will be relatively small, leaving the numerator of ROE (ROA) little changed, while the denominator is highly understated due to the absence of the intangible capital.

in the late '80s and early '90s was around 50-55%; but if Merck had instead capitalized and amortized its R&D, its ROE in that period would have ranged from 35-40%.[50]

Moreover, in a recent study, Bharat Sarath, Theodore Sougiannis, and I analyzed the impact of R&D expensing on reported earnings *growth*, which is the primary focus of many investors.[51] Our study demonstrated that firms whose growth rate of R&D falls below their growth in earnings will report higher earnings momentum when R&D is fully expensed than when R&D is capitalized and amortized. Thus, in this case as well—typical of mature companies— the expensing of R&D is far from conservative.

These biases in the reported performance of R&D-intensive companies are aggravated by the fact that U.S. firms expense not only *internally generated* R&D, but also *acquired* R&D. As noted earlier, acquired R&D amounts to 75%, on average, of the total acquisition price in those deals in which it is involved.[52] Obviously, the immediate expensing of the lion's share of the acquisition price substantially inflates the reported profitability of acquiring firms in the years after the acquisition. Post-acquisition earnings from the acquired entity are unencumbered by the previously expensed R&D, and the reported total assets or equity of the acquiring company reflects only a small portion of the total investment in the acquired entity. Thus, the full-expensing of R&D, internal as well as acquired, tends to inflate the reported profitability of R&D-intensive enterprises as well as the rate of growth of their reported earnings.

Financial analysts can partly correct for the reporting biases and distortions discussed above by a systematic reversal of R&D expensing—that is, by capitalizing and amortizing both internal and acquired R&D.[53] This adjustment involves adding back to earnings the expensed R&D and subtracting from earnings the amortization of the capitalized R&D. On the balance sheet, the R&D capital (net of amortization) should be added to total assets and equity (book value).[54]

To perform such a capitalization adjustment, the value of acquired R&D, which is provided in financial statement footnotes, should first be added to assets and equity. In contrast, the capitalized value of internal R&D has to be estimated. The key to the capitalization and amortization of internal R&D is the assumed *amortization rate*, or *average expected life*, of R&D projects, which is not reported by firms. As mentioned earlier, in estimating firms' R&D capital economists often use uniform annual amortization rates that range between 10% and 15%. But it is obviously preferable, whenever possible, to use industry- or firm-specific rates that reflect differences in technology and the appropriability of R&D benefits (relatively high in chemicals and drugs, where R&D is effectively protected by patents, and low in software and instruments) across industries and companies. Using the industry-specific amortization rates estimated by Lev and Sougiannis (1996) and other sources,[55] the following annual amortization rates seem suitable for R&D capitalization in the process of financial analysis:

- 8-10% (or amortization periods of 10-12 years) for pharmaceutical companies;
- 12-15% (6-8 years) for chemicals;
- 17-20% (5-6 years) for computer hardware, electronic equipment, and transportation vehicles; and
- 25% (4 years) for scientific instruments and software.

Despite the coarseness of the proposed capitalization and amortization estimates, it is inconceivable that investment analysis based on the uniform 100% amortization of R&D that now underlies reported earnings and book values could not be improved by the adjustment procedure outlined above.[56] Furthermore, the proposed capitalization procedure overcomes a disturbing inconsistency in accounting practices related to internally developed vs. acquired R&D products (e.g., scientific instruments). When a company acquires such a product it is recorded as an asset, whereas when the product is internally developed, all or most of the development costs are

---

50. Among the reasons for the increasing divergence between Merck's ROE (expensing) and ROE (capitalization) in the late 1980s (see Figure 4) is the considerable slowdown in its R&D growth. While Merck's average annual growth rate of R&D between 1977 and 1987 was close to 30%, its average annual R&D growth from 1987 to 1991 decreased to 18.6%. Ceteris paribus, the lower the growth rate of R&D, the larger the overstatement of reported profitability relative to profitability based on the capitalization of intangibles.

51. (Lev et al. 1999).

52. (Deng and Lev 1998); sample period ended in 1997.

53. Note that the EVA performance evaluation system also reverses the immediate expensing of intangibles.

54. For firms whose R&D expenditures are stationary (zero growth), capitalization will not affect earnings (in a steady state), but will affect book value and total assets. For all other firms, the proposed capitalization will affect both earnings and book values. For details of the capitalization procedure, see Lev and Sougiannis (1996, Appendix).

55. See, for example, Deloitte & Touche 1996 annual survey of the software industry.

56. This conclusion is also supported by Chambers et al. (1997), which shows that the explanatory power of earnings and book values with respect to stock prices increases when the financial variables are adjusted to reflect the capitalization of R&D.

expensed. The comparability of financial information between purchasing and developing companies can be restored by capitalizing the development costs of the latter companies.

Finally, it should be noted that the capitalization procedure outlined above is no substitute for the procedure for capitalizing intangibles that is currently required for software companies. Because such capitalization begins only after projects under development pass a technological feasibility test, the capitalization data provide investors with important information about the progress and probable success of firms' development programs. Furthermore, the writeoff of capitalized assets that are no longer commercially viable provides additional important information to investors. Such information, needless to say, is not reflected in the mechanical capitalization procedure proposed above.

In-Depth Assessment of Innovative Capabilities

The valuation and due diligence of R&D-intensive enterprises performed for corporate control transactions or IPOs require a thorough understanding and assessment of the innovative capabilities of the examined enterprise and its capacity to produce and market the developed products. Such assessment should begin with an analysis of the enterprise's R&D *strategy*—an analysis that determines the extent to which the firm primarily *develops* products and services, *shares* development with others through alliances, or *acquires* R&D. The strategy analysis should then attempt to ascertain the proportions of resources devoted to basic research vs. product development and cost reduction ("process R&D"), and to an assessment of the firm's capability to *use* rather than to *perform* R&D—that is, its record of learning from other companies' (and universities') innovations and adapting quickly to external technological changes. Learning from others requires an adequate scientific and engineering capacity as well as flexibility of organizational design. An examination of an enterprise's research strategy and capabilities will also shed light on the riskiness of investment in R&D. Obviously, the heavier the investment in basic vs. applied research, and the larger the proportion of in-house R&D vs. that developed in alliance with other firms, the riskier are the firm's R&D activities.

Research capability should be assessed primarily by *output* measures, such as the number of new products that have emerged from the development process, as well as the number of patents, patent citations, and trademarks registered (as discussed earlier, each of these measures of R&D output have been demonstrated to have a strong positive correlation with stock-price performance). Most important, efforts should be made to quantify the contribution of R&D activities to sales, cost savings, and earnings. Various quantitative measures can be used to gauge research output, such as citations to the firm's patents and measures indicating the share of current revenues coming from products developed within the last three or five years. The latter measure indicates the firm's ability to quickly "bring products to the market," a capacity which often differs from the ability to develop products.

R&D strategy should be evaluated in the context of the firm's overall strategic position. Is the firm an industry leader, reaping the advantages of a "first mover"; or is it a "follower" in introducing new products and innovations? What is the firm's record in appropriating the benefits of its innovative activities, such as successfully defending its patents from infringement and maximizing licensing revenues? Answers to these and similar questions will shed light on the firm's innovative capabilities.

Finally, the firm's product *pipeline* has to be considered. Even when accompanied by an impressive historical record of developing and marketing products, an impoverished pipeline of projects does not bode well for the future. This calls for a thorough examination of products under development, such as drugs in FDA approval process, as well as patents and trademarks pending registration. Also to be examined are current and expected revenues from licensing agreements and the activity level of research and development performed within alliances and joint ventures. When *valuation* of R&D-in-process is required (as in the case of corporate acquisitions), the future cash flows from pipeline projects should be estimated, accounting among other things for synergies with the acquiring entity's R&D. Such cash flow-based valuations of R&D-in-process are now common, given the large volume of technology company acquisitions.

An assessment of firms' product development and marketing capacity should also take into consideration managers' incentives to "manage" reported performance. As mentioned earlier, research indicates that under certain circumstances managers will change periodic R&D expenditures to

Efforts should be made to quantify the contribution of R&D activities to sales cost savings, and earnings. Various quantitative measures can be used to gauge research output, such as citations of the firm's patents and measures indicating the share of current revenues coming from products developed within the last three or five years.

achieve earnings targets or conform with investors' expectations.[57] Such "management" of R&D and the resulting effect on reported earnings should be adjusted for in the evaluation of R&D capabilities and consequences.[58]

SUMMARY

Although R&D is the major productive factor and the principal asset of high-tech and science-based companies, public information about firms' R&D activities and their benefits is wholly inadequate for investment research and analysis. This paper begins with a brief review of statistics that show the growth of U.S. corporate R&D expenditures outstripping the growth of corporate investment in tangible assets. Next, in comparing R&D disclosure regulations among industrialized nations, I show that U.S. rules are the least flexible in allowing management

discretion in the measurement and reporting of R&D (e.g., capitalization vs. expensing). Then I survey the large and growing body of empirical research on R&D, which demonstrates unequivocally that (1) the contribution of R&D to productivity and shareholder value is substantial and (2) that capital markets reflect such contributions in stock prices. But if investors clearly demonstrate a willingness to take the "long view" of R&D in many cases, there is also some evidence of undervaluation of R&D-intensive companies as well as other potential costs to some corporations and investors stemming from inadequate public information about R&D. In the final section, I offer some operating guidelines for investors and analysts that follow R&D-intensive companies, suggesting a number of adjustments of financial data (in particular, capitalizing instead of expensing some forms of R&D) designed to better reflect corporate performance and value.

---

57. See, for example, Perry and Grinaker (1994), Baber et al. (1991), Bushee (1998).

58. Incentive compensation plans, such as EVA, that capitalize R&D expenditures reduce but do not eliminate incentives to manage earnings via R&D.

RELATIONSHIP INVESTING

AND

SHAREHOLDER COMMUNICATION

JOEL STERN: Good morning, and welcome to this discussion of relationship investing and shareholder communication. The general purpose of the Roundtable will be to consider the recent rise of institutional investor activism and the opportunities it holds for corporate management to increase their share values by cultivating relationships with "longer-term" investors.

Some finance and legal scholars have proposed that companies give institutional investors greater voice in corporate strategic decisions, perhaps by inviting them into the boardroom. But another possibility—probably somewhat less troubling to management—is to improve the quality of their communication to investors by providing information that goes beyond what is provided by conventional accounting statements. Thus, one of the major themes in the discussion will be the limitations of current financial reporting. We would like to consider ways to improve the quality of corporate shareholder communications by devising new financial measures, or perhaps non-financial measures, that would give a more realistic picture of long-run corporate profitability.

■ In fact, there are no fewer than five major issues that we would like to address this morning. **First** is the longstanding controversy about the relationship between market efficiency and accounting disclosures. As most of you are aware, Chicago-school financial economists tend to think that by the time the information is released by the auditors, investors have already found alternative sources for that information. According to this view, most accounting information is already reflected in stock prices when disclosed, and thus there's not much point in improving accounting if nobody pays much attention to it. So we want to start by exploring what role, if any, more realistic accounting could play in improving the efficiency of capital markets.

■ The **second** major subject is a very intriguing one called "relationship investing." Stated in brief, the underlying proposition is that publicly traded companies can increase their share values by targeting a particular group of "patient" (or, as I prefer to call them, "value-based") investors. We at Stern Stewart have long argued that there are "lead steers" who effectively dominate the pricing process on Wall Street. Some obvious names that come to mind are Warren Buffett and Peter Lynch, but there are many others. And it may well be worth a considerable corporate effort to enlist such investors among the firm's major shareholders.

■ The **third** issue is whether and how we can improve existing financial measures of performance. The current search for relationship investors may reflect in large part the inadequacy of the accounting information that is regularly disclosed by companies to sell-side analysts—the largely meaningless quarterly compilation and reporting of earnings per share. To the extent this is so, better financial measures could help stimulate relationship investing. Such measures could become a new language, in effect, for communicating with and thus attracting sophisticated investors.

■ **Fourth**, corporate IR efforts may also want to make use of *non-financial* performance measures—of things like product quality, and customer and employee satisfaction—that could help investors better evaluate future corporate performance. Ned Regan, who has been kind enough to join us this morning, is leading a research effort in that direction, and I'm confident he will tell us about the promise these kinds of measures hold out for improving the dialogue between management and shareholders.

■ **Fifth** and last is the broader issue of corporate governance and board supervision, and how it interacts will all these other issues I've just mentioned.

To discuss these timely and provocative matters, we have assembled a very distinguished group of participants, and I will mention them now in alphabetical order:

BASIL ANDERSON is the Chief Financial Officer of Scott Paper Co. Basil has just succeeded in instituting at Scott a major change in the financial measures that guide the company's investment planning, periodic performance evaluation, and executive compensation decisions.

CAROLYN BRANCATO is executive director of the Columbia Institutional Investor Project at Columbia Law School. Carolyn, who runs her own economic consulting firm called Riverside Economic Research, also recently completed work as staff director of the Competitiveness Policy Council's study of corporate governance and financial markets.

GEOFFREY COLVIN is Assistant Managing Editor of *Fortune*, and a member of the magazine's Board of Editors.

JUDITH DOBRZYNSKI is a senior writer at *Business Week*. Judy wrote the magazine's recent cover story on "Relationship Investing" and, some time before that, the cover story on "Corporate Governance."

ALEX LEHMANN was formerly Vice President of investor relations at Whitman Corporation, and now is a consultant specializing in valuation issues. While at Whitman, Alex developed a very proactive approach to corporate IR—one that I think you'll find quite interesting.

NELL MINOW is one of the principals (another is Robert Monks) of The Lens Fund, a highly-publicized active investor that takes large positions in underperforming companies. Their role in spurring the break-up of Sears is probably their major accomplishment to date, but they are also hard at work at American Express, Kodak, and Westinghouse.

KRISHNA PALEPU is Professor of Accounting and Finance at the Harvard Business School. Krishna, along with Harvard colleague Robert Kaplan, is in the process of putting together a symposium on non-financial measures of corporate performance.

EDWARD REGAN has been New York State Controller for the past 14 years—and a remarkably effective one, judging from the performance of the State's pension fund over that period. Starting midnight tomorrow, however, Ned will cease to be a politician and will become President of the Jerome Levy Institute, an economics thinktank at Bard College. There he will lead a research project on corporate governance.

JOSEPH SHENTON is President of OLC Corporation, a corporate investor relations consulting firm that studies the behavior of institutional investors and now has close to 150 corporate clients. Joe is in the business of trying to help corporations choose the appropriate investor clienteles and then help ensure that such clienteles are heavily represented in the shareholder base.

DEREK SMITH is Executive Vice President of Equifax, Inc. in charge of insurance information services. Besides adopting a new internal financial measurement system, Equifax recently announced a leveraged Dutch auction share repurchase that was widely applauded by Wall Street. It should be interesting to hear the thinking behind that *financial* strategy—and the message Derek thinks it has sent to the company's investors.

EUGENE VESELL is Senior Vice President of Oppenheimer Capital. Gene and his colleagues, who have about $25 billion under management, have been practicing relationship investing long before anyone thought to give it a name. They have $18 billion invested in the equities of some 65 companies, giving Oppenheimer Capital an average position of about $250 million, and a 10% or greater ownership stake in about half their portfolio companies.

JEROLD ZIMMERMAN is Professor of Accounting at the University of Rochester's Simon School of Business. He is also the founding co-editor of the *Journal of Accounting and Economics*, a distinguished publication produced at the University of Rochester. Jerry has been among the four or five superstars in accounting research over the last 15 to 20 years. Last but not least are my Stern Stewart colleagues, **BENNETT STEWART**, who will serve as my co-moderator in this discussion, and **DON CHEW**, a founding partner of Stern Stewart and Editor of the Continental Bank *Journal of Applied Corporate Finance*. With that introduction, let me turn the floor over to Bennett Stewart.

What Accounting Was Never Meant to Be

STEWART: Thanks, Joel. Well, as you can see, we've been remarkably successful in narrowing the focus of this discussion.

Let's begin with this issue of the accounting framework that seems to underlie a lot of the concern expressed about the "short termism" of corporate America. Accounting conventions require corporations to expense much of their long-term investment, their R&D, their outlays for employee training, software investments, and so forth. The concern expressed by corporate managers is that investors focus myopically on near-term accounting results, thus placing an excessive discount on payoffs expected from promising long-run investment. Such allegedly systematic undervaluation of corporate investment then forces corporate managers to underinvest in the corporate future, or at least to invest in the wrong projects.

Let me begin by asking Professor Jerry Zimmerman to give us an academic perspective on these issues. Jerry, how is it that we have ended up with the current accounting system? And has it accomplished what it was really intended to do, or is it failing us in some important sense?

ZIMMERMAN: In the interest of full disclosure, let me preface my remarks with a disclaimer. The view I am about to offer is not widely held among my accounting colleagues, many of whom would likely argue that my views are speculative—that is, not sufficiently backed up by the existing body of accounting research. But, in fact, there is quite a bit of evidence that supports what I'm about to say.

Bennett Stewart has written an article called "Market Myths" in the *Journal of Applied Corporate Finance* that does a wonderful job of summarizing the ways in which accounting conventions fail to measure economic reality. I agree with almost everything Bennett has to say in that article, but I think he's left out probably the most important market myth of them all—namely, the notion that accounting numbers were ever demanded, or *intended* for use, by shareholders for the purpose of valuing companies. Although accounting numbers do provide some information to investors, they are not a primary source of information for our capital markets. And, as long as institutions like the SEC and FASB continue to regulate disclosure, I suspect reported accounting numbers will never be very useful for investors in setting stock values.

The accounting systems that we have today—the historical-cost-based numbers that we all love to hate—have developed over hundreds of years. They can be traced back to the first "joint stock" or publicly owned companies of the 14th century and even earlier. The problem that the accounting and auditing systems were originally designed to solve was the very basic problem of stewardship. Take the case of the East India Trading Company, which was an early joint stock company. Let's say they had a manager 4000 miles away running a trading post, and they shipped that person a boatload of goods. The purpose of accounting was to ensure that the manager used those goods to serve the company's interests and not just his own.

Another important function of accounting—one that developed somewhat later with the rise of public debt markets—was to control conflicts of interest between a company's bondholders and its shareholders. The problem was this: How could managers, as representatives of the shareholders, make credible promises to the bondholders that they would not pay out excessively high dividends or invest in excessively risky projects? To reduce these conflicts, companies contracted privately with their bondholders to hire reputable, third-party accounting firms to gather and report certain kinds of information that would be useful in monitoring management's compliance with debt covenants. This was all done privately; there was no SEC, no public regulatory body, to demand that this information be provided. And the system worked.

STEWART: At this point, though, Jerry, the companies were closely held, right? The owners were not widely dispersed as they are today?

ZIMMERMAN: No, these joint stock companies had lots of owners. The East India Company had hundreds of shareholders.

Today, of course, the SEC would have us believe—and this is another part of that same market myth your article fails to mention—that the 1929 stock market crash was caused by inadequate financial disclosure and that the existence of the SEC now somehow protects us from further stock market crashes. But, having recently experienced the Crash of 1987, we now know that the SEC and mandated financial disclosure do not prevent stock market declines.

So, the *primary* function of the financial accounting system was never—and nor is it today—to provide information for valuation decisions. It was designed to provide *internal* measures of performance to serve as guides in running companies, and to protect outside investors from opportunistic managers. It's basically an auditing function: Count the cash and make sure the inventories are what they're supposed to be. It's a basic control system. It is not *primarily* a system for shareholder valuation of companies as going concerns.

Of course, many people still believe the primary function of these systems is to provide information for valuation, but this expectation has created an enormous problem for the public accounting profession. Those who bought into this accounting myth 50 years ago are now in a Catch 22: The partners of what used to be the Big Eight firms (it's now down to the Big Six, of course) are saying to themselves today: "Yes, we can provide this information for valuation. But every time the stock market crashes, we get sued for poor financial disclosure. We are being litigated out of existence."

Today, the legal costs of Big Six firms are running at about 10 to 15% of their total revenue. Because they can't get insurance any more, they're self-insuring. If we have a few more big lawsuits, we will no longer have a Big Six audit industry. In that event, the SEC may eventually end up requiring American corporations to be audited by a government body like the GAO.

STERN: Jerry, you mentioned that one objective of accounting statements was to provide information for lenders to the company. If this information helps lenders make better judgments about credit risk, why wouldn't that kind of information also be useful to shareholders?

ZIMMERMAN: For one thing, lenders are really insiders in a way that, at least in the U.S., outside shareholders can never be. As part of their credit evaluation, lenders routinely ask corporate borrowers to provide extensive financial disclosures that they then keep privately. That kind of confidential exchange of private information is not permissible between management and shareholders in the U.S. This private exchange of information can be valuable because there is often important strategic information that companies don't want to disclose to their competitors, but only to certain investors.

Although accounting numbers do provide some information to investors, they are not a primary source of information for our capital markets. And, as long as institutions like the SEC and FASB continue to regulate disclosure, I suspect reported accounting numbers will never be very useful for outside investors in setting stock values.

—Jerold Zimmerman

Another important difference between lenders and shareholders is that lenders care primarily only about downside risk. Lenders are much less interested than shareholders in going concern values, and much more concerned about liquidation values. They want to know what the assets will be worth if the company can't meet its interest payments.

STEWART: But, Jerry, isn't it possible that a perception could become a reality? You're saying that the accounting system was never *intended* to be a system for measuring value by the stock market. But isn't it conceivable that, through the efforts of the SEC, it could have become one. After all, the research you have published in your own *Journal of Accounting and Economics* has shown that stock prices respond in fairly predictable ways to earnings "surprises." Doesn't that partly contradict your position?

ZIMMERMAN: No. Going back to the seminal research of Ray Ball and Phil Brown in 1968, the stock market anticipates *most* of the news in accounting earnings by the time the numbers are released. The market has more timely sources of information than accounting numbers, including voluntary management disclosures and financial analysts' reports. Joel described the importance of "lead steers" in the pricing process. I doubt these people use accounting earnings as their primary source of information about companies' future cash flows.

Keeping Three Sets of Books: The Case of Scott Paper

STEWART: Let me turn now to Basil Anderson. Basil, as CFO of Scott Paper, would you say that Jerry's view of the "irrelevance" of accounting to the stock market valuation process is one that is shared by your senior manage-

ment colleagues at Scott? And what do you find when you talk to your investors? Are they greatly interested in your quarterly financial results?

ANDERSON: One of the big challenges for us as a company is trying to reconcile the internal management information we need to run our business with the kind of information we *think* is required by investors on the outside. Of course, what we think investors want is to some extent dictated by SEC disclosure requirements. But, if we can believe people like Joel Stern and Bennett Stewart, there may well be kinds of information required by investors that are different from what is required by the SEC. To the extent this is true, companies could end up seeing a need to keep three different sets of books. And keeping three sets of books is not only costly and time-consuming, it can create lots of internal confusion about what the company is trying to achieve.

At Scott, we have developed an information system and financial performance measures that we feel are appropriate across a range of corporate decisions: capital budgeting, evaluation of divisional performance, management compensation awards, and so forth. And the financial measures we use to guide those decisions are quite different from what we're required to report to the SEC.

Communicating with investors, however, continues to pose the greatest challenge for us. Although the securities analysts and other representatives of the investment community I interact with tend to ask questions very much consistent with what the SEC and the accounting profession requires, these numbers have very little to do with how we manage and evaluate our own performance internally. Without any definite sense of the kind of information investors want from us, we simply try to do the best we can to respond.

STEWART: Basil, let's suppose you are rolling out a major new product line in Europe, and the costs associated with that investment will be expensed for two or three years before any benefits begin to show up in your financial statements. According to accounting conventions, much of that investment must be treated as an expense that reduces reported earnings. Yet, viewed from the perspective of a business person or an owner, it really represents an investment in the future.

How do you reconcile those two perspectives? How do you prevent yourself from underinvesting?

ANDERSON: Our own history of investment and capital spending would show that the perceived short-term focus of Wall Street has not prevented us from embarking on big expansion projects with longer-term payoffs. We do the best we can to inform Wall Street about the expected payoffs from our investment. But, as I said earlier, the disparity between how public accountants treat this investment and how we regard it internally creates a challenge for us in communicating with investors.

ALEX LEHMANN: Communicating effectively with investors is indeed a challenge. But it also represents a continuous opportunity to provide the kinds of information investors need to value a company. Basil referred to the expected payoffs from Scott's capital projects. Clearly that is what investor relations is all about: helping investors get a feel for the expected payoffs from both existing and new investment, and creating realistic expectations about the level of future cash flow and the investment necessary to provide that growth.

The Case for Accounting Reform

STEWART: Let me turn now to Krishna Palepu of the Harvard Business School. Krishna, you have a perspective on this issue that is somewhat different from Jerry Zimmerman's.

PALEPU: I would say my view of the world complements more than it contradicts Jerry's view, but I strongly disagree with part of his opening statement. The original intent of the accounting system may well have been the internal control and monitoring functions that Jerry described, but the limitation of this kind of historical analysis is that it may obscure important evolutionary change. In 1993, it may not be all that useful to be looking at the East India Company. The world economy has changed significantly over the past 300 years, and it's not implausible to me that the basic function of the accounting system could have evolved along with it. Part of the job of academic accountants like Jerry and me is of course to *describe* the past, and to explain why the existing accounting system looks the way it does. But another role for us academics is to suggest the possibility for change, to take a role in *prescribing* changes in the accounting system that would make accounting information more useful to investors.

For this reason, I welcome the SEC's challenge to the accounting profession to provide better measures of performance, non-financial as well as financial. Such measures ought to be designed to help investors monitor the value of their investments and keep track of how well management is using the capital they have committed. In fact, I believe the FASB has explicitly adopted this aim as their top priority in their ongoing redesign of the accounting system.

But despite the FASB's professed aim of facilitating communications between managers and investors— and here I'm about to agree with Jerry—the great majority of the FASB's actual rulings are really done with the mentality of a traffic cop: They just want the road to be clear; they don't seem to care as much whether any-

Even if the market is pretty good in valuing companies in the aggregate, individual companies may well be either overvalued or undervalued because of "information asymmetries" between managers and outside shareholders. If I were the CFO of an undervalued company, one of my principal responsibilities would be to figure out a way to get my story out. And one way to accomplish that would be to devise useful leading indicators and then make them the centerpiece in the voluntary or non-SEC part of my investor communications program.

—Krishna Palepu

body drives on it or not. For this reason, the FASB basically doesn't want to play an active role in addressing a problem like the one Bennett is talking about—that is, the treatment of long-term investment and R&D. If you look at the items on the FASB agenda at any point in time, there will always be a lot more items that relate to either expenses or liabilities, and a lot fewer to revenues and assets.

So there's a definite bias in terms of what the FASB is trying to do. As Jerry suggested, the accounting standards are designed more to protect the interests of creditors than to shed light on the going-concern value that accrues largely to shareholders. Creditors are interested primarily in the downside, but shareholders are interested in the upside as well. Shareholders are interested in assets as well as liabilities, future revenues as well as current expenses. So I think we need to move toward

an accounting system that aims to tell more of the complete story— while still keeping in mind, of course, who is telling the story and their incentives to get the story right.

STEWART: But, it seems to me that accounting still has one necessary and inescapable limitation. It is based upon historical results, it is a recording of past events. Since investors are by their nature forward looking, I don't see how we can expect an accounting-based system to play a major role in the dialogue that needs to take place between management and investors.

PALEPU: I disagree. In many cases, a company's recent history may well be the most reliable guide to the future and, hence, to its going concern value. At the same time, you could supplement these historical disclosures with some leading indicators that might actually tell investors where the company is going.

STEWART: Would you give us some examples of what you mean by leading indicators?

PALEPU: Well, suppose a company is making an investment in the design and marketing of a new product. When evaluating the progress of that investment for internal purposes, management will generally have a set of intermediate goals or milestones they use to assess whether they are on track. Companies could disclose some of these internal goals to the investment community without giving away the store.

Now, it's true some managers are worried that disclosure of strategic information could undermine their firms' competitive position. But while such concerns are valid, they are probably overstated—because competitors typically cannot replicate a really innovative strategy just by reading about it. For example, take the case of Wal-mart. Its strategy has become a matter of public knowledge, but very few competitors have been able to replicate it.

Indeed, I would argue that if a company's strategy can be readily replicated by another company, then it is not a source of sustainable competitive advantage. Much of the value of corporate strategy, I suspect, comes not from strategy *per se*, but rather from how effectively the strategy is implemented.

STEWART: Krishna, that reminds me of the message of your Harvard colleague Amar Bhide, who wrote a great *Harvard Business Review* article called "Hustle as Strategy." Amar's argument is that strategic brilliance is becoming less important to corporate success than execution and efficiency.

For example, I recently read in *Business Week* that whereas it took Chrysler two and a half years and $1.7 billion to come up with a new compact model, it took General Motors five or six years and some $3 billion

to develop its own compact, the Saturn. It's not hard to see from these two numbers why GM is having such problems. But what really struck me about this story is that I was learning about these time-to-market and investment cost measures—things that are really critical to evaluating the operating efficiency of auto manufacturers—*not* from the company's annual or quarterly reports, but from reading *Business Week*. This is precisely the kind of information investors need to know to gain a competitive edge.

So, it's no wonder investors don't expect to learn much from reading a company's annual report. Even if companies did disclose such information in their quarterly or annual reports—which they typically don't, unless it puts them in a consistently favorable light—it's already stale information by the time it comes out.

PALEPU: But there are many ways of communicating with shareholders that can be far more effective than the annual report. The annual report is simply the culmination of the financial reporting process; it's often more a ceremonial event than a source of information. Some companies use quarterly reports to provide management discussions of capital spending and progress toward meeting stated corporate goals. For example, if your internal corporate objectives include an increase in customer service and a decrease in new product cycle times, then it makes a lot of sense for management to tell the investment community about these goals, and about its progress in meeting them. It makes sense to give investors a roadmap, if you will, and then promise that you will faithfully chart your progress in bad times as well as good.

Credibility is, of course, a very important part of this whole disclosure process. To the extent you succeed in establishing credibility with

the investment community, a corporate IR program may have far more ability to supplement its financial disclosures with information about some of the nonfinancial leading indicators I mentioned earlier.

STERN: Krishna, let me present an alternative hypothesis, perhaps in a somewhat extreme form. Let's assume that all this accounting information is of absolutely no value to investors at all; it plays no role in determining the price of a company's shares. Assume further that you know the management of a poorly performing company was about to be replaced by a management team with a reputation for delivering results. Would that alone be sufficient basis for committing investment funds to such a company?

PALEPU: Management reputation certainly plays a major role. But if I were putting $100 million into a company, I would also like to know something about the new management's plan for reforming the business, for creating new growth, and for funding that growth. For example, if I were going to invest in IBM, I would need to know more than just that Lou Gerstner was coming in to run IBM and that he had a lot of stock options.

STERN: I would argue that top management's reputation represents a very important part of this market valuation process. Take the case of Eastman Kodak reported in today's *Wall Street Journal*. The article announced that Chris Steffen, the CFO hired a few months ago to push forward the restructuring of the company, is now leaving. There was a 15% drop in the price of Kodak's shares as soon as the announcement was made. When it was first announced he was coming on board, there was an almost identically large *increase* in the price of the shares.

I would argue that Steffen's reputation for doing what needs to be done significantly altered investors' expectations of future performance at Kodak. No accounting system that measured historical performance would have helped investors make the decision to buy when Steffen came on or to sell when he left. All you needed to know was whether he was coming or going.

NED REGAN: I think the shares would have dropped even if Steffen hadn't resigned. Yesterday's *Wall Street Journal* showed clearly that two people were trying to run the same company. I read that story and said to myself: "Goodbye Kay or goodbye Steffen."

Old-Fashioned Relationship Investing: The Case of Oppenheimer Capital

STERN: Well, I suspect we will come back to Kodak later in this discussion. But now let me turn to Eugene Vesell of Oppenheimer Capital. As I said earlier, Gene started practicing a kind of relationship investing long before anybody thought to give it a name.

Gene, would you tell us about Oppenheimer Capital and how it works? For example, do you use accounting-based information in evaluating investment candidates, or do you place more emphasis on other non-financial, perhaps more forward-looking, indicators?

VESELL: Joel, before I answer your last question, let me respond to the point you just made about reputation. You suggested that all you need to know about a company is management's reputation. Well, I essentially agree with that statement, but I would add that there's one other important consideration: the extent to which management's compensation is tied to shareholder value.

We at Oppenheimer have about $26 billion in assets under management. Our total equity investments are in the $17-$18 billion range. So we're fairly large, but not one of the

We like companies that are run as if they were private; maximization of cash flow and minimization of taxable reported earnings are the goals we want management to pursue. The fact that the company is run to maximize cash flow, not earnings, sends a very powerful signal to us that they are managing like owners. Our own firm, Oppenheimer Capital, is owner-managed; we're a publicly traded MLP with significant management ownership. And we look for other companies that are owner-managed...We want managers to be owners with us.

—Eugene Vesell

giants. And, unlike the giants, we tend to take very concentrated positions. As you mentioned earlier, we have about 65 positions (though a typical account will own only 35-40 stocks). Hence, an average position is about $250 million. However, we do have a dozen holdings over $400 million.

STEWART: What percentage of the stock does that typically represent?

VESELL: We often own 10% or more of a company's shares. In our larger companies, that obviously tends to be a little smaller; for example, we own only about 5-6% of Sprint. But, in our smaller companies, our stakes are quite large. We own 20% of Dole, over 15% of Sundstrand, 14% of Transamerica, and over 15% of Freeport McMoran.

STEWART: Let me stop you with Freeport McMoran. That's a very difficult company to analyze from the outside because of the depletion allowances and the diverse kinds of

assets. How do you evaluate a company like that? Their accounting statements are virtually meaningless.

VESELL: I couldn't agree more. Well, as Joel was suggesting, it's the reputation and the incentive compensation of the top management that were perhaps the most important factors driving our investment decision. The quality of the board of directors was also important.

With respect to the assets themselves, the best we could do was to assess their value using very imprecise, essentially qualitative judgments—although we did have some hard numbers on "proven reserves." The company's principal asset is a copper and gold mine in New Guinea, and we used those estimates of reserves to make a present value calculation of the value of those assets. And after making some back-of-the-envelope adjustments for their other assets and liabilities, we said to ourselves:

"Gee, what you can touch here is worth 50% to 75% above the current stock price."

But, once more, what we were really banking on was the reputation and incentives of management. In the case of Freeport McMoran, management had a record for both finding new assets and then, once they found them, of managing those assets very efficiently.

STEWART: But how would you know they were managing assets efficiently if you couldn't make sense of the financial statements?

VESELL: Well, as you say, historical accounting numbers were not much of a guide. The company has dual incorporation in Indonesia and Delaware, which even complicates the accounting more, because Indonesian tax laws allow you to write off a fair amount of the capital spending. And let me stop here and point out that we *want* our companies to write off their investment as quickly as possible. We like companies that are run as if they were private; maximization of cash flow and minimization of *taxable* reported earnings are the goals we want management to pursue.

So, in this case, we were able to look through the accounting statements to find the cash flows generated by the mining operations. And the fact that the company is run to maximize cash flow, not earnings, sends a very powerful signal to us that they are managing like owners. We also used the very solid stock price performance following the merger of McMoran Oil and Freeport Sulphur as another useful indicator of their ability to manage assets.

STEWART: I understand that, although the company is very adept at finding mineral reserves, they don't insist on taking them out of the ground.

VESELL: That's right. Unlike many natural resource companies, they have specialized in doing only what they do best. If they find new mineral reserves, they're not committed to developing them. They will sell the reserves if they can find a buyer willing to pay a high price for those reserves, presumably because the buyer brings more value added to the mining process. As managers, their aim is not to maximize assets under control, as so many American companies have done, but rather to maximize rates of return on capital and thus shareholder value. They really know how to manage investor capital.

And, as I mentioned earlier, we invest in companies where there's clearly a strong bond of common interest between management and the shareholders. Our own firm, Oppenheimer Capital, is owner-managed; we're a publicly traded MLP with significant management ownership. And we look for other companies that are owner-managed, either directly or through incentive compensation schemes like Stern Stewart's leveraged stock purchase plan. We want managers to be owners with us.

STERN: Gene, would it also make a difference if boards of directors had significant stock ownership?

VESELL: It may make a difference in some cases, but I'm not as convinced. Because of our large positions, I'm often asked the question, "Do you like inside or outside boards?" My answer is always, "A plague on both their houses." I know a lot of CEOs who serve as directors on other companies' boards. When I have asked them about their role on these other boards, they tell me quite candidly: "We don't have the information and the time to be very useful."

STERN: But, perhaps the reason they don't have time is that they don't have much of a personal stake in the outcome. They simply receive the fees and the reputational enhancement of sitting on another company's board.

But what if you could get board members to invest their annual directors' fees in, say, slightly out-of-the-money options that are taxless to them until exercise, and on the same basis as the managers? Would that make you feel better about their level of commitment to shareholders?

VESELL: It would, but I'm not sure it's practical from a time point of view. I'm on the board of a private company, and I've got 30,000 options. We had a board meeting in which we were contemplating an acquisition, and the material we were asked to review in preparation for the meeting was several inches thick. I just don't have time to do this. So I agree with Jack Welch's position at GE; he sits on no boards other than GE's.

But I agree with you 100% in principle. If you could get people who would serve as full-time, professional directors—people who really have something to offer—then your board incentive system could become very important.

STEWART: So, Gene, what you seem to be saying is that the corporate governance issue we've heard so much about is a phoney.

VESELL: Totally. The real issue is getting the managers inside the company to run the company in the interests of shareholders. You've got to provide *management* with the right incentives to add value.

GEOFF COLVIN: I couldn't agree more that the key is to provide management with the right incentives. But who is going to provide those incentives? Only one body: the board. And since these incentives almost always increase the risk of management's pay package, imposing them may be a disagreeable task. I would argue that, for obvious reasons, outside directors have a somewhat better shot at doing this than insiders—and for this reason, the outsiders versus insiders debate is important.

Back to Accounting

STERN: Jerry, what's your response to the suggestion that we can improve our accounting system?

ZIMMERMAN: In the enthusiasm to improve financial disclosures, there's something important that's being left out of this discussion. We have a set of institutions in place in this country that have a good deal of control over these disclosures. We can sit around this table and dream up the world's best financial disclosures, but the critical question is: "What will the SEC do? What will the FASB do? And what will the plaintiff bar do?"

In Bennett's article called "Market Myths," he shows quite clearly that accounting numbers do not reflect economic reality, and that sophisticated investors—the people who dominate the price-setting process at the margin—quite sensibly pay little attention to accounting numbers. At the very least, our capital markets are quite capable of correcting the distortions built into our accounting framework.

In place of conventional accounting numbers, Bennett proposes making several modifications of accounting conventions to arrive at a financial measure he calls "economic value added," or EVA. Now, how does he do it?

STEWART: Actually, Jerry, in fairness to Joel, I should confess here that most of these ideas were originally his.

ZIMMERMAN: Okay, how do *they* do it? Well, they capitalize corporate R&D instead of expensing it all immediately; they use the full-cost accounting method rather than the successful efforts method; and they add back non-cash expenses like deferred taxes and amortized goodwill to the income statement.

But what are they really doing in the process? Where did these num-bers originally come from? They came from the SEC and FASB. It is these same institutions, and the incentives of the people running them, that are at the heart of the problem. They are not really interested in becoming part of the solution. So why do we think that, if Krishna and his colleagues derive better accounting numbers, the SEC and FASB will sanction them? It's these very same institutions that for 60 years now have been mandating accounting disclosures that Joel Stern and Bennett Stewart then have to undo.

STEWART: I too have little hope for acceptance of these measures by the SEC and the FASB. In fact, an endorsement by the SEC would almost necessarily limit their usefulness to the most sophisticated investors—the kind most companies ought to be attempting to reach. In my experience, the most effective shareholder communications are those that focus on performance measures that companies have devised for their own *internal* purposes and to fit their own special circumstances. And when management volunteers to tell the market about those customized measures—especially when such a communication strategy is combined with significant management stock ownership—then I can see investors responding very strongly to such disclosures. But, again, I don't think it's either necessary for, or realistic to expect, the SEC to endorse these more customized kinds of performance measures.

PALEPU: Well, I think the SEC and the FASB can play a positive role in this process. I recently attended a conference on "Financial Reporting in the 21st Century" that had as its declared goal a fundamental rethinking of the U.S. financial reporting system. That conference, I would also point out, was sponsored by one of the Big Six accounting firms and had the blessing of the FASB.

ZIMMERMAN: That may be so, Krish. But I think the overriding concern of professional accountants today is to change the financial reporting system in ways that will reduce their exposure to lawsuits. That's the main thing public accountants are thinking about right now, not improved numbers for valuation purposes.

PALEPU: Well, I agree that we also need to revise auditors' legal liabilities and the excessive litigation our system invites. But that doesn't preclude the possibility of changing accounting measures for the better. We could solve the legal problem in part by restricting private rights of action to only the most minimal set of disclosures. And, by so doing, we could then provide corporate managers with much more freedom to customize their disclosures in a way that sheds light on the value added by their own activities.

Now, of course, you could still object that there's little need for better accounting if the market is already efficient. But I disagree. My view of market efficiency is that, on average, the value of the market portfolio consisting of all companies is probably priced correctly. But even if the market is pretty good in valuing companies in the aggregate, individual companies may well be either over-valued or undervalued for long periods of time because of what academics refer to as "information asymmetries" between managers and outside shareholders. So although a *portfolio* might be correctly valued, many of the individual stocks that make up their value could be significantly undervalued. Because managers could know more about their firm's prospects than outsiders, the market will automatically discount the value of those shares to reflect their informational disadvantage.

So, if I were the CFO of an under-valued company, I think one of my principal responsibilities would be to figure out a way to get my story out. And one way to accomplish that, as I suggested earlier, would be to devise useful leading indicators and then make them the centerpiece in the voluntary or non-SEC part of my investor communications program.

DON CHEW: Krishna, Joel was suggesting earlier that the most effective shareholder communication is the kind targeted for a small, highly sophisticated group of investors—the lead steers, if you will. But there are major regulatory barriers to sharing information privately with only certain investors. Have you thought of a way of getting around these SEC barriers to talking privately to a small group of investors? Or should companies instead design all-purpose communications that seek to reach all investors at their own levels of sophistication?

PALEPU: Well, I agree there are legal barriers, not to mention competitive risks, to sharing certain kinds of information with outside investors. But I think such risks have been greatly exaggerated. Even within the current institutional framework, there is much that could be done. In fact, I have done a number of case studies describing innovative disclosures some American companies have recently devised. For example, Home Depot, a retailer with an innovative strategy, discloses in its annual report a lot of data about the way its stores are managed. And Comdisco, the world's largest computer leasing company, provides detailed information on how it assesses and manages the residual values of its leased computer equipment. In both these cases, the information disclosed is critical for investors in assessing management performance and estimating share values.

STEWART: I too think the competitive risks of sharing strategic information have been overstated. As you said earlier, Krishna, strategy itself has

been devalued by technological advances in information and the increasing pace of change; and, as a consequence, execution and flexibility are becoming the keys to success.

What really matters to investors today is not corporate strategy, but the management *process* and the incentives that go along with them. For this reason, I think companies could benefit greatly just by focusing their disclosures on how they manage, what their goals are, how they monitor their progress in meeting those goals, and what their incentives are to bring it all off. So, it's not the specifics of strategy that are important—indeed, in some sense, a company's strategy is changing everyday—but rather the corporate process that would give investors a sense of management's alertness and incentives to respond to continuous change.

Abolish the SEC?

VESELL: As a long-time value-based investor, I was delighted to hear Professor Zimmerman's view about the irrelevance of accounting for stock market investors. I don't mean to suggest that accounting is completely useless. Accounting is sort of the language that you have to learn to get started. But then, as an outsider, you have to learn to translate those numbers in a way that allows you to get a sense of what's going on inside the company.

ZIMMERMAN: That's right. We know that investors are always looking for profits in undervalued or overvalued stocks. And we also know that accounting numbers do have some information content. When they're announced, whether it's in Jakarta or elsewhere, the stock market reacts. But that isn't what accounting numbers were designed to do.

The fundamental difference between Krishna and me is that he has a

lot more faith in the SEC than I do. My view is that if I've gone to the same witch doctor for the last 60 years and he's killed off every one of my relatives, I think it's time to shoot the witch doctor. If you want to have improved financial disclosures in this country, the best way is to abolish these blocking institutions and let the companies innovate and invent disclosures that make sense.

STEWART: You think we should abolish the SEC...entirely?

VESELL: I would agree with that.

STEWART: So what you're advocating is essentially a free-market, voluntary, unregulated system of disclosure?

ZIMMERMAN: That's right. And I would also eliminate the insider trading laws. You really can't communicate effectively with the lead steers under the existing insider trading laws. Even if Basil at Scott Paper has the world's best story, he can't whisper it to somebody like Gene Vesell.

STERN: Ned, as New York State Controller until midnight tomorrow, what do you think about these outrageous statements from Professor Zimmerman that we don't need any regulation of disclosure at all?

REGAN: Well, it's less outrageous than having Congress appoint the GAO to audit Scott Paper. But that's about all I can say for the proposal. I can't go along with the idea of an unregulated, completely voluntary market in corporate disclosure. It seems obvious to me we need regulation of disclosure.

ZIMMERMAN: Capital markets worked fine before 1933. Stocks were bought and sold...

REGAN: And a lot of little people were left with worthless paper.

ZIMMERMAN: A lot of people were left with significantly less valuable paper in 1987, too. Stock markets go up and down, despite the best intentions and efforts of auditors and regulators.

Prior to the founding of the SEC in 1933, most NYSE companies issued audited financial statements. Firms have an incentive to do that without the SEC. But look at what the SEC and the FASB have done to our accounting systems. It's because the accounting numbers do not reflect economic reality that people like Joel Stern and Bennett Stewart can make a living advising companies how to undo the harmful effects that come from using those numbers to make decisions.

REGAN: But the SEC doesn't prevent a company from disclosing its strategy, from disclosing its level of customer satisfaction, and the quality of its goods and services relative to that of its peers. They could do all that today, but they don't. The CEO of Scott talks about all these things with his division chiefs, but he doesn't talk about them with his board and with his shareholders. There's nothing in the world to prevent all of this from being discussed in the boardroom and communicated to investors in language they can understand.

So, you can still have your regulatory framework to provide a minimum amount and type of disclosure. But management can exceed that minimum whenever they wish. If they don't, at some point, some Scott shareholders are going to file a resolution to demand to see how the company judges the quality of its product as compared to its competitors. Shareholders know that that issue is discussed everyday on the shop floor at Scott Paper and they would like to know that information.

The Promise of Nonfinancial Measures

STERN: Ned, you are directing a taskforce of sorts to develop nonfinancial performance measures. Would you share with us some of your findings and recommendations?

The SEC doesn't prevent companies from disclosing their strategies, from disclosing their levels of customer satisfaction, and the quality of their goods and services relative to that of their peers. They could do all that today, but they don't. There's nothing in the world to prevent all of this from being discussed in the boardroom and communicated to investors in language they can understand.

—Edward Regan

REGAN: There is a lot of work going on today on nonfinancial measures of corporate performance. There is a study being conducted by an AICPA group headed by Ed Jenkins, the Chicago partner of Arthur Anderson. Another is a group led by Bob Eccles and Jim McGee in Cambridge that is being sponsored by Ernst and Young and the FEI, the Financial Executives Institute. A third study is being done in Toronto by a group of former business people and scholars to assess how these nonfinancial factors—including, interestingly, the corporation's social reputation—correlate with financial results and stock market performance. And Bob Reich at the Labor Department has started a fourth study that will attempt to measure employee satisfaction and involvement and correlate those measures with stock price. So that's at least four groups, and there are probably others doing it.

The AICPA study, like the FEI study, is looking to develop nonfinancial measures such as the ones I've just mentioned—quality of goods and services, employee satisfaction, and customer satisfaction; there are at least a dozen items on the agenda at the moment. Essentially what they are trying to do is to develop industry standards and norms for, say, the paper industry. (And, Basil, I'm making things up here a little bit, but I'm still a politician until midnight.) For example, there might be a measurable standard for customer satisfaction in the paper products industry that could be compiled and reported to investors like the New York State pension system.

And I think it's important to note that this study is being sponsored by the official institution of CPAs and undertaken by some of its members. Some of these CPAs have declared, at least in private to me, that their primary motive for conducting the study is their level of dissatisfaction with existing financial measures as indicators of future performance and value. They have told me that the current financial reporting system doesn't work—and that's, of course, exactly what we're hearing now from people around the table who are far better versed than I on this subject.

Now, I'm not saying this dissatisfaction with current accounting measures is the *prevailing* view among CPAs. Ed Jenkins doesn't necessarily have smooth sailing among his colleagues in conducting this study. STEWART: So we all agree, then, that quarterly reports don't mean very much to investors?
REGAN: That's right. And, frankly, few people in the public pension system industry are even capable of understanding such reports. You're wrong if you think politicians who run public pension funds are capable of understanding this stuff.
STEWART: Well, why couldn't public pension funds retain investment advisers like Institutional Shareholders Services to do the research for them? REGAN: They can't pay what somebody would pay a Morgan Stanley or Oppenheimer Capital to do due diligence on a company. And that's one reason I think this research on nonfinancial measures is important. These measures could be especially valuable to public institutional investors, to institutions like us that can't afford to have financial experts on their payroll and who don't relate well—and I put myself at the head of this list—to narrowly focused financial information. This is private-sector-oriented information, but public pension funds are run by public-sector, civil-service-oriented individuals. And it seems to me that a promising way to enhance the ability of what I refer to as the "new" or "reawakened" public-sector shareholder is to give the

people that run those institutions a corporate performance report on something to which they can relate.

Marty Lipton recently proposed the idea of an internal business audit; it's really a revival of something Peter Drucker has been proposing for years. It would not be a financial audit, but a business audit. My guess is that, if the companies themselves began to experiment with the disclosure of these kinds of nonfinancial performance measures, such disclosures would be widely accepted and encouraged by the investment community.

More on Nonfinancial Measures

STERN: Let me turn to Carolyn Brancato, who is staff director of this project with Ned Regan. Carolyn, would you summarize the major findings and proposals of this work to date?
BRANCATO: I want to add a couple of observations to Ned's comments.

One of the key nonfinancial measures of performance whose development we hope to encourage is some method of assessing how much, and how effectively, companies are spending to reposition themselves strategically to compete in world markets. As in the Scott Paper example mentioned earlier, I'm thinking of capital expenditures with longer-term payoffs, not something that will show up immediately in the bottom-line EPS.

Why do I think there's a need or demand for such measures? Let me explain by offering a brief recent history of Wall Street. I started my career in 1967 as a securities analyst. In those days we used slide rules, we read Graham & Dodd, and we were fundamentalists. In the late '60s, the institutional investors as we now know them—the pension funds, the mutual funds, and so on—accounted for only about 28% of the equity holdings in the country. (They now

account for upwards of 55%.) Most of the money that was managed came through large investment banking and brokerage houses, and it was managed for large individual accounts. Even the retail money was sort of herded together, and so there was a group of houses that engaged in quite a lot of fundamental analysis.

Brokerage commissions at that time were fixed, not negotiated as they are today. The move to floating commissions in the early 1970s led to a major change in the way Wall Street did business. Many of the big research houses phased out much of their fundamental research activities.

But, as fundamental analysts in the late '60s, we routinely attempted to look through accounting statements to get at normalized, cash-flow-based measures of corporate performance. We never simply took the income statement and the balance sheet at face value. We started with reported accounting numbers, then examined the footnotes, and ended up adding our own layers of information—some of which we got from talking directly to company CFOs. There was also, of course, a whole cadre of technical analysts—the "head and shoulders" people, if you will—but we sort of looked down our noses at them and said, "No, we're fundamentalists and we really know the company."

But today things are different on Wall Street. Consider the consequences of the tremendous flows of money into institutional investors. The large pension funds simply don't have the ability to make these fundamental decisions; in fact, their portfolios are indexed as often as not. In short, the money has moved away from these fundamental-oriented houses that were dominant in the late '60s.

So, largely as a result of these changes, we are now looking to groups like Oppenheimer Capital and The Lens Fund to reinvigorate the old-fashioned kind of fundamental analysis we once practiced. At the same time, as Ned just mentioned, we're also looking for new, particularly nonfinancial, measures of corporate performance. Such measures will help those kinds of investors who can't do the sophisticated financial analysis themselves. For example, we're looking for new ways to reflect R&D, and worker training and education— and for proxies for employee and customer satisfaction—that tend to correlate strongly with current and future corporate performance.

STERN: Are you arguing, then, that the shift from fixed to floating commissions and the increasing flow of funds to institutional investors was a bad thing?

BRANCATO: The consequences have been mixed, good and bad. On the one hand, the growth of pension funds means that our economy has become more effective in distributing wealth throughout the system. On the other hand, there are many companies that feel very constrained by having their shares in the hands of large institutions. They don't know quite how to deal with some of these large pension funds that are sitting on huge piles of money, but whom they believe lack the financial sophistication to understand their financial reporting. Twenty-five years ago, companies felt they could sit down with a relatively small group of analysts and tell their story to a receptive, fundamentally-oriented audience. That's no longer true today.

LEHMANN: I would like to add a different perspective here. On the domestic equity side, only about 10% of all tax-exempt funds managed are indexed. In my experience as a director of corporate IR, index managers typically do not have the need to talk to corporate IR people. But I have found many more fundamental managers who are quite receptive to direct contact with the corporations they invest in. I would also point out that

We are now looking for new, particularly nonfinancial, measures of corporate performance to help those investors who can't do the sophisticated financial analysis themselves. For example, we're looking for new ways to reflect R&D, and worker training and education—and for proxies for employee and customer satisfaction— that tend to correlate strongly with current and future corporate performance. Such measures, by closing the information gap between the lead steers and more passive indexed investors, can serve to extend the informational basis for relationship investing to a much broader base of investors.

—*Carolyn Brancato*

the active buyside manager is way ahead of all but a handful of sellside analysts when it comes to valuing businesses. And corporate IR practices have adapted to this reality by seeking much more direct contact with the buyside than when I entered the field ten years ago.

In Search of the Lead Steers

STERN: Let's turn now to Joe Shenton, who is an adviser to corporations on targeting investor clienteles. Joe, what do you think about what Carolyn just told us about Wall Street?

SHENTON: We have studied the effects of changing the commission structure on Wall Street, and our basic conclusion is that the market was much more efficient with respect to information flows in 1967 than it is today—and precisely for the reason Carolyn just mentioned: without fixed commissions, many brokerage houses lost their finan-

cial incentive to do fundamental research. In 1967 brokers earned 35 to 50 cent commissions for moving a share of stock. Today they earn only four to six cents a share.

For this reason, the quality of sellside research has fallen off dramatically over the past 25 years; indeed, the sellside has become essentially irrelevant to the major lead steer investors—to people like Gene Vesell, for example.

VESELL: I was one of those brokers in the 1970s. And there was a very good economic reason for allowing the brokerage commissions to float. In the old days, investors were being forced by regulation to subsidize the research activities of my brokerage firm and others. I think we're far better off with market-based commissions. This way, investors who are willing to pay their broker for fundamental research can volunteer to pay them directly, without having it built into the commission schedule.

SHENTON: I don't dispute that floating commissions are a better deal for investors. But it has affected corporate disclosure and investor relations in some sense for the worse. If I were a company in the late '60s or early '70s and I wanted to communicate effectively to the investment community, I would visit the ten to twelve sellside analysts that covered my industry, tell them my story, and they in turn would spread the word for me. They had every incentive to do so in those days.

Take Otis Bradley, who was a very well-known and widely-followed analyst of computer stocks in the '60s. When Otis announced a buy recommendation, that company's stock would go flying off the charts. Bradley was the epitome of a lead steer investor—and he was a sellside analyst! When an Otis Bradley research report came out, the information would be all over Wall Street and reflected in the stock price within minutes.

Today, by contrast, the best research is clearly being done by people far removed from the sellside. I was very interested in hearing Gene Vesell's account of how he gets his information. As Gene just told us, it has almost nothing to with the quarterly reports required by the SEC. The issue here is not who's mandating the information, it's who's smart enough to supplement the publicly available information with other, more reliable and useful kinds of information. In my experience, the smartest investors tend to find alternative, often nonfinancial, kinds of information—and they use that information to earn higher rates of return.

STERN: Where do they get the information from?

SHENTON: They dig it. And they get some of it from management.

STERN: If that is so, then why are you maintaining that markets are less efficient today than they were in 1967?

SHENTON: Because the best research is not shared, it is not spread around Wall Street the way it once was.

STERN: Why would that make any difference? I thought stock prices were set at the margin.

CHEW: In fact, a recent study—by Jeremy Stein of MIT and Ken Froot and Andrei Shleifer of Harvard—shows that stock prices now respond far more quickly to corporate news than they did in the '60s and '70s. And, given the advances in information technology, it would be very surprising to find that markets were less efficient today than 25 years ago.

SHENTON: Well, I agree with you both that the information is reflected quickly in the price of the stock. But I'm not talking about prices here, but about information flows. The information flows between companies and the investment community are not nearly as direct as they once were. As I said, a corporate IR director can no longer send his message to ten or twelve sellside analysts and be confident that the market is getting the word. And, deprived of these customary channels, many companies today just choose not to make the effort to tell their story. Instead, they fall back on the SEC safe harbor and disclose just the bare minimum.

But let me also say this. Before I started my consulting firm, I worked in corporate investor relations for 17 years; and, in spite of what you may be reading in the press, there's nothing new about relationship investing. John Neff was giving me heartaches in 1973, when I was director of IR at Northwest Industries. He was the most active investor I have ever seen. Relationship investing has been around in the same way venture capital has been around. It's the same model of corporate governance that is also used in LBOs, which of course came out of the venture capital industry. It's simply the model of highly sophisticated investors buying large stakes in companies and then having very good channels of communication (often including board seats) and very strong incentives to get information.

STEWART: So, even if the brokerage firms no longer have a strong interest in doing fundamental research today, the high rates of return promised by relationship investing have provided a new incentive for gathering fundamental information.

SHENTON: I agree. But, as I said earlier, there's nothing new about relationship investing; it's been there all the time. The brightest investors have always found ways to get information that give them a real competitive edge.

And for those companies worried about legal liability from providing unorthodox types of disclosure, I have another message: You don't need written disclosures to communicate with lead steer investors. There are lots of other ways to do so that don't violate the securities laws.

But, to reach lead steers, the first thing you have to do is to find out who they are. As Joel suggested earlier, there may be 50 investors who really determine the stock price of Scott Paper at the margin. These are the people who buy or sell in large quantities when the price falls too low or rises too high. All the other 5,000 investors may increase your trading volume, but they don't have any material effect on the stock price.

STEWART: But doesn't this sort of contradict Ned's point about the importance of this passively managed money sitting in public pension funds?

SHENTON: Yes, it does. I'm saying that the corporate IR strategy ought to aim for the highest common denominator. If you aim your financial communications for the most sophisticated investors, they will take care of the share price. Don't worry about the mass of investors. Instead seek out the 50 investors that are going to make a difference to your stock and communicate with them.

STEWART: That's part of the reason why I am very uncomfortable about *mandating* the use of nonfinancial information. I'm not saying that nonfinancial information is unimportant. It's clearly very important for *internal* management purposes.

Three years ago I was doing some work with Whirlpool on performance measurement, and they had put together a very sophisticated system for measuring customer satisfaction, product quality, employee commitment, degree of innovation—and it was all summarized on a single page. It was spontaneously developed by the company for their internal purposes. That makes all the sense in the world; and it may even make sense to share some of this information with outside investors. But to standardize these measures across all companies and then *mandate* their disclosure to investors seems pointless.

BRANCATO: Our commission has never suggested that such disclosures be mandated. We recommended that they be developed to close this information gap between the small groups of very sophisticated investors doing fundamental analysis and the large pension funds indexing huge blocks of money. As Ned said, these funds simply don't have the resources to do sophisticated financial analysis. And the nonfinancial measures we're now experimenting with—even if the most sophisticated investors do not need them to value the shares—could provide useful information to guide the investment decisions of the less sophisticated investors.

STEWART: But that's precisely my point. If investors are unwilling to pay for the information in the form of a higher stock price, then why do it? I just don't see how disclosure of these *standardized* nonfinancial measures

can help companies increase their stock prices—which, to me, is the true test of effective disclosure.

BRANCATO: My point is this: These nonfinancial measures of performance, by closing the information gap between the fundamentalist lead steers and more passive indexed investors, can serve to extend this informational basis for relationship investing in a way that involves a much broader base of investors.

VESELL: I should point out, however, that we at Oppenheimer manage a lot of public pension money, including some of New York State's. We're talking about $5 or $6 billion of public money that we're delighted to manage. So this information gap may not be as large as we are making it out to be.

STERN: So, even though commissions have disappeared, it would seem from Gene's comment that we have evolved into a system where 50 to 100 lead steers now do the work that some 1,000 security analysts were doing 25 years ago. And this system seems to work quite well—so much so that Oppenheimer Capital is winning over the business of public pension funds because of its ability to generate superior returns.

A Corporate IR Perspective

ALEX LEHMANN: There is another kind of information gap that divides even the fundamentalists. As I said earlier, there is a tremendous divergence between most brokerage or sellside research—which is based on the accounting model and geared toward predicting next quarter's EPS—and the approach of sophisticated buyside institutional investors, as represented by somebody like Gene Vesell.

I represented Whitman Corporation for about eight years starting in 1983. It's a fairly complex company, a

conglomerate. At that time, the company was comprised of six independent, freestanding businesses. My job was first and foremost to communicate one on one with the buyside. I set myself the task of identifying our 50 largest shareholders, getting to know them, and maintaining an ongoing dialogue with them. We discussed the company's goals and strategies—typically in terms of cash flows rather than conventional EPS. And, in the course of many discussions, it was always my aim to clarify any corporate actions or decisions that might have led to misunderstanding or uncertainty.

Put a little differently, our purpose was to create an appropriate or realistic set of investor expectations. The key was to establish and then maintain credibility and, by so doing, to try to make a complex company as simple as possible for investors to understand. As I said, most of our communications effort was directed at the buyside investment community, the people who owned our stock. The sellside analysts came in later in the process and proved very useful in leveraging our buyside efforts.

I discovered a few things along the way. First, to communicate effectively, you have to value the company's businesses regularly; such regular exercises in valuation give you the ammunition for productive discussions with investors. Then you have to be timely and consistent. Maintaining a sense of continuity is key, for example, when there is a change at the top. I served three CEOs during my eight years and, as you would expect, they each had different views about what the company should be or become. Also, maintaining reasonable expectations is difficult when management deviates from a carefully explained strategy or when it makes overly optimistic earnings predictions. The result is a credibility gap.

When you look at the portfolio turnover of different institutional investors, you will find that there are many who are interested in little more than higher EPS next quarter. Knowing my lead-steer investors, I had to decide how much time I wanted to spend with each of them. Most important, though, 35 of the 50 largest holders in 1983 were still with us when I left the company in 1991. Investors like nothing better than holding on, provided management performs and creates value.

STERN: Judy, from your vantage point at *Business Week*, what do you make of Alex Lehmann's approach to corporate investor relations at the Whitman Corporation? Is it something that many other companies might be able to borrow?

DOBRZYNSKI: I find the approach very interesting. In my experience, companies pay far too much attention to the sellside analysts. And I think it's the companies themselves that are inviting the investment community to focus on the quarterly numbers. If companies want the analysts to focus on longer-term performance measures, they ought to start talking to the buyside people—and perhaps they could even attempt to educate the sellside in the process. Maybe the sellside isn't as limited as we're all making it out to be.

So, in an important sense, then, companies are really getting the kinds of investors they deserve. If you appeal to the lowest common denominator, that's what you'll wind up getting—at least that's the message that Alex and Joe Shenton seem to be giving us.

The Case of Equifax

STEWART: Derek, as the former CFO of Equifax, and now an Executive Vice President running one of its major business lines, you have faced this kind of issue of being evaluated periodically on an EPS basis. Your company now seems to be undergoing a transformation of sorts, a significant change in both its internal management process and in its disclosures to the investment community. Could you tell us a little about what prompted these changes?

SMITH: Let me start by saying that much of U.S. accounting and regulatory process is counterproductive and archaic. As a consequence, it is reducing the competitiveness of U.S. companies in the global marketplace. Many poor management decisions are made in order to make public companies look good in terms of improved financial results. Fortunately, some companies such as Scott and Equifax are trying to manage *value* by creating new performance measures, a "second set of books." But I contend that too many important business decisions of U.S. companies continue to be driven by short-term accounting results—by management's belief that the investment community forces them to maximize reported earnings—and by executive compensation systems that reward management according to EPS instead of long-term value.

The issue I've heard everyone discuss is how we ought to *measure* value. But, frankly, I'm not as interested in measuring value as I am in how we're going to *create* value. It's this focus on creating value, and our level of dissatisfaction with the effectiveness of conventional measurement systems in driving value, that prompted Equifax to implement a new financial framework. We wanted to redirect our overall process toward the pursuit of value—or, more precisely, to minimize any temptation provided by our accounting system to interfere with rather than encourage the creation of value.

VESELL: Could you say a little more about the difference between creating value and measuring value?

SMITH: The accounting system reflects historical performance. But, given the pace of change today and the power of on-line information technologies, these accounting *statistics* have minimal value as real-time decision tools. As CFO, I couldn't wait for reported financial results. By the time those numbers were calculated and consolidated, new market developments, competitive events, and changing conditions usually had made them obsolete.

Management at Equifax has determined that there are two critical success factors in creating value—possibly the two most important—that traditional reporting methods ignore. The first is people. We must have superior people focused on the right issues, and we must be able to monitor their performance in meeting our most critical goals. The second is the business, or management, processes Bennett mentioned earlier.

This second critical factor made us face the realities of the problems created by the accounting systems. There are simply too many ways to produce better accounting results by making business decisions that fail to add value or, even worse, reduce value. Our old system was not encouraging the kind of value-creating behavior in our operating executives that we wanted.

But, try as we might to free ourselves from the traditional system and decision rules, traditional methods and habits of behavior die hard. For every relationship investor that really will give you a long enough time horizon, there are a whole slew of conventional EPS investors who, even if they don't ultimately set your price, can certainly divert your attention.

Accounting for Marketing: The Case of CUC International

STEWART: Well, let me give you an example I came across recently where this kind of conflict between accounting and economics comes into play. Take the case of a cellular phone business that pays Radio Shack $500 for each new cellular subscriber it signs up. The $500 amounts to a finder's fee, a marketing outlay that will take the company about two years to recoup.

Now, because of this heavy initial outlay, which the accounting system forces you to expense entirely in the year incurred, fourth-quarter earnings would be significantly reduced by a sharp growth in new sign-ups in that quarter. And what tends to happen, I'm told, is that in the fourth quarter of every year, sales come to a standstill because people are beginning to look at the year-end earnings figures that drive their bonuses. So here's an example where an accounting policy and incentives tied to the earnings are clearly having a material adverse impact on the business.

PALEPU: But, in fact, Bennett, companies can and do capitalize some of their marketing expenditures. Paul Healy at MIT and I just finished writing a case about a company with an accounting problem very similar to the one you just described. The company, which is called CUC International, is also in an annual subscription kind of business. It's also the kind of business where you spend a lot of money signing up somebody; and then if they stay with you, you make a lot of money because the service itself doesn't cost much to deliver.

Therefore, to the extent you can retain your subscribers, you have what amounts to an annuity for a significant period of time. The problem faced by CUC's management was finding a way to communicate to the market that its marketing outlays had a promising payoff down the road.

The way CUC initially chose to communicate its prospects was to capitalize a significant portion of their marketing outlays. But when they did so, a number of highly vocal sellside analysts criticized the accounting practice as too aggressive. So the company was faced with the choice of flouting the accounting norms endorsed by the analysts or finding some alternative method of convincing the investment community it was really creating value through these marketing outlays.

STEWART: But if they're using more conservative accounting methods, and everybody knows that, then shouldn't the higher "quality" of earnings be acknowledged by the market in the form of a higher P/E ratio? Isn't that what the theory says should happen?

PALEPU: Well, there are two reasons why that might not happen in this case. For one thing, CUC is a somewhat smaller company; and, at the time it was facing this problem, it had a relatively limited institutional following. And I happen to believe that such companies still operate in what I would call "pockets" of market inefficiency—in less efficient segments of the market.

My second point is that the problem is not just one caused by accounting distortions. There is a real economic uncertainty surrounding the payoff from these marketing outlays. That is, when you sign up new subscribers, there is no guarantee they are going to stay with you beyond a quarter or two. CUC's managers have a better handle on this than outsiders, but it is difficult to communicate this kind of information effectively.

So, to overcome this communication problem, CUC went back to conservative accounting and then undertook a very bold change in the *financial* structure of the company. They went out and borrowed a lot of money to pay a special dividend and repurchase their shares in the open market. And although this dramatic recapitalization did not lead to an immediate increase in its share value—

this took place over the next year or so—it did achieve one very notable change: It led to a very sharp increase in institutional ownership of CUC's shares, from 5% to 88%. And, interestingly, more active and sophisticated institutions like Tiger Management and Fidelity began reporting purchases of very large stakes.

So I would describe this as using financial change to "signal" management's confidence in the firm's prospects. And, over the two years following the recap, the value of the shares—including the large cash distribution—rose by some 96%.

BRANCATO: That story illustrates perfectly the existence of the information gap between sophisticated, fundamentals-driven investors and more passive institutions. If CUC had been able to devise an effective measure of its subscribers' satisfaction, it might not have had to resort to such a financial solution—and it might have retained its less sophisticated investor clientele in the process.

The Equifax Recap: Signalling Through Capital Structure

STERN: Derek, while you were still CFO at Equifax, the company did a somewhat similar financial recapitalization—a Dutch auction share repurchase—that was very well received by the market. What were you thinking when you did that, and what message did that send to your shareholders?

SMITH: That decision was part of a comprehensive change in the financial philosophy and measurement systems that guide our corporate decision processes at Equifax. We needed to find a way to communicate the value implications of these changes, and so our new financial structure was intended to be a powerful signal of these changes in the operating approach of the company. In effect, we used a major change in financial structure, including a significant repurchase of our stock, to accomplish two important value cre-

ation initiatives internally and to communicate that information to investors.

One, we were reducing our cost of capital through increased financial leverage. Two, we were indicating our internal commitment to increasing the capital efficiency of our ongoing businesses.

The *internal* message sent by our leveraged recapitalization was probably even more important than the external one. I was more concerned about signalling to our own management team the importance of making management decisions consistent with increasing value for our shareholders. I believe that if we do the right things internally, the market will figure out what we're doing, even it does take some time to get the point across.

STERN: Well, it didn't take much time for the market to react. My understanding is that your shares went up by some 20% within a month or two of the announcement.

VESELL: How did you decide on your capital structure? Were you driven by the rating agencies or by the economics of the business?

SMITH: We wanted to maintain a prudently leveraged capital structure—one that would enable us to command an investment-grade rating. The second part of your question is more difficult to answer. I hesitate to say that our leverage ratio was dictated entirely by the economics of the business because the rating agency decisions are driven only partly by pure economics or cash flows. As you know, there are some rating agency criteria that don't seem completely consistent with the economics of an information technology business.

To illustrate my point, a lot of Equifax's market assets are not on our books. We're in the financial and insurance information reporting business. The value of these businesses is not driven by hard assets, but by databases and information gateways that don't show up on the balance sheet. If you were using only the traditional financial ratios to assess our credit risk, none of our important assets would show up in the analysis.

STERN: If you can't kick it, how can you borrow against it?

SMITH: That's certainly the old formula. So, to keep our rating consistent with our true risk profile, we had to communicate to the agencies the unique nature of Equifax. We proved to be successful in telling our story, in part because there is a somewhat new appreciation of the ability of certain intangible assets to generate cash flow to service debt over the long term. To make your case with the rating agencies, you really have to take the initiative to educate them. But, if you take the time and do the job well, they are an intelligent and responsive audience.

VESELL: I'm frankly surprised you've succeeded in doing that; the rating agencies have a strong conservative bias.

SMITH: It wasn't easy, but we achieved a mutual understanding.

STERN: Well, Derek, if you were as persuasive with the rating agencies as you were in making the case in your most recent annual report, I can see why you were able to succeed. Equifax's new annual report provides very effective discussions of the company's new financing policy and financial measurement system.

Clientele Effects

STEWART: Joe, how would you expect the market to react to that kind of fundamental change communicated by Equifax? Would the investor base change? And what has your research shown about how different kinds of investment clienteles affect share prices?

SHENTON: Let me start by responding to the last question first. As you know,

There may be 50 investors who really determine the stock price of Scott Paper at the margin. These are the people who buy or sell in large quantities when the price falls too low or rises too high. Corporate IR strategy ought to aim for those 50 investors. If you aim your financial communications for the most sophisticated investors, they will take care of the share price.

—Joseph Shenton

Bennett, we at OLC have done some research demonstrating not only the existence of very different investor clienteles, but also that different kinds of investors tend to seek out different kinds of companies to invest in.

We started by taking ten of the most popular investment approaches and then assigned each of some 5,000 institutional investors to one of those ten categories. At one end of the spectrum is the Miller and Modigliani discounted cash flow approach that Stern Stewart has transformed into its EVA corporate performance measure—the kind that LBO investors were presumably using throughout the '80s. At the other extreme are technical analysis, indexation, and other purely computer-driven methods of trading. Between these extremes, and ranging from active to passive, are strategies like earnings momentum models, sector rotation models, and a variety of others.

Our next step was then to attempt to determine whether these different investor clienteles were attracted to different kinds of companies. For example, we used your Stern Stewart performance 1,000 rankings to come up with the following insight: As companies move up in your ranking system—thus becoming more profitable and more valuable in the view of the stock market—the more active, value-based investors increase their percentage holdings. And when companies move down in your MVA ranking system, the value-based investors bail out and the passive investors come in and take their place. (And, incidentally, I should point out that when we tried to find these clientele effects using other ranking systems like *Fortune*'s or *Business Week*'s—ranking systems that essentially measure size rather than profitability or value added— the clientele effects disappeared.)

Now, what are these clientele effects I'm talking about? Well, think about the story Derek just told us about Equifax. That story, quite frankly, wouldn't mean much to the average sellside analyst. Of course, you can talk to sellside analysts and try to educate them that the company is moving to manage for long-term economic value, but you won't get much of a response. The sellside has a vested interest in stimulating a lot of short-term trading, not in encouraging long-term investing. Consequently, their principal interest is in forecasting next quarter's EPS. To make an effect on sellside people, you really have to talk in standard EPS terms.

Early in the process of contemplating this fundamental change in its financial measurement system, Equifax decided that they were going to appeal to a fairly small group of investors—say, the 50 most sophisticated institutions out of a potential 5,000. They targeted their presentations to that group of 50, and half of those investors eventually became investors in Equifax. And this was certainly not a serendipitous event; these were the lead steer investors.

Now, what did Equifax accomplish by this? Well, what they really did was to shorten the time it took the market to place the proper value on the firm's shares. Without such a targeted IR program, it probably would have happened naturally anyway. But it would have taken much more time, and there likely would have been a lot more volatility in getting there.

The fact of the matter is, the market's ability to value shares properly depends greatly on the quality of the information management is providing. If you do a poor job of communicating with investors, you're much more likely to be undervalued at any given time. But if you instead design your communication to appeal to the people who are going to set the price—and you can figure out who they are—then you can influence the valuation of your shares.

STERN: But what about the other investors? Do you make any attempt to court them?

SHENTON: I have nothing against passive investors, but they're just not equipped to respond to fundamental issues. And it's far more cost-effective to devote a company's IR budget to influencing the views of the most sophisticated, value-based investors—most of whom, in my experience, tend to be long-term investors. In fact, such investors make their money by taking advantage of some of the short-term "noise" trading, by profiting from the fluctuations caused by less sophisticated investors' trading on the last quarter's earnings.

So, when Equifax set about communicating its story, it chose 50 investors from the active investor categories. In helping companies choose their investors, we look for investors that have taken similar risks, but without a large concentration in the given industry. For example, I would examine Gene's portfolio at Oppenheimer to evaluate whether Equifax represents a good fit. And if there were few other information services companies in the portfolio, and Oppenheimer had showed a willingness to take on companies with a moderate degree of financial risk—or, more pointedly, it had shown itself to be attracted to companies volunteering to increase their financial leverage—then we might have a nice fit.

STEWART: Joe, are you saying that relationship investors by and large fall into this top category of value-based, sophisticated, fundamentals-oriented investors?

SHENTON: Absolutely. Gene Vesell is clearly a value-based, fundamental investor. So is Warren Buffett. When I was at Northwest Industries in the '70s, Buffett was a 5% holder and that was relationship investing.

And let me make one very critical point about shareholder communications. Disclosure is not a one-way communication; it's really about establishing a two-way channel. Effective corporate IR means seeking out and listening to influential investors. This can help management design the performance measures that investors find useful. It's this kind of two-way communication and beneficial exchange that is the ultimate goal of relationship investing.

STEWART: If a company finds that it has an inordinately high proportion of passive investors, does that tell you anything?

SHENTON: If you have mostly passive or short-term investors—and a lot of companies do—it's either because your company is reasonably well run and has taken the attitude the market will take care of itself, or it is poorly run and value-based investors have bailed out. One thing our research has disclosed is that a "passive neglect" approach to corporate IR—as reflected by an increasing proportion of passive, short-term investors—is associated with an *increase* in a company's beta. That's very clear from our data. On the other hand, having lots of value investors can be bad news as well as good. A sharp increase in value investors could mean they sense a change of management control in the offing.

But, in general, it's good to have value-based investors. For example, look at what is happening in healthcare today. The most sophisticated investors are seizing profit opportunities created by the general devastation of healthcare stocks. These investors were not short-term earnings momentum or sector types; they were long-term investors taking advantage of the opportunities created by such short-term trading strategies.

STEWART: Does having more active, sophisticated investors typically lead to a better dialogue with management, and thus to better corporate governance?

SHENTON: Well, that's likely to be true if management's primary objective is to maximize the value of the company's shares. If your interests as a manager are identical with those of investors, then you clearly want to communicate regularly and clearly with investors. They should be viewed as your partners in the enterprise.

But if management is not completely committed to maximizing value, then they're not likely to want to get too close to investors. In such cases, the long-term, sophisticated investors are not likely to hold your shares. And the short-term, passive types that will hold your shares will effectively keep the firm on a very tight tether, responding to every blip in quarterly earnings.

Superactive Investors: The Case of The Lens Fund

STEWART: Let's now turn to Nell Minow, who, together with Bob Monks, recently launched The Lens Fund. Nell, how would you characterize The Lens Fund? Are you just an ordinary active investor, or does your style take you off the charts?

MINOW: We're very much off the charts. Normally, when you talk about active versus passive investors, you're really just talking about whether they're buying or selling. We are in the business of active management of the ownership rights conferred by common stock. Most money managers buy stock that they hope will go up. We buy stock and then we try to make it go up ourselves by exercising the rights that come with share ownership.

Our first case study was at Sears, where we used our initial purchase of

Relationship investing is not something new; it's been with us since the days of the joint stock companies and Adam Smith. Whether we're talking about venture capital for start-ups, LBOs for mature companies, or the management of large public companies, the essence of relationship investing is the same: it's having large-stake investors, and supplying them with information about and some measure of influence over corporate strategic decisions.

—Nell Minow

100 shares to initiate a process that led eventually to the break-up of a company that had become too large and lost its focus. By the time that break-up took place, we had accumulated enough shares to make up all of our costs (including a full page ad in *The Wall Street Journal* that called the board of directors a "nonperforming asset") and then some.

I would like to comment on a couple of the things that have been said. I was especially interested in Professor Zimmerman's opening point that the fundamental purpose of accounting was to monitor the stewardship function of corporate management. It seems to me that the real issue underlying this discussion is that of stewardship: Are managers doing the best possible job for the shareholders whom they supposedly represent, or are there signficant agency costs arising from conflicts of interest between management and shareholders?

Now, in order to answer this question, investors need good information. When I'm looking for information, I want the kind of information that will best help me to evaluate what the CEO and directors are doing. I don't need to hear everything that they hear in the boardroom; my agenda as a shareholder is limited, which is one consequence of my limited liability. But, as Bob Monks and I said in our book *Power and Accountability*, there is a reason accounting principles are called "generally accepted" and not "certifiably accurate." The best you can say is that they provide some consistency. You may be comparing apples and apples, but that does not answer your question about tomatoes. For this reason, Bennett, I think you are wrong to dismiss the relevance of nonfinancial measures for shareholders—I think that Carolyn Brancato and Ned Regan are on to something potentially quite valuable.

I also have another major objection to something I heard earlier. In communicating with investors, companies should not underestimate the importance of index investors. Information is not just about buying and selling, gentlemen. Information is about how you behave as an owner. And index investors can become very active as owners. Certainly that's been true of CALPERS, Wells Fargo, and a number of institutions I've worked with. And let me tell you that these institutions, even the indexers, want all the information they can get. If institutional investors didn't want information and influence, Bob Monks and I would not have started The Lens Fund.

What kinds of information do they want? Well, one thing they clearly value is all the information they can get about executive compensation plans. One piece of information that is not currently required, but one I find immensely useful, is the dilution impact of stock option plans. And my old firm, Institutional Shareholder Services, helps a lot of institutional investors by providing them with this information.

Now, I agree with Joe Shenton that relationship investing is not something new; it's been with us since the days of the joint stock companies and Adam Smith. Relationship investing has in fact been crucial to economic development (if it had not taken hold, we would be living in a socialist society today). As an entrepreneur myself, when I go to seek venture capital, the first thing the venture capitalist asks me is, how many seats can he have on the board? And this is the essence of relationship investing, whether we're talking about venture capital for start-ups, LBOs for mature companies, or the management of large public companies. It's having large-stake investors, and supplying them with information about and

some measure of influence over corporate strategic decisions.

In the case of Eastman Kodak, we intend to stay with Kodak to see through some major changes. We put our money where our mouth is. And if you get our money, you're going to get our mouth. And Joe Shenton is quite right, by the way, in saying that the best corporate executives will want to listen to what we have to say.
STERN: How long have you been in Kodak?
MINOW: Since the fund began—that is, about a year ago.
STERN: Why did you get into Kodak in the first place? Or, more generally, how do you choose to make your investments?
MINOW: We have invested in four companies to date. It's our intention to be substantial investors in no more than four companies at any given time, so that we can pay very careful attention to each of them.

One of our investment criteria is significantly substandard rates of return over several time horizons: one-year, three-year, and five-year periods. We work with Batterymarch, which provides all kinds of numbers for us on strategic momentum. We want to know if they're drifting downward or if they've already started to go back up.

We also do things like NEXIS searches on management to see whether we can isolate management as the variable that is depressing the stock. We're looking for companies where there's the largest possible gap between the value that could be there and the value that the market is showing. And it has to be a gap that we can influence. If it's a company that has industry-wide problems, if it's in a heavily regulated industry, or if management has a substantial number of shares, then we're not going to get into it. It has to be something where we can affect the outcome by

acting as shareholders, within the authority and by using the rights that accompany stock ownership.
STERN: How do you decide when it's time to get out? Kodak, for example, recently took a very positive step by encouraging its managers to buy stock in the company.
MINOW: Yes, we were thrilled about it.
STERN: And the stock price has since gone up by more than 25%. What else do you think they might do to enhance its value?
MINOW: We continue to believe that Kodak is highly susceptible to change if pushed. The imaging technology in their business is changing very dramatically and they have invested heavily in it. But their efforts to diversify have been disastrous, and we think that there's money to be made by reversing the process.
STEWART: I think there's two major changes Kodak can make. One, as you suggest, they can unwind the diversification. They have a very large chemical company, they have imaging, they have photography, and they have the pharmaceuticals company. Simply splitting the company into pieces—whether as independent companies through spin-offs to shareholders or by selling some of the businesses to other companies—should create considerable value.

The second thing you could do would be to stop using the huge gross profit margins on film to subsidize other businesses. As in so many conglomerates I've observed, the cash flows from the profitable businesses end up being wasted on organizational inefficiencies; they never make it down to the bottom line. Kodak has a huge management infrastructure that is crying out to be rationalized by going through the kind of core process redesign that has been laying off middle managers across America. Either Kodak's top management just can't make the hard decisions, or they've lost sight of the fact that it's execution that matters. It's not grandiose strategic thinking, but process redesign that makes the difference these days.

MINOW: That's right. And results are what the compensation scheme has to be designed to promote. And that's what the board has to be designed to promote.

STERN: Nell, are there certain kinds of nonfinancial measures you have asked Kodak to provide?

MINOW: We wrote Kodak a 22-page letter filled with questions about options we wanted them to consider. All but one page described strategic and financial initiatives; one page related to governance issues, focusing on the relationship between shareholders and directors. We did not say we wanted them to make those changes immediately. Rather, we said we were intelligent people with a significant financial investment at stake. And that, given the limits of *publicly available information*, we had certain questions that we wanted to explore with management. We met with Whitmore and Steffen several times, and we continue to be in close contact with the company.

PALEPU: Would you make public the brief that you wrote Kodak?

MINOW: It's not public at the moment, and won't be unless our communication with management breaks down.

PALEPU: But, if you're convinced your analysis is correct, why not make the document public and rally the support of other investors? This may give you even more leverage with management than you have now.

MINOW: True, but until we feel that leverage is needed, our approach is less confrontational. First we go to the CEO. If that works, fine; then we don't need to go farther. If that doesn't work, then we go to the board of directors. And if that doesn't work, and only then, do we go to the shareholders, and the press.

VESELL: What is your exit strategy?

MINOW: We have an exit price in mind when we go in—although that is subject to continuous revision. In fact, we have already taken some gains in Kodak because the price run-up made it more than 25% of our portfolio. We are designed to be an enhancement to an indexed portfolio. At the moment, it's all our own money, but we hope to change that fairly soon.

VESELL: How do you determine the price at which you're going to sell?

MINOW: Based on a sort of a traditional investment-banker, break-up-value analysis. This is not going to continue to be our strategy forever, but all the companies in our portfolio at the moment are there because they are conglomerates. That's one thing shareholders really have the information and the power to change in underperforming companies; they get to decide whether this should really be one big, diversified company or three separate companies. That's where there's the biggest opportunity to add value.

STEWART: Nell, what you are saying is that the '80s ended too soon. The deconglomeration wave reached as far as R.J. Reynolds; but, when it receded, we still had companies like Procter & Gamble and Sears and GM that needed to be restructured back into their basic parts. So, what you and Bob Monks are really now doing is the unfinished work of the restructuring of the '80s.

MINOW: Well, I think of what we're doing as a refinement of the takeover era. The takeover era brought some very important corrections, but it did so in a brutal and scattershot way. I think that we can do it in a more humane and, ultimately, more efficient way.

STERN: Four at a time? It may take forever at that rate. I would hope that just the threat of The Lens Fund owning stock would prompt many underperforming companies to reform from within—even if you never arrive. That would be a true sign of your effectiveness.

MINOW: I agree. In fact, I think the most telling measure of our success will be when the announcement of our investment becomes itself a buy signal to the general market. And I think that will happen. When Steffen's departure was announced yesterday, we got about a dozen phone calls from institutional investors with substantial stakes in Kodak asking us what we were going to do and if we wanted their help.

VESELL: What have been the results of your approach to date?

MINOW: As we near the end of the first year, we have substantially outperformed the S&P index with a 20.5% return. It would be about twice that if Westinghouse hadn't continued to be so recalcitrant. But keep your eyes on Westinghouse.

Incentive Compensation as a Substitute for Takeovers

STEWART: In 1985, CEOs or CFOs would likely have been concerned about their stock prices in large part because of the threat of hostile takeover. That threat seems to have all but disappeared. Basil, are you still concerned about Scott Paper's stock price? And are you more or less concerned than, say, back in the mid-1980s?

ANDERSON: In fact, I would argue that, because of fairly recent changes in our incentive compensation plan, the management and employees of Scott Paper are probably *more* concerned about our stock price today than they were five or ten years ago. In the past, our company's compensation philosophy was to pay higher-than-average salaries and modest bonuses. Today, our salaries are set at roughly the median level for large companies, but there is lots more incentive-based pay and stock options. So my own personal compensation, as well as that of most of our top executives, now depends significantly on how the stock performs.

STEWART: Nell, do you find now that the new SEC disclosures on management compensation are helpful to you as an investor? Do you think that's a productive change?

MINOW: Yes, I'm absolutely delighted about it. In fact, I think the disclosures provided by the compensation committee are the most important ones of all for investors. I want to know what companies are trying to achieve with the compensation plan. It's not how much the CEO gets paid, but the goals the company is setting for him. Are they trying to maximize earnings per share or long-term economic value? I like to see these goals spelled out clearly. But if I instead see just a lot of boilerplate in the compensation report, then I become very suspicious.

STEWART: Then you would agree with Michael Jensen that it's not how much we pay our CEOs that really matters, but rather how they are paid?

MINOW: Very much so. I want to see that the interests of the shareholders and the managers are closely aligned. If that's the case, then I'm delighted if the CEO makes a bundle.

But, at the same time, let me repeat a recent remark by Bud Crystal that really struck me. He said that if you go short on every company that gives restrictive stock grants to the CEO, you're going to make out like crazy. Why? Because that company is effectively saying, "We don't think the stock's going to go up, but we want the CEO to get something anyway." It reminds me of Sears' grant to Mr. Martinez of yet another "guaranteed bonus." A guaranteed bonus—which,

incidentally, is my favorite oxymoron—really tells you something about whether the man is willing to bet on himself or not.

CHEW: The same thing seems to hold for relationship investors. There's a study that demonstrates that when Warren Buffett and other relationship investors buy common stock, then that's a buy signal for the other stockholders—the stock will outperform market averages over the next few years. But if Buffett takes a convertible preferred instead of the common, then that's a sell signal. The signal, as you suggest, Nell, is in the structure of the contract.

MINOW: Yes, and that's the reason that the compensation committee report is going to be tremendously important.

As for other potentially valuable nonfinancial disclosures, I was very much influenced by Dick Crawford's book about human capital. I'd like to know from companies how much money they're spending on training and their employee turnover rate. I also look at the quality of the products and the extent to which there is a commitment to total quality management. If somebody gets the Baldridge Award, I think that's very useful information.

I also love to see disclosures about the governance component of the company. I want to make sure that they have a governance system that encourages listening. This includes having a majority of independent directors, an independent nominating committee, and, perhaps most important, regular private meetings of the independent directors without the CEO or other company employees. And I look to see the level of activism in the company. If I bought every company that CALPERS targeted, I would be making terrific returns. Last year, on an investment of $500,000, CALPERS made $137 million in extraordinary

returns in their shareholder initiative program. And I would defy anybody in the room to find another investment that made that kind of return.

Investing for the Long Run

STEWART: Gene, how do you contrast your approach in investing with that of The Lens Fund? It seems there's some similarities in that you both take major stakes—but you're not quite as provocative.

VESELL: Well, I'd say we're not quite as *vocal*. We may in fact be equally provocative.

STEWART: Do you make recommendations to companies that they make certain changes?

VESELL: We certainly do. We are not at all hesitant to talk about things that we think we know something about. Such things would generally be financial rather than operational, often involving management compensation.

But incentive compensation is by no means a panacea. We've found, to paraphrase Buffett, that if you have good assets but you're not in bed with good people, the people will win out. It's very hard to make money if you've got a really bad management. Most of the scars I have acquired during my years in this business have come from situations where we attempted to combine good assets and bad people.

STEWART: But you don't have an investment in Kodak or Sears. Why is that?

VESELL: It's not our cup of java. We try, in general, to invest in good businesses; and, in some instances, the businesses are better than the accounting results would suggest. We know Chris Steffen very well because we own about 10% of Honeywell, and we're very familiar with what he did there. We're just not knowledgeable enough about Kodak. We don't swing at every pitch.

DOBRZYNSKI: Do you have a predetermined exit point? How and when do you decide to get out and take a gain?

VESELL: When we go into a company, we establish what we think is the rational economic value of the enterprise; and we buy if that value is significantly higher than the current stock price. But once we buy a company, our time horizon—as Buffett said when he bought his stake in Coca-Cola—is forever. We don't want to sell.

In fact what we want to achieve is the continuous value creation, if you will, that can be achieved by a management intent on maximizing cash flow over the long haul. If the assets are managed correctly, and if the free cash is either reinvested in projects above the cost of capital or returned to shareholders (if there are no promising projects), then management can achieve continuous value creation. And that's the process we try to foster at Oppenheimer-owned companies. But, when we live with our investments for a long time, we constantly monitor the price/value relationships of our companies very carefully.

STEWART: Gene, you heard Derek Smith talk about share repurchase earlier, and you just mentioned it now. How do you look at dividends, which are just another way of distributing cash to investors? Does dividend yield or dividend payout enter into your valuation method?

VESELL: No, not really. Dividends are just one of several ways you can return your excess capital to investors—and we prefer stock repurchase.

STEWART: Do you typically tender your shares into repurchase offers?

VESELL: Only if the offer is made at a large premium over the stock price. Otherwise, and provided we feel it's a company in which want to increase our investment, we almost always choose to increase our proportional ownership instead of tendering our shares.

STERN: Gene, are there big risks to you from having to pay a huge premium to take a large equity position to get in, or from having to take a huge discount to get out?

VESELL: Not if we're correct in our buying or selling decisions. Because we're typically buying things that are out of favor and other people are selling, it's surprisingly easy to buy them. And if the company does well, then it should be relatively easy to get out.

Let me give you an example. At one time we owned as much as 25% of Fruit of the Loom. We started buying it at $12 or $13, and then it went down to six or seven. So we had no trouble buying all we wanted. We own somewhere between 5% and 10% of the company now. We started selling it in the high 30s and then sold more in the high 40s. There was no problem selling it at that point in time.

So if you're right, there's no problem. And even if you're wrong—we have owned a lot of American Express and haven't done very well with it—there can still be plenty of liquidity.

Indexed Activists: The Case of New York State

STERN: Let me turn back to Ned Regan, who, as I mentioned earlier, is now serving out his next to last day as a public servant. Ned, Joe Shenton has sort of suggested that it may not be worth companies' spending much time with indexers like your New York State fund. Yet you've defied his expectations in a way by becoming an active investor in a number of cases. Would you tell us why you've chosen this unusual blend of activeness and passivity?

REGAN: Well, it's not just New York State. There are other pension funds getting involved in corporate governance on a selective basis. This in-

volves hundreds of billions of dollars of assets, and it's growing.

Our own system for investing is quite different from what we've heard described today. We don't look at compensation and most other governance issues. I don't care about inside boards or outside boards. In fact, there are just two important considerations for us— and what I'm about to say is probably true of many of the large public pension funds. First, we are virtually permanent owners; we don't sell— and so we are concerned only about the long-term performance *prospects* of corporations. Second, we try to identify chronic underperformers. Having done so, we then attempt to determine if and how their strategy, their culture, and ultimately their performance can be improved— and, most important, whether the board understands this. After we identify these companies, we don't play the chase-the-headlines-and-gang-up-on-them game, provided they understand what needs to be done.

STEWART: Is that because you're convinced that these more forceful actions would not work?

REGAN: It's because we are permanent owners and have a fiduciary duty to do something constructive about the egregious underperformers in the portfolio.

STERN: Isn't it true, though, Ned, that your forebearance could partly reflect something else? It may be dictated in part by the fact that your own personal net worth is not affected by the potential increases in the value of the portfolio if you became even more active? You don't get paid based on the performance of the portfolio.

REGAN: Of course not. But I do get elected based on it. The taxpayers contribute next to nothing to our pension fund, and they like that. I could get re-elected on that alone.

STERN: Well, let me put it this way. Let's say you knew that if the value of the New York State portfolio went up by 20% during your tenure, you would have a very strong assurance of being re-elected. Now, the question I'm asking is this: What if you could double that amount to 40% by becoming even more activist than you are now? Would you consider doing it? Or would you acquire a reputation as a trouble maker among your political colleagues?

REGAN: Well, these are not matters that I really think about much. Again, our approach is very simple: We're permanent owners (and, as I said, there are hundreds of billions managed by funds like ours). And we have a fiduciary duty to do something about the clearly identified underperformers in the permanent portfolio.

We have developed our own system for picking the underperformers. And, on the basis of that system, we recently identified National Medical Enterprises and A&P. In the case of National Medical Enterprises, we had become quite involved with the company well before its problems made the headlines. And we're now in the midst of discussions with A&P as to whether we will solicit votes against their board. We also came across A&P before *Forbes* or anyone else ran stories on them.

Of course, two swallows a spring don't make, but we think we're on the right track. And, from my vantage point, it appears that some of the large public pension funds are headed in a very similar direction—and for the very simple reason I just mentioned: If you're not going to sell that underperforming stock, what are you going to do about it?

STERN: Why don't you sell it?

REGAN: Because we're indexed, we're permanent owners. There are probably no more than 200 people in

the country who understand the biggest investment movement in the country—and thousands of well-informed people who don't. I am continually amazed by the level of ignorance about the large public institutional investors in this country. We've been indexed, permanent owners for twelve years, it's no secret. Ten or eleven years ago we were the largest indexer in the country. We had more assets indexed than all the rest combined. But all that's changed. Now there's some $300 or $400 billion being indexed in this way.

But, to come back to your original question, Joel, we don't sell stocks because we are civil-servant oriented; we're a long way from being professional stock pickers. And, as you know, over the long run, indexed funds outperform 75 or 80% of all professional money managers.

I would also tell you that, when running an indexed fund, it is very important to maintain the discipline of the index—in our case, we index against the S&P 500 and 400 and the Russell 2000. By selling just one stock, I would be undermining the discipline of the index. In fact I once discovered that, when I turned my back, my staff at the other end of the hall just couldn't resist doing the same thing—deviating from the index. They wanted to create their own "enhanced" S&P 500 in the worst way, but I quickly stopped that.

So we rode IBM down but we rode everything else up. And, as most of you probably know, New York State has been very well served by just matching billions of dollars against the S&P 500. We pay about $20,000 a year to manage the $20 billion we have in indexed equities—and we have simply ridden the market up over the past 12 years. If we hadn't been indexing, our asset management fees would have run $30-$40 million per year.

So, we don't deviate from the index. Adhering to the discipline is essential. And I think my staff's the best in the country.

STERN: But what does that mean when you say they're the best in the country? They're the best at earning the market rate of return?

REGAN: We have the lowest transaction costs of any of the pension funds. The annual costs of running our $60 billion fund are well below a million dollars. As a consequence, New York taxpayers have gotten what amounts to a free ride on the stock market boom of the last 12 years.

STEWART: Ned, could you tell us more how you would go about energizing poorly performing companies?

REGAN: It's a fairly deliberate process. In the case of National Medical Enterprises, we filed a resolution with the company just last week—but this was after lengthy analysis that revealed to us that the company is in trouble. Similarly, in the case of A&P, we started to analyze their problems at least six months ago.

STEWART: So, although you can't pick stocks that are undervalued in the classic Graham and Dodd fundamental sense, you can pick stocks that have underperformed. And then you can use the voting power that comes with your shares, together with the voting power of the other funds, to bring management to the table. Like Nell Minow, you serve as catalyst investors to bring about dramatic change in those companies.

REGAN: But many large public investors do this, although we don't make a lot of noise about it. In fact, we deliberately avoid publicity when doing this. When I told the *Wall Street Journal* and the *New York Times* about A&P, they ran awful stories saying that I was waging a "proxy war." As a consequence, I didn't say a word to them about National Medical Enterprises.

VESELL: I know something about A&P. We used to own 10% of the shares. A German family owns 51% of it.

REGAN: That's right. We think that family has one idea in mind, and it is not the minority shareholders. So, we are planning to mount a solicitation of the 50 largest minority shareholders to withhold the vote from the board of directors.

STEWART: Is this Joe Grundfest's "just vote no" approach?

REGAN: That's right. We've done some very elaborate analysis of the company, which we have shared with the company and will share with the other shareholders. And we'll probably do something similar with National Medical Enterprises when their shareholders' meeting comes around, which is not for another six months or so.

So what is our motivation here for doing all this? I get satisfaction—and there are dozens of public pension fund trustees like myself—just from my sense of doing my job correctly. It has nothing to do with money. When we saw the problem at National Medical Enterprises, we acted to uphold our fiduciary duty to our beneficiaries to maximize the return to the fund. And you're going to see a lot more public pension funds doing the same thing in the next few years. I don't know what name you people will give that kind of investing, but that's what's coming.

STEWART: Ned, it seems to me that your two levers to promote change are the vote and the publicity that comes with public office.

REGAN: But I have never sought public attention for this activity; in fact, I've discouraged it.

STEWART: But, without some kind of a threat, aren't you just a paper tiger?

BRANCATO: I don't see how you could view somebody with $60 billion under management as a paper tiger.

REGAN: Our approach is to influence companies through relatively private dialogue, at least initially. What we are doing is to file resolutions with individual companies asking for changes in the corporate by-laws that would require the proxy to be opened to long-term shareholders to put in a couple of hundred words analyzing the performance of the company. The independent directors would then have the right to counter with their own couple of hundred words. By putting this dialogue in the corporate proxy, we could limit the excesses of the media that I prefer to avoid. Of course, we need some media exposure, but this would enable us to contain the excesses that come with a telephone call or a press release.

STEWART: Forgive me for pressing this point, but I just don't see how such indirect means can force really recalcitrant managements to move.

REGAN: Well, let me put it this way. We do a report showing chronic underperformance, and then we share that with management and the board. If they don't respond, then we send this report to other fiduciaries with a cover letter that says: "We have determined that you hold this stock in your portfolio. Here's a 20-page study that shows that this company is underperforming and, most important, has no interest in reforming. You, as a fiduciary, should withhold your vote from this board. If you don't, you are breaching your duty because the value of your portfolio is going to remain unnecessarily low unless you help us initiate change." So hopefully they vote with us and we end up with, say, a 35% vote against the board.

STEWART: Fantastic. That's just what I wanted to hear you say.

STERN: Well, this is a most fortunate ending to this discussion—because I really wanted to give Ned Regan the last word before going off to his new assignment. It also gives us the opportunity to salute him for a job well done.

REGAN: Joel, you may take this as my last word as a public official.

II. CORPORATE STRATEGY AND STRUCTURE

One of the major tasks of corporate financial management is to evaluate investment opportunities. In many companies, this investment function is separated from the financing decisions typically performed by the corporate treasury, and is instead entrusted to a corporate "planning" or "strategy" group. Perhaps partly as a result of this separation of the investment and financing functions within the corporation, corporate strategy has developed for the most part independently of the discipline of financial economics. But some financial economists have attempted to bring principles of corporate finance to bear directly on matters of corporate strategy.

One source of contention between financial analysts and strategists is the heavy reliance of the former on quantitative methods. In the early 1980s, the Harvard Business Review ran a series of articles assailing the shortsightedness of American corporate investment practices. The blame for this alleged myopia was placed, in large part, on the widespread use of the analytical technique known as discounted cash flow analysis, or "DCF." And because DCF has long been advocated by financial economists as the most reliable method for assessing economic value, the whole of finance theory seems to have been implicated.

In "Finance Theory and Financial Strategy," Stewart Myers sheds welcome light on this controversy by separating what may be valid in such claims from what is not. As Myers points out, much of the criticism of DCF involves a misreading of the underlying theory, and is indeed aimed not at "finance theory, but at habits of financial analysts that financial economists are attempting to reform"—and the article offers a list of the most prominent abuses of the DCF method.

Nevertheless, as Myers acknowledges, part of the "gap" that has long divided the disciplines of finance and corporate strategy can be attributed to the real (as opposed to imagined) limitations of the DCF method. When properly applied, DCF remains the best available technique for evaluating certain kinds of investments: namely, those companies or investments producing fairly predictable cash flow streams. Where the DCF method falls down, however, are in those kinds of investments that offer significant operating or strategic options—that is,

the right, but not the obligation, to, say, build on a vacant property, develop an oil reserve, expand or contract a mining operation, or to shift the use of existing capabilities among a variety of different markets. It is impossible to capture the value of such "real options" using the simple DCF technique; and options pricing theory, as Myers suggests, seems to hold out the best solution to this problem.

In the 1980s and especially in the 1990s, dramatic changes in the business environment have required major changes in corporate strategy. And such changes in strategy have in turned forced many companies to rethink their organizational structure. As one notable example, deregulation, global competition, and the rush of technological change and new product development have been driving large organizations to push decision-making down through the ranks to managers and employees closer to the company's operations and customers. But, as organizational theorists have long understood, there are significant costs associated with decentralizing decision-making. As one of the articles in this section points out,

"Today's information systems may now be capable of providing top management with real-time monitoring of the revenues and profits of the most farflung operations. But what software is programmed to report opportunities lost by operating heads too comfortable with the status quo? And what accounting systems are capable of distinguishing reliably between profitable and unprofitable corporate investment decisions at the time the decisions are being made?"

The answer, of course, is that much of the information necessary to seize business opportunities cannot be captured and passed on by computer systems. It is rather "specific" or "idiosyncratic" knowledge—the kind that comes out of the daily experience of line managers and employees. But if decentralization seems an obvious way for a company to make the best use of such knowledge, it's equally clear that giving line managers and employees more decision-making authority will pay off only if such people are highly motivated and focused on the right goals.

And so, as some organizational theorists are now coming to understand, companies that choose to decentralize must also change their performance evaluation and reward systems to help ensure that operating managers and employees use their expanded decision-making powers in ways that increase the value of the firm. In this sense—to borrow a phrase from another article in this section—decentralization, performance evaluation, and incentive compensation can be viewed as a "three-legged stool" of effective organizational design.

The original formulators of this three-part concept of corporate organization were Michael Jensen and William Meckling. In an article (not included here) entitled "Specific and General Knowledge, and Organizational Structure," Jensen and Meckling argued that there are two principal challenges in designing the structure of organizations: (1) the "rights assignment" problem—namely, ensuring that decision-making authority is vested in managers and employees with the "specific knowledge" necessary to make the best decisions; and (2) the "control" or "agency" problem—designing performance evaluation and reward systems that give decision-makers strong incentives to exercise their decision rights in ways that contribute to the goals of the organization.

In "The Economics of Organizational Architecture," James Brickley, Clifford Smith, and Jerold Zimmerman provide a number of instructive applications and extensions of the Jensen-Meckling organizational framework. Using a series of brief case studies that range from the recent Barings' debacle and the decade-long restructuring of ITT to McDonald's and Century 21, the authors demonstrate the importance of designing performance measurement and reward systems that are consistent with the assignment of decision rights. The authors also attempt to dispel the notion, popular among many TQM advocates, that widespread use of performance measures and incentives undermines efforts to promote teamwork within large organizations. Indeed, brief case histories of Xerox and Mary Kay Cosmetics show the critical role of performance measurement and individual rewards in reinforcing a quality-centered corporate "culture." As the authors conclude, "It is a mistake to think of the 'soft' and 'hard' aspects of organizations as mutually exclusive or even as competing."

One method of reducing manager-shareholder conflicts that has received considerable recent interest is the EVA® performance measurement and incentive compensation system designed by Stern Stewart & Co. In "The EVA Financial Management System," my colleagues Joel Stern, Bennett Stewart, and I begin by describing the shortcomings of the top-down, EPS-based model of financial management that has long dominated corporate America. Next we explain the rise of hostile takeovers and the phenomenal success of LBOs in the 1980s as capital market responses to the deficiencies of the EPS model. In the second half of the article, we show how the EVA financial management system borrows important aspects of the LBO movement—particularly, its focus on capital efficiency and ownership incentives—but without the high leverage and concentration of risk that limit LBOs to the mature sector of the U.S. economy. We close by presenting the outlines of an EVA-based incentive compensation plan that is designed to simulate for managers and employees the rewards of ownership.

If EVA seems particularly well-designed to discourage corporate overinvestment, it can also be used to address underinvestment problems. In "Capabilities and Capital Investments: New Perspectives on Capital Budgeting," Carliss Baldwin and Kim Clark note that U.S. companies face both external (capital market) and internal (corporate) pressures to underinvest in relatively intangible assets—things like stronger supplier relationships, market penetration, process improvements, employee training, and other corporate "capabilities." Not only are such assets difficult for investors on the outside to appreciate (and reflect in higher share prices), but their value also tends to elude measurement by most internal corporate capital budgeting and management compensation systems. And whereas the benefits of such investments take time to materialize and are generally shared throughout the company, the costs are expensed immediately rather than capitalized and are generally charged to particular units. Such a tendency to underinvest could be counteracted, as Baldwin and Clark propose, in two ways: by partly "centralizing" authority and by using an EVA-type of accounting that capitalizes instead of expensing corporate investments in capabilities.

In "Total Compensation Strategy," Steven O'Byrne argues that the design of the executive compensation plans found in most Fortune 500 companies contains a fundamental flaw. Even though a large proportion of an executive's current year's compensation may be "at risk," companies' commitment to maintaining "competitive" levels of compensation in every year effectively ensures that a large proportion of the executive's company-related wealth (that is, total expected compensation over the executive's entire tenure) is not really at risk. To create a total wealth incentive that replicates the incentives of a significant owner of the company's stock, O'Byrne argues, total compensation strategy must be based on policies that make a substantial proportion of an executive's future compensation depend more heavily on current performance. These policies include (1) front-loaded, fixed-share option grants rather than the widely-used annual, variable-share option grants; and (2) formula-based rather than negotiated bonus plans.

The section closes with the "Stern Stewart EVA Roundtable," in which Joel Stern and Bennett Stewart discuss the strengths and limitations of EVA with a group of corporate CFOs, financial academics, and representatives of the investment and legal community.

DHC

FINANCE THEORY AND FINANCIAL STRATEGY

by Stewart Myers,
*Massachusetts Institute of Technology**

S trategic planning is many things, but it surely includes the process of deciding how to commit the firm's resources across lines of business. The financial side of strategic planning allocates a particular resource, capital.

Finance theory has made major advances in understanding how capital markets work and how risky real and financial assets are valued. Tools derived from finance theory, particularly discounted cash-flow analysis, are widely used. Yet finance theory has had scant impact on strategic planning.

I attempt here to explain the gap between finance theory and strategic planning. Three explanations are offered:

1. Finance theory and traditional approaches to strategic planning may be kept apart by differences in language and "culture."
2. Discounted cash flow analysis may have been misused, and consequently not accepted, in strategic applications.
3. Discounted cash flow analysis may fail in strategic applications even if it is properly applied.

Each of these explanations is partly true. I do not claim that the three, taken together, add up to the whole truth. Nevertheless, I will describe both the problems encountered in applying finance theory to strategic planning, and the potential payoffs if the theory can be extended and properly applied.

The first task is to explain what is meant by "finance theory" and the gap between it and strategic planning.

THE RELEVANT THEORY

The financial concepts most relevant to strategic planning are those dealing with firms' capital investment decisions, and they are sketched here at the minimum level of detail necessary to define "finance theory."

Think of each investment project as a "mini-firm," all-equity financed. Suppose its stock could be actively traded. If we know what the mini-firm's stock would sell for, we know its present value. We calculate net present value (NPV) by subtracting the required investment.

In other words, we calculate each project's present value to investors who have free access to capital markets. We should therefore use the valuation model which best explains the prices of similar securities. However, the theory is usually boiled down to a single model, discounted cash flow (DCF):

$$PV = \sum_{t=1}^{T} \frac{C_t}{(1+r)^t},$$

where PV = present (market) value;

C_t = forecasted incremental cash flow after corporate taxes—strictly speaking the mean of the distribution of possible C_t's;

T = project life (C_T includes any salvage value);

r = the opportunity cost of capital, defined as the equilibrium expected rate of return on securities equivalent in risk to the project being valued.

NPV equals PV less the cash outlay required at t=0.

---

* This article was first published in *Interfaces* 14:1 January-February 1984 (pp.126-137). It is reprinted with permission of The Institute of Management Science.

Since present values add, the value of the firm should equal the sum of the values of all its mini-firms. If the DCF formula works for each project separately, it should work for any collection of projects, a line of business, or the firm as a whole. A firm or line of business consists of intangible as well as tangible assets, and growth opportunities as well as assets-in-place. Intangible assets and growth opportunities are clearly reflected in stock prices, and in principle can also be valued in capital budgeting. Projects bringing intangible assets or growth opportunities to the firm have correspondingly higher NPVs. I will discuss whether DCF formulas can capture this extra value later.

The opportunity cost of capital varies from project to project, depending on risk. In principle, each project has its own cost of capital. In practice, firms simplify by grouping similar projects in risk classes, and use the same cost of capital for all projects in a class.

The opportunity cost of capital for a line of business, or for the firm, is a value-weighted average of the opportunity costs of capital for the projects it comprises.

The opportunity cost of capital depends on the use of funds, not on the source. In most cases, financing has a second-order impact on value: you can make much more money through smart investment decisions than smart financing decisions. The advantage, if any, of departing from all-equity financing is typically adjusted for through a somewhat lowered discount rate.

Finance theory stresses cash flow and the expected return on competing assets. The firm's investment opportunities compete with securities stockholders can buy. Investors willingly invest or reinvest cash in the firm only if it can do better, risk considered, than the investors can do on their own.

Finance theory thus stresses fundamentals. It should not be deflected by accounting allocations, except as they affect cash taxes. For example, suppose a positive-NPV project sharply reduces book earnings in its early stages. Finance theory would recommend forging ahead, trusting investors to see through the accounting bias to the project's true value. Empirical evidence indicates that investors do see through accounting biases; they do not just look naively at last quarter's or last year's EPS. (If they did, all stocks would sell at the same price-earnings ratio.)

All these concepts are generally accepted by financial economists. The concepts are broadly consistent with an up-to-date understanding of how capital markets work. Moreover, they seem to be accepted by firms, at least in part: any time a firm sets a hurdle rate based on capital market evidence and uses a DCF formula, it must implicitly rely on the logic I have sketched. So the issue here is not whether managers accept finance theory for capital budgeting (and for other financial purposes). It is why they do not use the theory in strategic planning.

THE GAP BETWEEN FINANCE THEORY AND STRATEGIC PLANNING

I have resisted referring to strategic planning as "capital budgeting on a grand scale" because capital budgeting in practice is a bottom-up process. The aim is to find and undertake specific assets or projects that are worth more than they cost.

Picking valuable pieces does not ensure maximum value for the whole. Piecemeal, bottom-up capital budgeting is not strategic planning.

Capital budgeting techniques, however, ought to work for the whole as well as the parts. A strategic commitment of capital to a line of business is an investment project. If management does invest, they must believe the value of the firm increases by more than the amount of capital committed—otherwise they are throwing money away. In other words, there is an implicit estimate of net present value.

This would seem to invite application of finance theory, which explains how real and financial assets are valued. The theory should have direct application not only to capital budgeting, but also to the financial side of strategic planning.

Of course it has been applied to some extent. Moreover, strategic planning seems to be becoming more financially sophisticated. Financial concepts are stressed in several recent books on corporate strategy.[1] Consulting firms have developed the concepts' strategic implications.[2]

1. See, for example, W. E. Fruhan, Jr., *Financial Strategy: Studies in the Creation Transfer and Destruction of Shareholder Value,* (Homewood, Illinois: Richard D. Irwin, Inc., 1979); M. S. Salter and W. A. Weinhold, *Diversification Through Acquisition* (New York: The Free Press, 1979); and H. Bierman, *Strategic Financial Planning,* (New York: The Free Press, 1980).

2. See Alberts, W. A. and McTaggart, James M. 1984, "Value-based Strategic Investment Planning," *Interfaces,* Vol.14, No.1 (January-February), pp.138-151.

Nevertheless, I believe it is fair to say that most strategic planners are not guided by the tools of modern finance. Strategic and financial analyses are not reconciled, even when the analyses are of the same major project. When low net present value projects are nurtured "for strategic reasons" the strategic analysis overrides measures of financial value. Conversely, projects with apparently high net present values are passed by if they don't fit in with the firm's strategic objectives. When financial and strategic analyses give conflicting answers, the conflict is treated as a fact of life, not as an anomaly demanding reconciliation.

In many firms, strategic analysis is partly or largely directed to variables finance theory says are irrelevant. This is another symptom of the gap, for example:

■ Many managers worry about a strategic decision's impact on book rate of return or earnings per share. If they are convinced the plan adds to the firm's value, its impact on accounting figures should be irrelevant.

■ Some managers pursue diversification to reduce risk—risk as they see it. Investors see a firm's risk differently. In capital markets, diversification is cheap and easy. Investors who want to diversify do so on their own. Corporate diversification is redundant; the market will not pay extra for it.

If the market were willing to pay extra for diversification, closed-end funds would sell at premiums over net asset value, and conglomerate firms would be worth more to investors than their components separately traded. Closed-end funds actually sell at discounts, not premiums. Conglomerates appear to sell at discounts, too, although it is hard to prove it since the firm's components are not traded separately.

Much of the literature of strategic planning seems extremely naive from a financial point of view. Sometimes capital markets are ignored. Sometimes firms are essentially viewed as having a stock of capital, so that "cash cows" are needed to finance investment in rapidly growing lines of business. (The firms that pioneered in strategic planning actually had easy access to capital markets, as do almost all public companies.) Firms may not like the price they pay for capital, but that price is the opportunity cost of capital, the proper standard for new investment by the firm.

The practical conflicts between finance and strategy are part of what lies behind the recent criticism of U.S. firms for allegedly concentrating on quick payoffs at the expense of value. U.S. executives, especially MBAs, are said to rely too much on purely financial analysis, and too little on building technology, products, markets, and production efficiency. The financial world is not the real world, the argument goes; managers succumb to the glamour of high finance. They give time and talent to mergers, spinoffs, unusual securities, and complex financing packages when they should be out on the factory floor. They pump up current earnings per share at the expense of long-run values.

Much of this criticism is directed not against finance theory, but at habits of financial analysis that financial economists are attempting to reform. Finance theory of course concentrates on the financial world—that is, capital markets. However, it fundamentally disagrees with the implicit assumption of the critics who say that the financial world is not the real world and that financial analysis diverts attention from, and sometimes actively undermines, real long-run values. The professors and textbooks actually say that financial values rest on real values and that most value is created on the left-hand side of the balance sheet, not on the right.

Finance theory, however, is under attack, too. Some feel that any quantitative approach is inevitably short-sighted. Hayes and Garvin, for example, have blamed discounted cash flow for a significant part of this country's industrial difficulties. Much of their criticism seems directed to misapplications of discounted cash flow, some of which I discuss later. But they also believe the underlying theory is wanting; they say that "beyond all else, capital investment represents an act of faith."[3] This statement offends most card-carrying financial economists.

I do not know whether "gap" fully describes all of the problems noted, or hinted at, in the discussion so far. In some quarters, finance theory is effectively ignored in strategic planning. In others, it is seen as being in conflict, or working at cross-purposes, with other forms of strategic analysis. The problem is to explain why.

---

3. R. H. Hayes and D. A. Garvin, "Managing as if Tomorrow Mattered," *Harvard Business Review*, Vol.60, No. 3 (May-June), 1982, pp.70-79.

TWO CULTURES AND ONE PROBLEM

Finance theory and strategic planning could be viewed as two cultures looking at the same problem. Perhaps only differences in language and approach make the two appear incompatible. If so, the gap between them might be bridged by better communication and a determined effort to reconcile them.

Think of what can go wrong with standard discounted cash flow analyses of a series of major projects:

■ Even careful analyses are subject to random error. There is a 50 percent probability of a positive NPV for a truly borderline project. Firms have to guard against these errors dominating project choice.

■ Smart managers apply the following check. They know that all projects have zero NPV in long-run competitive equilibrium. Therefore, a positive NPV must be explained by a short-run deviation from equilibrium or by some permanent competitive advantage. If neither explanation applies, the positive NPV is suspect. Conversely, a negative NPV is suspect if a competitive advantage or short-run deviation from equilibrium favors the project. In other words, smart managers do not accept positive (or negative) NPVs unless they can explain them.

Strategic planning may serve to implement this check. Strategic analyses look for market opportunities—that is, deviations from equilibrium—and try to identify the firm's competitive advantages.

Turn the logic of the example around. We can regard strategic analysis which does not explicitly compute NPVs as showing absolute faith in Adam Smith's invisible hand. If a firm, looking at a line of business, finds a favorable deviation from long-run equilibrium, or if it identifies a competitive advantage, then (efficient) investment in that line must offer profits exceeding the opportunity cost of capital. No need to calculate the investment's NPV: the manager knows in advance that NPV is positive.

The trouble is that strategic analyses are also subject to random error. Mistakes are also made in identifying areas of competitive advantage or out-of-equilibrium markets. We would expect strategic analysts to calculate NPVs explicitly, at least as a check; strategic analysis and financial analysis ought to be explicitly reconciled. Few firms attempt this. This suggests the gap between strategic planning and finance theory is more than just "two cultures and one problem."

The next step is to ask why reconciliation is so difficult.

MISUSE OF FINANCE THEORY

The gap between strategic and financial analysis may reflect misapplication of finance theory. Some firms do not try to use theory to analyze strategic investments. Some firms try but make mistakes.

I have already noted that in many firms capital investment analysis is partly or largely directed to variables finance theory says are irrelevant. Managers worry about projects' book rates of return or impacts on book earnings per share. They worry about payback, even for projects that clearly have positive NPVs. They try to reduce risk through diversification.

Departing from theoretically correct valuation procedures often sacrifices the long-run health of the firm for the short, and makes capital investment choices arbitrary or unpredictable. Over time, these sacrifices appear as disappointing growth, eroding market share, loss of technological leadership, and so forth.

The non-financial approach taken in many strategic analyses may be an attempt to overcome the short horizons and arbitrariness of financial analysis as it is often misapplied. It may be an attempt to get back to fundamentals. Remember, however: finance theory never left the fundamentals. Discounted cash flow should not in principle bias the firm against long-lived projects, or be swayed by arbitrary allocations.

However, the typical mistakes made in applying DCF do create a bias against long-lived projects. I will note a few common mistakes.

Ranking on Internal Rate of Return

Competing projects are often ranked on internal rate of return rather than NPV. It is easier to earn a high rate of return if project life is short and investment is small. Long-lived, capital-intensive projects tend to be put down the list even if their net present value is substantial.

The internal rate of return does measure bang per buck on a DCF basis. Firms may favor it because they think they have only a limited number of bucks. However, most firms big enough to do formal strategic planning have free access to capital markets. They may not like the price, but they can get the money. The limits on capital expenditures are more often set inside the firm, in order to control an

The non-financial approach taken in many strategic analyses may be an attempt to
overcome the short horizons and arbitrariness of financial analysis
as it is often misapplied.

organization too eager to spend money. Even when a firm does have a strictly limited pool of capital, it should not use the internal rate of return to rank projects. It should use NPV per dollar invested, or linear programming techniques when capital is rationed in more than one period.[4]

Inconsistent Treatment of Inflation

A surprising number of firms treat inflation inconsistently in DCF calculations. High nominal discount rates are used but cash flows are not fully adjusted for future inflation. Thus accelerating inflation makes projects—especially long-lived ones—look less attractive even if their real value is unaffected.

Unrealistically High Rates

Some firms use unrealistically high discount rates, even after proper adjustment for inflation. This may reflect ignorance of what normal returns in capital markets really are. In addition:
- Premiums are tacked on for risks that can easily be diversified away in stocknolders' portfolios.
- Rates are raised to offset the optimistic biases of managers sponsoring projects. This adjustment works only if the bias increases geometrically with the forecast period. If it does not, long-lived projects are penalized.
- Some projects are unusually risky at inception, but only of normal risk once the start-up is successfully passed. It is easy to classify this type of project as "high-risk," and to add a start-up risk premium to the discount rate for all future cash flows. The risk premium should be applied to the start-up period only. If it is applied after the start-up period, safe, short-lived projects are artificially favored.

Discounted cash flow analysis is also subject to a difficult organizational problem. Capital budgeting is usually a bottom-up process. Proposals originate in the organization's midriff, and have to survive the trip to the top, getting approval at every stage. In the process political alliances form, and cash flow forecasts are bent to meet known standards. Answers—not necessarily the right ones—are worked out for anticipated challenges. Most projects that get to the top seem to meet profitability standards set by management.

According to Brealey and Myers's Second Law, "The proportion of proposed projects having positive NPV is independent of top management's estimate of the opportunity cost of capital."[5]

Suppose the errors and biases of the capital budgeting process make it extremely difficult for top management to verify the true cash flows, risks, and present value of capital investment proposals. That would explain why firms do not try to reconcile the results of capital budgeting and strategic analyses. However, it does not explain why strategic planners do not calculate their own NPVs.

We must ask whether those in top management—the managers who make strategic decisions—understand finance theory well enough to use DCF analysis effectively. Although they certainly understand the arithmetic of the calculation, they may not understand the logic of the method deeply enough to trust it or to use it without mistakes.

They may also not be familiar enough with how capital markets work to use capital market data effectively. The widespread use of unrealistically high discount rates is probably a symptom of this.

Finally, many managers distrust the stock market. Its volatility makes them nervous, despite the fact that the volatility is the natural result of a rational market. It may be easier to underestimate the sophistication of the stock market than to accept its verdict on how well the firm is doing.

FINANCE THEORY MAY HAVE MISSED THE BOAT

Now consider the firm that understands finance theory, applies DCF analysis correctly, and has overcome the human and organizational problems that bias cash flows and discount rates. Carefully estimated net present values for strategic investments should help significantly. However, would they fully grasp and describe the firm's strategic choices? Perhaps not.

There are gaps in finance theory as it is usually applied. These gaps are not necessarily intrinsic to finance theory generally. They may be filled by new approaches to valuation. However, if they are the firm will have to use something more than a straightforward discounted cash flow method.

---

4. See R. A. Brealey and S.C. Myers, *Principles of Corporate Finance* (New York: McGraw-Hill Book Company, 1981), pp.101-107.

5. Brealey and Myers, *Principles of Corporate Finance*, cited in note 4, p. 238.

Many managers distrust the stock market. Its volatility makes them nervous, despite the fact that the volatility is the natural result of a rational market. It may be easier to underestimate the sophistication of the stock market than to accept its verdict on how the firm is doing.

An intelligent application of discounted cash flow will encounter four chief problems:

- Estimating the discount rate,
- Estimating the project's future cash flows,
- Estimating the project's impact on the firm's other assets cash flows—that is, through the cross-sectional links between projects, and
- Estimating the project's impact on the firm's future investment opportunities. These are the time-series links between projects.

The first three problems, difficult as they are, are not as serious for financial strategy as the fourth. However, I will review all four.

Estimating the Opportunity Cost of Capital

The opportunity cost of capital will always be difficult to measure, since it is an expected rate of return. We cannot commission the Gallup Poll to extract probability distributions from the minds of investors. However, we have extensive evidence on past average rates of return in capital markets and the corporate sector.[6] No long-run trends in "normal" rates of return are evident. Reasonable, ballpark cost of capital estimates can be obtained if obvious traps (for example, improper adjustments for risk or inflation) are avoided. In my opinion, estimating cash flows properly is more important than fine-tuning the discount rate.

Forecasting Cash Flow

It's impossible to forecast most projects' actual cash flows accurately. DCF calculations do not call for accurate forecasts, however, but for accurate assessments of the mean of possible outcomes.

Operating managers can often make reasonable subjective forecasts of the operating variables they are responsible for—operating costs, market growth, market share, and so forth—at least for the future that they are actually worrying about. It is difficult for them to translate this knowledge into a cash flow forecast for, say, year seven. There are several reasons for this difficulty. First, the operating manager is asked to look into a far future he is not used to thinking about. Second, he is asked to express his forecast in accounting rather than operat-

ing variables. Third, incorporating forecasts of macroeconomic variables is difficult. As a result, long-run forecasts often end up as mechanical extrapolations of short-run trends. It is easy to overlook the long-run pressures of competition, inflation, and technical change.

It should be possible to provide a better framework for forecasting operating variables and translating them into cash flows and present value—a framework that makes it easier for the operating manager to apply his practical knowledge and that explicitly incorporates information about macroeconomic trends. There is, however, no way around it: forecasting is intrinsically difficult, especially when your boss is watching you do it.

Estimating Cross-Sectional Relationships Between Cash Flows

Tracing "cross-sectional" relationships between project cash flows is also intrinsically difficult. The problem may be made more difficult by inappropriate project definitions or boundaries for lines of businesses. Defining business units properly is one of the tricks of successful strategic planning.

However, these inescapable problems in estimating profitability standards, future cash returns, and cross-sectional interactions are faced by strategic planners even if they use no financial theory. They do not reveal a flaw in existing theory. Any theory or approach encounters them. Therefore, they do not explain the gap between finance theory and strategic planning.

The Links Between Today's Investments and Tomorrow's Opportunities

The fourth problem—the link between today's investments and tomorrow's opportunities—is much more difficult.

Suppose a firm invests in a negative-NPV project in order to establish a foothold in an attractive market. Thus a valuable second-stage investment is used to justify the immediate project. The second stage must depend on the first: if the firm could take the second project without having taken the first, then the future opportunity should have no

6. For estimates of capital market returns over the period 1926 to the present, see R. G. Ibbotson and R. A. Sinquefield, *Stocks, Bonds, Bills, and Inflation: The Past and the Future*, Financial Analysts Research Foundation, Charlottesville, Virginia, 1982. For estimates of historical returns on capital from a corporate perspective, see D. M. Holland and S.C. Myers, "Trends in Corporate Profitability and Capital Costs," in R. Lindsay, ed., *The Nation's Capital Needs: Three Studies*, Committee on Economic Development, Washington, DC, 1979.

impact on the immediate decision. However, if tomorrow's opportunities depend on today's decisions, there is a time-series link between projects.

At first glance, this may appear to be just another forecasting problem. Why not estimate cash flows for both stages, and use discounted cash flow to calculate the NPV for the two stages taken together?

You would not get the right answer. The second stage is an option, and conventional discounted cash flow does not value options properly. The second stage is an option because the firm is not committed to undertake it. It will go ahead if the first stage works and the market is still attractive. If the first stage fails, or if the market sours, the firm can stop after Stage 1 and cut its losses. Investing in Stage 1 purchases an intangible asset: a call option on Stage 2. If the option's present value offsets the first stage's negative NPV, the first stage is justified.

The Limits of Discounted Cash Flow

The limits of DCF need further explanation. Think first of its application to four types of securities:
1. DCF is standard for valuing bonds, preferred stocks and other fixed-income securities.
2. DCF is sensible, and widely used, for valuing relatively safe stocks paying regular dividends.
3. DCF is not as helpful in valuing companies with significant growth opportunities. The DCF model can be stretched to say that Apple Computer's stock price equals the present value of the dividends the firm may eventually pay. It is more helpful to think of Apple's price, P_0, as:

$$P_0 = \frac{EPS}{r} + PVGO,$$

where EPS = normalized current earnings
r = the opportunity cost of capital
PVGO = the net present value of future growth opportunities.
Note that PVGO is the present value of a portfolio of options—the firm's options to invest in second-stage, third—stage, or even later projects.

4. DCF is never used for traded calls or puts. Finance theory supplies option valuation formulas that work, but the option formulas look nothing like DCF.

Think of the corporate analogues to these securities:

There are few problems in using DCF to value safe flows, for example, flows from financial leases.
■ DCF is readily applied to "cash cows"—relatively safe businesses held for the cash they generate rather than for strategic value. It also works for "engineering investments," such as machine replacements, where the main benefit is reduced cost in a clearly-defined activity.
■ DCF is less helpful in valuing businesses with substantial growth opportunities or intangible assets. In other words, it is not the whole answer when options account for a large fraction of a business's value.
■ DCF is no help at all for pure research and development. The value of R&D is almost all option value. Intangible assets' value is usually option value.

The theory of option valuation has been worked out in detail for securities—not only puts and calls, but warrants, convertibles, bond call options, and so forth. The solution techniques should be applicable to the real options held by firms. Several preliminary applications have already been worked out, for example:
■ Calculations of the value of a federal lease for offshore exploration for oil or gas. Here the option value comes from the lessee's right to delay the decisions to drill and develop, and to make these decisions after observing the extent of reserves and the future level of oil prices.[7]
■ Calculating an asset's abandonment or salvage value: an active second-hand market increases an asset's value, other things equal. The second-hand market gives the asset owner a put option which increases the value of the option to bail out of a poorly performing project.[8]

The option "contract" in each of these cases is fairly clear: a series of calls in the first case and a put in the second. However, these real options last longer and are more complex than traded calls and

---

7. See the article in this issue by James Paddock, Daniel Siegel, and James Smith, which deals with the use of option pricing models in valuing offshore petroleum leases.

8. See S.C. Myers and S. Majd, "Applying Option Pricing Theory to the Abandonment Value Problem," Sloan School of Management, MIT, Working Paper, 1983.

puts. The terms of real options have to be extracted from the economics of the problem at hand. Realistic descriptions usually lead to a complex implied "contract," requiring numerical methods of valuation.

Nevertheless, option pricing methods hold great promise for strategic analysis. The time-series links between projects are the most important part of financial strategy. A mixture of DCF and option valuation models can, in principle, describe these links and give a better understanding of how they work. It may also be possible to estimate the value of particular strategic options, thus eliminating one reason for the gap between finance theory and strategic planning.

LESSONS FOR CORPORATE STRATEGY

The task of strategic analysis is more than laying out a plan or plans. When time-series links between projects are important, it's better to think of strategy as managing the firm's portfolio of real options.[9] The process of financial planning may be thought of as:
■ Acquiring options, either by investing directly in R&D, product design, cost or quality improvements, and so forth, or as a by-product of direct capital investment (for example, investing in a Stage 1 project with negative NPV in order to open the door for Stage 2).
■ Abandoning options that are too far "out of the money" to pay to keep.
■ Exercising valuable options at the right time—that is, buying the cash-producing assets that ultimately produce positive net present value.

There is also a lesson for current applications of finance theory to strategic issues. Several new approaches to financial strategy use a simple, traditional DCF model of the firm.[10] These approaches are likely to be more useful for cash cows than for growth businesses with substantial risk and intangible assets.

The option value of growth and intangibles is not ignored by good managers even when conventional financial techniques miss them. These values may be brought in as "strategic factors," dressed in non-financial clothes. Dealing with the time-series links between capital investments, and with the option value these links create, is often left to strategic planners. But new developments in finance theory promise to help.

BRIDGING THE GAP

We can summarize by asking how the present gap between finance theory and strategic planning might be bridged.

Strategic planning needs finance. Present value calculations are needed as a check on strategic analysis and vice versa. However, the standard discounted cash flow techniques will tend to understate the option value attached to growing, profitable lines of business. Corporate finance theory requires extension to deal with real options. Therefore, to bridge the gap we on the financial side need to:
■ Apply existing finance theory correctly.
■ Extend the theory. I believe the most promising line of research is to try to use option pricing theory to model the time-series interactions between investments.

Both sides could make a conscious effort to reconcile financial and strategic analysis. Although complete reconciliation will rarely be possible, the attempt should uncover hidden assumptions and bring a generally deeper understanding of strategic choices. The gap may remain, but with better analysis on either side of it.

---

9. See W. C. Kester, "Today's Options for Tomorrow's Growth," *Harvard Business Review* (March-April 1984).

10. See, for example, chapter 2 of W. E. Fruhan, Jr., *Financial Strategy: Studies in the Creation Transfer and Destruction of Shareholder Value*, (Homewood, Illinois: Richard D. Irwin, Inc., 1979).

THE ECONOMICS OF ORGANIZATIONAL ARCHITECTURE

*by James Brickley,
Clifford Smith, and
Jerold Zimmerman,
University of Rochester**

F rancis Baring with his brother John established Barings Bank in London in 1762. Their bank prospered by facilitating international trade. Barings helped finance the British effort in the American Revolutionary War, and thereafter Barings credit reopened trade with the United States. In 1803, Barings helped the U.S. finance the Louisiana Purchase; it also helped finance Britain's wars against Napoleon. In 1818, the bank's influence was such that Duc de Richelieu observed, "There are six great powers in Europe: England, France, Prussia, Austria, Russia, and Barings Brothers."

The bank was shaken in 1890 when loans that it had made in Argentina defaulted. But it survived with the help of a bailout engineered by the Bank of England. The family rebuilt the bank and, although it never regained its former preeminence, Barings remained a gilt-edged institution run largely by members of the family, and owned primarily by a charitable foundation. In the first half of the 1990s, its influence grew significantly, in part due to its substantial Far East securities business.

In late February of 1995, Barings' board of directors met to review the 1994 results. The bank had a small rise in profits—a quite reasonable result in what had been a dreadful year for most of its competitors. One big contributor to those results had been a very profitable securities operation in Singapore. But that afternoon, things changed dramatically. The Singapore office trading star, Nick Leeson, unexpectedly walked out of the office and disappeared. As senior management examined the bank's records, it became clear that something was very wrong.

In principle, Leeson was engaged in a simple arbitrage operation. He traded futures contracts on the Nikkei 225 (the main Japanese stock market index) on both the Osaka Stock Exchange and the Singapore International Monetary Exchange (SIMEX). He should have been able to lock in a virtually riskless profit by selling the security on the exchange with the higher price while simultaneously buying it on the exchange with the lower price. In this arbitrage business, although Barings would accumulate large positions on both exchanges, those securities it bought and those it sold should balance; there was supposed to be no net exposure.

Yet what management found as they reviewed the bank's records was that Leeson had bought securities in both markets; in effect, he had made an enormous bet that the Nikkei would rise. But it had fallen, and now the solvency of the bank was threatened.

How could this have happened? It appears that Leeson circumvented the bank's internal controls. The Singapore branch was small and Leeson had effective authority over both trading *and* the firm's back office systems. He used that power to conceal losses and disguise the true nature of his activities— and thus he was able to "cook the books." For example, he apparently told senior management that a number of his trades were on behalf of clients and not the bank. And the bank's internal control systems did not expose the deceit.

By early March, the bank's aggregate losses totaled $1.4 billion. Leeson, who had been arrested by German police at the Frankfurt Airport, was fighting extradition to Singapore. And Barings, Britain's oldest merchant bank, had been sold to ING, the large

*This article draws on Chapters 1, 8, and 15 of *Organizational Architecture: A Managerial Economics Approach* (Irwin, forthcoming). We owe a significant debt to our colleagues, Michael C. Jensen and William H. Meckling. Their work has profoundly affected our thoughts on these issues.

Dutch financial institution, for £1. Thus, Barings' owners had lost their entire investment.

The collapse of Barings was ultimately caused by a poorly designed organization. As the *Wall Street Journal* noted:

> *What is emerging from the documents and from interviews with current and former Barings executives is a fatally flawed organization: one that ignored at least several warning signs going back not just weeks and months, but years; one that so wanted to ensure the continuation of profits from Singapore—which boosted bonuses—that it was reluctant to impose tight controls; one that had a deeply split staff, which ultimately may have contributed to its downfall.*[1]

Three general aspects of the bank's organization contributed to the failure: (1) the broad range of authority and responsibilities granted to Leeson; (2) gaps in the bank's systems for evaluating, monitoring, and controlling its employees; and (3) aspects of the firm's compensation system. Let's examine each in more detail.

First, Leeson had responsibility for both proprietary and customer trading as well as effective control of the settlement of trades in his unit. This broad assignment of decision-making authority created the opportunity to circumvent the bank's internal controls. As the *Financial Times* noted:

> *In Singapore, Mr. Leeson was in the process of settling transactions as well as initiating them. A watertight line between dealing and operational responsibility, crucial to internal control, was missing.*[2]

In reaction to the Barings collapse, SIMEX changed its rules to require that member firms ensure that proprietary traders not handle customer business and that the head of the dealing section not take charge of the settlement process.

Second, Leeson compromised the firm's performance evaluation system. He misrepresented trades for the bank as customer trades and hid losses. A better designed and executed monitoring system would have identified these problems before the solvency of the institution was threatened.

Third, the bank's compensation system encouraged Leeson to speculate while providing senior managers with limited incentives to exercise tight control over their star trader. Barings traditionally had paid out approximately 50% of gross earnings as annual bonuses. Yet a system where managers participate in annual profits—but not in losses—can encourage excessive risk-taking. This incentive can be most pronounced when a small bet loses and the employee tries to make it up by doubling the bet. If this second bet also loses, there can be a strong incentive to double up again and "go for broke."

This tale of Barings' untimely end serves to illustrate a critical idea—namely, that the organization of the firm matters.[3] A poorly designed organization can result in lost profits and even in the failure of the institution. And competition in the marketplace provides strong pressures for more efficiently designed organizations. A company that clings to an inefficient, high-cost organizational design is eventually forced either to adapt or close.

With the benefit of hindsight, it seems easy to identify aspects of Barings' organization that, if changed, might have prevented this debacle. But the critical managerial question is whether one could reasonably have identified the potential problems *before* the fact and designed a more productive organization. We believe the answer to this managerial question is a resounding yes.

We are not, of course, the first to recognize the importance of corporate organization or to offer advice on how to improve it. The business section of any good bookstore displays an array of titles featuring many of the following: *Benchmarking, Empowerment, Total Quality Management, Reengineering, Outsourcing, Teaming, Corporate Culture, Venturing, Matrix Organizations, Just-In-Time Production,* and *Downsizing.* The authors of all these books would strongly agree with the proposition that the firm's organization and the associated policies chosen by management can have profound effects on performance and firm value. And they all buttress their recommendations with

1. M. Branchli, N. Bray, M. Sesit, "Barings PLC Officials May Have Been Aware of Trading Position," *Wall Street Journal*, March 6, 1995, p. 1.
2. "The Box That Can Never Be Shut," *Financial Times*, February 28, 1995, p. 17.
3. It is an idea that most economists tend to lose sight of. Economists have given surprisingly little attention to questions of the firm's organization. In traditional economic analysis, the firm is generally characterized simply as a "black box" that transforms inputs (like labor, capital, and raw materials) into outputs. Although more attention has been given in recent years to the ways in which companies are organized, there has been little effort devoted to synthesizing the material in an accessible way that emphasizes the managerial implications of the analysis.

> **Although competition tends to produce efficiently organized firms *over the longer run*, uncritical experimentation with the organizational innovation *du jour* can expose the firm to an uncomfortably high risk of failure.**

selected stories of firms that followed their advice and achieved fabulous successes.

The problem with such approaches, however, is that each tends to focus on a particular facet of the organization, whether it be quality control or worker empowerment or the compensation system, to the virtual exclusion of all others. As a consequence, the suggestions offered by the business press are often mutually inconsistent. These publications tend to offer little guidance as to which tools are most appropriate in which circumstances; the implicit assumption of most is that their technique can be successfully adopted by *all* companies. This assumption, however, is usually wrong.

For example, if the cover article in the next *Business Week* reports an innovative inventory control system at Toyota, managers around the globe will see it and ask, "Would that work in my company, too?" Undoubtedly the managers with the strongest interest in trying it will be those in firms with current inventory problems. Some will achieve success, but others may experience disastrous results caused by unintended, though largely predictable, organizational "side-effects" (like Leeson's unchecked appetite for risk-taking).

....

ECONOMIC DARWINISM:
THE CASE OF FRANCHISING

As described in Charles Darwin's *The Origin of Species*, natural history illustrates the principle of "survival of the fittest." In industry, we see Economic Darwinism in operation as competition weeds out those organizations that fail to adapt. There is an important difference, however, between these two evolutionary processes. In the biological systems that Darwin studied, the major forces at work were random mutations in organisms and shocks to the external environment. Within economic systems, voluntary purposeful changes are also possible. Indeed, managers are quick to imitate the organizational innovations of other successful firms.

As one illustration of Economic Darwinism, consider the rise of franchising in the 1950s. In those days, most quick-service restaurants in the U.S. were local "mom and pop" businesses. Similarly, small independent businesses tended to dominate industries such as motels, convenience stores, and auto repair. Individual businesses in these industries competed with one another and the most profitable tended to survive. Nevertheless, there was room for improvement. In particular, the quality across businesses was not uniform and consumers bore risks in trying new establishments. Vacationers, for example, were not sure what to expect when patronizing out-of-town restaurants and motels, and the importance of these issues increased as improved highways expanded travel.

Entrepreneurs responded to this opportunity by developing a relatively untried form of organization—franchising. For example, during the 1950s Ray Kroc, Bill Rosenberg, and Kemmons Wilson founded McDonald's, Dunkin' Donuts, and Holiday Inn, respectively. (Other franchise companies formed during this period include H&R Block, Midas Muffler, and Pizza Hut, to name a few.) The idea in each case was to establish a national chain to provide customers with uniform quality and service at all outlets.

One important advantage of franchising over conventional corporate ownership is that franchisees are more highly motivated than typical corporate managers to increase long-term sales and profits because franchisees pay for the franchise, keep much of the profits, and can sell the franchise. At the same time, franchising retains the "corporate" advantages of group affiliation for national advertising, quantity discounts for input purchases, and quality control.

The success of franchising has been immense. There are now over 500,000 franchised units operating in this country with sales of nearly $800 billion, representing about one-third of the nation's retail sales. Franchising now dominates industries such as fast food, auto repair and motels. Thus, many small independently owned companies were either driven out of business by franchise companies or joined franchise systems themselves.

Although competition tends to produce efficiently organized firms *over the longer run*, uncritical experimentation with the organizational innovation *du jour* can expose the firm to an uncomfortably high risk of failure. For this reason, it is important to be able to analyze the likely consequences of a contemplated change in organization for the *entire* firm.

In contrast to the approach of most business bestsellers, then, we seek to provide a systematic framework for addressing such issues—an approach that can be applied consistently in analyzing organizational problems and designing more effective organizations. This framework identifies three critical aspects of corporate organization:

(1) the assignment of decision rights within the firm;

(2) the structure of systems to evaluate the performance of both individuals and business units; and (3) the methods of rewarding individuals.[4]

We introduce the term *organizational architecture* to refer specifically to these three key aspects of the firm. Although we could instead have simply used "organization" to refer to these three corporate features, common usage of that term refers only to the hierarchical structure (that is, reporting relationships and decision right assignments), but it ignores the performance evaluation and reward systems. We thus use "organizational architecture" to help focus attention on all three of these key aspects of the organization.

Stated as briefly as possible, our argument is that successful firms assign decision rights in ways that effectively link decision-making authority with the relevant information for making good decisions. When assigning these decision rights, however, top management must also ensure that the company's performance evaluation and reward systems provide decision makers with appropriate incentives to make value-increasing decisions.

Our approach to corporate organization is "integrative" in the sense that it draws on a number of disciplines: accounting, finance, marketing, management, political science. But what also distinguishes this approach most clearly from that of the bestsellers is its central reliance on the basic principles of economics. In essence, economics provides a theory of how individuals make choices. For example, in designing organizations, one must always keep in mind that individuals respond to incentives. Managers and employees can be incredibly resourceful in devising methods to exploit the opportunities they face. This also means, however, that when their incentives are structured improperly, they can act in ways that reduce firm value. For this reason, in choosing corporate policies it is critical that managers anticipate potential responses by customers, suppliers, or employees that might produce undesirable outcomes. Failure to do so invites individuals to "game" the system and can result in the complete failure of well-intentioned policies.

More generally, this approach to corporate organization uses the basic tools of economics to examine the likely effect on firm value of decisions such as centralization versus decentralization, the bundling of tasks into specific jobs within the firm, the use of objective versus subjective performance measures, compensating employees through fixed versus variable (or "incentive") compensation, and retaining activities within the firm versus outsourcing. In sum, we examine how managers can design their organizational architecture to motivate individuals to make choices that increase firm value.

THE FUNDAMENTAL PROBLEM

The primary goal of any economic system is to produce the output customers want at the lowest cost possible. The challenge of discovering customer demands while reducing costs, both for economic systems and *within* individual firms, is complicated by the fact that important information for economic decision-making is generally held by many different individuals. Furthermore, this information is often expensive to transfer (that is, the information is *specific* as opposed to *general*).[5] For example, a scientist is likely to know more about the potential of a new research project than people higher up in the firm. Similarly, a machine operator may know more about how to use a particular machine than his supervisor. In both cases, a decision-making process that requires the communication of such information to headquarters for approval is likely to be cumbersome, resulting in many lost opportunities.

A second complication is that decision makers might not have appropriate incentives to make value-increasing decisions even if they have the relevant information (that is, there are *agency problems*).[6] For example, a scientist might want to complete a research project out of scholarly interest even if the project is unprofitable. Similarly, machine operators might not want to use machines efficiently if this means more work for them.

4. We thank Mike Jensen and Bill Meckling for impressing upon us the importance of these three features of organizations. See M. C. Jensen, "Organization Theory and Methodology," *Accounting Review* 58 (1983), pp. 319-339; and M. C. Jensen and W. H. Meckling, "Specific and General Knowledge and Organizational Structure," in *Contract Economics*, Lars Werin and Hans Wijkander, eds., Basil Blackwell Ltd., Oxford, U.K., 1992, chapter 9. These three features are identified throughout the economics and management literature on organizational design. For example, see P. Milgrom and J. Roberts, *Economics, Organization and Management*, Prentice Hall, Englewood Cliffs, NJ, 1992. A representative example, from the management literature is D. Robey, *Designing Organizations*, Richard D. Irwin Inc., Burr Ridge, IL, 1991.

5. Our discussion in this section closely parallels M. C. Jensen and W. H. Meckling, "Specific and General Knowledge and Organizational Structure," in *Contract Economics*, Lars Werin and Hans Wijkander, eds., Basil Blackwell Ltd., Oxford, U.K., 1992, chapter 9.

6. In this corporate context, the agency problem refers to conflicts of interest between shareholders and corporate managers and employees that reduce the value of the firm. For the original formulation of this problem, see Michael C. Jensen and William H. Meckling, "Theory of the Firm: Managerial Behavior, Agency Costs and Ownership Structure," *Journal of Financial Economics*, Vol. 4, No. 4 (October 1976).

In sum, the principle challenge in designing both firms and economic systems is to maximize the likelihood that decision-makers have (1) the relevant information to make good decisions and (2) the incentives to use the information productively.

The Right Architecture Is Built into Markets. The price system helps solve agency problems in markets. In market economies, individuals have private property rights. If a person owns a piece of property, an automobile, or a building, that person decides how to use it. Furthermore, this right can be sold to others. If someone else knows how to make better use of the resource, the owner can sell it and keep the proceeds. Owners thus have strong incentives to use resources productively because they bear the wealth effects of their decisions.

Hence, the market provides an architecture that promotes efficient resource use. First, through market transactions, decision rights for resources are rearranged so that they are held by individuals with the relevant specific knowledge. Second, the market provides a mechanism for evaluating and rewarding the performance of resource owners—owners bear the wealth effects of their decisions. This mechanism generates strong incentives to take efficient actions.

Organizational Architecture Must Be Designed for Firms. One especially valuable feature of markets is that the organizational architecture is created *automatically* with little conscious thought or human direction. Within firms, however, there are no automatic systems either for assigning decision rights to individuals with information or for motivating individuals to use information to promote the firm's objectives. Organizational architecture must be created.

Although transfer prices are used to allocate some resources within firms,[7] most resources are allocated by administrative decisions. For example, the CEO typically transfers a manager from one division to another by a simple command. Similarly, how a plant is used can be changed by administrative order. The top management of an organization must decide how to assign the decision rights among employees. For instance, does the top management make most major decisions or are these decisions delegated to lower-level managers? As another example, are machine operators permitted to deviate from procedures outlined in company manuals?

Through this assignment of decision rights, employees are granted authority over how to use company resources. But employees are not owners—they cannot sell company property and keep the proceeds. Thus, employees have fewer incentives to worry about the efficient use of company resources than the owners. To help control such agency problems, the firm must develop a *control system*. That is, it must develop both (1) performance evaluation systems and (2) reward systems that align the interests of decision-makers with those of the owners.

It is important to recognize, moreover, that *the control system must be consistent with the assignment of decision rights*. While the optimal control system depends on how decision rights are assigned in the firm, the assignment of decision rights depends in part on management's ability to devise an effective control system. For example, if employees are given greater decision-making authority, it will usually make sense to develop new performance evaluation and reward systems that tie the employees' compensation more closely to the new performance measures. By the same token, if a firm adopts a compensation plan to motivate employees, it is important to ensure that workers have decision rights that enable them to respond to such incentives.

In this sense, the three components of organizational architecture—the assignment of decision rights, the performance evaluation system, and the reward system—are all highly interdependent. Indeed, organizational architecture is like a "three-legged stool": changing one of the three legs without careful consideration of the other two is typically a mistake—they must be designed together to keep the stool level.

....

WHEN THE LEGS OF THE STOOL DON'T BALANCE

A plane owned by a major airline company was grounded for repairs at one airport, with the nearest qualified mechanic stationed at another. The decision right to allow the mechanic to work on the airplane was held by the manager of the second airport. But because that manager's compensation was tied to meeting his own budget rather than to the profits of the overall organization, he refused to send the mechanic immediately to fix the plane because the mechanic would have had to stay overnight at a hotel and the hotel bill would have been

---

7. One reason for the existence of firms is that coordinating related transactions through the market price mechanism can be expensive. Nevertheless, some firms use internal transfer prices in resource allocation decisions. See our discussion of "Transfer Pricing" later in this issue.

charged to the manager's budget. The mechanic was dispatched the next morning so that he could return the same day. Thus, a multi-million dollar aircraft was grounded, costing the company thousands of dollars, so that a manager's budget would avoid a $100 hotel bill.

Suggested by M. Hammer and J. Champy, *Reengineering the Corporation*, Harper Business, New York, 1993.

Once the firm grows beyond a certain size, the CEO is unlikely to have the relevant information for all major decisions. Consequently, this CEO has three basic choices in designing the organization.

First, the CEO can continue to make most major decisions even if he does not have the relevant information. The benefits of this choice are limited agency problems and hence little need for a detailed control system.[8] The costs of such centralization, however, will come in the form of suboptimal decisions resulting from the lack of specific information.

Second, the CEO can attempt to acquire the relevant information to make better decisions. But obtaining and processing the relevant information can be very time-consuming and costly.

Third, the CEO can decentralize decision rights to individuals with better information. This choice assigns decision-making authority to employees with the relevant specific information. But delegating decision rights gives rise to agency problems, which means that control systems must be developed.

Another potential drawback of decentralization is the cost of transferring information *from top management to the decentralized decision makers* in coordinating efforts throughout the firm. (In the story of the grounded airplane above, the CEO would certainly have sent the mechanic had the matter been brought to his attention.)

Of course, managers can choose a mix of these basic alternatives. For example, top managers are likely to choose to retain some decisions while delegating others. The optimal choice, as we discuss below, depends primarily on the business environment and strategy of the firm. In some cases—especially smaller firms in relatively stable industries—top managers are likely to have most of the relevant information for decision-making, and thus decision rights are more likely to be centralized at headquarters. In other cases—especially larger firms experiencing rapid change—top managers and their corporate staff often will not be in the best position to make many decisions. And, in such cases, decision rights are more likely to be decentralized with corresponding control systems put in place.

....
THE ORGANIZATIONAL ARCHITECTURE OF CENTURY 21

Century 21 International is the largest real estate firm in the world, operating throughout the United States and in ten countries, including Japan, the United Kingdom, and France. Given the geographic and cultural diversity of its operations, it would not make sense for the U.S. headquarters to make all major decisions. Such centralized decision-making would be especially problematic for the international operations, where laws and cultures can be far different than those in the U.S. To quote Century 21's management: "We provide the international regions with whatever knowledge we possess on how they can help their franchisees develop better offices. What they use is basically up to them and will reflect their housing market and real estate traditions. We allow our master subfranchisors a great deal of flexibility in running their regions, and internationally we want them to be able to accommodate their services to their culture."

Decentralized decision-making, however, requires a control system that promotes productive effort. At Century 21, most of the local operators are franchisees. Franchisees are essentially owners of their units and keep a large share of their units' profits. This ownership provides strong incentives to increase sales and Century 21's value. But Century 21 also reserves the right to terminate individual franchises that fail to maintain acceptable levels of service.

Suggested by C. Shook and R. L. Shook, *Franchising: The Business Strategy that Changed the World*, Prentice Hall, NJ, 1993.

DETERMINANTS OF ORGANIZATIONAL ARCHITECTURE

As suggested above, then, the optimal architecture will be different for different companies. Such

---

8. We assume for simplicity he is also the sole owner of the business. In small firms, top management and owners are often the same. In large firms, however, the owners (the shareholders) delegate most decision rights to the board of directors and the CEO. These parties are charged with developing the organizational architecture for the firm. For purposes of this discussion, we treat top managers and owners as the same.

> In general, deregulation causes firms to decentralize decision-making and to redesign their performance evaluation and reward systems to give lower-level workers stronger incentives to make the best use of their expanded decision rights.

FIGURE 1
DETERMINANTS OF
ORGANIZATIONAL
ARCHITECTURE

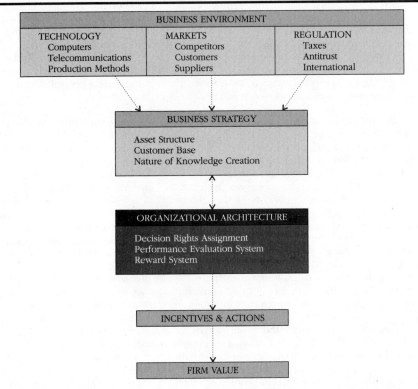

structural differences are not random, however, but vary in *systematic* ways with differences in certain underlying characteristics of the companies themselves. To illustrate the point, companies operating in the same industry tend to develop similar organizational architectures. Furthermore, if an important aspect of an industry changes, many companies in that industry end up making major changes in decision rights and internal control systems.

In Figure 1, we summarize those factors that are likely to be most important in designing the optimal architecture for a given firm. At the top of the figure are three key aspects of the firm's *external* business

environment: *technology, markets,* and *regulation.*[9] For any firm, these three factors—(1) the technology that affects both its products, its methods of production, and its information systems, (2) the structure of its markets (competitors, customers, suppliers, etc.), and (3) the regulatory constraints on its activities—are likely to have the greatest influence on the *business strategy.* By business strategy, we mean the answers to a broad set of questions: What are the firm's primary goals, non-financial as well as financial? What products and services is it providing, and to what customers? And what are the firm's sources of comparative advantage in so doing?

9. Although we can point to cases that contradict this generalization, Figure 1 treats the business environment as *exogenous,* or beyond the managers' control. By contrast, the business strategy and organizational structure are *endogenous* variables—that is, they are policy choices made by the management *in response to* the business environment.

By treating the business environment as exogenous, our analysis does not focus on potential feedback effects among the environment, business strategy, and

organizational structure. Consider, for example, how the organizational structure at Microsoft encourages innovation that, in turn, alters the basic technology facing the firm. Large firms also often have political power that can be used to influence government regulation. Although these types of feedback effects can sometimes be important, in most circumstances managers essentially must take the business environment as outside their control.

Take the case of AT&T before it was broken up in the early 1980s. Regulation dictated many aspects of the firm's business strategy—what services it could offer, what customers it could serve and how much it could charge them, and what technologies it could employ. After the break-up of AT&T and the deregulation of the telecommunications industry, both the Baby Bells and the new AT&T were forced to devise new strategies to provide new products, serve new customer bases, and develop new pricing structures.

To return to Figure 1, the ultimate goals of the firm, as reflected in its business strategy, in turn affect its optimal organizational architecture. As the celebrated architect Louis H. Sullivan once observed, "Form ever follows function." Applying the same principle to industry, we see that significant changes in corporate business strategies typically call for major changes in decision-making authority, performance measures for evaluating managers and employees, and management incentive compensation systems.

Returning to our telecommunications example, in the early 1980s a regulated AT&T faced little competition or pressure for technological innovation. It operated in a reasonably stable environment—one where it made sense for a huge formal bureaucracy to make the most important decisions "from the top down." Since the break-up of the company, however, the telecommunications industry has experienced almost continuous upheaval, with deregulation, increased competition, and rapid technological change. And, in 1992, after a nearly decade-long series of incremental moves toward decentralization, AT&T established a large number of fairly autonomous profit centers run by managers on pay-for-performance plans tied to economic value added (or EVA®).[10]

In general, deregulation causes firms to decentralize decision-making and to redesign their performance evaluation and reward systems to give lower-level workers stronger incentives to make the best use of their expanded decision rights. The impact of technological change on organization, however, is less clearcut than the effect of deregulation. Take the case of advances in information technology. More powerful corporate management information systems (MIS) could lead to greater *centralization* of decision-making by increasing the ability of corporate headquarters to monitor line managers' performance. But such advances could also allow for greater *decentralization* by allowing corporate staffs to implement more sophisticated and effective internal control systems. Advances in corporate MIS can also facilitate decentralization by channeling important information in the opposite direction: namely, *from the corporate center to line managers and employees.*

....

INFORMATION TECHNOLOGY AND CHANGES IN ORGANIZATIONAL ARCHITECTURE AT CYPRESS SEMICONDUCTOR

By allowing top management to communicate more directly with lower-level employees, computer technology makes it less expensive for managers to control and coordinate their actions. It thus has reduced the demand for middle managers, who traditionally have played an important role in transmitting information from the top of the corporation to lower levels.

An example of this took place at Cypress Semiconductors. T. J. Rodgers, CEO of Cypress, uses a computer system to rack the daily objectives of every employee in the company. The company has essentially no middle management. As noted in a *Fortune* article,

The computer system allows the CEO to stay abreast of every employee and team in his fast-moving organization. Each employee maintains a list of ten to 15 goals like "Meet with marketing for new product launch," or "Make sure to check with Customer X." Noted next to each goal is when it was agreed upon, when it's due to be finished, and whether it's finished or not.

This way, it doesn't take layers of expensive bureaucracy to check who's doing what, whether someone has got a light enough workload to be put on a new team, and who's having trouble. Rodgers says he can review the goals of all 1,500 employees in about four hours, which he does each week.

Suggested by Brian Dumaine, "The Bureaucracy Busters," *Fortune*, June 17, 1991, p. 46.

Another pronounced effect on organizational architecture has come from increases in foreign competition. Before the 1980s, many large American companies (for example, ITT, IBM, General Motors,

---

10. For an introduction to EVA®, see the next article in this issue, Joel Stern, Bennett Stewart, and Don Chew, "The EVA® Financial Management System."

In the past decade, a dramatic increase in foreign competition caused many large firms to push decision rights lower in the company, where specific knowledge about customer demand was located. Such firms also developed new performance evaluation systems focusing more on quality and customer service and increased their use of pay-for-performance compensation plans.

Eastman Kodak, and Xerox) faced limited competition in their product markets. Indeed, many of these companies had substantial market power, and thus they had little incentive to focus on rapid product development, high-quality production, or competitive pricing. Quite predictably, they had become highly bureaucratic with very centralized decision-making and limited incentive compensation.

In the past decade, however, a dramatic increase in foreign competition (notably, from Japanese producers) caused many of these large firms to rethink their basic strategies. In particular, such companies were forced to increase their emphasis on quality, customer service, and competitive pricing. To accomplish these objectives, such companies also typically found it necessary to redesign their organizations. Many chose to push decision rights lower in the company, where specific knowledge about customer demand was located. These firms also developed new performance evaluation systems focusing more on quality and customer service and increased their use of pay-for-performance compensation plans.

··
LESSONS FROM ITT

In 1984, ITT Corporation was the largest manufacturer of telecommunications equipment in the world, operating in over 80 different countries. It was also broadly diversified with operations in industrial and consumer products, insurance, automotive parts, telephone service, natural resources, food processing and utilities. ITT, however, faced a variety of market pressures that made 1984 an especially trying year. To quote *Moody's Handbook of Common Stocks* (Winter 1984-85):

ITT's telecommunications operations continued to suffer from soft market conditions in the U.S., a personal computer glut and competitive pricing. European operations are being hurt by the strength of the U.S. dollar.

In 1984, ITT's earnings per share were only $2.97 (down from $4.50 a year earlier), dividends were cut by nearly $1.00 per share, and the company was rumored to be a takeover target.

Part of ITT's problem was that it had become too large and unfocused. Decision-making in the organization was highly formalized and bureaucratic. This system made it difficult for ITT to respond rapidly to changing customer demands and competitive pressures. This inability to act quickly was especially problematic given the dramatic changes occurring in telecommunications and computers. ITT responded by announcing its plan to sell over $2 billion in assets in order to focus on its core strengths and major lines of business.

As one example of this "asset redeployment program," ITT sold O. M. Scott & Sons Company, the largest producer of lawn-care products in the U.S., to Clayton & Dubilier in a divisional leveraged buyout in December 1986. The buyout was accompanied by organizational changes at Scott that were designed to enhance performance.[11] These changes involved all three aspects of organizational architecture:

1. The Assignment of Decision Rights within the Organization. After the LBO, managers at Scott were given substantial authority to make and implement decisions, including major capital expenditures. As part of ITT, by contrast, these managers often had to seek approval from a number of levels at ITT headquarters and approval was frequently denied.

2. The Performance Evaluation System. The company's new performance-evaluation system placed a heavy emphasis on financial performance. For example, specific targets were established for corporate, divisional and individual performance that stressed generation of operating cash flow and efficient use of working capital.

3. The Reward System. To motivate value-enhancing decisions, coverage under the bonus plan was expanded to include additional managers. Payouts for exceeding performance targets were increased substantially from the old plan. For example, average bonuses as a percent of salary for the ten top managers increased from 10% and 17% in the two years before the buyout to 66% and 39% in the two years after. In addition, managers and employees had substantial financial interests in the firm through stock ownership. After the buyout, they owned 17% of Scott's equity. Before the buyout, managers and employees had no meaningful stock ownership.

These organizational changes at Scott were accompanied by a dramatic increase in operating performance. For example, in the two-year period following the buyout, sales increased by 25%, and earnings before interest and taxes increased by 56%. Moreover, these increases were not caused by slashing expenditures on either R&D or on marketing and distribution. In fact, expenditures in both categories increased, as did spending on capital projects.

11. Our discussion of O. M. Scott relies heavily on a paper entitled "Organizational Changes and Value in Leveraged Buyouts: The Case of the O. M. Scott & Sons Company," by George P. Baker and Karen H. Wruck, *Journal of* *Financial Economics,* December 1989. See also the less technical version of the same article that appeared in the *Journal of Applied Corporate Finance,* Vol. 4 No. 1 (Spring 1991).

CHANGING ORGANIZATIONAL ARCHITECTURE

As we have seen, changes in market conditions, technology, or government regulation can change the optimal design of organizations. But organizational change is by no means a costless process.

First there are direct costs. The new structure has to be designed and communicated to employees throughout the organization. Moreover, organizational changes frequently require costly changes in the firm's accounting and information systems. Often what appears to be a straightforward change in the performance evaluation system imposes a major and costly project on the firm's data processing and accounting departments. Literally hundreds of computer programs might have to be changed to alter the accounting and information systems.

Second, and perhaps more important, are indirect costs. Organizational changes are likely to affect some workers positively (say, by increasing their responsibilities and possibilities for rewards) and other workers negatively. Thus, reactions to a change are likely to vary among employees. Dealing with the associated politics of implementing change in an organization can be expensive. Finally, frequent organizational changes can have undesirable incentive effects. For instance, workers have limited incentives to invest in learning new job assignments, devising more efficient production processes, and developing relations with coworkers if they expect to change assignments in the near future. In general, frequent restructuring causes uncertainty about job assignments and will promote actions that focus more on short-run payoffs and less on long-run investments.

....

COSTS OF ORGANIZATIONAL CHANGE—NOT A NEW PHENOMENON

"We trained hard, but it seemed that every time we were beginning to form into teams we would be reorganized. I was to learn later in life that we tend to meet any new situation by reorganizing, and what a wonderful method it can be for creating the illusion of progress while producing confusion, inefficiency, and demoralization."

Petronius Arbiter, 210 BC

Unfortunately, too many firms appear to undertake organizational changes without a careful analysis of the relevant costs and benefits. At any point in time, as we noted earlier, there are a number of prominent management techniques being touted as the key to success. Among the most popular techniques of the 1990s are reengineering, benchmarking, total quality management, broadbanding, worker empowerment, and skill-based pay. Most of these techniques involve fundamental organizational change. For example, many advocates of total quality management recommend delegating decision rights to teams and not paying incentive compensation based on individual performance.

Adopting the most recent "business trend" can get a firm in trouble, however, unless the change is warranted by the actual circumstances facing the firm. As a *Wall Street Journal* article observed, "many companies try management fads, only to see them flop."[12] Furthermore, surveys indicate that a majority of companies are dissatisfied with the results of organizational changes.

CORPORATE CULTURE AND ORGANIZATIONAL CHANGE

One widely cited reason for the failure of such programs for change is that the proposed changes fail to mesh with, and are eventually defeated by, the existing *corporate culture*. "Corporate culture" is another term that appears often in the organizational design literature. Corporate culture usually encompasses the ways work and authority are organized, the ways people are rewarded and controlled, as well as organizational features such as customs, taboos, company slogans, heroes, and social rituals. But, although managers are regularly encouraged to develop high-powered, productive cultures, little concrete guidance is typically provided on how they might accomplish this goal.

A focus on organizational architecture helps identify the role of corporate culture in creating value. Indeed, our definition of architecture corresponds to some key aspects of what is often called corporate culture. For example, a company's architecture specifies how authority (or decision rights) is distributed among employees and how rewards are determined. The advantage of this economic approach is that it

---

12. *Wall Street Journal*, July 6, 1993.

helps managers identify the key components of a firm's corporate culture and analyze how they might affect culture in purposeful ways.

Most companies do not write down all the features of their organization in detailed procedures manuals. Rather, much of the structure is communicated to employees in less formal and potentially less costly ways. In this sense, corporate slogans, role models, and social rituals can be viewed as efficient, cost-effective methods of *communicating* important aspects of the organization to employees. For example, a slogan like "at Ford, quality is *Job One*" emphasizes that workers are expected to focus on quality and that this focus will be rewarded by the firm. Similarly, social rituals such as training sessions and company parties can help to disseminate information by increasing the interaction among employees who might not see each other on a frequent basis. Singling out role models or heroes for special awards is another way of credibly communicating what the corporation values.

······································

CORPORATE CULTURE AT MARY KAY COSMETICS

Total sales at Mary Kay Cosmetics increased from about $198,000 in 1963 to over $613 million in 1993. Mary Kay has built a sales force of 300,000 and has helped to create 74 millionaires (women who have earned commissions of $1 million or more over their careers).

The organizational architecture at Mary Kay focuses directly on sales. All sales consultants purchase products directly from Dallas at the same price. Rewards are based solely on sales and recruiting additional sales consultants. There is no cap on what sales consultants earn. As sales and the recruiting of consultants rise, so do commissions.

What is interesting about Mary Kay is how many features of the firm's culture reinforce each other in a consistent manner. For example, stories of role models are prevalent throughout the organization. Almost every employee knows the story of Mary Kay Ash, who started out as a young saleswoman for Stanley Home Products. She was so poor that she had to borrow $12 to travel from her Houston home to Stanley's 1937 convention in Dallas. Through hard work, she built the Mary Kay Cosmetic Company and amassed a family fortune of over $300 million. This story and those of other successful sales consultants permeate the organization, reinforcing the firm's architecture, and helping

to motivate hard work and increased sales. The company is also famous for lavishly rewarding its successful sales consultants in a very public manner. The annual sales meeting is an extravaganza where individuals are crowned as "queens" and rewarded with complementary pink Cadillacs, jewelry, color-coded suits, badges, and emblems.

The message at Mary Kay is clear. Success is measured by sales and recruiting efforts. Do these things well and you will be rewarded, both financially and through public recognition.

Suggested by A. Farnham, "Mary Kay's Lessons in Leadership," *Fortune*, September 20, 1993.

"Softer" features of organizations such as rituals and role models can be effective in reinforcing and communicating the goals of the firm; and they thus have the potential to provide important aspects of a coherent organizational architecture. Their effectiveness in certain cases has led some management experts to claim that a productive corporate culture can be molded without paying *any* attention to formal evaluation and compensation schemes. (Indeed, some argue that incentive-based pay is actually detrimental to a productive organization.) But it is a mistake to think of the "hard" and "soft" aspects of the organization as mutually exclusive or in competition with each other; both can play a valuable, if not an essential, role in increasing firm value.

CHANGING CORPORATE CULTURE: THE CASE OF XEROX[13]

In 1982, David Kearns was appointed CEO of Xerox Corporation, the major producer of copy machines in the world. At that time, the company was in significant trouble. Between 1976 and 1982, Xerox's share of installations of copiers in the United States dropped from about 80 percent to 13 percent. Japanese companies such as Canon, Minolta, Ricoh, and Sharp had become major players in this market, and were then selling copiers at prices that were lower than Xerox's costs for producing competing machines.

A primary reason for Xerox's decline in market share was poor product quality. As Kearns put it:

---

13. This discussion is based on David T. Kearns and David A. Nadler, *Prophets in the Dark*, Harper Business Press, New York, 1992.

Our customer cancellations were rapidly on the rise, our response to the problem was to try to outrun them by pushing hard to get enough new orders to offset the customers we had lost. Customers were fed up with our copiers breaking down and our service response.

Kearns reasoned that if something was not done that "Xerox was destined to have a fire sale and close down by 1990." The "only hope for survival was to urgently commit the company to vastly improving the quality of its products and services."

According to Kearns, however, most Xerox employees understood neither how bad the problem was nor the importance of enhancing product quality. He realized that even as CEO he could not implement his vision of improving product quality simply by ordering 100,000 employees to focus on quality. First, the employees were not trained to produce quality products. Second, unless employees were convinced that it was in their interests to focus on quality, the problems in motivating them to alter their behavior would be enormous. Certainly, Kearns did not have the time to monitor each employee to see if his vision was carried out. Third, he feared that painting too dismal of a picture would induce some key people to leave the company.

In response to these concerns, Kearns (with the help of outside consultants) initiated a strategy to shift corporate direction. He began by convincing a select group of key managers that focusing on quality was essential. These people in turn helped to refine the quality vision and to convince other employees of the potential benefits of this change in focus. Employees throughout the company received substantial training in quality techniques. And the importance of quality, as well as the potential crisis posed by the Japanese, was stressed at every opportunity (in media releases, management speeches, signs on bulletin boards, and so forth).

After much training and promotion, however, the desired change in culture still was not occurring. It was then that Kearns came to the recognition that to affect employee behavior, top management had to do more than just cajole and plead—the performance evaluation and incentive systems also had to change. As Kearns says:

Unless people get rewarded and punished for how they behave, no one will really believe that this is anything more than lip service. A widespread problem [with implementing cultural change] that was singled out was that people said we were still promoting and rewarding employees who weren't true believers and users of the quality process. This was creating noise in the system and sending mixed signals. It had to stop.

Kearns accordingly initiated changes in the criteria for promotions and salary decisions placing major emphasis on customer satisfaction and quality. Senior managers who did not buy into the changes left the firm. Eventually, the culture at Xerox changed. In 1989, Xerox won the Malcolm Baldridge National Quality Award, and the company's shareholders have been well rewarded.

Kearns displayed important leadership skills during his tenure as Xerox CEO. But effective leadership is more than developing an appropriate vision for the company. It is also necessary to be effective in motivating people to follow the vision. As this example illustrates, changes in the firm's organizational architecture—the assignment of decision rights, and the performance evaluation and reward systems—can play an important role in motivating significant organizational change.

CONCLUSION: SURVIVAL OF THE FITTEST

The fundamental economic problem facing individual firms (as well as entire economic systems) is trying to ensure that decision-makers have the relevant information to make good decisions and that these decision-makers have incentives to use information productively. In addressing this problem, all firms develop what we call an organizational architecture. There are three important components of organizational architectiture:

- the assignment of decision rights (rights to decide and take actions) among individuals,
- the performance evaluation system, and
- the reward system.

The factors that are likely to be particularly important determinants of a firm's architecture are *market conditions, technology,* and *the regulatory environment.* In heavily regulated firms—or in smaller firms in fairly stable industries—top management is likely to have more of the relevant information for decision-making. In such cases, centralized decision-making is more likely to be adopted with relatively less emphasis on formal performance evaluation and pay-for-performance systems. By

After much training and promotion, the desired change in Xerox's culture was not occurring. Kearns then came to the recognition that, to affect employee behavior, top management had to do more than just cajole and plead—the performance evaluation and incentive systems also had to change.

contrast, in larger companies—particularly those in unregulated industries or facing stiff foreign competition—decision rights are more likely to be decentralized among managers and employees. In such cases, performance evaluation and reward systems must be designed to control agency problems and promote better decision-making.

Like the process of "natural selection" in the theory of evolution, economic competition determines which organizations survive by weeding out inefficient firms. This principle of Economic Darwinism implies that companies increase their chance of survival by adapting their organizational architecture to changes in their particular economic environments.

The concept of survival of the fittest has important implications. First, existing architectures are not random; there are sound economic explanations for the dominant organization of firms in most industries. Second, surviving architectures at any point in time are optimal in a *relative* rather than an *absolute* sense; that is, they are best among the competition, though not necessarily the best possible. These two observations together suggest that, although improvements in architecture are certainly always possible, a manager should not be too quick to condemn the prevailing organization without careful analysis. Before undertaking major organizational changes, top managers should thus have a good understanding of how the firm arrived at its existing architecture and, more generally, of why particular types of organizations work well in particular settings. Such an understanding is important if only because the costs of organizational change can be so large.

EVA® is a registered trademark of Stern Stewart & Co.

CAPABILITIES AND CAPITAL INVESTMENT: NEW PERSPECTIVES ON CAPITAL BUDGETING

by Carliss Y. Baldwin and Kim B. Clark, Harvard Business School*

I n the half century since World War II, U.S. companies have lost their dominant position in virtually every major industry. While some loss of market power was inevitable as other economies rebuilt and reached their own potential, today there is widespread concern that the U.S. has lost its competitive edge in technology and manufacturing.[1] Among those who believe a problem exists, the most frequently cited cause of corporate America's lack of competitiveness is its failure to invest.

Underinvestment by U.S. companies is generally attributed to two related causes. First, the U.S. is said to have a higher cost of capital than competitor nations, which naturally leads U.S. companies to prefer shorter-term investments. Second, U.S. bankers and portfolio managers are said to be unduly sensitive to reported profits, which in turn causes U.S. managers to forgo long-term investments that reduce short-term earnings. However, the evidence in support of each of these theories is mixed. While the cost of capital and investor myopia may explain part of the loss of market share by U.S. companies, such factors do not explain why competitive performance varies so radically across companies and industries.

Pronounced differences in the shrinkage of worldwide market share since the end of the 1950s provide a clear indication of disparities in performance across U.S. industries. As shown in Table 1, between 1960 and 1986, the U.S. steel industry saw its world market share drop from 74% to 16%; at the same time, however, the U.S. aerospace industry actually *increased* its market share from 85% to 91%.[2] Neither a high cost of capital nor investors' short time horizons can explain such differences in performance. Steel companies have very long-lived capital (a blast furnace lasts over 50 years), but so do paper and aircraft manufacturers (it takes 50 to 70 years to harvest a forest, and two or more decades to reap the returns on a new generation of aircraft). Why, then, have steel companies given up most of the world market to foreign competitors, while paper and aircraft manufacturers have managed to hold their own?

Our goal in these pages is to explore the extent to which U.S. companies' investment practices have contributed to their loss of market position. In other words, do U.S. companies experiencing problems in competition invest differently than their competitors? How are such differences translated into long-run success or failure?

*Prepared for the Project on Capital Choices, sponsored by the Harvard Business School and the Council on Competitiveness. The authors wish to thank Alan Blinder, Alfred Chandler, Jr., Warren Farb, Thèrése Flaherty, Robert Hayes, Robert C. Merton, James McKenney, Richard Nelson, Michael Porter, Richard Rosenbloom, Jeremy Stein, John Sutton, John Sviokla, and the Advisory Board of the Council on Competitiveness for comments and discussions that led to significant improvements in this paper. We also thank Don Chew for very useful

editorial suggestions. Any errors or omissions are ours alone. The financial support of the Harvard Business School and the Alfred P. Sloan Foundation is gratefully acknowledged.

1. For discussions of U.S. technological disadvantages, see, for example, Lynn (1982), Jaikumar (1989), Clark and Fujimoto (1991), and Flaherty (1992). Full references for all citations appear at the end of this article.

2. These calculations are based on Franko (1989).

TABLE 1 ▪ CHANGES IN "WORLD MARKET SHARE" OF U.S. COMPANIES BY MAJOR INDUSTRY, 1960-1986

Industry	Percentage
Iron and Steel	−58 %
Non-Ferrous Metals	−47
Electrical Equipment and Electronics	−44
Chemicals	−38
Autos and Trucks	−33
Tire and Rubber	−26
Pharmaceuticals	−24
Textiles	−19
Petroleum Products	−18
Computers and Office Equipment	−11
Industrial and Farm Equipment	−10
Food and Beverage Products	−8
Paper and Paper Products	−4
Aerospace	6

Source: Franko (1989). Franko collected data on worldwide sales by the twelve largest firms in each industry, and calculated percentage revenue share by country of origin.

In this article we argue that investment practices have indeed contributed to the competitive decline of some U.S. companies. Field studies that focus on companies competing with one another show startling variations in operating performance across firms. The differences are significant not only between U.S. and Japanese companies, but also among companies within each nation, thus suggesting that the underlying causes are firm-specific rather than cultural or geographical.

The same field studies demonstrate that superior operating performance arises because the companies in question have organizational capabilities that allow them to exploit market opportunities more effectively than their competitors. Organizational capabilities are combinations of human skills, organizational procedures and routines, physical assets, and systems of information and incentives that improve performance along particular dimensions. Such capabilities are indeed organizational *assets*. Just as a well-designed machine increases a worker's productivity, the capability to move quickly, reduce cost, or improve quality increases a company's productivity and the value of its opportunities.[3]

But productivity-enhancing capabilities do not arise by chance. Investments in specialized information, education and training, physical assets, and systems for coordination and integration are necessary to achieve superior performance in terms of speed, quality, flexibility, and innovation.

Unfortunately, however, the corporate capital budgeting systems employed by U.S. companies in evaluating investment opportunities are often biased against expenditures on building capabilities. In theory, such systems are designed to screen investments and select any and all that are valuable, regardless of the timing of returns. In practice, however, for reasons discussed below, the systems exclude from consideration investments in competitive assets, such as speed or quality, that do not directly generate higher profits or cash flow.

Underinvestment in capabilities often appears in the guise of a time horizon problem. But the problem likely stems more from general lack of understanding about the long-run value of capabilities, and about how they are achieved. In general, investments in capabilities do not stand alone, but are intertwined with other investments and embedded in other capital budgeting proposals. When such proposals are rejected or cut back, it appears as if "the system" is biased against long-term investment. The real problem, however, is that managers do not have objective tools to value the embedded capabilities, and thus proponents and opponents of such investments have no way to reach a common understanding. Without agreement on the best course to follow, investment decisions will be based not on the project's merit, but on the sponsor's power or political clout within the organization.

What can companies do to remedy these problems? We believe that exempting capabilities investments from the control of the financial systems is potentially self-defeating, although this solution is often adopted in practice. Our recommendations, therefore, focus on both a strategic framework and on appropriate financial systems. First, senior management should identify the firm's critical organizational capabilities, and their connection to the business strategy. Senior managers must then translate this framework into specific goals and compensation targets that people throughout the organization can understand and use in making decisions.

---

3. The idea that organizational capabilities are assets is, of course, not new. In business history, Chandler (1990) shows that large-scale corporations achieved market dominance by being first movers in building capabilities for production, distribution, and marketing. In strategy, a number of theorists have focused on knowledge, competence, and capabilities, as the basis of competitive advantage.

See, for example, Wernerfelt (1984) or Prahalad and Hamel (1990). Resources that are the source of competitive advantage are, by definition, assets. In economics, Winter (1987) has proposed that competence, knowledge, and learned routines are "unconventional" assets that contribute to the value of a company.

At the operating levels of a company, capabilities should be recognized as an investment category, and resources should be explicitly allocated to their development. Performance in key dimensions such as speed, quality, and flexibility should be measured and rewards for improvement incorporated into compensation. Accounting systems should track the use of resources and measure them against results.

THE ROLE OF CAPABILITIES IN COMPETITION

Over the last decade, a number of studies have investigated performance differences among companies within the same industry. Overall, the research shows that there is wide variation in the productivity of capital among companies competing in the same markets. In many cases, U.S. companies are at a dramatic disadvantage: on dimensions of quality, efficiency, speed, flexibility, and innovation, a dollar invested by a U.S. company often buys less than one invested by its competitors abroad.

A sampling of the field studies shows that making U.S. companies competitive is not simply a matter of giving them more capital or reducing their cost of capital. To equal the performance of their foreign competitors, many need to improve their basic operating methods to achieve higher levels of quality, efficiency, speed and flexibility.

■ *A study of room air-conditioner plants in the U.S. and Japan measured quality on dimensions such as defect rates and service calls. It found startling differences between U.S. and Japanese factories. For example, assembly line defects ranged from 8 per hundred units in the best U.S. plants to 165 (more than one per unit) in the worst; the comparable range in Japan was 0.15 to 3 defects per hundred units.[4]*
■ *A study of the global machine tool industry documented significant differences in productivity among flexible manufacturing systems (FMS) installed in the U.S. and Japan. Whereas U.S. companies operated their systems about 40-50% of the time, the Japanese installations operated 90-95% of the time.[5]*
■ *A study of automobile product development found that U.S. and Japanese companies spent equivalent amounts on R&D. However, between 1982 and 1987, Japanese firms introduced 72 new models while U.S. firms launched only 21. To develop a comparable*

vehicle, a Japanese auto company used half as many engineering hours and came to market in two-thirds the time of a U.S. company.[6]
■ *A study of automobile manufacturing found that Japanese companies had a 50% productivity and quality advantage (on average) over U.S. companies, although the range in each country was very large. Higher productivity and quality were not related to age, capital or automation of a plant, but were correlated with operating modes that focused on continuous improvement of the production process.[7]*

The field studies consistently showed that superior operating performance did not arise because of luck, culture, or genius. On the contrary, superior performance was based on capabilities—that is, identifiable combinations of human skills, organizational procedures, physical assets, and information systems. Such complex combinations of resources are achieved because companies allocate resources (both human and financial) to their development in the expectation of future reward. In this respect, capabilities are like any other investment.

Nevertheless investments in capabilities pose unique problems, especially in companies with hierarchical or decentralized financial planning and capital budgeting systems. To see how such problems arise, we must first describe what capabilities are and show how they function as organizational assets. Although there are doubtless others, we shall focus here on five specific capabilities:
■ External integration leading to *quality*;
■ Internal integration leading to *speed* and *efficiency*;
■ Flexibility leading to *responsiveness* and *variety*;
■ The capacity to experiment leading to *continuous, incremental improvement*; and
■ The capacity to cannibalize leading to *radical innovation*.

External Integration

In the study of the air-conditioner industry mentioned above, David Garvin found that high-quality plants had clearly identifiable systems that provided for extensive gathering and processing of information, and active feedback from customer experience to engineering design. The systems included design processes and test procedures that

---

4. Garvin (1988).
5. Jaikumar (1989).

6. Clark and Fujimoto (1991).
7. Krafcik (1989); Krafcik and MacDuffie (1989).

established rigorous standards of product reliability, and communication links between plants and their suppliers that explicitly focused on quality. At the time of their creation (prior to his study), these systems were costly investments for the companies involved. They are at the core of the capability we have labeled "external integration."

External integration is the ability to link knowledge of customers with the details of engineering design in creating and improving products. The capability requires, first, market research to identify customer needs and, second, procedures that translate information about customers into product designs and, ultimately, products. Companies with this capability develop products that match customers' expectations down to the smallest details. The products not only satisfy customers, but often surprise and delight them.

The particular goals of external integration can be broken down into two subgoals. First, systems must be built to gather, collate, and analyze information about customers and the way they use the product. This means developing a sales and/or service organization that actively pursues in-depth knowledge of the customer. The second subgoal is to translate customer wants into specific technical and design choices. Firms with this capability develop detailed methodologies for accomplishing this translation.[8]

The other critical element linking customer needs and product outcomes is testing. Product testing simulates customer usage, and can confirm whether the product satisfies the goals established in its design. Effective testing must therefore mimic actual usage but with a limited sample and at a reasonable cost. This requires carefully designed protocols as well as skilled individuals to carry out the tests.

Investments in the linkage between customer needs and product outcomes are diverse and multifaceted. They range from travel budgets to send design engineers out to talk to customers, to designs that make products easier to modify (see the discussion of "flexibility" below), to sophisticated test engineers, methodologies and equipment.

The two necessary parts of an external integration investment—the creation of detailed knowledge and the linkage of such knowledge to the design—illustrate an important aspect of capabilities investments: the need for complementary action. A company might invest in developing a sales force and information systems; but if its product designers do not understand the customers, it will not achieve external integration. Another company might have highly qualified product engineers, capable of creating responsive and flexible designs; but without investment in knowledge about specific customers, their designs might never find a market.

The returns to investment in external integration are likely to be highest when the product is complex. With a complex product, consumer research can reveal many opportunities for enhancement, and product design can affect a myriad of details. Dominance on two or three key dimensions of perceived quality can be a very significant competitive advantage. In addition, information on customer usage of complex products may suggest new product variations that can be introduced later.[9]

Internal Integration

In their study of automobile product development, Kim Clark and Taka Fujimoto found that approaches to design and engineering differed substantially at U.S. and Japanese auto companies. The most successful of the Japanese firms had much smaller development teams than their competitors in the U.S. or Europe (for example, 300 vs. 1200). As a result, problem solving was more simultaneous in the Japanese companies and communication was more reciprocal and intense. Thus, the Japanese companies' efficiency in product development was the result of an organizational capability we refer to as "internal integration."

Internal integration enables a company to accelerate and reduce the cost of significant parts of an investment process. It makes companies faster and more efficient in performing functions such as new product development, prototyping, facilities engineering, and capacity expansion. Internal integration

---

8. For example, in their study of automobile product development, Clark and Fujimoto (1991) found striking differences in the ways U.S. and Japanese companies were connected with the market. The U.S. firms relied extensively on formal market research filtered through reports and meetings to discern the values and preferences of customers. The best (but not all) of the Japanese firms supplemented market research with direct personal interaction between design-

ers, engineers, and customers. From their multi-level contacts with consumers, the engineers obtained a very detailed understanding of how the products were used and performed in the field.

9. Sony has made effective use of the strategy of introducing many variants of successful new products. See Sanderson and Uzumeri (1990) on the Walkman and Sanchez (1991) on the video camcorder.

> **In the absence of internal integration, actions and decisions are taken first by the upstream function and then by the downstream function using the upstream group's output. Typically, the joint product will require two or more cycles of problem-solving to remedy the initial failures of coordination.**

is achieved when problem-solving is tightly connected across departmental boundaries. Decisions in one function then take into account the skills and concerns of the other function.

However, such integrated problem-solving requires specialists in different parts of the organization to develop common vocabularies, concepts, and objectives. The specialists must also have tools that facilitate cross-functional interaction, including computer simulation and testing equipment, redundant fabrication capacity (for the purpose of quickly building prototypes), and data bases that capture the relevant experience in different functions. Finally, internal integration requires communication and collaboration across functions and groups, which in turn grow out of education, training programs, career paths, and appropriate incentives.

In the absence of such internal integration, actions and decisions are taken first by the upstream function and then by the downstream function using the upstream group's output. Typically, then, the joint product will require two or more cycles of problem-solving to remedy the initial failures of coordination. Multiple cycles use up resources and delay the arrival of the final product.

The primary benefits derived from an investment in internal integration are efficiency and speed. Greater efficiency confers a cost advantage, which the company may use to increase profits or to gain market share. Speed is also a potent competitive weapon, which can be used to create value in many ways. For example, consider an industry such as electronics with declining unit costs (a "learning curve").[10] Suppose, through investment, Southern Electronics achieves the capability to develop new products in 12 months compared to 18 months for its principal rival, Northern Electronics.

To exploit its advantage, Southern first introduces a new generation of product (say, a stereo system) six months sooner than expected (the normal cycle was 24 months). With advanced features and performance, this creates an opportunity for premium pricing which Southern does not fully exploit. The effect is to increase Southern's market share even more than the performance advantage warrants. Although Northern follows six months later with its new generation product, it fails to recoup its lost share (and profits) because Southern

brings out its next generation 12 months later (still on its new 18-month cycle) and prices it above Northern's price, but below its warranted premium.

All of this has the effect of increasing Southern's effective volume and, because of learning effects, lowering its costs. But the *coup de grace* for Northern comes with its next generation product. Having mounted a "beat Southern" campaign but without changing its fundamental capabilities, Northern brings out what it thinks will be an excellent product only to discover that Southern has shortened its product cycle to 12 months. Southern thus brings to market a product that is a whole generation ahead of Northern, and continues with a 12-month cycle over the next few years. The impact on Northern can be disastrous. It is not only at a performance disadvantage in the market and thus unable to charge the same prices as Southern, but it also has higher manufacturing costs because of the learning effect. And Southern's capabilities for internal integration give it a further cost advantage, because it can develop new products with fewer engineering hours and less investment in tools and equipment than Northern.

Examples of such competition can be found in the recent histories of industries as diverse as automobiles, consumer electronics, medical technology (e.g., angioplasty), semiconductor production equipment, personal computers, workstations, and many others. In these industries, firms with capabilities for speed and efficiency in product development not only lowered their costs, but also changed the basic structure of their markets.

Flexibility

In his study of flexible manufacturing systems (FMS),[11] Jai Jaikumar found that Japanese and U.S. firms had different approaches to investment, which in turn significantly affected the performance of the FMS installations. The highest levels of performance were achieved by companies that made sustained commitments to internal systems over long periods of time. For example, at Hitachi Seki, a leading Japanese machine-tool manufacturer, the development of flexible manufacturing systems extended over 20 years.[12] During that time, the company invested in a series of projects that began with single

---

10. This example is adapted from Wheelwright and Clark (1992).
11. Jaikumar (1989).

12. Jaikumar (1986).

machines and culminated with the introduction of three flexible manufacturing systems capable of virtually untended, round-the-clock operation (the paradigmatic "factories with the lights turned off"). In contrast, U.S. firms in the study did not make sustained investments in software, tool design and system architecture; they invested more in the equipment (hardware), and relied on outside consultants and information specialists to install and implement their systems.

Flexibility comes in many forms. A company may have the capability to manufacture a wide range of products and change its mix on short notice. It may have the ability to respond to changes in volume, or it may have the ability to introduce new products rapidly and efficiently. As an asset, flexibility clearly has option-like characteristics. Just as the value of a financial option increases with the variability of an underlying price or quantity, so does the value of this capability.[13] Thus, if consumers will buy any car so long as it is black, product mix flexibility is worth very little. If oil prices vary only slightly from year to year, then there is little benefit to building facilities that can handle different feedstocks or varying levels of throughput.

In the last decade, many technologies have vastly increased their potential flexibility as a result of the informational capacity of microprocessors. Flexible manufacturing systems (FMS) are an example of one such technological advance. But as Jaikumar's study showed, there is often a wide gulf between potential and actual flexibility. Spanning the gulf requires investments in software, human skills, and organizational processes that complement the machinery.

Several kinds of investment are needed to build the capability of flexibility. To achieve product flexibility, for example, products and processes may need to be designed in a "modular" fashion. Designers pursuing this approach must have the skills (and incentives) to create components and sub-components that can serve as building blocks within a basic architecture. Modular design allows the end product to achieve very high variety while maintaining a

fairly focused effort and hence lower costs in engineering and manufacturing.[14]

To achieve process flexibility, companies need to invest in operating procedures and software that embed various rules and contingencies, and thus allow rapid and easy changeovers. Embedding contingencies in standard operating procedures requires significant investments in design, costing, and testing of software.[15] But, having the contingencies "wired" allows changes in tools, patterns, equipment, and routing to take place in seconds and minutes, where they might otherwise take hours or days. Again, the up-front investment must be weighed against the value of flexibility in terms of both variety and responsiveness.

The Capacity to Experiment

The value of detailed and specific knowledge about a product, process, or market is a recurring theme in our analysis of capabilities. Knowledge about consumer tastes is the first step in achieving external integration. Knowledge about process lies at the core of internal integration. Knowledge about the range of tastes or prices establishes the value of flexibility. However, many questions about complex phenomena cannot be answered by deduction and thus an important tool in developing knowledge is the capacity to experiment.

Modern manufacturing processes are inherently complex. Continuous incremental improvement—the process known in Japanese as *kaizen*—is often at the core of productivity and quality differences among otherwise similar companies.[16] Continuous improvement is the end product of organizational learning, which in turn is made possible by experimentation.

The capacity to experiment requires two complementary types of investment. The first involves development of knowledge, the second dissemination of results and their adoption in practice. The first set of expenditures may include extra manufacturing capacity to allow experimentation in the plant; appropriate sensors and tools for collecting data;

---

13. Financial options were first valued analytically by Black and Scholes (1973) and Merton (1975). Options involve truncations of probability distributions, thus virtually any option increases in value as underlying risk increases. For applications of option pricing to real investments (as opposed to financial securities), see Pindyck (1990) and the citations therein.

14. On the use of modularity in product design, see Eppinger et al. (1990), Cusumano (1990), and Baldwin and Clark (1992).

15. On investments in knowledge necessary to achieve process flexibility, see Jaikumar (1990).

16. See, for example, the previously cited study of automobile manufacturing, Krafcik and MacDuffie (1989); Imai (1986) provides many examples drawn from Japanese industry.

and people and systems that can organize, report, and analyze data. The second includes systems for communication between scientific and operating personnel; training for individuals in diagnosis and debugging; testing equipment and protocols; and procedures to facilitate rapid problem-solving and the coordination of schedules and supplies.

The value of the capacity to experiment tends to vary over time. In a study of semiconductor fabrication plants, for example, Therese Flaherty found that the start-up period of a new plant is a particularly critical period in which to foster experimentation.[17] If the production system is frozen too early, inefficient, unreliable subsystems tend to become embedded in the overall process, leading to chronic bottlenecks, backlogs, and work stoppages. Thus allocating resources to experimentation during the start-up period pays large dividends in efficiency and reliability later on.

The Capacity to Cannibalize

A company cannibalizes itself when it replaces an existing product or process with another that is potentially worth less. Two classic examples of cannibalistic investments are replacing old equipment and introducing a new product that decreases the sales of existing products. One of the oldest rules of resource allocation is a prohibition against cannibalization. Traditional analysis, however, does not take account of the impact of cannibalization on long-run product market structure.

For example, in the 1970s, the owner-managers of established semiconductor companies often were reluctant to introduce new products because they would reduce the current profits and market values.[18] Their unwillingness to cannibalize meant that new generation products were introduced by startups instead of by established firms. In the long run, the established companies could not stay competitive; eventually many were forced to exit the industry. This pattern of events has also been documented in the steel industry, the photolithographic alignment equipment industry, the videorecorder industry, and various segments of the chemicals and plastics industries.[19]

Self-cannibalization is a dominant (best) strategy when a company seeks to prevent competitors from entering a market. Interestingly, though, the strategy is "time inconsistent"—that is, when it comes time to introduce the new product or process, it will not be in the established firms' financial interest to do so.[20] Thus strategies of self-cannibalization are not feasible if managers must maximize the financial value of the company at all times.

The introduction of a cannibalistic new product or process is more than just a strategy, however. Actually identifying the particular innovations that ought to be undertaken and successfully implementing them is a capability on par with the others described in this section. As such, it requires a significant investment in procedures, information systems, and human skills, as well as physical assets.

There are two parts to the capacity to cannibalize. First is the ability to recognize which opportunities have competitive value and thus should be pushed forward more rapidly than a simple financial analysis would indicate. While everything may look obvious in retrospect, innovative products and processes are fraught with uncertainty and ambiguity. To recognize crucial opportunities, a company must have the ability to scan the environment, both commercially and technologically. It must be able to experiment with attractive opportunities at low cost, and to relate potential opportunities to the larger markets in which it operates. All of this tentative scanning, exploring, and opportunity-generating must go on while the firm is actively pushing its existing product line. Thus, the internal control systems, the information systems and the organizational structure must allow for surveillance of new opportunities while the company simultaneously extends existing markets and pursues incremental improvements of its current product.

The second major aspect of the capacity to cannibalize is the ability to implement a new direction once it has been chosen. Implementation involves not just new product design and process engineering, but also the ability to follow through with a radically new initiative while phasing out the old. Knowing how to price the new product, how

---

17. M.T. Flaherty (1992), private communication.
18. Ferguson (1987).
19. Crandall (1981); Henderson and Clark (1990); Rosenbloom and Freeze (1985); Foster (1986).

20. Gilbert and Newbery (1982); and Reinganum (1983).

to ramp up manufacturing capacity, and how to sustain revenues on the old product until the new one is ready to be shipped are all critical to achieving the highest possible value in the switchover.

In addition, an organization focused on supporting an existing product has built-in forces that will strongly resist change. Thus, implementation of a cannibalistic new product or process will be opposed within the established hierarchy. Companies that have the capacity to cannibalize must therefore build procedures, systems, and routines that not only support the existing structure, but also anticipate the need to phase it out. Without that understanding, a decision to cannibalize is likely to be followed by procrastination, delay, inappropriate action, and outright mistakes.

VALUING CAPABILITIES

The role of finance in the resource allocation process is to predict the value of significant corporate investments and strategic initiatives. The tools for such evaluation are normally labelled "capital budgeting" analysis. In many large, decentralized organizations, these tools are deployed as part of capital budgeting systems, which are hierarchical procedures for the approval of capital expenditures.

In theory, the tools of financial valuation should be able to cope with any investment that creates value, regardless of the pattern of returns. Thus when companies fail to invest in critical, value-enhancing capabilities, either their valuation methods or their resource allocation systems have failed. In sections that follow, we first describe the problems that arise in valuing capabilities and then turn to the problem of allocating resources in a large, decentralized corporation.

A tenet of economic theory is that *any* investment can be characterized in terms of its cash inflows and outflows. This is also true of capabilities investments; the ultimate, hoped-for product is a cash flow. However, the *intermediate* outputs of such investments are *skills*, *systems*, and *procedures*. Such skills, systems, and procedures create competitive advantage in the form of quality, speed, efficiency, flexibility, incremental improvement, and innovation, and thus are organizational assets.

Capabilities enhance the value of investments in the future. In the technical parlance of finance, they change one or more characteristics of the company's "opportunity set." Specifically, external integration reduces product risk. Internal integration increases the frequency of encountering opportunities, and reduces the cost of exploiting them. Flexibility increases the range of options associated with a given investment. The capacity to experiment allows systematic improvement and thus reduces cost over time. Finally, the capacity to cannibalize deters entry and thus increases the value of a company's market position.

Because they affect groups of opportunities, the expected returns to investment in capabilities are not easily translated into a series of cash flows. Nevertheless, the outputs of capabilities are measurable, and their values can be estimated by reframing the valuation in terms of the capability's impact on revenue. For example, in valuing an increase in external integration, one might ask: How much would revenue change if we reduced defects by a factor of ten? To value internal integration, one might ask: How would revenue change if we accelerated product introductions by half a year? In the case of flexibility: How much would we earn by building ten additional products off of Platform A? To value experimentation: How much would we reduce our manufacturing cost by incremental process improvements year to year? And finally, in the case of cannibalization: When will competitors enter our markets if we are unwilling to innovate?

There are tools that can be used to answer each of these questions and convert the results into cash flows.[21] They are not often used, however, because it is very difficult to get the answers "right" in practice. Many companies respond to this analytic difficulty simply by not subjecting capabilities to rigorous formal valuation. Instead, they develop internal rules of thumb designed to preserve whatever capabilities have been most critical to their past success.[22]

If such rules of thumb worked perfectly, we would be comfortable leaving the valuation of

---

21. On the value of quality, see Shapiro (1983) and Shaked and Sutton (1987). On the value of speed, see the technology "race" literature, e.g., Reinganum (1989) and the citations therein. On the value of flexibility, see He and Pindyck (1989). On the value of continuous improvement, see, for example, Spence (1981, 1984) or Lieberman (1984). On cannibalization, see Gilbert and Newbery (1982) or Baldwin (1989).

22. On the differences between rules of thumb ("principles") and cost-benefit analysis ("values"), see Prelec (1990). For examples of rules of thumb used in resource allocation, see Baldwin (1991).

> **Positive complementarities are part of what make capabilities so valuable; unfortunately, they also complicate both the valuation and the acquisition of capabilities. Many companies respond to this analytic difficulty simply by not subjecting capabilities to rigorous formal valuation.**

capabilities to academics. But the field studies we cited earlier show that for many U.S. companies the prevailing rules of thumb have not worked very well; resources have not been channeled to the development of organizational assets that enhance quality, speed, and flexibility. A better understanding of how capabilities create value is thus a necessary first step toward developing procedures that can direct more resources to the formation of capabilities.

Capabilities are difficult to value for two reasons. First, they change the way different units of a company work together. As system-level investments, capabilities are subject to threshold effects and positive complementarities that may dramatically affect their returns. Second, capabilities may be used to change the structure of a product market, in which case the value of the investment cannot be separated from the competitor's response.

Threshold Effects and Positive Complementarities

Threshold effects arise when benefits are not realized until a full system has been installed. For example, attempts to upgrade quality may fail because product designs are too inflexible; attempts to implement flexible manufacturing techniques may fail because of rigid price lists. Threshold effects make capabilities investments vulnerable to failure in early stages of their implementation. At this point, resources—often the "big ticket" items like computers or machinery—have been acquired, but the projected benefits have not materialized. The opponents of the investment can then point to its disappointing results, and it may be abandoned.

Obviously, it is best to identify as many threshold effects as possible before making an investment. However, in any complex system, there will be unperceived thresholds; and thus, before abandoning a capabilities investment, the company should examine its implementation in detail to see if complementary actions—such as modular designs or more frequent pricing—are what is needed to remedy the problem.

Positive complementarities are the converse of threshold effects. When two capabilities interact, they enhance a company's competitiveness along several dimensions and the return on investment increases commensurately. The most successful Japanese auto companies have both tight links with customers (external integration) and a highly efficient design

process (internal integration). The highest level of quality in air conditioners was achieved when feedback from service centers (external integration) was coupled with flexibility in design. And cannibalization is most effective at deterring entry when combined with speed and efficiency in design and engineering—the results of internal integration.

Positive complementarities are part of what make capabilities so valuable; unfortunately, they also complicate both the valuation and the acquisition of capabilities. Figuring out the incremental value of quality as opposed to speed or efficiency—say, for an auto company—may seem impossible; but acquiring all capabilities simultaneously is equally impossible for a company starting at ground zero.

In our view, this problem can be addressed only by decomposing capabilities into a small number of organizational assets with measurable outputs. Each of the capabilities we have defined can be quantified in terms of defect rates, engineering hours, time elapsed between changeovers, products derived from one platform, etc. Managers can estimate the value of these outputs, and list the actions and expenses associated with improving on each dimension. These three elements—measurable changes in performance, their impact on value, and lists of required actions—are the essential core of any resource allocation system. We shall consider how traditional capital budgeting systems deal with the allocation of resources to capabilities later. But before turning to this question, we describe the most potent way in which capabilities create value—through their impact on product markets and competition.

The Impact of Capabilities on Product Markets

In discussing the value of internal integration earlier, we described the evolution of a market over three successive generations of product competition. Southern's investment in internal integration, coupled with a learning curve, put Northern at a grave competitive disadvantage. The value of Southern's investment in capabilities thus included both the incremental profits (cash flows) over three rounds of competition *and* the value of "owning the market" if, as is likely, Northern decides to pull out. Strategic investments that cause reallocations of market share are clearly very valuable, but their value depends on the competitor's probable actions—in this case, what Northern does.

When capabilities are likely to affect product market structure, it is especially important to separate the measurable outputs of a capability from its impact on cash flow and value. From a managerial perspective, the outputs of capabilities in terms of speed, efficiency, etc., can be quantified, thus making it possible to set goals and track results. In contrast, the effect of capabilities on cash flow and value depend on what the competition does (or does not do), and thus are not under managers' control. Furthermore, it is always easy to disagree about what the competition is likely to do, and small changes in such assumptions will have large effects on the estimated value of any particular capability. (Competitive assessments do need to be made and communicated among units of the company, but burying them in the cash flow forecasts is not the most effective way to disseminate them.)

A competitor's response depends on, among other things, the amount of time it would need to duplicate a particular capability. But, as we discuss below, the acquisition of a capability is not as simple as acquiring a financial asset like a bond or even a tangible asset like a plant. The process cannot be planned and executed perfectly; there will always be threshold effects that must be remedied after the fact. In addition, capabilities generally involve the training of individuals whose learning cannot be accelerated. All of this implies that *competitors cannot duplicate capabilities easily or rapidly.* The problems and lags in implementation may be so formidable that competitors will choose to exit rather than attempting to recreate capabilities in their own organizations. Ironically, therefore, the very aspect of capabilities that makes them so difficult to value and to manage also makes them a major barrier to entry and hence a source of competitive advantage.

INVESTING IN CAPABILITIES

As we have shown, organizational capabilities involve the *system-level* characteristics of making or selling a product. To be effective, such capabilities must actually carry down to the working levels of the organization, and must involve both formal and informal procedures. Therefore, as a group, capabilities require different types of outlays than other types of investments. Many of these outlays are not normally classified as capital expenditures. Some examples of expenditures needed to build capabilities include: common languages and channels of communication; skills, training, and experience; facilities, software, and support services; and managerial attention. Of these, only facilities qualify as assets in most accounting systems.

The investments necessary to build a capability have two interesting properties. First, *they range widely in scale and scope.* They do not come in a neatly-wrapped package confined to one operating group or functional area. Instead, upgrading a capability generally requires many different kinds of investment, in different parts of the organization. If the company does not give individuals the discretion to make small investments, but instead requires all appropriations to move up through a compartmentalized, hierarchical capital budgeting process, some of the necessary investments will not be made.

Investing in a capability also means that a company must in the short run allocate people and resources explicitly to development of the capability. If a company takes the time and the people necessary to build a capability through training, experience, development of databases, etc., it necessarily pulls those people off of current programs and activities. While the incremental costs are visible (and on someone's budget), the benefits may accrue only to the company as a whole, or only after a significant amount of time. Thus, *managers of profit centers have incentives to skimp on capabilities.* This tendency is exacerbated by the fact that most of the necessary expenditures are not accounted for as capital, but are charged directly to expenses. If the key measure of performance is profitability, expenditures on capabilities will decrease performance and hence bonuses. Moreover, successful development of a capability may require new organizational structures that directly threaten those whose cooperation is critical to the capability's implementation.[23]

In view of the "scale and scope" problem and the inherent conflicts between individual operating units and the company as a whole, it is a challenging task to design decentralized systems to encourage capabilities investments. Few U.S. companies can

---

23. Kaplan (1990) describes a series of investments to enhance manufacturing quality and efficiency at Analog Devices. The unforeseen end result was to create overcapacity in the functions that improved the most.

While the incremental costs [of developing capabilities] are visible (and on someone's budget), the benefits may accrue only to the company as a whole, or only after a significant amount of time. Thus, managers of profit centers have incentives to skimp on capabilities.

claim to have succeeded in doing so. In the remainder of this section, we show how traditional capital budgeting systems subvert attempts to invest in capabilities.

Nevertheless, exempting capabilities investments from the control of these systems—as many companies have done—is not a satisfactory alternative. Thus, we conclude with recommendations that are designed to preserve the strengths of formal capital budgeting systems without excluding capabilities from the set of possible investments.

Capital Budgeting and Capabilities

Large U.S. corporations began to adopt decentralized profit planning and capital budgeting systems soon after World War II. In virtually all companies, the "business planning" and the "capital budgeting" systems evolved as complementary systems for organizing data and making decisions. The business planning system was used to project detailed revenues and expenses for the coming year. With the advent of computers, revenues and expenses could be disaggregated into very small units. The result was decentralized "responsibility accounting," wherein a manager's evaluation was tied to "making a plan."

The capital budgeting system served as a check on the business planning system. Planning was broken down by products, regions or facilities, while capital budgeting was organized around projects. Project analysis was based on economic theories of resource allocation, particularly the concept of the time value of money. According to this theory, cash invested at one time can be compared to cash returned at another time by adjusting for interest. The resulting cash inflow-cash outflow view of investment is still the core of most capital budgeting systems used today.

A number of innovations in the 1970s attacked problems of incoherence and lack of coordination that were prevalent in business planning in the 1950s and 1960s. The first step toward an "architecture" of planning was Boston Consulting Group's practice of locating businesses on a simple two-by-two matrix. Using this tool, top managers could quickly rank dissimilar businesses according to their growth potential and need for funds. But, in order to use this "portfolio planning" approach, corporations had to organize revenue and cost data to correspond to whole businesses. Thus, in the 70s, many companies reorganized into strategic business units, or SBUs.[24]

But even with these improvements, the traditional business-planning-cum-capital-budget system was still a very imperfect method of resource allocation. Not all the compelling motives for making an investment can be translated into specific revenue and cost projections even by the most skilled adepts of discounted cash flow methodology. As a result, large, strategic investments have almost always been exempt from the standard review procedures. Such investments do not fit into pre-established categories, do not have fixed time horizons, and often cannot satisfy corporate standards for payback or return on investment.[25]

In the highest echelons of most companies, formal capital budgeting systems are viewed as a means to an end. Most top managers understand very well the limits of formal discounted cash flow analysis, and accordingly use it as a "partial discipline" within a more complex resource allocation process. The impact of an investment on competitors, on the organization, and on the capital markets may equal or exceed the importance of DCF calculations in the eyes of top managers.[26]

At lower levels of most corporations, however, the formal capital budgeting system does impose real constraints on investment. The systems are designed to filter information upward through a series of screens.[27] To economize on top managers' time and to be comprehensible to managers in parallel functions, the information must be standardized. But certain types of information are not easily captured within the standard format. Such information then becomes virtually impossible to convey up through the hierarchy or across functions.

The critical information that falls between the cracks often relates to capabilities. Bower's classic study of capital budgeting in a large chemical company contains a telling example.[28] In this case, a group of operating managers had the idea to build a flexible facility. The plant they envisioned would

---

24. Porter (1980) proceeded from there to link portfolio planning to microeconomic (oligopoly) theory.

25. Bierman (1988) surveyed 102 chief financial officers on the problems of implementing capital budgeting analysis. Difficulty in incorporating strategic considerations was the problem most frequently cited.

26. See Donaldson (1984).

27. See Sah and Stiglitz (1986), Bull and Ordover (1987), and Thakor (1990) for theoretical explanations of this structure based on human fallibility or asymmetric information.

28. Bower (1970), Chapter 5.

allow easy switchovers in response to shifting demand, as well as small batch production of new compounds in early stages of commercial development. Bower vividly depicts the problems the managers faced as they attempted to justify this investment. First, the project resisted all efforts to classify it into one of the standard categories. When the issue of categorization was resolved, the project's sponsors had difficulty specifying the *base case*—in other words, the impact of *not* taking the project. The products of the new facility were already being made using spare capacity. The managers, who were engineers, asserted that current procedures reduced efficiency and made it impossible to guarantee purity (which was important to many customers). But they could not translate inefficiency and lower quality into cash flows, and thus had no way to counter the assertion (by the corporate staff) that the current cost of producing products in question was virtually zero.

It was equally hard for the managers to describe what the new plant would contribute. The key feature of the facility was its flexibility. Its volume and mix of products would vary, and thus—by definition—could not be predicted in advance. However, to conform to the company's capital budgeting format, the project's sponsors needed to project future cash flows. They did so by assuming a standard mix of products, and then had to explain (1) why this mix of products would not necessarily *ever* be produced; and (2) why the proposed facility was *not efficiently configured* for this mix.

Managers several levels below the top of the company wrestled with the issues of project classification, the base case, and the facility's contribution for almost two years. They found, however, that as the project moved up the levels of the corporate approval process, it became easier to justify. The issue of classification became less important and the project's strategic rationale carried more weight. Nevertheless, approvals were delayed, key sponsors were promoted to other responsibilities, and the project was never funded.

The concept of capabilities allows us to characterize the contributions of the flexible facility in more detail. The project would have contributed to *internal integration* by removing a distracting element in the current production system and by speeding the transition of new products from the lab to commercial production. The project promised to increase *external integration* by making it possible to sell small lots of new products to customers interested in developing applications. The project would have enhanced *flexibility* by allowing production plans to be revised in response to changing market conditions. And, finally, the project promised to increase opportunities for incremental innovation by facilitating *experimentation* with products and processes.

The company's capital budgeting system was not well-equipped to handle the investment, however. It was crammed into a DCF framework so that it could be reviewed through normal channels. But, as we argued earlier, capabilities do not conform to the basic cash inflow-cash outflow model of investment. Instead, they enrich the value of opportunities the company will encounter in the future (in this case, on several dimensions simultaneously).

Experiences like the one Bower describes often lead managers to abandon financial systems of resource allocation. Sometimes a particular class of projects is made exempt from normal evaluation, or a different approval process is invented for "strategic" investments. In high-tech industries such as electronics, companies may abandon financial systems altogether in favor of technologically-driven rules of thumb. And most often, top managers simply preempt the financial systems and fund investments they believe are essential to the company's competitive survival.

Unfortunately, overriding the formal resource allocation system creates as many problems as it solves. When top managers short-circuit the system, they do little to encourage capabilities investments at lower levels of the organization. Yet, threshold effects, complementarities, and the "scale and scope" problem all imply that the success of a capabilities investment depends on cooperation among groups at the operating levels of the company. Financial planning and capital budgeting analysis are important channels of communication across functions and groups, and provide a framework through which to coordinate the process of investment. Without such a framework, critical complementary actions, such as price changes or training expenditures, may not occur. The company will then be left with many dollars spent on expensive systems and very little increase in overall profitability.

An investment in a continuous heat treating line (CHTL) in a steel mill provides an example of this phenomenon. The CHTL investment resembled the flexible factory in Bower's study in many ways. It offered advantages over the old process in the quality of the product, but customer reaction to

The valuation of capabilities cannot be decentralized to the same degree as that of more traditional investments. Translating speed, quality, or flexibility into value cannot be done without taking into account threshold effects, complementarities, and the impact of the capability on competitors.

those advantages was uncertain. In addition, the new process could make steel with previously unavailable combinations of strength and weight, and thus opened up possibilities of new markets and applications. Finally, the line was highly flexible in its ability to change quickly from one product to another. Thus the advantages of the process lay in capabilities related to new product development and high variety production in a continuous-flow, cost-effective process. However, the new process had little direct cost advantage over the old.

Once again, lower level managers struggled to fit the investment into their standard capital budgeting framework. They worked with the numbers on cost and revenue (without assuming dramatic changes in the product line), until the financial returns were satisfactory. Once again the investment became easier to "sell" as it moved up through the corporate approval process. Indeed, at the very top of the corporation, some senior executives were excited about the CHTL investment's potential for new products and new markets.

The shortcomings of the review procedures only became apparent after the project was completed. The new system did not perform as planned because the company failed to take complementary actions. Historically it had relied upon a sales force that could explain the existing product line, process orders, and negotiate prices. In order to exploit the new line's potential, however, the company had to understand potential customer needs, translate them into new product specifications, and develop those products on the new line. While senior officers understood this, complementary investments in applications engineering and sales force development were never undertaken.[29,30]

In criticizing capital budgeting systems, it is very easy to lose sight of what they do well. One of their strengths is their capacity to organize information and decision-making. Many large and small items need to be purchased and many skills deployed to construct a plant or launch a product. To address these problems, the capital budgeting process starts with a project definition, a list of necessary expenditures, and a set of accounts. Organizing expenditures in this fashion is a significant first step that makes later implementation of the project smoother and more effective. Therefore, the true challenge for

a company is to develop an investment approval process that can accommodate capabilities investments, and yet preserves the positive contributions of a capital budgeting system to the organization.

RECOMMENDATIONS

In this paper, we have argued that U.S. companies underinvest in a set of organizational assets called "capabilities," and that their capital budgeting systems generally make the problem worse. We now describe the actions companies need to take to identify, implement, and foster investments in capabilities.

One of the critical assumptions of traditional capital budgeting is that both the valuation and the implementation of investments can be performed by decentralized units. But the valuation of capabilities cannot be decentralized to the same degree as that of more traditional investments. Translating speed, quality, or flexibility into value cannot be done without taking into account threshold effects, complementarities, and the impact of the capability on competitors. The information needed to address these issues simply is not present below the top levels of a business, and thus it is unrealistic (and often counterproductive) to expect functional units to carry out a full analysis of a capabilities investment.

Some companies go to the opposite extreme, and adopt a pure, top-down approach. But, as we have argued, capabilities are complex and, because of threshold effects, easy to derail. Thus a wholly centralized investment process will not work either.

Our approach therefore involves the development of a "mixed" resource allocation system—one in which the process of identifying and implementing specific investments is decentralized, while valuation, goal-setting, and performance measurement are carried out centrally. Linking the central and operating units of the company are accounting, information, and compensation systems that fund investments and reward improvements in capabilities over time.

Valuation

The valuation of critical capabilities and the choice of which to focus on in the short run are inherently the task of senior managers. Top managers,

---

29. Hayes, Wheelwright, and Clark (1988).

30. Kaplan (1990) describes a similar sequence of events at Analog Devices.

however, must have detailed knowledge of the technology and the manufacturing process in order to know what is possible. And they must have access to both competitive intelligence and relevant cost-accounting data to judge the revenue and cost impacts of any particular investment.[31]

The choice of which capabilities to pursue and what resources to allocate to their development is a critical element of a company's overall strategy. Capabilities are expensive, complex, and risky investments. Although it is tempting to try to improve on all dimensions at once, to do so is to invite disaster. Furthermore, there are instances where the organization is so rigid and the competitors' headstart so formidable, that leaving the market is preferable to investing in the capabilities necessary to compete. Many restructurings, recapitalizations, and hostile takeovers are directed at reversing investments in capabilities that outside investors view as beyond the company's capacity to implement.

Once top managers have selected which capabilities to develop, they must articulate their reasoning and gain commitment from the organization. They can do so only if they translate the desired capabilities into goals and rewards that people throughout the organization can understand and use in decision-making. It is relatively easy to identify the capabilities a company needs to compete. It is much harder to convert this analysis into resource allocation systems that foster consistent investment in appropriate capabilities at all levels of a corporation.

Systems

The first necessary step in building such systems is to set up appropriate accounting and budgeting procedures for capabilities investments. The place to start is with a *capabilities capital budget* that lists *all* expenditures needed. Expenditures on training, communications, and data, which are normally counted as expenses, should be incorporated into the capabilities budget. The list of expenditures is closely related to the list of necessary actions, and thus the budget serves to focus discussions across functions and groups about who is responsible for doing what and when.

Companies should also create authorized accounts against which capabilities-related expenses may be charged. Such accounts reduce conflicts of interest between the operating unit and the company as a whole. Many operating managers admit to deferring the "soft" parts of capabilities investments because they "can't afford the expense." A budgetary account removes some of the temptation to skimp on these costs to increase a unit's profits and bonus pool. The account also provides a detailed record against which managers can measure progress and efficiency in achieving the goals of the investment.

Goals are the second critical part of the system. As we have emphasized, capabilities deliver measurable changes in operating performance along the dimensions of quality, speed, efficiency, variety, responsiveness, and innovation. These measures can be translated into goals for particular operating units—for example, a reduction in processing time of 50% may be the desired end result of an investment in internal integration.[32] The efficiency and effectiveness of the investment can then be assessed by comparing actual expenditures against the budget and the achieved improvements. Unanticipated threshold effects and the need for complementary actions can also identified through analysis of the budget vs. the performance goals.

Goals are most powerful if they enter into compensation and thus the third step in system building is to tie the compensation of operating managers to the achievement of targeted improvements in speed, quality, flexibility, etc. The process of managing compensation is very difficult because threshold effects and complementarities imply that each individual or group's marginal contribution will exceed their average contribution. Thus compensating individuals according to their marginal contribution—as the theory of optimal incentives recommends—is not collectively feasible. But the other extreme of rewarding managers solely on the basis of their unit's profitability sets up strong incentives to skimp. The fact that many expenditures necessary to the development of capabilities are relatively small (hence invisible) and accounted for as expenses (hence subtracted directly from profits) practically guarantees that operating managers will underinvest unless they are rewarded directly for improvements in operating performance.

Finally, managers at all levels must be prepared for both positive and negative complementarities in

---

31. On measurement of relevant costs, see Kaplan (1989), and the articles in Kaplan, ed. (1990).

32. On the decomposition of capabilities investments into specific projects and detailed goals, see Garvin (1990).

Because of threshold effects and complementarities, compensating individuals according to their marginal contribution—as the theory of optimal incentives recommends—is not collectively feasible. But the other extreme of rewarding managers solely on the basis of their unit's profitability sets up strong incentives to skimp.

implementing capabilities investments. Negative complementarities mean that achieving the targeted goals will never be a smooth nor a predictable process: there will always be unanticipated threshold effects and learning along the way. Without losing sight of the rationale for the investment or the need to contain its cost, companies must be ready to change their initial plans as new knowledge develops. This does not make the original budget less meaningful; the more costs a company can forecast at the outset, the better its decision-making and the smoother its implementation will be.

At the opposite end of the spectrum, positive complementarities mean that concentrating on one capability alone will not be sufficient in the long run. Quality may be critical to survival today, but a company with high quality will eventually lose out to another that combines high quality with speed and efficiency.

Positive complementarities pose a major challenge for successful companies as their markets evolve. Often, companies achieve initial success through the implementation of one or two capabilities in a particular and limited context. For example, an electronics company may have the ability to develop high-quality products rapidly—that is, capabilities of internal and external integration in new product development. The investments that pre-

serve and enhance these capabilities then tend to become enshrined in the corporate culture and protected via rules of thumb, such as, "we always budget 15% of sales to new product R&D." Other capabilities do not have comparable status within the organization and often do not get funded, even when their rates of return are attractive by capital market standards.[33]

The crucial issue then is how to recognize the next cluster of necessary capabilities and how to shift from one set to another. High rates of return in unfunded opportunities are one early warning sign of an impending shift in critical capabilities. Changes in competitors' investment patterns are another. But fundamentally managers must develop their own concept of the potential value of specific capabilities, and then consider the best ways to develop them.

In the long run, the evolution of a company's capabilities determines the markets it enters, the products it sells, and the customers it serves. Investments in capabilities are thus among the most forward-looking commitments a company must make. Whether the industry's time horizon is five years or 50, managers must look beyond their present competitive environment to the capabilities that will deliver future advantage, and make those organizational assets the target of their investment programs.

---

33. Hayes, Wheelwright, and Clark (1988) and Flaherty (1992) each provide examples of process investments with rates of return of 30% to 50% that were not funded by companies accustomed to competing on the basis of new product development.

THE EVA® FINANCIAL MANAGEMENT SYSTEM

by Joel M. Stern, G. Bennett Stewart III, and Donald H. Chew, Jr., Stern Stewart & Co.

T he information revolution, along with the pace of technological change of all kinds and the rise of a global economy, is leading to major changes in the structure and internal control systems of large organizations. Centrally-directed economies are failing, state-owned enterprises are being privatized, and non-profits are experimenting with new ways of motivating employees and "selling" their services. At the same time, the huge conglomerates built up during the 1960s and '70s—the epitome of central planning in the private sector—are being steadily pulled apart and supplanted by more focused competitors.

In each of these spheres of activity—private, public, and non-profit—the spread of powerful computer and telecommunications networks is contributing to a worldwide move toward decentralization or, to use the more fashionable term, "empowerment." With the flattening of management hierarchies, corporate decision-making is being driven down through the ranks to managers and employees closer to the company's operations and customers.

But, as organizational theorists have long understood, there are significant costs associated with decentralizing decision-making. Today's information systems may now be capable of providing top management with real-time monitoring of the revenues and profits of the most farflung operations. But what software is programmed to report opportunities lost by operating heads too comfortable with the status quo? And what accounting systems are capable of distinguishing reliably between profitable and unprofitable corporate investment decisions *at the time* the decisions are being made?

The answer, of course, is that this kind of information cannot be passed on by computer systems. Such information resides with experienced line managers and employees—those who are posi-

tioned to serve as the nerve-endings of the organization—and it will be used to benefit the firm only insofar as those managers and employees are highly motivated and focused on the right goals.

And so, as some organizational theorists are now coming to understand, companies that push decision-making down into lower levels of the organization must also change their *internal control* systems. Such companies will typically find it necessary to rethink both their performance measurement and their reward systems to help ensure that operating managers use their expanded decision-making powers in ways that increase the value of the firm. In this sense, decentralization, performance measurement, and compensation policy constitute a "three-legged stool" of effective corporate control.[1]

In this article, we argue that for many large companies the top-down, earnings per share-based model of financial management that has long dominated corporate America is becoming obsolete. The most serious challenge to the long reign of EPS is coming from a measure of corporate performance called "Economic Value Added," or EVA. As Peter Drucker noted in a recent *Harvard Business Review* article, EVA is by no means a new concept. Rather it is a practical, and highly flexible, refinement of economists' concept of "residual income"—the value that is left over after a company's stockholders (and all other providers of capital) have been adequately compensated. As Drucker also observed, EVA is thus a measure of "total factor productivity"—one whose growing popularity reflects the new demands of the information age. For companies that aim to increase their competitiveness by decentralizing, EVA is likely to be the most sensible basis for evaluating and rewarding the periodic performance of empowered line people, especially those entrusted with major capital spending decisions.

EVA® is a registered trademark of Stern Stewart & Co.

1. The term is borrowed from James Brickley, Clifford Smith, and Jerold Zimmerman, "The Economics of Organizational Architecture," in this issue. For the original derivation of the concept, see Michael Jensen and William Meckling, "Specific and General Knowledge, and Organizational Structure," also in this issue.

EVA, moreover, is not just a performance measure. When fully implemented, it is the centerpiece of an *integrated financial management system* that encompasses the full range of corporate financial decision-making—everything from capital budgeting, acquisition pricing, and the setting of corporate goals to shareholder communication and management incentive compensation. By putting all financial and operating functions on the same basis, an EVA system effectively provides a common language for employees across all corporate functions, linking strategic planning with the operating divisions, and the corporate treasury staff with investor relations and human resources.

In the pages that follow, we begin by describing the shortcomings of the top-down, EPS-based model of financial management. Next we explain both the rise of hostile takeovers and the phenomenal success of LBOs in the 1980s as capital market responses to the deficiencies of the EPS model. The EVA financial management system, we go on to argue, borrows important aspects of the LBO movement—particularly, its focus on capital efficiency and ownership incentives—but without the high leverage and concentration of risk that limit LBOs to the mature sector of the U.S. economy. In the final section, we present the outlines of an EVA-based incentive compensation plan that is designed to simulate for managers and employees the rewards of ownership.

THE OLD SYSTEM: EPS-BASED FINANCIAL MANAGEMENT

As Alfred Chandler has argued, the centralized top-down approach to managing large corporations was well suited to the relatively stable business environment that prevailed during the first two or three decades after World War II. The principal challenge of top management then was to achieve the huge economies of scale in manufacturing and marketing that were available to firms finding opportunities for growth in the same or closely related businesses.

In this age of stability, the top managements of most large U.S. companies aimed to report steady increases in earnings per share by calling on each of their operating divisions to produce a given amount of profits each year. Because new capital appropriations for all the divisions (the total amount of which effectively determined the denominator in the EPS calculation) were usually tightly controlled from the top, a given amount of profits aggregated across all the divisions (the numerator) enabled top management to hit the target barring a sharp economic downturn.

The strategy of corporate diversification that became popular in the late 1960s and 1970s—that is, the acquisition of businesses in completely unrelated industries (which Chandler has called "both a disaster and an historical aberration")[2]—can also be explained in part as an attempt by top management to increase its ability to "manage" reported earnings. For one thing, the popular practice of buying companies with lower P/Es in stock-for-stock exchanges automatically boosted reported EPS (such "EPS bootstrapping," as the practice was called, was pure accounting artifice with no economic substance whatsoever). And, to the extent a portfolio of unrelated businesses produced less variable operating cash flows for the entire firm, such corporate diversification served to smooth reported earnings.[3]

Also contributing to top management's ability to deliver smoothly rising earnings—at least for a time—was the annual rite of negotiating divisional budget targets. In a time-honored practice known as "sandbagging," division heads with greater knowledge of their businesses' prospects than corporate staffers would underestimate the profit potential of their own units when negotiating their budgets with headquarters. And, having "low-balled" their estimates and negotiated easy targets, such operating heads also often found it in their own interest to "bank" excess profits for a rainy day—for example, by shifting revenues or costs.

This kind of "satisficing" behavior by division heads can be readily explained by standard features of the corporate reward system. In most companies, division heads' annual bonus awards were capped at a fairly modest fraction (say, 20-30%) of base salary, thus limiting their participation in exceptional profits. And really extraordinary divisional performance in any one year could have the unwanted

---

2. Alfred Chandler, in "Continental Bank Roundtable on Corporate Strategy in the '90s," *Journal of Applied Corporate Finance*, Vol. 6 No. 3 (Fall, 1993), p. 44.

3. Finance theory says that shareholders should be unwilling to place significant value on *corporate* diversification because they can achieve such diversification more cheaply on their own simply by diversifying their portfolio.

And the fact that unrelated businesses must be acquired at large premiums over their fair market value (which we like to describe as "charitable contributions to random passers by") tends to make corporate diversification a doubly losing strategy for the firm's shareholders.

effect of sharply raising future years' budgeted targets (as well as casting doubt on the integrity of the manager's forecasts).

But if the problems arising from budget negotiations were that obvious, then why didn't CEOs abandon the practice altogether and just give their division heads a fixed percentage of the divisional profits? After all, this system has reportedly served Warren Buffett well at a number of his companies.

As some economists and management experts have rightly pointed out, excessive reliance on divisional profit-sharing plans can discourage cooperation among divisions. Purely "objective" divisional performance measures have the potential not only to undermine attempts to exploit synergies among different business units (presumably the reason they are under the same corporate umbrella in the first place), they can even create internal conflicts that end up reducing overall firm value.

But another, more compelling explanation for the widespread use of negotiated budgets is that many top managements were content to tolerate, if not actually encourage, such counterproductive practices. For, besides making the life of division heads easier, the budgeting process also helped top management produce the smoothly rising EPS intended to satisfy shareholders. Thus, while division heads were "sandbagging" their estimates for headquarters, top managements were in some sense sandbagging their shareholders, managing investors' expectations while concealing the true profit potential of the business.

As Gordon Donaldson has argued, the understanding implicit in this management philosophy of the '60s and '70s was that a company's shareholders are only one of several important corporate constituencies whose interests must be served. Top managers saw their primary task not as *maximizing* shareholder value, but rather as achieving the *proper balance* among the interests of shareholders and those of other "stakeholders" such as employees, suppliers, and local communities.[4] In this view of the world, reporting steady increases in EPS was equivalent to giving shareholders their due. And, in fact, such a management approach worked reasonably well—at least as long as product markets were

relatively stable, and international competitors and corporate raiders remained dormant.

·······

THE CASE OF RJR NABISCO

In his last year as CEO of RJR Nabisco, Ross Johnson reportedly ordered John Greeniaus, the head of RJR's tobacco unit, to spend the excess profits of his division on additional advertising and promotion. Greeniaus later shared this information about the potential profitability of his unit with Henry Kravis of Kohlberg Kravis & Roberts, which reportedly played a major role in KKR's $25 billion bid for and eventual purchase of RJR Nabisco, the largest LBO to date.[5]

In the early 1980s, however, the deficiencies of the top-down, EPS-based system began to show in several ways. Strategically diversified conglomerates such as General Mills (which proudly called itself the "all-weather growth company"),[6] Northwest Industries, Beatrice Foods, and ITT saw their stock prices underperforming market averages even as the companies were producing steady increases in EPS. The operations of such diversified firms began to be outperformed by smaller, more specialized companies. And, as it became progressively more clear that large, centralized conglomerates were worth far less than the sum of their parts, corporate raiders launched the deconglomeration movement.

At the heart of the failure of the top-down, EPS-based control system was its refusal to empower divisional managers, to make them feel and act as if they were stewards of investor capital. One important consequence of this "lack of ownership" was that business units evaluated mainly on the basis of operating profits had little reason to be concerned with the level of investment required to achieve their profits. The primary incentive of operating managers was to achieve (moderate) growth in profits, which could be accomplished in two ways: (1) improve the efficiency of existing operations or (2) win more capital appropriations from headquarters. Because most corporate measurement systems did not hold corporate managers accountable for new capital, it did not take managers long to recognize that it was easier to "buy" additional operating profits with

---

4. See Gordon Donaldson, "The Corporate Restructuring of the 1980s and Its Import for the 1990s," *Journal of Applied Corporate Finance*, Vol. 6 No. 4 (Winter 1994).

5. Source: Brian Burrough and John Helyar, *Barbarians at the Gate* (Harper & Row, 1991), pp. 370-371.

6. See Gordon Donaldson, "Voluntary Restructuring: The Case of General Mills," *Journal of Applied Corporate Finance*, Vol. 4 No. 3 (Fall 1993).

capital expenditures—even if the investment did not promise anything like an acceptable rate of return[7]—than to wring out efficiencies with cutbacks.

This standard capital budgeting procedure led in turn to what might be called the "politicization" of corporate investment, a process in which persuasive and well-positioned business unit managers received too much capital while their less favored counterparts received too little. The top-down EPS system also tolerated the widespread practice of corporate cross-subsidization, in which the surplus cash flow of profitable divisions was wasted in futile efforts to shore up unpromising divisions or in diversifying acquisitions.[8] The result of this politicization of corporate decision-making was chronic overinvestment in some areas and underinvestment in others. In many cases, moreover, it was the potentially more profitable, but capital-starved business units that ended up being sold in LBOs to their own management teams, with the financial backing of outsiders like KKR and Clayton & Dubilier.

CORPORATE RAIDERS AND CAPITAL EFFICIENCY

As noted, the widespread corporate misallocation and waste of capital under the EPS-based system did not escape the attention of corporate raiders in the 1980s.[9] In making their own assessments of potential value, the raiders used a performance metric that was quite different from EPS. They were concerned primarily with companies' ability to generate cash flow (as opposed to earnings) and with their efficiency in using capital.

....
LESSONS FROM THE SAFEWAY LBO

Consider the following testimony from Peter Magowan, who was CEO of Safeway Stores both before and after the company's LBO by KKR in 1986:

"When Safeway was a public company, our profits grew at 20% per year for five years in a row, from 1981 to 1985...

We thought all the while that we were doing quite well. Our stock tripled during that period of time, we raised the dividend four years in a row, and 20% percent earnings growth seemed pretty darn good...

But we were still subjected to a hostile takeover [in 1986]—and deservedly so. We were not earning adequate rates of return on the capital we were investing to achieve that 20% growth. We were not realizing the values that were there for someone else to realize for our shareholders.... For this reason, and with hindsight, it now seems clear why outsiders could come in and see a way of buying our company for $4.2 billion—way above its then current market value—and improving it so it was worth $5.2 billion a few years later. And I think that's an important lesson for corporate America."[10]

In many cases, as takeover critics have argued, the push for capital efficiency led to cutbacks in corporate employment and investment. In the vast majority of such cases, however, "downsizing" was a value-adding strategy precisely because of the natural tendency of corporate management in mature industries to pursue growth at the expense of profitability, to overinvest in misguided attempts to maintain market share or, perhaps worse, to diversify into unrelated businesses.[11] This is why the vast majority of leveraged restructurings took place in industries with excess capacity—oil and gas, tires, paper, packaging, publishing, commodity chemicals, forest products, and retailing.

In an article published in this journal called "The Causes and Consequences of Hostile Takeovers,"[12] Harvard professor Amar Bhide compared the economic motives and consequences of 47 hostile takeovers of companies larger than $100 million attempted in 1985 and 1986 to those of a control group of 30 "friendly" takeovers in the same years. Whereas most of the friendly deals were designed to take advantage of vaguely defined "synergies" or to diversify the corporate "strategic" portfolio, the large majority of hostile deals were motivated by profits expected from "restructuring"—that is, from cutting

---

7. Just before KKR took over RJR, Ross Johnson reportedly approved a $2.8 billion dollar outlay for a state-of-the-art cookie manufacturing facility with a projected pre-tax rate of return of only 5%. (From Peter Waldman, "New RJR Chief Faces a Daunting Challenge at Debt-Heavy Firm," *Wall Street Journal*, March 14, 1989, p. A1:6).

8. The shareholder value destroyed by such unprofitable reinvestment of corporate cash flow has been described by Michael Jensen as the "agency costs of free cash flow." For the original formulation of this argument, see "The Agency Costs of Free Cash Flow: Corporate Finance and Takeovers," *American Economic Review* Vol. 76 No. 2, (May, 1986).

9. For estimates of the extent of the corporate misuse of capital and of the resulting gains from corprate control transactions, see Michael Jensen, "Corporate Control and the Politics of Finance," *Journal of Applied Corporate Finance*, Vol. 4 No. 2 (Summer, 1991).

10. Peter Magowan, "Continental Bank Roundtable on Performance Measurement and Management Incentives," *Journal of Applied Corporate Finance*, Vol. 4 No. 3, p.33.

11. See footnote 8.

12. Amar Bhide, "The Causes and Consequences of Hostile Takeovers," *Journal of Applied Corporate Finance*, Vol. 2 No. 2 (Summer 1989).

overhead, improving focus by selling unrelated businesses, and ending unprofitable reinvestment of corporate profits.

The targets of hostile and friendly deals were accordingly very different. Whereas the targets of friendly mergers tended to be single-industry firms with heavy insider ownership that had performed quite well (as measured by earnings growth, ROE, and stockholder returns), the targets of hostile deals were typically low-growth, poorly performing, and often highly diversified companies in which management had a negligible equity stake. (A *Fortune* magazine poll also ranked their managements as among the worst in their industries, as judged by their management peers.)

There were also notable differences between the *consequences* of friendly and hostile deals, although some differences were not as dramatic as they have been made out to be. Contrary to the claims of takeover critics, hostile deals did not typically lead to large cutbacks in investment or blue-collar employment.[13] And when they did—again, usually in consolidating industries with excess capacity—the cutbacks were roughly proportional to those made by other industry competitors not subjected to takeover. Those layoffs that did take place after hostile takeovers tended to be concentrated in corporate headquarters and not on the factory floor. And, as for the R & D issue, the targets of hostile takeovers didn't spend much on R & D to begin with—and this was also true of LBO firms (as we discuss later).

So, if they were not laying off rank-and-file workers and gutting investment and research programs in the drive to make a quick buck, how were corporate raiders—after paying large premiums over market and hefty fees to lawyers and investment bankers—paying the rent? The answer Bhide offers is that, besides making cutbacks in overhead and unprofitable corporate reinvestment, the raiders played a "limited, but significant arbitrage role" in buying large diversified conglomerates, dismantling them, and then selling the parts for a sum greater than the value of the conglomerate whole. Of the 81 businesses sold by the 47 targets of hostile offers in Bhide's sample, at least 78 had been previously acquired rather than developed from within. And roughly 75% of those divested operations were sold

off either to single-industry firms or to private investment groups in combination with operating management. Which brings us to the subject of leveraged buyouts, or LBOs.

THE RISE OF THE LBO: AN INTERIM STAGE IN THE PUSH FOR A NEW CORPORATE GOVERNANCE SYSTEM

Contrary to popular opinion, LBOs are one of the remarkable success stories of the 1980s. So impressive were the results of the first wave of LBOs that Harvard professor Michael Jensen was moved to write an article in 1989 for the *Harvard Business Review* entitled, "The Eclipse of the Public Corporation." There Jensen observed that LBO partnerships like KKR and Forstmann Little, which acquire and control companies across a broad range of industries, represent a "new form of organization"—one that competes directly with corporate conglomerates. With staffs of fewer than 50 professionals, LBO partnerships were said to provide essentially the same coordination and monitoring function performed by corporate headquarters staffs numbering, in some cases, in the thousands. As Jensen put it, "The LBO succeeded by substituting incentives held out by compensation and ownership plans for the direct monitoring and often centralized decision-making of the typical corporate bureaucracy."[14] For operating managers, in short, the LBO held out a "new deal": greater decision-making autonomy and ownership incentives in return for meeting more demanding performance targets.

The Important Differences

Let's look more closely at the differences between LBO firms and the way most public companies were run in the 1980s.

First of all, as newly private companies, LBO firms no longer had any motive for *reporting* higher EPS. Thus, LBOs effectively increased their *after-tax* cash flow by choosing accounting methods that would *minimize* reported earnings—and hence taxes paid—for a given level of pre-tax operating profits. Many public companies, when confronted with the same choice, would routinely choose accounting methods designed to boost reported

---

13. For macro data that confirm this finding about the 1980s in general, see Michael Jensen (1992), cited above.

14. Michael Jensen, "Active Investors, LBOs, and the Privatization of Bankruptcy," *Journal of Applied Corporate Finance*, Vol. 2 No. 1 (Summer 1988).

earnings, even if this resulted in higher taxes and hence lower after-tax cash flow.[15]

More important, where operating managers in many large U.S. companies tend to treat investor capital as a "free" good, a major concern of LBO firms was to produce sufficient operating cash flow to meet their high required interest and principal payments. In the average LBO of the 1980s, the debt-to-assets ratio increased from about 20% to 90%. Such heavy debt financing had the effect of making the cost of capital in LBO companies highly visible and, indeed, *contractually binding.* Failure to service debt could mean loss of operating managers' jobs (as well as their own equity investment); and it would almost certainly mean a reduction of the LBO partnership's financial (and reputational) capital.

The heavy use of debt financing also provided what amounted to an automatic internal monitoring-and-control system. That is, if problems were developing, top management would be forced by the pressure of the debt service to intervene quickly and decisively. By contrast, in a largely equity-financed firm, management could allow much of the equity cushion to be eaten away before taking the necessary corrective action.[16]

In addition to this explicit cost-of-capital target, operating managers were also provided—if not required to purchase—a significant equity stake. Such ownership was designed in part to encourage managers to resist the temptation, potentially strong in cases of high leverage, to produce "short-term" profits at the expense of the corporate future. For, even in those LBOs with exit strategies clearly defined at the outset, managers who are also significant owners have incentives to devote the optimal level of corporate capital—neither too much nor too little—to expenditures with longer-run payoffs such as advertising and plant maintenance. Regardless of how an LBO is eventually cashed out—whether by means of an IPO, a sale to another firm, or a recap involving another private investment group or management team—it is still true that the greater the level of *productive* investment undertaken by operating managers, the higher the value of their shares when traded in.

···

THE CASE OF DURACELL

Consider, for example, what Robert Kidder, CEO of Duracell, had to say about the firm's goals after it was purchased from Dart & Kraft by KKR in an LBO:

"The debt schedule is very effective in forcing management to attend to profitability in the near term. But, let me emphasize that another *important consideration—in some sense, more important than short-term cash flow—is carrying through on strategic commitments. There is a widespread public misconception that because you're an LBO, you have to do everything possible to generate short-term cash flow, and that LBOs thus simply represent a means of sacrificing future profit for immediate gain....*

Now, I don't mean to suggest that we don't do everything possible to reduce waste and cut costs. But, when I talk with Henry Kravis at lunch, we don't spend our time talking about cost reductions. We talk about how we're increasing the strategic value of the company—and by that I mean our long-term cash flow capability."[17]

In the average Fortune 1000 firm, as Jensen notes, the CEO's total compensation changes by less than $3 for every $1000 change in shareholder value. By comparison, the average operating head in an LBO firm in the '80s experienced a change of roughly $64 per $1000; and the entire operating management team owned about 20% of the equity, and thus earned close to $200 per $1000 change in value.[18] Moreover, the partners of the LBO firm itself (the KKRs of this world), which is the proper equivalent of a conglomerate CEO, controlled about 60% of the equity through their buyout funds.

Given such dramatic concentrations of ownership and improvements in the pay-for-performance correlation, researchers were not surprised to find major operating improvements in companies that were taken private through LBOs. There is now a large body of academic evidence on LBOs in the 1980s that attests to the following:[19]

- *shareholders earned premiums of 40% to 50% when selling their shares into LBOs;*
- *operating cash flow of LBOs increased by about 40%, on average, over periods ranging from two to four years after the buyout;*

---

15. Corporate managers persist in such EPS-boosting practices even in the face of academic evidence that the stock market rewards higher cash flow rather than reported earnings in cases—such as LIFO vs. FIFO inventory accounting and purchase vs. pooling accounting for acquisitions—where the two measures go in opposite directions.

16. For a demonstration of this point, see Jensen (1989), cited earlier.

17. "CEO Roundtable on Corporate Structure and Management Incentives," *Journal of Applied Corporate Finance,* Vol. 3 No. 3 (Fall 1990), pp. 8-9.

18. Jensen (1989).

19. For a review of research on LBOs, their governance changes, and their productivity effects, see Krishna Palepu, "Consequences of Leveraged Buyouts," *Journal of Financial Economics* 27, No. 1 (1990), 247-262.

- in cases where LBOs later went public or were sold to another company or investor group, the average firm value (that is, the market value of debt plus equity) increased by 235% (96%, when adjusted for general market movements) from two months prior to the buyout offer to the time of going public or sale (a holding period of three years, on average);
- there is little evidence in LBOs of a drop in employment levels or average wages of blue-collar workers;
- LBO firms were not doing much R & D to begin with; only about 10% of LBO firms were engaging in enough R & D before the LBO to report it separately in their financial statements;
- LBO boards, with typically eight or fewer members, represent about 60% of the equity, on average.

As the last finding suggests, however, it was not just better-designed performance measures and stronger ownership incentives that lay behind the success of LBOs. The LBO *governance* system is also fundamentally different from that of most public corporations. In fact, LBOs borrow several of the central governance features of venture capital firms.

Much as in venture capital firms like Kleiner Perkins, the boards of companies owned by LBO partnerships like KKR and Clayton & Dubilier are designed in large part to overcome many of the information problems facing boards of directors in public companies. The directors of a typical LBO don't merely represent the outside shareholders, they *are* the principal shareholders. Moreover, they have become the principal owners only after having participated in an intensive "due diligence" process intended to reveal the true profit potential of the business. And, as in the case of venture capital firms, the board members in LBOs also typically handle the corporate finance function, including negotiations with lenders and the investment banking community. If operating companies get into financial or operating difficulty, the board intervenes quickly, often appointing one of its members to step in as CEO until the crisis passes.

THE CASE OF THE BLACKSTONE GROUP

James Birle, General Partner of the Blackstone Group, comments as follows on the differences between the LBO governance process and that of most public companies:

"Unlike the boards of public companies, our board members come to the table already knowing a great deal about the operations and expected behavior of the businesses in various economic and competitive situations. This knowledge comes from the extensive due diligence process we have conducted just prior to the acquisitions. So we are able to determine when management has really gotten off the track far more quickly and confidently than most public company directors....

We [also] have a much tighter performance measurement system, by necessity, than most public companies I'm familiar with. The pressure to ensure that goals are being met is just far greater than that which exists in most public companies. At the same time, this sense of urgency does not prevent us from setting and pursuing long-term goals. Our goal at the Blackstone Group is maximizing shareholder value, and you can't command a high price for a business if all you've been doing is liquidating its assets and failing to invest in its future earnings power. And since management are also major equity holders in the company, we are confident that they are constantly attempting to balance short-term and long-term goals in creating value." [20]

What Went Wrong with the LBOs?

All this is not to suggest that the LBO movement was without flaws, or to deny that mistakes were made in structuring many of the deals. Beginning in 1989, there was a sharp increase in the number of defaults and bankruptcies of LBOs. Most of the problems, it turns out, came in the deals transacted in the latter half of the 1980s. Of the 41 LBOs with purchase prices of $100 million or more transacted between 1980 and 1984, only one defaulted on its debt. By contrast, of the 83 large deals done between 1985 and 1989, at least 26 defaulted and 18 went into bankruptcy. [21]

What went wrong with the later deals? Just as Jensen was the first economist to see the value-adding potential of LBOs, he was also the first to identify the source of the problems that were arising in the later transactions. Stated in brief, Jensen's analysis pointed to a "gross misalignment of incentives" between the dealmakers who promoted the transactions and the lenders and other investors who funded them. Such a "contracting failure" led to a

---

20. James Birle, "Continental Bank Roundtable on the Role of Corporate Boards in the 1990s," *Journal of Applied Corporate Finance*, Vol. 5 No. 3 (Fall 1992), pp. 68.

21. Steven Kaplan and Jeremy Stein, "The Evolution of Buyout Pricing and Financial Structure in the 1980s," *Journal of Applied Corporate Finance*, Vol. 6 No. 1 (Spring 1993).

concentration of overpriced, poorly structured deals in the second half of the '80s.[22]

Jensen's diagnosis was supported, moreover, by an important study by Steven Kaplan and Jeremy Stein demonstrating that (1) buyout prices as multiples of cash flow rose sharply in LBOs completed in the period 1986-1988, especially in junk-bond-financed transactions; (2) junk bonds displaced much of both the bank debt and the private subordinated debt in the later LBOs, thereby sharply raising the costs of reorganizing troubled companies; and (3) management and other interested parties, notably the dealmakers, put in less equity and took out more money up front in later deals.[23]

The Limitations of LBOs

A private market correction to the contracting problem noted by Jensen and others was already underway when regulators intervened heavily in the summer of 1989. There was already a general movement toward larger equity commitments, less debt, lower transaction prices, and lower upfront fees when S&L legislation (FIRREA) and HLT regulations created a downward spiral in high-yield bond prices (and, some would argue, in business activity in general). And much tightened oversight by bank regulators made it virtually impossible to reorganize troubled companies outside of Chapter 11 (by contrast, low-cost, expeditious private work-outs were a common event for the first wave of LBOs during the severe recession of 1981-82).[24]

As a consequence, LBOs and other HLTs underwent a sharp decline during the early 1990s. But, in the past few years, LBOs have begun to show signs of a resurgence. Nevertheless, even with the contracting problems of the late '80s largely corrected, there are still inherent limitations in the LBO form that are likely to ensure them at most a fairly specialized role in the U.S. economy.

First, of course, is their reliance on high leverage. The role of debt financing in LBOs limits their use primarily to mature industries with modest capital requirements, tangible assets, and highly stable cash flows. Although some steady-state service companies may prove suitable for LBOs, high-growth and high-tech companies will generally not. In the latter case, the expected costs of debt financing in the form of lost investment opportunities are just too large.[25]

The second limitation of LBOs stems from one of their principal benefits: the concentration of equity ownership. Concentration of ownership also means a concentration of risk-bearing. One of the main advantages of the public corporation is its efficiency in *spreading* risk among well-diversified investors. At some point, increasing the "firm-specific" risk borne by the management team becomes self-defeating because such managers will require sufficiently higher compensating rewards (in the form of stock or profit sharing) that there will be less left over for shareholders, even after considering the incentive benefits of such concentrated ownership.[26]

It is this heavy concentration of risk, not managerial shortsightedness, that explains why so many LBOs return to public ownership in five years or less. When they enter into an LBO, both owners and operating managers are betting on their ability to increase the value of the organization. But, in order to limit the scope of their bet and minimize their exposure to risks beyond their control, they typically have an exit or cash-out strategy. In his study of "The Staying Power of Leveraged Buyouts," Steven Kaplan reported that, as of early 1993, roughly half of the large LBOs ($100 million or more) of the 1980s had reverted to public ownership. Even so, some 90% of the 2,500 LBOs (large and small) transacted since the late 1970s still remain private; and, as Kaplan also reported, those LBOs that had gone public through IPOs retained two distinguishing features of the LBO

22. See the comments by Michael Jensen in "The Economic Consequences of High Leverage and Stock Market Pressures on Corporate Management: A Roundtable Discussion," *Journal of Applied Corporate Finance* Vol. 3 No. 2 (Summer 1990), pp. 8-9. For a more formal elaboration of this argument, see Michael Jensen, "Corporate Control and the Politics of Finance," *Journal of Applied Corporate Finance*, Vol. 4 No. 2 (Summer, 1991), pp. 25-27.

23. As reported in Kaplan and Stein (1993).

24. See Michael Jensen, "Corporate Control and the Politics of Finance," *Journal of Applied Corporate Finance*, Vol. 4 No. 2, pp. 27-29. As Jensen writes, "Such regulations...reduced the flexibility of lenders to work with highly leveraged companies who could not meet lending covenants or current debt service payments. These changes, coming on top of the departure of Drexel, the principal market maker, caused a sharp increase in defaults."

25. Although some observers have predicted an extension of the LBO form to high-growth, high-tech companies, the lower leverage and greater dispersion of equity that is best suited to such riskier companies will ultimately work to undermine the very sources of financial discipline that have helped to make LBOs so effective. For a discussion of corporate debt capacity that bears on this issue, see Michael Barclay, Clifford Smith, and Ross Watts, "The Determinants of Corporate Leverage and Dividend Policies," *Journal of Applied Corporate Finance*, Winter 1995.

26. See the article in this issue by Randy Beatty, "Management Incentives, Monitoring, and Risk-bearing in IPO Firms," which shows that riskier IPOs actually tend to have lower percentage ownership.

form: (1) considerably higher leverage (though below buyout levels) compared to that of their public competitors; and (2) significantly more concentrated equity ownership by insiders (over 40%, on average).[27]

EVA: A NEW FINANCIAL MODEL FOR PUBLIC COMPANIES

The accomplishments of the LBO movement have some important lessons for the structure and governance of public companies. For most large public companies, of course, it will not make sense to raise leverage ratios to 90%. Nor will it generally be cost-effective to provide significant stock ownership for most operating managers. In such cases, top management must design a performance measurement and reward system that simulates the feel and payoff of ownership. This is the principal aim of an EVA financial management system.

Like LBOs, but without the costs of high leverage or excessive risk-bearing, an EVA-based performance measurement system makes the cost of capital explicit. In its simplest form, EVA is net operating profit after taxes less a charge for the capital employed to produce those profits. The capital charge is the required, or minimum, rate of return necessary to compensate all the firm's investors, debtholders as well as shareholders, for the risk of the investment.[28]

To illustrate, a company with a 10% cost of capital that earns a 20% return on $100 million of net operating assets has an EVA of $10 million. This says the company is earning $10 million more in profit than is required to cover all costs, including the opportunity cost of tying up scarce capital on the balance sheet. In this sense, EVA combines operating efficiency and balance sheet management into one measure that can be understood by operating people.

For operating heads and top management alike, EVA holds out three principal ways of increasing shareholder value:

- First, increase the return derived from the assets already tied up in the business. Run the income statement more efficiently without investing any more capital on the balance sheet.
- Second, invest additional capital and aggressively build the business so long as the return earned exceeds the cost of that new capital. (Targets based on rates of return such as ROE or ROI, incidentally, can actually discourage this objective when divisions are earning well above their cost of capital, because taking on some EVA-increasing projects will lower their average return.)
- Third, stop investing in, and find ways to release capital from, activities that earn substandard returns. This means everything from turning working capital faster and speeding up cycle times to consolidating operations and selling assets worth more to others.

Besides making the cost of capital explicit, the EVA performance measure can also be designed to encourage tax-minimizing accounting choices and to incorporate a number of other adjustments intended to eliminate distortions of economic performance introduced by conventional accounting measures like earnings or ROE. For example, one notable shortcoming of GAAP accounting stems from its insistence that many corporate outlays with longer-term payoffs (like R & D or training) be fully expensed rather than capitalized and amortized over an appropriate period. While well-suited to creditors' concerns about liquidation values, such accounting conservatism can make financial statements unreliable as guides to going-concern values. More important, to the extent GAAP's conservatism is built into a company's performance measurement and compensation system, it can unduly shorten managers' planning horizon.

In setting up EVA systems, we sometimes advise companies to capitalize portions of their R&D, marketing, training, and even restructuring costs. In cases of other "strategic" investments with deferred payoffs, we have also developed a procedure for keeping such capital "off the books" (for internal

---

27. As Steven Kaplan has noted, there appear to be two distinct species of LBOs: (1) a "shock-therapy" variety, in which the LBO provides a vehicle for largely "one-time" improvements; and (2) a relatively permanent, "incentive-intensive" type, in which the company's investors and managers become convinced that the company is fundamentally more valuable as a private company than public. See Steven Kaplan, "The Staying Power of the Leveraged Buyouts," *Journal of Applied Corporate Finance*, Spring 1993. This article is a shorter, less technical, and partly updated version of another article with the same title published in the *Journal of Financial Economics* 29 (1991).

28. EVA is charged for capital at a rate that compensates investors for bearing the firm's explicit business risk. The assessment of business risk is based upon the

Capital Asset Pricing Model, which allows for a specific, market-based evaluation of risk for a company and its individual business units using the concept of "beta." In addition, the tax benefit of debt financing is factored into the cost of capital, but in such a way as to avoid the distortions that arise from mixing operating and financing decisions. To compute EVA, the operating profit for the company and for each of the units is charged for capital at a rate that blends the after-tax cost of debt and equity in the *target* proportions each would plan to employ rather than the actual mix each actually uses year-by-year. Moreover, operating leases are capitalized and considered a form of debt capital for this purpose. As a result, new investment opportunities are neither penalized nor subsidized by the specific forms of financing employed.

evaluation purposes) and then gradually readmitting it into the manager's internal capital acount to reflect the expected payoffs over time. As these examples are meant to suggest, EVA can be used to encourage a more far-sighted corporate investment policy than traditional financial measures based upon GAAP accounting principles.

In defining and refining its EVA measure, Stern Stewart has identified over 120 shortcomings in conventional GAAP accounting. In addition to GAAP's inability to handle R&D and other corporate investments, we have addressed performance measurement problems associated with standard accounting treatments of the following: inventory costing and valuation; depreciation; revenue recognition; the writing-off of bad debts; mandated investments in safety and environmental compliance; pension and post-retirement medical expense; valuation of contingent liabilities and hedges; transfer pricing and overhead allocations; captive finance and insurance companies; joint ventures and start-ups; and special issues of taxation, inflation, and currency translation. For most of these accounting issues, we have crafted a series of cases to illustrate the performance measurement problem, and devised a variety of practical methods to modify reported accounting results in order to improve the accuracy with which EVA measures real economic income.

Of course, no one company is likely to trigger all 120 measurement issues. In most cases, we find it necessary to address only some 15 to 25 key issues in detail—and as few as five or ten key adjustments are actually made in practice. We recommend that adjustments to the definition of EVA be made only in those cases that pass four tests:

- Is it likely to have a material impact on EVA?
- Can the managers influence the outcome?
- Can the operating people readily grasp it?
- Is the required information relatively easy to track or derive?

For any one company, then, the definition of EVA that is implemented is highly customized with the aim of striking a practical balance between simplicity and precision.

To make the measure more user-friendly, we have also developed a management tool called "EVA Drivers" that enables management to trace EVA through the income statement and balance sheet to key operating and strategic levers available to them in managing their business. This framework has proven to be quite useful in focusing management's attention, diagnosing performance problems, benchmarking with peers, and enhancing planning. More generally, it has helped people up and down the line to appreciate the role they have to play in improving value. It can also help guard against an excessive preoccupation with improving individual operational metrics to the detriment of overall performance. For example, a drive to increase productivity—or, say, a single-minded obsession with winning the Malcolm Baldridge Award—could lead to unwarranted capital spending or to shifts in product mix that result in less EVA and value, not more. In the end, management must be held accountable for delivering value, not improving metrics.[29]

THE EVA FINANCIAL MANAGEMENT SYSTEM

As we suggested at the beginning of this article, the real success of business today depends not on having a well-thought-out, far-reaching strategy, but rather on re-engineering a company's business systems to respond more effectively to the new business environment of continuous change. Our contention at Stern Stewart is that just as this information revolution has created a need for business process re-engineering, it has also precipitated a need to re-engineer the corporate *financial management system.*

What do we mean by a financial management system? A financial management system consists of all those financial policies, procedures, methods, and measures that guide a company's operations and its strategy. It has to do with how companies address such questions as: What are our overall corporate financial goals and how do we communicate them, both within the company and to the investment community? How do we evaluate business plans when they come up for review? How do we allocate resources—everything from the purchase of an individual piece of equipment, to the acquisition of an entire company, to opportunities for downsizing and restructuring? How do we evaluate ongoing operating performance? Last but not least, how do we pay our people, what is our corporate reward system?

---

29. Nevertheless, our research suggests a remarkably strong correlation between a company's EVA performance, its shareholder value added (or "MVA"), and its standing in *Fortune's* *Most Admired* survey, a ranking based upon an assessment of such criteria as customer responsiveness, innovation, time-to-market, and management quality. See Bennett Stewart, "EVA: Fact and Fantasy," *Journal of Applied Corporate Finance*, Vol. 7 No. 2 (Summer 1994).

Many companies these days have ended up with a needlessly complicated and, in many respects, hopelessly obsolete financial management system. For example, most companies use discounted cash flow analysis for capital budgeting evaluations. But, when it comes to other purposes such as setting goals and communicating with investors, the same companies tend to reach for accounting proxies—measures like earnings, earnings per share, EPS growth, profit margins, ROE, and the like. To the extent this is true, it means there is already a "disconnect" between the cash-flow-based capital budget and accounting-based corporate goals. To make matters worse, the bonuses for operating people, as we noted earlier, tend to be structured around achieving some annually negotiated profit figure.

This widespread corporate practice of using different financial measures for different corporate functions creates inconsistency, and thus considerable confusion, in the management process. And, given all the different, often conflicting, measures of performance, it is understandable that corporate operating people tend to throw their hands in the air and say, "So, what are you really trying to get me to do here? What is the real financial mission of our company?"

With EVA, all principal facets of the financial management process are tied to just one measure, making the overall system far easier to administer and understand. That is, although the process of coming up with the right definition of EVA for any given firm is often complicated and time-consuming, the measure itself, once established, becomes the focal point of a simpler, more integrated overall financial management system—one that can serve to unite all the varied interests and functions within a large corporation.

Why is it so important to have only one measure? As we noted earlier, the natural inclination of operating managers in large public companies is to get their hands on more capital in order to spend and grow the empire. This tendency in turn leads to an overtly political internal competition for capital—one in which different performance measures are used to gain approval for pet projects. And because of this tendency toward empire-building, top management typically feels compelled to intervene excessively—not in day-to-day decision making, but in capital spending decisions. Why? Because they don't trust the financial management system to guide their operating managers to make the right decisions. There's no real accountability built into the system, there's no real incentive for operating heads to choose only those investment projects that will increase value.

....

THE CASE OF BRIGGS AND STRATTON

At the annual shareholders' meeting in 1991, Chairman Fred Stratton of Briggs & Stratton noted that the company's stock was up 70% from the previous year, having outperformed the S&P 500 by about 40%. Stratton attributed the company's success in large part to the company's newly adopted "performance measurement and compensation system" based on EVA.

"Part of our problem in the early 1980s," comments president and chief operating officer John Shiely, *"was an antiquated functional 'top-down' structure. Nobody other than the CEO and the president was being held accountable for the profitability of our various lines. Under Chairman Fred Stratton's direction, we developed a plan to totally revamp the organization into discrete operating divisions. While the initial move was painful, the positive results were almost immediate. By pushing operating responsibility, including capital decisions, down to the level where they could be effectively managed, we accomplished a dramatic improvement in earnings and cash flow. Each of our seven new divisions now has its own functional management, resources, and capital. Each must develop very detailed strategic business unit plans. And each has an EVA incentive based on value created by the division.*

Before moving to an EVA system, the company took pride in making almost all components in-house. We now buy premium engines, at significantly lower cost, from outside sources. Molded plastics and other components, once made in small batches in-house, now flow from suppliers in huge quantities. As a result, operating profits have risen while the amount of capital required to generate them has fallen sharply.

EVA is the internal measure management can decentralize throughout the company and use as the basis for a completely integrated financial management system. It allows all key management decisions to be clearly modelled, monitored, communicated, and rewarded according to how much value they add to shareholders' investment. Whether reviewing a capital budgeting project, valuing an acquisition, considering strategic plan alternatives, assessing performance, or determining bonuses, the goal of

> *Although the process of coming up with the right definition of EVA for any given firm is often complicated and time-consuming, the measure itself, once established, becomes the focal point of a simpler, more integrated financial management system—one that can serve to unite all the varied interests and functions within a large corporation.*

increasing EVA over time offers a clear financial mission for management and a means of improving accountability and incentives. In this sense, it offers a new model of internal corporate governance.

EVA AND THE CORPORATE REWARD SYSTEM

Incentive compensation is the anchor of the EVA financial management system. The term "incentive compensation" is not quite right, however, for in practice too much emphasis gets placed on the word "compensation" and not enough on the word "incentive." The proper objective is to make managers behave as if they were owners. Owners manage with a sense of urgency in the short term but pursue a vision for the long term. They welcome change rather than resisting it. Above all else, they personally identify with the successes and the failures of the enterprise.

Extending an ownership interest is also the best way to motivate managers in the information age. As the pace of change increases and the world becomes ever less predictable, line managers need more general as opposed to specific measures of performance to which they will be held accountable. They need more leeway to respond to changes in the environment. They need a broader and longer-range mandate to motivate and guide them. Maximizing shareholder value is the one goal that remains constant, even as the specific means to achieve it are subject to dramatic and unpredictable shifts.

Making managers into owners should not be undertaken as an "add-on" to current incentive compensation methods. Rather, it should replace them. In place of the traditional short-term bonus linked to budget and ordinary stock option grants, the EVA ownership plan employs two simple, distinct elements: (1) a cash bonus plan that simulates ownership; and (2) a leveraged stock option (LSO) plan that makes ownership real.

The EVA Bonus Plan: Simulating Ownership

The cash bonus plan simulates ownership primarily by tying bonuses to *improvements* in EVA

over time. Paying for improvements in rather than absolute levels of EVA is designed mainly to solve the problem of "unequal endowments." This way, managers of businesses with sharply negative EVA can be given a strong incentive to engineer a turnaround—and those managers of businesses already producing large positive EVA do not receive a windfall simply for showing up.

Besides leveling the playing field for managers inheriting different circumstances, bonuses tied to improvements in rather than levels of EVA are also "self-financing" in the following sense: to the extent that a company's current stock tends to reflect current levels of EVA, it is only *changes* in current levels of EVA that are likely to be correlated with changes in stock price.[30] And, to the extent the managers of a given company succeed in increasing a company's EVA and so earn higher bonus awards for themselves, those higher bonuses are more than paid for by the increase in shareholder value that tends to accompany increases in EVA.

As with a true ownership stake, EVA bonuses are not capped. They are potentially unlimited (on the downside as well as upside), depending entirely on managerial performance. But, to guard against the possibility of short-term "gaming" of the system, we have devised a "bonus bank" concept that works as follows: Annual bonus awards are not paid out in full, but instead are banked forward and held "at risk," with full payout contingent on continued successful performance. Each year's bonus award is carried forward from the prior year and a fraction—for example, one third—of that total is paid out, with the remainder banked into the next year.

Thus, in a good year, a manager is rewarded—much like a shareholder who receives cash dividends and capital appreciation—with an increase in both the cash bonus paid out and in the bonus bank carried forward. But, in a poor year—again, much like a shareholder—the penalty is a shrunken cash distribution and a depletion in the bank balance that must be recouped before a full cash bonus distribution is again possible. Because the bonus paid in any one year is an accumulation of the bonuses earned over time, the distinction be-

---

30. Our own research indicates that the changes in companies' EVAs over a five-year period account for nearly 50% of the changes in their market value added, or MVAs, over that same time frame. (MVA, which is a measure of the shareholder value added by management, is roughly equal to the difference between the total market value and the book value of the firm's equity.) By comparison, growth in

sales explained just 10% of the MVA changes, growth in earnings-per-share about 15% to 20%, and return on equity only 35%. For a description of this research, see Bennett Stewart, "Announcing the Stern Stewart Performance 1,000," *Journal of Applied Corporate Finance* Vol. 3 No. 2 (Summer 1990).

tween a long-term and a short-term bonus plan becomes meaningless.

When combined with such a bonus bank system, EVA incentive plans tied to continuous improvement also help to break the counterproductive link between bonuses and budgets that we described earlier. EVA targets are automatically reset from one year to the next by formula, not annual negotiation. For example, if EVA should decline for whatever reason, management will suffer a reduced, possibly negative bonus in that year. In the following year, however, the minimal standard of performance for the next year's bonus will be set somewhat lower—again, by a pre-set formula. This automatic lowering of expectations is designed to help companies retain and motivate good managers through bad times by giving them a renewed opportunity to earn a decent bonus if they can reverse the company's fortune. At the same time, however, it avoids the problem—inherent in the stock option "repricing" practices of so many public companies—of rewarding managers handsomely when the stock drops sharply and then simply returns to current levels.

In combination with a bonus bank, then, the use of objective formulas to reset targets eliminates the problems of "sandbagging" on budgets and encourages collaborative, long-range planning. Instead of wasting time managing the expectations of their supervisors, managers are motivated to propose and execute aggressive business plans. Moreover, because it compensates the end of creating value rather than the means of getting there, the EVA bonus plan is entirely consistent with the movement to decentralize and empower.

In sum, the banking of bonuses tied to continuous improvements in EVA helps companies to smooth cyclical bumps and grinds, extends managers' time horizons, and encourages good performers accumulating equity in their bank accounts to stay and poor performers running up deficits to go. In so doing, the EVA bonus bank functions as both a long-term and short-term plan at one and the same time.

Leveraged Stock Options: Making Ownership Real

The annual EVA cash bonus is intended to simulate an owner's stake. In many cases, however, it will often be valuable to supplement the bonus plan with actual stock ownership by management. Pursuit of that goal, however, runs headlong into this fundamental contradiction: How can managers with limited financial resources be made into significant owners without unfairly diluting the current shareholders? Showering them with stock options or restricted stock is apt to be quite expensive for the shareholders, notwithstanding the incentive for the managers. And asking the managers to buy lots of stock is apt to be excessively risky for them.

One approach we recommend to resolve this dilemma is to encourage (or require) managers to purchase common equity in the form of special leveraged stock options (LSOs). Unlike ordinary options, these are initially in-the-money and not at-the-money, are bought and not granted, and project the exercise price to rise at a rate that sets aside a minimal acceptable return for the shareholders before management participates.

Although managers' purchase of LSOs could be funded by them as a one-time investment, we typically recommend that managers be allowed to buy them only with a portion of their EVA bonuses. Besides providing even more deferred compensation, this practice helps ensure that only those managers who have added value in their own operations are allowed to participate in the success of the entire enterprise.

To illustrate how an LSO operates, consider a company with a current common share price of $10. The initial exercise price on the LSO is set at a 10% discount from the current stock price, or $9, making the option worth $1 right out of the gate. But instead of just handing the LSOs to management, managers are required to purchase them for the $1 discount, and that money is put at risk. Another difference between LSOs and regular options is that the exercise price is projected to increase at a rate that approximates the cost of capital (less a discount for undiversifiable risk and illiquidity)—let's say 10% per annum. In this case, over a five-year period (and ignoring compounding for simplicity), the exercise price will rise 50% above the current $9 level to $13.50. In sum, management pays $1 today for an option to purchase the company's stock (currently worth $10) for $13.50 five years down the road.

Only if the company's equity value grows at a rate faster than the exercise price will management come out ahead. Indeed, if the exercise price rises at a rate equal to the cost of capital (less the dividend yield), then the LSOs wll provide exactly the same incentives as an EVA bonus plan. It rewards management for generating a spread between the company's rate of return on capital and the cost of that capital (as reflected by the rate of increase in the exercise price) times the capital employed by management to purchase the shares.

Perhaps a better comparison, however, is between the incentives held out by LSOs and those provided by leveraged buyouts. LSOs can be seen as putting management in the position of participating in an LBO, but without requiring an actual LBO of the company. By virtue of their being purchased 10% in the money, LSOs effectively replicate the 90% debt and 10% equity that characterized the structure of the LBOs of this past decade. Companies ranging from Briggs & Stratton, Centura Bank, CSX, Fletcher Challenge (the largest industrial company in New Zealand), R.P Scherer, and Varity have adopted LSO plans.

At bottom, then, LSOs (and LBOs, as we have seen) also boil down to EVA, to the idea that management should participate only in those returns in excess of a company's required rate of return. But while conceptually identical to an EVA bonus plan, LSOs are likely to be an even more powerful motivator because they amplify the risks and rewards for management. Any improvement in EVA that investors think will be sustained is capitalized into the value of the shares; for example, a company with a cost of capital of 10% that increases its EVA by $1 million will see its value appreciate by $10 million. For managers holding the LSOs, such capitalized increases in value are themselves further leveraged 10 to 1, thus creating $100 of added managerial wealth for each $1 improvement in EVA. This leveraging effect makes LSOs a potent way to get management to concentrate on building EVA over the long haul.

BACK TO BRIGGS & STRATTON

Having tasted success with their initial EVA bonus plan, management's appetite was whetted for taking more risk in return for the prospect of an even greater return. In August 1993, the board approved a revised Stock Incentive Plan *"to reward executives based on their ability to continuously improve the amount of EVA earned on behalf of shareholders."* Under the new plan, the company's annual stock option grants were replaced with an equivalent increase in target EVA bonus awards, but with the requirement that one half of actual bonuses earned each year would automatically be used to purchase leveraged stock options (LSOs) at a cost equal to 10% of the company's prevailing stock price.

The net effect was to increase the cash portion of the EVA bonus, and to increase significantly management's interest in upside stock performance, but in exchange for taking more risk. In particular, LSOs are purchased only if earned (whereas before options were granted to management each year as a matter of course), and the LSOs will come into the money only after a significant appreciation of the stock price.

Investors reacted favorably to this restructuring of incentive pay. From a price of $65 a share at the close of the 1993 fiscal year (June 30), B & S's shares rose to $85 over a period of just several months as the market began to appreciate the powerful new incentives for management represented by the plan.

In sum, the EVA ownership plan replaces the traditional short-term bonus linked to budget and ordinary stock option grants with two components: (1) a cash bonus plan that simulates ownership; and (2) a leveraged stock option plan that confers actual ownership. The cash bonus plan simulates ownership by tying bonuses to sustained improvements in EVA over time, with a large portion of awarded bonuses held in escrow and subject to loss to ensure that improvements are permanent. The LSO plan corrects the deficiencies of normal stock option plans in two ways: the leverage factor allows managers to purchase significantly more stock for a given amount of dollars (thus replicating an LBO's effect on ownership); and a steadily rising exercise price ensures that managers win only if shareholders do.

IN CLOSING

An EVA financial management system represents a way to institutionalize the running of a business in accordance with basic microeconomic and corporate finance principles. When properly implemented, it is a closed-loop system of decision-making, accountability, and incentives—one that has the potential to make the entire organization and not just the CEO responsible for the successes and failures of the enterprise. It can result in a self-regulated and self-motivated system of "internal" governance.

As a concept, EVA starts simple, but in practice it can be made as comprehensive as necessary to accommodate management's needs and preferences. EVA is most effective, however, when it is more than just a performance measure. At its best, EVA serves as the centerpiece of a completely integrated framework of financial management and incentive compensation. When used in that manner, the experience of a lengthening list of adopting companies throughout the world strongly supports the notion that an EVA system can refocus energies and redirect resources to create sustainable value—for companies, customers, employees, shareholders, and for management.

The anchor of the EVA financial management system is a powerful incentive compensation plan that consists of two parts: (1) a cash bonus plan tied to continuous improvement in EVA, in which a significant portion of the awarded bonuses are carried forward in a "bonus bank" and held at risk; and (2) a leveraged stock option (LSO) plan, in which managers use part of their cash bonus awards to make highly leveraged purchases of company stock.

Such an EVA reward system holds out major benefits over more conventional compensation plans:
■ Rewarding managers for continuous improvement in (rather than levels of) EVA means that new managers neither receive windfalls for inheriting already profitable divisions, nor are they penalized for stepping into turnaround situations.
■ In contrast to compensation plans that continually revise performance criteria to provide "competitive" compensation levels *each year*, the EVA bonus plan has a "long-term memory" in the form of a bonus bank that ensures that only consistent, sustainable increases in value are rewarded.
■ EVA bonuses are tied to a performance measure that is highly correlated with shareholder value, thus aligning managers' with shareholders' interests.
■ The strength of the correlation between changes in EVA and in shareholder value also means that the EVA compensation system is effectively "self-financing"; that is, managers win big only when shareholders are winning—and managers are truly penalized when shareholders lose.

Proper internal governance is certainly no guarantee of success, and it is no substitute for leadership, entrepreneurism, and hustle. But an EVA financial management and incentive system can help. We like to say that EVA works like the proverbial Trojan Horse: What is wheeled in appears to be an innocuous new financial management and incentive program, but what jumps out is a new culture that is right for times of rapid change and decentralized decision-making. By increasing accountability, strengthening incentives, facilitating decentralized decision-making, establishing a common language and integrated framework, and fostering a culture that prizes building value above all else, it significantly improves the chances of winning. That's all any shareholder can reasonably expect from governance in today's business environment of continuous change.

TOTAL COMPENSATION STRATEGY

by Stephen F. O'Byrne,
Stern Stewart & Co.

"Total compensation shall represent competitive levels of compensation...

Performance-related pay shall be a significant component of total compensation

---

placing a substantial portion of an executive officer's compensation at risk."

These statements from a recent Compensation Committee Report aptly express the dominant total compensation strategy of public companies today. This strategy is widely accepted as the most reasonable way to limit retention risk and control shareholder cost while still providing a strong incentive for management to maximize shareholder value.

The commitment to competitive compensation levels limits retention risk—that is, the risk that key managers will leave the firm for a better offer elsewhere—because total compensation opportunities are not allowed to fall below competitive levels. The same commitment also limits shareholder cost because total compensation opportunities are not allowed to rise above competitive levels. The commitment to maintaining a substantial proportion of total compensation "at risk"—that is, in the form of bonuses, stock options, and other incentive compensation—is thought to provide a strong incentive to maximize shareholder value—an incentive comparable to that of an owner with a substantial proportion of his wealth in company stock.

This article argues that the dominant total compensation strategy is fundamentally flawed and can never provide incentives comparable to those of an owner/entrepreneur who holds a large proportion of his wealth in company stock. The critical flaw in the strategy is that, even though a very large proportion of *the current year's* compensation may be "at risk," the commitment to maintaining competitive levels of compensation in all future years effectively ensures that a large proportion of the executive's *wealth* is not at risk. Incentives that approach entrepreneurial levels can be achieved only by total compensation strategies that make *the value of future compensation opportunities sensitive to current performance.*

But, strategies that provide strong wealth incentives will always lead to greater retention risk for poor performance or higher shareholder cost for superior performance than the dominant total compensation strategy. And this means that managers and directors who seek stronger wealth incentives must be prepared to make difficult trade-offs between stronger wealth incentives, greater retention risk, and higher potential cost to the shareholders. To help managers and directors in evaluating these trade-offs, this paper presents a new analytical framework—one that I call *total wealth incentive analysis*. This analytical framework can be used both to reveal the hidden and ill-considered trade-offs that typically underlie the dominant total compensation strategy, and to design compensation plans that provide strong, sustainable, and cost-effective wealth incentives.

TABLE 1		Competitive Percentile	Market Pay Mix	Target Pay Mix
Salary	$300	50	40%	30%
Target Bonus	$200		20%	20%
Target Cash Compensation	$500	60		
Target Option Value	$500		40%	50%
Target Total Compensation	$1,000	75		

THE DOMINANT TOTAL COMPENSATION STRATEGY

The foundation of the dominant total compensation strategy is the concept of annual recalibration to a competitive position target. The company adopts a competitive position target—say, the 75th percentile total compensation—and each year recalibrates its salaries, bonus plan targets, and number of option grant shares to provide a total compensation opportunity at the targeted percentile. Base salary and cash compensation can be targeted at the same percentile as total compensation, or, more commonly, at lower percentiles in order to provide higher leverage and a mix of pay that is more attractive to management and the directors than the market mix.

The company's total compensation strategy can be (and in fact often is) summarized in a table (much like Table 1) that expresses the company's target compensation percentiles and target pay mix. For example, in the case illustrated in Table 1, the firm has targeted the 50th percentile for salary, the 60th percentile for cash compensation, and the 75th percentile for total compensation. These targeted percentiles provide a targeted *pay mix* of 30% salary, 20% bonus, and 50% stock options. Despite the fact that these targets put 70% of total compensation at risk, the practice of annual recalibration, as I show below, leaves the company with a weak wealth incentive.

Recalibrating the total compensation program each year to maintain the target competitive percentiles requires adjusting the bonus plan performance target to a new level that represents current expected performance, and changing the number of option shares granted to reflect the current stock price. If, for example, the target operating profit for the first year is $10 million, but performance deteriorates to a level where the expected operating profit for the second year is only $5 million, the target operating profit for the second year must be reduced to $5

million to ensure that the target bonus is the expected value of the bonus. Similarly, if the initial option grant required to provide an expected value of $500K was 20,000 shares based on a stock price of $50 (and a Black-Scholes value of 50%, or $25 per option), and the stock price declines in the second year to $25, the number of option shares granted must be increased to 40,000 to provide an option grant with an expected value of $500K (because new at-the-money options are now worth only $12.50 per share). If performance improves instead of deteriorates, the target operating profit must be increased and the number of option shares reduced to maintain the expected value of the bonus and option grant at the targeted competitive level.

These annual adjustments required to maintain the target competitive position have two important consequences. The first, and intended, consequence is that the expected value of the total compensation opportunity remains at a competitive level. The second, unintended but unavoidable, consequence is that *poor performance is rewarded* by an increase in management's percentage interest in operating profit and stock price appreciation, while *superior performance is penalized* by a reduction in management's percentage interest in operating profit and stock price appreciation. When performance deteriorates and the target operating profit is reduced from $10 million to $5 million, the target bonus share of operating profit is increased from 2% ($200K/$10 million) to 4% ($200K/$5 million). When the stock price declines from $50 to $25, the number of option shares granted is increased from 20,000 to 40,000. When performance improves and the target operating profit is increased to $20 million, the target bonus share of operating profit is reduced from 2% ($200K/$10 million) to 1% ($200K/$20 million). When the stock price rises from $50 to $100, the number of option shares granted is reduced from 20,000 to 10,000.

As I demonstrate later, the "performance penalty" inherent in annual recalibration to competitive

The critical flaw in the dominant total compensation strategy is that, even though a very large proportion of the current year's compensation may be "at risk," the commitment to maintaining competitive levels of compensation in all future years effectively ensures that a large proportion of the executive's wealth is not at risk.

compensation levels makes it impossible for the dominant total compensation strategy to provide incentives that approach those of an owner who holds a large portion of his wealth in the form of a *fixed* percentage interest in the dividends and stock price appreciation of the company. It can also lead, as the compensation history of John Akers at IBM illustrates, to huge discrepancies between management compensation and shareholder gain. In Akers' first year as CEO, the IBM board gave him an option on 19,000 shares exercisable at $145. In subsequent years, as the stock price declined, they gave him larger and larger option share grants to offset the decline in the stock price and maintain the value of his annual compensation package at a competitive level. In 1990, the board gave him an option on 96,000 shares exercisable at $97. By the end of 1992, the board had put him in a position where he would have realized an option gain of $17.6 million just for getting the stock price back to the $145 level at which he received his first option grant as CEO!

THE OBJECTIVES OF EXECUTIVE COMPENSATION

The dominant total compensation strategy is, as any total compensation strategy must be if it seeks to maximize the wealth of current shareholders, an attempt to balance four conflicting objectives:

■ *Alignment:* giving management an incentive to choose strategies and investments that maximize shareholder value;

■ *Leverage:* giving management sufficient incentive compensation to motivate them to work long hours, take risks, and make unpleasant decisions, such as closing a plant or laying off staff, to maximize shareholder value;

■ *Retention:* giving managers sufficient total compensation to retain them, particularly during periods of poor performance due to market and industry factors; and

■ *Shareholder cost:* limiting the cost of management compensation to levels that will maximize the wealth of current shareholders.

Each of these objectives is critical to the success of total compensation strategy, but every total compensation strategy must make trade-offs between leverage, retention risk, and shareholder cost. A strategy that relies on large stock grants can achieve substantial leverage with minimal retention risk, but only by accepting higher shareholder cost

than a strategy that relies on stock option grants. A strategy that relies on large stock option grants can achieve substantial leverage with limited shareholder cost, but only by accepting greater retention risk than a strategy that relies on stock grants. A strategy that relies on a high proportion of guaranteed compensation can achieve limited retention risk and limited shareholder cost, but only by accepting modest leverage.

Most companies and directors believe that the dominant total compensation strategy provides a reasonable balance between the four conflicting objectives of executive compensation. Indeed, the rationale for the dominant corporate compensation practice can be summarized as follows:

■ It provides alignment because bonus and stock compensation is tied to operating and market measures of shareholder value;

■ It provides substantial leverage because a large proportion of pay is at risk and gives the executive incentives comparable to those of an owner who holds a large proportion of his wealth in company stock;

■ It provides retention because it gives the executive competitive compensation opportunities every year; and

■ It controls shareholder cost because compensation opportunities are limited to a given percentile of the competitive pay distribution.

TOTAL WEALTH LEVERAGE

To understand why having a large proportion of the current year's pay at risk does not provide incentives comparable to those of an owner who holds a similar proportion of his wealth in company stock, we need to focus on the value of management *wealth*, as opposed to current *income*, and its relationship to shareholder wealth. Management wealth is the value of its investment capital plus the value of its human capital. In other words, management wealth is the sum of (1) the value of current stock and option holdings; and (2) the present value of expected future compensation, including (a) salary, (b) bonus, (c) long-term incentive grants, and (d) pension.

Managers, like shareholders, try to maximize their wealth, not their current income. The true measure of the wealth *incentive* provided by a compensation plan is the sensitivity of management wealth to changes in shareholder wealth. More specifically, for any given change in shareholder wealth, it is the ratio of the percentage change in management wealth to the percentage change in shareholder wealth. To illustrate, if a 10% change in shareholder wealth changes management wealth by 10%, management's *total wealth leverage* is 1.0. This is the total wealth leverage of a "pure" entrepreneur—one whose entire wealth is held in company stock; in such case, any percentage change in shareholder wealth causes the same percentage change in the entrepreneur's wealth.

If a 10% change in shareholder wealth causes a 7% change in management wealth, then management's total wealth leverage is 0.7. This would be the wealth leverage of a manager whose wealth consisted of 70% company stock and 30% the present value of future salary and benefits. This would also be the wealth leverage of an investor who holds a portfolio of 70% stock and 30% bonds in the same company. In this case, wealth leverage is easy to calculate. If the investor holds $700,000 of equity and $300,000 of debt, a 10% increase in shareholder wealth increases the value of the investor's equity by 10% to $770,000 and the value of the investor's portfolio by 7% to $1,070,000. The investor's total wealth leverage is 0.7 (= 7%/10%), which is equal to equity leverage (1.0) times the proportion of the investor's wealth held as equity, 1.0 × 70%.

The total wealth leverage of a typical executive, however, is more difficult to calculate because the executive holds a more complicated portfolio—one that includes stock options, future bonus payments, and future option grants. Before I illustrate the use of wealth analysis in total compensation design, it will be helpful to lay some groundwork by first explaining:
■ the need to measure wealth leverage on a present value basis,
■ the leverage of options, and
■ the importance of expected future compensation in management wealth.

The Important Distinction Between Present and Future Values

Total wealth leverage must be measured on a present value basis since wealth is a risk-adjusted present value that reflects different discount rates for future stock and option gains as well as for future salary, bonus, and long-term incentive payouts. "Future value" wealth changes do not provide a meaningful measure of leverage.

To illustrate this point, suppose that an executive holds a ten-year option exercisable at the current market price of $50, and that the stock price increases by 10% over five years to $55. The value of the option at the time of grant is $31.82 (using the Black-Scholes model with a volatility of .350, a dividend yield of zero, and a risk-free interest rate of 8%), but declines by 17% to $26.33 at the end of five years. These two price changes over the five-year period imply that the option has a future value leverage of –1.7 since the 10% change in shareholder wealth reduces the option value by 17%. That is, option values appear to move in the opposite direction of shareholder value.

This paradoxical result arises because the future value leverage calculation ignores the fact that the option has greater risk, and hence a higher expected rate of return, than the stock. To calculate a meaningful measure of leverage, we need to compare the change in the present value of the option with the change in the present value of the stock. The present value of the $55 future stock price, assuming a 14% expected stock return, is $28.57, or 43% less than the initial $50 market price. The present value of the option, based on a 16.4% expected option return (from the Black-Scholes model), is $12.31, or 61% less than its initial value of $31.82.

This set of calculations reveals that the option's leverage is in fact a positive 1.4 (not a negative 1.7) since the percentage change in the present value of the option, –61%, is 1.4 times the percentage change in the value of the stock, –43%. This kind of present value analysis, unlike the future value analysis, confirms our intuitive sense that the option is more, not less, leveraged than the stock.

The Wealth Leverage Provided by Stock Options

The leverage of an option differs from the leverage of the stock in two basic ways. The leverage of an option can be much greater than 1.0 (and never less than 1.0), while the leverage of the stock is always 1.0. The leverage of the option also changes, unlike the leverage of the stock, as the stock price changes and also as the option comes closer to expiration. The leverage of an option declines as the option comes into the money and increases as the option falls out of the money and as the option comes closer to expiration. Table 2 shows the leverage of several different options for

The "performance penalty" inherent in annual recalibration to competitive compensation levels makes it impossible for the dominant total compensation strategy to provide incentives that approach those of an owner who holds a large portion of his wealth in the form of company stock.

TABLE 2	Exercise Price	Market Price	Option Term	Option Leverage
	$50	$50	10	1.5
	$50	$50	5	2.0
	$50	$50	1	4.2
	$50	$40	1	5.7
	$50	$25	1	10.0

a company with an average volatility (.35) and dividend yield (3%).

The higher leverage of options plays a critical role in designing strong total wealth incentives because it makes it possible to design a total compensation program that offsets the effect of base salary (which has zero leverage) and provides total wealth leverage that equals or exceeds that of an entrepreneur. For example, if 30% of the executive's total wealth is the present value of future salary, but the remaining 70% is held in options with a leverage of 1.45, total wealth leverage will be 1.02 (= .7 × 1.45 + .3 × 0).

Incorporating the Present Value of Future Compensation

The present value of expected future compensation can be a very large component of management wealth. It includes the present value of total compensation for the executive's expected job tenure plus the present value of the executive's future pension. Assuming a 5% growth in competitive compensation levels (and a risk-free rate of 8%), the present value of ten future years of competitive total compensation is more than 8 times the value of current total compensation. Adding the value of a pension equal to 50% of cash compensation increases the present value of expected future compensation to more than 10 times the value of current total compensation.

The size of expected future compensation is important because the recalibration feature of the dominant total compensation strategy makes expected future compensation completely independent of current performance. That is, the wealth leverage of the present value of expected future compensation is zero. And, when the present value of expected future compensation is 10 times the value of current total compensation and the company's total compensation strategy makes the value of expected future compensation totally independent of current performance, total wealth leverage will be very small even when current total compensation is highly sensitive to changes in shareholder wealth. For example, even if the leverage of current total compensation were designed to be 1.0, with annual recalibration *total wealth leverage* would be only 0.09 because current total compensation represents only 1/11, or 9%, of total wealth.

And this problem affects managers nearing retirement as well as those with longer time horizons. For, although the present value of total compensation for the executive's expected job tenure diminishes as she approaches retirement, the present value of the executive's pension increases. The present value of a pension equal to 50% of cash compensation can still be five times the value of current total compensation when an executive is close to retirement.

This basic analysis of the mix of management wealth and the leverage of options is helpful in understanding the fundamental flaw in the dominant total compensation strategy. But it is not powerful enough to guide the development of a new total compensation strategy. For that purpose, we need the ability to simulate the impact of *all* the key elements of total compensation strategy on total wealth leverage as well as their impact on retention risk and shareholder cost.

TOTAL WEALTH INCENTIVE ANALYSIS

To assess the leverage, retention risk, and shareholder cost implications of a total compensation program, we need to simulate the future payouts of the total compensation program across a set of future performance scenarios that reflect the range, variability, and probability of the company's stock price and operating performance and then calculate total wealth leverage as well as measures of retention risk and shareholder cost. In practice, we can do this by creating a Monte Carlo simulation of 100 (or more) five-year future performance scenarios and then simulating the five-year payouts

TABLE 3	Percentile of Future Shareholder Wealth	5th Year Shareholder Wealth	Percent Change in Shareholder Wealth	PV of Total Wealth	Percent Change in Management Wealth	Total Wealth Leverage
	30	$49		$3,050		
	50	$79	59%	$3,790	24%	0.41
	70	$123	57%	$4,670	23%	0.41

under the total compensation program for each scenario. The Monte Carlo simulations of future market value and operating performance are derived from—and thus are consistent with—the underlying assumptions of option pricing theory and discounted cash flow valuation.

For a company with a publicly traded stock, the future performance simulations are based on the current stock price, the historical volatility of shareholder return, the expected level of improvement in EVA® (that is, profit in excess of the cost of capital) reflected in the current stock price, and the historical volatility of year-to-year changes in EVA. For a private company or a business unit of a public company, performance simulations are based on the estimated market value of the company or business unit, the historical volatility of peer company shareholder returns, the level of the expected improvement in EVA that is reflected in the estimated market value, and the historical volatility of changes in EVA.

We use the future performance scenarios to simulate the future payouts under the total compensation program based on the actual bonus plan design and the specific provisions and grant guidelines of the stock option plan. We use the compensation simulations to measure *total wealth leverage* as well as *future retention risk* and *shareholder cost*. Total wealth leverage is based on a present value analysis using discount rates that reflect the risk of each element of the total compensation program. In some cases, especially where the expected job tenure of the management team is relatively short, our calculation of total wealth is based only on the present value of five-year total compensation. In other cases—for example, where the expected job tenure of the management team is much longer than five years and the company provides generous retirement benefits—our calculation of total wealth includes the present value of expected future compensation beyond five years as well as the present value of retirement benefits.

In either case, we measure *total wealth leverage* at each quintile or decile of the 100 future performance scenarios by calculating *the ratio of the percentage change in management wealth to the percentage change in shareholder wealth*. We measure future *retention risk* by calculating the expected value of total compensation at the end of the fifth year (based again on the actual bonus plan design and the specific provisions and grant guidelines of the stock option plan) and computing the *shortfall, if any, between expected and competitive compensation*. We measure *shareholder cost* by calculating *five-year total compensation* including salary, bonus, and long-term incentive payouts.

The Implications of the Dominant Total Compensation Strategy

These simulations allow us to assess the long-term implications of the dominant total compensation strategy. Let's assume, to begin, that the expected job tenure of the management team is relatively short and, hence, that the present value of five-year total compensation is a reasonable proxy for management wealth. Table 3 shows the total wealth leverage for the dominant total compensation strategy with a 30%/20%/50% mix of salary, bonus, and stock option value:

As shown in Table 3, the dominant total compensation strategy with 70% of pay "at risk" does not provide a total wealth incentive comparable to that of an owner who holds 70% of his total wealth in company stock. Under the most favorable assumptions, it provides a total wealth incentive comparable to that of an owner who holds only 40% of his wealth in company stock.

And if we lengthen the managerial time horizon, the plan provides even weaker wealth incentives. When we include the present value of expected future compensation for years 6-10 in the calculation of total wealth, the total wealth incentive provided by the same total compensation strategy (with 70% of

Managers, like shareholders, try to maximize their wealth, not their current income. The true measure of the wealth *incentive* provided by a compensation plan is the sensitivity of management wealth to changes in shareholder wealth.

TABLE 4

Percentile of Future Shareholder Wealth	5th Year Shareholder Wealth	Percent Change in Shareholder Wealth	PV of Total Wealth	Percent Change in Management Wealth	Total Wealth Leverage
30	$49		$5,770		
50	$79	59%	$6,510	13%	0.21
70	$123	57%	$7,390	14%	0.24

TABLE 5

Percentile of Future Shareholder Wealth	5th Year Shareholder Wealth	Percent Change in Shareholder Wealth	PV of Total Wealth	Percent Change in Management Wealth	Total Wealth Leverage
30	$49		$5,120		
50	$79	59%	$7,100	37%	0.62
70	$123	57%	$9,860	41%	0.72

TABLE 6

Percentile of Future Shareholder Wealth	5th Year Shareholder Wealth	Percent Change in Shareholder Wealth	PV of Total Wealth	Percent Change in Management Wealth	Total Wealth Leverage
30	$49		$4,550		
50	$79	59%	$6,890	51%	0.86
70	$123	57%	$10,880	58%	1.02

pay nominally "at risk") provides a wealth incentive comparable to that of an owner who holds only 20% of his total wealth in company stock (see Table 4).

Designing Entrepreneurial Incentives

To create a total wealth incentive that approaches entrepreneurial incentives, total compensation strategy must be based on policies that make a substantial proportion of management wealth sensitive to current performance. These policies include *front-loaded* option grants, *fixed-share* option grant guidelines, and formula bonus plans.

As shown in Table 5, substituting fixed-share annual stock option grants for the conventional fixed-dollar, variable-share grants provides a total wealth incentive that is comparable to that of an owner who holds 70% of his total wealth in company stock. Thus, just taking this step alone has the effect of tripling the proportion of management's wealth that is truly variable or "at risk."

This stronger incentive, however, comes with higher retention risk for poor performance and higher shareholder cost for superior performance. Retention risk increases for poor performance be-

cause the expected value of the fixed-share options will decline below competitive option grant values as the stock price declines. If a 24,500 share grant provides a competitive option grant value when the stock price is $50, it will only provide half of the competitive option grant value when the stock price is $25. Shareholder cost for superior performance will also increase because management will still get a 24,500 share grant when the stock is $100 or $200.

To demonstrate how an entrepreneurial incentive can be designed and to highlight the retention and shareholder cost implications of a strong wealth incentive, it will be useful to take our program redesign one step further and show the implications of a front-loaded option grant of 245,000 shares (in effect, granting 10 years' worth of options at the beginning of the manager's tenure). As shown in Table 6, a total compensation strategy based on a formula-driven, fixed-target EVA bonus and a front-loaded option grant can provide a total wealth incentive comparable to that of an entrepreneur whose total wealth varies in exact proportion to changes in shareholder value.

But what are the retention and shareholder cost implications of providing such an entrepreneurial

TABLE 7	Percentile of Future Shareholder Wealth	5th Year Shareholder Wealth	Year 6 Market Total Comp	Year 6 Expected Total Comp	Percentage Difference
	10	$28	$1,000	$610	−39%
	30	$49	$1,000	$830	−17%
	50	$79	$1,000	$1,260	+26%
	70	$123	$1,000	$2,030	+103%
	90	$208	$1,000	$3,610	+261%

TABLE 8	Percentile of Future Shareholder Wealth	5th Year Shareholder Wealth	5 Year Total Comp (A)	5 Year Total Comp (B)	Percentage Difference
	10	$28	$2,200	$1,800	−18%
	30	$49	$3,300	$2,700	−18%
	50	$79	$4,600	$7,700	+57%
	70	$123	$6,700	$18,100	+170%
	90	$208	$10,700	$38,200	+257%

incentive? If we assume that the front-loaded option grant vests pro-rata under this program, the expected value of total compensation in the sixth year is the sum of base salary, the target bonus, and expected value of the option shares vesting in the sixth year. And, as shown in Table 7, there are substantial differences between competitive total compensation and the expected value of the executive's total compensation in the sixth year. In fact, if the firm performs very poorly, and the stock price falls to $28 after five years, there will be an almost 40% difference between competitive levels and managers' expected total compensation.

Moreover, if we use the five-year sum of base salary and bonus payouts plus the spread on outstanding option grants as a measure of the total shareholder cost of the total compensation program, this alternative compensation strategy (column "B" in Table 8) has significantly higher shareholder cost than the dominant total compensation strategy (column "A" in Table 8). The higher cost will be incurred, however, when the shareholders are best able to afford it—when their shares have appreciated significantly.

As these comparisons of future retention risk and shareholder cost clearly show, there is no "free lunch" in total compensation strategy. The entrepreneurial leverage provided by the front-loaded option grant and EVA bonus plan implies both greater retention risk for poor performance and higher shareholder cost for average and superior performance. While future retention risk can be reduced by increasing the size of the initial option grant, an increase in the size of the option grant will increase the shareholder cost of the total compensation program. Such difficult trade-offs are unavoidable despite the illusions fostered by the dominant total compensation strategy. The real issue is how to make the trade-offs wisely—that is, in such a way that they will maximize the wealth of current shareholders.

A NEW APPROACH TO TOTAL COMPENSATION STRATEGY

The real issues in total compensation strategy are not competitive position targets and total compensation mix. The real issues are:
- What are the wealth incentives created by the current/proposed program?
- What is a desirable wealth incentive?
- How should a stronger wealth incentive be "financed?"
  - Through greater retention risk?
  - Through higher shareholder cost?

We have already explained the analysis necessary to address the first issue, so let's now turn to the second and third.

To create a total wealth incentive that approaches entrepreneurial incentives, total compensation strategy must be based on policies that make a substantial proportion of management wealth sensitive to current performance. These policies include *front-loaded* option grants, *fixed-share* option grant guidelines, and formula bonus plans.

In an ideal world, the determination of the optimal wealth incentive would be based on the empirical relationship between wealth incentive and shareholder return. This would identify the point at which the incremental cost of a stronger wealth incentive exceeds the incremental increase in shareholder wealth.

Unfortunately, there is no systematic research on this relationship, in large part because few companies publicly disclose their policies for adjusting performance targets and option grant levels. In the real world, decisions about optimal wealth incentives still require thoughtful director judgment about the expected effects of stronger incentives on management performance. While many directors are convinced that entrepreneurial leverage has a dramatic impact on management performance, others—particularly those with small stockholdings—remain skeptical that stronger incentives will make management work harder or smarter.

While there is no controlled statistical study that proves that entrepreneurial leverage has a dramatic impact on management performance, there is relevant evidence for these uncertain directors to consider. One important piece of evidence are the internal studies of chain restaurant companies that operate both company-owned and franchised units. These studies suggest that wealth incentives that approach or exceed entrepreneurial levels have a very significant effect on performance. More specifically, the studies show that franchised units, which provide wealth incentives at entrepreneurial levels, significantly outperform company-owned units with total compensation strategies tied to competitive pay objectives.

A second important piece of evidence in thinking about desirable wealth incentives is the wealth incentives agreed to in circumstances where there is substantial "arm's-length" bargaining over the terms of compensation. One important case of arm's-length bargaining occurs when outside directors and significant shareholders play the lead role in negotiating a long-term compensation contract for a new CEO hired from outside the company. In these situations, we often find compensation contracts that provide wealth incentives that approach or exceed entrepreneurial leverage. Consider, for example, Michael Eisner's original contract at Walt Disney. As I discussed in an earlier article in this journal ("What Pay for Performance Looks Like: The Case of Michael Eisner," Summer 1992), Eisner was given a contract at the outset of his tenure that gave him a large front-loaded stock option grant and a bonus equal to 2% of Disney's profits after shareholders had been provided with a 9% return on equity. The total wealth leverage provided by the contract was 1.4. And, during a period in which the market value of Disney increased by $12 billion, Eisner received some $200 million.

Another instructive case of arm's-length bargaining is the determination of the general partner's compensation in private placement investment funds, such as leveraged buyout funds and venture capital funds. The general partner's compensation typically consists of a 1% management fee, based on the total assets invested by the limited partners, plus a 20% interest in the ultimate profits from the fund. In addition, the limited partners normally demand that the general partner make an equity investment in the fund. (KKR, for example, typically committed about 1-4% of the equity in the funds for which it served as general partner.) The management fee is essentially the general partner's "base salary" since it is based on the limited partners' initial investments rather than the current value of their investments. When we model the general partner's total wealth leverage, we find that it slightly exceeds entrepreneurial leverage even though the present value of the management fee represents 25% of the general partner's fund related wealth (including the value of a 20% profit interest and a 4% equity interest).

Making the Trade-Off

Once the directors come to a consensus about a desirable wealth incentive, they must decide what combination of greater retention risk and greater shareholder cost should be used to "finance" it. Unfortunately, it is difficult to generalize about the optimal way to "finance" a stronger wealth incentive. The optimal trade-off between retention risk and shareholder cost depends on the difficulty of replacing the management team and the shareholders' willingness to accept higher retention risk to limit the cost of management compensation.

To illustrate the process of making such trade-offs, consider the following case. The shareholders of a closely held corporation wanted to strengthen management incentives to ensure the continued success of the company as the original shareholders retired from active participation in management. The original shareholders had had very strong wealth incentives during the period they had built up the company, and they were eager to give the new management team a total compensation program that would make them feel, and act, like entrepreneurs. But entrepreneurial incentives were not the only objective of the shareholders. They didn't want to "give the company away" and felt that a 5% option interest was the most they should reasonably have to sacrifice to motivate the management team. They were also concerned about the volatility of the business and the retention risks of forcing management to make a big bet on the current value of the company.

Given these concerns, their initial preference was for a total compensation program that provided annual fixed-share option grants, building up to a 5% management team option interest over five years, plus an annual EVA bonus with a target opportunity of 30% of salary. To their surprise, however, our analysis showed that the total wealth incentives provided by this program were only half the level of entrepreneurial incentives. This finding created a difficult dilemma for the original shareholders. They could provide the new management team with a far weaker incentive than the one that had motivated them to build the business, but that was at odds with their basic objective of motivating management to replicate and extend their own success. Or they could increase the incentive by providing a much larger cash bonus opportunity, but they were afraid that management would then lose its focus on maximizing *long-term* shareholder value. Or they could reduce management's guaranteed compensation to enhance the relative impact of the stock option grants, but they immediately decided that that would alienate, not motivate, their management team. Or, finally, they could increase their "investment" in management compensation by agreeing to surrender more than a 5% option interest in the company.

After much thought, analysis, and discussion, they decided that the last alternative was the best.

CONCLUSIONS

The dominant total compensation strategy has a very strong appeal for "fiduciary directors" with small stockholdings because it minimizes the risk of highly visible failure. Total compensation strategy can fail to maximize shareholders' wealth because it fails to provide a strong wealth incentive, but highly visible failures (the great concern of the fiduciary director) almost always involve retention or shareholder cost. When key managers leave to join a competitor, it is hard to convince skeptical shareholders that the company's total compensation strategy was based on a reasonable decision to accept more retention risk to limit shareholder cost. When managers receive very large incentive compensation payouts, it is hard to convince a skeptical public that strong incentives played a key role in the company's success. But failures of leverage (or alignment) are rarely attributed to total compensation strategy; they are lost in a multitude of other explanations for poor performance—bad strategy, tough competition, product development failures, adverse market trends, etc.

Directors who are large shareholders are far more aware that inadequate wealth incentives can be a much greater threat to shareholder value than management turnover or large incentive compensation payouts. The successful history of LBOs and the entrepreneurs who leave big companies to start small ones is largely a history of inadequate wealth incentives. It is time for all directors to abandon the illusions of the dominant compensation strategy and face up to the difficult decisions required to create the strong wealth incentives needed to maximize shareholder value.

JOEL STERN: Good afternoon, and welcome to this roundtable on EVA and corporate performance measurement.

As many of you know, last September *Fortune* magazine ran a cover story called "The Key to Creating Wealth for Shareholders." The subject of that article was a measure of corporate performance called Economic Value Added, or EVA, that Bennett Stewart and I have refined and popularized over almost 20 years of working together.

The financial concepts underlying EVA were not, of course, invented at Stern Stewart & Co. Economists since Adam Smith have been telling us that the social mission of the individual business enterprise is to maximize its value to its owners. And financial economists such as Nobel laureate Merton Miller have translated Smith's prescription into the goal of maximizing Net Present Value, or NPV. Our aim at Stern Stewart has been to decompose NPV, which is fundamentally a multi-year or long-term capital budgeting tool, into annual (or even monthly) installments called EVA that can be used to evaluate the periodic performance of corporate managers and their businesses.

The purpose of this roundtable will be to discuss EVA in relation to more conventional measures of corporate performance—to examine its strengths, the advantages it confers over traditional EPS and ROE measurement systems, as well as any potential drawbacks (though I feel obliged to warn you from the start that we have found very few). We will consider EVA not only as a measure of operating performance, but also as the basis for the entire range of corporate financial management functions, from capital budgeting and the setting of corporate goals to shareholder communication and, my favorite subject, management incentive compensation.

To discuss these matters with us, we have assembled a first-rate panel that includes three corporate CFOs (each of whom is now using EVA in their companies), three representatives from the investment and legal community, and two distinguished financial academics. I will now introduce them in alphabetical order.

■ **CARM ADIMANDO** is Vice President-Finance and Administration and Treasurer of Pitney Bowes. As the company's chief financial officer, Carm is responsible for all treasury and pension-related functions, corporate accounting and strategic financial planning, corporate facilities and administrative activities, and investor relations.

■ **ROBERT BUTLER** is Senior Vice President and Chief Financial Officer of International Paper, and has served in that capacity since joining the company in 1988. Prior to that, Bob served as group executive president and CFO of National Broadcasting Corporation—at a time when NBC was a subsidiary of RCA.

■ **SUSAN MALLEY** is the Chief Investment Officer for Citicorp Investment Services. As such she is responsible for economic, equity, and fixed income research, market allocation and investment strategy, bond trading, and product development. Dr. Malley holds a Ph.D. in finance from New York University's Stern Business School, and was previously a professor at Fordham University's Business School.

■ **S. ABRAHAM RAVID** is Associate Professor of Management at Rutgers University. He received his Ph.D. in Business Economics from Cornell University, has taught at NYU, UCLA, and Columbia, and published over 20 academic papers in top finance and economics journals. He has done consulting work for the U.S. Congress, the World Bank, and consumer organizations. Before becoming an academic, Professor Ravid was a professional journalist with the Israeli National Radio network.

■ **RICHARD SHEPRO** is a Partner of the Chicago law firm Mayer, Brown & Platt. He advises clients on matters related to acquisitions and other complex business transactions. In 1990, he published a book with Leo Herzl entitled *Bidders & Targets: Mergers and Acquisitions in the U.S.* Rick also holds the position of Lecturer at the University of Chicago Law School.

■ **BENNETT STEWART** is my colleague and founding partner of Stern Stewart & Co. Bennett has been a constant source of inspiration (as well as occasional vexation) throughout the almost twenty years that we have worked together, and I am confident that both aspects of our relationship will reveal themselves during the next two hours.

■ **R. HUTCHINGS VERNON** is a Vice President at Alex Brown Investment Management. Prior to joining Alex Brown in 1993, he previously held portfolio management and research positions at T. Rowe Price Associates, Legg Mason, and Wachovia Bank. In the name of full disclosure, I should tell you that Hutch is a big fan of EVA.

■ **JOSEPH WILLETT** is Senior Vice President and Chief Financial Officer of Merrill Lynch & Co., Inc. Prior to joining Merrill Lynch in 1982, Joe served seven years in the Chase Financial Policy Division of the Chase Manhattan Bank. And since I happened to have been President of the Financial Policy group at the time, I want to extend an especially warm greeting to Joe, and thank him for joining us.

■ **JEROLD ZIMMERMAN** is Professor of Accounting at the University of Rochester's Simon School of Business. He is also the founding co-editor of the *Journal of Accounting and Economics*, a distinguished publication produced at the University of Rochester. Jerry has been among the four or five superstars in accounting research over the last 15 to 20 years.

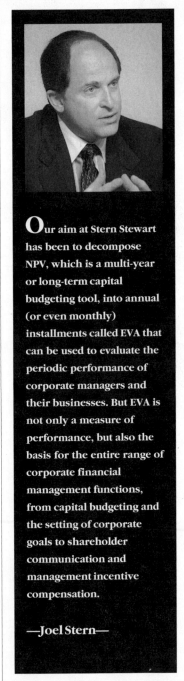

EVA and Management Incentives

STERN: I'd like to begin by discussing briefly why it is that an EVA-based incentive system makes managers behave as if they were owners of the enterprise. In most current corporate reward systems, executive pay is so dominated by the "fixed" elements of the total pay package—that is, salary and benefits—that managers behave more like lenders to the firm than the representatives of the shareholders they are supposed to be. By increasing the proportion of the "variable" element of managerial pay—bonuses, stock, and stock options—and by tying that variable pay to a more reliable proxy for shareholder value, an EVA incentive plan can go a long way toward aligning the interests of managers and shareholders.

As our friend Michael Jensen stated the issue in the title of a *Harvard Business Review* article several years ago, "It's Not How Much You Pay, But How." Jensen was so pessimistic about the ability of public companies to solve the manager-shareholder conflict—a conflict he referred to as "the agency costs of outside equity"—that he wrote another *HBR* article in 1989 called "The Eclipse of the Public Corporation." And although we continue to believe that Jensen and his collaborator Bill Meckling will eventually earn a Nobel Prize for their theory of agency costs, our aim at Stern Stewart is to eliminate—or at least to reduce significantly—the agency problem that Jensen and Meckling have identified at the core of the large public corporation. The alignment of managerial and shareholder interests is precisely what an EVA system is designed to accomplish.

But, before I begin telling you what EVA is, let me first attempt to correct a general misconception. The mission of the corporation is not to maximize its market value, as economists like to say, but rather its "market value added," or what we at Stern Stewart call MVA. Although this is a bit of an oversimplification, MVA is essentially the difference between a company's current market value, as determined by its stock price, and its "economic book value." A company's economic book value can be thought of as the amount of capital that shareholders (and, in the technically more correct version of EVA, lenders and all the other capital providers) have committed to the firm throughout its existence, including earnings that have been retained within the business.

Now, all this is not quite as simple as it sounds. Calculating a firm's economic book value, in particular, requires a number of adjustments that I will just mention briefly. At Stern Stewart, for example, we do not use pooling accounting for acquisitions; all acquisitions are treated as purchases—that is, as if they involved outlays of cash. Further unlike the accountants, we do not write off the goodwill that arises from purchase acquisitions of companies for amounts greater than their book value. That goodwill stays on the balance sheet more or less indefinitely, unless there is a real decline of economic value. As an example of another adjustment to conventional accounting statements, we also add back the balance sheet provision for deferred taxes to book equity, because it represents a reserve of cash on which the firm is expected to earn an adequate return. And there are a variety of other adjustments that can be made to get a better estimate of how much investor capital is really tied up in a firm.

To illustrate the importance of this distinction between market value and MVA, consider the case of General Motors. At the end of 1988, the company had a total market value of equity of $25 billion and an economic book value of roughly $45 billion. That is, the company had invested $45 billion of shareholder funds to produce an enterprise worth only $25 billion. GM thus had an MVA of *negative* $20 billion!

Interestingly, Merck also had a market equity value of $25 billion at the end of 1988. But because Merck's economic book value value was only $5 billion (even after adding back a considerable amount of already expensed R & D into the equity base, as our adjustments call for), the company had an MVA of positive $20 billion. So, although Merck and GM had almost the same market value at the end of 1988, Merck's management had succeeded in creating $20 billion of shareholder value while GM's had destroyed roughly the same amount.

To repeat what I said earlier, then, the corporate mission is not to maximize market value—this can be accomplished, as the case of GM illustrates, simply by retaining a large fraction of your earnings and raising more capital from outsiders—but rather to maximize the *difference* between a firm's market value and outside capital contributions. MVA, I should also point out, is the basis for our corporate ranking system known as the Stern Stewart Performance 1,000, which *Fortune* featured in an issue this past December.

Now, how does a company increase its MVA? The short answer is, by increasing its economic value added, or EVA. EVA is the *internal* measure of year-to-year corporate operating performance that best reflects the success of companies in adding value to their shareholders' investment. As such, EVA is strongly related to both the level of MVA at any given time and to changes in MVA over time. EVA is the "residual income" left over from operating profits after the cost of capital has been subtracted. So, for example, a firm

with a 10% cost of capital that earns $20 million on $100 million of net assets would have an EVA of $10 million.

To the extent a company's EVA is greater than zero, the firm is creating value for its shareholders. As I mentioned earlier, EVA is a kind of annual installment of the multi-year Net Present Value (NPV) that is calculated by using the standard discounted cash flow (or DCF) capital budgeting technique. Like NPV, EVA measures the degree to which a firm is successful in earning rates of return that exceed its cost of capital. But, as my colleague Bennett Stewart and I hope to convince you, EVA is a far better all-purpose corporate tool than NPV or DCF, even though both methods properly applied give you the same answer over an extended period of time.

We have done a number of studies to see which measures of performance are most closely linked *not* with market value, but with market value added—this *premium* value that's being created by management. Measures like earnings, earnings per share, and earnings growth all have some trivial relationship to MVA. When you bring in the balance sheet as well as the income statement—with measures such as ROE and return on net assets, or RONA—the significance of the relationship improves a great deal. But the correlation is not anywhere near as strong as what happens when you use EVA. And one reason for the greater strength of that correlation is that EVA, unlike ROE or RONA, takes into account the amount as well as the quality of corporate investment, corrects for accounting distortions in GAAP income statements and balance sheets, and specifies a minimum or required rate of return that must be earned on capital employed. To have a *positive* EVA, your rate of return on capital or net assets *must* exceed the required rate of return.

I'd like to describe very briefly what happens when you use EVA as a measurement device instead of more conventional measures. A senior manager recently asked me, "Why can't I use just RONA itself as a basis for evaluating and rewarding my people?" I said, "You shouldn't do that, for two reasons. One, if a company or a division is currently earning substandard returns, managers can increase RONA simply by taking projects with higher, but still inadequate returns. In this case, you would actually be rewarding managers for reducing shareholder value and further reducing MVA."

At the other extreme, consider a company with a 12% cost of capital that earns 25% after tax. In such cases, managers might be discouraged from taking on *all* projects below 25% because that will lower their *average* RONA. For that reason, the firm could be passing up value-adding investment opportunities.

Neither of these distortions of corporate investment incentives occurs under an EVA framework. In an EVA system, you improve EVA as long as you take on new projects where the rate of return on net assets exceeds the threshold.

In fact, there are three different ways to increase EVA. The first, as just mentioned, is to grow the business by taking on new investments that promise to earn more than the cost of capital. The second way to improve EVA is by not growing the business, but improving efficiency and so increasing returns on existing capital. And the third way is by getting rid of those parts of your business that offer no promise for improvement. EVA encourages managers to engage in a periodic culling of their businesses, discouraging them from wasting more time and money on clear losers.

Conventional corporate reward systems often do not encourage managers to take such steps. By making the lion's share of managerial compensation take the form of wages and wage-related items, such compensation plans lead managers to maximize not EVA or shareholder value, but rather their number of "Hay points." The way you do that is to maximize the *size* of your operation.

Now, the question is: To what extent can we change this kind of behavior that encourages size or empire-building at the expense of profitability? You will not succeed in changing behavior simply by changing corporate performance objectives *without also changing the compensation scheme*. If you set the performance objective with EVA over here, and you set the incentive compensation on some other basis over there, all your people will bow down to the performance objective and then march off in whatever direction the incentive structure calls for.

So, what do you need to do? Without going into great detail at this point, let me just say that there are four properties for any successful incentive compensation system. If you don't have these four properties, your plan won't work.

First, you need objectivity, not subjectivity. Most corporate bonus plans set targets based on negotiations between senior people and their juniors. The result is that the juniors have a tremendous incentive to "low ball" their budgets—because their bonus depends just on beating the budget (though not by too much, because that casts doubt on their credibility in setting the budget in the first place). Instead of stimulating managers to stretch—to expand the size of the pie, if you will—negotiated budgets reward managers for their success in carving out a larger share of the existing pie for themselves, often at the expense of the shareholders.

The second essential quality of an effective comp plan is simplicity. Incentive compensation should be carried down into the organization at least as far as the level of middle management, and many of our clients are extending it to all salaried employees. And the farther down you go, in my opinion, the more dramatic and durable the benefits seem to be.

Third, the plan has got to be significant. That means that the bonus potentials that come from improving EVA have to be large enough to affect people's behavior.

Fourth, the plan must be honored; it must not be subject to *ex post* adjustments. This means that if the board of directors and senior management find some employees doing *very* well and then *very, very* well, they must resist the inclination to pull the rug out from underneath them and change the rules. We have to permit people to do very well, *provided* the shareholders are also doing very well.

There are also three other distinctive features of a Stern Stewart incentive compensation program. One is that there are no caps on the upside. The more EVA people produce, the greater their reward, with no limitation on the size of the bonus awards.

At the same time, however, our system has a hold-back or bonus bank feature. To illustrate, when bonus plans are based on *improvements in* EVA as opposed to absolute EVA, we typically hold hostage as much as two-thirds of declared bonuses tied to EVA. And managers will lose the two-thirds held hostage if they don't at least maintain the level of performance that caused the declaration of the bonus in the first place.

The consequence of this bonus bank feature is to lengthen the managerial decision-making horizon beyond one year. It's very important to think of this as an ongoing cycle of value creation with one-third payable now, two-thirds later. For a successful manager under this plan, each new year brings steadily increasing payouts, new declarations, and new hold-backs. And if you do the calculations the way we do them, it takes you about six years to get 90% of your bonus declarations fully paid out.

We also have an unusual stock option program. Without going into too much detail, managers are asked to purchase stock options with a part of each year's bonus payments. What makes these options unusual is that they have an exercise price that is adjusted each year for the level of the broad stock market or, if management chooses, an industry group of the firm's primary competitors. If the S&P 500 or industry composite goes up by 10% in a given year, then the exercise price goes up by 10%. This way, shareholders have to get their rewards *before* the managers participate in any gains.

But consider also what happens if the market or industry goes down, even while the firm continues to churn out positive EVA. In those circumstances, the EVA bonuses can be used to buy options at a lower price, thus insulating high-performance operating managers from adverse industry or market events beyond their control. Take the case of our host company, Johnson & Johnson. If J & J's stock price drops because of exogenous factors such as announcements about impending health care reform, those people who are still creating EVA inside the firm will get their just deserts by being allowed to buy options with a lower exercise price.

So those are the major issues of corporate performance measurement as I see them. I'm interested not just in the performance measurement itself, but in how it motivates people to behave differently. Talking about increasing shareholder value and setting the right corporate objectives are necessary but not sufficient conditions for corporate success. Managerial incentives must also be changed along with the goals to make the system work.

With that as introduction, I will now turn the floor over to my colleague Bennett Stewart, who has his own story about EVA.

The EVA Financial Management System

BENNETT STEWART: Before opening up the floor to our panelists, let me take a little bit more of your time to give you my point of view as to why this is all happening now. Why all of a sudden EVA?

There are some profound changes going on in the world. There's an information revolution that is manifesting itself in many ways. Management hierarchies are flattening, large companies are being broken down into smaller firms, and vertical integration is giving way to outsourcing. Dramatic reductions in the costs of gathering and processing information have led to widespread corporate downsizing and outsourcing. And contracting with outsiders to perform functions once performed inside the company has allowed for a sharpening of corporate focus, for greater specialization and all the associated benefits.

And it's this information revolution that is really driving the whole business process re-engineering movement. Whether it's just-in-time inventory management or time-cycle compression, companies are increasingly recognizing that the real success of business today depends not on having a well-thought-out, far-reaching strategy, but rather on re-engineering a company's business systems to respond more effectively to the new business environment of continuous

change. And our contention at Stern Stewart is that just as this information revolution has created a need for business process re-engineering, it has also precipitated a need to re-engineer the corporate *financial management system*.

Now, let me describe what we mean by a financial management system. To us, a financial management system consists of all those financial policies, procedures, methods, and measures that guide a company's operations and its strategy. It has to do with how companies address such questions as: What are our overall corporate financial goals and how do we communicate them, both within the company and to the investment community? How do we evaluate business plans when they come up for review? How do we allocate resources—everything from the purchase of an individual piece of equipment to the acquisition of an entire company to the evaluation of opportunities to downsize and restructure? How do we evaluate ongoing operating performance? And, last but not least, how do we pay our people, what's our corporate reward system?

Many companies these days have ended up with a needlessly complicated and, in many respects, hopelessly obsolete financial management system. For example, most companies use discounted cash flow analysis for capital budgeting evaluations. But, when it comes to other purposes such as setting goals and communicating with investors, the same companies tend to reach for accounting proxies—measures like earnings, earnings per share, earnings growth, profit margins, ROE, and the like. Well, to the extent this is true, it means there is already a "disconnect," if you will, between the cash-flow-based capital budget and accounting-based corporate goals. To make matters worse, the bonuses for

Many companies have ended up with needlessly complicated and hopelessly obsolete financial management systems. For example, most companies use discounted cash flow for capital budgeting. But, when it comes to setting goals and communicating with investors, the same companies use measures like earnings, earnings per share, and ROE. This widespread corporate practice of using different financial measures for different corporate functions creates inconsistency, and thus considerable confusion, in the management process.

—Bennett Stewart—

operating people tend to be structured around achieving some annually negotiated profit figure.

This widespread corporate practice of using different financial measures for different corporate functions creates inconsistency, and thus considerable confusion, in the management process. And, given all the different, often conflicting, measures of performance, it is understandable that corporate operating people tend to throw their hands in the air and say, "So, what are you really trying to get me to do here? What is the real financial mission of our company?"

Take the case of DuPont. Back in the 1920s, DuPont had a very clear standard for assessing its performance. It was called return on investment, or ROI. In fact, this was known as the "DuPont Formula." DuPont then had "the Chart Room," a very large room in which they posted diagrams of the ROI trees for all of their businesses. From the early '20s until well after World War II, the Executive Committee met every Monday in the Chart Room with a division head and his staff to review the division's operating performance and discuss its capital expenditures and strategic plan. They would evaluate their progress using these ROI diagrams; and then they would break down the ROI calculation into more manageable components such as profit margin and sales turnover, and then analyze these components even further.

But, as the company began to acquire more businesses in unrelated industries, DuPont began to use EPS and EPS growth as its metric for evaluating corporate performance. And that change introduced a new level of complexity into the financial management process. It became impossible to reconcile internal ROI measures used for investment planning on the inside with the EPS measures reported to the investment community.

Then, in 1982, DuPont acquired Conoco, the oil and gas company, reportedly in part to take advantage of a "cash flow play." Operating cash flow became one of the major justifications for the acquisition, and thus another metric of performance further complicated the situation. And so the outcome at DuPont, as in so many large U.S. companies, has been the proliferation of financial measures.

Why is it important to have only one measure? The natural inclination of operating managers in large public companies is to get their hands on more capital in order to spend and grow the empire. This tendency in turn leads to an overtly political internal competition for capital—one in which different performance measures are used to gain approval for pet projects.

Because of this tendency toward empire-building, top management typically feels compelled to intervene excessively—not in day-to-day decision making, but in capital spending decisions. Why? Because they don't trust the financial management system to guide their operating managers to make the right decisions. There's no real accountability built into the system, there's no real incentive for operating heads to choose only those investment projects that will increase value.

So that's really what an EVA financial management system is designed to do. And, in this sense, I think the *Fortune* article was somewhat misleading. It seemed to give the impression that if a company simply calculates EVA, and begins to use it as just one of the dials on its financial navigation system, then that's enough to align the interests of management with shareholder value. But, as Joel was suggesting at the outset, that is not enough. EVA is a financial management *system*. It is a *framework* for all aspects of financial management decision-making that are

anchored by the incentive compensation plan.

Besides changing the performance measures, then, establishing an EVA system involves a number of other challenges: changing the capital budgeting process to emphasize the projecting and discounting of EVA instead of cash flow; tracing EVA back to key drivers in the business so operating managers understand how their decisions affect it; adopting continuous improvement in EVA as both the main financial goal internally and in communications with the investment community; and, finally, as Joel emphasized, designing an EVA-based annual cash bonus plan that has the effect of simulating ownership.

Integrating Disciplines in the Business Schools

So, with that introduction to EVA, let me turn to Professor Jerry Zimmerman, who is an expert on accounting systems and organizational theory at the University of Rochester. Jerry, when I graduated from the University of Chicago back in the 1970s, it seemed to me there was an excessive compartmentalization of the different disciplines. There were a number of required courses—corporate finance, investments, accounting, marketing, operations research—but there was no course designed to pull all these disciplines together into a single cohesive system. And that's really, I think, the major challenge that most large companies confront today: How should they go about designing and implementing an integrated, cohesive, but nevertheless simple and readily understandable financial management system?

Jerry, do you think the academic community has missed this point? Where does the issue of aligning business decisions with shareholder value manifest itself in a consistent and integrated way in our business schools?

ZIMMERMAN: Most business schools do not do a very good job of integrating and aligning business decisions with the corporate aim of maximizing shareholder value. Business schools are just starting to try and integrate the various disciplines. Some schools—Stanford, Harvard, and Rochester, to name a few—now offer courses that emphasize the linkage among business decision-making, performance evaluation, and compensation policy. Important research by finance and accounting scholars is beginning to break down the black box we call the firm and to provide insights into these linkages.

But I don't think you want to lay all the blame on the business schools for the failure of the business community to align all the various aspects of the financial management system with shareholder value. In fact, let me say that I don't think Stern Stewart has succeeded in pulling it all together with EVA. I think you and Joel have solved two-thirds of the problem. You have succeeded in putting the NPV/DCF valuation method we teach in business schools into a form that can be used by some corporations for ongoing performance measurement. But EVA is not right for every company, and we need to gain a better understanding of where EVA works well and where it may cause problems and should not be used.

So, there is still a missing third; there is still a critical element of this problem of integrating systems that I don't believe your approach addresses. And rather than telling you what I think that third is at this point, I'll let you see if you can figure it out. That's the final exam for today.

STERN: But, Jerry, even if we are missing something, and even if it represents one-third, then why is it that when companies today simply

announce their *intention* to go on to an EVA performance measurement and incentive compensation system, they experience substantial increases in the prices of their shares?

ZIMMERMAN: Don't misunderstand me, Joel. I think EVA clearly has the potential to add significant value in many corporate circumstances. At least for some companies, it holds out major improvements over the conventional accounting systems that form the basis for SEC disclosures. But there are other cases—cases that I think will come out in this discussion—in which a straightforward application of EVA to different operating businesses within a large company may create more problems than it solves, raise more questions than it answers.

As an academic historical footnote to this discussion, let me also point out that EVA is not new. I've been able to trace it back to a 1955 monograph by General Electric's management. GE was worried about some of the incentive problems with Return on Net Assets, or RONA, that Joel just described. And the GE people actually proposed a measure they called "residual income," which is operating income less a capital charge.

David Solomons, who had a long and industrious career at Wharton, wrote a 1965 monograph called "Divisional Performance" that is devoted to the subject of measuring residual income or EVA. And all managerial accounting textbooks since then include discussions of RONA versus residual income.

So, EVA is not new. What Joel and Bennett have accomplished with EVA, however, is primarily to make more precise estimates of cost of capital and better adjustments of conventional accounting statements. EVA corrects a lot of the accounting distortions—problems like those that arise from leasing and deferred taxes—that

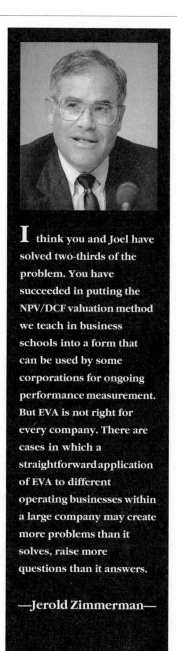

I think you and Joel have solved two-thirds of the problem. You have succeeded in putting the NPV/DCF valuation method we teach in business schools into a form that can be used by some corporations for ongoing performance measurement. But EVA is not right for every company. There are cases in which a straightforward application of EVA to different operating businesses within a large company may create more problems than it solves, raise more questions than it answers.

—Jerold Zimmerman—

weren't really around when David Solomons wrote his book in 1965. **STEWART**: In fact, Jerry, EVA actually goes back much farther than 1965. Alfred Sloan's book *My Years at General Motors* describes how in the 1920s General Motors had a system where they set aside a 15% rate of return on net assets as the required rate of return in their business. Ten percent of all operating profits after the 15% capital charge became the bonus pool to be shared by management.

And, much like our leveraged equity purchase plan, GM's managers would then be required to use part of their bonus to buy stock in the company on a leveraged basis. So, in this sense, everything we at Stern Stewart have done to refine and apply EVA is merely an afterthought to a system General Motors had in place in the 1920s. Now, how GM went from that system to their focus on EPS under Roger Smith during the 1980s is a sad story I will not regale you with.

The Case of Pitney Bowes

STEWART: While we're wondering about Jerry's other one-third, let me turn to Carm Adimando, the CFO of Pitney-Bowes. Carm, as a long-time user of EVA, can you tell us about the benefits—and limitations—of such a system?

ADIMANDO: As you know, Bennett, we have been measuring EVA by division for the last ten years. We measure the performance of each operation every month. And those monthly EVA numbers are sent to the board of directors as well as each of the divisional heads.

Perhaps our greatest challenge in implementing an EVA system was convincing our chairman and board of directors to go along with it. But we've been able to accomplish that, and our EVA program has led to

dramatic improvements in the efficiency with which our operating heads manage capital. During the time the plan has been in place, we've had great improvement in our share price, and we've moved up to number 79 this past year on your Stern Stewart 1,000 hit list. Between 1982 and 1992, we averaged a 24.5% rate of return to our investors.

STEWART: Carm, can you offer any concrete examples of how EVA has changed the behavior of operating managers?

ADIMANDO: It has affected not only our operating managers, but our sales managers, R & D personnel, financial managers, and division presidents. When considering a major decision, whether it be a strategic investment, a new product or marketing strategy, or a production plan, our people thoroughly evaluate its projected EVA *before* embarking on the plan. As a consequence, our returns have improved, margins have increased, new products have been more successful—and management bonuses and our share price have increased accordingly.

But, having mentioned the benefits, let me also describe some of the costs associated with starting an EVA program. In addition to selling the board on the merits of such a program, getting your operating people to understand that every little thing they do has an effect on shareholder value is a very difficult task—particularly when you start bringing people in from different companies with different ideas and methods. Take the case of a successful operating guy who has been around for 20 or 25 years and is fairly set in his ways. He knows he has achieved a certain level of accomplishment during those 20 years, and trying to convince him there's a better way is not easy.

The rapid obsolescence of products also makes EVA, or any financial

measurement system, very difficult to apply. Think about the difficulty of convincing people in production that they don't need that old product any more, even though it has been selling like hotcakes, because we've got a new product coming out. At the same time, you've got to convince the sales force that this new product is now the product to sell, when they've spent the last three years learning how to sell the older product and convinced three-quarters of corporate America that the older product is the one they need.

On the finance side, meanwhile, you're trying to guess how quickly the new product is going to cannibalize the old product, and how much profit you're going to sacrifice, especially since you're now producing the old product at the lowest cost in the last three years. Given that the new product will likely be produced inefficiently at the outset, and in the face of all the other uncertainties surrounding this process of substituting new products for old, financial systems don't offer much guidance.

The challenge of top management in such cases is to convince the factory floor person, the manufacturing person, the division head, the head of sales, the head of marketing, and, most important, the sales force that the new product is the way we have to go. If you can sit there and take them through EVA, it may make a lot of sense. But, at the beginning of this process, there are large hurdles. Your salespeople, who are on straight commission, are having a tough time because they aren't allowed to sell the old product any more. The factory floor worker is being criticized by the head of the factory for failing to make the conversion. And the division head is worrying about trying to make up with a new product what he's losing by cannibalizing the old.

At the same time, planning and financial personnel are trying to calculate how much has to be invested, not only in this product, but in the next generation of products. At our company, we have already budgeted three percent of our revenues for R & D over the next five years, and we have no way of estimating—at least not with any precision—what kind of value is being created by this R & D spending.

So, these are some of the uncertainties facing corporate financial management that do not seem to lend themselves to any financial system, EVA or otherwise.

STEWART: Well, I certainly sympathize with some of these problems, especially in evaluating the long-run payoff from R & D expenditures (although we do have a way of handling that, which I'm sure will come up later in the discussion). But let me just address this problem you cited about educating your line managers and employees.

At Quaker Oats, they have really driven their EVA program all the way down to the shop floor. In fact, I'm now holding up a picture of a fellow named Steve Brunner. He's a 23-year veteran of Quaker Oats, and here you can see him alongside his granola bars on the shop floor in Danville, Illinois.

The way Quaker has pushed EVA down through the ranks to the factory floor is by introducing a program called EVA *drivers*. This has meant breaking down EVA into its components and linking it, in this case, to variables like machine set-up times, operating uptimes, inventory levels, and defect rates. In this way, the EVA drivers create a bridge linking day-to-day actions and decisions with EVA itself and hence with the creation of shareholder value.

And those EVA drivers have allowed people like Steve Brunner to see that if they are willing to incur the costs of setting up their machines more fre-

quently, they can run their machines in smaller batches and so reduce their inventory. Besides the reduced capital charge associated with lower inventory, the greater consistency in the level of inventories also leads to better coordination with suppliers and lower defect rates.

So, the whole focus on EVA and EVA drivers allowed this guy to see how he could make what is essentially an investment—that is, a reduction in his income statement—that had as its principal payoff a benefit that took place largely on the balance sheet—that is, a reduction in the base of net assets under his control.

ADIMANDO: EVA also creates another problem, or at least a challenge, for management. As Joel pointed out, when you announce you're going on an EVA plan, or that you're going to spin off or sell a subsidiary, your stock price is likely to go up. The problem that creates for management is this: Because the stock market is forward looking, that stock price represents expected *future* value. Internally, however, we haven't achieved that value yet. And, given the market's higher expectations, we then have to spend the next two years achieving that expected value just to keep our stock price from falling. If we don't succeed in creating that value, our stock price will fall. The market is always pushing you, in effect asking you what's the next project that's going to push your market value above and beyond the level of shareholder capital invested in the company.

Let me give you another example of a similar problem. Pitney Bowes is part of a group of Fortune 500 computer and office equipment companies. For the last four years prior to this one, we have been ranked first in ten-year total return to investors. And that group includes companies like Compaq, Hewlett Packard, and

You have to push EVA all the way down to the individual operating units to get people's attention and produce results. You've got to convince everyone that increasing shareholder value is the one overarching goal of the organization, and that EVA is the main internal yardstick for evaluating your progress toward meeting that goal. You must also make clear the role of customer satisfaction in sustaining higher EVA—because if you don't have satisfied customers, your market share, your EVA, and your market value will all fall.

—**Carm Adimando**—

Xerox—and half of these companies, incidentally, are now talking EVA.

But, at any rate, we have achieved very high shareholder returns and a very high MVA. The problem is, our market valuation is so high that, unless we substantially increase our returns or our price/earnings multiple, there is no place for us to go but down in these rankings. And, in fact, this year Compaq, which is a very highly rated firm, achieved number one, and we fell to number two. Not because we slipped on returns—in fact our returns are even better—but because Compaq really got their act together and has created even more value.

Joel suggested that if a company is currently achieving a 25% return on capital, it should accept new projects earning less than 25% as long as they're earning more than the cost of capital. But I want to take issue with that. If you accept returns substantially lower than 25%, then your average return is going to fall. And the more you let projects bring that total return down, the more those returns start getting reflected into your stock price.

STEWART: Well, Carm, I think the problem you face is an enviable one; it arises from your extraordinary success. I'm even tempted to say that your stock price may be in some sense "overvalued." That is, you have done such a good job in the past that you may have succeeded in persuading the market you can continue earning 25% returns for longer than you can. But that's still not a good reason to walk away from new projects that promise to earn 15% or 20%.

But, as you say, the market is forward looking; it's always attempting to capture future profits in current prices. And, for this reason, I can see where having a very high stock price today could create problems for managers being rewarded on the basis of year-to-year stock price returns, or on

the basis of year-to-year changes in MVA. That's one reason we use EVA instead of MVA in measuring internal operating performance; it helps eliminate the unwanted effects of market volatility or unrealistic shareholder expectations.

This problem of market volatility could also affect an EVA system that attempted to mark net assets to market continuously. A sharp and sudden increase in market value, to the extent it was translated immediately into higher capital charges for operating managers, could end up holding those managers to unrealistically high standards of performance. And that's one reason why we typically end up recommending that companies use modified book values of net assets rather than some estimate of fair market values in calculating EVA.

EVA at Merrill Lynch

STEWART: But let me turn now to Joe Willett. Joe, as CFO of Merrill Lynch, you have developed a version of EVA that is designed for a financial institution as opposed to the industrial companies we typically advise. Would you mind describing what you have done and why you did it?
WILLETT: Sure. The standard approach for industrial companies using EVA is to look at the after-tax but pre-interest return on *total* capital in relation to the weighted average cost of capital. For financial institutions levered 25 to 30 times, that approach is analytically messy because the weighted average cost of capital (or WACC) is dominated by the after-tax cost of debt financing, and it will be very low in relation to normally observed market rates of return. For this reason, WACC is not very useful for us as a performance measurement tool.

So the approach that we've adopted—which I think, Bennett, is analytically equivalent to the way you

calculate EVA—is to look at the after-tax, *after*-interest operating returns in relation to the equity capital used in the business. Our performance measurement approach is to look at return on *equity* capital in relation to the cost of *equity* capital as the hurdle rate. For each of 50 or so different businesses in Merrill Lynch, we've assigned equity capital based on the risks of those businesses, and we calculate EVA based on the return on equity, the cost of equity, and the amount of equity capital employed in the business. For each of these businesses, an EVA level of zero is considered break-even economic performance.
STEWART: What do you see as the benefits of such an EVA system?
WILLETT: The appeal of EVA is that it encourages people to look for profitable growth opportunities while, at the same time, looking for ways to economize on the use of capital—not only by reducing capital needs in existing businesses, but also by eliminating unprofitable lines of business. Those are the most important benefits of the EVA approach.

Let me add that I think a good performance measurement system, such as one based on EVA, is necessary nowadays because most corporations have become too big and complex to be managed from one central place, and so you need to decentralize decision-making and controls. This is certainly true of Merrill Lynch, and it's probably true of the other companies represented on the panel. And, if you're going to decentralize the organization—if you're going to have real empowerment down through levels of the organization—then you're also going to have to align the incentives of the operating managers with those of top management and the shareholders. People with line authority are going to have to be focused on the right objectives.

I think it's fair to begin with the premise that individuals will do what they perceive to be in their own self-interest. At Merrill Lynch, we have learned that we get what we measure and what we pay people to do. If you go back in our history, there was a time when we emphasized revenues in our compensation system—and, not surprisingly, what we got then was revenues and not profits. Over time our system evolved to put more emphasis on profits and, ultimately, on both profits and returns, or what amounts to EVA. Our current EVA system captures both the quantity and quality dimensions of earnings. EVA, we think, gives our managers the proper incentive to achieve the right balance between profitability and growth.

As I said earlier, our company is too complex to be managed centrally. Having an EVA system combined with a compensation system that reinforces the emphasis on EVA allows us to decentralize while knowing that the interests of the people running our different businesses are consistent with those of our shareholders.

STERN: Your comment reminds me of an experience we recently had in working for a large company overseas. In January, they made their decision to go onto an EVA plan effective April 1st. The chairman of the company called me in February and said, "Something has happened, you must hear about this. Back in December, our operating managers submitted $570 million in capital expenditures for this fiscal year. But after we announced we were going on the EVA program, the very same people cut back on their requests for capital by $180 million. Why do you think they did that?"

I said, "My guess is that the rate of return on that extra $180 million of net assets was not going to earn the cost of capital, and that taking on those

extra projects was going to reduce management bonuses."

He said, "I think you're right. In the past, we had about an 80/20 wage-to-bonus structure, fixed-to-variable pay. Under your system, we're going to have 50/50; so our managers can really benefit if they do well and sustain that performance over time. They can't afford to have that extra $180 million dragging down their performance."

And that's the kind of thing that companies can accomplish with EVA. That is, we want a police function that stops dead in its tracks the incentive of corporate managers to overinvest in ways that hurt shareholders.

The Case of International Paper

STERN: Let's now turn to Robert Butler, CFO of International Paper. Bob, could you tell us a little about your experience with EVA?
BUTLER: One of the major attractions of EVA for us is that it's simple. That's what I especially like about it. During my own career, I've experimented with a variety of performance measures. For example, for years we tried to relate the returns on individual facilities with shareholder returns. We assigned debt-equity ratios to all divisions and calculated divisional returns on capital. We have also tried to allocate some part of earnings per share to all our businesses.

But I think EVA accomplishes this aim much more effectively. With this system, you simply say to the person running the facility, I want you to deliver $100,000 of EVA. So, if the facility has net assets of, say, $1 million, and the cost of capital is 10%, then the guy knows he's got to produce $200,000 of operating profit to earn his bonus. Nothing could be more straightforward. So, our experience with EVA is that it is very easy to budget and understand—it's just the

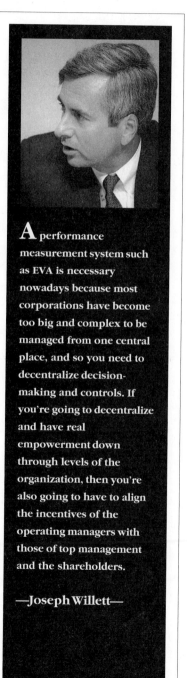

A performance measurement system such as EVA is necessary nowadays because most corporations have become too big and complex to be managed from one central place, and so you need to decentralize decision-making and controls. If you're going to decentralize and have real empowerment down through levels of the organization, then you're also going to have to align the incentives of the operating managers with those of top management and the shareholders.

—Joseph Willett—

There are a number of
factors that go into
corporate investment
decisions that are difficult
to handle with EVA. If
you're thinking about
building a new paper
facility, you're going to base
your decision on some
assumptions of economic
growth—and, as the result
of globalization, the
relevant growth measure
today is worldwide rather
than just domestic or U.S.
growth. But you also have
to factor in the response of
your competitors. We don't
announce our plans—and
the Justice Department
doesn't encourage us to talk
to our competitors about
these matters.

—Robert Butler—

amount that you're going to contribute over and above the company's
cost of capital.

STERN: Bob, could you tell us what
the response of the operating people
has been to this new performance
measure?

BUTLER: As you know, Joel, we
have only recently introduced EVA
into our performance measurement
system, and we are using it on an
experimental basis. At this point,
managerial compensation isn't tied
to EVA; we're just trying to get our
managers comfortable with and accustomed to using the measure. But
I think our EVA system is going to
work well for us, and tying managers' compensation to EVA is a likely
next step.

I can also tell you that over two-
thirds of my company is producing
negative EVA right now. The paper
industry is highly cyclical and, as you
know, we've been in the down part of
the paper cycle for the last three or
four years.

STEWART: I'm kind of fascinated by
your industry because it does go through
these cycles, and some part of that
cyclical market behavior seems to be
self-inflicted. When times are tough,
the industry as a group tends to hold
back, thus causing demand to rise very
abruptly. Then, when demand does
rise, all the companies tend to throw
piles of money into new capacity in
attempts to maintain market share.

Now, Bob, let's suppose you're back
at the top of the cycle, demand is
outrunning supply, and prices are rising, and it's time to consider reinvesting in the business. But you also know
that if you invest along with everybody
else, you face the following prisoner's
dilemma: If you don't invest, and many
other companies choose the same strategy, you will end up losing out on a
profitable investment opportunity; but
if you do invest, and everybody else
follows suit, then you will all suffer

together from excess capacity. How
do you think you're going to handle
that situation under an EVA framework?

BUTLER: Well, I don't know; that's
hard to answer. If you're thinking
about building a new paper facility,
you're going to base your decision
on some assumptions of economic
growth—and, by the way, as the result
of globalization, the relevant growth
measure today is worldwide rather
than just domestic or U.S. growth.

What we never seem to factor in,
however, is the response of our competitors. Who else is going to build a
plant or machine at the same time? We
don't announce our plans—and the
Justice Department doesn't encourage
us to talk to each other about these
matters.

There are also a number of other
factors that go into corporate investment decisions, particularly when you're
dealing with very large companies,
that are difficult to handle with EVA. In
our industry, cutting capital expenditures could be very counterproductive. In the first place, you've got to
maintain the plant. That's sort of a
given, because you're not going to get
any EVA after a while if the mill roof
comes in on you.

And what about the expenditures
necessary to comply with environmental regulations? We have to spend
a lot of money these days on non-
return projects to meet new regulations of all kinds. How does EVA evaluate those expenditures? And how does
it take into account things like accidents in the plant, lost work days,
incident rates, and so forth. Minimizing
these things must be part of the corporate reward system.

STEWART: There are clearly costs to
safety and environmental compliance
that end up showing up in your
financial results. But, given that you're
making these expenditures, there must
be potential benefits—a strong plant

safety record, for example, which would help you attract better employees—that are not being reflected in your financial statements.

In one of our consulting assignments, we actually devised a measurement system as part of an EVA program that would take account of not only explicit costs of unsafe plants such as higher workmen's compensation premiums, but also implicit costs such as lost time. We asked management to rank different kinds of safety infractions and then built penalty surcharges for such infractions into the EVA calculation. And we could do the same thing for a failure to comply fully with environmental laws—that is, establish penalty surcharges at levels top management viewed as appropriate to encourage the desired kind of behavior.

So, under this system, if managers spend money on improving safety or reducing environmental violations, then there really is a return to them from so doing. Having such a measurement and incentive system forces the corporate debate to focus on the right issue: Namely, what is the real marginal cost/benefit tradeoff of spending an additional dollar to improve safety. And it's important that this calculation be part and parcel of the overall performance framework, as opposed to the common corporate practice of putting these outlays into a separate category called mandatory expenditures. I feel very strongly that putting these expenditures *within* the framework of managerial financial accountability and incentives is the right way to go.

EVA and Corporate Governance

STEWART: Let me turn now to Richard Shepro. Rick, as a partner of the law firm Mayer Brown & Platt, you get involved in advising boards of directors on questions of proxy contests, takeovers, and all the other legal aspects of corporate governance. What do you think about the potential of an EVA financial management system for helping to eliminate the so-called U.S. corporate governance problem?

SHEPRO: Well, the main problem in corporate governance that people have been talking about for at least the last decade is how to align managers' interests with shareholders' interests. And that's a very, very difficult thing to do. The recent court decisions in takeover battles that have surprised so many people have all been the result of the courts' continued interest in the conflict of interest between managers and shareholders.

There are a number of ways for companies to assure the courts that the conflict of interest is being minimized. One is simply having managers hold a lot of stock, because courts tend to focus on the manager-shareholder conflict at the top of the organization. But, from a business perspective, you don't want something that just minimizes the conflict of interest, you want something that also produces profits for the company over the long run. And that's where a system such as EVA can have a real benefit. The courts respect companies that have a long-term point of view, and that are able to provide a credible explanation of why their policies were put in place.

In fact, that's one of the major reasons the courts reacted so differently to Paramount's attempt to challenge the Time-Warner merger and to its subsequent attempt to lock up its deal with Viacom. The critical difference between the two cases was that Time and Warner were able to articulate a long-term strategic vision in which their shareholders would ultimately benefit—and Paramount and Viacom were not.

So, long-term planning is just one more one way of demonstrating busi-

To the extent EVA does a better job of reflecting economic reality than GAAP accounting, it may provide a better language for communicating with institutional investors. It's a second set of books, in effect—one that gives management much more latitude to discuss the expected future payoff from its current investment policies. Having this alternative accounting framework should encourage more and better communication both between management and shareholders and among shareholders themselves.

—Richard Shepro—

ness judgment to a court, and having an EVA plan in place may well be construed as evidence of long-term planning.

STEWART: Rick, what do you think will be the effect of the new rules allowing institutional shareholders to talk to one another and make their voices heard? And can EVA play a role in dealing with investor activism?

SHEPRO: A system like EVA produces very different results from the SEC accounting rules, which are based on GAAP. To the extent it does a better job of reflecting economic reality, EVA may provide a better language for companies to use in communicating with institutional investors. It's a second set of books, in effect—one that gives management much more latitude to discuss its policies and the expected future payoff from its current investment policies. Having this alternative accounting framework should encourage more and better communication both between management and shareholders, and among shareholders themselves.

STEWART: I agree with you, Rick. You see, there seem to be two prominent schools of strategy today that divide the world between them. One school of strategy I'll call the Michael Porter school. Michael Porter argues in his tomes that top management should agonize over market conditions and exhaustively analyze industry structure in order to arrive at top-down strategies. After being designed by an army of strategic planners, such strategies can then be imposed on the divisions and orchestrated from the top.

At the other extreme you have Tom Peters, whose highly decentralized approach is suggested by the titles of his two most recent books: *Managing With Chaos* and *Liberation Management*. Peters's books emphasize the empowerment of people throughout the organization. The basic strategy

is really not to have a carefully formulated strategy at all, but rather to have the organizational structure sufficiently loose and managers sufficiently motivated to seize opportunities as they arise. We don't really know in advance what the opportunities will turn out to be, but we want to have the flexibility and incentives to respond when they come.

This devaluation of strategic thinking and emphasis on organizational responsiveness has important implications not only for how companies evaluate and reward their managers, but also for how they communicate with investors. What really matters to investors today is not corporate strategy, but the management *process* and the incentives that go along with it. For this reason, I think companies could benefit greatly just by focusing their disclosures on how they manage, what their goals are, how they monitor their progress in meeting those goals, and what their incentives are to bring it all off.

So, it's not the specifics of strategy that are important—indeed, in some sense, a company's strategy is changing every day—but rather the corporate process that would give investors a sense of management's alertness and incentives to respond to continuous change.

STERN: One way to promote such communication is simply to send a special letter to your shareholders from the chairman or chief executive officer spelling out the details of your EVA program in a page or two. Another method—used by firms like Coca-Cola and Quaker Oats—is to devote part of your annual report to explaining your results and expectations in terms of EVA. For example, the firm might attempt to show the correlation between their past five years' EVA and MVA as part of an explanation of why they are adopting an EVA program.

And, once having started the program, they can then report their EVA results on a regular basis along with the earnings measures required by the SEC.

SHEPRO: Given the new requirements on disclosure of executive pay and stock price performance, I think the SEC would welcome those additional kinds of explanation.

EVA and Investors

STEWART: Well, instead of our prating on about what might be done in the area of shareholder communication, why don't we consult our two representatives from the investment community? Susan, as Chief Investment Officer and head of research at Citicorp Investment Services, what do you think about EVA and its potential role in communicating corporate strategy to investors?

MALLEY: I'd like to comment on this from two perspectives. One is from the perspective of a corporate manager, the other is from the perspective of a securities analyst.

As some of my colleagues have mentioned, the ideas of net present value, discounted cash flow, and residual income have all been around for a while. But I think that EVA's contribution from a managerial point of view is that it has provided a method of taking those concepts and turning them into a simple, "actionable" framework that can be pushed down into the corporation.

Now, the flip side of that is the securities analysis perspective. Based on my knowledge and experience, analysts have always attempted to look at cash flow rather than earnings.

STEWART: Really?

MALLEY: Yes. In fact, I think that most analysts understand clearly that earnings are basically serving as a proxy for cash flow. But what I think EVA does for securities analysts is provide them with a look at the *process* of corporate decision-making. The most difficult problem in securities analysis is estimating the cash flows beyond two years or so. Creating a common language that would allow management to communicate its decision-making process could go a long way toward solving this problem, toward overcoming the information gap between managment and investors with regard to decisions that are being made today that will affect cash flows in the future.

Aside from EVA, there's really no financial language that allows management to communicate its longer-run prospects. When securities analysts are probing for this kind of information, they tend to ask: "What's the business strategy?" And I think EVA could help corporate managements provide a useful answer to that question.

So, I think EVA can make two important parallel contributions. On the managerial side, it takes an unconventional performance measure designed to promote capital efficiency and makes it simple and straightforward enough for use by operating people. On the securities analysis side, it provides a new language, if you will, that allows for discussion of longer-term corporate decision making and strategy.

STEWART: Are you now having more or better dialogue with companies that are using EVA? Or is this something you expect to happen?

MALLEY: I think it's already happening in certain cases. What remains to be done, though—and I understand you folks are addressing this to some extent—is to make EVA analysis available in automated form in standard data bases. This will allow EVA to become part of the ongoing evolution of the financial analyst community toward quantitative processes. If EVA isn't integrated into the data bases and information infrastructure, the quants

will ignore it and so will many fundamental analysts.

The second important missing element is what I would call "measures along the way." Although companies may say they're adopting EVA, there can still be major disagreements between management and analysts about the company's future prospects, implementation issues, and the intensity of competitive pressures. Take the case of high-technology firms like Intel, where analysts are always asking about the future payoff from research. Analysts want to know, for example, when the Pentium chip is going to take off, how much of the market it's going to win, and what the competitive response is going to be.

There is likely to be considerable uncertainty, and thus considerable disagreement, among analysts about the answers to these questions. And I think interim performance measures could help resolve part of this uncertainty.

STEWART: One of the companies that we're looking at right now is Polaroid. When Polaroid sells a Captiva camera, the company does not make an acceptable profit on that sale. They are willing to use camera sales as a "loss leader" because they expect to make it back on subsequent film sales. Under EVA, and in contrast to conventional GAAP accounting, we don't penalize them for selling more cameras; we make an internal adjustment to capture the expected payoff from those sales.

So, how would you and most analysts look at a company where the more cameras they sell in the fourth quarter of the year, the lower their reported returns? Does the market make this EVA kind of adjustment, or does it just take the accounting numbers at face value?

MALLEY: Most securities analysts, I think, would view the camera sales as producing a future stream of film

The most difficult problem in securities analysis is estimating the cash flows beyond two years or so. EVA provides securities analysts with a look at the *process* of corporate decision-making. Creating a common language that allows management to communicate its decision-making process could go a long way toward overcoming the information gap between management and investors with regard to decisions that are being made today that will affect cash flows in the future.

—Susan Malley—

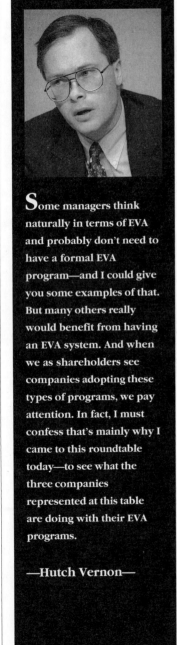

profits. And I think the market clearly understands the limitations of conventional accounting in such cases.

But let me change the subject and say something about the relationship between EVA and total quality management, or TQM, because I've heard people say that the two disciplines are incompatible. I don't think they're incompatible at all; in fact, I think that EVA actually reinforces and strengthens TQM. EVA provides management with a financial decision-making framework—one that deals very well with the management of *financial* capital. TQM deals effectively with management process and implementation— that is, with the management of *human* capital. So, when you put EVA and TQM together, I think you get a much more substantial management system.

BUTLER: Like EVA, TQM depends on empowerment. TQM works only if you've empowered your employees to improve themselves and the quality of their work.

STEWART: We try to make TQM and EVA parts of the same message. TQM largely boils down to the continuous improvement of products and processes. The goal of an EVA financial management system is, of course, continuous improvement in EVA. So, we too think that the goals of EVA and TQM are highly consistent with each other. EVA motivates and reinforces the TQM quest for operating efficiencies. An EVA system that focuses on incremental improvement allows the organization to relish its progressive successes and so institutionalize the dynamic of continuous change.

Another Investor Perspective

STEWART: Let me turn to our other representative of the investment community, Hutch Vernon of Alex Brown in Baltimore. Hutch, what's your interest in EVA?

VERNON: The reason we like EVA is that it encourages the kind of behavior among managers that we, as investors, like. We think the primary job of management is to produce a high return on the capital that has been entrusted to them by the shareholders. If the company is performing well, management must continue making the investment necessary to create high returns in the future. If the company is performing poorly, they need to make the changes, however painful, that will bring the return on capital back to acceptable levels. Or, if they've completely exhausted the possibilities of earning their cost of capital, then they should return that capital to the shareholders so that we can put it to some other productive use.

Some managers think naturally in terms of EVA and probably don't need to have a formal EVA program—and I could give you some examples of that. But many others really would benefit from having an EVA system. And when we as shareholders see companies adopting these types of programs, we pay attention. In fact, I must confess that's mainly why I came to this roundtable today—to see what the three companies represented at this table are doing with their EVA programs.

STEWART: You say some companies don't need EVA because there's an instinctive focus on value at the top. Can you give me examples?

VERNON: We like companies where the folks that run them think like owners.

STEWART: Is that because they *are* owners?

VERNON: Because they are owners or that's just their nature. Now, that's a small percentage of the population, but that's the way some people are.

STEWART: Can you give me a good example?

VERNON: Warren Buffett is one.

STEWART: He's a big owner.

VERNON: Travelers.

STEWART: Sandy Weill is a big owner.

VERNON: Well, I can think of some companies where managers also have significant ownership, but they really don't understand capital efficiency and shareholder value. One of the benefits of an EVA program in a situation like that—whether management owns the stock or not—is that it forces them to do the right thing by its shareholders.

STEWART: In your way of looking at companies, if a firm simply managed its assets more efficiently, or began to turn its assets faster or speed up its cycle times—even if that didn't show up in higher earnings—how would that cause you to increase its value?

VERNON: One way is by returning cash to the investor. If a company in a sorry business manages just to speed up the asset turnover and so produce some cash, and they can get that cash out of the company and into my hands, then I can plow that cash back into a company with better prospects. This kind of transfer of capital from mature to promising businesses, and from inefficient to more efficient managements, not only increases returns to private investors like us, but it has the social benefit of increasing the overall growth of the economy.

EVA vs. Cash Flow

STERN: We haven't heard yet from Professor Ravid. As a financial academic, could you tell us what you think of this EVA business?

RAVID: As Jerry Zimmerman was saying earlier, EVA is not new. In fact, the analysis of EVA is part of a much broader analysis I've been teaching in various universities for the last 15 years under the name of discounted cash flow and net present value. And, in fact, if you look at some other

people who are trying to implement a similar kind of analysis, you see that the market reacts the same way. For example, my friends at McKinsey have discovered a very high correlation between changes in discounted cash flow and changes in market value. So EVA is really just a kind of discounted cash flow analysis.

The concept of market value added, or MVA, is also not new. It is very similar to the concept of Tobin's Q, which is the ratio of the market value of assets to their replacement cost or book value. So, it's very nice that people are finally using these methods that we've been teaching our students for the last 20 or 30 years. If they buy it as EVA, that's great. And if they buy it as DCF, that's okay, too. Furthermore, nobody can argue with goals such as making better use of capital and getting rid of unproductive assets.

At the same time, however, one should also remember that EVA has the same problems that we have always had with discounted cash flow. For one thing, getting a precise estimate of the cost of capital is very difficult, especially in decentralized companies with many different business units. Also, estimating expected future cash flows is more of an art than a science. Because you are investing today and hoping that something will happen a few years hence, there is a great deal of uncertainty about those estimates. You can't escape this imprecision, whether you use EVA or discounted cash flow.

STEWART: In answer to your first objection about imprecision in the cost of capital, let me say this. From a practical perspective, we have found that just by charging managers for the use of capital, and by making their bonuses depend in a big way on covering that capital charge, that step alone goes a lot farther in motivating efficiency than in making subtle dis-

EVA has the same problems that we have always had with discounted cash flow. For one thing, getting a precise estimate of the cost of capital is very difficult, especially in decentralized companies with many different business units. Also, estimating expected future cash flows is more of an art than a science. Because you are investing today and hoping that something will happen a few years hence, there is a great deal of uncertainty about those estimates. You can't escape this imprecision, whether you use EVA or discounted cash flow.

—Abraham Ravid—

tinctions among levels of risk and cost of capital.

In fact, these days when people ask me what's the cost of capital, I often tell them just to use 12%. Why? Because it's one percent a month.

STERN: The other problem with DCF, as I mentioned earlier, is the difficulty in using it to come up with an interim or periodic performance measure. That is, if you have large cash outlays in time period zero, and the benefits begin in years two, three, and four, you need some way of holding people accountable for their performance on a year-by-year basis.

Under an EVA framework, we attempt to solve this problem by putting large capital expenditure items into a suspense account that, instead of being amortized on a standard depreciation schedule, bears interest at the required rate of return. The operating head responsible for the outlay is given what amounts to a customized, back-end-loaded amortization schedule built into his or her year-to-year performance measure that avoids penalizing large investments with heavy upfront depreciation charges. At the same time, however, the operating heads still have the incentive to bring the revenues onstream as quickly as possible because, in so doing, they reduce the interest costs for all that capital tied up in the suspense account.

And I think this ability to use EVA as an interim performance measure makes it far more useful than DCF.

STEWART: I would go farther, Joel, and say that not only is discounted cash flow not the answer, cash flow is *the problem.* Companies typically cast their capital budgets in cash flow terms. The problem, however, is they can't use cash flow for any other corporate function; it doesn't work as a year-to-year performance measure nor does it provide a useful basis for incentive compensation.

In most companies, the only time all the numbers in a capital budgeting exercise are ever put down on one piece of paper is when the project is first proposed. After the project is launched, the capital gets buried back in the balance sheet and no one gives it a second thought. At that stage, managers are not being held accountable for their use of additional capital but are being judged instead largely on the basis of the profit target negotiated in their budgets. The original discounted cash flow capital budget is just totally divorced from everything else that's happening in the financial management system.

For this reason, I think that the companies that use EVA most effectively are those that literally rewrite their capital budgeting manuals, valuation procedures, and strategy reviews from scratch so as to emphasize the projecting and discounting of EVA instead of cash flow. You're going to get the exact same NPV either way; but if the bonuses are also based upon increasing EVA, then you will have a completely integrated financial management system, including an automatic post-audit of project performance versus expectations.

Another virtue of EVA is that the calculation is based on earnings, which makes it easier for operating managers to grasp. To get a monthly EVA for an operation, you simply take sales, subtract all operating expenses, and then subtract a capital charge equal to one percent times the net assets employed in the balance sheet. The one percent represents a corporate charge to the operating head for renting him the assets. And what's left over after the capital charge is EVA.

So, EVA is simpler, it's more focused, and it's integrated. And that's why I tell companies to abandon discounted cash flow.

RAVID: But, Bennett, don't you think managers would quickly learn to understand discounted cash flow if their bonuses were based upon it?

STEWART: It wouldn't work. Wal-Mart, which by our estimates was perhaps the biggest wealth creator in corporate America during the '80s, had a negative cash flow during the entire decade—they were investing more than they were earning. In fact, there's likely to be a *negative* correlation between contemporaneous changes in corporate cash flow and market value because companies that are investing the most to build their business sell for the highest prices.

RAVID: But there is surely a strong positive correlation between current market value and *projected* future cash flow.

STEWART: But that's precisely my point; that's why you can't use cash flow as a measure of interim performance. It's useful only looking forward, not backwards. EVA is useful looking forward and looking backwards.

Rewriting the Corporate Constitution

SHEPRO: Joel stated in his introduction that an effective compensation system has to be perceived as objective. But think about your Polaroid example, the case where the company loses money on each camera, but makes it up on subsequent film sales. My question is, When you make these accounting adjustments to capture future benefits from film sales, don't you risk introducing a new kind of agency cost? We know that conventional accounting understates the future benefits of the film sales, but what prevents operating management from overestimating those benefits in order to win bigger bonuses for themselves, at least in the short term?

STEWART: Well, that's an excellent point. What we're really calling for is rewriting a company's constitution.

It's a one-time exercise of sitting down, understanding the business, understanding the accounting, and literally rewriting a set of ground rules that are not renegotiable.

And you're right. The integrity of the accounting system depends upon a careful thinking through of as many as 164 different EVA performance measurement issues. How do you account for acquisitions, start-ups, joint ventures? How do you account for inventories and depreciation? What about warranty reserves and overfunded pension plans? There's a whole laundry list of items where our conventional GAAP accounting system clearly fails to capture economic reality.

WILLETT: Bennett, what happens if you get your new system up and running, and then you suddenly discover you overlooked something? Do you then open up the system to further renegotiation?

STEWART: No, you just have to live with it.

STERN: I would answer you differently. When we take on an assignment with a firm, we typically start by looking at the historical performance of all the units to get some idea as to how far down into an organization EVA can be constructively and reliably measured. You can only carry the new incentive structure as far down as you can sensibly identify and measure separate EVAs or EVA drivers.

The second stage of our work is to set up a steering committee to work with us—one that represents every major discipline in the firm. In the case of a manufacturing firm, the committee would include representatives from operations, manufacturing, sales and marketing, human resources, finance, and the CEO. And we would hold several all-day sessions in which we explore all the major issues that go into the process of measuring EVA.

WILLETT: But, Joel, I thought one of the virtues of the system was that it was supposed to be simple. What happened to simplicity as an objective?

STERN: Well, although the analysis is complex and time-consuming, the final product is simple. The accounting adjustments that end up being introduced into the system are only those that have a material impact on performance. For example, in the case of a company like Johnson & Johnson, the two biggest adjustments would be for advertising and R & D. Although these are both major sources of future value, GAAP forces the company to write them off completely. But that makes absolutely no sense from an economic measurement standpoint.

Under EVA, the people at Johnson & Johnson would capitalize their R & D and write it off over a more sensible period. We would turn to the head of R & D and ask, "What do you think is the right period for amortizing R & D? Give us some average number that you can live with, is consistent with shareholder value, and will be approved by the compensation committee of your board." And we would come up with an adjustment on that basis.

We're actually doing this for a pharmaceutical company at this moment. And I think Professor Zimmerman would agree with the logic of what we're proposing here.

ZIMMERMAN: Well, yes and no. I agree that investments in both advertising and R & D have future payoffs that are not reflected in GAAP accounting. But, at the same time, you've got to keep in mind why GAAP has this conservative bias. As I said in an earlier Stern Stewart roundtable, GAAP accounting was not really designed to help shareholders value companies; its fundamental purpose was to help people such as creditors monitor debt agreements and to establish liquidation values, not going-concern values.

But what happens, Joel, if you put in this EVA program and the Clinton plan succeeds three years from now in turning the whole pharmaceutical industry on its head—or if the FDA changes the whole new drug application process, either shortening or lengthening it in such a way that it makes all of those prior assumptions that you built into the capitalization of R & D totally obsolete. Do you go back and reopen the discussion?

STERN: I would say yes, because the world has been changed and managers should be insulated against these kinds of shocks. You see—and I'm about to disagree with my colleague Bennett Stewart on this one—I don't necessarily believe that corporate managers should have large stock holdings in their company. The problem with having a large block of stock in their hands is that somewhere between 50% and 75% of changes in value are not company specific, and I wouldn't want managerial rewards to be determined largely by factors that have no relationship to their own efforts or decisions. For example, if the connection between managerial effort and stock returns becomes tenuous—as it has become in the case of Johnson & Johnson and Merck over the last 18 months or so—we feel that it's important for managers to spend their time doing what they know how to do best.

STEWART: But, Joel, what happened to our conception of managers as owners with payoffs aligned with those of the shareholders? If there's an external shock, shareholders don't get to reopen the discussion about the value of the stock. I think you want to aim at establishing a rule of laws, not a rule of men.

STERN: You're missing an important point, Bennett. If you rewrite the laws to reflect the new circumstances, managers will not be penalized for events beyond their control, but they will still have the right incentives *going forward*—that is, on all new investments. And I think it makes sense even from a shareholder perspective to offer that kind of protection to management.

STEWART: Yes, but Joel, there's no need to go in and rewrite the system a second time. Under our EVA improvement system, a major shock will lead to a one-time drop in EVA, and management will forgo its bonus in that year. But, as a result of that reduction in EVA, the level of future targeted EVA will be reduced accordingly, the bonus will effectively recalibrate itself from the new lower base, and the company will be able to reward continuous improvement *after adjusting for that shock.*

And that's precisely what happens to the shareholders in those circumstances. They take a one-time hit and, after the share price adjusts downward, the future is fair game. Why treat managers any differently from shareholders?

ZIMMERMAN: A similar debate has been going on in the accounting and organization literature for the last 50 years, and it has to do with a problem that every controller has probably had to deal with since we invented something called standard costs. When do you revise the standards? Does anyone here ever reopen the standards in the middle of the year?

ADIMANDO: We would change standards in mid-year if we added, let's say, a new component at a significantly lower cost.

ZIMMERMAN: Okay, but once you allow the standards to be reopened, then you run into the problem that Bennett is alluding to. You create a set of incentives for managers to avoid accountability every time the world changes.

BUTLER: We don't change standards in the middle of a year.

ZIMMERMAN: Okay, so Carm changes standards, but Bob doesn't. You're facing essentially the same issue of accountability with respect to changing standard costs that Joel and Bennett have just been debating in the context of changing asset amortization schedules. And I suspect if I asked a hundred people, I'd get roughly the same split of opinion. Unfortunately, there is no single right answer to this question.

If you don't allow *any* flexibility to change the system, you create inaccuracies and inequities. But once you allow flexibility, you give rise to what economists call "influence costs," the costs people impose on organizations in trying to change the rules of the game. Once people know the rules are flexible, they will work hard to change them if it serves their interests to do so.

A Role for Subjectivity

WILLETT: Well, I think it's possible to build too much objectivity into the system, and so I would argue there is a lot of room for the exercise of judgment by top management in performance evaluation and compensation. Even with the most careful planning in the world, when you put into place a system that has 164 components, it is likely that you will discover that you forgot one or two. And it seems to me that you ought to build in a fair amount of subjectivity not only into the measurement system, but also into the compensation system that reinforces the measurement system. This will allow you to make the inevitable adjustments that you're going to want to make once the system is put into place.

STEWART: Well, the most objective measure of all is the stock price. Take the case of a company operating in one line of business in which management and employees own all the stock. In that event, the stock price would be the perfectly objective measure; you wouldn't need surrogates like EVA in that case.

WILLETT: That's true, Bennett. But if you're managing a large and somewhat diverse collection of businesses under rapidly changing circumstances, the current stock price is certainly not going to provide a useful indicator of the performance of the person running one of the businesses.

STEWART: Well, for that same reason, I say that the right answer is not to pay for performance, but to make managers into owners. Pay-for-performance schemes are based on the notion that you can somehow isolate what it is that management is doing from everything else that's happening in the world around them. But what often happens with such systems is that somebody will come in and say, "It's true we had a bad year last year. But we were digging ditches, we were draining swamps, we were shooting crocodiles, we never worked so hard in our life—and we deserve our reward." And, to the extent you allow this kind of ex post adjustment, you leave room for endless debate and the discipline of the whole system is lost.

So I think you want to push this idea of surrogate ownership as far as you can. You say to your operating heads, we've thought about all the excuses, and they're built into the system. And if something horrendous happens, you'll lose that year. But the target will automatically adjust to give you a level playing field in the following year. If you don't like bearing the risk of ownership, there's the door. And that's what works, that's why LBOs have worked so well.

SHEPRO: Yes, but that's an awful lot of risk to impose on a manager. If you're an owner and things turn bad, you no longer have the option of moving to another company.

STEWART: Yes, that's true. But we are also offering a total compensation with a considerably higher *expected level* of compensation than the typical plan, because we're asking people to assume more risk. Most companies have both too little risk *and* too little reward. We want more risk and more reward.

In most companies, they not only debate the annual bonus targets, they even allow changes in the time horizon of already established plans. Even in the most far-sighted companies, a bonus plan generally lasts no more than three years. So what you find is that the bonus plans all end up being deferred, but guaranteed, compensation in disguise. There really isn't any sense of ownership understood as a fixed, long-term interest in a company.

Now, there is an entire spectrum of management incentive plans ranging from loose pay-for-performance schemes with lots of subjectivity on the one end to highly rigid and objective schemes on the other. Probably the most disciplined and objective form of managerial ownership is that achieved by an LBO. In that case, the capital charge in our EVA system becomes a contractually binding commitment to meet an *unyielding* schedule of interest and principal. If you don't pay it back, you're out; you've lost your investment and maybe your job.

Of course, that is likely to be too much risk for most managers, especially those operating in growth companies with lots of investment requirements. But the right question to ask is this: Where along that spectrum of flexibility and rigidity, of subjectivity and objectivity, is it optimal to design a management incentive system for this particular company? And while it will almost certainly vary from company to company, I feel very strongly that most companies err on the side of subjectivity and too little risk-

bearing. In the vast majority of companies, there are too many ways for corporate managers to earn bonuses that are not justified by shareholders' returns.

You see, what we're really attempting to achieve with EVA is a unified, coherent financial management system. And systems always involve trade-offs. That is, you establish policies designed to handle the most likely cases, even while recognizing that there will always be cases that might cause you to want to deviate from that policy. But, you have to maintain the discipline of the system; you don't want to be constantly changing the rules of the game.

The Missing Third: Accounting for Synergies

STEWART: But let me return to the point Joe Willett was making about accounting for the performance of different businesses. When you examine a large corporation, when you take the lid off the pot and look inside, you'll many times find a complex organization with lots of different product lines. In such cases, there will be shared costs and benefits, with the need to make transfers of costs or revenues among them. And while this is not specifically an EVA issue, it begs the question: How far down in an organization can we calculate individual EVAs until we begin to undermine any sense of common cause within the organization?
ADIMANDO: To make EVA effective, I think you have to push it all the way down to the individual operating units to get people's attention and produce results. And the best way to do that is to give them some level of targets, including an EVA target.

And, by the way, Bennett, I disagree with your characterization of EVA as just a financial management system; I think it's a way of life. You've

got to convince everybody that increasing shareholder value is the one overarching goal of the organization, and that EVA is the main internal yardstick for evaluating your progress toward meeting that goal. You must also make clear the role of customer satisfaction in sustaining higher EVA— because if you don't have satisfied customers, you won't be able to increase prices; you won't be able to sustain the market share you've achieved; and your EVA and market value will fall. I think stock market analysts, and especially the institutions that invest their money in public companies' stock, clearly understand this.

So, I think EVA has got to go down to the level of the operating units; they all have to buy into the plan.
STEWART: Can you measure EVA at the level of the individual plant?
ADIMANDO: Yes, you can. But, rather than go through 164 adjustments, you have to start off with something very simple. You take the assets operating people are familiar with—things like receivables, inventory, fixed assets, and rental equipment—and then figure out the cost of capital for that business. The cost of capital becomes the minimum rate of return they have to achieve on these working assets they have under their control. A given unit's EVA is its net profits minus the capital charge.

Once division heads and plant managers become accustomed to the process, you can begin using more sophisticated adjustments to get a better measure of operating cash flow and net assets employed. If you're a division manager or plant manager in our company, you're held responsible for creating EVA on the company's investment in your operation.
ZIMMERMAN: But how do you recognize profitability or value at the level of the plant?
ADIMANDO: By the value of the products coming out of that plant. We

measure that value by setting our actual production costs against our standard costs.

ZIMMERMAN: I agree that you can measure the plant's performance using standard costs. The question is: Do you get a number that really tells you anything? It's very difficult to come up with standard costs that provide a useful basis for measuring profitability, especially in cases where there are joint costs or benefits associated with the product.

Just think about a very simple firm that has two divisions. Presumably, you have one firm with two divisions as opposed to two separate firms because there are some synergies between the two operations. There are either some joint costs that are being shared, or there are joint benefits that would not be realized if the operations were independent. To illustrate the difficulty of accounting for joint costs or benefits, take a company like Coca-Cola with a lot of brand-name capital. How do you charge each of the product lines within Coca-Cola for that joint benefit?

Or consider the hamburger and hide problem of joint costs that appears in virtually every accounting textbook I've ever seen. The cow walks in the door and gets bopped over the head, and so you have a pile of hides and a pile of hamburger. Do you allocate the costs of raising the cow to the hamburger or the hides?

The accounting system can do that allocation, right down to the penny. But the answer will be wrong; it will be at best meaningless and it may even cause you to make bad business decisions. Allocating costs to the hides and the hamburger based on weight, for example, might cause you to decide to stop making hamburger. But, if you do that, you will suddenly discover that hides have become much less profitable than you thought they were.

And that's ultimately the conundrum that you have with EVA or any other performance measure. You can allocate costs down to the penny, and they will be right in an arithmetic sense. But they don't tell you anything about the real economic profitability of producing that joint product. Neither EVA nor any accounting system is set up to handle this kind of problem that arises from synergies.

But let me go back to the beginning of the discussion, because we're closing in on this missing third that I mentioned earlier. In his opening remarks, Joel described EVA as a performance measure *and* a compensation scheme. He said that putting in EVA as a performance measure without changing the compensation plan "isn't going to buy you anything."

But, as I stated earlier, I think Stern Stewart's got the problem two-thirds right, but there's one critical element missing from the story. The other third, which has been floating around in comments here and there, has to do with the notion of empowerment. Bennett earlier showed us a picture of a Quaker Oats plant manager on EVA. But what Bennett failed to mention is that when this guy sets up his machines, he is now able, perhaps for the first time, to determine the batch sizes. The *Fortune* article on EVA also mentioned that, after putting his company on an EVA program, the CEO of AT&T *starting last year* encouraged his operating heads to divide their businesses into profit centers resembling independent companies. And Joe Willett also mentioned the notion of empowerment in connection with Merrill Lynch's 50 different businesses.

My point, then, is that when you think about using EVA, it's not just a matter of linking performance measurement to the comp plan. For EVA to be effective, you have to be willing to decentralize the firm and "em-power" the operating managers. If you put in an EVA performance measurement system and incentive plan but keep all the decision rights at the top of the organization, then an EVA system may not accomplish much.

For some firms, however—particularly those in stable, mature, low-tech industries that are not facing much competition—decentralization is probably not optimal. The agency costs associated with delegating decisions to line managers in such cases probably outweigh the benefits. In these cases, you don't want to go to EVA—because lower-level managers just don't have the decision-making authority.

STEWART: Well, I agree with you that there's an iron triangle between decentralized decision-making, accountability, and incentives. And, as I said earlier, the information revolution and globalization are driving the need to decentralize decision-making, to vest decision-making closer to the action so that the organization is flexible, responsive, and really takes continuous improvement to heart. If that's the case, then to decentralize decision-making without also decentralizing the risk and reward of ownership is a formula for empire building as opposed to value building.

ZIMMERMAN: I agree with you, Bennett, that there's a lot more outsourcing and downsizing going on as companies realize that the costs of doing everything internally, of being a fully integrated firm, often outweigh the benefits. But there are still lots of large companies that operate in a variety of different businesses. Johnson & Johnson is one. And Merrill Lynch, as Joe said, has some 50 operating divisions that are each presumably more valuable as part of Merrill Lynch than as independent businesses.

So, there is still lots of evidence of valuable synergies in the corporate world. You can measure the EVA of the whole firm. But when you try and divide it up, you've got the classic hamburger and hide problem of joint costs. And activity-based costing won't solve that problem. It's not just the allocation of the joint costs, it's the allocation of the joint benefits as well, such as Coca-Cola's brand name capital. It's a very contentious matter, and it's bound to involve subjective judgment by top management overseeing the entire organization.

Think about your own firm, Bennett. Stern Stewart is basically a two-part firm: it has the consulting side of the business, as represented by you and Joel. And it has the *Journal of Applied Corporate Finance*, which is edited by Don Chew.

STEWART: That's an oversimplification. In fact, we have about ten lines of business.

ZIMMERMAN: Let's just keep it to those two for my example. Now, why do these two activities exist within the same firm? Well, presumably, because there are joint benefits. In fact, there are synergies that are evident in this room right now: the *Journal* benefits from the reputation of the consulting practice and its ability to bring practitioners into this kind of meeting, and the consulting side benefits from the prestige and advertising value of the *Journal*.

Now, how do you measure the EVA of the *Journal*? Does Don Chew have an EVA target?

STEWART: Yes, in effect.

ZIMMERMAN: And how do you allocate the joint benefits of having them both in the same firm?

STEWART: As I said, we have about ten different product lines. And if we get a consulting assignment, that consulting revenue can be divided up into five different pies internally.

ZIMMERMAN: But is it garbage in, garbage out?

STEWART: No, I determine the proper allocation—and, as you know,

Jerry, I have an automatic marginal cost calculator in my head.

ZIMMERMAN: Well, Bennett, that just goes to prove my point: there is likely to be an important role for subjectivity and judgment by top management, particularly in cases involving joint costs and benefits.

STEWART: Well, perhaps my answer was overly simple. A good example of what I have in mind is what AT&T has done with Bell Labs. Bell Labs, as you know, has been a fountain of basic and applied research that has benefitted the reputation and profitability of the entire firm. As such, Bell Labs was treated entirely as corporate overhead. Under their new EVA system, however, only basic research remains in overhead, while all the engineers and researchers working on applied research must now "sell" their services to internal operating units, with explicit goals and deliverables clearly spelled out. The cost of those services are charged to the operating unit or units, and this has transformed Bell Labs' applied research into an EVA center—one that is accountable for generating economic profits. And this in turn has led to a more effective allocation of those research resources to promising uses.

More on Synergies

RAVID: I would like to ask a somewhat technical question. When you measure EVA, how do you measure the value of net assets? Is it historical accounting cost, or is it replacement cost? If you're using replacement cost or market value, then EVA is telling you something about how much absolute economic value you're creating. But, if you're using historical costs—which, in one sense, are sunk costs—then you're really better off just asking managers to increase their economic earnings or cash flow.

STERN: This is an important issue: For example, what do you do with a mining company most of its assets you acquired a hundred years ago? Our answer would be that it depends on how large the differences are between historical and replacement costs. If the differences are not material, or there's no way of confidently establishing replacement costs, then we recommend using historical costs.

STEWART: In the case of the mining firm with 100-year-old assets, you may actually be better off setting up a performance measurement system by assuming there is *no* balance sheet and hence *no* capital. Then you would simply define EVA as the operating earnings. And you would charge people only for new capital that goes in, while giving them a credit for any additional capital that comes out.

You see, if you keep the old balance sheet and attempt to correct that on a piecemeal basis, you then fall prey to the fallacy that sunk costs are relevant; but they are not. That's why if you merely get people to focus on the *increase* in EVA, then it really doesn't matter if you haven't gotten the value of the assets correct the first time. It doesn't matter where you begin; only that you maintain consistency after beginning the measurement process.

RAVID: But that wouldn't tell me how to make a decision on the initial investment—whether the economic earnings were adequate to justify buying the assets in the first place.

STEWART: That's true. But consider this: If you sell an asset and you recognize a book gain or loss, that gain or loss does not go through EVA. In our system, that book gain or loss is taken off the income statement, and put back onto the balance sheet. In this sense, we're using cash accounting.

ZIMMERMAN: But, Bennett, that statement gives me even more concern about how you handle this issue of synergies. Take Coca-Cola again, with its huge investment in its brand name. It's an intangible asset; it can't be sold to a third party without selling the whole firm and the products that go along with it. It's not like a plant, it's not like a deposit of ore that they can sell.

Let's assume that Coca-Cola has just two product lines: Diet Coke and Classic Coke. How does your system work? Assuming there are no assets in Coca-Cola other than its brand name, how do you value its capital stock? Do you value the brand name?

STEWART: No, we don't care about that.

ZIMMERMAN: You don't care? But if I'm running Diet Coke on an EVA plan, I could earn large bonuses at the expense of Classic Coke by making low-quality Diet Coke and cutting back on advertising. I can enrich myself while ruining the brand name and imposing a large cost on Classic Coke.

STEWART: Yes, I know. There you have a joint product, so what you have to do is to create a keiretsu-like structure with what amounts to cross ownership among products. That is, you have to say that while the larger part—say, 70%—of your bonus is based on your own operation's EVA, the other 30% is based on the EVA of the entire firm.

ZIMMERMAN: But that won't make the problem disappear. Think about advertising decisions. This is also a case where if I decide to advertise Diet Coke, I'm also advertising Coca-Cola's name, which is going to add to the value of that corporate name.

STEWART: Right. So what we would do in such a case is to figure out what is a reasonable apportionment of value among divisions. For example, we might say that two thirds of the advertising costs in that case are borne by Diet Coke and the remaining third is unallocated and held at corporate. At any rate, you can address this problem by devising some sensible allocation rule.

In Closing

STERN: Well, I don't think we're going to solve this problem in the next five minutes. In bringing this discussion to an end, I would just like to offer a modest proposal—one that holds up EVA as a means of taking a step toward not just managerial ownership, but employee ownership throughout a large organization.

Because of its simplicity, one of the great benefits of EVA is that it can make employees throughout an organization conscious of what they're doing and why they're doing it. If you "incentivize" people on a clear and simple basis, you can impound the corporate objective into their very being. And even if some individuals don't get it right away, peer pressure alone should compel most to behave as value-maximizers.

We instituted an EVA plan at a government agency in South Africa in July of '93. The agency spent four months implementing this program, which included our participation in a two-hour tape that was shown to 11,000 employees—principally laboratory technicians. More than 85% of the employees have not graduated from high school, and we were told they would never be able to understand this.

And we were amazed at the outcome. Their EVA for the first six months exceeded by five times what they had forecast for the entire year. And they are now planning to pay out bonuses to all 11,000 employees that are more than twice what they originally expected.

The lesson from this experience appears to be that, in many cases, all you have to do to improve people's performance is to get them to understand how superior performance can have an impact on themselves. Their performance measure is not a consolidated measure. These people are deep down in their units. But once a month they get a line from the CFO telling them how well their unit is doing on EVA year-to-date. And, as the director of the agency told me, that is the day of the month when these employees tell their families they won't be home for dinner; instead they sit around the table at work trying to figure out what they can do to improve things even more.

So, from the implementation side, I'm not concerned about employees' ability to understand the concept of EVA. I recognize that there are some issues and mechanics of getting it done that we have not addressed in the last two hours—particularly, the issue of empowerment and the problem of accounting for synergies that Jerry Zimmerman was raising at the end. But these are issues that can be resolved, as Bennett was suggesting, through cross-ownership schemes and—as reluctant as I am to concede this—perhaps even some subjective judgment by top management. But, having made this concession, let me say that our ultimate aim with EVA is to eliminate altogether the need for subjectivity in the financial management (and incentive) system.

III. CAPITAL STRUCTURE AND PAYOUT POLICY

The articles in this section are devoted largely to questions like the following: Are there good reasons to believe there is such a thing as an "optimal" capital structure—a proportion of debt to equity that can be expected to maximize a company's market value? And is there likely to be an optimal percentage of corporate earnings to pay out as dividends? Further, assuming the answer is yes to the above, what are the critical factors in setting the leverage and payout ratios for a given company? Or, to put the same matter a little differently, what are the most important benefits and costs associated with the use of more debt and the payment of higher dividends?

In the 1980s, these questions attained a prominence, and indeed an urgency, unprecedented in our corporate history. For, along with the wave of corporate restructuring activities—acquisitions, divestitures, leveraged buyouts, spin-offs, and major stock repurchases—many companies underwent dramatic changes in capital structure. In the LBO movement, for example, newly private companies were launched with debt-to-asset ratios upwards of 90%. Large public companies, traditionally leveraged at 20% to 30%, resorted to the junk bond market to make large acquisitions and, in so doing, raised their debt ratios well above 50%. At the same time, many corporate restructurings have included major stock repurchase programs that seem to reflect a more explicit, permanent decision to leverage the capital structure.

As I said in my "Introduction," after the dramatic recapitalizations of the 1980s, typically accompanied by large increases in stock prices, it may seem odd to begin this section with Merton Miller's reassessment of the "The Modigliani-Miller Propositions After Thirty Years." For it was Miller who, with Franco Modigliani, formulated in 1958 the classic "M&M" capital structure "irrelevance" proposition—stated baldly, the argument that a corporation's debt-equity ratio should not affect the value of its shares. A few years after came its equally venerated companion—the M&M dividend irrelevance proposition—the notion that share values are influenced primarily by a corporation's expected earnings power, and not by the percentage of those earnings paid out as dividends.

The empirical import of the M&M propositions—and thus their central message to corporate practitioners—can be seen by turning the propositions "on their heads." That is, if changes in corporate capital structure or dividends do increase stock values, they are likely to do so only for the following reasons: (1) they reduce taxes or transaction costs: (2) they provide a reliable "signal" to investors of management's confidence in the firm's earnings prospects; or (3) they increase the probability that management will undertake only profitable investments.

In this article, after recounting the thinking behind the propositions, Professor Miller goes on to consider the contribution of each of these three factors to an explanation of the leveraged restructuring movement of the '80s. Part of the discussion focuses on the beneficial effect of debt finance on managerial efficiency and corporate reinvestment decisions—especially in companies in mature industries with too much "free cash flow" (for more on this, see Michael Jensen's comments in the roundtable at the end of this section). But the greatest stress falls on the tax advantage of debt over equity, an argument put forth by Miller and Modigliani in 1963. In brief, the "tax-adjusted" M&M proposition says that the benefits of substituting tax-deductible interest payments for non-deductible (and thus twice-taxed) dividend payments could push the optimal capital structure toward 100% debt (provided, of course, the offsetting costs of high leverage are not too great).

In "The Capital Structure Puzzle: Another Look at the Evidence," the University of Rochester's Michael Barclay and Clifford Smith begin by observing that the academic finance profession has failed to provide corporate CFOs and treasurers with useful, much less definitive, answers to these questions. Financial economists in the tradition of the University of Chicago long argued that both capital structure and dividends are largely "irrelevant"; that is, they have no important, predictable effects (with the possible exception of tax consequences) on corporate market values. The conventional view of capital structure—or, at least the one most often professed by practicing financial executives—says that companies attempt to balance the tax advantages of increased debt financing against the higher expected "bankruptcy costs." But, responding to the limitations of this static trade-off theory (particularly its inability to explain why more profitable companies seem to have lower, not higher, debt ratios), Stewart Myers' 1984 Presidential Address to the American Finance Association presented a competing pecking order theory. Stated in brief, the pecking order justifies managers' preference for internal funds (retained earnings) over outside capital, and for debt over equity when outside funding is required, as a financing strategy that aims to minimize "information costs."

In their article, Barclay and Smith argue that management incentives, taxes, bankruptcy costs, and information costs all appear to play important roles in corporate financing decisions. The key to reconciling the different theories—and thus to solving the capital structure puzzle—lies in achieving a better understanding of the relation between corporate financing stocks (leverage ratios) and flows (specific choices between debt and equity). According to the authors, the bulk of the evidence on leverage ratios is consistent with the idea that companies have target leverage ratios, and that such targets depend primarily on one key variable: the company's investment opportunities. As a general rule, the larger the percentage of a firm's value that consists of intangible "growth options," the lower the leverage ratio. The authors explain this pattern as follows: For high-growth firms, the "underinvestment problem" associated with heavy debt financing can end up destroying significant value. For mature companies, however, high leverage is likely to add value by strengthening incentives for efficiency and controlling the managerial tendency to overinvest.

But if the evidence on leverage ratios is largely consistent with the idea that companies set leverage targets, other research suggests that firms often deviate widely from their targets, particularly firms experiencing changes in profitability. Although such findings are generally viewed as evidence that corporate managers do not set target leverage ratios—or do not try very hard to achieve them—Barclay and Smith suggest another interpretation: Precisely because the information (and other) costs of issuing riskier securities can be very large, "even if companies have target leverage ratios, there will be an optimal deviation from those targets—one that depends on the costs associated with adjusting back to the target relative to the costs of deviating

from it." As the authors note in closing, "The next major step forward in solving the capital structure puzzle is almost certain to involve a more formal weighing of these two sets of costs."

In "On Financial Architecture," Barclay and Smith present the findings of their more recent study of two important features of corporate debt: maturity and priority. After examining over 6,000 firms during the period 1981-1993, Smith and Barclay conclude that a company's investment opportunities are also the most important factor in determining both the maturity and priority of its debt. Besides having less debt to begin with, growth companies tend to choose debt with shorter maturities and higher priority than mature firms. According to the authors, growth companies make such choices not only to give lenders protection against the greater uncertainty associated with such businesses, but also to preserve their own future financing flexibility and ability to make strategic investments.

In "Who Wins in Large Stock Buybacks—Those Who Sell or Those Who Hold?," William McNally discusses the findings of his recent study of fixed-price and dutch auction self-tender offers in the 1980s. Shareholders who tender into fixed-price offers earn higher returns than those selling into dutch auctions, reflecting the larger premiums offered in fixed-price repurchases. Nevertheless, the two types of offers produce roughly the same total returns to the shareholders who do not tender (about 10%, on average, during the two-to-four-week offering period).

In "The Dividend Cut 'Heard 'Round the World,' " Professor Eugene Brigham and two practitioners, Paul Evanson, president of Florida Power and Light, and Stern Stewart's Dennis Soter collaborate in describing an interesting innovation in corporate practice—one that lends support to the M&M "dividend irrelevance" proposition. In May 1994, the FPL Group, the parent company of Florida Power & Light, announced a 32% reduction in its dividend, thereby becoming the first profitable utility to take this step. Although the initial market reaction was negative, FPL's stock has outperformed the S&P Electric Utility index by a significant margin in the two years following the announcement. Within six weeks of the dividend cut (but after a series of "roadshows" explaining FPL's decision to the investment community), at least 15 major brokerage houses had added the stock to their "buy" lists. And, by the end of 1995, FPL's institutional ownership had increased from about 33% to 47%.

At the same time it announced the dividend cut, FPL also announced its intent to repurchase up to 10 million shares of its common stock. Besides providing a more tax-efficient means of distributing excess capital, FPL's partial substitution of stock repurchases for dividends was justified as a way of increasing the company's financial flexibility in advance of further deregulation and heightened competition among utilities. And, although few utilities have followed FPL's example to date, a remarkable number of U.S. companies now appear to be choosing stock repurchases in place of larger dividend increases—an appropriate response, as the authors suggest, to an increasingly competitive business environment.

In the "Bank of America Roundtable on the Link Between Capital Structure and Shareholder Value," Michael Jensen explores with three senior corporate executives a number of ways in which corporate financial policies and performance measures can be designed to provide the managers of public companies with stronger incentives to make value-increasing investment and operating decisions. For companies in mature industries with significant overcapacity, Jensen argues that an LBO-like structure combining high leverage with concentrated equity ownership can add value by encouraging the payout of excess capital and reduction of capacity. But, for firms with significant growth opportunities and limited debt capacity, Jensen holds out another solution: an "EVA-based" internal performance measurement and incentive compensation system (see articles in the previous section). Where LBOs make the cost of capital "both explicit and contractually binding" by converting most of the old equity into debt, an EVA financial management system simulates the conditions of an LBO by charging operating managers for their use of all investor capital, equity as well as debt. And although such simulated incentives may be less powerful than the real ones, EVA has one advantage over the LBO that will often prove decisive, especially for growth firms: it provides the "feel" of ownership without imposing the costs of high leverage.

DHC

THE MODIGLIANI-MILLER PROPOSITIONS AFTER THIRTY YEARS

by Merton H. Miller, University of Chicago*

I t has now been 30 years since the Modigliani-Miller Propositions were first presented in "The Cost of Capital, Corporation Finance and the Theory of Investment," which appeared in the *American Economic Review* in June 1958. I have been invited, if not to celebrate, at least to mark, the event with a retrospective look at what we set out to do on that occasion and an appraisal of where the Propositions stand today after three decades of intense scrutiny and often bitter controversy.

* This article is a shortened version of an article that appeared in the *Journal of Economic Perspectives* (Fall 1988) and is reprinted here with permission of the American Economic Association the journal's publisher The author would like to acknowledge helpful comments on an earlier draft made by George Constantinides, Melvin Reder, Lester Telser, Hal Varian, Robert Vishny and by the editors of the *Journal of Economic Perspectives*, Carl Shapiro, Joseph Stiglitz, and Timothy Taylor.

> *The view that capital structure is literally irrelevant or that "nothing matters" in corporate finance, though still sometimes attributed to us,...is far from what we ever actually said about the real-world applications of our theoretical propositions.*

Some of these controversies can by now be regarded as settled. Our Proposition I, which holds the value of a firm to be independent of its capital structure (its debt/equity ratio), is accepted as an implication of equilibrium in perfect capital markets. The validity of our then novel arbitrage proof of that proposition is also no longer disputed, and essentially similar arbitrage proofs are now common throughout finance.[1] Propositions analogous to, and often even called, M and M propositions have spread beyond corporation finance to the fields of money and banking, fiscal policy, and international finance.[2]

Clearly Proposition I, and its proof, have been accepted into economic theory. Less clear, however, is the empirical significance of the MM value-invariance Proposition I in its original sphere of corporation finance.

Skepticism about the practical force of our invariance proposition was understandable given the almost daily reports in the financial press, then as now, of spectacular increases in the values of firms after changes in capital structure. But the view that capital structure is literally irrelevant or that "nothing matters" in corporate finance, though still sometimes attributed to us (and tracing perhaps to the very provocative way we made our point), is far from what we ever actually said about the real-world applications of our theoretical propositions. Looking back now, perhaps we should have put more emphasis on the other, upbeat side of the "nothing matters" coin: showing what *doesn't* matter can also show, by implication, what *does*.

This more constructive approach to our invariance proposition and its central assumption of perfect capital markets has now become the standard one in teaching corporate finance. We could not have taken that approach in 1958, however, because the analysis departed too greatly from the then accepted way of thinking about capital structure choices. We first had to convince people (including ourselves!) that there could be *any* conditions, even in a "frictionless" world, where a firm would be indifferent between issuing securities as different in legal status, investor risk, and apparent cost as debt and

equity. Remember that interest rates on corporate debts were then in the 3 to 5 percent range, with equity earnings/price ratios—then the conventional measure of the "cost" of equity capital—running from 15 to 20 percent.

The paradox of indifference in the face of such huge spreads in the apparent cost of financing was resolved by our Proposition II, which showed that when Proposition I held, the cost of equity capital was a linear increasing function of the debt/equity ratio. Any gains from using more of what might seem to be cheaper debt capital would thus be offset by the correspondingly higher cost of the now riskier equity capital. Our propositions implied that the *weighted average* of these costs of capital to a firm would remain the same no matter what combination of financing sources the firm actually chose.

Though departing substantially from the then conventional views about capital structure, our propositions were certainly not without links to what had gone before. Our distinction between the real value of the firm and its financial packaging raised many issues long familiar to economists in discussions of money illusion and money neutrality...

In the field of corporate finance, however, the only prior treatment similar in spirit to our own was by David Durand in 1952 (who, as it turned out, also became our first formal critic).[3] Durand had proposed, as one of what he saw as two polar approaches to valuing shares, that investors might ignore the firm's then-existing capital structure and first price the whole firm by capitalizing its operating earnings *before* interest and taxes. The value of the shares would then be found by subtracting out the value of the bonds. But he rejected this possibility in favor of his other extreme, which he believed closer to the ordinary real-world way of valuing corporate shares. According to this conventional view, investors capitalized the firm's net income *after* interest and taxes with only a loose, qualitative adjustment for the degree of leverage in the capital structure.

That we too did not dismiss the seemingly unrealistic approach of looking through the momentary capital structure to the underlying real flows may

1. Examples include Cornell and French (1983) on the pricing of stock index futures, Black and Scholes (1973) on the pricing of options, and Ross (1976) on the structure of capital asset prices generally. For other, and in some respects, more general proofs of our capital structure proposition see among others, Stiglitz (1974) for a general equilibrium proof showing that individual wealth and consumption opportunities are unaffected by capital structures; Hirshleifer (1965) and (1966) for a state preference, complete-markets proof; Duffie and Shafer (1986) for extensions to some cases of incomplete markets; and Merton (forthcoming) for a spanning proof.

Full citations for all articles mentioned are listed in the References section at the end of this article.
2. See, for example, Wallace (1981) on domestic open-market operations; Sargent and Smith (1986) on central bank foreign-exchange interventions: Chamley and Polemarchakis (1984) on government tax and borrowing policies; and Fama (1980), (1983) on money, banking, and the quantity theory.
3. Durand (1939).

well trace to the macroeconomic perspective from which we had approached the problem of capital structure in the first instance. Our main concern, initially, was with the determinants of *aggregate* economic investment by the business sector. The resources for capital formation by firms came ultimately from the savings of the household sector, a connection that economists had long found convenient to illustrate with schematic national income and wealth T-accounts, including, of course, simplified sectoral balance sheets such as:

BUSINESS FIRMS		HOUSEHOLDS	
Assets	**Liabilities**	**Assets**	**Liabilities**
Productive capital	Debts owed to households	Debts of firms	Household net worth
	Equity in firms owned by households	Equity in firms	

Consolidating the accounts of the two sectors leads to the familiar national balance sheet in which the debt and equity securities no longer appear:

Assets	**Liabilities**
Productive capital	Household net worth

The value of the business sector to its ultimate owners in the household sector is thus seen clearly to lie in the value of the underlying capital. And by the same token, the debt and equity securities owned by households can be seen not as final, but only as intermediate, assets serving to partition the earnings (and their attendant risks) among the many separate individual households within the sector.

Our value-invariance Proposition I was in a sense only the application of this macroeconomic intuition to the microeconomics of corporate finance; and the arbitrage proof we gave for our Proposition I was just the counterpart, at the individual investor level, of the consolidation of accounts and the washing out of the debt/equity ratios at the sectoral level. In fact, one blade of our arbitrage proof had the arbitrager doing exactly that washing out. If levered firms were undervalued relative to unlevered firms, our arbitrager was called on to "undo the leverage" by buying an appropriate

portion of both the levered firm's debt and its shares. On a consolidated basis, the interest paid by the firm cancels against the interest received and the arbitrager thus owned a pure equity stream. Unlevered corporate equity streams could in turn be relevered by borrowing on individual accounts if unlevered streams ever sold at a discount relative to levered corporate equity. That possibility of "homemade leverage" by individual investors provided the second and completing blade of our arbitrage proof of value invariance.

Our arbitrage proof drew little flak from those who saw it essentially as a metaphor—an expository device for highlighting hidden implications of the "law of one price" in perfect capital markets. But whether the operations we called arbitrage could *in fact* substitute for consolidation when dealing with real-world corporations was disputed. Could investors, acting on their own, really replicate and, where required, wash out corporate capital structures—if not completely, as in the formal proof, then by enough, and quickly enough, to make the invariance proposition useful as a description of the central tendency in the real-world capital market? These long-standing and still not completely resolved issues of the empirical relevance of the MM propositions will be the primary focus of what follows here.

Three separate reasons (over and above the standard complaint that we attributed too much rationality to the stock market) were quickly offered by our critics for believing that individual investors could not enforce the corporate valuations implied by Propositions I and II. These lines of objection, relating to dividends, debt defaults, and taxes, each emphasized a different, distinctive feature of the corporate form of business organization. And each in turn will be reexamined here, taking full advantage this time, however, of the hindsight of thirty years of subsequent research and events.

■ ARBITRAGE, DIVIDENDS, AND THE CORPORATE VEIL

The law of one price is easily visualized in commodity settings where market institutions deliberately provide the necessary standardization and interchangeability of units. But to which of the many features of an entity as complex as an operating business firm would our financial equilibration extend?

We opted for a Fisherian rather than the standard Marshallian representation of the firm. Irving Fisher's view of the firm—now the standard one in finance, but

> The dividend invariance proposition stated only that, *given* the firm's investment decision, its dividend decision would have no effect on the value of the shares.

then just becoming known—impounds the details of technology, production, and sales in a black box and focuses on the underlying net cash flow. The firm for Fisher was just an abstract engine transforming current consumable resources, obtained by issuing securities, into future consumable resources payable to the owners of the securities. Even so, what did it mean to speak of firms or cash flow streams being different, but still "similar" enough to allow for arbitrage or anything close to it?

Some of the answers would be provided, we hoped, by our concept of a "risk class," which was offered with several objectives in mind. At the level of the theory, it defined what today would be called a "spanning" set; the uncertain underlying future cash flow streams of the individual firms within each class could be assumed perfectly correlated, and hence perfect substitutes. But the characteristics of those correlated streams could be allowed to differ from class to class. Hence, at the more practical level, the risk class could be identified with Marshallian industries—groupings around which so much academic and Wall Street research had always been organized.[4] We hoped that the earnings of firms in some large industries such as oil or electricity generation might vary together closely enough not just for real-world arbitragers to carry on their work of equilibration efficiently, but also to offer us as outside observers a chance of judging how well they were succeeding. Indeed, we devoted more than a third of the original paper (plus a couple of follow-up studies) to empirical estimates of how closely real-world market values approached those predicted by our model. Our hopes of settling the empirical issues by that route, however, have largely been disappointed.[5]

INVESTOR ARBITRAGE WHEN DIVIDENDS DIFFER: THE DIVIDEND-INVARIANCE PROPOSITION

Although the risk class, with its perfect correlation of the underlying real cash streams, may have provided a basis for the arbitrage in our formal proof, there remained the sticking point of how real-

world market equilibrators could gain access to a firm's operating cash flows, let alone to two or more correlated ones. As a matter of law, what the individual equity investor actually gets on buying a share is not a right to the firm's underlying cash flow but only to such cash dividends as the corporation's directors choose to declare. Must these man-made payout policies also be assumed perfectly correlated along with the underlying cash flows to make the equilibration effective? If so, the likely empirical range of the value-invariance proposition would seem to be narrow indeed.

A second MM-invariance proposition—that the value of the firm was independent of its dividend policy—was developed in part precisely to meet this class of objections. The essential content of the dividend-"irrelevance" argument was already in hand at the time of the original leverage paper and led us there to dismiss the whole dividend question as a "mere detail" (not the last time, alas, that we may have overworked that innocent word "mere"). We stated the dividend-invariance proposition explicitly, and noted its relation to the leverage proof in the very first round of replies to our critics.[6] But because dividend decisions were controversial in their own right, and because considering them raised so many side issues of valuation theory and of practical policy, both private and public, we put off the fuller treatment of dividends to a separate paper that appeared three years after the first one.[7]

That the close connection in origin of the two invariance propositions has not been more widely appreciated traces not only to their separation in time, but probably also to our making no reference to arbitrage (or even to debt or equity) in the proof of the dividend-invariance proposition. Why bring in arbitrage, we felt, when an even simpler line of proof would serve? The dividend invariance proposition stated only that, *given* the firm's investment decision, its dividend decision would have no effect on the value of the shares. The added cash to fund the higher dividend payout must come from somewhere, after all; and with investment fixed, that somewhere could only be from selling off part of the firm. As long as

---

4. Remember, in this connection, that the capital asset pricing models of Sharpe (1964) and Lintner (1965) and their later extensions that now dominate empirical research in finance had yet to come on the scene. For some glimpses of how more recent asset pricing frameworks can accommodate the MM propositions without reference to MM risk classes or MM arbitrage, see Ross (1988).

5. Direct statistical calibration of the goodness of fit of the MM value-invariance propositions has not so far been achieved by us or others for a variety of reasons, some of which will be noted further in due course below.

6. See Modigliani and Miller (1959), especially pages 662-668.

7. See Miller and Modigliani (1961).

*If the tale is actually one of cutting back unprofitable investments and paying out
the proceeds as dividends, followed by a big run-up in price,
then the MM invariance proposition may seem to be failing,
but is really not being put to the test.*

the securities sold off could be presumed sold at their market-determined values, then, whether the analysis was carried out under conditions of certainty or uncertainty, the whole operation of paying dividends, again holding investment constant, could be seen as just a wash—a swap of equal values not much different in principle from withdrawing money from a pass-book savings account.

The Informational Content of Dividends

Managerial decisions on dividends thus might affect the cash component of an investor's return; but they would not affect the *total* return of cash plus appreciation, and the total is what mattered. In practice, of course, even changing the cash-dividend component often seemed to matter a great deal, at least to judge by the conspicuous price jumps typically accompanying announcements of major boosts or cuts in dividends. These highly visible price reactions to dividend announcements were among the first (and are still the most frequently mentioned) of the supposed empirical refutations of the MM value-invariance principle. By invoking the dividend-invariance proposition to support the leverage-invariance proposition, we seemed to have succeeded only in substituting one set of objections for another.

But, as we suggested in our 1961 dividend paper, these price reactions to dividend announcements were not really refutations. They were better seen as failures of one of the key assumptions of both the leverage and dividend models, *viz.* that all capital market participants, inside managers and outside investors alike, have the same information about the firm's cash flows. Over long enough time horizons this all-cards-on-the-table assumption might, we noted, be an entirely acceptable approximation, particularly in a market subject to S.E.C. disclosure rules. But new information is always coming in; and over shorter runs, the firm's inside managers were likely to have information about the firm's prospects not yet known to or fully appreciated by the investing public at large. Management-initiated actions on dividends or other financial transactions might then serve, by implication, to convey to the

outside market information not yet incorporated in the price of the firm's securities.

Although our concern in the 1961 dividend paper was with the observed announcement effects of dividend decisions, informational asymmetry also raised the possibility of strategic behavior on the part of the existing stockholders and/or their management agents. Might not much of the price response to dividend (and/or other capital structure) announcements simply be attempts by the insiders to mislead the outsiders; and if so, what point was there to our notion of a capital market equilibrium rooted solely in the fundamentals? Our instincts as economists led us to discount the possibility that firms could hope to fool the investing public systematically. But, at the time, we could offer little more support than a declaration of faith in Lincoln's Law—that you can't fool all of the people all of the time.

By the 1970s, however, the concept of an information equilibrium had entered economics, and came soon after to the field of corporate finance as well.[8] In 1978, for example, Stephen Ross showed how debt/equity ratios might serve to signal, in the technical sense, managements' special information about the firm's future prospects.[9] But the extent to which these and subsequent asymmetric information models can account for observed departures from the "invariance" propositions has not so far been convincingly established.[10]

The Interaction of Investment Policy and Dividend Policy

The dividend-invariance proposition, as we initially stated it, highlights still another way in which the corporate form of organization, and especially the separation it permits between ownership and management, can have effects that at first sight at least seem to contradict the MM value-invariance predictions. Recall that the dividend-invariance proposition takes the firm's investment decision as given—which is just a strong way of saying that the level of investment, whatever it might be, is set by management *independently* of the dividend. Without imposing such an "other-things-equal" condition, there would, of course, be no way of separating

---

8. Bhattacharya (1979) noted the formal similarity between Spence's (1973) job-market signaling model and the MM dividend model with asymmetric information.

9. Ross (1977).

10. For a recent survey of results on dividend signaling, see Miller (1987). For a more general survey of asymmetric information models in finance, see Stiglitz (1982).

the market's reaction to real investment events from reactions to the dividend and any associated, purely financial events.

In the real world, of course, the financial press reports single-company stories, not cross-sectional partial regression coefficients. In these single company tales, the investment decision and the dividend/financing decisions are typically thoroughly intertwined. But if the tale is actually one of cutting back unprofitable investments and paying out the proceeds as dividends, followed by a big run-up in price, then the MM invariance proposition may seem to be failing, but is really not being put to the test. Nor is this scenario only hypothetical. Something very much like it appears in a number of the most notorious of recent takeover battles, particularly in the oil industry where some target firms had conspicuously failed to cut back their long-standing polices of investment in exploration despite the drastic fall in petroleum prices.

In a sense, as noted earlier, these gains to shareholders from ending a management-caused undervaluation of the firm's true earning power can also be viewed as a form of capital-market arbitrage, but not one that atomistic MM investors or arbitragers can supply on their own. Once again, the special properties of the corporate form intrude, this time the voting rights that attach to corporate shares and the majority-like rules (and sometimes supermajority rules) in the corporate charters that determine the control over the firm's decisions. Much of the early skepticism, still not entirely dispelled, about the real empirical force of inter-firm arbitrage (MM-arbitrage included) traces to these properties of corporate shares beyond their purely cash-flow consequences. A particular example of the obstacle they offered to effective capital market equilibrium was that of closed-end investment funds. In 1958, as still today, closed-end funds often sold at a substantial discount to net asset value—a discount that could be recaptured only by the shareholders merely (that word again) by getting enough of them to vote to convert to open-end fund status . . .

[Omitted here from the original is a section entitled "MM Invariance with Limited Liability and Risky Debt."]

■ THE MM PROPOSITIONS IN A WORLD WITH TAXES

We have no shortage of potential candidates for forces that might well lead the market to depart systematically and persistently from the predictions of the original MM value-invariance propositions. One such likely candidate, the third of the original lines of objection, has loomed so large in fact as to have dominated academic discussions of the MM propositions, at least until the recent wave of corporate takeovers and restructurings became the new focus of attention. That candidate is the corporate income tax, the one respect in which everyone agreed that the corporate form really did matter.

The U.S. Internal Revenue Code has long been the classic, and by now is virtually the world's only, completely unintegrated tax system imposing "double taxation" of corporate net income. A separate income tax is first levied directly on the corporation; and, except for certain small and closely held corporations, who may elect to he taxed as partnerships under Subchapter S of the Code, a second tax is then levied at the personal level on any income flows such as dividends or interest generated at the corporate level. Double taxation of the interest payments is avoided because interest on indebtedness is considered a cost of doing business and hence may he deducted from corporate gross income in computing net taxable corporate earnings. But no such allowance has been made for any costs of equity capital.[11]

If the separate corporate income tax were merely a modest franchise tax for the privilege of doing business in corporate form, as was essentially the case when it was introduced in the early years of this century, the extra burden on equity capital might be treated as just one more on the long list of second-order differences in the costs of alternative sources of capital for the firm. But, at the time of our 1958 article, the marginal tax rate under the corporate income tax had been close to and sometimes over 50 percent for nearly 20 years, and it remained there for almost another 30 years until dropped to 34 percent by the recent Tax Reform Act of 1986. The cost differentials of this size were just too big to be set aside in any normative or empirical treatments of real-world capital structure choices.

---

11. Two exceptions should be noted for the record. An undistributed profits tax from which dividends were deductible was in force for two years in the late 1930s. The excess-profits tax during World War II also allowed a deduction not for dividends, but for the "normal profits" of the firm.

> **The tax-adjusted MM proposition...suggested that the high bond ratings of such companies, in which the management took so much pride, may actually have been a sign of their incompetence; that the managers were leaving too much of their stockholders' money on the table in the form of unnecessary corporate income tax.**

Strictly speaking, of course, there is one sense, albeit a somewhat strained one, in which the basic value-invariance does go through even with corporate taxes. The Internal Revenue Service can be considered as just another security holder, whose claim is essentially an equity one in the normal course of events (but which can also take on some of the characteristics of secured debt when things go badly and back taxes are owed). Securities, after all, are just ways of partitioning the firm's earnings: the MM propositions assert only that the sum of the values of all the claims is independent of the number and the shapes of the separate partitions.

However satisfying this government-as-a-shareholder view may be as a generalization of the original model, the fact remains that the government, though it sometimes gives negative taxes or subsidies for some kinds of investment, does not normally buy its share with an initial input of funds that can serve to compensate the other stockholders for the claims on income they transfer to the Treasury. Nor are we talking here of taxation-according-to-the-benefits or of the rights of eminent domain or even of whether the corporate tax might ultimately be better for the shareholders, or for the general public, than alternative ways of raising the same revenue. For the nongovernment equity claimholders, the government's claim to the firm's earnings is a net subtraction from their own.

THE MM TAX-ADJUSTED LEVERAGE PROPOSITION

Allowing for that subtraction can lead to a very different kind of MM Proposition, though one, as we showed in our Tax Correction article (1963), that can still be derived from an arbitrage proof along lines very similar to the original.[12] This time, however, the value of the firm (in the sense of the sum of the values of the private, nongovernmental claims) is *not* independent of the debt/equity division in the capital structure. In general, thanks to the deductibility of interest, the purely private claims will increase in value as the debt ratio increases. In fact, under conditions which can by no means be dismissed out of hand as implausible, we showed that the value of the private claims might well have no well-defined interior maximum. The optimal capital structure might be all debt!

In many ways this tax-adjusted MM proposition provoked even more controversy than the original invariance one—which could be, and often was, shrugged off as merely another inconsequential paradox from some economists' frictionless dream-world. But this one carried direct and not very flattering implications for the top managements of companies with low levels of debt. It suggested that the high bond ratings of such companies, in which the management took so much pride, may actually have been a sign of their incompetence; that the managers were leaving too much of their stockholders' money on the table in the form of unnecessary corporate income tax payments—payments which in the aggregate over the sector of large, publicly-held corporations clearly came to many billions of dollars.

We must admit that we too were somewhat taken aback when we first saw this conclusion emerging from our analysis. The earlier modeling of the tax effect in our 1958 paper, which the 1963 paper corrected, had also suggested tax advantages in debt financing, but of a smaller and more credible size. By 1963, however, with corporate debt ratios in the late 50s not much higher than in the low tax 1920s,[13] we seemed to face an unhappy dilemma: either corporate managers did not know (or perhaps care) that they were paying too much in taxes; or something major was being left out of the model. Either they were wrong or we were.

The Offsetting Costs of Debt Finance

Much of the research effort in finance over the next 25 years has been spent, in effect, in settling which it was. Since economists, ourselves included, were somewhat leerier then than some might be now in offering mass ineptitude by U.S. corporate management as an explanation for any important and long-persisting anomalies, attention was naturally directed first to the possibly offsetting costs of leveraging out from under the corporate income tax. Clearly, leveraging increased the riskiness of the shares, as we ourselves had stressed in our Proposition II and its tax-adjusted counterpart. A sequence of bad years, moreover, might wipe out the firm's taxable income and, given the very ungenerous treatment of losses in our tax law, that could reduce, possibly quite substantially, any bene-

---

12. Modigliani and Miller (1963).

13. See Miller (1963).

> In sum, many finance specialists, myself included, remained unconvinced that the
> high-leverage route to corporate tax savings was either technically unfeasible or
> prohibitively expensive in terms of expected bankruptcy or agency costs.

fits from the interest tax shields. A run of very bad years might actually find a highly-levered firm unable (or, as the option theorists might prefer, unwilling) to meet its debt-service requirements, precipitating thereby any of the several processes of recontracting that go under the general name of bankruptcy. These renegotiations can be costly indeed to the debtor's estate, particularly when many separate classes of creditors are involved. [14]

The terminal events of bankruptcy are not the only hazards in a high-debt strategy. Because the interests of the creditors and the stockholders in the way the assets are managed need not always be congruent, the creditors may seek the additional protection of restrictive covenants in their loan agreement. These covenants may not only be costly to monitor but may foreclose, if only by the time delay in renegotiating the original terms, the implementation of valuable initiatives that might have been seized by a firm less constrained. Nor should the transaction and flotation costs of outside equity financing be neglected, particularly in the face of information asymmetries. Prudence alone might thus have seemed to dictate the maintenance of a substantial reserve of untapped, quick borrowing power, especially in an era when those managing U.S. corporations (and the financial institutions buying their debt securities) still had personal memories of the debt refinancing problems in the 1930s.

We dutifully acknowledged these well-known costs of debt finance, but we were hard put at the time to see how they could overweigh the tax savings of up to 50 cents per dollar of debt that our model implied. Not only did there seem to be potentially large amounts of corporate taxes to be saved by converting equity capital to tax-deductible interest debt capital, but there appeared to be ways of doing so that avoided, or at least drastically reduced, the secondary costs of high-debt capital structures. The bankruptcy risk exposure of junior debt could have been blunted with existing hybrid securities such as income bonds, to take just one example, under which deductible interest payments could be made in the good years, but passed or deferred in the bad years without precipitating a technical default.

For reducing the moral hazards and agency costs in the bondholder-stockholder relation, the undoing-of-leverage blade in the original MM proof offered a clue: let the capital suppliers hold some of each— equity as well as debt—either directly or through convertible or exchangeable securities of any of a number of kinds. In sum, many finance specialists, myself included, remained unconvinced that the high-leverage route to corporate tax savings was either technically unfeasible or prohibitively expensive in terms of expected bankruptcy or agency costs.

JUNK BONDS, LEVERAGED BUY-OUTS AND THE FEASIBILITY OF HIGH-LEVERAGE STRATEGIES

A number of recent developments in finance can be seen as confirming the suspicions of many of us academics in the early 1960s that high-leverage strategies to reduce taxes were indeed entirely feasible. Among these, of course, is the now large outstanding volume of what are popularly known as "junk bonds." The very term is a relic of an earlier era in which the distinguishing characteristic of bonds as investments was supposedly their presence at the low-risk end of the spectrum. High-risk, high-yield bonds did exist, of course, but were typically bonds issued initially with high ratings by companies that had subsequently fallen on hard times. The significant innovation in recent years—and it is still a puzzle as to why it took so long—has been in the showing that, contrary to the conventional wisdom, junk bonds could in fact be issued and marketed successfully by design, and not just as "fallen angels."

The designs utilizing new risky-debt securities have often taken the very conspicuous form of "leveraged buyouts" of the outside shareholders by a control group typically led by the existing top management. The device itself is an old one, but had been confined mainly to small firms seeking both to assure their continuity after the death or retirement of the dominant owner-founder, and to provide more liquidity for the entrepreneur's estate. The new development of recent years has been the ability, thanks in part to the market for junk bonds, to apply the technique to a much wider range of publicly-held, big businesses with capitalizations

---

14. The perceived complexity of the present bankruptcy code (and perhaps even the very reason for having such a code) reflect mainly the need for resolving conflicts within and between the various classes of creditors. The difficulties parallel those encountered elsewhere in "common pool" problems. (See Jackson (1987).)

The significant innovation in recent years—and it is still a puzzle
as to why it took so long—has been in the showing that,
contrary to the conventional wisdom, junk bonds could in fact be issued and
marketed successfully by design, and not just as "fallen angels."

now routinely in the billions, and with new size records being set almost every year.

The debt/equity ratios in some recent LBOs have reached as high as 9 to 1 or 10 to 1 or even more—far beyond anything we had ever dared use in our numerical illustrations of how leverage could be used to reduce taxes. The debtor/creditor incentive and agency problems that might be expected under such high leverage ratios have been kept manageable partly by immediate asset sales, but over the longer term by "strip financing"—trendy investment banker argot for the old device of giving the control and most of the ownership of the equity (except for the management incentive shares) to those providing the risky debt (or to the investment bankers they have designated as monitors). The same hold-both-securities approach, as in our arbitrage proof, has long been the standard one in Japan where corporate debt ratios are, or are at least widely believed to be, substantially higher than for their U.S. counterparts.

Some Possible Non-tax Gains from Leveraging

The recent surge of leveraged buyouts not only shows the feasibility of high-leverage capital structures for reducing corporate income taxes, but also suggests at least two other possible sources for the gains to the shareholder that may accompany a major recapitalization with newly-issued debt. The firm may, for example, already have had some long-term debt outstanding when the additional debt needed to accomplish the buyout was arranged. Even in a world without taxes, the no-gain-from-leverage implication of the original MM invariance proposition might fail if the new debt was not made junior in status to the old, if the old bond covenant was "open ended," as many still are, and if the new bonds were issued under it. Assuming no change in the underlying earning power from the recapitalization, the original creditors would then find the value of their claim diluted. The benefits of this dilution of the old bondholders accrue, of course, to the stockholders, which is why it has often been labeled "theft," particularly by the adversely affected bondholders. (Finance specialists prefer the less emotionally charged term "uncompensated wealth transfer.")

The high debt ratios in LBOs also redirect attention to the assumption, shown earlier to be crucial to the MM dividend-invariance proposition, that the firm's financial decisions can be taken as independent of its real operating and investment decisions. That assumption never sits well and certainly the notion that heavy debt burdens might indeed lead to overcautious business behavior has long been part of the folk wisdom on the dangers of debt. The new wrinkle to the interdependence argument brought in recently by the defenders of LBOs has been to stress the positive *virtues* of having managers face large debt obligations. Managements in such firms must work hard and diligently indeed to achieve any earnings above interest to enhance the value of the residual equity they hold in the firm. By accepting such heavy debt-service burdens, moreover, the managers are making a binding commitment to themselves and to the other residual equity holders against yielding to the temptations, noted earlier, to pour the firm's good money down investment ratholes.[15]

Voluntary Recapitalizations and the MM Dividend Proposition

High debt ratios have been installed in some U.S. firms in recent years, not just by outside-initiated LBOs but through voluntary recapitalizations—sometimes, it is true, merely for fending off an imminent hostile takeover, but sometimes also with the tax benefits very clearly emphasized. Even apart from the tax angles, nothing in the practice of finance these days could be more quintessentially MM than these often highly visible "self takeovers," as some wag has dubbed them. Leverage-increasing recapitalizations of this kind do indeed raise the firm's debt/equity ratio, but because the proceeds of the new bonds floated are turned over to the shareholders, the self takeovers also reunite in a single operation the two Siamese-twin MM propositions, the leverage proposition and the dividend proposition (joined together originally at birth, but soon parted and living separate lives thereafter).

The dividend proposition, as noted earlier, was put forward initially to overcome a line of objection to the leverage proof. But how dividends might actually affect real-world prices raises other issues which in turn have led to as much controversy, and to an even larger

---

15. This view of debt service as a device for reining in managerial discretion is a major strand in what has come to be called the "free cash flow" theory of corporate finance. For an account of that theory, see Jensen (1988).

> *Defenders of LBOs have stressed the positive virtues of having managers face large debt obligations...the managers are making a binding commitment to themselves and to the other residual equity holders against yielding to the temptations, noted earlier, to pour the firm's good money down investment ratholes.*

number of discordant empirical findings, than for the leverage propositions. Once again, moreover, major tax differentials intruded, this time the gap between rates on dividends and capital gains under the personal income tax, with again what seemed in the late 50s and early 60s to be strikingly unorthodox policy implications. Some high-income stockholders clearly would have been better off if the firm paid no dividends and simply reinvested its earnings or bought shares in other corporations. That much every real-world conglomerator and every public finance specialist surely knew.

But the value-for-value presumption of the MM dividend proposition carried within it some further advice. There were better ways to avoid taxes on dividends than pouring the firm's money down ratholes: use the money to buy back the firm's shares! For the taxable shareholders, buybacks at market-determined prices could transform heavily taxed dividends into less-heavily taxed capital gains and, better yet, into unrealized capital gains for shareholders who choose not to sell or trade their shares. Unlike a declared regular dividend, moreover, an announced share repurchase, whether by tender or by open market purchases, carried no implied commitments about future payouts.

PERSONAL-CORPORATE TAX INTERACTIONS AND CAPITAL MARKET EQUILIBRIUM

These tax-advantaged dividend-substitution properties of share repurchase may also offer a clue as to why the leveraging of corporate America out from under the corporate income tax may have been so long delayed. The point is not so much that share repurchase by itself has been a major vehicle deliberately invoked by corporations to reduce the personal income taxes of their shareholders, though its potential for that purpose certainly has not been lost on corporate treasurers and directors.[16] But the very presence of such a possibility at the corporate level serves as a reminder that the U.S. tax system has not one but two distinct taxes that bear on capital structure choices. Any model of capital market equilibrium must allow for both, and for their interactions.

In particular, under reasonable assumptions, the joint corporate-personal tax gains from corporate leverage, G_L, can be expressed in the following relatively transparent formula:

$$G_L = [1 - \frac{(1-t_c)(1-t_{PS})}{(1-t_{PB})}] B_L$$

where B_L is the value of the levered firm's interest-deductible debts, t_c is the marginal corporate tax rate, and t_{PS} and t_{PB} are the marginal investor's personal marginal tax rates on, respectively, income from corporate shares and income from interest-bearing corporate debts.[17] In the special case in which the personal income tax makes no distinction between income from debt or from equity (i.e., $t_{PS} = t_{PB}$), the gain from leverage reduces to $t_c B_L$, which is precisely the expression in the MM tax model.[18] But in the contrasting extreme special case in which (a) the capital gains provisions or other special reliefs have effectively eliminated the personal tax on equity income, (b) full loss offsets are available at the corporate level, and (c) the marginal personal tax rate on interest income just equals the marginal corporate rate ($t_{PB} = t_c$), the purely tax gains from corporate leverage would vanish entirely. The gains from interest deductibility at the corporate level would be exactly offset by the added burden of interest includability under the personal tax—an added burden that, in equilibrium, would be approximated by risk-adjusted interest rate premiums on corporate and Treasury bonds over those on tax-exempt municipal securities.

This somewhat surprising special case of zero net gain from corporate leverage has inevitably received the most attention, but it remains, of course, only one of the many potentially interesting configurations for market equilibrium. Stable intermediate cases are entirely possible in which some gains to corporate leverage still remain, but thanks to the capital gains or other special provisions driving t_{PS} below t_{PB}, or to limitations on loss offsets, those gains at the corporate level are substantially below those in the original MM tax model. The tax

---

16. Most economists, upon first hearing about share repurchase as an alternative to dividend payments assume that the Internal Revenue Service must surely have some kind of magic bullet for deterring so obvious a method of tax avoidance. It doesn't, or at least not one that will work in the presence of even minimally-competent tax lawyers.

17. See Miller (1977).

18. That special case assumes, among other things, that debt, once in place, is maintained or rolled over indefinitely. For valuing the tax savings when debts are not perpetuities, see the comment on this paper by Franco Modigliani that appears in the same issue of *Journal of Economic Perspectives* (Fall 1988) as this article originally appeared in.

Congressional hopes of substantially increasing the yield of the
corporate income tax—that is to say, their hopes of reinstating the double taxation
of corporate profits—may well be disappointed.[20] Our capital markets and legal
institutions offer too many ways for averting the double hit.

gains from leverage might, in fact, even be small enough, when joined with reasonable presumed costs of leverage, to resolve the seeming MM anomaly of gross underleveraging by U.S. corporations.[19]

THE MM PROPOSITIONS AND THE RECENT TAX REFORM ACT

Any such "debt and taxes" equilibrium, however, that the corporate sector might have reached in these early 1980s by balancing costs of debt finance against MM tax gains from leverage must surely have been shattered by the Tax Reform Act of 1986. That act sought, among other things, to reverse the long steady slide, accelerating in the early 1980s, in the contribution of corporate income taxes to total federal tax revenues. But, in attempting to increase the load on corporations, Congress seemed to have overlooked some of the interactions between corporations and individual investors that lie at the heart of the MM propositions and their later derivatives. For shareholders taxable at high marginal rates on interest or dividends under the personal income tax, for example, maintaining assets in corporate solution and suffering the corporate tax hit might make sense, provided enough of the after-corporate tax earnings could be transmuted into long-deferred, low-taxed capital gains by profitable reinvestment in real assets. In fact, over much of the life of the income tax, when shares were held largely by wealthy individuals and hardly at all by pension funds or other tax-exempt holders, the corporate form of organization for businesses with great growth potential may well have been the single most important tax shelter of all.

But the pattern of tax advantages that encouraged the accumulation of wealth in corporate form appears to have been altered fundamentally by the Tax Reform Act of 1986. The Investment Tax Credit and related tax subsidies to fixed investment have been phased out. The marginal rate on the highest incomes under the personal income tax has now been driven to 28 percent and, hence, below the top corporate rate of 34 percent. The long-standing personal income tax differential in favor of long-

term realized capital gains has been eliminated, though income in that form still benefits from a variety of timing options and from the tax-free write-up of any accumulated gains when the property passes to heirs. The analogous tax free write-up privileges for corporate deaths or liquidations, however, formerly allowed under the so-called *General Utilities* doctrine, have now been cut back by the TRA and some of its recent predecessors, reducing still further the tax benefits of the corporate form.

To finance specialists familiar with the MM propositions, these combined changes suggest that Congressional hopes of substantially increasing the yield of the corporate income tax—that is to say, their hopes of reinstating the double taxation of corporate profits—may well be disappointed.[20] Our capital markets and legal institutions offer too many ways for averting the double hit. Corporations can split off their cash-cow properties into any of a variety of non-corporate "flow-through" entities such as master limited partnerships or royalty trusts. And, as has been the running theme of this entire section, firms retaining corporate form can always gut the corporate tax with high-leverage capital structures. In fact, under not entirely implausible conditions (notably that the marginal bondholder is actually a tax-exempt pension fund rather than a taxable individual investor, implying that the t_{PB} is zero) the incentive to leverage out from under the corporate tax may now actually be as high or higher than it was back in 1963. The statutory top corporate tax rate has indeed been cut; but with the Investment Tax Credit and Accelerated Depreciation also blown away by the Tax Reform Act of 1986, many capital-intensive corporations may now, for the first time in a very long while, be facing the unpleasant prospect of actually paying substantial corporate taxes.

And perhaps that observation can serve as a fitting note of uncertainty, or at least of unfinished business, on which to close this look back at the MM propositions. The open questions about those propositions have long been the empirical ones, as noted here at many points. Are the equilibria the propositions imply really strong enough attractors to demand the attention of those active in the capital

---

19. For some recent empirical tests of such an intermediate equilibrium using the premium over municipals, see Buser and Hess (1986). Kim (1987) offers a wide-ranging survey of recent theoretical and empirical research on capital market equilibrium in the presence of corporate-personal income tax interactions.

20. For some recent signs of Congressional concerns on this score, see Brooks (1987) and Canellos (1987).

markets either as practitioners or as outside observers? In the physical or biological sciences, one can often hope to answer such questions by deliberately shocking the system and studying its response. In economics, of course, direct intervention of that kind is rarely possible, but nature, or at least Congress, can sometimes provide a substitute. The U.S. tax system is a pervasive force on business decisions of many kinds, but especially so on the class of financial decisions treated in the MM propositions. Tax considerations have for that reason always figured prominently in the field of finance. Occasionally, the profession may even see changes in the tax regime drastic enough for the path of return to a new equilibrium to stand out sharply against the background of market noise. Whether the Tax Reform Act of 1986 is indeed one of those rare super shocks that can validate a theory remains to be seen.

REFERENCES

Bhattacharya, Sudipto, "Imperfect Information, Dividend Policy and the 'Bird in the Hand' Fallacy." *Bell Journal of Economics* 10.1 (Spring 1979): 259-70.

Black, Fischer, and John Cox, "Valuing Corporate Securities: Some Effects of Bond Indenture Provisions." *Journal of Finance* 31.2 (May 1976): 351-67.

Black, Fischer, and Myron Scholes, "The Pricing of Options and Corporate Liabilities." *Journal of Political Economy* 81.3 (May-June 1973): 637-54.

Brooks, Jennifer J. S., "A Proposal to Avert the Revenue Loss from 'Disincorporation.'" *Tax Notes* 36.4 (July 27, 1987): 425-28.

Buser, Stephen A., and Patrick J. Hess, "Empirical Determinants of the Relative Yields on Taxable and Tax-exempt Securities," *Journal of Financial Economics* 17 (May 1986): 335-56.

Canellos, Peter C., "Corporate Tax Integration: By Design or by Default?" *Tax Notes* 35.8 (June 8, 1987): 999-1008.

Chamley, Christopher, and Heraldis Polemarchakis, "Assets, General Equilibrium and the Neutrality of Money." *Review of Economic Studies* 51.1 (January; 1984): 129-38.

Cornell, Bradford, and Kenneth French, "Taxes and the Pricing of Stock Index Futures." *Journal of Finance* 38.3 (June 1983): 675-94.

Duffie, Darrell, and Wayne Shafer, "Equilibrium and the Role of the Firm in Incomplete Markets." Manuscript, (August 1986).

Durand, David, "Costs of Debt and Equity Funds for Business: Trends and Problems of Measurement." In Conference on Research in Business Finance. National Bureau of Economic Research. New York. (1952): 215-47.

Durand, David, "The Cost of Capital. Corporation Finance and the Theory of Investment: Comment." *American Economic Review* 49.4 (September 1959): 639-55.

Fama, Eugene, "Banking in the Theory of Finance." *Journal of Monetary Economics* 6.1 (January 1980): 39-57.

Fama, Eugene, "Financial Intermediation and Price Level Control." *Journal of Monetary Economics* 12.1 (January 1983): 7-28.

Hirshleifer, Jack, "Investment Decision under Uncertainty: Choice Theoretic Approaches." *Quarterly Journal of Economics* 79 (November 1965): 509-36.

Hirshleifer, Jack, "Investment Decision under Uncertainty: Applications of the State Preference Approach." *Quarterly Journal of Economics* 80 (May 1966): 611-17.

Jackson, Thomas H., *The Logic and Limits of Bankruptcy Law*. Cambridge, Mass.: Harvard University Press. 1986.

Jensen, Michael C., "Takeovers: Their Causes and Consequences." *Journal of Economic Perspectives* 2 (Winter 1988): 21-48.

Kim, E. Han, "Optimal Capital Structure in Miller's Equilibrium." In *Frontiers of Financial Theory*. Edited by Sudipto Bhattacharya and George Constantinides [Totowa. N.J.: Renan and Littlefield. 1987]. Forthcoming.

Linmer, John, "The Valuation of Risk Assets and the Selection of Risky Investments in Stock Portfolios and Capital Budgets." *Review of Economics and Statistics* 47 (February 1965): 13-37.

Merton, Robert C., "Capital Market Theory and the Pricing of Financial Securities." In *Handbook of Monetary Economics* edited by Benjamin Friedman and Frank Hahn. Amsterdam: North Holland. Forthcoming.

Merton, Robert C., "On the Pricing of Corporate Debt: The Risk of Interest Rates." *Journal of Finance* 29.3 (May 1974): 449-70.

Miller, Merton H., "The Corporate Income Tax and Corporate Financial Policies." In *Stabilization Policies*, The Commission on Money and Credit, Prentice Hall. Inc. New Jersey. (1963): 381-470.

Miller, Merton H., "Debt and Taxes."*Journal of Finance* 32.2 (May 1977): 261-75.

Miller, Merton H., "The Informational Content of Dividends." In *Macroeconomics and Finance: Essays in Honor of Franco Modigliani.* Editors Rudiger Dornbusch. Stanley Fischer and John Bossons. MIT Press. Cambridge, MA. (1987): 37-58.

Miller, Merton H., and Franco Modigliani, "Dividend Policy. Growth and the Valuation of Shares." *Journal of Business* 34.4 (October 1961): 411-33.

Miller, Merton H., and Franco Modigliani, "Some Estimates of the Cost of Capital to the Utility Industry, 1954-7." *American Economic Review* 56.3 (June 1966): 333-91.

Miller, Merton H., and Myron S. Scholes, "Dividends and Taxes."*Journal of Financial Economics* 6.4 (December 1978): 333-64.

Modigliani, Franco, "Debt, Dividend Policy, Taxes, Inflation and Market Valuation."*Journal of Finance* 37.2 (May 1982): 255-73.

Modigliani, Franco, and Merton H. Miller, "The Cost of Capital, Corporation Finance and the Theory of Investment: Reply." *American Economic Review* 48.3 (June 1958): 261-97.

Modigliani, Franco, and Merton H. Miller, "The Cost of Capital, Corporation Finance and the Theory of Investment: Reply." *American Economic Review* 49.4 (September 1959): 655-69.

Modigliani, Franco, and Merton H. Miller, "Corporate Income Taxes and the Cost of Capital: A Correction." *American Economic Review* 53.3 (June 1963).

Ross, Stephen, "The Determination of Financial Structure: The Incentive Signalling Approach." *Bell Journal of Economics* 8.1 (Spring 1977): 23-40.

Ross, Stephen, "Return, Risk and Arbitrage." In *Risk and Return in Finance.* Editors Irwin Friend and James Bicksler. Vol. 1. Ballinger. Cambridge, MA. (1976): 189-219.

Rubinstein, Mark, "Derivative Assets Analysis." *Journal of Economic Perspectives* 1 (Fall 1987): 73-93.

Sargent, Thomas J., and Bruce D. Smith, "The Irrelevance of Government Foreign Exchange Operations." Manuscript, 1986.

Sharpe, William F., "Capital Asset Prices: A Theory of Market Equilibrium under Conditions of Risk."*Journal of Finance* 19 (September 1964): 425-42.

Spence, Michael, "Job-Market Signaling," *Quarterly Journal of Economics* 87.3 (August 1973): 355-79.

Stiglitz, Joseph, "A Re-Examination of the Modigliani Miller Theorem." *American Economic Review* 59.5 (December 1969): 784-93.

Stiglitz, Joseph, "On the Irrelevance of Corporate Financial Policy." *American Economic Review* 64.6 (December 1974): 851-66.

Stiglitz, Joseph, "Information and Capital Markets." In *Financial Economics: Essays in Honor of Paul Cootner.* Editors William F. Sharpe and Cathryn Gootner, Prentice Hall, New Jersey (1982): 118-58.

Stoll, Hans R., "The Relationship Between Put and Call Option Prices."*Journal of Finance* 24 (December 1969): 801-24.

Wallace, Neil, "A Modigliani-Miller Theorem for Open Market Operations." *American Economic Review* 71.5 (June 1981): 267-74.

THE CAPITAL STRUCTURE PUZZLE: ANOTHER LOOK AT THE EVIDENCE

by Michael J. Barclay and Clifford W. Smith, Jr., University of Rochester

A perennial debate in corporate finance concerns the question of optimal capital structure: Given a level of total capital necessary to support a company's activities, is there a way of dividing up that capital into debt and equity that maximizes current firm value? And, if so, what are the critical factors in setting the leverage ratio for a given company?

Although corporate finance has been taught in business schools for almost a century, the academic finance profession has found it remarkably difficult to provide definitive answers to these questions—answers that can guide practicing corporate executives in making their financing decisions. Part of the difficulty stems from how the discipline of finance has evolved. For much of this century, both the teaching of finance and the supporting research were dominated by the case-study method. In effect, finance education was a glorified apprenticeship system designed to convey to students the accepted wisdom—often codified in the form of rules of thumb—of successful practitioners. Such rules of thumb may have been quite effective in a given set of circumstances, but as those circumstances change over time such rules tend to degenerate into dogma. An example was Eastman Kodak's longstanding decision to shun debt financing—a policy stemming from George Eastman's brush with insolvency at the turn of the century that was not reversed until the 1980s.

But this "anecdotal" approach to the study of finance is changing. In the past few decades, financial economists have worked to transform corporate finance into a more scientific undertaking, with a body of formal theories that can be tested by empirical studies of market and corporate behavior. The ultimate basis for judging the usefulness of a theory is, of course, its consistency with the facts—and thus its ability to predict actual behavior. But this brings us to the most important obstacle to developing a definitive theory of capital structure: namely, the difficulty of designing empirical tests that are powerful enough to distinguish among the competing theories.

What makes the capital structure debate especially intriguing is that the different theories represent such different, and in some ways almost diametrically opposed, decision-making processes. For example, some finance scholars have followed Miller and Modigliani by arguing that both capital structure and dividend policy are largely "irrelevant" in the sense that they have no significant, predictable effects on corporate market values. Another school of thought holds that corporate financing choices reflect an attempt by corporate managers to balance the tax shields of greater debt against the increased probability and costs of financial distress, including those arising from corporate underinvestment. But if too much debt can destroy value by causing financial distress and underinvestment, others have argued that *too little* debt—at least in large, mature companies—can lead to *over*investment and low returns on capital.

Still others argue that corporate managers making financing decisions are concerned primarily with the "signaling" effects of such decisions—for example, the tendency of stock prices to fall significantly in response to common stock offerings (which can make such offerings very expensive for existing shareholders) and to rise in response to leverage-increasing recapitalizations. Building on this signaling argument, MIT professor Stewart Myers has suggested that corporate capital structures are simply the cumulative result of individual financing decisions in which managers follow a financial *pecking order*—one in which retained earnings are preferred to outside financing, and debt is preferred to equity when outside funding is required. According to Myers, corporate managers making financing decisions are not really thinking about an optimal capital structure—that is, a long-run targeted debt-to-equity ratio they eventually want to achieve. Instead, they simply take the "path of least resistance" and choose what then appears to be the low-cost financing vehicle—generally debt—with little thought about the future consequences of these choices.

In his 1984 speech to the American Finance Association in which he first presented the pecking order theory, Professor Myers referred to this conflict among the different theories as the "capital structure puzzle." As we already suggested, the greatest barrier to progress in solving the puzzle has been the difficulty of devising conclusive tests of the competing theories. Over 30 years ago, researchers in the *capital markets* branch of finance, with its focus on portfolio theory and asset pricing, began to develop models in the form of precise mathematical formulas that predict the values of traded financial assets as a function of a handful of (mainly) observable variables. The predictions generated by such models, after continuous testing and refinement, have turned out to be remarkably accurate and useful to practitioners. For example, the Black-Scholes option pricing model—variations of which have long been widely used on options exchanges—has enabled traders to calculate the value of traded options of all kinds as a function of just six variables (all but one of which can be directly observed).

The key to financial economists' success in capital markets is this: Armed with specific hypotheses, they have been able to develop sophisticated and powerful empirical tests. The evidence from such tests has in turn allowed theorists to increase the "realism" of their models to the point where they have been used, and in some cases further refined, by practitioners. And while no one would argue that all major asset pricing issues have been resolved, the continuing interaction between theory and testing has yielded a richer understanding of risk-return tradeoffs than anyone might have imagined decades ago.

Empirical methods in corporate finance have lagged behind those in capital markets for several reasons. First, our models of capital structure decisions are less precise than asset pricing models. The major theories focus on the ways that capital structure choices are likely to affect firm value. But rather than being reducible, like the option pricing model, to a precise mathematical formula, the existing theories of capital structure provide at best qualitative or directional predictions. They generally identify major factors like taxes or bankruptcy costs that would lead to an association between particular firm characteristics and higher or lower leverage. For example, the tax-based theory of capital structure suggests that firms with more non-interest tax shields (like investment tax credits) should have less debt in their capital structures; but the theory does not tell us how much less.

Second, most of the competing theories of optimal capital structure are not mutually exclusive. Evidence consistent with one theory—say, the tax-based explanation—generally does not allow us to conclude that another factor—the value of debt in reducing overinvestment by mature companies—is unimportant. In fact, it seems clear that taxes, bankruptcy costs (including incentives for underinvestment), and information costs all play some role in determining a firm's optimal capital structure. With our current tests, it is generally not possible to reject one theory in favor of another.

Third, many of the variables that we think affect optimal capital structure are difficult to measure. For example, signaling theory suggests that the managers' "private" information about the company's prospects plays an important role in their financing choices. But, since there is no obvious way to identify when managers have such proprietary information, it is hard to test this proposition.

For all of these reasons and others, the state of the art in corporate finance is less developed than in asset pricing. Thus it is important for the academic community to continue to develop the theory to yield more precise predictions, and to devise more powerful empirical tests as well as better proxies for the key firm characteristics that are likely to drive corporate financing decisions.

In this paper, we offer our assessment of the current state of the academic finance profession's understanding of these issues and suggest some new directions for further exploration. We also offer in closing what we feel is a promising approach to reconciling the different theories of capital structure.

THE THEORIES[1]

Current explanations of corporate financial policy can be grouped into three broad categories: (1) taxes, (2) contracting costs, and (3) information costs. Before discussing these theories, it is important to keep in mind that they are not mutually exclusive and that each is likely to help us understand at least particular facets of corporate financing. Our aim is to determine the relative importance of the different theories and to identify those aspects of financial policy that each theory is most helpful in explaining.

Taxes

The basic corporate profits tax allows the deduction of interest payments but not dividends in the calculation of taxable income. For this reason, adding debt to a company's capital structure lowers its expected tax liability and increases its after-tax cash flow. If there were only a corporate profits tax and no individual taxes on corporate securities, the value of a levered firm would equal that of an identical all-equity firm plus the present value of its interest tax shields. That present value, which represents the contribution of debt financing to the market value of the firm, could be estimated simply by multiplying the company's marginal tax rate (34% plus state and local rates) times the principal amount of outstanding debt (assuming the firm expects to maintain its current debt level).

The problem with this analysis, however, is that it overstates the tax advantage of debt by considering only the corporate profits tax. Many investors who receive interest income must pay taxes on that income. But those same investors who receive equity income in the form of capital gains are taxed at a lower rate and can defer any tax by choosing not to realize those gains. Thus, although higher leverage lowers the firm's corporate taxes, it increases the taxes paid by investors. And, because investors care about their *after-tax* returns, they require compensation for these increased taxes in the form of higher yields on corporate debt—higher than the yields on, say, comparably risky tax-exempt municipal bonds.

The higher yields on corporate debt that reflect investors' taxes effectively reduce the tax advantage of debt over equity. In this sense, the company's shareholders ultimately bear all of the tax consequences of its operations, whether the company pays those taxes directly in the form of corporate income tax or indirectly in the form of higher required rates of return on the securities its sells. For this reason alone,[2] the tax advantage of corporate debt is almost certainly not 34 cents for every dollar of debt. Nor is it likely to be zero, however, and so a consistently profitable company that volunteers to pay more taxes by having substantial unused debt capacity is likely to be leaving considerable value on the table.

Contracting Costs

Conventional capital structure analysis holds that financial managers set leverage targets by balancing the tax benefits of higher leverage against the greater probability, and thus higher expected costs, of financial distress. In this view, the optimal capital structure is the one in which the next dollar of debt is expected to provide an additional tax subsidy that just offsets the resulting increase in expected costs of financial distress.

Costs of Financial Distress (or the Underinvestment Problem). Although the *direct* expenses associated with the administration of the bankruptcy process appear to be quite small relative to the market values of companies,[3] the *indirect* costs can be substantial. In thinking about optimal capital structure, the most important indirect costs are likely to be the reductions in firm value that result from cutbacks in promising investment that tend to be made when companies get into financial difficulty.

1. This section draws on the discussion of capital structure theory in Michael J. Barclay, Clifford W. Smith, Jr., and Ross L. Watts, "The Determinants of Corporate Leverage and Dividend Policies," *Journal of Applied Corporate Finance*, Vol. 7 No. 4 (Winter 1995).

2. The extent to which a company benefits from interest tax shields also depends on whether it has other tax shields. For example, holding all else equal, companies with more investment tax credits or tax loss carryforwards should have lower leverage ratios to reflect the lower value of their debt tax shields. See Harry DeAngelo and Ronald Masulis, "Optimal Capital Structure Under Corporate and Personal Taxation," *Journal of Financial Economics*, Vol. 8 No. 1 (1980), pp. 3-29.

3. Perhaps the best evidence to date on the size of direct bankruptcy costs comes from Jerry Warner's study of 11 railroads that declared bankruptcy over the period 1930-1955. (Jerold B. Warner, "Bankruptcy Costs: Some Evidence," *Journal of Finance*, Vol. 32 (1977), pp. 337-347.) The study reported that out-of-pocket expenses associated with the administration of the bankruptcy process were quite small relative to the market value of the firm—less than 1% for the larger railroads in the sample. For smaller companies, it's true, direct bankruptcy costs are a considerably larger fraction of firm value (about five times larger in Warner's sample). Thus there are "scale economies" with respect to *direct* bankruptcy costs that imply that larger companies should have higher leverage ratios, all else equal, than smaller firms. But, even these higher estimates of direct bankruptcy costs, when weighted by the probability of getting into bankruptcy in the first place, produce *expected costs* that appear far too low to make them an important factor in corporate financing decisions.

When a company files for bankruptcy, the bankruptcy judge effectively assumes control of corporate investment policy—and it's not hard to imagine circumstances in which judges do not maximize firm value. But even in conditions less extreme than bankruptcy, highly leveraged companies are more likely than their low-debt counterparts to pass up valuable investment opportunities, especially when faced with the prospect of default. In such cases, corporate managers are likely not only to postpone major capital projects, but to make cutbacks in R&D, maintenance, advertising, or training that end up reducing future profits.

This tendency of companies to underinvest when facing financial difficulty is accentuated by conflicts that can arise among the firm's different claimholders. To illustrate this conflict, consider what might happen to a high-growth company that had trouble servicing its debt. Since the value of such a firm will depend heavily on its ability to carry out its long-term investment plan, what the company needs is an infusion of equity. But there is a problem. As Stewart Myers pointed out in his classic 1977 paper entitled "Determinants of Corporate Borrowing,"[4] the investors who would be asked to provide the new equity in such cases recognize that much of the value created (or preserved) by their investment would go to restoring the creditors' position. In this situation, the cost of the new equity could be so high that managers acting on their shareholders' behalf might rationally forgo both the capital and the investment opportunities.

Myers referred to this as "the underinvestment problem." And, as he went on to argue, companies whose value consists primarily of intangible investment opportunities—or "growth options," as he called them—will choose low-debt capital structures because such firms are likely to suffer the greatest loss in value from this underinvestment problem. By contrast, mature companies with few profitable investment opportunities where most of their value reflects the cash flows from tangible "assets in place"

incur lower expected costs associated with financial distress. Such mature companies, all else equal, should have significantly higher leverage ratios than high-growth firms.

The Benefits of Debt in Controlling Overinvestment. If too much debt financing can create an underinvestment problem for growth companies, too little debt can lead to an *over*investment problem in the case of mature companies. As Michael Jensen has argued,[5] large, mature public companies generate substantial "free cash flow"—that is, operating cash flow that cannot be profitably reinvested inside the firm. The natural inclination of corporate managers is to use such free cash flow to sustain growth at the expense of profitability, either by overinvesting in their core businesses or, perhaps worse, by diversifying through acquisition into unfamiliar ones.

Because both of these strategies tend to reduce value, companies that aim to maximize firm value must distribute their free cash flow to investors. Raising the dividend is one way of promising to distribute excess capital. But major substitutions of debt for equity (for example, in the form of leveraged stock repurchases) offer a more reliable solution because contractually obligated payments of interest and principal are more effective than discretionary dividend payments in squeezing out excess capital. Thus, in industries generating substantial cash flow but facing few growth opportunities, debt financing can add value simply by forcing managers to be more critical in evaluating capital spending plans.[6]

Information Costs

Corporate executives often have better information about the value of their companies than outside investors. Recognition of this information disparity between managers and investors has led to two distinct but related theories of financing decisions—one known as "signaling," the other as the "pecking order."

4. Stewart C. Myers, "Determinants of Corporate Borrowing," *Journal of Financial Economics,* Vol. 5 (1977), pp. 147-175.

5. See Michael C. Jensen, "Agency Costs of Free Cash Flow, Corporate Finance, and Takeovers," *American Economic Review* 76 (1986), pp. 323-329.

6. More generally, the use of debt rather than equity reduces what economists call the agency costs of equity—loosely speaking, the reduction in firm value that arises from the separation of ownership from control in large, public companies with widely dispersed shareholders. In high-growth firms, the risk-sharing benefits of the corporate form are likely to outweight these agency costs. But, in mature industries with limited capital requirements, heavy debt financing has the added benefit of facilitating the concentration of equity ownership. To illustrate this

potential role of debt, assume that the new owner of an all-equity company with $100 million of assets discovers that the assets can support $90 million of debt. Reducing the firm's equity from $100 million to $10 million greatly increases the ability of small investor groups (including management) to control large asset holdings.

The concentration of ownership made possible by leverage appears to have been a major part of the value gains achieved by the LBO movement of the '80s, and which has been resurrected in the 1990s. And, to the extent there are gains from having more concentrated ownership (and, again, these are likely to be greatest for mature industries with assets in place), companies should have higher leverage ratios.

Signaling. With better information about the value of their companies than outside investors, managers of undervalued firms would like to raise their share prices by communicating this information to the market. Unfortunately, this task is not as easy as it sounds; simply announcing that the companies are undervalued generally isn't enough. The challenge for managers is to find a *credible* signaling mechanism.

Economic theory suggests that information disclosed by an obviously biased source (like management, in this case) will be credible only if the costs of communicating falsely are large enough to constrain managers to reveal the truth. Increasing leverage has been suggested as one potentially effective signaling device. Debt contracts oblige the firm to make a fixed set of cash payments over the life of the loan; if these payments are missed, there are potentially serious consequences, including bankruptcy. Equity is more forgiving. Although stockholders also typically expect cash payouts, managers have more discretion over these payments and can cut or omit them in times of financial distress.

For this reason, adding more debt to the firm's capital structure can serve as a credible signal of higher future cash flows.[7] By committing the firm to make future interest payments to bondholders, managers communicate their confidence that the firm will have sufficient cash flows to meet these obligations.

Debt and equity also differ with respect to their sensitivity to changes in firm value. Since the promised payments to bondholders are fixed, and stockholders are entitled to the residual (or what's left over after the fixed payments), stock prices are much more sensitive than bond prices to any proprietary information about future prospects. If management is in possession of good news that has yet to be reflected in market prices, the release of such news will cause a larger increase in stock prices than in bond prices; and hence current stock prices (prior to release of the new information) will appear more undervalued to managers than current bond prices. For this reason, signaling theory suggests that managers of companies that believe their assets are undervalued will generally choose to issue debt—and to use equity only as a last resort.

To illustrate this with a simple example, let's suppose that the market price of a stock is $25.00. Investors understand that its "real" value—that is, the value they would assign if they had access to the same information as the firm's managers—might be as high as $27.00 or as low as $23.00; but given investors' information $25.00 is a fair price. Now let's suppose that the managers want to raise external funds and they could either sell equity or debt. If the managers think the stock is really worth only $23.00, selling shares for $25.00 would be attractive—especially if their compensation is tied to stock appreciation. But if the managers think the stock is really worth $27.00, equity would be expensive at $25.00 and debt would be more attractive.

Investors understand this—and so if the company announces an equity offer, investors reassess the current price in light of this new information. Since it is more likely that the stock is worth $23.00 than $27.00, the market price declines. Such a rapid adjustment in valuation associated with the announcement thus eliminates much of any potential gain from attempting to exploit the manager's superior information.

Consistent with this example, economists have documented that the market responds in systematically negative fashion to announcements of equity offerings, marking down the share prices of issuing firms by about 3% on average. By contrast, the average market reaction to new debt offerings is not significantly different from zero.[8] The important thing to recognize is that most companies issuing new equity—those that are undervalued as well as those that are overvalued—can expect a drop in stock prices when they announce the offering. For those firms that are fairly valued or undervalued prior to the announcement of the offering, this expected drop in value represents an economic dilution of the existing shareholders' interest. Throughout the rest of this paper, we refer to this dilution as part of the "information costs" of raising outside capital.

The Pecking Order. Signaling theory, then, says that financing decisions are based, at least in part, on management's perception of the "fairness" of the market's current valuation of the stock. Stated as

---

7. Stephen Ross, "The Determination of Financial Structure: The Incentive Signaling Approach," *Bell Journal of Economics*, Vol. 8 (1977), pp. 23-40.

8. More generally, the evidence suggests that leverage-increasing transactions are associated with positive stock price reactions while leverage-reducing transactions are associated with negative reactions. In reaction to large debt-for-stock exchanges, for example, stock prices go up by 14% on average. The market also reacts in a predictably negative way to *leverage-reducing* transactions, with prices falling by 9.9% in response to common-for-debt exchanges and by 7.7% in preferred-for-debt exchanges. For a review of this evidence, see Clifford Smith, "Investment Banking and the Capital Acquisition Process," *Journal of Financial Economics*, Vol. 15 (1986), pp. 3-29.

A 1985 study showed that the five most highly leveraged industries—cement, blast
furnaces and steel, paper and allied products, textiles, and petroleum refining—
were all mature and asset-intensive. At the other extreme, the five industries with
the lowest debt ratios were all growth industries with high advertising and R&D.

simply as possible, the theory suggests that, in order to minimize the information costs of issuing securities, a company is more likely to issue debt than equity if the firm appears undervalued, and to issue stock rather than debt if the firm seems overvalued.

The pecking order theory takes this argument one step farther, suggesting that the information costs associated with issuing securities are so large that they dominate all other considerations. According to this theory, companies maximize value by systematically choosing to finance new investments with the "cheapest available" source of funds. Specifically, they prefer internally generated funds (retained earnings) to external funding and, if outside funds are necessary, they prefer debt to equity because of the lower information costs associated with debt issues. Companies issue equity only as a last resort, when their debt capacity has been exhausted.[9]

The pecking order theory would thus suggest that companies with few investment opportunities and substantial free cash flow will have low debt ratios—and that high-growth firms with lower operating cash flows will have high debt ratios. In this sense, the theory not only suggests that interest tax shields and the costs of financial distress are at most a second-order concern; the logic of the pecking order actually leads to a set of predictions that are *precisely the opposite* of those offered by the tax and contracting cost arguments presented above.

THE EVIDENCE

Having discussed the different theories for observed capital structure, we now review the available empirical evidence to assess the relative "explanatory power" of each.

Evidence on Contracting Costs

Leverage Ratios. Much of the previous evidence on capital structure supports the conclusion that there is an optimal capital structure and that firms make financing decisions and adjust their capital structures to move closer to this optimum. For example, a 1967 study by Eli Schwartz and Richard

Aronson showed clear differences in the average debt to (book) asset ratios of companies in different industries, as well as a tendency for companies in the same industry to cluster around these averages.[10] Moreover, such industry debt ratios seem to align with R&D spending and other proxies for corporate growth opportunities that the theory suggests are likely to be important in determining an optimal capital structure. In a 1985 study, Michael Long and Ileen Malitz showed that the five most highly leveraged industries—cement, blast furnaces and steel, paper and allied products, textiles, and petroleum refining—were all mature and asset-intensive. At the other extreme, the five industries with the lowest debt ratios—cosmetics, drugs, photographic equipment, aircraft, and radio and TV receiving—were all growth industries with high advertising and R&D.[11]

Other studies have used "cross-sectional" regression techniques to test whether the theoretical determinants of an optimal capital structure actually affect financing decisions. For example, in their 1984 study, Michael Bradley, Greg Jarrell, and Han Kim found that the debt to (book) asset ratio was negatively related to both the volatility of annual operating earnings and to advertising and R&D expenses. Both of these findings are consistent with high costs of financial distress for growth companies, which tend to have more volatile earnings as well as higher spending on R&D.[12]

Several studies have also reported finding that the debt ratios of individual companies seem to revert toward optimal targets. For example, a 1982 study by Paul Marsh estimated a company's target ratio as the average ratio observed over the prior ten years. He then found that the probability that a firm issues equity is significantly higher if the firm is above its target debt ratio, and significantly lower if below the target.[13]

As described in a 1995 article in this journal, we (together with colleague Ross Watts) attempted to add to this body of empirical work on capital structure by examining a much larger sample of companies that we tracked for over three decades.[14] For some 6,700 companies covered by Compustat, we calculated "market" leverage ratios (measured as the book value of total debt divided by the book

9. See Stewart Myers, "The Capital Structure Puzzle," *Journal of Finance*, 39 (1984), pp. 575-592.

10. Eli Schwartz and J. Richard Aronson, "Some Surrogate Evidence in Support of Optimal Financial Structure," *Journal of Finance*, Vol. 22 No. 1 (1967).

11. Michael Long and Ileen Malitz, "The Investment-Financing Nexus: Some Empirical Evidence," *Midland Corporate Finance Journal*, Vol. 3 No. 3 (1985).

12. Michael Bradley, Greg Jarrell, and E. Han Kim, "The Existence of an Optimal Capital Structure: Theory and Evidence," *Journal of Finance*, Vol. 39 No. 3 (1984).

13. Paul Marsh, "The Choice Between Equity and Debt," *Journal of Finance*, 37 (1982), pp. 121-144.

14. Barclay, Smith, and Watts (1995), cited above.

value of debt and preferred stock plus the *market* value of equity) over the period 1963-1993. Not surprisingly, we found considerable differences in leverage ratios, both across companies in any given year and, in some cases, for the same firm over time. Although the average leverage ratio for the 6700 companies over the 30-year period was 25%, one fourth of the cases had market leverage ratios that were higher than 37.5% and another one fourth had leverage ratios less than 10.3%.

To test the contracting cost theory described earlier in this paper, we attempted to determine the extent to which corporate leverage choices can be explained by differences in companies' investment opportunities. As suggested earlier, the contracting cost hypothesis predicts that the greater these investment opportunities (relative to the size of the company), the greater the potential underinvestment problem associated with debt financing and, hence, the lower the company's target leverage ratio. Conversely, the more limited a company's growth opportunities, the greater the potential overinvestment problem and, hence, the higher should be the company's leverage.

To test this prediction, we needed a measure of investment opportunities. Because stock prices reflect intangible assets such as growth opportunities but corporate balance sheets do not, we reasoned that the larger a company's "growth options" relative to its "assets in place," the higher on average will be its market value in relation to its book value. We accordingly used a company's market-to-book ratio as our proxy for its investment opportunity set.

The results of our regressions provide strong support for the contracting cost hypothesis. Companies with high market-to-book ratios had significantly lower leverage ratios than companies with low market-to-book ratios. (The t-statistic on the market-to-book ratio in the leverage regression was about 130.) To make these findings a little more concrete, our results suggest that, as one moves from companies at the bottom 10th percentile of market-to-book ratios (0.77) to the 90th percentile (2.59), the predicted leverage market ratio falls by 14.3 percentage points—which is a large fraction of the average ratio of 25%. (For further discussion of these results, see the box on the next page.)

Moreover, such a negative relation between corporate leverage and market-to-book ratios appears to hold outside the U.S. as well. In a 1995 study, Raghuram Rajan and Luigi Zingales examined capital structure using data from Japan, Germany, France, Italy, the U.K. and Canada, as well as the U.S. They found that, in each of these seven countries, leverage is lower for firms with higher market-to-book ratios and higher for firms with higher ratios of fixed assets to total assets.[15]

The above evidence on leverage ratios, it should be pointed out, is also generally consistent with the tax hypothesis in the following sense: The same low-growth companies that face low financial distress costs and high free-cash-flow benefits from heavy debt financing are also likely to have greater use for interest tax shields than high-growth companies. At the same time, the above evidence is inconsistent with the predictions of the pecking order theory—which, again, suggests that low-growth firms with high free cash flow will have relatively low debt ratios.

Debt Maturity and Priority. Like this article up to this point, most academic discussions of capital structure focus just on the leverage ratio. In so doing, they effectively assume that all debt financing is the same. In practice, of course, debt differs in several important respects, including maturity, covenant restrictions, security, convertibility and call provisions, and whether the debt is privately placed or held by widely dispersed public investors. Each of these features is potentially important in determining the extent to which debt financing can cause, or exacerbate, a potential underinvestment problem. For example, debt-financed companies with more investment opportunities would prefer to have debt with shorter maturities (or at least with call provisions, to ensure greater financing flexibility), more convertibility provisions (which reduce the required coupon payments), less restrictive covenants, and a smaller group of private investors rather than public bondholders (which makes it easier to reorganize in the event of trouble). By recognizing this array of financing choices, we can broaden the scope of our examination and raise the potential power of our tests, while at the same time increasing the relevance of

---

15. See Raghuram Rajan and Luigi Zingales, "What Do We Know About Capital Structure? Some Evidence From International Data," *Journal of Finance*, Vol. 50 No. 5 (1995). These relations are statistically significant for each country for the coefficient on growth options and for every country but France and Canada for the coefficient on assets in place.

As one moves from companies at the bottom 10th percentile of market-to-book ratios (0.77) to the 90th percentile (2.59), the predicted leverage market ratio falls by 14.3 percentage points—which is a large fraction of the average ratio of 25%.

ROBUSTNESS OF THE EVIDENCE ON CONTRACTING COSTS

A number of empirical tests of the contracting cost hypothesis have taken the form of a regression with market leverage (measured as the ratio of the book value of debt to the total market value of the firm) as the dependent variable and the corporate market-to-book ratio together with a few "control" variables as the independent variables. Because the market value of the firm appears on both the left and right hand sides of this regression (in the denominator of the leverage ratio and in the numerator of the market-to-book ratio), some researchers have questioned whether the strong negative relation between these variables really supports the theory or is simply the "artificial" result of large variations in stock prices.

To examine the robustness of these results, our 1995 study with Ross Watts used other proxies for the firms' investment opportunities (the independent variable) that do not rely on market values. For example, when we substituted a company's R&D and advertising as a percentage of sales for its market-to-book ratio, our results were consistent with the contracting cost hypothesis. The coefficients on both of our alternative proxies for the firm's investment opportunities had the correct sign, and the t-statistics, although lower than 130, were still impressive—about 65 in the R&D regression and 18 in the advertising regression.

In a more recent series of tests, we used two different proxies for leverage (the dependent variable): (1) the ratio of total debt to the *book* value of assets; and

(2) the interest coverage ratio (EBIT over interest). On purely theoretical grounds, these regressions are expected to produce less significant results. Recall that the contracting cost hypothesis predicts that tangible "assets in place" provide good collateral for loans while intangible investment opportunities do not. If leverage is measured as the ratio of total debt to the book value of assets, we are really measuring the extent to which the firm has leveraged just its tangible (book) assets while essentially ignoring the intangible assets. For this reason, the theory predicts less variation in leverage when measured in relation to book assets than when measured in relation to total market value.

Nevertheless, when we re-estimated the leverage regression substituting book leverage as the dependent variable, the results again supported the contracting cost hypothesis. The regression coefficient on the market-to-book ratio in the book-leverage regression was smaller (with a somewhat lower t-statistic), as predicted. But the coefficient was still reliably negative, with a t-statistic greater than 45.

A similar problem arises with the coverage ratio. In this case, the benefits of intangible growth opportunities (in the form of higher expected future cash flow) are not reflected in current earnings when we use the coverage ratio as our proxy for leverage. Yet, even so, the correlation coefficient was positive; that is to say, companies with higher market-to-book values tended to have significantly higher interest coverage ratios (the t-statistic exceeded 70).

---

the analysis for managers who must choose the design of their debt securities.

As described in our 1996 article in this journal,[16] we designed an empirical test of the suggestion— offered by Stewart Myers in his 1977 article—that one way for companies with lots of growth options to control the underinvestment problem is to issue debt with shorter maturities. The argument is basically this: A firm whose value consists mainly of growth opportunities could severely reduce its future financing and strategic flexibility—and in the process destroy much of its value—by issuing long-

term debt. Not only would the interest rate have to be high to compensate lenders for their greater risk, but the burden of servicing the debt could cause the company to defer strategic investments if their operating cash flow turns down. By contrast, shorter-term debt, besides carrying lower interest rates in such cases, would also be less of a threat to future strategic investment because, as the firm's current investments begin to pay off, it will be able over time to raise capital on more favorable terms.[17]

When we tested this prediction (again using market-to-book as a measure of growth options),

---

16. Michael J. Barclay and Clifford W. Smith, Jr., "On Financial Architecture: Leverage, Maturity, and Priority," *Journal of Applied Corporate Finance*, Vol. 8 No. 4 (1996).

17. If the firm's debt matures before a company's growth options must be exercised, the investment distortions created by the debt is eliminated. Since these investment distortions are most severe, and most costly, for firms with significant growth options, high-growth firms should use more short-term debt.

we found that growth companies tended to have significantly less debt with a maturity greater than three years than companies with limited investment opportunities. More specifically, our regressions suggest that moving from companies at the 10th to the 90th percentile of market-to-book ratios (that is, from 0.77 to 2.59) reduces the ratio of long-term debt to total debt by 18 percentage points (a significant reduction, given our sample average ratio of 46%).

Moreover, we also found in the same study that the debt issued by growth firms is significantly more concentrated among high-priority classes. Consistent with our results indicating that firms with more growth options tend to have lower leverage ratios, we find that changing the market-to-book ratio from the 10th to the 90th percentile is associated with reductions in leasing of 89%, in secured debt of 71%, in ordinary debt of 78%, and in subordinated debt of almost 250%. Our explanation for this is as follows: When firms get into financial difficulty, complicated capital structures with claims of different priorities can generate serious conflicts among creditors, thus exacerbating the underinvestment problem described earlier. And because such conflicts and the resulting underinvestment have the greatest potential to destroy value in growth firms, those growth firms that do issue fixed claims are likely to choose mainly high-priority fixed claims.

The Evidence on Information Costs

Leverage. Signaling theory says that companies are more likely to issue debt than equity when they are undervalued because of the large information costs (in the form of dilution) associated with an equity offering. The pecking order model goes even farther, suggesting that the information costs associated with riskier securities are so large that most companies will not issue equity until they have completely exhausted their debt capacity. Neither the signaling nor the pecking order theory offers any clear prediction about what optimal capital structure would be for a given firm. The signaling theory seems to suggest that a firm's actual capital structure will be influenced by whether the company is perceived by management to be undervalued or overvalued. The pecking order model is more extreme; it implies that a company will not have a target capital structure, and that its leverage ratio will be determined by the gap between its operating cash flow and its investment requirements over time. Thus, the pecking order predicts that companies with consistently high profits or modest financing requirements are likely to have low debt ratios—mainly because they don't need outside capital. Less profitable companies, and those with large financing requirements, will end up with high leverage ratios because of managers' reluctance to issue equity.

A number of studies have provided support for the pecking order theory in the form of evidence of a strong negative relation between past profitability and leverage. That is, the lower are a company's profits and operating cash flows in a given year, the higher is its leverage ratio (measured either in terms of book or market values).[18] Moreover, in an article published in 1998, Stewart Myers and Lakshmi Shyam-Sunder added to this series of studies by showing that this relation explains more of the time-series variance of debt ratios than a simple target-adjustment model of capital structure that is consistent with the contracting cost hypothesis.[19]

Such findings have generally been interpreted as confirmation that managers do not set target leverage ratios—or at least do not work very hard to achieve them. But this is not the only interpretation that fits these data. Even if companies have target leverage ratios, there will be an *optimal deviation* from those targets—one that will depend on the transactions costs associated with adjusting back to the target relative to the costs of deviating from the target. To the extent there are fixed costs and scale economies in issuing securities, companies with capital structure targets—particularly smaller firms—will make infrequent adjustments and often will deliberately overshoot their targets. (And, as we argue in the closing section of this paper, a complete theory of capital structure must take account of these adjustment costs and how they affect expected deviations from the target.)

18. See, for example, Carl Kester, "Capital and Ownership Structure: A Comparison of Unites States and Japanese Manufacturing Corporations," *Financial Management*, Vol. 15 (1986); Rajan and Zingales (1995); and Sheridan Titman and Roberto Wessels, "The Determinants of Capital Structure Choice," *Journal of Finance*, 43 (1988), pp. 1-19.

19. Lakshmi Shyam-Sunder and Stewart Myers, "Testing Static Tradeoff Against Pecking Order Models of Capital Structure," *Journal of Financial Economics*, Vol. 51 No. 2.

> Even if companies have target leverage ratios, there will be an *optimal deviation* from those targets—one that will depend on the transactions costs associated with adjusting back to the target relative to the costs of deviating from the target.

In our 1995 paper with Ross Watts, we attempted to devise our own test of how information costs affect corporate financing behavior. According to the signaling explanation, undervalued companies will have higher leverage than overvalued firms. One major challenge in testing this signaling argument is coming up with a reliable proxy for undervaluation that can be readily observed. In devising such a measure, we began with the assumption that corporate earnings follow a random walk, and that the best predictor of a company's next year's earnings is thus its current year's earnings. We then classified firms as undervalued in any given year in which their earnings (excluding extraordinary items and discontinued operation and adjusted for any changes in shares outstanding) increased in the following year. We designated as overvalued all firms whose ordinary earnings decreased in the next year.

Our regressions showed a very small (but statistically significant) positive relation between a company's leverage ratio and its unexpected earnings, thus suggesting that this undervaluation variable has a trivial effect on corporate capital structure. For example, moving from the 10th percentile of abnormal earnings in our sample (those firms whose earnings decreased by 12%) to the 90th percentile (those whose earnings increased by 13%) raised the predicted leverage ratio by only 0.5 percentage points. Moreover, in our 1996 study (which also uses COMPUSTAT data, although for a somewhat different time period), we again found a small relation between leverage and unexpected earnings. In this regression, however, the relation was *negative*.

Maturity and Priority. Signaling theory implies that undervalued firms will have more short-term debt and more senior debt than overvalued firms because such instruments are less sensitive to the market's assessment of firm value and thus will be less undervalued when issued. The findings of our 1996 study are inconsistent with the predictions of the signaling hypothesis with respect to debt maturity. Companies whose earnings were about to increase the following year in fact issued less short-term debt and more long-term debt than firms whose earnings were about to decrease. And, whereas the theory predicts more senior debt for firms about to experience earnings increases, the ratio of senior debt to total debt is lower for overvalued than for undervalued firms.

In sum, the results of our tests of managers' use of financing choices to signal their superior information to the market are not robust, and the economic effect of any such signaling on corporate decision-making seems minimal.

According to the pecking order theory, the firm should issue as much of the security with the lowest information costs as it can. Only after this capacity is exhausted should it move on to issue a security with higher information costs. Thus, for example, firms should issue as much secured debt or capitalized leases as possible before issuing any unsecured debt, and they should exhaust their capacity for issuing short-term debt before issuing any long-term debt. But these predictions are clearly rejected by the data. For example, when we examined the capital structures of over 7,000 companies between 1980 and 1997 (representing almost 57,000 firm-year observations), we found that 23% of these observations had no secured debt, 54% had no capital leases, and 50% had no debt that was originally issued with less than one year to maturity.

To explain these more detailed aspects of capital structure, proponents of the pecking order theory must go outside their theory and argue that other costs and benefits determine these choices. But once you allow for these other costs and benefits to have a material impact on corporate financing choices, you are back in the more traditional domain of optimal capital structure theories.

The Evidence on Taxes

Theoretical models of optimal capital structure predict that firms with more taxable income and fewer non-debt tax shields should have higher leverage ratios. But the evidence on the relation between leverage ratios and tax-related variables is mixed at best. For example, studies that examine the effect of non-debt tax shields on companies' leverage ratios find that this effect is either insignificant, or that it enters with the wrong sign. That is, in contrast to the prediction of the tax hypothesis, these studies suggest that firms with more non-debt tax shields such as depreciation, net operating loss carryforwards and investment tax credits have, if anything, *more* not less debt in their capital structures.[20]

---

20. See, for example, Bradley, Jarrell, and Kim (1984); Titman and Wessels (1988); and Barclay, Smith, and Watts (1995), all of which are cited above.

But before we conclude that taxes are unimportant in the capital structure decision, it is critical to recognize that the findings of these studies are hard to interpret because the tax variables are crude proxies for a company's effective marginal tax rate. In fact, these proxies are often correlated with other variables that influence the capital structure choice. For example, companies with investment tax credits, high levels of depreciation, and other non-debt tax shields also tend to have mainly tangible fixed assets. And, since fixed assets provide good collateral, the non-debt tax shields may in fact be a proxy not for limited tax benefits, but rather for low contracting costs associated with debt financing. The evidence from the studies just cited is generally consistent with this interpretation.

Similarly, firms with net operating loss carryforwards are often in financial distress; and, since equity values typically decline in such circumstances, financial distress itself causes leverage ratios to increase. Thus, again, it is not clear whether net operating losses proxy for low tax benefits of debt or for financial distress.

More recently, several authors have succeeded in detecting tax effects in financing decisions by focusing on incremental financing choices (that is, *changes* in the amount of debt or equity) rather than on the levels of debt and equity. For example, a 1990 study by Jeffrey Mackie-Mason examined registered security offerings by public U.S. corporations and found that firms were more likely to issue debt if they had a high marginal tax rate and to issue equity if they had a low tax rate.[21] In another attempt to avoid the difficulties with crude proxy variables, a 1996 study by John Graham used a sophisticated simulation method to provide a more accurate measure of companies' marginal tax rates.[22] Using such tax rates, Graham also found a positive association between changes in debt ratios and the firm's marginal tax rate.

On balance, then, the evidence appears to suggest that taxes play at least a modest role in corporate financing and capital structure decisions. Moreover, as mentioned earlier, the results of our tests of contracting costs reported above can also be interpreted as evidence in support of the tax explanation.

TOWARD A UNIFIED THEORY OF CORPORATE FINANCIAL POLICY

In addition to explaining the basic leverage (or debt vs. equity) decision, a useful theory of capital structure should also help explain other capital structure choices, such as debt maturity, priority, the use of callability and convertibility provisions, and the choice between public and private financing. As discussed above, the contracting-cost theory provides a unified framework for analyzing the entire range of capital structure choices while most other theories, such as the signaling and pecking order theories, are at best silent about—and more often inconsistent with—the empirical evidence on these issues.

We now take this argument one step further by suggesting that a productive capital structure theory should also help explain an even broader array of corporate financial policy choices, including dividend, compensation, hedging, and leasing policies. The empirical evidence suggests that companies choose coherent *packages* of these financial policies. For example, small high-growth firms tend to have not only low leverage ratios and simple capital structures (with predominantly short-maturity, senior bank debt), but also low dividend payouts as well as considerable stock-based incentive compensation for senior executives. By contrast, large mature companies tend to have high leverage, more long-term debt, more complicated capital structures with a broader range of debt priorities, higher dividends, and less incentive compensation (with greater reliance on earnings-based bonuses rather than stock-based compensation plans).[23] Thus, corporate financing, dividend, and compensation policies, besides being highly correlated with each other, all appear to be driven by the same fundamental firm characteristics: investment opportunities and (to a lesser extent) firm size. And this consistent pattern of corporate decision-making suggests that we now have the rudiments of a unified framework for explaining most, if not all, financial policy choices.

As mentioned earlier, proponents of the pecking order theory argue that the information costs

---

21. Jeffrey Mackie-Mason, "Do Taxes Affect Corporate Financing Decisions?", *Journal of Finance*, 45 (1990), pp. 1471-1494.

22. John Graham, "Debt and the Marginal Tax Rate," *Journal of Financial Economics*, 41 (1996), pp. 41-73.

23. See Clifford W. Smith and Ross L. Watts, "The Investment Opportunity Set and Corporate Financing, Dividend and Compensation Policies," *Journal of Financial Economics*, 32 (1992), pp. 263-292.

associated with issuing new securities dominate all other costs in determining capital structure. But, as we also noted, the logic and predictions of the pecking order theory are at odds with, and thus incapable of explaining, most other financial policy choices. For example, in suggesting that firms will always use the cheapest source of funds, the model implies that companies will not simultaneously pay dividends and access external capital markets. But this prediction can, of course, be rejected simply by glancing at the business section of most daily newspapers. With the exception of a few extraordinarily successful high tech companies like Microsoft and Amgen, most large, publicly traded companies pay dividends while at the same time regularly rolling over existing debt with new public issues. And, as already discussed, although the pecking order predicts that mature firms that generate lots of free cash flow should eventually become all equity financed, they are among the most highly levered firms in our sample. Conversely, the pecking order theory implies that high-tech startup firms will have high leverage ratios because they often have negative free cash flow and incur the largest information costs when issuing equity. But, in fact, such firms are financed almost entirely with equity.

Thus, as we saw in the case of debt maturity and priority, proponents of the pecking order must go outside of their theory to explain corporate behavior at both ends of the corporate growth spectrum. In so doing, they implicitly limit the size and importance of information costs; they concede that, at least for the most mature and the highest-growth sectors, information costs are less important than other considerations in corporate financing decisions.

Integration of Stocks and Flows

Although the pecking order theory is incapable of explaining the full array of financial policy choices, this does not mean that information costs are unimportant in corporate decision-making. On the contrary, such costs will influence corporate financing choices and, along with other costs and benefits, must be part of a unified theory of corporate financial policy.

In our view, the key to reconciling the different theories—and thus to solving the capital structure puzzle—lies in achieving a better understanding of the relation between corporate financing *stocks* and *flows*. The theories of capital structure discussed in this paper generally focus either on the stocks (that is, on the levels of debt and equity in relation to the target) or on the flows (the decision of which security to issue at a particular time). For example, the primary focus of the contracting-cost theories has been leverage ratios, which are measures of the *stocks* of debt and equity. By contrast, information-based theories like the pecking order model generally focus on flows—for example, on the information costs associated with a new issue of debt or equity. But, since both stocks and flows are likely to play important roles in such decisions, neither of these theoretical approaches taken alone is likely to offer a reliable guide to optimal capital structure.

In developing a sensible approach to capital structure strategy, the CFO should start by thinking about the firm's target capital structure in terms of stock measures—that is, *a ratio of debt to total capital that can be expected to minimize taxes and contracting costs* (although information costs may also be given some consideration here). That target ratio should take into consideration factors such as the company's projected investment requirements; the level and stability of its operating cash flows; its tax status; the expected loss in value from being forced to defer investment because of financial distress; and the firm's ability to raise capital on short notice (without excessive dilution).

If the company is not currently at or near its optimal capital structure, the CFO should come up with a plan to achieve the target debt ratio. For example, if the firm has "too much" equity (or too much capital in general), it can increase leverage by borrowing (or using excess cash) to buy back shares—a possibility that the pecking order generally ignores. (And the fact that U.S. corporate stock repurchases have been growing at almost 30% per year for most of this decade is by itself perhaps the single most compelling piece of evidence that corporate managers *are* thinking in terms of optimal capital structure.) But, if the company needs more capital, then managers choosing between equity and various forms of debt must consider not only the benefits of moving toward the target, but also the associated adjustment costs. For example, a company with "too much" debt may choose to delay an equity offering—or issue convertibles or PERCS instead—in order to reduce the cost of issuing securities that it perceives to be undervalued.

As a more general principle, the CFO should adjust the firm's capital structure whenever the costs of adjustment—including information costs as well as out-of-pocket transactions costs—are less than the costs of deviating from the target. Based on the existing research, what can we say about such adjustment costs? The available evidence on the size and variation of such costs suggests that there is a material fixed component—one that again includes information costs as well as out-of-pocket costs.[24] And, since average adjustment costs fall with increases in transaction size, there are scale economies in issuing new securities that suggest that small firms, all else equal, are likely to deviate farther from their capital structure targets than larger companies.

Although the different kinds of external financing all exhibit scale economies, the structure of the costs varies among different types of securities. Equity issues have both the largest out-of-pocket transactions costs and the largest information costs. Long-term public debt issues, particularly for below-investment-grade companies, are less costly.[25] Short-term private debt or bank loans are the least costly. And, because CFOs are likely to weigh these adjustment costs against the expected benefits from moving closer to their leverage target, it is not surprising that seasoned equity offerings are rare events, that long-term debt issues are more common, and that private debt offerings or bank loans occur with almost predictable regularity. Moreover, because of such adjustment costs, most companies—particularly smaller firms—are also likely to spend considerable time away from their target capital structures. Other things equal, larger adjustment costs will lead to larger deviations from the target before the firm readjusts.

In sum, to make a sensible decision about capital structure, CFOs must understand both the costs associated with deviating from the target capital structure and the costs of adjusting back toward the target. The next major step forward in solving the capital structure puzzle is almost certain to involve a more formal weighing of these two sets of costs.

---

24. See, for example, David Blackwell and David Kidwell, "An Investigation of Cost Differences Between Private Placements and Public Sales of Debt," *Journal of Financial Economics*, 22 (1988), pp. 253-278; and Clifford Smith, "Alternative Mehtods for Raising Capital: Rights vs. Underwritten Offerings," *Journal of Financial Economics*, 5 (1977), pp. 273-307.

25. See, in this issue, Sudip Datta, Mai Iskandar-Datta, and Ajay Patel, "The Pricing of Debt IPOs," *Journal of Applied Corporate Finance*, Vol. 12 No. 1 (Spring 1999).

ON FINANCIAL ARCHITECTURE: LEVERAGE, MATURITY, AND PRIORITY

by Michael J. Barclay and
Clifford W. Smith, Jr.,
University of Rochester

I n an article published in this journal a year ago, we reported the findings of our study of corporate financing and payout policies covering some 6,700 industrial companies over the past 30 years.[1] Our analysis suggests that the most important systematic determinant of a company's leverage ratio and dividend yield is the nature of its investment opportunities. Companies whose value consists largely of intangible growth options (as indicated by high market-to-book ratios and heavy R&D spending) have significantly lower leverage ratios and dividend yields, on average, than companies whose value is represented primarily by tangible assets (with low market-to-book ratios and high depreciation expense).

We explained this pattern of financing and dividend choices as follows: For high-growth firms, the "underinvestment problem" associated with heavy debt financing and the flotation costs of high dividends make both policies potentially quite costly. But, for mature firms with limited growth opportunities, high leverage and dividends can have substantial benefits from controlling the "free cash flow" problem—the temptation of managers to overinvest in mature businesses or make diversifying acquisitions. (Taxes, too, may play a role in this pattern since low-growth companies are likely to be generating more taxable income and thus have greater use for interest tax shields. But, because there are important managerial incentive benefits as well as costs to having higher debt and dividends, companies would have optimal leverage and dividend ratios even in a world without income taxes.)

Throughout our previous paper, we effectively assumed that all debt financing is the same. In practice, of course, debt can differ in several important respects, including maturity, covenant restrictions, convertibility, call provisions, security, and whether the debt is privately placed or held by widely-dispersed public investors. Each of these features is potentially important in determining the extent to which debt financing can help control (or exacerbate) problems. For example, as we argue below, companies with lots of investment opportunities can be expected to issue debt with shorter maturities, not only to protect lenders against the greater uncertainty associated with growth firms, but also to preserve their own financing flexibility and future ability to invest. Growth companies are also likely to choose private over public sources of debt because renegotiating a troubled loan with a banker (or a handful of private lenders) will generally be much easier than getting hundreds of widely dispersed bondholders to restructure the terms of a public bond issue.

In this paper, we expand the scope of our earlier study, examining broader facets of corporate financial architecture. Here we focus specifically on the maturity and priority structure of the firm's debt by looking at 6000 firms during the period 1981-1993. As in our earlier study, we test three basic explanations of these corporate financing choices. In addition to the incentive-contracting argument described above, we also test "signaling" and "tax" explanations. Consistent with our earlier findings, this study provides strong evidence for the incentive-contracting explanation, but only weak support for the signaling and tax arguments.

---

1. Michael J. Barclay, Clifford W. Smith, Jr. and Ross L. Watts (1995), "The Determinants of Corporate Leverage and Dividend Policies," *Journal of Applied Corporate Finance* 7: 4, 4-19. This article draws heavily on that article as well as two other recently published studies by Barclay and Smith: "The Maturity Structure of Corporate Debt," *Journal of Finance*, Vol. 50, No. 2 (1995); and "The Priority Structure of Corporate Liabilities," *Journal of Finance*, Vol. 50, No. 3 (1995).

TABLE 1
SOURCES OF CORPORATE
DEBT

	Commercial Paper	Bank Debt	Non–Bank Private Debt	Public Debt
AVERAGE MATURITY	35 days[a]	5.6 years[b]	15.3 years[b]	18.0 years[b]
COVENANTS				
■ Affirmative	Rare	Common	Common	Rare
■ Negative	Limited[d]	Common	Common	Common
ISSUE COSTS	Large	Small	Small[c]	Large[c]

a. J.O. Light and W. L. White (1979), *The Financial System* (Irwin: Homewood, IL). SEC rules exempt public debt with maturities less than 270 days from registration.
b. Average maturities reported in Christopher James (1987), "Some Evidence on the Uniqueness of Bank Loans," *Journal of Financial Economics* 19, 217–235.
c. David Blackwell and David Kidwell (1988), "An Investigation of Cost Differences Between Public Sales and Private Placements of Debt," *Journal of Financial Economics* 27, 253–278, estimate that average flotation costs per $1000 are $7.95 for private debt and $11.65 for public debt.
d. Commercial paper typically contains few covenants other than cross default provisions that protect lenders in the case of default on other loans.

CHARACTERISTICS OF CORPORATE LIABILITIES

Corporate debt claims differ in a number of dimensions in addition to maturity and priority. To the extent that maturity and priority structures are strongly correlated with other debt features (for example, whether the debt is public or private), it is important to recognize at the outset that corporate choices of maturity and priority may be effectively "bundled" into choices of other critical financial aspects. Thus, we begin by noting some of these correlations in order to provide a broader context for interpreting our empirical results.

Maturity

Sources of Debt. As Table 1 shows, maturity is correlated with whether the debt is held by banks or insurance companies (private placements) or public bondholders. Commercial paper, with its maximum maturity of 270 days, is of course the shortest-term instrument. Bank debt comes next, with an average maturity of 5.6 years, followed by (non-bank) private placements (15.3 years) and public debt (18 years). Which of these sources of debt the firm chooses, however, is likely to be influenced by two other important considerations: (1) *issue costs*, which in

turn are determined in large part by the *size of the firm*; and (2) the extent and kinds of *restrictive covenants* contained in the debt agreement.

Issue Costs (and Firm Size). The fixed issue costs of public debt issues and commercial paper programs are generally much higher than the fixed costs of a bank loan or private placement. One widely cited study of some 250 debt offerings over the period 1979-1983 estimates that the average issue cost per $1000 was $11.65 for public debt, but only $7.95 for private debt.[2] Public debt and commercial paper also have more pronounced scale economies than bank or other private debt. For example, borrowers issuing directly-placed commercial paper will usually borrow at least $1 billion per month to cover the substantial costs of distribution and marketing.[3]

Thus, larger firms are more likely to issue public debt and commercial paper than are smaller firms. The average size (total assets) of firms issuing public debt in the study cited above was $3.4 billion as compared to $2.3 billion for issuers of private debt. Moreover, the size of the average public debt issue was roughly twice the average private issue ($80 million as compared to just under $40 million).

Covenants. The alternative sources of debt listed in Table 1 also differ in their use of covenants. Debt contracts frequently contain covenants that

---

2. David W. Blackwell and David Kidwell, "An Investigation of Cost Differences Between Public Sales and Private Placements of Debt," *Journal of Financial Economics* 22 (1988).

3. P.S. Rose, *Money and Capital Markets* (Irwin: Homewood, IL, 1992).

TABLE 2 ■ CHARACTERISTICS OF CORPORATE LIABILITIES

Types of Corporate Liabilities	Capitalized Leases	Secured Debt	Ordinary Debt	Subordinated Debt	Preferred Stock	Common Stock
PRIORITY OF CLAIM	Highest					Lowest
■ Can Default Trigger Bankruptcy?	Yes				No	
CONTROL RIGHTS	Right to restrict use of leased asset	Right to limit activities specified in covenants			Right to limit activities and conditional voting rights	Voting rights
CORPORATE TAX SHIELDS:						
■ Cash Flows	Lease and interest payments are deductible				Dividend payments are not deductible	
■ Depreciation	Depends on the structure of the contract	Assets financed with debt or equity can be depreciated				
■ Flotation Costs	Flotation costs in lease payment	Flotation costs amortized over the life of the issue			Flotation costs not deductible	
TAX LIABILITY FOR CLAIMHOLDERS:						
■ Individuals	Lease and interest payments are ordinary income				Dividends are ordinary income	
■ Corporations					70% of dividends excluded from taxable income	

restrict the firm's investment, payout, and financing policies. The covenants can be either *affirmative* covenants (for example, those requiring the firm to maintain specific working capital balances) or *negative* covenants (those prohibiting the firm from issuing additional debt unless a specified financial ratio is maintained).

Bank debt generally contains the most extensive covenants, normally including both affirmative and negative covenants. Non-bank private debt also tends to include both affirmative and negative covenants. By contrast, public debt usually includes negative but rarely affirmative covenants; and commercial paper contains few covenants at all. Many firms, of course, borrow money from more than one source; for example, they may use both public debt issues and bank loans. In this case, public debt holders are typically protected by cross-default provisions that put the debt in default if the firm violates a covenant in any of its outstanding debt.

Priority

As illustrated in Table 2, differences in priority also tend to be associated with differences in other aspects of corporate claims. Specifically, in addition to their priority in bankruptcy, these claims have different control rights and tax implications.

Rights in Bankruptcy. Default on promises made in lease or debt contracts generally gives the claimholders the right to force the firm into bankruptcy. Of the claims that we examine, capital leases usually have the highest priority in bankruptcy. Default on a promised lease payment typically gives the lessor the right to repossess the leased asset. If the lessee files for bankruptcy and argues that the asset is essential to the ongoing operation of the firm, the court can prevent the lessor from repossessing the leased asset. However, if the lessee affirms the lease contract, the court requires that the lessee make the specified lease payments to the lessor throughout the bankruptcy process. In contrast, debtholders typically are not paid until the bankruptcy process is resolved.

Debt contracts contain provisions that specify the priority of the claim in bankruptcy. Secured debt gives the debtholders title to pledged assets until the bonds are paid in full. In liquidation, secured debtholders have first claim on the pledged assets. If the value of the pledged assets is less than the amount owed, secured debtholders have a claim on the firm's other assets for the shortfall. Subordinated debt generally specifies that with the occurrence of a stipulated event (such as bankruptcy or default on payments to senior debt), its claimholders are paid only after senior debtholders are paid in full. Thus, subordinated debtholders agree to stand at the back of the line of debtholders.

Common and preferred stockholders do not have the right to force a firm into bankruptcy. In bankruptcy, preferred stock has higher priority than common stock, but lower priority than debt.

Control Rights. Lease contracts generally restrict corporate decisions only with respect to the leased asset. For example, the lease contract might specify required maintenance activities or limit subleasing of the asset, but the contract normally would not include provisions restricting the firm's financing or payout policies. (Internal Revenue Service rules prohibit such provisions in lease contracts.)

Debt contracts generally include covenants limiting investment, financing, or dividend decisions, but normally do not give lenders the right to initiate policy. Such rights would be expensive under the U.S. bankruptcy code. If a debt issue were to give lenders such control rights and the firm were to default on other payments, the firm's other creditors could sue the lender, claiming the lender received an unfair preference, and have the effective priority of that lender's debt reduced.

Preferred stock issues also sometimes include covenants limiting corporate policy choices (for example, prohibiting dividend payments to common stockholders unless preferred dividends have been paid). However, such preferred-stock covenants are typically less extensive than those in debt contracts. Preferred stock also can convey certain voting rights, but these voting rights generally are conditioned on specific corporate events such as an omission of a preferred dividend or a merger.

Common stockholders have voting rights as specified in the corporate charter. They typically elect the board of directors, which in turn appoints corporate management. They also must approve certain corporate activities like mergers and corporate charter amendments.

Taxes. The various claims have materially different tax consequences for the parties to the contracts. Lease and interest payments are tax deductible expenses for the firm; but, under U.S. tax law, dividend payments are not. Assets financed with either debt or stock can be depreciated. There is greater flexibility in allocating depreciation tax shields in leases, which can be structured so that either the lessor or the lessee receives the depreciation expense.

In lease contracts, origination expenses are generally reflected in the schedule of lease payments and thereby deductible. Debt flotation costs are amortized over the life of the issue and are also deductible. Flotation costs are not tax-reducing expenses in either common or preferred stock issues; they are a direct charge to the capital account.

For lessors and bondholders, the lease and interest payments are ordinary income. The tax consequences of dividends for stockholders are different for individuals and corporations. If the stockholder is an individual, it is ordinary income; if the stockholder is a corporation, 70% of the dividend is excluded in the calculation of taxable income.

HISTORICAL EVIDENCE

Table 3 (see next page) summarizes our basic findings on leverage, maturity, and priority for the entire sample of industrial firms (SIC classifications between 2,000 and 5,999) listed on the COMPUSTAT data base for the years 1981-1994.

Leverage. For all the companies over this 14-year period, the average debt-to-total-capital ratio is 21%. COMPUSTAT balance-sheet data provides a broad view of corporate debt. In addition to bonds and mortgages, total debt also includes capitalized lease obligations, paper companies' timber contracts, publishing companies' royalty contracts payable, and similar long-term fixed claims. We also include short-term notes, bank acceptances and overdrafts, sinking funds and installments on loans, and the current portion of long-term debt.

In contrast to common corporate practice in defining leverage ratios, we define total capital as the current *market value* of total equity plus the book value of the firm's other liabilities. Although it introduces more variability into the leverage ratios (some of which may not reflect a conscious shift in

TABLE 3		Classes of Fixed Claims					
HISTORICAL EVIDENCE ON		Scaled by Total Capital			Scaled by Total Fixed Claims		
CORPORATE LEVERAGE, MATURITY, AND PRIORITY		Mean	Median	Standard Deviation	Mean	Median	Standard Deviation
LEVERAGE (n=55,713)		.21	.18	.17			
MATURITY (n=43,945)							
▪ More than one year		.16	.14	.15	.69	.80	.30
▪ More than two years		.14	.11	.14	.56	.65	.32
▪ More than three years		.12	.08	.13	.46	.51	.32
▪ More than four years		.10	.06	.12	.39	.39	.31
▪ More than five years		.08	.04	.11	.32	.28	.29
PRIORITY (n=37,147)							
▪ Capitalized Leases		.01	.00	.04	.11	.00	.19
▪ Secured Debt		.07	.02	.11	.40	.31	.37
▪ Ordinary Debt		.07	.02	.11	.38	.21	.40
▪ Subordinated Debt		.03	.00	.08	.10	.00	.23

corporate financing policy), our use of market equity in calculating total capital reflects our view that it is ultimately the long-term cash-generating ability of the firm (captured in its market value, not its balance sheet) that provides a better guide to corporate leverage.[4] The fact that our study covers 15 years of corporate experience should go far toward "washing out" the effects of such undesired variability on leverage ratios. As one example of the insights afforded by our method, while book leverage ratios have increased dramatically since the late 1970s, average debt-to-market capitalization ratios have remained roughly constant over this period.

Maturity. COMPUSTAT reports the amount of long-term debt payable in each of years one through five from the firm's fiscal year end. As shown in Table 3, the average amount of debt payable in more than one year is 16% of total capital (or, as we note below, about 75% of total debt claims). If maturity is extended to more than five years, this fraction falls to 8% of total capital (or just under 40% of total debt).

For purposes of our remaining analysis, we classify debt payments as long term if they are scheduled to occur in more than three years. Using this definition, we find that the average ratio of long-term debt to capital is 12%, and short-term debt to capital is 11%.[5] As a percentage of total debt, long-term debt is 46% for the average firm (and 51% for the median).

Priority. As reported in the lower part of Table 3, the average ratio of capital leases to total capital is 1%; secured debt to capital is 7%; ordinary debt to capital is 7%; and subordinated debt to capital is 3%. As a percentage of total fixed claims, capitalized leases represent 11%, secured debt 40%, ordinary debt 38%, and subordinated debt 10%.

THE INVESTMENT OPPORTUNITY SET AND FINANCIAL STRUCTURE

As we observed earlier, a company's financial structure can affect its managers' incentives to invest wisely (taking all positive-NPV projects and rejecting all others) and to operate efficiently. For some companies, heavy debt financing can improve managerial incentives and increase value; but, in other cases, it is more likely to distort incentives and reduce value.

More specifically, in mature firms with limited growth opportunities, high leverage can add value by controlling the "free cash flow" problem—namely, the temptation of managers to overinvest (or fail to

---

4. As we also pointed our in last article, however, book debt-to-capital ratios also contain useful information about corporate debt policy in the following sense: To the extent book values provide accurate assessments of the tangibility of assets, they too serve as useful indicators of corporate debt capacity.

5. The reason these two measures, 12% and 11%, do not add to the mean total leverage ratio of 21% is that the two calculations are performed on somewhat different samples.

High-growth companies face a steeply-sloped "term structure" for their debt, both because of the high probability of financial trouble and because of the value-reducing incentives that can arise if they get into trouble.

make necessary cutbacks) in mature core businesses or, what often proves worse, to make diversifying acquisitions. But, in the case of high-growth firms with many profitable investment opportunities, debt financing can lead to a very costly underinvestment problem.

To begin with the extreme case, companies that wind up in Chapter 11 face considerable interference from the bankruptcy court with their investment and operating decisions, not to mention the substantial direct costs of administration and reorganization. And, even in circumstances much less extreme than bankruptcy, debt-financed companies are more likely than their debt-free counterparts to pass up valuable investment opportunities. Especially when faced with the possibility of default, corporate managers are not only likely to put off major capital projects, but also to make short-sighted cutbacks in R&D, maintenance, advertising, or training that end up reducing the value of the firm. This is not just another allegation of the "myopic" behavior for which American managers are so often criticized in the popular press. As Stewart Myers demonstrated in his classic 1977 article, "Determinants of Corporate Borrowing,"[6] there is a rational basis for this shortsightedness.

Assume, just for the sake of illustration, that a high-growth technology firm manages to persuade its local bankers to fund its investment with a high percentage of bank debt.[7] Suppose further that sales fail to materialize as quickly as projected, and that management now is confronted with a dilemma: Either cut the R&D budget (which is expected to generate much of the future growth of the business) or face a very high probability of default on the loans.

What the firm really needs in such circumstances is an infusion of new equity. But potential new shareholders face a major obstacle: Much of the value created (or preserved) by their investment will go toward shoring up the creditors' position. To induce new equity players to participate, either the bank will be forced to write down the value of its loans substantially (which it would be understandably reluctant to do), or the new equity will come at a very high price (in the form of excessive dilution of ownership). Thus, as a consequence of its earlier financing choices, managers may pass up a valuable investment opportunity.

As this example is meant to illustrate, companies whose value consists primarily of investment opportunities (or "growth options," as Myers calls them) are likely to find debt financing very costly. For such companies, the lack of good collateral will make debt expensive to obtain in the first place. And, for those high-growth firms that do manage to get such funding, the costs of financial difficulty in the form of lost opportunities are likely to be substantial.

Conversely, for mature companies with few profitable investment opportunities whose value comes primarily from "assets in place" (tangible assets that provide good collateral for lenders), the indirect costs of financial distress or even bankruptcy are likely to prove quite low. The low costs of financial distress, together with the control *benefits* of debt cited earlier, will cause such companies to have significantly higher leverage ratios than high-growth firms.

Maturity and Investment Opportunities: The Theory

The above argument provides clear predictions for how leverage ratios should vary with a firm's investment opportunities. But what about the maturity and priority of its debt? Should the debt of high-growth firms be expected to have shorter or longer maturities than that of mature companies, and should it be predominantly secured or unsecured?

After discussing the underinvestment problem in his 1977 article, Myers goes on to suggest that the problem can be managed in a number of different ways. Besides the obvious solution of having high-growth firms use less debt, he also proposes that such companies will tend to use debt with shorter maturities. Rather than go through Myers's chain of reasoning here, we will try instead to capture the "intuition" of the argument by using another simple example.

Suppose you are the new CFO of a Silicon Valley firm, and you have decided to raise capital through a straight public debt issue. You have already determined the size and all other aspects of the issue—everything except its maturity. When you meet with your investment banker, you tell her that you are considering maturities of 5, 10, 20, and 30 years (and you are willing to forgo any call

---

6. Stewart C. Myers, "Determinants of Corporate Borrowing," *Journal of Financial Economics*, Vol. 5 (1977), pp. 147-175.

7. This example is reproduced from our earlier article cited in footnote 1.

provision to make the deal more attractive to investors). Her first impulse is to blurt out that even the thought of 20- or 30-year straight debt for a Silicon Valley firm is rank folly. Instead she calmly assures you that her firm can find investors for any of these issues, *provided the coupon is right*. Drawing on her knowledge of the market, she says that the required spreads over comparable-maturity Treasuries are likely to be 200 basis points for your 5-year bonds, 350 bp for 10-year bonds, 550 bp for 20-year bonds, and 750 bp for 30-year bonds. Faced with these alternatives, you quickly go for the 5-year issue.

But now consider the same discussion taking place with the CFO of a gas pipeline company. In this case, the investment banker quotes spreads that range from 100 basis points on the short end to 150 bp on the long end. Here the CFO is more than likely to end up choosing 30-year bonds.

As this example illustrates, corporate financing decisions reflect the outcome of negotiations between issuers and capital providers over pricing and terms. High-growth firms, because of the increased risk they pose for lenders, are likely to find it prohibitively expensive to obtain long-term (straight) debt. And it's not only the higher variability of the cash flows and the lack of good collateral that give lenders pause in such cases; it's also the problems that can arise if the firm's fortunes suddenly shift—for the worse or even for the better.

If things improve dramatically, the firm is going to want to get out of its debt-service commitment by refinancing as soon as possible (and, for this reason, will probably resist giving investors' more than a year or so of call protection). This is another example of the importance of preserving flexibility in financing companies with lots of growth options. But, if things take a sudden turn for the worse, then having long-term debt outstanding can exacerbate the underinvestment problem described earlier. Of course, the pressure of debt service alone, regardless of maturity, could cause management to defer valuable investments. But having longer-term debt actually makes the problem less tractable because the value of such debt will have fallen significantly more than the value of short-term debt.

As we noted in our earlier example, what growth companies typically need in such circumstances is an infusion of new capital, preferably equity. But new investors are likely to be put off (or charge very high prices for the capital) because so much of the value preserved by their investment will go toward restoring the value of the bonds. In short, new investors in such situations (unless they can get higher priority than the current bondholders) bear most of the risk, but receive only part of the expected return created by their investment.

And, so, to return to Myers's argument, the management of a high-growth firm that chooses to issue debt can better protect the firm's ability to make valuable investments by having the debt come due *before* the firm must "exercise" its growth options. In contrast to large, mature companies, the timing of investment opportunities for high-growth firms is less predictable—indeed, they are likely to come along at any time. But, when such opportunities present themselves, management typically needs to react quickly. In such cases, having 100% equity and large cash reserves on hand provides the most flexibility; but, if the firm has debt outstanding, short-term debt is more flexible than long-term debt.[8]

In sum, high-growth companies face a steeply-sloped "term structure" for their debt, both because of the high probability of financial trouble and because of the value-reducing incentives that can arise if they get into trouble. For these reasons, we would expect those growth companies that use debt to rely primarily on short-term bank loans (secured, say, by working capital) or perhaps medium-term convertibles (which overcome lenders' reluctance, and effectively reduce the coupon rate, by giving them a piece of the upside). By contrast, low-growth companies with lots of tangible assets face a relatively flat "term structure," and they can be expected to use public debt with its longer maturities.

Priority and Investment Opportunities: The Theory

Of course, high-growth firms might like to issue longer-term debt if it were offered to them with the same terms and conditions as short-term debt.

---

8. In this sense, Myers's analysis provides a rationale for value-maximizing firms to match effective maturities of their assets and liabilities. At the end of an asset's life, the firm faces a reinvestment decision. Issuing debt that matures at this time helps to establish the appropriate investment incentives when new invest- ment is required. More importantly, however, this analysis indicates that the maturity of a firm's tangible assets is not the sole determinant of its debt maturity. The firm's intangible assets—its growth options—play a critical role as well.

Complicated capital structures with claims of different priority can produce fierce conflicts among creditors when firms have difficulty servicing their debt. And it is precisely in the case of companies with promising investment opportunities that such creditor conflicts have the potential to destroy the most value.

Similarly, they might prefer to issue unsecured or subordinated debentures to maintain as much operating flexibility as possible. But potential lenders generally respond to the greater uncertainty in such situations by demanding security (typically in receivables or inventory, since there is little in the way of long-term, tangible assets) as well as shortening maturities. Of course, a CFO has considerable flexibility in structuring a public debt issue. But changing the priority of the issue will also change its reception in the marketplace. In general, attempts by high-growth firms to issue low-priority claims will attract little investor interest and low prices; and, hence, such firms will be forced to offer high promised rates. For this reason, the CFOs of most growth firms can be expected to choose high-priority claims such as secured debt.

Another reason high-growth firms can be expected to avoid low-priority debt is the destruction of value that can take place if the firm gets into financial trouble. Complicated capital structures with claims of different priority can produce fierce conflicts among creditors when firms have difficulty servicing their debt. *And it is precisely in the case of companies with promising investment opportunities that such creditor conflicts have the potential to destroy the most value.* This possibility, of course, will be reflected in the high cost of unsecured or subordinated public debt for such companies. But even those CFOs initially willing to pay the higher cost for the flexibility (lack of covenants) provided by public debt may be deterred by the prospect of the value lost through underinvestment.[9]

Tests of the Theory

To test these propositions, we ran a series of regressions designed to examine the strength of the correlations of a firm's leverage ratio, its debt maturity, and the priority of its debt with its investment opportunity set. To run such tests, however, we required a measure of growth opportunities. Because stock prices should reflect intangible assets

such as growth opportunities but corporate balance sheets do not, we reasoned that the larger a company's "growth options" relative to its "assets in place," the higher on average will be its market value in relation to its book value. We accordingly used a company's market-to-book-ratio as our proxy for its investment opportunity set.[10]

The Evidence on Leverage. The results of our regressions summarized in Table 4 provide strong support for the argument. Companies with high market-to-book ratios have significantly lower leverage than companies with low market-to-book ratios. The correlation between the market-to-book ratio and leverage is highly statistically significant (with a *t*-statistic of −103.03).

Perhaps more important than these measures of statistical significance, however, is the "economic" significance of this relation. We measure economic impact as the percentage change in the leverage ratio associated with changing the market-to-book ratio from the 10th to the 90th percentile in our sample. To illustrate, if the market-to-book ratio increases from 0.84 (the lowest 10th percentile) to 2.92 (the 90th percentile), the predicted leverage ratio falls by 12.84 percentage points, or 61.2% of the average leverage ratio of 21%. Put another way, an increase in the market-to-book ratio from about 0.8 to almost 3.0 is associated, on average, with a drop in the firm's leverage ratio from over 27% to under 15%.

The Evidence on Maturity. The coefficients are also negative and highly significant in a pair of regressions designed to test correlations between market-to-book and corporate use of short-term debt and long-term debt. (The *t*-statistic for this variable is −63.90 in the short-term debt regression and −64.82 in the long-term debt regression.) The negative coefficient indicates that, on average, firms with more growth options have less short-term *as well as* less long-term debt in their capital structures. The economic impact of the market-to-book ratio on debt maturity is also material (−54.5% in the short-term debt regression and −54.65% in the long-term debt regression).

---

9. Financing new investment projects with senior claims limits wealth transfers from stockholders to existing bondholders and thus reduces the incentives to underinvest. The underinvestment problem can also be reduced if the firm preserves the right to finance new investments with high priority claims, such as secured debt or leases. For a discussion of the role of secured debt in controlling the underinvestment problem, see René Stulz and Herbert Johnson, "An Analysis of Secured Debt," *Journal of Financial Economics*, Vol. 14 (1985), pp. 501-521.

10. We estimate the market value of the firm's assets as the book value of assets minus the book value of equity plus the market value of equity. The market-to-book

ratio is then calculated as the estimated market value of assets divided by the book value of assets. The estimated market-to-book ratio has several extreme observations. For example, 98 percent of the ratios are between 0.57 and 9.58. The range for this variable, however, is 0.19 to 260.30. To prevent extreme observations from having an undue influence on the regression results, we discard observations if the market-to-book ratio is greater than ten. Discarding these observations reduces the statistical significance of this variable in the regressions, but increases the size of the coefficient.

	Leverage	Maturity		Priority			
		Short-Term Debt	Long-Term Debt	Capitalized Leases	Secured Debt	Ordinary Debt	Subordinated Debt
Intercept	27.44	23.72	12.13	0.17	16.72	−0.42	−18.72
	(122.15)	(125.21)	(62.14)	(1.34)	(74.20)	(−1.97)	(−35.34)
INVESTMENT OPPORTUNITIES							
■ Market-to-Book	−6.16	−3.24	−3.39	−0.65	−2.53	−2.69	−2.87
	(−103.03)	(−63.90)	(−64.82)	(−18.78)	(−41.10)	(−44.78)	(−19.51)
	[−61.15]	[−54.46]	[−54.65]	[−89.32]	[−70.99]	[−78.80]	[−248.67]
■ Regulation	11.76	−1.31	11.49	−3.84	3.76	7.76	0.31
	(38.07)	(−5.93)	(50.52)	(−6.85)	(4.47)	(10.26)	(0.19)
	[55.37]	[−11.54]	[101.27]	[−253.64]	[51.23]	[110.09]	[12.60]
SIGNALING							
■ Abnormal Earnings	(−0.11)	−0.98	0.32	(−0.02)	−0.10	−0.62	0.30
	(−4.46)	(−7.93)	(2.49)	(−0.24)	(−0.69)	(−4.40)	(1.02)
	[−1.03]	[−2.67]	[0.86]	[−0.46]	[−0.46]	[−2.93]	[4.11]
TAX							
■ Tax-Loss Carryforward	6.06			0.49	2.04	0.64	6.12
	(35.36)			(5.37)	(12.53)	(4.23)	18.76)
	[28.52]			[32.31]	[27.73]	[9.09]	[256.72]
■ Term-Structure		−0.12	−0.47				
		(−2.59)	(−9.89)				
		[−3.01]	[−11.77]				
SIZE							
■ Firm Value	0.36	−1.42	1.08	−0.07	−1.46	2.02	1.63
	(10.41)	(−53.41)	(39.63)	(−3.58)	(41.24)	(62.44)	(22.52)
	[9.82]	[−70.58]	[54.12]	[−25.61]	[−109.12]	[156.97]	[372.38]
Adjusted R²	0.23	0.16	0.24	0.02	0.10	0.15	0.02
No. of Observations	45,906	36,297	36,297	30,566	30,566	30,566	30,566

1. Dependent variables expressed as percentages of total debt.
2. *t*-statistics in parentheses; economic impact measures in brackets.

These findings largely reinforce our earlier cited leverage results—namely, that high-growth firms use less debt in general, and so both short-term and long-term debt are reduced. But what about such companies' *relative* use of short-term and long-term debt?

To gain some insight into this question, we also express the maturity variables as a percentage of total debt instead of total capital. Consistent with Myers's argument that the underinvestment problem can be controlled by shortening debt maturity, we find that firms with more more growth options (higher mar-

TABLE 5
THE DETERMINANTS OF
CORPORATE FINANCIAL
ARCHITECTURE[1,2]

	Maturity	Priority			
	Long-Term Debt	Capitalized Leases	Secured Debt	Ordinary Debt	Subordinated Debt
Intercept	26.47	0.73	83.63	−14.06	−72.39
	(53.92)	(1.13)	(102.58)	(−14.10)	(37.75)
INVESTMENT OPPORTUNITIES					
■ Market-to-Book	−4.56	1.54	1.02	−3.53	−5.73
	(−34.69)	(9.15)	(4.66)	(−12.99)	(−11.55)
	[−17.94]	[28.87]	[5.16]	[−18.24]	[−113.62]
■ Regulation	14.70	−20.11	4.12	7.40	−0.80
	(25.72)	(−7.09)	(1.36)	(2.07)	(−0.13)
	[31.63]	[−182.73]	[10.21]	[18.51]	[−7.69]
SIGNALING					
■ Abnormal Earnings	0.92	0.45	1.04	−216	1.67
	(2.83)	(1.05)	(1.94)	(−3.28)	(1.58)
	[0.60]	[1.35]	[0.85]	[−1.82]	[5.42]
TAX					
■ Tax-Loss Carryforward		1.42	−2.47	−3.69	19.71
		(3.09)	(−4.22)	(−5.19)	(16.73)
		[12.91]	[−6.12]	[−9.24]	[189.52]
■ Term-Structure	−0.93				
	(−7.67)				
	[−5.60]				
SIZE					
■ Firm Value	5.69	−1.11	−9.48	11.06	5.75
	(82.70)	(−1.18)	(−73.70)	(71.58)	(22.02)
	[69.56]	[−55.20]	[−128.54]	[151.57]	[301.95]
Adjusted R²	0.23	0.02	0.17	0.18	0.01
No. of Observations	36,297	30,566	30,566	30,566	30,566

1. Dependent variables expressed as percentages of total debt.
2. *t*-statistics in parentheses; economic impact measures in brackets.

ket-to-book ratios) use larger proportions of short-term debt (see Table 5). This result is both statistically significant ($t = −34.7$) and economically material (moving from the 10th to the 90th percentile of market-to-book reduces the ratio of long-term debt to total debt by 17.9 percentage points).

Lessons on Capital Structure from LBOs. In a discussion of recent changes in the financial structure of LBOs (in the article immediately following), Jay Allen, Senior Managing Director of Bank of America, makes the following observation: "*In contrast to the LBOs of the '80s, [in the 90s] there has been considerably more more attention paid to the appropriate debt-to-equity ratio for specific deals. For example, in financing the LBO of a standard manufacturing company in a relatively mature industry, Bank of America will typically structure a 6-7 year senior bank term loan and revolving credit facility. The amount of the senior debt will typically be 3-4 times EBITDA, with sponsor-controlled capital composing 20-25% of the capital structure. By contrast, in financing recent LBOs of higher-growth, technology-driven investments by Welsh, Carson, Anderson, & Stowe and DLJ Merchant Banking, we provided senior bank facilities with 3-4 year maturities and senior debt-to-EBITDA multiples of under 2.5; and sponsor-controlled capital represented more than 35% of the capital structure.*"

Priority. The regressions in Table 4 also indicate that firms with more growth options in their investment opportunity sets issue fewer fixed claims of all priority classes. This, too, is consistent with previous results on leverage ratios indicating that firms with more growth options tend to have less debt in their capital structures. The economic impact appears material. Changing the market-to-book ratio from the 10th to the 90th percentile reduces leasing by 89%, secured debt by 71%, ordinary debt by 78%, and subordinated debt by almost 250%.

Findings reported in Table 5 indicate that firms with more growth opportunities issue a significantly larger proportion of higher-priority fixed claims—or, alternatively, a lower proportion of unsecured or junior debt—than low-growth firms.

The Structure of Debt Financing in Silicon Valley.
Founded in 1983, Silicon Valley Bancshares has traditionally served the needs of high-tech companies in California and elsewhere. Recently, it has expanded into industry "niches" most commercial banks tend to avoid—telecommunications and software start-ups, bio-tech firms, and small manufacturers of medical devices. "*In lending to small, high-risk businesses,*" comments former CFO Dennis Uyemura, "*there are a few very basic rules to observe: (1) Keep the debt ratios very low, of course, and try to ensure the borrower has substantial cash reserves; (2) Keep the maturities short, to preserve flexibility for lender and borrower alike; and (3) Secure everything you can. Attaching assets not only increases your chances of getting paid back, but also deters borrowers from bringing in junior creditors. Junior creditors are likely to cause big problems if the firm has trouble servicing the debt.*"

Maturity and Priority in Regulated Companies

Another way of testing the effect of investment opportunities on corporate choices of leverage, maturity, and priority is to look at the special case of regulated companies. Regulation effectively reduces the possibility for corporate underinvestment simply by transferring much of management's discretion over investment decisions to regulatory authorities. State utility commissions, for example, oversee utilities' investments in maintenance and capacity. Given such limits on managerial discretion, and the stability of cash flows ensured by the regulatory process, we would expect regulated firms to have more leverage and use longer-maturity debt than unregulated firms.

To estimate the effects of regulation, we constructed a "dummy variable" that was set equal to one for firms in regulated industries and zero otherwise. The regulated industries we examine are two: gas and electric utilities (as represented in SIC codes 4900 to 4939) and telecommunications (SIC 4812 and 4813) through 1982.

Consistent with our argument about the investment opportunity set, regulation has both a statistically and economically material impact on leverage. Based on the coefficient from the regression reported in Table 4, regulation is expected to increase leverage ratios by about 11 percentage points ($t = 34.87$), which amounts to a 55% increase in the average leverage ratio of our entire sample. Other things equal, regulation increases long-term debt by 11.5 percentage points while reducing short-term debt by 1.3 percentage points. These effects are statistically significant ($t = 50.52$ for long-term debt and $t = -5.93$ for short-term debt) and economically material (101% for long-term debt and −11.54% for short-term debt). Finally, regulated firms use fewer leases, but more secured debt and ordinary debt. These effects are also economically material (−254% for capitalized leases, 51% for secured debt, and 110% ordinary debt).

If we examine maturity and priority classes as a fraction of total fixed claims, we get a similar picture. As reported in Table 5, regulated firms use higher proportions of long-term debt and ordinary debt, but lower proportions of capitalized leases.

SIGNALING AND FINANCIAL STRUCTURE

Some corporate finance scholars have argued that corporate managers making financing decisions are concerned primarily with the "signaling" effects of such decisions—for example, the tendency of stock prices to fall significantly in response to common stock offerings, but only slightly in response to straight debt offerings. According to signaling theory, outside capital is expensive (that is, firms are effectively forced to issue new capital at an "information discount") because managers are in a position to know more than outside investors about the firm's prospects. And the more risky the security, the larger the information discount is likely to be.

Consider the plight of a CFO who wishes to raise additional capital by selling additional debt or equity, but who believes that both of these securities are currently undervalued. If the undervaluation is

> *Contrary to the predictions of signaling theory, firms whose earnings were about to increase the following year issued less short-term debt and more long-term debt than firms whose earnings were about to decrease.*

Deregulation of the Telecommunications Industry. In 1982, the telecommunications industry was deregulated. Our theory would predict that this would cause leverage to fall and debt maturity to shorten. As shown in the adjacent figure, leverage ratios have fallen from almost 46% before 1980 to 23.6% after 1985. The ratio of long-term debt to total debt has also fallen from 76% before 1980 to 57% after 1985. (We would also expect deregulation to affect firms' debt-priority mix. But, since COMPUSTAT does not report debt-priority information before 1981, we are unable to investigate this prediction for the telecommunications industry.)

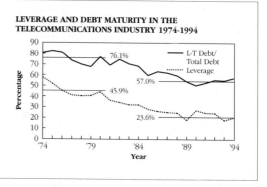

LEVERAGE AND DEBT MATURITY IN THE TELECOMMUNICATIONS INDUSTRY 1974-1994

sufficiently large, he might choose to forgo the issue altogether. If he chooses to proceed, however, a CFO intent on preserving value would choose to sell the security that is least undervalued. In this case, he will issue debt rather than equity because debt is less sensitive to changes in firm value than equity; and he will issue short-term, senior debt rather than long-term, junior debt because the former is less undervalued. But, if the firm is overvalued, he is more likely to issue the most overvalued security—in this case, equity over debt, and long-term, subordinated rather than short-term, senior or secured debt.

According to the signaling theory, then, undervalued (or "high-quality") companies will have higher leverage, more short-term debt, and higher priority claims than overvalued ("low-quality") firms. To test these propositions, we classified as "high quality" all firms in a given year whose earnings (excluding extraordinary items and discontinued operations and adjusted for any changes in shares outstanding) increased in the following year; and we designated as low quality all firms whose ordinary earnings decreased in the next year.

Leverage. In our leverage regression in Table 4, we find a negative relation between the size of the company's earnings increase and its leverage ratio, a result that is inconsistent with the signaling hypothesis. The economic impact of this quality variable, however, is negligible (0.6%).

Maturity. The evidence in Table 4 also appears inconsistent with the predictions of the signaling hypothesis with respect to debt maturity. Firms whose earnings were about to increase the following year in fact had less short-term debt and more long-term debt than firms whose earnings were about to decrease. Similarly, the evidence in Table 5 suggests that undervalued firms have a higher

proportion of long-term debt instead of the lower proportion predicted by the theory. But, again, the economic impact appears immaterial in both cases.

Priority. The evidence in Table 4 also offers little support for the signaling hypothesis. Whereas the theory predicts higher ordinary debt for firms about to experience earnings decreases, ordinary debt for such firms in fact turns out to be lower (although, again, the economic impact is small—less than −3%); and the use of the other priority classes we examine is insignificantly different from that of the average firm in the sample. As shown in Table 5, the ratio of ordinary debt to total debt is lower for low-quality than for high-quality firms (although, again, the economic impact is small—less than 2%).

TAXES AND FINANCIAL STRUCTURE

Leverage. The tax hypothesis predicts that companies with low effective marginal tax rates and high non-interest tax shields should have less debt in their capital structure. We use a "dummy" variable that identifies firms with tax-loss carryforwards to proxy for corporate tax status. Here we assume that firms with tax-loss carryforwards have the lowest effective marginal tax rates.

The tax hypothesis predicts a negative coefficient for the tax-loss carryforward variable in the leverage regression. In contrast to the prediction, however, the coefficient on the tax-loss carryforward variable in the leverage regression is actually positive and statistically significant (see Table 4). Nevertheless, this apparent anomaly can be readily explained as a case of "reverse causality." That is, companies with lots of tax-loss carryforwards generally acquire them by reporting losses, which reduce their market values and increase their leverage ratios.

Maturity. Whenever the term structure of interest rates is not flat, the expected value of the firm's interest tax shields depends on the maturity structure of its debt. Maturity structure can affect the value of tax shield because, if the firm defaults on its promised debt payments, it may never get to use those interest deductions.

When the yield curve is upward sloping, the expected interest expense from issuing long-term debt is greater in the early years of the contract than the expected interest expense from rolling short-term debt (and the opposite is true in later years of the contract). To the extent the probability of default increases over time, a firm intent on maximizing the present value of its interest tax shield will use the longest maturity possible. Conversely, if the term structure is downward sloping, issuing short-term debt will maximize the value of the interest tax shield. Thus, the tax hypothesis implies that companies will employ more long-term debt when the term structure has a positive slope.[11]

The results reported in Tables 4 and 5, however, provide no support for this tax hypothesis. The coefficient for the term-structure variable is significantly negative in the long-term debt regression; that is, the more steeply-upward-sloping the yield curve, the more likely are companies to issue not long-term, but short-term debt.

Priority. There are two principal ways in which the priority of debt is likely to affect corporate taxes. On the one hand, firms with low effective marginal tax rates (perhaps because of non-interest tax shields like tax-loss carryforwards) are likely to prefer leasing because it effectively allows the benefits of the tax shields to be shifted from the lessee/borrower back to the lessor/lender. At the same time, the tax system encourages firms facing higher effective marginal tax rates to issue the lowest priority (and thus most risky) debt claims because interest payments on risky debt include a default premium that is tax deductible as paid. As a proxy for the firm's marginal tax rate, we include a dummy variable that is equal to one if the firm has any tax-loss carryforwards and thus has a low effective marginal tax rate.

The evidence in Table 4 indicates that firms with more tax-loss carryforwards have significantly more fixed claims of each priority class. Table 5 suggests that firms with more tax-loss carryforwards issue a higher proportion of both capitalized leases and subordinated debt, but less secured debt and ordinary debt. Although consistent with the argument about leasing, our results provide no support for the argument that firms with high marginal tax rates issue riskier debt.

Overall, then, our tests provide little support for the proposition that taxes have an important impact on corporate leverage choices. We should add, however, that this does not prove that tax considerations do not affect financing decisions. When companies are faced with financing alternatives that are close substitutes (for example, the choice between secured debt and leasing), tax consequences often prove to be the deciding factor.

FIRM SIZE AND FINANCIAL STRUCTURE

As one final test, we examined whether company size (measured as total capitalization) has a systematic effect on the firm's financial architecture. As noted earlier, it is important to control for firm size in this analysis to guard against the possibility that it is firm size—and say, the issue costs and debt sources associated with a given firm size—that is "driving" our earlier findings. For example, a skeptic might argue that the earlier-noted tendency of high-growth firms to have secured debt with shorter maturities may well just reflect that, for many small firms, banks are the only available source of funds. And banks, for reasons related more to regulation than to their borrowers' needs, tend to provide only relatively short-term, senior loans.

Leverage. The positive firm-size coefficient in the leverage regression is statistically significant, thus implying that bigger firms have more leverage. However, the economic impact of firm size on leverage is relatively small. For example, the largest firms had leverage ratios that were only about one percentage point higher than the average of 21%.

Maturity. Firm size is also likely to be potentially correlated with debt maturity for several reasons. As discussed earlier, issuance costs for public issues have a large fixed component, resulting in

---

11. This tax hypothesis is presented in Ivan Brick and S. Abraham Ravid, "On the Relevance of Debt Maturity Structure," *Journal of Finance* 40 (1985). The argument assumes that the probability of default increases with time, and the value of the firm's interest tax shield is reduced upon default. This would occur, for example, if in reorganization the firm faces binding constraints on the use of tax-loss carrybacks.

> **While providing little support for signaling and tax theories, our findings provide strong support for the argument that a firm's financial architecture can be expected to be determined primarily by its investment opportunities.**

significant scale economies. Smaller firms are less able to take advantage of these scale economies; and, partly for this reason, they typically opt for private debt with its lower fixed costs. And, just by virtue of choosing bank debt over public debt for its lower flotation costs, smaller firms will have more short-term debt.

As expected, the coefficient for the log of firm value is positive and significant in the long-term debt regression in Table 4, but negative and significant in the short-term debt regression. The economic significance of this variable is also material: the two coefficients imply that moving from the 10th to the 90th percentile for firm size increases the fraction of long-term debt by 54% and reduces the fraction of short-term debt by 70%. Similarly, the evidence in Table 5 suggests that larger firms issue more long-term debt as a fraction of total debt.

Priority. We also expect firm size to affect corporate priority choices. Because public securities have large fixed costs and substantial scale economies, large firms should have a comparative advantage in issuing securities publicly. For example, this would imply that large firms would issue more preferred stock, since it is rarely privately placed, and fewer capital leases, since they are never issued publicly.

The evidence in Table 4 indicates that larger firms issue significantly more ordinary debt and subordinated debt, but significantly less capitalized leases and secured debt. The findings reported in Table 5 suggest that larger firms use less ordinary debt as a percentage of total debt, but there is no significant difference in their use of capitalized leases, secured debt, or subordinated debt as a fraction of total debt.

In sum, there are discernible size effects that contribute to the significance of our results—particularly those suggesting the tendency of high-growth firms to issue high-priority debt with shorter maturities. Nevertheless, even after controlling for such size effects, the variables intended to proxy for a firm's investment opportunity set—market-to-book ratio and whether the firm is regulated or not—still appear to play a major role in corporate choices of debt maturity and priority.

CONCLUSION

Most academic discussions of capital structure are based on the implicit assumption that all debt is the same. In reality, of course, corporate debt instruments vary considerably with respect to features such as maturity, covenants, priority, and whether the debt is public or private. In this article, we present the results of our recent efforts to extend empirical studies of capital structure into two relatively new areas: maturity and priority.

While providing little support for signaling and tax theories, our findings provide strong support for the argument that a firm's financial architecture is determined primarily by its investment opportunities. In brief, we find that companies with high market-to-book ratios ("growth firms") tend to use less debt than companies with low market-to-book ratios ("mature firms"). Moreover, the lesser debt raised by growth firms also tends to have shorter maturity and higher priority than the debt issued by mature firms. We interpret such financing patterns as the result of efforts to preserve financing flexibility and proper investment incentives in growth firms while providing stronger managerial incentives for efficiency (and reducing taxes) in mature firms.

But if our results are suggestive, many important questions remain. As just one example, although we find a strong positive correlation between market to book and the proportion of short-term, secured debt in the capital structure, our tests do not allow us to distinguish how much of this correlation results from growth firms' inability—because of their smaller size alone—to use unsecured, longer-term public debt. We would really like to be able to distinguish between two separate effects: (1) how much of the variation in debt maturity and priority can be attributed to the choice of a given debt source; and (2) *given* that a certain firm has chosen bank debt or public debt, how much of the remaining variation can be explained using our proxies for the firm's investment opportunity set, signaling opportunities, and tax position? Future research will undoubtedly tell us more about why firms choose public vs. private debt, and how they choose the call, convertibility, and other provisions attached to their debt.

WHO WINS IN LARGE STOCK BUYBACKS— THOSE WHO SELL OR THOSE WHO HOLD?

*by William McNally, University of Victoria**

Fixed-price and dutch auction repurchases feature large price premiums to tendering shareholders and large increases in firm value. Despite the premiums, a substantial proportion of shareholders choose not to tender; indeed, in most offers, the inside shareholders (senior management and directors) commit to hold onto their shares. Non-tendering shareholders don't just forgo the premium; they pay for it directly because the premium transfers wealth from non-tendering to tendering shareholders. The good news for non-tendering shareholders, however, is that self-tender offers are accompanied by an increase in the intrinsic value of the firm that greatly exceeds the cost of the premium.

"Signalling" is widely regarded by academics as the explanation for the increase in intrinsic firm value that accompanies self-tender offers.[1] The signalling hypothesis—loosely stated, the idea that only a management confident about its company's prospects would volunteer to buy back its own shares at a premium over market—is supported by the tendency of repurchasing firms to cite "undervaluation" as their primary motive for the offer. In signalling models, the premium wealth transfer is a cost borne by inside shareholders—and it is the very willingness of such insiders to bear these costs that in turn "signals" the true value of the firm to outside shareholders, thereby increasing the value of the company's shares.

In this sense, the wealth transfer from insiders to outsiders is an investment and not a cost. To get the signalling benefit, inside shareholders must put some wealth "at risk." That is, inside shareholders must commit not to tender, and the offer must include a premium over not just the pre-announcement market value but, as I show later, over insiders' estimates of the fair value of the shares.[2] Insiders are at risk in the sense that, if the firm's intrinsic value does not rise upon announcement of the offer, the premium paid over the fair value of the shares will represent a significant transfer of value from their shares (and those of other nontendering shareholders) to the tendering shareholders.

But how large is the benefit to signalling and how great is the risk? Using a sample of self-tender offers from the 1980s, this study measures and compares wealth transfers, premiums, increases in intrinsic value, and the returns to tendering and non-tendering shareholders. It attempts to answer the following questions: Are non-tendering shareholders fully compensated for the premium wealth transfer by the increase in the intrinsic value of their shares? Do non-tendering shareholders do better in fixed-price offers or dutch auctions? Is the premium wealth transfer a big component of the returns to the two shareholder groups—and what percentage of firm value does the transfer amount to? Since fixed-price offers feature larger premiums, are they accompanied by larger increases in intrinsic value (or do insiders have a tendency to "overpay" in fixed-price offers)? Do tendering shareholders do better in fixed-price offers or dutch auctions?

*I thank Justin Pettit and the editor, Don Chew, for their helpful comments. I am grateful for the financial support of the Social Sciences and Humanities Research Council of Canada.

1. For empirical evidence of signalling, see Robert Comment and Gregg Jarrell, "The Relative Signalling Power of Dutch-Auction and Fixed-Price Self-Tender Offers and Open-Market Share Repurchases," *Journal of Finance* 46 (September 1991) 1243-1271. There have been a number of theoretical models of signalling with fixed-price and dutch auction offers. See, for example, William J. McNally,

"Multi-Dimensional Signalling with Fixed-Price Repurchase Offers," *Managerial and Decision Economics*, forthcoming; and Donald B. Hausch, and James K. Seward, "Signaling with Dividends and Share Repurchases: A Choice between Deterministic and Stochastic Cash Disbursements," *Review of Financial Studies* 6 (1993) 121-154.

2. My model shows that a premium over the full-information value and some non-tendering shareholders are both necessary conditions to support a signalling equilibrium with fixed-price offers.

My findings, which are quite different from those reported by earlier studies, suggest that the two types of offers generate roughly the same total return (about 10-11%, on average) to shareholders who do not tender. While fixed-price offers involve a considerably larger wealth transfer from non-tendering to tendering shareholders, fixed-price repurchases compensate the non-tendering shareholders for the larger wealth transfer with larger increases in intrinsic value, thus generating the same total return as dutch auctions. Because of the equivalent total return, I suspect that the attraction of dutch auctions lies not in their smaller wealth transfer or efficiency but in other factors, particularly their reduced risk that the offer will be undersubscribed and the signal will fail to produce the desired effect.

The study described in this paper also extends previous research by using a different method for defining and dissecting the returns to the two different stockholder groups ("non-tendering" and "tendering"). In addition to the new empirical results just mentioned, this new method also yields two other important insights. The first, although not original, bears repeating: the relevant premium is the excess over not the pre-announcement value, but over the "full-information value" of the firm (and I also show that a full-information premium is necessary for a wealth transfer).[3] The second insight—one that should be especially interesting from a non-tendering management's point of view—is that the wealth transfer from non-tendering to tendering shareholders is equal not to this full-information premium, but rather to the premium *less* a portion of that premium that is effectively paid by tendering shareholders.

AN EXAMPLE AND SOME DEFINITIONS

The following presents a simplified example of a dutch auction that will be used to illustrate some of the main points of the paper.[4] Consider a firm that has five shareholders: four outside shareholders and one inside shareholder who controls the firm and does not tender into the offer. (The inside shareholder rules by force of character rather than majority control!) Assume that each of the five shareholders holds 20 of the firm's 100 outstanding shares, and that the current share price is $10.

Now assume the firm proposes a dutch auction self-tender offer for 20% of the firm's outstanding shares at prices between $13 and $17. In dutch auctions, the firm announces a range of prices within which investors may make offers to sell shares to the firm. The firm sorts the offers in ascending order by price and then accepts each offer, starting at the cheapest, until it has met its target quantity. It pays the same price for all purchased shares, and that price is equal to the asking price of the last offer accepted. Since our interest is in the effect of the offer on the wealth of the average shareholder rather than on the bidding process, let's assume that the outside investors all have the same view of the firm's prospects and therefore each chooses to tender five shares at a price of $15.

Assume further that the firm has cash holdings of $500 and has future expected annual after-tax earnings of $25 in perpetuity. The market value of the firm is the sum of the cash and the present value of future earnings (assume a 5% discount rate for the firm's risk class): $500 + $25/0.05 = $1000 or $10 per share. Because the minimum repurchase price of $13 represents a premium of 30% over the pre-announcement price—and the maximum price a premium of 70%—the offer should look very attractive to tendering shareholders.

The typical dutch auction self-tender offer takes from two to four weeks between announcement and execution of the offer. To the extent the market views repurchases as positive signals conveying insiders' confidence about the firm's prospects, the market will raise its estimate of future earnings during this period—and let's assume that the new expected level is $38 per annum. In this case, as I show in a calculation that follows shortly, the stock price will rise from $10 to $12 from the date of announcement through the expiration of the offer.

Before calculating the returns to tendering and non-tendering shareholders, let's first define some values that are important for the subsequent analysis. The first is the *post-repurchase firm value*, which is equal to the cash remaining after the repurchase plus the present value of the new level of earnings:

3. The full-information premium was first identified by Theo Vermaelen in his seminal study of stock repurchases, "Common Stock Repurchases and Market Signalling: An Empirical Study," *Journal of Financial Economics* 9 (1981) 139-183.

4. An analogous example of a fixed-price offer could easily be constructed with a tender price of $15. For fixed-price offers, we would assume that all outside shareholders tender all of their shares and that each has an equal proportion—five shares—purchased.

$$P_E^*N_E = \text{Initial Cost} - \text{Cost of Repurchase} + \frac{\text{New Earnings}}{0.05}$$

$$= \$500 - (15*20) + \frac{38}{0.05}$$

$$= \$960$$

where P_E is the price post-expiration, and N_E is the number of shares outstanding post-expiration. This post-expiration value, $960, can then be divided by the remaining 80 shares to arrive at the post-offer share price of $12.

Alternatively, the post-expiration firm value can be expressed as the value of the firm before the offer ($P_o^*N_o$) less the cost of the repurchase plus the change in value implied by the offer:

$$P_E^*N_E = P_o^*N_o - P_T^*(N_o - N_E) + \Delta V$$

$$= \$10*100 - (15*20) + 260 \qquad (1)$$

$$= \$960$$

where ΔV is the change in the firm's intrinsic value implied by the repurchase. ΔV can also be thought of as the amount by which the firm's value would have increased had the new information about earnings been costlessly transmitted to the market. In this example, ΔV is the increase in the present value of the firm's earnings = $\$38 - \$25/0.05$, or $260. The increase in intrinsic value is an important concept and central to four variables that we now define below.

The first is the stock's *intrinsic value*—that is, the price that would have prevailed prior to the repurchase if the new information about the firm's future earnings had been known (also known as the full-information price, which we will use synonymously with intrinsic value):

$$P_{FI} = \frac{P_o^*N_o + \Delta V}{N_o} = \frac{1000 + 260}{100} = \$12.60 \qquad (2)$$

The second is the *information return*[5]—the increase in the firm's intrinsic value as a proportion of the pre-announcement value:

$$\text{info} = \frac{P_{FI} - P_o}{P_o} = \frac{\Delta V}{P_o^*N_o} = \frac{260}{1000} = 26\% \qquad (3)$$

The last two are measures of the tender premium. The first is the tender premium in excess of the pre-announcement price as proportion of the pre-announcement price:

$$\text{tenprm} = \frac{P_T - P_o}{P_o} = \frac{15 - 10}{10} = 50\% \qquad (4)$$

The second is the tender premium in excess of the full-information price as a proportion of the pre-announcement price:

$$\text{fullprm} = \frac{P_T - P_{FI}}{P_o} = \frac{15 - 12.60}{10} = 24\% \qquad (5)$$

The full-information premium is only about half of the size of the tender premium. Because the repurchase signals an increase in intrinsic value of 26%, over half of the tender premium can be thought of as representing payment for the fair value of the share and the relevant premium is the excess over fair value. The excess over fair value is measured by the full-information premium. (As I show later, a positive full-information premium is both a key component of the returns to the two shareholder groups and a necessary condition for a wealth transfer from non-tendering to tendering shareholders.)

Now let's look more closely at the returns to tendering and non-tendering shareholders. The return to a tendered share is measured by the tender premium in excess of the pre-announcement price: 50% in this example. There is also a substantial return to non-tendered shares, which increase in value from $10 to $12 for a return of 20%. The return to tendering outside shareholders is a weighted average of the return to their tendered and non-tendered shares, since each has 5 shares repurchased and retains 15. The post-repurchase wealth of the tendering shareholders is $255, which is an increase of 27.5% over their pre-repurchase wealth of $200.

Despite the fact that the premium transfers wealth from the non-tendering to tendering shareholders, the non-tendering insiders experience a net gain of 20% (over a period that, as noted, runs two to four weeks in a typical self-tender offer). The non-tendering insiders' return is less than the information return (the increase in intrinsic value of 26%) because of the wealth transfer implicit in the premium. But the increase in intrinsic value is so large that it swamps the cost of the wealth transfer, and so the non-tendering shareholders earn a return that is almost as large as the return to tendering shareholders.

---

5. As noted in footnote 3, the full-information premium was first identified by Theo Vermaelen in his 1981 study of stock repurchases.

My findings, which are quite different from those reported by earlier studies, suggest that the two types of offers generate roughly the same total return (about 10-11%, on average) to shareholders who do not tender.

One might be tempted to estimate the tendering shareholders' return as the sum of the information return and the full-information premium because the tendering shareholders experience an increase in the intrinsic value of their shares (both tendered and non-tendered) and receive the full-information premium. But this would be a mistake (their actual return of 27.5% is less than this sum of the information return, 26%, and the full-information premium, 24%) because the tendering shareholders hold an interest in the firm after the repurchase that is reduced in value by the premium, and so they effectively pay for part of the full-information premium. As I argue in more detail below, because tendering shareholders pay for part of the premium, the wealth transfer from non-tendering shareholders to them is considerably less than the full-information premium.

A number of other insights come out of this example. The first is that both a full-information premium and a group of non-tendering shareholders are necessary conditions for a repurchase to transfer wealth to tendering shareholders. If the firm offers to repurchase shares but at a price that represents a zero full-information premium (in this case, a price of $12.60), then there is no advantage to tendering; the return to tendering is equal to the return to not tendering, and tendering shareholders simply move wealth from shares to cash. For example, open market repurchases can be thought of as self-tender offers with a zero full-information premium. Moreover, if a firm repurchases at a premium to fair value and everyone tenders, there is also no net transfer of wealth. (These conditions can easily be confirmed simply by re-working the above example with a tender price of $12.60 or by assuming that all five investors tender four shares each.)

A second insight is that the wealth transfer is not equal to the full-information premium. The cost of the premium reduces the value of the firm after the repurchase. Non-tendering shareholders obviously bear some of that cost because the value of their holdings in the firm decline after the repurchase. However, tendering shareholders, to the extent they maintain an ownership share, effectively also bear

TABLE 1 ■ SELF-TENDER OFFER SAMPLE BY YEAR

	Fixed-Price	Dutch Auction
1980	10	—
1981	10	—
1982	14	—
1983	6	—
1984	22	2
1985	14	3
1986	9	4
1987	18	7
1988	15	12
1989	11	13
Total	129	41

part of the cost. Thus, to the extent tendering shareholders retain an ownership interest, the wealth transfer from non-tendering insiders is smaller than the premium.[6]

A FIRST LOOK AT DIFFERENCES BETWEEN FIXED-PRICE OFFERS AND DUTCH AUCTIONS

In performing my study, I examined a sample of 170 self-tenders that consisted of 129 fixed-price offers between 1980-1989 and 41 dutch auctions between 1984-1989.[7] (See Table 1 for a year-by-year breakdown of the sample.) Stock prices, returns, and shares outstanding were obtained from the Centre for Research in Securities Prices (CRSP) tapes and the stock holdings of Officers and Directors were obtained from the firms' proxy statements.

As shown in Table 2, there are a number of fundamental differences between fixed-price offers and dutch auctions. Companies making fixed-price offers were smaller, on average, with average capitalization of $800 million, as compared to the average market cap of $2.1 billion for firms effecting dutch auctions. Insiders held 28.6% of the shares in firms executing fixed-price repurchases, considerably larger than the 10.9% inside ownership in firms executing dutch auctions. Moreover, fixed-price offers targeted a significantly larger proportion of shares (22.4%) than dutch auctions (17.7%). The percentage change

---

6. Previous studies of returns to self-tenders incorrectly identify the full-information premium as a measure of the wealth transfer. See Sreenivas Kamma, George Kanatas, and Steve Raymar, "Dutch Auctions versus Fixed-Price Self-Tender Offers for Common Stock," *Journal of Financial Intermediation* 2, (1992) 277-307; and Josef Lakonishok and Theo Vermaelen. "Anomalous Price Behaviour Around Repurchase Tender Offers," *Journal of Finance*, (June 1990) 455-477.

7. More precisely, my sample combines the fixed-price samples of Lakonishok and Vermaelen (1990) with the fixed-price and dutch auction samples of Comment and Jarrell (1991). Dutch auctions were not widely used prior to 1984, but fixed-price offers were. I extended the fixed-price sample to span the 1980s to increases the sample size. The results with the smaller sample are not reported but are qualitatively equivalent to those shown here.

TABLE 2
SUMMARY OF SELF-
TENDER OFFER DATA*

	Fixed-price		Dutch Auction		Prob Value for Difference of	
	Mean	Std Dev	Mean	Std Dev	Means	Medians
Size ($M)	799.90	1,415.60	2,084.10	2,560.70	0.004	0.000
Shares Sought (%)	22.44	13.65	17.74	11.08	0.028	0.049
Insider Holdings (%)	28.55	21.37	10.85	12.67	0.000	0.000
Announcement Return	11.09	11.21	8.02	6.49	0.032	0.049
Beta	0.85	0.56	0.83	0.44	0.816	0.849
Info — raw (%)	12.88	16.75	11.21	9.05	0.416	0.371
Info — Exc.1(%)	10.38	12.68	7.70	9.00	0.171	0.183
Info — Exc.2 (%)	10.54	16.40	8.06	8.45	0.208	0.108
Fullprm (%)	7.11	14.36	2.37	4.57	0.001	0.000
Tenprm (%)	19.99	19.15	13.58	8.85	0.004	0.020
Minprm (%)	n.a.	n.a.	2.76	6.90	n.a.	n.a.
Maxprm (%)	n.a.	n.a.	16.70	8.56	n.a.	n.a.

*129 fixed-price observations and 41 dutch auctions. *Size* is market capitalization prior to announcement. *Insider holdings* are holdings of officers & directors from Proxy statements. *Announcement Return* is the 7-day announcement period return. *Beta* is the OLS beta from the market model estimated with 120 days of data prior to the announcement (VWR as market proxy). *Info* is information return. Raw indicates unadjusted return, Exc.1 is return in excess of Beta times market return (93 FP and 39 DA observations), and Exc. 2 is in excess of raw market return. *Minprm* and *Maxprm* are the dutch range prices expressed as a percentage of the pre-announcement price. Prob Value for Difference gives the p-values from the difference of means (t-test assuming different variances) and difference of medians tests between the fixed-price sample value and the corresponding dutch auction sample value.

in stock price around the announcement was 11.1% for fixed-price offers, and 8% for dutch auctions.[8]

ANALYZING PREMIUMS, RETURNS, AND THE WEALTH TRANSFER

This section presents estimates of the premiums, wealth transfers, information returns, and shareholder returns for the sample of fixed-price offers and dutch auctions summarized above. In evaluating these returns, keep in mind that the typical self-tender offer lasts from two to four weeks. And since the returns reported below are measured from three days before the announcement to three days following the expiration, they span a relatively short period of time. Thus, my study does not address the returns earned by shareholders in the months and years following repurchases. But, as I discuss briefly at the end of this article, there are at least two reputable studies that have measured longer-run rates of returns earned by non-tendering shareholders after fixed-price and open market

repurchases.[9] And both studies conclude that investors who retain their shares after the repurchase go on to earn substantial excess returns.

Premiums and the Increase in Intrinsic Value

As we can see in Table 2, the premiums for tendering into fixed-price offers are significantly larger than the premiums for dutch auctions. The average tender price premium over the pre-announcement price is about 20% in fixed-price offers. In dutch auctions, the firm does not commit to a tender price, but instead announces a range of prices within which offers are accepted. As also reported in Table 2, the minimum range price averages 2.75% above the pre-announcement price and the maximum range price 16.7% above. The final "buy" price of dutch auctions represents an average premium of 13.6% above the pre-announcement price.

But, as suggested earlier, the variable of greater interest to corporate management is likely to be the tender price premium in excess of the intrinsic value

---

8. This difference cannot be attributed to differences in risk since the two samples have equivalent systematic risk.

9. See Josef Lakonishok and Theo Vermaelen, "Anomalous Price Behavior Around Repurchase Tender Offers," *Journal of Finance*, (1990) 455-477; and David Ikenberry, Josef Lakonishok and Theo Vermaelen, "Market Underreaction to Open Market Share Repurchases," *Journal of Financial Economics*, (1995) 181-208.

Insiders held 28.6% of the shares in firms executing fixed-price repurchases, considerably larger than the 10.9% inside ownership in firms executing dutch auctions. The percentage change in stock price around the announcement was 11.1% for fixed-price offers, and 8% for dutch auctions.

Times Mirror's Fixed-Price Offer

On July 1, 1985 Times Mirror Inc. announced a fixed-price repurchase for 10.4% of its shares at a price of $60. The average price in the week preceding the announcement was $51.6 and the average price in the week after the expiration of the offer (July 15) was $55.0. From these values, the full-information price of the shares was $55.50 (0.104 * $60 + (1 − 0.104) * $55). The information return was thus 7.7% [($55.5/$51.6) − 1] * 100. The tender price represents a premium of 16.3% above the pre-announcement price, and a premium of 8.7% (100*($60 − $55.5)/$51.6) above the full-information price. The Officers and Directors held 36% of the shares outstanding prior to the offer, and if we assume that they are the non-tendering shareholders, then their return was 6.7% around the period of the offer. The tendering shareholders did better and earned a return of 8.3%. (The calculations of the returns to shareholders are shown later.)

Schlumberger's Dutch Auction

On September 20, 1988 Schlumberger announced a dutch auction for 11.2% of their shares at prices between $32 and $37. The offer expired on October 18 and the company paid $34.7 per share. The average price in the week preceding the announcement was $32.1 and the average price in the week after the expiration of the offer was $34. From these values, the full-information price of the shares is $34.1 (0.112 * $34.7 + (1 − 0.112)*$33.9). The information return was thus 6.2% ([($34.1/$32.1) − 1]*100). The purchase price represents a premium of 8.3% above the pre-announcement price, and a premium of 2.1% (100*($34.7 − $34.1)/$32.1) above the full-information price. The Officers and Directors held 3.3% of the shares outstanding prior to the offer; and if we assume that they are the non-tendering shareholders, then their return was 5.9% around the period of the offer. The tendering shareholders earned a return of 6.2%. (The calculations of the returns to shareholders are shown later.)

---

of the shares. In fixed-price offers, the average full-information premium is 7.1%, as compared to only 2.4% for tendering into dutch auctions.

The increase in intrinsic value of the repurchasing firms is measured by the full-information return (as calculated using Equation 3 earlier). Table 2 reports an increase in intrinsic value of 12.9% for firms engaging in fixed-price offers, and 11.2% for firms using dutch auctions (though this difference in mean returns is not statistically significant).[10] But when these "raw" information returns are adjusted for movements in the broad market, the return is statistically significantly larger for fixed-price offers (10.5% vs. 8.1% for dutch auctions, as reported on the line "info-Exc.2" in Table 2).[11]

Returns to Non-Tendering Shareholders

If the non-tendering shareholders (later I will assume that these are the firm's insiders) own a proportion of the equity prior to the repurchase, and

the firm offers to buy back b percent of the shares, then their proportionate holdings after the repurchase are a/(1–b). For example, if they own 25% before the repurchase and the firm buys back half of the outstanding shares, then their proportionate holdings after the repurchase are 25%/50% = 50%. The non-tendering shareholders' return around a repurchase can be calculated in two ways: (1) the percentage change in the stock price from pre-announcement to post-expiration; or, equivalently, (2) the change in their wealth from pre-announcement to post-expiration. I adopt the latter approach because it provides better insights into the determinants of the change in their wealth.

With a little algebraic manipulation (which is presented in Appendix I), non-tendering shareholders' change in wealth can be partitioned into the sum of three parts: (1) the increase in intrinsic value of their share of the firm; (2) the reduction in firm value due to the premium over intrinsic value paid for the repurchased shares; and (3) the portion

---

10. The relative magnitudes are consistent with the findings of previous studies. For example, Kamma, Kanatas, and Raymar (1992) also find that average information return for fixed-price offers is larger than the average for dutch auction, 8.63% vs. 7.92%, but the difference is not significant. Comment and Jarrell (1991) find that fixed-price repurchases feature significantly larger announcement period

returns than dutch auctions, 12.3% vs. 8.3%. Announcement returns are equal to the information returns if the proportion of shares sought equals the proportion actually repurchased.

11. Based on a difference of medians test at the 10.8% level.

TABLE 3
THE RETURNS TO SELF-
TENDERS*

Variable	Fixed-Price		Dutch Auction		Prob Value for Difference of	
	Mean	Std Dev	Mean	Std Dev	Means	Medians
PANEL A: RETURNS TO NON-TENDERING SHAREHOLDERS						
Raw total return (r_N–RAW)	10.24	18.58	10.15	10.78	0.971	0.592
Excess total return (r_N–Excess.1)	8.34	14.79	6.65	10.61	0.464	0.342
Excess total return (r_N–Excess.2)	7.89	17.72	6.99	9.97	0.685	0.108
Wealth transfer loss (r_{NW})	–2.65	5.78	–1.07	3.84	0.047	0.007
PANEL B: RETURNS TO TENDERING SHAREHOLDERS						
Raw total return (r_T–RAW)	13.77	16.74	11.28	8.99	0.224	0.211
Excess total return (r_T–Excess.1)	10.89	12.43	7.77	8.95	0.109	0.183
Excess total return (r_T–Excess.2)	11.43	16.46	8.13	8.40	0.094	0.108
Wealth transfer gain (r_{TW})	0.89	2.67	0.07	0.22	0.001	0.001
PANEL C: MISCELLANEOUS RETURNS						
% Wealth Transfer (WTRAN)	0.51	1.44	0.05	0.18	0.001	0.001
Long-run excess return — Prior	1.20	24.03	–0.66	14.53	0.589	0.567
Long-run excess return — Post	2.72	31.24	–4.93	11.94	0.046	0.567

*129 fixed-price observations and 41 dutch auctions. Raw indicates unadjusted return, Excess.1 is return in excess of Beta times market return, and Excess.2 is in excess of raw market return. The market return is measured with the CRSP VWR. Long-run excess returns are buy and hold returns for stock for 160 trading days less concurrent return on market. Prior period ends 7 days before announcement and post period starts 7 days after expiration of offer. Long-run returns based on 91 observations for fixed-price sample and 39 for dutch auction sample. Prob Value for Difference gives the p-values from the difference of means (t-test assuming different variances) and difference of medians tests difference between medians of the fixed-price sample and the corresponding dutch auction sample.

of the premium paid for by the tendering share-holders through the loss in value of their post-repurchase share of the firm. The important insight here (and demonstrated more formally in Appendix I) is that the wealth transfer from insiders (and other non-tendering shareholders) is not equal to the premium, but rather to the difference between parts (2) and (3)—that is, the difference between the full-information premium and the portion of that premium borne by the tendering shareholders. Another implication of this insight is that if there is no full-information premium (e.g., $P_T = P_{FI}$), then the wealth transfer is zero. If a firm offers no full-information premium, then it is simply paying the fair price for the shares, which means no extraordinary gain for tendering shareholders (except for the increase in intrinsic value) and no loss to the non-tendering shareholders.

The rate of return the non-tenderers earn across the repurchase is equal to their change in wealth (from Appendix I) expressed as a percentage of the initial value of their shares, denoted r_N. A little simplification yields the following expression:

$$r_N = \text{info} - \frac{\delta}{1-\delta}\text{fullprm} = r_{Ninf} + r_{NW} \qquad (6)$$

The return to non-tendered shares (Equation 6) comprises two parts: the first is the gain from the increase in intrinsic firm value (r_{Ninf}), and the second is the loss associated with the wealth transfer implicit in the premium (r_{NW}). The second term is the net cost to non-tenders: the cost of the premium less the portion paid by tendering shareholders (where δ is the fractional proportion repurchased).

Panel A of Table 3 shows the size of the returns to non-tendering shareholders for both fixed-price and dutch auction self-tenders. These results are quite different from those obtained by previous studies. The returns to non-tendering shareholders in dutch auctions are numerically and statistically equivalent to the returns in fixed-price offers, 10.15% vs. 10.24%.[12] Since fixed-price offers feature a larger tender premium than

---

12. Kamma, Kanatas and Raymar (1992) analyze cumulative abnormal returns over the tender period and show that non-tenderers in dutch auctions achieve an extra 173 basis point over their counterparts in fixed-price offers (although the difference is not statistically significant).

In fixed-price offers, the average full-information premium is 7.1%, as compared to only 2.4% for tendering into dutch auctions. The average tender price premium over the pre-announcement price is about 20% in fixed-price offers, whereas the final "buy" price of dutch auctions represents an average premium of 13.6% above the pre-announcement price.

dutch auctions, it is not surprising that the proportionate loss due to the wealth transfer is larger for fixed-price offers, a loss of 2.65% versus 1.07% for dutch auctions (the difference is statistically significant). The benefit to not tendering into a premium repurchase offer is the increase in the intrinsic value of the firm that accompanies the repurchase. As noted earlier (and shown in Table 2), the increase in intrinsic value is 12.9% for fixed-price offers and 11.2% for dutch auctions. The larger increase in intrinsic value in fixed-price offers offsets the bigger premium wealth transfer and yields a return for non-tendering shareholders that is equivalent to their return in dutch auctions. This data suggests that inside shareholders would be indifferent (from an expected wealth standpoint) between dutch auctions and fixed-price offers.

Panel A of Table 3 also presents the returns net of the concurrent change in the market to isolate the effects of the repurchase. Two market adjusted returns are calculated: (1) the raw return less beta times the concurrent return on the market (the return on the CRSP value weighted index), and (2) the raw return less the concurrent market return.[13] Contrary to some previous results, the excess returns imply that non-tendering shareholders do better in fixed-price offers than dutch auctions: the second measure (Excess.2) indicates that non-tendering shareholders earn an excess return of 7.89% in fixed-price offers but only 6.99% in dutch auctions (the difference in means is not significant but the difference in medians is significant at the 11% level).

This evidence suggests that non-tendering shareholders in fixed-price offers get a total return at least as large, if not larger than, the total return in dutch auctions. As stated earlier, the total return is the information return less the wealth transfer. Therefore, if both the total return and the wealth transfer are significantly larger for fixed-price offers, then the information return must also be significantly larger. This finding, in combination with the fact that the median excess information return is significantly larger for fixed-price offers (see Table 2), strongly implies that fixed-price offers generate greater increases in intrinsic value than dutch auctions.

Returns to Tendering Shareholders

To measure the returns to tendering shareholders we need to know the proportion of non-tendering shareholders. Because that proportion cannot be directly observed, it must be estimated.[14] We make the reasonable assumption that insiders (officers and directors) do not tender.[15]

The calculation of returns to non-tendering shareholders is based on the further assumption that all tendering shareholders retain an interest in the firm after the repurchase.[16] Tendering shareholders retain an interest if they choose not to tender all of their shares, or if the offer is oversubscribed and results in a *pro-rata* repurchase. If the offer is undersubscribed, or in the special case where a sub-set of shareholders is bought out entirely (a targeted repurchase), the tendering shareholders earn a return equal to the premium over the pre-announcement price.

Given the assumption that the tendering shareholders retain an interest in the firm, we could simply express their returns as a weighted average of the returns to tendered and non-tendered shares, where the weights are the proportion of shares repurchased and the proportion retained. Tendered shares earn a return equal to the pre-announcement tender premium, and the return to non-tendered shares was explained above. This approach, while correct, does not highlight the fundamental sources of the wealth gains to the tendering shareholders.

There are two basic sources of wealth gain for the tendering sharheolders: the transfer of wealth from the non-tendering shareholders and the increase in the firm's intrinsic value. Specifically, Appendix I dissects the tendering shareholders' return into three components: (1) the increase in intrinsic value of the shares kept after the repurchase; (2) the gain on tendered shares (which in turn consists of two parts—the increase in intrinsic value of the tendered shares and the premium over intrinsic value received for tendered shares); and (3) the share of the premium (over intrinsic value) paid by the tendering shareholders due to the reduction in value of the shares they continue to hold after the repurchase.

13. Beta is simply the daily OLS beta measured over a one hundred and twenty day window preceding the repurchase. The market is proxied by the CRSP value weighted market index.

14. Kamma, Kanatas, and Raymar (1992) do not address this issue and so do not compute the returns to tendering shareholders.

15. Vermaelen's 1981 study of fixed-price offers found that insiders commit not to tender into 85% of the sample firms. Comment and Jarrell's more recent

(1991) study of both fixed-price and dutch auctions found the same to be true in 88% of their sample of fixed-price offers, but in only 41% of their sample of dutch auctions.

16. Thus, I explicitly ignores the case of a targeted repurchase. For an analysis of the wealth effects of targeted repurchases, see Michael Bradley and L. MacDonald Wakeman, "The Wealth Effects of Targeted Share Repurchases," *Journal of Financial Economics* 11 (1983).

These three components can be combined to yield the following expression for the tendering shareholders' return (see Appendix I for the derivation):

$$r_T = \text{info} + \frac{\delta\alpha}{(1-\alpha)(1-\delta)}\text{fullprm} = r_{Tinf} + r_{TW} \qquad (7)$$

The return is a function of the two basic sources of wealth gain: intrinsic value and wealth transfer. The first part of the return, r_{Tinf}, is the sum of the increase in intrinsic value of the shares retained and the shares tendered, and the second term, r_{TW}, is the net wealth transfer from the non-tendering shareholders—it is the full-information premium received for tendered shares less the part of the premium paid by tendering shareholders.

Panel B of Table 3 shows that shareholders tendering into dutch auctions received an average return of 11.3% and shareholders tendering into fixed-price auctions received an average of 13.8% (the difference, although it seems quite large, is not significant at standard levels). In dutch auctions, tendering shareholders earn a little bit more than non-tendering shareholders, 11.3% v. 10.1% (but, again, the difference is not statistically significant). In fixed-price offers, tendering shareholders do considerably better, earning 13.8% to the non-tenderer's 10.2% (and this difference is statistically significant).[17]

When taken as a whole, however, these results suggest that non-tendering shareholders do almost as well as tendering shareholders despite the transfer of wealth implicit in the premium tender price. The equivalence in returns can be attributed to the following: (1) the increase in intrinsic value, which is the chief determinant of returns for both groups, significantly exceeds the size of any wealth transfer; and (2) the wealth transfer is reduced by the fact that the tendering shareholders pay for part of the premium.

How big are the wealth transfers, then? Using Equation (7) and estimates of r_{TW}, I found the wealth transfer to tendering shareholders was quite small in fixed-price offers—representing only 0.9% of their initial investment—and significantly smaller (just 0.07%) in dutch auctions. But, again, this is not surprising when one realizes that tendering shareholders end up paying for a large part of the premium. Thus, the bulk of the tendering shareholders' return is due to the increase in intrinsic firm value, which, as discussed above, is larger for fixed-price offers, 12.9% v. 11.2%.

Panel B of Table 3 also presents the returns to tendering shareholders net of concurrent changes in the market. Consistent with the raw returns, both excess return measures indicate that shareholders tendering into fixed-price offers do better than shareholders tendering into dutch auctions (and the difference is statistically significant at the 10% level).

Another way of assessing the relative size of the wealth transfers is to look at the total value of the wealth transfer as a proportion of the initial firm value, denoted Wtran. Panel C of Table 3 shows that the wealth transfer represents only *one half of one percent* (0.5%) of the initial value of the firm for fixed-price offers—and just one tenth of that amount, or 0.05%, for dutch auctions. The wealth transfers in self-tender offers are small no matter how they are expressed.

The returns to tendering and non-tender shareholders are large, especially when contrasted with the returns earned in the period preceding and succeeding the offer. The buy-and-hold returns for the preceding and succeeding eight-month periods are shown in Panel C of Table 3. The return is expressed in excess of the concurrent buy-and-hold return on the CRSP value weighted index. For fixed-price offers, there is no significant excess return either during the eight-month periods before or after the repurchase (whereas, during the two- to four-week period surrounding the offer, shareholders experience excess returns between 7% and 12%. In the case of dutch auctions, although there are no significant excess returns prior to the offers, there is a significant average negative excess return (of almost 5%) in the eight months following.

Longer-Run Returns

How the inside shareholders expect the stock to perform over not just the next eight months, but over the next three to five years is also likely to play a role in management's decision to repurchase shares—and in investors' decisions whether or not to tender. As we showed above, the return to non-tendering shareholders is substantial even over the relatively short period around the actual repurchase because of the increase in the firm's intrinsic value. If, in addition, positive excess returns are expected in the future, then there is very little cost to not

---

17. The difference is significant at the 11% level using a two-tail t-test.

tendering—and it is thus not surprising that officers and directors choose not to tender.

Although there is no published evidence on the longer-run performance of companies executing dutch auctions, there are studies of firms conducting open market repurchases and fixed-price offers. In a study published in 1990, Josef Lakonishok and Theo Vermaelen studied the long-run returns of companies following fixed-price offers and reported that their average return exceeded the average return on a benchmark portfolio by more than 8% over a 21-month period starting three months after the announcement. In a 1995 study, David Ikenberry along with Lakonishok and Vermaelen reported that the average return of companies announcing open market repurchase programs exceeded a benchmark portfolio by more than 12% over the four-year period following the announcements.[18]

Thus, at least in the case of open market repurchases and fixed-price offers, investors who retain their shares go on to earn substantial excess returns. Besides providing strong support for the signalling hypothesis cited at the outset of this article, this finding also explains why most shareholders do not tender all of their shares into premium offers—and why many shareholders beyond the officers and directors choose not to tender *any* of their shares.

CONCLUSIONS

Self-tender offers pay substantial premiums for tendered shares. In fixed-price offers, the premium is 20% over the pre-announcement price and 7.1% over the "full-information" price; in dutch auctions, it is 13.6% over the pre-announcement price and 2.4% over the full-information price. Consistent with the argument that the premiums in self-tender offers are signals of higher future earnings, this article documents that the market increases its estimate of firm value by almost 13% around fixed-price offers, and by just over 11% around dutch auctions.

A necessary condition for signalling is that the self-tender transfer wealth from non-tendering to tendering shareholders. I show that a premium over full-information value is necessary for a wealth transfer, though the transfer is equal not to the full-information premium, but to that premium net of the portion paid for by the tendering shareholders.

Despite the large premiums offered in both types of offers, the wealth transfer implicit in the premium is only a small part of the total return to tendering shareholders. It also represents a small cost (less than 1% in fixed-price offers, and less than 0.1% in dutch auctions) to non-tendering shareholders. The increase in intrinsic value, measured by the information return, is the major component of the return for both tendering and non-tendering shareholders, dominating the wealth transfer for both offer types.

Empirical estimates from a sample of self-tender offers spanning the 1980s show that, consistent with other studies, fixed-price repurchases offer significantly larger premiums than dutch auctions. Some observers have suggested that these premiums are overpayments and that dutch auctions are cheaper and so more efficient than fixed-price offers. But my study (unlike previous ones) finds that non-tendering shareholders do as well in fixed-price as in dutch auctions. Fixed-price offers feature larger wealth transfers than dutch auctions, but also larger increases in intrinsic value so that the total returns to non-tendering shareholders are equivalent to those in dutch auctions.

For inside shareholders who are choosing between offer types, the main difference is not in their respective returns to insiders, but rather in the degree of commitment each requires from insiders who do not tender and, thus, in the degree of risk borne by insiders. Fixed-price offers allow the inside shareholders to signal more persuasively because they make a commitment to a specific tender price—a commitment that entails the practical risk that the price and quantity of the firm's shares demanded by outside shareholders may lie below the supply curve for the firms shares. If this proves to be the case, the offer will be undersubscribed and fail to convey management's confidence about future earnings.

Dutch auctions do not require a commitment to a price and so are less powerful signals, but they remove the risk of undersubscription. Thus, dutch auctions are better for insiders who suspect that their shares are undervalued but are unsure of their share's true intrinsic value; they are also the more likely choice for insiders who have greater uncertainty about the position of the supply curve for the company's shares.

---

18. See the studies cited in footnote 9.

The Return to Non-Tendering Shareholders

The change in wealth of non-tendering shareholders is given by:

$$\Delta Wealth_N = \frac{\alpha}{1-\delta} {}^*P_E{}^*N_E - \alpha{}^*P_O{}^*N_O$$

$$= \alpha{}^*N_O{}^*(P_{FI}-P_O) - \delta N_O(P_T-P_{FI}) +$$

$$\left[\frac{(1-\alpha-\delta)}{1-\delta}\right]\delta N_O(P_T-P_{FI})$$

This can be expressed in proportionate terms as a percentage of the non-tenderer's initial wealth:

$$r_N = \frac{\Delta Wealth_N}{\alpha N_O P_O} = info - \delta fullprm + \left[\frac{(1-\alpha-\delta)}{1-\delta}\right]\delta fullprm$$

$$r_N = info - \frac{\delta}{1-\delta} fullprm = r_{Ninf} + r_{NW}$$

The Return to Tendering Shareholders

The return to tendering shareholders across the repurchase is given by:

$$\Delta Wealth_T = \frac{(1-\alpha-\delta)}{1-\delta}{}^*P_E{}^*N_E +$$

$$\delta{}^*N_O{}^*P_T - (1-\alpha){}^*P_O{}^*N_O$$

This profit can be disaggregated into three component parts:

$$\Delta Wealth_T = (1-\alpha-\delta)\,\Delta V + \alpha N_O[(P_T-P_{FI}) + (P_{FI}-P_O)] - \frac{(1-\alpha-\delta)}{1-\alpha}{}^*[\delta N_O(P_T-P_{FI})]$$

Dividing this gross return by the value of the tendering shareholders' initial shares, gives their total return. Simplification of the resulting expression yields:

$$r_T = \frac{(1-\alpha-\delta)}{1-\alpha} {}^* info + \frac{\delta}{1-\alpha} fullprm + \frac{\delta}{1-\alpha} info - \left[\frac{(1-\alpha-\delta)}{1-\delta}\right]\left[\frac{\delta}{1-\alpha}\right]{}^* fullprm$$

Further simplification yields the tendering shareholders' returns as a function of two components:

$$r_T = info + \frac{\delta\alpha}{(1-\alpha)(1-\delta)} fullprm = r_{Tinf} + r_{TW}$$

Wealth Transfer as a Proportion of Initial Firm Value

The dollar value of the wealth transfer is simply the return to non-tendering shareholders due to the wealth transfer, r_{NW}, times the value of their initial holdings (aN_OP_O). Taking the total dollar value of the wealth transfer as a proportion of the initial value of the firm, denoted Wtran, yields:

$$WTran = \frac{1}{P_O N_O}\left[\alpha N_O P_O \frac{\delta}{1-\delta} fullprm\right] = \frac{\alpha\delta}{1-\delta} fullprm$$

THE DIVIDEND CUT "HEARD 'ROUND THE WORLD": THE CASE OF FPL

by Dennis Soter,
Stern Stewart & Co.,
Eugene Brigham,
University of Florida, and
Paul Evanson,
Florida Power & Light Company

[FPL's decision was] "the dividend cut heard 'round the world."

— Morgan Stanley analyst report, June 1994

On May 9, 1994, FPL Group, the parent company of Florida Power & Light Company, announced a 32% reduction in its quarterly dividend payout, from 62 cents per share to 42 cents. This was the first-ever dividend cut by a healthy utility. A number of utilities had reduced their dividends in the past, but only after cash flow problems—often associated with nuclear plants—had given them no other choice.

In its announcement, FPL stressed that it had studied the situation carefully and that, given the prospect of increased competition in the electric utility industry, the company's high dividend payout ratio (which had averaged 90% in the past four years) was no longer in its stockholders' best interests. The new policy resulted in a dividend payout of about 60% of the prior year's earnings. Management also announced that, starting in 1995, the dividend payout would be reviewed in February instead of May to reinforce the linkage between dividends and annual earnings. In so doing, the company wanted to minimize unintended "signaling effects" from any future changes in the dividend.

At the same time it announced this change in dividend policy, FPL Group's board authorized the repurchase of up to 10 million shares of common stock over the next three years; and FPL's management indicated that 4 million shares would be repurchased over the next 12 months, depending on market conditions. (In fact, the company repurchased 4 million shares in the last eight months of 1994 and 1.9 million shares in 1995, at a total cost of $193 million.) In adopting this strategy, the company noted that changes in the U.S. tax code since 1990 had made capital gains more attractive than dividends to shareholders. Whereas dividends are taxed at ordinary income rates, gains from stock sales are taxed at lower capital gains rates. Furthermore, capital gains are taxed only when realized, thus providing each shareholder the opportunity to defer that tax.

Besides providing a more tax-efficient means of distributing excess capital to its stockholders, FPL's substitution of stock repurchases for dividends was also designed to increase the company's financial flexibility in preparation for a new era of deregulation and heightened competition among utilities. Although much of the cash savings from the dividend cut would be returned to investors in the form of stock repurchases, the rest would be used to retire debt at Florida Power & Light and so reduce the company's leverage ratio. This deleveraging and strengthening of FPL's financial condition were intended both to prepare the company for an increase in business risk and to provide the financial resources to take advantage of future growth opportunities.

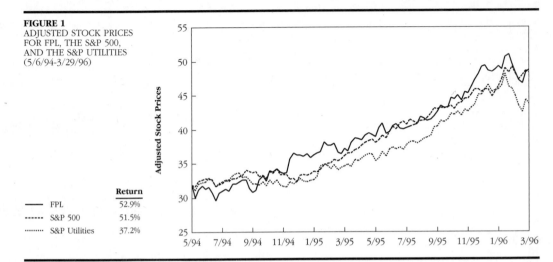

FIGURE 1
ADJUSTED STOCK PRICES
FOR FPL, THE S&P 500,
AND THE S&P UTILITIES
(5/6/94-3/29/96)

	Return
—— FPL	52.9%
------ S&P 500	51.5%
········ S&P Utilities	37.2%

The stock market's initial reaction to FPL's announcement was negative. On the day of the announcement, the company's stock price fell from $31.88 to $27.50, a drop of nearly 14%. (Given that FPL's average stock price during the prior month was about $33.75, and that the stock underperformed the S&P Utilities Index by about 4% during that month, a better estimate of the market's negative response is probably about 18-20%.) But, as analysts digested the news and considered the reasons for the reduction, they concluded that the action was not a signal of financial distress but rather a strategic decision that would improve the company's long-term financial flexibility and prospects for growth. This view spread throughout the financial community, and FPL's stock began to recover.

On May 31, less than a month after the announcement, FPL's stock closed at $32.17 (adjusted for the quarterly dividend of 42 cents), or about 30 cents higher than the pre-announcement price. By the middle of June, at least 15 major brokerage houses had placed FPL's common stock on their "buy" lists. On May 9, 1995—exactly one year after the announcement of the cut—FPL's stock price closed at $37.75, giving stockholders a one-year post-announcement return (including dividends) of 23.8%,[1] more than double the 11.2% of the S&P 500 Index and well

above the 14.2% of the S&P Utilities Index over the same period. As this article went to press (April 1, 1996), FPL's stock was trading at $45.25 (or $48.73 adjusted for dividends), providing stockholders with a two-year post-announcement return of 52.9%—again, well above the 37.2% return of the S&P Utilities Index over the same period. (For a graphic illustration of FPL's stock return relative to the S&P Utilities Index, see Figure 1.)

Management's decision, however, was not an easy one. FPL had achieved the longest record of continuous annual dividend increases of any electric utility—47 years—and the third longest of any company traded on the New York Stock Exchange. Moreover, dividend cuts are almost invariably followed by sharp reductions in stock price. Anticipating that the market's initial reaction would be negative, management undertook a major investor relations campaign to explain the company's change in dividend policy as a critical part of its overall business and financial strategy. That campaign took the form of a series of "road shows" comparable to those used in launching IPOs. The comparison seems apt because, in an important sense, FPL was becoming a *new* company—or at least it was a company in the process of transforming itself to confront a new competitive business environment.

---

1. Measured from the $31.88 stock price prior to the announcement. If we measure the return instead from the prior month's average of $33.75, the return would have been about 17%, still above the S&P return of 14.2%.

FPL was not alone, however, either in reconsidering its dividend policy, or in making a partial substitution of stock repurchases for dividends. With companies in many industries facing greater competition, boards of directors are increasingly deciding that stock buybacks are a more effective means than dividends of committing management to distribute excess cash to stockholders. In the past three years, the dividend payout ratio of the S&P 500 has fallen from a 70-year historical average of about 55% to under 40%.[2] Stock market "bears" continue to point to a market dividend yield that has fallen from an historical average of about 4% to below 2.4%. What such analysis typically fails to recognize is the growing extent to which stock repurchases are being used to supplement dividends as a method of paying out excess cash. Between 1991 and 1995, total corporate dividends increased from $82.6 billion to an estimated $98.7 billion, an average annual growth rate of about 4%. Over the same period, the total amount of stock repurchased by U.S. companies grew from $21.3 billion to $55.3 billion, an average annual growth rate of over 30%.[3] (For an illustration of the growth of stock repurchases relative to dividends since 1976, see Figure 2.)[4] In 1995 alone, over 800 U.S. companies announced plans to repurchase a total of $98 billion of stock—a 42% increase over the prior year.

THE CASE OF GE

In the first five years of the eighties...GE returned to its share owners about $840 million a year in dividends. Throughout the following five years, ending in 1990...we returned nearly double that—about $1.4 billion in annual dividends and repurchased $2.6 billion of stock. During the past five years, we've returned to share owners about $2.3 billion a year in dividends and repurchased an additional $5.5 billion of our stock. The pace continued to accelerate in 1995 when...[we paid] $2.8 billion in dividends and [repurchased] $3.1 billion [of our stock].

—Jack Welch
1995 Annual Report of General Electric

Other utilities, as well as companies in other rapidly changing industries, are wrestling with the dividend issue. Neither financial economists nor Wall Street operators have a magic formula for establishing the optimal payout policy. Indeed, many academics are still engaged in a 35-year-old debate as to whether dividend policy matters at all. The FPL case can be seen as contributing to the dividend debate in the following sense: It suggests that while there may not be a single dividend payout ratio that maximizes a company's value, the wrong policy may end up reducing value. More important, it makes clear that the right dividend policy for an individual company depends primarily on the business environment in which the firm operates—and that changes in the business environment are likely to dictate changes in financial policy. As the FPL story also shows, making the right dividend decision is not a trivial undertaking.

THE CHANGING ECONOMIC ENVIRONMENT

Dividend policy cannot be established in a vacuum. It must be viewed as part of an integrated financial strategy that includes a company's target capital structure and its expected future requirements for outside capital. The most important determinants of a company's financial strategy, as we will argue below, are its business strategy and the nature and extent of its investment opportunities. When the dynamics of the business change, as the case of FPL will illustrate, corporate strategy and financial policies—including dividends—also must change.

Under traditional rate-of-return regulation, FPL and other utilities had relatively stable earnings and paid out a high percentage of earnings as dividends. Largely because of the stability of their earnings, dividends on utility stocks tended to be quite predictable, much like the interest earned on corporate bonds. For this reason, utility stocks were typically purchased as "income" stocks and, like bonds, are highly sensitive to changes in interest rates. In fact, many utilities maintained their dividends throughout the Great Depression and, as a result, attracted income-oriented investors—the so-

---

2. See Jean Helwege, David Laster, and Kevin Cole, "Stock Market Valuation Indicators: Is This Time Different?" *Financial Analysts Journal* (forthcoming, 1996).
    3. Ibid.

4. As the figure shows, the first major spurt of growth in stock repurchases begins in 1984 and then rises to a peak in 1989. Much of these repurchases in the 1980s, however, were part of defensive recapitalizations and were thus not entirely "voluntary" decisions on the part of management. In the 1990s, by contrast, stock repurchases have been largely voluntary—that is, undertaken without pressure from a hostile bidder.

> With companies in many industries facing greater competition, more and more boards of directors have decided that stock repurchases are a more effective means than dividends of committing management to distribute excess cash to stockholders.

FIGURE 2
TOTAL DIVIDEND
PAYMENTS AND
REPURCHASES*

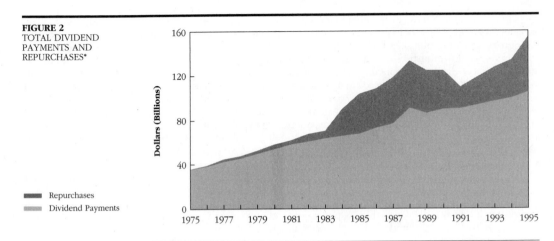

Repurchases
Dividend Payments

Source: Compustat. 1995 repurchases are estimated based on first three quarters.
*This figure is taken from Jean Helwege, David Laster, and Kevin Cole, "Stock Market Valuation Indicators: Is This Time Different?," *Financial Analysts Journal* (forthcoming, 1996).

called widow and orphan clientele, who are said to place a special value on high payouts and high dividend yields.

Historically, utilities have been natural monopolies and have been granted monopoly franchises for their service areas. In return, they are required to provide customers with power on demand. They have operated subject to a "regulatory compact" under which regulators are supposed to allow them to earn a rate of return on their invested capital that is "commensurate with returns on investments in other enterprises having corresponding risks." That means, in effect, that the utility can earn its cost of capital on funds supplied by investors, but no more. Because of regulation, utilities have limited upside potential, but they have also been thought to have relatively little downside risk.

However, the regulatory compact began to be revamped during the 1970s and 1980s when many utilities were charged, with 20-20 hindsight, with having made "imprudent" investments, especially in nuclear plants. Regulatory actions during those years made it clear that a utility could no longer make investments with the assurance that revenues would be sufficient to provide a reasonable rate of return.

The most significant federal legislation affecting the electric utility industry was the Energy Policy Act of 1992. This act required utilities to open their transmission lines for wholesale transactions to any utility or independent power producer, and it allowed any company to build, own, and operate power plants. While the act specifically precluded the Federal Energy Regulatory Commission (FERC) from ordering transmission access for "retail wheeling"—that is, sales directly to retail customers—it did not prevent states from allowing retail competition.

Since the passage of this act, there has been growing pressure at both the federal and state levels for customer choice. In Washington, Republican Congressman Dan Schaefer of Colorado, the chairman of the House Commerce Subcommittee on Energy and Power, has been strongly advocating a rapid transition to full retail competition. Bills have already been introduced in both the House and the Senate that would require states to prescribe some form of retail competition. At present, 35 states are considering regulatory or legislative proposals for retail competition.

To illustrate the significance of wheeling for the industry, on April 20, 1994 (just two weeks before the FPL dividend announcement), the California Public Utilities Commission released its proposal to phase in retail wheeling beginning in 1996. In the week following that proposal, California's three largest utilities together lost over $1.8 billion of market value—an average loss of 8%.

This announcement was by no means the first sign that the electric utility industry was becoming a riskier place in which to operate and invest. Perhaps the most dramatic statement about the financial future of the industry came in October 1993—six months prior to the FPL dividend action—when Standard & Poor's took the unprecedented step of revising its bond rating outlook on 22 utilities (representing about one-third of all utilities with rated debt) from "stable" to "negative." To reflect the more competitive environment, S&P also announced that it was changing its rating guidelines for the industry to take greater account of factors such as revenue dependencies and vulnerabilities, fuel diversity, and the regulatory environment.[5]

In sum, FPL and other utilities today find themselves increasingly subject to competition and so can no longer make investments with the expectation that they will earn a "fair" rate of return because of their status as a regulated monopoly. The shift in utilities' position from low-risk, regulated monopolies to riskier, competitive companies began in the late 1960s and is still going on today. Furthermore, different utilities have been affected in different ways and at different times. Still, FPL and all other utilities now face a drastically different future than under the old rules of the game, and this new situation requires new and different financial policies.

FINANCIAL IMPACTS

Panel A of Figure 3 shows dividend payout ratios for FPL, the utility industry, and the S&P 400 industrials over the past 30 years. The two most striking features of the figure are (1) the high payouts of utilities relative to other industries' and (2) the fact that FPL's payout, although below that of the average utility in the early years, had become substantially higher than the industry average by 1993.

As shown in Panel B, FPL's dividends grew at roughly the same rate as earnings in the years from 1965 until the beginning of the 1990s. During the second half of the 1980s, for example, earnings were trending upward, dividends were increasing at about 4% annually, and FPL's payout ratio fell within a fairly narrow range of 60-70%. Over the period 1990-1993, however, earnings fell about 10% from their late '80s levels; and, even though dividend increases were held to less than 2% per year, FPL ended up paying out an average of 90% of its earnings over this four-year period.

In short, FPL's dividends were increasing faster than its earnings. Under the old regulatory regime, the company might have chosen to maintain the dividend growth rate by resorting to new stock or bond issues.[6] (In fact, over the five-year period 1989-1993, FPL's total dividend payments were roughly equivalent to the company's proceeds from new equity issues[7]—and thus the company was effectively just recycling equity capital, paying out cash with one hand that it would soon take back with another in the form of a new stock offering.) Facing the prospect of greater competition and less predictable earnings, FPL's management wanted to increase its financial flexibility and end its past dependence on regular infusions of outside equity capital, especially since access to capital could be limited in the future.

FPL was not alone in wanting to escape from this pattern of dividends financed by new debt and equity offerings. Many utilities suspected that their payout ratios were getting too high, but they also felt compelled to maintain or even increase their dividends. Partly completed plants were in the pipeline, and capital was needed to finish these plants. Debt was being used aggressively, which in turn required additional equity. Most companies debated internally and with their investment bankers the pros and cons of getting the needed equity by cutting dividends versus issuing new stock.

5. See Ben Esty, "Dividend Policy at FPL Group, Inc. (A)," Harvard Business School Case 9-295-059, p. 6.

6. A major potential drawback to issuing stock is the fact that the announcement of a stock offering is generally taken by investors to be a negative signal about management's outlook for the future. If future prospects looked brighter to management than to investors, and hence the stock was in management's view undervalued, then the company would want to finance with debt rather than stock so as to avoid unnecessary dilution. On the other hand, if management was more pessimistic than investors, it would view the stock as overvalued; and in this situation management would tend to choose stock rather than debt financing. Because investors know that this is the way management can be expected to act, the announcement of a stock offering is construed as a negative signal, on average, and stock prices tend to decline when stock offerings are announced.

Under the old regulatory compact, however, this announcement effect probably did not apply to most utilities. The size of the market's negative response to a stock offering announcement is likely to depend on the extent of the

"information asymmetry" between management and investors. That is, if investors know a great deal about a company and its operations, then the announcement (and the reasons for it) will have been anticipated, and there will be relatively little pressure on the stock price. Because of regulation, investors know more about utilities than about most other companies, so the price pressure when utilities issue stock is relatively small. Therefore, other things equal, utilities are better able to provide stockholders with cash dividends and then raise equity by issuing stock.

As we argue in this article, in the new competitive environment for utilities a new financing rule is likely to prevail—namely, "cash is king." Because the managements of utilities can no longer count on equity capital being available on favorable terms, they are likely to see a greater need to "control their own destiny" by conserving equity capital, maintaining higher cash balances, and reducing their target debt-to-capital ratios.

7. We are indebted to Ben Esty's Harvard case study, cited earlier, for this observation.

In the week following release of the California Public Utilities Commission's proposal to phase in "retail wheeling" beginning in 1996, California's three largest utilities together lost over $1.8 billion, or 8%, of their market value.

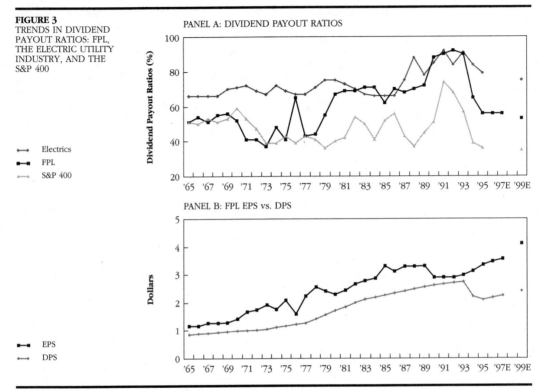

FIGURE 3
TRENDS IN DIVIDEND PAYOUT RATIOS: FPL, THE ELECTRIC UTILITY INDUSTRY, AND THE S&P 400

Electrics
FPL
S&P 400

PANEL A: DIVIDEND PAYOUT RATIOS

PANEL B: FPL EPS vs. DPS

EPS
DPS

The conclusion that was invariably reached—one that reflects the conventional wisdom of the utility industry and its financial advisers—can be summarized as follows: Investors in utilities *expect* annual dividend increases (that is why they buy the stocks in the first place), and so a dividend cut by a utility would immediately, drastically, and perhaps even permanently lower the stock price. The subsequent drop in stock price would in turn make it virtually impossible for the utility to issue new stock in the future—or, at best, the new stock could be sold only at a very low and dilutive price. That dilution would in turn lead to lower future earnings, which would lead to still lower stock prices in subsequent issues. In this fashion, a dividend cut would lead to a downward spiral in the market value of utilities.

The upshot of this conventional reasoning for FPL, and for most other utilities, was a series of dividend increases in the early '90s that exceeded earnings growth and, hence, high and rising payout ratios. As we have observed, the typical utility entered the 1990s with a payout ratio much higher than most industrials', even as the industry was facing rapidly increasing competition. Many utility executives were concerned about this situation. They wanted to improve the alignment of their financial policies with the new market realities, but they were afraid of what might happen to stock prices if they cut the dividend or held the increase to less than what was expected by investors.

In 1994, FPL's management concluded that its dividend payout was too high. But determining the best course of action, and getting agreement from the Board, required further work and study, along with considerable input from Stern Stewart & Co.

THE THEORY OF DIVIDENDS

Financial economists have been producing studies of dividend policy for at least 30 years; but, as often happens, different researchers have come to different conclusions. There are three major theories that attempt to explain investors' "demand" for dividends.

The traditional justification for high dividends is that stockholders want current income. They could sell a portion of their shares each year to get that income, but in doing so they would incur transactions costs and possibly capital gains taxes. Stockholders are also commonly said to prefer dividends to retained earnings because "a dollar of dividends in the hand is better than a dollar of hoped-for capital gains in the bush." In other words, dividends are less risky and, hence, more valuable to investors than retained earnings.

A second theory maintains that investors as a group care only about total returns, not about whether they receive them in the form of dividends or price appreciation. This "dividend irrelevance" proposition, formulated by Nobel Prize winners Franco Modigliani and Merton Miller in the early '60s, is based on the argument that dividend policy is "merely a financing decision," a way of dividing up the pie of corporate earnings. In this view, the only important determinant of a company's value is its future earnings power. Thus, whether companies choose to pay low dividends and finance themselves with retained earnings, or pay high dividends and retrieve the capital with new stock or debt, is largely a matter of indifference to investors.

A third theory says that investors care about how their total returns are divided between dividends and price appreciation primarily because of the tax code. To the extent dividends are taxed at higher rates than capital gains, investors collectively will prefer a lower payout policy.

Empirical studies have been conducted to test these three theories, but statistical problems make the results inconclusive. For example, studies of announcements of dividend changes confirm, without exception, that the market responds positively to dividend increases, on average, and negatively to dividend cuts.[8] On the other hand, there are also studies that show that companies announcing dividend cuts outperform the market significantly in the year following the dividend cut.[9] None of the existing studies provides a conclusive answer to the issue confronted by FPL—namely, whether companies that choose to pay out higher proportions of their earnings as dividends end up producing higher (or lower) total returns for their stockholders.[10]

There are, however, a number of insights from academic research on dividends that managers should at least take into account when thinking about dividend policy. We review them (in order of ascending importance) below.

Dividend Policy and Signaling

Perhaps the most obvious is the "signaling" effect of dividends that is said to arise from "information asymmetries" between managers and outside investors. The argument in brief is this: Managers are extremely reluctant to cut dividends, and so they generally increase the dividend only if they are confident that future earnings and cash flows will enable them to maintain the new, higher payout. Investors are aware of this behavior (indeed, they have been conditioned to respond to it by decades of experience). Because investors also know that managers are likely to have a clearer view of their companies' prospects than outsiders, a dividend increase functions as a fairly reliable signal that managers foresee a rosy future, and a dividend reduction signals a gloomy forecast.[11]

In most cases, however, providing investors with accurate signals about the company's future will not be the *primary* purpose of a change in financial

8. See, for example, among many others, Paul Asquith and David W. Mullins, "The Impact of Initiating Dividend Payments on Stockholders' Wealth," *Journal of Business*, vol. 56, January 1983, pp. 77-96; Terry E. Dielman and Henry R. Oppenheimer, "An Examination of Investor Behavior During Periods of Large Dividend Changes," *Journal of Financial and Quantitative Analysis*, vol. 19, June 1984; and Robert H. Litzenberger and Krishna Ramaswamy, "The Effects of Dividends on Common Stock Prices: Tax Effects or Information Effects," *Journal of Finance*, Vol. 37, May 1982, pp. 429-443.

9. See Randall Woolridge and Chinmoy Ghosh, "Dividend Cuts: Do They Always Signal Bad News," *Midland Corporate Finance Journal*, Vol. 3 No. 2 (Summer 1985).

10. The first major broad-based study of the relationship between dividends and stock prices was published in 1974 by the late Fischer Black and Myron Scholes. (See "The Effects of Dividend Yield and Dividend Policy on Common Stock Prices and Returns," *Journal of Financial Economics*, Vol. 1 No. 1 (May 1974).) For each

year between 1935 and 1966, Black and Scholes grouped all NYSE stocks into one of 25 portfolios on the basis of dividend yield and risk, and then attempted to test whether stock returns varied in any systematic fashion with yields (holding risk constant). Finding no significant relationship between yield and return, the study concluded that the market is essentially "neutral" toward dividends.

11. Note that since a dividend increase requires that an optimistic forecast be backed up with cash, managers are limited in their ability to mislead investors with higher-than-sustainable dividends. For this reason, a dividend increase is regarded as a more credible signal of future good times than just, say, a management forecast of higher future earnings. On the other hand, some companies might increase dividends because of a decline in available investment opportunities, which would not generally be regarded by investors as good news. Thus, while dividend actions can be used to convey useful information, they are by no means perfect signals, and their expected role may change in the future as more companies substitute stock repurchases for dividends.

Under the old regulatory regime, the company might have chosen to maintain the dividend growth rate by resorting to new stock or bond issues. Facing the prospect of greater competition, FPL's management wanted to increase its financial flexibility and end its past dependence on regular infusions of outside equity capital.

policy. In the case of FPL's dividend cut, management did not of course intend to send a negative signal (companies sometimes do, for example, when they alert analysts to an expected downturn in earnings). Moreover, the company attempted to offset the negative signal from the dividend with the simultaneous announcement of a major stock repurchase, which typically communicates management's confidence about the future. However, management's principal aim in changing dividend policy was not to provide accurate signals to the market, but rather, as we discuss below, to establish the right financial structure for a more competitive environment.

Managing Clientele Effects

A second, related, consideration is the "clientele effect" associated with changing dividend policy. The argument here is that companies, by virtue of their past dividend payouts, attract investors whose characteristics cause them to prefer a particular company's dividend policy. Thus, utilities have traditionally attracted investors who like high dividend payouts. Such investors want regular cash income, are in relatively low tax brackets, and seek relatively safe, "defensive" investments. "Growth" companies, on the other hand, pay lower dividends, reinvest more of their earnings, and provide a greater percentage of their total returns in the form of capital gains. Investors in high tax brackets with no pressing need for cash income tend to be attracted to such companies.

Clientele theory suggests that management should attempt to maintain a stable dividend policy because change could require stockholders to switch companies, which would involve brokerage costs, and, possibly, capital gains taxes. Perhaps the best definition of a stable dividend policy would include two elements: (1) avoid if at all possible reducing the dividend, both to avoid giving investors incorrect signals and also to provide investors with a stable flow of cash income; (2) if conditions permit, increase the dividend at some reasonable rate, because the combination of inflation and earnings retention should lead to rising earnings and an increased capacity to pay dividends.

On the other hand, in well-functioning capital markets, there is no compelling reason for companies to prefer one investor clientele to another. If the stock price drops because of selling by one group of investors, the theory says that "value-based" bargain hunters should be attracted to the firm's stock.[12] The case history of FPL appears to bear out this logic.

Of course, it would have been desirable to have been able to accommodate FPL's high-dividend clientele—and, yes, those investors who sold undoubtedly incurred transactions costs. However, as we argued earlier, the primary aim of FPL's management was not to avoid sending unintended signals, nor was it necessarily to preserve its existing clientele—it was to achieve the right financial structure going forward.

ARE CLIENTELE EFFECTS IMPORTANT?: THE CASE OF EQUIFAX

In 1992, Stern Stewart & Co. advised Equifax on a major leveraged recapitalization involving the repurchase of 12% of the company's common stock. This case was somewhat different from FPL's in that Equifax was *increasing* its leverage ratio to take advantage of unused debt capacity.

What Equifax has in common with FPL is that a dramatic shift in the company's financial strategy led to a major change in the company's investor clientele. As in the case of FPL, when Equifax announced its leveraged recap, many of its traditional investors sold while a number of larger, "value-based" investors became significant buyers. As in the case of FPL, the experience of Equifax suggests that clientele effects are at most "second-order" concerns, and they should not prevent companies from taking actions that improve their long-run competitive position.

Nevertheless, the existence of clientele effects may have one important implication for FPL. Given that the company had decided that a 90% payout ratio no longer made sense, management should make a sufficiently large cut in the dividend that the

---

12. Indeed, more recent developments in corporate investor relations—in particular, the practice of targeting large, sophisticated investors—suggest that companies may increase their values by seeking out and cultivating more active and better-informed investors. See John Bird et al., "Finance Theory and the New Investor Relations," *Journal of Applied Corporate Finance*, Vol. 6 No. 2 (Summer 1993). See also the "Stern Stewart Roundtable on Relationship Investing and Shareholder Communication," in the same issue of the *JACF*.

probability of future cuts is low. In the case of FPL, as we suggest later, reducing the company's dividend payout by 32% in 1994 may well have been the only way of ensuring *future* dividend stability. In this sense, FPL's dividend action was designed to accommodate those dividend-seeking investors who chose not to sell their shares and to attract new income-seeking investors looking for consistent dividend growth from an electric utility even in the face of industry uncertainties. The dividend reduction, while significant, nevertheless kept FPL's payout and yield within the range of electrics generally. This way, traditional utility investors could continue to invest in FPL for current income, but with the expectation of greater stock appreciation.

Balancing Agency Costs and Flotation Costs

Economists have tended to dismiss the notion that dividends are more valuable than capital gains because they are more reliable and hence less risky. What this bird-in-the-hand theory fails to recognize is that dividends can ultimately be paid only out of future cash flow, and it is the riskiness of the future cash flow stream that determines the degree of certainty with which investors can view future dividends.

More recent academic thinking, however, has provided an interesting variation of this "bird-in-the-hand" argument. As Michael Jensen has observed, companies in mature industries with excess capital have a tendency to retain and then waste that capital, either by overinvesting in core businesses or diversifying through acquisitions.[13] High dividends represent one solution to this "free cash flow" problem. Other possible solutions are special dividends or open market stock repurchase programs—and, in more extreme cases of excess capital, large tender offers for the firm's own stock financed with new borrowings.

One recent study provides strong empirical support for this argument. After examining 6,700 companies over the period 1961-1991, Michael Barclay, Clifford Smith, and Ross Watts conclude that "mature" companies—those with few promising investment opportunities (as indicated by low

market-to-book ratios and high depreciation expense)—tend to have significantly higher dividend yields and leverage ratios than "growth" companies (with high market-to-book ratios and heavy R & D spending).[14] With few investment opportunities and thus limited requirements for new capital, mature companies pay high dividends in part to prevent themselves from wasting their excess cash, or from becoming a takeover target as a consequence of having too much cash.

Conversely, growth companies tend to have lower dividend payouts and debt ratios not only because there is no temptation to waste capital (after all, such firms by definition have many profitable investment opportunities), but because raising outside capital can be very costly. Though there are exceptions to this rule, growth companies tend to be in riskier businesses than mature companies, and higher business risk is likely to mean a greater likelihood of not having access to capital at reasonable cost across market cycles. In such cases, a policy of high dividends can lead to high flotation costs (including dilution of equity as well as investment banker fees) or, still worse, an inability to capitalize upon valuable investment opportunities. For this reason, high-risk companies tend to use equity-dominated capital structures and to conserve their equity capital by retaining rather than paying out earnings.

Barclay, Smith, and Watts also find that regulation—and, by implication, a change from regulated to unregulated status—has predictable effects on a company's dividend (and overall financing) policy. Specifically, their study shows that regulated companies have systematically higher dividend payouts and leverage ratios than unregulated firms. The study also furnishes evidence (see Figure 4) that the deregulation of the telecommunications industry that began in the early 1980s has led to a significant reduction in the dividend yields and leverage ratios of those companies.

Both of these findings, as we discuss below, have a direct bearing on FPL because management was anticipating a change in its fundamental business from that of a heavily regulated, low-risk enterprise to a competitive, riskier one.

---

13. See Michael C. Jensen, "Agency Costs of Free Cash Flow, Corporate Finance, and Takeovers," *American Economic Review* 76 (1986), 323-329.

14. Michael J. Barclay, Clifford W. Smith, Jr. and Ross L. Watts (1995), "The Determinants of Corporate Leverage and Dividend Policies," *Journal of Applied Corporate Finance* Vol. 7 No. 4 (Spring 1995), 4-19.

> In well-functioning capital markets, there is no compelling reason for companies to prefer one investor clientele to another. If the stock price drops because of selling by one group of investors, the theory says that "value-based" bargain hunters should be attracted to the firm's stock.

FIGURE 4
CHANGES IN LEVERAGE
AND DIVIDEND YIELD
IN RESPONSE TO
DEREGULATION OF THE
TELECOMMUNICATIONS
INDUSTRY:
1970-1993

—— Leverage
········· Dividend Yield

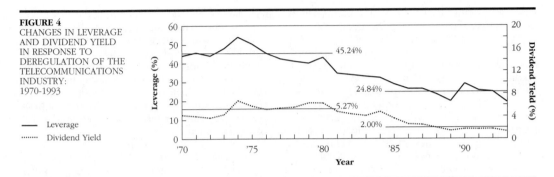

BACK TO FPL

The academic thinking summarized above—buttressed by the findings of Smith, Barclay, and Watts just described—suggests that a company's target dividend payout ratio should reflect primarily the following considerations:

(1) its expected capital requirements (that is, the amount of projected capital expenditures and strategic investments over and above its expected level of operating cash flow);

(2) the riskiness of its business (as reflected in the expected *variability* of its cash flow);

(3) the company's target capital structure (also partly a function of risk); and

(4) the availability and cost of outside capital (which are both a function of and important factors in setting target capital structure).

According to its own financial projections, FPL was not expecting a sharp increase in its investment requirements in the foreseeable future. In fact, management was projecting a large and growing cash operating *surplus* (net income plus depreciation minus capital expenditures) in each of the next five years. FPL was thus not a traditional "growth" company in the sense of having profitable growth opportunities requiring outside funding.

But if greater competition would not increase FPL's investment requirements in the near term, it was expected to lead to a significant increase in business risk and, hence, in the variability of its earnings and operating cash flows. An increase in cash flow variability in turn implies reductions in both the company's optimal leverage ratio and dividend payout.

As stated earlier, FPL chose to reduce its dividend payout ratio from over 90% to about 60% of annual earnings. Management's decision-making process can be summarized as follows:

■ FPL's operating cash flows and investment requirements were projected over each of the next five years (1994-1998). Operating cash flow (net income plus depreciation) was projected to increase at a steady rate while capital expenditures were projected to fall sharply. With this decline in capital spending, the amount of cash flow available to pay dividends was projected to turn positive in 1994, and to exceed the projected dividend in 1995.

■ Having thus projected both the level of its operating cash flows and its funding requirements, FPL's next step was to determine its target capital structure. Here the critical consideration was the expected increase in management's uncertainty about future operating cash flows due to deregulation. In the past, FPL had operated with a capital structure composed of about 48% long-term debt, 6% preferred, and 46% common equity. The expected increase in business risk caused management to raise its targeted percentage of common equity to 50%.

■ After having decided on a target capital structure, the final step was to determine the dividend payout ratio. The company looked at the payout ratios of other electric utilities, of companies in other industries that had recently been deregulated (telecommunications and trucking, for example), and of competitive industries generally. Management's goal was to set a dividend level that would increase in tandem with the expected growth in earnings and that the company would be able to maintain in almost any business environment, including that of full competition. At the same time, the payout was designed to preserve management's ability to invest in growth opportunities in preparation for worldwide deregulation of the electric utility industry.

STOCK REPURCHASES AS A SUBSTITUTE FOR CASH DIVIDENDS

What if management significantly underestimated FPL's future earnings power and, as a consequence of cutting the dividend, the firm became awash in excess cash? FPL's decision to cut its dividend was announced simultaneously with an authorization to buy back up to 10 million shares over the next three years. From the company's point of view, dividends and stock repurchases represent alternative means of distributing excess capital to stockholders. There are two basic reasons why stock repurchases may be a more efficient means of returning capital to stockholders.

The first has to do with taxes. Stock repurchases substitute returns in the form of capital gains for returns in the form of dividends, and taxable investors typically pay higher rates on dividend income than on capital gains. Since 1990, the spread between the marginal tax rate on dividends and capital gains has widened from zero to 11.6% (39.6% vs. 28%). Moreover, those stockholders who choose to tender their shares pay capital gains only on the difference between the repurchase price and their tax basis in the stock. Of course, those stockholders who choose not to sell their shares can defer taxes indefinitely. For all these reasons, investors as a group are likely to pay lower taxes on corporate distributions when stock repurchases take the place of dividends.

The second motive for substituting stock repurchases for dividends—and by far the more important in FPL's case—is the financial flexibility that a policy of selective stock buybacks can be expected to provide management in the future. As we just observed, although the firm's capital requirements are projected to decline in the next five years, the increase in competition is expected to reduce the stability of FPL's operating cash flows over time. In addition, deregulation in the U.S. and around the world may present attractive investment opportunities for the company. As a result, there is greater uncertainty about how much "free cash flow" will be left over to pay dividends.

Substituting a policy of selective stock repurchases for roughly one third of FPL's past dividend payout effectively provided management an option—execute the repurchase or, if management has better uses for the capital, wait until a better time. The value of this option can be viewed as rising in tandem with increases in the expected variability of future operating cash flow and with the emergence of new investment opportunities. As stated earlier, one clear aim of FPL's new financial policy is to reduce its past dependence on new equity issues. Under the old funding regime, FPL, like other utilities, paid out ever higher dividends and then simply raised more capital as necessary through new stock and debt issues. The new competitive environment is giving rise to a new financing rule that can be summed up in the expression "cash is king." Because equity capital will not always be available on favorable terms, companies in competitive industries are likely to see a greater need to "control their own destiny" by conserving equity capital, maintaining higher cash balances, and reducing their target debt-equity ratios. Substituting a policy of discretionary stock repurchases for regular cash dividends contributes to each of these objectives.

INVESTOR REACTION

As noted earlier, the initial market reaction to the announcement of FPL's dividend cut was decidedly negative. Because of the market's strong past association of dividend cuts with reduced profitability, the announcement clearly signaled diminished earnings prospects to some of FPL's stockholders. What seems equally clear from the FPL story, however, is the willingness of other investors to accept the idea that a dividend cut *by a profitable company* can be a value-increasing financial strategy, a move to be applauded rather than condemned. It is interesting to note that FPL's institutional ownership has increased since the dividend action—from 34% at the end of 1993 to 47% at the end of 1995.

Could FPL have avoided the initial price drop, and should it have done more to prepare the market for the announcement? In fact, management did inform analysts early in 1994 that it was reviewing its dividend payout level, pointing out that FPL's payout was high relative to other utilities', and that industry payouts were high relative to historic industry standards. Moreover, the company did attempt to stabilize its price by announcing the dividend cut and stock repurchase program simultaneously. But the fact that this measure had only limited effect, at least initially, is not surprising. FPL was a pioneer in this undertaking—the first utility to cut its dividend for strategic reasons—and there are bound to be costs as well as benefits from being ahead of the market's learning curve. Our financial markets, as sophisticated as they are, must to some extent learn "by doing." Trial and error may be a necessary prelude to valuable innovation.

The good news for other companies is that the market appears to catch on very quickly. For example, after the market closed on October 13, 1995, Texas Utilities cut its dividend by 35%. On the next morning, the company's stock price opened *higher*, and its price has since remained above its pre-announcement level. Our prediction is that when other profitable utilities follow FPL's lead, as some surely will, the market's immediate response will be positive in more cases than not.

CONCLUSION: DO THE RIGHT THING

Since the formulation of the celebrated M & M "dividend irrelevance" proposition in 1961, financial economists—and an increasing number of industry practitioners and money managers—have been arguing that dividends "do not matter." That is, whether a company pays out 10% or 100% of its earnings in the form of dividends is likely to have no material effect on its long-run market value.

In one sense, the FPL story can be viewed as confirming the validity of the M & M logic. After experiencing an initial drop of some 20% in value, FPL's shares quickly recovered their lost value and went on to outperform the S&P Utility Index by a significant margin over the two-year period following the announcement.

To say that investors collectively do not care whether they receive their returns in the form of dividends or capital appreciation is not the same as saying that the dividend policies of individual companies do not matter. In fact, dividend policy may matter greatly in certain circumstances. For mature companies with highly stable cash flows, paying out too little of operating cash flows may cause managers to overinvest—for example, through value-destroying diversifying acquisitions or misguided attempts to maintain market share at the expense of profitability. On the other hand, for companies in higher-growth or riskier businesses, paying out too much may reduce financial flexibility to the point that management is forced to pass up valuable investment opportunities.

As the case of FPL demonstrates, stock repurchases are likely to be a superior alternative to dividends for distributing excess capital to investors, especially for companies confronting a riskier business environment. Besides potential tax advantages for investors, a policy of substituting stock repurchases for dividends increases a company's financial flexibility. In the case of FPL, the improvement in financial condition was designed to provide management with the financial flexibility to respond to increased competition, and to make strategic acquisitions in an industry expecting further consolidation.

BANK OF AMERICA ROUNDTABLE ON

THE LINK BETWEEN CAPITAL STRUCTURE AND SHAREHOLDER VALUE

PHOTOGRAPHS BY GARY GEIGER

Bennett Stewart • Jay Allen • Cheryl Francis • Michael Jensen • Mike O'Neill • Dennis Soter

Pebble Beach, California *June 25, 1997*

BENNETT STEWART: Good afternoon, and, on behalf of our hosts Jerry Fair and Bank of America, let me welcome you all to this roundtable discussion of corporate capital structure. I'm Bennett Stewart, senior partner of Stern Stewart & Co., and I will be serving as moderator.

A number of leading business magazines have recently run cover stories on the "return of leverage." "Like it or not," it says on the cover of this *Institutional Investor* that I'm now holding up, "Leverage is back." And the cover story presents two startling facts: In 1996, new junk bond issues reached a record-high $73 billion; and, over the period 1995-1996, leveraged buyout funds amassed $40 billion in new capital. When you put debt on top of that $40 billion—leveraged, say, at three to one—that means there are now $160 billion of funds out there ready to buy your company.

These developments raise a number of interesting questions: Are we witnessing a return to the debt and leveraged transactions of the 1980s? Why would leveraged restructuring come back now? And what does this all say about the optimal, or value-maximizing, corporate capital structure? To put the same question a little differently, are there reliable ways for corporate managers to manage their capital structure so as to add value for their shareholders?

It's also true that equity markets are at all-time highs, and dividend yields are at all-time lows. So it's tempting to think that equity is cheap if not free. But is equity cheap? If you make an acquisition by issuing new shares, is that cheaper than using debt? If so, why? Does it matter whether you use purchase or pooling accounting? Does accounting matter? These are some of the questions we'll address this afternoon.

And because major changes in capital structure are often accompanied by changes in ownership structure—in fact, debt financing is one of the principal means for accomplishing such changes—we will also find ourselves talking about corporate ownership structure. LBOs, of course, involve major changes in ownership as well as debt structure—and so do large leveraged recaps. And while we're addressing the subject of ownership structure, we might also look briefly at the issues raised by spin-offs. Just yesterday, the Whitman Corporation announced its intention to spin off its Hussman and Midas Muffler businesses. The stock rose almost 10%, in spite of an accompanying announcement of bad earnings and more restructuring charges to follow. This is equivalent to saying that when you take a pie and cut it into slices and put them on separate plates, you suddenly have a bigger pie. It's curious; it appears to defy the laws of physics—and of economics as well. But the market reaction to spin-offs, together with the subsequent performance of spun-off businesses, suggests that ownership structure matters. Who owns the assets, the form of the ownership, and the composition of the right-hand side of the balance sheet—all these seem to be capable of having large effects on firm performance and value.

So, these are the kinds of questions that we want to investigate today. We have assembled a distinguished group of panelists to help us explore these issues, and I will introduce them in alphabetical order:

JAY ALLEN is the President of Tosco Corporation, which is the largest independent refiner and marketer of oil in America. Tosco, as we will hear, has been actively acquiring other refining operations and using considerable amounts of debt financing to fund the acquisitions. In the process, the company has seen its stock price go up fivefold in the past four and a half years.

CHERYL FRANCIS is the Chief Financial Officer of the R.R. Donnelley & Sons Co. For the past two years, and with the assistance of Stern Stewart, Donnelley has been implementing an EVA performance measurement and incentive compensation program. Prior to joining Donnelley about a year ago, Cheryl was Treasurer of the FMC Corporation, which undertook a very dramatic leveraged recapitalization in 1986—and I think this audience will find Cheryl's account of this experience an interesting and instructive one.

MICHAEL JENSEN is the Edsel Bryant Ford Professor of Business Administration at the Harvard Business School. Mike has to be at the top of the list of leading academic scholars in the area of corporate finance and its relationship to corporate governance. He will talk at length about the implications of a paper he published in the *American Economic Review* in 1986 setting forth his "free cash flow" theory of takeovers. "Free cash flow," for those of you who are unfamiliar with the term, is the amount by which a company's operating cash flow exceeds what can be profitably reinvested in its basic businesses—and the emphasis here is on the word "profitably." In his 1993 Presidential Address to the American Finance Association, Mike gave this theory new life by arguing that we are now in the midst of a "Third Industrial Revolution"—an era of rapid technological change that, by speeding up product obsolescence, is continuing to create still more excess capacity and free cash flow, and so more demand for leveraged restructuring and downsizing. As Mike will tell us, there are persistent economic forces, now operating on an increasingly global basis, that are making the 1990s look a lot like the '80s—and the resulting pressures on corporate management can be expected to continue well into the next century.

MICHAEL O'NEILL is Chief Financial Officer and a Vice Chairman of Bank of America. As most of you are aware, Bank of America has created an extraordinary amount of shareholder value since Dave Coulter took over as CEO 18 months ago. What is probably less well known is the role financial management has played in the process. Under Mike O'Neill, B of A has been using its substantial "free cash flow" to buy back very large amounts of its stock. And, as Mike I'm sure will also mention, the bank has put in place an innovative performance measurement scheme that draws on and resembles the RAROC system for allocating capital to individual business units that was developed by Banker's Trust. B of A's system also makes use of a measure called "economic profit" that looks a lot like EVA. And, like our EVA system, the bank's new performance measurement system is designed to hold managers accountable for the capital tied up in their businesses.

Last but not least is **DENNIS SOTER**, my colleague and fellow partner at Stern Stewart. Dennis runs our corporate finance advisory activity and also oversees implementations of EVA in middle-market companies. In the past several months, Dennis has served as financial adviser in three highly successful leveraged recapitalizations. The companies executing the transactions were an Indianapolis utility called IPALCO, the engine manufacturer Briggs & Stratton, and auto parts maker SPX Corporation. Each of these three deals involved borrowing substantial amounts of new debt to buy back shares—and two cases involved major changes in dividend policy as well.

Capital Structure and the Theory of Corporate Finance

STEWART: So, with that brief introduction of the panelists, let me just say a few more words to introduce the subject. The beginnings of the current academic thinking on capital structure and shareholder value can be traced to two papers published over 35 years ago by professors Franco Modigliani and Merton Miller, both of whom won Nobel Prizes. The two papers argued that both capital structure and dividend policy are "irrelevant"—that is, incapable of affecting the total value of the firm. In the M & M view, the public corporation is a cash-generating engine whose market value is determined only by the investment and operating decisions that generate the cash flows. These are what economists refer to as the "real" decisions, those that affect the left-hand side of the balance sheet. Capital structure and dividend decisions, by contrast, are merely "financial" decisions—that is, ways of dividing up those operating cash flows among different groups of investors. And if financial markets are doing their job and arbitrageurs are exploiting all profit opportunities, there should be little opportunity for financing decisions to add value.

On the day it was announced that he won the Nobel Prize, Merton Miller was asked during a press interview to explain the M & M theory. After a series of failed attempts to compress the theory into a sound byte, Mert threw out, "Let me give you a *very simple* analogy. Whether you cut a pizza into six or eight slices doesn't change the size of the pie, right? Well, it's the same with corporations." As Mert likes to tell the story, the interviewer then looked at him and said, "And you got a Nobel Prize for *that*?"—and, with that, the press crew took down the cameras and lights and went away.

The message of the M & M irrelevance propositions is that there is no "magic" in leverage or dividends. M & M showed that, if we make some simplifying assumptions—if we ignore taxes and bankruptcy costs, and if we assume managers behave the same way if the firm is leveraged with 10% debt or 90% debt—there is no good reason to expect changes in corporate leverage and dividend payout ratios to affect the total market value of the firm's debt and equity.

One interesting experiment to test the logic of the M & M propositions took place about three years ago. In late 1994, a profitable utility called Florida Power & Light, with counsel from my colleague Dennis Soter, announced that it was cutting its dividend by 33%. No profitable utility had ever done such a thing. The conventional wisdom was that utility investors *require* dividends—and the more the better.

After FPL announced the cut, the stock price immediately fell from about 32 to 27, or about 15%, just as its investment banker had predicted. The banker also warned that the discount might last as long as two years. But, as it turned out, most of the discount disappeared in the following two weeks! And FPL's stock has outperformed the electric utility index since that time.

But the practical import of the M & M propositions is not in these isolated events, but in what they say about why financing decisions might matter. The M & M propositions say, in effect, that *if* corporate financing and dividend decisions are going to increase corporate values, they are likely to do so only for the following reasons: (1) they reduce the taxes paid by the corporation or its investors; (2) they reduce the probability of a costly bankruptcy; (3) they send a positive signal to investors about management's view of the firm's pros-

pects; or (4) they provide managers with stronger incentives to invest wisely and operate efficiently. It is in this sense that the M & M framework laid the groundwork for the modern theory of corporate finance; it showed future scholars where to look for the *real* effects of financial decisions.

It was Merton Miller himself who started the process of relaxing some of the assumptions underlying M & M by exploring issues like the tax benefit of debt and the "signaling effect" of dividends. But the most important attempt to take finance theory beyond the M & M propositions—to show why capital structure and dividend policy matter—was a 1976 paper by Mike Jensen and Bill Meckling called "Theory of the Firm: Managerial Behavior, Agency Costs, and Capital Structure." Mike and Bill's accomplishment was to focus the attention of the academic finance profession on the potential loss in value caused by the separation of ownership from control in large public corporations. As Jensen and Meckling observed, conflicts of interest between management and shareholders could be controlled—or made worse—by corporate capital structure and dividend choices.

Then, as if to confirm the thinking of Jensen and Meckling, there came the leverage revolution of the 1980s—the expansion of the junk bond market and the remarkable successes of the LBO movement. And, in 1986, Mike published the *American Economic Review* article I mentioned earlier called "The Agency Costs of Free Cash Flow: Corporate Finance and Takeovers." That article, in my opinion, offers the single most powerful explanation of the leveraged takeover movement of the 1980s. Stated in brief, the free cash flow theory says that highly leveraged acquisitions, stock buybacks, and management buyouts of public compa-

I t is the contractual obligation to repay the debt, the fact that they've borrowed money and pre-committed to paying it back, that forces companies to pay out cash, to sell unrelated businesses, or to take other value-increasing steps they might otherwise be reluctant to take. And there is likely to be another kind of benefit of debt financing in these leveraged transactions: Having more debt and less equity makes it easier to concentrate the equity in the hands of the insiders so that not only do they have the discipline of debt, they have the stronger incentives to create value that come with significant equity ownership.

nies were all adding value by squeezing excess capital out of organizations with few profitable growth opportunities. Jensen observed that managers in mature industries have a natural tendency to hoard capital, to reinvest corporate earnings rather than paying them out to shareholders. And the massive substitution of debt for equity in the '80s provided a solution to this free cash flow problem by converting smaller, discretionary dividend payments into much higher, and contractually binding, payments of interest and principal.

Jensen's free cash flow analysis also does a nice job of explaining the problems with the Japanese economy in the 1990s. As early as 1989, Mike was writing in our *Journal of Applied Corporate Finance* that Japanese managers were in the same position as U.S. managers in the late 1960s. Japanese companies in the late '80s were flush with cash from their successes in the product wars, they were paying only nominal dividends, and

stock repurchase was forbidden by law. As a result, they were either overinvesting in their core businesses in misguided attempts to maintain market share, or they were diversifying through acquisition into completely unrelated businesses. In many cases, they were doing both—and both are symptoms of the same free cash flow problem.

In 1991, we ran a piece in our journal by Carl Kester of the Harvard Business School called "The Hidden Costs of Japanese Success" that pointed directly to this problem. And soon after that my colleague Don Chew, who is the editor of the *Journal*, received a visit from four representatives of the Nomura Research Institute, the well-known private Japanese thinktank. The subject they wanted to discuss was stock repurchase. And it appears that the Ministry of Finance has finally taken the free cash flow problem seriously because Japanese stock repurchases were legalized in 1995.

So, it's hard to overstate the importance of Michael Jensen's work on the role of management incentives in corporate financial decisions. And, since he's sitting here with us, let me now turn the floor over to him. Mike, you have written extensively about the debt wave of the 1980s. You have put this into the context of corporate governance. You see an ongoing free cash flow problem coming out of this broad new modern industrial revolution. Can you give us your perspective on the forces that are now shaping corporate capital structure?

The Restructuring of the '80s

JENSEN: Thank you, Bennett, for that very generous account of my work— and I think Bill Meckling would be happy to hear it, too. I have a number of things I want to chat about. I want to begin by talking a little about why capital structure does matter, even though Merton Miller got a Nobel Prize for saying it didn't. Mert, by the way, was one of my teachers back at Chicago. I learned a great deal from him, and he is rightly identified as the "father" of modern finance. Mert, more than anyone else I can think of, has been responsible for whatever claim the academic finance profession can now make to being a hard science.

After I talk about the M & M propositions, I'm going to talk about what I have called "the agency costs of free cash flow." It is an endemic problem in large organizations. Solving that problem has been a big challenge for capital markets and companies for the last 20 years, and it will continue to be a major challenge for a long time. I'll talk a bit about the decade of the '80s, and show how most of the leveraged transactions, although very controversial, served the interests of the U.S. economy by providing a solution to this free cash flow problem.

Then I want to step back and talk for a few minutes about what I call the modern industrial revolution. It has been going on for several decades now; if I had to pick a starting point, I would choose the oil crisis of 1973 and all the changes that set off. This revolution is affecting all of our lives by making products obsolete with incredible speed, generating excess capacity, substantial free cash flow, and the necessity for downsizing. These forces are going to continue to operate in our lives for at least the next 20 years or so.

If there's still time at the end, I will also say a few things about the current environment. The bankers here—people like Mike Murray and Mike O'Neill—are much closer to these issues than I am. But I can at least open up that discussion with a few thoughts. Finally, I will mention in passing how new performance measurement and compensation systems like EVA act to resolve some of these free cash flow issues and in fact substitute for changes in capital structure.

So that's what I'm going to do, all in 15 minutes. We're going to move right along.

Why, then, does capital structure matter? The famous Modigliani-Miller theorems said that, in well-functioning capital markets, changes in capital structure and dividend policy should not have any predictable effects on the profitability and value of the organization. There are a number of restrictive assumptions on which this argument rests—things like perfect information, no taxes or transactions costs, and no bankruptcy costs. But far and away the most important assumption underlying M & M is that corporate real investment and operating decisions are not affected by corporate capital structure and dividend policies. That is, regardless of whether the company operates with 10% debt or 90% debt, and whether it commits to pay out all or none of its earnings, M & M effectively assume that a company's real investment policy and thus the operating cash flows of the organization do not change.

Now, as logical propositions, the M & M irrelevance theorems are absolutely correct. Under those assumptions, changes in capital structure and payout policy should not affect value. But what we know from the 1980s—and from the vast amount of theoretical and empirical work that's been done since the original M & M theory—is that it is precisely this last condition that is not fulfilled. When companies make dramatic changes in their capital structure, their ownership structure, or their payout ratios, we tend to see major changes in the performance and value of those organizations. We see changes in real investment policy, changes in efficiency, and therefore big changes in value, either up or down, depending on how the financial policies are changing. And these real effects of financial decisions, as I said, have

been well documented by studies published in the *Journal of Financial Economics*—the journal I founded in 1973, and which I recently stepped down from as managing editor—and in other reputable academic journals.

So what is this thing called the "agency cost of free cash flow?" It occurs in the following environment: You have an organization generating lots of cash, more than managers can possibly reinvest in positive net present value projects. In that kind of an environment, we have a serious problem in the capital markets, a serious organizational control problem: How do we motivate managers and organizations to get rid of the cash, to pay it back to investors? By the late '70s and early '80s, it reached the point where companies could destroy as much as one half of their value by failing to pay out their free cash flow and instead reinvesting in low-return projects or diversifying acquisitions. The failure of organizations right and left to pay out their excess capital led to the invention—or, more precisely, the "reinvention"—of hostile takeovers and leveraged acquisitions. And it led to the LBO movement in the mid-1970s, which then roared right along through the 1980s.

The net result of the leveraged restructurings of the '80s was close to a trillion dollars worth of gains in the equity market. Ironically, this was all being accomplished at the very time when so many people were saying that corporate America was being stripped of its competitive potential by financial markets. I think most economists and businessmen now understand that what went on during the '80s ended up leaving corporate America lean and mean. But not as lean and mean as it could have been; the process was stopped too soon. But, even so, U.S. companies today are faring very well in the international competitive markets in large

MICHAEL JENSEN

I agree that if you have the wrong business strategy, or if you hire the wrong people, you're going to destroy value. Finance cannot solve those problems. My point is this: You can do all those things right, but if you screw up these financial issues at the top of the organization where the cash comes pouring in, the company can destroy much of the value that's been created on the real side of the business. You can have everything done right at the lower levels in the organization. But if you don't get the right governance structure at the top—and finance can be a critical part of that governance structure—the operating value of the company can be frittered away.

part as a result of the changes that went on then.

So how does debt play a role in this? Think of an organization that has huge amounts of excess cash. Rather than paying out the cash, managers have a natural tendency to spend it on projects that have very low or even negative rates of return. There are several ways to solve that problem. First of all, managers can just pay out the excess cash by declaring increases in the dividend, or by making a large special or one-time dividend. An alternative to dividends is to pay out free cash flow in a regular series of stock buybacks. But a consistent policy of paying out free cash flow is very hard to maintain. There are large organizational pressures from middle managers and others who want to get to bat, who want to have their favorite projects funded—and so we get this gold-plating of organizations at the expense of massive reductions in value.

But now consider what happens when the firm issues a lot of new debt and uses it to buy back a significant fraction of its stock. In that case, contractual debt service payments substitute for the promised dividend payments. Dividends can be cut—or at least not increased—without too much difficulty. But if you don't make the debt service payments, the trustee can eventually put you into bankruptcy court. So, the use of debt puts some incentives and some bite behind that contract. And that sharpening of incentives to pay out excess cash and capital is an important source of value in leveraged restructurings. It's not the only thing going on in LBOs and other leveraged deals, but it's a very important part of it.

Now, let's look a little more closely at what happens in highly leveraged transactions. One of the things they accomplish is to make the cost of capital both explicit and contractually binding. Before the 1980s, large, mature organizations could operate with 20% debt and 80% equity and think that they were making lots of money—

at least that's what their accounting statements were telling them—when in fact they were destroying value by failing to earn their cost of capital every single year. When dividend yields are low and the cost of equity doesn't show up in the accounting statements, managers can easily get into the habit of thinking that equity is costless when, in fact, it's the most costly source of finance. That was certainly one factor behind IBM's failure to take decisive action in response to competitive threats in the mid-80s, and it is clearly a big part of the problem still facing many Japanese and European companies today. They continue to think that equity is free.

So, in the process of converting most of that old equity into debt, LBOs make the cost of capital explicit. Besides being an actual cash cost, it's now in the accounting statements. And, in this sense, it's very much like Stern Stewart's EVA financial management system. Under EVA, if you don't earn the cost of capital, you don't get a bonus. But there's also an importance difference between the simulated ownership of EVA and the actual ownership of an LBO. If you can't make the interest payments in an LBO, not only will managers' bonuses and equity values be reduced, but there will be some unhappy debtholders or bankers to put you into bankruptcy.

So, what happened during the 1980s was a dramatic increase in leveraged transactions that brought about the exit of trapped equity in organization after organization throughout corporate America. To give you a typical example, let's say you have an oil company with a billion dollars worth of cash floating around in corporate headquarters that is targeted for exploration projects or refineries that the market expects to be worth only $600 million. And we know from our research, by the way, that even though investors generally react positively to announcements of capital spending projects, the market had a systematically *negative* response to announcements of big oil projects in the early '80s.

Now, if the capital market is expecting the firm's marginal investments to generate a net economic loss of $400 million, then the company's share price will sell at a large discount to net asset value. You might recall that oil executives were then complaining that you could buy oil on Wall Street more cheaply than drilling for it. But Wall Street was being perfectly rational by discounting the shares. And this price discounting by the market invited the attention of outside investors, corporate raiders. People like Boone Pickens saw that they could add $400 million in value simply by shutting off the investment spigot.

And this same phenomenon of overcapacity, stock market discounting of corporate assets below replacement cost, and corrective leveraged

restructurings took place in industry after industry in America. Besides oil and gas, it happened in paper and forest products, it happened in tires, in publishing and broadcasting, commodity chemicals, financial services, and the list goes on. So, these leveraged restructurings were by and large a productive, value-adding response by our capital markets to this free cash flow problem—to the excess capacity generated by managers' natural tendency to pursue growth instead of the necessary downsizing.

The 1990s—What Went Wrong?

Then, of course, came the problems with the leveraged deals in the late 1980s. Starting in 1989, there was a sharp increase in the number of defaults and bankruptcies of LBOs. Most of the problems, it turns out, came in the deals done in the latter half of the 1980s. Of the 41 LBOs with purchase prices of $100 million or more completed between 1980 and 1984, only one defaulted on its debt. But, of the 83 deals larger than $100 million between 1985 and 1989, at least 26 defaulted and 18 went into bankruptcy.

So what went wrong with the later deals? The problem started with what I have described as a "contracting failure," a gross misalignment of the incentives between the dealmakers who promoted the transactions and the lenders and other investors who provided most of the funding for the deals. By the end of the '80s, dealmakers like Bruce Wasserstein were essentially being paid just to do deals; they were taking out more in upfront fees than they were putting back into the deals. And this arrangement was a sure prescription for too many deals—for deals that were overpriced and structured with too much debt, or with the wrong kind of debt. Now, as Bennett mentioned earlier,

LBOs are back today, and with a different structure. Sponsors are required to put in much more equity, and the deals themselves are less highly leveraged.

But, having said this, there is also some evidence that a private market correction to this contracting problem was already underway when regulators intervened heavily in the summer of 1989. There was already a general move toward larger equity commitments, less debt, lower transaction prices, and lower upfront fees when S&L legislation like FIRREA and HLT regulations created a downward spiral in high-yield bond prices. And when combined with changes in the tax law penalizing private work-outs, tightened oversight by bank regulators made it virtually impossible to reorganize troubled companies outside of Chapter 11. Few people seem to be aware of this, but private work-outs—many of them by Drexel under Mike Milken—were a common event for the first wave of LBOs during the bad recession of 1981-82. But by the time the troubles in the leveraged markets began to emerge in the late '80s, Milken was under investigation and Drexel was in the process of being "RICO'd" out of existence.

So, as a consequence of the tanking of the junk bond markets, the destruction of Drexel, and changes in the bankruptcy laws, the optimal leverage ratio for corporate America suddenly went way down. And, in fact, Milken saw much of this coming because he was advising companies in the late '80s to put equity back into their capital structures. But because of this contracting problem I mentioned, most of the participants in the HLT markets kept going, pushing purchase prices higher and increasing leverage ratios.

Interestingly enough, by the way, the banks seem to have recognized what was going on, because they responded to the higher purchase prices by funding smaller portions of the deals and accelerating their repayment schedules. As a result, their losses on HLTs were remarkably small—so small in fact that the Comptroller of the Currency dropped the HLT category altogether in 1992. The real losers in the overpriced deals turned out to be the junk bondholders. But, again, you have to keep this all in perspective. Total creditors' losses in all the deals of the '80s probably did not exceed $30 billion—a number that seems trivial when set against the trillion or so dollars of value that was added by leveraged restructurings over this period.

Now, what about the '90s? Coming on top of the new constraints on leveraged lending, we saw state takeover laws that basically shut down the old-style corporate control market. And that sharply limited the capital markets' ability to curb the value-destruction that was going on inside many organizations with too much capital. But other forces then came in to fill the vacuum left by takeovers and LBOs. There was a sharp increase in the activism of institutional investors like CALPERS and the United Shareholders Association. And, although much of this was sound and fury with little significance, some of it succeeded in putting pressure on boards to get rid of underperforming CEOs. About the same time, a lot of companies began to show interest in adopting EVA-type systems that attempt to reproduce internally the capital discipline exerted by takeover markets. And, perhaps most important, there was heightened foreign competition in the product markets, which is guaranteed to work if none of these other forces kicks in.

So, given these different pressures on management for efficiency that are operating today, most companies are now in a situation where, if they don't make the necessary adjustments themselves, they're going to have a hard time just staying in business.

The Modern Industrial Revolution

Now, let me say a little bit about the broader environment within which all of this has been taking place. In my 1993 speech to the American Finance Association that Bennett mentioned earlier, I argued that there are striking parallels between what's happened in America in the past 20 years and what went on in the second half of the 19th century—a period historians have called "the Second Industrial Revolution." In both periods, technological advances resulted in huge increases in productivity and dramatic reductions in prices. But, at the same time these changes were increasing productivity, they were causing massive obsolescence and overcapacity in many industries. After the Civil War, for example, there were reductions of as much as 80% to 90% in the prices of important industrial commodities such as kerosene, aluminum, and chemicals. And much as the great M & A wave of the 1890s served to reduce capacity—between 1890 and 1910, some 1,800 U.S. firms were consolidated into about 150—the leveraged takeovers, LBOs, and other leveraged recapitalizations of the 1980s provided a solution to overcapacity building in many sectors of the U.S. economy.

To give you one modern example, think about what happened in the tire industry in the '80s. The introduction of steel radial tires, which last several times longer than the old bias ply tires, suddenly made much of the tire industry obsolete. And leveraged restructurings, like Bridgestone's takeover of Firestone and James Goldsmith's run at Goodyear Tire, succeeded in removing much of the resulting overcapacity. In fact, every U.S. tire company with the possible exception of Cooper has either merged or been restructured.

But, to give you a more dramatic example, think about what has happened to the price of computer chips and computing power in the last 20 years. If we had seen the same kind of price/performance changes in the automobile industry that we've seen in the computer business since 1980, a $20,000 automobile in 1980 would be selling for about two bucks today. And these advances, coupled with advances in communications technology, have had profound changes on how our organizations are run. You can't have that kind of change in such a basic commodity as computer chips and processors without dramatically affecting the ways in which we live and interrelate to each other, both in the social dimension and in the work dimension. Just ask a lot of the people that used to work for the old IBM or, more recently, for DEC.

So what we're seeing are major changes in technology—and it's not just in computers and telecommunications—that are being implemented over and over again in various organizations. The huge increases in output that are being brought about by such advances are driving down market prices. But many managers are not paying attention to the fact that these changes result in excess capacity and huge amounts of free cash flow. In those industries where the overcapacity is really chronic—and commercial banking comes to mind—a large number of firms will have to go out of business. But, of course, nobody wants to volunteer to leave.

So, today we have the same phenomenon going on that we saw both in the 1890s and the 1980s. But there is also another important factor driving today's restructuring activity—and this one promises to be with us well into the next century. In addition to the burst of technological change that's generating excess capacity, we now have political revolutions taking place throughout the world that are compounding the problem. The decline of socialism as a way of organizing business activity is now pretty obvious. And, with the failure of closed, centrally-planned economic systems, we are now seeing Russia and other nations in central and eastern Europe moving in fits and starts toward open capitalist systems. The same thing is going in parts of Latin America, and in India and other Asian countries.

How does all this translate into excess capacity and a free cash flow problem? Over the next 30 years, we're going to see something on the order of 1.2 billion laborers coming into world labor markets. About a billion of those people currently earn less than $3 a day; 250 million earn less than 10 bucks a day. To put that in comparison, average daily wages in the West are about $85, and the total labor force is about 250 million people. What we have discovered in recent years is that you can take relatively modern, up-to-date technology, install it in developing countries, and get 85% to 100% of the productivity of those same plants in the West. Without larger differences in productivity, you can't have these kind of wage differences across national economies surviving for very long. That's why, for example, so much of the U.S. textile industry has moved to Asia. And it's not just textiles; there are lots of other industries where U.S. and European and Japanese facilities have been made obsolete by these wage differentials. There are big implications in all of this for labor union activity, for political conflict, for trade wars.

So, all of these forces that were in play in the '80s are being intensified by the political revolutions around the world. In the end, the migration of some Western facilities and capital to emerging economies is going to make both the industrialized and the developing economies better off. But it's going to require major adjustments—lots of dislocations and downsizings and restructurings—to accomplish such changes.

What do we see going on in the current U.S. financial environment? Well, LBO's have not gone away. They've come back stronger than ever, as many of us predicted they would. The junk bond market did not go away after the destruction of Drexel and the jailing of Mike Milken. As Bennett said earlier, they're at all-time records. As I mentioned earlier, LBOs have got a somewhat different structure now than they had in the '80s. LBO sponsors are putting up much more equity; and besides having less debt, today's LBOs seem to be making greater use of bank debt than public junk debt, especially in the leveraged build-ups. The rise of the leverage buildup is to me an especially interesting development; it's kind of a new version of the focused conglomerate. They seem to growing up everywhere, and they're changing the industrial landscape in another way by consolidating fragmented industries—and reducing excess capacity in the process.

Now, it's hard to imagine that every industry worldwide is afflicted with this problem of overcapacity. There's got to be growth companies out there exploiting profitable investment opportunities—and this is certainly true of much of the high-tech sector in the U.S. And perhaps there are lots of large, mature companies that are finding ways to "reinvent" their businesses, new growth opportunities that are sufficiently related to their core businesses that they can find uses for some of their internal cash. But it's really hard to find an industry where at least some parts of the business are not experiencing overcapacity.

Before I close, let me say that EVA is another way of accomplishing the central features of an LBO or leveraged acquisition. I am a big fan of EVA as a performance measurement and management compensation system. It is a way of changing internal management accounting statements to simulate many of the benefits of a leveraged buyout without any of the financial risks. It simply prices out what the capital costs for every division in the organization, and then bases management compensation on the extent to which operating profits exceed the capital costs. Making managers' conscious of the cost of capital in this way can have a huge impact on organizational efficiency and values.

So, there's no reason why our public companies can't imitate the effect of virtually all of these highly leveraged capital market transactions that resolve the free cash flow and governance problems. Even if they can't do an LBO, they can make greater use of debt and use it to concentrate ownership. Or, if debt financing is too risky, they can simulate ownership with an EVA-type system. And I'll stop there.

The Distinction between Overpayment and Overleveraging

STEWART: Thank you, Michael. I can't imagine that everyone in the room feels as warmly as you do about the benefits of debt financing. So let me just play the devil's advocate. Let's take the case of Robert Campeau's highly leveraged acquisition of Federated Department Stores in 1988. The whole deal blew up in his face. How can you say that such transactions are so wonderful when we see a deal like that? JENSEN: Steve Kaplan has done an excellent analysis of the Campeau case, which was published in the *JFE*.

Contrary to what we were told by the business press, the Campeau transaction—or at least the change of control initiated by that transaction—actually created about $1.5 billion in value. What do I mean by that? When Federated and the associated companies eventually emerged from bankruptcy, the value of the total debt and equity was about $1.5 billion higher—even after adjusting for the time value of money and broad market movements over the period—than what they were selling for just before the Campeau bid was announced.

So what was the problem, then? It turns out that Campeau paid a $4 billion premium over market value for the right to run those companies, and you can't make that up on volume. People confuse the overpayment with the fact that the deal was structured with a very large amount of debt. But one of the beneficial effects of structuring an overpaid deal with debt is that it reveals the mistake very clearly, both to the market, and to the managers and to the board of directors. As a result of the bankruptcy filing, Campeau was forced out and replaced by a highly respected bankruptcy trustee, Allen Questrom, who by all accounts did a very creditable job of restoring the company to profitability. In fact, a *New York Times* article made the point that Bloomingdales had never been run as well outside of Chapter 11.

But now let me give you an example of a deal that was done with equity—a vast overpayment involving massive value destruction even though there was nothing in the accounting statements that would indicate that. It was the Time-Warner merger that took place a number of years ago, which was an utter disaster. The loss of value from that deal never showed up in the accounting statements because it was done with equity.

Now, I'm not saying that you can't overleverage an organization, and I'm not advocating that you do it. But it's very important to keep separate overleveraging from overpayment. If you overpay for anything, as I said before, it's real hard to make it up in volume.

A "Public LBO": The Case of FMC

STEWART: You're saying that it is the contractual obligation to repay the debt, the fact that they've borrowed money and pre-committed to paying it back, that forces companies to pay out cash, to sell unrelated businesses, or to take other value-increasing steps they might otherwise be reluctant to take. And, you've also suggested that there is likely to be another kind of benefit of debt financing in these leveraged transactions: Having more debt and less equity makes it easier to concentrate the equity in the hands of the insiders so that not only do they have the discipline of debt, but they have the stronger incentives to create value that come with significant equity ownership.

And this brings me to a question for Cheryl Francis. Cheryl, in your former life as Treasurer at FMC, FMC went through a very dramatic leveraged recapitalization. Essentially, FMC's management said to its shareholders: "Look, our stock is now trading at $70. We'll pay you $70 in cash for each of your shares and give you one share in the new FMC. But management insiders will get a different deal: for each of our shares, we will get no cash but five and two thirds shares in the new company. This way, if the new shares were to be valued by the market at $15, both groups—outsiders and insiders—will come out with a total value of $85, which is obviously a nice premium over $70."

FMC had to borrow $2 billion to make this cash distribution. And al-though the company remained public, insiders' ownership increased dramatically in relation to the ownership of outsiders. In effect, FMC did a "public LBO." And, as in private LBOs, you have the combination of the discipline of debt with greater concentration of the equity in the hands of insiders.

Cheryl, from your insider's experience, can you provide us with some insights as to why this transaction happened? Was the expected incentive effect important in your decision? And what were the consequences of this dramatic change in capital and ownership structure?

CHERYL FRANCIS: You explained the transaction pretty well. There were also some nice tax structures that were in place at the time that allowed us to get some extra cash that you couldn't get today—for example, we had a $300 million surplus in our pension fund that we were able to use to pay down the debt.

But the transaction was essentially as you described it, Bennett. FMC basically chose to borrow $2 billion one day and then turn around and pay it out to shareholders the next day. And, within four months of the announcement of the transaction, FMC's share price had risen not to $85, but to $97. So, this transformation of FMC's capital structure and ownership structure ended up creating a lot of value for shareholders.

But let me also mention—and I'm surprised you didn't take credit for this, Bennett—that the leveraged recap was the second stage of a shareholder value program that we started at FMC several years earlier. The first stage was the creation of an EVA-like measurement system—a process that was started in 1979, but not fully implemented until 1982. Our leveraged recap affected the right-hand side of the balance sheet; but the left-hand side is extremely important, of course, and you have to keep the two aligned. The leveraging concept worked well at FMC because our EVA-type system had already forced us to run the company for cash and for value. And I believe that's one major reason why FMC's recapitalization proved to be more successful than several others that came along later.

Running the company for cash flow and value prior to the recap also had the benefit of providing us with valuable perspective when evaluating several strategic alternatives that we were considering at the same time. As alternatives to the leverage recap, we were also looking at three very large acquisitions in related businesses. But, after weighing the risks and expected benefits of each alternative, we chose to do the leveraged recap. That is, we chose to stick with the company that we knew how to run, and to run it even more effectively for cash.

So, it's important to understand that we were embedding the capital charge into the business for at least three years prior to the time that we did the recap. Two years before the recap, we bought back a third of our shares, which means that we were already paying out lots of cash well in advance of the recap. But when we looked forward, we saw that we would have to disgorge far more cash because we did not have profitable opportunities for reinvestment inside the company. Thus, our choices were either to acquire or to lever up. We chose to borrow extensively and give it back to the shareholders—and it was a rewarding experience for management as well as the shareholders.

This brings me to the last part of your question: Did the change in leverage and ownership structure change people's behavior? As Mike Jensen said earlier, the EVA concept gets you *part* of the way there with less of the risk. It makes managers conscious of the fact that capital is costly and that value can be created by running the business for cash as opposed to just earnings. But when you actually go out and put the leverage on, it does two things: You now have the financial risk, and it's staring you in the face every day. As a result, the sense of urgency goes up several notches. The second effect comes from management's highly concentrated stock and option ownership, which gives them a much stronger incentive for value creation.

The Case of R.R. Donnelley

FRANCIS: Interestingly enough, my present company, R.R. Donnelley, has adopted an EVA measurement and reward system. It's been in place for about a year-and-a-half. And, although we are facing less risk, there is also less of a sense of urgency about increasing cash flow and value than if we had a highly leveraged capital structure. So, there is a tradeoff that you make between EVA and high leverage in terms of how quickly you want to bring about the change.

STEWART: Why wouldn't R.R. Donnelley pursue a leveraged recap?

FRANCIS: Well, at some point, we may choose to do that. But we haven't reached that point because we haven't proven to ourselves how much cash can really be generated by the company.

And, this is not an idle question, by the way. When John Walter left us to go to AT&T, our stock was depressed, and we felt vulnerable without leadership at the top. So, with the help of some investment bankers, our finance team at Donnelley spent a very long weekend figuring out whether we were now a target for financial buyers. What we then concluded was that a leveraged recap didn't work for Donnelley at that time. But if we succeed in changing our business model so that we can become much more profitable, and produce much higher returns and cash flows, a leveraged recap may become a real choice for us.

STEWART: Mike Jensen pointed to excess capacity as a cause of much of the leveraged activity. Is excess capacity a feature of your business at Donnelley?

FRANCIS: Very much so. It's happening in our business, and in just the ways that Michael explained it. We have market impacts, and we have technology impacts—and we have them both in spades. These two sets of forces have been affecting the company for five years, and the company is only now catching up with that.

But let me step back and say just a little about R.R. Donnelley so people can put this into context. Donnelley is primarily a printing company. We produce magazines, catalogues, telephone directories, and books. We also do financial printing, but this is actually more of a service than a product these days. The company has $6-1/2 billion in revenues; but though we have some overseas operations, I would not describe the company as "global."

The printing industry is a low-growth industry. And, although it has been that way for the past five to seven years, the internal management team did not view it as such. Instead we continued to invest heavily in new capacity. And, compounding this problem of industry-wide overinvestment, the printing industry has also been impacted by technology in the base business. In fact, as a result of some recent technological advances, the replacement of old presses by new ones has the effect of increasing existing capacity. So, just by replacing assets, managers in the industry are effectively choosing to add significant capacity. And, besides this source of overcapacity, we are facing the additional threat from other technologies that could displace some uses of print.

CHERYL FRANCIS

T he leveraged recap was the second stage of a shareholder value program that we started at FMC several years earlier. The first stage was the creation of an EVA-like measurement system. The leveraging concept worked well at FMC because our EVA-type system had already forced us to run the company for cash and for value. And I believe that's one major reason why FMC's recapitalization proved to be more successful than several others that came along later.

STEWART: Why wouldn't you just add fewer presses, then?

FRANCIS: You would do that, if you were acting *intelligently*, or *rationally*.

JAY ALLEN: Yes, but it doesn't pay to be the only rational competitor in an *irrational industry*.

FRANCIS: Well, no industry can be irrational for long periods of time. You're much better off by acting rationally, by attempting to understand the economics of what's driving your business and positioning yourself accordingly.

STEWART: Jay, I don't understand what you're saying. Are you saying that if everyone else is being irrational by adding capacity in a low-growth market, then you should be irrational, too?

ALLEN: I am not saying you should be irrational. What I'm suggesting is that you don't benefit from your own rational behavior if all your competitors are irrational. You have to adopt a different strategy.

STEWART: Well, one strategy would be to buy your irrational competitors and turn them into rational ones.

JENSEN: There's a better strategy than that. *Sell* your firm to your irrational competitors. If they're willing to build excess capacity, they're also likely to overpay for your company.

FRANCIS: Yes, that's the ultimate strategy. But few management teams are willing to volunteer to leave the business.

The Case of Tosco

ALLEN: The industry I'm most familiar with is the oil refining business. It's a business that has long been plagued with overcapacity. It's endemic to the business for lots of reasons, including some regulatory factors. The irrational competitors in our business are happy to build new capacity, but they will not even consider buying *existing* capacity. In fact, Tosco is one of the very few oil refiners that will buy capacity from other companies.

So, yes, there is some classical consolidation going on in the industry. There have been a few mergers among players at public market prices that will result in fewer and bigger—though not necessarily more rational—players. But we know of no one else besides Tosco that is buying up other refineries in private market transactions.

STEWART: Let me ask you this, Jay. Michael's theory would suggest that if you're willing to buy other companies in a mature industry that generates a lot of excess cash, then you want to turn off the investment spigot. And to do that, you should make aggressive use of debt finance to fund those acquisitions. Is that what you've done?

ALLEN: We use a fair amount of debt in our acquisitions. Our industry is not one that generates lots of "free cash flow" as you would typically measure it. The uses of cash are driven by outside forces. The Clean Air Act of 1990 effectively mandated $3 or $4 billion of investment by the U.S. oil industry. California's change in specifications for gasoline mandated at least another $5 billion of investment. And those requirements reduced the amount of free cash flow that could be paid out to investors.

STEWART: Okay, but that doesn't really *eliminate* the free cash flow problem. Let me ask you the following question: Why wouldn't the obligation to make such investments already be reflected in the stock prices of the companies that you buy? And if the prices of the companies are now lower to reflect those mandates, why wouldn't you acquire those companies at the lower prices and still use debt to finance the acquisition? You can still finance the transaction with debt because the current stock price has already been reduced by the future investment necessary to comply with the regulatory requirements.

ALLEN: I agree. In fact, Tosco has bought several companies after they already made those investments. And other companies are choosing to leave the industry rather than make such investments—but these companies are few and far between. So, we borrow to the extent we think is reasonable, which is usually 50%, 60%, or sometimes 70%, of the purchase price. And if you want to include working capital, the leverage gets as high as 80% of the transaction. We use such leverage because we know of no other way to get a decent return on our equity investment.

But you have to understand something about our situation. Mike Jensen said, "Why not sell out to your competitors?" Well, we are buying assets at pennies on the dollar. To give you an example, while we were buying a refinery in New Jersey from the Exxon Corporation and paying $175 million for the fixed assets, Amerada Hess was spending a billion dollars to build a comparable facility that was only about two-thirds the size of the refinery we had just purchased.

Now, why wouldn't Amerada Hess have bought that plant instead of us and saved themselves more than $800 million? Well, you'll have to ask them. But this kind of thing happens all the time in our industry.

JENSEN: That's right, and it's called the agency cost of free cash flow. Many managers don't seem to understand that when you're in an industry that is low-growth, and your competitors are clearly reducing their own value by overinvesting, you can make money by downsizing. Provided you do it rationally, there's always a way to pick up some of the money that's on the table or being poured down an investment rathole.

As I said earlier, the managers of oil companies were all complaining in the early '80s that it was much cheaper to buy oil "on Wall Street" than it was to drill for it. But though managers pointed to this as evidence of market irrationality, it was in fact completely rational. The market was recognizing the amount of excess capacity that was being put in place by unwise competitors by putting a value on the shares that was well below the replacement cost of the net assets. And, in this situation, a value-conscious management ought to be able to buy up its less efficient competitors, even at premiums over their current market value, and then cut down on the capital investment, extract the resources from the industry by letting the assets depreciate, and make a lot of money in the process.

ALLEN: That sounds like a good strategy in a stand-alone industry. But the refining industry is by and large part of a larger integrated business. Our main competitors are not independent refiners, but integrated producers like Exxon, Shell, BP, and Amoco. Those integrated oil companies treat our part of the business—refining and marketing—as merely an adjunct to their basic business, which is to produce and sell

crude oil at a huge margin. And, by deciding to be in the refining business, they are choosing to give up a piece of that margin. They tax themselves by maintaining overcapacity in the downstream side of their business, which in turn kills everybody in the downstream side of the business.

So, for the business to really be rationalized will require the integrated companies to separate their downstream business from their upstream business. If and when that happens, the downstream business will rationalize itself very quickly because there's not enough profit to go around. But, until then, the large integrated producers will simply continue to subsidize their downstream operations and to overbuild capacity in anticipation of some future demand that will almost certainly never materialize. These are all common mistakes that a capital-intensive business with unequaled access to capital can be expected to make. And management doesn't really even need to raise outside capital, or to make a conscious choice of debt or equity. The capital just flows in from the business.

JENSEN: You mean it's internally generated?

ALLEN: It's internally generated. At the same time, though, we are seeing some movement toward a solution. Some of the majors are beginning to say to themselves, "Maybe we don't want to be in a downstream business in the U.S. any longer." The downstream business outside of Europe and the U.S. is highly profitable.

JENSEN: But Jay, in the situation you describe, you should be able to make them an offer to buy some of their downstream capacity that they should find attractive—at least if they're doing their calculations correctly.

ALLEN: Well, we have, and we will continue to do so. Indeed, we have purchased two-thirds of what the company is today from integrated com-

O ur main competitors are not other independent refiners, but integrated producers like Exxon, Shell, BP, and Amoco. For the business to really be rationalized will require the integrated companies to separate their downstream business from their upstream business. But, until that happens, the large integrated producers will simply continue to subsidize their downstream operations and to overbuild capacity in anticipation of some future demand that will almost certainly never materialize. These are all common mistakes that a capital-intensive business with unequaled access to capital can be expected to make. And management doesn't really even need to raise outside capital, or to make a conscious choice of debt or equity: the capital just flows in from the business.

panies that either wanted to get rid of a certain plant or, in some cases, became convinced that they shouldn't be fully integrated. In each such case, we have been able to take that plant and make it highly profitable within our own system.

But, remember, this is not a growth industry. It's a very typical, commodity, low-growth business. And getting the large oil companies to sell their refineries requires nothing less than a cultural change at the very highest level. If I'm CEO of Exxon, I am asking myself, "Why should I sell to these guys who're going to make more money with my assets than I did? We've been integrated like this for 60 years. We invented this business, and so what if I've got some assets that aren't earning adequate rates of return."

But Exxon's not a good example of this thinking. They pay attention to returns on *all* their assets. But a lot of other large oil companies don't.

JENSEN: So, one way to view organizations like your own is as entrepre-neurs who are going about the business of restructuring the industry.

ALLEN: We're rationalizing our industry, but we can't do it unless they're willing to sell.

JENSEN: And you're making money at it.

ALLEN: We make money at it because we buy cheap. Because of this over-capacity problem, it's almost always cheaper in commodity-based industries to buy the assets rather than build them. So, the strategy in our business is to find the guy who's got a nice asset that you can either talk into selling or a guy who's just thrown his hands up in the air, and says, "I want out." That's what we look for. And when we find what we want, we go to Bank of America and borrow to fund a large part of the purchase.

The Case of General Dynamics

JENSEN: Cheryl said earlier that few managements volunteer to go out of business. And that, of course, is one of the major sources of the free cash flow problem we've been talking about. In shrinking industries, it becomes a game of musical chairs—and nobody wants to be the first to leave.

But I do know of at least one case where management found a way to maximize value for its shareholders under those conditions. There is a very careful study published in the *Journal of Financial Economics* that describes how General Dynamics created enormous value for its share-holders in a shrinking industry. When Bill Anders took over as CEO, it was shortly after the Cold War ended, not a very auspicious time for defense contractors. Anders saw the implications of reduced government spending on defense—the need for mas-sive downsizing—and he went around and tried to buy up a lot of his competitors in the industry. But nobody would sell to him. As Anders put it, he was "hanged on his own theory." So, he had to go back and rethink his strategy.

His next move was to initiate a strategy to shrink the company. Over a two-and-a-half-year period, General Dynamics went from having 98,000 people to less than 27,000. Anders took a company with a backlog of $25 billion that was selling on the market for $1 billion, and he created $4 billion of additional shareholder wealth over the next three years by downsizing. At the end of the three years, he fired himself because they were too small to justify keeping him on.

STEWART: What sort of incentive compensation plan did he have?

JENSEN: Anders recruited a new management team, and he put in a high-powered incentive compensation plan for the top 18 managers. The price of General Dynamics was at $25 when they approved the plan. The plan specified that, for every $10 increase in the stock price, Anders and his top managers got a bonus that was equal to double their annual salary. And, since Anders was then being paid $800,000, he was promised a payment of $1.6 million for every $10 increase in the stock price that stayed there for five or ten days.

When this plan was made public, it caused a lot of heat because the plan triggered a large payment a week after the stockholders approved the plan. It wasn't very long before it triggered the next payment and then the next payment. And, by December of the year the plan was adopted, the Compensation Committee canceled the compensation plan in the face of fierce criticism from the press and commentators—a group from which shareholders were conspicuously absent.

Now, what happened next is a very interesting lesson for those of us who pay attention to compensation. When the board soon after substituted for the old plan a conventional stock option plan that effectively paid him

$1.6 million for every $10 increase in the stock price, the controversy over compensation died out completely. The lesson here is that apparently it's okay if you take performance-based pay in the form of equity, but it's not okay if you take it in cash. The cosmetics of this stuff is very important. You cannot be laying people off, selling divisions, shrinking the enterprise—even though it's very hard to get top managers to do that—and be paying top managers large cash bonuses. It just won't wash in the press.

Managerial Incentives and Debt Capacity

STEWART: Mike, do you think there's a relationship between the amount of money a company can borrow and the kind of incentive plan or stock ownership interest that the management has in the company? Do lenders or rating agencies consider management incentives at all in their decision-making?

JENSEN: I think the capital markets are becoming much more sophisticated in how they respond to compensation plans and management incentives. There are lots of examples in the past where organizations implemented high-powered compensation plans and the capital markets didn't pay much attention to it until the cash flows were delivered in the market. The capital markets now appear to understand the import of an announced change in compensation, and they often reflect that in the stock price well before the improvements materialize.

But, having said that, I still think we're a long way from the capital markets seeing it as well as they should.

DENNIS SOTER: I would put this issue of incentives and debt capacity a little differently. I would argue that the *willingness* of companies to as-

sume debt in the first place is a function of the compensation structures that are in place. I agree with Mike that there has been an increase in the sophistication of institutional investors—and, to a lesser extent, in the sophistication of the rating agencies—in responding to corporate incentive structures. But the willingness of management to take on debt is very much a function of the compensation plan and the incentives it provides.

STEWART: Can you give us some examples of that, Dennis?

SOTER: In 1997, we have been involved as adviser in three highly publicized leveraged recapitalizations. The first involved IPALCO Enterprises, which is the holding company for Indianapolis Power & Light. That was followed by SPX Corporation, which is an automotive components manufacturer in Muskegon, Michigan. And the third was Briggs & Stratton in suburban Milwaukee. In each instance, management is working under EVA compensation plans—and, in the case of both SPX and Briggs & Stratton, management has leveraged stock options as well. So, especially in the last two cases, management has a highly-leveraged compensation plan that is pegged to sustainable increases in the stock price. As a consequence, it was far easier to convince those managements that debt is good—and more debt is even better—than it would have been if their compensation structures weren't so closely tied to increases in stock prices.

STEWART: Let's take the example of SPX. Here's a company that announced a decision to make a permanent change in its capital structure, in its mix of debt and equity. Management was going to borrow money to buy back stock. And they were completely eliminating the dividend so as to retain more cash in the firm to service the debt. When they communicated this new financial policy to the mar-

DENNIS SOTER

I would argue that the *willingness* of companies to assume debt in the first place is a function of the compensation structures that are in place. In 1997, we were involved as adviser in three highly publicized leveraged recapitalizations. In each instance, management is working under EVA compensation plans—and, in the case of both SPX and Briggs & Stratton, management has leveraged stock options as well. As a consequence, it was far easier to convince those managements that debt is good—and more debt is even better—than it would have been if their compensation structures weren't so closely tied to increases in stock prices.

ketplace, I think the stock went from $43 to $53 a share.

Now, why did the stock price go up so much? Is the market saying that it views debt as being that much cheaper than equity? If so, why is debt cheaper than equity?

SOTER: Well, let me first say that your question may be as much a subject for psychoanalysis as economic analysis. But the market clearly interpreted the change as a very strong positive signal about the future performance of the company.

SPX is a particularly interesting example because it was already a highly-leveraged company when it announced the transaction. It had one issue of senior subordinated notes outstanding rated "B" and a corporate credit rating of "BB–." Even in these circumstances, we were able to convince management—and later the board—that the company would add value by borrowing an additional $100 million to buy back common stock. And I might add that the re-

purchase, which was structured as a Dutch auction to buy up to 21% of the outstanding common stock, eliminated the entire accounting net worth of the company.

STEWART: That also happened in FMC's case, as I recall.

FRANCIS: That's right. Our accounting net worth went to a negative $600 million.

SOTER: The stock price on the day we priced the Dutch auction was $45-7/8. We set the range at $48 to $56. The transaction cleared at $56, which meant that we were not successful in buying back all of the shares we sought. And the stock continued to go up. In fact, within a few weeks, it peaked at just over $70.

As Bennett mentioned, along with this recapitalization the company also announced that it was eliminating cash dividends. There were two important considerations behind this decision. Because dividends are effectively taxed twice, share repurchases are more efficient from a tax

standpoint. And substituting a major stock repurchase for a future series of dividend payments adds to debt capacity by removing an additional layer of fixed costs. Think about it this way: To pay one dollar in cash dividends, a company must earn about $1.60 pre-tax since dividends are paid with after-tax cash. And if the company can borrow at, say, 8 percent, it means that the $1.60 in pre-tax income that has to be generated to pay $1 in cash dividends could instead service interest expense on $20 of debt. This means that every dollar in dividends paid represents a reduction in debt capacity of at least $20 in today's capital market environment. So, by eliminating SPX's dividend, we effectively increased its debt capacity enough to fund the stock buyback.

A Brief Digression on EPS vs. Economic Profit

STEWART: Let me ask Mike O'Neill a question. Mike, Bank of America has been buying back a lot of stock lately. Do you share the conviction that dividends don't matter to your shareholders?

O'NEILL: When we ask them, most of our investors say they want both port and brandy, dividends and share repurchases. But we clearly have a preference for share repurchases because, as Dennis just suggested, for those investors that are not institutional there is a tax advantage to selling your stock and getting capital gains treatment versus ordinary income.

I know you're going to hate this, Bennett, but we also think that stock repurchases help support our stock price through their effect on our earnings per share. This does not mean that we manage the company to maximize EPS, or that we use it as the primary measure for evaluating our performance. But it is something we look at.

STEWART: Why?

O'NEILL: Because our investors look at it. Aren't we strange?

But, again, Bennett, share repurchase is something we do for more fundamental economic reasons. It just happens to have this nice EPS side-effect that can prove useful in certain circumstances—including meetings with some securities analysts.

ALLEN: We too feel that we need to manage the company for EPS. We do that because that's what our shareholders tell us they want. But, at the same time, we are also highly leveraged because the business doesn't generate adequate returns to shareholders if you don't leverage. We understand that equity is expensive. In fact, we find that equity is *super*-expensive, because you're spreading a fixed amount of earnings power over more and more shares.

So when we buy in shares—and we've done a good deal of it in the past—that helps our EPS. And EPS matters. It matters an awful lot.

STEWART: Well, let me ask you a question. Suppose your earnings are $10, you sell for 10 times earnings, and so your stock price is $100. And let's say you earn a five percent return on investment, and you reinvest all the earnings back in the business. This means next year's earnings are $10.50. Now, according to the accounting model of the firm, you should still sell for 10 times earnings, and so your stock price should go to $105.

But what have you really accomplished in all this? The stock price went up by $5, but you invested $10. In effect, you destroyed $5 in value. That's what we refer to as a loss of $5 of Market Value Added, or MVA. It's the difference between the value that you create and the capital that you invest back in the business. Now, Jay, is that kind of growth in earnings per share a good deal for the shareholders?

ALLEN: I agree completely with your analysis. But let me also say that, if you grow the earnings by only five percent a year, you're not going to have a P/E of 10.

STEWART: Well, let me put it a little differently. You can increase earnings per share by earning any positive rate of return whatsoever on your retained earnings. My question is this: Is there some minimum rate of return on capital your company must earn so that your market value will increase by at least as much as the capital you retain in your business? As Warren Buffett put it, any moron can increase earnings. If you just put more money in a savings account, you get more earnings.

ALLEN: Taken to its logical conclusion, though, doesn't your argument suggest that growth in earnings per share is a *bad* thing for shareholders?

STEWART: No, not at all. Earnings per share is simply a misleading measure. It's often the case that when earnings per share is up, the EVA is up, too.

O'NEILL: That's right. And I think it is possible to triangulate between the two measures, EPS and economic profit, while using economic measures as the driver. But, at the same time, you have to look at EPS because there are people out there—misguided though they may be—who continue to rely on it as their primary measure of performance.

STEWART: We ran an interesting experiment several years ago. We looked at 1,000 U.S. companies and found that, over a three- to five-year period, the change in the company's MVA had a much higher correlation with the change in EVA than with the change in earnings or earnings per share.

O'NEILL: I absolutely agree. We've done the same work.

STEWART: Well, then what's the argument?

O'NEILL: I guess I'm just a little less messianic than you are.

STEWART: Well, when you have a good thing, run with it. But, more seriously, Mike, as I'm sure you're aware, the research departments at places like Goldman Sachs, Smith Barney, First Boston, and Morgan Stanley are now paying a lot of attention to our EVA concept.

Dividends and Stock Buybacks: The Case of Bank of America

O'NEILL: But, as I was saying, in this business of repurchasing our shares, the EPS effect is essentially just a by-product, a sideshow. What we're really trying to do at Bank of America is to manage the company on the premise that equity capital is in fact the most expensive source of funding. Using a now pretty well-established technique called "RAROC"—which is shorthand for "risk adjusted return on capital"—we allocate eq-

MIKE O'NEILL

Bank of America is now generating about $3-1/2 billion a year in net operating cash flow, and we are investing only about $600 to $700 million back in our businesses. So that leaves us with a large excess. We are in an industry that's been characterized by overcapitalization and overcapacity. In the past, bankers have had the hubris to think that they could all expand and make money across a broad range of financial services and markets. So, the agency costs of free cash flow have been alive and well in the banking industry.

What we're trying to do at Bank of America is to manage the company on the premise that equity capital is the most expensive source of funding. We say to ourselves, "If we can't put this money to use by earning returns above our cost of capital, we're going to give it back."

uity capital to all of our businesses and try to hold the people running those businesses accountable for that capital. If we find a business that is generating returns below our cost of capital, we withdraw funds from that business. At the same time, we invest as aggressively as prudence will allow in the businesses that are generating returns above the cost of capital.

Bank of America is now generating about $3-1/2 billion a year in net operating cash flow, and we are investing only about $600 to $700 million back in our businesses. So that leaves us with a large excess. Like the other companies represented at this table, we are in an industry that's been characterized by overcapitalization and overcapacity. In the past, bankers have had the hubris to think that they could all expand and make money across a broad range of financial services and markets. So, the agency costs of free cash flow have been alive and well in the banking industry. Bankers as a group took their excess

cash and reinvested it, often with pretty poor results.

What we're trying to do today at BAC is to be more disciplined. We say to ourselves, "If we can't put this money to use productively—that is, by earning returns above our cost of capital—we're going to give it back." That is what we have done for the last couple of years at B of A. And the payoff from that strategy has been showing up in our stock price over the last two years.

STEWART: But, Mike, it still sounds like you have kind of a hedging strategy with respect to dividends and stock repurchase. You continue to pay dividends, and you also buy back stock. You're trying to give investors both. But, if you believe there's a tax benefit to buying back stock instead of paying dividends, why wouldn't you do what SPX did and just completely eliminate the dividend? This way you can buy back even more stock, and enhance your debt capacity in the process? If that

strategy works a little, why doesn't it work a lot?

O'NEILL: We are a large-cap company, with a market cap approaching $50 billion. We've got a lot of institutional investors, and a number of them continue to have dividend requirements that we just try to meet. Many of our institutional investors will not invest in a company that doesn't have at least a 2 percent dividend yield. We think there is value to having a broad investor base, and so we attempt to pay the minimum required level of dividends.

But having said that, I will also concede that our largest institutional investors are showing an increasing preference for buybacks over dividends. Fidelity, for instance, is a good example of an investor that likes share repurchases. Now, if I wanted Fidelity as my only shareholder, I might consider eliminating our dividend. But I think it's a value-adding strategy for a large-cap company to attract a broad range of shareholders.

Leverage, Dividends, and Investor Clientele

JENSEN: Dennis, what happened to the shareholder base in SPX after the elimination of the dividend and the leveraged recap? When Sealed Air did a similar transaction and eliminated the dividend, about 75% of its shareholders turned over within a couple of weeks of the announcement of the transaction. And the net effect was a large increase in value.

But Sealed Air had a market cap of less than $1 billion. And I agree with Mike O'Neill that, if you tried this with a company like Bank of America with a $50 billion equity base, the company's market value could take a big hit because of institutional constraints demanding all kinds of things like a positive book value of equity and a minimum dividend yield.

SOTER: Let me first say that if all SPX did was to eliminate the dividend, the market reaction would have been much less positive. Three years ago, as Bennett mentioned earlier, we were adviser to FPL Group, the parent company of Florida Power & Light, when it announced a cut in its dividend. Like many utilities, its dividend payout ratio had crept up over 90%, and management felt that a 90% payout was simply not sustainable in an era of increased competition. We convinced them to cut the dividend by just under one-third.

Now, in that particular case, there was no change in the company's capital structure policy. Upon the announcement of the dividend cut, the stock fell from about $32 to $27-1/2, a drop of about 15%. But, as new investors replaced those who were selling, it took less than three weeks for the stock to recover. And, as Bennett told you earlier, FPL's stock ended up outperforming the S&P electric index over the next year.

JENSEN: What was the total market cap of FPL at the time of the elimination of the dividend?
SOTER: It was probably around $2.5 to $3 billion.
JENSEN: But, as Mike O'Neill was suggesting, if you do that with a company that has a $50 billion market cap, you could take a huge hit during the time it takes for the EPS and institutionally-constrained crowd to drop your stock and for the value-based and cash flow sharpies to move in.
SOTER: But there's a way to limit that clientele effect. It's one that we used when one of our clients, IPALCO, became the second profitable utility to voluntarily cut its dividend. In this case, as with FPL, the cut was about 33% At the same time it announced its dividend cut, IPALCO also announced a Dutch auction stock repurchase that would be financed with additional debt. In effect, management said to its stockholders: "If you don't like our new dividend policy, we're giving you the opportunity to get out at a premium."

And let me share with you an interesting aspect of the IPALCO situation. No industry prizes its investment-grade ratings more than utilities because they are constantly in the marketplace raising capital. In the course of borrowing $400 million to buy back 21% of its stock, we leveraged the company from a debt-to-capital ratio of 42% to 68%. At 42% debt to capital, IPALCO's ratings were "AA−" by Standard & Poor's and "AA" by Moody's. And the fascinating thing is that, when the company moved to 68%, its bond ratings were reaffirmed by both rating agencies. Absolutely nothing happened to the bond rating because we were able to demonstrate to the rating agencies that the book-debt-to-capital ratio had no economic significance. In fact, Standard & Poor's was even considering *increasing* the

company's rating to "AA" because we were able to demonstrate that the after-tax cash savings from cutting the dividend would be significantly greater than the after-tax interest expense that would be incurred in financing the stock buyback.

Now, one question that invariably arises is: How much can you afford to pay when you buy back your own stock? Our answer is this: It doesn't matter how much you pay to buy back your stock so long as after the expiration of the tender offer, the stockholders that don't tender are at least as well off as the stockholders who tender. And, in fact, in all three of the situations that I've described—IPALCO, Briggs & Stratton, and SPX—the nontendering stockholders ended up at least as well off as the stockholders who did tender.

STEWART: And it's important to keep in mind that the managements of those companies were among the non-tendering stockholders. For example, both John Blystone at SPX and Fred Stratton and the top management team at Briggs & Stratton have large stock or leveraged stock option positions. And, especially in such cases, management's decision not to tender their shares can send a very powerful signal to the market.

So one of the reasons why the market price would not go down is that you're buying your stock back at the higher price and management is not selling. What stronger signal of management confidence could you provide to the marketplace?
FRANCIS: Bennett, I think there are some other practical considerations that might keep you from cutting the dividend. At Donnelley I have a problem that maybe you can help me with. Regardless of what the general market thinks about the inefficiency of dividends relative to stock repurchase, 18% of my company's shares are held by the Donnelley family. And, be-

cause of restrictions in their trust agreements, they can't sell those shares. They want income, and so reducing the dividend in our case is not likely to happen.

STEWART: Well, you could say to them, "Look, let's calculate the present value of the dividends we would pay for the next five years. And, instead of paying it for the next five years, we'll go out and borrow that amount, and we'll pay you today the present value of the dividend." Now, it's true, that this would force them to pay today the same tax that they would have paid over the five years. But this way the company can borrow money and benefit from the tax deductibility of the interest payments. What's more, the company's financing capacity will not be affected because the additional debt can be serviced by the forgone dividend payments.

So this way the company is better off and the family is no worse. In fact, they will be better off, too, to the extent the stock price is higher as a result. What's the matter with that?

FRANCIS: Well, that's an option we might consider.

STEWART: And this strategy will become all the more attractive if capital gains tax rates are cut. It seems to me that every company in the U.S. will have to reexamine its capital structure and their choice of dividends and share repurchases if capital gains tax rates are dropped in some significant way.

Growth Companies and the Limits of Debt Financing

STEWART: When I visit companies and make the arguments for debt that you have heard this afternoon, some CFOs will say to me, "Well, Bennett, I hear your argument. But, to tell you the truth, we look out over the next three to five years, and we see ourselves generating internally a lot more

cash than we can productively reinvest. So, for us, debt is just unnecessary." My typical response to them is, "The less you need to borrow, the more you ought to borrow. Debt is advantageous both from a tax point of view and from an incentive or control point of view. You should borrow money if you're able to, not because you need to."

MICHAEL DE BLASIO: So far, we've only been talking about low-growth companies, about companies that generate more cash than they can reinvest in their basic business. But what about companies that are growing at 30% or 40% a year? Do any of these arguments apply to these kind of companies?

STEWART: About five years ago, we worked with a company called Equifax. They had recently made a number of acquisitions, and it was part of their strategy to continue to grow aggressively through acquisition. But they also had a very conservative capital structure, with only about 20% debt. At the same time, they were paying lots of dividends.

In that case, the company ended up making two major changes: it adopted our EVA performance measurement and incentive compensation, and it did a leveraged recapitalization in the form of a Dutch auction share repurchase. The company's debt to capital ratio went up significantly. And, even though this was a service business without much in the way of tangible assets or other collateral, management was able to persuade the rating agencies that the company's creditworthiness was largely unaffected. True, its bond rating was dropped from A to BBB. But, as Dennis was suggesting, this was likely to be closer to the optimal capital structure than their A-rated structure with 20% debt.

JENSEN: That case is really the essence of the leverage build-up strat-

egy that we've been hearing a lot about lately. These are by some measures very rapidly growing companies that are growing through highly-leveraged acquisitions in the same business. They typically occur in fragmented industries that are consolidating. And they seem to be creating large amounts of value very quickly in industries that are actually shrinking—again, because of the existence of too many players and the need for consolidation.

The leverage is playing an important role in this process. Although leverage build-ups don't operate with the same amount of debt as the LBOs of the 80s—they tend to run with leverage ratios around 50-60%—the debt is soaking up the excess cash flow and thus adding value in these industries in much the same way as the leveraged deals of the '80s. And, as I suggested earlier in the case of Campeau, the use of debt makes it a "razor-edged" strategy in the sense that, if you overpay for those acquisitions, it's going to show up very quickly in the accounting statements and in your ability to make the debt service payments.

DE BLASIO: Yes, but these leveraged build-ups are a very different animal from the kind of classic high-growth companies that I'm thinking about. Take the case of a company whose basic business is growing very rapidly—and let's say the stock is selling at about 40 times earnings to reflect that growth. What is the role of debt, or stock repurchase, in these kinds of situations?

STEWART: Stewart Myers once said that all corporate assets can be classified as one of two kinds: "assets in place" and "growth options." And Stew went on to argue that while assets in place should be financed with lots of debt, growth options generally should be funded with equity.

So, I agree with you, Mike, that if much of your company's current value consists of growth options, and if that value is premised on management's ability to "exercise" those options by continuing to make strategic investments, then the high-leverage strategy could end up imposing large costs and destroying value.

And, in fact, some of the best empirical work on capital structure would seem to bear this out. About two years ago, our journal ran an article summarizing a study by Michael Barclay, Clifford Smith, and Ross Watts of the University of Rochester. After looking at both the capital structures and dividend policies of some 6,800 companies—all the companies covered by COMPUSTAT—over a 30-year period, they concluded that the most important factor in determining both a company's leverage ratio and its dividend payout was the extent of its profitable investment opportunities. The study found that companies whose value consisted largely of intangible growth options—as measured by high market-to-book ratios and high R & D-to-value ratios—had significantly lower leverage ratios and dividend yields than firms whose value was represented mainly by tangible assets—as indicated by low market-to-book and high depreciation-to-value ratios.

So, it seems to me we need to be more careful in making distinctions about which kinds of companies will benefit from high leverage. As Mike De Blasio was suggesting, companies whose value consists largely of attractive reinvestment or growth opportunities are going to stay away from debt. For these companies, the tax and control benefits of debt are going to be much less important than the need to maintain continuous access to the capital markets.

Take Yahoo!, for example, a company with the exclamation point built right into its name. That company is so risky that management goes out and raises equity and then parks it in marketable securities. It's really negative debt, if you will. And this strategy has a major tax disadvantage: the returns on those securities are taxed twice, once inside the company and then again on distribution—though such companies typically don't pay much in the way of dividends. But for these companies with vast growth opportunities and high business risk, incurring this tax disadvantage is probably a small price to pay for the increase in financial flexibility.

Do you agree with that, Michael? We're close to Silicon Valley, and I see you've got your Apple computer here for your lecture. Would a lot more debt be good for Apple Computer or a high-tech Silicon Valley company?
JENSEN: Well, I agree that high leverage can impose big costs on companies with high operating risk and lots of investment opportunities. But such companies, by definition, do not have a free cash flow problem. They have lots of *profitable* investment opportunities. The companies that will benefit most from debt are those that don't have profitable investment opportunities. The problem I see, though, is the willingness of managers to see profitable growth opportunities where they just don't exist—and where the markets are clearly telling them not to do it.

But let me add one more reason to your argument about why companies should be careful in using debt. A company's capital structure can also affect its ability to sell its products. Financial firms like Bank of America operate with very high credit ratings because their customers—their depositors, their relationship borrowers with lines of credit, and their swap counterparties—put a high value on the assurance that the bank will be around to make good on its commitments down the road. Many of a bank's customers have effectively made an investment in the bank, and a high credit rating can help "bond" the bank's commitment to making the payoff.

And the same argument applies to the product warranties provided by some industrial companies. For example, I'm going to hold Apple personally responsible for the decline in the value of my PowerBook 3400 if the company goes under. So, even if the capital markets allowed Apple to borrow a lot, management has got to pay very careful attention to how consumers like me are going to view that financing decision. The capital markets aren't perfect, and in some cases too much leverage can absolutely kill the company by reducing demand for its products.

Capital Structure, Incentives, and Performance: More on Bank of America

SOTER: In the course of advising companies on recapitalization strategies, we've analyzed almost 25 different industries. And in virtually all of those industries, we have found that the optimal capital structure—that is, the mix of debt and equity that results in the lowest weighted-average cost of debt and equity capital—is *below* an investment-grade rating.
FRANCIS: Then why do you suppose there are so few companies operating there now?
SOTER: I think the primary reason has to do with the incentive structures at most large public companies. Most compensation plans don't motivate that kind of behavior on the part of management.
STEWART: Well, let me turn to Mike O'Neill and put that question to him. Mike, what real incentives are there for the chief financial officer, or the treasurer of a company, to promote

this kind of recapitalization? After all, it does appear—at least on the surface—to be a much riskier strategy. It is also often a value-adding strategy, but think of the personal risk if it doesn't work out. What are the incentives for the chief financial officer to push the capital structure and dividend policy issue to the point where you do in fact minimize the cost of capital? What's the dynamic of all this in an organization?

O'NEILL: Generally, the motivating force is self-interest, *enlightened* self-interest. People like to get rewarded for doing a good job. And if you link their pay to shareholder returns, people get on the bandwagon pretty quickly.

We've been at this for a couple of years at Bank of America. It has not been easy because it is a departure from the way things were done in the past. Historically, our mission was to grow. We were very successful in accomplishing that goal under Dick Rosenberg. The investments in expanding our franchise undertaken during that period really laid the basis for our future growth and profitability. But our overarching mission now is the creation of value for our shareholders.

Our biggest challenge in this undertaking has been to impress on our people that capital has a cost—and that if you do not generate returns above that cost, your stock is unlikely to do very well. The beauty of the argument is that when investors believe that you are going to do better, those expectations get built into your current stock price. This way, you are often rewarded even before you have achieved the expectation. So if you do a reasonable job of communicating the strategy and implementing it in the early stages, the market will often give you the benefit of the doubt, particularly in the benign environment that we've been blessed with recently.

STEWART: Mike, it's also my impression that when companies go through major policy changes—such as B of A's move to economic profit or through a leveraged restructuring like the one Cheryl went through at FMC—one of the critical determinants of success is the active involvement and complete commitment by the chief executive officer.

O'NEILL: That has absolutely been the case at Bank of America. In fact, it's really *all* his fault. Dave Coulter has pushed it through, and he's done a terrific job of getting the board and other constituencies convinced that this is the right way to go.

What I'm talking about is our use of "economic profit" to evaluate the performance of our different operations and, to some extent, as a basis for rewarding managers. Like your EVA system, Bennett, our economic profit measures the dollar amount by which the operating earnings of each of our profit centers—and, in some cases, our individual customer relationships—exceeds its capital charge. The capital charge in turn is calculated by multiplying our corporate-wide cost of capital, which we estimate to be about 12%, by the amount of capital that has been assigned to the profit center. What is different for us, as a financial institution as opposed to an industrial firm, is the extent to which the *implicit* capital backing our operations is different from our actual cash or regulatory capital.

So, we are now doing economic value-based management. As far as our capital structure goes, we've got regulators who sort of limit what our capital structure can look like within a fairly narrow range. Moreover, we are involved in a number of businesses where we feel it is essential to maintain a credit posture no lower than AA. This means that, in managing our capital structure, we have a limited range of options for replacing our equity by issuing more debt. Given the constraints put on us both by regulators and by our customers, we have not found it a good idea to borrow much more than our principal competitors.

But what we have done is to use our cash flow to buy back some of our excess equity, and to get the most out of the equity that we are operating with. And our attempt to maximize economic profit, as suggested, has led us to look at all the businesses that we're in, assign capital based on the risk, and make judgments about where we can and where we can't make a go of it. Based on this analysis, we have also made decisions to get out of businesses where there appeared to be little chance of ever earning our cost of capital.

An Alternative to LBOs: Leveraged Stock Options

STEWART: Well, Mike, you say that you are constrained in your ability to use high leverage. But there is a way that bankers can experience the thrill of victory and agony of defeat of a leveraged buyout without leveraging the bank at all. It's by using a concept called "leveraged stock options," or LSOs.

To illustrate how an LSO operates, consider a company with a current share price of $10. The initial exercise price on the LSO is set at a 10% discount from the current stock price, or $9, making the option worth $1 right out of the gate. But instead of just handing the LSOs to management, managers are required to purchase them—generally with a portion of their EVA cash bonus—for the $1 discount, and that money is put at risk.

Besides requiring managers to make an initial investment, another important difference between LSOs and regular options is that the exercise price is projected to increase at a rate that approximates the cost of capital, less a discount for undiversifiable risk and illiquidity. Now, let's just assume that rate of increase is 10% per annum. In this case, over a five-year period—and ignoring compounding for simplicity—the exercise price will rise 50% above the current $9 level to $13.50. This way, management pays $1 today for an option to purchase the company's stock, currently worth $10, for $13.50 five years down the road.

Only if the company's equity value grows at a rate faster than the exercise price will management come out ahead. In fact, if the exercise price rises at a rate equal to the cost of capital (less dividends), then the LSOs will provide exactly the same incentives as an EVA bonus plan.

O'NEILL: Bennett, we've done essentially the same thing with our own stock option plan.

STEWART: What do you use as the growth rate for the exercise price?

O'NEILL: We looked at the performance of the S&P 500 banks over the past ten years, and we found that total shareholder returns increased about 9% per year, on average, over that ten-year period. Then we made the simplifying assumption that the next ten years would be like the last ten, and we essentially increased the strike price over the eight-year life of our options by roughly 9%.

STEWART: Per year?

O'NEILL: Effectively, yes. We have three different tranches of options, each with higher exercise prices. So these are *premium-priced* stock options. It's a variation on the leveraged stock option. Transamerica has a similar plan. But, to my knowledge, we are the only large bank in America using such a program. And although we put it in fairly recently, it is clearly having quite an impact on the way our people behave.

The Internal LBO

STEWART: Besides leveraged stock options, there's another strategy for replicating the incentives of LBOs within companies that have multiple operating units. Suppose you run a company with lots of different divisions; and, though you would like to use the incentive effect of leverage to motivate your operating heads, you don't want to subject your company to the financial risk. In that case, you can take an individual business unit and have it borrow money nonrecourse to the parent, and then have the unit pay the money out to the parent company. In effect, you're substituting nonrecourse unit debt for corporate debt. And, if you at the same time grant or sell the operating managers an equity stake in the business unit, then you have what I call an "internal LBO."

Why would you want to do this? In the 1980s, I was struck by the fact that KKR and other buyout firms were buying business units from conglomerates and getting fantastic returns. And I asked myself, "Why wouldn't a company want to do that on its own?" What's more, you don't even actually have to borrow the money. You can just simulate the transaction on a piece of paper. You can just pretend that the business unit borrowed the money, and the only real part of this transaction is that the managers of the business unit will be required to buy an equity stake. The value of the unit will be appraised each year according to the firm's success in earning a return over and above the imputed debt service on the fictional debt.

But, again, we're trying to find ways to compete with the KKRs of the world by simulating *inside the firm* what otherwise can be very expensive and risky to do from an external point of view.

O'NEILL: Again, we have done that at Bank of America, at least in a limited way. We have a private equity business with a little over $2 billion of investments. These are KKR-type buyout investments, but obviously smaller than KKR's because of our regulatory limitations. But, essentially, we force the people who arrange the deals at B of A to *coinvest* in the deals that they do. These deals are pretty highly leveraged, and our success rate in this business has been nothing short of terrific.

ALLEN: Mike, how do you manage the cultural differences between the more traditional commercial bankers in your organization, and the investment and merchant bankers you're trying to attract and keep satisfied? How do you manage that cultural diversity?

I ask the question because I wonder what would happen to a lot of corporate divisions if they went through an LBO, or allowed some of their managers to act as if they were LBO'd. Would such changes really affect their behavior? Or would you, in most cases, have to change management? Regardless of which way you do it, though, it seems to me that everybody who isn't in on that type of plan will soon be unhappy with those who are in on it.

STEWART: Jay, you suggested that you might have to change the management if you were to LBO, or even pretend to LBO, a division. Doesn't that suggest that you might not have the right people running your divisions?

ALLEN: My impression is that most of the LBOs were done either with a new management team, or by the exceptional managers that either chose to stick around, or were asked by the buyout firm to stay on. And it's also my impression that those managers who stayed became exceptional performers in large part because they had to shove in their own personal equity.

Now, the question you're asking is: Do we have the right managers for our divisions? It's a question we ask each other every day. But big companies have trouble hiring and firing at great speed, and that can be a big obstacle to doing this kind of internal LBO. And, if you do carve out parts of your company and provide ownership incentives, then you're bound to run into problems in integrating an entrepreneurial LBO culture with the more traditional corporate culture.

JENSEN: I think this issue of mixing cultures is a big potential problem. In fact, it's the one of the major costs of becoming a large organization. Small companies can pick off pieces of large organizations just by paying people in a way that large companies can't because of these pressures for equity in compensation. And, except in cases where there are large economies of scale and scope, we see small companies taking business from large ones all the time.

But even so, I still think large organizations would benefit from doing more of these internal LBOs than they have done to date. And I feel certain that if we required divisional managers to coinvest in their projects, we would see a lot more projects turned down that are now routinely approved based on the typical hockey-stick projections. Because now they're betting their families' wealth on it.

ALLEN: Well, let me give you the other side of that theory. We're old fashioned at Tosco, and we continue to leave the major capital spending decisions to senior management. Division heads can propose but they don't dispose. So the discipline is really the CEO's, and he's already laid down the law on that.

JENSEN: That kind of centralization can work in an industry that's fairly

mature, and where there is little technological change and market conditions are relatively stable. In those cases, the "specific knowledge" necessary to make the right investment and production decisions may well be at the top of the organization. On the other hand, we have all kinds of evidence from studies of Harold Geneen's ITT and other conglomerates that centralized decision-making will fail if you're in a lot of different businesses, and your businesses are highly dynamic. As has been strongly suggested in the case of ITT, too much centralization can easily lead a company to underinvest in potentially profitable businesses while overinvesting in mature businesses.

So, in many organizations, the critical issue has been to get those decision rights out of corporate headquarters and down to the divisions.

ALLEN: What you're saying, at bottom, is that diversified companies typically don't work well because top management is incapable of managing all of them equally well.

JENSEN: That's right, or at least that's one of the main implications. The traditional conglomerate with centralized controls and decision-making is bound to fail in today's environment.

ALLEN: I agree completely. I've seen it in my own life, and I've seen it in others'. We all took on businesses saying, "We're smart people, we can do this." And the typical outcome was that the new operation you thought you could manage ended up taking nine-tenths of your time, even though it was only three-tenths of your total business—and you never made a dent in it. And the worst thing about this kind of diversification is that it forces you to ignore your good businesses.

So, my feeling, based on both my own experience and that of many others I've observed, is that corporate diversification is a bad idea.

Broadening the Issue

ANIRUDDHA ROY: Up to this point, we have been discussing corporate governance as if the resolution of agency costs were the only major problem confronting corporate managers and their boards of directors. But surely there are other issues that are at least as important, if not more important, than paying out free cash flow and preventing managements from overinvesting. Surely management must spend at least as much time thinking about whether they have the right technology and the right supplier networks as they do about having the right dividend and financial policy. Successful managements must devote as much effort to ensuring they have the optimal level and kinds of *human* capital as they do to figuring out the optimal mix of financial capital. As C.K. Prahalad likes to say, capital is not the scarce resource these days; it's human talent and technology that are most likely to distinguish the exceptional value creators from the mediocre.

So, these are all aspects of corporate decision-making that strike me as contributing more to future corporate value than financial policies and whether you choose EVA or some other measure to evaluate your performance. And, what concerns me about this discussion is that an *exclusive* focus on stock price performance or some financial measure can end up reducing value, especially in the case of high-growth companies. Such measures are also likely to discourage mature companies from seeking out new sources of growth and so transforming themselves into growth companies.

JENSEN: Well, I agree with you completely in one sense. And that is, if you have the wrong business strategy, or if you hire the wrong people, you're going to destroy value. My point is this: You can do all those things right, but if you screw up these financial issues at the top level of the organization where the cash comes pouring in, the company can destroy much of the value that's been created on the real side of the business. Top management can go out on elephant hunts—acquisition campaigns that systematically destroy value—or make major investment decisions without actually looking at the numbers. So, you can have everything done right at the lower levels in the organization. But if you don't get the right governance structure at the top—and finance can be a critical part of that governance structure—the operating value of the company can be frittered away.

Now, if you want to push this discussion beyond finance, let me say that I think there are non-financial aspects of corporate governance where corporate America is continuing to make serious mistakes. We tend to have systematically overcentralized organizations. As I said earlier, we now have evidence of the enormous destruction of value by conglomerates before many of them were taken apart in the '80s. And there's still a lot of that centralized, conglomerate mentality lingering in corporate America. What we have found in our field work at Harvard is that, in large diversified enterprises, the decision rights migrate to the top where uninformed people—not stupid people, but *uninformed* people—lose track of what's going on lower down. As Jay was suggesting earlier, although you may have the most intelligent top management team in the world, top management in large organizations can't possibly have sufficient "specific" knowledge to make the right decisions at the division level.

In contrast to large organizations, the LBO associations, private equity groups, and venture capitalists that I've studied seem to know very well how to assign decision rights so as to strike the proper balance of decentralization and centralization. But, once you start moving into larger organizations, getting the decision-making authority in the right place becomes a very difficult problem. And, again, that's one of the big problems with large organizations. Even after all the downsizing, I would say that we still have too many large, diversified public corporations in this country. After all these years, ITT is still attempting to get down to the right structure.

So, let me endorse your comment that, in a full-ranging discussion of organizational policy, all of those things you mentioned are critically important. I started out my remarks by saying that the reason capital structure matters is not because of any financial alchemy; as Bennett put it, there is no magic in leverage. The reason finance matters is because it affects real operating decisions; it affects what actually goes on at lower levels in the organization.

To give you just one example, I visited FMC about two years after they had done their buyout in 1986. And I was astonished at how the middle managers I was talking to understood, and felt threatened by, the possibility of bankruptcy. My recollection, Cheryl, was that your employees owned about 45% of the company through an ESOP plan...

FRANCIS: It was 40%.

JENSEN: 40% of the company. And that ownership was playing a big role in the decisions that were being made. People at all levels of the organization suddenly became concerned about the level of capital expenditures and began paying attention to expected returns. In fact, I remember being led by a secretary from one meeting to another; and, as we were going down the elevator, she remarked that yesterday the company's stock price had reached an all-time high. She added that it didn't *close* at an all-time high, but it reached the high during the day. And when I asked her why she was interested in this, she mentioned the ESOP and her concerns about the company's future.

Now, if you walk into the typical corporate environment, you will find that only people at the very top are concerned with those kinds of decisions and their consequences. When you use financial changes to make a significant change in ownership, that can affect awareness and decision-making throughout the organization.

And it is that kind of decentralized decision-making, combined with highly concentrated ownership, that explains the success of LBOs in this country. We've had well over 3,000 LBOs since the mid-1970s. Although the business press gives you the opposite impression, very few of them ever come back public. And very few of them, except for some very large ones at the end of the 1980s, went into bankruptcy. It has been the most successful wave of restructuring in American history. And it continues to go on.

The LBO represents a new organizational "technology," if you will. And those of you in corporate America who are running old-style companies and not paying attention to what this new LBO technology can do for you could be blind-sided by changes in the product market and the competition by people who are taking advantage of the technology. As I said before, public companies can imitate these firms in lots of ways without going private. Besides levering up, they can get more equity ownership, shrink their board size, and even persuade large investors to become long-term owners in their companies, if not part of their board.

The Balanced Scorecard vs. Shareholder Value

ROY: But, I am still concerned about the effect of an exclusive focus on shareholder value. If you look at companies like General Motors, IBM, Phillips, and Wang that have gone through very difficult periods, the stock market was the last to see the troubles that were coming on. The management literature reveals that not only people inside the company, but also some outside observers, foresaw these difficulties long before the market.

So, given that the stock market often seems to function as a lagging rather than a leading indicator, do we really want to rely so heavily on stock prices—and on market-value proxies like EVA—in evaluating managers' performance? Shouldn't we also be focusing on customer and employee satisfaction, and on a whole host of strategic performance variables?

Once a company's stock price crashes, it tends to be a crisis situation. It reminds of something my son told me the other day: As long as he gets good grades, everything's fine. But, by the time the poor performance shows up in his grades, the problem has probably gotten out of hand.

JENSEN: Well, you're making at least one very good point. And let me agree with you while trying to put your argument in a slightly different way. I agree with you in the sense that I feel the U.S. corporate governance system lets companies go on destroying value too long before intervening in a meaningful way. And I'm prepared to accept your view that the capital markets are not always the first to see the problems. But, after all, the capital market investors in our large public companies are *outsiders*. That's the way we've set up our system in this country. And outsiders don't always have the information—much less the

control—to bring about change when it's necessary.

So, for this reason I agree that we don't want to focus on the stock price in the sense that I think I heard you say. But we do want to focus on the stock price in another way. We want to hold up stock price maximization—or, more generally, maximizing the total value of the enterprise—as the main objective function, the overarching goal, for corporate management. If you're interested in maximizing efficiency and social welfare, then total enterprise value is the correct number for managers to aim to maximize. If you pick any other number or any other index or any other multiple of indexes or indices, you're going to screw it up. You will end up destroying value.

This is my major concern over the use of the so-called balanced scorecard. It never puts it altogether in a single overall number. The reason I find EVA so attractive is that it converts what is essentially a "stock" number—that is, the total market value added—into a "flow" number that managers can look at year by year to assess the extent to which they're adding or destroying value.

Now, given that you're going to maximize the total market value added of the company, how do you do that? You've got to look at the business strategy, you've got to look at HR policies, you've got to look at R&D, and the list goes on. These are the things that somebody in the organization actually gets to decide on. But nobody gets to decide on what the stock price is. That is the result of all those millions of decisions that get made in any organization.

So if your point is that the stock price is an imperfect index of year-to-year performance—and that in some cases it can fail to indicate problems where problems exist—then I'm in 100% agreement. But it's the market

value added—which, again, is determined largely by changes in your stock price—that should serve as your longer-run index of success. And what I think we're talking about today is how corporate financial policies—pay-out ratios, leverage ratios, and to some extent ownership structure—can be used to encourage investment and production decisions that increase EVA and MVA. If financial decisions don't end up affecting these real decisions inside organizations, then I agree with Merton Miller that they're essentially irrelevant.

STEWART: To expand on what Michael said, we have an expression that says, "Metrics without mission is madness." And this relates back to the balanced scorecard. A number of years ago, before Briggs & Stratton went on EVA, they would manage according to a process they now describe as "squeezing on a balloon." One month was inventory-management month, and the head office would trumpet out, "Drive-down-inventory day is at hand." And, sure enough, inventories would go down; but then they would have stock-outs of key parts and products. So the next month was total customer satisfaction month. With the marketers in charge, the company extended the receivables, dropped prices, and offered delivery of any part or product anytime you wanted—and, quite predictably, the manufacturing department screamed bloody murder. So the next month was manufacturing efficiency month, and they drove down unit costs of production with long runs of standardized products. But this succeeded only in bringing them full circle to the excess inventory problem that they started with.

And this is a large part of my problem with the balanced scorecard. It has all these metrics and a flat landscape, but there's no measure of total factor productivity.

Another good example of this is Coca-Cola, which is a longstanding EVA company. For years, they sent their concentrates to their bottlers in stainless steel containers. The cost of the containers was written off against earnings over a long period of time, which had the effect of increasing reported profits and profit margins. But, after they switched to EVA, somebody lower down in the organization—and this bears on Michael's point about the difficulty of transferring good information to the top of the organization—came up with a new idea. He said, "What if we switch to cardboard containers? Now, it's true that because cardboard containers are not reusable, they have to be expensed against the earnings, which reduces profit and profit margins. But, because cardboard costs much less than steel containers, our investment on our balance sheet goes way down."

So, the manager faces a trade-off here. The company could have faster inventory turns and higher returns on assets with cardboard, or a juicier profit margin with stainless steel. Which is the right answer?

The balanced scorecard doesn't give you any means for evaluating such trade-offs. If you have to choose between two desirable, but conflicting objectives that are both rewarded by the balanced scorecard—and, after all, this is often what management decision-making comes down to—there's no single scale that allows you weigh those trade-offs?

Coke solved this problem simply by saying that EVA *is* the balanced scorecard. Run the numbers, and tell us what gives us more EVA. And what they found was that when they switched from stainless steel to cardboard, the savings on the balance sheet ended up being far more valuable than what they gave up on the income statement.

So, that's why we feel metrics without mission is madness. But metrics *with* mission is marvelous! If you have a well-defined mission like increasing economic profit, then that can enable you to evaluate the trade-offs among the other less quantifiable goals of the company.

Too Much Stock Ownership?

ROY: Professor Jensen, are you concerned that when senior management has a lot of stock in their own company, such holdings could actually cause them to behave in ways that run against the shareholder interest? We have a client with an outstanding track record based on growth through acquisitions. The managers are people in their late 30s and early 40s who are sitting on $40-50 million of value in their stock. And, although the company would appear to have more opportunities for growth, the managers are saying, "It's time to slow down; we really don't need to take those kind of risks anymore."

So, my question is, can too much stock ownership lead to an undesirable amount of risk aversion on the part of the managers? And are you concerned about this effect?

JENSEN: You're absolutely right; it can have that effect. Gene Fama and I wrote a paper on that very topic that was published in the *Journal of Business* about ten years ago. As we show there, as the total amount of equity by the top management team rises, you can get exactly the effect you're talking about, which is excessively risk-averse behavior.

But the answer to that problem is not to abandon stock, but rather to change the structure of the stock ownership. That's why I love Bennett's leveraged stock option concept. Unlike conventional options, these LSOs involve a sort of sharing at the margin with managers. So, even if you've

already got a large amount of equity in managers' hands, you can put leveraged stock options on top of that to give them incentives to take the right amount of risk.

Now, finding the right amount and structure for equity ownership by managers is a delicate process, and we're never going to get it exactly right. But I agree with you completely that as we move to more and more equity-based and option-based plans, we will need to think carefully about these issues.

And let me also say, by the way, that I would eliminate tomorrow all the traditional executive stock options and replace them with these leveraged stock options. The way conventional stock option plans work today induces very bad behavior on the part of managers. The cost of equity capital that is implied in the typical executive stock option is zero. And, given the way compensation plans are "recalibrated" each year, and new options are awarded with exercise prices at market each year, managers are effectively rewarded for lousy performance.

So, if we could just get rid of conventional stock option programs, we could have a big impact on the way managers behave.

The Effect of Financial Risk on Operating Risk

ROY: On a related issue, has anybody done any studies or simulations of what happens to the performance of EVA companies when the industry or the economy turns down?

STEWART: Well, since our EVA program really took off around 1992, there hasn't been a general bear market, but there have been downturns in various industries. George Harad, the Chairman & CEO of Boise Cascade, is here with us. Boise Cascade is a forest products and paper company that went on EVA several years ago. George, I understand that paper prices fell over 40% last year, which means you're going through a bear market in your business. Could you comment on this question about whether EVA has helped you weather the down part of your business cycle?

GEORGE HARAD: Well, I think there are really two different questions here: How does EVA work in bear markets? And how does it work in companies with volatile markets?

I think focusing on EVA works in either direction; in fact it may work better when your markets are falling away from you. It motivates people to do something, as opposed to just sitting on capital assets while the returns keep falling farther below the cost of capital.

The second question is: How does EVA work in a business or an industry where the volatility of cash flows makes the cash flows very unpredictable. In two of our businesses—the wood products business and the paper business—in the past five years we have seen prices go down as much as 50-60% in a single year, and then go up by as much as 130%. Now, given the size of those price swings, we really have to get on top of the other, more controllable elements of our business. Dealing with that kind of price volatility forces you to engineer close to the edge, and having an EVA system in place has helped us find ways to eliminate other fixed costs in our overall system.

JENSEN: That's an interesting comment. One of the results that we now have from our studies of leveraged transactions is that, when companies lever up and take on high financial risk, the people on the operating side

of the business find ways to reduce operating risk so that the companies are not operating so close to the edge. For example, a study by Steve Kaplan and Jeremy Stein examined the riskiness of the stub shares that remain after the the large leveraged restructurings like the one by FMC. And the measured risk of that equity was much lower than it should have been if the operating risk of the total assets had remained the same. This evidence is consistent with my own observation that the operating risk of the assets just plummets in these highly leveraged deals.

STEWART: Give me an example. How does somebody magically reduce the operating leverage in their business?

JENSEN: Well, in our Harvard field studies, we have found that managers in LBOs find all kinds of ways to reduce fixed costs, or to convert them into variable costs. You can subcontract or outsource a lot of activities. You can substitute stock or options for salary increases. These kinds of changes can have a dramatic effect on the riskiness of the business—one that helps highly leveraged firms to pull through in down markets.

Now I happen to think that these kinds of changes ought to be made by most companies, not just those with high leverage. And I'm not suggesting that companies should never pursue strategies with high operating risk. But what we have learned from studies of LBOs is that managers can generally do a lot more to increase value when given the right incentives and when facing the pressure of debt.

Some of the success stories are really dramatic, and I'll just tell you about one. There was a little company

I studied back in 1987 that did an LBO of 2,000 miles of railroad track in Wisconsin that the SOO Line couldn't make money on. And, as part of a new organization called Wisconsin Central Limited, a group of managers from Northwestern Railroad bought it out with a lot of debt and with some equity from an LBO firm in Boston called Berkshire Partners. And within a year and a half, Wisconsin Central was rated the number one regional railroad in the United States. Wisconsin Central and Berkshire Partners then went on to buy the New Zealand Rail and Shipping System when it was denationalized. They also recently bought a very substantial fraction of the British railroad system.

I should also point out that the LBO sponsor, Berkshire Partners, using the same operating and financial strategies, has also recently made large equity investments in a variety of other businesses such as cable and cellular tower construction. And the remarkable thing is that, while operating all of these different businesses, Berkshire Partners has never had a losing business. But you have to remember that this is not like a conventional U.S. conglomerate. This is a highly decentralized system in which the operating managers of each business get to make the operating decisions—and they own a significant fraction of their businesses. And that, in a nutshell, is why LBO firms have succeeded where companies like ITT have failed.

STEWART: Well, that sounds like a good note on which to bring this to an end. I would like to thank the panel for their participation, and to thank Jerry Fair once again for setting up this event—and for including me in it.

IV. RAISING CAPITAL

In "Raising Capital: Theory and Evidence," Clifford Smith begins this section with a concise review of academic research bearing on (1) the stock market's response to announcements by public companies of different kinds of securities offerings and (2) the relative efficiency of different methods of marketing corporate securities—that is, rights vs. underwritten offerings, negotiated vs. competitive bid contracts, and traditional vs. shelf registration. Somewhat surprisingly, at least to academics, the research confirms that the average market reaction to security offerings of all kinds—debt and equity, straight and convertible, and issued by utilities as well as industrials—is "consistently either negative or not significantly different from zero... Furthermore, the market's response to common stock issues is more strongly negative than its response to preferred stock or debt offerings. It is also more negative to announcements of convertible than non-convertible securities, and to offerings by utilities than industrials."

In the first half of the article, Smith evaluates a number of explanations that have been offered to account for these findings. For example, the expected dilutive effect of new equity and convertibles on EPS is dismissed as an "accounting illusion" that should have no effect on economic values. Skepticism is also expressed about the time-honored "price-pressure" argument that maintains that large issues of new securities must be offered at a discount from market prices, even in heavily traded markets like the New York Stock Exchange. In place of these traditional arguments, Smith suggests that the most plausible explanation of the market's systematically negative response to equity and convertibles is the "information asymmetry" hypothesis. In brief, the argument holds that, because of the possibility of inside information, and given the incentives of management as insiders to exploit outside investors by issuing overvalued securities, the mere act of announcing new equity or convertibles often releases a negative signal to the market about the firm's cash flow prospects (at least, relative to those reflected in its current stock price), thus causing stock prices to fall on average.

In the second part of the article, Smith uses this "information asymmetry" argument to explain why firm commitment underwritten offerings predominate over rights offerings, negotiated over competitive bids, and traditional registration over the new shelf registration procedure (although the latter is gaining ground, especially in debt issues). The mere possibility of insider information creates a demand by potential investors for the issuing firm to hire reputable underwriters to "certify" the value of the new securities. The guarantee of quality, as well as the commitment to maintain an after-market, provided to investors is much stronger in the case of firm underwritten offerings, especially those which are negotiated with a single investment banker rather than auctioned through a competitive bid and registered using the traditional rather than the new shelf procedure. In cases where such certification services are unnecessary, however, shelf registration can provide significant savings in transaction costs.

In "A Survey of U.S. Corporate Financing Innovations: 1970-1997," Kenneth Carow, Gayle Erwin, and John McConnell report increasing issuance of debt in overseas markets and denominated in foreign currencies, as well as large and growing use of innovative securities designed mainly to accomplish one of three ends: (1) manage interest rate and other financial exposures; (2) reduce "information costs"; and (3) increase the "tradability" of financial assets.

In "Initial Public Offerings," Roger Ibbotson, Jay Ritter, and Jody Sindelar attempt to explain a well-documented research finding that has puzzled finance scholars for years. IPOs are significantly "underpriced"—by as much as 18 percent on average, on the authority of Ritter's exhaustive study of the period 1960-1987. The research also shows that IPOs tend to run in cycles of "hot" and "cold" markets. That is, markets characterized by large average underpricing (large initial run-ups in the aftermarket) lead to a heavier volume of initial offerings, which in turn are associated with progressively lower underpricing over time. Lower underpricing in turn appears to lead to lower volume and thus the onset of "cold" markets. The authors review the explanations that have recently been offered to account for this peculiar pattern while also reporting some interesting new evidence on the pricing of venture-capital-backed and mutual fund IPOs, as well as "reverse" LBOs.

In "Internet Investment Banking," Bill Wilhelm suggests that this new phenomenon could dramatically reduce the transactions costs of raising capital in public markets. In establishing the demand curve for a new securities offering, investment bankers have long used "bookbuilding" methods that are designed to economize on search costs by eliciting bids from a small but influential group of institutional investors. The new "OpenIPO" procedure, by giving underwriters a low-cost means of canvassing all investors, is said to have the potential to cut underwriting fees on IPOs from the customary 7% of gross proceeds to as little as 3-5%—and the new technology is also expected to reduce costs on bond and seasoned stock offerings as well.

From IPOs, we move to the subject of bank loan financing, which, as mentioned above, may be the best debt financing alternative for those companies unable to tap the public debt markets. In a theoretical paper entitled "What's Different About Banks," the University of Chicago's Eugene Fama argued that banks have a comparative advantage over public investors and other financial institutions in making short-term loans because of their access to deposit histories and continuous customer relationships. In the article "Are Banks Still Special: New Evidence on Their Role in the Capital-Raising Process," Christopher James and David Smith review research over the past 15 years that suggests that bank loans possess some distinctive if not unique advantages over other forms of financing.

In "Convertible Bonds: Matching Financial and Real Options," David Mayers explains the appeal of convertible financing for companies with favorable but uncertain growth prospects. They argue that convertibles are likely to be the low-cost financing alternative for companies contemplating a sequence of future financings for investment opportunities ("real options") that may materialize, but may not.

One interesting variation of convertibles are the highly successful Liquid Yield Option Notes pioneered by Merrill Lynch in 1985. In "The Origin of LYONs: A Case Study in Financial Innovation," John McConnell of Purdue University and Eduardo Schwartz of UCLA provide an account—admittedly second-hand—of the thinking that went into their design. Such an account is "second-hand" because

Professors McConnell and Schwartz were not present at the creation of the security (Merrill's then Options Marketing Manager, Lee Cole, is credited with the original insight). Their role was rather to design a model to "price" the security—one that not only turned out to be remarkably accurate (it overestimated the first-trading-day closing price of the first LYON issue by only 1.5%), but also enabled Merrill to answer charges by a would-be competitor that Merrill was grossly underpricing the security.

LYONs are part of a broader class of debt securities known as hybrids—those that combine conventional, fixed-rate debt with an embedded forward, swap, or option. In "The Uses of Hybrid Debt in Managing Corporate Risk," Charles Smithson and I attempt to explain why the early 1990s proved to be a "Hot Times for Hybrids" (to borrow the title from a *New York Times* article). In the early 1980s, when interest rates were much higher than they are today, hybrids like Sunshine Mining's silver-linked bond issue were used by riskier companies to help reduce their interest costs to manageable levels. But though rates are much lower today, credit spreads have widened considerably for all but blue-chip borrowers. In many cases, companies are using hybrid debt to lower their risk profile and thus avoid the higher funding costs now associated with being a riskier corporate borrower.

In "Using Project Finance to Fund Infrastructure Investments," Richard Brealey, Ian Cooper, and Michel Habib argue that the complex web of contractual agreements underlying most project financings can be viewed as attempts to shift a variety of project risks—operating risks, political risks, currency risks—to the parties best able to appraise and control them. In this sense, risk management also involves structuring the incentives of the various parties in ways designed to increase efficiency. The equity investment by the project's operators is seen as working together with high debt ratios and the web of contracts to reduce "agency" problems that arise in the management of large projects (and, indeed, in all organizations, public and private). The authors also explain why most project financing takes the form of limited recourse bank loans rather than, say, public bonds with full recourse to the sponsors.

DHC

RAISING CAPITAL: THEORY AND EVIDENCE

*by Clifford W. Smith, Jr., University of Rochester**

C orporations raise capital by selling a variety of different securities. The *Dealers' Digest* (1985) reports that over $350 billion of public securities sales were underwritten between 1980 and 1984. Of that total, 63 percent was straight debt, 24 percent was common stock, 6 percent was convertible debt, 5 percent was preferred stock, and the remaining 2 percent was convertible preferred stock. Besides choosing among these types of securities, corporate management must also choose among different methods of marketing the securities. In issues that accounted for 95 percent of the total dollars raised between 1980 and 1984, the contracts were negotiated between the issuing firm and its underwriter; in only 5 percent of the offers was the underwriter selected through a competitive bid. Shelf registration, a relatively new procedure for registering securities, was employed in issues accounting for 27 percent of the total dollars raised; the remaining 73 percent was raised through offerings using traditional registration procedures.

Despite the critical role that capital markets play in both financial theory and practice, financial economists have only recently begun to explore the alternative contractual arrangements in the capital raising process and the effect of these choices on a company's cost of issuing securities. This article has two basic aims: (1) to examine the theory and evidence concerning the market's response to security offer announcements by public corporations; and (2) to evaluate the different methods of marketing corporate securities (rights versus underwritten offers, negotiated versus competitive bid contracts, traditional vs. shelf registration, etc.), with attention given to the special case of initial public equity offers.

MARKET REACTIONS TO SECURITY OFFER ANNOUNCEMENTS

A public company seeking external capital must first decide what type of claim to sell. In making that decision, it is important to understand the market's typical reaction to these announcements.

Presented in Table 1 is a summary of the findings of recent academic research on the market's response to announcements of public issues (grouped by industrial firms and utilities) of common stock, preferred stock, convertible preferred stock, straight debt and convertible debt. Perhaps surprisingly, the average abnormal returns (that is, the price movements adjusted for general market price changes) are consistently either negative or not significantly different from zero; in no case is there evidence of a significant positive reaction. Furthermore, the market's response to common stock issues is more strongly negative than its response to preferred stock or debt offerings. It is also more negative to announcements of convertible than non-convertible securities, and more negative to announcements of offerings by industrials than utilities.

I would first like to examine potential explanations of these findings. Let me start by briefly noting a number of arguments that have been

*This article is based on "Investment Banking and the Capital Acquisition Process," *Journal of Financial Economics* (1986). This research was supported by the Managerial Economics Research Center, Graduate School of Management, University of Rochester.

> **Management may possess important information about the company that the market doesn't share. Investors recognize this information disparity and revise their estimate of a company's value in response to management's announced decisions.**

TABLE 1
THE STOCK MARKET RESPONSE TO ANNOUNCEMENTS OF SECURITY OFFERINGS

In the columns below are the average two-day abnormal common stock returns and average sample size (in parentheses) from studies of announcements of security offerings. Returns are weighted averages by sample size of the returns reported by the respective studies listed below. (Unless noted otherwise, returns are significantly different from zero.) Most of these studies appear in the forthcoming issue of the University of Rochester's *Journal of Financial Economics* 15 (1986).

	Types of Issuer	
Type of Security Offering	**Industrial**	**Utility**
Common Stock	-3.14%[a]	-0.75%[b]
	(155)	(403)
Preferred Stock	-0.19% [c,*]	+0.08% [d,*]
	(28)	(249)
Convertible Preferred Stock	-1.44% [d]	-1.38% [d]
	(53)	(8)
Straight Bonds	-0.26% [e,*]	-0.13% [d]
	(248)	(140)
Convertible Bonds	-2.07%[e]	n.a.[g]
	(73)	

[a] Source: Asquith/Mullins (1986), Kolodny/Suhler (1985), Masulis/Korwar (1986), Mikkelson/Partch (1986), Schipper/Smith (1986)
[b] Source: Asquith/Mullins (1986), Masulis/Korwar (1986), Penway/Radcliffe (1985)
[c] Source: Linn/Pinegar (1986), Mikkelson/Partch (1986)
[d] Source: Linn/Pinegar (1986)
[e] Source: Dann/Mikkelson (1984), Eckbo (1986), Mikkelson/Partch (1986)
[f] Source: Eckbo (1986)
[g] Not available (virtually none are issued by utilities)
[*] Interpreted by the authors as not statistically significantly different from zero

proposed to account for at least parts of this overall pattern of market responses, and then go on to consider each in more detail.

EPS Dilution: The increase in the number of shares outstanding resulting from an equity (or convertible) offering is expected to reduce (fully diluted) reported earnings per share, at least in the near term. New equity is also expected to reduce reported ROE. It has been suggested that such anticipated reductions in accounting measures of performance reduce stock prices.

Price Pressure: The demand curve for securities slopes downward. A new offering increases the supply of that security relative to the demand for it, thus causing its price to fall.

Optimal Capital Structure: A new security issue changes a company's capital structure, thus altering its relationship to its optimal capital structure (as perceived by the market).

Insider Information: Management may possess important information about the company that the market doesn't share. Investors recognize this information disparity and revise their estimate of a company's value in response to management's announced decisions. This effect works through two channels:

Implied Cash Flow Change: Security offers reveal inside information about operating profitability; that is, the requirement for external funding may reflect a shortfall in recent or expected future cash flows.

Leverage Change: Increases in corporate leverage are interpreted by the market as reflecting management's confidence about the company's prospects. Conversely, decreases in leverage, such as those brought about by equity offers, reflect management's lack of confidence about future profitability.

Unanticipated Announcements: To the extent an offer is anticipated, its economic impact is already reflected in security prices. Thus, market reactions to less predictable issues should be greater, other things equal, than to more predictable issues.

Ownership Changes: Some security offerings accompany actual or expected changes in the ownership or organization of the company, which in turn can influence market reaction to the announcement.

Before considering each of these possibilities at greater length, let me emphasize that some of the above arguments have more explanatory power than others. But no single explanation accounts, to the exclusion of all others, for the complete pattern of market responses documented by the research.

EPS Dilution

Many analysts argue that announcements of new equity issues depress stock prices because the increase in the number of shares outstanding is expected to result in a reduction, at least in the near term, of reported earnings per share. The expected fall in (near-term) EPS causes stock prices to fall.

Underlying this argument is the assumption that investors respond uncritically to financial statements, mechanically capitalizing EPS figures at standard, industry-wide P/E multiples. Such a view is, of course, completely at odds with the theory of modern finance. In an efficient market, the value of a company's equity—like the value of a bond or any other investment—should reflect the present value of all of its expected future after-tax *cash flows* (discounted at rates which reflect investors' required returns on securities of comparable risk). This view thus implies that even if near-term EPS is expected to fall as the result of a new equity offering, the issuing company's stock price should not fall as long as the market expects management to earn an adequate rate of return on the new funds. In fact, if the equity sale is perceived by the market as providing management with the means of undertaking an exceptionally profitable capital spending program, then the announcement of an equity offering (combined perhaps with an announcement of the capital expenditure plan) should, if anything, cause a company's price to rise.

There remains a strong temptation, of course, to link the negative stock price effects of new equity announcements to the expected earnings reduction. But to accept this argument is to mistake correlation for causality. We must look to other events to assess whether it is the expected earnings dilution that *causes* the market reaction, or whether there are other, more important factors at work. I believe that studies of stock price reactions to accounting changes have provided convincing testimony to the sophistication of the market, which contradicts the claims of the EPS dilution argument.[1] Such studies provide remarkably consistent evidence that markets see through cosmetic accounting changes, and that market price reactions generally reflect changes in the expected underlying cash flows—that is, in the

long-run prospects for the business. In short, there is no plausible theoretical explanation—nor is there credible supporting evidence—that suggests that the reductions in expected EPS accompanying announcements of stock offerings should systematically cause the market to lower companies' stock prices.

Price Pressure

In a somewhat related explanation, some argue that the price reduction associated with the announcement of a new equity or convertible issue is the result of an increase in the supply of a company's equity. This price pressure argument is based on the premise that the demand schedule for the shares of any given company is downward sloping, and that new shares can thus be sold only by offering investors a discount from the market price. The greater the proportional amount of new shares, the larger the discount necessary to effect the sale.

Modern portfolio theory, however, attaches little credibility to the price pressure argument—not, at least, in the case of widely-traded securities in well-established secondary markets. The theory says that investors pricing securities are concerned primarily with risk and expected return. Because the risk and return characteristics of any given stock can be duplicated in many ways through various combinations of other stocks, there are a great many close substitutes for that stock. Given this abundance of close substitutes, economic theory says that the demand curve for corporate securities should more closely approximate a horizontal line than a sharply downward sloping one. A horizontal demand curve in turn implies that an issuing company should be able to sell large quantities of new stock without any discount from the current market price (provided the market does not interpret the stock sale itself as releasing negative insider information about the company's prospects relative to its current value).

What does the available research tell us about the price pressure hypothesis? I will simply mention a few studies bearing on this question.

The first serious study of price pressure was Myron Scholes's doctoral dissertation at the University of Chicago. Scholes examined the effect on share

---

1. For an excellent review of this research, see Ross Watts, "Does It Pay to Manipulate EPS?," *Chase Financial Quarterly* (Spring 1982). Reprinted in *Issues in Corporate Finance* (New York: Stern Stewart & Co., 1983).

prices of large blocks offered through secondary offerings. According to the price pressure hypothesis, the larger the block of shares to be sold, the larger the price decline would have to be to induce increasing numbers of investors to purchase the shares. By contrast, the intrinsic value view suggests that the stock price would be unaffected by the size of the block to be sold. It says that at the right price, the market would readily absorb additional shares.

Scholes found that while stock prices do decline upon the distribution of a large block of shares, the price decline appears to be unrelated to the size of the distribution. This finding suggests that the price discount necessary to distribute the block is better interpreted as a result of the adverse information communicated by a large block sale than as a result of selling pressure. This interpretation was reinforced by the additional finding that the largest price declines were recorded when the secondary sale was made by corporate officers in the company itself—that is, by insiders with possibly privileged information about the company's future.[2]

In another study on price pressure, Avner Kalay and Adam Shimrat recently examined bond price reactions to new equity offers. They reason that if price pressure (and not adverse information) causes the negative stock price reaction, there should be no reduction in the value of the company's outstanding bonds upon the announcement of the stock issue—if anything, the new layer of equity should provide added protection for the bonds and cause their prices to rise. The study, however, documented a significant drop in bond prices, suggesting that the market views an equity offering as bad news, reducing the value of the firm as a whole.[3]

Another recent study of price pressure was conducted by Scott Linn and Mike Pinegar. They examined the price reaction of outstanding preferred stock issues to announcements of new preferred stock issues by the same company. They found that the price of an outstanding preferred stock did not fall with the announcement of an additional new preferred issue, thus providing no support for the operation of price pressure in the market for preferred stock.[4]

In short, there is little empirical evidence in support of price pressure in the market for widely-traded stocks. The observed stock price declines, as I shall suggest later, are more plausibly attributed to negative "information" effects.

Optimal Capital Structure

Financial economists generally agree that firms have an optimal capital structure and a number of researchers have suggested that the price reactions documented in Table 1 reflect companies' attempts to move toward that optimum. This explanation might be useful if we found broad samples of firms experiencing positive market responses to their new security issues. But because the market reaction to most security offerings appears systematically negative (or at best neutral), it is clear that any attempt by firms to move toward a target capital structure is not the dominating factor in the market's response. If we were to use the market's reaction to new security offerings as the basis for any useful generalization about companies' relationship to their optimal structure, we would be put in the embarrassing position of arguing that new security offerings routinely move companies away from, not toward, such an optimum. Thus, I raise this possibility largely to dismiss it.

Information Disparity Between Management and Potential Investors

The documented reductions in firm value associated with security sales—which, after all, are voluntary management decisions—thus present financial economists with a puzzle. One possible explanation is that new security sales are optimal responses by management to changes for the worse in a company's prospects. Alternatively, a company's current market valuation may seem to management to reflect excessive confidence about the future, and it may attempt to exploit such a difference in outlook by "timing" its equity offerings. Investors habituated to stock offerings under such conditions will discount, as a matter of course, the stock prices of companies

---

2. For the published version of Scholes's dissertation, see "Market for Securities: Substitution versus Price Pressure and the Effects of Information on Share *Prices,"* Journal of Business 45 (1972), 179-211.

3. Avner Kalay and Adaen Shimrat, "Firm Value and Seasoned Equity Issue: Price Pressure, Wealth Redistribution, or Negative Information," New York University working paper, 1986.

4. See Scott Linn and J. Michael Pinegar, "The Effect of Issuing Preferred Stock on Common Stockholder Wealth," unpublished manuscript, University of Iowa, 1985.

announcing security offerings. In such circumstances, even if a security sale increases the value of the firm by allowing it to fund profitable projects, it could lead potential investors to suspect that management has a dimmer view of the company's future than that reflected in its current market value.

It is now well documented that managers have better information about the firm's prospects than do outside investors.[5] There is also little doubt that outsiders pay attention to insider trading in making their own investment decisions. Given these observations, I believe that the findings in Table 1 are driven in large part by this potential disparity of information between management and the market, and the incentives it offers management in timing the issue of new securities.

Furthermore, I would argue that, as a result of this potential information disparity, new security offerings affect investors outlook about a company through two primary channels: (a) the implied change in expected net operating cash flow and (b) the leverage change.

Implied Changes in Net operating Cash Flow. Investors, of course, are ultimately interested in a company's capacity to generate cash flow. Although a new security offering might imply that the company has discovered new investment opportunities, it might also imply a shortfall in cash caused by poor current or expected future operating performance. As accounting students learn in their first year of business school, "sources" must equal "uses" of funds. Consequently, an announcement of a new security issue must imply one of the following to investors: (1) an expected increase in new investment expenditure, (2) a reduction in some liability (such as debt retirement or share repurchase) and hence a change in capital structure, (3) an increase in future dividends, or (4) a reduction in expected net operating cash flow. If new security sales were generally used only in anticipation of profitable new investment or to move capital structure closer to an optimal target ratio, then we should expect positive stock price reactions to announcements of new offerings. But if unanticipated security issues come to be associated with reductions in future cash flows from operations, then investors would systematically interpret announcements of security sales as bad news.

This argument can be generalized to consider other announcements which do not explicitly link

sources and uses of funds. Using the above line of reasoning, we would interpret announcements of stock repurchases, increases in investment expenditures, and higher dividend payments as signaling increases in expected operating cash flow and, thus, as good news for investors. Conversely, security offerings, reductions in investment expenditures, and reductions in dividend payments all would imply reductions in expected operating cash flow.

The academic evidence on market responses to announcements of new securities sales, stock repurchases, dividend changes, and changes in capital spending (summarized in Table 2) is broadly consistent with this hypothesis. As shown in the upper panel of Table 2, announcements of security repurchases, dividend increases, and increases in capital spending are greeted systematically by increases in stock prices. The market responds negatively, as a rule, to announcements of security sales, dividend reductions, and decreases in new investment (an exception has been the oil industry in recent years, in which case the market's response to increases in capital spending has been negative, and positive to announced cutbacks in investment). On the basis of this evidence, the market appears to make inferences about changes in operating cash flow from announcements that do not explicitly associate sources with uses of funds.

I should point out, however, that although this explanation helps to explain non-positive price reactions to announcements of all security sales, it provides no insight into the questions of why investors respond more negatively to equity than debt sales, to convertible than non-convertible issues, and to sales by industrials rather than utilities.

Information Disparity and Leverage Changes. Suppose that a potential purchaser of securities has less information about the prospects of the firm than management. Assume, furthermore, that management is more likely to issue securities when the market price of the firm's traded securities is higher than management's assessment of their value. In such a case, sophisticated investors will reduce their estimate of the value of the firm if and when management announces a new security issue. Furthermore, the larger the potential disparity in information between insiders and investors, the greater the revision in expectations and the larger the negative price reaction to the announcement of a new issue.

---

5. See Jeffrey Jaffe's seminal study of insider trading, "Special Information and Insider Trading," *Journal of Business* 47 (1974), 410-420.

Because debt and preferred stock are more senior claims on corporate cash flows,
the values of these securities are generally less sensitive to changes in a company's
prospects than is the value of common stock.

TABLE 2
THE STOCK MARKET
RESPONSE TO
ANNOUNCEMENTS OF
CHANGES IN FINANCING,
DIVIDEND, AND
INVESTMENT POLICY

In the columns below are the average two-day common stock abnormal returns and average sample size from studies of changes in financing, dividend, and investment policy grouped by implied changes in corporate cash flows. Returns are weighted averages by sample size of the returns reported by the respective studies. (Unless otherwise noted, returns are significantly different from zero.) Full citations for all studies mentioned can be found in the reference section at the end of this issue.

Type of Announcement	Average Sample Size	Two-Day Announcement Period Return
Implied Increase in Corporate Cash Flow		
Common Stock Repurchases:		
Intra-firm tender offer[a]	148	16.2%
Open market repurchase[b]	182	3.6
Targeted small holding[c]	15	1.6
Calls of Non-Convertible Bonds[d]	133	-0.1*
Dividend Increases:		
Dividend initiation[e]	160	3.7
Dividend increase[f]	280	0.9
Specially designated dividend[g]	164	2.1
Investment Increases[h]	510	1.0
Implied Decrease in Corporate Cash Flow		
Security Sales:		
Common stock[i]	262	-1.6
Preferred stock[j]	102	0.1*
Convertible preferred[k]	30	-1.4
Straight debt[l]	221	-0.2*
Convertible debt[l]	80	-2.1
Dividend Decreases[f]	48	-3.6
Investment Decreases[h]	111	-1.1

[a] Source: Dann (1981), Masulis (1980), Vermalen (1981), Rosenfeld (1982)
[b] Source: Dann (1980), Vermalen (1981)
[c] Source: Bradley/Wakeman (1983)
[d] Source: Vu (1986)
[e] Source: Asquith/Mullins (1983)
[f] Source: Charest (1978), Aharony/Swary (1980)
[g] Source Brickley (1983)
[h] Source: McConnell/Muscarella (1985)
[i] Source: Asquith/Mullins (1986), Masulis/Korwar (1986), Mikkelson/Partch (1986), Schipper/Smith (1986), Pettway/Radcliff (1985)
[j] Source: Linn/Pinegar (1986), Mikkelson/Partch (1986)
[k] Source: Linn/Pinegar (1986)
[l] Source: Dann/Mikkelson (1984), Eckbo (1986), Mikkelson/Partch (1986)
* Interpreted by the authors as not significantly different from zero.

Because debt and preferred stock are more senior claims on corporate cash flows, the values of these securities are generally less sensitive to changes in a company's prospects than is the value of common stock. Thus, this problem of potential insider information that management faces whenever it issues a new security is most acute in the case of equity offerings. Similarly the values of convertible debt and convertible preferred stock are also generally more sensitive to changes in firm value than non-convertible debt and preferred because of their equity component—but less sensitive, of course, than common stock; hence the information disparity should be more problematic for convertible than for straight securities.

**The market responds positively to leverage-increasing transactions and negatively
to leverage-decreasing transactions; the larger the change in leverage,
the greater the price reaction.**

The case of utility offerings is somewhat different. In the rate regulation process, managers of utilities generally petition their respective regulatory authorities for permission to proceed with a new security issue. This petitioning process should reduce the price reaction of utilities announcements relative to industrials for three reasons: (1) it could reduce the differential information between manager and outsiders; (2) it could limit managers' discretion as to what security to sell; (3) it could reduce managers ability to "time" security offerings to take advantage of inside information. Because of this regulatory process, utilities do not face as great a problem in persuading the market to accept its securities at current prices.

Thus, while this information disparity hypothesis does not predict whether the response to announcements of debt and preferred issues will be negative or positive, it does predict that the reaction to common stock sales will be more negative than the response to preferred or debt, more negative to convertible than non-convertible issues, and to industrial than utility offers.[6]

This second, leverage-related channel through which the information disparity problem operates can be distinguished from the implied cash flow explanation by examining evidence from events that *explicitly* associate sources and uses of funds: namely, exchange offers, conversion-forcing calls of convertible securities, and security sales in which the proceeds are explicitly intended for debt retirement. Research on announcements of these transactions (summarized in Table 3) documents the following: (1) the market responds positively to leverage-increasing transactions and negatively to leverage-decreasing transactions; (2) the larger the change in leverage, the greater the price reaction. Accordingly, debt-for-common offers have larger positive stock price reactions than preferred-for-common offers, and common-for-debt offers have larger negative price reactions than common-for-preferred offers.

In Table 4 the analysis of the two channels is combined to provide additional insight into the information disparity explanation. The events to the upper left of the table tend to have positive stock price reactions, those in the lower right tend to have negative reactions, while those along the diagonal tend to be insignificant.

Hence, a common stock offering, which implies both a reduction in future operating cash flow and a reduction in leverage, prompts the largest negative market response of all the security offers. A stock repurchase, by contrast, suggests increases both in operating cash and leverage, and accordingly receives strong endorsement by the market. It seems to provide a credible expression to investors of management's confidence about the company's future performance (at least relative to its current value).

Unanticipated Announcements

Because stock price changes reflect only the unanticipated component of announcements of corporate events, the stock price change at the announcement of a security offering will be larger, all else equal, the more unpredictable is the announcement. For example, debt repayment (either from maturing issues or sinking-fund provisions) requires the firm to issue additional debt to maintain its capital structure. Given a target capital structure and stable cash flows, debt repayment must be matched with a new debt issue; hence the more predictable are principal repayments, the more predictable will be new debt issues. Similarly, the predictability of earnings (and thus internally generated equity) will determine the predictability of a new equity issue. Therefore, one should expect a new debt issue to be more predictable than a new equity issue because principal repayments are more predictable than earnings.

Another reason for the greater predictability of public debt offerings is related to the cost structures of public versus private debt. Flotation costs for publicly-placed debt appear to have a larger fixed component and more pronounced economies of scale than bank debt. Thus, a firm tends to use bank lines of credit until an efficient public issue size is reached; then the firm issues public debt and retires the bank debt. If investors can observe the amount of bank borrowing and the pattern of public debt issues, then more predictable announcements of public bond issues should have smaller price reactions.

Utilities use external capital markets with far greater frequency than industrials, thus making utility issues more predictable. For this reason alone we would expect utilities' stock prices to exhibit a

---

6. But if the evidence across classes of securities is consistent with the information asymmetry hypothesis, some data within security classes is apparently inconsistent. When Eckbo (1986) and Mikkelson/Partch (1986) disaggregate their bond data by rating class, neither study finds higher rated, less risky (and thus less sensitive to firm value) bonds to be associated with smaller abnormal returns. Eckbo also finds more negative abnormal returns to mortgage bonds than non-mortgage bonds. (References for studies are cited in full at the end of this issue.)

A stock repurchase, by contrast, suggests increases both in operating cash and leverage, and accordingly receives strong endorsement by the market.

TABLE 3
THE STOCK MARKET
RESPONSE TO
ANNOUNCEMENTS OF
PURE FINANCIAL
STRUCTURE CHANGES:
EXCHANGE OFFERS, SECURITY
SALES WITH DESIGNATED USES OF
FUNDS, AND CALLS OF
CONVERTIBLE SECURITIES

Below is a summary of two-day announcement effects associated with the events listed above. Because each of these transactions explicitly associate sources with uses of funds, they represent virtually pure financial structure changes. (Unless otherwise noted, returns are significantly different from zero.) Full citations for all studies mentioned can be found in the reference section at the end of the article.

Type of Transaction	Security Issued	Security Retired	Average Sample Size	Two-Day Announcement Period Return
Leverage-Increasing Transactions				
Stock Repurchases[a]	Debt	Common	45	21.9%
Exchange Offer[b]	Debt	Common	52	14.0
Exchange Offer[b]	Preferred	Common	9	8.3
Exchange Offer[b]	Debt	Preferred	24	2.2
Exchange Offer[c]	Income Bonds	Preferred	24	2.2
Transactions with No Change in Leverage				
Exchange Offer[d]	Debt	Debt	36	0.6*
Security Sale[e]	Debt	Debt	83	0.2*
Leverage-Reducing Transactions				
Conversion-forcing Call[c]	Common	Convertible	57	-0.4*
Conversion-forcing Call[c]	Common	Preferred	113	-2.1
Security Sale[f]	Convertible Debt	Convertible Bond	15	-2.4
Exchange Offer[b]	Common	Debt	30	-2.6
Exchange Offer[b]	Preferred	Preferred	9	-7.7
Security Sale[f]	Common	Debt	12	-4.2
Exchange Offer[c]	Common	Debt	20	-9.9
		Debt		

[a] Source: Masulis (1980)
[b] Source: Masulis (1983) (Note: These returns include announcement days of both the original offer and, for about 40 percent of the sample, a second announcement of specific terms of the exchange.)
[c] Source: McConnell/Schlarbaum (1981)
[d] Source: Dietrich (1984)
[e] Source: Mikkelson (1981)
[f] Source: Eckbo (1986) and Mikkelson/Partch (1986)
* Not statistically different from zero.

smaller reaction to announcements of new security sales. In short, the relative predictability of announcements of security offerings helps explain both the observed differences in market reactions to common stock versus debt issues and to the offerings of industrials versus those of utilities.

Changes in Ownership and Control

Some security sales involve potentially important changes in ownership or organizational structure. In such transactions, part of the observed price reaction may reflect important changes in the ownership and control of the firm. For example, equity carve-outs (also known as partial public offerings) are transactions in which firms sell a minority interest in the common stock

of a previously wholly-owned subsidiary. In contrast to the negative returns from the sale of corporate common stock reported earlier equity carve-outs are associated with significant *positive* returns of 1.8 percent for the five days around the announcement.

In this case, the problem of the potential information disparity which appears to plague equity offerings seems to be offset by positive signals to investors. What are these signals? As Katherine Schipper and Abbie Smith have argued in their important study, equity carve-outs may suggest to the market that management feels the consolidated firm is not receiving full credit in its current stock price for the value of one of its subsidiaries. If such is the information management communicates by offering separate equity claims on an "undervalued" subsidiary, then

TABLE 4

| | | IMPLIED CASH FLOW CHANGE | | |
		Negative	No Change	Positive
LEVERAGE CHANGE	**No Change**	Common Sale	Convertible Bond Sale to Retire Debt Common/Preferred E.O. Preferred/Debt E.O. Common/Debt E.O. Common Sale to Retire Debt Call of Convertible Bonds Call of Convertible Preferred	Calls of Non-Convertible Bonds
	Negative	Convertible Preferred Sale Convertible Debt Sale Investment Decrease Dividend Decrease	Debt E.O./Debt E.O.	Dividend Increases Investment Increases
	Positive	Preferred Sale Debt Sale	Common Repurchase Finance with Debt Debt/Common E.O. Preferred/Common E.O. Debt/Preferred E.O. Income Bond/Preferred E.O.	Common Repurchase

Significant Negative Stock Price Reaction

Insignificant Stock Price Reaction

Significant Positive Stock Price Reaction

carve-outs could provide a means of raising new equity capital that neutralizes the negative signal released by announcements of seasoned equity offerings. Also worth noting, the public sale of a minority interest in a subsidiary carries potentially important control implications. For example, the sale of subsidiary stock allows management of the subsidiary to have a market-based compensation package that more accurately reflects the subsidiary's operating performance. In fact, 94 percent of the carve-outs studied adopted incentive compensation plans based on the subsidiary's stock.[7]

Academic research in general suggests that changes in ownership and organization affect stock prices (see Table 5). The evidence summarized in the upper panel suggests that voluntary organizational restructuring on average benefits stockholders. The research findings summarized in the lower panel suggests that announcements of transactions that increase ownership concentration raise share prices while those that reduce concentration lower share prices. For example, in equity offers where a registered secondary offering by the firm's management accompanied the primary equity, the average stock price reaction was -4.5 percent, almost 1.5 percent more negative than the average response to

industrial equity offerings. This is the case, incidentally, in which the information problem becomes most acute: not only is the firm issuing new stock, but management is using the offering to further reduce its ownership stake—the reverse of a leveraged buyout.

Summing Up the Market's Reaction to Securities Offerings

Table 6 offers a pictorial summary of the various hypotheses and how each contributes to our understanding of the research findings on new security issues. Those arguments focusing on the information gap between management and investors appear to have the most explanatory power. The extent to which announcements are unanticipated helps explain differences in the market's response to debt vs. equity offerings, and to industrial vs. utility issues. And in the special cases when the offer accompanies ownership or organizational changes, there are important additional insights available. The price pressure hypothesis may have some validity, but for widely-traded securities I remain skeptical. The dilutive effects on EPS and ROE of new equity and convertible offerings are nothing more than accounting illusions; *given* that the security

7. See the article immediately following in this journal: Katherine Schipper and Abbie Smith, "Equity Carve-outs." See also the academic piece on which the above article is based, "A Comparison of Equity Carve-outs and Seasoned Equity

Offerings: Share Price Effects and Corporate Restructuring," *Journal of Financial Economics* 15 (1986), pp.153-186.

Carve-outs could provide a means of raising new equity capital that neutralizes the negative signal released by announcements of seasoned equity offerings.

TABLE 5
THE MARKET RESPONSE
TO ANNOUNCEMENTS OF
ORGANIZATIONAL AND
OWNERSHIP CHANGES

In the columns below are summaries of the cumulative average abnormal common stock returns and average sample size from studies of announcements of transactions which change corporate control or ownership structure. Returns are weighted averages by sample size of the returns reported by the respective studies. (Unless otherwise noted, returns are significantly different from zero.) Full citations for all studies mentioned can he found in the reference section at the end of this issue.

Type of Announcement	Average Sample Size	Cumulative Abnormal Returns
Organizational Restructuring		
Merger: Target[a]	113	20.0%
Bidder[a]	119	0.7*
Spin-Off[b]	76	3.4
Sell-Off: Seller[c]	279	0.7
Buyer[d]	118	0.7
Equity Carve-Out[e]	76	0.7*
Joint Venture[f]	136	0.7
Going Private[g]	81	30.0
Voluntary Liquidation[h]	75	33.4
Life Insurance Company Mutualization[i]	30	56.0
Savings & Loan Association Charter Conversion[j]	78	5.6
Proxy Fights[k]	56	1.1
Ownership Restructuring		
Tender Offer: Target[l]	183	30.0
Bidder[l]	183	0.8*
Large Block Acquisition[m]	165	2.6
Secondary Distribution: Registered[n]	146	-2.9
Non-Registered[n]	321	-0.8
Targeted Share Repurchase[o]	68	-4.8

[a] Source: Dann (1980), Asquith (1983), Eckbo (1983), Jensen/Ruback (1983)
[b] Source: Hite/Owers (1983), Miles/Rosenfeld (1983), Schipper/Smith (983), Rosenfeld (1984)
[c] Source: Alexander/Benson/Kampmeyer (1984), Rosenfeld (1984), Hite/Owers (1985), Jain (1985), Klein (1985), Vetsuypens (1985)
[d] Source: Rosenfeld (1984), Hite/Owers (1985), Jain (1985), Klein (1985)
[e] Source: Schipper/Smith (1986)
[f] Source: McConnell/Nantell (1985)
[g] Source: DeAngelo/DeAngelo/Rice (1984)
[h] Source: Kim/Schatzberg (1985)
[i] Source: Mayers/Smith (1986)
[j] Source: Masulis (1986)
[k] Source: Dodd/Warner (1983)
[l] Source: Bradley/Desai/Kim (1985), Jensen/Ruback (1983)
[m] Source: Holderness/Sheehan (1985), Mikkelson/Ruback (1985)
[n] Source: Mikkelson/Partch (1985)
[o] Source: Dann/DeAngelo (1983), Bradley/Wakeman (1983)
* Interpreted by the authors as not significantly different from zero.

is fairly priced at issue, and that management expects to earn its cost of capital on the funds newly raised, there is no real economic dilution of value caused by a new equity offering. Finally, optimal capital structure theories, at this stage of development, seem to offer little insight into the general pattern of price reactions to new security sales.

Alternative Methods of Marketing Security Offerings

Once having decided on the terms of a security to sell, management then must choose among a number of methods to market the issue. It can offer the securities on a pro rata basis to its own stock-

Despite evidence that the out-of-pocket expenses of an equity issue underwritten by
an investment banker are from three to 30 times higher than
the costs of a non-underwritten rights offering, over 80 percent of
equity offerings employ underwriters.

TABLE 6

			RESEARCH FINDING		
		Returns < 0	Common < Debt or Preferred	Convertibles < Non-Convertibles	Industrials < Utilities
POTENTIAL EXPLANATIONS	Optimal Capital Structure	No	No	No	No
	Implied Cash Flow Change	Yes	No	No	No
	Leverage Change	No	Yes+	Yes	Yes
	Unanticipated Announcements	No	Yes	No	Yes
	Ownership Changes	Yes*	Yes*	Yes*	No
	Price Pressure	No	No	No	No

+ But only for Debt, not Preferred
* In Special Cases

holders through a rights offering, it can hire an underwriter to offer the securities for sale to the public, or it can place the securities privately. If management chooses to use an underwriter, it can negotiate the offer terms with the underwriter, or it can structure the offering internally and then put it out for competitive bid. The underwriting contract can be a firm commitment or a best efforts offering. Finally, the issue can be registered with the Securities and Exchange Commission under its traditional registration procedures; or, if the firm qualifies, it can file a shelf registration in which it registers all securities it intends to sell over the next two years.

Let's look at the major alternatives for marketing securities to provide a better understanding of why certain methods predominate.

Rights versus Underwritten Offerings

The two most frequently used methods by which public corporations sell new equity are firm-commitment underwritten offerings and rights offerings. In an underwritten offering, the firm in effect sells the issue to an investment bank, which resells the issue to public investors (or forms a syndicate with other investment banks to do so). The initial phases of negotiation between the issuing company and the investment banker focus on the amount of capital, the type of security, and the terms of the offering. If the firm and its chosen underwriter agree to proceed, the underwriter begins to assess the prospects, puts together an underwriting syndicate, prepares a registration statement, and performs what is known as a "due diligence" investigation into the financial condition of the company.

In a rights offering, each stockholder receives options (or, more precisely, warrants) to buy the newly issued securities. One right is issued for each share held. Rights offerings also must be registered with the SEC.

Despite evidence that the out-of-pocket expenses of an equity issue underwritten by an investment banker are from three to 30 times higher than the costs of a non-underwritten rights offering,[8] over 80 percent of equity offerings employ underwriters. Perhaps the most plausible rationale for using underwriters is that they are effective in monitoring the firm's activities and thus provide implicit guarantees to investors when they sell the securities. This monitoring function would be especially valuable in light of the information disparity between managers and outside stockholders discussed in the first part of this article.

Thus, in addition to providing distribution channels between issuing corporations and investors, the investment banker performs a monitoring function analogous to that which bond rating

8. See my paper, "Alternative Methods for Raising Capital: Rights versus Underwritten Offerings," *Journal of Financial Economics* 5 (1977), 273-307.

agencies perform for bondholders and auditing firms perform for investors and other corporate claimholders. While such activities are expensive, such monitoring of management increases the value of the firm by raising the price investors are willing to pay for the company's securities

Negotiated versus Competitive Bid Contracts

The evidence also suggests that competitive bid offerings involve lower total flotation costs than negotiated offers.[9] In fact, it has been estimated that companies which use negotiated contracts can expect their total issue costs to be higher, on average, by 1.2 percent of the proceeds. Nevertheless, the primary users of competitive bids are regulated firms which are required to do so. Companies not facing this regulatory constraint (Rule 50 of the Public Utilities Holding Company Act) appear overwhelmingly to choose negotiated offers.

This behavior may be attributed partly to the fact that the variance of issuing costs has been found to be higher for competitive bid than for negotiated offers. Executives whose compensation is tied to accounting earnings might prefer a more stable, if somewhat lower, bottom line resulting from the use of negotiated offerings. Another potentially important problem with competitive bids is the difficulty in restricting the use of information received by investment bankers not awarded the contract. Hence, companies with valuable proprietary information are likely to find the confidentiality afforded by negotiated bids more attractive.

Probably most important, though, is that the monitoring, and thus the guarantee provided investors, is much more effective in the case of negotiated offerings than in competitive bids. With a negotiated offer, the issuing firm has less control over the terms and timing of the offer; hence, investors have fewer worries that the issue will be structured to exploit their information disadvantage.

This leads me to generalize about the kinds of companies which are likely to benefit from using competitive bids. The less the potential disparity between management's and the market's estima-

tion of the value of the company, the greater are the likely savings to a company from using the competitive bidding process. For this reason, regulated utilities (those not already subject to Rule 50) stand to benefit more from the use of competitive bids than unregulated firms. Also, in the case of more senior claims such as debt and preferred stock, the informational asymmetry problem is less pronounced, as I have suggested, because the value of the claim is less sensitive to firm value. Thus straight debt, secured debt and non-convertible preferred stock should all be sold through competitive bids more frequently than common stock, convertible preferred stock or convertible bonds. And this is apparently the case.[10]

Shelf versus Traditional Registration

Prior to any public security offering, the issue must be registered with the SEC. Using traditional registration procedures, the issuing firm, its investment banker, its auditing firm, and its law firm all typically participate in filing the required registration statements with the SEC (as well as with the appropriate state securities commissions). The offering can only proceed when the registration statement becomes effective.

In March of 1982, however, the SEC authorized Rule 415 on an experimental basis, and it was made permanent in November 1983. It permits companies with more than $150 million of stock held by investors unaffiliated with the company to specify and register the total dollar amount of securities they expect to offer publicly over the next two years. The procedure is called shelf registration because it allows companies to register their securities, "put them on the shelf" and then issue the securities whenever they choose.

After the securities are registered, management can then offer and sell them for up to two years on a continuous basis. Rule 415 also allows the company to modify a debt instrument and sell it without first filing an amendment to the registration Statement. Thus, shelf registration allows qualifying firms additional flexibility both in structuring debt issues and in timing all security issues.

---

9. See Sanjai Bhagat and Peter Frost, "Issuing Costs to Existing Shareholders in Competitive and Negotiated Underwritten Public Utility Equity Offerings," *Journal of Financial Economics* 15 (1986).

10. See the article which appears later in this issue, James R. Booth and Richard L. Smith, "The Certification Role of the Investment Banker in the Pricing of New Issues." The article is based on their study, "Capital Raising, Underwriting and the Certification Hypothesis," *Journal of Financial Economics* 15 (1986).

Because of the additional flexibility afforded management by the shelf procedure, there is greater opportunity for management to exploit its inside information and issue (temporarily) overvalued securities. Thus, the information disparity problem attending new issues should be especially great in cases of shelf registration. Potential investors anticipating this problem will exact an even larger discount in the case of shelf offerings than in offerings registered through traditional procedures. Hence stock price reactions to announcements of new offerings registered under Rule 415 could be more negative, other things equal, than those under traditional registration procedures.

It is largely for this reason, I would argue, that shelf registration has been used far more frequently with debt than with equity offerings.

A Special Case: Initial Public Offerings

Private firms that choose to go public typically obtain the services of an underwriter with which to negotiate an initial public equity offering (IPO). IPOs are an interesting special case of security offers. They differ from offerings previously discussed in two important ways: (1) the uncertainty about the market clearing price of the offering is significantly greater than for public corporations with claims currently trading; (2) because the firm has no traded shares, examination of stock price reactions to initial announcements is impossible. The first difference affects the way these securities are marketed; the second limits the ways researchers can study the offerings.

Underpricing

The stock price behavior of IPOs from the time the initial offer price is set until the security first trades in the aftermarket demonstrates unmistakably that the average issue is offered at a significant discount from the price expected in the aftermarket. In fact the average underpricing appears to exceed 15 percent. (For a summary of the results of studies of offer prices for initial public equity offerings as well as new issues of seasoned equity and bonds, see Table 7.) Once the issue has begun trading in the aftermarket, however, the returns to stockholders appear to be normal.

In an IPO, as suggested, there is a large amount of uncertainty about the market-clearing price. Furthermore, as some observers have argued, this uncertainty creates a special problem if some investors are considerably more knowledgable than others—for example, institutions relative to, say, individuals (especially since the Rules of Fair Practice of the NASD prohibit raising the price if the issue is oversubscribed). Assume, for the sake of simplicity, that we can divide all potential investors into two distinct groups: "informed" and "uninformed." Under these conditions, if the initial offer price were set at its expected market-clearing price, it is not difficult to demonstrate that uninformed investors would earn systematically below normal returns. If an issue is believed by informed investors to be underpriced, then those investors will submit bids and the issue will be rationed among informed and uninformed investors alike. If the issue is overpriced, however, informed investors are less likely to submit bids and the issue is more likely to be undersubscribed. In this process, uninformed investors systematically receive more of overpriced issues and less of under-priced issues.[11]

Recognizing their disadvantaged position in this bidding process, uninformed investors will respond by bidding for IPOs only if the offer price is systematically below their estimate of the aftermarket price in order to compensate them for their expected losses on overpriced issues. Such a bidding process would also account for the well-documented observation that underpricing is greater for issues with greater price uncertainty.

The above explanation has been tested using data from IPOs in the following way. Given that there is an equilibrium amount of underpricing (i.e., one which has proved to be acceptable to issuers in order to sell the issue), we can hypothesize that an investment banker that repeatedly prices issues below this equilibrium level will lose the opportunity for further business. If the investment banker repeatedly overprices (or does not underprice by enough), however, he loses investors.

A recent study by Randy Beatty and Jay Ritter estimated an underpricing equilibrium and then examined the average deviation from that level of underpricing by 49 investment bankers who handled

---

11. For a systematic formulation of this "informed-uninformed" investor dichotomy and its effects on IPO pricing, see Kevin Rock, "Why New Issues Are Underpriced," *Journal of Financial Economics* 15 (1986).

> **Recognizing their disadvantaged position in this bidding process, uninformed investors will respond by bidding for IPOs only if the offer price is systematically below their estimate of the after-market price to compensate them for their expected losses on overpriced issues.**

TABLE 7
THE UNDERPRICING OF
NEW SECURITY ISSUES

Presented below is a summary of estimates of the underpricing of new securities at issuance by type of offering. Underpricing is measured by the average percentage change from offer prices to aftermarket price. Full citations for all studies mentioned can be found in the reference section at the end of this issue.

Type of Offering	Study	Sample Period	Sample Size	Estimated Underpricing
Initial Public Equity Offering	Ibbotson (1974)	1960-1969	120	11.4%
Initial Public Equity Offering	Ibbotson/Jaffe (1975)	1960-1970	2650	16.8
Initial Public Equity Offering	Ritter (1984)	1960-1982	5162	18.8
		1977-1982	1028	26.5
		1980-1981	325	48.4
Initial Public Equity Offering	Ritter (1985)	1977-1982		
Firm Commitment			664	14.8
Best Efforts			364	47.8
Initial Public Equity Offering	Chalk/Peavy (1985)	1974-1982	440	13.8
Firm Commitment			415	10.6
Best Efforts			82	52.0
Equity Carve-Outs	Schipper/Smith (1986)	1965-1983	36	0.19
Seasoned New Equity Offering	Bhagat/Frost (1986)	1973-1980	552	-0.30
Negotiated			479	-0.25
Competitive Bid			73	-0.65
Primary Debt Issue	Weinstein (1978)	1962-1974	412	0.05
	Sorenson (1982)	1974-1980	900	0.50
	Smith (1986)	1977-1982	132	1.60

four or more initial public offerings during the period 1977-1981. When they compared the subsequent performance of the 24 underwriters whose average deviation from their estimated normal underpricing was greatest with that of the remaining 25 underwriters, the market share of those 24 firms fell from 46.6 to 24.5 percent during 1981-1982; and five of the 24 actually closed down. For those 25 with the smallest deviation from the estimated underpricing equilibrium, market share goes from 27.2 to 21.0 percent, and only one of the 25 ceases operation. (The remaining 54.5 percent of the business in 1981-1982 was underwritten by firms which did fewer than four IPOs from 1977-1981.)[12]

As Table 7 shows, security issues by public corporations are also typically underpriced, but much less so than in the case of IPOs Seasoned new equity issues have been found to be underpriced by 0.6 percent. There is some disagreement about the degree

of underpricing of seasoned bonds, with estimates ranging from 0.05 percent to as high as 1.2 percent of the offer price. Seasoned equity issues by utilities, however, appear to be *overpriced* by 0.3 percent.

Best Efforts versus Firm Commitment Contracts

There are two alternative forms of underwriting contracts that are typically used in IPOs The first is a firm commitment underwriting agreement, in which the underwriter agrees to purchase the whole issue from the firm at a specified price for resale to the public. The second is a "best efforts" agreement. In such an arrangement, the underwriter acts only as a marketing agent for the firm. The underwriter does not agree to purchase the issue at a predetermined price, but simply sells as much of the security as it can and takes a predetermined spread. The

---

12. See Randolph P. Beatty and Jay R. Ritter, "Investment Banking, Reputation, and the Underpricing of Initial Public Offerings," *Journal of Financial Economics* 15 (1986).

> In a best efforts contract, the firm provides potential investors not only with an implicit call option (because of the rule against raising the price), but also gives them the option to put the shares back to the firm if the issue is undersubscribed. The Green Shoe option is equivalent to granting the investment banker a warrant with an exercise price equal to the offer price in the issue.

issuing company gets the net proceeds, but without any guarantee of the final amount from the investment banker. This agreement generally specifies a minimum amount that must be sold within a given period of time; if this amount is not reached, the offering is cancelled. From 1977-1982, 35 percent of all IPOs were sold with best efforts contracts. Those issues, however, raised only 13 percent of the gross proceeds from IPOs over that period, implying that larger IPOs tend to use the firm commitment method.

The choice between firm commitment and best efforts comes down, once again I think, to resolving the problems created by the information disparity between informed and uninformed investors. The preceding argument for underpricing firm commitments can be contrasted with the incentives in a best efforts contract. Consider that in the case of a best efforts IPO, if the issue is overpriced and the issue sales fall short of the minimum specified in the underwriting contract, the offer is cancelled and the losses to uninformed investors are reduced. Structuring the contract in this manner reduces the problem faced by uninformed potential security holders, and thus reduces the discount necessary to induce them to bid.

Thus, the relative attractiveness of the two types of contracts will be determined, in part, by the amount of uncertainty associated with the price of the issue. The prohibition against raising prices for an oversubscribed issue (imposed by the NASD's Rules of Fair Practice) means that the company has effectively given a free call option to potential stockholders. Thus, relative to a best efforts contract, the expected proceeds to the issuer in a firm commitment IPO are reduced as the amount of uncertainty about after-market prices increases. In a best efforts contract, the firm provides potential investors not only with an implicit call option (because of the rule against raising the price), but also gives them the option to put the shares back to the firm if the issue is undersubscribed. Because of these implicit options provided investors in best efforts contracts, the greater the uncertainty about the after-market price of an IPO, the more attractive are best efforts contracts to investors; hence, the

more likely are issuers to choose that form over a firm commitment.

To summarize, firm commitment offerings are more likely the less the uncertainty about the market-clearing security price. Consistent with this hypothesis, one study found that the average standard deviation of the aftermarket rates of returns for 285 best efforts offerings was 7.6 percent in contrast to a 4.2 percent standard deviation for 641 firm commitment offerings.[13]

Stabilization Activity and the Green Shoe Option

Underwriters typically attempt to stabilize prices around the offer date of a security. In the case of primary equity offers by listed firms, this stabilization is accomplished by placing a limit order to purchase shares with the specialist on the exchange. I believe this activity represents a bonding mechanism by the investment banker—one that promises investors that if the issue is overpriced, they can sell their shares into the stabilizing bid, thereby cancelling the transaction.

The Green Shoe option (so named because it was originally used in an offering by the Green Shoe Company) is frequently employed in underwritten equity offers. It gives the underwriter the right to buy additional shares from the firm at the offer price. This is equivalent to granting the investment banker a warrant with an exercise price equal to the offer price in the issue. The total quantity of shares exercisable under this option typically ranges between 10 and 20 percent of the offer. Obviously, the option is more valuable if the offer price is below the market value of the shares; thus, the Green Shoe option is another potentially effective bonding mechanism by which the investment banker reassures investors that the issue will not be overpriced. That is, if a new offering prospectus contains a Green Shoe provision, potential investors (especially the less-informed) will reduce their forecast of the probability that the issue will be overpriced because the returns to the underwriter from the Green Shoe are lower if the warrant cannot be exercised.

---

13. See Jay Ritter, "The 'Hot Issue' Market of 1980," *Journal of Business* 57 (1984).

Implications for Corporate Policy

Recent research on the stock market response to new security offers consistently documents a significant negative reaction (on the order of 3 to 4 percent on average) to announcements of new equity issues by industrial companies. Convertible issues, both debt and preferred, also typically are greeted by a negative, though smaller, price change (of roughly 1 to 2 percent). By contrast, the market reaction to straight debt and preferred issues appears to be neutral.

The critical question, of course, is: Why does the market systematically lower the stock prices of companies announcing new stock and convertible offers? Such financing decisions, after all, are voluntary choices by management intended, presumably, to increase the long-run value of the firm by providing necessary funding.

After consideration of several possible explanations, I argue that the primary cause of this negative response is the potential for management to exploit its inside information by issuing overvalued equity (or convertibles, which of course have an equity component). Investors recognize their vulnerability in this process and accordingly reduce their estimate of the firm's value. The result, in the average case, is that the new equity is purchased by investors at a discount from the pre-announcement price.

This theory and evidence has a number of managerial implications. Perhaps the most important is that management should be sensitive to the way the market is likely to interpret its announcement of a new issue. For example, if the company is contemplating a primary equity offering and an executive asks to include a registered secondary in the offer, the board of directors should recognize that this can be a very expensive perk; in such cases the market price typically falls by almost 5 percent upon the announcement. This is probably the surest means of arousing the market's suspicion that insiders have a different view of the company's future than that reflected in the current stock price.

Perhaps the best way for management to overcome this information problem is to state, as clearly as possible, the intended uses for the funds. For example, if management intends to use the proceeds for plant expansion, management should say so—emphatically. We know that the market responds positively, on average, to announcements of increases in capital spending plans (with the exception of the case of oil companies in recent years, where the reverse has been true).[14] Consequently, short of revealing proprietary information which could compromise the firm's competitive position,[15] management should benefit from the attempt to be as forthright as possible in sharing with the investment community its investment opportunities, corporate objectives, capital structure targets, and so forth.

This strategy is not meant to contradict the obvious: namely, that current stockholders benefit when management issues stock or convertibles when the market price proves to have been high; and that debt or preferred stock is better if the company proves to be undervalued (though, in the absence of significant inside information, I would suggest that this can only be determined with hindsight). The problem, however, is that this kind of managerial opportunism may prove an expensive strategy for a firm that wants to maintain its access to capital markets. If management develops a reputation for exploiting inside information, the price discount the market exacts for accepting subsequent new issues could be even larger.

In the second part of the article, I attempt to show how the use of investment bankers as underwriters also helps to solve this financing problem arising from the possibility of insider information. The fact that management may have an incentive to issue overvalued securities causes a demand for "bonding" the firm's actions—that is, investors will offer more for the securities if they are provided a credible promise that they will not be exploited.

In those cases where the information disparity between management and investors is likely to be greatest, and to have the worst potential consequences for new investors (i.e., for equity holders, and especially in the case of smaller firms in less heavily traded markets), the demand for the bond-

---

14. A study by John McConnell and Chris Muscarella ("Corporate Capital Expenditure Decisions and the Market Value of the Firm," *Journal of Financial Economics* 14 (1985)) found that announcements of increases of corporate capital spending were accompanied by a 1 percent increase, on average, of the announcing company's stock price.

15. For example, when Texas Gulf Sulphur discovered substantial mineral deposits in Canada, immediate release of this information would have substantially increased the cost of adjacent mineral rights then under negotiation.

The largest price declines were recorded when the secondary sale was made by corporate officers in the company itself—that is, by insiders with possibly privileged information about the company's future.

ing or certification provided by the banker is also likely to be the greatest. For this reason I have argued that underwritten issues provide stronger guarantees to investors than rights offers; issues with negotiated underwriting contracts are more strongly bonded than competitive bid issues; issues registered using traditional procedures are more strongly bonded than those employing the new shelf registration procedures; and issues containing a Green Shoe option are more strongly bonded than those without. Therefore, for example, an industrial equity issue should more frequently be registered using traditional rather than shelf registration procedures, and sold under a negotiated, firm commitment rather than a competitive bid contract; it is also more likely to include a Green Shoe option. By contrast, a non-convertible debt issue by a utility is more likely to be sold under a competitive bid contract and registered using the new shelf registration procedures.

The above argument is not to deny that shelf registration procedures have significantly lowered the fixed costs of public issues for some industrial companies. In fact it should be especially cost-effective for large, well-established companies, especially in the case of public debt offers.

To take greatest advantage of the potential savings from shelf registration, I believe that management must change some of its practices with respect to debt offerings. Instead of using a line of credit at a bank until a large public issue can be made, qualifying companies could use the shelf registration process to place several smaller issues. In order to retain the additional liquidity in secondary markets associated with larger issues, I expect companies to begin offering multiple issues with the same coupon rate, coupon dates, maturity dates, and covenants—instead of designing all new issues to sell at par.

A SURVEY OF U.S. CORPORATE FINANCING INNOVATIONS: 1970-1997

by Kenneth A. Carow,
Indianapolis University,
Gayle R. Erwin,
University of Virginia,
and
John J. McConnell,
Purdue University

A n appropriate subtitle for this article might well be "The Evolution Lives! Long Live the Evolution!" Previous articles in this journal have described innovations in financial security design and the forces that give rise to such innovations.[1] In this article, we expand upon and update those articles by documenting changes over the past 30 years in the way U.S. public corporations finance themselves both in public and private security markets.[2]

The past articles have focused mainly on innovations in the kinds of securities issued. But major changes have also occurred in the *way* securities are issued, and in the national markets *where* they are issued. Traditional registered offerings have been partly displaced by shelf registered offerings and Rule 144A private offerings. And once exclusively domestic U.S offerings are increasingly being supplemented by foreign market offerings by U.S. companies, and by simultaneously domestic and foreign offerings. In the research summarized in this article, we tracked not only the kinds of securities (both by number and by dollar amount) issued each year by U.S. public companies between 1970 and 1997, but also their method of issuance and the locale of the offerings.

In a 1992 article in this journal entitled "An Overview of Corporate Securities Innovation," John Finnerty traced innovations (through the first half of 1991) in the design of securities issued by U.S. corporations by identifying the year in which the design first appeared.[3] Our study extends that article's findings in two ways: (1) by updating developments in the design of corporate securities through the end of 1997; and (2) by presenting an annual time series of security issues classified according to the design of the security from 1970 through 1997.

Our updating of new developments in security design provides clear evidence that the pace of innovation in securities design has not slackened. For example, whereas Finnerty identified 40 types of securities that were first issued by U.S. companies in the 1980s,[4] our study found 34 kinds that were first issued during the first eight years of the 1990s.[5] Among these securities were equity indexed bonds, commodity indexed preferred stock, convertible exchangeable notes, and dividend enhanced convertible securities.

Our study also attempted to identify which innovations have prospered over time and which have languished or even disappeared. For example, the first non-convertible floating rate note (FRN) was issued in 1974. The use of FRNs increased steadily throughout the next 24 years and, in 1997 alone, U.S. public companies issued 1,411 FRNs with an aggregate face value of $139.8 billion. By contrast, after the first convertible adjustable rate bond (CARB) came to market in 1981, ten additional CARBs were issued during the remainder of the 1980s, and none have been issued since. Our findings suggest that financial innovation is a trial and error process in which "failure is more likely than not."[6]

---

1. These include John Finnerty, "An Overview of Corporate Securities Innovation," *Journal of Applied Corporate Finance*, Vol. 4, No. 4 (1992), 25-39; Merton Miller, "Financial Innovation: Achievements and Prospects," *Journal of Applied Corporate Finance*, Vol. 4, No. 4 (Winter 1992), 4-11; and Peter Tufano, "Securities Innovations: A Historical and Functional Perspective," *Journal of Applied Corporate Finance*, Vol. 7, No. 4 (Winter 1995), 90-103.

2. Our data are obtained from Securities Data Corporation and include public and private offerings by U.S. companies whose common stock is publicly traded.

3. Finnerty (1992).

4. We excluded from this count various types of mortgage-backed securities and collateralized mortgage obligations because these more closely resemble asset sales than corporate financing.

5. Any classification system is subjective. For consistency, wherever possible, we adopt Finnerty's classification scheme. In some cases, that was not possible and in others, we determined that a slightly modified classification structure better captured the flavor of the data.

6. A finding that that echoes Tufano (1995), cited above.

CORPORATE FINANCING IN THE AGGREGATE— WHERE, HOW, AND HOW MUCH?

Publicly traded U.S. companies can issue securities exclusively to U.S. investors, exclusively to non-U.S. investors, or simultaneously to U.S. and foreign investors. The three panels of Table 1 display the number and dollar amount of security offerings for each year from 1970 through 1997. Panel A shows public and private offerings in the U.S.; Panel B shows public and private offerings made simultaneously in the U.S. and one or more foreign countries; and Panel C reports offerings made in one or more foreign countries. Before describing the different types of securities issued, we focus on the data in Table 1 to provide an overview of offerings in the aggregate by offering technique and locale.

U.S. Domestic Offerings

Within the U.S. market, securities can be issued in either the public or private market. Any security that is registered with the SEC is considered to be issued in the public security market. Unregistered securities are considered to be issued in the private security market.

Prior to March of 1982, once a company had decided to issue a security in the public market, the company prepared and filed with the SEC a registration statement and prospectus describing the terms of the security and the dollar amount of funds to be raised. The company then waited for completion of an SEC review before issuing the security.

In March of 1982, the SEC implemented Rule 415. Under Rule 415, public companies that meet certain size and credit requirements are allowed to register a "generic" statement with the SEC. This generic registration statement (form S-3) includes the company's basic financial information and the amount of securities the firm expects to issue within the next two years, although the life of the registration statement is indefinite. At the time the company decides to issue a specific security, the company is required to file a prospectus supplement that discloses the specific terms and dollar amount of the security to be issued and incorporates by reference other financial information filed by the company with the SEC. Upon filing this information, the security can be issued. This procedure is popularly known as

shelf registration because, in effect, the issuer puts its new securities "on the shelf" until the funds are actually needed.

As shown in Panel A of Table 1, in 1983 shelf registered issues accounted for 20% of the number of securities offered and 37% of the total dollar amount of funds raised in public offerings. In 1997, shelf registered offerings accounted for 49% of the securities issued and 46% of the dollar amount of funds raised in the *public* market.

A similar transformation occurred in the private security market with the introduction of Rule 144A in 1990. Securities issued in the private security market cannot be traded on an organized exchange. Furthermore, prior to Rule 144A, the original investor in an unregistered security could not trade the security in any venue for at least two years. Following that two-year period, the security could only be traded among "sophisticated" investors. Rule 144A allows unregistered securities to be traded among "sophisticated" investors immediately after issuance. According to SEC guidelines, a sophisticated investor is one who has the capacity to (1) evaluate the risk and return characteristics of the security and (2) bear the financial risk contained in the security.

As shown in Panel A of Table 1, in 1991 Rule 144A offerings accounted for 13% of the number of private securities issued and 19% of the total dollar amount of funds raised in private offerings. In 1997 Rule 144A offerings accounted for 64% of the securities issued privately and 83% of the dollar amount of funds raised in the private market.

Simultaneous U.S. Domestic and Foreign Market Offerings

Panel B parallels Panel A in that offerings made simultaneously in the U.S. and one or more foreign countries are classified according to whether the offering is public or private and whether it is a shelf or 144A offering. This panel illustrates that, although simultaneous offerings have grown over time in both absolute number and dollar amount, they still amount to only a modest fraction of purely domestic offerings. In 1997, the $855 billion raised by U.S. public companies through purely domestic offerings was 18 times the $47 billion raised through simultaneous offerings. Additionally, this panel illustrates that the growth in shelf and 144A simultaneous offerings mirrors that shown in Panel A.

TABLE 1 ■ NUMBER AND DOLLAR AMOUNTS (IN $ BILLIONS) OF SECURITY ISSUES BY U.S. CORPORATIONS CLASSIFIED BY METHOD OF ISSUANCE[1, 2]

	70/71	72/73	74/75	76/77	78/79	80/81	82/83	84/85	86/87	88/89	90/91	92/93	94/95	96/97
PANEL A: US CORPORATE OFFERINGS IN THE US DOMESTIC MARKET														
■ All Offerings/Number of Issues	1125/1561	**1692/566**	492/708	**669/525**	547/554	**1015/1605**	1706/2755	**1752/2401**	3479/2850	**2645/2508**	2140/3652	**4176/5501**	4051/5232	**6747/9157**
/Proceeds ($ billions)	27.5/36.2	**31.5/21.1**	28.7/39.0	**34.7/27.3**	24.2/28.9	**51.9/58.0**	70.8/101.9	**85.6/144.0**	245.0/212.1	**221.1/245.3**	190.4/305.2	**377.4/494.2**	348.6/481.1	**639.1/855.0**
■ Public Offerings (Excludes Shelf)/Number of Issues	1125/1561	**1692/566**	492/708	**669/525**	547/554	**1015/1140**	926/1640	**860/1200**	1797/1293	**728/834**	675/1680	**1978/2725**	1791/2579	**3270/4099**
(Excludes Shelf)/Proceeds ($ billions)	27.5/36.2	**31.5/21.1**	28.7/39.0	**34.7/27.3**	24.2/28.9	**51.9/47.3**	40.8/51.9	**33.6/60.5**	98.1/83.1	**74.8/80.9**	71.1/145.9	**186.0/234.6**	167.8/232.2	**293.9/390.0**
■ Shelf Registered Public Offerings/Number of Issues							193/406	**255/386**	631/490	**397/396**	394/635	**913/1213**	1394/1906	**2686/3972**
/Proceeds ($ billions)							15.7/30.0	**27.7/44.6**	88.5/66.8	**58.0/64.5**	62.4/107.4	**142.9/196.9**	148.3/208.3	**274.8/330.1**
■ Private Offerings (Excludes Rule 144A)/Number of Issues						Beginning of SDC data −/465	587/709	**637/815**	1051/1067	**1520/1278**	1057/1168	**1006/1036**	696/452	**336/394**
/Proceeds ($ billions)						Beginning of SDC data −/10.7	14.2/20.0	**24.3/38.8**	58.4/62.1	**88.3/99.9**	54.9/42.1	**32.6/30.2**	20.1/17.8	**19.3/22.3**
■ Rule 144A Private Offerings/Number of Issues										14/169	**279/527**	170/295	**455/692**	
/Proceeds ($ billions)										1.9/9.7	**15.9/32.5**	12.5/22.8	**51.1/112.6**	
PANEL B: US CORPORATE OFFERINGS MADE SIMULTANEOUSLY IN THE US AND IN ONE OR MORE FOREIGN MARKETS														
■ All Offerings/Number of Issues								**1/4**	35/55	**37/51**	84/175	**196/233**	190/184	**226/230**
/Proceeds ($ billions)								**0.0/0.6**	6.8/7.3	**3.7/5.3**	14.5/31.5	**36.3/42.4**	39.0/40.3	**41.4/47.3**
■ Public Offerings (Excludes Shelf)/Number of Issues								**1/3**	35/55	**37/50**	82/169	**192/202**	137/144	**185/165**
(Excludes Shelf)/Proceeds ($ billions)								**0.0/0.6**	6.8/7.3	**3.7/5.1**	14.0/31.1	**35.9/35.8**	23.3/31.7	**35.1/34.7**
■ Shelf Registered Public Offerings/Number of Issues										−/1	−/1	**3/21**	44/22	**10/36**
/Proceeds ($ billions)										−/0.2	−/0.1	**0.4/6.0**	14.2/7.7	**4.5/11.2**
■ Private Offerings (Excludes Rule 144A)/Number of Issues								−/1			1/2	**1/−**	3/1	
/Proceeds ($ billions)								−/0.0			0.3/0.2	**0.0/−**	0.1/0.0	
■ Rule 144A Private Offerings/Number of Issues											1/3	**−/10**	6/17	**31/29**
/Proceeds ($ billions)						0.1/0.1	**−/0.6**	1.3/0.8	**1.8/1.5**					
PANEL C: US CORPORATE OFFERINGS IN FOREIGN MARKETS (EXCLUDES SIMULTANEOUS OFFERINGS IN US)														
■ All International Market Offerings (Excluding Offerings Simultaneously in US)/Number of Issues							Beginning of SDC data −/17	**97/325**	322/172	**122/111**	103/124	**114/158**	223/326	**340/306**
/Proceeds ($ billions)							Beginning of SDC data −/1.0	**10.2/35.5**	37.8/17.9	**15.0/14.8**	10.5/15.0	**16.0/22.7**	26.9/38.2	**50.0/57.8**
■ International Market Offerings in US Dollars/Number of Issues							−/7	**68/190**	182/97	**52/58**	29/48	**49/92**	81/133	**104/96**
/Proceeds ($ billions)							−/0.5	**8.6/26.9**	26.8/12.2	**8.5/9.9**	4.7/7.2	**9.0/14.9**	13.7/21.2	**21.5/26.6**
■ International Market Offerings Not in US dollars/Number of Issues							−/10	**29/135**	140/75	**70/53**	74/76	**65/66**	142/193	**236/210**
/Proceeds ($ billions)							−/0.5	**1.6/8.7**	11.1/5.8	**6.5/4.9**	5.8/7.8	**7.0/7.8**	13.2/17.0	**28.5/31.3**

1. For Private Offerings SDC began collecting data in 1981.
2. For the international offerings, SDC began collecting data in 1978 for Japan, 1983 for Euro and Foreign Markets, 1986 for Canada, 1989 for the United Kingdom, 1990 for India, 1991 for Asia Pacific, Australia, Continental Europe, and Latin America, and 1994 for Korea.

U.S. Corporate Foreign Offerings

In Panel C, offerings made outside the U.S. (starting in 1983, the first year for which SDC data are available) are classified according to whether they are denominated in U.S. dollars or a foreign currency. To expand the geographic scope of their offerings, U.S. companies can offer securities in international markets exclusively or they can simultaneously issue securities in both domestic and international markets. Total international market offerings grew quickly during the mid-1980s, slowed during the late 1980s and early 1990s, and have shown continued growth in the mid-1990s. In 1997, U.S. companies raised $58 billion in 306 bond issues outside the U.S. When international offerings are combined with simultaneous offerings, the volume of these offerings totaled $105 billion, or 11% of the total funds raised by U.S. corporations in that year.

Besides expanding the geographic scope of their securities offerings, U.S. companies have also changed their currency denomination. In the seven-year interval from 1983-1989, U.S. corporations raised $93.4 billion in U.S. dollar-denominated international market offerings, but only $39.1 billion in non-U.S. denominated issues. Then, for the first time, in 1990 the volume of foreign currency-denominated international offerings exceeded dollar-denominated overseas issues. And, from 1990-1997, the $237 billion raised by international offerings has been almost equally divided between foreign-currency and dollar-denominated issues. Of the total amount issued in 1997, 54% were denominated in a currency other than U.S. dollars.

Why the growing use of foreign-currency debt? For companies with significant international revenues, issuing debt with interest and principal denominated in matching currencies can reduce cash flow volatility stemming from exchange rate movements.

CHANGES IN SECURITY DESIGN

In tracking the process of securities innovation, we started by classifying all securities employed by corporate issuers since 1970 into six generic categories: (1) common stock, (2) non-convertible debt, (3) convertible debt, (4) non-convertible preferred stock, (5) convertible preferred stock, and (6) asset-backed securities. Then, within each of the six categories, all securities were identified as either "traditional" or "innovative."

For our purposes, a traditional non-convertible debt is any callable or noncallable non-convertible bond or note with a fixed periodic cash coupon payment, a fixed final maturity date, and fixed repayment schedule. A traditional convertible debt is defined similarly, except that the security is convertible into the common stock of the issuer at the option of the investor. Convertible and non-convertible bonds or notes with any other feature are categorized as innovative.

A traditional non-convertible preferred stock is any callable or noncallable non-convertible preferred stock with a fixed periodic cash dividend and no fixed maturity date.[7] A traditional convertible preferred stock is defined similarly, except that the security is convertible into the common stock of the issuer at the option of the investor. Convertible and non-convertible preferred stock with any other feature are considered innovative.

Asset-backed securities do not fit neatly into our classification scheme because of the absence of a "traditional" asset-backed security. Thus, by definition, all asset-backed securities are innovative. Conversely, all common stocks, because of their homogeneity, are treated as traditional.[8]

The results of our classification scheme are presented in Table 2. In 1970, of the 1,124 securities issued, only one—an offering of zero coupon convertible debt—is classified as innovative. Over the period 1970 through 1975, 12 of 6,132 issues are identified as innovative. But, as we move into the 1980s, the pace of innovation begins to quicken. In 1985, 317 of 2,405 (or 13%) issues are classified as innovative. And, in 1997, 2,644 of the 9,387 (28%) issues fall into the non-traditional category. Expressed in dollar terms, $314.5 billion of the $902.3 billion (or 35%) raised through all 1997 offerings were accounted for by innovative securities.

The fraction of securities classified as traditional and innovative securities varies across the six generic categories. As we noted, there are no innovative

---

7. We do allow one deviation from this definition. Some preferred stocks do have modest sinking fund requirements. One example is a preferred with a fixed coupon rate and a sinking fund requirement of 2% per year. Given the minimal requirements of the sinking fund, we classify this as a traditional preferred.

8. Finnerty (1992) documents several innovations in common stocks. Several common stock innovations failed prior to issuance; however, two innovations that were brought to market include puttable common stock and callable common stock. The combined offerings of these securities includes only five offerings raising $200 million in capital.

The $237 billion raised by U.S. companies in overseas corporate debt offerings from 1990-1997 was almost equally divided between foreign-currency and dollar-denominated issues. For firms with significant international revenues, issuing debt with interest and principal denominated in matching currencies can reduce cash flow volatility stemming from exchange rate movements.

TABLE 2 ■ NUMBER AND DOLLAR AMOUNTS (IN $ BILLIONS) OF SECURITY ISSUES IN THE DOMESTIC U.S. MARKET CLASSIFIED BY TYPE OF SECURITY

	70/71	72/73	74/75	76/77	78/79	80/81	82/83	84/85	86/87	88/89	90/91	92/93	94/95	96/97
ALL OFFERINGS														
■ Traditional/Number of Issues														
	1124/1559	1689/564	492/704	665/499	519/512	971/1539	1539/2606	1483/2088	3150/2564	2249/2057	1796/3309	3606/4518	2821/3991	5028/6743
/Proceeds ($ billions)														
	27.5/36.2	31.3/21.1	28.7/38.9	34.5/25.6	21.7/24.3	47.5/53.5	59.1/88.9	58.4/116.7	214.3/183.5	171.0/169.5	128.7/240.0	298.8/378.7	204.9/332.8	415.6/587.8
■ Non-Traditional/Innovative/Number of Issues														
	1/2	3/2	0/4	4/26	28/42	44/66	167/149	270/317	364/341	433/502	428/518	766/1216	1420/1425	1945/2644
/Proceeds ($ billions)														
	0.0/0.1	0.2/0.0	0.0/0.2	0.2/1.8	2.4/4.6	4.4/4.5	11.7/13.0	27.2/27.9	37.5/36.0	53.7/81.1	76.2/96.7	114.9/157.9	182.7/188.5	264.9/314.5
COMMON STOCK														
■ Traditional/Number of Issues														
	611/989	1222/289	119/205	251/185	249/251	515/769	585/1506	620/795	1236/854	477/535	437/908	1115/1518	1057/1148	1501/1240
/Proceeds ($ billions)														
	4.3/11.5	12.4/6.5	2.7/6.6	7.9/6.0	5.9/5.5	12.5/14.9	16.6/37.1	9.6/25.2	41.9/35.8	30.1/28.8	21.0/54.3	69.7/95.4	53.9/73.3	99.0/102.1
NON-CONVERTIBLE DEBT														
■ Traditional/Number of Issues														
	389/379	319/214	312/405	327/246	211/182	299/588	749/831	712/1084	1637/1463	1691/1395	1284/2243	2239/2646	1629/2746	3298/5183
/Proceeds ($ billions)														
	19.6/18.9	14.8/11.8	23.9/28.3	23.7/16.8	13.9/16.3	28.0/31.5	34.6/41.2	43.0/83.9	160.4/132.8	136.5/132.5	104.4/171.9	203.8/258.0	140.2/254.2	283.7/444.9
■ Non-Traditional/Innovative/Number of Issues														
	–/1	–/1	–/3	26/32	27/42	39/64	149/89	224/200	223/223	276/361	254/301	513/915	1185/1082	1408/1815
/Proceeds ($ billions)														
	–/0.1	–/0.0	–/0.1	1.8/2.2	2.3/4.6	4.2/4.4	10.2/7.9	24.0/18.3	22.3/22.2	32.7/50.8	29.0/38.6	63.7/104.5	132.4/117.3	154.0/203.7
CONVERTIBLE DEBT														
■ Traditional/Number of Issues														
	72/117	73/12	8/15	24/16	18/29	89/105	79/127	66/149	207/149	33/56	26/53	78/105	46/39	95/94
/Proceeds ($ billions)														
	2.4/3.7	1.8/0.4	0.4/1.2	0.9/0.4	0.3/0.6	4.0/4.6	3.1/6.0	3.5/6.2	9.4/9.5	1.3/2.9	1.4/4.5	6.3/6.4	3.1/1.7	10.3/11.3
■ Non-Traditional / Innovative/Number of Issues														
	1/1	3/1				4/2	4/5	10/16	13/6	11/14	14/16	12/25	10/26	31/23
/Proceeds ($ billions)														
	0.0/0.0	0.2/0.0				0.2/0.1	0.2/0.2	0.6/1.4	0.9/0.2	2.1/2.6	3.7/3.8	1.8/6.3	2.6/5.4	3.9/7.7
NON-CONVERTIBLE PREFERRED STOCK														
■ Traditional/Number of Issues														
	50/71	71/49	52/74	57/44	28/32	41/56	94/76	42/17	34/61	40/41	30/68	119/178	53/37	101/189
/Proceeds ($ billions)														
	1.2/1.9	2.3/2.3	1.6/2.4	1.8/1.9	1.3/1.3	1.8/1.8	4.3/2.2	1.4/0.7	0.8/2.9	2.3/2.3	1.3/6.0	13.3/12.3	4.7/2.3	19.8/26.6
■ Non-Traditional / Innovative/Number of Issues														
			–/1		–/1	1/–	13/33	22/66	72/62	86/58	62/58	124/120	30/65	90/128
/Proceeds ($ billions)														
			–/0.1		0.1/–	0.0/–	1.2/3.5	1.8/4.5	5.9/4.2	5.6/5.2	4.2/3.8	7.4/6.2	4.5/8.9	21.5/19.6
CONVERTIBLE PREFERRED STOCK														
■ Traditional/Number of Issues														
	2/3	4/–	1/5	6/8	13/18	27/21	32/66	43/43	36/37	8/30	19/37	55/71	36/21	33/37
/Proceeds ($ billions)														
	0.0/0.2	0.0/	0.0/0.4	0.3/0.4	0.3/0.6	1.3/0.6	0.5/2.4	0.8/0.6	1.8/2.5	0.9/3.0	0.6/3.2	5.7/6.6	3.0/1.2	2.8/2.9
■ Non-Traditional/Innovative/Number of Issues														
						1/22	14/28	41/25	10/14	5/17	18/33	17/15	29/32	
/Proceeds ($ billions)														
						0.1/1.4	0.8/2.4	3.2/2.5	0.6/0.9	0.9/5.1	5.8/4.0	2.5/2.3	6.3/6.3	
ASSET-BACKED SECURITIES														
■ Non-Traditional/Innovative/Number of Issues														
							–/7	15/25	50/55	93/126	99/123	178/237	387/646	
/Proceeds ($ billions)														
							–/1.2	5.3/6.9	12.7/21.6	38.3/45.3	36.3/36.9	40.8/54.6	79.2/77.2	

securities in the common stock category and there are no traditional securities in the asset-backed category. Among debt securities, traditional offerings outnumber innovative offerings every year in both number and dollar amount. In 1997, the $456.2 billion of traditional non-convertible and convertible debt offerings was 2.2 times the $211.4 billion issued in innovative debt securities. In the case of preferred stocks, by contrast, there are some years in which innovative offerings exceed traditional offerings. Between 1982 and 1997, $153 billion in straight and convertible preferred stock issues qualified as innovative issues while only $142 billion qualified as traditional issues. The tax advantage of preferred stock securities (i.e., 70% of dividends received are not taxable) may play an important role in the dominance of innovative preferred stock issues relative to traditional preferred stock issues. In addition to their tax advantage, preferred stock innovations like MIPS and QUIPS also feature variable dividend payments that reduce price volatility for investors and may allow issuers to manage interest rate risk.

Innovative Features

An innovation in the design of a security occurs when one of the basic features of the security is altered. According to our definition, a traditional debt security has a fixed periodic payment in U.S. dollars, a fixed repayment schedule payable in U.S. dollars, and a fixed maturity date. A change in any of these features gives rise to an innovative security.

For example, when the fixed periodic payment is denominated in a foreign currency, a new security has been created. Similarly, in the case of preferred stock, any security that deviates from a fixed periodic dividend payable in U.S. dollars, or from a perpetual life, constitutes a new security. For example, when the dividend payment is linked to commodity prices or when the investor may shorten the life through a put feature, a new security is created. In practice, most innovative securities represent a combination of changes in the basic features of the security. For example, a puttable floating rate bond alters both the periodic payment (by making it adjust with the level of interest rates) and the maturity date (by providing investors with the option to sell the bonds back to the firm before maturity).

Presumably corporations issue these new securities to enable the issuer or investors to accomplish something they could not achieve with existing securities—or to replicate opportunities currently available but at lower cost. Some innovations, such as commodity-linked debt, have been designed to reduce financial distress costs (by reducing interest payments when corporate cash flows are expected to be lower) and to shift risks to market participants (say, investors seeking oil price risk in oil-linked bonds) who are willing to bear them. Other innovations, such as asset securitization, aim to benefit investors more directly by, for example, increasing liquidity and reducing transactions costs. New securities may also be designed to meet the combined demands of the issuer and the investor. For example, securities such as zero coupon bonds and monthly income preferred stock (MIPS) have been designed to reduce the combined taxes of the issuer and the investors. Alternatively, innovations can be designed to accomplish in a single transaction what might have previously required multiple transactions. For example, a dual currency bond combines a fixed rate bond and a long-dated forward contract on foreign exchange.

Tables 3 through 6 present the number and dollar amounts of the different types of innovative non-convertible debt (Table 3), convertible debt (Table 4), non-convertible preferred stock (Table 5), and convertible preferred stock (Table 6). In each table, the securities are classified according to their specific features. Each security issued is represented only once. That is, the categories are meant to be mutually exclusive. For example, Table 3 contains a category called "floating rate notes" and another called "puttable floating rate notes." Although a puttable floating rate note is clearly also an FRN, it is not counted in the floating rate note category in order to avoid double counting.

Innovations in Periodic Payments

The most common alteration of the fixed periodic payment is to link the payment to an index such as interest rates or foreign exchange rates. For example, floating rate notes have coupon payments that equal a specific interest rate index, such as LIBOR, plus a spread that reflects the risk of the issuer and the liquidity of the security. Auction rate-preferred stock and auction rate notes link the coupon or dividend payments to the issuer's current market interest rate through a process of periodic auctions. Remarketed preferred stock and remarketed notes use a remarketing agent to reset the coupon or dividend payments to the issuer's current market interest rate.

Some innovations, such as commodity-linked debt, have been designed to reduce financial distress costs by reducing interest payments when corporate cash flows are expected to be lower and to shift risks to market participants who are willing to bear them.

TABLE 3 ■ NUMBER AND DOLLAR AMOUNT (IN $ BILLIONS) OF NON-CONVERTIBLE DEBT SECURITIES ISSUED BY U.S. CORPORATIONS CLASSIFIED BY FEATURES

Security Name/Description		70-75	76/77	78/79	80/81	82/83	84/85	86/87	88/89	90/91	92/93	94/95	96/97
INTEREST RATE LINKED SECURITIES													
Floating Rate Notes (FRN): Coupon rate floats with an interest rate index or the CPI.	No. issued	2		1/17	3/16	28/20	113/109	70/90	106/151	154/195	317/579	908/893	1153/1502
	Proceeds	0.0		0.2/2.6	0.3/0.5	2.0/1.1	11.0/7.5	4.9/7.9	8.3/17.3	14.4/22.2	31.8/57.3	96.5/88.3	112.0/150.7
Puttable Floating Rate Bonds: Coupon rate floats with an interest rate index. Bonds are puttable at the option of the investor.	No. issued				1/1	4/1	1/6	3/–	13/10	6/5	4/9	13/2	7/3
	Proceeds				0.3/0.3	0.2/0.1	0.1/0.5	0.3/–	1.6/1.2	0.5/0.3	0.7/1.1	3.0/0.2	1.5/0.5
Perpetual Floating Rate Notes: A bond without a maturity whose coupon rate floats with an interest index or whose rate is periodically reset.	No. issued							7/–	–/1				–/2
	Proceeds							2.1/–	–/0.1				–/0.5
Step-Up/Step-Down Floating Rate Notes: FRN whose spread over an interest rate index increases or decreases at a future date.	No. issued								6/4	2/–	30/67	88/23	44/31
	Proceeds								1.0/1.7	0.6/–	7.3/8.8	8.9/1.0	2.0/2.2
FRN Exchangeable for Fixed Rate Notes: FRN that can be exchanged for a fixed rate note at the investor's option.	No. issued							2/–		1/–			
	Proceeds							0.1/–		1.0/–			
Fixed/Floating Rate Bonds: Coupon rate is fixed during the bonds early life and floats thereafter.	No. issued										–/1	8/4	9/3
	Proceeds										–/0.4	0.3/0.2	0.4/0.6
Auction/Remarketed Notes: Interest rate is reset so the security sells at par by an auction process or a remarketing agent.	No. issued							–/1	8/8	1/1	2/3	2/3	3/5
	Proceeds							–/0.1	0.6/0.0	0.4/0.4	0.2/0.4	0.6/0.3	1.0/0.7
Yield Curve Notes/Maximum Rate Notes/Power Notes: Coupon rate equals a specified rate less an interest rate index.	No. issued									–/2	1/2	–/5	
	Proceeds								–/0.4	0.0/0.1		–/0.3	
Indexed Sinking Fund Debentures: The amount of each sinking fund payment is indexed to a specified interest rate index (overlaps with other securities).	No. issued	1	20/28	22/20	30/26	28/21	23/15	46/35	23/24	26/32	39/52	29/5	5/–
	Proceeds	0.1	1.2/1.9	1.8/1.7	3.5/2.4	2.3/1.7	2.4/1.5	5.1/3.8	2.0/2.2	2.3/3.8	6.4/5.0	2.5/0.4	0.2/–
PAYMENTS LINKED TO OTHER ASSETS													
Rate Sensitive Securities: Coupon rate increases (decreases) if the issuer's credit rating deteriorates (improves).	No. issued								–/2	–/4			
	Proceeds								–/0.2	–/1.1			
Dual Currency Bonds: Interest and/or principal is payable in a currency other than US dollars.	No. issued						–/2	32/32	7/13	7/3	1/1	2/1	2/8
	Proceeds						–/0.2	2.3/2.0	0.4/1.1	0.5/0.2	1.0/0.0	0.1/0.4	0.3/1.5
Principal Exchange Rate Linked Securities (PERLS) and Reverse PERLS: Principal and/or coupon payments are payable in US dollars, but payments are linked to the exchange rate.	No. issued						–/6	4/7	7/1	3/3			
	Proceeds						–/0.5	0.3/0.4	0.5/0.1	0.2/0.2			
Index, Equity, and Commodity Linked Securities: Payments linked to a stock (Chips, Elks, Percs, Yeelds), a basket of stocks (Cubs, Suns, Mitts, Smarts), a stock index (S&P500, NASDAQ), or a commodity (gas, oil, gold).	No. issued				3/1	2/2	–/3	6/2	5/2	–/8	5/16	21/14	9/16
	Proceeds				0.1/0.0	0.3/0.1	–/0.3	0.6/0.2	0.7/0.2	–/0.7	0.4/1.2	1.1/0.5	0.7/1.8
FIXED RATE SECURITIES													
Puttable Bonds and Poison Put Bonds: Bond is redeemable at a pre-specified price at the holder's option.	No. issued	2	2/3	4/5	2/4	8/5	26/6	32/28	41/110	38/35	96/165	106/86	126/146
	Proceeds	0.0	0.2/0.0	0.3/0.3	0.0/0.3	0.1/0.1	2.3/0.3	2.7/3.3	6.3/20.3	6.4/6.6	13.7/27.3	16.7/17.4	24.5/27.7
Extendible Bonds and Resettable Bonds: Interest rate adjusts periodically. At each interest rate reset period, the holder has the option to redeem the bonds.	No. issued					16/33	50/44	19/19	44/18	7/7	6/4	1/2	3/2
	Proceeds					2.0/4.9	6.8/6.7	3.8/2.8	8.4/4.0	1.2/0.7	0.7/1.5	0.3/0.1	0.2/0.1
Step-Up/Step-Down Fixed Rate Notes: Coupon rate is adjusted up or down at a predetermined point in the future.	No. issued								5/9			–/2	–/1
	Proceeds								1.3/1.8			–/0.0	–/0.0
Zero Coupon Bonds: Non-interest bearing bonds. Payment in one lump sum is made at maturity.	No. issued				–/16	61/7	9/15	8/5	7/2	1/11	7/6	3/8	12/65
	Proceeds				–/1.0	3.2/0.1	1.3/1.3	0.5/0.4	0.5/0.3	0.0/3.2	0.9/0.5	0.8/1.0	2.4/8.5
Payment-In-Kind Notes: Notes on which the interest payments can be made in cash or additional notes, at the option of the issuer.	No. issued							–/4	5/–	–/1	–/2	1/–	–/1
	Proceeds							–/0.7	1.1/–	–/0.0	–/0.3	0.2/–	–/0.0
Monthly/Quarterly Income Debt Securities (Mids, Quids, Qids, or Quics): A foreign subsidiary issues the security. The subsidiary then lends the funds back to the parent.	No. issued											–/11	4/1
	Proceeds											–/0.9	0.7/0.1
OTHER DEBT INNOVATIONS													
Depositary Debentures: Debentures issued using depository receipts.	No. issued	1	4/1			2/–	–/2	–/1			2/4	1/–	1/–
	Proceeds	0.0	0.3/0.2			0.0/–	–/0.1	–/0.5			0.3/0.5	0.0/–	0.0/–
Global Bonds: Bonds issued with debt structured to qualify for simultaneous offering in more than one market.	No. issued										–/1	2/23	30/29
	Proceeds										–/0.0	1.5/6.3	8.1/8.7

TABLE 4 ■ NUMBER AND DOLLAR AMOUNTS (IN $ BILLIONS) OF CONVERTIBLE DEBT ISSUED BY U.S. CORPORATIONS CLASSIFIED BY FEATURE

Security Name / Description		70-75	76/77	78/79	80/81	82/83	84/85	86/87	88/89	90/91	92/93	94/95	96/97
INTEREST RATE LINKED SECURITIES													
Convertible Adjustable Rate Bonds (CARBs): Convertible bond with coupon payments adjusted based on an interest rate index.	No. issued				–/1	1/3	2/–		4/–				
	Proceeds				–/0.1	0.1/0.2	0.1/–		0.3/–				
Adjustable Rate Convertible Debt: Coupon interest varies directly with the dividend rate on the underlying common stock.	No. issued									1/–			
	Proceeds									0.2/–			
FIXED RATE SECURITIES													
Extendible Convertible Bonds: Convertible bonds with a maturity date that is extendible.	No. issued					–/1	1/1	–/1			–/2		
	Proceeds					–/0.0	0.0/0.1				–/0.1		
Puttable Convertible Bonds: Convertible bond that can be redeemed prior to maturity, at the option of the holder.	No. issued					2/1	6/3	7/4		2/–		–/2	5/5
	Proceeds					0.0/0.1	0.4/0.1	0.4/0.1		0.7/–		–/0.2	0.2/0.9
Liquid Yield Option Notes (LYONs): Puttable, callable, convertible, zero coupon debt.	No. issued						–/7	2/1	4/11	6/10	7/10	3/4	3/3
	Proceeds						–/0.9	0.3/0.1	1.0/2.1	1.9/3.0	1.3/3.0	0.5/1.4	0.5/2.2
Zero Coupon Convertible Debt: Non-interest bearing convertible debt issues.	No. issued	5			–/1				1/1	4/5	2/2	1/–	1/1
	Proceeds	0.2			–/0.0				0.1/0.4	1.0/0.8	0.2/0.5	0.1/–	0.1/0.4
Investment Company Convertible Notes (ICONs): If the bond is selling for less than 95% of par value, the convertible price must be adjusted downward or interest rate upward.	No. issued											1/–	
	Proceeds											0.0/–	
Convertible Exchangeable Notes: Convertible bond that allows the issuer to substitute convertible preferred shares with an identical yield.	No. issued										–/1	1/1	1/–
	Proceeds										–/0.0	0.0/0.1	0.1/–
Exchangeable Debt: Debt Convertible into the common stock of a third party's stock (not the issuer's stock).	No. issued	1/–			4/–	1/–	1/5	4/–	2/2	–/1	1/7	3/13	15/8
	Proceeds	0.0/–			0.2/–	0.1/–	0.1/0.5	0.2/–	0.7/0.1	–/0.0	0.1/1.5	1.1/2.5	2.1/2.7
Step-Up Income Redeemable Equity Notes	No. issued										2/3		
	Proceeds										0.2/0.5		
MANDATORY CONVERSION													
Exchangeable DECS (STRYPES, SAILS): A DEC that has a mandatory conversion into a third party's stock.	No. issued											1/4	4/3
	Proceeds											0.7/1.0	0.6/1.0
Dividend Enhanced Convertible Securities (DECS): Debt that must be converted at a specified date. Generally pays a cash dividend above that on the underlying common stock and has capped share value.	No. issued									1/–	–/1	1/3	3/3
	Proceeds									0.0/–	–/0.8	0.2/0.4	0.5/0.5

As examples of exchange rate-indexed securities, principal exchange rate securities have coupon payments that are linked to foreign currency exchange rates and payable in U.S. dollars, and dual currency bonds have coupon and/or principal payments denominated in a currency other than U.S. dollars.

Interest rate and exchange rate-linked securities can enable the investor and the issuer to match their asset and liability structures more closely so as to reduce the volatility of cash flows. Reducing the volatility of cash flows may reduce taxes and financial distress costs, as well as costs arising from conflicts of interest between stockholders and bondholders in highly leveraged firms. Index-linked securities like floating rate, auction rate, and remarketed securities reduce cash flow volatility by hedging interest rate risk. In similar fashion, exchange rate-linked securities and dual currency bonds can provide a hedge for firms who are involved in international commerce. Rather than issuing a dual currency bond, companies could achieve much the same effect by issuing bonds in the foreign market.

Auction rate securities, remarketed securities, and resettable securities also reduce investor uncertainty and information costs by resetting interest rates to adjust for changes in the issuer's credit quality. As the firm's credit rating improves (or deteriorates), each of these securities reduces (increases) the firm's financing costs. And, although such a provision can end up increasing financing costs, it reduces the credit spread the firm must pay when the securities are issued.[9]

Other innovativons in bond design include the exclusion of any periodic payments (as in zero coupon bonds), payments that increase or decrease over time in a predetermined schedule (step-up and

---

9. This may also reassure investors by reducing any incentive the firm might have to increase the firm's future risk.

TABLE 5 ■ NUMBER AND DOLLAR AMOUNTS (IN $ BILLIONS) OF NON-CONVERTIBLE PREFERRED STOCK ISSUED BY U.S. CORPORATIONS CLASSIFIED BY FEATURE

Security Name / Description		70-75	76/77	78/79	80/81	82/83	84/85	86/87	88/89	90/91	92/93	94/95	96/97
INTEREST RATE LINKED SECURITIES													
Adjustable Rate Preferred Stock: Dividend rate is reset each period based on an interest rate index.	No. issued					13/31	13/14	12/7	8/4	1/−	−/5	11/1	4/17
	Proceeds					1.2/2.8	1.1/0.8	0.6/0.5	0.4/1.0	0.1/−	−/0.2	1.5/0.1	1.0/3.2
Variable Term Floating Rate Preferred Stock	No. issues										6/2	−/18	−/4
	Proceeds										0.3/0.8	−/1.2	−/0.2
Auction Rate Preferred Stock (MMP, DARTS, AMPS, STAR): Dividend rate is reset by an auction process every period.	No. issued						6/48	57/37	45/40	53/52	107/92	3/7	12/12
	Proceeds						0.5/3.4	4.0/2.4	2.8/3.1	3.7/3.6	6.5/3.8	0.2/0.7	1.6/0.8
Remarketed Preferred Stock: Dividend rate is reset every period by a remarketing agent.	No. issued						−/1	1/14	25/9	6/5	5/13		−/1
	Proceeds						−/0.0	0.1/0.9	2.0/0.5	0.3/0.2	0.3/0.3		−/0.1
Fixed/Adjustable Rate Preferred: Fixed rate preferred that becomes adjustable or auction rate after a specified period.	No. issued								1/2	1/−		−/1	5/1
	Proceeds								0.1/0.3	0.1/−		−/0.1	0.9/0.3
Step-Up/Step-Down Preferred Stock: An adjustable preferred stock security who's dividend spread over an index increases or decreases.	No. issued									−/1	2/−		1/4
	Proceeds									−/0.0	0.1/−		0.2/4.3
PAYMENTS LINKED TO OTHER ASSETS													
Commodity-Indexed Preferred Securities (COMPS): Preferred security whose coupon and/or principal payments are tied to a commodity price index.	No. issued										−/1	1/−	1/−
	Proceeds										−/0.2	0.1/−	0.5/−
Indexed Sinking Funds Preferred: The amount of each sinking fund payment is indexed to a specified interest rate index.	No. issued	1	1/−	1/−	−/1	2/1			1/−		3/−		1/−
	Proceeds	0.1	0.1/−	0.0/−	−/0.1	0.1/0.0			0.1/−		0.1/−		0.6/−
FIXED RATE SECURITIES													
Payment-In-Kind Preferred: Preferred in which the payments can be made in cash or additional preferred shares at the option of the issuer.	No. issued											−/1	1/6
	Proceeds											0.8	0.2/1.0
Exchangeable Preferred Stock: Preferred stock exchangeable into the debt with similar characteristics at the option of the issuer.	No. issued			−/1	1/2	2/4	6/3	1/−			−/4	1/2	3/10
	Proceeds			−/0.6	0.1/0.2	1.2/0.5	0.3/0.3	0.2/−			−/0.2	0.5/0.3	1.8/1.7
Monthly/Quarterly Income Preferred Stock (MIPS, QUIPS): A foreign subsidiary issues preferred stock. The subsidiary then lends the proceeds to the parent corporation.	No. issued										−/2	14/25	19/13
	Proceeds										−/0.6	2.2/3.7	4.3/2.0
Trust Monthly Income Preferred Stock (TOPrS, TRUPS, HYTOPS): A version of MIPs issued by a trust.	No. issued											−/8	44/60
	Proceeds											−/1.3	11.1/6.0
Preferred Purchase Units: Debt obligation requiring the holder to buy the parents' future preferred stock issue.	No. issued									1/1		−/1	
	Proceeds									0.1/0.2		−/0.1	

step-down securities), payments in an asset other than cash (payment-in-kind securities), and payments linked to the credit quality of the issuer (credit sensitive securities). Specifically, zero coupon bonds, zero coupon convertible bonds, and liquid yield option notes (LYONs) have no payments until the maturity date; however, at maturity both the principal and accrued interest are due in a single payment. The coupon rate for step-up fixed rate notes increases by a specified amount at a stated future date. In the case of step-up floating rate notes, the spread above an interest rate index increases at a stated future date—and the converse holds for step-down securities. Payment-in-kind notes and payment-in-kind preferred stock provide the issuer with the option of making coupon or dividend payments either in cash or additional securities. Credit-sensitive bonds require an increase in coupon payments if the issuer's credit rating decreases.

Tax advantages also influence the decision to issue a new security. Prior to the passage of the Tax Equity and Fiscal Responsibility Act of 1982, the U.S. tax code allowed an issuer of zero coupon bonds to amortize the original discount on a straight line basis for tax purposes. This feature allowed corporations to deduct interest for tax purposes at a rate faster than interest actually accrued on the debt. The 1982 Tax Act requires that corporations deduct interest as it actually accrues. Not coincidentally, the number of zero coupon bonds issued subsequent to 1982 declined dramatically.

A relatively recent innovation is the tax-deductible preferred stock categorized in Table 5 as monthly income preferred stock and trust monthly income preferred stock. The innovation with the tax deductible preferred has to do with the structure of the offering more than the features of the security. In particular, with tax deductible preferred a parent company establishes a trust that issues preferred stock.[10] The proceeds from the preferred stock offering are used to buy a bond issued by the parent company, and the interest payments on the debt are deductible by the issuer. With this structure, the parent receives the flexibility of preferred stock with the tax deduction of interest payments on traditional debt.

Companies facing large costs of financial distress can benefit from issuing obligations that do not require intermediate cash payments, such as zero coupon bonds, preferred stock (whose dividends can be deferred), or payment-in-kind securities.[11] Postponing intermediate cash payments until maturity with any of these financing options may allow issuers with strong growth potential but limited current cash flow to fund that growth while avoiding a costly default or dilutive equity issue. Of course, the security's price in such cases will be more sensitive to the firm's credit rating. Payment-in-kind features transfer additional risk from shareholders to bondholders, especially in an environment of deteriorating credit risk or increasing interest rates. If rates increase,[12] reducing the security's market value, the issuer can (and will) make the interest payments in additional payment-in-kind securities. The newly issued securities will have the same maturity and coupon payments as the existing payment-in-kind security. Even though the market value of the payment-in-kind securities is less than par value, the par value determines the number of additional securities necessary to meet the interest payments.

A step-up bond or step-up preferred security changes the security's periodic payment, but its primary effect is on the expected maturity of the security. A step-up security increases the interest rate payment on fixed rate securities (or the spread in the case of floating rate securities) relative to the initial interest rate. Combining a step-up with the call feature provides the firm with added incentive to call the bond or preferred stock, since the interest rates on such securities are likely to be below market in the early part of the security's life and above-market in latter periods.

Tables 3 through 6 illustrate the ebbs and flows of securities that alter the periodic payments. The evidence indicates that some innovations have prospered, others have stagnated, and still others have dwindled away. To date, the most widely employed innovation has been the floating rate note. For instance, during the 1970s, a total of 20 FRNs were issued, raising a total of $2.9 billion in gross proceeds. During the 1980s, 706 FRNs raised proceeds of $60.8 billion; and in the first eight years of the 1990s, 5,701 issues accounted for a total of $573.2 billion in proceeds. No other innovative security compares to either the volume or proceeds associated with floating rate notes.

In contrast, the use of zero coupon bonds, zero coupon convertible bonds, and auction remarketed notes has been steady but modest. For instance, with the exception of 1982 and 1997, the number of zero coupon bond issues has not exceeded 15 since they were introduced in 1981. The use of zero coupon convertible bonds and auction remarketed notes has never exceeded eight in any one year. Finally, the use of auction rate-preferred stock, principal exchange rate-linked securities, and convertible adjustable rate preferred stock has deteriorated over time. Specifically, the number of auction rate-preferred stock issues has ranged from six when first introduced in 1984, to a peak of 107 issues in 1992, to 12 or fewer offerings during 1994 to 1997. The use of principal exchange rate-linked securities and convertible adjustable rate-preferred stock has never exceeded seven issues in any year since their introduction and no issues have been made during the last four years.

Innovations in Repayment Schedule and Maturity Dates

According to our definition, traditional debt has a predetermined repayment schedule payable in U.S. dollars and a fixed maturity date. Traditional preferred stock has perpetual life. Any alterations of

---

10. For an account of such securities published in this journal, see Arun Khanna and John McConnell, "MIPs, QUIPs, and TOPrs: Old Wine in New Bottles," *Journal of Applied Corporate Finance*, Vol. 11, No.1 (Spring 1998), 39-44.

11. Sankar De and Jayant Kale, "Contingent Payments and Debt Contracts," *Financial Management*, 22, 2 (1993), 106-122.

12. When interest rates decline, the corporation is less likely to make the interest payments in additional payment-in-kind securities. In this case, the market value of the securities exceed the par value, but the par value is still used to determine the number of additional securities necessary to meet the interest payments.

Security Name / Description		70-75	76/77	78/79	80/81	82/83	84/85	86/87	88/89	90/91	92/93	94/95	96/97
INTEREST RATE LINKED SECURITIES													
Convertible Floating Rate Preferred: Convertible preferred stock with dividend payments based upon an interest rate index.	No. issued					–/3	**3/4**	1					**1**
	Proceeds					0.1	**0.1/0.0**	0.0					**0.0**
Convertible Auction Rate Preferred: Convertible preferred stock with dividend payments set via an auction.	No. issued							–/3					
	Proceeds							–/0.2					
FIXED RATE SECURITIES													
Convertible Adjustable Preferred Stock: Issue convertible into the issuer's common stock with a value equal to the par value of the preferred.	No. issued					–/2	**4/–**	1/1	**1/–**				
	Proceeds					–/0.1	**0.2/–**	0.0/0.0	**0.1/–**				
Convertible Exchangeable Preferred Stock (CEPS): Convertible preferred that is exchangeable, at the issuer's option, for convertible debt with similar rate and conversion terms.	No. issued					1/14	**6/22**	38/21	**8/13**	4/8	**6/17**	3/2	**5/9**
	Proceeds					0.1/1.0	**0.2/1.8**	3.2/2.2	**0.5/0.6**	0.9/0.3	**0.6/1.7**	0.1/0.3	**1.4/1.8**
Convertible Monthly Income Preferred Stock: MIPs which have a conversion feature.	No. issued											3/3	**11/9**
	Proceeds											0.7/0.6	**3.2/2.4**
Depository Convertible Preferred: Convertible preferred stock issued using depository receipts.	No. issued							–/3	**1/1**	–/3	**7/7**	–/1	**2/–**
	Proceeds							–/0.2	**0.3/0.6**	2.1/2.1	**1.2/**	–/0.2	**0.1/–**
Payment-in-Kind Convertible Preferred Securities: Convertible preferred stock on which the interest payments can be made in cash or additional shares, at the option of the issue.	No. issued												**–/1**
	Proceeds												**–/0.2**
MANDATORY CONVERSION													
Mandatory Convertible Preferred Stock (PERCS): Preferred stock that must be converted at a specified date. Generally pays a cash dividend above that on the underlying common stock and has capped share value.	No. issued						–/1	1/–	**1/1**	1/6	**5/4**	2/6	**7/3**
	Proceeds						–/0.0	0.0/–	**0.0/0.3**	0.0/2.7	**3.1/0.4**	0.0/0.7	**0.9/0.2**
Preferred Redeemable Increased Dividend Equity Securities (PRIDES): The investor gives up the first 20-25% of the stock's appreciation in return for a higher dividend rate.	No. issued										–/2	5/2	**2/4**
	Proceeds										–/0.3	0.9/0.2	**0.3/0.8**
Automatically Convertible Equity Shares (ACES): Similar in structure to DECs. Preferred stock coupled with a contract obligating the holder to buy a future stock issue.	No. issued										–/2	3/1	**–/2**
	Proceeds										–/0.4	0.5/0.1	**–/0.2**
Term Convertible Preferred Shares	No. issued											1/–	**2/4**
	Proceeds											0.2/–	**0.3/0.8**

these features give rise to an innovative debt security or preferred stock. Securities making changes in the standard repayment schedule include securities that can be exchanged for another security of the issuer (such as exchangeable preferred stock and mandatory convertible securities), securities that can be exchanged for a security of a company other than the issuer (exchangeable debts), commodity linked securities (commodity indexed preferred securities), and stock index linked securities (Standard & Poor's 500 Index notes). For instance, exchangeable preferred stock and convertible exchangeable preferred stock provide *the issuer* the option to exchange the securities for a bond with similar characteristics. Mandatory convertible preferred stock and mandatory convertible bonds *require* that the preferred stockholder exchange the security for the issuer's common stock at the maturity date. Exchangeable debt allows the investor to convert the security into the stock of a third party, but not that of the issuer. Commodity indexed preferred securities pay a fixed dividend and have a principal value that is linked to the value of a commodity. Standard and Poor's 500 Index notes pay the principal amount plus accrued interest plus the excess (if any) of the S&P 500 index value over the initial value of the index times some predetermined multiplier.

Exchangeable securities give the issuer the flexibility to time when to issue debt or preferred stock without incurring the cost of refinancing. For issuers, preferred stock has a tax disadvantage relative to debt because interest expense is tax deductible while preferred dividends are not. However, preferred stock has one important tax advantage for corporate investors—only 30% of dividends received are treated as taxable income to the corporation. Part of the dividend-received deduction is passed through to the issuer by the willingness of corporate investors to accept a lower dividend rate. The disadvantage of non-deductible dividends is small for a zero- or low-taxed corporation, providing a greater incentive to issue preferred stock.

Should the issuer's marginal tax rate increase in the future, exchangeable preferred stock enables the issuer to replace the preferred stock with notes on which the interest payments are tax deductible. Alternatively, for issuers that currently have a high marginal tax rate and expect a reduction in the future, exchangeable notes provide the issuer the option to replace the note with preferred stock that has the same terms and dividend payments as the note.

The conversion feature also affects the security's maturity. The conversion feature can add value by reducing conflicts of interest between bondholders and shareholders that can take the form of corporate underinvestment and risk-shifting.[13] The conversion feature provides bondholders with the assurance that they will participate in any increase in shareholder value that results from an increase in the firm's risk. Furthermore, by lowering current interest rates, convertibles reduce the probability that cash-constrained companies will be forced to forgo valuable investment opportunities.

Mandatory convertible bonds (such as DECS) and mandatory convertible preferred stock (ACES) are similar to other convertible securities, except that conversion into the common stock is required at maturity.[14] Unlike ordinary convertibles, DECS and ACES reduce the investor's downside protection, since the bondholder must convert into the common stock even if the conversion value is less than the bond's par value. Mandatory conversion implies a perpetual life for the security that typically allows it to be treated as equity for balance sheet and regulatory purposes.

Alterations of the maturity date include bonds that do not mature (such as perpetual floating rate notes), bonds that provide the investor with the option to sell the security back to the issuer (puttable bonds), and bonds with the option to extend the life of the security (extendible bonds). In the case of perpetual floating rate notes, the security has an infinite life and the coupon payment is linked to an interest rate index. Puttable bonds and puttable convertible bonds include either a general put or a limited put. The general put provides the investor with the option to sell the security back to the issuer at a specific price and time prior to the security's maturity date. In contrast, the limited put may specify the conditions under which the security can be sold back to the issuer and/or the number of securities that can be sold back to the issuer at a specified put date. Extendible bonds and extendible convertible bonds enable the holder to lengthen the life of the security.

Puttable bonds and extendible bonds provide investors with protection against declining interest rates and against the possible losses from deteriorating operating performance or a leveraged recapitalization. The put can be viewed as an option on changes in the firm's creditworthiness as well as on changes in interest rates. When interest rates increase or credit quality declines, bonds with a put option decline less than bonds without a put option. When the bond price falls below the put value (i.e., when interest rates rise), the investor can sell the bond back to the issuer at a fixed price. If the firm can meet the cash flow requirement, puttable bondholders are able to avoid further wealth reductions. If the firm is unable to meet the cash flow requirement, the firm is forced to restructure or declare bankruptcy.

When reduced to fundamentals, an extendible bond is the same as a puttable bond. For example, a three-year fixed-rate bond with an extension feature for an additional three years is the same as a six-year puttable fixed-rate bond with an option to exercise the put at the end of the third year. In either case, if the coupon rate on the bond does not exceed the current required return for a security with the same risk and features, investors will return the bond to the corporation at the end of the third year.

Liquid yield option notes (LYONs) combine several innovative features into a single security. LYONs are puttable, callable, convertible, zero coupon securities. The put, call, and conversion feature each have an effect on the repayment

---

13. For a financially troubled firm, the underinvestment problem arises when a larger portion of the returns from a new project must go to restore the value of debt securities before the shareholders receive any value. Asset substitution can occur when management can choose to invest in riskier projects after the debt is issued. Leveraged recapitalization can occur when management can reduce the value of outstanding bonds by increasing debt or adding debt senior to that in question. By increasing firm risk, both asset-substitution and leveraged recapitalization can transfer wealth from bondholders to stockholders.

14. In general, these securities pay a higher dividend than common stock and have limited potential for appreciation (either a cap on the price appreciation or a limit to a percentage of the price appreciation).

TABLE 7 ■ NUMBER AND DOLLAR AMOUNT (IN $ BILLIONS) OF ASSET-BACKED SECURITIES ISSUED BY U.S. CORPORATIONS CLASSIFIED BY ASSET TYPE

		85	86	87	88	89	90	91	92	93	94	95	96	97
Automobile Loans /	No. issued	6	**14**	16	**21**	15	**14**	31	**29**	39	**21**	30	**61**	76
Receivables	Proceeds	1.0	**5.1**	4.2	**4.6**	7.5	**9.0**	16.6	**17.6**	17.5	**9.4**	12.6	**14.7**	14.5
Boat Loans	No. issued				**3**	1	1		1		**2**		1	
	Proceeds				**0.6**	0.3	**0.1**		0.2		**0.1**		0.2	
Charge Cards	No. issued								2	1	**3**			
	Proceeds								1.0	0.6	**0.9**			
Commercial Loans	No. issued										**2**		1	
	Proceeds										**0.2**		0.1	
Consumer Loans	No. issued							1					6	
	Proceeds							0.2					0.2	
Credit Card Receivables	No. issued			5	**15**	20	**46**	46	**20**	31	**65**	96	**100**	74
	Proceeds			2.2	**6.5**	10.0	**22.2**	20.4	**9.3**	12.8	**21.7**	33.1	**40.2**	26.9
Equipment Loans	No. issued									3	**2**		5	
	Proceeds									0.3	**0.1**		0.6	
Equipment Leases	No. issued	1	**1**		**1**			2	1	1	**5**	4	**2**	9
	Proceeds	0.2	**0.2**		**0.1**			0.3	**0.1**	1.0	**0.4**	0.2	**0.2**	1.0
Home Improvement Loans	No. issued										**8**	11	**19**	35
	Proceeds										**0.2**	0.2	**0.4**	1.3
Installment Receivables	No. issued										**2**			4
	Proceeds										**0.8**			0.4
Insurance Receivables	No. issued												**2**	
	Proceeds												**0.5**	
Leases	No. issued													3
	Proceeds													0.2
Manufactured Housing	No. issued			2	**8**	9	**11**	18	**19**	15	**33**	49	**61**	66
Certificates	Proceeds			0.2	**0.8**	1.1	**1.0**	1.3	**1.2**	1.0	**1.5**	1.8	**2.4**	2.5
Recreational Vehicle Loans	No. issued				**1**	3	**5**	3	**1**	2	**3**	8	**4**	23
	Proceeds				**0.1**	0.4	**1.4**	0.4	**0.1**	0.2	**0.2**	0.7	**0.4**	1.8
Revolving Credit / Home	No. issued					6	**15**	26	**20**	28	**22**	29	**107**	319
Equity	Proceeds					2.2	**4.4**	6.3	**3.1**	3.0	**3.2**	2.7	**13.0**	19.8
Small Business Loans	No. issued													3
	Proceeds													0.1
Student Loans	No. issued										**3**	6	**14**	18
	Proceeds										**0.4**	1.9	**4.4**	6.9
Truck Receivables	No. issued			1	**1**	1	**1**			1	**4**	1	**2**	6
	Proceeds			0.1	**0.0**	0.1	**0.1**			0.1	**0.9**	0.2	**0.1**	0.6
Wholesales Auto Receivables	No. issued								**5**	1	**1**	2	**2**	
	Proceeds								**0.4**	3.5	**0.3**	0.6	**1.1**	1.8

schedule and the maturity date of LYONs. The zero coupon feature eliminates the periodic payments, while the put, call, and conversion feature influence the final maturity and final payment.

Among securities that alter the repayment schedule and maturity dates, the use of puttable bonds has increased dramatically since they were introduced in 1973. In the 1970s U.S. corporations floated 16 puttable bonds issues that raised a total of $800 million. In the 1980s there were 262 issues of puttable bonds yielding $35.7 billion in proceeds. From 1990 to 1997, 798 puttable bond issues have raised $140.3 billion. By comparison, the use of exchangeable preferred stock and mandatory convertible preferred stock has been modest, but steady (neither security type has exceeded ten issues in any given year). And the use of convertible exchangeable preferred stock and extendible bonds has fallen over time. In the 1980s, there were 123 issues of convertible exchangeable preferred stock raising $9.6 billion in proceeds. From 1990 to 1997, 54 issues of convertible exchangeable preferred stock raised $7.1 billion. In the 1980s, 243 extendible bonds were issued for $39.4 billion, as compared to only 32 issues for $4.8 billion in the 1990s.

Asset-backed Securities

In Table 7, we present the number and dollar amounts of asset-backed securities classified by asset type. Asset-backed securities create a secondary market that increases the security's liquidity.

Intermediaries can purchase portfolios of assets, place them in trusts or special purpose corporations, and resell the securities through a process called securitization.

For corporations with a low credit rating, securitization may be able to reduce borrowing costs on that debt. The credit rating of the underlying pool of securities is based on the underlying assets, not the issuer's credit quality. Thus, an issuer benefits from issuing a security with a credit rating that is superior to its own.[15]

The concept of asset-backed financing is relatively new in U.S. corporate financial markets. Asset-backed securities were introduced in 1985. Since that time, this market has grown from 7 issues to 646 issues in 1997 ($1.2 billion to $77.2 billion in proceeds, respectively). The types of assets used to back these securities have also increased over this period. For instance, in 1985 only automobile loans and equipment leases were securitized. By 1997, there were 19 different categories of securitized assets. Three of them—credit card receivables, automobile loans, and revolving credit/home equity loans—dominate the asset-backed market. In 1997, these three categories accounted for 469 (or 73%) out of the 646 asset-backed securities that were issued—and these 469 issues raised $61.2 billion (79%) of the $77.2 billion raised in the asset-backed security market.

CONCLUSION

This article examines the financing of publicly traded U.S. corporations in public and private security markets from 1970 through 1997. We document significant changes during this time period in the method of issuance (traditional registered offerings, shelf registered offerings, private offerings, and Rule 144A private offerings), the national locale of the offerings (domestic, simultaneous domestic and foreign market offerings, and foreign market offerings), and the kinds of securities issued.

The Securities Exchange Commission (SEC) implemented Rule 415 (shelf registration) in 1982 and Rule 144A in 1990. Based on volume, these new procedures have been very successful. In 1997,

nearly half of all publicly offered securities were issued as shelf registered offerings. Of private market offerings made by U.S. corporations in 1997, Rule 144A offerings accounted for 83% of proceeds.

The internationalization of capital markets is also evident. In 1997, 11% of all proceeds raised by U.S. corporations were issued in one or more foreign markets. Of the $105 billion raised in these offerings, $31 billion was denominated in currencies other than the U.S. dollar. For corporations with foreign currency cash receipts, foreign currency debt payments provide a long-term hedge against exchange rate volatility.

Since 1970, publicly traded U.S. corporations have used 76 different varieties of innovative securities to raise over $1.7 trillion in the domestic capital markets. While traditional securities still dominate the market, our research indicates that the pace of financial innovation increased markedly during the 1980s and has continued strong throughout the 1990s. In 1997, the 2,644 issues of innovative securities accounted for almost 30% of total domestic offerings; and these 2,644 issues raised 37% ($315 billion) of the total proceeds from all U.S. offerings.

Three of the most common objectives of innovative security design have been to (1) manage the interest rate (and other financial price) risk faced by investors and issuers; (2) reduce information costs faced by investors when buying securities from issuers with better information about their own prospects (a condition known as information asymmetry); and (3) increase the tradability of financial assets.

Interest rate-linked coupon payments such as those used in floating rate notes are the most common features used to reduce both the interest rate risk faced by investors and hence the *real* interest cost to the issuer.[16] Interest rate-linked securities account for 63% of all innovative issues and 48% of proceeds between 1970 and 1997. Although such securities may seem to transfer interest rate risk from the investor to the issuing corporation, some issuers may have a comparative advantage in bearing such risk—particularly those whose revenues tend to increase with higher inflation and interest rates and inflation.

---

15. As in any risk transfer, this advantage is not without costs. That is, since the remaining assets in the firm will be riskier, the existing bondholders and stockholders will be left with riskier assets. Whether the net cost of capital is reduced is unclear. The lower cost of securitized debt may very well be offset by a higher cost of equity and outstanding bonds.

16. For a nice statement of this argument, see Brad Cornell, "The Case for Floating-Rate Bonds," *Chase Financial Quarterly*, Vol. 1, No. 1 (Spring 1981).

Another popular security, puttable notes or bonds (which in 1997 raised $32 billion, or 10% of total proceeds from innovative issues), also reduces investors' exposure to increasing rates by allowing them to put their bonds back to the issuer. But a more important attraction for investors is the protection puttable securities offer against a deterioration of the issuer's credit quality. In this sense, puttable securities may enable somewhat riskier issuers to overcome the information costs arising from investor uncertainty about the firm's future prospects.

Another entire category of securities innovation, namely asset-backed securities (ABS), has also been used by lower-rated issuers to reduce asymmetric information costs.[17] Asset-backed securities (not including mortgage-backed securities) have grown substantially, with proceeds ratcheting up from $1.2 billion in 1985 to $77 billion in 1997 (and representing 25% of innovative security proceeds).

Because the ABS process segregates a set of high-quality assets (typically receivables) into a special purpose security, the values of ABS are based solely on the cash flows and risk of the underlying asset class, not on the expected cash flow performance of the issuing firm. Besides reducing investor uncertainty in this manner, asset securitization may also add value by increasing the tradability of financial assets. Increasing the tradability of financial assets may reduce investors' required rates of return and hence issuers' overall financing costs.

In sum, U.S. capital markets in the 1980s and 1990s were distinguished by both innovation and internationalization. While some securities have languished or even disappeared, others have prospered. As securities continue to be redesigned to meet the specific needs of issuing firms and investors, we expect further internationalization of the capital markets and continued growth in the quantity and dollar volume of innovative securities.

---

17. See Claire Hill, "Asset Securitization: A Low Cost Sweetener for Lemons," *Journal of Applied Corporate Finance*, Vol. 10 No. 1 (Spring 1997).

INITIAL PUBLIC OFFERINGS

by Roger G. Ibbotson and
Jody L. Sindelar, Yale University, and
Jay R. Ritter, University of Michigan*

A privately held firm or successful venture capital project raises capital and achieves greater liquidity by going public. These initial public offerings are almost always quite risky. Risks are faced by each of the three major parties involved: issuer, investment banker, and investors. The pricing of initial public offerings (IPOs) is difficult, both because there is no observable market price prior to the offering and because many of the issuing firms have little or no operating history. If the price is set too low, the issuer does not get the full advantage of its ability to raise capital. If it is priced too high, then the investor would get an inferior return and consequently might reject the offering. Investors, moreover, would be unwilling to purchase offerings from an investment banker with a record of overpriced offerings. Without accurate pricing, the market could wither as one side or the other is unsatisfied. Without a healthy market for IPOs, young growth companies would have only limited access to the public in raising capital.

The empirical evidence on the pricing of IPOs provides a puzzle to those who otherwise believe in efficient financial markets. Numerous empirical studies have shown that unseasoned new issues are significantly underpriced, on average.[1] For example, a study by one of the present authors found positive initial stock price performance of 11.4 percent, while a more recent study by another of us found an average initial return of 18.8 percent.[2] Given the level of competition in financial markets, this is a surprising result. A number of hypotheses have been offered to explain the underpricing, but to date there is still no persuasive, widely accepted, and test-supported explanation of IPO underpricing.

To add to this surprising underpricing phenomenon, there is also strong evidence of a recurring pattern of alternating "hot" and "cold" new issue markets.[3] Hot issue markets have average initial returns that sometimes reach unbelievable levels; for example, new issues were underpriced, on average, by 48 percent during the 15-month period starting in January 1980. These markets also tend to be associated with increasing volume. Following these hot periods, there tend to be periods of "heavy" volume accompanied by relatively low initial returns (and thus less underpricing).

These heavy issue markets then frequently give way to periods of poor initial performance and "light" volume. For example, in 1971 there were 391 offerings with relatively high average initial returns, followed by 562 offerings in 1972 with moderate returns, which in turn were followed by 105 offerings in 1973 with negative returns. In the mid-1970s, there were very few offerings, but by 1980 life returned to the new issues market with a spate of oil and gas offerings.

This paper updates previous research on IPOs using data through the end of 1987 and then reviews the related literature that attempts to explain these puzzling results. We try to explain why new issues have been underpriced and how to interpret hot and cold, and heavy and light markets. We conclude with some words of advice to issuers and investors, who may be able to gain from knowledge of these market phenomena.

* The authors gratefully acknowledge the financial support of the J. Ira Harris Center for the Study of Corporate Finance at the Michigan Business School.

1. These studies are summarized in Table 7 of Clifford W. Smith, Jr., "Raising Capital: Theory and Evidence," *Midland Corporate Finance Journal*, 4 (Spring 1986), pp. 6-22.

2. The two studies cited are, respectively, Roger G. Ibbotson, "Price Performance of Common Stock New Issues," *Journal of Financial Economics* 2, (September 1975), pp.235-272; and Jay R. Ritter, "The 'Hot Issue' Market of 1980," *Journal of Business* 57 (April 1984), pp. 215-240. The difference between Ibbotson's 11.4 percent and Ritter's 18.8 percent can be attributed to differing sample selection criteria. Ibbotson excludes issues with an offering price of less than $3.00 per share, whereas Ritter includes them. These low-priced issues (penny stocks) tend to be the riskiest, and have the highest initial performance.

3. These hot and cold issue markets were first documented by Roger G. Ibbotson and Jeffrey F. Jaffe in "Hot Issue' Markets," *Journal of Finance* 30 (September 1975), pp.1027-42, which analyzes the 1960-70 period. The continued existence of this phenomenon is documented in Ritter (1984), cited in footnote 2, for the 1960-82 period.

INSTITUTIONAL ASPECTS
The Process

Going public provides the firm with more capital while at the same time allowing the original owners to diversify their holdings. The publicly traded price also provides management and shareholders with important outside information about the firm's value.

The issuer of the stock decides to sell a portion of his firm and presumably wants to receive as much as possible in return. The price at which the company can trade ownership for cash depends upon overall market conditions, the specifics of the firm, and the policies of investment bankers.

The firm that wants to go public will generally seek an underwriter, or syndicate of underwriters. The issuer prefers a more prestigious underwriter because this prestige provides a favorable signal to the market. However, prestigious investment banking firms remain that way only by using discretion in choosing the firms that they will bring public. They may refuse more speculative issues. Thus, new issuers search for the best underwriter and the most favorable conditions possible.

The initial public offerings can be made by either of two methods: "best efforts" or "firm commitment."[4] In best efforts contracts the issuer and underwriter negotiate an offering price. The underwriter uses its "best efforts" to raise all of the desired capital at the negotiated price, usually receiving a percentage of the capital raised as its fee. If there is not enough demand at this price, the offer is withdrawn from the market and the issuer does not raise any capital. It is unlikely that a second offering will be made at a lower price. The best efforts offering reduces the risk faced by the underwriter and leaves much of the risk to be borne by the issuer.

By contrast, in the case of the firm commitment offering, the underwriter guarantees that the agreed-upon amount of capital will be raised. In effect, the underwriter buys all of the stock issued at an agreed-upon price (with a price spread to compensate the underwriter) and is then responsible for selling it all.

The underwriter may later reduce the public offering price, but nonetheless delivers to the issuer the entire sum that was previously specified. Thus, it is crucial to the underwriter that the price is set appropriately.

When the issuer and underwriter agree to an initial public offering, the parties must comply with the Securities Act of 1933. The Act was designed to disclose information to potential investors, giving investors the right to sue if there is misleading information or material omission of fact. The restrictions are stricter for S-1 offerings (greater than $7.5 million in gross proceeds) than they are for S-18 offerings (less than $7.5 million). The smallest offerings (less than $1.5 million in gross proceeds) are eligible for a Regulation A offering, which involves even fewer requirements. In this paper, we confine our attention to the two larger classes of IPOs.[5]

According to SEC regulations the underwriter, after investigating the issuing firm, files the necessary information (e.g., type of business, nature of security, financial statements) in the preliminary prospectus. Then there is a period of at least twenty days in which the SEC reviews the submitted material. During this "cooling off" period the underwriter surveys the market. Information is sent to prospective investors and, in a firm commitment offering, the investors are asked to indicate their willingness to purchase shares at some price (to "circle" their demand). This information is used by the underwriter to set the offering price. The final price is usually set at a pricing meeting the afternoon before the formal initial public offering.

Setting the Price

Setting the price of an initial public offering is crucial to a successful offering. But even after the underwriters' surveys of the market and investigation of the issuer, considerable uncertainty remains about how the broader market will receive the issue. The difficulty in pricing arises from the fact that IPO firms, by definition, have no price history (although "reverse

4. On an institutional basis, it happens that firm commitment offerings are typically conducted by the more prestigious underwriters and the size of the offering is on average more than four times as large as best efforts offerings. See Jay R. Ritter, "The Costs of Going Public," *Journal of Financial Economics* 19 (December 1987), pp. 269-81. Both Ritter and Gershon Mandelker and Artur Raviv, "Investment Banking: An Economic Analysis of Optimal Underwriting Contracts," *Journal of Finance* 32 (June 1977), pp .683-694, suggest that the best efforts method is used when there is greater

uncertainty about the issuing firm. Various studies have found that the degree of underpricing declines as the prestige of the underwriter increases. See, for example, Richard Carter and Steven Manaster, "Initial Public Offerings and Underwriter Reputation," unpublished Iowa State and University of Utah working paper (1988).

5. For an analysis of Regulation A Offerings, see Hans R. Stoll and Anthony J.Curley, "Small Business and the New Issues Market for Equities," *Journal of Financial and Quantitative* Analysis 5(1970), pp. 309-322.

The cycles in underpricing allow one to predict next month's average intial return
based upon the current month's average with a high degree of accuracy...
[Moreover] the monthly data show that average initial returns lead volume
by roughly 6 to 12 months.

LBOs," as will be seen later, provide an interesting exception). Yet the underwriter has to set the price to satisfy both his clienteles, the issuer and the investors.

If the price is set too low, the issuer does not realize his full potential to raise capital. Although initial public offerings are one-time-only events for specific firms, the reputation of the underwriter is important in helping other new issuers choose their underwriters. Consequently, the underwriter has the incentive to keep the initial price relatively high.

On the other hand, if the price is set too high, the firm commitment underwriter has a financial loss because he has to lower the price (break the syndicate) to sell the entire issue. In the best efforts case, if the price is too high, the issue is withdrawn and the issuer raises no capital and the investment banker receives no commissions. On the other hand, if the price is set too low, the issuer suffers excessive dilution of ownership.

EMPIRICAL FINDINGS

The results of our collective research on IPOs are summarized in two figures and a table. In Figures 1 and 2, we present the monthly average initial returns (or percentage underpricing) and the monthly volume of IPOs over the period 1960-1987. The extent of the underpricing and the hot-and-cold, heavy-and-light cycles are clearly demonstrated.

The monthly average initial returns are calculated by taking an equally-weighted average of the initial returns on all the offerings in a given calendar month. Because daily stock prices of OTC stocks (where almost all IPOs begin trading) are more readily available in recent years than in periods prior to NASDAQ, we chose to use two different methods of calculating the initial returns for the periods 1960-76 and 1977-87. For the 1960-76 period, the initial returns are computed as the percentage return from the offering price to the bid price at the end of the month following the offering, net of the market return (as measured by the dividend-inclusive S&P 500 return). For the 1977-87 period, the initial returns are measured as the percentage return from the offering price to the first closing bid price, a period that is normally one day; these returns are not adjusted for market movements.[6]

Table 1 presents the contents of the two figures on a year-by-year basis. The first column presents the number of IPOs, the second column the average initial return, and the third column the gross proceeds raised, with the vast majority of the funds going to the firms, and only a small part going to selling shareholders. During this 28-year period, 8668 companies have gone public. (Actually, this understates the number by several thousand, since we exclude small Regulation A offerings from our count, and our data sources undoubtedly have omitted some smaller offerings.) This number gives an indication of the dynamic nature of the U.S. economy. It is far in excess of the number of publicly traded firms that have disappeared through bankruptcy, mergers, or takeovers during this period.

Several aspects of these exhibits are striking, especially the pronounced cycles in volume and underpricing. The cycles in underpricing allow one to predict next month's average intial return based upon the current month's average with a high degree of accuracy. (In technical terms, the first-order autocorrelation of monthly average initial returns displayed in Figure 1 is 0.62 for the full 28-year period.) Furthermore, the persistence of underpricing shows no signs of abating: the average initial return for the decade of the 1960s was 21.25 percent, for the 1970s it was 8.95 percent, and for the 1980s (through 1987), it has been 16.09 percent. In the 1970s, it should be pointed out, there was a sustained period of light volume in which average initial returns were negative.

The persistence of volume from month to month is even stronger (the first-order autocorrelation of monthly volume is 0.88). High-volume months are almost always followed by high-volume months, with the exceptions being associated with sharp market drops, such as the October 1987 crash.

Using the data in Table 1, we also measured the correlation between the average initial return and the number of new offerings. The correlation using contemporaneous yearly data is 0.12, while the correlation of the average initial return with the following year's number of new offerings is 0.49. We interpret these numbers as evidence that initial returns lead volume. Further, inspection of the monthly data shows that average initial returns lead volume by roughly 6 to 12 months.[7]

---

6. The conclusions regarding underpricing seem to he fairly insensitive to the length of the initial return interval, and whether (or how) market risk adjustments are made. For evidence on this, see, for example, R. E. Miller and F. R. Reilly, "An Examination of Mispricing, Returns, and Uncertainty for Initial Public Offerings," *Financial Management* (Summer 1987), pp. 33-38.

7. The correlation coefficient between monthly volume and lagged average initial returns is maximized for a lag of 8 months, although there is also a strong relation for other lags in the 5 to 16 month range.

FIGURE 1
AVERAGE INITIAL RETURNS BY MONTH FOR S.E.C.-REGISTRED INITIAL PUBLIC OFFERINGS.[1]

percentage average initial returns

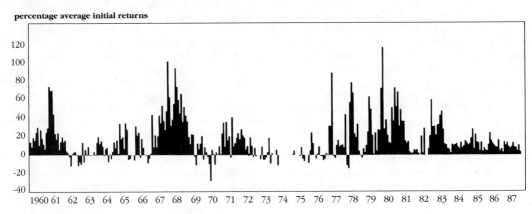

FIGURE 2
NUMBER OF OFFERINGS BY MONTH FOR S.E.C.-REGISTERED INITIAL PUBLIC OFFERINGS.[2]

volume

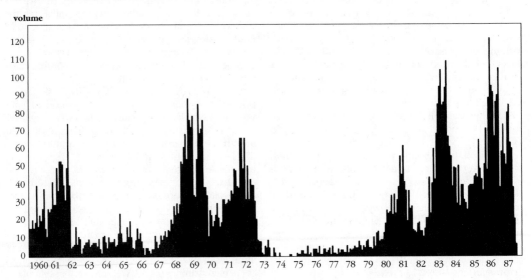

1. Returns for January 1960-October 1970 are from Ibbotson and Jaffe (1975). Returns for November 1970-December 1987 constructed by authors. See text for definitions.
2. Volume for January 1960-October 1970 taken from Ibbotson and Jaffe (1975). Volume for November 1970-December 1974 from the "New Market Names" section of *Investment Dealer's Digest*. Volume for January 1975-December 1987 from *Going Public–The IPO Reporter*.

TABLE 1
NUMBER OF OFFERINGS, AVERAGE INITIAL RETURN AND GROSS PROCEEDS OF INITIAL PUBLIC OFFERINGS IN 1960-87

Year	Number of Offerings	Average Initial Return,%[2]	Gross Proceeds $ Million[3]
1960	269	17.83	553
1961	**435**	**34.11**	**1,243**
1962	298	-1.61	431
1963	**83**	**3.93**	**246**
1964	97	5.32	380
1965	**146**	**12.75**	**409**
1966	85	7.06	275
1967	**100**	**37.67**	**641**
1968	368	55.86	1,205
1969	**780**	**12.53**	**2,605**
1970	358	-0.67	780
1971	**391**	**21.16**	**1,655**
1972	562	7.51	2,724
1973	**105**	**-17.82**	**330**
1974	9	-6.98	51
1975	**14**	**-1.86**	**264**
1976	34	2.90	237
1977	**40**	**21.02**	**151**
1978	42	25.66	247
1979	**103**	**24.61**	**429**
1980	259	49.36	1,404
1981	**438**	**16.76**	**3,200**
1982	198	20.31	1,334
1983	**848**	**20.79**	**13,168**
1984	516	11.52	3,932
1985	**507**	**12.36**	**10.450**
1986	953	9.99	19,260
1987	**630**	**10.39**	**16,380**
TOTAL	8,668	16.37	83,984

[1]. The number of offerings excludes Regulation A offerings (small issues, raising less than $1.5 million currently). Data are from Ibbotson and Jaffe (1975) for 1960-70, Ritter (1984) for 1971-82, *Going Public: The IPO Reporter* for 1983-85, and *Venture* magazine for 1986-87. The authors have excluded real estate investment trusts (REITs) and closed-end mutual funds.

[2]. Initial returns are computed as the percentage return from the offering price to the end-of-the-calendar-month bid price, less the market retorn, for offerings in 1960-76. For 1977-87 initial returns are calculated as the percentage return from the offering price to the end-of-the-first-day bid price, without adjusting for market movements. Data are from Ibbotson and Jaffe (1975) for 1960, Ritter (1984) for 1971-82, and prepared by the authors for 1983-87. The latter numbers have been prepared w'ith the assistance of Choo-Huang Teoh, using data supplied by Robert F. Millet.

[3]. Gross proceeds data comes from various issues of the *SFG Monthly Statistical Bulletin* and *Going Public: The IPO Reporter*. The gross proceeds nombers reported here have been adjusted to remove REIT and closed-end motual fund offerings.

Because it takes at least several months from the decision to go public until the offering is consummated, it appears that many firms initiate the process when they observe a very receptive market to the offerings of other firms, especially for firms in their own industry.

The Effects of Investor Uncertainty on Underpricing

Table 2 presents average initial returns for 2,439 IPOs in 1975-84 that were listed in *Going Public: The IPO Reporter*. (These 2,439 firms exclude closed-end mutual funds, REITs, and offerings not using an investment banker.) Here the IPO firms are categorized according to their annual sales, with the idea that sales may serve as a proxy for the degree of investor uncertainty about a firm's value. As shown in the table, larger firms are underpriced less. This pattern has been noted in many recent studies, using a variety of measures of investor uncertainty (for example, age of the firm, gross proceeds, assets, and the number of uses for the proceeds specified by the offering).

TABLE 2 AVERAGE INITIAL RETURNS CATEGORIZED BY ANNUAL SALES OF ISSUING FIRM	Annual sales of issuing firm, $[1]	Number of firms[2]	Average initial return, %[3]
	0	386	42.9
	1 – 999,999	678	31.4
	1,000,000 – 4,999,000	353	14.3
	5,000,000 – 14,999,999	347	10.7
	15,000,000 – 24,999,000	182	6.5
	25,000,000 and larger	493	5.3
	All	2439	20.7

1. Annual sales are measured as the 12-month revenue for the year prior to going public. No adjustments for the effects of inflation have been made.
2. Firms included are those using S-1 or S-18 registration forms, or with Federal Home Loan Bank Board approval, and listed in *Going Public: The IPO Reporter* for 1975-84. Issues not using an investment banker are excluded.
3. Initial returns are calculated as the percentage return from the offering price to the first recorded closing bid price. No adjustments for market movements have been made.

More speculative issues also tend to have offering prices below $3.00 per share. Whether or not these "penny stocks" are included in the sample has a large effect on the equally-weighted average initial return calculations. For example, of the 2439 issues used in constructing Table 2, the average initial return on those firms priced at less than $3.00 per share is 42.8 percent, while the average initial return on the higher-priced issues is only 8.6 percent.

Another piece of evidence suggesting the effect of investor uncertainty on IPO underpricing is the recent experience of "reverse LBOs." In the 1980s, dozens of firms, or divisions of firms, have gone private in leveraged buyouts, only to go public again within a few years. These reverse LBOs present a unique opportunity to examine IPOs with a more established track record. A study by Chris Muscarella and Michael Vetsuypens finds that for 76 firms converting first from public to private and then back to public ownership during the period 1976-87, the average initial return to IPO investors was only 2.1 percent.[8]

In summary, these results suggest that (1) initial public offerings arc significantly underpriced, on average; (2) the more established an issuer and hence the less investor uncertainty about the firm's real value, the lower the amount of underpricing;

(3) hot and cold performances come in waves, the persistence of which is predictable; (4) cold issue markets have average initial returns that are not necessarily positive; (5) the number of new offerings also comes in waves of heavy and light activity which are highly serially correlated; and (6) underpricing appears to lead the number of new offerings by roughly six to twelve months.

SOME IDEAS ON NEW ISSUES: UNDERPRICING, HOT, COLD, HEAVY, AND LIGHT MARKETS

Most of the theories put forward to explain IPO underpricing rest on assumptions about differences of information between parties (or "information asymmetries") about the value of the new issue. One such theory is built on the premise that the underwriter has significantly better information than the issuer.[9] In firm commitment offerings, the underwriter has the incentive to set a relatively low price to ensure that the entire issue sells at the predetermined price. Because of its information advantage, the underwriter may be able to convince the issuer that a relatively low price is appropriate if the issuer is unable to ascertain its own underlying value. This view is based on the reasoning that,

8. See Chris J. Muscarella and Michael R. Vetsuypens, "The Underpricing of 'Secondary' Initial Public Offerings," unpublished Southern Methodist University working paper (1988). A study of closed-end mutual fund IPOs sheds additional light on the hypothesis. Since these offerings have very little uncertainty about the underlying value, the hypothesis predicts little underpricing. A study by J. W. Peavy ("Closed-end Fund New-Issues: Pricing and Aftermarket Trading Considerations," 1987 Southern Methodist University working paper) finds that, for 45 closed-end mutual fund IPOs in 1986 and 1987, the average initial return was only 1.0 percent.

9. Baron and Holmstrom analyze how to devise a contract such that the relatively less informed issuer can delegate the pricing and marketing of the new issue without being taken advantage of by the underwriter. See David P. Baron and Bengt Holmstrom, "The Investment Banking Contract for New Issues Under Asymmetric Information: Delegation and the Incentive Problem," *Journal of Finance* 35 (1980), pp. 1115-1138.

**The extent to which the underwriter can take advantage of issuers is
limited by the underwriter's desire to protect its reputation and thus its future
business with other potential issuers.**

although issuers know more about the specifics of their businesses, the underwriters may be more informed about the market-clearing prices—because the underwriter surveys the markets, conducts "due diligence" investigations of the issuing company, receives proprietary information from the issuer, and has substantial experience in new issues.

To be sure, the extent to which the underwriter can take advantage of issuers is limited by the underwriter's desire to protect its reputation and thus its future business with other potential issuers. Competition among underwriters should also limit the ability of one underwriter to take advantage of an issuer.

One recent study casts doubt on this notion of systematic exploitation of issuers by underwriters. In this study, Muscarella and Vetsuypens, mentioned earlier, examined the underpricing of IPOs of another special group of issuers: investment banks going public.[10] They find that, for the 38 investment banks that went public during 1970-87, the average initial return was 7.1 percent—an amount of underpricing comparable to that of other similar size IPOs. The fact that presumably well-informed investment bankers also appear to underprice their own IPOs suggests that there may indeed be an "equilibrium" level of underpricing—a level which issuers, underwriters, and investors thus appear to accept as necessary to the process.

An alternative explanation of underpricing, developed by Kevin Rock, emphasizes the asymmetry of information among potential investors.[11] According to this view, some investors become informed about the true value of a new issue, while others remain uninformed because it is more difficult or costly for them to become informed. The underwriter is assumed not to know for certain how much the market would be willing to pay for the issue. Thus the underwriter (and the issuer) generally *err* in setting the price: some stocks are overvalued and others are undervalued. The informed investors line up to buy the undervalued stock and avoid the overvalued issues. As a consequence, the uninformed investors will, on average, end up buying less of the undervalued and more of the overvalued issues, thereby earning a less than average return. Because issuers must continue to attract uninformed as well as informed investors, new issues must be underpriced on average to provide uninformed investors with acceptable rates of return.

One of the present authors extends this reasoning to try to explain the hot and cold periods of new issues. Hot markets, this argument goes, occur when issues are characterized by great uncertainty and issues have to be discounted even more than usual to attract uninformed investors.[12] Cold markets occur when there is comparatively less uncertainty and therefore less discounting. Empirical support for this hypothesis, however, is relatively weak, as variations in the riskiness of new issues appear to explain only a small portion of the cycles in average initial returns. Even if this hypothesis had been supported, moreover, it does not provide any explanation of the cycles in volume.

These theories of IPO underpricing based on information asymmetries are all fairly recent, and have met with partial acceptance by financial economists. Some of the more traditional explanations—all of which are viewed with skepticism—are as follows:[13]

1. Regulations require underwriters to set the offering price below the expected value. (But note that while regulatory constraints may be important in explaining underpricing in countries such as Korea and Japan, there is no explicit regulation that seems to require underpricing in the U.S.)

2. Underwriters collude to exploit inexperienced issuers and to favor investors. The large number of underwriters makes collusion seem unlikely at best. However, a single prestigious underwriter might conceivably be able to achieve a somewhat monopsonistic position with respect to a single issuer if there were high fixed costs of search on the part of the issuer.

3. Underpriced new issues "leave a good taste" with investors so that future underwritings from the same issuer can be sold at attractive prices. While it is unusual for established companies to issue equity with any regularity (with the possible exception of utilities), one study has found that approximately

10. See Chris J. Muscarella and Michael R. Vetsuypens, "A Simple Test of Baron's Model of IPO Underpricing," unpublished Southern Methodist University working paper (1988).

11. See Kevin F. Rock, "Why New Issues Are Underpriced," *Journal of Financial Economics* 15 (1986), pp. 187-212.

12. See Ritter (1984), cited in note 2. Beatty and Ritter also investigate the idea that the greater is the uncertainty about the value of the firm on the part of the investors, the more discounting is necessary to attract uninformed investors. Their empirical analysis suggests that greater disclosure by the issuer will reduce the underpricing necessary to attract investors. See Randolph P. Beatty and Jay R. Ritter, "Investment Banking, Reputation, and the Underpricing of Initial Public Offerings," *Journal of Financial Economics* 15 (1986), pp. 213-232.

13. Roger Ibbotson [1975], cited in note 2.

one-third of the companies that went public in the late 1970s and early 1980s have issued additional equity to the public at least once since then.[14]

One way of testing this hypothesis is to look at issues financed with venture capital money. Venture capital firms invest in many companies that they expect to go public in the future; and they may accordingly wish to underprice current new issues if it makes it easier to sell other new issues that they have financed in the future. However, a recent study has found that venture capital-backed IPOs are underpriced by approximately the same amount as other IPOs of comparable size.[15] This finding is inconsistent with the argument that IPOs are deliberately underpriced to maintain continued investor participation in IPO markets, which would predict steeper discounting of venture capital-backed issues. Because venture capitalists are sophisticated financial advisors, the study results also contradict the earlier argument that underpricing reflects the systematic exploitation of disadvantaged issuers by underwriters, which would predict lower underpricing of venture capital-backed issues.

4. "Firm commitment" underwriting spreads do not cover all of the risks, so that the underwriter underprices new issues to compensate. In this case investors would benefit and would be expected to have to pay for this benefit. And it seems, in fact, they did pay for it before "May Day" (the May 1975 decontrol of brokerage commissions), when large or active investors were overpaying for brokerage. In that environment, brokers might be expected to rebate excessive commissions, perhaps by providing access to underpriced new issues.

5. Through tradition or some other arrangement, the underwriting process consists of underpricing offerings with full (or partial) compensation via side payments from investors to underwriters to issuers.

6. The issuing corporation and underwriter perceive that underpricing constitutes a form of insurance against legal suits. The SEC Act of 1933 allows civil liability suits in the case of misinformation. If there is misinformation, but a cushion of safety in the underpricing, then the probability of losses followed by a law suit is diminished.

While this explanation is logically sound, it does not account for the size of the initial discounts that are sometimes observed in the new issue market. Furthermore, it appears that the more prestigious underwriters typically compensate their preferred customers for losses prior to a lawsuit. Just the implicit threat of a suit and a tarnished reputation seem incentive enough to elicit compensation.

As shown above, then, there are several possible explanations of the underpricing of initial public offerings. None taken alone, however, is entirely satisfactory. The question remains why, in a competitive market where it is reasonable to believe that most stocks are fairly priced, is there persistent and systematic underpricing of IPOs? Furthermore, why are there hot and heavy cycles of underpricing and volume followed by cold spells having zero or negative initial performance and light volume? A completely convincing theory would be able to explain both the underpricing on average and the cycles in both volume and underpricing.

POLICY IMPLICATIONS

The unseasoned new issue market is unusual in a variety of ways, demonstrating apparent deviations from the otherwise efficient market. Although we have not been able to offer completely satisfying explanations of our findings, we can offer tentative advice to investors and issuers.

What should investors do? They should buy new issues during a hot issue market when they are generally underpriced. They ought to suspect, however, that the more underpriced an issue, the harder it is to get. Not all issues are underpriced, even during "hot" markets. In cold markets, conversely, significantly underpriced issues are much less likely, but they do exist.

According to one view, "outsiders" that regularly participate in the IPO process will only get enough of the underpriced issues to compensate for any overpriced issues they might get. Thus, only "insiders" should buy new issues since they are the only ones who should expect to come out ahead. According to another view, though, no investor receives abnormal gains after all accounts are settled; even informed investors and preferred clients must rebate their apparent gains.

14. See Ivo Welch, "Seasoned Offerings, Imitation Costs, and the Underpricing of Initial Public Offerings," unpublished University of Chicago working paper.

15. See Christopher Barry, Chris Muscarella, John Peavy, and Michael Vetsuypens, "Venture Capital and Initial Public Offerings," unpublished Southern Methodist University working paper.

Neither of these arguments comes to terms, however, with the puzzling but well-established fact that there have been high-volume, high-performance markets in which it was both hard to lose and relatively easy to find something to buy. It appears to be extremely unlikely that one had to be an insider to gain or had to rebate all the profits. Thus, if another hot issue market emerges, we recommend that investors buy, and buy most in the early part of the cycle when stocks are the most underpriced. On average, the more speculative offerings have the greatest initial run-ups.

One other observation: It also seems possible to predict which issues are most likely to appreciate by comparing the final offering price with the offering price range listed on the front page of the preliminary prospectus of a firm commitment offering. The preliminary prospectus is generally issued about three weeks prior to the offering date, and during this interval the underwriters conduct pre-selling activities, achieving better knowledge about the demand for an issue in the process. As an example, in the March 1986 offering of Microsoft, the preliminary prospectus indicated an offering price range of $16-$19 per share. The actual offering price was $21 per share. The stock closed at $27.75 on its first day of trading.[16]

While this is an extreme example, when investment bankers find unanticipatedly strong or weak demand, they adjust the offering price, but only partially. If they adjust the offering price up, it is because they have found exceptionally strong demand. But since they only adjust partially, there seems to be an extremely high probability of a positive initial return when the offering price is increased from the range indicated in the preliminary prospectus. Similarly, if the offering price is lowered, it is very likely that there will be a low or even negative initial return. Thus, we recommend that investors pay attention to the direction of the price change in deciding whether or not to submit a purchase order.

What should issuers do? They should issue in the heavy markets that typically follow hot issue markets. In these periods, issuers get the highest price for their securities relative to the efficient (after-market) publicly traded price at a time when the market is still willing to pay high multiples for unseasoned new issues. The low number of offerings during cold issue markets may be due to a perceived lack of buyers and to the lower multiples received by issuers. The issuer should try to make its initial public offering during a heavy spell when issues are less severely underpriced.

If possible, issuers should use a firm commitment offering with a prestigious underwriter. To some degree, the quality of the underwriter "certifies" the quality of the issuer, thus increasing the price that investors are willing to pay. A best efforts transaction may expose the firm to too great a risk that the offering is undersubscribed and then withdrawn, thus denying capital to the would-be issuer. Furthermore, best efforts issues tend to be more severely underpriced.

Finally, issuers should disclose as much information as possible about their firm—short of divulging valuable competitive secrets—at the time of issue. As the recent case of the "reverse LBOs" suggests, the less uncertainty investors have about the value of the issuing firm, the lower the amount of underpricing necessary to attract them.

---

16. For an informative account of the Microsoft offering, see Bro Uttal, "Inside the Deal that Made Bill Gates $350,000,000," *Fortune* 114 (July 21,1986), pp. 23-33.

INTERNET INVESTMENT BANKING: THE IMPACT OF INFORMATION TECHNOLOGY ON RELATIONSHIP BANKING

by William J. Wilhelm, Jr., Boston College*

T he banker's network of personal relationships is perhaps the central element of the production technology of the 20th-century investment bank. In his classic history of *Investment Banking in America* (1970), Vincent Carosso argued that investor networks began to take shape in the 1870s as the evolution of the corporation increasingly required banks to distribute large blocks of securities.[1] More recently, in an article published in this journal, Charles Calomiris and Carlos Ramirez traced bank relationships with client firms to the rise of "financial capitalism" in the late 19th century. A distinguishing feature of this form of capitalism was the presence of powerful financiers on corporate boards, which provided companies with the "certification" necessary to raise capital from outside investors.[2] And, in their 1988 book on investment banking, Harvard professors Robert Eccles and Dwight Crane added to this general argument by showing how the banks' relationships with corporate clients have provided them with a constant flow of information that has shaped the design of products and services.[3]

Given the relatively primitive state of information technology for much of this century, this *relationship-based production technology* appears to have been a remarkably effective institutional adaptation to the information-intensive nature of the investment banking industry. When these financial networks were suppressed in the wake of New Deal financial reforms, the activity and amount of capital raised in public securities markets fell dramatically—and, perhaps more surprisingly, took decades to rebound. Indeed, it was not until the 1960s, when investment bank relationships were able to restore their ties to institutional investors, that U.S. public debt and equity markets returned to their former prominence.[4] And yet, in spite of the historical success of this relationship-based production technology, evidence is mounting that it could be displaced—at least in part.

In this article, I provide an economic perspective on how recent advances in information technology have begun to lay siege to the relationship-based technology. Most of the discussion takes place in the context of recent applications of Internet technology to the pricing and distribution of securities. In particular, I focus on strategies pioneered by Wit Capital and, more recently, W.R. Hambrecht + Co. in the market for initial public offerings (IPOs) of equity. Then, near the close of the article, I broaden the focus by sketching some implications of my analysis for other aspects of the investment banking business.

*I am grateful to Thomas Chemmanur and Alec Petro for discussions that have helped to clarify my thoughts on several of the issues at hand. Bruno Biais, Walid Busaba, Alexander Ljundqvist, Alan Marcus, Pegaret Pichler, and Patrick Schumacher also provided helpful comments. My e-mail address is william.wilhelm@bc.edu.

1. Vincent P. Carosso, *Investment Banking in America: A History*, Harvard University Press, Cambridge, Massachusetts, 1970.

2. Charles W. Calomiris and Carlos D. Ramirez, "The Role of Financial Relationships in the History of American Corporate Finance," *Journal of Applied Corporate Finance*, Summer, 1996.

3. Robert G. Eccles and Dwight B. Crane, *Doing Deals: Investment Banks at Work*, Harvard Business School Press, Boston Massachusetts, 1988.

4. See Calomiris and Ramirez (1996).

SECURITIES PRICING AND DISTRIBUTION

Securities offerings feature a complex series of events that are orchestrated by the issuing company's investment bank. In part, these events reflect regulatory demands for full and complete disclosure of information that might be relevant to prospective investors. The bulk of these activities consist of the due diligence effort conducted by the issuing firm's bank, auditors, and legal advisors followed by the registration of the offering with the Securities and Exchange Commission and the distribution of a preliminary prospectus account. Although not required, a series of roadshows aimed at the institutional investor community is a common supplementary source of information.[5]

A subtle intermediation problem arises as investors gain access to information and begin forming opinions about the value of the firm's offering. Historically, investment banks have attempted to assess these opinions as accurately and efficiently as possible by "building a book" for the offering. The book contains institutional investor responses to the bank's request for "indications of interest." These indications typically take the form of offers to purchase a certain number of shares at the market price or, alternatively, the number of shares the investor is willing to purchase at a particular price or range of prices.[6] *Although indications of interest are legally non-binding, they are offered in the context of an ongoing relationship between the bank and its institutional investor network.* Failure to stand by an implicit commitment can lead to an investor's exclusion from future deals managed by the bank.

Ideally, the bank would canvass the entire investor population to establish the demand curve for a securities offering. Until very recently, however, it would have been folly to even consider such an undertaking. Faced with relatively primitive information technology, *bookbuilding methods economized on search costs by seeking the opinions of a relatively narrow but influential pool of institutional investors.* In this capacity, investment bank-

ers have long employed a strategy analogous to that of the modern-day political pollster who seeks the opinions of a representative sample of the population at large.

But there is an important difference between these two polling processes. Participants in an opinion poll are most likely indifferent about the outcome of the polling effort. In contrast, institutional investors have a significant financial stake in the outcome of the poll conducted by the investment bank. The manager of a large mutual fund, for example, knows that providing a strong indication of interest can drive up the offer price both directly and perhaps indirectly by influencing the beliefs of other investors.[7] For this reason, institutional investors have an incentive to *understate* their interest and thereby compromise the bank's effort to accurately assess market demand conditions.

In a 1997 article published in this journal, Lawrence Benveniste and I explained how the collection of practices that make up a bookbuilding effort can be understood to diminish this incentive distortion.[8] In short, we interpret the favored treatment enjoyed by institutional investors in IPOs as the "payoff" necessary to obtain accurate indications of interest.

In recent years, the steadily increasing share of assets controlled by institutional investors has probably strengthened their bargaining power relative to banks and, in so doing, increased the cost of doing business with the relationship-based technology. For this reason alone, investment banks have recently sought to deepen their retail investor channels. A deep retail network provides a credible fallback during (implicit) bargaining with institutional investors over the "price" at which they will provide accurate indications of interest. Recent consolidations and strategic alliances between wholesale and retail organizations represent a traditional response to the shifting balance of power. But even such alliances cannot alter the reality that, *as the cost of direct communication with individual investors has plummeted, the relative cost of the relationship-based production technology has increased.*

---

5. In an earlier article in this journal, Lawrence Benveniste and I point out that roadshow dissemination of information not contained in the prospectus can trigger a delay in an offering by the SEC. In spite of this threat, there is at least the perception among both institutional and retail investors that roadshows provide institutional investors with an informational advantage, most likely related to earnings forecasts. See "Initial Public Offerings: Going by the Book," *Journal of Applied Corporate Finance*, Spring, 1997.

6. See David Goldreich and Francesca Cornelli, "Bookbuilding and Strategic Allocation," London Business School working paper, December, 1998.

7. In fact, some management firms formally respond to the latter threat with internal policies of withdrawing from offerings where it is determined that the issuing firm's bank has shared the management firm's indication of interest with other prospective investors.

8. See Lawrence Benveniste and William Wilhelm, "Initial Public Offerings: Going by the Book," *Journal of Applied Corporate Finance*, Spring, 1997.

In establishing the demand curve for a securities offering, investment bankers have long used bookbuilding methods that economize on search costs by seeking the opinions of a relatively narrow but influential pool of institutional investors. This strategy is analogous to that of the modern-day political pollster who seeks the opinions of a representative sample of the population.

OFFERING SECURITIES VIA THE INTERNET

Andrew Klein was the first to exploit this shift in relative costs with the 1996 founding of Wit Capital, now widely known as "the Internet investment bank." Wit coordinates an "e-syndicate" of retail investors who are offered first-come first-served access to IPOs. The price of admission to the e-syndicate is a willingness to refrain from "flipping" allocations in the immediate secondary market for the offering; investors who sell their allocations within 60 days are excluded from future offerings.[9] The firm seeks to develop this reliable network of retail investors both directly and through relationships with online brokerage firms.

Although Wit was founded to serve firms too small to bear the fixed costs of the traditional underwritten securities offering, it has increasingly sought to provide e-syndicate members with access to larger offerings underwritten by the bulge-bracket banks. To date, Wit has participated in about 30 offerings in this capacity—and it soon expects to achieve co-manager status.

It is noteworthy that Wit's strategy of providing retail investors with access to IPOs in exchange for a commitment to refrain from flipping is very much consistent with the perspective developed in the preceding section. In this respect, *Wit's pioneering efforts in Internet investment banking thus far have mainly complemented rather than substituted for the existing production technology.*[10] The question remains whether this is the logical endpoint of innovation or simply a means of establishing the presence necessary to supplant the existing technology.

In contrast to Wit's complementary strategy, *the success of the OpenIPO auction mechanism recently introduced by W.R. Hambrecht + Co. will be measured by its capacity for displacing the networks of investor relationships that have been central to the pricing and distribution of securities.* Through OpenIPO, Hambrecht accepts bids from the public at large for 100% of the shares in IPOs that it manages. Any investor can place a bid through the Internet for up to 10% of the shares being offered. Based on these bids, the offer price will be set at the highest price at which all shares can

be sold. Finally, there are no restrictions or penalties related to the sale of initial allocations. In short, the only price of admission is a brokerage account.

Although narrow in its current focus, William Hambrecht's status as founder and former CEO of Hambrecht and Quist has led to characterizations of OpenIPO as a harbinger of the future of investment banking. Hambrecht's fundamental insight has been to recognize that the technology that enables Wit Capital to coordinate retail investors also enables individual retail investors to speak for themselves. By offering individual investors an alternative to voicing their preferences through an institutional representative, Hambrecht's technology attempts to "divide and conquer" the institutional investor network at the core of the relationship-based technology. The success of this strategy will depend in part on continued efficiency gains in online discount brokerage and the willingness of individual investors to take back the responsibility for investment decisions that so many have delegated to institutional representatives. But the recent interest in online-brokerage technology shown by Merrill Lynch and Goldman Sachs, among others, suggests that bulge-bracket banks take this prospect seriously.[11]

THE CHALLENGE TO THE RELATIONSHIP-BASED TECHNOLOGY

Thus far, I have suggested that the traditional relationship-based technology for pricing and distributing securities offerings evolved in response to the high cost of communicating with the investor community at large. Relationships with institutional investors provided banks with summary statistics for market demand conditions and efficient means of distributing large blocks of securities. Strategic pricing and allocation features of the bookbuilding process responded to the bargaining power these investors enjoyed as a consequence of their central role in the marketplace. In this setting, the seemingly large 7% fee commonly paid to investment banks might simply reflect the cost of doing business with relatively primitive information technology.[12]

---

9. For a discussion of "penalty bids" and other such price stabilization practices, see William J. Wilhelm, Jr., "Secondary Market Stabilization of IPOs," *Journal of Applied Corporate Finance*, 1999.

10. Incremental change from a base of established practice is the more common path of technological innovation. See R. R. Nelson and S. G. Winter, *An Evolutionary Theory of Economic Change*, Harvard University Press, Cambridge, Massachusetts, 1982.

11. See *The Wall Street Journal*, p. C1, February 22, 1999)

12. For documentation of the near universality of the 7% underwriting spread, see Hsuan-Chi Chen and Jay R. Ritter, "The Seven Percent Solution," University of Florida working paper (http://bear.cba.ufl.edu/ritter/index.html), February 1999. In a recent Oxford University working paper, Michel Habib and Alexander Ljungqvist emphasize that fees are just one dimension of issuance costs that the issuing firm optimally weighs along with expected underpricing against firm-specific and bank-specific characteristics.

But more fee-based competition seems likely to reduce those spreads in the very near future. Hambrecht predicts that OpenIPO will place IPOs for 3-5% of gross proceeds. More extreme predictions have suggested that existing technology could reduce an implicit underwriting fee of 150 basis points for a $100 million corporate bond issuance to about 30 basis points. Although cost savings projections of this size suggest that we take seriously the prospect that new technologies for securities pricing and distribution are simply more efficient, it remains to be seen whether the benefits of the relationship-based technology can be matched. To gain further insight into this question, it is useful to probe more deeply into the differences between historical practices and those built on recent advances in information technology.

First, we should note that, at an abstract level, the auction mechanism proposed by Hambrecht is simply a set of rules by which the market's valuation of an asset is determined; the price-revealing bidding behavior depends upon the specific pricing and allocation rules that define the auction. Similarly, bookbuilding practices can be characterized as a set of well-understood, albeit informal, rules for achieving the same goal.[13]

Auctions for items with a "true" but unknown value (such as the present value of a firm's future cash flows) commonly suffer from a *winner's curse*. That is, if nothing else, at the end of the auction, the winning bidder knows that his or her estimate of the item's value was greater than that of any other bidder. Kevin Rock has argued that this problem arises in IPOs because some investors (presumably institutional investors) are invariably better informed about the issuing firm than others.[14] Those who are relatively well-informed avoid offerings they perceive as being overpriced while demanding large allocations of those selling at an apparent discount. This behavior will tend to crowd relatively poorly informed investors out of discounted offerings and leave them holding the bag for overpriced offerings. Faced with this threat, poorly informed (perhaps retail) investors will bid cautiously or not at all. The net result is that the expected proceeds from an issuing firm's IPO are diminished.

Lawrence Benveniste and I have shown that bookbuilding practices respond to this problem by encouraging the release of private information that well-informed investors would otherwise prefer to keep to themselves.[15] Two practices deserve special attention in this regard because they are less commonly featured in proposals to replace the bookbuilding technology. First, we showed in a 1996 paper (with Walid Busaba) that a strategic commitment to secondary market price stabilization can promote efficiency in the bookbuilding process.[16] Wit Capital's requirement that its investors hold initial allocations for at least 60 days is consistent with the strategy that we propose (although I would also point out that OpenIPO explicitly disavows penalties and constraints on secondary market activity).

Moreover, Benveniste and Paul Spindt suggest in their 1989 paper that a bank's longstanding relationships with a stable pool of investors can provide a more subtle source of efficiency.[17] Specifically, they suggest that, in the context of a longstanding relationship, a bank and its investors can implicitly agree to bundle IPOs rather than treating each as an independent transaction. Doing so provides greater pricing flexibility because investor concerns about any single deal being overpriced are reduced. As a consequence, issuing firms on average can expect to achieve greater proceeds from their offerings. I am not aware of any proposal to date that attempts to replace this element of linkage among deals that the relationship-based technology makes possible.

Of course, the fact that such practices have not yet been observed in online banking efforts does not mean they are impossible. Indeed, both require little more than some form of memory. Clearly, Wit Capital has demonstrated the capacity for conditioning investors' IPO allocations on their past behavior in the secondary market. The bundling of transactions envisioned by Benveniste and Spindt traditionally would have relied on "institutional memory." But,

---

13. Lawrence Benveniste and Paul Spindt (in "How Investment Banks Determine the Offer Price and Allocation of Initial Public Offerings," *Journal of Financial Economics*, Vol. 24 (1989)) provide the first such characterization of bookbuilding practices. In a 1998 Université de Toulouse working paper entitled "IPO Auctions" Bruno Biais and Anne Marie Faugeron-Crouzet demonstrate that the optimal mechanism identified by Benveniste and Spindt can be implemented in the auction-like "mise en vente" used for many French IPOs.

14. Kevin Rock, "Why New Issues are Underpriced," *Journal of Financial Economics*, 1986, 15.

15. "A Comparative Analysis of IPO Proceeds Under Alternative Regulatory Environments," *Journal of Financial Economics*, 1990, 28.

16. "Price Stabilization as a Bonding Mechanism in New Equity Issues," *Journal of Financial Economics*, 1996, 42.

17. Lawrence Benveniste and Paul Spindt, "How Investment Banks Determine the Offer Price and Allocation of Initial Public Offerings," *Journal of Financial Economics*, Vol. 24 (1989).

with recent advances in digital storage and access, the benefits of institutional memory should be easily replicable if they indeed promote efficiency.

Finally, it is worth considering the possibility that the information problem bookbuilding practices address may arise in part because of the special status accorded institutional investors. As individual investors have placed their assets under the control of institutional investors, incentives for information production related to firms going public have improved. Delegating this responsibility to institutional investors reduces duplication of effort and the incentive of individuals to "free ride" on the information production effort of others. Thus, the relationship-based technology that evolved in response to a primitive information technology may have widened the gulf between relatively informed and uninformed investors. Although bookbuilding practices can help to place investors on more nearly equal footing, a simple mechanism like OpenIPO coupled with advanced information technology might prove superior.

Of course, that depends on how one defines a "superior" outcome. If online investment opportunities diminish the relative private benefits of delegating asset management to institutional investors, they may also reduce the *public* benefits associated with the production of information by institutional investors. If so, primary equity market prices could become less useful guides for capital allocation decisions in the economy at large. Unfortunately, it will be difficult to predict how technological innovation will influence the delicate balance between public and private interests that presumably contributes to the vibrancy of U.S. primary equity markets.

In sum, the present state of information technology is such that the relative private benefits of the traditional relationship-based technology for pricing and distributing securities are about to be substantially reduced. The technical hurdles to investors speaking as individuals rather than through the common voice of an institutional representative are few and rapidly shrinking. Auction theory is sufficiently well-developed that codifying best practices for assessing market demand conditions is straightforward. Finally, even subtle benefits of the relationship-based technology such as institutional memory are now amenable to approximation if not replication. Add to these developments the widespread concerns about discrimination and lack of transparency in bookbuilding practices, and it appears that the stage is set for a serious challenge to the traditional production technology.

TRADING, PRODUCT INNOVATION, AND M&A ADVISORY SERVICES

Is this an isolated threat or will technological advances have similar consequences throughout investment banks? To gain insight into this question, note first that the preceding argument was based only in part on the reduced importance of maintaining a network of relationships as a means of economizing on the costs of communicating with investors at large. Of perhaps greater importance than technological change, as I have suggested, are the advances in economic theory cited above that have essentially codified the critical collateral function of correcting incentive distortions that would otherwise prevent investors from accurately conveying their demands. In my view, it is these continuing advances in economic theory—aided, to be sure, by better information technology—that represent the most serious threat to the demand for the continuous human judgment embodied in banking relationships.

Obvious parallels exist in other areas of investment banking. As the *science* of portfolio theory and contingent claims analysis becomes standard fare in the training of every MBA, activities such as trading, market making, and money management continue to become more systematic. Derivatives trading desks, for example, have long relied on option pricing theory codified in computer software to monitor and coordinate trading in real time across many different marketplaces. Similarly, passive and quantitative money management techniques increasingly substitute for human judgment, particularly in the management of fixed income portfolios.

Perhaps less obvious are the implications for product innovation. Historically, the design of new securities products has been more an art than a science—an undertaking that, as Eccles and Crane suggest, benefited from day-to-day client interaction and experimentation. This in turn led to longstanding client-bank relationships based on an informal understanding that a banker's time spent understanding and responding to a client's needs would eventually be rewarded by compensation received from that client from a transaction of some kind. One rationale for this business model is that financial products are relatively easy to reverse engineer, represent intellectual property that is difficult to prevent others from using, and yet, as Peter Tufano has documented, have relatively high development costs.[18] In the absence of strong relationships, client firms might share an innovative bank's ideas with a competing bank that has not borne development costs with the expectation that the latter will provide the product or service at a lower price. By preventing such behavior, *client/bank relationships provided a mechanism for efficient sharing of R&D costs.* This interpretation is supported by Tufano's finding that innovative banks, although able to underwrite a median of only one deal before a competitor develops a comparable product, are able to capture larger market share in the new products.

Obviously, many recent product innovations were made possible by low-cost, high-speed computers. Perhaps more important to the future shape of the industry, however, are technological advances related to the continued codification of advances in the practice of "financial engineering" and the increasingly wide array of publicly traded "building blocks" for risk management and security design. Both should reduce production costs—the former by reducing the need for learning by trial and error and the latter by commoditizing basic inputs to production. Moreover, the codification of product design implies that the production technology itself is more nearly a public good, which in turn opens the door to greater competition among banks and client firms developing their own solutions. Consistent with this interpretation is the pronounced shift toward a more transactional orientation between banks and client firms documented by Eccles and Crane[19]—a shift that suggests the industry is far along in replacing a traditional relationship-based production technology that supported sharing of R&D costs.

But does all this mean we will soon see an end to relationship banking? Not likely. For one thing, the mergers and acquisition side of the business will remain dependent on a relationship-based technology for the foreseeable future. So, too, will the financing of small and middle-market companies, and corporate finance advisory work, including risk management, for large corporations. The banker's network in this capacity provides for continuous measurement of the "pulse" of the marketplace. It is unlikely that information technology will soon substitute for considerations of trust and confidentiality central to the free flow of information. Moreover, because the science of corporate (financial) structure remains relatively immature, the typical corporate restructuring is a "poorly defined problem" with no clear solution or solution strategy. Even if corporate restructuring becomes highly systematized, the division of any value created by a restructuring will be determined by bargaining among the various interested parties. Thus we should expect the central role of the banker in this part of corporate finance to persist.

CONCLUSION

Historically, the production technology of investment banking has depended heavily on the capacity of investment bankers to maintain networks of relationships with institutional investors and client firms. In this article, I have suggested that advances in information technology, together with increased understanding and codification of investment banking practices, have and will continue to diminish the importance of these relationships. Relationships with institutional investors that have long formed the foundation for the pricing and distribution of securities offerings appear particularly vulnerable to recent efforts to conduct securities offerings via the Internet.

In the past, the scale of a bank's network of relationships has been limited by the processing capacity of individual bankers and their ability to coordinate with one another. The existence of the underwriting syndicate, which temporarily brings together the networks of many banks for a single firm's offering, suggests that the network of any single bank has not been broad enough to support efficient pricing and distribution of the typical IPO. If the use of information technology to communicate more directly with individual investors takes hold, we might expect to observe both a (continued) decline in the role of the syndicate and fewer, more dominant intermediaries in the securities underwriting business.[20]

18. Peter Tufano, "Financial Innovation and First-Mover Advantages," *Journal of Financial Economics*, 1989, 25.

19. Robert G. Eccles and Dwight B. Crane, *Doing Deals: Investment Banks at Work*, Harvard Business School Press, Boston, Massachusetts, 1988.

20. Recent years have witnessed a decline in syndicate size. This is likely a consequence of the sharply diminished risk-sharing role the syndicate played when firms were private partnerships and opportunities for laying off risk in the marketplace were limited. For a more detailed discussion of the syndicate and the coordination problems it may help to resolve, see Pegaret J. S. Pichler and William J. Wilhelm, Jr., "A Theory of the Syndicate: Form follows Function," Boston College working paper, 1999.

Perhaps a more likely path of development, particularly in the short run, is one in which a technology like Wit Capital's continues to complement the traditional technology for "firm-commitment" offerings and a Hambrecht-like technology displaces "best efforts" offerings of smaller IPOs by less prestigious, regional banks.

In the extreme, low-cost direct communication, memory, and data-processing capacity might lead to something more like a "direct marketing" business model. Already, Wit Capital seeks to identify "affinity groups" for a firm's offering and electronically alerts potential investors to impending offerings. This business model derives scale economies not only from its dependence on information technology but also because the benefits from "data mining" for client tendencies increase with scale.[21] Both factors would support further consolidation within the industry.[22]

Perhaps a more likely path of development, particularly in the short run, is one in which a technology like Wit Capital's continues to complement the traditional technology for "firm-commitment" (underwritten) offerings and a Hambrecht-like technology displaces "best efforts" offerings of smaller IPOs by less prestigious, regional banks. This more conservative prediction rests on the idea that there will never be a sufficiently large fraction of the individual investor population that chooses to take responsibility for asset management decisions. Clearly, declines in transactions costs and timely, low-cost dissemination of information are quickly taking us to a point where the individual can compete on more equal footing with institutional investors. However, as Herbert Simon observed, "a wealth of information creates a poverty of attention."[23] We must ask how many individual investors will sift through the mass of information being placed at their fingertips. So long as there remains a strong incentive for delegating asset management decisions to institutional representatives, we might expect these representatives to be treated "more equally" than other individual investors.

In any event, investment banks will continue in the information brokerage role I have described in this article. However, we should expect information technology to reduce the degree to which banker networks are embodied in individual investment bankers.[24] Although space constraints do not permit me to go into detail here, further codification of the knowledge base (or "human capital") at the core of production will alter industry structure and the organization of banking firms and will probably lower the relative wage in certain areas of investment banking.[25] The relative cost to individual investors of not delegating responsibility for asset management will continue to fall—a development that most will welcome. But, as I argued earlier, information production in the overall economy, and therefore the informational efficiency of the marketplace, could suffer as a consequence. Obviously, not every investor will choose to participate in this brave new world—and constraints like those imposed by Wit Capital on the secondary market sale of share allocations can force those who do to make some investment in firm-specific research. But we might hope that the future of securities offerings is not foreshadowed by the recent Internet-related IPOs, with their unprecedented price runups and volatility.

---

21. This model also gives rise to a variety of privacy and property rights concerns that remain largely unresolved. For a discussion of these issues, see Anne Wells Branscomb, *Who Owns Information?*, Basic Books, 1994.

22. Goldman Sachs recently agreed to purchase a 22% stake in Wit Capital for an estimated $25 million. Public statements reported in *The Wall Street Journal* (March 30, 1999) identify the complementary nature of the firms' networks as the motivating force behind the agreement.

23. For further development of this point, see Carl Shapiro and Hal R. Varian, *Information Rules: A Strategic Guide to the Network Economy*, Harvard Business School Press, Boston, Massachusetts, 1998.

24. Bharat N. Anand and Alexander Galetovic provide a formal development of this idea in "A Theory of Financial Market Structure," Harvard Business School working paper, May 1998.

25. An example of the latter is the steady demise of the partnership, which can be interpreted as an organizational form that served the development and retention of human capital, in favor of the corporate form of organization to better meet the growing demands for large-scale risk capital investments.

ARE BANK LOANS DIFFERENT?: SOME EVIDENCE FROM THE STOCK MARKET

by Christopher James and Peggy Wier, University of Oregon

T raditionally, economists have focused on the role of commercial banks in the payment system. Banks are unique, the argument goes, because unlike other financial institutions, they provide transaction services by taking demand deposits. This involvement in the money supply process has been the basis for regulations, such as reserve requirements, designed to facilitate monetary control and for regulations intended to preserve the soundness of banks and the payment system.

But banks, of course, do more than gather deposits. And they are more than passive investors—as the older research tends to suggest—which simply channel their deposits into a pool of assets earning slightly higher rates of return than those paid out to depositors. In fact, commercial banks constitute a major source of capital for U.S. public corporations. Indeed, as shown in Table 1, in any given year over the ten-year period from 1977 to 1986, at least a third—and in several years more than half—of the new debt raised by all American industrial corporations was provided by financial institutions, chiefly banks.

Securities sales, after all, are voluntary management decisions, and, provided the
proceeds are used to finance profitable new investment opportunities,
the change in the market value of the firm should be positive, if anything, in
response to such announcements.

TABLE 1
LOANS FROM FINANCIAL INSTITUTIONS TO
NON-FINANCIAL CORPORATIONS AS A
PERCENTAGE OF NEW DEBT FINANCING,
1977 THROUGH 1986

Year	Percentage
1977	50.73
1978	52.64
1979	54.60
1980	37.32
1981	49.51
1982	52.24
1983	43.68
1984	46.81
1985	34.44
1986	38.38
Average	46.02

Source: Federal Reserve Statistical Release Z.7, various years.

In somewhat belated recognition of this role, the attention of academic economists has recently shifted away from the payment system and toward the distinctive contribution by banks and other financial institutions to the process of providing capital for corporate investment. For example, in 1985 the University of Chicago's Eugene Fama published a paper in the *Journal of Monetary Economics* entitled "What's Different About Banks?" In that paper Professor Fama argued that banks have a comparative advantage in gathering information about, and in monitoring, corporate borrowers.[1] In another paper published two years later, Christopher James (one of the present authors) described an intriguing empirical "regularity" uncovered by his work: namely, announcements by public firms of new bank lending agreements elicit, on average (and in a very strong majority of cases), a significantly positive reaction from the stock market.[2] This finding offers a pointed contrast to the neutral to negative responses that have recently been found to accompany almost all other kinds of securities offerings:

private placements of debt, straight public debt, preferred stock, convertible debt, convertible preferred, and common stock.[3]

This pronounced difference between the market reaction to announcements of bank loans and public securities raises the question of whether there is indeed anything "different" about bank loans. In this paper we present the findings of recent studies in more detail and explore the possibility that banks have some unique advantages in their role as providers of capital.

THE MARKET REACTION TO SECURITIES OFFERINGS

Table 2 provides a summary of recent academic research on the market's reaction to announcements of public securities offerings. The major findings of this research are as follows: (1) the market response to companies issuing common stock is significantly negative (on the order of 3 percent, on average); (2) the response to convertible offerings, both debt and preferred, is also significantly negative (although less so than in the case of common); and (3) the response to straight debt and preferred offerings, although slightly negative on average, is not significantly different from zero.[4]

These results came as something of a surprise, at least to the academic finance profession. Securities sales, after all, are voluntary management decisions. And provided the proceeds are used to finance profitable new investment opportunities, the change in the market value of the firm should be positive, if anything, in response to such announcements. Thus, we were confronted with a puzzle in need of an explanation.

The explanation now most widely accepted, at least by financial economists, originates in a paper by Stewart Myers and Nicholas Majluf entitled, "Corporate Financing and Investment Decisions When Firms Have Information That Outsiders Do Not Have."[5] The paper begins by observing that new

1. Eugene Fama, "What's Different About Banks?," *Journal of Monetary Economics* 15 (1985).

2. Christopher James, "Some Evidence on the Uniqueness of Bank Loans," *Journal of Financial Economics* 19 (1987).

3. The lone exception is "equity carve-outs," or partial public offerings by the subsidiaries of U.S. public companies. As documented by Katherine Schipper and Abbie Smith ("A Comparison of Equity Carve-Outs and Seasoned Equity Offerings: Share Price Effects and Corporate Restructurings," *Journal of Financial Economics* 15 (1986), announcements of these offerings are accompanied by a roughly 3 percent increase in the value of the parent corporation's stock price.

4. For an excellent review of this literature see Clifford Smith, "Investment Banking and the Capital Acquisition Process," *Journal of Financial Economics* 15 (1986). For a less technical version of the same paper, see Clifford Smith, "Raising Capital: Theory and Evidence," *Midland Corporate Finance Journal*, Spring 1986.

5. See Stewart Myers and Nicolas Majluf, "Corporate Financing and Investment Decisions When Firms Have Information that Outsiders Do Not Have," *Journal of Financial Economics* 13 (1985). See also Clifford Smith (1986), cited in note 4.

TABLE 2
STOCK PRICE RESPONSE TO ANNOUNCEMENTS OF
PUBLIC SECURITIES OFFERINGS[a]
(SAMPLE SIZE IS IN PARENTHESES)

Type of Security Offering	Two Day Abnormal Returns
Common Stock	-3.14%
	(155)
Preferred Stock	-.19%
	(28)
Convertible Preferred Stock	-1.44%*
	(53)
Straight Bonds	-.26%
	(248)
Convertible Bonds	-2.07%*
	(73)

a. The information contained in this table is from Clifford Smith's article entitled,
"Raising Capital: Theory and Evidence," *Midland Corporate Finance Journal*
(Spring 1986). The returns reported are for industrial corporations. The studies
reporting these results are cited in Smith (1986).
* Significantly different from zero.

securities offerings are not the primary method
which firms use to finance new investment projects.
Most corporate capital requirements are instead
financed with internally generated funds—that is,
retained earnings. And this has been especially true
of the 1980s. Since 1980, for example, the proportion of capital raised internally has exceeded 60
percent. During the same period net new equity has
been negative; that is, in the aggregate, firms have
repurchased more equity than they have issued.
Public and private borrowing account for the rest of
the capital raised.[6]

This set of financing preferences—starting with
internal funds, moving next to debt, and then finally
to the riskiest security, common stock—is now
known as the financial "pecking order." To account
for this pattern, Myers and Majluf point to the well-
known (and now well-documented) observation
that a corporation's managers often have better
information about the firm's prospects, and hence
about its actual current value, than do outside
investors. Thus, while a new security offering might
mean that the firm has profitable new investment
opportunities, it also might suggest that management thinks that the firm's earnings will be lower
than previously expected; that is, management's
expectation of a shortfall in cash profits may be the
real reason for the new offering.

Potential investors cannot confidently distinguish between these two possible signals from
management. Investors do know, however, that if
management's aim is to maximize the wealth of their
current stockholders, it will try to issue new securities when it believes the firm is *overvalued* relative
to its prospects. Put a little differently, managers are
more likely to offer securities when they expect a
fall in firm profits after the offering (and thus think
the firm is "overvalued") than when they anticipate
a subsequent rise in profits (and think the firm is
"undervalued").

For this reason a new issue is likely to signal
management's belief that the firms' outstanding securities are currently overvalued. Recognizing
management's incentives to issue overvalued securities,
the market systematically discounts the value of firms
announcing new offerings. And this discount is largest
in the cases of common stock and convertible offerings
because the value of these securities. is most sensitive
to changes in the expected profitability of the firm.

Given this rational market "bias" against new
offerings (which in turn explains management's
preference for internal funds over, especially, new
equity issues), some companies with genuinely
profitable investment opportunities may have a
financing problem. If it is costly for management to
convey information about these opportunities in a
detailed and reliable fashion (since investors know
that all firms have an incentive to exaggerate the
promise of new projects), such firms are likely to
find themselves undervalued in the market (again,
at least relative to insiders' expectations). Unless
investors can be convinced of the profitability of
these opportunities, firms that possess them are in
the uncomfortable position of penalizing their existing stockholders by selling underpriced securities or
seeking other, private sources of funds. As noted
earlier, the most commonly used source is internally
generated cash. But what of the firm whose retained
earnings are insufficient to fund its projects?

THE ROLE OF BANKS AND OTHER FINANCIAL INSTITUTIONS

In the paper cited earlier, "What's Different
About Banks?," Eugene Fama makes the distinction
between "inside" and "outside" debt. Inside debt is

---

6. These data are reported by Richard Brealey and Stewart Myers in *Principles
of Corporate Finance*, 3rd ed. McGraw-Hill (1988), pp. 312-313.

defined as a loan for which the lender has access to information about the borrower that is not otherwise publicly available. For example, the lender may participate in the firm's decision-making as a member of executive committees or as a member of the board of directors. Outside debt, by contrast, is a publicly-traded claim, for which the debtholder relies on publicly available information generated by bond rating agencies, independent audits, or analyst reports. Bank loans and privately placed loans are inside debt, and publicly-traded bonds and commercial paper are examples of outside debt.

Inside debt, moreover, appears to be a major source of financing for smaller public corporations as well as privately held firms. As presented in Table 1 earlier, bank loans represented some 46 percent of all debt financing by U.S. (non-financial) corporations between 1977 and 1986. Private placements of bonds, which are essentially loan sales to a limited number of investors (typically insurance companies and pension funds), accounted for about 30 percent of all bond issues over the same period.

There are several possible advantages to using inside debt. First, inside debt may provide a possible solution to the problem of "information asymmetry" that attends all public securities offerings. For example, to the extent banks have better information about, and thus greater confidence in, a given firm's future than outsiders, they would price their loans to reflect this information advantage. For firms with strong relationships with local bankers, but no chance of gaining an investment grade bond rating (perhaps for reasons of size alone), the cost of a bank loan or private placement can be substantially lower than the cost of borrowing through a public securities offering.

Second, inside debtholders are in a better position to monitor the firm after the debt is issued. Private placements and bank loans typically contain detailed restrictive covenants, often custom-tailored to the specific problems and opportunities of the borrower. Renegotiating the credit in response to unexpected developments is much easier when there is only one or several lenders than when there are several hundred or even thousands of anonymous investors. Also, in the case of bank loans, firms may be able to lower their debt costs by borrowing from banks with which they maintain a deposit relationship, because these banks already have information useful for evaluating and monitoring credit quality.

Third, there may be an advantage to maintaining confidentiality about the firm's investment op-

portunities. Companies may not wish to reveal to the public the information that lenders require. For example, suppose a firm is raising capital for an investment that involves a new marketing strategy, the value of which would be reduced if competitors learn of it prior to its introduction. Borrowing from insiders permits the firm to keep its strategy secret.

Finally, the use of inside debt allows borrowers to avoid the costly and time-consuming process of registering issues with the Securities and Exchange Commission. It should be noted, however, that there are also costs to negotiating inside debt, and while the fixed costs of public issues are relatively large, variable costs are small. For this reason, inside debt is more likely to be used for smaller borrowings— that is, when the size of the issues are not large enough to benefit from the considerable economies of scale in floating new public issues.

A testable implication of the hypothesis that bank loans and other types of private debt avoid the negative signal associated with public offerings is that announcements of such inside debt transactions will have a positive effect on the stock prices of the borrowing firms. The loan approval process itself may convey positive information to market participants about the financial strength of the firm, especially in the case of smaller firms without access to public capital markets. Loan renewals and new extensions may provide a credible "seal of approval" to equity investors and other claimants of the firm, who therefore need not undertake similar costly evaluations of the firm's financial condition.

Bank Loans versus Private Placements

Thus far we have looked at some possible advantages of inside over outside debt. But is there any reason to believe that bank loans differ in important ways from "inside" debt provided by other financial institutions? One possibility is the difference in the quality and timeliness of information that results from an ongoing deposit and customer relationship. The history of a borrower as a depositor (and, more generally, as a customer for a variety of the bank's services) may provide banks with a significant cost advantage in evaluating and monitoring the risks of loans. This special information, although not especially privileged in the case of Fortune 500 companies, is likely to be particularly valuable in making short-term loans to smaller firms without established credit histories.

If the access to a deposit history and a continuous customer relationship does indeed provide banks with a comparative advantage over other inside lenders, one would expect banks to dominate the market for short-term lending. Moreover, one would expect the stock market reaction to announcements of bank loans to be more favorable than price reactions to announcements of private placements of debt. In announcing a loan agreement, a company declares its willingness to subject itself to periodic evaluations by a reputable bank; and this willingness is likely to provide a positive signal to the market about management's view of the firm's prospects.

Two observations tend to support the argument that a deposit history gives banks a comparative advantage. First, banks often require that borrowers maintain compensating balance requirements (i.e., have a deposit account at the lending institution), which suggests that both borrowers and lenders view the deposit account as an integral part of the lending relationship. Second, commercial banks are the dominant suppliers of short-term debt, particularly to smaller corporate borrowers. At the end of 1986, commercial banks held $541 billion in commercial and industrial loans, most of which had a maturity of less than one year. The next largest source of short-term financing is the commercial paper market with $79 billion in paper issued by industrial firms outstanding. The commercial paper market is limited, however, to relatively large well-known borrowers.

THE MARKET REACTION TO BORROWING ANNOUNCEMENTS

As mentioned at the beginning, a recently published study by one of the present authors examines the stock price reactions to announcements of new bank loans, private placements of debt, and straight public debt offerings.[7] The test sample consists, more specifically, of all public straight debt offerings, private placements of debt with nonbanking institutions (primarily insurance companies), and new commercial loans announced (in *The Wall Street Journal*) by 300 randomly selected nonfinancial companies over the period 1973-1983. All 300 firms are traded either on the New York or American Stock Exchanges.

The bank loan agreements in the sample consist of new credit agreements as well as the expansion of existing agreements. They also include both term loans and extensions of lines of credit (that is, commitments to lend). The most common agreement, however, involves a line of credit whereby the borrowing can be converted, at the firm's option, into a term loan. The private placements consist of debt sold for cash to a restricted number of institutional investors. Approximately 70 percent of the agreements involved an insurance company as the principal lender.

For the random sample of 300 companies, the study produced 207 financing announcements, which can be broken down as follows: 80 bank loan agreements, 37 private debt placements, and 90 public straight debt offerings. As shown in Table 3, the amount of capital raised by public debt offerings is considerably larger than private borrowing agreements. And, not surprisingly, the firms using private placements and bank loans are significantly smaller than companies issuing public straight debt. In fact, the average size of both the private placement and bank loan sample is about 25 percent of the average size in the straight debt sample. These findings merely confirm the widely-held view that private placements and bank loans typically involve small- and medium-size firms.

As also presented in Table 3, bank loans have considerably shorter maturities than either privately placed debt or straight debt. Indeed, the longest term bank loan is twelve years, which is less than the median maturity of either privately placed or public debt.

The Results

For each of 207 financing announcements, the percentage change in the firm's stock price was calculated over the two days surrounding the announcement date. The price changes were then adjusted for the firm's risk and for general market movements in order to provide an estimate of the return attributable to the financing announcement.

As summarized in Table 4, the market responded to 80 announcements of bank loan arrangements by raising the stock prices of the borrowing companies by 2 percent on average; positive responses

---

7. See Christopher James, "Some Evidence on the Uniqueness of Bank Loans," cited before in note 2.

TABLE 3
DESCRIPTIVE STATISTICS FOR COMMERCIAL BANK LOANS, PRIVATELY PLACED DEBT, AND PUBLICLY PLACED STRAIGHT DEBT FOR A RANDOM SAMPLE OF 300 NYSE- AND AMEX-TRADED NONFINANCIAL FIRMS (1974-1983)[a]

	Type of Borrowing					
	Commercial bank loans (sample size = 80)		Privately placed debt (sample size = 37)		Public straight debt (sample size = 90)	
Descriptive measure	**Mean**	**Median (Range)**	**Mean**	**Median (Range)**	**Mean**	**Median (Range)**
Debt amount (millions of dollars)	72.0	35.0	32.3	25.0	106.2	75.0
		(4-800)		(5-120)		(10-10,000)
Firm size (millions of dollars)[b]	675	212	630	147	2,506	1,310
		(28.6-10,311)		(20.2-6,365)		(47-59,540)
Debt amount/market value of common stock	0.72	0.46	0.52	0.25	0.26	0.15
		(0.04-2.6)		(0.04-2.6)		(0.02-1.5)
Maturity of debt (years)[c]	5.6	6.0	15.34	15.0	17.96	20.0
		(0.6-12)		(3-25)		(1-40)
Number of firms	52		34		43	
Number of firms with publicly traded debt outstanding[d]	25		16		30	

a. Statistics given in the first row are the mean followed by the median. The range is provided in the second row.
b. Firm size is for December 31 of the year immediately preceding the security offering or borrowing. Firm size equals the book value of all liabilities and preferred stock plus the market value of common stock outstanding. The market value of common stock is the product of the number of shares outstanding and the closing price per share at year-end preceding the announcement. Closing prices are from the *Security Owners Stock Guide*. The book value of liabilities and the number of shares outstanding are from *Moody's* manuals.
c. Maturity of the loan or debt offering is from *The Wall Street Journal* article. No information on maturity was provided for twenty-four bank loans, two private placements, and nine straight debt offerings. For bank loans that are convertible to term loans, the maturity of the term loan is used.
d. Firms are classified as having publicly traded if the *Moody*'s manuals report the firm had rated debt outstanding at year-end preceding the financing announcements.

were recorded in 66 percent of the announcements. Moreover, the market responded more strongly to the nine cases in which no actual borrowing was announced (3.7%) than to the 71 cases in which borrowing was announced (1.7%).

By contrast, the market response to the 37 private placements averaged -0.9 percent (significantly different from zero at the 10% level), with 56 percent of the announcements eliciting a negative response. Consistent with the findings of other studies reported in Table 2, the average market reaction to the 90 announcements of public straight debt offerings was -0.1 percent and thus indistinguishable from zero; 56 percent of these issues were also associated with a negative reaction.

If the positive price response to bank loan announcements reflected some benefit associated with borrowing through a financial intermediary,

TABLE 4
STOCK PRICE RESPONSE TO ANNOUNCEMENTS OF CORPORATE BORROWING[a]
(SAMPLE SIZE IS IN PARENTHESES)

Type of Borrowing Arrangement	Two Day Abnormal Returns
Bank Loan Agreement	1.93%*
	(80)
Private Placement of Debt	-91%
	(37)
Public Straight Debt	-11%
	(90)

a. The information contained in this table is from Christopher James's article entitled "Some Evidence on the Uniqueness of Bank Loans," *Journal of Financial Economics* 19 (1987).
* Significantly different from zero.

The fact that the price reaction to the announcements of private placements is negative suggests that commercial banks may indeed have a lending advantage over insurance companies and pension funds, and that bank loans may well be a special form of "inside" debt.

		Type of Borrowing					
TABLE 5 PERCENTAGE STOCK PRICE REACTION TO CORPORATE BORROWING, GROUPED BY THE STATED PURPOSE OF THE BORROWING[a] (SAMPLE SIZE IS IN PARENTHESES)	**Purpose**	**Bank Loans**		**Private Placements**		**Public Straight Debt**	
		Avg.% Ret.	**Avg.% Mat.**	**Avg.% Ret.**	**Avg. Mat.**	**Avg.% Ret.**	**Avg. Mat.**
	Repay Debt	1.14 (17)	6.5	.51 (5)	14.2	-.35 (32)	17.4
	Capital Expenditures	1.20* (24)	5.9	.23 (5)	16.6	.55 (34)	18.9
	General Purposes	4.67* (8)	4.6	.26 (9)	17.1	.07 (9)	17.1
	Repay Bank Loans	3.10 (11)	5.8	-2.07* (18)	14.4	-1.63* (12)	18.4
	No Purpose Given	1.74 (20)	4.7	na	na	.69 (3)	14.0

a. The information contained in this table is from Christopher James's article entitled, "Some Evidence on the Uniqueness of Bank Loans," *Journal of Financial Economics* 19 (1987).
* Significantly different from zero.

we would expect to see a similar price reaction for the announcement of private placements. But the fact that the price reaction to the announcements of private placements is negative suggests that commercial banks may indeed have a lending advantage over insurance companies and pension funds, and that bank loans may well be a special form of "inside" debt.

INTERPRETING THE STOCK PRICE REACTION

This pronounced difference in price reactions to bank loans and private placements may also arise, however, from differences in important aspects of the borrowing arrangement—such as maturity of the issue, purpose of the borrowing, or the risk of the borrower—that may have nothing to do with the identity of the lender. To examine this possibility, the study also tested whether the market reaction varied systematically with the stated purpose of the borrowing, the maturity of the offering, the default risk of the borrower, and the size of the borrower.

With regard to the stated purpose of the borrowing, we classified all 207 financing announcements (based on Wall Street Journal articles) into five categories: (1) debt refinancing, (2) capital expenditures,

(3) "general corporate" purposes, (4) repayment of bank loans, and (5) no purpose given. As presented in Table 5, the average response to bank loan announcements was positive for all of the purpose categories. By contrast, the average reaction to both private placements and public debt offerings was not significantly different from zero for all categories except one. Somewhat surprisingly, in the 18 cases of private placements and 12 cases of public debt where the funds were to be used expressly to repay bank loans, the average market responses were -2.1 percent and -1.6 percent respectively. Given this adverse reaction, why do managements choose to replace bank debt with private placements and public debt?

The most obvious explanation for the use of private placements and straight debt to repay bank loans is that management wants to lengthen the maturity of its debt. As shown in Table 3, the average maturity of the 80 bank loans in the sample was 6 years, as compared to 15 years for the 37 private placements and 20 years for the 80 public debt offerings. But why, then, would longer maturities have a more negative effect on the market reaction?

A company's choice of maturity may send a signal to the market about management's view of the firm's earnings prospects. When a company seeks financing, whether it involves the renewal of a loan or the issuance of new securities, the process of raising capital triggers a review of the borrowing company's current condition (and presumably its prospects) by reputable financial intermediaries (whether an investment bank, insurance company, or commercial bank). Corporate managements, by virtue of their willingness to submit themselves to the more frequent, periodic reviews required by loan arrangements, effectively signal their confidence in the firm's future. That is, when management expects the firm's credit condition to improve tomorrow (and feels that the firm is undervalued today), then it has an incentive to use shorter maturities today and to refinance after the improvement takes place. By contrast, the management of a company that expects its credit position to deteriorate (and whose equity may thus be overvalued) is more likely to attempt to extend the maturity of its debt.[8]

This raises a different, but nonetheless interesting issue: Why do banks specialize to such a degree in shorter maturities?[9] If a continuing relation between a bank and its customer results in lower costs of refinancing, commercial banks should also have a comparative advantage in making long-term loans to their existing customers. In particular, while a change in a firm's earnings prospects may result in a shift in its maturity preference, it is not clear why this action should result in a change in the intermediary used (for example, from banks to insurance companies). We have no good answers to this puzzle. Perhaps banks are reluctant to make long-term loans because of regulatory pressures, or perhaps they want to avoid a mismatch with liabilities that are principally often short-term.

A second factor that may explain the difference in the stock price reactions to the various borrowing arrangements are differences in the risk of the debt issued. The financing problem caused by the potential for inside information is expected to be most acute for smaller, riskier firms.[10] For, in cases where the perceived default risk of the new issue is appreciably higher, the price of the debt is expected to be more sensitive to changes in the firm's expected cash flows.

To examine the possible effect of default risk on the market reaction, the study used bond ratings as a proxy for risk. As shown in the top half of Table 6, companies issuing straight debt are far more likely to have rated debt outstanding—no surprise here—than the companies using bank loans and private placements. More than half of the firms announcing bank loans and private placements did not have a bond rating. Thus, to the extent we can rely on the rating agencies, firms announcing bank loans and private placements have considerably higher default risk.

In the lower half of Table 6, we present results showing that for each type of borrowing agreement, the market response is more positive the higher the debt rating. This result both confirms and contradicts the arguments we have made in this paper. On the one hand the fact that the riskiest private placements and public debt offerings elicit significant negative responses supports the "information asymmetry" hypothesis presented earlier. On the other hand, the fact that the largest positive market response attends announcements of bank loans by the highest-rated companies (and thus presumably those firms least in need of a bank's implicit "seal of approval") remains something of a puzzle.

In considering this puzzle, though, it is important to keep in mind two things. First, the sample of bank loans rated A or better contains only nine companies, and is thus hardly sufficient to provide a basis for generalization. Second, unlike the cases of private placements and public debt offerings, where the market reaction becomes markedly more negative with increases in default risk, the positive reaction to bank loans remains consistently and significantly positive over all risk categories.

Viewed in this light, the results seem to suggest that the use of bank financing is an effective means for management to overcome the "information problem"—one that is especially troublesome for small companies trying to raise capital for new investment.

---

8. See Mark Flannery, "Asymmetric Information and the Risky Debt Maturity Choice," *Journal of Finance* 41 (1986).

9. The Federal Reserve Board's "Survey of the Terms of Bank Lending" confirms this specialization by banks in short-term lending. The May 1987 survey reports that only 13 percent of commercial loans have a maturity of more than one year; and these loans had an average maturity of four years.

10. It is well known, for example, that smaller companies tend to rely on bank loans and private placements; and, as shown in Table 3, the median market value of the bank loan sample was $212 million, compared to $147 million for the private placement firms and $1.31 billion for companies issuing public debt.

TABLE 6
STOCK PRICE REACTION
TO CORPORATE
BORROWING
GROUPED BY THE
RATING OF
OUTSTANDING DEBT[a]

PANEL A: DEBT RATING[b]

Type of event	Proportion of firms rated AA or better[b]	Proportion of firms rated A	Proportion of firms rated BAA or below	Proportion of firms with rated debt
Bank loan agreements	0.12 (5)	0.10 (4)	0.78 (25)	0.48 (34)
Private placements	0.12 (2)	0.20 (3)	0.68 (11)	0.47 (16)
Public straight debt offerings	0.31 (20)	0.41 (27)	0.28 (18)	0.69 (65)

PANEL B: AVERAGE TWO-DAY PREDICTION ERRORS BY DEBT RATING[c]

Type of event	Rated A or better	Rated BAA or below	Not rated
Bank loan agreements	3.89% (2.82)	1.77% (1.92)	1.76% (2.18)
Private placements	1.18% (1.68)	0.30% (0.21)	-2.03% (-2.90)
Public straight debt offerings	0.40% (1.72)	-0.32% (-1.42)	-1.08% (-1.45)

a. Rating refers to the bond rating of the most recently issued debt prior to announcement. Ratings were obtained from *Moody's* manuals.
b. Sample size is in parentheses.
c. Z-value in parentheses: the null hypothesis is that the average standardized prediction error equals zero. $Z = N (ASPE^t)$, where $ASPE^t$ is the average standardized prediction error and N is the number of firms in the sample.

SUMMARY

One explanation for the neutral to negative reaction associated with the announcement of public securities offerings is the potential for management to exploit inside information by issuing securities when they believe that the firm is overvalued. Investors recognize this incentive and interpret announcements of public offerings accordingly.

One way for managers to acquire new financing without sending this message to the market is to issue "inside debt." By arranging a bank loan or, alternatively, a private placement, management may be able to mitigate the problem of "information asymmetry" that attends all financing by substituting commercial bankers or a small group of institutional investors for a large, diffuse body of investors.

In this article, we present evidence from the stock market that bank loans are the most effective form of inside debt. We also suggest that banks have an advantage over other inside lenders in evaluating and in monitoring the borrowing firm—in large part because of an ongoing deposit and customer relationship. The evidence suggests that, in some respects, bank loans are indeed unique.

CONVERTIBLE BONDS: MATCHING FINANCIAL AND REAL OPTIONS

by David Mayers,
*University of California at Riverside**

W hy do companies issue convertible bonds instead of, say, straight bonds or common stock? The popular explanation is that convertibles provide the best of both worlds: they provide issuers with "cheap" debt in the sense that they carry lower rates than straight debt; and, if the firm performs well and the bonds convert into equity, they allow issuers to sell stock "at a premium" over the current share price. Take the case of MCI Communications Corp. In August of 1981, the company issued 20-year-convertible subordinated debentures with a 10 1/4% coupon rate (as compared to the 14 1/8% it was paying on 20-year sub bonds issued just four months earlier). The conversion price of $12.825 was set at an 18% premium over MCI's then current price of $10.875. Eighteen months later, when the stock price had risen to $40, the issue was called, the convertible bondholders chose to become stockholders, and MCI received an infusion of equity in the midst of a major capital investment program.

But, as finance professors Michael Brennan and Eduardo Schwartz pointed out in an article published in the same year as MCI's first convertible bond issue,[1] the argument that convertibles represent cheap debt and the sale of equity at a premium involves a logical sleight of hand. It compares convertibles to straight debt in one set of circumstances (when the company's stock doesn't rise and there is no conversion) and to common stock under another (when the stock price rises and the issue converts). What the argument fails to point out is that convertible issuers may well have been better off issuing stock in the first set of circumstances and straight debt in the second. That is, if the firm performs very well, straight debt may have preserved more value for the existing shareholders by not cutting new investors into future appreciation. And, if the

*This research received support from the Charles A. Dice Center for Research in Financial Economics at Ohio State University. I thank Steve Buser, Peter Chung, Larry Dann, Tom George, Dan Greiner, Jeff Harris, Herb Johnson, Wayne Mikkelson, Tim Opler, John Persons, Cliff Smith, René Stulz, Ralph Walkling, Jerry Warner, and especially Paul Schultz for helpful comments. I thank Arnold Cowan, Nandkumar Nayar, and Ajai Singh for graciously providing me the use of their listing of convertible bond calls.

1. Michael Brennan and Eduardo Schwartz, "The Case for Convertibles," *Chase Financial Quarterly* (Fall 1981). Reprinted in *Journal of Applied Corporate Finance* (Summer 1988).

firm's stock performs poorly after the new issue, then common stock would have been better than convertibles—not only because there is no dilution of value, but because the firm may then have had the greatest need for equity.

As Brennan and Schwartz went on to say in their 1981 article, convertibles do not provide issuers with the financing equivalent of a "free lunch." Investors are willing to accept a lower coupon rate on convertibles than on straight bonds *only because* the issuer is also granting them a valuable option on the company's stock—an upside participation that can dilute the value of existing stockholders' claims. And provided the company's stock is fairly valued at the time of issue, there are no obvious reasons why convertibles should be less expensive than straight debt or equity.

But there are some less obvious reasons why convertibles may be a value-conserving financing strategy—reasons that depend on market "imperfections" such as transaction and information costs, and managerial incentives that are not fully consistent with maximizing stockholder wealth. Beginning with the pioneering paper on agency cost theory by Jensen and Meckling in 1976,[2] financial academics have proposed a number of ways that convertibles can reduce the costs arising from such imperfections. And, in a study published in 1998 in the *Journal of Financial Economics* (*JFE*), I presented yet another rationale for convertibles that shows how they reduce new issue costs and agency problems facing certain kinds of companies.[3] Put as simply as possible, my explanation views convertibles as the most cost-effective way for companies with promising growth opportunities to finance a *sequence* of major corporate investments of uncertain value and timing. Financial economists, along with a steadily increasing number of corporate practitioners, refer to such future investment opportunities as "real options." Such investments are options in the sense that, although they may not be worth undertaking today (i.e., they are currently "out-of-the-money"), they may become so in the future. And if and when such options move "into the money," the company will need to have sufficient capital (or at least access to capital) to "exercise" its real options and carry out its strategic plan. Convertible bonds are likely to prove

a cost-effective financing approach for companies with major growth options because of the ability they offer management to match capital inflows with expected investment outlays. In particular, as the company's real options move into the money and its stock price rises to reflect that, the call provision in convertibles effectively gives management the option to call the bonds and so force conversion into equity. And, besides eliminating the cash flow drain from servicing the debt, the new infusion of equity can in turn be used to support additional debt (or convertible) financing.

In this article, after reviewing the theory and evidence on convertibles, I show how my own explanation and findings are both consistent with and extend the previous research. Like other theories—notably, Jeremy Stein's "backdoor equity" hypothesis—my argument suggests that convertibles can be viewed as "deferred equity" offerings that add value for companies with promising future growth opportunities (that may not be fully reflected in current share prices). Unlike past theories, I show how convertibles are uniquely suited to the sequential financing problem faced by management in funding real investment options. Although there is considerable empirical support for my explanation in the past research, the most persuasive evidence comes from my recent study of the investment and financing activity of a large sample of U.S. companies around the time their convertible bonds are converted into common stock. In brief, my study of 289 conversion-forcing calls of convertible debt over the period 1971-1990 shows significant increases in corporate investment activity beginning in the year of the call and continuing for the following three years. This investment activity is matched with increased financing activity, principally new long-term debt, that is significant primarily in the year of the call. Thus, although equity is being brought in "through the back door" by the conversion process, new debt is being brought in along with it. To return to our earlier example, one month after MCI forced conversion of its first ($250 million) convertible bond issue, it floated its second convertible issue, this time raising almost $400 million. In short, my study suggests that convertibles are designed to facilitate the future financing of valuable real investment options.

---

2. See Michael C. Jensen and William H. Meckling, "Theory of the Firm: Managerial Behavior, Agency Costs, and Capital Structure," *Journal of Financial Economics* (1976), pp. 305-360.

3. See my article, "Why Firms Issue Convertible Bonds: The Matching of Financial and Real Investment Options," *Journal of Financial Economics* 47 (1998), pp. 83-102, from which article all tables and figures in this article are taken.

THEORETICAL ARGUMENTS FOR CONVERTIBLES[4]

Given that financial markets are reasonably efficient and that convertibles are a fair deal for investors and issuers alike, finance theory says that the issuance of convertibles should not increase the value of the issuing company. In fact, there is even reason to believe that the market's response to the announcement of new convertible offerings should be negative, on average.

Convertibles and the Market's "Information Asymmetry" Problem

In a 1984 paper entitled "Corporate Financing and Investment Decisions When Firms Have Information That Investors Do Not Have," Stewart Myers and Nicholas Majluf offered an explanation for why the announcement of a convertibles issue is generally not good news for the company's stockholders.[5] A company's managers have at least the potential to know more about their firm's prospects than outside investors and, as representatives of the interests of existing stockholders, the managers have a stronger incentive to issue new equity when they believe the company is overvalued. Because part of a convertible issue's value consists of an option on the company's stock, the same argument holds for convertibles, although to a lesser degree. Recognizing managers' incentives to issue overpriced securities, investors respond to announcements of both equity and convertible offerings by lowering their estimates of the issuers' value to compensate for their informational disadvantage.

This argument is supported by empirical studies that show that, in the two-day period surrounding the announcement of new equity issues, a company's stock price falls by about 3%, on average. In response to announcements of convertibles, the average market response is roughly a negative 2%.[6] (By contrast, the market response to straight debt offerings is not reliably different from zero.) The negative market reactions to announcements of new equity and convertible offerings cause the new securities to be issued at a lower price than otherwise. And in those cases where management believes the firm is fairly valued (or even undervalued) prior to the announcement of the convertible offering, the negative market response effectively dilutes the value of the existing stockholders' claims. In this sense, the negative market reaction represents a major cost of issuing the security (potentially much larger than the investment banker fees and other out-of-pocket costs). For example, if the stock price of a (fairly valued) firm with an equity market cap of $1 billion drops by 5% upon the announcement of a new $500 million common stock issue, the "information costs" associated with the new issue amount to 3.3% of the value of the firm (or 10% of the funds raised)—possibly a good reason not to issue common equity.

The Risk Insensitivity Hypothesis

Up to this point, we have mentioned the information costs associated with issuing convertibles. And such costs come on top of out-of-pocket flotation costs that are estimated to run around 3.8% (of funds raised) for the median convertible issue of $75 million.[7] What are the benefits of convertibles that would make companies willing to incur such costs? And what kinds of companies are likely to find the cost/benefit ratio for convertibles to be most favorable?

The first theoretical justification for convertibles consistent with modern finance theory was provided by Michael Jensen and William Meckling in their much-cited 1976 paper on agency costs. Among the sources of agency problems described by Jensen and Meckling are potential conflicts of interest between

4. This section draws heavily on Frank C. Jen, Dosoung Choi, and Seong-Hyo Lee, "Some New Evidence on Why Companies Use Convertible Bonds," *Journal of Applied Corporate Finance*, Vol. 10 No. 1 (Spring 1997).

5. S. Myers and N. Majluf, "Corporate Financing and Investment Decisions When Firms Have Information That Investors Do Not Have," *Journal of Financial Economics* 13 (1984).

6. See L. Dann and W. Mikkelson, "Convertible Debt Issuance, Capital Structure Change, and Financing-Related Information," *Journal of Financial Economics* 13 (1984); D. Asquith and P. Mullins, "Equity Issues and Offering Dilution," *Journal of Financial Economics* 15 (1986); E. Eckbo, "Information Asymmetries and Valuation Effects of Corporate Debt Offerings," *Journal of Financial Economics* 15 (1986); R. Masulis and A. Kowar, "Seasoned Equity Offerings: An Empirical Investigation," *Journal of Financial Economics* 15 (1986);

W. Mikkelson and M. Partch, "Valuation Effects of Security Offerings and the Issuance Process," *Journal of Financial Economics* 15 (1986); C. Smith, "Investment Banking and the Capital Acquisition Process," *Journal of Financial Economics* 15 (1986); R. Hansen and C. Crutchley, "Corporate Earnings and Financing: An Empirical Analysis," *Journal of Business* 63 (1990); and E. Pilotte, "Growth Opportunities and Stock Price Response to New Financing," *Journal of Business* 65 (1992), among others.

7. See I. Lee, S. Lochhead, J. Ritter, and Q. Zhao, "The Costs of Raising Capital," *The Journal of Financial Research* 19 (1996), pp. 59-74. In addition to the out-of-pocket flotation costs, there also is evidence that convertibles, like IPOs, are underpriced, by about 1% on average. See J. Kang and Y. Lee, "The Pricing of Convertible Debt Offerings," *Journal of Financial Economics* 41 (1996), pp. 231-248.

> *Convertibles do not provide issuers with the financing equivalent of a "free lunch." Investors are willing to accept a lower coupon rate on convertibles than on straight bonds* only because *the issuer is also granting them a valuable option on the company's stock—an upside participation that can dilute the value of existing stockholders' claims.*

a company's bondholders and its stockholders (or managers acting on behalf of stockholders). In normal circumstances—that is, when operations are profitable and the firm can comfortably meet its debt service payments and investment schedule—the interests of bondholders and shareholders are united. Both groups of investors benefit from managerial decisions that increase the total value of the firm. But, in certain cases, corporate managements find themselves in the position of being able to increase shareholder value *at the expense of* bondholders. For example, management can reduce the value of outstanding bonds by increasing debt or adding debt senior to that in question. (In professional circles, this is known as "event risk"; in academic terms it is the *claims dilution problem*.) Or, in highly leveraged companies, management could also choose—as did many S&L executives—to invest in ever riskier projects after the debt is issued (the *risk-shifting* or *asset substitution problem*). Finally, a management squeezed between falling revenues and high interest payments might choose to pass up value-adding projects such as R&D or, if things are bad enough, basic maintenance and safety procedures (the *underinvestment problem*).[8]

Debtholders, of course, are aware that such problems can arise in leveraged firms, and they protect themselves by lowering the price they are willing to pay for the debt. For corporate management, such lower prices translate into higher interest payments, which in turn further raise the probability of financial trouble. And for high-growth firms, in particular, financial trouble can mean a large loss in value from underinvestment.

Convertibles help to control such shareholder-bondholder conflicts in two ways: First, by providing bondholders with the right to convert their claims into equity, management gives bondholders the assurance that they will participate in any increase in shareholder value that results from increasing the risk of the company's activities—whether by further leveraging, or by undertaking riskier investments. Second, by reducing current interest rates and so

reducing the likelihood of financial trouble, convertibles also reduce the probability that financially strapped companies will be forced to pass up valuable investment opportunities.[9]

The Role of Convertibles in Reducing Information Costs

As Brennan and Schwartz argued in their 1981 paper, convertibles also are potentially useful in resolving any disagreements between managers and bondholders about how risky the firm's activities are. As suggested above, the value of convertibles is relatively insensitive to changes in company risk. Unexpected increases in company risk reduce the value of the bond portion of a convertible, but at the same they increase the value of the embedded option on the company's stock (by increasing the "volatility" of the stock price). And, as Brennan and Schwartz went on to show, it is largely because of this risk-neutralizing effect of convertibles that convertible issuers tend to be smaller, riskier, growth firms characterized by high earnings volatility.[10]

The Backdoor Equity Financing Hypothesis

The next major development in the theory came in 1992, when Jeremy Stein published a paper in the *JFE* entitled "Convertibles Bonds as Backdoor Equity Financing."[11] Beginning with the recognition that many convertible bond issuers build equity through forced conversion of convertibles, Stein developed a model that uses information asymmetry between managers and investors, and the resulting information costs, to explain why growth firms in particular find it attractive to issue convertibles. As Stein suggests, companies with limited capital and abundant growth opportunities often find themselves in a financing bind. On the one hand, they are reluctant to use significant amounts of straight debt because they face high expected costs of financial distress. Often lacking an investment-grade bond rating, the kinds of companies that issue convertibles are likely

---

8. For an account of the underinvestment problem, see Stewart Myers, "The Determinants of Corporate Borrowing," *Journal of Financial Economics* (1977). For a more detailed examination of these sources of shareholder/debtholder conflict, see Clifford W. Smith and Jerold B. Warner, "On Financial Contracting: An Analysis of Bond Covenants," *Journal of Financial Economics* 7 (1979), pp. 117-161.

9. More technically, the underinvestment problem arises from the fact that, in financially troubled firms, an outsized portion of the returns from new investments must go to helping restore the value of the bondholders claims before the

shareholders receive any payoff at all. This has also been dubbed the "debt overhang" problem.

10. In his 1991 Ph.D. dissertation at the University of Chicago, "Convertible Securities and Capital Structure Determinants," Stuart Essig reported that convertible bond financing tends to be used by risky firms, high-tech firms, and firms with a limited track record.

11. J. Stein, "Convertibles Bonds as Backdoor Equity Financing," *Journal of Financial Economics* 32 (1992).

to face high coupon rates on straight debt. And, even if they are able to issue high-yield bonds or raise a significant amount through bank loans, a temporary shortfall in cash flow could force their managers to cut back on strategic investment—and tripping a covenant or failing to meet an interest payment could even mean relinquishing much of the value of the firm to creditors or other outsiders.

But if straight debt financing is very costly in these circumstances, conventional equity financing could also have significant costs. For one thing, the management of some growth firms—particularly, those in a fairly early stage of a growth trajectory—may not feel the current stock price fairly reflects the firm's growth opportunities, and so the issuance of equity would be expected to cause excessive dilution of existing stockholders' claims. And, even if the firm is fairly valued, the information asymmetry problem described earlier might cause investors to reduce the value of the company's shares upon announcement of the offering, thereby diluting value.

In such circumstances, where both straight debt and equity appear to have significant costs, managers with a great deal of confidence in their firm's growth prospects may choose to build equity by issuing convertibles and planning to use the call provision to force conversion when the stock price rises in the future. Moreover, the stock market may actually encourage the use of convertibles in the following sense: If investors are persuaded that convertible issuers have promising growth prospects but no other viable financing options (i.e., there is little additional debt capacity and a straight equity issue has been ruled out by management as too dilutive), the market is likely to respond less negatively (or, in some cases, even positively) to the announcement of a new convertible issue. That is, management's choice of a convertible bond financing may function as a "signal" to investors that management is highly confident about the firm's future, thus allowing the issuer to avoid much of the negative information costs that attend conventional equity announcements. And there is some interesting evidence to support this view. In a 1997 study published in this journal, Frank Jen, Dosoung Choi, and Seong-Hyo Lee showed that the stock market responds more favorably to announcements of convertible issues by companies with high post-issue capital expenditures and high market-to-book ratios (both plausible proxies for growth opportunities), but low credit ratings and high (post-offering) debt-equity ratios.[12] And since high capital expenditures and market-to-book ratios are also reasonable proxies for the presence of the real options I discussed earlier, such findings also provide support for my own theory of convertibles.

A NEW RATIONALE

In my 1998 article in the *JFE*, I offered a rationale for convertibles that both is consistent with and extends Stein's "backdoor equity" argument.[13] Stein's model addresses itself mainly to the financing problem that growth companies face at a given point in time. That is, given that the firm needs financing and cannot easily service a large amount of straight debt, how does management raise a form of equity financing that minimizes the dilution ("information costs") suffered by the current stockholders *at the time of issue?*

The problem I address is somewhat different: Given that the firm needs financing today to fund current activities and *may* also require significantly more capital in the future (depending on how things turn out in the next few years), how does management minimize dilution and other costs over the expected *sequence* of current and future financings. To cite once more the case of MCI, how does management minimize not just the costs associated with its present convertible bond issue, but also that of the issue that is expected to follow its conversion, and, if the latter issue is likely to be a convertible, too, perhaps even the issue that is expected to follow it? Thus, a key consideration in my theory is the extent of both managers' and investors' uncertainty about both the value and the timing of the firm's future investment opportunities. As I suggested earlier, the presence of such uncertainty means that today's future investment opportunities are really "growth options" that may (or may not) be "exercised" at some point in the future—in most cases, by raising more outside capital.

---

12. Jen, Choi, and Lee (1997), cited above.
13. My explanation is also similar to recent explanations for other special financing arrangements: unit initial public offerings, where warrants are issued with shares (Schultz (1993)), and venture capital arrangements, where equity is provided sequentially (Sahlman (1990)).

> My explanation views convertibles as the most cost-effective way for companies with promising growth opportunities to finance a *sequence* of major corporate investments of uncertain value and timing. Financial economists refer to such future investment opportunities as "real options."

The Analysis

To show how convertibles can minimize costs over a sequence of financings, my study used a "two-period model" that works essentially as follows. At time 0, the company has a (clearly) positive-NPV investment project that requires immediate funding, and it also has an investment "option" that may require funding at time 1, depending on what happens between time 0 and time 1. In addition to its positive-NPV project and investment option, the company also has an abundant supply of negative-NPV projects (think of them as diversifying acquisitions) that management might choose to take if it has excess capital and no positive-NPV projects. All investment projects are assumed to have a life of one period.

Given these conditions, the challenge for management is to devise a financing strategy at time 0 that minimizes the costs associated with funding *both* the initial project *and* the investment option. My model assumes that there are only two major categories of costs: (1) new issue costs and (2) overinvestment costs. By new issue costs I mean not only the transactions costs associated with floating a new issue, but also the "information costs" discussed above.[14] Overinvestment costs can be described as the reduction in value that results from companies having too much capital—more than they can profitably reinvest in their core businesses. Excess capital is assumed to lead to corporate investment in negative-NPV projects because of the managerial tendency to pursue size at the expense of profitability. In my model, investors automatically assume that managers will invest excess capital in negative-NPV projects. Thus, if the firm announces its intent to raise more capital than investors think it can profitably use, investors effectively charge a higher cost for such capital by reducing the value of the firm's shares in advance of the offering.

My model also assumes that the company can choose among three debt financing alternatives available at time 0 (an equity offering is ruled out from the start as "too expensive," making some form of debt the preferred choice). It can issue two-period straight debt (that is, debt issued at time 0 and

maturing at time 2); this way, the profits from the initial project can be used to help fund the second-period investment if the prospects materialize. Alternatively, the firm can finance both projects separately by sequentially issuing single-period straight debt (and forgoing the second issue if the investment option proves "out of the money"). The third possibility is that the firm can issue a convertible bond that matures at the end of the first period and must either be redeemed or converted into equity at that point.

First, let's consider the two-period straight-debt issue. The advantage of this financing arrangement is that the proceeds from the first-period investment are left in the firm to help finance the second-period project if it turns out to be profitable (and this would also be true of an equity offering). For example, if the proceeds from the first project are sufficient, the two-period contract provides complete financing for both projects up front and saves the entire second-period issue cost. The problem with this financing alternative, however—and this would be even more true of equity—is that the second-period project will be financed, regardless of whether the investment option turns out to be valuable or not. And because the market anticipates this behavior, the firm's securities are priced at a discount to reflect investors' uncertainty about management's use of the proceeds.

The second financing alternative—sequential issues of single-period straight debt—avoids this overinvestment problem of two-period debt (and equity) by forcing managers to return to the market to fund the second project. But this choice also has a problem: if the investment option proves profitable, the firm may be forced to bear heavy new issue costs, particularly if managers have a more optimistic view of the new investment than the market.[15] And if it turns out that the firm really needs equity to fund the investment option, such new issue costs will be even higher.

The optimal solution to this sequential financing problem—the one that both economizes on second-period issue costs and helps control the overinvestment problem—is to issue a convertible bond at time 0 that matures at the end of the first period. The bond is designed such that its equity component is "out of the money" at issue

---

14. The issue (or "information") cost function is assumed to contain fixed and variable components, so that issue costs exhibit economies of scale, and the function is the same in each period.

15. Short-term debt typically has issue costs that are quite low, and the reader may wish to solve the cost-of-issue problem by sequentially issuing short-term debt. However, the periods are assumed long term, and long-term contracts are less costly.

and becomes "in the money" only if and when the NPV of the investment option is revealed (to investors as well as managers) to be positive. If the second-period project looks sufficiently profitable at time 1, the bondholders will convert their bonds into equity at the bond maturity date. This leaves the funds both inside the firm and transformed into equity that can then be used to finance the second-period project. But if the project turns out not to be profitable, the bondholders do not exercise the conversion option; instead they submit their bonds for redemption, thus controlling the overinvestment problem.

The Special Role of the Call Provision. Of course, like all models, this one is clearly unrealistic in many respects. To cite one of its most artificial assumptions, the model assumes that the maturity date of the investment option occurs at the end of the first period. But what if the investment opportunity materializes before then? If the stock price has appreciated sufficiently (in part to reflect the emergence of the new opportunity) to make the bond in the money, then management can use the call provision to force the bondholders to convert into equity.[16]

Forcing conversion has a number of benefits in this situation. First of all, the bonds no longer have to be redeemed at the end of time 1, thus eliminating the need to raise new capital (and the associated issue costs) to fund the new investment project. Second, since dividend yields are typically much lower than convertible coupon rates, forcing conversion halts the cash flow drain on the firm from required interest payments and allows the savings to be channeled into the new project. Third, the resulting addition to the firm's equity base allows it to raise additional debt financing for the new project unencumbered by the outstanding debt issue. As mentioned earlier, one month after MCI forced conversion of its August 1981 10 1/4% convertible, the company issued a new 20-year convertible carrying a coupon of 7 3/4%. Thus, a major advantage of convertible debt is that immediate conversion reduces leverage, thus making it less costly to sell additional securities when more financing is required.

Extension to Debt with Warrants and Convertible Preferreds. My model of convertible bonds—and to some extent those of Stein and Brennan and Schwarz as well—can also be applied to the cases of debt with warrants and convertible preferreds. Like convertible bonds, issues of debt with warrants and convertible preferreds also include options that provide additional financing (by allowing the firm to retain funds it would otherwise pay out) if the options are exercised; if not, the funds are returned to investors. (And it's interesting to note that MCI issued both convertible preferreds and debt with warrants before issuing its first convertible bonds.) Indeed, the attachment of these financing options may make sense whenever a real investment option exists, regardless of whether debt, common, or preferred stock is the initial choice. Thus, for any initial security type (debt, equity, or preferred), it can be advantageous to add a financial option as a hedge against incurring additional issue costs.

THE EVIDENCE

What evidence do we have to back this theory? Consistent with the MCI story, my own recent study found striking evidence of increased investment and financing activity around the time convertible bonds are converted. But, before reporting the results of my own recent study, let me briefly review some of the relevant findings of other studies of convertibles.

The focus of past research on convertibles can be classified into the following four categories: (1) managers' professed motives for issuing convertibles; (2) the frequency and timing of convertible calls and conversions; (3) the kinds of companies that choose to issue convertibles; and (4) the stock market's reaction to announcements of new convertible issues.

The first academic research on convertibles took the form of surveys of corporate issuers. Each of the three best-known surveys, published in 1955, 1966, and 1977,[17] reported that about two-thirds of the responding managers believed that their stock prices would rise in the future and accordingly viewed their convertible offerings as ways of obtain-

---

16. The Stein model explains the purpose of the call provision as helping to avoid possible financial distress. The call provision allows companies "to get equity into their capital structures 'through the backdoor' in situations where... informational asymmetries make conventional equity issues unattractive." Stein (1992, pp. 3-4).

17. C.J. Pilcher, "Raising Capital with Convertible Securities," *Michigan Business Studies*, 21/2 1955); Eugene Brigham, "An Analysis of Convertible Debentures: Theory and Some Empirical Evidence," *Journal of Finance* 21 (1966); and J.R. Hoffmeister, "Use of Convertible Debt in the Early 1970s: A Reevaluation of Corporate Motives," *Quarterly Review of Economics and Business* 17 (1977).

ing deferred equity financing. Management's belief that the convertible feature will be exercised because the stock price will rise is, of course, consistent with my argument that convertible issuers have future investment "options" that will require funding if they turn out to be profitable.

And management's expectations appear to be borne out by the subsequent experience of convertible issuers. For, as shown in a 1991 study by Paul Asquith, roughly two-thirds of all convertible bonds issued (and not subsequently redeemed in a merger) are eventually converted.[18] Moreover, a 1991 study by Asquith and David Mullins showed that essentially all companies call their convertibles if the conversion value exceeds the call price and if there are cash savings from the conversion (that is, if the after-tax interest payments on the debt exceed the dividends on the new equity).[19] The fact that such a large fraction of convertible bonds is ultimately converted is consistent with my view of convertibles as part of an anticipated financing sequence.

Among studies of the kinds of companies that issue convertibles, Stuart Essig's 1991 Ph.D. dissertation showed that convertible issuers tend to have higher-than-average R&D-to-sales ratios, market-to-book ratios, and long-term debt-to-equity ratios (when the convertible issue is counted as debt).[20] They also tend to have more volatile cash flows than issuers of straight debt. At the same time, convertible issuers have lower ratios of tangible assets (property, plant and equipment, and inventories) to total assets. The association of convertibles with volatility, intangible assets, and high R&D and market-to-book ratios is consistent with convertible issuers having significant future growth opportunities, as well as considerable uncertainty about the value and timing of those opportunities. The higher leverage ratios also are consistent with my argument since higher leverage means larger potential cash flow savings from calling the bonds and replacing them with equity when additional financing is required for new investment.

As noted earlier, the stock market reaction to announcements of convertible bonds is significantly negative, on average, though less negative than in the case of equity issues. Such a finding in and of

itself neither supports nor contradicts my explanation. But, as also mentioned earlier, the 1997 study by Jen, Choi, and Lee found considerable variation in the market's response to convertible offerings. The market reaction was significantly less negative to announcements of convertibles by companies with high market-to-book ratios and high (post-offering) capital expenditures. These are the kinds of companies that fit my thesis—firms with significant investment options that may pan out and require future funding, but may not.

New Evidence on After-Issue Investment and Financing Activity

In my 1998 study of convertibles, I tested my sequential financing hypothesis by comparing the post-issue investment and financing activity of convertible issuers with that of their industry competitors. I began by compiling a sample of all (436) calls of convertible bonds by NYSE or AMEX companies during the period 1968-1990. After combining multiple calls by the same companies within the same year (there were 35 such cases) and deleting cases without Cusip numbers (5) or call announcement dates (2), the sample fell to 394. Finally, I was forced to drop an additional 105 cases because some firms are not listed in *Standard and Poor's Industrial Compustat* data files—my source of information about the company's investment and financing. The final sample contains 289 events that occur during the period 1971 to 1990.

Table 1 lists the (two-digit) industrial classification codes of the companies making the 289 calls. As the table shows, convertible issuers are not confined to just a few industries, nor are they randomly distributed among all sectors. For example, both the oil and gas extraction and computer equipment industries have large concentrations of companies calling their convertibles. The firms in such industries would seem to fit the profile of companies with large ongoing financing requirements combined with significant investment options.

Table 2 contains summary statistics comparing the sample firms with their industry medians at the close of the year prior to the call. Like the findings

18. Paul Asquith, "Convertible Debt: A Dynamic Test of Call Policy," Working paper, Sloan School of Management (1991).

19. Paul Asquith and David Mullins, Jr., "Convertible Debt: Corporate Call Policy and Voluntary Conversion," *Journal of Finance* 46 (1991), 1273-1289.

20. Stuart Essig, "Convertible Securities and Capital Structure Determinants," Ph.D. dissertation (Graduate School of Business, University of Chicago, 1991).

TABLE 1 ■ DISTRIBUTION OF TWO-DIGIT INDUSTRY AFFILIATION OF 289 FIRMS CALLING CONVERTIBLE BONDS DURING THE PERIOD 1971 THROUGH 1990

Two-Digit Code	Industry	No.	Two-Digit Code	Industry	No.
01	Agriculture Production-Crops	1	48	Communications	7
10	Metal Mining	1	49	Electric, Gas, Sanitary Serv.	7
13	Oil and Gas Extraction	18	50	Durable Goods-Wholesale	7
15	Operative Builders (Bldg. Const.)	2	51	Nondurable Goods-Wholesale	7
16	Heavy Construction-Not Bldg. Const.	2	52	Bldg. Matl., Hardwr., Garden-Retl.	6
20	Food and Kindred Products	5	53	General Merchandise Stores	9
21	Tobacco Products	1	54	Food Stores	4
22	Textile Mill Products	2	56	Apparel and Accessory Stores	1
23	Apparel & Other Finished Pds.,	2	57	Cmp. and Cmp. Software Stores	1
24	Lumber and Wood Pds. - Ex. Furn.	2	58	Eating Places	4
25	Wood-Hshld. Furniture	1	59	Miscellaneous Retail	3
26	Paper and Allied Products	5	60	Depository Institutions	9
27	Printing, Publishing & Allied Products	2	61	Nondepository Credit Instn.	4
28	Chemicals & Allied Products	12	62	Security Brokers and Dealers	6
29	Petroleum Refining	10	63	Insurance Carriers	3
30	Rubber & Misc. Plastics Products	2	65	Real Estate	5
32	Abrasives, Asbestos, Misc. Minrls.	1	67	Real Estate Investment Trust	5
33	Primary Metal Industries	6	70	Hotels, Other Lodging Places	1
34	Fabr. Metal	9	73	Business Services	12
35	Indl., Comml. Machy., Computer Eq.	21	75	Auto Rent and Lease	3
36	Electr., Oth. Elec. Eq., Ex. Cmp.	12	78	Motion Pic., Videotape Prodtn.	2
37	Transportation Equipment	16	79	Misc. Amusement & Rec. Services	3
38	Meas. Instr.; Photo. Gds.; Watches	16	80	Hospitals	5
39	Misc. Manufacturing Industries	3	82	Educational Services	1
40	Railroad Transportation	2	83	Social Services	1
44	Water Transportation	1	87	Engineering Services	1
45	Transportation by Air	17		Total	289

TABLE 2 ■ SUMMARY STATISTICS COMPARING CHARACTERISTICS OF FIRMS CALLING CONVERTIBLE BONDS DURING THE PERIOD 1971 THROUGH 1990 WITH MATCHING INDUSTRY MEDIANS

	Calling Firms Mean/Median	N	Matching Industry Mean/Median	N	Two-sample Test p-values	
					t-test	Wilcoxon
Leverage (LTD/Equity)	0.94/0.47	286	0.53/0.30	248	0.0001	0.0012
Convertible Debt/Total Debt	0.30/0.23	263	0.01/0.00	238	0.0001	0.0001
Total Convertible/Total Debt & Preferred	0.31/0.24	261	0.01/0.00	238	0.0001	0.0001
Market/Book of Equity	2.12/1.60	289	1.64/1.40	250	0.0090	0.0002
R&D/Sales	0.03/0.02	119	0.04/0.01	224	0.1842	0.0986
Tangible/Total Assets	0.97/0.99	228	0.99/1.00	250	0.0001	0.0001

reported in Essig's 1991 study (cited earlier), my sample of convertible-calling companies had higher leverage ratios, higher market-to-book ratios, more R&D to sales, and lower tangible to total assets than the median values in their industries. Moreover, for these sample firms, convertible bonds were an

Companies that call their convertibles show somewhat higher levels of capital expenditures than their industry competitors in the years leading up to the call, but sharply higher levels in the years following the call. By far the largest changes in capital expenditures are reported in the year of the call and the year immediately following.

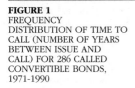

FIGURE 1
FREQUENCY DISTRIBUTION OF TIME TO CALL (NUMBER OF YEARS BETWEEN ISSUE AND CALL) FOR 286 CALLED CONVERTIBLE BONDS, 1971-1990

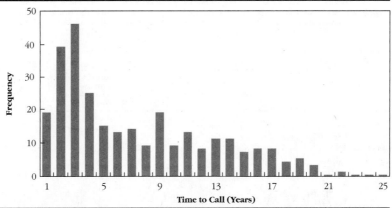

important part of the capital structure, representing on average 30% of total debt.[21]

The next issue my study addressed was the amount of time that elapses between the issuance and call of convertibles. Figure 1 presents a frequency distribution of the number of years between issue and call (time to call) for the 286 called convertible bonds that are identified in *Moody's Industrial Manual*. Although the original maturities of the called convertible bonds ranged from 10 to 35 years, with a median of 25 years, the time period between issue and call was relatively short. The mean and median time to call were 6.8 and 5 years, and the mode was 3 years. (MCI's 1981 convertible had a maturity of 20 years and was called in 18 months.)

I also examined the stated uses of funds reported in *Moody's* (by 279 issuers) at the time of issue. Although the most common is to repay other indebtedness (cited by 162 of the 279 issuers), most issuers mention other uses. And, in the majority of cases where debt repayment is cited, there is another use that can be interpreted as providing funding for corporate investment. For example, 95 issuers mentioned a desire to fund increases in working capital (including accounts receivable), 38 cited funding for acquisitions, and 74 mentioned various forms of investment, a category that includes "exploration," "expansion," "capital expenditure," and "new equipment." Thus, considering the relatively short time-to-

call together with the stated uses of funds, it seems highly plausible that most convertible issuers were considering the possible need to fund future investment options when raising capital for current activities.

Post-Call Investment Activity. Having looked at corporate statements of intent and the timing of convertible calls, the next step in my study was to examine both actual investment and further financing activity around the time of the convertible bond calls. For each of the 289 companies in my sample, I collected annual data from *Standard & Poor's Industrial Compustat* files on capital expenditures (a category which represents the funds used for additions to the company's property, plant, and equipment, but excludes amounts arising from acquired companies). My data collection began five years before the convertible call (year –5) and ended four years after the year of the call (year +4). For each of the 10 years (year 0 counts as the year of the call) and for all 289 companies, I calculated (1) the level of capital expenditures as a percentage of total assets and (2) (for nine of the ten years) the change in capital expenditures as a percentage of total assets from the prior year. Then I performed the same calculations for a control sample of companies in the same four-digit industrial classification.

As shown in Table 3 (see columns 2 and 3), companies that call their convertibles show somewhat higher levels of capital expenditures than their

21. These companies also tended to be among the larger firms in their industries; however, I think that the more useful comparison is that between convertible issuers and issuers of straight bonds in the same industry. Other studies (e.g., Essig (1991)) have shown that across industries small firms tend to have the greatest proportion of convertible securities. This fact is also consistent with the sequential-financing hypothesis since issue costs are more important for smaller issues, and issue size should be correlated with firm size.

TABLE 3 ■ MEAN AND MEDIAN CAPITAL EXPENDITURES AND CHANGES IN CAPITAL EXPENDITURES (LEVELS AND CHANGES SCALED BY TOTAL ASSETS FOR YEAR –1) FOR YEARS RELATIVE TO THE CALL OF CONVERTIBLE DEBT BY 289 FIRMS DURING THE PERIOD 1971 THROUGH 1990*

| | Capital Expenditures/Total Assets (%) | | | | Changes in Capital Expenditures/Total Assets (%) | | | |
| | Conversion Sample | Industry Match | | | Conversion Sample | Industry Match | Two-sample Test p-values | |
Year (1)	Mean/Median (2)	Mean/Median (3)	N(Sample) (4)	N(Match) (5)	Mean/Median (6)	Mean/Median (7)	t-test (8)	Wilcoxon (9)
–5	5.0/3.7	4.7/4.0	227	228				
–4	5.8/4.2	5.1/4.5	241	233	$1.0^a/0.5^a$	$0.4^a/0.4^a$	0.0967	0.2106
–3	6.8/5.8	5.7/4.8	245	241	$0.8^a/0.4^a$	$0.5^a/0.4^a$	0.4285	0.6412
–2	7.6/6.4	6.6/5.7	264	253	$0.8^a/0.7^a$	$0.8^a/0.6^b$	0.9377	0.9618
–1	9.2/7.1	7.8/6.2	276	268	$1.3^a/0.6^a$	$0.8^a/0.4^a$	0.1720	0.4009
0	13.4/8.8	9.5/7.2	273	268	3.4 /1.3	1.5 /0.5	0.0023	0.0019
1	18.3/11.6	11.5/8.1	261	268	$5.0^c/1.8^a$	1.6 /0.5	0.0001	0.0001
2	18.8/12.4	12.7/9.5	252	268	$1.0^b/0.9$	$0.3^a/0.2$	0.5132	0.0274
3	20.5/12.5	13.4/9.6	238	257	$1.8^c/0.9$	$-0.1^b/0.2$	0.0929	0.0138
4	23.2/12.2	14.6/9.7	224	249	$1.3^b/0.5^b$	0.7/0.2	0.5033	0.5719

*Tests reported in columns 6 and 7 (and indicated by the letters a, b, and c as described below) are paired mean and median tests comparing year-zero changes with the changes in other years. Thus, for example, the 3.4 mean value reported in column 6, year 0 is significantly different from the other mean values of that column in all years. The tests reported in columns 8 and 9 are the indicated two-sample tests comparing the sample and matching mean changes and distributions of changes for each year. Thus, for example, both the means and distributions differ in years 0 and 1 between the conversion sample (column 6) and the industry matches (column 7).
a. indicates significance at the 0.01 level.
b. indicates significance at the 0.05 level.
c. indicates significance at the 0.10 level.

industry competitors in the years leading up to the call, but sharply higher levels in the years following the call. Moreover, as can be seen most clearly in column 6, by far the largest changes in capital expenditures are reported in the year of the call (3.4%) and the year immediately following (5.0%). (MCI's increases in capital expenditures were 40.9% and 25.8% in the year of and the year following the call of its first convertible issue in 1983.) As shown in column 7, the industry-matched control firms also show their largest increases in years 0 and 1 (although the increases were only 1.5% and 1.6%). (And, to return to the MCI example, the capital spending of other telecommunications firms changed by –1.1% and 0.6% in 1983 and 1984.) Increased investment by competitors is not surprising since the profitability of investment options for firms within industries should be correlated. That is, when one oil company decides to undertake a major expansion, the same factors are likely to drive other oil companies to do the same. But even so, both the levels of capital expenditures, and their rates of growth, are significantly higher for the companies that force conversion of their convertibles.

Financing activity. Using the same *Compustat* source for the same sample of 289 firms, I next calculated the amount of funds received from (1) the sale of common and preferred stock, (2) the issuance of long-term debt, and (3) total sources—each as a percentage of total assets—over the same ten-year period. As shown in Table 4, long-term debt, common and preferred stock, and total funding sources all experience significant increases during the year of the call. For example, as shown in Panel A, the average increase in long-term debt for convertible-calling firms was 6.66% of total assets (as compared to less than 1% for the industry matched sample). And, as shown in Panel B, the increase in common and preferred stock in year 0 also is about 6%, which reflects mainly the conversion of the called convertibles into stock.[22] But then in year 1, the percentage of equity drops sharply (by about

22. I inferred this from the following procedure: Using the fractions of outstanding shares into which the bonds are convertible (about 14%), as reported in Singh, Cowan, and Nayar (1991), and the equity capitalization and total asset means from Table 3, I estimate that shares added through conversions on average represent 5.5% of assets. See A.K. Singh, A.R. Cowan, and N. Nayar, "Underwritten Calls of Convertible Bonds," *Journal of Financial Economics* 29 (1991), 173-196.

Long-term debt, common and preferred stock, and total funding sources all experience significant increases during the year of the call. Debt is clearly the preferred instrument for financing after convertible bond calls.

TABLE 4 ■ MEAN AND MEDIAN ISSUANCES OF LONG-TERM DEBT, COMMON AND PREFERRED, AND TOTAL SOURCES OF FUNDS (LEVELS AND CHANGES SCALED BY TOTAL ASSETS FOR YEAR −1) FOR YEARS RELATIVE TO THE CALL OF CONVERTIBLE DEBT BY 289 FIRMS DURING THE PERIOD 1971 THROUGH 1990*

| | Financing Activity Level/Total Assets (%) | | | | Changes in Financing Activity/Total Assets (%) | | | |
| | Conversion Sample Mean/Median | Industry Match Mean/Median | | | Conversion Sample Mean/Median | Industry Match Mean/Median | Two-sample Test p-values | |
Year (1)	(2)	(3)	N(Sample) (4)	N(Match) (5)	(6)	(7)	t-test (8)	Wilcoxon (9)
PANEL A: ISSUANCES OF LONG-TERM DEBT								
−5	4.4/2.6	3.6/1.3	195	224				
−4	5.0/2.8	3.9/1.6	205	229	0.8a/0.0a	0.7 /0.0	0.8398	0.3640
−3	7.5/4.9	3.4/1.8	214	233	2.7b/0.5	−0.3c/0.0	0.0003	0.0012c
−2	7.9/5.6	3.2/1.9	220	241	0.5a/0.0a	−0.2a/0.0	0.4828	0.5194b
−1	8.9/5.0	4.3/2.3	230	253	1.3b/0.8a	0.4 /0.0	0.3020	0.1939c
0	15.5/9.0	4.9/2.3	243	268	6.6 /1.6	0.9 /0.0	0.0001	0.0004
1	21.0/8.6	7.2/3.0	229	268	5.4 /0.0	1.9c/0.0	0.1410	0.2694
2	18.1/8.5	6.7/2.6	225	268	−2.3a/0.0a	−1.5b/0.0	0.7622	0.6488c
3	20.9/7.6	9.0/2.8	219	257	2.3b/0.0a	0.6 /0.0	0.4578	0.9114
4	22.4/9.1	9.6/3.2	207	250	0.2b/0.0	1.1 /0.0	0.7038	0.7552
PANEL B: ISSUANCES OF COMMON AND PREFERRED								
−5	0.9/0.1	0.3/0.0	200	224				
−4	1.4/0.1	0.6/0.0	212	229	0.4a/0.0a	0.2 /0.0	0.5335	0.3864
−3	1.7/0.2	0.6/0.0	219	233	0.3a/0.0a	0.0c/0.0 a	0.4362	0.0072
−2	1.8/0.2	0.6/0.0	227	241	0.0a/0.0a	0.1 /0.0	0.7142	0.2078
−1	2.4/0.5	0.7/0.0	238	253	0.6a/0.0a	0.0b/0.0 a	0.2119	0.0071
0	9.4/5.4	0.9/0.1	250	268	6.7 /3.5	0.2 /0.0	0.0001	0.0001
1	5.4/0.5	0.6/0.1	239	268	−4.0a/−2.4a	−0.3b/0.0a	0.0002	0.0001
2	3.5/0.2	0.6/0.1	232	268	−1.8a/0.0	−0.2 /0.0 a	0.1662	0.0037
3	4.1/0.3	0.9/0.0	220	257	0.7a/0.0a	0.1 /0.0	0.5740	0.8634
4	3.8/0.2	0.7/0.0	206	250	−0.6a/0.0	0.0 /0.0 b	0.6038	0.3575
PANEL C: TOTAL SOURCES OF FUNDS								
−5	13.1/11.2	14.1/11.6	210	224				
−4	15.4/12.7	16.0/12.6	219	228	2.4a/1.3a	2.2b/1.7a	0.8455	0.5159
−3	19.4/15.4	16.3/14.4	219	231	4.2a/3.1a	1.8b/1.7a	0.0180	0.0127
−2	22.8/18.5	18.3/17.2	212	236	4.0a/3.3a	1.8b/2.2a	0.0748	0.0773
−1	27.4/21.9	21.9/19.9	208	240	4.7a/2.8a	2.3 /2.8c	0.1112	0.7692
0	43.0/34.3	29.1/22.6	212	252	16.1 /12.4	7.3 /3.0	0.0043	0.0001
1	47.6/33.4	31.0/24.4	185	244	3.3a/−1.4a	4.3 /1.8c	0.7505	0.0012
2	48.1/36.7	32.9/26.1	169	221	1.8a/2.2a	0.4a/1.9a	0.6850	0.5429
3	52.9/36.9	38.7/29.4	150	200	5.0a/0.8a	3.8 /2.9	0.7025	0.2585
4	60.2/38.9	40.5/32.8	129	186	7.4 /2.8a	4.0 /2.2	0.4198	0.7757

*Tests reported in columns 6 and 7 (and indicated by the letters a, b, and c as described below) are paired mean and median tests comparing year 0 changes with the changes in other years. Thus, for example, the 6.6 mean value reported in column 6, year 0 of Panel A is significantly different from the other mean values of that column and Panel in all years except year 1. The tests reported in columns 8 and 9 are the indicated two-sample tests comparing the sample and matching mean changes and distributions of changes for each year. Thus, for example, both the means and distributions differ in year 0 of Panel A between the conversion sample (column 6) and the industry matches (column 7).
a. indicates significance at the 0.01 level
b. indicates significance at the 0.05 level
c. indicates significance at the 0.10 level

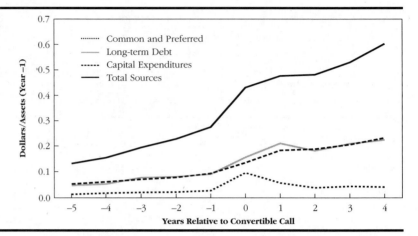

FIGURE 2
MEAN CAPITAL
EXPENDITURES AND NEW
FINANCING (SCALED BY
ASSETS IN YEAR −1) FOR
YEARS RELATIVE TO THE
CALL OF CONVERTIBLE
DEBT BY 289 FIRMS,
1971-1990

4%)—and the reason for this sudden drop will shortly become clear.

In the final part of my study, I also collected data from *Investment Dealer's Digest* (which reports all issues of public securities by corporations) on the financing activity of a somewhat larger sample of 365 convertible-calling companies around the time of the call. Of the 365 firms, 110 obtained new financing during the year prior to the call, while 144 raised new capital the year after the call, a significant increase of 31%. Moreover, of the 144 firms with new post-call financings, 86 issued only debt, 28 only equity, and seven only preferred—while 23 issued some combination of debt and either preferred or equity. Thus, debt is clearly the preferred instrument for financing after convertible bond calls.[23]

Another way to capture the relative importance of debt in post-call financing is to examine leverage ratios (LTD/Equity), which reflect private as well as public debt. As a result of conversion, there are significant reductions in leverage ratios by the end of year 0, the mean and median leverage ratios are 0.63 and 0.36, as compared with 0.94 and 0.47 at the end of the preceding year. But at the end of year 1, the mean and median leverage ratios have risen significantly to 0.81 and 0.39. Moreover, by the end of year 2, mean and median leverage are 1.00 and 0.43, which are indistinguishable from their values at year end −1. (And the same result is obtained using

total debt rather than long-term debt in measuring the leverage ratio.) This rapid increase in leverage ratios after the call explains the sharp drop in common and preferred in year 1.

In summary, Figure 2 illustrates the changes in both capital expenditures and funding sources of the 289 companies over the 10-year period surrounding their conversions. As shown in the figure, both the level of investment and total sources of outside funding experience notable increases in the year of the call and the year after. Nevertheless, equity funding, after rising sharply in the year of conversion, declines sharply in the next two years as companies follow with new debt (or convertible) issues.

CONCLUSION

In the "new economy," a rapidly growing proportion of corporate value appears to derive not from the profits generated by companies' current activities, but from their real investment options that may prove worth pursuing, but may not. For companies whose value consists in large part of real options (and Internet and biotech stocks are likely to fall into this category), convertible bonds may offer the ideal financing match (as long as the coupon rate can be kept low enough) because of the matching financial option that they provide.

23. Further, these estimates of the relative number of firms with new debt financings are likely biased down by the omission of private financings by the *Digest.*

> **For companies whose value consists in large part of real options (and Internet and biotech stocks are likely to fall into this category), convertible bonds may offer the ideal financing match because of the matching financial option they provide.**

In this paper, I propose that corporations use convertible debt as a key element in a financing strategy that aims not only to fund current activities, but to enable them to "exercise" their real options by giving them access to low-cost capital should the options turn out to be valuable. In this sense, convertibles can be seen as the most cost-effective solution to a sequential financing problem—that is, how to fund not only today's activities, but also tomorrow's opportunities. According to my analysis, the sequential financing approach is designed to control an overinvestment incentive that can arise if financing is provided before an investment option's maturity (i.e., before an investment opportunity materializes). The key considerations in my analysis are new issue costs (which include the "information costs" associated with selling underpriced securities) and the degree of uncertainty about the profitability of the firm's real investment options. The higher the new issue costs, and the greater the degree of uncertainty about the size and timing of the firm's future capital requirements, the more effective are convertibles both in controlling the overinvestment problem and minimizing costs associated with raising capital in the future.

As my analysis also shows, the critical feature of convertibles is the call provision that, provided the stock price is "in the money," effectively enables managers to force conversion of the bonds into equity. As option pricing theory suggests, the value of this call option increases directly with increases in uncertainty about both the eventual value and the maturity date of the real option. If and when the investment opportunity does materialize, exercise of the call feature gives the firm an infusion of new equity that enables it to carry out its new investment and financing plan unencumbered by the debt issue.

Because my analysis suggests the convertible feature is the key to solving a sequential-financing problem, my study examines the investment and financing activities of 289 companies around the time their convertible bonds are called and converted. Such companies made significant increases in capital expenditures (as compared to those by an industry-matched control group) starting in the year of the call and extending through three years after. These companies also showed increased financing activity following the call, mainly new long-term debt that is issued in the year of the call. These new issues of debt, which are often themselves convertible into equity, suggest that financing the exercise of real investment options is an important consideration in the design of convertible bonds.

THE ORIGIN OF LYONs: A CASE STUDY IN FINANCIAL INNOVATION

*by John J. McConnell,
Purdue University, and
Eduardo S. Schwartz,
University of California at Los Angeles*

Viewed at a distance and with scholarly detachment, financial innovation is a simple process. Some kind of "shock"— say, a sudden increase in interest rate volatility or a significant regulatory change—is introduced into the economic system. The shock alters the preferences of either investors or issuers in such a way that there then exists no financial instrument capable of satisfying a newly-created demand. Observing the unsatisfied demand, an entrepreneur moves quickly to seize the opportunity by creating a new financial instrument. In the process, the entrepreneur reaps an economic reward for his efforts, investors and issuers are better served, and the entire economic system is improved.

On closer inspection, however, the actual process of financial innovation turns out, like most other human endeavors, to be a lot less tidy than economists' models would have it. In this article, we provide an "up-close" view of the origin and evolution of one financial instrument—the Liquid Yield Option Note (LYON™).

The LYON is a highly successful financial product introduced by Merrill Lynch in 1985. Between April 1985 and December 1991, Merrill Lynch served as the underwriter for 43 separate LYON issues, which together raised a total of $11.7 billion for corporate clients. LYON issuers include such well-known firms as American Airlines, Eastman Kodak, Marriott Corporation, and Motorola. In 1989, other underwriters entered the market and have since brought an additional 13 LYON-like issues to market. In the words of a recent *Wall Street Journal* article, the LYON is "one of Wall Street's hottest and most lucrative corporate finance products."[1]

As academics examining a new security, we begin by posing the questions: What does the LYON provide that was not available previously? Does the LYON really increase the welfare of investors and issuers, or is it simply a "neutral mutation"—that is, a now accepted practice that serves no enduring economic purpose, but is sufficiently harmless to avoid being extinguished by competitive forces.[2]

In the spirit of full disclosure, however, we must admit that we are not entirely disinterested observers. Our association with the LYON is longstanding. When the early LYON issues were being brought to market in April 1985, questions arose about LYON pricing. We were hired by Merrill Lynch to develop a model for analyzing and pricing this new financial instrument. A by-product of this assignment was the opportunity to learn about the train of events that led to the creation of the LYON, and we have since followed the evolution of this market with interest. In the pages that follow, we relate what we have observed, thought, and contributed during the development of this new security.

WHAT IS A LYON?

The LYON is a complex security. It is a *zero coupon, convertible, callable, and puttable* bond. None of these four features is new, it is only their combination that makes the LYON an innovation. These general features of the instrument are perhaps best illustrated by considering a specific issue. Because it was the first one, we consider the LYON issued by Waste Management, Inc. on April 12, 1985.

According to the indenture agreement, each Waste Management LYON has a face value of $1,000

LYON™ is a trademark of Merrill Lynch & Co.

1. Randall Smith, "Tax Status of LYONs, One of Street's Hottest Products, Gets IRS Challenge," Dec. 17, 1991, p. C1.

2. Merton H. Miller introduced this Darwinian metaphor in "Debt and Taxes," *Journal of Finance* (May 1977), p. 273.

and matures on January 21, 2001. There are, by definition, no coupon interest payments. If the security is not called, converted, or redeemed (i.e., put to the issuer) prior to that date, and if the issuer does not default, the investor will receive $1,000 per bond. If this turns out to be the case, moreover, and based on an initial offering price of $250 per bond, the investor will receive an effective yield-to-maturity of 9%.

The Investor's Conversion Option. At any time prior to maturity (or on the maturity date), the investor may convert the bond into 4.36 shares of Waste Management common stock. Given a stock price of about $52 at the time of issue, this conversion ratio would appear to indicate an initial conversion "premium" of about 10% ($250/4.36 = $57.34). But, because the LYON is a *zero coupon* convertible and thus issued at a large discount from par value, the conversion "premium" is not fixed. That is, as we discuss in more detail later, the minimum share price at which holders would willingly exchange their bonds for 4.36 shares effectively increases throughout most of the life of the bond.

The Investor's Put Option. Although not entirely new, the most unfamiliar feature of the LYON is the right it gives investors to put the bond to Waste Management beginning on June 30, 1988, and on each subsequent anniversary date, at pre-determined exercise prices that increase through time, as shown below:

Date	Put Price	Implied Yield	Date	Put Price	Implied Yield
6/30/88	$301.87	6 %	6/30/95	$613.04	9 %
6/30/89	333.51	7	6/30/96	669.45	9
6/30/90	375.58	8	6/30/97	731.06	9
6/30/91	431.08	9	6/30/98	798.34	9
6/30/92	470.75	9	6/30/99	871.80	9
6/30/93	514.07	9	6/30/00	952.03	9
6/30/94	561.38	9			

Based on the issue price of $250.00 per bond, this schedule of put exercise prices provides investors with a minimum 6% rate of return at the date of first exercise, rising in three 1% increments to a level of 9% over the next three years.

The Issuer's Call Option. Finally, Waste Management has the right to call the LYON at fixed exercise prices that also increase through time. Although the issuer may call the LYON immediately after issuance, the investor does receive some call protection because Waste Management may not call the bond prior to June 30, 1987 unless the price of the Waste Management common stock rises above $86.01. The schedule of call prices is as shown below:[3]

Date	Call Price	Date	Call Price
Issuance	$272.50	6/30/94	$563.63
6/30/86	297.83	6/30/95	613.04
6/30/87	321.13	6/30/96	669.45
6/30/88	346.77	6/30/97	731.06
6/30/89	374.99	6/30/98	798.34
6/30/90	406.00	6/30/99	871.80
6/30/91	440.08	6/30/00	952.03
6/30/92	477.50	Maturity	1,000.00
6/30/93	518.57		

As in the case of convertibles generally, investors may respond to the call by choosing either to accept redemption payment from the issuer or convert their bonds into stock.

As mentioned earlier, although the LYON is a complex security, it is not entirely new. Callable convertible bonds certainly existed prior to the LYON, as did zero coupon bonds. And so did put and call options on a wide array of common stocks. What demand, then, did the LYON fulfill that was not being adequately met by an already existing financial instrument?

THE SEEDS OF THE IDEA

To address that question, it is useful to trace the history of the LYON. This history begins with Merrill Lynch and Mr. Lee Cole. During the mid-1980s, Merrill Lynch was the largest broker of equity options for retail (that is, non-institutional) investors. During that period, owing to the success of its Cash Management Accounts (CMAs), Merrill Lynch was also the largest manager of individual money market accounts. Individuals had over $200 billion invested in CMAs. CMAs are funds invested essentially in short-term government securities and, for this reason, are subject to little interest rate risk and virtually no default risk.

---

3. The imputed interest is computed by increasing the call prices at a rate of 9.0% per year compounded semiannually. If the LYON is called between the dates shown above, the call price is adjusted to reflect the "interest" accrued since the immediately preceding call date shown in the schedule.

During 1983, Lee Cole was Options Marketing Manager at Merrill Lynch. Cole discerned (or, more aptly, divined) a pattern in the transactions of individual retail customers. As Options Marketing Manager, Cole observed that individuals' primary activity in the options market was to buy calls on common stocks. The most active calls had a maximum term to maturity of 90 days and often expired unexercised. Viewed in isolation, this strategy appeared to be very risky.

In reviewing customers consolidated accounts, however, Cole observed that many options customers also maintained large balances in their CMA accounts while making few direct equity investments. From these observations, Cole deduced a portfolio strategy: Individuals (or at least some individuals) were willing to risk a fraction of their funds in highly volatile options as long as the bulk of their funds were largely safe from risk in their CMA accounts. They also avoided direct equity investment. He leaped to the further inference that funds used to buy options came largely from the interest earned on CMA accounts. In short, individuals were willing to risk all or a fraction of the interest income from their CMAs in the options market so long as their principal remained intact in their CMA account.

With these observations and deductions in hand, Cole drafted a memorandum describing in general terms a corporate security that would appeal to this segment of the retail customer market. In drafting his memo, Cole's intent was to design a security that would allow corporations to tap a sector of the retail market whose funds were currently invested in government securities and options. The security described therein eventually turned into the LYON. Because it is convertible into the stock of the issuer, the LYON effectively incorporates the call option component of the portfolio strategy perceived by Cole. Because of the put option, the investor is assured his principal can be recovered by putting the bond back to the issuer at pre-specified exercise prices. The LYON thus approximates the features of the trading strategy as perceived by Cole.

If Cole's theory were correct, the LYON would be a desirable security for individual investors and would give corporation issuers access to an untapped sector of the retail market. As with most theories, however, Cole's rested upon a number of unproven assumptions. The ultimate question, of course, was whether the security would pass the market test.

THE SEARCH FOR THE IDEAL ISSUER

It takes two sides to make a market. And while Cole had identified what he perceived to be a demand by investors, that demand could not be satisfied by every issuer. The ideal issuer would have to satisfy at least two, and perhaps three, criteria: First, because of the put feature and the downside protection desired by investors, issuers would have to have an investment-grade bond rating—and the higher the rating the better. At the same time, however, the issuer's equity would have to exhibit substantial volatility, otherwise the security would not provide the "play" desired by option investors. These two features were critical. Because the initial target market for the security was to be individuals, a third highly desirable characteristic of the issuer would be broad name recognition.

Beginning in mid-1984, the investment banking department of Merrill Lynch began the search for the first LYON issuer. That task turned out not to be a simple one. First, the population of candidates was obviously limited to those firms that needed to raise funds. Second, every issuer, even those issuing already tried and true securities, is anxious about the possibility that an issue might "fail." That anxiety is compounded when a new instrument is proposed—especially one as complex as the LYON. Third, because investment-grade credit ratings tend to be assigned firms with less volatile earnings (and thus, presumably, less volatile stock prices), the subset of companies with investment-grade ratings and volatile stock prices is a fairly small one.

After repeated presentations to a variety of potential issuers and after repeated rejections, Waste Management, Inc. expressed an interest in the security and authorized Chuck Lewis and Thomas Patrick, the Merrill Lynch representatives, to move forward with a proposal. Furthermore, Waste Management exhibited most (perhaps all) of the requisite characteristics of the ideal issuer. Its debt was rated Aa. In terms of volatility, the annual variance of its common stock of 30% placed it in the top half of all NYSE stocks. The only question was whether Waste Management had sufficient name recognition to attract Merrill Lynch's retail customers.

Its stock was traded on the NYSE and it operated in communities throughout the country. It specialized in the disposal of industrial and household waste; but it was not necessarily a well-known consumer product. The Waste Management name

Over time, the fraction of LYONs purchased by retail customers has averaged roughly 50%. Furthermore, the zero coupon, puttable, convertible bond apparently has staying power. Of the total proceeds raised through convertible bonds during 1991, roughly half were zero coupon, puttable convertibles.

was by then a familiar one, however, to the extensive Merrill Lynch brokerage network. Over the period 1972 through 1985, Merrill Lynch had managed four separate new equity issues for Waste Management, a number of secondary equity issues, and nine issues of industrial revenue bonds. All of these raised the broker and customer awareness of the company.

Over the same 1972-1985 time period, Merrill Lynch had also arranged a private placement of $50 million in debt for Waste Management and had represented the company in two hostile takeovers. This working relationship may have been the key factor necessary to overcome "first-issuer anxiety."

In any event, Merrill Lynch finally brought the first LYON to market in April 1985, roughly two years after Lee Cole drafted his outline memorandum. The issue sold out quickly and Cole turned out to be at least partly right. In the case of a traditional convertible bond issue, roughly 90% of the issue is typically purchased by institutional investors with only a tiny fraction taken by retail customers. In the case of the first LYON, approximately 40% was purchased by individual investors. Apparently Merrill Lynch had designed a corporate convertible that appealed to an otherwise untapped sector of the market.

And the appeal of the LYON to the retail sector of the market has persisted. For example, Euro Disney raised $965 million with a LYON issue in June 1990. Of that issue, 60% was purchased by individual investors and 40% by institutions. Individuals accounted for over 45,000 separate orders. Over time, the fraction of LYONs purchased by retail customers has varied from issue to issue, but has averaged roughly 50% of the total. Furthermore, the zero coupon, puttable, convertible bond apparently has staying power. Of the total proceeds raised through convertible bonds during 1991, roughly half were zero coupon, puttable convertibles.

Merrill Lynch, moreover, as the entrepreneurial source of this successful innovation, has profited handsomely from the LYON. In the case of the typical convertible bond, the underwriter's spread is about 1.7% of the dollar amount of funds raised. For the earliest LYONs, the spread was 3% and, at the present time, continues to be about 2.5% of the amount of funds raised. Additionally, Merrill Lynch

was able to "corner" the market for almost five years before other investment bankers brought LYON-like securities to market. According to the *Wall Street Journal* article cited earlier, since 1985 Merrill Lynch has earned some $248 million from sale of LYONs.

THE CASE FOR CONVERTIBLES (or, Financing Synergies from Combining Debt with Call Options)

But this brings us to the obvious question: What was the source of the gains to issuers and investors from the LYON that would allow Merrill Lynch to earn such large rewards?

Because the LYON is a variant of the convertible, let's begin by revisiting the "case for convertibles" made by Michael Brennan and Eduardo Schwartz in an article published in 1981.[4] The popular argument for convertible bonds is that they provide "cheap debt" (that is, they carry coupon rates below those on straight debt) and allow companies to sell stock "at a premium" relative to the current market price. But, as Brennan and Schwartz demonstrate, this reasoning conceals a logical sleight of hand: It effectively compares convertibles with a debt issue under one set of circumstances (when the firm's stock price doesn't rise and there is no conversion) and with a stock issue under another (the stock price rises and the issue converts). What it fails to point out is that the convertible issuer would have been better off issuing stock in the first set of circumstances and straight debt in the second. In short, convertibles do not provide the average issuer with a financing "bargain."

After exposing this popular fallacy, Brennan and Schwartz go on to argue that the real source of convertibles' effectiveness is that *their value is relatively insensitive to the risk of the issuing company.* Increases in company risk reduce the value of the bond portion of a convertible, but at the same time increase the value of the built-in option (by increasing the volatility of the stock price). Because of this risk-neutralizing effect, convertibles are useful in resolving disagreements (arising from what academics refer to as "information asymmetries") between management and would-be investors about the risk

4. Michael Brennan and Eduardo Schwartz, "The Case for Convertibles," *Chase Financial Quarterly*, Vol. 1 No. 3 (Fall 1981). Reprinted in *Journal of Applied Corporate Finance*, Vol. 1 No. 2 (Summer 1988). This article extends insights about the role of convertibles formulated earlier by Michael C. Jensen and William H.

Meckling, "Theory of the Firm: Managerial Behavior, Agency Costs, and Capital Structure," *Journal of Financial Economics* (1976), pp. 305-360. See also Clifford W. Smith and Jerold B. Warner, "On Financial Contracting: An Analysis of Bond Covenants," *Journal of Financial Economics*, 7 (1979), pp. 117-161.

of a company's operations. And it is largely for this reason that the use of convertibles tends to be concentrated among relatively smaller, high-growth companies with volatile earnings—the kind of companies, in short, that ordinary fixed-income investors shy away from. Convertibles are also well-suited to such issuers because the lower current interest payments reduce the risk of financial distress, which is likely to be especially disruptive for companies on a high-growth track.

Convertibles are also effective in cases where management has significant opportunity to increase the risk of the firm's activities. When such risk-shifting is a real possibility, the firm will be required to pay an especially high premium to issue straight debt, far more than management believes is warranted given its true intentions for the company. Convertible debt, because it can be exchanged for common stock, provides the bondholder with built-in insurance against such risk-shifting behavior.

But what has all this to do with the LYON—which, after all, is intended for investment-grade companies? To the extent the equity values of LYON issuers are more volatile than those of other investment-grade issuers, LYON issuers also presumably benefit from this risk-neutralizing effect that comes from combining debt with options.

To have succeeded in the manner it has, the LYON must also provide benefits that go well beyond those of conventional convertibles. The success of the LYON, as suggested earlier, has much to do with Merrill Lynch's ability to design a convertible that would appeal to individual investors.

RETAILING CONVERTIBLES
(or, the Value of the Put Option)

Lee Cole was apparently correct in his assessment that there was a latent demand among retail investors for a convertible-like payoff structure—one combining, in the case of the LYON, a *zero-coupon*, fixed-income component with an equity call option. By offering what amounts to a continuous option position, such a convertible would have the added appeal to investors of potentially large transactions costs savings. Recall that, under the call-option-cum-CMA strategy perceived by Cole, investors were purchasing a series of calls that expire at 90-day (or shorter) intervals, thereby incurring commission costs at least four times a year.[5] By buying and holding a newly issued LYON, the retail investor could maintain continuous ownership of an option position over the life of the bond without paying any brokerage fees.

But, to allow retail investors to take advantage of these long-dated, low-transaction-cost options, Cole realized the new security would have to be designed to overcome retail investors' normal resistance to convertibles. This could be accomplished, in part, by choosing only issuers with investment-grade bond ratings and with "name-recognition." But, to reduce the principal risk to levels acceptable to retail investors, the new security would also have to include a stronger, contractual assurance.

Hence the put option. By giving investors the right to put the notes back to the company after three years (and at one-year intervals thereafter), the Waste Management LYON greatly reduced the exposure of investors' principal to a sharp increase in interest rates as well a drop in the issuer's credit standing. In so doing, it dramatically increased the value of the security. (As we show later, the put option accounted for almost 20% of the value of the Waste Management LYON at the time of issue.)

Of course, granting investors such an option could turn out to be costly to the LYON issuer. A jump in rates or fall in operating cash flows could force the company to retire the bonds at the worst possible time. For this reason, LYONs issuers are likely to "self-select" in the following sense: Among companies with sufficient market volatility to provide LYONs investors with the desired option "play," LYONs issuers will also tend to be those with greatest confidence in the ability of their operations to weather a sharp rate increase, and the need to raise new capital under those conditions.

In short, ideal LYONs issuers are companies for which the benefit of granting the put option (and thereby gaining a retail following) most outweighs the expected cost of having to deliver on that option.

A Retail Clientele Effect?

But this brings us back to the alleged benefits of appealing to a retail clientele. Generally speaking, the "modern theory" of finance has offered little

---

5. Traded equity options are available with maturities as long as 270 days, but such options are much less liquid than their 90-day counterparts.

The popular argument for convertible bonds conceals a logical sleight of hand: It compares convertibles with a debt issue when the stock price fails to go up and with a stock issue when the price goes up. What it fails to point out is that the convertible issuer would have been better off issuing stock in the first set of circumstances and straight debt in the second.

encouragement to explanations of securities designed for specific kinds of investors. But there are notable exceptions. Robert Merton, in his 1987 Presidential Address to the American Finance Association, developed a model of asset pricing in which the size of the firm's investor base is an important determinant of the price of the firm's securities.[6] Starting from the assumption that investors invest only in a limited set of securities about which they have information, Merton's proposed model suggests that securities markets may effectively be "segmented"—that is, companies lacking retail investors may be selling at a sharp "information discount" relative to their retail-owned counterparts. To the extent such segmentation exists—and this is still a matter of sharp contention—management actions that expand the firm's investor base would increase the firm's value.

Moreover, a recent study by Greg Kadlec and John McConnell provides empirical support for the predictions of Merton's model.[7] Their study reports that the prices of stocks newly listed on the NYSE during the 1980s increased in value by 5% to 6% at the time of listing. Also suggestive, this increase in value is significantly correlated with the increase in the *number of investors* in the firm's stock from the year before to the year after listing. In sum, if we extend Merton's argument and this supporting evidence to the case of the LYON, it is plausible that the LYON's extension of convertibles to a previously untapped sector of the market could be providing significant value for issuers.

The Appeal to Institutional Investors

But what about institutional investors? Why would they "pay up" for a convertible with a put option relative to an otherwise identical convertible bond without one? To this question, our answer is again tentative and follows from the form of potential payoffs under the LYON.

During the mid-1980s, portfolio insurance began to flourish as a popular tool for portfolio managers. The general objective of portfolio insurance is to provide upside potential while limiting downside risk. And that is essentially the payoff pattern presented by the LYON. If the underlying stock price increases, the value of the LYON increases accordingly. If the stock price falls or interest rates increase, the LYON holder is protected by the floor provided by the put exercise price.

To the extent some institutional investors are willing to "pay" for portfolio insurance, then those investors might also be willing to pay a slight premium for the "insurance" provided by the LYON. Over time, however, as more LYON-like securities are brought to market, and as more investment bankers produce competing products, the spread commanded by underwriters should decline. In the meantime, Merrill would have earned its "reward."

ENTER THE MODEL BUILDERS

It was only after the Waste Management LYON had been brought to market successfully that Merrill Lynch asked us to build a model to value the security. Why the need for a model? The answer has as much to do with marketing as with the need of traders and issuers to analyze and price the security. The answer is also reassuring to those like us who view modern finance theory as a powerful, but practical, scientific discipline with important implications for corporate managers and investors.[8]

Following the issuance of the Waste Management LYON, Merrill Lynch intensified its effort to bring additional issues to market, both to increase the liquidity of the market for the security and to demonstrate that the security was not just a passing curiosity.[9] Following the success of the first LYON, other potential issuers showed more interest, but also asked more questions.

Three questions typically came up: First, what was a "fair" price for a specific LYON given the characteristics of the company and security in question?[10] Second, how would the security react under different market conditions? Third, under what

---

6. See Robert Merton, "A Simple Model of Capital Market Equilibrium with Incomplete Information," *Journal of Finance*, Vol. 42 (July 1987).

7. Greg Kadlec and John J. McConnell, "The Effect of Market Segmentation and Illiquidity on Asset Prices: Evidence from Exchange Listings," unpublished manuscript, Krannert School of Management, Purdue University (1992).

8. The model can also be used to determine the appropriate LYON hedge ratio.

9. It goes without saying that generating a fee for bringing the security to market was also an important consideration, but to continue generating fees from LYON issues it was necessary to demonstrate the continued viability of the security.

10. Interest in this question was motivated, at least in part, by critics who used a crude option pricing model to argue (to potential issuers) that the Waste Management LYON was underpriced by roughly 30%. The likely cause of such underpricing, as this article goes on to explain, was its failure to take account of the interaction of the values of the various components of the LYON.

conditions would investors elect to convert the security to common stock? This last question was asked by managers concerned about the dilutive effect of conversion on the company's EPS.

Pricing the LYON

The model we developed to answer those questions is based on the Brennan-Schwartz (1977) model for analyzing convertible bonds—which is based in turn upon the classic Black-Scholes (1973) option pricing model.[11] Interestingly, with some minor modifications, this model is still used by Merrill Lynch to analyze LYONs today.

Given the similarity between a LYON and an call-option-cum-CMA strategy, the great temptation in developing a model to analyze this security is simply to sum the value of the components: to add the values of the put and call options to that of a zero-coupon (callable) bond issued by the same firm. The problem with such an approach, however, is that it ignores the *interactions* between these values. For example, both the issuer's call option and the investor's conversion rights reduce the value of the put option (by reducing the expected maturity of the put). The value of the conversion option is similarly reduced by the issuer's call option and the put option, both of which reduce the probability of eventual conversion. Because of these interactions, the value of the LYON depends both on the conversion and redemption strategies followed by the investor and the call strategy followed by the issuer.

Our model makes the by-now standard assumptions of the option pricing literature that the investor follows conversion and redemption strategies that maximize the value of the security, while the issuer adheres to a call strategy that minimizes the security's value.[12] These assumptions, coupled with the assumptions that the value of the LYON depends upon the issuer's stock price and that securities are all priced to eliminate arbitrage profits, yield a fairly complicated differential equation for valuing and analyzing the LYON. Despite its complicated appearance, the equation can be solved numerically on a personal computer in a few minutes.

The "intuition" underlying the model is this: The higher the general level of interest rates, the lower the value of the LYON; the higher the volatility and the level of the issuer's stock price, the greater the value of the LYON; the lower the LYON call price and the sooner the call can be exercised, the lower the value of the LYON; the higher the dividend on the issuer's stock, the lower the value of the LYON (since higher dividends imply less stock price appreciation and less chance of conversion); and, of course, the higher the put exercise prices, the higher the value of the LYON.

For purposes of illustration, consider the Waste Management LYON described earlier. The table below presents the basic market characteristics, the characteristics of the firm, and the features of the bond as of the issue date. Given these characteristics, our model predicted that the market value of the bond as of the issue date should be $262.70. In fact, at the close of the first day of trading, the bond's price was $258.75. We tracked the bond over the next 30 days and determined that the model's predicted prices closely tracked the actual closing prices, but were typically slightly above the closing price. Apparently, the model has a slight upward bias in valuing the LYON.

Interest rate of intermediate term bond	11.21%
Stock price	$52.25
Stock price volatility	30.0%
Dividend yield	1.6%
LYON maturity	15 years
Face value	$1,000/bond
Conversion ratio	4.36 shares/bond
Call prices	In text
Put prices	In text

Sensitivity Analysis

In the following table, we show the effects of changes in market conditions, the issuing company, and feaures of the security on the value of Waste Management's LYON. There are a number of interesting insights from this "sensitivity analysis." The value of the Waste Management LYON is highly

---

11. For the formulation of the Black-Scholes option pricing model, see Fischer Black and Myron Scholes, "The Pricing Options and Corporate Liabilities," *Journal of Political Economy*, Vol. 81, No. 3 (May-June 1973). For the extension of that model to the valuation of convertible bonds, see Michael Brennan and Eduardo Schwartz, "Convertible Bonds: Valuation and Optimal Strategies for Call and Conversion," *Journal of Finance*, Vol. 32, No. 5 (December 1977).

12. This discussion draws heavily on our article "LYON Taming," *Journal of Finance* (July 1986). Whether investors and issuers follow these strategies is an issue of some contention. For a discussion of this controversy see Michael Brennan and Eduardo Schwartz, "Convertible Securities," *Palgrave Dictionary of Accounting and Finance* (MacMillan, 1992).

Given the features of the bond, the characteristics of the firm, and market
conditions as of the issue date, our model predicted that the market value of the
bond as of the issue date should be $262.70. In fact, at the close of the first day of
trading, the bond's price was $258.75.

insensitive to interest rate changes (a 200 basis point increase in yields would cause less than a 4% decline in the value of the LYON). But this insensitivity to rates is caused by the put option, which our analysis indicates accounts for almost 20% of the security's value. That is, *without* the put option, the LYON's value would be reduced from roughly $260 to under $215 per bond. At the same time, however, the *issuer's* call option reduces the value of the LYON by roughly $20 per bond (or 8% of its total value). It does so, as mentioned, by reducing both the probability of the investor exercising his conversion rights and the likely length of time that option is allowed to remain outstanding.

	Bond Value	Effect of Change on Bond Value
Basic features	$262.70	
Stock price to $56.00	271.68	+8.98
Stock price volatility to 40.00%	271.89	+9.19
Dividend yield to 3.0%	260.78	-1.92
Interest rate to 13.21%	252.38	-10.32
Without call	283.29	20.59
Without put	215.04	-47.66

The Question of Conversion

As noted, one question of frequent concern to LYON issuers is the stock price at which investors will choose to convert the bond to stock. In deciding whether to convert, the investor weighs the value of dividends forgone by holding the LYON against the downside protection provided by the put. Thus, if the dividend yield is relatively low, the benefits of conversion (to obtain the dividend) are also relatively low. But, even for low-dividend paying stocks, if the stock price rises high enough, it will be so far above the put price that the protection provided by the investor's put option becomes negligible.

Our model assumes the critical conversion stock price is the price at which the investor becomes indifferent between holding the LYON and converting to common stock. As illustrated in the next table, the critical conversion stock price for the

Waste Management LYON changes throughout its life, increasing steadily throughout the first 13 years, and declining sharply thereafter. There are two opposite effects driving these changes—one that is present in all convertibles and one that is unique for the LYON. As in the case of a conventional, current-coupon convertible, the optimal conversion price of the LYON is reduced because the value of the conversion option is shrinking along with the remaining time to maturity. But, unlike conventional convertibles, the conversion price in the case of the LYON is also *increased* through time by the fact that the redemption price increases while the conversion ratio remains constant (4.36 shares per bond)—which, of course, reduces the value of the conversion option. In all but the last two years, the latter effect dominates the former.

Date	Conversion Stock Price	Date	Conversion Stock Price
Issue	$129.50	6/30/93	$273.00
6/30/85	132.00	6/30/94	287.00
6/30/86	145.50	6/30/95	301.50
6/30/87	158.50	6/30/96	316.00
6/30/88	173.50	6/30/97	329.50
6/30/89	194.50	6/30/98	339.00
6/30/90	217.00	6/30/99	340.00
6/30/91	238.50	6/30/00	317.50
6/30/92	257.00	1/21/01	229.36

IN CLOSING

It is difficult to generalize from a single observation—and the Liquid Yield Option Note is just one of many successful financial innovations of the 1980s. The case history of the LYON does illustrate, however, that successful financial innovation requires ingenuity, perseverance, and, perhaps, a measure of good fortune. It also illustrates the potential practical power of modern financial theory in assisting in the development of new financial products and strategies. As practitioners of the science of modern finance, we were fortunate enough to be present at the creation of what now appears to be a successful financial innovation.

THE USES OF HYBRID DEBT IN MANAGING CORPORATE RISK

by Charles W. Smithson,
Chase Manhattan Bank, and
Donald H. Chew, Jr.,
Stern Stewart & Co.

T he corporate use of hybrid debt securities—those that combine a conventional debt issue with a "derivative" such as a forward, swap, or option—increased significantly during the 1980s. And, while many of the more esoteric or tax-driven securities introduced in the last decade have disappeared, corporate hybrids now seem to be flourishing. In so doing, they are helping U.S. companies raise capital despite the restrictive financing climate of the '90s.

Hybrid debt, to be sure, is not a new concept. Convertible bonds, first issued by the Erie Railroad in the 1850s, are hybrid securities that combine straight debt and options on the value of the issuer's equity.[1] What is distinctive about the hybrid debt instruments of the 1980s is that their payoffs, instead of being tied to the issuing company's stock price, are linked to a growing variety of *general* economic variables. As illustrated in Figure 1, corporate hybrids have appeared that index investor returns to exchange rates, interest rates, stock market indices, and the prices of commodities such as oil, copper, and natural gas.

The recent wave of corporate hybrids began in 1973, when PEMEX, the state-owned Mexican oil producer, issued bonds that incorporated a *forward contract* on a commodity (in this case, oil). In 1980, Sunshine Mining Co. went a step further by issuing bonds incorporating a commodity *option* (on silver). In 1988, Magma Copper made yet another advance by issuing a bond giving investors a *series of commodity options* (on copper)—in effect, one for every coupon payment.

Other new hybrids, as mentioned, have had their payoffs tied to interest rates, foreign exchange rates, and the behavior of the stock market. In 1981, Oppenheimer & Co., a securities brokerage firm, issued a security whose principal repayment is indexed to the volume of trading on the New York Stock Exchange. Notes indexed to the value of equity indexes appeared in 1986, and inflation-indexed notes (tied to the CPI) were introduced in 1988.

---

1. The date for the introduction of convertible bonds is reported by Peter Tufano in "Financial Innovation and First-Mover Advantages," *Journal of Financial Economics*, 25, pp. 213-240.

FIGURE 1 ■ DEVELOPMENT OF HYBRID SECURITIES: 1973-1991

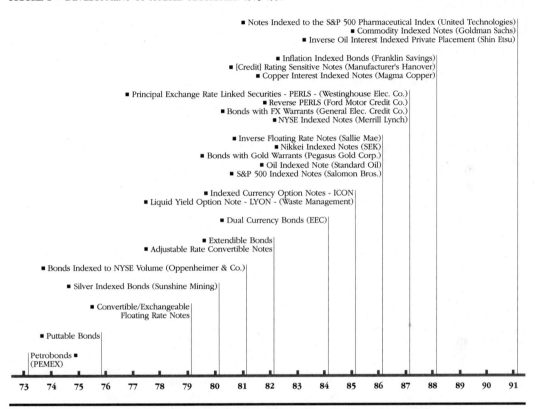

The 1980s also saw new hybrids with payoffs that, like those of convertibles, are tied to company-specific performance. For example, the Rating Sensitive Notes issued by Manufacturer's Hanover in 1988 provide for increased payments to investors if Manny Hanny's creditworthiness declines. And the LYON pioneered and underwritten by Merrill Lynch in 1985 grants investors not only the option to convert the debt into equity, but also the right to "put" the security back to the firm.

The pace of hybrid innovation peaked around 1987. But hybrids are now staging a comeback. As the title of a recent *Wall Street Journal* article put it, 1991 was "A Boom Year for Newfangled Trading Vehicles."[2] The past year witnessed the introduction of notes indexed to a subset of a general equity index, Goldman Sachs' notes indexed to a commodity index, private placements incorporating options on commodities, and a boom in convertible debt.

Why do companies issue, and investors buy, such complex securities? Before the development of derivative products in the 1970s, investors may have been attracted by the prospect of purchasing a "bundle" of securities—say, debt plus warrants—that they could not duplicate themselves by purchasing both of the components separately. And this "scarce security" or "market completion" argument also holds for some of today's debt hybrids (especially those that provide longer-dated forwards and options than those available on organized exchanges).

---

2. December 26, 1991, p. C1. The *Journal* article dealt more with exchange-traded products than with hybrids.

But, because active exchanges now provide low-cost futures and options with payoffs tied to all variety of interest rates, exchange rates, and commodity prices, markets are becoming increasingly "complete," if you will. Given the existence of well-functioning, low-cost markets for many of the components making up the hybrid debt instruments, we have to ask the following question: Is there any reason investors should be willing to pay more for these securities sold *in combination* rather than separately?

In this article, we argue that hybrid debt offers corporate treasurers an efficient means of managing a variety of financial and operating risks—risks that, in many cases, cannot be managed if the firm issues straight debt and then purchases derivatives. By hedging such risks and thereby increasing the expected stability of corporate cash flows, hybrids may lower the issuer's overall funding costs.[3] At the same time, though, part of the present corporate preference for managing price risks with hybrids rather than derivative products stems from current restrictions on the use of hedge accounting for derivatives, as well as tax and regulatory arbitrage opportunities afforded by hybrids.

PRICE VOLATILITY: THE NECESSARY CONDITION FOR HYBRIDS

The stability of the economic and financial environment is a key determinant of the kinds of debt instruments that dominate the marketplace. When prices are stable and predictable, investors will demand—and the capital markets will produce—relatively simple instruments.

In the late 1800s, for example, the dominant financial instrument in Great Britain was the *consol*, a bond with a fixed interest rate and no maturity—it lasted forever. Investors were content to hold infinite-lived British government bonds because British sovereign credit was good and because inflation was virtually unknown. General confidence in price level stability led to stable interest rates, which in turn dictated the use of long-lived, fixed-rate bonds.

But consider what happens to financing practices when confidence is replaced by turbulence and

uncertainty. As one of us pointed out in an earlier issue of this journal, in 1863 the Confederate States of America issued a 20-year bond denominated not in Confederate dollars, but in French Francs and Pounds Sterling. To allay the concern of its overseas investors that the Confederacy would not be around to service its debt with hard currency, the issue was also convertible at the option of the holder into cotton at the rate of six pence per pound. In the parlance of today's investment banker, the Confederate States issued a *dual-currency, cotton-indexed* bond.[4]

The Breakdown of Bretton Woods and the New Era of Volatility

Throughout the 1950s and most of the 1960s, economic and price stability prevailed in the U.S., and in the developed nations generally. Investment-grade U.S. corporations responded predictably by raising capital in the form of 30-year, fixed-rate bonds (yielding around 3-4%). But, toward the end of the '60s, rates of inflation in the U.S. and U.K. began to increase. There was also considerable divergence among developed countries in monetary and fiscal policy, and thus in rates of inflation. Such pressures led inevitably to the abandonment, in 1973, of the Bretton Woods agreement to maintain relatively fixed exchanged rates. And, during the early 1970s and thereafter, the general economic environment saw higher and more volatile rates of inflation along with unprecedented volatility in exchange rates, interest rates, and commodity prices. (For evidence of such general price volatility, see Figure 2.)

In response to this heightened price volatility, capital markets created new financial instruments to help investors and issuers manage their exposures. Indeed, the last 20 years has seen the introduction of (1) futures on foreign exchange, interest rates, metals, and oil; (2) currency, interest rate, and commodity swaps; (3) options on exchange rates, interest rates, and oil; and (4) options on the above futures and options. Flourishing markets for these products in turn helped give rise to corporate hybrid debt securities that effectively incorporate these derivative products.

---

3. For preliminary evidence of the impact of issuing hybrid debt on the firm's cost of capital, see Charles Smithson and Leah Schraudenbach, "Reflection of Financial Price Risk in the Firm's Share Price," Chase Manhattan Bank, 1992.

4. Waite Rawls and Charles Smithson, "The Evolution of Risk Management Products," *Journal of Applied Corporate Finance*, Vol. 1 No. 4 (1989).

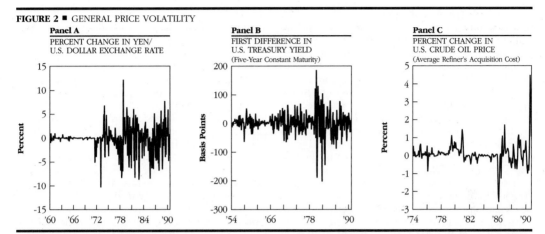

FIGURE 2 ■ GENERAL PRICE VOLATILITY

Panel A
PERCENT CHANGE IN YEN/
U.S. DOLLAR EXCHANGE RATE

Panel B
FIRST DIFFERENCE IN
U.S. TREASURY YIELD
(Five-Year Constant Maturity)

Panel C
PERCENT CHANGE IN
U.S. CRUDE OIL PRICE
(Average Refiner's Acquisition Cost)

USING HYBRIDS TO MANAGE COMMODITY RISK

Unlike foreign exchange and interest rates, which were relatively stable until the 1970s, commodity prices have a long history of volatility. Thus, it is no surprise that hybrid securities designed to hedge commodity price risks came well before hybrids with embedded currency and interest rate derivatives.

As mentioned earlier, the Confederacy issued a debt instrument convertible into cotton in 1863. By the 1920s, commodity-linked hybrids were available in U.S. capital markets. A case in point is the gold-indexed bond issued by Irving Fisher's Rand Kardex Corporation in 1925. Similar to the PEMEX issue described earlier, the principal repayment of this gold-indexed bond was tied directly to gold prices.[5] Fisher realized that he could significantly lower his firm's funding costs by furnishing a scarce security desired by investors—in this case, a long-dated forward on gold prices. And Fisher's successful innovation was imitated by a number of other U.S. companies during the '20s.

Like so many of the financial innovations of the 1920s, however, that wave of hybrid debt financings was ended by the regulatory reaction that set in during the 1930s.[6] Specifically, the "Gold Clause" Joint Congressional Resolution of June 5, 1933

virtually eliminated indexed debt by prohibiting "a lender to require of a borrower a different quantity or number of dollars from that loaned." And it was not until October 1977, when Congress passed the Helms Amendment, that the legal basis for commodity-indexed debt was restored.

Hybrids with Option Features

The hybrids issued by Rand Kardex and PEMEX represent combinations of debt securities with forward contracts; that is, the promised principal repayments were designed to rise or fall directly with changes in the prices, respectively, of gold and oil. In the case of PEMEX, moreover, this forward-like feature reduced the risk to investors that the issuer wouldn't be able to repay principal; it did so by making the *amount* of the principal vary as directly as possible with the company's oil revenues.

Unlike the PEMEX and Rand Kardex issues, Sunshine Mining's 15-year silver-linked bond issued in 1980 combined a debt issue with a *European option*[7] on silver prices. In this case, the promised principal repayment could not fall below a certain level (the face value), but would increase proportionally with increases in the price of silver price above $20 per ounce at maturity.[8] Because most of

5. See J. Huston McCulloch, "The Ban on Indexed Bonds," *American Economic Review* 70 (December 1980), pp. 1018-21.

6. See Merton Miller's account of financial innovation in the 1920s and 1930s in the first article of this issue.

7. European options can be exercised only at maturity, as distinguished from American options, which can be exercised any time before expiration.

8. From the perspective of 1991, during which the silver price has averaged $4.00 per ounce, this exercise price of $20 per ounce may seem bizarre. But keep in mind that this bond was issued in early 1980. During the period October 1979-January 1980, the price of silver averaged $23 per ounce.

**In return for being granted this upside participation, bondholders will reduce
the risk premium they charge. Indeed, the greater the expected volatility
of the commodity price in question, the more valuable is that
embedded option to the bondholders.**

the commodity-linked hybrids that followed the Sunshine Mining issue in the '80s contain embedded options rather than forwards, let's consider briefly how the embedding of options within debt issues manages risk and lowers the issuer's cost of capital.

How Hybrids with Options Manage Risk. Corporate bondholders bear "downside" risk while typically being limited to a fixed interest rate as their reward. (In the jargon of options, the bondholder is "short a put" on the value of the firm's assets.) Because of this limited upside, they charge a higher "risk premium" when asked to fund companies with more volatile earnings streams. Like the forward contract embedded in the PEMEX issue, options also provide bondholders with an equity-like, "upside" participation. In return for this upside participation, bondholders will reduce the risk premium they charge. Indeed, the greater the expected volatility of the commodity price in question, the more valuable is that embedded option to the bondholders.[9]

Unlike hybrids with forwards, hybrids with embedded options provide investors with a "floor"—that is, a minimum principal repayment or set of coupons. And, though options therefore effect a less complete transfer of risk than in the case of forwards (in the sense that the firm's financing costs don't fall below the floor in the event of an extreme decline in commodity prices), investors should be willing to pay for the floor in the form of a reduced base rate of interest. To the extent they lower the rate of interest, option-like hybrids reduce the probability of default, thus reassuring bondholders and the rating agencies.

A good example of corporate risk management with options was a 1986 issue of Eurobonds with detachable gold warrants by Pegasus Gold Corporation, a Canadian gold mining firm. In effect, this issue gave investors two separable claims: (1) a straight debt issue with a series of fixed interest payments and a fixed principal repayment; and (2) European options on the price of gold. By giving bondholders a participation in the firm's gold revenues, the inclusion of such warrants reduced the coupon rate on the bond—which in turn lowered the issuer's financial risk.

Probably the most newsworthy hybrid in 1986, however, was Standard Oil's *Oil-Indexed Note*. This hybrid combines a zero-coupon bond with a European option on oil with the same maturity. The issue not only aroused the interest of the IRS, but also succeeded in rekindling regulatory concerns about the potential for "speculative abuse" built into hybrid securities.[10]

Commodity Interest-Indexed Bonds. The commodity hybrids mentioned thus far are all combinations of debt with forwards or options with a single maturity. In effect, they link only the principal repayment to commodity prices, but not the interim interest payments. But, in recent years, hybrids have also emerged that combine debt with a *series of options* of different maturities—maturities that are typically designed to correspond to the coupon dates of the underlying bond.

In 1988, for example, Magma Copper Company issued *Copper Interest-Indexed Senior Subordinated Notes*. This 10-year debenture has embedded within it 40 option positions on the price of copper—one maturing in 3 months, one in 6 months, ..., and one in 10 years. The effect of this series of embedded option positions is to make the company's quarterly interest payments vary with the prevailing price of copper, as shown below:

Average Copper Price	Indexed Interest Rate
$2.00 or above	21 %
1.80	20
1.60	19
1.40	18
1.30	17
1.20	16
1.10	15
1.00	14
0.90	13
0.80 or below	12

In 1989, Presidio Oil Company issued an oil-indexed note with a similar structure, but with the coupons linked to the price of natural gas. And, in 1991, Shin Etsu, a Japanese chemical manufacturer,

---

9. For a discussion of how the equity option embedded in convertibles could make convertible bondholders indifferent to increases in the volatility of corporate cash flow, see Michael Brennan and Eduardo Schwartz, "The Case for Convertibles," *Chase Financial Quarterly* (Fall 1981). Reprinted in *Journal of Applied Corporate Finance* (Summer 1988).

10. See James Jordan, Robert Mackay, and Eugene Moriarty, "The New Regulation of Hybrid Debt Instruments," *Journal of Applied Corporate Finance*, Vol. 2 No. 4 (Winter 1990).

issued a hybrid with a similar structure; however, the issue was a private placement and the coupon payment floated *inversely* with the price of oil.

The Case of Forest Oil:
The Consequences of Not Managing Risk

It was Forest Oil, however, and not Presidio, that first considered issuing natural gas-linked debt. But Forest's management was confident that natural gas prices would go higher in the near future and thus decided that the price of the natural gas-linked debt would turn out to be too high. Unfortunately, the company's bet on natural gas prices ended up going against them. Natural gas prices since the issue was contemplated have fallen dramatically, and the company has been squeezed between high current interest costs and reduced revenues. Indeed, the squeeze has been so tight that Forest has been forced to restructure its debt.

USING HYBRIDS TO MANAGE FOREIGN EXCHANGE RISK

As Figure 2 suggests, exchange rates became more volatile following the abandonment of the Bretton Woods agreement in 1973. As a result, many companies have experienced foreign exchange risk arising from transaction, translation, and economic exposures.

The simplest way to manage an exposure to foreign exchange risk is by using a forward foreign exchange contract. If the firm is long foreign currency, it can cover this exposure by selling forward contracts. Or if it has a short position, it can buy forwards.

Dual Currency Bonds. Similar to PEMEX's oil-indexed issue, the simplest FX hybrid debt structure is a *Dual Currency Bond*. Such a bond combines a fixed-rate, "bullet" (that is, single) repayment bond and a long-dated forward contract on foreign exchange. For example, in 1985, Philip Morris Credit issued a dual-currency bond in which coupon payments are made in Swiss Francs while principal will be repaid US Dollars.

PERLs. A variant of the dual currency structure is the *Principal Exchange Rate Linked Security*. In 1987, Westinghouse Electric Company issued *PERLs*

wherein the bondholder received at maturity the principal the USD value of 70.13 million New Zealand dollars. The issuer's motive in this case was likely to reduce its funding costs by taking advantage of an unusual investor demand for long-dated currency forwards. Earlier in the same year, and presumably with similar motive, Ford Motor Credit Company issued *Reverse PERLs*. In this case, the principal repayment varied inversely with the value of the yen.[11]

Creating a Hybrid by Adding Options

As in the case of commodity-linked hybrids, forward-like FX hybrids seemed to have given way to structures containing warrants or other option-like features. In 1987, for example, General Electric Credit Corporation made a public offering made up of debt and yen-USD currency exchange warrants.

Bonds with Principal Indexed (Convertible) to FX. Like bonds with warrants, convertible bonds are made up of bonds and equity options. But there is one important difference: In the case of bonds with warrants, the bondholder can exercise the option embodied in a warrant and still keep the underlying bond. With convertibles, the holder must surrender the bond to exercise the option. Sunshine Mining's Silver-Indexed Bonds and Standard Oil's Oil Indexed Notes are similar constructions. The bondholder can receive either the value of the bond or the value of the option, but not both.

When this debt structure appeared with an embedded foreign currency option, the hybrid was called an *Indexed Currency Option Note* (or *ICON*). This security, which was first underwritten by First Boston in 1985, combines a fixed rate, bullet repayment bond and a European option on foreign exchange.[12]

USING HYBRIDS TO MANAGE INTEREST RATE RISK

Some companies have significant exposures to interest rates. Take the case of firms that supply inputs to the housing market. When interest rates rise, the revenues of such firms tend to fall. The use of standard, floating-rate bank debt in such cases would likely increase the probability of default.

---

11. See Michael G. Capatides, *A Guide to the Capital Markets Activities of Banks and Bank Holding Companies*, (Browne & Co.), 1988, p. 132.

12. In his article in this issue, "Securities Innovation: An Overview," John Finnerty notes that ICONs "were introduced and disappeared quickly."

Corporate hybrids reduce shareholder-bondholder conflicts by reducing current
interest rates, shifting debt service payments to periods when firms are better able
to pay, stabilizing cash flow, and thereby reducing the likelihood of financial
distress.

Creating a Hybrid with Embedded Swaps

To manage interest rate risk, such companies may be best served by a debt instrument wherein the coupon payment actually declines when interest rates rise. Such an *Inverse Floating Rate Note*—or a *Yield-Curve Note*, as it was called when first issued by the Student Loan Marketing Association (Sallie Mae) in the public debt market in 1986—can be decomposed into a floating-rate, bullet repayment note and a plain vanilla interest rate swap for twice the principal of the loan.

Creating a Hybrid by Adding Options

Just as bondholders can be provided options to exchange their bonds for a specified amount of a commodity or foreign currency, hybrid securities have been issued that give bondholders the option to exchange a bond (typically at maturity) for another bond (typically with the same coupon and maturity).

Convertible/Exchangeable Floating Rate Notes. These hybrids, which give the holder the right to convert to (or exchange for) a fixed-rate bond at a pre-specified interest rate, first appeared in 1979. Such notes contain embedded "put" options on interest rates; that is, investors are likely to exercise their conversion or exchange rights only if interest rates fall below a certain level.

Extendible Notes. The same, moreover, is true of extendible notes, which give the holder the right to exchange the underlying bond for a bond of longer maturity. Such bonds first appeared in 1982.

USING HYBRIDS TO REDUCE CONFLICTS BETWEEN BONDHOLDERS AND SHAREHOLDERS

In "normal" circumstances—that is, when operations are profitable and the firm can comfortably meet its debt service payments and investment schedule—the interests of bondholders and shareholders are united. Both groups of investors benefit from managerial decisions that increase the total value of the firm.

In certain cases, however, corporate managements find themselves in the position of being able to increase shareholder value *at the expense of bondholders*.[13] For example, as happened in a number of leveraged recapitalizations, management could reduce the value of outstanding bonds by increasing debt or adding debt senior to that in question. (In professional circles, this is known as *event risk*; in academic parlance it is the *claims dilution problem*.) Or, if the firm were in danger of insolvency, management could choose—as did some S&L executives—to invest in ever riskier projects in desperate attempts to save the firm (the *asset substitution problem*). Finally, a management squeezed between falling revenues and high interest payments could choose to pass up value-adding projects such as R&D or, if things are bad enough, basic maintenance and safety procedures (the *underinvestment problem*).[14]

Corporate debtholders are well aware that such problems can arise, and they accordingly protect themselves by lowering the price they are willing to pay for the debt. For corporate management, such lower prices translate into higher interest payments, which in turn further raise the probability of financial trouble.

Hybrids reduce these shareholder-bondholder conflicts by reducing current interest rates, shifting debt service payments to periods when firms are better able to pay, stabilizing cash flow, and thereby reducing the likelihood of financial distress. In so doing, they also raise the price of the corporate debt to investors and lower the overall corporate cost of capital.

Using Hybrids to Reduce the Claims Dilution Problem (or, Protect Against "Event Risk")

Puttable Bonds. Introduced in 1976, these bonds give their holders the option to "put" the bond back to the issuer. Such an option would be exercised only if interest rates rise or the issuer's

13. For the seminal discussion of the effect of conflicts between shareholders and debtholders (and between management and shareholders as well) on the behavior of the firm, see Michael C. Jensen and William H. Meckling, "Theory of the Firm: Managerial Behavior, Agency Costs, and Capital Structure," *Journal of Financial Economics* (1976), pp. 305-360.

14. For an account of the underinvestment problem, see Stewart Myers, "The Determinants of Corporate Borrowing," *Journal of Financial Economics* (1977).

For a more detailed examination of these sources of shareholder/debtholder conflict, see Clifford W. Smith and Jerold B. Warner, "On Financial Contracting: An Analysis of Bond Covenants," *Journal of Financial Economics*, 7 (1979), pp. 117-161.

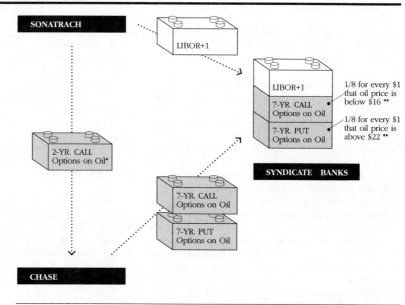

FIGURE 3
OIL-LINKED CREDIT-
SENSITIVE SYNDICATE

SONATRACH

LIBOR+1

LIBOR+1

7-YR. CALL
Options on Oil

7-YR. PUT
Options on Oil

1/8 for every $1
that oil price is
below $16 **

1/8 for every $1
that oil price is
above $22 **

2-YR. CALL
Options on Oil*

SYNDICATE BANKS

7-YR. CALL
Options on Oil

7-YR. PUT
Options on Oil

CHASE

*During the first two years, if the price of oil exceeds $23, Sonatrach will pay a supplemental coupon to Chase.
**In the first year, the syndicate receives additional interest if the price of oil falls outside the range of $16-$22. In year 2, the range widens to $15-$23, then to $14-$24 in year 3, and to $13-$25 in years 4 through 7.

credit standing falls. In this sense, puttable bonds give bondholders both a call option on interest rates and an option on the credit spread of the issuer.[15] Such put options thus protect bondholders not only against increases in interest rates, but also against the possibility of losses from deteriorating operating performance or leveraged recapitalizations. In the wake of the widely publicized bondholder losses accompanying the KKR buyout of RJR Nabisco in 1989, the use of put options to protect against such "event risk" enjoyed a new vogue.

Floating Rate, Rating Sensitive Notes. These notes, issued by Manufacturer Hanover in 1988, contain explicit options on the issuer's credit standing. In this security, Manufacturer's Hanover agreed to pay investors a spread above LIBOR that increased with each incremental decline in the bank's senior debt rating.

From the standpoint of risk management, however, there is an obvious flaw in the design of this security. Although it may partially compensate investors for increases in risk, it actually increases the probability of default instead of reducing it. The security increases the corporate debt service burden precisely when the issuing firm can least afford it—when its credit rating has fallen and, presumably, its operating cash flow declined.

A hybrid structure designed to overcome this problem was a syndication of oil-indexed bonds created by Chase Manhattan for Sonatrach (the state hydrocarbons company of Algeria) in 1990. As illustrated in Figure 3, the transaction was structured so that Chase accepted two-year call options on oil from Sonatrach and then transformed those two-year calls into seven-year calls and puts that were passed on to the syndicate members. Investors were compensated for a below-market interest by a payoff structure that would provide them with higher payoffs in the event of significantly *higher or lower* oil prices.

---

15. Extendible notes also provide bondholders with an option on the firm's credit standing. But, unlike puttable debt, it represents the opportunity to benefit from increases in the firm's credit standing, or decreases in the spread. In the case of extendible notes, if the credit spread of the issuer decreases, the right to extend the maturity of the note (at the old credit spread) has value.

The combination of the put and conversion features are especially useful in controlling the asset substitution, or risk-shifting, problem. For this reason, the LYONs structure should be particularly attractive to issuers with substantial capital investment opportunities and a wide range of alternative investment projects.

For the issuer, however, the security requires higher payments to Chase *only in the event of higher oil prices.* If the price of oil declines, although the syndicate members receive a higher yield, the increase comes from Chase, not Sonatrach.

Using Hybrids to Reduce the Asset Substitution and Underinvestment Problems

Convertibles. At the outset, we noted that convertible bonds contain embedded options on the company's equity. By providing bondholders with the right to convert their claims into equity, management provides bondholders with the assurance that they will participate in any increase in shareholder value that results from increasing the risk of the company's activities—whether by leveraging up or undertaking riskier investments. By lowering current interest rates and thus reducing the likelihood of financial trouble, convertibles also reduce the probability that financially strapped companies will be forced to forgo valuable investment opportunities.[16]

Convertibles (and debt with warrants, their close substitutes) are also potentially useful in resolving disagreements between bondholders and shareholders about just how risky the firm's activities are. The value of convertibles are risk-neutral in the following sense: Unexpected increases in company risk reduce the value of the bond portion of a convertible, but at the same time increase the value of the embedded option (by increasing volatility). It is largely because of this risk-neutralizing effect—and for their role in reducing the "underinvestment problem" mentioned below—that convertible issuers tend to be smaller, newer, riskier firms characterized by high growth and earnings volatility.[17]

The Case of LYONs

While a number of bonds are puttable or convertible, the Liquid Yield Option Note (LYON) introduced by Merrill Lynch in 1985 is both puttable and convertible. The combination of the put and conversion features are especially useful in controlling the asset substitution, or risk-shifting, problem just described.[18] For this reason, the LYONs structure should be particularly

attractive to issuers with substantial capital investment opportunities and a wide range of alternative investment projects (with varying degrees of risk).

It is thus interesting to note that the LYON structure was first used to fund companies where the asset substitution problem was acute. Take the case of Waste Management, the first issuer of LYONs. Although Waste Management is today a household name among even small investors, in 1985 the company could best be viewed as a collection of "growth options." As such it posed considerable uncertainty for investors.

THE ECONOMIC RATIONALE FOR ISSUING A HYBRID SECURITY

We are still left with a fundamental question: Given the well-functioning, low-cost markets for derivative products available today, why should a corporate issuer ever prefer the "bundled" hybrid to simply issuing standard debt and buying or selling the derivatives. We now discuss the following three reasons why corporate management might choose hybrids:

(1) If the firm issuing the hybrid can provide investors with a "play" not available otherwise—that is, a derivative instrument not available in the traded derivatives markets—the issuing firm will consequently be paid a premium for "completing the market."

(2) The hybrid may enable the issuer to take advantage of tax or regulatory arbitrages that would lower the cost of borrowing.

(3) By embedding a risk management product into a hybrid, the issuer may be able to obtain hedge accounting treatment, which may not be allowed if the derivative was bought or sold separately.

Using Hybrids to Provide Investors with a "Play"

The most straightforward reason for issuing a hybrid is to provide investors with a means of taking a position on a financial price. If the issuer provides a "play" not otherwise available, the investor will be willing to pay a premium, thereby reducing the issuer's cost of funding. (And, if the hybrid provides

---

16. More technically, the underinvestment problem arises from the fact that, in financially troubled firms, an outsized portion of the returns from new investments must go to help restore the value of the bondholders' claims before the shareholders receive any payoff at all. This has also been dubbed the "debt overhang" problem.

17. For an exposition of this argument, see Michael Brennan and Eduardo Schwartz, "The Case for Convertibles," *Chase Financial Quarterly* (Fall 1981). Reprinted in *Journal of Applied Corporate Finance* (Summer 1988).

18. As described at length in the next article in this issue, the put feature also enabled Merrill Lynch to tailor the security for its network of retail investors.

investors with a "scarce security" not otherwise obtainable, it may also provide corporate issuers with a hedge they can't duplicate with derivative products.)

The "play" can be in the form of a forward contract. Perhaps the best example of such is dual currency bonds, which provided investors with foreign exchange forward contracts with longer maturities than those available in the standard market. The forward contracts embedded in dual currency bonds have maturities running to 10 years, whereas liquidity in the standard foreign exchange forward market declines for maturities greater than one year, and falls very significantly beyond five years.

The "play," however, has more commonly been in the form of an option embedded in the bond—generally an option of longer maturity than those available in the standard option market. Sunshine Mining's Silver Indexed Bond fits this category, as do Standard Oil's Oil Indexed Note and the gold warrants issued by Pegasus Gold Corporation. In 1986 long-dated options on stock market indices were introduced with the development of hybrid debt in which the principal was indexed to an equity index. While the first such debt issues were indexed to the Nikkei, Salomon Brothers' "S&P 500 Index Subordinated Notes (SPINs)" have probably received more public attention. A SPIN is convertible into the value of the S&P 500 Index, rather than into an individual equity. Since then, debt has been issued that is indexed to other equity indices (for example, the NYSE index) or subsets of indices. For example, in 1991, United Technologies issued a zero-coupon bond indexed to the S&P Pharmaceutical Index.

Using Hybrids to "Arbitrage" Tax and/or Regulatory Authorities

Hybrid debt has also been used to take advantage of asymmetries in tax treatment or regulations in different countries or markets. One classic example is a case of "arbitrage" reported in *Business Week* under the provocative title, "A Way for US Firms to Make 'Free Money'." The "free money" came from two sources:

(1) A difference in tax treatment between the U.S. and Japan—the Japanese tax authorities ruled

that income earned from holding a zero-coupon bond would be treated as a capital gain, thereby making interest income on the zero non-taxable for Japanese investors. In contrast, U.S. tax authorities permitted any U.S. firm issuing a zero coupon bond to deduct from current income the imputed interest payments.

(2) A regulatory arbitrage—the Ministry of Finance limited Japanese pension funds' investments in non-yen-dominated bonds issued by foreign corporations to at most 10% of their portfolios. The Ministry of Finance also ruled that dual currency bonds qualified as a yen issue, thus allowing dual currency bonds to command a premium from Japanese investors.

Consequently, U.S. firms issued zero-coupon yen bonds (to realize the interest rate savings from the tax arbitrage), and then issued a dual currency bond to hedge the residual yen exposure from the yen zero, while realizing a further interest savings from the regulatory arbitrage.

Tax-Deductible Equity. Perhaps the most thinly disguised attempt to issue tax-deductible equity was the *Adjustable Rate Convertible Debt* introduced in 1982.[19] Such convertibles paid a coupon determined by the dividend rate on the firm's common stock; moreover, the debt could be converted to common stock at the current price at any time (i.e., there was no conversion premium). Not surprisingly, once the IRS ruled that this was equity for tax purposes, this structure disappeared.

On a less aggressive level, hybrid structures like Merrill Lynch's LYON take advantage of the treatment of zero coupon instruments by U.S. tax authorities—that is, zero coupon bonds allow the issuer to deduct deferred interest payments from current income (although the holder of the bond must declare them as income). Given the impact of the IRS ruling on adjustable rate convertible debt, it is not surprising that a great deal of attention has been given to the tax status of the LYON.

Using Hybrids to Obtain Accrual Accounting Treatment for Risk Management

If a U.S. company uses a forward, futures, swap, or option to hedge a specific transaction (for example, a loan or a purchase or a receipt), it is

---

19. This point is made by John Finnerty in his article in this issue.

> **Except for the highest-rated companies, most firms today face *non-price* credit restrictions that have greatly enlarged credit spreads. Many such companies are using hybrid debt to lower their risk profile and thus avoid the higher funding costs now associated with being a riskier borrower.**

relatively simple to obtain accrual accounting treatment for the hedge. (Changes in the market value of the hedging instrument offset changes in the value of the asset being hedged, so there is no need to mark the hedging instrument to market.)

If, however, the firm wishes to use one of the risk management instruments to hedge expected net income or an even longer-term economic exposure, the current position of the accounting profession is that the hedge position must be marked to market. Some companies have been reluctant to use derivatives to manage such risks because this accounting treatment would increase the volatility of their reported income—*even while such a risk management strategy would stabilize their longer-run operating cash flow.*

With the use of hybrids, by contrast, which contain embedded derivatives, the firm may be able to obtain accrual accounting treatment for the entire package. Accountants are accustomed to valuing convertible debt at historical cost; and, given this precedent, they can extend the same treatment to hybrids.[20]

CONCLUDING REMARKS

Beginning in 1980 with Sunshine Mining's issue of silver-linked bonds, U.S. corporations have increasingly chosen to raise debt capital by embedding derivatives such as forwards or options into their notes and bonds. In the early '80s, such hybrids typically provided investors with payoffs (at first only principal, but later interest payments as well) indexed to commodity prices, interest rates, and exchange rates. But, in recent years, companies have begun to issue debt indexed to general stock market indices and even subsets of such indices.

Critics of such newfangled securities view them as the offspring of "supply-driven" fads. According to this view, profit-hungry investment banks set their highly-paid "rocket scientists" to designing new securities that can then be foisted on unsuspecting corporate treasurers and investors.

As economists, however, we begin with the assumption that capital market innovations succeed only to the extent they do a better job than existing products in meeting the demands of issuers and investors. The evidence presented in these pages, albeit anecdotal, suggests that hybrid debt is a capital market response to corporate treasurers' desire to manage pricing risks and otherwise tailor their securities to investor demands. In some cases, especially those in which hybrids feature long-dated forwards or options, hybrids are furnishing investors with securities they cannot obtain elsewhere.

Like the remarkable growth of futures, swaps, and options markets beginning in the late '70s, the proliferation of corporate hybrids during the '80s is fundamentally an attempt to cope with increased price volatility. The sharp increase in the volatility of exchange rates, interest rates, and oil prices—to name just the most important—during the 1970s provided the "necessary condition" for the rise of hybrids.

But another important stimulant to hybrids has come from other constraints on companies' ability to raise debt. In the early '80s, for example, when interest rates were high, hybrid debt was used by riskier firms to reduce their interest costs to manageable levels. Given the current level of interest rates today, most companies would likely choose to borrow as much straight debt as possible. But except for the highest-rated companies, many firms also now face *non-price* credit restrictions that have greatly enlarged credit spreads. In some such cases, companies are using hybrid debt to lower their risk profile and thus avoid the higher funding costs now associated with being a riskier corporate borrower. In other cases, hybrids are providing access to debt capital that would otherwise be denied on any terms.

---

20. See J. Matthew Singleton, "Hedge Accounting: A State-of-the-Art Review," *Journal of Banking and Finance*, 5 (Fall 1991), pp. 26-32.

USING PROJECT FINANCE TO FUND INFRASTRUCTURE INVESTMENTS

*by Richard A. Brealey,
Ian A. Cooper, and
Michel A. Habib,
London Business School**

T hroughout most of the history of the industrialized world, much of the funding for large-scale public works such as the building of roads and canals has come from private sources of capital. It was only toward the end of the 19th century that public financing of large "infrastructure" projects began to dominate private finance, and this trend continued throughout most of the 20th century.

Since the early 1980s, however, private-sector financing of large infrastructure investments has experienced a dramatic revival. And, in recent years, such private funding has increasingly taken the form of project finance. The principal features of such project financings have been the following:

- A project is established as a separate company, which operates under a concession obtained from the host government.
- A major proportion of the equity of the project company is provided by the project manager or sponsor, thereby tying the provision of finance to the management of the project.
- The project company enters into comprehensive contractual arrangements with suppliers and customers.
- The project company operates with a high ratio of debt to equity, with lenders having only limited recourse to the government or to the equity-holders in the event of default.

The above characteristics clearly distinguish project finance from traditional lending. In conventional financing arrangements, projects are generally not incorporated as separate companies; the contractual arrangements are not as comprehensive, nor are the debt-equity ratios as high, as those observed in the case of project finance; and the vast majority of loans offer lenders recourse to the assets of borrowers in case of default.

Our purpose in this paper is to explore some possible rationales for the distinctive characteristics of project finance, from the viewpoint of both the project sponsor and the host government. We do so in the specific context of infrastructure investments. After providing some information about the growth of project finance in funding such investments, we note that project finance is but one of several mechanisms for involving the private sector in funding and managing infrastructure projects. We show how project finance, and the complex web of contractual arrangements that such funding entails, can be used to address "agency problems" that reduce efficiency in large organizations, private as well as public. We also view the contracts among the multiple parties to project financings as risk management devices designed to shift a variety of project risks to those parties best able to appraise and control them. In closing, we discuss what we believe are some common misconceptions about the benefits and costs of project finance—particularly, the notion that project finance represents "expensive finance" for governments—and we contrast project finance with other private-sector options such as privatization and the use of service contracts with private-sector companies.

*We would like to thank Joseph Blum, Carlo Bongianni, Don Lessard, Gill Raine, Mary Wan and Adam Wilson for helpful discussions. The third author would like to acknowledge the financial support of the International Programme on the Management of Engineering and Construction.

THE GROWTH IN PROJECT FINANCE: SOME EVIDENCE

Comprehensive data on the financing of infrastructure projects do not appear to be available. Table 1 does, however, provide information about the growth in the value of those projects in developing countries that have been partially financed by the International Finance Corporation (the World Bank's private sector affiliate).

TABLE 1
VALUE OF PROJECTS INVOLVING IFC PARTICIPATION IN DEVELOPING COUNTRIES

Year of approval	No. of projects	Value of projects $ million
1966-1987	7	517
1988	2	409
1989	6	704
1990	4	1279
1991	6	1103
1992	8	1384
1993	15	3699
1994(1st 6 months)	30	5512

Source: G. Bond and L. Carter, "Financing Private Infrastructure Projects; Emerging Trends from IFC's Experience," International Finance Corporation, Discussion Paper 23, 1994.

Over 80 percent (by value) of the projects involving the IFC have been in the power and telecommunication industries, with the remainder in transportation (roads, railroads, and ports), water, and pipelines. About 50% of the projects have been in Latin America, with the bulk of the remainder in Asia.

The use of project finance has not been restricted to infrastructure investments in developing countries. Indeed, over 40 percent of the project finance loans reported in the 1995 survey conducted by *IFR Project Finance International* were for projects in the United States, Australia, or the United Kingdom. In the United States, the passage of the Public Utility Regulatory Power Act (PURPA) in 1978 provided a major stimulus to the use of project finance by requiring that electric utilities purchase power from independent power producers. This encouraged the formation of stand-alone power producers able to borrow large sums on the basis of the long-term power purchase agreements they had entered into with electric utilities. Since these projects do not directly involve a government or a government agency, they are somewhat beyond the scope of this article. So are projects in Australia, which have primarily been in extractive industries rather than in infrastructure.

In the U.K. by contrast, the government has been directly involved in a growing number of infrastructure projects since it announced in 1992 the establishment of the Private Finance Initiative (PFI). The PFI is designed to involve the private sector in the financing and the management of infrastructure and other projects. Private finance has so far been used principally for transportation projects such as the £320 million rail link to Heathrow Airport, the £2.7 billion Channel Tunnel Rail Link, a £250 million scheme to build and maintain a new air traffic control center in Scotland, and projects worth more than £500 million to design, build, finance, and operate (DBFO) trunk roads. But the potential scope of the PFI is wide. Over 1,000 potential PFI projects have been identified, and the government has signed contracts to build and maintain such diverse assets as prisons, hospitals, subway cars, and the National Insurance computer system.[1]

SOME ALTERNATIVES TO PROJECT FINANCE

A government need not involve the private sector in either the financing or the management of projects, and may choose to undertake both itself. As we will argue below, the desirability of private-sector involvement in infrastructure projects depends in large part on the extent to which (1) the provision of high-powered incentives is necessary to the success of the project and (2) such incentives can be specified in a verifiable contract.

It is important to note that high-powered incentives need not always be beneficial. For example, consider the hypothetical case of privatized parking enforcement agencies. Such organizations would probably be subject to severe moral hazard problems if provided with high-powered incentives, for they may then have an incentive to claim an offence has been committed even where none has.

1. See Standard & Poor's, *Global Project Finance*, July 1996, pages 24-28, and OXERA, *Infrastructure in the UK*.

The desirability of private sector involvement in infrastructure projects depends in large part on the extent to which the provision of high-powered incentives is necessary to the success of the project. The dominant reason for the growing importance of project finance in funding infrastructure investment is that it addresses agency problems in a way that other forms of financing do not.

It should further be noted that public-sector organizations are not entirely devoid of incentives, and that these are often of the same nature as the incentives found in private-sector companies. Both voters and shareholders have an interest in efficient management, the former as taxpayers and the latter as owners. Both use their votes to discipline inefficient management, the former by voting for a new government, and the latter by voting for a new management. Nonetheless, the greater power and prevalence of incentives in private-sector organizations suggests an important role for these organizations when high-powered incentives are desired.

A government that uses project finance to fund a project obtains both private-sector funding and private-sector management. Project finance therefore reduces the need for government borrowing, shifts part of the risks presented by the project to the private sector, and aims to achieve more effective management of the project. But, as we indicate in Table 2, there are a number of other means of involving the private sector in infrastructure investment. The government can do so through privatization, for example, in which case the private sector provides capital and management services to an entire industry rather than to individual projects. Thus, the government can privatize a public utility that generates and distributes electric power, rather than grant a concession to a private company to generate power that is then sold to the public utility.

If the government simply wishes to benefit from private-sector management expertise, it can contract with the private sector for the provision of management services while continuing to finance the project and retaining ownership of the project's assets. Conversely, the government can simply secure finance by leasing the project's assets from the private sector, while continuing to be responsible for the management of the project.

TABLE 2
WAYS THAT INFRASTRUCTURE PROJECTS CAN BE FUNDED AND MANAGED

Arrangement	Finance	Management
Project finance	Private	Private
Privatization	Private	Private
Service contracts	Government	Private
Leases	Private	Government
Nationalization	Government	Government

In view of these alternatives to project finance, it is natural to ask why it has developed into such an important mechanism for funding infrastructure investments. We argue that the dominant reason for the growing importance of project finance in funding infrastructure investment is that it addresses agency problems in a way that other forms of financing do not.

PROJECT FINANCE AS A RESPONSE TO AGENCY PROBLEMS

Agency problems arise from the differing, and sometimes conflicting, interests of the various parties involved in any large enterprise. Success of the enterprise therefore requires that these parties be provided with incentives to work together for the common good. This can be achieved, to some extent at least, by the appropriate choice of a company's financial structure.

Consider, for example, the problem faced by shareholders in a public corporation who wish to motivate the CEO to work hard to increase firm value. Shareholders would like the CEO to do her utmost to increase shareholder wealth, and they may wish to write a contract that specifies what she should do in all the various circumstances that she may encounter. But such a contract would be impossible to write, if only because of the difficulty of envisaging and describing these various circumstances. Any contract between shareholders and corporate managers will therefore inevitably be incomplete. Furthermore, even if it were possible to write a complete contract that specified exactly what the CEO were to do in every circumstance, it would be very costly for shareholders to monitor the manager to ensure that she was keeping to the contract.

One solution to these problems of incomplete contracting and costly monitoring is to arrange for the manager to take an equity stake in the business. Such a stake ties the manager's wealth to her actions, thus rewarding her for hard work and penalizing her for sloth. The "residual claimancy" associated with the ownership of equity therefore serves to motivate the manager, to some extent at least, in the cases where contracts fail to do so.

The above example illustrates the role of financial structure in solving agency problems. Notice that the CEO's equity stake in the business provides her with the incentive to act in the shareholders'

FIGURE 1
PARTIES TO PROJECT
FINANCING

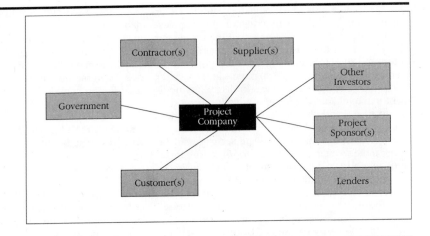

interest by exposing her to part of the risk of the business. The creation of incentives and the transfer of risk from the shareholders to the manager are therefore two sides of the same coin. This transfer of risk is not beneficial in itself; for the manager, unlike the shareholders, does not hold a diversified portfolio. She therefore requires a higher return than do the shareholders for bearing this risk. The transfer of risk is beneficial *only* to the extent that it improves efficiency.

In the case of project finance, a complex series of contracts and financing arrangements distributes the different risks presented by a project among the various parties involved in the project. As in the case of our simple example of the management compensation contract, these transfers of risk are rarely advantageous in themselves, but have important incentive effects. To see how this occurs, we need to look at the structure of a typical project financing.

THE MAIN PARTIES

There are numerous parties involved in the structuring of a typical project financing. As shown in Figure 1, besides the lenders and the project company, these parties typically include one or more project sponsors, contractors, suppliers, major customers, and a host government.

Sponsors and Investors. A separate company is established for the purpose of undertaking the project. A controlling stake in the equity of that company will typically be owned by a single project sponsor, or by a group of sponsors, who will generally be involved in the construction and the management of the project. Other equity-holders may be companies with commercial ties to the project, such as customers and suppliers, or they may be financial investors. For example, the shareholders of the PT. Paiton Energy Co. (PEC), which is building the Paiton 7 and 8 power stations in Indonesia, are Edison Mission Energy (40%), General Electric Capital Corp. (12.5%), Mitsui & Co. Ltd. (32.5%), and PT. Batu Hitam Perkasa (15%). As is typical of such projects, the main shareholders of the project company are the main contractor of the plant, Mitsui, and its operator, Edison Mission Energy, which will operate and maintain the plant through PT. MOMI Indonesia, the local affiliate of Mission Operation & Maintenance Inc. General Electric Co., of which General Electric Capital Corp. is the finance affiliate, will supply the steam turbine generators. The Indonesian company PT. Batu Hitam Perkasa appears to have no operational involvement in the project, but may carry political clout.

Lenders. Infrastructure projects involve substantial investments. A large fraction of the needed finance is generally raised in the form of debt from a syndicate of lenders such as banks and specialized lending institutions and, less frequently, from the bond markets. In the case of PEC, for example, equity-holders provided $680 million in equity and subordinated debt. $1.8 billion was provided in the form of senior debt, of which 90 percent was bank debt and 10 percent was senior secured bonds.

Most infrastructure projects are financed by bank loans. The concentrated ownership of bank debt encourages lenders to devote considerable resources to evaluating the project, and to monitoring its progress on a continuing basis. It also facilitates the renegotiation of the debt should the project company experience difficulties in servicing it.

Project companies will sometimes enter into production payment arrangements instead of issuing ordinary debt. These arrangements are functionally equivalent to borrowing: a bank provides cash up-front as advance payment for a project's output, and the project company undertakes to deliver the output to the bank and arranges for the output to be repurchased at a guaranteed price.

Most infrastructure facilities have very long lives. This suggests that they should be financed with long-term debt. Yet, most infrastructure projects are financed by bank loans, which have maturities that rarely exceed 10 to 12 years, rather than by long-term bonds.

Some observers have suggested that the difficulty in arranging long-term bond financing is due to the fact that bondholders are particularly risk-averse. But, since most bondholders also hold substantial portfolios of equities, this seems improbable. Our explanation for the widespread use of bank finance, and the correspondingly limited role of bond finance, focuses instead on the ownership structures of these two forms of financing. The concentrated ownership of bank debt encourages lending banks to devote considerable resources to evaluating the project, and to monitoring its progress on a continuing basis. It also facilitates the renegotiation of the debt should the project company experience difficulties in servicing it. By contrast, the more diffuse nature of bond ownership reduces the incentives of bondholders to evaluate and monitor the progress of the project, and makes it difficult to take concerted action if covenants are breached or require modification. Thus, it does not seem surprising that many bond issues, such as the $180 million issue made by PEC, have been privately placed under rule 144a. This ensures that ownership remains in the hands of a limited number of qualified institutional buyers (or QIBs).

A bond issue to fund a green-field project is likely only in the case of a low-risk project. Even then, it is commonly enhanced by a credit guarantee from an insurance company, or a political risk guarantee from a national or supranational agency. For example, a project company established to upgrade two major roads in England was able to raise the majority of its debt by an issue of bonds that were enhanced by a Aaa/AAA guarantee from AMBAC Indemnity Corporation.

Bonds are also commonly used in project finance in one other set of circumstances. Once construction is completed and project facilities become operational, bond financing is often used to replace existing bank debt. This can be explained by the fact that the need for monitoring falls upon completion of the construction phase.

Government. The project company will in most cases need to obtain a concession from the host government to build a road or a railway, for example, or to operate a telecommunication service. The government may also need to establish a new regulatory framework, guarantee currency convertibility, and provide environmental permits.

In many cases, the project company retains ownership of the project's assets. Such arrangements are known as "build-own-operate" projects (BOOs). In other cases, ownership of the project's assets is transferred to the government at the end of the concession period. These arrangements are known as "build-operate-transfer" projects (BOTs).[2]

Contractors. As noted above, the main contractor of the plant will often hold a stake in the equity of the project company. Other contractors may also do so, although generally to a lesser extent.

Suppliers and Customers. Once the project facility has been built and has become operational, the project company will need to purchase the supplies it requires, and to sell the products it produces or the services it provides. Sometimes, as in the case of a pipeline, there will be in effect only one customer. Often in this case the customer will be a government-owned utility, or the government itself. For example, the sole customer for the electricity produced by the Paiton 7 and 8 power stations will be the Indonesian state-owned electric utility. In other cases, as in that of a toll road, there may be many possible customers.

CONTRACTUAL ARRANGEMENTS

Although a project company is unusual in that it is established to undertake a single project, there is nothing unusual about the identity of the parties involved in the project. All companies have owners, lenders, suppliers, and customers, and all have dealings with the government. The difference in the case of project finance lies in the overriding impor-

---

2. It should however be noted that the terms BOO and BOT are sometimes used interchangeably.

tance of the contractual and financing arrangements that exist between these various parties. These are more than a series of independent bilateral arrangements. In particular, the complete package of contracts needs to be put in place before debt finance can be secured.

We discuss the contractual arrangements first. These are designed to allocate every major risk presented by a project to the party that is best able to appraise and control that risk. Because a party to a project will agree to bear a given risk at a non-prohibitive price only if it has a clear understanding of that risk, most projects involve established technologies, as is the case for power stations, roads, and airports. Project finance is less appropriate for projects that involve complex or untried technologies, as evidenced by the failure of the U.K. government to secure project financing for research and development projects.

Let us look briefly at the various ways in which contractual arrangements distribute risk among the various parties to a project:

- The project sponsors bear the risks of project completion, operation, and maintenance. This is achieved through a facility management contract that includes guarantees that the project facility will be completed on time, and that it will be built and operated to the desired specifications. The project sponsor may also enter into a "working capital maintenance" agreement or a "cash deficiency" agreement with the lending banks. Such agreements ensure adequate funding for the project in its early years.

- The lenders to the project will require the usual assurances from the project company, including security for their loans. But, especially in the early stages of the project, lenders will also have recourse to the project sponsors in the event of specific problems such as cost overruns. Lenders will particularly want to ensure that cash that can be used to service the debt is not paid out to equity-holders. The amount of debt service may therefore be linked to the project's output, and any earnings in excess of debt service requirements may be placed in a "reclaim" account and drawn on if subsequent earnings do not suffice to service the debt.

- The main contractor is obviously best able to ensure that construction is completed within cost and on schedule. He will therefore often enter into a turnkey contract that specifies a fixed price and

penalties for delays, and he will usually be required to post a performance bond.

- When there is a major supplier to the project, there will be a contract with that supplier to ensure that (1) he does not abuse his possible monopoly power and (2) he produces efficiently. For example, if the project company is a major purchaser of energy from a monopolistic state-owned enterprise (SOE), the project company will enter into a long-term supply contract with the SOE. The contract purchase price will often be fixed, or indexed to inflation or some other variable that affects project revenues; and the contract may require the SOE to compensate the project company if the SOE fails to supply the contracted energy.

- When there are only a few potential customers for the project's output, revenue risk is likely to be transferred to those customers by means of long-term sales contracts. These will often include a take-or-pay clause or, as in the case of a pipeline, a throughput agreement that obliges the customer to make some minimum use of the pipeline. Another arrangement for transferring revenue risk to a customer is a tolling contract, whereby the customer agrees to deliver to the project company materials that it is to process and return to the customer. Some power projects, such as Navotas in the Philippines, have been structured in a similar way: the purchasing utility provides the fuel and the project company is simply paid for converting it to electricity. The purpose of transferring revenue risk to customers is to provide them with the incentive to estimate their demand for the project's output as carefully and honestly as possible.

The contract between project company and customers will as much as possible seek to ensure that the prices of the product are indexed to its costs; and, where there is considerable currency uncertainty, prices may also be indexed to exchange rates as in the case of the Paiton power project.

- When there are many customers, as in the case of a toll road, long-term purchase contracts with these customers may be impossible. Indeed, if alternative routes are not subject to a toll, it may be infeasible to set a price that provides the project company with a satisfactory return. For example, one of the problems in attracting private finance to the funding of rail projects within central London has been that the revenues from such projects are likely to be highly dependent on transport policy towards *other* means of transportation in the capital. In such cases, it may be possible to attract project finance only if the government guarantees some minimum payment to investors.

- When the government grants a concession to a project company, there will need to be a concession agreement that gives the company the right to build and operate the project facility. The concession agreement may also require the government to construct supporting facilities such as access roads. Failure to do so may lead to the failure of the project, or may decrease the return on the project. For example, the profitability of Eurostar, the company that operates rail services through the Channel Tunnel, has suffered from the delays in the construction of a promised high-speed rail link in England and a new railway station south of London. The government may also need to guarantee the performance of state-owned companies. For example, if a project sells electricity to a state-owned power utility, the government may need to guarantee the contractual obligations of that utility.

The project company will also be concerned about currency convertibility, in particular its ability to service its foreign currency debt and pay dividends to its equity-holders. The government may therefore be asked to provide guarantees or comfort letters; and, if the project has hard currency revenues, it may have to consent to having these revenues paid into an offshore escrow account.

As we have already observed, this web of contractual arrangements, which may vary over time in line with the progress of a project, is designed to allocate the various risks presented by the project to those parties that can best appraise and control those risks. An attempt to allocate a given risk to a party that is not best able to control that risk will generally fail. For example, the private financing of prisons in the U.K. ran into difficulties when the government sought to link its payments to private prisons to the number of prisoners that were sent to these prisons. The problem, of course, was that the number of prisoners was outside the control of the project companies, but at least partially within that of the government. Conversely, failure to allocate a given risk to the party that is best able to control that risk will lead to a loss in efficiency. As one example, government guarantees of fair rates of return to utilities or project companies remove any incentive for these organizations to reduce their costs.

OWNERSHIP, CAPITAL STRUCTURE, AND INCENTIVES

We now turn to the financing arrangements observed in the case of project finance. Among the questions we address are the following:

- Why are projects incorporated in separate companies?
- Why are the operators and the main contractors of the project typically the main equity-holders in that company?
- Why are project companies highly leveraged?
- Why does this leverage take the form of non-recourse financing?

The object of the contractual arrangements that we have described above is to ensure that a project company is not exposed to an abuse of monopoly power, and to provide all parties to the project with the incentives to act efficiently by transferring the risk of poor performance to those best able to manage it. Construction risk is thus borne by the contractor, the risk of insufficient demand by the purchaser, and similarly for the other risks presented by the project.

But this does not explain the widespread practice of incorporating the project in a separate company, and tying the management of a project to its financing. Indeed, a government could easily raise money directly for infrastructure investment and contract with each party to provide the required services. But, as we pointed out earlier, there is a limit to how much can be written into a contract and how efficiently that contract can be monitored. Contractual arrangements therefore need to be complemented by financing arrangements.

Think, for example, why the operator and the main contractor of a project should be made to be equity-holders in the project. These equity holdings would not be needed if it were possible to write and monitor complete contracts with the contractor and the operator. The operation of the project could then be separated from its financing. This sometimes happens—most recently, in the case of a South African road project. But it is usually not possible to write and monitor sufficiently comprehensive contracts. In such cases, the equity holdings that the contractor and the operator have in the project company provide them with an incentive to be efficient by making them residual claimants whose profits depend on how well the project facility is built and operated.

Project companies are highly levered: the average debt ratio for IFC-financed projects, for example, is around 60 percent. Such leverage is used despite the fact that there is reputed to be a shortage of potential lenders for project finance, and that it is costly to structure the project to make these high debt levels possible. Furthermore, lenders lend directly to the project company rather than to the sponsors, and they have only limited recourse to the sponsors in case of default by the project company. This last observation suggests that the motive for the high leverage observed cannot be that debt is a "cheap" source of finance. If that were the case, the loans could equally well be made to the sponsors.

In their classic paper on capital structure, Miller and Modigliani showed that, in perfectly competi-

tive capital markets, company value would be independent of the degree of leverage. Similar arguments can be used to show that, under the same restrictive set of conditions, value cannot be enhanced simply by concentrating debt in a subsidiary or an associated company. As illustrated in Exhibit 1 below, the total cash flow to all security holders is independent of whether debt is located in a project company or in its parent company.

Why, then, do we observe a high concentration of debt in the project company? As happens so often in discussions of capital structure, there is an abundance of possible explanations, none of which appears to be capable of explaining all the facts.

EXHIBIT 1 ■ THE IMPACT OF PROJECT FINANCE IN AN M&M WORLD

The example below illustrates (a) that, in a Miller-Modigliani world, project finance does not affect the total value of the firm and (b) that project finance can potentially affect value when debt default is costly.

Panel 1 shows a firm with existing assets and debt undertaking a large project. Both the assets and the project give a single cash flow and have pure discount debt. Panel 2 shows the payoffs in different states of the world to debt and equity if the project is undertaken as part of the general activities of the firm. Panel 3 shows the payoffs to project debt, existing debt, and parent equity if the project is undertaken as a separate entity (project finance).

In a Miller-Modigliani world without taxes, project finance has no impact on the total value of the firm. This can be seen by comparing the final columns of Panel 2 and Panel 3, where the total cash flows accru-

ing to all security holders are identical in all states. In a complete securities market, this guarantees that the total value of the firm is independent of the way that financial claims on the firm are structured.

The impact of project finance on default risk can be seen by comparing Panel 3 (project finance) with Panel 2. The net impact of project finance on default is to:

A. Prevent the existing assets bringing down the project in state 2.

B. Prevent the project bringing down the existing assets in state 3.

C. Make the project default in state 5 because the coinsurance of the existing assets is lost.

By thus rearranging the states of the world in which default occurs, project finance can change the associated costs of default.

	CHARACTERISTICS OF EXISTING ASSETS AND PROJECT				SECURITY PAYOFFS IN THE CASE OF TRADITIONAL FINANCE			SECURITY PAYOFFS IN THE CASE OF PROJECT FINANCE						
State	PANEL 1	Debt Face Value: Existing Assets	Debt Face Value: Project	Cash Flow: Existing Assets	Cash Flow: Project	PANEL 2	Debt	Equity	Total Cash Flow	PANEL 3	Project Debt	Project Equity	Total Cash Flow to Sponsor	Parent Debt	Parent Equity	Total Cash Flow: Project Debt + Existing Debt + Parent Equity
1		100	100	50	50		100*	0	100		50*	0	50	50*	0	100
2		100	100	50	130		180*	0	180		100	30	80	80*	0	180
3		100	100	130	50		180*	0	180		50*	0	130	100	30	180
4		100	100	130	130		200	60	260		100	30	160	100	60	260
5		100	100	300	50		200	150	350		50*	0	300	100	200	350
6		100	100	300	130		200	230	430		100	30	330	100	230	430

*Indicates default.

If the bankruptcy costs of the sponsor are higher than those of the project company, it could be more efficient to isolate the debt in the project company to ensure that the sponsor's business is not damaged by a possible bankruptcy of the project.

Many of these explanations are related to the incompleteness of contracts. We discuss below some of the more common explanations (and summarize in Exhibit 2 four of the principal theoretical models of project finance).

Bankruptcy Costs. The example in Exhibit 1 shows that the total cash flows to investors are independent of whether the firm employs project financing when bankruptcy costs are assumed to be zero, as in an M & M world. The example also shows, however, that project finance changes the states of the world in which the debt is in default. In so doing, project finance changes the expected costs of default.

The projects undertaken by project companies typically have low bankruptcy costs. This is because their assets are largely tangible assets, which are likely to go through a bankruptcy process largely unscathed. For example, a change in ownership is unlikely to affect the efficiency with which a power station or a toll road is operated. In addition, if the bankruptcy costs of the sponsor are higher than those of the project company, it could be more efficient to isolate the debt in the project company to ensure that the sponsor's business is not damaged by a possible bankruptcy of the project.[3] A trading and construction company such as Mitsui, for example, is likely to lose much more of its operating value than the project company building the Paiton power stations, and it should therefore attempt to contain the effects of a possible project failure through the use of project finance. The low cost of bankruptcy for project companies may therefore help to explain why project companies carry heavy, non-recourse debt loads, but it does not explain why these companies enter into a variety of credit-enhancing contracts, such as insurance and hedging contracts (we return to this issue later).

Taxes. When a project is located in a high-tax country, and the project company in a lower-tax country, it may be beneficial for the sponsor to locate the debt in the high-tax country. The company maximizes its interest tax shields in so doing. But the difference in tax rates does not explain why the debt has limited recourse, nor does it explain the

concentration of debt in the project company when both the sponsor and the project company are located in the same jurisdiction.

Myopia. Some of the arguments for placing the debt in the project company assume that the lenders are blinkered. For example, it is sometimes suggested that the limited recourse of the debt holders to the project sponsors provides the sponsors with a free lunch, and that project finance allows the debt to be "off-balance-sheet" to the sponsors (for example, by structuring the contractual obligation as a production payment rather than as a loan). However, it is very doubtful that lenders are misled by such stratagems.

Political Risk. We have argued that the difficulty of writing complete contracts with operators and contractors provides the motive for tying project financing and management. Similarly, the difficulty of writing a comprehensive and binding concession agreement with a host government provides the need for financing arrangements that make it difficult for the government to take actions that may render the project unprofitable.

One such arrangement is for the host government to take equity in the project company. Another is an extensive reliance on limited recourse financing. By arranging for the project company to issue such debt, the sponsors ensure that the cost of adverse government action falls directly on the lending banks and agencies. These generally consist of a syndicate of major banks from a wide range of countries, together with national or supranational bodies such as the export-import banks of the main industrial countries, the World Bank, the International Finance Corporation, the Asian Development Bank, and the Inter-American Development Bank. All have considerable political clout, and can bring pressure to bear upon the host government if necessary. Moreover, the national and supranational agencies commonly hold subordinated debt that further exposes them to the consequences of adverse government actions. In contrast, the commercial banks tend to hold senior debt in the project.

In addition, the national and supranational agencies also provide loan guarantees, which are

---

3. See Michel Habib and D. Bruce Johnsen, "User Specialisation and Asset Financing," working paper, London Business School, 1996. It may not simply be the sponsor's business that is damaged by bankruptcy. The management of the sponsoring company may have valuable control rights such as perquisites and an enhanced reputation, and the project may have synergies with other projects run

by the same management. Management may therefore wish to isolate the project to protect its control rights. See T. Chemmanur and K. John, "Optimal Incorporation, Structure of Debt Contracts, and Limited-Recourse Project Financing," working paper, New York University, 1992.

generally intended to protect lenders against political risk, but rarely provide protection against commercial risk, again illustrating the principle that risk should be allocated to those that can best manage it. For example, the World Bank may assist the project company in raising debt by offering a partial risk guarantee that covers the host government's contractual obligations and political *force majeure* risks, as in the case of the Hub power project in Pakistan. Similarly, one level of government may guarantee the performance of another. For example, the Indian central government was contractually liable for any loss to the sponsor of the Dabhol power project that was a consequence of government action. This encouraged the Indian central government to put pressure on the state government of Maharashtra to resume construction of the plant, in spite of the electoral promises of the new state government to cancel the project.

Protection against political risk may go far towards explaining the debt structure of project companies in developing countries. It does not explain why projects in politically stable countries are also heavily levered. Of course, such countries are not free from political risk. Environmental legislation or court awards in liability suits may sometimes pose serious threats to business. However, these risks generally threaten the sponsors of the project as much as the project company, and are therefore unlikely to explain the concentration of debt in the project company.

Information Costs. The granting of a loan clearly requires that the lenders evaluate the creditworthiness of the borrower, and monitor his use of the assets financed by the loan. A possible benefit

---

EXHIBIT 2 ■ THEORETICAL MODELS OF PROJECT FINANCE

Model	Benefit of Debt	Cost of Debt	Benefit of Project Finance	Cost of Project Finance
Habib and Johnsen (1996)[a]: Asset specific investment by the initial user and the alternative user of an asset.	Induces both users to make the first-best investment in case the asset is to be transferred over some range of states.	May distort the asset-specific investment made by the initial user in case the asset is not to be transferred.	Avoids the distortion of asset-specific investment in the case of many assets and many alternative users.	
Chemmanur and John (1992)[b]: Private benefits of control	Avoids selling outside equity, thus lowering the probability of losing control to outsiders	Increases the probability of bankruptcy and the monitoring of management by debt-holders.	Avoids having a high-risk project bankrupt a low-risk project.	Loses the coinsurance property of debt.
John and John (1991)[c]: Tax benefits and agency costs of debt.	Tax savings.	Foregone growth opportunities (Myers underinvestment).	Enables trade-offs between the costs and the benefits of debt that are specific to the project and to existing assets.	
Shah and Thakor (1987)[d]: Signalling with debt.	Tax savings.	Signals high risk.	Lowers the cost of information gathering by creditors. Avoids the joint credit evaluation of the projects and existing assets.	Precludes optimal leverage for the entire firm.

a. M. Habib and D.B. Johnsen, "User Specialisation and Asset Financing," Working Paper, London Business School, 1996.
b. T. Chemmanur and K. John, "Optimal Incorporation, Structure of Debt Contracts, and Limited-Recourse Project Financing," Working Paper, New York University, 1992.
c. T. John and K. John, "Optimality of Project Financing: Theory and Empirical Implications in Finance and Accounting," *Review of Quantitative Finance and Accounting* 1 (1991), 51-74.
d. S. Shah and A. Thakor, "Optimal Capital Structure and Project Financing," *Journal of Economic Theory* 42 (1987), 209-243.

> By arranging for the project company to [fund itself heavily with debt], the sponsors ensure that the cost of adverse government action falls directly on the lending banks and agencies. These generally consist of a syndicate of major banks from a wide range of countries, together with national or supranational bodies such as the World Bank... All have considerable political clout.

of project finance, and of the associated lack of recourse, is that it allows lenders to the project to confine their evaluation and monitoring to the project only, and saves them from having to evaluate and monitor the sponsors as well.

Free Cash Flow. Michael Jensen has argued that companies with a surplus of cash and a lack of worthwhile projects have a tendency to invest this cash in negative NPV projects rather than return it to shareholders. Leverage ensures that cash is needed to service debt, and is not frittered away. That is, heavy debt financing can provide stronger incentives both to generate more cash, and to pay out what cash cannot be profitably reinvested in the company.

The above argument leaves open the question as to why the debt is located in the project company rather than in the parent companies. After all, if the parent companies assumed the debt, they would have an equally great incentive for ensuring that cash was distributed to them rather than reinvested unproductively.

There are two possible reasons why the location of the debt could matter. One is that the parent companies may find it difficult or costly to monitor the efficiency with which cash is used within the project company, and therefore cannot prevent the waste of free cash flow. The other is that, when there is more than one parent company, the owners may have different views about how to use cash. For example, if one parent is a potential supplier to the project company while another has a purely financial interest in it, the two parents may disagree about the desirability of having the company reinvest its free cash flow. By ensuring that cash flows are used to service debt, such disagreements are avoided.

INSURANCE AND HEDGING

The risk transfer contracts that we described earlier have the effect of transferring many of the project risks from the project sponsor to the other parties to the project. Further risks are transferred by a variety of insurance contracts, such as completion insurance, insurance against *force majeure*, and insurance against political risks.

Although an insurance company may have particular expertise at pricing these risks and may

possibly be skillful at monitoring them, it has no control over them. An insurer cannot control whether there will be a flood, a hurricane, or other natural catastrophes. Insurance contracts therefore should have no beneficial effect, and may well have detrimental effects, on incentives, as they reduce the incentives of the project company to exert effort that would minimize the effects of such disasters. Therefore, the probable purpose of such risk transfers is simply to enable the project company to operate at higher debt ratios than it otherwise could.

In addition to the protection against firm-specific risks they purchase from insurance companies, project companies may also undertake to hedge themselves against market risks, such as any remaining currency risk, interest rate risk, and commodity price risk. These contracts too enable the project company to operate at high debt ratios.

BIDDING

Project finance is expensive to arrange. It involves establishing the project company, forming a consortium of equity-holders and lenders, gaining agreement to a complex set of contractual arrangements between the parties involved, and arranging costly documentation.

Governments commonly advertise for competing bids. Of course, in preparing their bid, companies recognize both the cost of doing so and the probability that they will not be awarded the contract. For this reason, an open auction will not necessarily result in the optimal number of bidders, or the lowest cost to the government. For example, a common complaint by contractors in the U.K. has been that they have incurred large bidding costs under the Private Finance Initiative, with a low probability of success. Bidding costs are reputed to have been up to five times higher than for private sector projects.[4]

Where each potential bidder has access to the same technology and is equally well-equipped to undertake the project, there is no gain in social welfare from inviting a large number of bids. The government needs to invite only a sufficient number of bids to avoid collusion or the exercise of monopoly power.

---

4. *The Financial Times*, 10 November 1995.

BUILD-OPERATE-TRANSFER

In the case of BOT (build-operate-transfer) as opposed to BOO (build-own-operate) projects, ownership of a project's assets is transferred to the government at the end of the concession period. For example, ownership of privately financed toll roads and bridges is often eventually transferred to the government.

Of course this is not a free lunch: sponsors will recognize the limited nature of the concession in their bidding. Since project sponsors need to recover their investment within the limited period of the concession, it may not be possible to arrange BOT finance even for projects that provide a satisfactory return over their complete life. An often-cited example is the early Mexican toll road program, where a 10-year concession period obliged sponsors to charge such high tolls that motorists avoided using the roads. The other danger with BOT contracts is that, as the end of the concession period approaches, there is little incentive for the sponsor to invest more in the project, and every incentive for him to take as much cash out as he can. For example, oil rights with a limited life encourage the franchisee to extract oil earlier than may be desirable.

Why, then, are some projects organized as BOT contracts? We suggest that such an arrangement makes sense where there is a need for the government to support the project by continuing infrastructure investments that cannot easily be specified by contract. Knowing that the project will eventually revert to government ownership provides an incentive for the government to invest in the supporting infrastructure.

The government sometimes has an option to terminate the concession before the end of the concession period. This may be particularly important when the original concession agreement may prevent government policy changes in (say) the regulatory framework.

CONCLUDING REMARKS

We conclude this paper by discussing what we believe are some common misconceptions about project finance, and by briefly contrasting project finance with the alternatives of privatization and service contracts.

It is sometimes argued that project finance is attractive simply because "the mobilisation of private capital is the only way in which public service is likely to be maintained,"[5] or because it saves the government money by transferring the investment expenditure from the public to the private sector. For example, the British government recently agreed to sell homes occupied by military personnel to private firms which would manage those homes and lease them back to the government. This, it was asserted, would reduce government spending by £500 million, thus cutting the government's borrowing requirements. While this is literally correct, the sale of the homes also makes the government liable for a series of future rental payments. Unless the private sector is more efficient at managing these homes, the cash flows paid out by the government in the sale-and-leaseback arrangement can be exactly replicated by government borrowing. Of course, by using project finance rather than direct government borrowing, a government may reduce its apparent deficit and avoid contravening IMF requirements on borrowing, or rules for admission to European Monetary Union. But it is difficult to believe that such transparent dodges provide a reliable long-term basis for the use of project finance.[6]

Some *critics* of the use of project finance for infrastructure investment argue that the cheaper financing available to the government could well outweigh the gains in efficiency made possible by private-sector management. The government is said to have a lower cost of capital than do private-sector companies because it is able to borrow at blue-chip rates, whereas a project company is likely to pay a higher rate of interest on its debt and may need to offer the project sponsors a prospective return of 20 or 30 percent on their equity investment in the company. For example, *The Economist* quotes a report on a Scottish water project by Chemical Bank, which estimates that "if the works were privately built, owned and operated, interest rates and the need to achieve a return on equity investment would make the finance costs 50% more expensive than the

---

5. As Ross Goobey argued in *The Times* (22 June 1996).

6. It may however be the case that project finance, by allocating the revenues from a project to the project company, serves to remove these revenues from the reach of the government, which may otherwise divert them to uses other than the repayment of the debt. This may justify the view of project finance as "off-balance-sheet" finance in the case of governments, but it does not explain why such projects should be highly leveraged.

> While governments can borrow more cheaply than corporations and do not have to provide a return to shareholders, this does not imply that the total cost of capital is lower to governments than it is to the private sector. Indeed, because the capital markets share risk better than does the tax system, the cost of capital for the government could well be *higher* than for corporations.

£201 million costs that would be incurred under the normal public-borrowing rules. There would be no chance... to recoup the higher financing costs through the greater efficiency of a private operator, because the costs of running a £100m sewage work is only about £5m a year."[7] The World Bank, too, appears to subscribe to the view that governments have a lower cost of capital than private sector companies, commenting that "[i]n infrastructure projects, the cheaper credit available to governments needs to be weighed against possible inefficiencies in channelling funds through government."[8]

The notion that the government enjoys a lower cost of capital than private sector companies is misleading. While it is certainly the case that governments can borrow more cheaply than corporations and do not have to provide a return to shareholders, this does not imply that the total cost of capital is lower to governments than it is to the private sector. The lower interest rate paid by a government simply reflects the guarantee provided by taxpayers to lenders. In the case of private sector companies, the bulk of the risk presented by a project is borne by the equity-holders, who demand a correspondingly higher rate of return. A smaller part of the risk goes to the debt-holders, who bear the risk that the firm may default on its debt payments. In contrast, government debt is risk-free in nominal terms, a characteristic that is reflected in the low rate of interest on the debt. But the risk presented by the projects does not disappear when the project is financed by the government. If cash flows from the project are unexpectedly low and do not suffice to service the debt raised by the government to finance the project, the shortfall is met by taxpayers, who play a role similar to that of equity-holders in a private sector company (but without the benefit of limited liability). Indeed, because it seems likely that the capital markets share risk better than does the tax system, the cost of capital for the government could well be *higher* than for corporations.

We believe that the argument for transferring ownership as well as management revolves around the difficulty of writing contracts that ensure that managers maximize efficiency. We have described above how contractual arrangements provide in-

---

7. "Something Nasty in the Water," *The Economist*, 9 September 1995, page 32.

8. World Development Report 1994, World Bank.

EXHIBIT 3 ■ THE BENEFITS AND COSTS OF PROJECT FINANCE*

WHEN PROJECT FINANCE

MAKES SENSE

AGENCY EFFECTS:
- Specializes and decentralizes management.
- Makes possible the provision of separate incentives for project managers.
- Precludes the waste of project free cash flow.
- Increases the outside scrutiny of projects.
- Improves incentives for the production of information.

OWNERSHIP STRUCTURE:
- Permits joint ventures without requiring the exhaustive mutual evaluation of the creditworthiness of potential partners.
- Limits the liability of parents to projects.
- Limits the exposure of creditors to well-defined project risks.
- Allows project-specific debt ratios.

OTHER EFFECTS:
- Crystallizes project costs for regulatory purposes.
- Allows the provision of services to several companies rather than just to sponsors.
- Partially transforms a sponsor from an equity-holder in the project into a supplier to the project, thus improving the sponsor's priority ranking in case of default.
- May avoid double taxation.

WHEN PROJECT FINANCE

DOES *NOT* MAKE SENSE
- *There are complex interactions of the project with the rest of the firm.*
- *Default of the project is costly (lost coinsurance).*
- *The optimal leverage of the project is low.*
- *The costs of contracting for the project are high.*

---

*This exhibit, along with some of the arguments presented in this paper, adapt and extend arguments made by John Kensinger and John Martin in "Project Finance: Raising Money the Old-Fashioned Way," *Journal of Applied Corporate Finance*, Vol. 1 No. 3 (Fall 1988).

centives for efficiency by transferring risks to those best able to control them. At the same time, we have also argued that, because the vast majority of contracts are incomplete and imperfectly monitored, an exclusive reliance on service contracts is unwise. The ultimate incentive for project managers to maximize efficiency is for them to be made residual claimants who capture the benefits of any improvements they make. Thus, it is desirable to tie ownership and the provision of management services whenever it is difficult to specify *ex ante* the required level of services, or the acceptable level of costs, and to monitor them. This can be achieved through the use of project finance.

Rather than living off individual projects in order to attract private-sector funding and management expertise to a given industry, a government can do so by privatizing the industry. Indeed, it seems likely that the growth in privatization and in the use of project finance for infrastructure investments have both been prompted by the same concerns about the efficiency of government-owned enterprises and the appropriateness of government funding for large, risky investments. However, while the recent popularity of project finance and privatization may have similar causes, there are three reasons why project finance may sometimes be preferred to privatization. First, privatization is a more complex undertaking, particularly since it involves both existing and new plant. While project finance relies on a one-off set of contractual undertakings for each plant, privatization needs a regulatory framework for the entire industry. Second, there are a number of areas, such as health or education, where it may be possible to involve private funding for particular projects but where full-scale privatization is deemed inappropriate. Third, unless the industry is to be entirely foreign-owned, privatization requires a large local capital market, in contrast to project financings, which take place piecemeal and over a period of time.

V. RISK MANAGEMENT

Wall-Street bashing is a time-honored practice, even among economists. In the lead article in this section, "Financial Innovation: Achievements and Prospects," Merton Miller traces the popular skepticism about Wall Street and financial innovation to an 18th-century economic doctrine known as "Physiocracy." According to this theory, the ultimate source of national wealth lies in the production of physical commodities. All other forms of commercial activity are considered nonproductive, if not parasitic. "Modern-day Physiocrats," as Miller says, "automatically and enthusiastically consign to that nonproductive class all the many thousands on Wall Street and LaSalle Street now using the new instruments."

The subject of Miller's article is "the new instruments"—that is, the proliferation since the early 1970s of all variety of futures, swaps, and options. It is Miller's contention—and indeed the underlying thesis of this book—that the social benefits accruing from financial innovation far outweigh the costs.

What are these benefits? Perhaps the principal source of gain from the many securities innovations over the past 20 years has been an improvement in the allocation of risk within the financial system— which in turn has enabled the capital markets to do a better job of performing their basic task of channeling investor savings into productive corporate investment of all kinds. The foreign exchange futures market started in 1972, together with the host of "derivative" products that have risen up since then, have dramatically reduced the cost of transferring risks to those market participants with a comparative advantage in bearing them. "Efficient risk-sharing," as Miller says, "is what much of the futures and options revolution has been all about." By functioning much like "a gigantic insurance company," the options, futures, and other derivative markets also effectively raise the price investors pay for corporate securities, thus adding to corporate investment and general economic growth.

Consider, for example, the development of a national mortgage market made possible by investment bankers' pooling and repackaging of individual mortgages into securities. Such asset securitization, which in turn was made possible by

the development of financial futures necessary to hedge the investment bankers' interest rate and prepayment exposures, has accomplished a massive transfer of interest rate risk away from financial institutions to well-diversified institutional investors. Besides lowering interest rates for homeowners (by as much as 100 basis points, according to some estimates), such risk-shifting should also help prevent a repeat of the S&L debacle.

Futures and options continue, of course, to have a big PR problem—one that stems mainly from the fact that they are used by "speculators" as well as "hedgers." But economists know that speculators serve a purpose: Besides keeping markets "efficient" by channeling information rapidly into prices, they also help supply the liquidity essential to these markets. And, as Miller argues further, the widespread charges that index futures and options are the cause of growing stock price volatility (including the crash of 1987) are contradicted by a growing weight of academic evidence. In short, popular indictments of the "new instruments" confound the "messenger" with the "message." What price volatility shows up within the system (and today's volatility is by no means high by historical measures) is largely the reflection of fundamental events; index futures and options are simply methods allowing companies and investors to cope with it.

In "Strategic Risk Management," Charles Smithson and Clifford Smith provide a broad survey of the theory and current practice of corporate risk management. There is still a good deal of confusion in the corporate world about what constitutes—and thus about the extent of—real, economic corporate exposures to exchange rates, interest rates, and commodity prices. American corporations are accustomed to hedging accounting-based exposures that arise from contractual commitments to make future sales or purchases (known as "transaction exposures"). Many companies also attempt to smooth their earnings by hedging "contingent" exposures—that is, operating net cash flows that are relatively predictable, but not yet bound by contract and booked. Relatively new, however, are corporate efforts to quantify and manage "competitive" exposures—the longer-run effects of changes in financial variables on corporate revenues and net operating margins. Such competitive exposures are the most elusive, and potentially the most damaging, of all the corporate exposures the authors refer to collectively as "strategic risk."

The article then describes a variety of techniques for identifying and quantifying such exposures. Although gap and duration analysis are now widely used by financial institutions to measure interest rate exposures, the methods for evaluating industrial companies' exposures to interest rates and other financial variables are still in an early stage of development. Some companies such as Merck (as described in another article in this section) are using sophisticated quantitative methods to simulate the effect of exchange rate changes on long-run currency earnings and cash flows. Others evaluate specific exposures by means of statistical regressions that measure the strength of correlation between stock price movements and changes in financial variables.

But, as Smithson and Smith go on to argue, not all corporate exposures should be hedged. From the perspective of modern portfolio theory (MPT), foreign exchange risk, interest rate risk, and commodity price risk are all "diversifiable" risks. Stockholders, according to MPT, are able to manage such risks on their own simply by holding large, diversified portfolios. And thus active corporate management of these risks does not increase share values by reducing a company's cost of capital. (This would suggest, for example, that a multinational's success in reducing the volatility of its overseas earnings would not by itself cause investors to raise the P/E multiple on the stock.) There are, however, other important benefits from hedging that are likely to increase corporate market values: (1) a reduction in expected tax liabilities; (2) a lowering of the probability (and hence expected costs) of financial difficulty (or, alternatively, an increase in the firm's debt capacity); and (3) an improvement of management's incentives to undertake valuable long-run investments.

In the latter part of the article, Smithson and Smith go on to provide an introduction to the four basic instruments for managing financial risks: forwards, futures, swaps, and options. After demonstrating the close relationships among these four "financial building blocks," the article goes on to demonstrate the potential for combining these to achieve virtually any desired risk position. The framework also lends itself to the analysis and pricing of complex hybrid securities by breaking them down into the basic components.

In "Rethinking Risk Management," Rene Stulz presents a theory of corporate risk management that uses the idea of comparative advantage in risk-bearing to go beyond the "variance-minimization" model that dominates most academic discussions. It argues that the primary goal of risk management is not to dampen swings in corporate cash flows or value, but rather to provide protection against the possibility of costly lower-tail outcomes—situations that would cause financial distress or make a company unable to carry out its investment strategy. By reducing the odds of financial trouble, risk management has the power to change not only the optimal capital structure of the firm, but its optimal ownership structure as well. For besides increasing corporate debt capacity, the reduction of downside risk also facilitates larger equity stakes for managers by shielding their investments from "uncontrollables."

The article's most significant departure from the standard theory, however, is in Stulz's suggestion that some companies may have a comparative advantage in bearing certain financial market risks—an advantage that could derive from information acquired through normal business activities. Although such specialized market information may lead some companies to take speculative positions in commodities or currencies, it is more likely to encourage "selective" hedging, a practice in which the risk manager's "view" of future price movements influences the percentage of the exposure that is hedged. But, if such view-taking becomes an accepted part of a company's risk management program, managers' "bets" should be evaluated on a risk-adjusted basis and relative to the market. As Stulz notes in closing, "If risk managers want to behave like money managers, they should be evaluated like money managers."

In "Identifying, Measuring, and Hedging Currency Risk at Merck," Judy Lewent and John Kearney describe the company's effort to understand and manage the effect of exchange rate volatility on worldwide revenues and earnings. In a thought process that parallels the one laid out by Smithson and Smith in the preceding article, Merck's treasury arrived at the following conclusions: (1) the home currency value of cash flows regularly repatriated by its many overseas subsidiaries was vulnerable to a strengthening of the U.S. dollar; (2) although stock market analysts and investors do not appear much concerned about the exchange-related volatility of reported earnings, volatility in repatriated cash flows could interfere with the company's ability to make long-term investments in R&D and marketing (the principal sources of the company's future earnings); and (3) consistent with Stulz's argument that risk management should be designed to eliminate the lower tail of the distribution (and not to minimize variance), hedging (only part of) its currency options was the most cost-effective means of ensuring the company's ability to carry out its long-range strategic plan.

In "Theory of Risk Capital for Financial Firms," Nobel laureate Robert Merton and Andre Perold present a concept of risk capital that can be used to guide the capital structure, performance measurement, and strategic planning decisions of commercial and investment banks, insurance companies, and other firms engaged in principal financial activities. In the wake of the new BIS capital guidelines, not only banks but most financial institutions have been forced to revisit the issue of capital adequacy. The concept of risk capital presented in these pages differs significantly, however, from "both regulatory capital, which attempts to measure risk capital according to a particular accounting standard, and from cash capital, which represents the up-front cash required to execute a transaction." (And, given that Bob Merton is a principal in Long Term Capital Management, Inc., the highly publicized trading venture formed by ex-Salomon Brothers executive John Meriwether, we can infer that at least some of the principles described here are now being applied on Wall Street.)

After illustrating their concept of risk capital with a series of examples, Merton and Perold go on to demonstrate its application to a number of challenging problems faced by financial firms—specifically, allocating the costs of risk capital to individual businesses or projects in performance measurement and accounting for the benefits of internal diversification among business units in strategic planning.

In "How to Use the Holes in Black-Scholes," the late Fischer Black, co-originator of the Black-Scholes(-Merton) option pricing model, discusses each of the ten "unrealistic assumptions" underlying the model. The purpose of this exercise is twofold: first, to suggest how the model might be made to better reflect market prices by making the assumptions more "realistic"; second, to point out

profitable trading strategies that depend on the user's having better knowledge than the market's in making specific assumptions. Such trading strategies typically focus on expectations about the volatility of the underlying asset (in part because volatility is the only variable in the Black-Scholes formula that cannot be directly observed, but also because option values are so sensitive to estimates of volatility). But, giving a somewhat new twist to the argument, the article also shows how the presence of "mean reversion" in the stock market (the tendency for the expected return on stocks to fall as the market rises) points to profitable trading strategies using options. This same "mean reversion" tendency, accentuated by the widespread use of portfolio insurance, also furnishes the author with an interesting theory about the stock market crash of 1987.

In "Value at Risk: Uses and Abuses," Merton Miller, Chris Culp, and Andrea Neves use a number of derivatives disasters to illustrate some pitfalls in using the popular risk measurement technique called "VAR."

In "Corporate Insurance Strategy," Neil Doherty and Clifford Smith describe a radical shift in British Petroleum's approach to insuring property and casualty losses, product liability suits, and other insurable events. Conventional corporate practice—and until recently the longstanding risk management policy of BP—has been to insure against large losses while "self-insuring" against smaller ones. In this article, Doherty and Smith explain why BP has chosen to flout the conventional wisdom and now insures against most smaller losses while self-insuring larger ones.

The BP decision came down to factors affecting the market supply of insurance as well as the corporate demand for it. On the demand side, the authors demonstrate that the primary source of demand for insurance by large public companies is not, as standard insurance textbooks assume, to transfer risk away from the corporation's owners (corporate stockholders and bondholders, it turns out, have their own means of neutralizing the effect of such risks). The demand stems rather, at least in BP's case, from insurance companies' comparative advantage in assessing and monitoring risk and in processing claims. On the supply side, the authors explain why the capacity of insurance markets to underwrite very large or highly specialized exposures is quite limited—and can be expected to remain so.

In the "Bank of America Roundtable on Derivatives and Corporate Risk Management," four corporate financial executives discuss their companies' approaches to hedging interest rate, foreign exchange, and commodity price exposures. While all the participants firmly rejected the idea that their companies used derivatives to enlarge existing risks or create new ones, most described themselves as pursuing a policy of "selective" hedging informed by the corporate "view" of future market prices. (The panelists' comments, the reader will recognize, do a nice job of reinforcing Rene Stulz's argument about the departure of corporate risk management practice from the academic theory of variance minmization.) One contributing motive—though not the only one—for selective as opposed to "full-cover" hedging appears to stem from how derivatives positions are accounted for and reported. As one participant put the matter,

"We all have friends in the financial community who say they wouldn't hedge because derivatives are bad things to use. The irony, of course, is that by making that statement, they've effectively made a decision that they're going to accept the risk. But this hypocrisy, or at least confusion, persists in part because the two kinds of losses don't get accounted for in the same way. Unhedged losses don't show up anywhere, they aren't broken out into a separate account; and so the board never sees it, and the media never report it. But hedging losses are reported separately—typically independently of the position they're being used to hedge—and they are now being held up for very strong scrutiny."

DHC

FINANCIAL INNOVATION: ACHIEVEMENTS AND PROSPECTS

*by Merton H. Miller, University of Chicago**

T he wonderment of Rip Van Winkle, awakening after his sleep of 20 years to a changed world, would pale in comparison to that felt by one of his descendants in the banking or financial services industry falling asleep (presumably at his desk) in 1970 and waking two decades later. So rapid has been the pace of innovation in financial instruments and institutions over the last 20 years that nothing could have prepared him to understand such now commonplace notions as swaps and swaptions, index futures, program trading, butterfly spreads, puttable bonds, Eurobonds, collateralized-mortgage bonds, zero-coupon bonds, portfolio insurance, or synthetic cash—to name just a few of the more exotic ones. No 20-year period has witnessed such a burst of innovative activity.

What could have produced this explosive growth? Has all this innovation really been worthwhile from society's point of view? Have we seen the end of the wave of innovations, or must we brace for more to come? These are the issues I now address.

---

*This article will appear in *Japan and the World Economy*, Vol. 4 No. 2 (June, 1992).

WHY THE GREAT BURST OF FINANCIAL INNOVATIONS OVER THE LAST TWENTY YEARS?

Several explanations have been offered for the sudden burst of financial innovations starting some 20 years ago.[1]

The Move to Floating Exchange Rates

A popular one locates the initiating impulse in the collapse of the Bretton Woods, fixed-exchange rate regime. In the early 1970s, the U.S. government, with strong prodding from academic economists, notably Milton Friedman, finally abandoned the tie of gold to the dollar. The wide fluctuations in exchange rates following soon after added major new uncertainty to all international transactions. One response to that uncertainty was the development of exchange-traded foreign-exchange futures contracts by the Chicago Mercantile Exchange—an innovation that spawned in turn a host of subsequent products as the turbulence spread from exchange rates to interest rates.

But cutting the tie to gold cannot be the whole story because financial futures, influential as they proved to be, were not the only major breakthrough of the early 1970s. Another product introduced only a few months later, and almost equally important to subsequent developments, was not so directly traceable to the monetary events of that period. The reference, of course, is to the exchange-traded options on common stock of the CME's cross-town rival, the Chicago Board of Trade. That the CBOT's options did not precede the CME's financial futures was mainly luck of the bureaucratic draw. Both exchanges started the process of development at about the same time, impelled to diversify by the same stagnation in their traditional agricultural markets. Both needed the cooperation, or at least the toleration, of the appropriate regulators to break out in such novel directions.

The CME was the more fortunate in having to contend only with the U.S. Treasury and the Federal Reserve System—at a time, moreover, when both those agencies were strongly committed to the Nixon administration's push for floating exchange rates.[2] The CBOT, alas, faced the U.S. Securities and Exchange Commission, a New Deal reform agency always hypersensitive to anything smacking of speculative activity.[3] By the time the SEC had finished its detailed review of option trading, the CME had already won the race.

Computers and Information Technology

Another explanation for the sudden burst of financial innovation after 1970 finds the key in the information revolution and, especially, in the electronic computer. Computers in one form or another had been available since the 1950s. But only in the late 1960s, with the perfection of transistorized circuitry, did computers become cheap and reliable enough to design new products and strategies such as stock index arbitrage and collateralized mortgage obligations. And certainly the immense volume of transactions we now see regularly could not have been handled without the data-processing capacities of the computer.

But the basic and most influential innovations, financial futures and exchange-traded options, did not require computers to make them commercially feasible. Options on commodities in fact had been traded regularly on the CBOT until the U.S. Congress, in one of its periodic bouts of post-crash, anti-speculative zeal, ended the practice in 1934. That this long prior history of option trading is not better known may trace to the arcane CBOT terminology under which options were known as "privileges." But traded instruments designated with the modern terms puts and calls go back much further than that, to the Amsterdam Stock Exchange of the late 17th century.[4] Routine exchange trading of futures contracts has a history almost as long.

---

1. See, for example, my article, "Financial Innovation: The Last Twenty Years and the Next," *Journal of Financial and Quantitative Analysis* 21 (December 1986), 459-71; and James C. Van Horne, "Of Financial Innovations and Excesses," *Journal of Finance* 40 (July 1985), 621-36.

2. The then Secretary of the Treasury was George P. Shultz, a former colleague and long-time friend of Milton Friedman. The Chairman of the Federal Reserve Board was Arthur Burns, another old friend. With Milton Friedman's blessing, both gave a cordial audience to Leo Melamed of the CME and at least a *nihil obstat* to his proposal for an International Monetary Exchange. (See Leo Melamed, "The International Monetary Market," in *The Merits of Flexible Exchange Rates*, ed. Leo Melamed, George Mason University Press, Fairfax, Virginia, 1988, 417-29.)

3. Under the SEC's original dispensation, only calls could be traded because puts were regarded as potentially destabilizing. Word of the put-call parity theorem had apparently not yet reached the SEC staff.

4. Joseph de la Vega, *Confusion de Confusiones*, Amsterdam, 1688, translated by Hermann Kellenbenz, 1957, reprinted by Baker Library, Harvard Business School, 1988.

Innovation and World Economic Growth

Still another possibility, and the one I find most persuasive,[5] is that the seeming burst of innovation in the 1970s was merely a delayed return to the long-run growth path of financial improvement. The burst seems striking only in contrast to the dearth of major innovations during the long period of economic stagnation that began in the early 1930s and that for most of the world continued well into the 1950s.

The shrinkage in the world economy after 1929 was on a scale that few not actually experiencing it can readily imagine. The prolonged depression undermined any demand pull for developing new financial instruments and markets, and the increased regulatory role of the state throttled any impulses to innovate from the supply side. Much of this new regulation, particularly in the U.S., was in fact a reaction to the supposed evils—notably the Crash of 1929—flowing from the development of exchange-traded, and hence relatively liquid, common stock as a major investment and financing vehicle in the 1920s. Prior to the 1920s, U.S. companies had relied almost exclusively on bonds and preferred stock for raising outside capital.

Even in the depressed '30s, of course, financial innovation, though muted relative to the 1920s, did not come to a halt. But the major novelties tended to be government sponsored, rather than market induced. Examples are the special housing-related instruments such as the amortizing mortgage and the Federal Home Administration loan guarantees. Another government initiative of the '30s was the support direct and indirect of what later came to be called, rather unprophetically we now know, "thrift institutions." New U.S. Treasury instruments were developed, or at least used on a vastly expanded scale, notably Series E savings bonds for small savers and, at the other extreme, U.S. Treasury bills. Indeed, T-bills quickly became the leading short-term liquid asset for banks and corporate treasurers, displacing the commercial paper and call money instruments that had previously served that function.

Financial innovation by the private sector might perhaps have revived by the 1940s had not the War intervened. The War not only drained manpower

and energy from normal market-oriented activity, but led to new regulatory restrictions on financial transactions, particularly international transactions.

Regulation and Deregulation as Stimuli to Financial Innovation

By a curious irony, the vast structure of financial regulation erected throughout the world during the 1930s and 1940s, though intended to and usually successful in throttling some kinds of financial innovation, actually served to stimulate the process along other dimensions. Substantial rewards were offered, in effect, to those successfully inventing around the government-erected obstacles. Many of these dodges, or "fiddles" as the British call them, turned out to have market potential far beyond anything dreamed of by their inventors; and the innovations thrived even after the regulation that gave rise to them was modified or abandoned.

The most striking example of such a regulation-propelled innovation may well be the swap in which one corporation exchanges its fixed-rate borrowing obligation for another's floating-rate obligation; or exchanges its yen-denominated obligations for another's mark-denominated obligations; and so on in an almost unimaginable number of permutations and combinations. Some swaps are arranged by brokers who bring the two counterparties directly together; others by banks who take the counterparty side to a customer order and then either hedge the position with forwards and futures or with an offsetting position with another customer.

The notional amount of such swaps, interest and currency, currently outstanding is in the trillions of dollars and rising rapidly. Yet, according to legend at least,[6] the arrangement arose modestly enough as vacation-home swapping by British overseas travelers, who were long severely limited in the amount of currency they could take abroad. Two weeks free occupancy of a London flat could compensate a French tourist for a corresponding stay in a Paris apartment or compensate an American for the use of a condominium at Aspen. If the ingenious British innovator happened to work for one of the merchant banks in the City, as is likely, the extension of the

---

5. See Miller (1986), cited in note 1.

6. The first currency swap appears to have been arranged by Continental Illinois' London merchant bank in 1976. The precise dates and places remain problematic because the originators sought secrecy in a vain attempt to maintain their competitive advantage. See Henry T. C. Hu, "Swaps, the Modern Process of Financial Innovation and the Vulnerability of a Regulatory Paradigm," *University of Pennsylvania Law Review* 128 (December 1989), pp. 333-435 (see especially note 73, p. 363).

The burst of innovations in the past 20 years seems striking only in contrast
to the dearth of major innovations during the long period of economic stagnation
that began in the early 1930s and that for most of the world continued well
into the 1950s.

notion to corporate currency swaps was a natural one. The rest, as they say, is history.

The list of similar, regulation-induced or tax-induced innovations is long, and includes the Eurodollar market, the Eurobond market, and zero-coupon bonds, to name just some of the more far-reaching loopholes opened in the restrictive regulatory structure of the 1930s and 1940s.[7] Whether the private sector processes that produced the seemingly great wave of innovations after 1970 will continue to produce innovations if left unchecked is a topic to be taken up later. First let's consider some of the arguments currently being advanced for not leaving them unchecked.

HAS THE WAVE OF FINANCIAL INNOVATIONS MADE US BETTER OR WORSE OFF?

Free market economists have a simple standard for judging whether a new product has increased social welfare: are people willing to pay their hard-earned money for it? By this standard, of course, the new products of the 1970s and '80s have proved their worth many times over. But why have they been so successful? Whence comes their real "value added"? The answer, in large part, is that they have substantially lowered the cost of carrying out many kinds of financial transactions.

Consider, for example, a pension fund or an insurance company with, say, $200 million currently in a well-diversified portfolio of common stocks. Suppose that, for some good reason, the sponsors of the fund believe that the interests of their beneficiaries would be better served at the moment by shifting funds from common stocks to Treasury bills. The direct way would be first to sell the stock portfolio company by company, incurring commissions, fees, and "market impact" on each transaction. The cash proceeds, when collected, could then be put in Treasury bills, again incurring transaction costs. A second and much cheaper alternative, however, is simply to sell about 1,000 (at present price levels) S&P 500 index futures contracts. Thanks to the way the futures contracts must be priced to maintain intermarket equilibrium, that one transaction has the same consequences as the two transactions along the direct route. And at a fifth or even less of the cost in fees, commissions, and market impact!

Or, to take other kinds of financial costs, consider a bank maintaining an inventory of government bonds for resale. The availability of that inventory, like the goods on the shelf in a supermarket, means better and faster service for the bank's customers when they come to shop. But it also means considerable risk for the bank. Bond prices can fall, sometimes very substantially, even in the course of a single day.

To protect against such losses, the bank can hedge its inventory by selling Treasury bond futures. Should the price of the bonds fall during the life of the futures contract, the gain on that contract will offset the loss on the underlying inventory. Without this opportunity to shift the risk via futures, the bank must seek other and more costly ways of controlling its inventory exposure. Some banks might find no better solution than to shrink their inventory and, hence, the quality and immediacy of the services they offer. Others might well abandon the activity altogether.

Insurance and Risk Management

A bank's use of futures to hedge its own inventory does not, of course, eliminate the price risk of the underlying bonds. It merely transfers that risk to someone else who *does* want to bear the risk, either because he or she has stronger nerves, or more likely, because another firm or investor somewhere wants to hedge against a *rise* in bond prices. The futures and options exchanges have greatly reduced the time (and hence cost) that each risk-shifter might otherwise have spent searching for a counterparty with the opposite risk exposure.

The combined set of futures and options contracts and the markets, formal and informal, in which they are transferred has thus been likened to a gigantic insurance company—and rightly so. Efficient risk-sharing is what much of the futures and options revolution has been all about. And that is why the term "risk management" has come increasingly to be applied to the whole panoply of instruments and institutions that have followed in the wake of the introduction of foreign exchange futures in CME's International Money Market in 1972. Honesty requires one to acknowledge, however, that this essentially benign view of the recent

---

7. For a fuller account of tax- and regulation-induced innovations, see Miller (1986), cited in note 1.

great innovative wave is not universally shared by the general public or even by academic economists.

The Case Against the Innovations

Some of the complaints about the harmful social consequences of the financial innovations appear to be little more than updated versions of a once-popular 18th-century economic doctrine known as Physiocracy, which located the ultimate source of national wealth in the production of physical commodities, especially agricultural commodities. Occupations other than commodity production were nonproductive. Modern-day Physiocrats, disdaining consumer sovereignty, automatically and enthusiastically consign to that nonproductive class all the many thousands on Wall Street and LaSalle Street now using the new instruments.

A related complaint is that the new instruments, by lowering transactions costs, have led to too much short-term trading—trading that not only wastes resources, but which has unduly shortened the planning horizons of both firms and investors. That the volume of trading has in fact skyrocketed in recent years there can be no doubt. But the key stimulus to the surge in trading in the underlying stocks appears to have been less the introduction of index futures and options than the ending of the regime of high fixed commissions in 1974. For Treasury bonds, the spur was the huge expansion of federal government debt beginning in 1981.

But the critics are surely right in believing that lower trading costs will induce more trading. More trading, however, need not mean more waste from society's point of view. Trading is part of the process by which economic information, scattered as it necessarily is in isolated bits and pieces throughout the whole economy, is brought together, aggregated, and ultimately revealed to all. The prospect of trading profits is the bribe, so to speak, that society uses to motivate the collection, and ultimately the revelation, of the dispersed information about supply and demand.

Index Futures and Stock Market Volatility. Although many of the complaints against the new financial investments are merely standard visceral reactions against middlemen and speculators, some

are specific enough to be tested against the available data. Notable here is the widespread view, expressed almost daily in the financial press, that stock market volatility has been rising in recent years and that stock-index futures and options are responsible. The evidence, however, fails to support this widespread public perception of surging volatility.

Volatility, measured as the standard deviation of rates of return (whether computed over monthly, weekly or even daily intervals), is only modestly higher now than during the more placid 1950s and 1960s, and is substantially below levels reached in the 1930s and 1940s.[8] Even the 1950s and 1960s had brief, transitory bursts of unusually high volatility, with a somewhat longer-lasting major burst occurring in the mid-1970s. The number of large, one-day moves (that is, moves of 3% or more in either direction) has indeed been higher in the 1980s than in any decade since the 1930s, but almost entirely due to the several days of violent movements in the market during and immediately following the crash of October 1987. Such increased volatility seems to accompany every major crash (as the Japanese stock market showed through much of 1990).

In fact, the tendency of volatility to rise after crashes and fall during booms is one of the few, well-documented facts researchers have been able to establish about the time-series properties of the volatility series. These bursts of post-crash volatility typically die out within a few months, and that has been basically the case as well for the crash of 1987. Indeed, what makes the 1930s so different from more recent experience is that the high levels of post-1929-crash volatility persisted so long into the next decade.

Index Products and the Crash of 1987. The failure to find a rising trend in volatility in the statistical record suggests that the public may be using the word volatility in a different and less technical sense. They may simply be taking the fact of the crash of 1987 itself (and the later so-called mini-crash of October 13, 1989) as their definition of market volatility. And without doubt, the 20% decline during the crash of 1987 was the largest one-day shock ever recorded. (The mini-crash of October 13, 1989, at about 6%, was high, but far from record-breaking.) If the crash of 1987 is the source of the public perception of increased volatility, the

---

8. See G. William Schwert, "Why Does Stock Market Volatility Change over Time?", *Journal of Finance* 44 (December 1989), 1115-53.

The combined set of futures and options contracts and the markets, formal and informal, in which they are transferred has been likened to a gigantic insurance company—and rightly so. Efficient risk-sharing is what much of the futures and options revolution has been all about.

task of checking for connections between the innovative instruments and volatility becomes the relatively straightforward one of establishing whether index futures and options really were responsible either for the occurrence or the size of the crash. On this score, signs of a consensus are emerging, at least within academia, with respect to the role of two of the most frequently criticized strategies involving futures and options, portfolio insurance and index arbitrage.

For portfolio insurance, the academic verdict is essentially "not guilty of causing the crash," but possibly guilty of the lesser charge of "contributing to the delinquency of the market." Portfolio insurance, after all, was strictly a U.S. phenomenon in 1987, and the crash seems to have gotten under way in the Far East, well before trading opened in New York or Chicago. The extent of the fall in the various markets around the world, moreover, bore no relation to whether a country had index futures and options exchanges.[9] Even in the U.S., nonportfolio insurance sales on the 19th, including sales by mutual funds induced by the cash redemptions of retail investors, were four to five times those of the portfolio insurers.

Still, portfolio insurance using futures, like some older, positive-feedback strategies such as stop-loss orders or margin pyramiding, can be shown, as a matter of theory, to be potentially destabilizing.[10] The qualification "using futures" is important here, however, because the potentially destabilizing impact of portfolio insurance is much reduced when carried out with index options (that is, essentially, by buying traded puts rather than attempting to replicate the puts synthetically with futures via craftily-timed hedges). With exchange-traded puts, the bearishness in portfolio insurance would make its presence known immediately in the market prices and implicit volatility of the puts. With futures, by contrast, or with unhedged, over-the-counter puts, the bearishness may be lurking in the weeds, only to spring out on a less-than-perfectly forewarned public.[11]

Index Arbitrage: The New Villain. Whatever may or may not have been its role in the crash of 1987, portfolio insurance using futures rather than options has almost entirely vanished. Certainly it played no role in the mini-crash of October 13, 1989. Its place in the rogues' gallery of the financial press has been taken over by computerized "program trading" in general and by index arbitrage program trading in particular.

Why index arbitrage should have acquired such an unsavory public reputation is far from clear, however. Unlike portfolio insurance, which can be destabilizing when its presence as an information-less trade in the market is not fully understood, intermarket index arbitrage is essentially neutral in its market impact. The downward pressure of the selling leg in one market is always balanced by the equal and opposite buying pressure in the other. Only in rather special circumstances could these offsetting transactions affect either the level or the volatility of the combined market as a whole.

Index arbitrage might, possibly, increase market volatility if an initial breakout of the arbitrage bounds somehow triggered sales in the less-liquid cash market so massive that the computed index fell by more than needed to bring the two markets back into line. A new wave of arbitrage selling might then be set off in the other direction.

Despite the concerns about such "whipsawing" often expressed by the SEC, however, no documented cases of it have yet been found.[12] Careful studies find the market's behavior after program trades entirely consistent with the view that prices are being driven by "news," not mere speculative "noise" coming from the futures markets as the critics of index futures have so often charged.

Nor should these findings be considered in any way remarkable. The low cost of trading index futures makes the futures market the natural entry port for new information about the macro economy. The news, if important enough to push prices through the arbitrage bounds, is then carried from the futures market to the cash market by the program trades of the arbitragers. Thanks to the electronic order routing systems of the NYSE, the delivery is fast. But arbitrage is still merely the medium, not the message.

9. See Richard Roll, "The International Crash of October 1987," *Financial Analysts Journal* 22 (September 1988), 19-35.

10. See Michael J. Brennan and Eduardo S. Schwartz, "Portfolio Insurance and Financial Market Equilibrium," *Journal of Business* 62 (October 1989), pp. 455-72. Particularly interesting in their demonstration, however, is how small the destabilization potential really is, provided the rest of the investing public understands what is going on.

11. See Sanford J. Grossman, "An Analysis of the Implications for Stock and Futures Price Volatility of Program Trading and Dynamic Hedging Strategies," *Journal of Business* 61 (July 1988), 275-98.

12. See, for example, the very thorough searches described in Gregory Duffie, Paul Kupiec, and Patricia White, "A Primer on Program Trading and Stock Price Volatility: A Survey of the Issues and Evidence," Working Paper, Board of Governors, Federal Reserve System, Washington, D.C., 1990.

That so much recent criticism has been directed against the messenger rather than the message may reflect only the inevitably slow reaction by the public to the vast changes that have transformed our capital markets and financial services institutions over the last 20 years. Index futures, after all, came of age less than 10 years ago. The shift from a predominantly retail stock market to one dominated by institutional investors began, in a big way, less than 15 years ago. In time, with more experience, the public's understanding of the new environment will catch up. Unless, of course, new waves of innovation are about to sweep in and leave the public's perceptions even further behind.

FINANCIAL INNOVATIONS: ANOTHER WAVE ON THE WAY?

Will the next 20 years see a continuation, or perhaps even an acceleration, in the flow of innovations that have so vastly altered the financial landscape over the last 20 years? I think not. Changes will still take place, of course. The new instruments and institutions will spread to every country in the developed world (and possibly even to the newly liberalized economies of Eastern Europe). Futures and options contracts will be written on an ever-widening set of underlying commodities and securities. But the process will be normal, slow, evolutionary change, rather than the "punctuated equilibrium" of the recent past.[13]

Long-range predictions of this kind are rightly greeted with derision. Who can forget the U.S. Patent Office Commissioner who recommended in the early 1900s that his agency be closed down because all patentable discoveries had by then been made? We know also that regulation and taxes, those two longstanding spurs to innovation, are still very much with us despite the substantial progress, at least until recently, in deregulation and in tax rate reduction. But something important has changed. In the *avant garde* academic literature of economics and finance today, few signs can be seen of new ideas and concepts like those that bubbled up in the '60s and '70s and came to fruition later in specific innovations.

The extent to which academic thinking and criticism prefigured the great wave of financial innovations of the 1970s and 1980s is still too little appreciated. Calls for the creation of a foreign exchange futures market and analysis of the economic benefits that would flow from such an institution were common in the 1950s and 1960s, as noted earlier, in the writings of the academic supporters of floating exchange rates, especially Milton Friedman. On the common-stock front, major academic breakthroughs in the 1950s and 1960s were the Mean-Variance Portfolio selection model of Harry Markowitz and, building on it, the so-called Capital Asset Pricing Model of William Sharpe and John Lintner in which the concept of the "market portfolio" played a central role.

The notion of the market portfolio ultimately became a reality by the early 1970s when the first, passively-managed index funds were brought on line. That the world would move from there to the trading of broad market portfolios, either as baskets or as index futures and options, was widely anticipated. The fundamental Black-Scholes and Robert Merton papers on rational option pricing were published in the early 1970s, though manuscript versions of them had been circulating informally among academics well before then. These and other exciting prospects abounded in the academic literature 20 years ago. At the moment, however, that cupboard seems bare of new concepts and ideas waiting for the day of practical implementation.

Such hints of future developments as the current literature does relate more to the structure of the exchanges themselves than to the products they trade. For academics, accustomed to spending their workdays staring at the screens of their PCs, the near-term transition of the markets from floor trading to electronic trading is taken for granted. Frequent references can be found in the many articles on the crash of 1987 to the presumed failings of the current exchange trading systems during that hectic period. Those systems are typically characterized pejoratively as "archaic" and "obsolete," in contrast to the screen-based trading systems in such non-exchange markets as government bonds or inter-bank foreign exchange.

That screen-based trading will someday supplant floor trading seems more than likely, but whether that transition will occur even by the end of

---

13. Evolution also involves "extinctions." Some of the recent innovations will inevitably fail in the competitive struggle. Others may be killed by heavy-handed regulation.

this century is far from clear. The case of the steamship is instructive. The new steam technology was clearly superior to sail-power in its ability to go up river and against winds and tides. Steam quickly took over inland river traffic but not, at first, ocean traffic. There steam was better, but vastly more expensive. Steam thus found its niche in military applications and in the high-unit-value fast passenger trade. Only as fuel costs dropped did steam take over more and more of the low-unit-value bulk trade in ocean freight. For some bulk commodities such as lumber, in fact, sail was often the lower-cost alternative up until the start of the first World War, more than 100 years after the first practical steamboat.

The same laws of comparative advantage apply to electronic trading systems. The open-outcry trading pits of the major futures exchanges may seem hopelessly chaotic and old-fashioned; but they are, for all that, a remarkably cheap way of handling transactions in large volume at great speed and frequency in a setting of high price volatility. Until recently, at least, electronic trading could not have come close to being cost-competitive in this arena. Screen trading found its niche elsewhere. And electronic computer systems found their niche in futures in tasks such as order routing, data processing and some kinds of surveillance rather than on the trading floor.

But screen-trading technology, like that of computing technology generally, continues to advance and a possibly crucial watershed for the trading systems in futures may soon be crossed. By mid-1992 the Chicago exchanges hope finally to bring on line the long-delayed Globex electronic network for after-hours trading of futures contracts. Unlike some past experiments with screen trading of futures, the test this time will be a valid one. The contracts to be traded, Eurodollars and foreign exchange rates, have long proven viable; the underlying spot markets are themselves screen traded; and substantial potential trading demand for the contracts might well exist outside the U.S. and after U.S. trading hours.

Even a successful Globex, however, need not doom the exchanges to disappear as functioning business entities. The transactions facilities the exchanges provide through their trading floors are currently the major and certainly the most glamorous, but by no means the only, services they offer. The exchanges also provide such humdrum but critical functions as clearing and settlement, guarantees of contract performance, record-keeping and audit trails, and the collection and dissemination of price information. The market for these services in supporting financial transactions not currently carried out via exchanges is potentially huge. The futures exchanges, by virtue of their expertise and their substantial existing capital investments, are well positioned to enter and to capture a significant share of these new markets, just as they were 20 years ago when the shrinkage in their agricultural business propelled them into financial futures and options.

STRATEGIC RISK MANAGEMENT

*by Charles W. Smithson,
Chase Manhattan Bank and
Clifford W. Smith, Jr.,
University of Rochester **

As we have listened to managers discuss their companies' exposures to financial price risk, we have heard them talk about several very different kinds of risk. Virtually every manager considers *accounting exposures*, and the accounting exposures that receive the most attention are transaction exposures—those that arise from direct expenses or sales to which the firm is contractually committed. In the foreign exchange environment, transaction exposures are defined very specifically by FAS 52. In the case of interest rates, the guidance is less formal, but most companies focus on managing their interest expense. In addition to transaction exposures, some companies, especially multinationals with large foreign holdings, are concerned about translation exposures—that is, possible changes in the value of the firm from converting the value of foreign assets into the home currency.

Beyond such accounting exposures, managers realize that while transaction exposures defined by FAS 52 deal only with "firm commitments," changes in exchange rates, interest rates, or commodity prices can affect the value of the firm through future transactions. Hence, some managers actively manage their *contingent exposures*—those resulting from the effects of financial price changes on transactions expected, but not yet booked.

Finally, some managers have begun to assess their firm's competitive exposures. Such an assessment attempts to evaluate the impact of changes in foreign exchange rates, interest rates, or commodity prices on the firm's sales market share and, ultimately, net profits (or, more precisely, net cash flows).

In this article, we use the term *strategic exposure* to encompass the other three. A company has a strategic exposure to the extent that changes in foreign exchange rates, interest rates, or commodity prices affect its market value—that is, the present value of the expected future cash flows.[1] The increased volatility of exchange rates and interest rates in the 1970s has led more companies to recognize their strategic exposures. Unfortunately, many firms have been forced to recognize their exposures the hard way: Strategic exposures have put them out of business. In some cases, the exposure was a transaction exposure, arising from a mismatch in revenues and expenses. . .

HOW SIR FREDDIE SHOT HIMSELF DOWN

In the late 1970s, Laker Airlines was doing well—so well that their existing fleet of aircraft simply couldn't handle the volume of British vacationers. So, Freddie Laker bought five more DC10s, financing them in U.S. dollars. The problem was that, since the airline's revenues were primarily in pounds while the payments for the new DC10s were in dollars, Laker Airlines had a mismatch between revenues and expenses. When the dollar strengthened in 1981, revenues declined because British travelers could no longer afford the resulting higher cost of trans-Atlantic travel; and the increased liabilities sent Laker into bankruptcy.[2]

In other cases, the exposure was a competitive exposure, arising from the impact of a financial price on the firm's ability to compete. . .

CATERPILLAR'S FX WHAMMY

Throughout the early 1980s, Caterpillar cited the strong dollar as the primary cause of its difficulties. When the dollar strengthened relative to the yen, the price of Caterpillar equipment rose relative to the price of Komatsu equipment, giving Komatsu a competitive advantage on Caterpillar. And Caterpillar's sales, domestic as well as international, fell off sharply.[3]

---

* This section of the article draws on *Managing Financial Risk*, a book Charles Smithson co-authored with Clifford W. Smith, Jr. and D. Sykes Wilford, Institutional Investor Series in Finance, New York: Harper & Row, (1990).

1. There are some accounting exposures that offset others. Moreover, some accounting exposures have no impact on the value of the firm. Hence, while the firm's strategic exposure does represent the firm's total economic exposure, this measure is *not* simply the sum of the other exposures.

2. This illustration is taken from a story by the same title which appeared in *Business Week* (Febmary 22,1982), and from "How Smart Competitors Are Locking in the Cheap Dollar," Gregory J. Millman, *Corporate Finance,* (December 1988).

3. From "Caterpillar's Triple Whammy," Dexter Hutchins, *Fortune,* (October 27, 1986).

FIGURE 1A ■ THE IMPACT OF RISK MANAGEMENT HEDGING IS TO REDUCE THE VARIANCE IN THE DISTRIBUTION OF FIRM VALUE

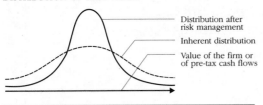

- Distribution after risk management
- Inherent distribution
- Value of the firm or of pre-tax cash flows

As illustrated in Figure 1A, the practice of risk management-that is, hedging exposures—reduces the volatility of the firm's pre-tax cash flows (and hence reduces the volatility of the value of the firm). Before a company decides to undertake a risk management program, however, two questions need to be answered:
1. To what extent does my firm face strategic exposures to interest rates, foreign exchange rates, or commodity prices?
2. Would a risk management program increase the value of the firm? And, if so, how?

In the pages that follow, we address these two questions. And, besides discussing how we think management ought to examine and deal with corporate exposures, we also focus on a third question:
3. What are firms actually doing with respect to risk management?

HOW TO MEASURE A FIRM'S STRATEGIC EXPOSURE

When confronted in the 1970s with the impact of volatile interest rates on their income, banks began using financial risk management techniques. A bank or a financial institution measures its exposure to interest rate changes using either a maturity gap approach or duration analysis. Maturity gap measures the sensitivity of an institution's net interest income to changes in the interest rate. Duration, by contrast, measures the sensitivity of the value of assets to changes in interest rates (as follows):[4]

$$D = \frac{\text{Percentage Change in V}}{\text{Percentage Change in } (1 + r)}$$

Moreover, because duration is "additive," the duration technique can be expanded to deal with the impact of changes in interest rates on the value of a portfolio or the value of the entire firm. The technique can also be used to

calculate the duration of the firm's equity—that is, the sensitivity of the value of the firm to changes in interest rates.

Although gap and duration work well for financial institutions, they are not helpful if we want to examine the interest rate sensitivity of a nonfinancial institution. Neither gap nor duration, moreover, is useful in examining a firm's sensitivity to movements in other financial prices such as foreign exchange rates or commodity prices. We thus require a more general method for measuring financial price risk—one that can handle firms other than financial institutions and financial prices other than interest rates.

To get a measure of the sensitivity of the value of the firm to changes in the financial prices, we must first define the basis for the measure. It can be a "flow" (or single-period) measure like the maturity gap analysis above or a "stock" (or multi-period capitalized present value) measure such as duration.

Flow Measures. Within a specific company, the corporate treasury can evaluate the sensitivity of income flows to changes in financial prices as part of the budgeting/planning process. Some firms have begun using simulation models ("what-if" analyses) that allow them to evaluate the sensitivity of their pre-tax income to changes in interest rates, exchange rates, and commodity prices.

QUANTIFYING KODAK'S STRATEGIC RISK

Kodak is well aware that changes in the yen-dollar exchange rate affect its value. As the value of the dollar gets stronger, Kodak's competitive position deteriorates relative to Fuji's. Articles in the trade press suggest that Kodak begins with a base-case set of assumptions about the yen-dollar exchange rate and other financial prices to obtain a base-case forecast of revenues, costs, and pre-tax income. Then, using alternative values for interest rates, exchange rates, or commodity prices, alternate forecasts of revenues, costs, and pre-tax income are simulated. By observing how forecasts of sales, costs, and income move in response to changes in the financial prices, the risk managers at Kodak are able to quantify their exposures.

As David Fiedler, Kodak's Director of Foreign Exchange Planning, puts it, in managing "the real problem—the economic problem—I have to make an estimate of its magnitude." Mr. Fiedler recognizes that there is a large margin of error; but, by using simulations, they are "quite a bit closer to a real solution than saying we can't be precise about it; so, we'll ignore the problem. The latter response effectively estimates the problem at zero."[5]

---

4. This equation holds only as an approximation. For the equation to be a true equality. we would be talking about "modified duration."

5. This illustration is based on "Daring to Hedge the Unhedgeable," Paul Dickins, *Corporate Finance*, (August 1988) and "Strategic Risk Management," William Millar and Brad Asher, *Business International*, (January 1990).

In accomplishing such an evaluation, however, the analyst faces two major difficulties: (1) the approach requires substantial data and (2) it relies on the ability of the researcher to make accurate forecasts of sales and costs under alternative assumptions about the financial prices. Thus, such an approach is generally possible only for analysts inside a specific firm.

Stock Measures. Given the data requirements noted above, analysts outside the company generally rely on market valuations—typically, the value of the firm's equity. A good starting point for evaluating the risk of a given firm's equity is with the "market model," a statistical regression equation that reveals the sensitivity of a company's stock price movements to changes in the general market. Specifically, the market model regresses the rate of return on the firm's equity against the rate of return on the market portfolio; and the resulting correlation coefficient, known as "beta," is a measure of market (or "undiversifiable") risk.

The number of variables in the market model can then be expanded to measure "diversifiable" risks such as foreign exchange rate, interest rate, and commodity price exposures; and the resulting correlation coefficients can serve as estimates of the sensitivity of the firm's value to changes in each of these financial prices.

MEASURING WESTINGHOUSE'S STRATEGIC EXPOSURES

To estimate a firm's sensitivity to interest rates, exchange rates, and the price of oil, we would estimate an equation like the following:

$$R_t = \alpha + b_1(\Delta\ 3ML/3ML) + b_2(\Delta\ 10YT/10YT) + b_3(\Delta\ P_{\pounds}/P_{\pounds}) + b_4(\Delta\ P_{\yen}/P_{\yen}) + b_4(\Delta\ P_{OIL}/P_{OIL})$$

where

R_t = rate of return for holding the firm's stock,

$\Delta 3_{ML}/3_{ML}$ = percentage change in three month LIBOR;

$\Delta 10_{YT}/10_{YT}$ = percentage change in the 10-year Treasury rate;

$\Delta P_{\pounds}/P_{\pounds}, \Delta P_{\yen}/P_{\yen}$ = percentage changes in dollar prices of pounds and yen;

$\Delta P_{OIL}/P_{OIL}$ = percentage change in crude oil price. The coefficients b_1 and b_2 provide measures of the sensitivity of the value of the firm to changes in the three-month LIBOR rate and 10-year Treasury rate, while b_3 and b_4 estimate the sensitivity to the exchange rates and b_5 estimates the sensitivity to the oil price.

To estimate Westinghouse's price sensitivities, we calculate the rate of return on the firm's equity using daily data on share prices and dividends for the period

October 1987 to October 1989. Likewise, we calculate the daily percentage changes in three-month LIBOR, the 10-year Treasury rate, the dollar prices of pounds and yen, and the price of West Texas Intermediate crude oil.

Sensitivity to	Parameter Estimate
3-month LIBOR	-0.263*
10-Year T-Bond Yield	-0.681*
Price of Sterling	-0.517
Price of Yen	0.098*
Price of Oil	0.023

* Statistically significant at the 95% confidence level.

The resulting estimates indicate that, over the two-year period, there is a statistically significant inverse relation between both 3-month LIBOR and the 10-year Treasury rate and the value of Westinghouse equity That is, increases in (short or long) interest rates are associated with decreases in the value of Westinghouse shares. Conversely there is a significant positive relation between the price of yen and the value of Westinghouse shares. Looking at each one-year period separately we find that Westinghouse's exposure to LIBOR has decreased over time.[6]

WHY WOULD A FIRM WANT TO MANAGE STRATEGIC RISK?

If the value of a firm is sensitive to movements in interest rates, foreign exchange rates, or commodity prices, a tantalizing conclusion is that the value of the firm will necessarily rise if this exposure is managed. Albeit tantalizing, this conclusion does not follow directly. The fact that a firm is confronted with strategic risk is only a necessary condition for the firm to manage that risk. The sufficient condition is that the risk management strategy increase the expected value of the firm.

The value of a firm (V) can be thought of as the sum of all future expected net cash flows (E(NCF)), discounted by the company's cost of capital (r). Expressed in the form of an equation,

$$V = \sum_{t=0}^{T} \frac{E(NCF_t)}{(1+r)^t}$$

The insight provided by this equation is that, if the value of the firm is to increase, it must result from either an increase in expected net cash flows or a decrease in the discount rate.

---

6. This approach extends the analyses of Flannery/James(1984) ("The Effect of Interest Rate Changes on Common Stock Returns of Financial Institutions," *Journal of Finance*, (Vol. 39 No.4) and Sweeney/Warga (1986) ("The Pricing of Interest Rate Risk: Evidence from the Stock Market," *Journal of Finance*, (Vol. 41 No. 2). The approach used here is described more completely in "Identifying and Quantifying Financial Risk," Charles W. Smithson and Leah Sonnenschein, working paper, Continental Bank, (1990).

IF risk management policies are going to increase the value of the firm,
THEN such policies must either reduce the firm's transaction costs or taxes or
improve its investment decisions.

Since we are talking about risk, the most obvious place to look for an effect is through a decrease in the discount rate. But, from the perspective of modern portfolio theory, foreign exchange rate risk, interest rate risk, and commodity price risk are all diversifiable risks; and shareholders can manage such risks effectively on their own simply by holding diversified portfolios. Therefore, actively managing these risks should have no effect on the company's cost of capital.[7] So, unless the firm is held by undiversified owners (as is the case, for example, in most private or closely held firms), risk management is not going to increase the expected value of the firm through a reduction in the discount rate.

Consequently, in the case of a company held by well-diversified investors, risk management can be expected to increase the value of the firm only by increasing expected net cash flows. But, this of course begs the question: How can hedging, or any other financial policy for that matter, have any impact on the real cash flows of the organization?

In 1958, Franco Modigliani and Merton Miller formally proposed that in a world with no taxes, no transaction costs, and fixed corporate investment policies, a company's value is unaffected by financial policies.[8] That is, whether management decides to fund its operations with debt or equity, and what kinds of debt or equity securities it chooses to issue, should have no effect on the value of the company's shares. In such a world, financial decisions would be nothing more than ways of repackaging the company's operating cash flows for distribution to investors. The insight provided by M & M is that investors can efficiently repackage corporate earnings on their own. And just as investors can use "home-made" leverage to lever up debt-free companies, they can also create their own home-made risk management strategy by holding diversified portfolios.

The important message of the M & M proposition for corporate practitioners becomes evident only when the argument is turned upside down:

IF risk management policies are going to increase the value of the firm,

THEN such policies must either reduce the firm's transaction costs or taxes or improve its investment decisions.

FIGURE 1B ■ THE IMPACT OF HEDGING ON THE PROBABILITY OF FINANCIAL DISTRESS

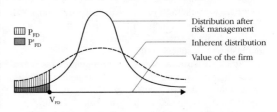

Define V_{FD} as that value of the firm below which financial distress is encountered. Risk management reduces the probability of V_{FD} from P_{FD} to P'_{FD}.

Transaction Costs: Expected Costs of Financial Distress[9]

In Figure 1A, we noted that risk management reduces the volatility of the cash flows of the firm. Figure 1B goes further to show that, by reducing cash flow volatility, risk management reduces the probability of the firm getting into financial difficulty and bearing the consequent costs.

How much risk management can reduce these costs depends on two obvious factors: (1) the probability of encountering financial distress if the firm does not hedge and (2) the costs imposed by such financial problems. The reduction in expected costs, and thus the expected benefit from risk management, will be larger the higher is the probability of distress and the greater are the associated costs.

Financial distress—the precursor of default—results when a firm's income is insufficient to cover its fixed claims. The probability of financial distress is thus determined by two factors: (1) fixed claims coverage (because the probability of default rises as the coverage of fixed claims declines); and (2) income volatility (the probability of default rises as the firm's income becomes more volatile).

If financial distress actually leads to bankruptcy and then to reorganization or liquidation, the firm would face substantial direct legal and accounting costs. But, even short of bankruptcy, financial distress can impose substantial indirect costs on the firm.[10] Such costs include higher contracting costs with customers, employees, and suppliers.

---

7. In the context of the market model as long as interest rate, foreign exchange rate, and commodity price risks are diversifiable managing these risk will have no impact on the firm's "beta." However, in actuality, interest rate, foreign exchange rate, and commodity price movements also influence the rate of return to the market portfolio: so managing financial price risk can change the firm's beta, albeit marginally.

8. The original M&M proposition was presented in, "The Cost of Capital, Corporation Finance and the Theory of Investment," *American Economic Review,* 48 (June 1958), pp. 261-97. The M&M proposition was extended to dividends in 1961, "Dividend Policy, Growth and the Valuation of Shares," *Journal of Business,* 34 (October 1961), pp. 411-33, arguing that "homemade" dividends can be created as the investor sells the firm's stock.

9. While we concentrate on the expected costs of financial distress, risk management could reduce other transaction costs as well. For instance, the cost of hedging by the management of the firm could be less than the cost of the shareholders' constructing a diversified portfolio, particularly in the case where the firm has access to information not disclosed to the shareholder.

10. The work of Jerry Warner suggests that the direct costs of bankruptcy are small in relation to the value of the firm. See "Bankruptcy, Absolute Priority, and the Pricing of Risky Debt Claims," *Journal of Financial Economics,* 13 (May 1977), pp. 239-76. But the indirect costs are significant. See "Bankruptcy Costs: Some Evidence," *Journal of Finance,* 32 (May 1977), pp. 337-47.

For example, companies that provide service agreements or warranties have made a longer-term contract with their customers. The value consumers place on the service agreements and warranties depends on their perception of the financial viability of the firm. If the future of the firm seems in doubt, consumers will place less value on the service agreements and warranties and are likely to turn to a competitor.

THE IMPACT OF FINANCIAL DISTRESS ON SALES[11]
THE CASE OF WANG

As reported in the *Wall Street Journal*, "the biggest challenge any marketer can face is selling the products of a company that is on the ropes." For Wang's customers, the guarantees and warranties (both explicit and implicit) are extremely important. As *The Journal* put it, "Wang's customers . . .want to be sure that their suppliers are stable, well-run companies that will be around to fix bugs and upgrade computers for years to come." Consequently, when Wang got into financial trouble, sales turned down. One of Wang's customers put it best when she noted that "before the really bad news, we were looking at Wang fairly seriously [but] their present financial condition means that I'd have a hard time convincing the vice president in charge of purchasing . . . At some point we'd have to ask 'How do we know that in three years you won't be in Chapter 11?'"

Taxes

Reducing the volatility of earnings through risk management can reduce corporate taxes if the firm's effective tax schedule is "convex." As shown in Figure 1C, a convex tax schedule is one in which the firm's average effective tax rate is rising as pre-tax income rises.

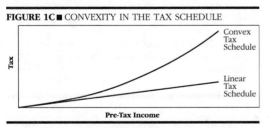

FIGURE 1C ■ CONVEXITY IN THE TAX SCHEDULE

REDUCING TAXES WITH RISK MANAGEMENT

Suppose that, without hedging, the distribution of the firm's pre-tax income is as shown in below For any given year, the firm could have a low pre-tax income (PTI_1) or a high pre-tax income (PTI_2), either with probability 50%.

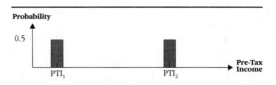

If the firm has pre-tax income PTI_1, it will pay tax $T(1)$; if its pre-tax income is PTI_2, the tax will be $T(2)$. Hence, if the firm does not hedge, expected tax will be $IE(T) = [0.5 \times T(1)] + [0.5 \times T(2)]$.

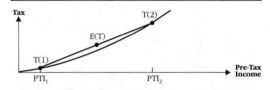

If this firm hedges, the volatility of its pre-tax income will decline; and both PTI_1 and PTI_2 will move toward the mean income. For purposes of illustration, suppose that the firm hedges completely such that the distribution of the firm's pre-tax income becomes a single point at the mean (PTI_{MEAN}).

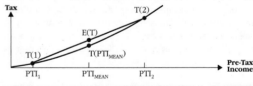

With income PTI_{MEAN}, the firm will pay a tax of $T(PTI_{MEAN})$.

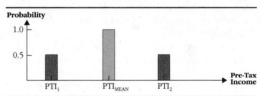

As is obvious, the tax on the hedged is strictly less than the expected tax if the firm does not hedge.

As the preceding example illustrates, if the tax schedule is convex, risk management can lead to a reduction in the firm's expected taxes. The more convex is the tax schedule, and the more volatile the firm's pre-tax income stream, the greater are the tax benefits.

---

11. This illustration is based on "Tough Pitch: Marketing on the Defense," William H. Bulkely, *The Wall Street Journal*, October 18, 1989.

One obvious factor that would make a tax schedule convex is the degree of progressivity (a tax schedule in which the statutory tax rate rises as income rises). Although the range of progressivity for corporation income taxes in the United States is relatively small, the Alternative Minimum Tax and tax shields like tax loss carryforwards and tax credits also make the tax schedule more convex. [12, 13]

Improving the Investment Decision and Increasing the Firm's Debt Capacity

As mentioned earlier, the MM "irrelevance" proposition rests on the assumption that corporate financial decisions do not affect investment and operating decisions. But, as we shall suggest here, reducing the volatility of cash flows by means of risk management can increase the value of the firm by improving management's incentives to undertake all profitable (positive NPV) projects while rejecting unprofitable ones. By so doing, risk management effectively expands the firm's "debt capacity" (or, put a little differently, reduces the firm's cost of borrowing).

How does risk management increase debt capacity? By reducing the volatility of cash flows, risk management also reduces the conflict of interest that can arise between stockholders and lenders in highly leveraged firms.[14] The conflict results from differences in the kind of claims each hold: bondholders hold fixed claims (and thus bear most of the downside risk) whereas shareholders hold claims that are equivalent to a call option on the value of the firm (and thus accrue the upside gains). Financial managers intent on maximizing stockholder value may have incentives to take actions that reduce the value of the fixed claims while increasing the value of the stock. Actions that increase the variability of the firm's cash flows such as undertaking riskier investments or further increasing financial leverage will "transfer" wealth from bondholders to stockholders. (Recall the effect of the KKR buyout proposal on RJR-Nabisco's bondholders.) The mere possibility of such action (popularly referred to as "event risk") should cause current lenders to limit the firm's future borrowings or to raise the coupon rate to compensate for bearing greater risk.

One determinant of the severity of the conflict between the shareholders and bondholders is the debt-equity ratio—the more debt in the capital structure, the sharper is the conflict.[15] The conflict between shareholders and bondholders is also determined by factors such as the range of investment opportunities available to the firm. Like the value of any other option, the value of shareholders' equity rises as the variance in the returns to the underlying asset increases. By switching from low-variance investment projects to high-variance projects, management can transfer wealth from bondholders to shareholders.[16]

At the end of the day, the bondholder (let's make that the potential bondholder) is concerned about the probability that he or she will be left holding the bag—i.e., the value of the assets of the firm will be insufficient to cover the face value of the debt. In addition to general concerns about future market conditions, the potential bondholder is concerned about opportunistic behavior on the part of the shareholder—the shareholders might declare a liquidating dividend, load the firm up with extra debt, or select risky investment projects. But, since potential bondholders realize that this opportunistic behavior could occur, they protect themselves by lowering the price they are willing to pay for the firm's bonds.

To get the bondholders to pay more for the bonds, the shareholders must assure the bondholders that the wealth transfers will not take place. Such assurances can be provided by attaching restrictive covenants to debt issues (restrictions on dividends and debt coverage ratios), issuing a mortgage bond (to preclude shifts into riskier projects), making the debt convertible (to align the interest of bondholders with those of the shareholders), or issuing preferred stock instead of debt (to reduce the probability that future market conditions will lead to default).

The shareholder-bondholder conflict can also be reduced by risk management. As we will show at the end of this article on page 477, a bond issue can be combined with one of the hedging instruments to reduce the probability of default and thereby increased the debt capacity of the firm.

---

12. There exists a substantial body of evidence on the convexity of the tax function and the factors which make it convex beginning with J.J. Siegfried "'Effective Average U.S. Corporation Income Tax Rates," *National Tax Journal,* (June 1974), pp. 245-59 through papers like J.L. Zimmerman "Taxes and Firm Size," *Journal of Accounting and Economics,* (August 1983), pp. 119-49 to recent papers like P.J. Wilkie "Corporate Average Effective Tax Rates and Inferences about Relative Tax Preferences," *Journal of American Taxation Association,* (Fall 1988), pp. 75-88.

13. Moreover, since the Alternate Minimum Tax (AMT) gives tax authorities a claim which is similar to a call option on the pre-tax income of the firm, the AMT also makes the tax schedule more convex.

14. This situation is one aspect of the agency problem which refers to the conflicts of interest which occur in virtually all cooperative activities among self-interested individuals. The agency problem was introduced by Michael C. Jensen and William

H. Meckling in "Theory of the Firm: Managerial Behavior, Agency Costs and Ownership *Structure," Journal of Financial Economics,* 3(1976), pp. 305-60.

15. While the optimal investment policy is to accept all positive NPV projects and reject all negative NPV projects, the *underinvestment problem* (introduced by S.C. Myers in "The Determinants of Corporate Borrowing," *Journal of Financial Economics,* 5 (November 1977), pp. 147-75) is proposed as an instance in which a firm will turn down a positive NPV project. If the firm has a large amount of debt in its capital structure and if the value of the firm's assets is low, shareholders may opt not to undertake a positive net present value project, because the gains accrue to the bondholders.

16. The problem referred to as *asset substitution* is a case in point. A firm can increase the wealth of its shareholders at the expense of its bondholders by (1) issuing debt with the promise of investing in low-risk projects and (2) then investing the proceeds in high-risk projects.

THE TOOLS FOR MANAGING FINANCIAL RISK: A BUILDING BLOCK APPROACH[17]

If it turns out that a firm is subject to significant financial price risk, management may choose to hedge that risk.[18] One way of doing so is by using an "on-balance-sheet" transaction. For example, a company could manage a foreign exchange exposure resulting from overseas competition by borrowing in the competitor's currency or by moving production abroad. But such on-balance sheet methods can be costly and, as firms like Caterpillar have discovered, inflexible.[19]

Alternatively, financial risks can be managed with the use of off-balance-sheet instruments. The four fundamental off-balance-sheet instruments are forwards, futures, swaps, and options.

When we first began to attempt to understand these financial instruments, we were confronted by what seemed an insurmountable barrier to entry. The participants in the various markets all seemed to possess a highly specialized expertise that was applicable in only one market to the exclusion of all others (and the associated trade publications served only to tighten the veil of mystery that "experts" have always used to deny entry to novices). Options were discussed as if they were completely unrelated to forwards or futures, which in turn seemed to have nothing to do with the latest innovation, swaps. Adding to the complexities of the individual markets was the welter of jargon that seems to have grown up around each, thus further obscuring any common ground that might exist. (Words such as "ticks" "collars," "strike prices," and "straddles" suddenly had acquired a remarkable currency.) In short, we seemed to find ourselves looking up into a Wall Street Tower of Babel, with each group of market specialists speaking in different languages.

But, after now having observed these instruments over the past several years, we have been struck by how little one has to dig before superficial differences give way to fundamental unity. And, in marked contrast to the specialized view of most Wall Street practitioners, we take a more "generalist" approach—one that treats forwards,

FIGURE 2 ■ PAYOFF PROFILE FOR FORWARD CONTRACT

futures, swaps, and options not as four unique instruments and markets, but rather as four interrelated instruments for dealing with a single problem: managing financial risk. In fact, we have come up with a little analogy that captures the spirit of our conclusion, one which goes as follows: The four basic off-balance-sheet instruments—forwards, futures, swaps, and options—are much like those plastic building blocks children snap together. You can either build the instruments from one another, or you can combine the instruments into larger creations that appear (but appearances deceive) altogether "new."

Forward Contracts

Of the four instruments, the forward contract is the oldest and, perhaps for this reason, the most straightforward. A forward contract obligates its owner to buy a specified asset on a specified date at a price (known as the "exercise price") specified at the origination of the contract. If, at maturity, the actual price is higher than the exercise price, the contract owner makes a profit equal to the difference; if the price is lower, he suffers a loss.

In Figure 2, the payoff from buying a forward contract is illustrated with a hypothetical risk profile. If the actual price at contract maturity is higher than the expected price, the inherent risk results in a decline in the value of the firm; but this decline is offset by the profit on the forward contract. Hence, for the risk profile illustrated, the forward contract provides an effective hedge. (If the risk profile were positively instead of negatively sloped, the risk would be managed by selling instead of buying a forward contract.)

17. This section of the article is adapted from Charles W. Smithson, "A LEGO Approach to Financial Engineering: An Introduction to Forwards, Futures, Swaps, and Options," *Midland Corporate Finance Journal* 4 (Winter 1987).

18. In this paper we do not address the question of why public corporations hedge. For a discussion of the corporate decision whether or not to hedge financial price exposures, see Alan Shapiro and Sheridan Titman, "An Integrated Approach to Corporate Risk Management," *Midland Corporate Finance Journal* 3 (Summer 1985). For other useful theoretical discussions of the corporate hedging decision, see David Mayers and Clifford Smith, "On the Corporate Demand for Insurance," *Journal of Business* 55 (April 1982) (a less technical version of which was published as "The Corporate Insurance Decision," *Chase*

Financial Quarterly (Vol. 1 No. 3) Spring 1982); René Stulz, "Optimal Hedging Policies," *Journal of Financial and Quantitative Analysis* 19 (June 1984); Clifford Smith and René Stulz, "The Determinants of Firms' Hedging Policies," *Journal of Financial* and *Quantitative Analysis* 20 (December 1985).

For some empirical tests of the above theoretical work, see David Mayers and Clifford Smith, "On the Corporate Demand for Insurance: Some Empirical Evidence," working paper, 1988; and Deana Nance, Clifford Smith, and Charles Smithson, "The Determinants of Off-Balance-Sheet Hedging: An Empirical Analysis," working paper, 1988.

19. See Caterpillar's Triple Whammy," Fortune, October 27, 1986.

This daily settlement feature combined with the margin requirement allows futures contracts to eliminate the credit risk inherent in forwards.

Besides its payoff profile, a forward contract has two other features that should be noted. First, the default (or credit) risk of the contract is two-sided. The contract owner either receives or makes a payment, depending on the price movement of the underlying asset. Second, the value of the forward contract is conveyed only at the contract's maturity; no payment is made either at origination or during the term of the contract.

Futures Contracts

The basic form of the futures contract is identical to that of the forward contract; a futures contract also obligates its owner to purchase a specified asset at a specified exercise price on the contract maturity date. Thus, the payoff profile for the purchaser of a forward contract as presented in Figure 2 could also serve to illustrate the payoff to the holder of a futures contract.

But, unlike the case of forwards, credit or default risk can be virtually eliminated in a futures market. Futures markets use two devices to manage default risk. First, instead of conveying the value of a contract through a single payment at maturity, any change in the value of a futures contract is conveyed at the end of the day in which it is realized. Look again at Figure 2. Suppose that, on the day after origination, the financial price rises and, consequently, the financial instrument has a positive value. In the case of a forward contract, this value change would not be received until contract maturity. With a futures contract, this change in value is received at the end of the day. In the language of the futures markets, the futures contract is "marked-to-market" and "cash settled" daily.

Because the performance period of a futures contract is reduced by marking to market, the risk of default declines accordingly. Indeed, because the value of the futures contract is paid or received at the end of each day, Fischer Black likened a futures contract to "a series of forward contracts [in which] each day, yesterday's contract is settled and today's contract is written."[20] That is, a futures contract is like a sequence of forwards in which

the "forward" contract written on day 0 is settled on day 1 and is replaced, in effect, with a new "forward" contract reflecting the new day 1 expectations. This new contract is then itself settled on day 2 and replaced, and so on until the day the contract ends.

The second feature of futures contracts which reduces default risk is the requirement that all market participants—sellers and buyers alike—post a performance bond called the "margin."[21] If my futures contract increases in value during the trading day, this gain is added to my margin account at the day's end. Conversely, if my contract has lost value, this loss is deducted from my margin account. And, if my margin account balance falls below some agreed-upon minimum, I am required to post additional bond; that is, my margin account must be replenished or my position will be closed out.[22] Because the position will be closed before the margin account is depleted, performance risk is eliminated.[23]

Note that the exchange itself has not been proposed as a device to reduce default risk. Daily settlement and the requirement of a bond reduce default risk, but the existence of an exchange (or clearinghouse) merely serves to transform risk. More specifically, the exchange deals with the two-sided risk inherent in forwards and futures by serving as the counterparty to all transactions. If I wish to buy or sell a futures contract, I buy from or sell to the exchange. Hence, I need only evaluate the credit risk of the exchange, not of some specific counterparty.

The primary economic function of the exchange is to reduce the costs of transacting in futures contracts. The anonymous trades made possible by the exchange, together with the homogeneous nature of the futures contracts—standardized assets, exercise dates (four per year), and contract sizes—enables the futures markets to become relatively liquid. However, as was made clear by recent experience of the London Metal Exchange, the existence of the exchange does not in and of itself eliminate the possibility of default.[24]

In sum, a futures contract is much like a portfolio of forward contracts. At the close of business of each day,

---

20. See Fischer Black, "The Pricing to Commodity Contracts," *Journal of Financial Economics* 3 (1976), 167-179.

21. Keep in mind that if you buy a futures contract, you are taking a long position in the underlying asset. Conversely, selling a futures contract is equivalent to taking a short position.

22. When the contract is originated on the U.S. exchanges, an "initial margin" is required. Subsequently, the margin account balance must remain above the "maintenance margin." If the margin account balance falls below the maintenance level, the balance must be restored to the initial level.

23. Note that this discussion has ignored daily limits. If there are daily limits on the movement of futures prices, large changes in expectations about the underlying asset ran effectively close the market. (The market opens, immediately moves the limit, and then is effectively closed until the next day.) Hence, there could exist an instance in which the broker desires to close outs customer's position but is not able to immediately because the market is experiencing limit moves. In such a case, the statement that performance risk is "eliminated" is too strong.

24. In November of 1985, the "tin cartel" defaulted on contracts for tin delivery on the London Metal Exchange, thereby making the exchange liable for the loss. A description of this situation is contained in "Tin Crisis in London Roils Metal Exchange," The *Wall Street Journal,* November 13, 1985.

From the point of view of the market, the exchange does not reduce default risk. The expected default rate is not affected by the existence of the exchange. However, the existence of the exchange can alter the default risk faced by an individual market participant. If I buy a futures contract for a specific individual, the default risk I face is determined by the default rate of that specific counterparty. If I instead buy the same futures contract through an exchange, my default risk depends on the default rate of not just my counterparty, but on the default rate of be entire market. Moreover, to the extent that the exchange is capitalized by equity from its members, the default risk I perceive is further reduced because I have a claim not against some specific counterparty, but rather against the exchange. Therefore, when I trade through the exchange, I am in a sense purchasing an insurance policy from the exchange.

> **A swap contract is in essence nothing more complicated than a series of forward contracts strung together.**

FIGURE 3

Panel A: An Interest Rate Swap

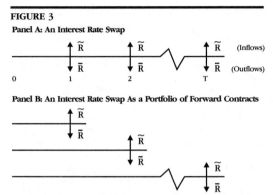

Panel B: An Interest Rate Swap As a Portfolio of Forward Contracts

in effect, the existing forward-like contract is settled and a new one is written.[25] This daily settlement feature combined with the margin requirement allows futures contracts to eliminate the credit risk inherent in forwards.

Swap Contracts[26]

A swap contract is in essence nothing more complicated than a series of forward contracts strung together. As implied by its name, a swap contract obligates two parties to exchange, or "swap," some specified cash flows at specified intervals. The most common form is the interest rate swap, in which the cash flows are determined by two different interest rates.

Panel A of Figure 3 illustrates an interest rate swap from the perspective of a party who is paying out a series of cash flows determined by a fixed interest rate ($\bar{R}$) in return for a series of cash flows determined by a floating interest rate ($\tilde{R}$).[27]

Panel B of Figure 3 serves to illustrate that this swap contract can be decomposed into a portfolio of forward contracts. At each settlement date, the party to this swap contract has an implicit forward contract on interest rates: the party illustrated is obligated to sell a fixed-rate cash flow for an amount specified at the origination of the contract. In this sense, a swap contract is also like a portfolio of forward contracts.

In terms of our earlier discussion, this means that the solid line in Figure 2 could also represent the payoff from a swap contract. Specifically, the solid line in Figure 3 would be consistent with a swap contract in which the party illustrated receives cash flows determined by one price (say, the U.S. Treasury bond rate) and makes payments determined by another price (say, LIBOR). Thus, in terms of their ability to manage risk, forwards, futures, and swaps all function in the same way.

But identical payoff *patterns* notwithstanding, the instruments all differ with respect to default risk. As we saw, the performance period of a forward is equal to its maturity; and because no performance bond is required, a forward contract is a pure credit instrument. Futures both reduce the performance period (to one day) and require a bond, thereby eliminating credit risk. Swap contracts use only one of these mechanisms to reduce credit risk; they reduce the performance period.[28] This point becomes evident in Figure 3. Although the maturity of the contract is T periods, the performance period is generally not T periods long but is instead a single period. Thus, given a swap and a forward contract of roughly the same maturity, the swap is likely to impose far less credit risk on the counterparties to the contract than the forward.

At each settlement date throughout a swap contract, the changes in value are transferred between the counterparties. To illustrate this in terms of Figure 3, suppose that interest rates rise on the day alter origination. The value of the swap contract illustrated has risen. This value change will be conveyed to the contract owner not at maturity (as would be the case with a forward contract) nor at the end of that day (as would be the case with a futures contract). Instead, at the first settlement date, part of the value change is conveyed in the form of the "difference check" paid by one party to the other. To repeat, then, the performance period is less than that of a forward, but not as short as that of a futures contract.[29] (Keep in mind that we are comparing instruments with the same maturities.)

25. A futures contract is like a portfolio of forward contracts; however, a futures contract and a portfolio of forward contracts become identical only if interest rates are "deterministic" -that is, known with certainty in advance. See Robert A. Jarrow and George S. Oldfield, "Forward Contracts and Futures Contracts, *Journal of Financial Economics* 9 (1981), 373-382; and John A. Cox, Jonathan E. Ingersoll, and Stephen A. Ross, The Relation between Forward Prices and Futures Prices, *Journal of Financial Economics* 9 (1981), 321-346.

26. This section is based on Clifford W. Smith, Charles W. Smithson, and Lee M. Wakeman, 'The Evolving Market for Swaps," *Midland Corporate Finance Journal* Winter (1986), 20-32.

27. Specifically, the interest rate swap cash flows are determined as follows: The two parties agree to some notional principal, P. (The principal is notional in the sense that it is only used to determine the magnitude of cash flows; it is not paid or received by either party.) At each settlement date, 1, 2,....T the party illustrated makes a payment R = rP, where r is the T-period fixed rate which existed at origination. At each settlement, the party illustrated receives R = rP, where r is the floating rate for that period (e.g., at settlement date 2, the interest rate used is the one-period rate in effect at period 1).

28. There are instances in which a bond has been posted in the form of collateral. As should be evident, in this case the swap becomes very like a futures contract.

29. Unlike futures, for which all of any change in contract value is paid/ received at the daily settlements, swap contracts convey only part of the total value change at the periodic settlements.

**Black and Scholes took what might be described as a "building block"
approach to the valuation of options...They demonstrated that a call option could
be replicated by a continuously adjusting portfolio of two securities:
forward contracts and riskless securities.**

FIGURE 4 ■ PAYOFF PROFILES OF PUTS AND CALLS

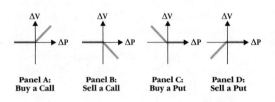

| Panel A: | Panel B: | Panel C: | Panel D: |
| Buy a Call | Sell a Call | Buy a Put | Sell a Put |

Let us reinforce the two major points made thus far. First, a swap contract, like a futures contract, is like a portfolio of forward contracts. Therefore, the payoff profiles for each of these three instruments are identical. Second, the primary difference among forwards, futures, and swaps is the amount of default risk they impose on counterparties to the contract. Forwards and futures represent the extremes, and swaps are the intermediate case.

Option Contracts

As we have seen, the owner of a forward, futures, or swap contract has an *obligation* to perform. In contrast, an option gives its owner a *right,* not an obligation. An option giving its owner the right to buy an asset at a predetermined price—a call option—is provided in Panel A of Figure 4. The owner of the contract has the right to purchase the asset at a specified future date at a price agreed-upon today. Thus, if the price rises, the value of the option also goes up. But because the option contract owner is not obligated to purchase the asset if the price moves against him, the value of the option remains unchanged (at zero) if the price declines.[30]

The payoff profile for the party who sold the call option (also known as the call "writer") is shown in Panel B. In contrast to the buyer of the option, the seller of the call option has the *obligation* to perform. For example, if the owner of the option elects to exercise his option to buy the asset, the seller of the option is obligated to sell the asset.

Besides the option to buy an asset, there is also the option to sell an asset at a specified price, known as a put option. The payoff to the buyer of a put is illustrated in Panel C of Figure 4, and the payoff to the seller of the put is shown in Panel D.

Pricing Options: Up to this point, we have considered only the payoffs to the option contracts. We have side-stepped the thorniest issue-the valuation of option contracts.

The breakthrough in option pricing theory came with the work of Fischer Black and Myron Scholes in 1973.[31] Conveniently for our purposes, Black and Scholes took what might be described as a "building block" approach to the valuation of options. Look again at the call option illustrated in Figure 4. For increases in the financial price, the payoff profile for the option is that of a forward contract. For decreases in the price, the value of the option is constant—like that of a "riskless" security such as a Treasury bill.

The work of Black and Scholes demonstrated that a call option could be replicated by a continuously adjusting ("dynamic") portfolio of two securities: (1) forward contracts on the underlying asset and (2) riskless securities. As the financial price rises, the "call option equivalent" portfolio contains an increasing proportion of forward contracts on the asset. Conversely, the replicating portfolio contains a decreasing proportion of forwards as the price of the asset falls.

Because this replicating portfolio is effectively a synthetic call option, arbitrage activity should ensure that its value closely approximates the market price of exchange-traded call options. In this sense, the value of a call option, and thus the premium that would be charged its buyer, is determined by the value of its option equivalent portfolio.

Panel A of Figure 5 illustrates the payoff profile for a call option which includes the premium. This figure (and all of the option figures thus far) illustrates an "at-the-money" option—that is, an option for which the exercise price is the prevailing expected price. As Panels A and B of Figure 5 illustrate, an at-the-money option is paid for by sacrificing a significant amount of the firm's potential gains. However, the price of a call option falls as the exercise price increases relative to the prevailing price of the asset. This means that if an option buyer is willing to accept larger potential losses in return for paying a lower option premium, he would then consider using an "out-of-the-money" option.

An out-of-the-money call option is illustrated in Panel C of Figure 5. As shown in Panel D, the out-of-the-money option provides less downside protection, but the option premium is significantly less. The lesson to be

---

30. For continuity, we continue to use the ΔV, ΔP convention in figures. To compare these figures with those found in most texts, treat ΔV as deviations from zero ($\Delta V = V - 0$) and remember that P measures deviations from expected price ($\Delta P = P - P_e$).

31. See Fischer Black and Myron Scholes, "The Pricing of Options and Corporate Liabilities," *Journal of Political Economy* 1973. For a less technical discussion of the model, see "The Black-Scholes Option Pricing Model for Alternative Underlying Instruments," *Financial Analysts Journal,* November-December, 1984, 23-30.

FIGURE 5

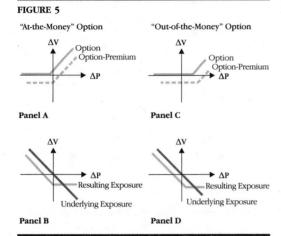

"At-the-Money" Option

Panel A

Panel B

"Out-of-the-Money" Option

Panel C

Panel D

FIGURE 6

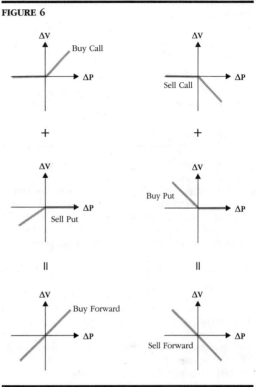

learned here is that the option buyer can alter his payoff profile simply by changing the exercise price.

For our purposes, however, the most important feature of options is that they are not as different from other financial instruments as they might first seem. Options do have a payoff profile that differs significantly from that of forward contracts (or futures or swaps). But, option payoff profiles can be duplicated by a combination of forwards and risk-free securities. Thus, we find that options have more in common with the other instruments than was first apparent. Futures and swaps, as we saw earlier, are in essence nothing more than portfolios of forward contracts; and options, as we have just seen, are very much akin to portfolios of forward contracts and risk-free securities.

This point is reinforced if we consider ways that options can be combined. Consider a portfolio constructed by buying a call and selling a put with the same exercise price. As the left side of Figure 6 illustrates, the resulting portfolio (long a call, short a put) has a payoff profile equivalent to that of buying a forward contract on the asset. Similarly, the right side of Figure 6 illustrates that a portfolio made up of selling a call and buying a put (short a call, long a put) is equivalent to selling a forward contract.

The relationship illustrated in Figure 6 is known more formally as "put-call parity." The special import of this relationship, at least in this context, is the "building block construction" it makes possible: two options can be "snapped together" to yield the payoff profile for a forward contract, which is identical to the payoff profile for futures and swaps.

At the beginning of this section, then, it seemed that options would be very different from forwards, futures, and swaps—and in some ways they are. But we discovered two building block relations between options and the other three instruments: (1) options can be replicated by "snapping together" a forward, futures, or swap contract together with a position in risk-free securities; and (2) calls and puts can be combined to become forwards.

The Financial Building Blocks

Forwards, futures, swaps, and options—they all look so different from one another. And if you read the trade publications or talk to the specialists that transact in the four markets, the apparent differences among the instruments are likely to seem even more pronounced.

But it turns out that forwards, futures, swaps, and options are not each unique constructions, but rather more like those plastic building blocks that children combine to make complex structures. To understand the off-balance-

FIGURE 7

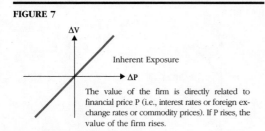

Inherent Exposure

The value of the firm is directly related to financial price P (i.e., interest rates or foreign exchange rates or commodity prices). If P rises, the value of the firm rises.

sheet instruments, you don't need a lot of market-specific knowledge. All you need to know is how the instruments can be linked to one another. As we have seen, (1) futures can be built by "snapping together" a package of forwards; (2) swaps can also be built by putting together a package of forwards; (3) synthetic options can be constructed by combining a forward with a riskless security; and (4) options can be combined to produce forward contracts—or, conversely, forwards can be pulled apart to replicate a package of options.

Having shown you all the building blocks and how they fit together in simple constructions, we now want to demonstrate how they can be used to create more complicated, customized financial instruments that in turn can be used to manage financial risks.

ASSEMBLING THE BUILDING BLOCKS

Using The Building Blocks to Manage an Exposure

Consider a company whose market value is directly related to unexpected changes in some financial price, P. The risk profile of this company is illustrated in Figure 7. How could we use the financial building blocks to modify this inherent exposure?

The simplest solution is to use a forward, a futures, or a swap to neutralize this exposure. This is shown in Panel A of Figure 8.

But, the use of a forward, a futures, or a swap eliminates possible losses by giving up the possibility of profiting from favorable outcomes. The company might want to minimize the effect of unfavorable outcomes while still allowing the possibility of gaining from favorable ones. This can be accomplished using options. The payoff profile of an at-the-money option (including the premium paid to buy the option) is shown on the left side of Panel B. Snapping this building block onto the inherent exposure profile gives the resulting exposure illustrated on the right side of panel B.

FIGURE 8

Use a forward or futures or swap... to neutralize the risk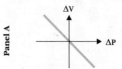

Resulting Exposure

Or, use an at-the-money option... to minimize adverse outcomes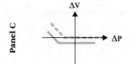

Buy Put

Or, use an out-of-the-money option... to get lower cost insurance

Or, buy and sell options... 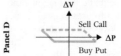 to eliminate out-of-pocket costs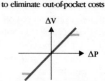

Sell Call

Buy Put

Or, use a forward/futures/swap with options... to provide customized solutions

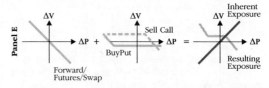

Forward/Futures/Swap   BuyPut   Sell Call   Inherent Exposure   Resulting Exposure

A common complaint about options—especially at-the-money options—is that they are "too expensive." To reduce the option premium, you can think about using an out-of-the-money option. As Panel C of Figure 8 illustrates, the firm has thereby given up some protection from adverse outcomes in return for paying a lower premium.

But, with an out-of-the-money option, some premium expense remains. Panel D illustrates how the out-of-pocket expense can be *eliminated*. The firm can sell a call option with an exercise price chosen so as to generate premium income equal to the premium due on the put option it wishes to purchase. In building block parlance, we snap the "buy-a-put" option onto the inherent risk profile to reduce downside outcomes; and we snap on the "sell-a-call" option to fund this insurance by giving up some of the favorable outcomes.

Panel E reminds us that forwards, futures, and swaps can be used in combination with options. Suppose the treasurer of the company we have been considering comes to you with the following request:

I think that this financial price, P, is going to fall dramatically. And, while I know enough about financial markets to know that P could actually rise a little, I am sure it will not rise by much. I want some kind of financial solution that will let me benefit when my predictions come to pass. But I don't want to pay any out-of-pocket premiums. Instead, I want this financial engineering product to pay me a premium.

If you look at the firm's inherent risk profile in Figure 7, this seems like a big request. The firm's inherent position is such that it would lose rather than gain from big decreases in P.

The resulting exposure profile shown on the right side of Panel E is the one the firm wants: it benefits from large decreases in P, is protected against small increases in P (though not against large increases) and receives a premium for the instrument.

How was this new profile achieved? As illustrated on the left side of Panel E, we first snapped a forward/futures/swap position onto the original risk profile to neutralize the firm's inherent exposure. We then sold a call option and bought a put option with exercise prices set such that the income from selling the call exceeded the premium required to buy the put.

No high level math was required. Indeed, we did this bit of financial engineering simply by looking through the box of financial building blocks until we found those that snapped together to give us the profile we wanted.

Using the Building Blocks to Redesign Financial Instruments

Now that you understand how forwards, futures, swaps, and options are all fundamentally related, it is a relatively short step to thinking about how the instruments can be combined with each other to give one financial instrument the characteristics of another. Rather than talk about this in the abstract, let's look at some examples of how this has been done in the marketplace.

FIGURE 9

Pay Fixed, Receive Floating for Periods 1 through T

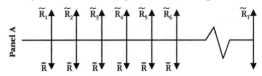

PLUS Pay Floating, Receive Fixed for Periods 1 through 4

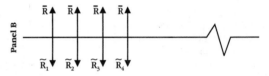

EQUALS A Four-Period Forward Contract on a Pay Fixed, Receive Floating Swap

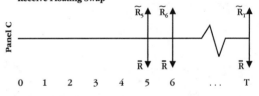

Combining Forwards with Swaps: Suppose a firm's value is currently unaffected by interest rate movements. But, at a known date in the future, it expects to become exposed to interest rates: if rates rise, the value of the firm will decrease.[32] To manage this exposure, the firm could use a forward, futures, or swap commencing at that future date. Such a product is known as *a forward* or *delayed start* swap. The payoff from a forward swap is illustrated in Panel C of Figure 9, where the party illustrated pays a fixed rate and receives floating starting in period 5.

Although this instrument is in effect a forward contract on a swap, it also, not surprisingly, can be constructed as a package of swaps. As Figure 9 illustrates, a forward swap is equivalent to a package of two swaps:

Swap 1—From period 1 to period T, the party pays fixed and receives floating.

Swap 2—From period 1 to period 4, the party pays floating and receives fixed.

---

32. For example, the firm may know that, in one year, it will require funds which will be borrowed at a floating rate, thereby giving the firm the inverse exposure to interest rates. Or, the firm may be adding a new product line, the demand for which is extremely sensitive to interest rate movements—as rates rise, the demand for the product decreases and cash flows to the firm decrease.

33. This discussion is adapted from Warren Edwardes and Edmond Levy, "Break Forwards: A Synthetic Option Hedging Instrument," *Midland Corporate Finance Journal* 5 (Summer 1987), 59-67.

**In this break forward construction, the premium is effectively
being paid by the owner of the break forward contract in the form of the
above market contract exchange rate.**

FIGURE 10

Panel A: Standard Forward

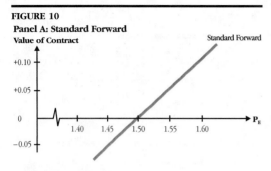

Panel B: Break Forward

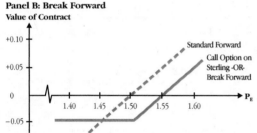

Panel C: Range Forward

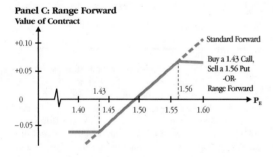

Forwards with Option-like Characteristics: The addition of option-like characteristics to forward contracts first appeared in the foreign exchange markets. To see how this was done, let's trace the evolution of these contracts.

Begin with a standard forward contract on foreign exchange. Panel A of Figure 10 illustrates a conventional forward contract on sterling with the forward sterling exchange rate (the "contract rate") set at $1.50 per pound sterling. If, at maturity, the spot price of sterling exceeds $1.50, the owner of this contract makes a profit (equal to the spot rate minus $1.50). Conversely, if at maturity the spot price of sterling is less than $1.50, the owner of this contract suffers a loss. The owner of the forward contract, however, might instead want a contract that allows him to profit if the price of sterling rises, but limits his losses if the price of sterling falls.[33] Such a contract would be a call option on sterling. Illustrated in Panel B of Figure 10 is a call option on sterling with an exercise price of $1.50. In this illustration we have assumed an option premium of 5 cents (per pound sterling).

The payoff profile illustrated in Panel B of Figure 10 could also be achieved by altering the terms of the standard forward contract as follows:

1. Change the contract price so that the exercise price of the forward contract is no longer $1.50 but is instead $1.55. The owner of the forward contract agrees to purchase sterling at contract maturity at a price of $1.55 per unit; and

2. Permit the owner of the contract to break (i.e., "unwind") the agreement at a sterling price of $1.50.

This altered forward contract is referred to as a *break forward* contract.[34] In this break forward construction, the premium is effectively being paid by the owner of the break forward contract in the form of the above market contract exchange rate.

From our discussion of options, we also know that a call can be paid for with the proceeds from selling a put. The payoff profile for such a situation is illustrated in Panel C of Figure 10. In this illustration, we have assumed that the proceeds of a put option on sterling with an exercise price of $1.56 would carry the same premium as a call option on sterling with an exercise price of $1.43.[35]

A payoff profile identical to this option payoff profile could also be generated, however, simply by changing the terms of a standard forward contract to the following:
■ at maturity, the buyer of the forward contract agrees to purchase sterling at a price of $1.50 per pound sterling;
■ the buyer of the forward contract has the right to break the contract at a price of $1.43 per pound sterling; and
■ the seller of the forward contract has the right to break the contract at a price of $1.56 per pound sterling.
Such a forward contract is referred to as a *range forward*.[36]

34. According to Sam Srinivasulu in "Second-Generation Forwards: A Comparative Analysis," *Business International Money Report*, September 21, 1987, break forward is the name given to this construction by Midland Bank. It goes under other names: Boston Option (Bank of Boston), BOX-Forward with Optional Exit (Hambros Bank), and Cancelable Forward (Goldman Sachs)

35. These numbers are only for purposes of illustration. To determine the exercise prices at which the values of the puts and calls are equal, one would have to use an option pricing model.

36. As Srinivasulu, cited in note 34, pointed out, this construction also appears under a number of names: range forward (Salomon Brothers), collar (Midland Montagu), flexible forward (Manufacturers Hanover), cylinder option (Citicorp), option fence (Bank of America) and mini-max (Goldman Sachs).

FIGURE 11 ■ PAYOFF PROFILE FOR FLOOR-CEILING SWAPS

Panel A:
Floating Floor-Ceiling Swap

Cash Flows from Swap

Panel B:
Fixed Floor-Ceiling Swap

Cash Flows from Swap

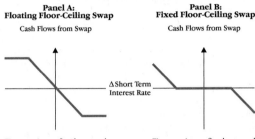

Δ Short Term
Interest Rate

Firm receives a fixed rate and pays a floating rate between the limits set by the floor and ceiling rates

Firm receives a fixed rate and pays a floating rate outside the limits set by the floor and ceiling rates

Swaps with Option-like Characteristics: Given that swaps can be viewed as packages of forward contracts, it should not be surprising that swaps can also be constructed to have option-like characteristics like those illustrated for forwards. For example, suppose that a firm with a floating-rate liability wanted to limit its outflows should interest rates rise substantially; at the same time, it was willing to give up some potential gains should there instead be a dramatic decline in short-term rates. To achieve this end, the firm could modify the interest rate swap contract as follows:

As long as the interest rate neither rises by more than 200 basis points nor falls more than 100 basis points, the firm pays a floating rate and receives a fixed rate. But, if the interest is more than 200 basis points above or 100 basis points below the current rate, the firm receives and pays a fixed rate.

The resulting payoff profile for this floating floor-ceiling swap is illustrated in Panel A of Figure 11.

Conversely, the interest rate swap contract could have been modified as follows:

As long as the interest rate is within 200 basis points of the current rate, the firm neither makes nor receives a payment; but if the interest rate rises or falls by more than 200 basis points, the firm pays a floating rate and receives a fixed rate.

The payoff profile for the resulting fixed floor-ceiling swap is illustrated in Panel B of Figure 11.

Redesigned Options: To "redesign" an option, what is normally done is to put two or more options together to change the payoff profile. Examples abound

in the world of the option trader. Some of the more colorfully-named combinations are *straddles, strangles,* and *butterflies.*[37]

To see how and why these kinds of creations evolve, let's look at a hypothetical situation. Suppose a firm was confronted with the inherent exposure illustrated in Panel A of Figure 12. Suppose further that the firm wanted to establish a floor on losses caused by changes in a financial price.

As you already know, this could be done by purchasing an out-of-the-money call option on the financial price. A potential problem with this solution, as we have seen, is the premium the firm has to pay. Is there a way the premium can be eliminated?

We have already seen that buying an out-of-the-money call can be financed by selling an out-of-the-money put. However, suppose that this out-of-the-money call is financed by selling a put with precisely the same exercise price—in which case, the put would be in-the-money. As illustrated in Panel B of Figure 12, the proceeds from selling the in-the-money put would exceed the cost of the out-of-the-money call. Therefore, to finance one out-of-the-money call, one would need sell only a fraction of one in-the-money put.

In Panel B, we have assumed that the put value is twice the call value; so, to finance one call, you need sell only 1/2 put. Panel C simply combines the payoff profiles for selling 1/2 put and buying one call with an exercise price of X. Finally, Panel D of Figure 12 combines the option combination in Panel C with the inherent risk profile in Panel A.

Note what has happened. The firm has obtained the floor it wanted, but there is no up-front premium. At the price at which the option is exercised, the value of the firm with the floor is the same as it would have been without the floor. The floor is paid for not with a fixed premium, but with a share of the firm's gains above the floor. If the financial price rises by X, the value of the firm falls to the floor and no premium is paid. If, however, the financial price rises by less, say Y, the value of the firm is higher and the firm pays a positive premium for the floor. And, if the financial price falls, say, by Z, the price it pays for the floor rises.

What we have here is a situation where the provider of the floor is paid with a share of potential gains, thereby leading to the name of this option combination—a participation. This construction has been most widely used in the foreign exchange market where they are referred to as *participating forwards.*[38]

---

37. For a discussion of traditional option strategies like straddles, strangles, and butterflies, see for instance chapter 7 of Richard M. Bookstaber, *Option Pricing and Strategies in Investing* (Addison-Wesley, 1981).

38. For more on this construction, see Srinivasulu cited in notes 34 and 36.

> **Our position with respect to "financial engineering" is that there is little new under the sun. The "new" products typically involve nothing more than putting the building blocks together in a new way.**

FIGURE 12

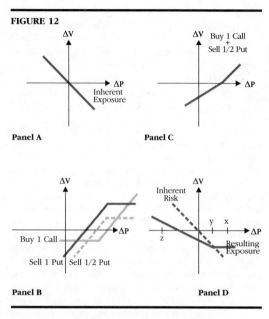

Panel A

Panel B

Panel C

Panel D

FIGURE 13 ■ USING A SWAP TO CREATE A REVERSE FLOATING RATE LOAN

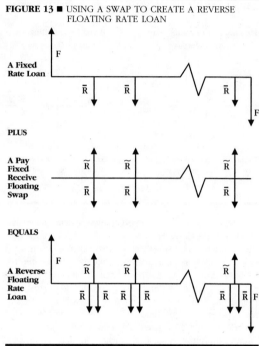

Options on Other Financial Instruments

Options on futures contracts on bonds have been actively traded on the Chicago Board of Trade since 1982. The valuation of an option on a futures is a relatively straightforward extension of the traditional option pricing models.[39] Despite the close relation between futures and forwards and futures and swaps, the options on forwards *(options on forward rate agreements)* and options on swaps *(swaptions)* are much more recent.

More complicated analytically is the valuation of an option on an option, also known as a *compound option*.[40] Despite their complexity and resistance to valuation formulae, some options on options have begun to be traded. These include options on foreign exchange options and, most notably, options on interest rate options (caps), referred to in the trade as *captions*.

Using the Building Blocks to Design "New" Products

It's rare that a day goes by in the financial markets without hearing of at least one "new" or "hybrid" product.

But, as you should have come to expect from us by now, our position with respect to "financial engineering" is that there is little new under the sun. The "new" products typically involve nothing more than putting the building blocks together in a new way.

Reverse Floaters: One example of a hybrid security is provided in Figure 13. If we combine the issuance of a conventional fixed rate loan and an interest rate swap where the issuing party pays fixed and receives floating, the result is a reverse floating-rate loan. The net coupon payments on the hybrid loan are equal to twice the fixed rate ($\bar{r}$) minus the floating rate ($\tilde{r}$) times the principal (P), or

$$\text{Net Coupon} = (2\bar{r} - \tilde{r})P = 2\bar{R} - \tilde{R}$$

If the floating rate ($\tilde{r}$) rises, the net coupon payment falls.

Bonds with Embedded Options: Another form of hybrid securities has evolved from bonds with warrants.

39. Options on futures were originally discussed by Fischer Black in "The Pricing of Commodity Options," *Journal of Financial Economics* 3 (January-March 1976). A concise discussion of the modifications required in the Black-Scholes formula is contained in James F. Meisner and John W. Labuszewski,

"Modifying the Black-Scholes Option Pricing Model for Alternative Underlying Instruments," *Financial Analysts Journal*, November/December 1984.
40. For a discussion of the problem of valuing compound options, see John C. Cox and Mark Rubinstein, *Options Markets* (Prentice Hall, 1985), 412-415.

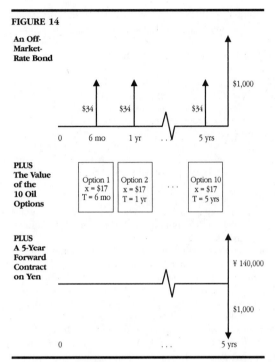

FIGURE 14

An Off-Market-Rate Bond

$1,000

$34 $34 $34

0   6 mo   1 yr . . . 5 yrs

PLUS The Value of the 10 Oil Options

| Option 1 x = $17 T = 6 mo | Option 2 x = $17 T = 1 yr | . . . | Option 10 x = $17 T = 5 yrs |

PLUS A 5-Year Forward Contract on Yen

¥ 140,000

$1,000

0   . . .   5 yrs

Bonds with warrants on the issuer's shares have become common. Bond issues have also recently appeared that feature warrants that can be exercised into foreign exchange and gold.

And, in 1986, Standard Oil issued a bond with an oil warrant. These notes stipulated that the principal payment at maturity would be a function of oil prices at maturity. As specified in the Prospectus, the holders of the 1990 notes will receive, in addition to a guaranteed minimum principal amount, "the excess...of the Crude Oil Price...over $25 multiplied by 170 barrels of Light Sweet Crude Oil." What this means is that the note has an embedded four-year option on 170 barrels of crude oil. If, at maturity, the value of Light Sweet Oklahoma Crude Oil exceeds $25, the holder of the note will receive (Oil

Price – $25) × 170 plus the guaranteed minimum principal amount. If the value of Light Sweet Oklahoma Crude is less than $25 at maturity, the option expires worthless.[41]

The building block process has also been extended to changes in the timing of the options embedded in the bond. For a traditional bond with an attached warrant, there is only one option exerciseable at one point in time. More recent bonds have involved packages of options which can be exercised at different points in time.

The first time we saw this extension was in Forest Oil Corporation's proposed *Natural Gas Interest Indexed Debentures*. As set forth in the issue's red herring prospectus of July 1988, Forest Oil proposed to pay a stipulated base rate plus four basis points for each $0.01 by which the average gas spot price exceeds $1.76 per MMBTU (million British Thermal Units). In effect, then, this proposed 12-year "hybrid" debenture is a package consisting of one standard bond plus 24 options on the price of natural gas with maturities ranging from 6 months to 12 years.[42]

And, if we want to get a little fancier, we can consider the possibility of an *Oil Interest-Indexed, Dual-Currency Bond*.[43] Assume that the maturity of this issue is 5 years, with the semi-annual coupon payments indexed to the price of crude oil and the final principal repayment indexed to the value of yen. More specifically, assume that, for each $1000 of principal, the bondholder receives the following:

(1) the greater of $34 or the value of two barrels of Sweet Light Crude Oil at each coupon date; and

(2) 140,000 yen at maturity.

How would we value such a complicated package? The answer, again, is by breaking it down into the building blocks. As shown in Figure 14, this oil-indexed, dual currency bond consists of three basic components: (1) a straight bond paying $34 semi-annually; (2) 10 call options on the price of oil with an exercise price of $17 per barrel ($34/2) maturing sequentially every six months over a five-year period; and (3) a five-year forward contract on yen with an exercise price of 140 yen/dollar. As it turns out, then, this complicated-looking bond is nothing more than a combination of a standard bond, a series of options, and a forward contract.

---

41. Note that this issue did have a cap on the crude oil price at $40. Hence, the bondholder actually holds two options positions: long a call option at $25 per barrel and short a call option at $40 per barrel.

42. As reported in the *Wall Street Journal* on September 21, 1988, Forest Oil withdrew its Natural Gas Indexed Bond in favor of a straight issue. However, in November of 1988, Magma Copper did issue senior subordinated notes on which the coupon payments were linked to the price of copper in much the same way as Forest's coupons would been linked to the price of natural gas.

43. Unlike the other structures discussed, this one has not yet been issued.

CONCLUDING REMARKS

The world is more volatile today than it was two decades ago. Today's corporate risk manager must deal with the potential impact on the firm of significant month-to-month (and sometimes day-to-day) changes in exchange rates, interest rates, and commodity prices. Volatility alone could put a well-run firm out of business, so financial price risk deserves careful attention. As this summary has demonstrated, there now exist techniques and tools for accomplishing this task.

This article makes three major points:

First, there are simple techniques that allow management (and outsiders as well) to identify and measure a firm's exposures. Besides managing "one-off" exposures (such as interest rate exposures from floating-rate borrowings or foreign exchange transaction and translation exposures), many firms are now recognizing their economic exposures. To measure such economic exposures, we have introduced the concept of the *risk profile*. Using this concept, we have proposed simple methods for quantifying the extent of an individual firm's exposures to interest rates, foreign exchange rates, and commodity prices. In the case of a financial firm's exposure to interest rate risk, the techniques of "gap" and "duration" analysis can be applied directly. For the more general case, we demonstrate how simple regression analysis (the same technique used in calculating a firm's "beta") can be used to measure a variety of exposures.

Second, the tools for managing financial risk are more simple than they appear. These financial instruments can be viewed as building blocks. The basic component is a forward contract. Both futures and swaps are like bundles of forward contracts; forwards, in fact, can be combined to yield futures and swaps. The primary differences between, these two instruments are the way they deal with default risk and the degree of customization available.

Even options, moreover, can be related to forward contracts. An option on a given asset can be created by combining a position in a forward contract on the same asset with a riskless security; in short, forwards and T-bills can be combined to produce options.[44] Finally, options can be combined to create forward positions; for example, buying a call and shorting a put produces the same position as buying a forward contract.

Third, once you understand the four basic building blocks, it is a straightforward step to designing a customized strategy for managing your firm's exposure. Once the exposure is identified, it can be managed in a number of ways:

■ by using one of the financial instruments—for example, by using an interest rate swap to hedge a building products firm's exposure to rising interest rates;
■ by using combinations of the financial instruments—for example, buying a call and selling a put to minimize the out-of-pocket costs of the hedge; or
■ by combining financial instruments with a debt instrument, to create a hybrid security—for example, issuing an oil-indexed bond to hedge a firm's exposure to oil prices.

Our final point in all of this is very simple. Managing financial price risk with "financial engineering" sounds like something you need a degree from Caltech or M.I.T. to do. Designing effective solutions with the financial building blocks is easy.

---

44. This is most often referred to as a synthetic option or as dynamic option replication.

* Based on an article by the same title by Michael Quint in "Talking Deals," *The New York Times*, February 16, 1989.

CUTTING RATE RISK ON BUYOUT DEBT
Reducing Shareholder-Debtholder Conflict in the RJR Nabisco Deal

When Kohlberg, Kravis, Roberts and Co. got ready to issue the senior bank debt for the RJR-Nabisco deal, they ran head-on into the shareholder-debtholder conflict. The use of risk management tools enabled them to reduce the conflict and increase their debt capacity.

The market was concerned about the interest rate risk caused by such a large amount of debt. If the debt was floating and if rates rose substantially, the probability of default would rise dramatically. Therefore, to reduce the shareholder-debtholder conflict, KKR was required to purchase interest rate insurance. (In fact, the Vice Chairman of Chase Manhattan Bank indicated that, before committing any money to finance a corporate takeover, Chase routinely insists that steps be taken to reduce the interest rate risk.)

Consequently, KKR agreed to keep interest rate protection (in the form of swaps or caps) on half of the outstanding balance of its bank debt. In this way, KKR was able to borrow $13 billion. Without the rate insurance, the amount the banks would have been willing to lend would almost certainly have been substantially less.*

RETHINKING RISK MANAGEMENT

by René M. Stulz,
*The Ohio State University**

T his article explores an apparent conflict between the theory and current practice of corporate risk management. Academic theory suggests that some companies facing large exposures to interest rates, exchange rates, or commodity prices can increase their market values by using derivative securities to reduce their exposures. The primary emphasis of the theory is on the role of derivatives in reducing the variability of corporate cash flows and, in so doing, reducing various costs associated with financial distress.

The actual corporate use of derivatives, however, does not seem to correspond closely to the theory. For one thing, large companies make far greater use of derivatives than small firms, even though small firms have more volatile cash flows, more restricted access to capital, and thus presumably more reason to buy protection against financial trouble. Perhaps more puzzling, however, is that many companies appear to be using risk management to pursue goals other than reducing variance.

Does this mean that the prevailing academic theory of risk management is wrong, and that "variance-minimization" is not a useful goal for companies using derivatives? Or, is the current corporate practice of risk management misguided and in urgent need of reform? In this paper, I answer "no" to both questions while at the same time suggesting there may be room for improvement in the theory as well as the practice of risk management.

The paper begins by reviewing some evidence that has accumulated about the current practice of corporate risk management. Part of this evidence takes the form of recent "anecdotes," or cases, involving large derivatives losses. Most of the evi-

dence, however, consists of corporate responses to surveys. What the stories suggest, and the surveys seem to confirm, is the popularity of a practice known as "selective" as opposed to "full-cover" hedging. That is, while few companies regularly use derivatives to take a "naked" speculative position on FX rates or commodity prices, most corporate derivatives users appear to allow their views of future interest rates, exchange rates, and commodity prices to influence their hedge ratios.

Such a practice seems inconsistent with modern risk management theory, or at least the theory that has been presented thus far. But there is a plausible defense of selective hedging—one that would justify the practice without violating the efficient markets tenet at the center of modern financial theory. In this paper, I attempt to explain more of the corporate behavior we observe by pushing the theory of risk management beyond the variance-minimization model that prevails in most academic circles. Some companies, I argue below, may have a comparative advantage in bearing certain financial risks (while other companies mistakenly think and act as if they do). I accordingly propose a somewhat different goal for corporate risk management—namely, the *elimination of costly lower-tail outcomes*—that is designed to reduce the expected costs of financial trouble while preserving a company's ability to exploit any comparative advantage in risk-bearing it may have. (In the jargon of finance specialists, the fundamental aim of corporate risk management can be viewed as the purchase of "well-out-of-the-money put options" that eliminate the downside while preserving as much of the upside as can be justified by the principle of comparative advantage.)

*I am grateful for extensive editorial assistance from Don Chew, and for comments by Steve Figlewski, Andrew Karolyi, Robert Whaley, and participants at a seminar at McKinsey, at the Annual Meeting of the International Association of Financial Engineers, and at the French Finance Association.

Such a modified theory of risk management implies that some companies should hedge all financial risks, other firms should worry about only certain kinds of risks, and still others should not worry about risks at all. But, as I also argue below, when making decisions whether or not to hedge, management should keep in mind that risk management can be used to change both a company's capital structure and its ownership structure. By reducing the probability of financial trouble, risk management has the potential both to increase debt capacity and to facilitate larger equity stakes for management.

This paper also argues that common measures of risk such as variance and Value at Risk (VaR) are not useful for most risk management applications by non-financial companies, nor are they consistent with the objective of risk management presented here. In place of both VaR and the variance of cash flows, I suggest a method for measuring corporate exposures that, besides having a foundation in modern finance theory, should be relatively easy to use.

I conclude with a discussion of the internal "management" of risk management. If corporate risk management is focused not on minimizing variance, but rather on eliminating downside risk while extending the corporate quest for comparative advantage into financial markets, then much more attention must be devoted to the evaluation and control of corporate risk-management activities. The closing section of the paper offers some suggestions for evaluating the performance of risk managers whose "view-taking" is an accepted part of the firm's risk management strategy.

RISK MANAGEMENT IN PRACTICE

In one of their series of papers on Metallgesellschaft, Chris Culp and Merton Miller make an observation that may seem startling to students of modern finance: "We need hardly remind readers that most value-maximizing firms do not hedge."[1] But is this true? And, if so, how would we know?

Culp and Miller refer to survey evidence—in particular, to a Wharton-Chase study that sent questionnaires to 1,999 companies inquiring about their risk management practices.[2] Of the 530 firms that responded to the survey, only about a third answered "yes" when asked if they ever used futures, forwards, options, or swaps. One clear finding that emerges from this survey is that large companies make greater use of derivatives than smaller firms. Whereas 65% of companies with a market value greater than $250 million reported using derivatives, only 13% of the firms with market values of $50 million or less claimed to use them.

What are the derivatives used to accomplish? The only uses reported by more than half of the corporate users are to hedge contractual commitments and to hedge anticipated transactions expected to take place within 12 months. About two thirds of the companies responded that they never use derivatives to reduce funding costs (or earn "treasury profits") by arbitraging the markets or by taking a view. Roughly the same proportion of firms also said they never use derivatives to hedge their balance sheets, their foreign dividends, or their economic or competitive exposures.

The Wharton-Chase study was updated in 1995, and its results were published in 1996 as the Wharton-CIBC Wood Gundy study. The results of the 1995 survey confirm those of its predecessor, but with one striking new finding: Over a third of all derivative users said they sometimes "actively take positions" that reflect their market views of interest rate and exchange rates.

This finding was anticipated in a survey of Fortune 500 companies conducted by Walter Dolde in 1992, and published in this journal in the following year.[3] Of the 244 companies that responded to Dolde's survey, 85% reported having used swaps, forwards, futures, or options. As in the Wharton surveys, larger companies reported greater use of derivatives than smaller firms. And, as Dolde notes, such a finding confirms the experience of risk management practitioners that the corporate use of derivatives requires a considerable upfront investment in personnel, training, and computer hardware and software—an investment that could discourage small firms.

---

1. Christopher Culp and Merton Miller, "Hedging in the Theory of Corporate Finance: A Reply to Our Critics," *Journal of Applied Corporate Finance* Vol. 8 No. 1 (Spring 1995), p. 122. For the central idea of this paper, I am indebted to Culp and Miller's discussion of Holbrook Working's "carrying-charge" theory of commodity hedging. It is essentially Working's notion—and Culp and Miller's elaboration of it—that I attempt in this paper to generalize into a broader theory of risk management based on comparative advantage in risk-bearing.

2. The Wharton School and The Chase Manhattan Bank, N.A., "Survey of Derivative Usage Among U.S. Non-Financial Firms" (February 1994).

3. Walter Dolde, "The Trajectory of Corporate Financial Risk Management," *Journal of Applied Corporate Finance,* Vol. 6 No. 4 (Fall 1993), 33-41.

But, as we observed earlier, there are also reasons why the demand for risk management products should actually be greater for small firms than for large—notably the greater probability of default caused by unhedged exposures and the greater concentration of equity ownership in smaller companies. And Dolde's survey provides an interesting piece of evidence in support of this argument. When companies were asked to estimate what percentages of their exposures they chose to hedge, many respondents said that it depended on whether they had a view of future market movements. *Almost 90% of the derivatives users in Dolde's survey said they sometimes took a view.* And, when the companies employed such views in their hedging decisions, the smaller companies reported hedging significantly greater percentages of their FX and interest rate exposures than the larger companies.

Put another way, the larger companies were more inclined to "self-insure" their FX or interest rate risks. For example, if they expected FX rates to move in a way that would increase firm value, they might hedge only 10% to 20% (or maybe none) of their currency exposure. But if they expected rates to move in a way that would reduce value, they might hedge 100% of the exposure.

Like the Wharton surveys, the Dolde survey also found that the focus of risk management was mostly on transaction exposures and near-term exposures. Nevertheless, Dolde also reported "a distinct evolutionary pattern" in which many firms "progress from targeting individual transactions to more systematic measures of ongoing competitive exposures."[4]

The bottom line from the surveys, then, is that corporations do not systematically hedge their exposures, the extent to which they hedge depends on their views of future price movements, the focus of hedging is primarily on near-term transactions, and the use of derivatives is greater for large firms than small firms. Many of the widely-reported derivative problems of recent years are fully consistent with this survey evidence, and closer inspection of such cases provides additional insight into common risk management practices. We briefly recount two cases in which companies lost large amounts of money as a result of risk management programs.

Metallgesellschaft

Although the case of Metallgesellschaft continues to be surrounded by controversy, there is general agreement about the facts of the case. By the end of 1993, MGRM, the U.S. oil marketing subsidiary of Metallgesellschaft, contracted to sell 154 million barrels of oil through fixed-price contracts ranging over a period of ten years. These fixed-price contracts created a huge exposure to oil price increases that MGRM decided to hedge. However, it did not do so in a straightforward way. Rather than hedging its future outflows with offsetting positions of matching maturities, MGRM chose to take "stacked" positions in short-term contracts, both futures and swaps, and then roll the entire "stack" forward as the contracts expired.

MGRM's choice of short-term contracts can be explained in part by the lack of longer-term hedging vehicles. For example, liquid markets for oil futures do not go out much beyond 12 months. But it also appears that MGRM took a far larger position in oil futures than would have been consistent with a variance-minimizing strategy. For example, one study estimated that the minimum-variance hedge position for MGRM would have required the forward purchase of only 86 million barrels of oil, or about 55% of the 154 million barrels in short-maturity contracts that MGRM actually entered into.[5]

Does this mean that MGRM really took a position that was long some 58 million barrels of oil? Not necessarily. As Culp and Miller demonstrate, had MGRM adhered to its professed strategy and been able to obtain funding for whatever futures losses it incurred over the entire 10-year period, its position would have been largely hedged.[6]

But even if MGRM's net exposure to oil prices was effectively hedged over the long haul, it is also clear that MGRM's traders had not designed their hedge with the aim of minimizing the variance of their net position in oil during the life of the contracts. The traders presumably took the position they did because they thought they could benefit from their specialized information about supply and demand—and, more specifically, from a persistent feature of oil futures known as "backwardation," or the long-run

---

4. Dolde, p. 39.

5. Mello, A., and J.E. Parsons, "Maturity Structure of a Hedge Matters: Lessons from the Metallgesellschaft Debacle," *Journal of Applied Corporate Finance*, Vol. 8 No. 1 (Spring 1995), 106-120.

6. More precisely, Culp and Miller's analysis shows that, ignoring any complications arising from basis risk and the daily mark-to-market requirement for futures, over the 10-year period each rolled-over futures contract would have eventually corresponded to an equivalent quantity of oil delivered to customers.

tendency of spot prices to be higher than futures prices. So, although MGRM was effectively hedged against changes in spot oil prices, it nevertheless had what amounted to a long position in "the basis." Most of this long position in the basis represented a bet that the convenience yields on crude oil—that is, the premiums of near-term futures over long-dated futures—would remain positive as they had over most of the past decade.

When spot prices fell dramatically in 1993, MGRM lost on its futures positions and gained on its cash positions—that is, on the present value of its delivery contracts. But because the futures positions were marked to market while the delivery contracts were not, MGRM's financial statements showed large losses. Compounding this problem of large "paper losses," the backwardation of oil prices also disappeared, thus adding real losses to the paper ones. And, in response to the reports of mounting losses, MG's management chose to liquidate the hedge. This action, as Culp and Miller point out, had the unfortunate consequence of "turning paper losses into realized losses" and "leaving MGRM exposed to rising prices on its remaining fixed-price contracts."[7]

Daimler-Benz

In 1995, Daimler-Benz reported first-half losses of DM1.56 billion, the largest in the company's 109-year history. In its public statements, management attributed the losses to exchange rate losses due to the weakening dollar. One subsidiary of Daimler-Benz, Daimler-Benz Aerospace, had an order book of DM20 billion, of which 80% was fixed in dollars. Because the dollar fell by 14% during this period, Daimler-Benz had to take a provision for losses of DM1.2 billion to cover future losses.

Why did Daimler-Benz fail to hedge its expected dollar receivables? The company said that it chose not to hedge because the forecasts it received were too disperse, ranging as they did from DM1.2 to DM1.7 per dollar. Analysts, however, attributed Daimler-Benz's decision to remain unhedged to its view that the dollar would stay above DM1.55.[8]

These two brief case studies reinforce the conclusion drawn from the survey evidence. In both of these cases, management's view of future price movements was an important determinant of how (or whether) risk was managed. Risk management did not mean minimizing risk by putting on a minimum-variance hedge. Rather, it meant choosing to bear certain risks based on a number of different considerations, including the belief that a particular position would allow the firm to earn abnormal returns.

Is such a practice consistent with the modern theory of risk management? To answer that question, we first need to review the theory.

THE PERSPECTIVE OF MODERN FINANCE

The two pillars of modern finance theory are the concepts of efficient markets and diversification. Stated as briefly as possible, market efficiency means that markets don't leave money on the table. Information that is freely accessible is incorporated in prices with sufficient speed and accuracy that one cannot profit by trading on it.

Despite the spread of the doctrine of efficient markets, the world remains full of corporate executives who are convinced of their own ability to predict future interest rates, exchange rates, and commodity prices. As evidence of the strength and breadth of this conviction, many companies during the late '80s and early '90s set up their corporate treasuries as "profit centers" in their own right—a practice that, if the survey evidence can be trusted, has been largely abandoned in recent years by most industrial firms. And the practice has been abandoned with good reason: Behind most large derivative losses—in cases ranging from Orange County and Baring Brothers to Procter & Gamble and BancOne—there appear to have been more or less conscious decisions to bear significant exposures to market risks with the hope of earning abnormal returns.

The lesson of market efficiency for corporate risk managers is that the attempt to earn higher returns in most financial markets generally means bearing large (and unfamiliar) risks. In highly liquid markets such as those for interest rate and FX futures—and in the case of heavily traded commodities like oil and gold as well—industrial companies are unlikely to have a comparative advantage in bearing these risks. And so, for most industrial corporations, setting up the corporate treasury to

---

7. Culp and Miller, Vol. 7 No. 4 (Winter 1995), p. 63.
8. See *Risk Magazine*, October 1995, p. 11.

trade derivatives for profit is a value-destroying proposition. (As I will also argue later, however, market efficiency does not rule out the possibility that management's information may be better than the market's in special cases.)

But if the concept of market efficiency should discourage corporations from *creating* corporate exposures to financial market risks, the companion concept of diversification should also discourage some companies from *hedging* financial exposures incurred through their normal business operations. To explain why, however, requires a brief digression on the corporate cost of capital.

Finance theory says that the stock market, in setting the values of companies, effectively assigns minimum required rates of return on capital that vary directly with the companies' levels of risk. In general, the greater a company's risk, the higher the rate of return it must earn to produce superior returns for its shareholders. But a company's required rate of return, also known as its cost of capital, is said to depend only on its non-diversifiable (or "systematic") risk, not on its total risk. In slightly different words, a company's cost of capital depends on the strength of the firm's tendency to move with the broad market (in statistical terms, its "covariance") rather than its overall volatility (or "variance").

In general, most of a company's interest rate, currency, and commodity price exposures will not increase the risk of a well-diversified portfolio. Thus, most corporate financial exposures represent "non-systematic" or "diversifiable" risks that shareholders can eliminate by holding diversified portfolios. And because shareholders have such an inexpensive risk-management tool at their disposal, companies that reduce their earnings volatility by managing their financial risks will not be rewarded by investors with lower required rates of return (or, alternatively, with higher P/E ratios for given levels of cash flow or earnings). As one example, investors with portfolios that include stocks of oil companies are not likely to place higher multiples on the earnings of petrochemical firms just because the latter smooth their earnings by hedging against oil price increases.

For this reason, having the corporation devote resources to reducing FX or commodity price risks makes sense only if the cash flow variability arising

from such risks has the potential to impose "real" costs on the corporation. The academic finance literature has identified three major costs associated with higher variability: (1) higher expected bankruptcy costs (and, more generally, costs of financial distress); (2) higher expected payments to corporate "stakeholders" (including higher rates of return required by owners of closely-held firms); and (3) higher expected tax payments. The potential gains from risk management come from its ability to reduce each of these three costs—and I review each in turn below.[9]

Risk Management Can Reduce Bankruptcy Costs

Although well-diversified shareholders may not be concerned about the cash flow variability caused by swings in FX rates or commodity prices, they will become concerned if such variability materially raises the probability of financial distress. In the extreme case, a company with significant amounts of debt could experience a sharp downturn in operating cash flow—caused in part by an unhedged exposure—and be forced to file for bankruptcy.

What are the costs of bankruptcy? Most obvious are the payments to lawyers and court costs. But, in addition to these "direct" costs of administration and reorganization, there are some potentially larger "indirect" costs. Companies that wind up in Chapter 11 face considerable interference from the bankruptcy court with their investment and operating decisions. And such interference has the potential to cause significant reductions in the ongoing operating value of the firm.

If a company's shareholders view bankruptcy as a real possibility—and to the extent the process of reorganization itself is expected to reduce the firm's operating value—the expected present value of these costs will be reflected in a company's *current* market value. A risk management program that costlessly eliminates the risk of bankruptcy effectively reduces these costs to zero and, in so doing, increases the value of the firm.

The effects of risk management on bankruptcy costs and firm value are illustrated in Figure 1. In the case shown in the figure, hedging is assumed to

9. For a discussion of the benefits of corporate hedging, see Clifford Smith and René Stulz, "The Determinants of Firms' Hedging Policies," *Journal of Financial and Quantitative Analysis* 20 (1985), pp. 391-405.

Because shareholders have such an inexpensive risk-management tool, companies that reduce their earnings volatility by managing financial risks will not be rewarded with a lower "cost of capital." But if shareholders are not concerned about the cash flow variability caused by swings in FX rates or commodity prices, they will become concerned if such variability materially raises the probability of financial distress.

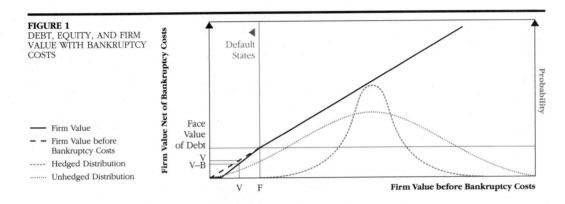

FIGURE 1
DEBT, EQUITY, AND FIRM VALUE WITH BANKRUPTCY COSTS

—— Firm Value
– – Firm Value before Bankruptcy Costs
----- Hedged Distribution
········ Unhedged Distribution

reduce the variability of cash flow and firm value to the degree that default is no longer possible. By eliminating the possibility of bankruptcy, risk management increases the value of the firm's equity by an amount roughly equal to Bc (bankruptcy costs) multiplied by the probability of bankruptcy if the firm remains unhedged (pBU). For example, let's assume the market value of the firm's equity is $100 million, bankruptcy costs are expected to run $25 million (or 25% of current firm value), and the probability of bankruptcy in the absence of hedging is 10%. In this case, risk management can be seen as increasing the current value of the firm's equity by $2.5 million (10% x $25 million), or 2.5%. (Keep in mind that this is the contribution of risk management to firm value *when the company is healthy*; in the event that cash flow and value should decline sharply from current levels, the value added by risk management increases in absolute dollars, and even more on a percentage-of-value basis.)

This argument extends to distress costs in general. For instance, as a company becomes weaker financially, it becomes more difficult for it to raise funds. At some point, the cost of outside funding—if available at all—may become so great that management chooses to pass up profitable investments. This "underinvestment problem" experienced by companies when facing the prospect of default (or, in some cases, just a downturn in earnings[10]) represents an important cost of financial distress. And, to the extent that risk management succeeds in reducing the

perceived *probability* of financial distress and the costs associated with underinvestment, it will increase the current market value of the firm.

Risk Management Can Reduce Payments to "Stakeholders" (and Required Returns to Owners of Closely Held Firms)[11]

Although the shareholders of large public companies can often manage most financial risks more efficiently than the companies themselves, the case may be different for the owners—or owner-managers—of private or closely-held companies. Because such owners tend to have a large proportion of their wealth tied up in the firm, their required rates of return are likely to reflect all important sources of risk, those that can be "diversified away" by outside investors as well as those that cannot. In such circumstances, hedging financial exposures can be thought of as adding value by reducing the owners' risks and hence their required rates of return on investment.

And it's not just the owners of closely held companies that value the protection from risk management. In public companies with dispersed ownership, non-investor groups such as managers, employees, customers, and suppliers with a large stake in the success of the firm typically cannot diversify away large financial exposures. If there is a chance that their "firm-specific" investments could be lost because of financial distress, they are likely to require added compensation for the greater risk.

---

10. This argument is made by Kenneth Froot, David Scharfstein, and Jeremy Stein in "Risk Management: Coordinating Corporate Investment and Financing Policies," *Journal of Finance* 48, (1993), 1629-1658.

11. The discussion in this section and the next draws heavily on Smith and Stulz (1985), cited in footnote 9.

Employees will demand higher wages (or reduce their loyalty or perhaps their work effort) at a company where the probability of layoff is greater. Managers with alternative opportunities will demand higher salaries (or maybe an equity stake in the company) to run firms where the risks of insolvency and financial embarrassment are significant. Suppliers will be more reluctant to enter into long-term contracts, and trade creditors will charge more and be less flexible, with companies whose prospects are more uncertain. And customers concerned about the company's ability to fulfil warranty obligations or service their products in the future may be reluctant to buy those products.

To the extent risk management can protect the investments of each of these corporate stakeholders, the company can improve the terms on which it contracts with them and so increase firm value. And, as I discuss later in more detail, hedging can also facilitate larger equity stakes for managers of public companies by limiting "uncontrollables" and thus the "scope" of their bets.

Risk Management Can Reduce Taxes

The potential tax benefits of risk management derive from the interaction of risk management's ability to reduce the volatility of reported income and the progressivity (or, more precisely, the "convexity") of most of the world's tax codes. In the U.S., as in most countries, a company's effective tax rate rises along with increases in pre-tax income. Increasing marginal tax rates, limits on the use of tax-loss carry forwards, and the alternative minimum tax all work together to impose higher effective rates of taxation on higher levels of reported income and to provide lower percentage tax rebates for ever larger losses.

Because of the convexity of the tax code, there are benefits to "managing" taxable income so that as much of it as possible falls within an optimal range—that is, neither too high nor too low. By reducing fluctuations in taxable income, risk management can lead to lower tax payments by ensuring that, over a complete business cycle, the largest possible proportion of corporate income falls within this optimal range of tax rates.

RISK MANAGEMENT AND COMPARATIVE ADVANTAGE IN RISK-TAKING

Up to this point, we have seen that companies should not expect to make money consistently by taking financial positions based on information that is publicly available. But what about information that is not publicly available? After all, many companies in the course of their normal operating activities acquire specialized information about certain financial markets. Could not such information give them a comparative advantage over their shareholders in taking some types of risks?

Let's look at a hypothetical example. Consider company X that produces consumer durables using large amounts of copper as a major input. In the process of ensuring that it has the appropriate amount of copper on hand, it gathers useful information about the copper market. It knows its own demand for copper, of course, but it also learns a lot about the supply. In such a case, the firm will almost certainly allow that specialized information to play some role in its risk management strategy.

For example, let's assume that company X's management has determined that, when it has no view about future copper prices, it will hedge 50% of the next year's expected copper purchases to protect itself against the possibility of financial distress. But, now let's say that the firm's purchasing agents persuade top management that the price of copper is far more likely to rise than fall in the coming year. In this case, the firm's risk manager might choose to take a long position in copper futures that would hedge as much as 100% of its anticipated purchases for the year instead of the customary 50%. Conversely, if management becomes convinced that copper prices are likely to drop sharply (with almost no possibility of a major increase), it might choose to hedge as little as 20% of its exposure.[12]

Should the management of company X refrain from exploiting its specialized knowledge in this fashion, and instead adhere to its 50% hedging target? Or should it, in certain circumstances, allow its market view to influence its hedge ratio?

Although there are clearly risks to selective hedging of this kind—in particular, the risk that the

---

12. For a good example of this kind of selective hedging policy, see the comments by John Van Roden, Chief Financial Officer of Lukens, Inc. in the "Bank of America Roundtable on Corporate Risk Management," *Journal of Applied Corporate Finance*, Vol. 8 No. 3 (Fall 1995). As a stainless steel producer, one of the company's principal inputs is nickel; and Lukens' policy is to allow its view of nickel prices to influence how much of its nickel exposure it hedges. By contrast, although it may have views of interest rates or FX exposures, such views play no role in hedging those exposures.

How can management determine when it should take risks and when it should not?
The best approach is to implement a *risk-taking audit*—a comprehensive review of
the risks to which the company is exposed, both through its financial instruments
and liability structure as well as its normal operations.

firm's information may not in fact be better than the market's—it seems quite plausible that companies could have such informational advantages. Companies that repurchase their own shares based on the belief that their current value fails to reflect the firm's prospects seem to be vindicated more often than not. And though it's true that management may be able to predict the firm's future earnings with more confidence than the price of one of its major inputs, the information companies acquire about certain financial markets may still prove a reasonably reliable source of gain in risk management decisions.

The Importance of Understanding Comparative Advantage

What this example fails to suggest, however, is that the same operating activity in one company may not necessarily provide a comparative advantage in risk-bearing for another firm. As suggested above, the major risk associated with "selective" hedging is that the firm's information may not in fact be better than the market's. For this reason, it is important for management to understand the source of its comparative advantages.

To illustrate this point, take the case of a foreign currency trading operation in a large commercial bank. A foreign currency trading room can make a lot of money from taking positions provided, of course, exchange rates move in the anticipated direction. But, in an efficient market, as we have seen, banks can reliably make money from position-taking of this sort only if they have access to information before most other firms. In the case of FX, this is likely to happen only if the bank's trading operation is very large—large enough so that its deal flow is likely to reflect general shifts in demand for foreign currencies.

Most FX dealers, however, have no comparative advantage in gathering information about changes in the value of foreign currencies. For such firms, management of currency risk means ensuring that their exposures are short-lived. The most reliable way to minimize exposures for most currency traders is to enlarge their customer base. With a sufficient number of large, highly active customers, a trading operation has the following advantage: If one of its traders agrees to buy yen from one customer, the firm can resell them quickly to another customer and pocket the bid-ask spread.

In an article entitled "An Analysis of Trading Profits: How Trading Rooms Really Make Money," Alberic Braas and Charles Bralver present evidence suggesting that most FX trading profits come from market-making, not position-taking.[13] Moreover, as the authors of this article point out, a trading operation that does not understand its comparative advantage in trading currencies is likely not only to fail to generate consistent profit, but to endanger its existing comparative advantage. If the source of the profits of the trading room is really the customer base of the bank, and not the predictive power of its traders, then the bank must invest in maintaining and building its customer base. A trading room that mistakenly believes that the source of its profits is position-taking will take large positions that, on average, will neither make money nor lose money. More troubling, though, is that the resulting variability of its trading income is likely to unsettle its customers and weaken its customer base. Making matters worse, it may choose a compensation system for its traders that rewards profitable position-taking instead of valuable coordination of trading and sales activities. A top management that fails to understand its comparative advantage may waste its time looking for star traders while neglecting the development of marketing strategies and services.

How can management determine when it should take risks and when it should not? The best approach is to implement a *risk-taking audit*. This would involve a comprehensive review of the risks to which the company is exposed, both through its financial instruments and liability structure as well as its normal operations. Such an audit should attempt to answer questions like the following: Which of its major risks has the firm proved capable of "self-insuring" over a complete business cycle? If the firm chooses to hedge "selectively," or leaves exposures completely unhedged, what is the source of the firm's comparative advantage in taking these positions? Which risk management activities have consistently added value without introducing another source of volatility?

Once a firm has decided that it has a comparative advantage in taking certain financial risks, it must then determine the role of risk management

---

13. See Albéric Braas and Charles Bralver, "An Analysis of Trading Profits: How Most Trading Rooms Really Make Money," *Journal of Applied Corporate Finance*, Vol. 2 No. 4 (Winter 1990).

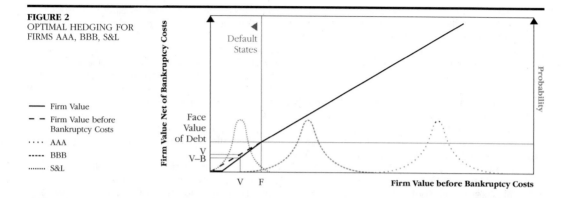

FIGURE 2
OPTIMAL HEDGING FOR
FIRMS AAA, BBB, S&L

—— Firm Value

– – Firm Value before
Bankruptcy Costs

···· AAA

----- BBB

········ S&L

in exploiting this advantage. As I argue below, risk management may paradoxically enable the firm to take *more* of these risks than it would in the absence of risk management. To illustrate this point, let's return to our example of company X and assume it has valuable information about the copper market that enables it to earn consistently superior profits trading copper. Even in this situation, such trading profits are by no means a sure thing; there is always the possibility that the firm will experience significant losses. Purchasing far-out-of-the-money calls on copper in such a case could actually serve to increase the firm's ability to take speculative positions in copper. But, as I argue in the next section, a company's ability to withstand large trading losses without endangering its operating activities depends not only on its risk management policy, but also on its capital structure and general financial health.

THE LINK BETWEEN RISK MANAGEMENT, RISK-TAKING, AND CAPITAL STRUCTURE

In discussing earlier the benefits of risk management, I suggested that companies should manage risk in a way that makes financial distress highly unlikely and, in so doing, preserves the financing flexibility necessary to carry out their investment strategies. Given this primary objective for risk management, one would not expect companies with little or no debt financing—and, hence, a low probability of financial trouble—to benefit from hedging.

In this sense, risk management can be viewed as a direct substitute for equity capital. That is, the more the firm hedges its financial exposures, the less equity it requires to support its business. Or, to put it another way, the use of risk management to reduce exposures effectively increases a company's debt capacity.

Moreover, to the extent one views risk management as a substitute for equity capital—or, alternatively, as a technique that allows management to substitute debt for equity—then it pays companies to practice risk management only to the extent that equity capital is more expensive than debt. As this formulation of the issue suggests, a company's decisions to hedge financial risks—or to bear part of such risks through selective hedging—should be made jointly with the corporate capital structure decision.

To illustrate this interdependence between risk management and capital structure, consider the three kinds of companies pictured in Figure 2. At the right-hand side of the figure is company AAA, so named because it has little debt and a very high debt rating. The probability of default is essentially zero; and thus the left or lower tail of AAA's distribution of potential outcomes never reaches the range where low value begins to impose financial distress costs on the firm. Based on the theory of risk management just presented, there is no reason for this company to hedge its financial exposures; the company's shareholders can do the same job more cost-effectively. And, should investment opportunities arise, AAA will likely be able to raise funds on an economic basis, even if its cash flows should decline temporarily.

Should such a company take bets on financial markets? The answer could be yes, provided management has specialized information that would give it a comparative advantage in a certain market. In

AAA's case, a bet that turns out badly will not affect the company's ability to carry out its strategic plan.

But now let's consider the company in the middle of the picture, call it BBB. Like the company shown in Figure 1 earlier, this firm has a lower credit rating, and there is a significant probability that the firm could face distress. What should BBB do? As shown earlier in Figure 1, this firm should probably eliminate the probability of encountering financial distress through risk management. In this case, even if management feels that there are occasional opportunities to profit from market inefficiencies, hedging exposures is likely to be the best policy. In company BBB's case, the cost of having a bet turn sour can be substantial, since this would almost certainly imply default. Consequently, one would not expect the management of such a firm to let its views affect the hedge ratio.

Finally, let's consider a firm that is in distress—and let's call it "S&L." What should it do? Reducing risk once the firm is in distress is not in the interest of shareholders. If the firm stays in distress and eventually defaults, shareholders will end up with near-worthless shares. In these circumstances, a management intent on maximizing shareholder value will not only accept bets that present themselves, but will *seek out* new ones. Such managers will take bets even if they believe markets are efficient because introducing new sources of volatility raises the probability of the "upper-tail" outcomes that are capable of rescuing the firm from financial distress.

Back to the Capital Structure Decision. As we saw in the case of company AAA, firms that have a lot of equity capital can make bets without worrying about whether doing so will bring about financial distress. One would therefore not expect these firms to hedge aggressively, particularly if risk management is costly and shareholders are better off without it.

The major issue that such companies must address, however, is whether they have too much capital—or, too much equity capital. In other words, although risk management may not be useful to them *given their current leverage ratios*, they might be better off using risk management and increasing leverage. Debt financing, of course, has a tax advantage over equity financing. But, in addition to its

ability to reduce corporate taxes, increasing leverage also has the potential to strengthen management incentives to improve efficiency and add value. For one thing, the substitution of debt for equity leads managers to pay out excess capital—an action that could be a major source of value added in industries with overcapacity and few promising investment opportunities. Perhaps even more important, however, is that the substitution of debt for equity also allows for greater concentration of equity ownership, including a significant ownership stake for managers.

In sum, the question of what is the right corporate risk management decision for a company begs the question of not only its optimal capital structure, but optimal *ownership* structure as well. As suggested above, hedging could help some companies to increase shareholder value by enabling them to raise leverage—say, by buying back their shares—and increase management's percentage ownership. For other companies, however, leaving exposures unhedged or hedging "selectively" while maintaining more equity may turn out to be the value-maximizing strategy.

CORPORATE RISK-TAKING AND MANAGEMENT INCENTIVES

Management incentives may have a lot to do with why some firms take bets and others do not. As suggested, some companies that leave exposures unhedged or take bets on financial markets may have a comparative advantage in so doing; and, for those companies, such risk-taking may be a value-increasing strategy. Other companies, however, may choose to take financial risks without having a comparative advantage, particularly if such risk-taking somehow serves the interests of those managers who choose to expose their firms to the risks.

We have little convincing empirical evidence on the extent of risk-taking by companies, whether public or private. But there is one notable exception—a study by Peter Tufano of the hedging behavior of 48 publicly traded North American gold mining companies that was published in the September 1996 issue of the *Journal of Finance*.[14] The gold mining industry is ideal for studying hedging behav-

---

14. Peter Tufano, "Who Manages Risk? An Empirical Examination of the Risk Management Practices of the Gold Mining Industry," *Journal of Finance* (September, 1996).

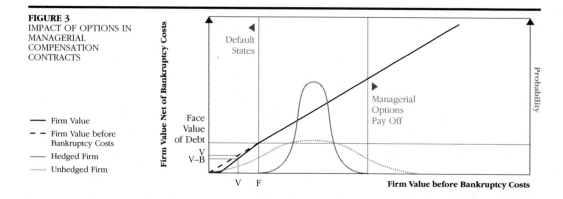

FIGURE 3
IMPACT OF OPTIONS IN
MANAGERIAL
COMPENSATION
CONTRACTS

——— Firm Value

– – Firm Value before
    Bankruptcy Costs

——— Hedged Firm

········· Unhedged Firm

Firm Value Net of Bankruptcy Costs (vertical axis label)

Default
States

Managerial
Options
Pay Off

Face
Value
of Debt

V
V–B

V   F

Firm Value before Bankruptcy Costs

Probability (right vertical axis label)

ior in the sense that gold mining companies tend to be single-industry firms with one very large price exposure and a wide range of hedging vehicles, from forward sales, to exchange-traded gold futures and options, to gold swaps and bullion loans.

The purpose of Tufano's study was to examine the ability of various corporate risk management theories to explain any significant pattern of differences in the percentage of their gold price exposures that the companies choose to hedge. Somewhat surprisingly, there was considerable variation in the hedging behavior of these 48 firms. One company, Homestake Mining, chose not only to hedge none of its exposure, but to publicize its policy while condemning what it called "gold price management." At the other extreme were companies like American Barrick that hedged as much as 85% of their anticipated production over the next three years. And whereas about one in six of these firms chose to hedge none of its exposure and sold *all* of its output at spot prices, another one in six firms hedged 40% or more of its gold price exposure.

The bottom line of Tufano's study was that the only important systematic determinant of the 48 corporate hedging decisions was managerial ownership of shares and, more generally, the nature of the managerial compensation contract. In general, the greater management's direct percentage share ownership, the larger the percentage of its gold price exposure a firm hedged. By contrast, little hedging took place in gold mining firms where management owns a small stake. Moreover, managerial compen-

sation contracts that emphasize options or option-like features were also associated with significantly less hedging.

As Tufano acknowledged in his study, this pattern of findings could have been predicted from arguments that Clifford Smith and I presented in a theoretical paper in 1985.[15] Our argument was essentially as follows: As we saw in the case of closely held companies, managers with a significant fraction of their own wealth tied up in their own firms are likely to consider all sources of risk when setting their required rates of return. And this could help explain the tendency of firms with heavy managerial equity ownership to hedge more of their gold price exposures. In such cases, the volatility of gold prices translates fairly directly into volatility of managers' wealth, and manager-owners concerned about such volatility may rationally choose to manage their exposures. (How, or whether, such hedging serves the interests of the companies' outside shareholders is another issue, one that I return to shortly.)

The propensity of managers with lots of stock options but little equity ownership to leave their gold price exposures unhedged is also easy to understand. As shown in Figure 3, the one-sided payoff from stock options effectively rewards management for taking bets and so increasing volatility. In this example, the reduction in volatility from hedging makes management's options worthless (that is, the example assumes these are well-out-of-the-money options). But if the firm does not hedge, there is some

15. Clifford Smith and René Stulz, "The Determinants of Firms' Hedging Policies," *Journal of Financial and Quantitative Analysis* 20 (1985), pp. 391-405.

Given that the firm has chosen to concentrate equity ownership, hedging may well be a value-adding strategy. If significant equity ownership for managers is expected to strengthen incentives to improve operating performance, hedging can make these incentives even stronger by removing the "noise" introduced by a major performance variable that is beyond management's control.

probability that a large increase in gold prices will cause the options to pay off.

What if we make the more realistic assumption that the options are *at the money* instead of far out of the money? In this case, options would still have the power to influence hedging behavior because management gains more from increases in firm value than it loses from reductions in firm value. As we saw in the case of the S&L presented earlier, this "asymmetric" payoff structure of options increases management's willingness to take bets.[16]

But if these differences in hedging behavior reflect differences in managerial incentives, what do they tell us about the effect of risk management on shareholder value? Without directly addressing the issue, Tufano implies that neither of the two polar risk management strategies—hedging none of their gold exposure vs. hedging 40% or more—seems designed to increase shareholder value while both appear to serve managers' interests. But can we therefore conclude from this study that neither of these approaches benefits shareholders?

Let's start with the case of the companies that, like Homestake Mining, choose to hedge none of their gold price exposure. As we saw earlier, companies for which financial distress is unlikely have no good reason to hedge (assuming they see no value in changing their current capital structure). At the same time, in a market as heavily traded as gold, management is also not likely to possess a comparative advantage in predicting gold prices. And, lacking either a motive for hedging or superior information about future gold prices, management has no reason to alter the company's natural exposure to gold prices. In further defense of such a policy, one could also argue that such a gold price exposure will have diversification benefits for investors seeking protection against inflation and political risks.

On the other hand, as Smith and I pointed out, because stock options have considerably more upside than downside risk, such incentive packages could result in a misalignment of managers' and

shareholders' interests. That is, stock options could be giving managers a one-sided preference for risk-taking that is not fully shared by the companies' stockholders; and, if so, a better policy would be to balance managers' upside potential by giving them a share of the downside risk.

But what about the opposite decision to hedge a significant portion of gold price exposures? Was that likely to have increased shareholder value? As Tufano's study suggests, the managers of the hedging firms tend to hold larger equity stakes. And, as we saw earlier, if such managers have a large fraction of their wealth tied up in their firms, they will demand higher levels of compensation to work in firms with such price exposures. *Given that the firm has chosen to concentrate equity ownership*, hedging may well be a value-adding strategy. That is, if significant equity ownership for managers is expected to add value by strengthening incentives to improve operating performance, the role of hedging is to make these incentives even stronger by removing the "noise" introduced by a major performance variable—the gold price—that is beyond management's control. For this reason, the combination of concentrated ownership, the less "noisy" performance measure produced by hedging, and the possibility of higher financial leverage[17] has the potential to add significant value. As this reasoning suggests, risk management can be used to facilitate an organizational structure that resembles that of an LBO![18]

To put the same thought another way, it is the risk management policy that allows companies with large financial exposures to have significant managerial stock ownership. For, without the hedging policy, a major price exposure would cause the scope of management's bet to be too diffuse, and "uncontrollables" would dilute the desired incentive benefits of more concentrated ownership.

Although Tufano's study is finally incapable of answering the question, "Did risk management add value for shareholders?," the study nevertheless has an important message for corporate policy. It says

---

16. Additional empirical support for the importance of the relation between the option component of managerial compensation contracts and corporate risk-taking was provided in a recent study of S&Ls that changed their organizational form from mutual ownership to stock ownership. The study finds that those "converted" S&Ls where management has options choose to increase their one-year gaps and, hence, their exposure to interest rates. The study also shows that the greater the percentage of their interest rate exposure an S&L hedges, the larger the credit risk it takes on. The authors of the study interpret this finding to argue, as I do here, that risk management allows firms to increase their exposures to some risks by reducing other risks and thus limiting total firm risk. See C.M. Schrandt and H. Unal,

"Coordinated Risk Management: On and Off-balance Sheet Hedging and Thrift Conversion," 1996, unpublished working paper, The Wharton School, University of Pennsylvania, Philadelphia, PA.

17. Although Tufano's study does not find that firms that hedge have systematically higher leverage ratios, it does find that companies that hedge less have higher cash balances.

18. For a discussion of the role of hedging in creating an LBO-like structure, see my study, "Managerial Discretion and Optimal Financing Policies," *Journal of Financial Economics* (1990), pp. 3-26.

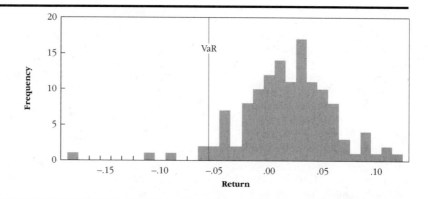

FIGURE 4
WORLD MARKET
PORTFOLIO RETURN
SEPTEMBER 1985-
DECEMBER 1995

that, to the extent that risk-taking within the corporation is decentralized, it is important to understand the incentives of those who make the decisions to take or lay off risks.

Organizations have lots of people doing a good job, and so simply doing a good job may not be enough to get promoted. And, if one views corporate promotions as the outcome of "tournaments" (as does one strand of the academic literature), there are tremendous incentives to stand out. One way to stand out is by volunteering to take big risks. In most areas of a corporation, it is generally impossible to take risks where the payoffs are large enough to be noticeable if things go well. But the treasury area may still be an exception. When organized as a profit center, the corporate treasury was certainly a place where an enterprising executive could take such risks and succeed. To the extent such possibilities for risk-taking still exist within some corporate treasuries, top management must be very careful in establishing the appropriate incentives for their risk managers. I return to this subject in the final section of the paper.

MEASURING RISK (OR, IMPROVING ON VaR)

As I mentioned at the outset, the academic literature has focused on volatility reduction as the primary objective of risk management, and on variance as the principal measure of risk. But such a focus on variance, as we have seen, is inconsistent with both most corporate practice and with the theory of risk management presented in this paper. Rather than aiming to reduce variance, most corporate risk management programs appear designed

just to avoid "lower-tail outcomes" while preserving upside potential. Indeed, as I suggested earlier, some companies will hedge certain downside risks precisely in order to be able to increase their leverage ratios or to enlarge other financial exposures in ways designed to exploit their comparative advantage in risk-taking.

Many commercial banks and other financial institutions now attempt to quantify the probability of lower-tail outcomes by using a measure known as Value at Risk, or VaR. To illustrate the general principle underlying VaR, let's assume you are an investor who holds a stock portfolio that is fully diversified across all the major world markets. To calculate your Value at Risk, you will need the kind of information that is presented graphically in Figure 4, which is a histogram showing the distribution of monthly returns on the Morgan Stanley Capital International world market portfolio from September 1985 through December 1995.

How risky is that portfolio? One measure is the standard deviation of the portfolio's monthly returns. Over that roughly 10-year period, the average monthly return was 1.23%, with a standard deviation of 4.3%. This tells you that, about two thirds of the time, your actual return would have fallen within a range extending from a loss of 3.1% to a gain of 5.5%.

But what if one of your major concerns is the size of your monthly losses if things turn out badly, and you thus want to know more about the bottom third of the distribution of outcomes? Let's say, for example, that you want to know the maximum extent of your losses in 95 cases out of 100—that is, within a 95% "confidence interval." In that case, you would calculate the VaR evaluated at the 5% level,

The question management would like to be able to answer is this: If we define financial distress as a situation where we cannot raise funds with a rating of BBB, or where our cash flows fall below some target, what is the probability of distress over, say, the next three years? VaR by itself cannot answer this question—nor can traditional measures of volatility.

which turns out to be a loss of 5.9%. This VaR, represented by the vertical line in the middle of Figure 4, is obtained by taking the monthly average return of 1.23% and subtracting from it 1.65 times the standard deviation of 4.3%. And, if you wanted to know the dollar value of your maximum expected losses, you would simply multiply 5.9% times the dollar value of your holdings. That number is your monthly VaR at the 95% confidence level.

Athough the VaR is now used by some industrial firms to evaluate the risks of their derivatives portfolios, the measure was originally designed by J.P. Morgan to help financial institutions monitor the exposures created by their trading activities. In fact, for financial institutions that trade in liquid markets, a *daily* VaR is likely to be even more useful for monitoring trading operations than the monthly VaR illustrated above. Use of a daily VaR would tell an institution that it could expect, in 95 cases out of 100, to lose no more than X% of its value before unwinding its positions.

The special appeal of VaR is its ability to compress the expected distribution of bad outcomes into a single number. But how does one apply such a measure to the corporate risk management we have been discussing? Despite its advantages for certain uses, VaR cannot really be used to execute the risk management goal presented in this paper—namely, the elimination of lower-tail outcomes to avoid financial distress. The fact that there is a 95% probability that a company's loss on a given day, or in a given month, will not exceed a certain amount called VaR is not useful information when management's concern is whether firm value will fall below some critical value *over an extended period of time*. The question management would like to be able to answer is this: If we define financial distress as a situation where we cannot raise funds with a rating of BBB, or where our cash flows or the value of equity fall below some target, what is the probability of distress over, say, the next three years? VaR by itself cannot answer this question—nor can traditional measures of volatility.

It is relatively simple to calculate VaR for a financial institution's portfolio over a horizon of a day or a week. It is much less clear how one would compute the VaR associated with, say, an airline's ongoing operating exposure to oil prices. In evaluating their major risks, most non-financial companies will want to know how much volatility in their cash flows or firm value an exposure can be expected to

cause over periods of at least a year, and often considerably longer. Unfortunately, there are at least two major difficulties in extending the VaR over longer time horizons that may not be surmountable.

First, remember that a daily VaR at the 99th percentile is one that is expected to occur on one day out of 100. The relative precision of such a prediction makes it possible to conduct empirical checks of the validity of the model. With the large number of daily observations, one can readily observe the frequency with which the loss is equal or greater than VaR *using reasonably current data*. But, if we attempt to move from a daily to, say, a one-year VaR at the same 99th percentile, it becomes very difficult to calculate such a model, much less subject it to empirical testing. Since an annual VaR at the 99th percentile means that the loss can be expected to take place in only one year in every 100, one presumably requires numerous 100-year periods to establish the validity of such a model.

The second problem in extending the time horizon of VaR is its reliance on the normal distribution. When one is especially concerned about "tail" probabilities—the probabilities of the worst and best outcomes—the assumption made about the statistical distribution of the gains and losses is important. Research on stock prices and on default probabilities across different classes of debt suggests that the tail probabilities are generally larger than implied by the normal distribution. A simple way to understand this is as follows. If stock returns were really normally distributed, as many pricing models assume, market declines in excess of 10% in a day would be extremely rare—say, once in a million years. The fact that such declines happen more often than this is proof that the normal distribution does not describe the probability of lower-tail events correctly.

Although this is not an important failing for most applications in corporate finance, including the valuation of most securities, it can be critical in the context of risk management. For example, if changes in the value of derivatives portfolios or default probabilities have "fatter tails" than those implied by a normal distribution, management could end up significantly understating the probability of distress.

An Alternative to VaR: Using Cash Flow Simulations to Estimate Default Probabilities. Moreover, even if we could calculate a one-year VaR for the value of the firm and be reasonably confident that the distribution was normal, the relevant risk measure for hedging purposes would not be the VaR computed at the one-year horizon. A VaR computed at the one-year horizon at the 99th percentile answers the question: What is the maximum loss in firm value that I can expect in 99 years out of 100? But when a company hedges an exposure, its primary concern is the likelihood of distress *during the year*, which depends on the value of the cumulative loss throughout the year. Thus, it must be concerned about the path of firm value during a period of time rather than the distribution of firm value at the end of the period.

Given this focus on cumulative changes in firm value during a period of time, perhaps the most practical approach to assessing a company's probability of financial distress is to conduct sensitivity analysis on the expected distribution of cash flows. Using Monte Carlo simulation techniques, for example, one could project the company's cash flows over a ten-year horizon in a way that is designed to reflect the combined effect of (and any interactions among) all the firm's major risk exposures on its default probability. The probability of distress over that period would be measured by the fraction of simulated distributions that falls below a certain threshold level of cumulative cash flow. Such a technique could also be used to estimate the expected effect of various hedging strategies on the probability of distress.[19]

One of the advantages of using simulation techniques in this context is their ability to incorporate any special properties (or "non-normalities") of the cash flows. As we saw earlier, the VaR approach assumes that the gains and losses from risky positions are "serially independent," which means that if your firm experiences a loss today, the chance of experiencing another loss tomorrow is unaffected. But this assumption is likely to be wrong when applied to the operating cash flow of a nonfinancial firm: If cash flow is poor today, it is more likely to be poor tomorrow. Simulation has the ability to build this "serial dependence" of cash flows into an analysis of the probability of financial distress.

MANAGING RISK-TAKING

As we have seen, a hedging strategy that focuses on the probability of distress can be consistent with an increase in risk-taking. With such a strategy, the primary goal of risk management is to eliminate lower-tail outcomes. Using risk management in this way, it is possible for a company to increase its volatility while also limiting the probability of a bad outcome that would create financial distress. One example of such a strategy would be to lever up the firm while at the same time buying way out-of-the-money put options that pay off if the firm does poorly. Focusing on lower-tail outcomes is also fully consistent with managing longer-term economic or competitive exposures, as opposed to the near-term transaction exposures that most corporate risk management seems designed to hedge.

But how would the firm decide whether the expected payoff from taking certain financial bets is adequate compensation for not only the risk of losses, but also the expected costs of financial distress? And, once management decides that it is a value-increasing proposition to undertake certain bets, how would the firm evaluate the success of its risk-taking efforts?

To evaluate if the bet is worth taking, let's start by supposing that we are willing to put an explicit cost on the increase in the probability of distress resulting from betting on certain markets. In that case, the trade-off for evaluating a bet for the company becomes fairly simple: The expected profit from the bet must exceed the increase in the probability of distress multiplied by the expected cost of distress.[20] Thus, a bet that has a positive expected value and no effect on the probability of distress is one that the firm should take. But a bet with positive expected profit that significantly increases the probability of financial distress may not appear profitable if the costs of a bad outcome are too large. In such cases, it makes sense for the firm to think

---

19. For an illustration of the use of Monte Carlo analysis in risk management, see René Stulz and Rohan Williamson, "Identifying and Quantifying Exposures," in Robert Jameson, ed., *Treasury Risk Management* (London, Risk Publications), forthcoming.

20. One possible approach to quantifying the *expected* costs of financial distress involves the concept of American "binary options" and the associated option pricing models. An example of a binary option is one that would pay a fixed amount, say, $10, if the stock price of IBM falls below $40. Unlike standard American put options, which when exercised pay an amount equal to (the strike price of) $40 minus the actual price, the holder of a binary option receives either $10 or nothing, and exercises when the stock price crosses the $40 barrier. Such options can be priced using modified option pricing models.

The connection between binary options and risk management is this: The present value of a binary option is a function of two major variables: the probability that firm value will fall below a certain level (in this case, $40) and the payoff in the event of such a drop in value ($10). By substituting for the $10 payoff its own estimate of how much *additional* value the firm is likely to lose *once its value falls to a certain level and gets into financial trouble*, management can then estimate the expected present value of such costs using a binary option pricing model. This is the number that could be set against the expected profit from the firm's bet in order to evaluate whether to go ahead with the bet.

> **To the extent that view-taking becomes an accepted part of a company's risk management program, it is important to evaluate managers' bets on a risk-adjusted basis and relative to the market. If managers want to behave like money managers, they should be evaluated like money managers.**

about using risk management to reduce the probability of distress. By hedging, management may be able to achieve a reduction in cash flow variability that is large enough that an adverse outcome of the bet will not create financial distress.

Given that management has decided the bet is worth taking, how does it evaluate the outcome of the strategy? Consider first the case of our firm AAA discussed earlier. Recall that this firm is not concerned about lower-tail outcomes and thus has no reason to hedge. When evaluating the outcome of the bet in this case, the appropriate benchmark is the expected gain *adjusted for risk*. It is not enough that the bet ends up earning more than the risk-free rate or even more than the firm's cost of capital. To add value for the company's shareholders, the bet must earn a return that is higher than investors' expected return on other investments of comparable risk.

For example, there is considerable evidence that holding currencies of high-interest rate countries earns returns that, on average, exceed the risk-free rate. This excess return most likely represents "normal" compensation for bearing some kind of risk—say, the higher inflation and interest rate volatility associated with high-interest-rate countries. And because such a strategy is thus *expected* to earn excess returns, it would not make sense to reward a corporate treasury for earning excess returns in this way. The treasury takes risks when it pursues that strategy, and the firm's shareholders expect to be compensated for these risks. Thus, it is only the amount by which the treasury exceeds the expected return—or the "abnormal return"—that represents *economic profit* for the corporation.

So, the abnormal or excess return should be the measure for evaluating bets by company AAA. But now let's turn to the case of company BBB, where the expected increase in volatility from the bet is also expected to raise the probability of costly lower-tail outcomes. In such a case, as we saw earlier, management should probably hedge to reduce the probability of financial trouble to acceptable levels. At the same time, however, top management should also consider

subjecting its bets to an even higher standard of profitability to compensate shareholders for any associated increase in expected financial distress costs.

How much higher should it be? One method would be to assume that, instead of hedging, the firm raises additional equity capital to support the expected increase in volatility associated with the bet. In that case, the bet would be expected to produce the same risk-adjusted return on capital as the bet taken by company AAA, but on a larger amount of imputed "risk" capital.[21]

In sum, when devising a compensation scheme for those managers entrusted with making the firm's bets, it is critical to structure their incentive payments so that they are encouraged to take only those bets that are expected to increase shareholder wealth. Managers should not be compensated for earning average returns when taking larger-than-average risks. They should be compensated only for earning more than what their shareholders could earn on their own when bearing the same amount of risk.

This approach does not completely eliminate the problem discussed earlier caused by incentives for individuals to stand out in large organizations by taking risks. But traditional compensation schemes only reinforce this problem. If a risk-taker simply receives a bonus for making gains, he has incentives to take random bets because he gets a fraction of his gains while the firm bears the losses. Evaluating managers' performance against a risk-adjusted benchmark can help discourage risk-taking that is not justified by comparative advantage by making it more difficult for the risk-taker to make money by taking random bets.

CONCLUSION

This paper presents a theory of risk management that attempts to go beyond the "variance-minimization" model that dominates most academic discussions of corporate risk management. I argue that the primary goal of risk management is to eliminate the probability of costly lower-tail outcomes—those that would cause financial distress or

---

21. The amount of implicit "risk capital" (as opposed to the actual cash capital) backing an activity can be calculated as a function of the expected volatility (as measured by the standard deviation) of the activity's cash flow returns. For the distinction between risk capital and cash capital, and a method for calculating risk capital, see Robert Merton and André Perold, "Theory of Risk Capital for Financial Firms," *Journal of Applied Corporate Finance*, Vol. 6 No. 3 (Fall 1993). For one company's application of a similar method for calculating risk capital, see Edward

Zaik et al., "RAROC at Bank of America: From Theory to Practice," *Journal of Applied Corporate Finance*, Vol. 9 No. 2 (Summer 1996). For a theoretical model of capital budgeting that takes into account firm-specific risks, see Kenneth Froot and Jeremy Stein, "Risk Management, Capital Budgeting, and Capital Structure Policy for Financial Institutions: An Integrated Approach," Working Paper 96-030, Harvard Business School Division of Research.

make a company unable to carry out its investment strategy. (In this sense, risk management can be viewed as the purchase of well-out-of-the-money put options designed to limit downside risk.) Moreover, by eliminating downside risk and reducing the expected costs of financial trouble, risk management can also help move companies toward their optimal capital and ownership structure. For, besides increasing corporate debt capacity, the reduction of downside risk could also encourage larger equity stakes for managers by shielding their investments from "uncontrollables."

This paper also departs from standard finance theory in suggesting that some companies may have a comparative advantage in bearing certain financial market risks—an advantage that derives from information it acquires through its normal business activities. Although such specialized information may occasionally lead some companies to take speculative positions in commodities or currencies, it is more likely to encourage selective hedging, a practice in which the risk manager's view of future price movements influences the percentage of the exposure that is hedged. This kind of hedging, while certainly containing potential for abuse, may also represent a value-adding form of risk-taking for many companies.

But, to the extent that such view-taking becomes an accepted part of a company's risk management program, it is important to evaluate managers' bets on a risk-adjusted basis and relative to the market. If managers want to behave like money managers, they should be evaluated like money managers.

IDENTIFYING, MEASURING, AND HEDGING CURRENCY RISK AT MERCK

*by Judy C. Lewent and A. John Kearney, Merck & Co., Inc.**

T he impact of exchange rate volatility on a company depends mainly on the company's business structure, both legal and operational, its industry profile, and the nature of its competitive environment. This article recounts how Merck assessed its currency exposures and reached a decision to hedge those exposures. After a brief introduction to the company and the industry, we discuss our methods of identifying and measuring our exchange exposures, the factors considered in deciding whether to hedge such risks, and the financial hedging program we put in place.

AN INTRODUCTION TO THE COMPANY

Merck & Co., Inc. primarily discovers, develops, produces, and distributes human and animal health pharmaceuticals. It is part of a global industry that makes its products available for the prevention, relief, and cure of disease throughout the world. Merck itself is a multinational company, doing business in over 100 countries.

Total worldwide sales in 1989 for all domestic and foreign research-intensive pharmaceutical companies are projected to be $103.7 billion. Worldwide sales for those companies based in the U.S. are projected at $36.4 billion—an estimated 35% of the world pharmaceutical market; and worldwide sales for Merck in 1989 were $6.6 billion. The industry is highly competitive, with no company holding over 5% of the worldwide market. Merck ranks first in pharmaceutical sales in the U.S. and the world, yet has only a 4.7% market share worldwide. The major

foreign competitors for the domestic industry are European firms and emerging Japanese companies.

Driven by the need to fund high-risk and growing research expenditures, the U.S. pharmaceutical industry has expanded significantly more into foreign markets than has U.S. industry as a whole. In 1987, the leading U.S. pharmaceutical companies generated 38% of their sales revenues overseas; and 37% of their total assets were located outside the U.S. In contrast, most U.S. industry groups report foreign sales revenues in the range of 20% to 30%. Merck, with overseas assets equal to 40% of total and with roughly half of its sales overseas, is among the most internationally-oriented of U.S. pharmaceutical companies.

The U.S. pharmaceutical industry also differs in its method of doing business overseas. In contrast to U.S. exporters, who often bill their customers in U.S. dollars, the pharmaceutical industry typically bills its customers in their local currencies. Thus, the effect of foreign currency fluctuations on the pharmaceutical industry tends to be more immediate and direct.

The typical structure is the establishment of subsidiaries in many overseas markets. These subsidiaries, of which Merck has approximately 70, are typically importers of product at some stage of manufacture, and are responsible for finishing, marketing, and distribution within the country of incorporation. Sales are denominated in local currency, and costs in a combination of local currency for finishing, marketing, distribution, administration, and taxes, and in the currency of basic manufacture and research—typically, the U.S. dollar for U.S.-based companies.

* The authors would like to thank Francis H. Spiegel, Jr., Senior Vice President and CFO of Merck & Co., Inc., and Professors Donald Lessard of M.I.T. and Darrell Duffie of Stanford for their guidance throughout.

The potential loss in dollar value of net revenues earned overseas represents the company's most significant economic and financial exposure.

EXHIBIT 1
MERCK SALES INDEX

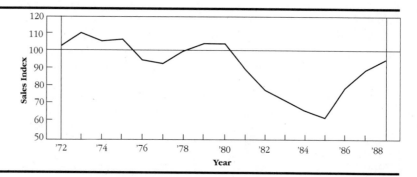

IDENTIFICATION AND MEASUREMENT OF EXPOSURE

It is generally agreed that foreign exchange fluctuations can affect a U.S. company's economic and financial results in three ways:

1. By changing the dollar value of net assets held overseas in foreign currencies (known as "translation" exposures) or by changing the expected results of transactions in non-local currencies ("transaction" exposures).

2. By changing the dollar value of future revenues expected to be earned overseas in foreign currencies ("future revenue" exposures).

3. By changing a company's competitive position—for example, a competitor whose costs are denominated in a depreciating currency will have greater pricing flexibility and thus a potential competitive advantage ("competitive" exposures).

Competitive exposures have been the subject of much of the recent academic work done on exchange risk management. Such exposures are best exemplified by the adverse effect of the strong dollar on the competitive position of much of U.S. industry in the early 1980s. This was true not only in export markets but also in the U.S. domestic market, where the strengthening U.S. dollar gave Japanese and European-based manufacturers a large competitive advantage in dollar terms over domestic U.S. producers.

For the pharmaceutical industry, however, the pricing environment is such that competitive exposure to exchange fluctuations is generally not significant. The existence of price controls through-out most of the world generally reduces flexibility to react to economic changes.

Hence, Merck's exposure to exchange tends to be limited primarily to net asset and revenue exposures. The potential loss in dollar value of net revenues earned overseas represents the company's most significant economic and financial exposure. Such revenues are continuously converted into dollars through interaffiliate merchandise payments, dividends, and royalties, and are an important source of cash flow for the company. To the extent the dollar value of these earnings is diminished, the company suffers a loss of cash flow—at least over the short term. And, as discussed in more detail later, the resulting volatility in earnings and cash flow could impair the company's ability to execute its strategic plan for growth.

With its significant presence worldwide, Merck has exposures in approximately 40 currencies. As a first step in assessing the effect of exchange rate movements on revenues and net income, we constructed a sales index that measures the relative strength of the dollar against a basket of currencies weighted by the size of sales in those countries.[1] When the index is above 100%, foreign currencies have strengthened versus the dollar, indicating a positive exchange effect on dollar revenues. When the index is below 100%, as was the case through most of the 1980s, the dollar has strengthened versus the foreign currencies, resulting in income statement losses due to exchange.

As Exhibit 1 illustrates, the index was relatively stable from 1972 to 1980. But, as the dollar strengthened in the early 1980s, the index declined to the

---

1. The index uses 1978 as its base year. The currency basket excludes hyperinflationary markets where exchange devaluation is measured net of price increases.

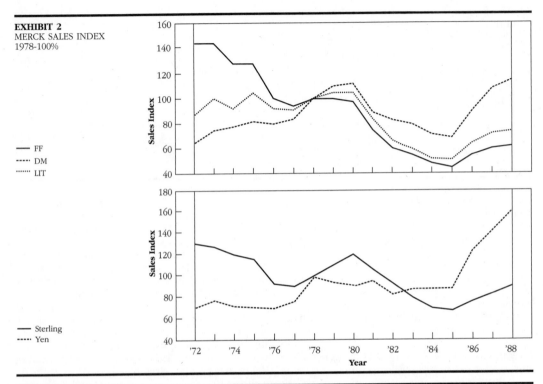

EXHIBIT 2
MERCK SALES INDEX
1978-100%

— FF
---- DM
······ LIT

— Sterling
---- Yen

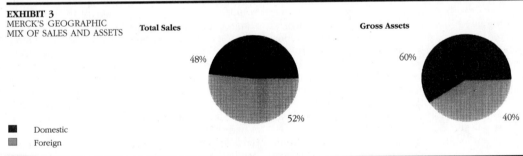

EXHIBIT 3
MERCK'S GEOGRAPHIC
MIX OF SALES AND ASSETS

Total Sales

48%

52%

Gross Assets

60%

40%

■ Domestic
▨ Foreign

60% level, resulting in a cumulative exchange reduction in sales of approximately $900 million. But, then, as the dollar weakened in the later 1980s, the index increased to roughly 97%, returning to its 1972-1980 range.

But, as Exhibit 2 also shows, although the overall index returned as of 1988 to the earlier range, not all currencies have moved together against the dollar. The strengthening in the yen and the deutschemark

has offset the decline of historically weaker currencies such as the Italian lira and French franc, while the British pound is very near 1978 levels.

RESOURCE ALLOCATION

Given the significant exchange exposure of our net overseas revenues as reflected by our experience in early 1980s, we next decided to review the company's global allocation of resources across currencies and, in the process, to determine the extent to which revenues and costs were matched in individual currencies. Our analysis (the main findings of which are illustrated in Exhibit 3) revealed that the distribution of Merck's assets differs somewhat from the sales mix, primarily because of the concentration of research, manufacturing, and headquarters operations in the U.S.

On the basis of this analysis, it was clear that Merck has an exchange rate mismatch. To reduce this mismatch, we first considered the possibility of redeploying resources in order to shift dollar costs to a different currency. This process would have involved relocating manufacturing sites, research sites, and employees such as headquarters and support staff. We soon reached the conclusion, however, that because so few support functions seemed appropriate candidates for relocation a move would have had only a negligible effect on our global income exposure. In short, we decided that shifting people and resources overseas was not a cost-effective way of dealing with our exchange exposure.

HEDGING MERCK'S EXPOSURES WITH FINANCIAL INSTRUMENTS

Having concluded that resource deployment was not an appropriate way for Merck to address exchange risk, we considered the alternative of financial hedging. Thinking through this alternative involved the following five steps:

1. Exchange Forecasts. Review of the likelihood of adverse exchange movements.

2. Strategic Plan Impact. Quantification of the potential impact of adverse exchange movements over the period of the plan.

3. Hedging Rationale. Critical examination of the reasons for hedging (perhaps the most important part of the process).

4. Financial Instruments. Selection of which instruments to use and how to execute the hedge.

5. Hedging Program. Simulation of alternative strategies to choose the most cost-effective hedging strategy to accommodate our risk tolerance profile (an ongoing process supported by a mathematical model we have recently developed to supplement our earlier analysis).

STEP 1: Projecting Exchange Rate Volatility

Our review of the probability of future exchange rate movements was guided by four main considerations:

(1) The major factors expected to affect exchange rates over the strategic plan period—for example, the U.S. trade deficit, capital flows, the U.S. budget deficit—all viewed in the context of the concept of an "equilibrium" exchange rate.

(2) Target zones or government policies designed to manage exchange rates. To what extent will government policies be implemented to dampen exchange rate volatility, particularly "overshooting," in the future?

(3) Development of possible ranges for dollar strength or weakness over the planning period.

(4) Summary of outside forecasters—a number of forecasters were polled on the outlook for the dollar over the plan period.

Our review of outside forecasters showed they were almost evenly split on the dollar's outlook. Although almost no one predicted a return to the extremes of the early 1980s, we nonetheless concluded that there was a potential for a relatively large move in either direction.

We developed a simple method for quantifying the potential ranges that reflects the following thought process:

■ Except for 1986, the upper limit of the year-to-year move in average exchange rates for the deutschemark and the yen has been about 20%. We used this as the measure of potential volatility in developing the probabilistic ranges in the forecast. (The deutschemark, incidentally, was used as a proxy for all European currencies.)

■ The widest ranges would likely result from one-directional movements—that is, 5 years of continued strengthening or weakening.

■ However, as the effect of each year's movement is felt in the economy and financial markets, the probability of exchange rates' continuing in the same direction is lessened. For example, if the dollar were to weaken, the favorable effects on the trade balance and on relative asset values would likely induce increased capital flows and cause a turnaround.

Based in part on this concept of exchange rate movements as a "mean-reverting" process, we developed ranges of expected rate movements (as shown in Exhibit 4) by assigning probabilities to the dollar continuing to move along a line of consecu-

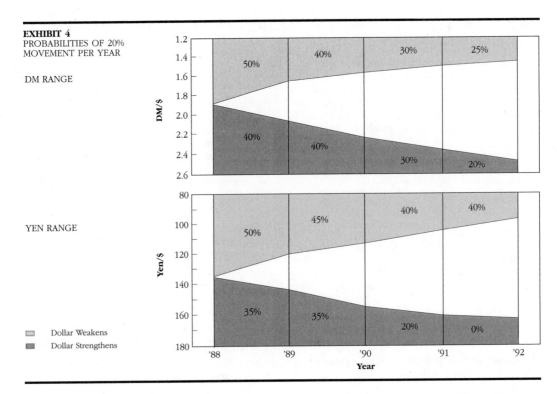

EXHIBIT 4
PROBABILITIES OF 20%
MOVEMENT PER YEAR

DM RANGE

YEN RANGE

☐ Dollar Weakens
■ Dollar Strengthens

tive years' strengthening or weakening. For example, the dollar was considered to have a 40% probability of strengthening by 20% versus the DM in 1989. If the dollar does appreciate by 20% in 1989, then we also assume that the probability of its strengthening by a further 20% in 1990 is also 40%, but that the chance of this pattern continuing in 1991 is only 30% and falls to 20% in 1992.

Such ranges represent our best guess about the likely boundaries of dollar strength or weakness. The actual probability of exchange rate movements reaching or exceeding these boundaries is small, but the use of such extreme rates allows us to estimate the extent of our exposure. These exchange boundaries were also used in quantifying the potential impact of unfavorable exchange rate movements on our Strategic Plan.

STEP 2: Assessing the Impact on the 5-Year Strategic Plan

To assess the potential effect of unfavorable exchange rates, we converted our Strategic Plan into U.S. dollars on an exchange neutral basis (that is, at the current exchange rate) and compared these cash flow and earnings projections to those we expected to materialize under both our strong dollar and weak dollar scenarios. (See Exhibit 5.)

Further, we measured the potential impact of exchange rate movements on a cumulative basis as well as according to the year-to-year convention that is standard in external reporting. Exhibit 6 shows the effect of translating the year-to-year data from Exhibit 5 on a cumulative basis. (The total bar represents the cumulative variance, while the top portion represents the variance as determined by the change in rates from one period to the next.) Because it looks beyond a one-year period, the cumulative exchange variance provides a more useful estimate of the size of the exchange risk associated with Merck's long-range plan. Use of a cumulative measure also provides the basis for the kind of multi-year financial hedging program that, as we eventually determined, is appropriate for hedging multi-year income flows.

Although exchange fluctuations clearly can have material effects on reported accounting earnings, it is not clear that exchange-related fluctuations in earnings have significant effects on stock price.

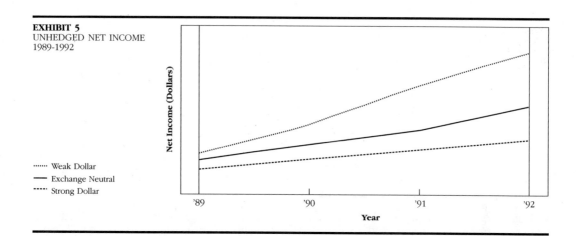

EXHIBIT 5
UNHEDGED NET INCOME
1989-1992

Net Income (Dollars)

······ Weak Dollar
——— Exchange Neutral
- - - - Strong Dollar

'89   '90   '91   '92

Year

EXHIBIT 6
EXCHANGE IMPACT
STRONG DOLLAR
SCENARIO

DM 2.45
DM 2.35
DM 2.21
DM/$
DM 2.03
DM 1.87

'88   '89   '90   '91   '92

Year

Total Bar represents cumulative exchange impact. Shaded area represents year-on-year impact.

STEP 3: Deciding Whether to Hedge the Exposure

Over the long term, foreign exchange rate movements have been—and are likely to continue to be—a problem of volatility in year-to-year earnings rather than one of irreversible losses. For example, most of the income statement losses of the early 1980s were recouped in the following three years. The question of whether or not to hedge exchange risk thus becomes a question of the company's own risk profile with respect to interim volatility in earnings and cash flows.

The desirability of reducing earnings volatility due to exchange can be examined from both external and internal perspectives.

External Concerns. These center on the perspective of capital markets, and accordingly involve matters such as share price, investor clientele effects, and maintenance of dividend policy. Although exchange fluctuations clearly can have material effects on reported accounting earnings, it is not clear that exchange-related fluctuations in earnings have significant effects on stock price. Our own analysis (as illustrated in Exhibit 7) suggests only a modest correlation in recent years between exchange gains and losses and share price movements, and a slight relationship in the strong dollar period—the scenario of greatest concern to us.

Industry analysts' reports, moreover, tend to support our analysis by arguing that exchange gains and losses are at most a second-order factor in determining the share prices of pharmaceutical companies. While invariably stressing the importance of new products as perhaps the most critical share price variable, analysts

**The key factors that would support hedging against exchange volatility are...
the large proportion of the company's overseas earnings and cash flows; and the
potential effect of cash flow volatility on our ability to execute our strategic plan.**

EXHIBIT 7
TRADE WEIGHTED
DOLLAR VERSUS
DRUG INDEX

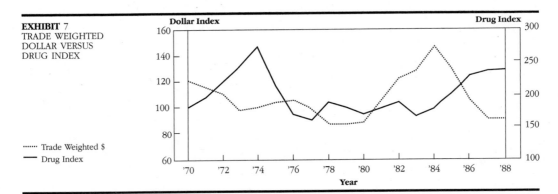

····· Trade Weighted $
—— Drug Index

also often comment on the regulated price environment overseas (which, as we pointed out earlier, limits competitive exposure by reducing the effect of exchange changes on sales volume).[2]

With respect to investor clientele, exchange would seem to have mixed effects. To the extent that some investors—especially overseas investors—see Merck's stock as an opportunity for speculating on a weak dollar, hedging would be contrary to investors' interests. But, for investors seeking a "pure play" on the stocks of ethical drug companies, significant exchange risk could be undesirable. Thus, given this potential conflict of motives among investors, and recognizing our inability to ascertain the preferences of all of Merck's investor clienteles (potential as well as current), we concluded that it would be inappropriate to give too much weight to any specific type of investor.

On the issue of dividend policy, we came to a somewhat different conclusion. Maintaining Merck's dividend, while probably not the most important determinant of our share price, is nevertheless viewed by management as an important means of expressing our confidence in the company's prospective earnings growth. It is our way of reassuring investors that we expect our large investment in future research (funded primarily by retained earnings) to provide requisite returns. And, although both Merck and the industry in general were able to maintain dividend rates during the strong dollar period, we were concerned about the company's ability to maintain a policy of dividend *growth*

during a future dollar strengthening. Because Merck's (and other pharmaceutical companies') dividend growth rates did indeed decline during the strong dollar 1981-1985 period, the effect of future dollar strengthening on company cash flows could well constrain future dividend growth. So, in considering whether to hedge our income against future exchange movements, we chose to give some weight to the desirability of maintaining growth in the dividend.

In general, then, we concluded that although our exchange hedging policy should consider capital market perspectives (especially dividend policy), it should not be dictated by them. The direct effect of exchange fluctuations on shareholder value, if any, is unclear; and it thus seemed a better course to concentrate on the objective of maximizing long-term cash flows and to focus on the potential effect of exchange rate movements on our ability to meet our internal objectives. Such actions, needless to say, are ultimately intended to maximize returns for our stockholders.

Internal Concerns. From the perspective of management, the key factors that would support hedging against exchange volatility are the following two: (1) the large proportion of the company's overseas earnings and cash flows; and (2) the potential effect of cash flow volatility on our ability to execute our strategic plan—particularly, to make the investments in R & D that furnish the basis for future growth. The pharmaceutical industry has a very long planning horizon, one which reflects the complexity

---

2. Some analysts have also claimed to detect an inverse relationship between drug stock prices and inflation that also acts to reduce currency exposure. Drug stocks, as this reasoning goes, are growth stocks and generally benefit from low inflation because the discount factor used to price growth stocks declines under low inflation which increases shareholder value. Likewise a high inflation environment will depress share prices for growth stocks. Since generally high inflation leads to a weaker dollar, the negative impact of high inflation would over time limit the positive effect of a weaker dollar and the reverse would also be true.

In the current competitive environment, success in the industry requires a continuous, long-term commitment to a steadily increasing level of research funding...the cash flow and earnings uncertainty caused by exchange rate volatility leads to a reduction of growth in research spending.

EXHIBIT 8
ALTERNATVE HEDGING
INSTRUMENTS

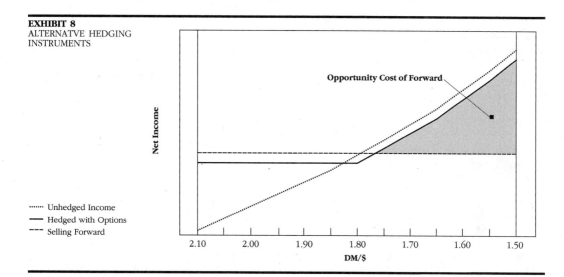

of the research involved as well as the lengthy process of product registration. It often takes more than 10 years between the discovery of a product and its market launch. In the current competitive environment, success in the industry requires a continuous, long-term commitment to a steadily increasing level of research funding.

Given the cost of research and the subsequent challenges of achieving positive returns, companies such as Merck require foreign sales in addition to U.S. sales to generate a level of income that supports continued research and business operations. The U.S. market alone is not large enough to support the level of our research effort. Because foreign sales are subject to exchange volatility, the dollar equivalent of worldwide sales can be very unstable. Uncertainty can make it very difficult to justify high levels of U.S. based-research when the firm cannot effectively estimate the pay-offs from its research. Our experience, and that of the industry in general, has been that the cash flow and earnings uncertainty caused by exchange rate volatility leads to a reduction of growth in research spending.

Such volatility can also result in periodic reductions of corporate spending necessary to expand markets and maintain supportive capital expenditures. In the early 1980s, for example, capital expenditures by Merck and other leading U.S. pharmaceutical companies experienced a reduction in rate of growth similar to that in R & D.

Our conclusion, then, was that we should take action to reduce the potential impact of exchange volatility on future cash flows. Reduction of such volatility removes an important element of uncertainty confronting the strategic management of the company.

STEP 4: Selecting the Appropriate Financial Instruments

While we will not discuss the various hedging techniques in detail, we do wish to share the thought processes that led us to choose currency options as our risk management tool. Our objective was to select the most cost-effective hedging instrument that accommodated the company's risk preferences.

Forward foreign exchange contracts, foreign currency debt, and currency swaps all effectively fix the value of the amount hedged regardless of currency movements. With the use of options, by contrast, the hedging firm retains the opportunity to benefit from natural positions—albeit at a cost equal to the premium paid for the option. As illustrated in Exhibit 8, under a strong dollar scenario (based on 1988 spot rates and forward points), Merck would prefer a forward sale because the contract would produce the same gains as the option but without incurring the cost of the option premium. But, under the weak dollar scenario, both the unhedged and the option positions would be preferred to hedging with the forward contract.

A certain level of option premiums could be justified as the cost of an insurance policy designed to preserve our ability to carry through with our strategic plan.

Given the possibility of exchange rate movements in either direction, we were unwilling to forgo the potential gains if the dollar weakened; so options were strictly preferred. We also concluded, moreover, that a certain level of option premiums could be justified as the cost of an insurance policy designed to preserve our ability to carry through with our strategic plan.[3]

STEP 5: Constructing a Hedging Program

Having selected currency options as our hedging vehicle and designated the 5-year period of our strategic plan as our hedging horizon, we then considered several implementation strategies, including:

Varying the term of the hedge. That is, using year-by-year rather than multi-year hedging.

Varying the strike price of the foreign exchange options. For example, out-of-the-money options were considered as a means of reducing costs.

Varying the amount. That is, different percentages of income could be covered, again, to control costs.

After simulating the outcome of alternative strategies under various exchange rate scenarios we came to the following decisions: (1) we would hedge for a multi-year period, using long-term options to protect our strategic cash flow; (2) we would not use far-out-of-the-money options to reduce costs; and (3) we would hedge only on a partial basis and, in effect, self-insure for the remainder.

We continue to refine this decision through our use of increasingly more sophisticated modeling. Recognizing this as a quantitative process whereby decisions can be improved by application of better techniques, Merck has been developing (with the guidance of Professor Darrell Duffie of Stanford University) a state-of-the-art computer model that simulates the effectiveness of a variety of strategies for hedging. The model is a Monte Carlo simulation package that presents probability distributions of unhedged and hedged foreign income for future periods (the shortest of which are quarters). By so doing, it allows us to visualize the effect of any given hedging policy on our periodic cash flows, thus permitting better-informed hedging decisions.

The model has six basic components:

1. Security Pricing Models: State-of-the-art financial analytics are used to calculate theoretical prices for various securities such as bonds, futures, forwards, and options.[4]

2. Hedging Policy: We can specify a variety of hedging policies, with each representing a portfolio of securities to buy or sell in each quarter. The number of hedging policies is essentially unlimited, reflecting a variety of hedge ratios, proxy currencies, accounting constraints, security combinations, etc. For example, the model permits us to compare a hedging program of purchasing options that cover the exposures of the 5-year planning period and holding them until maturity with the alternative of a dynamic portfolio revision strategy. A dynamic hedge would involve not only the initial purchase of options, but a continuous process of buying and selling additional options based on interim changes in exchange rates.

3. Foreign Income Generator: Before simulating changes in hedging policy, however, we start by building our strategic plan forecast of local currency earnings into the model. The model then generates random earnings by quarter according to a specified model of forecast projections and random forecast errors. This process provides us with an estimate of the variability of local currency earnings and thereby allows us to reflect possible variations versus plan forecasts with greater accuracy.

4. Exchange Rate Dynamics: The model uses a Monte Carlo simulator to generate random exchange rates by quarter. The simulator allows us to adjust currency volatilities, rates of reversion, long-term exchange rates, and coefficients of correlation among currencies. We can test the sensitivity of the simulator to stronger or weaker dollar exchange rates by modifying the inputs. We can also use the Monte Carlo simulation package to re-examine the development of exchange scenarios and ranges described earlier.[5]

3. It was also recognized that to the extent hedge accounting could be applied to purchased options, this represents an advantage over other foreign currency instruments. The accounting ramifications of mark-to-market versus hedge accounting were, and remain, an important issue and we have continued to monitor developments with respect to the ongoing controversy over accounting for currency options.

4. In pricing options, we have the choice of using the Black-Scholes model or an alternative highly advanced valuation model. These models provide reasonably reliable estimates of the expected true cost, including transaction fees, of the option program. Although Black-Scholes is the predominant pricing model in pricing many kinds of options, alternative models appear to have an advantage in the pricing of long-dated currency options. Black-Scholes implicitly assumes that the volatility of exchange rates grows exponentially with time to maturity. Generally speaking, the further out the expiry date, the higher the price. The alternative model has a sophisticated approach in its assumption of a dampened exponential relationship between time to maturity, expected volatility, and price. For this reason, in the case of long-dated options, the Black-Scholes model generally overstates option prices relative to the alternative model.

5. The model will also have the ability to simulate historic exchange trends. The model will have access to a large database of historic exchange rates. We will be able to analyze the impact of hedging on a selected time period, for example, the strong dollar period of the 1980s. Or, we can have the model randomly select exchange rate movements from a historical period, resulting in a Monte Carlo simulation of that period.

The simulator allows us to analyze a wide range (in fact, an infinite number) of exchange scenarios, hedging policies, and security combinations.

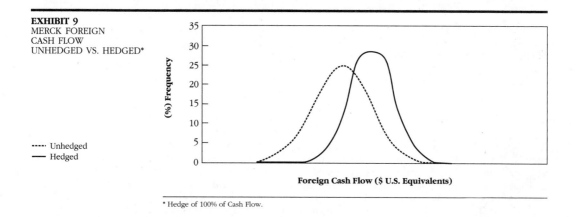

EXHIBIT 9
MERCK FOREIGN
CASH FLOW
UNHEDGED VS. HEDGED*

(%) Frequency

Foreign Cash Flow ($ U.S. Equivalents)

····· Unhedged
—— Hedged

* Hedge of 100% of Cash Flow.

5. Cash Flow Generator: The model collects information from each of the above four components so as to calculate total cash flow in U.S. dollars by quarter for each random scenario.

6. Statistical and Graphical Output: The quarterly cash flow information for each of a large number of scenarios is collected and displayed graphically in frequency plots, and in terms of statistics such as means, standard deviations, and confidence levels. Exhibit 9 provides an example of the graphical output from our simulator, comparing distributions of unhedged and hedged cash flows. In this case, the hedged curve assumes 100% of Merck's exposure has been covered through the purchase of foreign currency options. Given the pattern of exchange rate movements simulated, the hedging strategy has shifted the hedged cash flow distribution to the right, cutting off a portion of unfavorable outcomes. In addition, the hedged cash flow distribution has a higher mean value as well as a lower standard deviation. Therefore, in this scenario hedging would be preferable to not hedging, resulting in higher returns as well as lower risk. (Again, of course, the trade-off is the initial cost of the option premiums that would have to be bal-

anced against the improved risk/return pattern.) Other scenarios may indicate that a lower hedge ratio or not hedging is the preferred strategy.

In sum, the model provides Merck with a powerful tool to determine the optimal strategy for reducing our exposure to foreign currency risk. The simulator allows us to analyze a wide range (in fact, an infinite number) of exchange scenarios, hedging policies, and security combinations. This in turn gives us the ability to select the hedging policy that is both cost-effective and consistent with our desired risk profile.

CONCLUSION

Identifying a company's exchange risk and reaching a decision with respect to what action, if any, should be taken requires extensive analysis. We believe that, as a result of this kind of analysis of Merck's currency exposures, we have developed an appropriate financial hedging plan—one that provides management with what amounts to an insurance policy against the potentially damaging effect of currency volatility on the company's ability to carry out its strategic plan. We continue to refine the actual implementation process as we move forward.

THEORY OF RISK CAPITAL IN FINANCIAL FIRMS

by Robert C. Merton and André F. Perold, Harvard Business School*

T his paper develops a concept of risk capital that can be applied to the financing, capital budgeting, and risk management decisions of financial firms. The development focuses particularly on firms that act as a *principal* in the ordinary course of business. Principal activities can be asset-related, as in the case of lending and block-positioning; liability-related, as in deposit-taking and writing of guarantees (including insurance, letters of credit, and other contingent commitments); or both, as in the writing of swaps and other derivatives for customers.

For the purposes of this paper, principal financial firms have three important distinguishing features. The first is that their customers can be major liabilityholders; for example, policyholders, depositors, and swap counterparties are all liabilityholders as well as customers. By definition, a financial firm's customers strictly prefer to have the payoffs on their contracts as unaffected as possible by the fortunes of the issuing firm. Hence, they strongly prefer firms of high credit quality. Investors, by contrast, expect their returns to be affected by the profits and losses of the firm. Hence, they are less credit-sensitive provided, of course, they are compensated appropriately for risk. This means that A-rated firms, for example, can generally raise the funds they need to operate, but are at a disadvantage in competing with AAA-rated firms in businesses such as underwriting

insurance or issuing swaps. The presence of credit-sensitive customers thus greatly increases the importance of risk control of the overall balance sheet.[1]

A second distinguishing feature of principal firms is their *opaqueness* to customers and investors.[2] That is, the detailed asset holdings and business activities of the firm are not publicly disclosed (or, if disclosed, only with a considerable lag in time). Furthermore, principal financial firms typically have relatively liquid balance sheets that, in the course of only weeks, can and often do undergo a substantial change in size and risk.[3] Unlike manufacturing firms, principal financial firms can enter, exit, expand, or contract individual businesses quickly at relatively low cost. These are changes that customers and investors cannot easily monitor. Moreover, financial businesses—even non-principal businesses like mutual-fund management—are susceptible to potentially enormous "event risk" in areas not easily predictable or understood by outsiders.[4]

All of this implies that principal firms will generally experience high "agency" and "information" costs in raising equity capital and in executing various types of customer transactions.[5] (We later refer to these "dissipative" or "deadweight" costs collectively as *economic costs of risk capital*, in a manner to be made more precise.) Risk management by the firm is an important element in controlling these costs.

---

*An earlier version appears as "Management of Risk Capital in Financial Firms" in Samuel L. Hayes, III (1993), ed., *Financial Services: Perspectives and Challenges*, Boston: Harvard Business School Press: 215-245.

1. For an elaboration on the difference between "customers" and "investors" of the financial-service firm as a core concept, see Robert C. Merton, (1992), *Continuous-Time Finance*, Revised Edition, Oxford: Basil Blackwell; R.C. Merton (1993), "Operation and Regulation in Financial Intermediation: A Functional Perspective," in Peter Englund, ed., *Operation and Regulation of Financial Markets*, Stockholm: The Economic Council: 17-67; and R.C. Merton and Zvi Bodie, "On the Management of Financial Guarantees," *Financial Management*, 21 (Winter, 1992): 87-109.

2. The notion of "opaqueness" of financial institutions is developed by Stephen Ross in "Institutional Markets, Financial Marketing, and Financial Innovation," *Journal of Finance*, 44 (July, 1989): 541-556. For further discussion, see Merton (1993), cited in note 1.

3. As reported in *The Wall Street Journal*, October 24, 1991, the investment bank of Salomon Brothers reduced its total assets or "footings" by $50 billion in a period of approximately 40 days.

4. For example, consider the potentially large exposures from the "scandals" at E.F. Hutton (check writing), Merrill Lynch ("ticket in drawer"), Salomon Brothers (Treasury auction), Drexel Burnham Lambert (FIRREA/collapse of high-yield debt market), and T. Rowe Price Associates (money-market-fund credit loss).

5. For detailed development and review of the literature on asymmetric information and agency theory in a financial market context, see Amir Barnea, Robert Haugen, and Lemma Senbet (1985), *Agency Problems and Financial Contracting*, Englewood Cliffs, NJ: Prentice Hall; Michael Jensen, (1986), "Agency Costs of Free Cash Flow, Corporate Finance, and Takeovers," *American Economic Review*, 76 (May): 323-329, and especially N. Strong and M. Walker (1987), *Information and Capital Markets*, Oxford: Basil Blackwell.

A third distinguishing feature of principal financial firms is that they operate in competitive financial markets. Their profitability is thus highly sensitive to their cost of capital, and especially their cost of risk capital. Allocating the costs of risk capital to individual businesses or projects is a problem for organizations that operate in a more or less decentralized fashion. As we shall discuss, there is no simple way to do so. Moreover, any allocation must necessarily be *imputed*, if only because highly risky principal transactions often require little or no up-front expenditure of cash.

For example, an underwriting commitment can be executed with no immediate cash expenditure. However, the customer counterparty would not enter into the agreement if it did not believe that the underwriting commitment would be met. The commitment made by the underwriting business is backed by the entire firm. Therefore, the strength of this guarantee is measured by the overall credit standing of the firm. The problem of capital allocation within the firm is thus effectively the problem of correctly charging for the guarantees provided by the firm to its constituent businesses.

These three distinctive features of principal financial firms—credit-sensitivity of customers, high costs of risk capital (resulting from their opaqueness), and high sensitivity of profitability to the cost of risk capital—should all be taken into account explicitly by such firms when deciding which activities to enter (or exit), how to finance those activities, and whether to hedge its various market or price exposures.

What Is Risk Capital? We define *risk capital* as *the smallest amount that can be invested to insure the value of the firm's net assets against a loss in value relative to the risk-free investment of those net assets.* By *net assets*, we mean gross assets minus customer liabilities (valued as if these liabilities are default-free). Customer liabilities can be simple fixed liabilities such as guaranteed insurance contracts (GICs), or complex contingent liabilities such as property and casualty insurance policies. With fixed customer liabilities, the riskiness of net assets (as measured, for example, by the standard deviation of their change in value) is the same as the riskiness of gross assets. With contingent customer liabilities, however, the riskiness of net assets depends not only on the riskiness of gross assets, but also on the riskiness of customer liabilities and the covariance between changes in the value of gross

assets and changes in the value of customer liabilities. The volatility of the change in the value of net assets is the most important determinant of the amount of risk capital.

As defined, risk capital differs from both *regulatory capital*, which attempts to measure risk capital according to a particular accounting standard, and from *cash capital*, which represents the up-front cash required to execute a transaction. Cash capital is a component of *working capital* that includes financing of operating expenses like salaries and rent. Cash capital can be large, as with the purchase of physical securities—or small, as with futures contracts and repurchase agreements—or even negative, as with the writing of insurance.

The organization of the paper is as follows. In the next section, a series of examples is presented to show that the amount of risk capital depends only on the riskiness of net assets, and not at all on the form of financing of the net assets. These examples further establish how risk capital funds, provided mainly by the firm's shareholders (except in the case of extremely highly leveraged firms), are then either implicitly or explicitly used to purchase asset insurance from various sources. Besides third-party guarantors, other potential issuers of asset insurance to the firm are the firm's stakeholders, including customers, debtholders, and shareholders.

We next discuss how standard methods of accounting can fail to measure risk capital and its associated costs correctly in the calculation of firm profitability, and how this can lead to an overstatement of profitability. The economic costs of risk capital to the firm are shown to be the "spreads" on the price of asset insurance arising from information costs (adverse selection and moral hazard) and agency costs. We then use this framework to establish the implications for hedging and risk-management decisions.

Finally, for multi-business firms, we discuss the problems that arise in trying to allocate the risk capital of the firm among its individual businesses. It is shown that, for a given configuration, the risk capital of a multi-business firm is less than the aggregate risk capital of the businesses on a stand-alone basis. Therefore, full allocation of risk capital across the individual businesses of the firm is generally not feasible, and attempts at such a full allocation can significantly distort the true profitability of individual businesses.

MEASURING RISK CAPITAL

We now use a series of hypothetical but concrete examples to illustrate the concept of risk capital. In the first set of examples, there are no customer liabilities, so that gross assets equal net assets. After that, we consider two cases with customer liabilities, one with fixed liabilities and the other with contingent liabilities.

Consider the hypothetical newly-formed firm of Merchant Bank, Inc., a wholly owned subsidiary of a large AAAA-rated[6] conglomerate. The firm currently has no assets. Merchant Bank's one and only deal this year will be a $100 million participation in a one-year bridge loan promising 20% interest ($120 million total payment at maturity). It does not plan to issue any customer liabilities. Merchant Bank's net assets will thus consist of this single bridge loan.

The bridge loan is a risky asset. We assume in particular that there are only three possible scenarios: A likely "anticipated" scenario, in which the loan pays off in full the promised $120 million; an unlikely "disaster" scenario, in which the borrower defaults but at maturity the lender recovers 50 cents on the dollar—that is, collects $60 million; and a rare "catastrophe" scenario, in which the lender recovers nothing.

To invest in the bridge loan requires $100 million of *cash* capital. Because this asset is risky, the firm also needs risk capital.

Merchant Bank wants to finance the cash capital by means of a one-year note issued to an outside investor. The firm wants the note to be default free. If these terms can be arranged, then at the current riskless rate of 10%, $110 million would be owed the noteholder at maturity.

In general, a firm has essentially two ways to eliminate the default risk of its debt liabilities. Both involve the purchase of insurance: The first is to do so indirectly through the purchase of insurance on its *assets*; the second and more direct method is to purchase insurance on its (debt) *liabilities*. (Combinations of these would also work.) As we shall see, the two are economically equivalent. The risk capital of the firm is equal to the smallest investment that can be made to obtain complete default-free financing of its net assets.

Risk Capital and Asset Guarantees. Suppose that Merchant Bank buys insurance on the bridge loan from a AAAA-rated bond insurer. Suppose further that, for $5 million, Merchant Bank can obtain insurance just sufficient to guarantee a return of $110 million on the bridge loan.[7] With this asset insurance in place, the value of Merchant Bank's assets at the end of the year will equal or exceed $110 million. The noteholders of Merchant Bank are thus assured of receiving the full payment of their interest and principal, and the note will be default-free.

It follows from the definition of risk capital that the price of the loan insurance ($5 million) is precisely the amount of risk capital Merchant Bank requires if it holds the bridge loan. Merchant Bank would need to fund it with a $5 million cash equity investment from its parent. Once these transactions have been completed, Merchant Bank's accounting balance sheet will be as follows:

ACCOUNTING BALANCE SHEET A

Bridge loan	$100	Note (default free)	$100
Loan insurance	5	Shareholder equity	5
(from insurance company)			

If the bridge loan pays off as promised at the end of the year, Merchant Bank will be able to return a total of $10 million pre-tax to its parent ($20 million in interest income less $10 million in interest expense). If the bridge loan defaults, the asset insurance covers any shortfall up to $110 million, and Merchant Bank will just be able to meet its note obligations. There will be nothing to return to the parent. The risk capital used to purchase the insurance will have been just sufficient to protect the firm from any loss on the underlying asset (including financing expense of the cash capital). And, of course, the risk capital itself will have been lost. In this arrangement, the insurance company bears the risk of the asset; Merchant Bank's parent as shareholder bears the risk of loss of the risk capital itself.

The payoffs (cash flows) at maturity to the various stakeholders in Merchant Bank can be summarized in the following table:

---

6. By "AAAA-rated" we mean a firm with default-free liabilities that without question will stay that way.

7. That is, *full insurance*. The insurance would take the form of paying Merchant Bank the difference between the promised debt payments and actually received cash flows on the bridge loan.

Risk capital differs from both *regulatory capital*, which attempts to measure risk capital according to a particular accounting standard, and from *cash capital*, which represents the up-front cash required to execute a transaction.

TABLE A: PAYOFF STRUCTURE

Bridge Loan	Loan Insurance	Bridge Loan + Insurance	Firm Stakeholders Note	Firm Stakeholders Shareholder
ANTICIPATED SCENARIO				
120	0	120	110	10
DISASTER SCENARIO				
60	50	110	110	0
CATASTROPHE SCENARIO				
0	110	110	110	0

Note that, in this example, Merchant Bank's accounting balance sheet corresponds to what we shall call the firm's *risk-capital balance sheet*:

RISK-CAPITAL BALANCE SHEET A

Bridge loan	$100	Note (default free)	$100
Loan insurance	5	Risk capital	5
(from insurance company)			

By inspection of the two balance sheets, "shareholder equity" is equal to the firm's risk capital, and the non-equity liabilities are default free. We shall see, however, that the accounting and risk-capital balance sheets are in general quite different.

Risk Capital and Liability Guarantees. A parent guarantee of the note is an alternative, and perhaps the most common, form of credit enhancement for the debt of a subsidiary such as Merchant Bank.[8] This way, the parent makes no cash equity investment in Merchant Bank. At the outset, the firm's accounting balance sheet is as follows:

ACCOUNTING BALANCE SHEET B

Bridge loan	$100	Note (default free)	$100
		Shareholder equity	0

Here Merchant Bank again obtains the necessary $100 million in cash capital through issuance of a default-free note; however, all asset risk is now borne by the parent. Thus the risk capital is merely taking the form of the parent guarantee of the note. This guarantee is an additional asset of the subsid-

iary—one that does not appear on its balance sheet. Suppose that the value of this guarantee is worth $G million. Then the parent's (off-balance-sheet) equity investment in Merchant Bank is worth $G million, and Merchant Bank's balance sheet can be restated in terms of its risk-capital balance sheet as follows:[9]

RISK-CAPITAL BALANCE SHEET B

Bridge loan	$100	Note (default free)	$100
Note guarantee	G	Risk capital	G
(from parent)			

As in the previous example, if the bridge loan pays off as promised, Merchant Bank will be able to return a total of $10 million pre-tax to its parent ($20 million in interest income less $10 million in interest expense). If the bridge loan defaults, so too will Merchant Bank on its note, and the noteholder either collects any unpaid amounts from the parent, or the parent pays out the promised $110 million and receives back the value of the bridge-loan asset seized; either way the economic effect is the same. Merchant Bank of course will have nothing to return to its parent as equityholder. In this arrangement, the parent bears the risk of the asset as guarantor of its subsidiary's debt; the parent also bears the risk of loss of the risk capital as shareholder of Merchant Bank. Table B summarizes in terms of payoffs at maturity:

TABLE B: PAYOFF STRUCTURE

Bridge Loan	Note sans Guarantee	Note Guarantee	Note + Guarantee	Shareholder
ANTICIPATED SCENARIO				
120	110	0	110	10
DISASTER SCENARIO				
60	60	50	110	0
CATASTROPHE SCENARIO				
0	0	110	110	0

A comparison of Table A and Table B demonstrates the economic equivalence of liability insurance and asset insurance.[10] In both, the noteholder

---

8. This insurance could take the form of the parent either paying the noteholder the $110 million promised payment in the event of default, and then seizing Merchant Bank's assets, or paying the noteholder the difference between the promised payment and actual payments Merchant Bank is able to make. The parent guarantee avoids outside lenders becoming involved in any bankruptcy of the subsidiary, and gives the parent some "choice." For our purposes here, we can abstract from such details of structure.

9. For a real-world application of this "extended" balance-sheet approach to capture the "hidden" asset and corresponding equity investment arising from parent guarantees of its subsidiary's debt, see R.C. Merton, (1983), "Prepared Direct

Testimony of Robert C. Merton on Behalf of ARCO Pipe Line Company," Federal Energy Regulatory Commission, Washington, D.C., Docket No. OR78-1-011 (Phase II), Exhibits II N-C-34-0-34-4 (November 28). For a similar approach to analyze corporate pension assets and liabilities and the firm's guarantee of any shortfall on the pension plan, see Zvi Bodie (1990), "The ABO, the PBO, and Pension Investment Policy," *Financial Analysts Journal*, 46 (September/October): 27-34.

10. This equivalence may not apply exactly if one takes account of the various bankruptcy costs and delays in payments which could occur, for example, if Merchant Bank sought Chapter 11 bankruptcy protection.

bears no risk and the parent, solely in its capacity as shareholder of Merchant Bank, obtains the same cash flows: $10 million in the "anticipated" scenario and zero otherwise. Moreover, the note guarantee has the same cash flows as the bridge-loan insurance. The note guarantee therefore is also worth G = $5 million. Thus, risk capital is once again $5 million.[11]

Liabilities with Default Risk. We now turn to the more typical case where our hypothetical firm, Merchant Bank, is willing to issue liabilities with some default risk. Suppose it issues the same 10% note (promising $110 million at maturity), but without any of the credit enhancements of the previous case. This now risky note will sell at a discount $D to par (at a promised yield to maturity higher than 10%), leaving Merchant Bank $D short of its need for $100 million cash capital. The shortfall in initial funding must be supplied in the form of a cash equity investment. Merchant Bank's beginning balance sheet is as follows:

ACCOUNTING BALANCE SHEET C

| Bridge loan | $100 | Note (risky) | $100 – D |
| | | Shareholder equity | D |

Once again, if the bridge loan pays off as promised, Merchant Bank will be able to pay a total of $10 million pre-tax to its parent.[12] If the bridge loan defaults, so too will Merchant Bank default on its note, and the noteholder will be at risk for any shortfall on the bridge loan under $110 million. Merchant Bank will have nothing to return to its parent.

Merchant Bank's shareholder here receives the same payoffs as it did in the previous examples (see Table C). This economic equivalence implies that the firm's equity must be worth D = $5 million initially. Correspondingly, the risky note will have an initial value of $95 million (with a *promised* yield to maturity of $15 on $95, or 15.8%).

To see where risk capital enters, consider the position of the debtholder. The debtholder can interpret its purchase of the risky note as equivalent to the following three-step transaction: First, the purchase of default-free debt from Merchant Bank for $100 million; second, the sale to Merchant Bank of debt insurance for $5 million; and third, the netting of payments owed the debtholder on the default-free debt against payments owed the firm if the insurance is triggered. It is perhaps easiest to see this by observing the economic identity:[13]

Risky note + note insurance = Default-free note

so that

Risky note = Default-free note – note insurance.

As already shown (in Tables A and B), note insurance is economically equivalent to asset insurance. Thus, the debtholder can interpret its purchase of the risky note as equivalent to the purchase of default-free debt coupled with the *sale* to Merchant Bank of *asset* insurance (on the bridge loan) for $5 million. In other words:

Risky note = Default-free note – asset insurance.

This relation allows the restatement of the accounting balance sheet C in its risk-capital form:

RISK-CAPITAL BALANCE SHEET C

Bridge loan	$100	Note (default free)	$100
Asset insurance	5	Risk capital	5
(from note holder)			

The payoffs at maturity associated with this risk-capital balance sheet are shown in Table C:

TABLE C: PAYOFF STRUCTURE

Bridge Loan	Asset Insurance	Default-free Note	Risky Note = Default-free Note – Asset Insurance	Shareholder
ANTICIPATED SCENARIO				
120	0	110	110	10
DISASTER SCENARIO				
60	50	110	60	0
CATASTROPHE SCENARIO				
0	110	110	0	0

---

11. The assumption that economically-equivalent cash flows have the same value is made only for expositional convenience in this part of the paper. Later in the discussion of the management of risk capital, the assumption is relaxed to take account of differences in information and agency costs among alternative guarantors.

12. $20 million in interest income less $15 million in cash plus amortized interest expense plus $5 million return of capital.

13. For a full development and applications of this identity, see R.C. Merton, (1990), "The Financial System and Economic Performance," *Journal of Financial Services Research*, 4 (December): 263-300; and Merton and Bodie (1992), cited in note 1.

Each of the examples has a different accounting balance sheet. Yet all have very similar risk-capital balance sheets. They have the same amount of risk capital—because the underlying asset requiring the risk capital is the same in all cases.

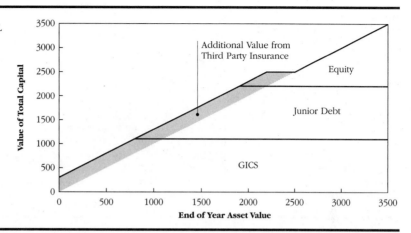

FIGURE 1
PAYOFFS TO FIRM CAPITAL PROVIDERS

Each of the examples (A,B,C) has a different accounting balance sheet. Yet all have very similar risk-capital balance sheets. They have the same amount of risk capital—because the underlying asset requiring the risk capital is the same in all cases. They differ only in which parties bear the risk of insuring the asset: the insurance company (example A), the parent (example B), or the noteholder (example C).

A More General Case. The concept of risk capital is now further expanded by analyzing a more general balance sheet. The goals here are to illustrate the case of fixed customer liabilities and the purchase of asset insurance from multiple sources.

Consider a firm with an investment portfolio of risky assets worth $2.5 billion. The firm has customer liabilities outstanding in the form of one-year guaranteed investment contracts (GICs) promising 10% on their face value of $1 billion. Because the riskless rate is also 10%, the *default-free* value of these customer liabilities is $1 billion. The net assets—equal to assets minus the default-free value of customer liabilities—are thus worth $1.5 billion.

The riskiness of the portfolio is assumed to be such that the price of insurance to permit the portfolio to be financed risklessly for a year is $500 million. Since the customer liabilities are fixed, it follows that the price of insurance to permit the *net* assets to be financed risklessly for a year is also $500

million.[14] Therefore, $500 million is the required risk capital based on a one-year horizon.

The firm's investor financings are in two forms: one-year junior debt promising 10% on its face value of $1 billion and shareholder equity. Thus, the total promised payment on fixed liabilities at the end of the year is $2.2 billion, comprised of $1.1 billion of GICs and $1.1 billion of debt that is junior to the GICs.

Suppose that the firm has formally obtained *partial* insurance on its investment portfolio, arbitrarily chosen to cover the *first* $300 million of decline of value of portfolio value below $2.5 billion. The insurance is thus structured to guarantee the portfolio value at $2.5 billion at year end, but is capped at a maximum payout of $300 million; therefore, the cap will be reached if the portfolio value falls below $2.2 billion. Assume, moreover, that the value of this "third-party" insurance is $200 million. The value of the policy appears as an additional asset on the firm's accounting balance sheet.

Figure 1 shows the payoffs on the various liabilities of the firm depending on the value of the investment portfolio at year end. Because the portfolio is only partially protected from loss by the firm-owned insurance policy, the junior debt and the customer liabilities are both potentially at risk to receive less than their promised payments.

14. By the end of the year, the *gross* assets will have experienced a loss relative to a risk-free investment if they fall below $2,750 million (110% of $2,500 million). The *net* assets will have experienced a loss relative to a risk-free investment if they fall below $1,650 million (110% of $1,500 million). Since year-end net assets always equals year-end gross assets minus $1,100 million, any shortfall in year-end *gross* assets is exactly equal to the shortfall in year-end *net* assets, and vice versa. Therefore, the loss to the insurer of gross assets is identical to the loss to the insurer of net assets, and the prices of the two policies are the same.

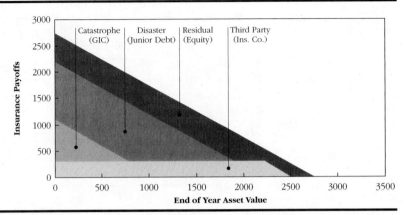

FIGURE 2
COMPONENTS OF ASSET
INSURANCE

[Chart with y-axis "Insurance Payoffs" from 0 to 3000, x-axis "End of Year Asset Value" from 0 to 3500. Labeled regions: Catastrophe (GIC), Disaster (Junior Debt), Residual (Equity), Third Party (Ins. Co.)]

As the senior liability, the GICs are most protected against a decline in the firm's asset values. As shown in Figure 1, customers holding the GICs are at risk only if the value of the firm's portfolio has fallen below $800 million at year end, a decline in value of more than 68%. Accordingly, the GICs trade at only a small percentage discount to par. In our example, we assume that this discount is 1%, thus implying a price of $990 million and a promised yield to maturity of 11% ($110 on $990).

The junior debt is considerably riskier: the holders are exposed to loss if the value of the firm's portfolio falls below $1.9 billion by year end, a decline of about 24%. This debt therefore will trade at a larger discount to par. In our example, we assume that the discount is 10% for a price of $900 million, with a promised yield to maturity of 22.2% ($200 on $900). The value of the firm's equity is equal to $810 million, the difference between the value of total assets ($2.7B) and the market value of customer- and investor-held liabilities ($990 + 900MM). The accounting balance sheet (valuing assets and liabilities at market) is thus as follows:

ACCOUNTING BALANCE SHEET D

Investment portfolio	$2,500	GICs (par $1,000)	$990
"Third-party" insurance	200	Debt (par $1,000)	900
(insurance company)		Equity	810
Total assets	2,700	Total liabilities	2,700

We now construct the risk-capital balance sheet for this firm. As in our earlier discussion of liabilities with default risk, the economic interpretation of the

GIC holders is that, in effect, they have purchased default-free GICs and simultaneously *sold* some asset insurance to the firm, with the two transactions netted against each other. GIC holders are at risk only in the least likely of circumstances, and so they provide a kind of "catastrophe" insurance. As shown in Figures 1 and 2, the catastrophe insurance pays off only if the portfolio value falls by more than 68%. The (implicit) price of this insurance is the discount from the default-free value of the GICs, or $10 million ($1 billion − $990 million). Similarly, the debtholders' position is as if they purchased default-free debt and simultaneously sold the firm asset insurance with a value of $100 million ($1 billion − 900 million). This insurance pays off if the firm's portfolio falls below $1.9 billion, but the maximum payoff is capped at $1.1 billion. The risk to the debtholders is greater than the risk to the GIC holders, but is still relatively small. As illustrated in Figure 2, it is a kind of "disaster" insurance.

We have so far accounted for total premiums of $310 million for asset insurance (third-party ($200mm) + debtholders ($100mm) + GICs ($10mm)). But we know that it takes $500 million in premiums to insure the portfolio fully. Hence, the balance of the insurance representing $190 million in premiums must effectively be provided by the equityholders. Because this insurance covers all the risks not covered by the other kinds of insurance, we call it "residual" insurance. (Figure 2 shows the combination of all sources of asset insurance.)

The total insurance has the same payoff structure as a *put option* on the portfolio with an exercise price equal to the current value of the portfolio ($2.5 billion) plus one year of interest at the riskless rate ($250 million), or $2.75 billion. The aggregate value of this asset insurance, or "put option," is equal to $500 million—as assumed at the outset. This is the risk capital of the firm.[15]

The equityholders can think of their $810 million investment as serving three functions: providing $500 million of default-free cash-capital financing (bringing the total cash capital to $2.5 billion), providing $500 million of risk capital to pay for asset insurance, and selling to the firm a portion of that asset insurance worth $190 million. The equityholders' net cash contribution is $500 plus $500 minus $190 million, which equals $810 million.

The risk-capital balance sheet of the firm is as follows:

RISK-CAPITAL BALANCE SHEET D

Asset portfolio	$2,500	Cash capital (default free)	
		Customers (GICs)	$1,000
Asset insurance		Debtholders	1,000
Equityholders ("residual")	190	Equityholders	500
Insurance Co ("third-party")	200	Total cash capital	2,500
Debtholders ("disaster")	100		
Customers ("catastrophe")	10	Risk capital (Equityholders)	500
Total insurance	500		
Total assets	3,000	Total Capital	3,000

This balance sheet encapsulates three basic functions of capital providers. First, *all provide cash capital*. Second, *all are sellers of asset insurance* to the firm, although in varying degrees. Customers and other senior providers of cash capital are typically sellers of catastrophe type insurance—the kind that is called upon to pay in only the rarest of instances. This level of exposure is typical because customers prefer to have their contract payoffs insensitive to the fortunes of the issuing firm.

Customers will buy contracts from the firm only if they perceive the risk of default on those contracts to be very low. "Mezzanine" debtholders and equityholders are investors who provide cash capital and sell to the firm almost all the insurance not purchased from third-party providers.

The third function is the provision of risk capital, which is the cash required for the purchase of asset insurance. It is almost always performed by equityholders, as in all our illustrations. (Non-equity liabilityholders and other stakeholders in the firm will also be providers of risk capital if the market value of the underlying assets is less than the value of promised liabilities, capitalized at the riskless rate.)

A comparison of the risk-capital balance sheet with the accounting balance sheet thus illustrates that the debt and equity values of the firm need not, and generally will not, sum to the firm's cash capital; nor does the value of the equity necessarily equal the firm's risk capital. Cash capital is determined by the *assets* of the firm. Risk capital is determined by the riskiness of the *net assets* of the firm. Debt and equity, defined in the *institutional* sense, represent the netting of asset insurance against the provision of riskless cash capital and risk capital.

Contingent Customer Liabilities. As mentioned earlier, with contingent customer liabilities, the riskiness of net assets will in general differ from the riskiness of gross assets. The following example illustrates this difference.[16]

Consider again a principal financial firm with no equity, but with liabilities fully guaranteed by a AAAA parent. Suppose the firm issues a contingent liability in the form of a one-year S&P 500 index-linked note that promises to pay $100 million times the total return per dollar on the S&P index over the year. The purchaser of the note is a customer, say, a pension fund, that wants the return on its $100 million portfolio to match exactly that of the S&P 500 stock index. The customer has chosen this method

---

15. An alternative interpretation of the coverage provided by the four sources of insurance is as follows: The equityholders fully insure the gross assets at a level of $2.75 billion by year end, but purchase reinsurance from the insurance company that insures the assets to a level of $2.5 billion by year end. The insurance company in turn purchases reinsurance from the debtholders that insures the gross assets to a level of $1.9 billion by year end. The debtholders then purchase reinsurance from the firm's GIC customers that insures the gross assets to a level of $1.1 billion by year end. Equivalently, this can be expressed in terms of *put options*: The equityholders sell to the firm, for $500 million, a put option on the gross assets with exercise price $2.75 billion. They in turn spend $310 million of the $500 million proceeds to buy a put option from the insurance company with exercise price $2.5 billion. The insurance company then spends $110 million to buy a put option from

the debtholders with exercise price $1.9 billion. Finally, the debtholders spend $10 million to purchase a put option from the GIC customers with exercise price $1.1 billion. The equityholders, insurance company, and debtholders have thus each sold a put option on the gross assets at one exercise price, and purchased reinsurance in the form of a second put option at a lower exercise price. For the formal development of the correspondence between loan guarantees and put options, see R.C. Merton (1977), "An Analytical Derivation of the Cost of Deposit Insurance and Loan Guarantees: An Application of Modern Option Pricing Theory," *Journal of Banking and Finance*, 1 (June): 3-11; see also R. C. Merton (1992,1993), cited in note 1.

16. For an illustration of this point in the case of gross and net assets of a corporate pension plan, see Bodie (1990), cited in note 9.

of investing as an alternative to investing in an S&P 500 index fund. At the instant the transaction is consummated, the firm's accounting balance sheet is as follows:

ACCOUNTING BALANCE SHEET E

| Cash | $100 | Index-linked Note | $100 |
| | | Shareholder equity | 0 |

How the firm chooses to invest the $100 million will determine its risk capital. For instance, the firm might invest in one-year U.S. Treasury bills paying 10%. If it does so, the *gross* assets are riskless, but the *net* assets are extremely risky. In fact, the net assets are equivalent to a short position in the S&P 500.[17] By year end, the parent as guarantor will have to make up a shortfall that is equal to the total return on $100 million worth of the S&P 500 minus $10 million, the return on U.S. Treasury bills, if this amount is positive. This shortfall payment is the same payoff as that promised by a European call option on $100 million worth of the S&P 500 with a strike price of $110 million.[18,19] The risk capital of the firm—the smallest amount that can be invested to insure the value of its net assets—is thus equal to the value of this call option.

As an alternative to U.S. Treasury bills, the firm might invest in the actual portfolio of stocks comprising the S&P 500. Assume it can do so costlessly. In this case, the *gross* assets are risky, but they exactly match the liabilities, so that the *net* assets are *riskless*. When the assets are invested this way, the firm's risk capital is zero.

As another alternative, the firm might invest in a customized portfolio of stocks that tracks fairly closely the S&P 500, but that omits the companies that the firm believes will underperform the S&P 500 index. In this case, the riskiness of the net assets is determined by the potential deviations in performance between the customized portfolio and the index. The risk capital of the firm will equal the value of a guarantee that pays the amount by which the customized portfolio underperforms the index, if it does so at all.[20]

These examples illustrate how the riskiness of the net assets can be significantly less than or greater than the riskiness of the gross assets. They also show that it is the riskiness of *net* assets that determines the type of insurance required to permit default-free financing for the firm, and hence it is the riskiness of net assets that determines the amount of the firm's risk capital.

ACCOUNTING FOR RISK CAPITAL IN THE CALCULATION OF PROFITS

As discussed above, risk capital is implicitly or explicitly used to purchase insurance on the net assets of the firm from a variety of potential providers. Insurance is a financial asset, and the gains or losses on this asset should be included along with the gains or losses on all other assets in the calculation of profitability. Standard methods of accounting often fail to do this, however. For example, as discussed earlier, when a parent guarantees the performance of a subsidiary, the guarantee is not usually accounted for as an asset on the balance sheet of the subsidiary.

To illustrate, consider a securities underwriting subsidiary of a principal financial firm. The subsidiary anticipates deriving $50 million in revenues from underwriting spreads over the next year. It anticipates customary expenses of $30 million, so that its profit before tax is anticipated to be $20 million. (This profit figure assumes no mishaps such as occurred, for example, in the underwriting of British Petroleum shares in 1986.)[21] The subsidiary has an ongoing net working-capital requirement of $10 million. It has no other formal assets or liabilities and so its equity capital is $10 million.

Thus, the subsidiary's pre-tax return on equity is anticipated to be 200% for the year, and its accounting balance sheet and income statement would appear as follows:

---

17. Assuming the firm receives full use of the proceeds of the short sale.

18. The option must be protected from dividend payouts.

19. We saw previously that the purchase of insurance was economically equivalent to the purchase of a put option on the net assets. That is also the case here since a European call option on the S&P 500 is equivalent to a European put option on a *short* position in the S&P 500, that is, a put option on the net assets.

20. Thus, the value of *perfect* stock-selection skills equals the value of the risk capital of the portfolio since *with such skills,* the portfolio *never* underperforms the index and its risk capital is thus reduced to zero. For a theory that equates the value of market timing to the value of a portfolio guarantee, see R.C. Merton (1981), "On

Market Timing and Investment Performance, Part I: An Equilibrium Theory of Value for Market Forecasts," *Journal of Business,* 54 (July): 363-406.

21. In October, 1987, prior to the stock market crash, the British government arranged to sell its $12.2 billion stake in British Petroleum to the public. The underwriting firms agreed to pay $65 per share, a full month before the offering would come to market. The shares fell to $53 post crash. According to *The New York Times,* October 30, 1987, the four U.S. underwriters collectively stood to lose in excess of $500 million. A subsequent price guarantee from the Bank of England reduced these losses to an estimated $200 million after tax.

ACCOUNTING BALANCE SHEET F

Net working capital	$10	Shareholder equity	$10

ACCOUNTING INCOME STATEMENT F

Revenues (underwriting spreads)	$50
Customary expenses	(30)
Profit before tax	20
Pre-tax ROE	200%

This accounting analysis, however, ignores risk capital, which in this case is the price of the insurance (implicitly provided by the parent) needed to ensure that the subsidiary can perform its underwriting commitments. Suppose such insurance would cost $15 million in premiums. Then the risk capital balance sheet of the subsidiary would include the insurance as an asset, and total shareholder equity would be $25 million, consisting of $10 million of cash capital and $15 million of risk capital.

RISK-CAPITAL BALANCE SHEET F

Net working capital	$10	Cash capital	$10
Underwriting guarantee	15	Risk capital	15
(from parent)			
Total Assets	25	Shareholder equity	25

After the fact, if the underwriting business performs as anticipated, the parent guarantee will not have been needed. Thus, the insurance that enabled the subsidiary to get the business in the first place will have expired worthless. As shown below in Table F, including the cost of this insurance (which expired worthless) in the income statement results in an anticipated net profit of $5 million, or a pre-tax return of 20% on *economic* equity of $25 million:

TABLE F
ANTICIPATED NET PROFIT INCLUDING RISK CAPITAL

Revenues (underwriting spreads)	$50
Customary expenses	(30)
Underwriting insurance	(15)
Profit before tax	5
Pre-tax ROE	20%

The expensing of the $15 million cost of insurance shown in Table F is standard accounting practice if the insurance is obtained from arms-length providers. The fact that the parent provides the insurance should not change the treatment. Thus, the proper internal accounting would book the $15 million insurance premium as an expense to the underwriting subsidiary, and as revenue to the parent in its role as guarantor. Correspondingly, any "claims" paid on the guarantee should be considered revenue to the sub and an expense to the parent.

Even though this treatment of revenue and expense does not affect consolidated accounting, it can materially affect the calculated profit rates of individual businesses within the firm. In particular, the omission of risk capital "expended" on insurance overstates profits when the underlying assets perform well (because the insurance expires worthless) and understates profits when the underlying assets perform poorly (because the insurance becomes valuable).

THE ECONOMIC COST OF RISK CAPITAL

Accounting for risk capital in the calculation of actual after-the-fact profits is important for reporting and other purposes, such as profit-related compensation. For the purposes of decision-making *before the fact*, however, *expected* profits must be estimated. This requires estimation of the *expected* or *economic* cost of risk capital. Since risk capital is used to purchase insurance, and insurance is a financial asset, risk capital will not be costly in the economic sense if the insurance can be purchased at its "actuarially" fair market value. For example, the purchase of $100 worth of IBM stock is not costly in this sense if it can be purchased for $100.

Usually, however, transacting is not costless. Typically, a spread is paid over fair market value. These spread costs are "deadweight" losses to the firm. In terms of traditional use of "bid-ask" spread, the bid price from the firm's perspective is the fair value and the ask price is the amount the firm must actually pay for the insurance. The *economic cost* of risk capital to the firm is thus the spread it pays in the purchase of this insurance.

The reasons for such spreads in insurance contracts vary by type of risk coverage, but the largest component for the type discussed here generally relates to the insurer's need for protection against various forms of information risks and agency costs:

■ *Adverse selection* is the risk insurers face in not being able to distinguish "good" risks from "bad."

Unable to discriminate perfectly, they limit amounts of coverage and set prices based on an intermediate quality of risk, and try to do so to profit enough from the good risks to offset losses incurred in the underpricing of bad risks.[22]

■ *Moral hazard* is the risk insurers face if they are not able to monitor the actions of the insured. Once covered, those insured have an incentive to increase their asset risk.

■ *Agency costs* are the dissipation of asset values through inefficiency or mismanagement. As residual claimants with few contractual controls over the actions of the firm, equityholders bear the brunt of these costs.

Because principal financial firms are typically opaque in their structure, insurers of such firms—capital providers included—are especially exposed to these information and agency risks. Spreads for providing asset insurance to these types of firms—and hence their economic cost of risk capital—will therefore be relatively higher than for more transparent institutions.

The cost of risk capital is likely to depend on the form in which the insurance is purchased. The spreads on each form of insurance are determined differently. For example, in an all-equity firm, the required asset insurance is "sold" to the firm by its shareholders. The cost of risk capital obtained in this way will tend to reflect high agency costs (given the extensive leeway afforded to management by this structure), but little in the way of moral-hazard costs since there is no benefit to management or the firm's shareholders from increasing risk for its own sake. Debt financing, on the other hand, can impose a discipline on management that reduces agency costs. But then moral-hazard spreads can be high, especially in highly leveraged firms in which debtholders perceive a strong incentive for management to "roll the dice." The task for management is to weigh the spread costs of the different sources of asset insurance to find the most *efficient* way of "spending" the firm's risk capital.

Managing the firm most efficiently does not necessarily imply obtaining the lowest cost of risk capital. Consider the case of *signaling costs*. Firms faced with high spread charges can try to obtain lower spreads by making themselves more transparent, signaling that they are "good" firms. For example, "good" firms can report on a mark-to-market basis knowing that the cost to "bad" firms of doing so would be prohibitive (they would be seized by creditors and/or lose their customers). Transparency, however, can also impose costs of its own. For example, increasing transparency could lead to greater disclosure of proprietary strategies or self-imposed trading restraints that prevent it from taking advantage of short-lived windows of opportunity. Thus, the principal firm has to trade off between paying higher spread costs of risk capital for opaqueness and paying signaling costs and sacrificing potential competitive advantages to achieve transparency.

In calculating expected profitability for the overall firm, risk-capital costs should be expensed along with cash-capital costs. To illustrate, consider the example of Balance Sheet D in which the firm required $2.5 billion of cash capital and $500 million of risk capital. Because the cash capital is riskless, its cost is the AAAA rate (a little less than LIBOR), assumed to be 10% per annum. Suppose that the spread or economic cost of one-year risk capital for this firm is $30 million.[23] That is, the fair value "bid price" of the insurance provided by risk capital is $470 million and the "ask price" is $500 million. The $30 million spread is thus 6% of the ask price. Then total economic capital costs for the firm will be as follows:

| Cash capital costs: | $250 | (10% of $2.5 billion) |
| Risk capital costs: | 30 | (6% of $500 million) |

The rate paid for cash capital is the same for all firms, the riskless rate, here 10%. Risk capital costs could vary considerably among firms, and in a few special cases they could be negligible.[24]

This example differs importantly from the previous securities underwriting example (Table F). In Table F, we deducted the full "premium" expended on the purchase of insurance, while here we consider only that portion of the premium attributable to the spread or economic cost. The full insurance premium is deducted when the purpose of the

---

22. For a general discussion of these risks and costs in the context of insurance contracts, see Karl H. Borch (1990), *Economics of Insurance*, Amsterdam: North-Holland.

23. For an explicit model of these spread costs, see Merton (1993), cited in note 1.

24. For example, an open-end mutual fund is highly transparent. Moreover, the liabilityholders are principally customers who can redeem shares daily. Enforced by the securities laws, the selection of assets matches the promised contingent payments on customer liabilities, as expressed in the fund's prospectus. Hence *net* assets are virtually riskless.

analysis is to measure profits after the fact, or *ex post*. But when the purpose of the analysis is to measure the cost of capital *ex ante*, only the economic cost is deducted because, *ex ante*, insurance purchased free of spread costs at its actuarial fair value is just that—costless.

We next apply our concept of risk capital to two important areas of firm management.

HEDGING AND RISK MANAGEMENT

The implications of our framework for hedging and risk-management decisions are straightforward. Exposures to broad market risk—such as stock market risk, interest rate risk, or foreign exchange risk—usually can be hedged with derivatives such as futures, forwards, swaps and options. By definition, hedging away these risk exposures reduces asset risk. Thus, hedging market exposure reduces the required amount of risk capital.

Firms that speculate on the direction of the market, and therefore maintain a market exposure, will require more risk capital. By purchasing put options to insure against these market risks, the firm can maintain its desired exposures with the least amount of risk capital.

If there were no spread costs for risk capital, larger amounts of risk capital would impose no additional costs on the firm. In this case, firms may well be indifferent to hedging or not.[25] But if there are spread costs, and if these costs depend on the amount of risk capital, then a reduction in risk capital from hedging will lead to lower costs of risk capital if the hedges can be acquired at relatively small spreads.[26] That will usually be the case with hedging instruments for broad market risks where significant informational advantages among market participants are unlikely.[27]

CAPITAL ALLOCATION AND CAPITAL BUDGETING

Financial firms frequently need to consider entering new businesses or getting out of existing businesses. The cost of risk capital can be a major influence on these decisions. As always, the marginal benefit must be traded off against the marginal cost. But to evaluate the net marginal benefit of a decision is difficult, because in principle it requires a comparison of total firm values under the alternatives being considered.

One simplifying assumption is that the incremental cost of risk capital is proportional to the incremental *amount* of risk capital. This might be reasonable, for example, if the decision does not lead to disclosures that materially change the degree of transparency or opaqueness of the firm. In this case, calculation of the economic cost of risk capital for a particular business is equivalent to the calculation of the risk capital applicable to that business.

Even if there are no economic costs of risk capital, calculation of the amount of risk capital of a particular business is still relevant. As discussed in example F, allocations of risk capital to individual businesses within the firm are necessary to calculate their after-the-fact profits. Such profit calculations can then serve, for example, as the basis for incentive compensation awards.

In general, the incremental risk capital of a particular business within the firm will differ from its risk capital determined on the basis of a stand-alone analysis. As we shall demonstrate, this results from a diversification effect that can dramatically reduce the firm's overall risk capital. The importance of this externality from risk-sharing depends on the correlations among the profits of the firm's various businesses. Its presence means that a full allocation of all the risk capital of the firm to its constituent businesses is generally inappropriate.

We illustrate with an example of a firm with three distinct businesses. Table 1 shows the current gross assets, customer liabilities, net assets (investor capital), and one-year risk-capital requirements of each business on a stand-alone basis.[28] The businesses all have the same amounts of gross assets, but different amounts of net assets because they have different amounts of customer liabilities. Business 1

---

25. Except if it changes the transparency or opaqueness of the firm, as discussed previously.

26. Merton (1993), cited in note 1, provides a model of spread costs that produces this result.

27. For example, for an explanation of the very narrow observed spreads on stock-index futures relative to the spreads on individual stocks, see James F. Gammill and and A.F. Perold (1989), "The Changing Character of Stock Market Liquidity," *The Journal of Portfolio Management*, 15 (Spring): 13-18.

28. Risk capital in this example is computed using the loan guarantee model in Merton (1977), cited in note 15, which is based on the Black-Scholes option-pricing model. Risk capital for this model will be roughly proportional to the standard deviation of profits. See the Technical Appendix for the precise calculations. See Merton (1993) and Merton and Bodie (1992), cited in note 1, for an extensive bibliography of more general models for valuing loan guarantees.

requires substantial amounts of investor capital but relatively little stand-alone risk capital. Business 3 is the riskiest, requiring the most stand-alone risk capital; however, it has the least investor capital. Business 2 is fairly risky and requires a moderate amount of investor capital.

TABLE 1 ($ MILLIONS)

	Gross Assets	Customer Liabilities	Investor Capital	Stand-Alone Risk Capital
BUSINESS 1				
	$1,000	$500	$500	$150
BUSINESS 2				
	1,000	600	400	200
BUSINESS 3				
	1,000	700	300	250
TOTAL				
	$3,000	$1,800	$,1200	$600

Table 2 shows how the profits of the three businesses are correlated. With a correlation coefficient of .5, the profit streams of Business 1 and Business 2 are fairly highly correlated. The profits of Business 3, by contrast, are completely uncorrelated with those of Businesses 1 and 2.

TABLE 2: CORRELATION AMONG BUSINESSES

	Business 1	Business 2
Business 2	.5	
Business 3	0	0

Because the businesses are not perfectly correlated with one another, there will be a diversification benefit: the risk of the portfolio of businesses will be less than the sum of the stand-alone risks of the businesses. Risk capital—the value of insurance on the portfolio of assets—will therefore mirror this effect, and the risk capital for the total firm will be less than the sum of the (stand-alone) risk capital necessary to support each of the three businesses. For example, based on the correlations in Table 2, the risk capital of the firm can be shown to be $394 million, a 34% reduction relative to the aggregate risk capital on a stand-alone basis (see Technical Appendix).

The reduction in risk capital derives from the interaction among the risks of the individual businesses. The less-than-perfect correlation among their year-to-year profits leaves room for one business to do well while another does poorly. In effect, the businesses in the portfolio coinsure one another, thus requiring less external asset insurance.

An important implication of this risk-reduction effect is that businesses that would be unprofitable on a stand-alone basis because of high risk-capital requirements might be profitable within a firm that has other businesses with offsetting risks. Thus, the true profitability of individual businesses within the multi-business firm will be distorted if calculated on the basis of stand-alone risk capital. A decision-making process based on this approach will forgo profitable opportunities.

The alternative approach of allocating the risk capital of the combined firm across individual businesses also suffers from this problem. To show why, we examine the *marginal* risk capital required by a business. This can be done by calculating the risk capital required for the firm without this business, and subtracting it from the risk capital required for the full portfolio of businesses. Doing so for the three businesses in our example produces the results in Table 3:

TABLE 3

Combination of Businesses	Required Risk Capital for Combination	Marginal Business	Marginal Risk Capital
1+2+3	$294		
2+3	320	1	$74
1+3	292	2	102
1+2	304	3	90
	Summation of marginals:		$266

The first line of Table 3 shows the required risk capital for the combination of all three businesses, taking into account the less than perfect correlations among the businesses. As already noted, this amounts to $394 million. The next three lines of Table 3 show the calculation of the marginal risk capital of each business. For example, in the second line, we calculate the required risk capital for a firm composed of just businesses 2 and 3, taking into account the zero correlation between these businesses. It amounts to $320 million. The difference between $320 million and the required risk capital for all three businesses is $74 million. This is the marginal risk capital for business 1. It is the reduction in risk capital that a firm in businesses 1, 2, and 3 would achieve by exiting business 1; or it is the additional risk capital required for a firm in businesses 2 and 3 to enter business 1.

Less-than-perfect correlations among the profits of a financial firm's different businesses can dramatically reduce the firm's risk capital. In effect, the businesses in the portfolio coinsure one another, thus requiring less external asset insurance.

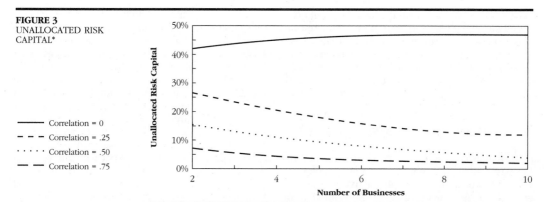

FIGURE 3
UNALLOCATED RISK CAPITAL*

Correlation = 0
Correlation = .25
Correlation = .50
Correlation = .75

*Percentage of total firm risk capital not accounted for by the marginal risk capital of the individual businesses. Calculations assume businesses are symmetrically correlated and have the same stand-alone risk capital.

For the purposes of making the marginal decision, the cost of marginal risk capital should be used. As shown in the last line of Table 3, however, the summation of marginal risk capital, $266 million, is only two thirds of the full risk capital of $394 million required for the firm. Thus, if marginal risk capital is used for allocation among businesses, $128 million (32% of total risk capital) will not be allocated to any business.[29]

The discrepancy between the total risk capital of the firm and the sum of the marginal risk capital of its businesses will of course depend on the specifics of those businesses, but it can be very large. Using the aggregate of marginal risk capital, Figure 3 illustrates how much of the firm's total risk capital goes unallocated as a function of the number of businesses in the firm, and the correlation among their profits. The analysis assumes that all businesses are the same size (in terms of stand-alone risk capital) and are symmetrically correlated. As shown in Figure 3, the unallocated capital is larger at lower correlations. Only at the extreme of perfect correlation among the businesses is all of the capital allocated. In all other cases, at least some is not allocated. In the case of no correlation among the businesses, for example, the marginal risk capital of the individual businesses can account for as little as

50% of firm risk capital, so that as much as 50% can (and should) go unallocated.

These conclusions hold quite generally. Full allocation of the firm's risk capital overstates the marginal amount of risk capital. And the risk capital of a business evaluated on a stand-alone basis overstates the marginal risk capital by an even greater amount.[30]

Taking into account correlations among profits of individual businesses in capital-budgeting analysis may seem at odds with the traditional CAPM-based notion that the only correlations that matter are those between individual business units and the broad market. Correlations among business units matter here because, by affecting the total amount of risk capital needed to support the businesses, they ultimately affect the total economic costs of risk capital. Per our earlier discussion, the economic cost of risk capital is the deadweight loss of spreads. The firm must expect to earn profits in excess of this cost as well as the cost of cash capital, which is the riskless rate of interest.

In traditional capital-budgeting procedures, estimates of cash flow correlations with the market portfolio are used to determine their stand-alone asset values. In our framework, these stand-alone asset values are assumed as given. Hence, correla-

29. "Grossing up" the marginal allocations (by 32 percent in the example) to "fully allocate" the firm's risk capital does not solve the problem. Instead, it overstates the benefits of reductions in risk capital from dropping businesses or not starting new ones.

30. See the Technical Appendix for a formal proof of these propositions. Merton (1993) provides another extensive example. The fact that risk capital cannot

be allocated stems from the "externality" arising out of the less-than-perfect correlations among the profits of individual businesses and the asymmetric risk faced by providers of insurance: limited upside and potentially large downside.

tions of business units with the broad market enter only indirectly—that is, in determining the amount of risk capital. As an insurance premium, risk capital is a function of the riskiness of the net assets as well as the value of the net assets. The *riskiness* of the net assets is affected by correlations among business units; the *value* of net assets is affected by their correlation with the broad market.

SUMMARY AND CONCLUSIONS

Financial firms that act as principal in the ordinary course of business do so in terms of asset-related as well as liability-related activities. Liability-related activities (such as deposit-taking and issuing guarantees like insurance and letters of credit) are mostly customer-driven, which makes such businesses credit-sensitive. Principal activities create a special set of financing, capital budgeting, and risk management decisions for the firm.

We have developed a framework for analyzing those decisions within the principal financial firm. The framework is built around a concept of risk capital, which we define as the smallest amount that can be invested to insure the *net* assets of the firm against loss in value relative to a risk-free investment. Using this definition of risk capital, the paper develops a number of important conclusions:

- The amount of risk capital is uniquely determined, and depends only on the riskiness of the net assets. It is not affected by the form of financing of net assets.
- Risk capital funds are provided by the firm's residual claimants, usually shareholders (except in the case of extremely highly leveraged firms). Implicitly or explicitly, this capital is used to purchase asset insurance. Potential issuers of asset insurance to the firm are third-party guarantors and the firm's stakeholders, including customers, debtholders, and shareholders.
- The economic costs of risk capital to the firm are the spreads on the price of asset insurance that stem from information costs (adverse selection and moral hazard) and agency costs.
- For a given configuration, the risk capital of a multi-business firm is less than the aggregate risk capital of the businesses on a stand-alone basis. Full allocation of risk-capital across the individual businesses of the firm therefore is generally not feasible. Attempts at such a full allocation can significantly distort the true profitability of individual businesses.

CALCULATION OF RISK CAPITAL IN TABLE 1 AND TABLE 3

For a given business, let the value of gross assets at time t be denoted by A_t, and the default-free value of customer liabilities be denoted by L_t, for $0 \leq t \leq T$. Gross assets and customer liabilities may both have uncertain, contingent payoffs. The value of the net assets at time t is $A_t - L_t$. If the net assets were invested risklessly, they would amount to $(A_0 - L_0)\exp(rT)$ at time T, where r is the continuously-compounded riskless rate of interest. The shortfall in net assets relative to a riskless return is thus $(A_0 - L_0)\exp(rT) - (A_T - L_T)$, so that insurance to permit default-free financing of the net assets must pay $\max\{(A_0 - L_0)\exp(rT) - (A_T - L_T), 0\}$ at time T. This is the same payoff structure as a European put option on the net assets with exercise price $(A_0 - L_0)\exp(rT)$. Under the assumption that the gross assets and customer liabilities both follow geometric Brownian motions, the value of this put option, and hence the amount of risk capital, is given by:

$$\text{Risk Capital} = A_0 F(1,1,0,T,\sigma)$$

where $F(S,E,r,T,\sigma)$ is the Black-Scholes (1973) formula[31] for a European call option on a stock with initial value S, exercise price E, riskless rate r, expiration date T, and volatility σ.[32] Here, σ is the volatility of profits as measured by the volatility of percentage changes in the ratio of gross assets to customer liabilities A_t/L_t (or simply the percent volatility of gross assets if customer liabilities are fixed or are non-existent). As shown by Taylor's expansion for $\sigma\sqrt{t}$ not too large, the formula for risk capital is closely approximated by:

$$\text{Risk Capital} \approx .4 A_0 \sigma\sqrt{T}.$$

The formula used here for the variance rate of profits for a combination of N businesses is given by

$\Sigma\Sigma w_i w_j \rho_{ij}\sigma_i\sigma_j$, where ρ_{ij} is the correlation between the profits of businesses i and j, and w_i is the fraction of gross assets in business i. The formula is an approximation that applies exactly only if investments in the businesses are continuously rebalanced so that the volatilities of the profits of the individual businesses maintain their relative proportions over the interval 0 to T. For the purposes here, this approximation has no material effect.

In Table 1, the volatility of business profits was assumed to be 37.5%, 50%, and 62.5% per annum, respectively. Using the above variance formula, the volatility of the profits of the combination of three businesses evaluates to 32.75% per annum. This low percentage volatility of the three businesses combined stems directly from the diversification effect. The pairwise combinations show a similar effect.

Table A shows that for the range of parameter values used here the approximation $.4 A_0 \sigma\sqrt{T}$ is very close to the exact Black-Scholes option value:

TABLE A ($ MILLIONS)

Gross Assets	Standard Deviation (σ)	Approximate Risk Capital ($.4 A_0 \sigma\sqrt{T}$)	"Exact" Risk Capital (Black-Scholes)
BUSINESS 1			
$1,000	37.5%	$150	$148.7
BUSINESS 2			
1,000	50.0%	200	197.4
BUSINESS 3			
1,000	62.5%	250	245.3
BUSINESSES 1+2			
2,000	38.0%	304	301.4
BUSINESSES 1+3			
2,000	36.4%	292	288.8
BUSINESSES 2+3			
2,000	40.0%	320	317.0
BUSINESSES 1+2+3			
3,000	32.8%	394	390.8

31. Set forth in F. Black and M. Scholes (1973), "The Pricing of Options and Corporate Liabilities," *Journal of Political Economy*, 81 (May-June): 637-654.

32. $\sigma^2 = \sigma^2{}_A + \sigma^2{}_L - \sigma_A\sigma_L\rho_{AL}$, where σ_A is the volatility of gross asset returns, σ_L is the volatility of customer liability "returns," and ρ_{AL} is the correlation between gross asset returns and customer returns. See Stanley Fischer, (1978), "Call Option Pricing When the Exercise Price Is Uncertain, and the Valuation of

Index Bonds," *Journal of Finance*, 33 (March): 169-176; William Margrabe, (1978), "The Value of an Option to Exchange One Asset for Another," *Journal of Finance*, 33 (March):177-186; and, especially, René Stulz, (1982), "Options on the Minimum or the Maximum of Two Risky Assets: Analysis and Applications," *Journal of Financial Economics*, 10 (July): 161-185.

THE RELATIONSHIP OF MARGINAL RISK CAPITAL TO COMBINED AND STAND-ALONE RISK CAPITAL

This section establishes the general propositions that a) the sum of the risk capital of stand-alone businesses exceeds the risk capital of the businesses combined in one firm; and b) the risk capital of a combination of businesses exceeds the sum of the marginal risk capital of each of those businesses.

As in the first part of this Appendix, let $X = (A_0 - L_0)\exp(rT) - (A_T - L_T)$ be the shortfall (or surplus if it is negative) in the net assets of a business at time T. Let there be N individual businesses, and let X_i be the shortfall for business i. From the above, insurance to permit default-free financing of the net assets of business i must pay $f(X_i) = \max\{X_i, 0\}$ at time T. Note that the function $f(.)$ is convex and satisfies $f(0) = 0$.

The sum of the insurance payoffs to the stand-alone businesses is $\Sigma f(X_i)$, and the insurance payoff to the combined businesses is $f(\Sigma X_i)$. Since $f(.)$ is convex, we can apply Jensen's inequality to obtain:

$$\Sigma f(X_i) \geq f(\Sigma X_i)$$

which establishes the first proposition.[33]

To establish the second proposition, we note that $f(\Sigma_{j \neq i} X_j)$ is the insurance payoff to the firm consisting of all businesses except i. Thus the marginal insurance payoff for business i is

$$f(\Sigma X_i) - f(\Sigma_{j \neq i} X_j).$$

We now observe the identity:

$$\Sigma X_i = \Sigma_i (\Sigma_{j \neq i} X_j)/(N - 1).$$

Therefore, by Jensen's inequality,

$$f(\Sigma X_i) \leq \Sigma_i f((\Sigma_{j \neq i} X_j)/(N - 1)).$$

Applying Jensen's inequality a second time and using the fact that $f(0) = 0$, we obtain

$$(N - 1)f(\Sigma X_i) \leq \Sigma_i f(\Sigma_{j \neq i} X_j)$$

from which it follows that

$$Nf(\Sigma X_i) - \Sigma_i f(\Sigma_{j \neq i} X_j) \leq f(\Sigma X_i)$$

or

$$\Sigma_k \{f(\Sigma X_i) - f(\Sigma_{j \neq k} X_j)\} \leq f(\Sigma X_i).$$

This proves that the sum of the marginal insurance payoffs is at most the insurance payoff to the combined firm. Therefore, the risk capital of a combination of businesses exceeds the sum of the marginal risk capital of each of those businesses.

---

33. This is the well-known proposition that a portfolio of options always returns at least as much as the corresponding option on a portfolio of underlying securities.

HOW TO USE THE HOLES IN BLACK-SCHOLES

*by Fischer Black, Goldman, Sachs & Co.**

T he Black-Scholes formula is still around, even though it depends on at least 10 unrealistic assumptions. Making the assumptions more realistic hasn't produced a formula that works better across a wide range of circumstances.

In special cases, though, we can improve the formula. If you think investors are making an unrealistic assumption like one of those we used in deriving the formula, there is a strategy you may want to follow that focuses on that assumption.

The same unrealistic assumptions that led to the Black-Scholes formula are behind some versions of "portfolio insurance." As people have shifted to more realistic assumptions, they have changed the way they use portfolio insurance. Some people have dropped it entirely, or have switched to the opposite strategy.

People using incorrect assumptions about market conditions may even have caused the rise and sudden fall in stocks during 1987. One theory of the crash relies on incorrect beliefs, held before the crash, about the extent to which investors were using portfolio insurance, and about how changes in stock prices cause changes in expected returns.

---

* This article is a revised version of an earlier article, "The Holes in Black-Scholes," which appeared in Vol. 1 No. 4 of *Risk* in March of 1988.

A higher expected return on the stock means a higher expected return on the option, but it doesn't affect the option's value for a given stock price.

THE FORMULA

The Black-Scholes formula looks like this:

$$w\ (x,t)\ =\ xN(d_1)\ -\ ce^{-r\ (t^*\ -\ t)}N(d_2)$$

where
$$d_1\ =\ \frac{\ln(x/c)\ +\ (r\ +\ 1/2v^2)\ (t^*\ -\ t)}{v\ \sqrt{t^*\ -\ t}}$$

and
$$d_2\ =\ \frac{\ln(x/c)\ +\ (r\ -\ 1/2v^2)\ (t^*\ -\ t)}{v\ \sqrt{t^*\ -\ t}}$$

In this expression, **w** is the value of a call option or warrant on the stock, **t** is today's date, **x** is the stock price, **c** is the strike price, r is the interest rate, **t*** is the maturity date, **V** is the standard deviation of the stock's return, and **N** is something called the "cumulative normal density function." (You can approximate **N** using a simple algebraic expression.)

The value of the option increases with increases in the stock's price, the interest rate, the time remaining until the option expires, and the stock's volatility. Except for volatility, which can be estimated several ways, we can observe all of the factors the Black-Scholes formula requires for valuing options.

Note that the stock's expected return doesn't appear in the formula. If you are bullish on the stock, you may buy shares or call options, but you won't change your estimate of the option's value. A higher expected return on the stock means a higher expected return on the option, but it doesn't affect the option's value for a given stock price.

This feature of the formula is very general. I don't know of any variation of the formula where the stock's expected return affects the option's value for a given stock price.

HOW TO IMPROVE THE ASSUMPTIONS

In our original derivation of the formula, Myron Scholes and I made the following unrealistic assumptions:

■ The stock's volatility is known, and doesn't change over the life of the option.
■ The stock price changes smoothly: it never jumps up or down a large amount in a short time.
■ The short-term interest rate never changes.
■ Anyone can borrow or lend as much as he wants at a single rate.
■ An investor who sells the stock or the option short will have the use of all the proceeds of the sale and receive any returns from investing these proceeds.

■ There are no trading costs for either the stock or the option.
■ An investor's trades do not affect the taxes he pays.
■ The stock pays no dividends.
■ An investor can exercise the option only at expiration.
■ There are no takeovers or other events that can end the option's life early.

Since these assumptions are mostly false, we know the formula must be wrong. But we may not be able to find any other formula that gives better results in a wide range of circumstances. Here we look at each of these 10 assumptions and describe how we might change them to improve the formula. We also look at strategies that make sense if investors continue to make unrealistic assumptions.

Volatility Changes

The volatility of a stock is not constant. Changes in the volatility of a stock may have a major impact on the values of certain options, especially far-out-of-the-money options. For example, if we use a volatility estimate of 0.20 for the annual standard deviation of the stock, and if we take the interest rate to be zero, we get a value of $0.00884 for a six-month call option with a $40 strike price written on a $28 stock. Keeping everything else the same, but doubling the volatility to 0.40, we get a value of $0.465.

For this out-of-the-money option, doubling the volatility estimate multiplies the value by a factor of 53.

Since the volatility can change, we should really include the ways it can change in the formula. The option value will depend on the entire future path that we expect the volatility to take, and on the uncertainty about what the volatility will be at each point in the future. One measure of that uncertainty is the "volatility of the volatility."

A formula that takes account of changes in volatility will include both current and expected future levels of volatility. Though the expected return on the stock will not affect option values, expected changes in volatility will affect them. And the volatility of volatility will affect them too.

Another measure of the uncertainty about the future volatility is the relation between the future stock price and its volatility. A decline in the stock price implies a substantial increase in volatility, while an increase in the stock price implies a substantial decrease in volatility. The effect is so strong that it is even possible that a stock with a price of $20 and a typical daily move

**To buy pure volatility, buy both puts and calls in a ratio that gives you
no added exposure to the stock; to sell pure volatility, sell both puts and
calls in the same ratio.**

of $0.50 will start having a typical daily move of only $0.375 if the stock price doubles to $40.

John Cox and Stephen Ross have come up with two formulas that take account of the relation between the future stock price and its volatility.[1] To see the effects of using one of their formulas on the pattern of option values for at-the-money and out-of-the money options, let's look at the values using both Black-Scholes and Cox-Ross formulas for a six-month call option on a $40 stock, taking the interest rate as zero and the volatility as 0.20 per year. For three exercise prices, the value are as follows:

Exercise Price	Black Scholes	Cox-Ross
40.00	2.2600	2.2600
50.00	0.1550	0.0880
57.10	0.0126	0.0020

The Cox-Ross formula implies lower values for out-of-the-money call options than the Black-Scholes formula. But putting in uncertainty about the future volatility will often imply higher values for these same options. We can't tell how the option values will change when we put in both effects.

What should you do if you think a stock's volatility will change in ways that other people do not yet understand? Also suppose that you feel the market values options correctly in all other respects.

You should "buy volatility" if you think volatility will rise, and "sell volatility" if you think it will fall. To buy volatility, buy options; to sell volatility, sell options. Instead of buying stock, you can buy calls or buy stock and sell calls. Or you can take the strongest position on volatility by adding a long or short position in straddles to your existing position. To buy pure volatility, buy both puts and calls in a ratio that gives you no added exposure to the stock; to sell pure volatility, sell both puts and calls in the same ratio.

Jumps

In addition to showing changes in volatility in general and changes in volatility related to changes in stock price, a stock may have jumps. A major news development may cause a sudden large change in the stock price, often accompanied by a temporary suspension of trading in the stock.

When the big news is just as likely to be good as bad, a jump will look a lot like a temporary large increase in volatility. When the big news, if it comes, is sure to be good, or is sure to be bad, the resulting jump is not like a change in volatility. Up jumps and down jumps have different effects on option values than symmetric jumps, where there is an equal chance of an up jump or a down jump.

Robert Merton has a formula that reflects possible symmetric jumps.[2] Compared to the Black-Scholes formula, his formula gives higher values for both in-the-money and out-of-the-money options and lower values for at-the-money options. The differences are especially large for short-term options.

Short-term options also show strikingly different effects for up jumps and down jumps. An increase in the probability of an up jump will cause out-of-the-money calls to go way up in value relative to out-of-the-money puts. An increase in the probability of a down jump will do the reverse. After the crash, people were afraid of another down jump, and out-of-the-money puts were priced very high relative to their Black-Scholes values, while out-of-the-money calls were priced very low.

More than a year after the crash, this fear continues to affect option values.

What should you do if you think jumps are more likely to occur than the market thinks? If you expect a symmetric jump, buy short-term out-of-the-money options. Instead of stock, you can hold call options or more stock plus put options. Or you can sell at-the-money options. Instead of stock, you can hold more stock and sell call options. For a pure play on symmetric jumps, buy out-of-the-money calls and puts, and sell at-the-money calls and puts.

For up jumps, use similar strategies that involve buying short-term out-of-the-money calls, or selling short-term out-of-the-money puts, or both. For down jumps, do the opposite.

Interest Rate Changes

The Black-Scholes formula assumes a constant interest rate, but the yields on bonds with different maturities tell us that the market expects the rate to change. If future changes in the interest rate are known, we can just replace the short-term rate with the yield on a zero-coupon bond that matures when the option expires.

---

1. See John Cox and Stephen Ross, *Journal of Financial Economics* (January/March 1976).

2. See John Cox, Robert Merton, and Stephen Ross, *Journal of Financial Economics* (January/March 1976).

Suppose you want to short a stock but you face penalties if you sell the stock short directly...You can short it indirectly by holding put options, or by taking a naked short position in call options.

But, of course, future changes in the interest rate are uncertain. When the stock's volatility is known Robert Merton has shown that the zero-coupon bond yield will still work, even when both short-term and long-term interest rates are shifting.[3] At a given point in time, we can find the option value by using the zero-coupon bond yield at that moment for the short-term rate. When both the volatility and the interest rate are shifting, we will need a more complex adjustment.

In general, the effects of interest rate changes on option values do not seem nearly as great as the effects of volatility changes. If you have an opinion on which way interest rates are going, you maybe better off with direct positions in fixed-income securities rather than in options.

But your opinion may affect your decisions to buy or sell options. Higher interest rates mean higher call values and lower put values. If you think interest rates will rise more than the market thinks, you should be more inclined to buy calls, and more inclined to buy more stocks and sell puts, as a substitute for a straight stock position. If you think interest rates will fall more than the market thinks, these preferences should be reversed.

Borrowing Penalties

The rate at which an individual can borrow, even with securities as collateral, is higher than the rate at which he can lend. Sometimes his borrowing rate is substantially higher than his lending rate. Also, margin requirements or restrictions put on by lenders may limit the amount he can borrow.

High rates and limits on borrowing may cause a general increase in call option values, since calls provide leverage that can substitute for borrowing. The interest rates implied by option values may be higher than lending rates. If this happens and you have borrowing limits but no limits on option investments, you may still want to buy calls. But if you can borrow freely at a rate close to the lending rate, you may want to get leverage by borrowing rather than by buying calls.

When implied interest rates are high, conservative investors might buy puts or sell calls to protect a portfolio instead of selling stock. Fixed-income investors might even choose to buy stocks and puts, and sell calls, to create a synthetic fixed-income position with a yield higher than market yields.

Short-Selling Penalties

Short-selling penalties are generally even worse than borrowing penalties. On U.S. exchanges, an investor can sell a stock short only on or after an uptick. He must go to the expense of borrowing stock if he wants to sell it short. Part of his expense involves putting up cash collateral with the person who lends the stock; he generally gets no interest, or interest well below market rates, on this collateral. Also, he may have to put up margin with his broker in cash, and may not receive interest on cash balances with his broker.

For options, the penalties tend to be much less severe. An investor need not borrow an option to sell it short. There is no uptick rule for options. And an investor loses much less interest income in selling an option short than in selling a stock short.

Penalties on short selling that apply to all investors will affect option values. When even professional investors have trouble selling a stock short, we will want to include an element in the option formula to reflect the strength of these penalties. Sometimes we approximate this by assuming an extra dividend yield on the stock, in an amount up to the cost of maintaining a short position as part of a hedge.

Suppose you want to short a stock but you face penalties if you sell the stock short directly. Perhaps you're not even allowed to short the stock directly. You can short it indirectly by holding put options, or by taking a naked short position in call options. (Though most investors who can't short stock directly also can't take naked short positions.)

When you face penalties in selling short, you often face rewards for lending stock to those who want to short it. In this situation, strategies that involve holding the stock and lending it out may dominate other strategies. For example, you might create a position with a limited downside by holding a stock and a put on the stock, and by lending the stock to those who want to short it.

Trading Costs

Trading costs can make it hard for an investor to create an option-like payoff by trading in the underlying stock. They can also make it hard to create a stock-like payoff by trading in the option.

---

3. Robert Merton, *Bell Journal of Economics and Management Science* (1977).

**If you pay taxes on gains and cannot deduct losses, you may want
to limit the volatility of your positions and have the freedom to control
the timing of gains and losses.**

Sometimes they can increase an option's value, and sometimes they can decrease it.

We can't tell how trading costs will affect an option's value, so we can think of them as creating a "band" of possible values. Within this band, it will be impractical for most investors to take advantage of mispricing by selling the option and buying the stock, or by selling the stock and buying the option.

The bigger the stock's trading costs are, the more important it is for you to choose a strategy that creates the payoffs you want with little trading. Trading costs can make options especially useful if you want to shift exposure to the stock after it goes up or down.

If you want to shift your exposure to the market as a whole, rather than to a stock, you will find options even more useful. It is often more costly to trade in a basket of stocks than in a single stock. But you can use index options to reduce your trading in the underlying stocks or futures.

Taxes

Some investors pay no taxes; some are taxed as individuals, paying taxes on dividends, interest, and capital gains; and some are taxed as corporations, also paying taxes on dividends, interest, and capital gains, but at different rates.

The very existence of taxes will affect option values. A hedged position that should give the same return as lending may have a tax that differs from the tax on interest. So if all investors faced the same tax rate, we would use a modified interest rate in the option formula.

The fact that investor tax rates differ will affect values too. Without rules to restrict tax arbitrage, investors could use large hedged positions involving options to cut their taxes sharply or to alter them indefinitely. Thus tax authorities adopt a variety of rules to restrict tax arbitrage. There maybe rules to limit interest deductions or capital loses deductions, or rules to tax gains and losses before a position is closed out. For example, most U.S. index option positions are now taxed each year—partly as short-term capital gains and partly as long-term capital gains—whether or not the taxpayer has closed out his positions.

If you can use capital losses to offset gains, you may act roughly the same way whether your tax rate is high or low. If your tax rate stays the same from year to year, you may act about the same whether you are forced to realize gains and losses or are able to choose the year you realize them.

But if you pay taxes on gains and cannot deduct losses, you may want to limit the volatility of your positions and have the freedom to control the timing of gains and losses. This will affect how you use options, and may affect option values as well. I find it hard to predict, though, whether it will increase or decrease option values.

Investors who buy a put option will have a capital gain or loses at the end of the year, or when the option expires. Investors who simulate the put option by trading in the underlying stock will sell after a decline, and buy after a rise. By choosing which lots of stock to buy and which lots to sell, they will be able to generate a series of realized capital losses and unrealized gains. The tax advantages of this strategy may reduce put values for many taxable investors. By a similar argument, the tax advantages of a simulated call option may reduce call values for most taxable investors.

Dividends and Early Exercise

The original Black-Scholes formula does not take account of dividends. But dividends reduce call option values and increase put option values, at least when there are no offsetting adjustments in the terms of the options. Dividends make early exercise of a call option more likely, and early exercise of a put option less likely.

We now have several ways to change the formula to account for dividends. One way assumes that the dividend yield is constant for all possible stock price levels and at all future times. Another assumes that the issuer has money set aside to pay the dollar dividends due before the option expires. Yet another assumes that the dividend depends in a known way on the stock price at each ex-dividend date.

John Cox, Stephen Ross, and Mark Rubinstein have shown how to figure option values using a "tree" of possible future stock prices.[4] The tree gives the same values as the formula when we use the same assumptions. But the tree is more flexible, and lets us relax some of the assumptions. For example, we can put on the tree the dividend that the firm will pay for each possible future stock price at each future time. We can also test, at each node of the tree,

---

4. John Cox, Mark Rubinstein, and Stephen Ross, "Option Pricing: A Simplified Approach," *Journal of Financial Economics* Vol.7 (1979), 229-263.

The true cost of portfolio insurance, in my view, is a factor that doesn't even affect
option values. It is the mean reversion in the market: the rate at which the
expected return on the market falls as the market rises.

whether an investor will exercise the option early for that stock price at that time.

Option values reflect the market's belief about the stock's future dividends and the likelihood of early exercise. When you think that dividends will be higher than the market thinks, you will want to buy puts or sell calls, other things equal. When you think that option holders will exercise too early or too late, you will want to sell options to take advantage of the opportunities the holders create.

Takeovers

The original formula assumes the underlying stock will continue trading for the life of the option. Takeovers can make this assumption false.

If firm A takes over firm B through an exchange of stock, options on firm B's stock will normally become options on firm A's stock. We will use A's volatility rather than B's in valuing the option.

If firm A takes over firm B through a cash tender offer, there are two effects. First, outstanding options on B will expire early. This will tend to reduce values for both puts and calls. Second, B's stock price will rise through the tender offer premium. This will increase call values and decrease put values.

But when the market knows of a possible tender offer from firm A, B's stock price will be higher than it might otherwise be. It will be between its normal level and its normal level increased by the tender offer. Then if A fails to make an offer, the price will fall, or will show a smaller-than-normal rise.

All these factors work together to influence option values. The chance of a takeover will make an option's value sometimes higher and sometimes lower. For a short-term out-of-the-money call option, the chance of a takeover will generally increase the option value. For a short-term out-of-the-money put option, the chance of a takeover will generally reduce the option value.

The effects of takeover probability on values can be dramatic for these short-term out-of-the-money options. If you think your opinion of the chance of a takeover is more accurate than the market's, you can express your views clearly with options like these.

The October 19 crash is the opposite of a takeover as far as option values go. Option values

then, and since then, have reflected the fear of another crash. Out-of-the-money puts have been selling for high values, and out-of-the-money calls have been selling for low values. If you think another crash is unlikely, you may want to buy out-of-the-money calls, or sell out-of-the-money puts, or do both.

Now that we've looked at the 10 assumptions in the Black-Scholes formula, let's see what role, if any, they play in portfolio insurance strategies.

PORTFOLIO INSURANCE

In the months before the crash, people in the U.S. and elsewhere became more and more interested in portfolio insurance. As I define it, portfolio insurance is any strategy where you reduce your stock positions when prices fall, and increase them when prices rise.

Some investors use option formulas to figure how much to increase or reduce their positions as prices change. They trade in stocks or futures or short-term options to create the effect of having a long-term put against stock, or a long-term call plus T-bills.

You don't need synthetic options or option formulas for portfolio insurance. You can do the same thing with a variety of systems for changing your positions as prices change. However, the assumptions behind the Black-Scholes formula also affect portfolio insurance strategies that don't use the formula.

The higher your trading costs, the less likely you are to create synthetic options or any other adjustment strategy that involves a lot of trading. On October 19, the costs of trading in futures and stocks became much higher than they had been earlier, partly because the futures were priced against the portfolio insurers. The futures were at a discount when portfolio insurers wanted to sell. This made all portfolio insurance strategies less attractive.

Portfolio insurance using synthetic strategies wins when the market makes big jumps, but without much volatility. It loses when market volatility is high, because an investor will sell after a fall, and buy after a rise. He loses money on each cycle.

But the true cost of portfolio insurance, in my view, is a factor that doesn't even affect option values. It is the mean reversion in the market: the rate at which the expected return on the market falls as the market rises.[5]

---

5. For evidence of mean reversion, see Eugene Fama and Kenneth French, "Permanent and Temporary Components of Stock Prices," *Journal of Political Economy* Vol. 96 No. 2 (April 1988), 246-273; and James Poterba and Lawrence Summers, "Mean Reversion in Stock Prices: Evidence and Implications," *Journal of Financial Economics* Vol. 22 No.1 (October 1988), 27-60.

If your view of mean reversion is higher than the market's, you can buy short-term
options and sell long-term options. If you think mean reversion is lower,
you can do the reverse.

Mean reversion is what balances supply and demand for portfolio insurance. High mean reversion will discourage portfolio insurers because it will mean they are selling when expected return is higher and buying when expected return is lower. For the same reason, high mean reversion will attract "value investors" or "tactical asset allocators," who buy after a decline and sell after a rise. Value investors use indicators like price-earnings ratios and dividend yields to decide when to buy and sell. They act as sellers of portfolio insurance.

If mean reversion were zero, I think that more investors would want to buy portfolio insurance than to sell it. People have a natural desire to try to limit their losses. But, on balance, there must be as many sellers as buyers of insurance. What makes this happen is a positive normal level of mean reversion.

THE CRASH

During 1987, investors shifted toward wanting more portfolio insurance. This increased the market's mean reversion. But mean reversion is hard to see; it takes years to detect a change in it. So investors did not understand that mean reversion was rising. Since rising mean reversion should restrain an increase in portfolio insurance demand, this misunderstanding caused a further increase in demand.

Because of mean reversion, the market rise during 1987 caused a sharper-than-usual fall in expected return. But investors didn't see this at first. They continued to buy, as their portfolio insurance strategies suggested. Eventually, though, they came to understand the effects of portfolio insurance on mean reversion, partly by observing the large orders that price changes brought into the market.

Around October 19, the full truth of what was happening hit investors. They saw that at existing levels of the market, the expected return *was* much lower than they had assumed. They sold at those levels. The market fell, and expected return rose, until equilibrium was restored.

MEAN REVERSION AND STOCK VOLATILITY

Now that we've explained mean reversion, how can you use your view of it in your investments?

If you have a good estimate of a stock's volatility, the stock's expected return won't affect option values. Since the expected return won't affect values, neither will mean reversion.

But mean reversion may influence your estimate of the stock's volatility. With mean reversion day-to-day volatility will be higher than month-to-month volatility, which will be higher than year-to-year volatility. Your volatility estimates for options with several years of life should be generally lower than your volatility estimates for options with several days or several months of life.

If your view of mean reversion is higher than the market's, you can buy short-term options and sell long-term options. If you think mean reversion is lower, you can do the reverse. If you are a buyer of options, you will favor short-term options when you think mean reversion is high, and long-term options when you think it is low. If you are a seller of options, you will favor long-term options when you think mean reversion is high, and short-term options when you think it's low.

These effects will be most striking in stock index options. But they will also show up in individual stock options, through the effects of market moves on individual stocks and through the influence of "trend followers." Trend followers act like portfolio insurers, but they trade individual stocks rather than portfolios. When the stock rises, they buy; and when it falls, they sell. They act as if the past trend in a stock's price is likely to continue.

In individual stocks, as in portfolios, mean reversion should normally make implied volatilities higher for short-term options than for long-term options. (An option's implied volatility is the volatility that makes its Black-Scholes value equal to its price.) If your views differ from the market's, you may have a chance for a profitable trade.

VALUE AT RISK: USES AND ABUSES

by Christopher L. Culp,
CP Risk Management LLC,
Merton H. Miller,
University of Chicago, and
Andrea M. P. Neves,
CP Risk Management LLC*

Value at risk ("VAR") is now viewed by many as indispensable ammunition in any serious corporate risk manager's arsenal. VAR is a method of measuring the financial risk of an asset, portfolio, or exposure over some specified period of time. Its attraction stems from its ease of interpretation as a summary measure of risk and consistent treatment of risk across different financial instruments and business activities. VAR is often used as an approximation of the "maximum reasonable loss" a company can expect to realize from all its financial exposures.

VAR has received widespread accolades from industry and regulators alike.[1] Numerous organizations have found that the practical uses and benefits of VAR make it a valuable decision support tool in a comprehensive risk management process. Despite its many uses, however, VAR—like any statistical aggregate—is subject to the risk of misinterpretation and misapplication. Indeed, most problems with VAR seem to arise from what a firm *does* with a VAR measure rather than from the actual computation of the number.

Why a company manages risk affects *how* a company should manage—and, hence, should measure—its risk.[2] In that connection, we examine the four "great derivatives disasters" of 1993-1995—Procter & Gamble, Barings, Orange County, and Metallgesellschaft—and evaluate how *ex ante* VAR measurements likely would have affected those situations. We conclude that VAR would have been of only limited value in averting those disasters and, indeed, actually might have been *misleading* in some of them.

---

*The authors thank Kamaryn Tanner for her previous work with us on this subject.

1. *See, for example,* Global Derivatives Study Group, *Derivatives: Practices and Principles* (Washington, D.C.: July 1993), and Board of Governors of the Federal Reserve System, *SR Letter 93-69* (1993). Most recently, the Securities and Exchange Commission began to require risk disclosures by all public companies. One approved format for these mandatory financial risk disclosures is VAR. For a critical assessment of the SEC's risk disclosure rule, *see* Merton H. Miller and Christopher L. Culp, "The SEC's Costly Disclosure Rules," *Wall Street Journal* (June 22, 1996).

2. This presupposes, of course, that "risk management" is consistent with value-maximizing behavior by the firm. For the purpose of this paper, we do not consider whether firms *should be* managing their risks. For a discussion of that issue, *see* Christopher L. Culp and Merton H. Miller, "Hedging in the Theory of Corporate Finance: A Reply to Our Critics," *Journal of Applied Corporate Finance*, Vol. 8, No. 1 (Spring 1995):121-127, and Rene M. Stulz, "Rethinking Risk Management," *Journal of Applied Corporate Finance*, Vol. 9, No. 3 (Fall 1996):8-24.

FIGURE 1

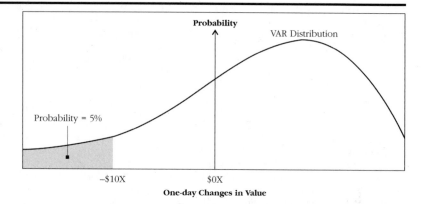

VAR Distribution

Probability = 5%

−$10X $0X

One-day Changes in Value

WHAT IS VAR?

Value at risk is a summary statistic that quantifies the exposure of an asset or portfolio to market risk, or the risk that a position declines in value with adverse market price changes.[3] Measuring risk using VAR allows managers to make statements like the following: "We do not expect losses to exceed $1 million on more than 1 out of the next 20 days."[4]

To arrive at a VAR measure for a given portfolio, a firm must generate a probability distribution of possible changes in the value of some portfolio over a specific time or "risk horizon"—*e.g.,* one day.[5] The value at risk of the portfolio is the dollar loss corresponding to some pre-defined probability level—usually 5% or less—as defined by the left-hand tail of the distribution. Alternatively, VAR is the dollar loss that is expected to occur no more than 5% of the time over the defined risk horizon. Figure 1, for example, depicts a one-day VAR of $10X at the 5% probability level.

The Development of VAR

VAR emerged first in the trading community.[6] The original goal of VAR was to systematize the measurement of an active trading firm's risk exposures across its dealing portfolios. Before VAR, most commercial trading houses measured and controlled risk on a desk-by-desk basis with little attention to firm-wide exposures. VAR made it possible for dealers to use risk measures that could be compared and aggregated across trading areas as a means of monitoring and limiting their consolidated financial risks.

VAR received its first public endorsement in July 1993, when a group representing the swap dealer community recommended the adoption of VAR by all active dealers.[7] In that report, the Global Derivatives Study Group of The Group of Thirty urged dealers to "use a *consistent measure* to calculate daily the market risk of their derivatives positions and compare it to market risk limits. Market risk is best measured as 'value at risk' using *probability analysis* based upon a common confidence interval (*e.g.,* two standard deviations) and *time horizon* (*e.g.,* a one-day exposure). [emphasis added]"[8]

The italicized phrases in The Group of Thirty recommendation draw attention to several specific features of VAR that account for its widespread popularity among trading firms. One feature of VAR is its *consistent* measurement of

---

3. More recently, VAR has been suggested as a framework for measuring credit risk, as well. To keep our discussion focused, we examine only the applications of VAR to market risk measurement.

4. For a general description of VAR, *see* Philippe Jorion, *Value at Risk* (Chicago: Irwin Professional Publishing, 1997).

5. The risk horizon is chosen exogenously by the firm engaging in the VAR calculation.

6. An early precursor of VAR was SPANTM—Standard Portfolio Analysis of Risk—developed by the Chicago Mercantile Exchange for setting futures margins.

Now widely used by virtually all futures exchanges, SPAN is a non-parametric, simulation-based "worst case" measure of risk. As will be seen, VAR, by contrast, rests on well-defined probability distributions.

7. This was followed quickly by a similar endorsement from the International Swaps and Derivatives Association. *See* Jorion, cited previously.

8. Global Derivatives Study Group, cited previously.

financial risk. By expressing risk using a "possible dollar loss" metric, VAR makes possible direct comparisons of risk across different business lines and distinct financial products such as interest rate and currency swaps.

In addition to consistency, VAR also is *probability-based*. With whatever degree of confidence a firm wants to specify, VAR enables the firm to associate a specific loss with that level of confidence. Consequently, VAR measures can be interpreted as forward-looking approximations of potential market risk.

A third feature of VAR is its reliance on a *common time horizon* called the risk horizon. A one-day risk horizon at, say, the 5% probability level tells the firm, strictly speaking, that it can expect to lose no more than, say, $10X on the next day with 95% confidence. Firms often go on to assume that the 5% confidence level means they stand to lose more than $10X on no more than five days out of 100, an inference that is true only if strong assumptions are made about the stability of the underlying probability distribution.[9]

The choice of this risk horizon is based on various motivating factors. These may include the timing of employee performance evaluations, key decision-making events (*e.g.,* asset purchases), major reporting events (*e.g.,* board meetings and required disclosures), regulatory examinations, tax assessments, external quality assessments, and the like.

Implementing VAR

To estimate the value at risk of a portfolio, possible future values of that portfolio must be generated, yielding a distribution—called the "VAR distribution"—like that we saw in Figure 1. Once the VAR distribution is created for the chosen risk horizon, the VAR itself is just a number on the curve—*viz.,* the change in the value of the portfolio leaving the specified amount of probability in the left-hand tail.

Creating a VAR distribution for a particular portfolio and a given risk horizon can be viewed as a two-step process.[10] In the first step, the price or return distributions for each individual security or asset in the portfolio are generated. These distributions represent possible value changes in all the component assets over the risk horizon.[11] Next, the individual distributions somehow must be aggregated into a portfolio distribution using appropriate measures of correlation.[12] The resulting portfolio distribution then serves as the basis for the VAR summary measure.

An important assumption in almost all VAR calculations is that the portfolio whose risk is being evaluated *does not change* over the risk horizon. This assumption of no turnover was not a major issue when VAR first arrived on the scene at derivatives dealers. They were focused on one- or two-day—sometimes *intra*-day—risk horizons and thus found VAR both easy to implement and relatively realistic. But when it comes to generalizing VAR to a longer time horizon, the assumption of no portfolio changes becomes problematic. What does it mean, after all, to evaluate the *one-year* VAR of a portfolio using only the portfolio's contents *today* if the turnover in the portfolio is 20-30% per day?

Methods for generating both the individual asset risk distributions and the portfolio risk distribution range from the simplistic to the indecipherably complex. Because our goal in this paper is not to evaluate all these mechanical methods of VAR measurement, readers are referred elsewhere for explanations of the nuts and bolts of VAR computation.[13] Several common methods of VAR calculation are summarized in the Appendix.

9. This interpretation assumes that asset price changes are what the technicians call "iid," independently and identically distributed—*i.e.,* that price changes are drawn from essentially the same distribution every day.

10. In practice, VAR is not often implemented in a clean two-step manner, but discussing it in this way simplifies our discussion—without any loss of generality.

11. Especially with instruments whose payoffs are non-linear, a better approach is to generate distributions for the underlying "risk factors" that affect an asset rather than focus on the changes in the values of the assets themselves. To generate the value change distribution of an option on a stock, for example, one might first generate changes in the stock price and its volatility and *then* compute associated option price changes rather than generating option price changes "directly." For a discussion, *see* Michael S. Gamze and Ronald S. Rolighed, "VAR: What's Wrong With This Picture?," unpublished manuscript, Federal Reserve Bank of Chicago (1997).

12. If a risk manager is interested in the risk of a particular financial instrument, the appropriate risk measure to analyze is *not* the VAR of that instrument. Portfolio effects still must be considered. The relevant measure of risk is the *marginal risk* of that instrument in the portfolio being evaluated. *See* Mark Garman, "Improving on VAR," *Risk*, Vol. 9, No. 5 (1996):61-63.

13. *See, for example,* Jorion, cited previously, and Rod A. Beckström and Alyce R. Campbell, "Value-at-Risk (VAR): Theoretical Foundations," in *An Introduction to VAR*, Rod Beckström and Alyce Campbell, eds. (Palo Alto, Ca.: CAATS Software, Inc., 1995), and James V. Jordan and Robert J. Mackay, "Assessing Value at Risk for Equity Portfolios: Implementing Alternative Techniques," in *Derivatives Handbook*, Robert J. Schwartz and Clifford W. Smith, Jr., eds. (New York: John Wiley & Sons, Inc., 1997).

Uses of VAR

The purpose of any risk measurement system and summary risk statistic is to facilitate risk reporting and control decisions. Accordingly, dealers quickly began to rely on VAR measures in their broader risk management activities. The simplicity of VAR measurement greatly facilitated dealers' reporting of risks to senior managers and directors. The popularity of VAR owes much to Dennis Weatherstone, former chairman of JP Morgan & Co., Inc., who demanded to know the total market risk exposure of JP Morgan at 4:15pm every day. Weatherstone's request was met with a daily VAR report.

VAR also proved useful in dealers' risk *control* efforts.[14] Commercial banks, for example, used VAR measures to quantify current trading exposures and compare them to established counterparty risk limits. In addition, VAR provided traders with information useful in formulating hedging policies and evaluating the effects of particular transactions on net portfolio risk. For managers, VAR became popular as a means of analyzing the performance of traders for compensation purposes and for allocating reserves or capital across business lines on a risk-adjusted basis.

Uses of VAR by Non-Dealers. Since its original development as a risk management tool for active trading firms, VAR has spread outside the dealer community. VAR now is used regularly by non-financial corporations, pension plans and mutual funds, clearing organizations, brokers and futures commission merchants, and insurers. These organizations find VAR just as useful as trading firms, albeit for different reasons.

Some benefits of VAR for non-dealers relate more to the exposure monitoring facilitated by VAR measurement than to the risk measurement task itself. For example, a pension plan with funds managed by external investment advisors may use VAR for policing its external managers. Similarly, brokers and account merchants can use VAR to assess collateral requirements for customers.

VAR AND CORPORATE RISK MANAGEMENT OBJECTIVES

Firms managing risks may be either *value risk managers* or *cash flow risk managers*.[15] A value risk manager is concerned with the firm's total value at a particular point in time. This concern may arise from a desire to avoid bankruptcy, mitigate problems associated with informational asymmetries, or reduce expected tax liabilities.[16] A cash flow risk manager, by contrast, uses risk management to reduce cash flow volatility and thereby increase debt capacity.[17] Value risk managers thus typically manage the risks of a *stock of assets*, whereas cash flow risk managers manage the risks of a *flow of funds*. A risk measure that is appropriate for one type of firm may not be appropriate for others.

Value Risk Managers and VAR-Based Risk Controls

As the term *value* at risk implies, organizations for which VAR is best suited are those for which *value* risk management is the goal. VAR, after all, is intended to summarize the risk of a stock of assets over a particular risk horizon. Those likely to realize the most benefits from VAR thus include clearinghouses, securities settlement agents,[18] and swap dealers. These organizations have in common a concern with the value of their exposures over a well-defined period of time *and* a wish to limit and control those exposures. In addition, the relatively short risk horizons of these enterprises imply that VAR measurement can be accomplished reliably and with minimal concern about changing portfolio composition over the risk horizon.

Many value risk managers have risks arising mainly from *agency* transactions. Organizations like financial clearing-houses, for example, are exposed to risk arising from intermediation services rather than the risks of proprietary position taking. VAR can assist such firms in monitoring their customer credit exposures, in

---

14. *See* Rod A. Beckström and Alyce R. Campbell, "The Future of Firm-Wide Risk Management," in *An Introduction to VAR*, Rod Beckström and Alyce Campbell, eds. (Palo Alto, Ca.: CAATS Software, Inc., 1995).

15. For a general discussion of the traditional corporate motivations for risk management, *see* David Fite and Paul Pfleider, "Should Firms Use Derivatives to Manage Risk?" in *Risk Management: Problems & Solutions*, William H. Beaver and George Parker, eds. (New York: McGraw-Hill, Inc., 1995).

16. *See, for example,* Clifford Smith and Rene Stulz, "The Determinants of Firms' Hedging Policies," *Journal of Financial and Quantitative Analysis*, Vol. 20 (1985):391-405.

17. *See, for example,* Kenneth Froot, David Scharfstein, and Jeremy Stein, "Risk Management: Coordinating Corporate Investment and Financing Policies," *Journal of Finance*, Vol. 48 (1993):1629-1658.

18. *See* Christopher L. Culp and Andrea M.P. Neves, "Risk Management by Securities Settlement Agents," *Journal of Applied Corporate Finance*, Vol. 10, No. 3 (Fall 1997):96-103.

setting position and exposure limits, and in determining and enforcing margin and collateral requirements.

Total vs. Selective Risk Management

Most financial distress-driven explanations of corporate risk management, whether value or cash flow risk, center on a firm's *total risk*.[19] If so, such firms should be indifferent to the *composition* of their total risks. *Any* risk thus is a candidate for risk reduction.

Selective risk managers, by contrast, deliberately choose to manage some risks and not others. Specifically, they seek to manage their exposures to risks in which they have no comparative informational advantage—for the usual financial ruin reasons—while actively exposing themselves, at least to a point, to risks in which they *do* have perceived superior information.[20]

For firms managing total risk, the principal benefit of VAR is facilitating explicit risk control decisions, such as setting and enforcing exposure limits. For firms that selectively manage risk, by contrast, VAR is useful largely for diagnostic monitoring *or* for controlling risk in areas where the firm perceives no comparative informational advantage. An airline, for example, might find VAR helpful in assessing its exposure to jet fuel prices; but for the airline to use VAR to analyze the risk that seats on its aircraft are not all sold makes little sense.

Consider also a hedge fund manager who invests in foreign equity because the risk/return profile of that asset class is desirable. To avoid exposure to the exchange rate risk, the fund could engage an "overlay manager" to hedge the currency risk of the position. Using VAR on the *whole position* lumps together two separate and distinct sources of risk—the currency risk and the foreign equity price risk. And *reporting* that total VAR without a corresponding expected return could have disastrous consequences. Using VAR to ensure that the currency hedge is accomplishing its intended aims, by contrast, might be perfectly legitimate.

VAR AND THE GREAT DERIVATIVES DISASTERS

Despite its many benefits to certain firms, VAR is not a panacea. Even when VAR is calculated appropriately, VAR *in isolation* will do little to keep a firm's risk exposures in line with the firm's chosen risk tolerances. Without a well-developed risk management infrastructure—policies and procedures, systems, and well-defined senior management responsibilities—VAR will deliver little, if any, benefits. In addition, VAR may not always help a firm accomplish its particular risk management objectives, as we shall see.

To illustrate some of the pitfalls of using VAR, we examine the four "great derivatives disasters" of 1993-1995: Procter & Gamble, Orange County, Barings, and Metallgesellschaft.[21] Proponents of VAR often claim that many of these disasters would have been averted had VAR measurement systems been in place. We think otherwise.[22]

Procter & Gamble

During 1993, Procter & Gamble ("P&G") undertook derivatives transactions with Bankers Trust that resulted in over $150 million in losses.[23] Those losses traced essentially to P&G's writing of a put option on interest rates to Bankers Trust. Writers of put options suffer losses, of course, whenever the underlying security declines in price, which in this instance meant whenever interest rates rose. And rise they did in the summer and autumn of 1993.

The put option actually was only one component of the whole deal. The deal, with a notional principal of $200 million, was a fixed-for-floating rate swap in which Bankers Trust offered P&G 10 years of floating-rate financing at 75 basis points below the commercial paper rate in exchange for the put and fixed interest payments of 5.3% annually. That huge financing advantage of 75 basis points apparently was too much for P&G's treasurer to resist, particularly because the put was well out-of-the-money

---

19. *See, for example,* Smith and Stulz, cited previously, and Froot, Scharfstein, and Stein, cited previously.

20. *See* Culp and Miller (Spring 1995), cited previously, and Stulz, cited previously.

21. In truth, Procter & Gamble was the only one of these disasters actually *caused* by derivatives. *See* Merton H. Miller, "The Great Derivatives Disasters: What Really Went Wrong and How to Keep it from Happening to You," speech presented to JP Morgan & Co. (Frankfurt, June 24, 1997) and Chapter Two in Merton H. Miller, *Merton Miller on Derivatives* (New York: John Wiley & Sons, Inc., 1997).

22. The details of all these cases are complex. We thus refer readers elsewhere for discussions of the actual events that took place and limit our discussion here only to basic background. *See, for example,* Stephen Figlewski, "How to Lose Money in Derivatives," *Journal of Derivatives,* Vol. 2, No. 2 (Winter 1994):75-82.

23. *See, for example,* Figlewski, cited previously, and Michael S. Gamze and Karen McCann, "A Simplified Approach to Valuing an Option on a Leveraged Spread: The Bankers Trust, Procter & Gamble Example," *Derivatives Quarterly,* Vol. 1, No. 4 (Summer 1995):44-53.

For firms that selectively manage risk, VAR is useful for controlling risk only in areas where the firm perceives no comparative informational advantage. An airline might find VAR helpful in assessing its exposure to jet fuel prices; but to use VAR to analyze the risk that seats on its aircraft are not all sold makes little sense.

when the deal was struck in May 1993. But the low financing rate, of course, was just premium collected for writing the put. When the put went in-the-money for Bankers Trust, what once seemed like a good deal to P&G ended up costing millions of dollars.

VAR would have helped P&G, *if* P&G also had in place an adequate risk management infrastructure—which apparently it did not. Most obviously, senior managers at P&G would have been unlikely to have approved the original swap deal if its exposure had been subject to a VAR calculation. But that presupposes a lot.

Although VAR would have helped P&G's senior management measure its exposure to the speculative punt by its treasurer, much more would have been needed to stop the treasurer from taking the interest rate bet. The first requirement would have been a system for measuring the risk of the swaps *on a transactional basis.* But VAR was never intended for use on single transactions.[24] On the contrary, the whole appeal of the concept initially was its capacity to aggregate risk *across* transactions and exposures. To examine the risk of an individual transaction, the *change* in portfolio VAR that would occur with the addition of that new transaction should be analyzed. But that still requires first calculating the total VAR.[25] So, for P&G to have looked at the risk of its swaps in a VAR context, its entire treasury area would have needed a VAR measurement capability.

Implementing VAR for P&G's entire treasury function might *seem* to have been a good idea *anyway.* Why not, after all, perform a comprehensive VAR analysis on the whole treasury area and get transactional VAR assessment capabilities as an added bonus? For some firms, that *is* a good idea. But for other firms, it is not. Many non-financial corporations like P&G, after all, typically undertake risk management in their corporate treasury functions for *cash flow* management reasons.[26] VAR is a *value* risk measure, not a cash flow risk measure. For P&G to examine value at risk for its *whole*

treasury operation, therefore, presumes that P&G was a *value* risk manager, and that may not have been the case. Even had VAR been in place at P&G, moreover, the assumption that P&G's senior managers would have been *monitoring* and *controlling* the VARs of individual swap transactions is not a foregone conclusion.

Barings

Barings PLC failed in February 1995 when rogue trader Nick Leeson's bets on the Japanese stock market went sour and turned into over $1 billion in trading losses.[27,28] To be sure, VAR would have led Barings senior management to shut down Leeson's trading operation in time to save the firm— *if they knew about it.* If P&G's sin was a lack of internal management and control over its treasurer, then Barings was guilty of an even more cardinal sin. The top officers of Barings lost control over the trading operation *not* because no VAR measurement system was in place, but because they let the same individual making the trades also serve as the recorder of those trades—violating one of the most elementary principles of good management.

The more interesting question emerging from Barings is why top management seems to have taken so long to recognize that a rogue trader was at work. For that purpose, a fully functioning VAR system would certainly have helped. Increasingly, companies in the financial risk-taking business use VAR as a monitoring tool for detecting unauthorized increases in positions.[29] Usually, this is intended for *customer* credit risk management by firms like futures commission merchants. In the case of Barings, however, such account monitoring would have enabled management to spot Leeson's run-up in positions in his so-called "arbitrage" and "error" accounts.

VAR measurements at Barings, on the other hand, would have been impossible to implement,

24. Recently, some have advocated that derivatives dealers should evaluate the VAR of specific transactions *from the perspective of their counterparties* in order to determine counterparty suitability. Without knowing the rest of the counterparty's risk exposures, however, the VAR estimate would be meaningless. Even with full knowledge of the counterparty's total portfolio, the VAR number still might be of no use in determining suitability for reasons to become clear later.

25. *See* Garman, cited previously.

26. *See, for example,* Judy C. Lewent and A. John Kearney, "Identifying, Measuring, and Hedging Currency Risk at Merck," *Journal of Applied Corporate Finance,* Vol. 2, No. 4 (Winter 1990):19-28, and Deana R. Nance, Clifford W. Smith, and Charles W. Smithson, "On the Determinants of Corporate Hedging," *Journal of Finance,* Vol. 48, No. 1 (1993):267-284.

27. *See, for example,* Hans R. Stoll, "Lost Barings: A Tale in Three Parts Concluding with a Lesson," *Journal of Derivatives,* Vol. 3, No. 1 (Fall 1995):109-115., and Anatoli Kuprianov, "Derivatives Debacles: Case Studies of Large Losses in Derivatives Markets," in *Derivatives Handbook: Risk Management and Control,* Robert J. Schwartz and Clifford W. Smith, Jr., eds. (New York: John Wiley & Sons, Inc., 1997).

28. Our reference to rogue traders is not intended to suggest, of course, that rogue traders are only found in connection with derivatives. Rogue traders have caused the banks of this world far more damage from failed real estate (and copper) deals than from derivatives.

29. *See* Christopher Culp, Kamaryn Tanner, and Ron Mensink, "Risks, Returns and Retirement," *Risk,* Vol. 10, No. 10 (October 1997):63-69.

given the deficiencies in the *overall* information technology ("IT") systems in place at the firm. At any point in time, Barings' top managers knew only what Leeson was telling them. If Barings' systems were incapable of reconciling the position build-up in Leeson's accounts with the huge wire transfers being made by London to support Leeson's trading in Singapore, no VAR measure would have included a complete picture of Leeson's positions. And without that, no warning flag would have been raised.

Orange County

The Orange County Investment Pool ("OCIP") filed bankruptcy in December 1994 after reporting a drop in its market value of $1.5 billion. For many years, Orange County maintained the OCIP as the equivalent of a money market fund for the benefit of school boards, road building authorities, and other local government bodies in its territory. These local agencies deposited their tax and other collections when they came in and paid for their own wage and other bills when the need arose. The Pool paid them interest on their deposits—handsomely, in fact. Between 1989-1994, the OCIP paid its depositors 400 basis points more than they would have earned on the corporate Pool maintained by the State of California—roughly $750 million over the period.[30]

Most of the OCIP's investments involved leveraged purchases of intermediate-term securities and structured notes financed with "reverse repos" and other short-term borrowings. Contrary to conventional wisdom, the Pool was making its profits *not* from "speculation on falling interest rates" but rather from an investment play on the *slope* of the yield curve.[31] When the Federal Reserve started to raise interest rates in 1994, the intermediate-term securities declined in value and OCIP's short-term borrowing costs rose.

Despite the widespread belief that the leverage policy led to the fund's insolvency and bankruptcy filing, Miller and Ross, after examining the

OCIP's investment strategy, cash position, and net asset value at the time of the filing, have shown that the OCIP was *not* insolvent. Miller and Ross estimate that the $20 billion in total assets on deposit in the fund had a positive net worth of about $6 billion. Nor was the fund in an illiquid cash situation. OCIP had over $600 million of cash on hand and was generating further cash at a rate of more than $30 million a month.[32] Even the reported $1.5 billion "loss" would have been completely recovered within a year—a loss that was realized only because Orange County's bankruptcy lawyers forced the liquidation of the securities.[33]

Jorion has taken issue with Miller and Ross's analysis of OCIP, arguing that VAR would have called the OCIP investment program into question long before the $1.5 billion loss was incurred.[34] Using several different VAR calculation methods, Jorion concludes that OCIP's one-year VAR at the end of 1994 was about $1 billion at the 5% confidence level. Under the usual VAR interpretation, this would have told OCIP to expect a loss in excess of $1 billion in one out of the next 20 years.

Even assuming Jorion's VAR number is accurate, however, his interpretation of the VAR measure was unlikely to have been the OCIP's interpretation—at least not *ex ante* when it could have mattered. The VAR measure in isolation, after all, takes no account of the *upside* returns OCIP was receiving as compensation for that downside risk. Remember that OCIP was pursuing a very deliberate yield curve, net cost-of-carry strategy, designed to generate high expected cash returns. That strategy had risks, to be sure, but those risks seem to have been clear to OCIP treasurer Robert Citron—and, for that matter, to the people of Orange County who re-elected Citron treasurer in preference to an opposing candidate who was criticizing the investment strategy.[35]

Had Orange County been using VAR, however, it almost certainly *would* have terminated its investment program upon seeing the $1 billion risk

---

30. Miller, cited previously.

31. When the term structure is upward sloping, borrowing in short-term markets to leverage longer-term government securities generates positive cash carry. A surge in inflation or interest rates, of course, could reverse the term structure and turn the carry negative. That is the real risk the treasurer was taking. But it was not much of a risk. Since the days of Jimmy Carter in the late 1970s, the U.S. term structure has never been downward sloping and nobody in December 1994 thought it was likely to be so in the foreseeable future.

32. Merton H. Miller and David J. Ross, "The Orange County Bankruptcy and its Aftermath: Some New Evidence," *Journal of Derivatives*, Vol. 4, No. 4 (Summer 1997):51-60.

33. Readers may wonder why, then, Orange County did declare bankruptcy. That story is complicated, but a hint might be found in the payment of $50 million in special legal fees to the attorneys who sued Merrill Lynch for $1.5 billion for selling OCIP the securities that lost money. In short, *lots* of people gained from OCIP's bankruptcy, even though OCIP was not actually bankrupt. *See* Miller, cited previously, and Miller and Ross, cited previously.

34. Philippe Jorion, "Lessons From the Orange County Bankruptcy," *Journal of Derivatives*, Vol. 4, No. 4 (Summer 1997):61-66.

35. Miller and Ross, cited previously.

Especially for institutional investors, a major pitfall of VAR is to highlight large potential losses over long time horizons without conveying any information about the corresponding expected return.

estimate. The reason probably would *not* have been the actual informativeness of the VAR number, but rather the fear of a public outcry at the number. Imagine the public reaction if the OCIP announced one day that it expected to lose more than $1 billion over the next year in one time out of 20. But that reaction would have far less to do with the actual risk information conveyed by the VAR number than with the lack of any corresponding expected profits reported *with* the risk number. Just consider, after all, what the public reaction would have been if the OCIP publicly announced that it would *gain* more than $1 billion over the next year in one time out of 20![36]

This example highlights a major abuse of VAR—an abuse that has nothing to do with the meaning of the value at risk number but instead traces to the presentation of the information that number conveys. Especially for institutional investors, a major pitfall of VAR is to highlight large potential losses over long time horizons *without conveying any information about the corresponding expected return.* The lesson from Orange County to would-be VAR users thus is an important one—for organizations whose mission is *to take some risks,* VAR measures of risks are meaningful *only* when interpreted alongside estimates of corresponding potential *gains.*

Metallgesellschaft

MG Refining & Marketing, Inc. ("MGRM"), a U.S. subsidiary of Metallgesellschaft AG, reported $1.3 billion in losses by year-end 1993 from its oil trading activities. MGRM's oil derivatives were part of a marketing program under which it offered long-term customers firm price guarantees for up to 10 years on gasoline, heating oil, and diesel fuel purchased from MGRM.[37] The firm hedged its resulting exposure to spot price increases with short-term futures contracts to a considerable extent. After several consecutive months of *falling* prices in the autumn of 1993,

however, MGRM's German parent reacted to the substantial margin calls on the losing futures positions by liquidating the hedge, thereby turning a paper loss into a very real one.[38]

Most of the arguments over MGRM—in press accounts, in the many law suits the case engendered, and in the academic literature—have focused on whether MGRM was "speculating" or "hedging." The answer, of course, is that like all other merchant firms, they were doing both. They were definitely speculating on the oil "basis"—inter-regional, inter-temporal, and inter-product *differences* in prices of crude, heating oil, and gasoline. That was the *business they were in.*[39] The firm had expertise and informational advantages far beyond those of its customers or of casual observers playing the oil futures market. What MGRM did not have, of course, was any special expertise about the level and direction of oil prices generally. Here, rather than take a corporate "view" on the direction of oil prices, like the misguided one the treasurer of P&G took on interest rates, MGRM chose to hedge its exposure to oil price *levels.*

Subsequent academic controversy surrounding the case has mainly been not whether MGRM was hedging, but whether they were *over*-hedging—whether the firm could have achieved the same degree of insulation from price level changes with a lower commitment from MGRM's ultimate owner-creditor Deutsche Bank.[40] The answer is that the day-to-day cash-flow volatility of the program *could* have been reduced by any number of cash flow variance-reducing hedge ratios.[41] But the cost of chopping off some cash drains when prices fell was that of losing the corresponding cash inflows when prices spiked up.[42]

Conceptually, of course, MGRM could have used VAR analysis to measure its possible financial risks. But why would they have wanted to do so? The combined marketing/hedging program, after all, was *hedged* against changes in the *level* of oil prices. The only significant risks to which MGRM's

---

36. Only for the purpose of this example, we obviously have assumed symmetry in the VAR distribution.

37. A detailed analysis of the program can be found in Christopher L. Culp and Merton H. Miller, "Metallgesellschaft and the Economics of Synthetic Storage," *Journal of Applied Corporate Finance,* Vol. 7, No. 4 (Winter 1995):62-76.

38. For an analysis of the losses incurred by MRGM—as well as why they were incurred—*see* Christopher L. Culp and Merton H. Miller, "Auditing the Auditors," *Risk,* Vol. 8, No. 4 (1995):36-39.

39. Culp and Miller (Winter 1995, Spring 1995), cited previously, explain this in detail.

40. *See* Franklin R. Edwards and Michael S. Canter, "The Collapse of Metallgesellschaft: Unhedgeable Risks, Poor Hedging Strategy, or Just Bad Luck?," *Journal of Applied Corporate Finance,* Vol. 8, No. 1 (Spring 1995):86-105.

41. *See, for example,* Froot, Scharfstein, and Stein, cited previously.

42. A number of other reasons also explain MGRM's reluctance to adopt anything smaller than a "one-for-one stack-and-roll" hedge. *See* Culp and Miller (Winter 1995, Spring 1995).

program was subject thus were basis and rollover risks—again, the risk that MGRM was *in the business of taking*.[43]

A much bigger problem at MGRM than the change in the *value* of its program was the large negative *cash flows* on the futures hedge that would have been offset by eventual gains in the future on the fixed-price customer contracts. Although MGRM's former management claims it had access to adequate funding from Deutsche Bank (the firm's leading creditor and stock holder), perhaps some benefit might have been achieved by more rigorous cash flow simulations. But even granting that, VAR would have told MGRM very little about its *cash flows* at risk. As we have already emphasized, VAR is a *value*-based risk measure.

For firms like MGRM engaged in *authorized* risk-taking—like Orange County and unlike Leeson/ Barings—the primary benefit of VAR really is just as an internal "diagnostic monitoring" tool. To that end, estimating the VAR of MGRM's basis trading activities *would* have told senior managers and directors at its parent what the basis risks were that MGRM actually was taking. But remember, MGRM's parent appears to have been fully aware of the risks MGRM's traders were taking *even without a VAR number*. In that sense, even the monitoring benefits of VAR for a proprietary trading operation would not have changed MGRM's fate.[44]

ALTERNATIVES TO VAR

VAR certainly is not the *only* way a firm can systematically measure its financial risk. As noted, its appeal is mainly its conceptual simplicity and its consistency across financial products and activities. In cases where VAR may *not* be appropriate as a measure of risk, however, other alternatives *are* available.

Cash Flow Risk

Firms concerned *not* with the value of a stock of assets and liabilities over a specific time horizon but with the volatility of a *flow of funds* often are better off eschewing VAR altogether in favor of a measure of cash flow volatility. Possible cash requirements over a *sequence* of future dates, for example, can be simulated. The resulting distributions of cash flows then enable the firm to control its exposure to cash flow risk more directly.[45] Firms worried about cash flow risk for preserving or increasing their debt capacities thus might engage in hedging, whereas firms concerned purely about liquidity shortfalls might use such cash flow stress tests to arrange appropriate standby funding.

Abnormal Returns and Risk-Based Capital Allocation

Stulz suggests managing risk-taking activities using abnormal returns—*i.e.,* returns in excess of the risk free rate—as a measure of the expected profitability of certain activities. Selective risk management then can be accomplished by allocating capital on a risk-adjusted basis and limiting capital at risk accordingly. To measure the risk-adjusted capital allocation, he suggests using the cost of new equity issued to finance the particular activity.[46]

On the positive side, Stulz's suggestion does not penalize selective risk managers for exploiting perceived informational advantages, whereas VAR does. The problem with Stulz's idea, however, lies in any company's capacity actually to implement such a risk management process. More properly, the difficulty lies in the actual estimation of the firm's equity cost of capital. And in any event, under M&M proposition three, all sources of capital are equivalent on a risk-adjusted basis. The source of capital for financing a particular project thus should not affect the decision to undertake that project. Stulz's reliance on equity only is thus inappropriate.

Shortfall Risk

VAR need not be calculated by assuming variance is a complete measure of "risk," but in practice this often *is* how VAR is calculated. (*See* the Appendix.) This assumption can be problematic when

---

43. The claim that MGRM was in the business of trading the basis has been disputed by managers of MGRM's parent and creditors. Nevertheless, the marketing materials of MGRM—on which the parent firm signed off—suggests otherwise. *See* Culp and Miller (Spring 1995), cited previously.

44. Like P&G and Barings, what happened at MGRM was, in the end, a *management* failure rather than a *risk management* failure. For details on how management failed in the MGRM case, *see* Culp and Miller (Winter 1995, Spring 1995). For a redacted version of the story, *see* Christopher L. Culp and Merton H. Miller, "Blame Mismanagement, Not Speculation, for Metall's Woes," *Wall Street Journal Europe* (April 25, 1995).

45. *See* Stulz, cited previously.

46. *See* Stulz, cited previously.

Firms concerned not with the value of a stock of assets and liabilities over a specific time horizon but with the volatility of a flow of funds often are better off eschewing VAR altogether in favor of a measure of cash flow volatility.

measuring exposures in markets characterized by non-normal (i.e., non-Gaussian) distributions—*e.g.,* return distributions that are skewed or have fat tails. If so, as explained in the Appendix, a solution is to generate the VAR distribution in a manner that does *not* presuppose variance is an adequate measure of risk. Alternatively, other summary risk measures can be calculated.

For some organizations, asymmetric distributions pose a problem that VAR on its own *cannot* address, no matter how it is calculated. Consider again the OCIP example, in which the one-year VAR implied a $1 billion loss in one year out of 20. With a symmetric portfolio distribution, that would also imply a $1 billion gain in one year out of 20. But suppose OCIP's investment program had a *positively skewed* return distribution. Then, the $1 billion loss in one year out of 20 might be comparable to, say, a $5 billion gain in one year of 20.

One of the problems with interpreting VAR thus is interpreting the confidence level—*viz.,* 5% or one year in 20. Some organizations may consider it more useful *not* to examine the loss associated with a chosen probability level but rather to examine the risk associated with a *given loss*—the so-called "doomsday" return below which a portfolio must *never* fall. Pension plans, endowments, and some hedge funds, for example, are concerned primarily with the possibility of a "shortfall" of assets below liabilities that would necessitate a contribution from the plan sponsor.

Shortfall risk measures are alternatives to VAR that allow a risk manager to define a specific target value below which the organization's assets must *never* fall and they measure risk accordingly. Two popular measures of shortfall risk are below-target probability ("BTP") and below-target risk ("BTR").[47]

The advantage of BTR, in particular, over VAR is that it penalizes large shortfalls more than small ones.[48] BTR is still subject to the same misinterpretation as VAR when it is reported without a corresponding indication of possible *gains*. VAR, however, relies on a somewhat arbitrary choice of a "probability level" that can be changed to exaggerate or to de-emphasize risk measures. BTR, by

contrast, is based on a real target—*e.g.,* a pension actuarial contribution threshold—and thus reveals information about risk that can be much more usefully weighed against expected returns than a VAR measure.[49]

CONCLUSION

By facilitating the consistent measurement of risk across distinct assets and activities, VAR allows firms to monitor, report, and control their risks in a manner that efficiently relates risk control to desired and actual economic exposures. At the same time, reliance on VAR can result in serious problems when improperly used. Would-be users of VAR are thus advised to consider the following three pieces of advice:

First, VAR is useful only to certain firms and only in particular circumstances. Specifically, VAR is a tool for firms engaged in *total value* risk management, where the consolidated values of exposures across a variety of activities are at issue. Dangerous misinterpretations of the risk facing a firm can result when VAR is wrongly applied in situations where total value risk management is *not* the objective, such as at firms concerned with *cash flow* risk rather than value risk.

Second, VAR should be applied very carefully to firms selectively managing their risks. When an organization deliberately takes certain risks as a part of its primary business, VAR can serve at best as a diagnostic monitoring tool for those risks. When VAR is analyzed and reported in such situations with no estimates of corresponding expected profits, the information conveyed by the VAR estimate can be extremely misleading.

Finally, as all the great derivatives disasters illustrate, no form of risk measurement—including VAR—is a substitute for good management. Risk management as a process encompasses much more than just risk measurement. Although judicious risk measurement can prove very useful to certain firms, it is quite pointless without a well-developed organizational infrastructure and IT system capable of supporting the complex and dynamic process of risk taking and risk control.

---

47. *See* Culp, Tanner, and Mensink, cited previously. For a complete mathematic discussion of these concepts, *see* Kamaryn T. Tanner, "An Asymmetric Distribution Model for Portfolio Optimization," manuscript, Graduate School of Business, The University of Chicago (1997).

48. BTP accomplishes a similar objective but does *not* weight large deviations below the target more heavily than small ones.

49. *See* Culp, Tanner, and Mensink, cited previously, for a more involved treatment of shortfall risk as compared to VAR.

To calculate a VAR statistic is easy *once you have generated the probability distribution for future values of the portfolio*. Creating that VAR distribution, on the other hand, can be quite hard, and the methods available range from the banal to the utterly arcane. This appendix reviews a few of those methods.

Variance-Based Approaches

By far the easiest way to create the VAR distribution used in calculating the actual VAR statistic is just to *assume* that distribution is normal (i.e., Gaussian). Mean and variance are "sufficient statistics" to fully characterize a normal distribution. Consequently, knowing the variance of an asset whose return is normally distributed is all that is needed to summarize the risk of that asset.

Using return variances and covariances as inputs, VAR thus can be calculated in a fairly straightforward way.[1] First consider a single asset. If returns on that asset are normally distributed, the 5th percentile VAR is always 1.65 standard deviations below the mean return. So, the variance is a sufficient measure of risk to compute the VAR on that asset—just subtract 1.65 times the standard deviation from the mean. The risk horizon for such a VAR estimate corresponds to the frequency used to compute the input variance.

Now consider two assets. In that case, the VAR of the portfolio of two assets can be computed in a similar manner using the variances of the two assets' returns. These variance-based risk measures then are combined using the correlation of the two assets' returns. The result is a VAR estimate for the portfolio.

The simplicity of the variance-based approach to VAR calculations lies in the assumption of normality. By *assuming* that returns on all financial instruments are normally distributed, the risk manager eliminates the need to come up with a VAR distribution using complicated modeling techniques. All that *really* must be done is to come up with the appropriate variances and correlations.

At the same time, however, by assuming normality, the risk manager has greatly limited the VAR estimate. Normal distributions, after all, are symmetric. Any potential for skewness or fat tails in asset returns thus is totally ignored in the variance-only approach.

In addition to sacrificing the possibility that asset returns may *not* be normally distributed, the variance-only approach to calculating VAR also relies on the critical assumption that asset returns are totally independent across increments of time. A multi-period VAR can be calculated only by calculating a single-period VAR from the available data and then extrapolating the multi-day risk estimate. For example, suppose variances and correlations are available for historical returns measured at the *daily* frequency. To get from a one-day VAR to a T-day VAR—where T is the risk horizon of interest—the variance-only approach requires that the one-day VAR is multiplied by the square root of T.

For return variances and correlations measured at the monthly frequency or lower, this assumption may not be terribly implausible. For daily variances and correlations, however, serial independence is a very strong and usually an unrealistic assumption in most markets. The problem is less severe for short risk horizons, of course. So, using a one-day VAR as the basis for a five-day VAR might be acceptable, whereas a one-day VAR extrapolated into a one-year VAR would be highly problematic in most markets.

Computing Volatility Inputs

Despite its unrealistic assumptions, simple variance-based VAR calculations are probably the dominant application of the VAR measure today. The approach is especially popular for corporate end users of derivatives, principally because the necessary software is cheap and easy to use.

All variance-based VAR measures, however, are not alike. The sources of inputs used to calculate VAR in this manner can differ widely. The next several subsections summarize several popular methods for determining these variances.[2] Note that these methods are *only* methods of computing *variances* on single assets. Correlations still must be determined to convert the VARs of individual assets into portfolio VARs.

---

1. A useful example of this methodology is presented in Anthony Saunders, "Market Risk," *The Financier*, Vol. 2, No. 5 (December 1995).
2. For more methods, *see* Jorion (1995), cited previously.

For more of a forward-looking measure of volatility, option-implied volatilities sometimes can be used to calculate VAR.

APPENDIX: CALCULATING VAR (Continued)

Moving Average Volatility. One of the simplest approaches to calculating variance for use in a variance-based VAR calculation involves estimating a historical moving average of volatility. To get a moving average estimate of variance, the average is taken over a rolling window of historical volatility data. For example, given a 20-day rolling window,[3] the daily variance used for one-day VAR calculations would be the average daily variance over the most recent 20 days. To calculate this, many assume a zero mean daily return and then just average the squared returns for the last 20 trading days. On the next day, a new return becomes available for the volatility calculation. To maintain a 20-day measurement window, the first observation is dropped off and the average is recomputed as the basis of the next day's VAR estimate.

More formally, denote the daily return from time t-1 to time t as r_t. Assuming a zero mean daily return, the moving average volatility over a window of the last D days is calculated as follows:

$$v_t^2 = \left[\frac{1}{D}\right]\sum_{i=0}^{D-1} r_{t-i}^2$$

where v_t is the daily volatility estimate used as the VAR input on day t.

Because moving-average volatility is calculated using equal weights for all observations in the historical time series, the calculations are very simple. The result, however, is a smoothing effect that causes sharp changes in volatility to appear as plateaus over longer periods of time, failing to capture dramatic changes in volatility.

Risk Metrics. To facilitate one-day VAR calculations and extrapolated risk measures for longer risk horizons, JP Morgan—in association with Reuters—began making available their RiskMetrics™ data sets. This data includes historical variances and covariances on a variety of simple assets—sometimes called "primitive securities."[4] Most other assets have cash flows that can be "mapped" into these simpler RiskMetrics assets for VAR calculation purposes.[5]

In the RiskMetrics data set, daily variances and correlations are computed using an "exponentially weighted moving average." Unlike the simple moving-average volatility estimate, an exponentially weighted moving average allows the most recent observations to be more influential in the calculation than observations further in the past. This has the advantage of capturing shocks in the market better than the simple moving average and thus is often regarded as producing a better volatility for variance-based VAR than the equal-weighted moving average alternative.

Conditional Variance Models. Another approach for estimating the variance input to VAR calculations involves the use of "conditional variance" time series methods. The first conditional variance model was developed by Engle in 1982 and is known as the autoregressive conditional heterskedasticity ("ARCH") model.[6] ARCH combines an autoregressive process with a moving average estimation method so that variance still is calculated in the rolling window manner used for moving averages.

Since its introduction, ARCH has evolved into a variety of other conditional variance models, such as Generalized ARCH ("GARCH"), Integrated GARCH ("IGARCH"), and exponential GARCH ("EGARCH"). Numerous applications of these models have led practitioners to believe that these estimation techniques provide better estimates of (time-series) volatility than simpler methods.

For a GARCH(1,1) model, the variance of an asset's return at time t is presumed to have the following structure:

$$v_t^2 = a_0 + a_1 r_{t-1}^2 + a_2 v_{t-1}^2$$

The conditional variance model thus incorporates a *recursive* moving average term. In the special case where $a_0=0$ and $a_1+a_2=1$, the GARCH(1,1) model reduces *exactly* to the exponentially weighted moving average formulation for volatility.[7]

Using volatilities from a GARCH model as inputs in a variance-based VAR calculation does not circumvent the statistical inference problem of presumed normality. By incorporating additional information

---

3. The length of the window is chosen by the risk manager doing the VAR calculation.

4. Jorion (1995), cited previously.

5. For a detailed explanation of this approach, *see* JP Morgan/Reuters, *RiskMetrics—Technical Document*, 4th ed. (1996).

6. Robert Engle, "Autoregressive Conditional Heteroskedasticity with Estimates of the Variance of United Kingdom Inflation," *Econometrica*, Vol. 50 (1982):391-407.

7. *See* Jorion (1995), cited previously.

into the volatility measure, however, more of the actual time series properties of the underlying asset return can be incorporated into the VAR estimate than if a simple average volatility is used.

Implied Volatility. All of the above methods of computing volatilities for variance-based VAR calculations are based on historical data. For more of a forward-looking measure of volatility, option-implied volatilities sometimes can be used to calculate VAR.

The implied volatility of an option is defined as the *expected future volatility* of the underlying asset over the remaining life of the option. Many studies have concluded that measures of option-implied volatility are, indeed, the *best* predictor of future volatility.[8] Unlike time series measures of volatility that are entirely backward-looking, option implied volatility is "backed-out" of actual option prices—which, in turn, are based on actual transactions and expectations of market participants—and thus is inherently forward-looking.

Any option-implied volatility estimate is dependent on the particular option pricing model used to derive the implied volatility. Given an observed market price for an option *and* a presumed pricing model, the implied volatility can be determined numerically. This variance may then be used in a VAR calculation for the asset underlying the option.

Non-Variance VAR Calculation Methods

Despite the simplicity of most variance-based VAR measurement methods, many practitioners prefer to avoid the restrictive assumptions underlying that approach—*viz.,* symmetric return distributions that are independent and stable over time. To avoid these assumptions, a risk manager must actually generate a full distribution of possible future portfolio values—a distribution that is neither necessarily normal nor symmetric.[9]

Historical simulation is perhaps the easiest alternative to variance-based VAR. This approach generates VAR distributions merely by "re-arranging" historical data—*viz.,* re-sampling time series data on the relevant asset prices or returns. This can be about as easy *computationally* as variance-based VAR, and it does *not* presuppose that everything in the world is normally distributed. Nevertheless, the approach is highly dependent on the availability of potentially massive amounts of historical data. In addition, the VAR resulting from a historical simulation is totally sample dependent.

More advanced approaches to VAR calculation usually involve some type of forward-looking simulation model, such as Monte Carlo. Implementing simulation methods typically is computationally intensive, expensive, and heavily dependent on personnel resources. For that reason, simulation has remained largely limited to active trading firms and institutional investors. Nevertheless, simulation does enable users to depart from the RiskMetrics normality assumptions about underlying asset returns without forcing them to rely on a single historical data sample. Simulation also eliminates the need to assume independence in returns over time—*viz.,* VAR calculations are no longer restricted to one-day estimates that must be extrapolated over the total risk horizon.

---

8. *See, for example,* Phillipe Jorion, "Predicting Volatility in the Foreign Exchange Market," *Journal of Finance,* Vol. 50 (1995):507-528.

9. Variance-based approaches avoid the problem of generating a new distribution by *assuming* that distribution.

CORPORATE INSURANCE STRATEGY: THE CASE OF BRITISH PETROLEUM

*by Neil A. Doherty, University of Pennsylvania, and Clifford W. Smith, Jr., University of Rochester**

I nsurable events such as product liability suits, toxic torts, and physical damage to corporate assets represent major production costs for industrial corporations. For large public companies, conventional practice is to buy insurance to hedge against large potential losses while self-insuring against smaller ones. The underlying logic of this strategy, which is reflected in insurance textbooks,[1] is essentially this: For large and medium-sized corporations, small losses—the kind that stem from localized fires, employee injuries, vehicle crashes, and so forth—occur with such regularity that their total cost is predictable. To the extent such losses are predictable in the aggregate, buying insurance amounts simply to exchanging known dollars of premium for roughly equivalent and relatively known dollars of loss settlements (a practice called "trading dollars" in the profession). Larger losses, by contrast, are rare and much less predictable. Because such losses are borne by the company's owners (mainly by its stockholders but also, if the losses are large enough, by its bondholders), they should be hedged with insurance.

Recently, however, British Petroleum, one of the largest industrial companies in the world, decided upon a major change in its insurance strategy that turns the conventional wisdom on its head. In this article, we analyze why BP now insures against most smaller losses while self-insuring against the larger ones. Our analysis focuses on factors affecting the market *supply* of insurance as well as the corporate demand for it. On the demand side, we demonstrate that the primary source of demand for insurance by widely held public companies is not, as standard insurance textbooks assume, to transfer risk from the corporation's owners, but rather to take advantage of insurance companies' efficiencies in providing risk-assessment, monitoring, and loss-settlement services. On the supply side, we explain why the capacity of insurance markets to underwrite very large (or highly specialized) exposures is quite limited. Given BP's size, when losses become large enough to be of concern, they exceed the capacity of the industry. In essence, BP has a comparative advantage relative to the insurance industry in bearing large losses.

* The authors wish to thank Judith Hanratty and Rodney Insall of British Petroleum for many discussions and insightful comments.

1. See, for example, G. E. Rejda, *Principles of Insurance* (Glenview, Ill.: Scott Foresman, 1989), pp. 52-53; and C. A. Williams, *Risk Management and Insurance* (New York: McGraw-Hill, 1989), Chapter 13.

A FRAMEWORK FOR EVALUATING CORPORATE INSURANCE

Before discussing the case of BP, we first provide a general framework for analyzing the corporate insurance decision—one that identifies the benefits and costs of insurance from the perspective of a corporate management intent on maximizing shareholder value.

The Important Difference Between Individual and Corporate Insurance[2]

Let's begin with the simplest case: the purchase of insurance by individuals. Insurance allows individuals to transfer risks to insurance companies, thus reducing uncertainty about their net worth and standard of living. In return for accepting the risk of losses, the insurance company charges a premium. The *expected cost* of the insurance, known as the "premium loading," is the difference between the premium and the present value of expected losses.

The decision to purchase insurance can be justified if the insurance company has a comparative advantage over the policyholder in bearing the risks in question. Such an advantage can derive from two sources: the reduction of risk accomplished by pooling a large portfolio of similar risks and better access to capital markets.

It is not hard to see that, relative to the risk-bearing capacity of insurance companies, the ability of most individuals to self-insure against large risks is quite limited. Private assets are not protected by the "limited liability" provision that shelters other assets of corporate stockholders. Thus, decisions by individuals to pay premiums to insure their hard assets and human capital are economically rational choices based primarily on insurance companies' advantages in pooling such risks.

Private or closely held corporations are likely to purchase insurance for the same reason—namely, their limited ability to bear certain risks relative to the risk-bearing capacity of insurance companies. The owners of such companies often have a large proportion of their wealth tied up in the firm; and, whether out of a desire to maintain control or some other motive, they choose not to diversify their own holdings fully. For most closely-held and private companies, then, logic and experience tell us that the companies' owners will self-insure only against those risks where they have specialized expertise and, hence, their own kind of comparative advantage.

The case of large, widely held public corporations, however, presents some important differences that standard insurance textbooks fail to acknowledge. The conventional wisdom says, in effect, that because the owners of corporations (their stockholders and bondholders) are individually risk-averse,[3] financial managers should attempt to minimize their exposure to large risks. What this explanation fails to recognize, however, is that the company's stockholders and bondholders generally diversify their own portfolios of corporate securities. In so doing, they effectively diversify away the kinds of risks insurable through insurance companies.

Now, it's true that the stock market effectively assesses corporations a risk premium when setting their minimum required rates of return on capital. In general, the greater a company's risk, the higher the rate of return it must earn, on average, to produce superior returns for its shareholders. But a company's required rate of return (also known as its cost of capital) depends only on its non-diversifiable risk.[4] And because most insurable risks can be readily managed by investors through diversification, capital markets will not reward companies for eliminating them.

In short, insurance purchases reduce the expected variance of a company's cash flows, but not

---

2. This discussion draws heavily on three articles by David Mayers and Clifford Smith, "On the Corporate Demand for Insurance," *Journal of Business* (1982), 281-296; "The Corporate Insurance Decision," *Chase Financial Quarterly* (Spring 1982), 47-65; "Corporate Insurance and the Underinvestment Problem," *Journal of Risk and Insurance*, LIV (1987), 45-54.

3. In the financial economics literature, risk aversion refers to an invidual who prefers the average outcome, or the "expected value" of a gamble, to taking a chance on the distribution of possible outcomes. Thus, a risk-averse individual would pay to get out of a risky situation or, alternatively, would demand a higher rate of return for holding a riskier security.

4. One of the cardinal principles of modern finance is that, on average and over long periods of time, investors both expect and receive rewards commensurate with the risks they bear. As the bulk of the academic evidence also shows,

however, average resturns on investment correlate most strongly with systematic or non-diversifiable risk. The measure of this risk, known as "beta," is a measure of the sensitivity of individual stock prices to market-wide and general economic developments; such risk cannot be eliminated by investors' diversification of their holdings. Nor is a company's systematic risk likely to be reduced by purchasing insurance—because insurable risks, to the extent they have no discernible correlation with broad economic cycles, are completely diversifiable for investors.

To the extent insurable losses do represent systematic risk, insurance will reduce the firm's cost of capital. But then insurance premiums paid must include an appropriate risk premium, which will offset any possible gain in terms of the firm's discount rate associated with competitively priced insurance. (See N. A. Doherty and S. M. Tinic, "A Note on Reinsurance under Conditions of Capital Market Equilibrium," *Journal of Finance*, 36 (1982), 949-953.)

its cost of capital. Thus, corporate purchases of insurance intended solely to reduce *investors'* exposures to such risks are negative-NPV projects; the loading built into insurance premiums represents a pure transfer from the company to the insurer.

The Real Benefits of Insurance

Why, then, do large corporations buy insurance? In this section, we describe a number of services and functions performed by insurance companies that provide the basis for a rational corporate demand for insurance—functions having nothing to do with stockholders' risk aversion. As described in sequence below, insurance purchases can increase shareholder value by:

■ avoiding underinvestment and other problems faced by companies whose financial solvency (or even just liquidity) could be threatened by uninsured losses;

■ transferring risk from non-owner corporate stakeholders—managers, employees, suppliers—at a disadvantage in risk-bearing;

■ providing efficiencies in loss assessment, prevention, and claims processing;

■ reducing taxes; and

■ satisfying regulatory requirements.

Avoiding the Underinvestment (and Associated Illiquidity) Problem. Although well-diversified shareholders and bondholders may not be concerned about the prospect of uninsured losses *per se*, they will become concerned if such losses materially raise the probability of financial insolvency. Shareholders are concerned about insolvency mainly because of its potential to cause significant reductions in companies' *operating* values—that is, reductions in the present value of expected operating cash flows.

There are two important things to keep in mind about a firm's operating cash flows in this context. First, large uninsured losses do not in and of themselves reduce ongoing operating values, but should be thought of instead as one-time reductions of a company's equity, or stock of capital (a point we return to below). Second, because operating cash

flows are before interest expense, a company's operating value can also be viewed as the sum of the bondholders' and the stockholders' claims on the company. This sharing of value between the two groups can create problems that end up reducing the operating value of the firm.

How does financial trouble, or just the prospect of trouble, reduce a company's operating value? To begin with the extreme case, companies that wind up in Chapter 11 face considerable interference from the bankruptcy court with their investment and operating decisions, not to mention substantial direct costs of administration and reorganization. But, even short of bankruptcy, financial difficulty can impose large indirect costs. One important source of such costs is a potential "underinvestment problem." This problem arises from conflicts of interest between stockholders and bondholders in companies with significant amounts of debt. As the example below illustrates, insurance can help manage this problem.

Consider a company with a large amount of debt outstanding that chooses not to purchase fire insurance for its plants. Suppose also that a large and highly profitable plant is destroyed at a time when a downturn in operating cash flow has depleted the company's cash reserves and driven down its stock price.

The company is then faced with a potentially difficult reinvestment decision—that is, whether and, if so, when to rebuild the plant. In these circumstances, the large casualty loss has the effect of cutting further into the firm's already deflated equity cushion, and so further raising its effective leverage ratio. This, needless to say, would be a difficult time for management to approach capital markets for funding.

In this situation, if the company's debt burden is heavy enough, a management acting on behalf of its shareholders would have an incentive to pass up such a positive-NPV investment. As Stewart Myers demonstrated years ago,[5] this would be a rational decision (not just the result of managerial shortsightedness) if enough of the value of the new investment went to shoring up the bondholders' position. The

---

5. More technically, insurance controls an aspect of Stewart Myers' underinvestment problem involving the joint effect of risk, limited liability, and leverage on project selection (see S. C. Myers, "Determinants of Corporate Borrowing," *Journal of Financial Economics*, 5 (1977), 147-176). With debt in the capital structure, the firm's stockholders can face incentives to turn down positive-NPV projects. An uninsured casualty loss reduces firm value, increasing the firm's

leverage and thereby exacerbating this incentive. Such behavior is anticipated by rational bondholders and will be reflected *ex ante* in the bond price. Thus the loss of value from distortions in project selection falls *ex ante* on shareholders. For a discussion of insurance can control such incentives, see Mayers and Smith (1987), cited in note 2.

new equity issue would amount to a major wealth transfer from stockholders to bondholders—and a shareholder-wealth-maximizing management would thus choose either not to rebuild the plant, or to defer it, thereby reducing overall firm value.[6]

Even if stockholders would end up sharing some of the benefits from reinvestment, such a severe liquidity problem could still tempt management to defer raising capital until the company's stock price increased. But, in this case, there would be a significant loss in operating value as a consequence of deferring the investment.

Now let's go back to the beginning of this story and assume that management instead purchases fire insurance. (In fact, debt covenants typically *require* companies to buy such insurance—in part to control this underinvestment incentive.) In that case, insurance effectively serves as a funding source. If the loss is large and the facilities must be replaced quickly, it provides a "leverage-neutral" source of financing that permits the company to avoid the costs of a hurried new issue. In so doing, insurance reduces the likelihood that management is confronted with this kind of decision.

A note on insurance and capital structure. An alternative solution to this underinvestment problem, of course, would be to reduce the amount of corporate debt. Indeed, one could argue that, as a general rule, corporate decisions to retain large exposures effectively reduce the optimal amount of debt—and, conversely, insurance purchases increase corporate debt capacity. But this conclusion, though correct as far as it goes, obscures an important feature of large casualty losses—their infrequency. Large uninsured losses, as suggested above, do not reduce ongoing operating values, but represent instead one-time reductions of a company's equity cushion. A company that chooses to self-insure such large exposures is thus making a decision that affects the adequacy of its *stock* of capital—including its ability to raise additional funds on short notice—rather than its ability to service a predictable *flow* of interest and principal payments out of regular operating cash flows.

Because large exposures are by definition infrequent events, an alternative way to manage them would be to arrange lines of credit available specifically in the event of a large uninsured loss. Such lines

of credit, at least for larger, more creditworthy companies that can obtain them at reasonable cost, potentially provide a more economical, custom-tailored solution to the problem of insuring against extreme illiquidity—while allowing the firm to use its remaining debt capacity more effectively.

For smaller companies, however, insurance is likely to be more valuable. To the extent such companies have lower liquidity and face higher transactions costs for new issues, they will find insurance to be both a lower-cost funding source and an indispensable means of increasing their corporate debt capacity.

Riskshifting within the Firm. Up to this point, we have viewed the corporation from the perspective of its investors and owners. Of course, the corporation is a vast network of contracts among various parties with conflicting as well as common interests. In addition to bondholders and stockholders, other corporate constituencies such as employees, managers, suppliers, and customers all have vested interests in the company's success.

Like the owners of private or closely-held companies, the corporation's managers, employees, suppliers, and customers may not be able to diversify insurable risks; and such risks, if not insured, can affect their future payoffs under their respective contracts. (In many cases, of course, these contracts are implied rather than explicit.) Because they are also risk-averse, these groups are likely to require extra compensation to bear any risk not assumed by the owners or transferred to an insurance company. Employees will demand higher wages (or reduce their loyalty or perhaps their work effort) at a company where the probability of layoff is greater. Managers with alternative opportunities will demand higher salaries (or maybe an equity stake in the company) to run firms where the risks of insolvency and financial embarrassment are significant. Suppliers will be more reluctant to enter into long-term contracts, and trade creditors will charge more and be less flexible, with companies whose prospects are more uncertain. And customers concerned about the company's ability to fulfil warranty obligations or service their products in the future may be reluctant to buy those products.

Because of limited liability, the amount of risk that can be allocated to the stockholders is limited

---

6. Such stories can be told about corporate decisions to invest in routine maintenance and safety projects; in highly leveraged or financially distressed firms, insurance purchases effectively force managements to make necessary maintenance investments by reducing their cash premiums for so doing.

by the capital stock of the company. Companies in service industries, for instance, are often thinly capitalized. And, for such companies, where the claims—and thus the risks—of managers and employees are likely to be very large relative to the claims of investors, there may be substantial benefits from transferring those risks to an insurance company.

Even if companies self-insure, the above argument can also be extended to the design of *management compensation* contracts. Effective compensation plans achieve an appropriate balance between two partly conflicting aims: strengthening managers' performance incentives and insulating them from risks beyond their control. Incentive considerations require that compensation be linked to performance measures such as share price and earnings. A potential problem with such performance proxies is that they contain significant variation (or "noise") that is unrelated to management's performance. Because uninsured losses are a potential source of such noise, companies may achieve economies in risk-bearing by excluding uninsured losses from performance measures that serve as the basis for managerial evaluations and bonuses. In so doing, though, companies should be mindful of avoidable losses and ensure that managers still have strong incentives to take sensible measures to control such risks.

Service Efficiencies. Besides transferring risk, insurance companies often provide a set of related services—and at a significantly lower cost than offered elsewhere. One obvious example, as mentioned earlier, is insurers' comparative advantage in processing and settling claims, an advantage that derives from specialization and economies of scale. Thus, we would expect part of the corporate demand for insurance to be explained by insurers' expertise and efficiency in providing low-cost claims administration.[7]

Other services for which insurance companies are likely to have a comparative advantage are the assessment of loss exposures (more precisely, estimation of the parameters of the loss distribution) and the design, administration, and auditing of safety and other loss-control programs. Although these services are occasionally priced and sold separately, they are typically bundled with insurance. When insurers accumulate large numbers of exposures, they not only reduce risks through pooling, but also achieve economies of scale and other benefits from specialization that economists typically refer to as "organizational capital."

The most tangible aspect of this organizational capital is the large data base built up by an insurance company over years of underwriting. The data base allows for extensive and precise actuarial analysis, which in turn enables the insurer to estimate and classify individual exposures more accurately and price their products appropriately.[8] Indeed, this data base constitutes one of an insurer's principal comparative advantages over its policyholders in insuring many corporate risks—namely, its greater confidence in forecasting its policyholder's loss distribution for events such as fires, vehicle collisions, and workers' injuries.

In general, then, it is the frequency of events that makes them amenable to statistical analysis. But, for exposures in which new or specialized technology is employed—especially if losses are infrequent—more subjective and hence less precise estimation techniques such as engineering risk assessment must take the place of statistical analysis. In these cases, the industrial companies that have developed the new technology can generally use their own organizational capital to assess the risks posed by the technology. (Also, if the company is better able to assess the risk than the insurer, adverse selection becomes a serious problem—a point we discuss below.) Hence, insurance companies are likely to operate at a competitive disadvantage in indemnifying those companies for such risks. In this sense, insurance companies' inability to apply actuarial analysis to the pricing of their products helps to define the limits of the insurance industry's products.

Similar issues of comparative advantage arise in connection with safety, loss control, and loss prevention. Insurers data bases permit them to identify common types of accidents, often enabling them to advise clients as to potential sources of risk and cost-

---

7. A striking confirmation of this general argument is the existence of "claims only" insurance contracts—those in which the insurance company provides only claims-management services while the insured firm pays all the claims. Claims only policies, moreover, represent only an extreme of a spectrum of insurance policies that allow the insured company to maintain a degree of self-insurance. More often employed are policies that use retrospective ratings that continually adjust the premium to reflect actual claims experience over the life of the policy. This means the insured is effectively bearing most of the risk of claims losses.

8. From the insurer's perspective, this is necessary to quote competitive insurance premiums. Failure of an insurer to categorize individuals accurately by loss expectation leads to adverse selection by policyholders.

For exposures in which new or specialized technology is employed, more subjective and hence less precise estimation techniques such as engineering risk assessment must take the place of statistical analysis. In these cases, insurance companies are likely to operate at a competitive disadvantage in indemnifying industrial firms.

effective means of reducing expected losses. Some specialist insurers—factory mutual insurance firms, for example—focus as much on safety audits as on the provision of insurance services. As suggested above, however, the more specialized and complex the technology, the more likely is the producer, not the insurer, to have a comparative advantage in designing and implementing a loss-prevention program. In such cases, producers are likely to perform these functions themselves.

One specific area, however, in which insurers are almost certain to have superior expertise is the defense of lawsuits. Access to the insurer's lawyers and other defense resources can reduce the expected costs of third-party liability claims. Insurers regularly defend such cases, whereas individual policyholders see them infrequently. Moreover, the adverse reputation effects that could come from vigorous defense of a lawsuit are partly shifted to the insurer that effectively conducts the case. This is particularly useful in cases where third-party claimants have a continuing relationship with the firm, as in the case of workers-compensation or product-liability claims.

Tax Benefits. The tax benefits of corporate insurance derive from the interaction of two factors: (1) the ability of corporate insurance to reduce the volatility of reported income and (2) the effective progressivity of most of the world's tax codes.

In the United States, and most other jurisdictions throughout the world, tax codes permit the deduction of both insurance premiums and of uninsured losses. Given (1) a constant marginal tax rate and (2) actuarially fair premiums, such provisions would have a neutral effect on the decision to purchase insurance. That is, the expected present value of tax deductions would be the same with insurance as without.

In practice, however, the marginal tax rate in the U.S. (and in most other jurisdictions) is not constant, but rather "convex"; that is, a company's effective tax rate rises along with increases in pre-tax income. Increasing marginal tax rates, tax shields such as depreciation allowances and interest expense, the inability to earn interest on tax-loss carry forwards, and the alternative minimum tax all work together to impose higher effective rates of taxation on higher levels of reported income and to provide lower percentage rebates for ever larger losses. Given U.S. tax treatment of insurance premiums and uninsured losses, the reductions in the volatility of taxable income resulting from insurance effectively reduce corporate taxes.

In the case of multinational corporations, tax liabilities are imposed by a number of different jurisdictions (the various countries in which they operate). Reductions in the expected tax liabilities in different jurisdictions can reduce expected taxes incurred in each, thereby reducing a multinational's overall worldwide taxes. For this reason, local purchases of insurance can add value by reducing expected local tax obligations, although they have little or no effect on the risk of aggregate corporate income.

Regulatory Requirements. Financial-responsibility laws sometimes require insurance coverage. For example, many jurisdictions require that an operator of motor vehicles have insurance or other evidence of financial capability to discharge third-party liability claims. Similar requirements are often found in workers-compensation insurance. A further example in the U.S. is the financial-responsibility requirement associated with handling hazardous materials under the Resource Control and Recovery Act of 1976.

These requirements are generally modest relative to the resources of medium to large companies. For example, in the U.S. the requirement for automobile liability insurance is typically in the range of $30,000 to $50,000. Such regulatory requirements tend to increase the demand for insurance covering relatively small losses.

The Supply Side of Corporate Insurance

As stated earlier, the gross profit to an insurer from underwriting a given policy, known as the premium loading, is defined as the difference between the expected loss and the premium. The insurance premium can be further decomposed into the expected indemnity payment, administrative costs (including the costs of providing services), a normal profit, and any rent, or "abnormal profit," that might be captured by the insurer.

Thus, some elements of the loading are not a cost to the policyholder—for example, the expected cost of various services bundled with the coverage. But other parts of the loading represent a transfer to the insurer and thus deter the purchase of insurance. This is true not only of insurer rents, but also of the component of expected indemnity payments attributable to moral hazard and adverse selection—two well-known problems confronting insurance underwriters that we discuss below. These factors affect the comparative advantage of insurance versus other risk-management strategies.

Effective Competition. Expected rents depend on the degree of competition. Some sectors of the insurance market are highly competitive; barriers to entry are low, insurers sell large numbers of homogenous policies with low correlation among payoffs, and expected losses are easily estimated. Since aggregate losses are fairly predictable, relatively little capital is required to ensure the solvency and maintain the creditworthiness of the insurer. Moreover, the routine nature of the business and the presence of established independent selling networks—that is, independent agents and brokers—serve to reduce the required investment in underwriters, actuaries, engineers, and individuals with other technical skills. Such markets include those for routine small property and liability losses incurred by large companies[9] as well as various kinds of insurance for small businesses and individuals.

In contrast, the markets for large losses and for certain specialized risks are characterized by significantly less competition. For example, writing pollution insurance requires a large investment in the ability to provide environmental audits and risk assessment; there are few U.S. insurers active in this market (A.I.G. and Reliance are the two best-known). There are also few insurers that offer coverage of very large exposures. Such business requires a large surplus—that is, equity—and substantial investment in establishing reinsurance facilities. Such an investment can be viewed as necessary reputational capital. Success in selling policies for such large exposures depends critically on the insurer's ability to assure the insured that the contract will be honored if losses occur. A large stock of equity capital may be the only credible means of backing that promise.

A significant portion of worldwide capacity for insuring very large and unusual exposures is provided by Lloyd's of London. In part, this is due to its distinctive organizational form. With unlimited liability, Lloyd's syndicates have additional implicit reserves in the form of a call on the wealth of their members. But since the value of this call depends on the net worth of the members, the ultimate capacity of Lloyd's is limited.[10] Thus, the markets for pollution and other unusual lines of insurance, for high-risk lines, and for very high levels of all lines of insurance are characterized by less competition and higher expected insurer rents.

The effective supply of insurance coverage is not limited by the financial capability of *individual* insurers. Insurance is commonly syndicated among several insurers. Alternatively, policyholders can "layer" insurance protection by purchasing separate policies from several insurers (known as "surplus-lines" insurers). In yet another alternative, the capacity of individual insurers can be extended by selling secondary claims on some of its policies—or on its entire portfolio—in the reinsurance market. In most cases, some combination of these mechanisms is used to spread coverage over the market through a complex network.

Yet, in spite of these possibilities for combining insurer capacity, there are still limits to the amount of insurance protection available in the marketplace for certain kinds of exposures. For example, it is difficult to place insurance for exposures in excess of $500 million, and virtually impossible to find protection for exposures in excess of $1 billion, even on restricted terms.

Even for policies well under $500 million, the "quality" of insurance is not constant. In insurance markets, the expected value of coverage falls with the size of the claim for a number of reasons. First, a large claim can cause an insurer to become insolvent, and insurance contracts are not fully enforceable against an insolvent insurer. Even if large claims do not trigger insolvency, they often cause significant financial difficulty for insurers, especially in the surplus-lines market where the variance of claims is usually high relative to the insurer's surplus (equity). Enforcing contracts against such insurers can be very costly since they can dispute their obligations under the contract and otherwise delay settlements. The costs of enforcing contracts include legal costs of the actions as well as increases in the costs of writing future contracts

---

9. For example, the fire insurer insuring 5,000 independently owned retail grocery stores will significantly improve its diversification by insuring one additional policyholder which is a chain owning 4,000 stores. It might further improve its diversification by insuring the smaller losses on much bigger risks, small fire losses (not exceeding $500,000) on department stores, electronics manufacturers, etc.

10. There is also some question concerning the enforceability of claims against members' wealth. Following recent catastrophic loss experience in a number of syndicates, Lloyds is facing a number of lawsuits from members who are alleging negligent underwriting and challenging the call on their wealth.

because reputational capital has depreciated. These problems can be particularly acute since the expected adverse reputation consequences of disputing claims are less of a restraint on an insurer facing a higher probability of insolvency.

Moral Hazard and Adverse Selection. Moral hazard and adverse selection arise naturally in insurance markets. Moral hazard—loosely speaking, the tendency for insured parties to exercise less care and thus to experience greater losses than the uninsured—is one factor that works against insurance purchase by all potential policyholders. The expected costs of the average policyholder's actions will be built into the insurance premium. Adverse selection—the likelihood that insurers will get a riskier-than-average sample, given the tendency of less risky parties to self-insure—discourages the purchase of insurance by those policyholders that are of low risk relative to their class. The industry practice of "experience rating"—in which the premiums for future insurance contracts are based on prior claim experience—is widely used to control moral hazard and adverse selection problems. In the case of insurable risks involving frequent losses, experience rating is an especially effective control device: it motivates the policyholder to reduce the risk of losses, thereby reducing moral hazard; and it quickly reveals loss characteristics, thus reducing the costs of adverse selection.

When losses are infrequent, however, experience rating is less useful. Simply because large losses occur much less often than small ones, the costs of adverse selection and moral hazard built into the premiums of very large insurance policies tend to be much larger than the same costs confronting purchasers of small policies.

THE CASE OF BRITISH PETROLEUM

BP comprises four operating companies. BP Exploration is the upstream company, which is responsible for exploration and development of new oil and gas resources. BP Oil is the downstream business, whose activities include refining, distribution, and retailing of petroleum products. The remaining two companies are BP Chemicals, which concentrates in petrochemicals, acetyl, and nitrates,

and BP Nutrition, a relatively small company in the animal-feed business.

Perhaps the most striking feature of BP is its size. It is the largest company in the U.K., and the second largest in Europe. BP's equity capital is approximately $35 billion, and its debt is approximately $15 billion. After-tax profit has averaged $1.9 billion over the previous five years with a standard deviation of $1.1 billion.[11]

BP's major assets include exploration and extraction licenses, and scientific and technical capital specific to the oil industry in the form of rigs, pipelines, refineries, ships, road tankers and filling stations. While the company has operations worldwide (for example, it has some 13,000 service stations in some 50 countries), it has two major concentrations of value: its production licenses and its facilities in the North Sea and on the Alaska North Slope. This concentration of value, together with the limited range of the company's activities, imply that significant aspects of its business risk are relatively undiversified.

BP's Loss Exposures

BP's loss exposure ranges from routine small losses to potential losses in the multi-billion-dollar range. At the low end of this scale, there are vehicle accidents, minor shipping accidents, industrial injuries, small fires, and equipment failures. On a larger scale, potential losses include refinery fires or explosions, minor environmental damage from oil spills, and loss of (nautical) oil tankers. Very large losses could result from clean-up costs arising from major oil spills, tort claims for widespread injuries caused by release of toxic chemicals, liability for defective fuel causing a major airline disaster, and loss of an offshore rig with major loss of life (as in the Piper Alpha case). Perhaps one of the largest foreseeable losses to an oil firm would be the withdrawal of operating licenses as a consequence of political backlash in response to environmental damage.

BP employed independent actuarial consultants to estimate its loss distribution. The actuaries had access to extensive industry and BP loss data. Table 1 provides a summary of BP's estimated loss exposure—one that is based not only on BP's

---

11. These numbers reflect BP's balance sheet and income statement as of year-end 1991, the last full year for which data were available when the authors were assisting in the analysis of the company's insurance strategy.

TABLE 1 ACTUARY'S ESTIMATE OF BP'S LOSS DISTRIBUTION AT 1990 (MILLIONS OF DOLLARS)	Loss Range	Number per Year	Average Loss	Expected Annual Loss	Standard Deviation
	$0-$10	1845.00	$0.03	$52	$12
	$10-$500	1.70	40.00	70	98
	$500 plus	0.03	1000.00	35	233
	Whole Distribution	1846.73	$0.66	$157	

Note: This table covers all insurable losses whether or not they were previously insured.

experience but also on that of other firms in the oil and chemical industries.[12]

A comparison of these figures with other BP financial statistics provides some useful insights. For example, assuming a corporate tax rate of 35%, an uninsured pretax loss of $500 million represents less than a 1% reduction of the market value of BP equity; it also amounts to only 17% of average annual after-tax earnings over the last five years, and about 30% of the standard deviation of average earnings.

Historically, BP has insured its property and liability exposures. It has also insured, to a very limited extent, business-interruption exposures where insurance coverage has been available. Liability insurance and business-interruption insurance has been placed largely with external insurers, though some insurance has been purchased from an oil-industry mutual called O.I.L. (of which BP was a joint owner). O.I.L. in turn reinsures the upper tail of its exposures. Some property has been insured directly by independent insurers, other property through a captive insurer, which also reinsures.

Thus, in the past, BP has purchased considerable external insurance protection. Virtually all of this insurance covers the first two loss ranges—those under $10 million and those between $10 and $500 million—and most has been in the $10-$500 million category. With only one or two exceptions, insurance has been unavailable above $500 million, and BP has historically self-insured in this range.

Using the cost-benefit framework presented earlier in this article, BP recently undertook a

comprehensive re-examination of its insurance strategy. In the pages that follow, we describe BP's new approach to each of the three loss categories.

Coverage for Losses Below $10 Million

Under the new approach, losses below $10 million are now the responsibility of the managers of the local operating unit. (Such decisions were previously made by BP's insurance subsidiary.) Where there is a demonstrable need for insurance, local managers may buy it from BP's captive insurer or seek competitive quotations in local markets.

Expected changes in firm value (and leverage ratios) resulting from uninsured losses at this level are small. The standard deviation of after-tax earnings for BP exceeds $1 billion. In comparison, self-insuring losses under $10 million increases the standard deviation of earnings by only $12 million. Thus, the expected benefits of insurance in controlling financial-distress costs are trivial at this level.

The decision to allow local managers to insure small losses reflects other considerations:
■ Because markets for losses at this level are very competitive, market forces effectively eliminate expected insurer rents.
■ Insurers have a comparative advantage in service-provision activities such as claims administration. Because losses within this range are frequent and routine, insurers have an informational advantage in loss assessment and control, and contract enforcement is reliable.

---

12. Curve fitting permits estimation of the tail of the loss distribution despite the absence (or virtual absence) of very large losses in the loss record. Distributions such as the compound poisson are found to fit reasonably well. In addition, loss scenarios are constructed for possible large and unusual events that are not in the loss record but which nevertheless are considered to be feasible. (Note also that it would be rare for an insurer to undertake a study of this intensity to estimate the loss distribution for an individual client.)

■ Insurance coverage satisfies local financial-responsibility requirements.

■ Insurance reduces noise in the performance measures employed for local managers, producing stronger incentives for good performance.

■ Because of the localized nature of some of BP's tax liabilities, there are potential tax-related benefits of insurance.

Coverage for Losses Between $10 Million and $500 Million

Losses above $10 million are not to be insured using external insurance markets except in specific circumstances (for example, in cases where insurance is required under existing bond indentures or joint-venture provisions). This represents a major change in policy, since most of the company's losses in the $10-$500 million range were previously insured. This strategy change reflects the following considerations:

■ At this level, effective competition in insurance markets is limited.

■ The costs of enforcing contracts are high.

■ Over this range of losses, insurers do not have a comparative advantage in supplying safety and other services that are bundled with financial indemnification.

■ The impact of such losses on total corporate value is quite limited (as shown in Table 1, self-insuring losses between $10 million and $500 million increases the standard deviation of annual earnings (and cash flow) by only $98 million).

Over the ten-year period ending in 1989, BP paid $1.15 billion in premiums and recovered $250 million in claims (both in present values). In effect, this amounts to a 360% loading on realized losses. This loading can be broken down into several components: (1) a reserve against catastrophe losses, (2) a payment for bundled insurance services, and (3) a payment for transaction costs, and (4) rents for the insurer. Transaction costs and bundled services typically account for 10% to 30% of premiums. We doubt that the size of this loading can be explained

as a catastrophe reserve. The difference of $900 million between premiums and losses is simply too large to be accounted for by the prospect of large losses that, owing to chance, failed to materialize over the ten-year span.[13] Thus, we can only conclude that insurers received extraordinary rents in insuring these losses.

The explanation for this rent is found partly in the limited competition in this market. Few insurers are willing to make a market in risks the size and nature of BP's. Much of the market capacity, as mentioned earlier, is provided by Lloyd's syndicates. A large loss, however, would have a material impact on Lloyd's financial position. For example, a $500 million loss would amount to about 8% of Lloyd's total annual premia, 90% of profits, and 4% of surplus. Moreover, these statistics reflect the combined numbers of all Lloyd's syndicates, even though only a subset made a market for BP. In short, the potential for a large loss to impose financial stress on BP's insurers is great.

This problem arising from limited competition is aggravated by several contractual and institutional features of insurance markets.

Enforcement Costs. In the case of large losses, enforcement problems are higher due to the low frequency of such losses, which in turn reduces the effectiveness of reputational restraints on opportunistic behavior by insurers. To illustrate potential enforcement costs, consider that in the only large liability loss BP has filed with its insurers, settlement with the insurers was not reached until several years after settlement with the plaintiff. The insurance settlement, moreover, was only 70% of the liability claim; and, to secure this 70%, BP estimated that its expenses, legal costs, and management time in resolving this dispute amounted to approximately $1 million.

There are good reasons to view this as a representative rather than an unusual experience. Small losses occur routinely but large losses are rare. Indeed, the data in Table 1 contain the implication that losses greater than $500 million occur only about once every 30 years. Although insurers are unlikely

---

13. Suppose the total premiums paid, $1.15 billion (present values), were competitively priced in the sense that they represent the expected value of losses of $880 million plus a typical expense loading of about 20%. We can approximate this as a sequence of ten annual expected losses each having a present value of $88 million. (We cannot compare this $88 million directly with the Table 1 estimate of $70 million for second-tier losses since not all losses in this tier were insured.) If we use the coefficient of variation from the second tier in the table (1.4), this yields an estimate for the standard deviation of annual aggregate losses actually insured of $108.4 million. If losses are time independent, the standard deviation of the aggregate losses for the ten-year period is $[(10)(108.4)^2]^{1/2} = \$342$ million. The realized losses for the period are $250 million, which is 1.84 standard deviations below the assumed total expected losses of $880 million. Using standard normal tables, there is only a .033 chance that revealed losses could be that low. This estimate is conservative since the loss distribution is skewed to the right. For such cases, use of the standard normal table will normally overestimate the probability mass in the left hand tail and underestimate the mass in the right hand tail.

to sacrifice their reputational investments with clients for modest savings in disputing small claims, concerns about reputation are a much less effective restraint on insurers' opportunism when faced with large, infrequent losses.

Small losses also tend to come from repetitions of similar events such as damage to cars at autowashers, customer accidents, or crashes of road tankers. Given the large body of accumulated experience in negotiating past claim settlements and the experience of courts in interpreting contracts, there is little room for disagreement on coverage. Larger losses, by contrast, often present unusual facts and challenges for which there is little experience. The scope for different legal interpretations and, hence, the expected enforcement costs are correspondingly larger.

For large losses, the unlimited liability structure of the Lloyd's syndicates can make contract enforcement difficult. Lloyd's closes its accounts after three years and distributes surplus. Thus, much of a syndicate's reserves for long-gestation losses, such as liability claims, takes the form of a call on the personal wealth of the underwriting members. In recent years, attempts to recover deficits from members have met legal challenges (such as malpractice suits against the underwriter). Costly access to reserves and surplus raises expected enforcement costs.

The potential for dispute under large claims can be further increased by insurers' practice of laying off risks through the purchase of reinsurance. If a primary insurer disputes a claim and loses the ensuing litigation, the primary insurer must settle the claim to its policyholder and the reinsurer is then bound to the primary firm. However, if the primary settles a claim without a challenge, but the reinsurer considers that the loss was not covered by the primary contract language, the reinsurer might dispute its settlement to the primary. Consequently, when deciding whether to settle or fight claims, primary firms have to anticipate both the chances of being successful in litigation with their policyholder and whether they can bind their reinsurer in any settlement. (Similarly, the threat of legal challenges to syndicates at Lloyds from their members may act as an important factor in resisting settlements.) Since large losses generally involve reinsurance contracts, this further raises enforcement costs for large losses.

Comparative Advantage in Risk Assessment. In operating its production, refining, and distribution activities, BP has considerable engineering and related skills. These are put to further use in safety programs that relate to design of facilities, inspection, *post mortem* on actual losses, and analysis of loss records. Given the scale and specialized nature of its operations, BP has a comparative advantage over its insurers in providing these services.

Management Incentives and Self-Insurance. The decision to self-insure against losses within this range has, however, created one problem that management has chosen to address. Uninsured losses, while posing little risk to aggregate firm value, can introduce significant "noise" into local and regional performance measures. Because such losses are infrequent and discrete events, the corporation has adopted a policy of eliminating this noise from performance measures on an *ad hoc* basis. That is, losses will not be charged against profit centers— and thereby reduce management bonuses—except insofar as the loss reflects poor management (say, a failure to enforce adequate safety standards).

Coverage for Losses Above $500 Million

BP has chosen to continue self-insuring very large losses—primarily for supply considerations: As the size of the loss becomes material for BP, it exceeds the capacity of the insurance market.

Such expected losses, moreover, are not necessarily as large as they look because of what amount to generous co-insurance provisions in many countries' tax codes, especially the U.K.'s. Uninsured casualty losses generate tax shields, thus allowing BP to share these losses with the tax authorities. The tax code thus provides an implicit insurance policy with a coinsurance rate equal to the effective tax rate.

Losses greater than $500 million are most likely to occur in BP's two major geographical concentrations, the North Sea and the North Slope of Alaska. BP's effective tax rate for income from its North Sea production is 87%. Thus a $2 billion North Sea loss would result in only a $260 million reduction in firm value (and the expected cost of negotiation with the Inland Revenue Service over the tax treatment for losses in this range appears modest).

Another consideration reinforcing BP's decision to self-insure very large losses is that such losses could actually lead to increases in oil prices. For example, an oilrig fire of the magnitude of the Piper Alpha disaster in the North Sea could result in new safety regulations; or a large tanker spill like the one experienced by the Exxon Valdez in Alaska could lead to the withdrawal of operating licenses. Be-

> The expected costs of financial distress can be reduced by combining a policy of self-insurance with lower financial leverage. However, the use of dedicated standby lines of credit can be used to provide additional liquidity while limiting the required reduction in financial leverage.

cause BP has what amounts to a very large long position in oil, the expected price increases from such supply reductions reduce BP's net exposure.

Work in Progress

To manage its remaining exposure more effectively, BP is considering some additional adjustments. As one example, the three-tiered insurance strategy described above makes use of the tendency for both the costs and the benefits of insurance to increase with loss size. The tax effects just noted, however, suggest the need for some refinement of this strategy. Given the wide variation in marginal tax rates for different jurisdictions (ranging from zero to the 87% rate for North Sea production), losses of the same pre-tax value can result in widely different after-tax costs to BP. The initial allocation of exposures to the various tiers was based on pre-tax losses. This strategy is being fine-tuned to reflect after-tax costs.

A second issue to be examined more carefully is the effect of self-insurance on BP's optimal capital structure. As we observed earlier, the expected costs of financial distress can be reduced by combining a policy of self-insurance with lower financial leverage. However, the use of dedicated standby lines of credit, especially in the case of a large, creditworthy firm like BP, can be used to provide additional liquidity while limiting the required reduction in financial leverage.

In addition to lines of credit, financial instruments that include financial "shock absorbers" could also be used to lower the cost of an uninsured casualty loss. Consider, for example, the effect of substituting a convertible for a straight bond issue. A convertible bond gives bondholders, in effect, both a non-convertible bond and a call option on the stock. In return for this option, bondholders reduce the rate of interest on the bonds, thereby reducing the probability of financial difficulty.

CONCLUSION

British Petroleum, one of the largest industrial companies in the world, recently revised its corpo-rate insurance strategy in a way that stands the conventional wisdom on its head. This change reflects recent developments in the theory of corporate finance and applications of the theory to the practice of corporate risk management.

In the past decade, financial economists have begun to re-examine the benefits and costs of corporate risk management from a shareholder-value perspective. To date, academic attention has been focused almost entirely on factors affecting the corporate *demand* for risk management products. But, in our analysis of British Petroleum's recent and marked shift in insurance strategy, we demonstrate that this new approach also depends critically on supply considerations across different sizes of potential claims.

Based on this supply-side analysis of the insurance industry as well as distinctive aspects of the *corporate* demand for insurance, this very large public company reached the conclusion that it has a substantial comparative advantage over the insurance industry in bearing the risk of its largest exposures. For this reason, BP purchases coverage only for their smallest tier of losses (under $10 million). Even in these cases, the primary motive for buying insurance is not to transfer risk, but rather to exploit the insurance industry's comparative efficiency in providing risk-assessment and claims-administration services.

Having completed and acted upon this re-thinking of its insurance strategy, BP is now in the process of reviewing the way its manages its other significant exposures. In addition to property and casualty risks, oil price changes, currency fluctuations, and interest rate changes all affect the value of BP in fairly systematic ways, thus imposing risk. Over the past decade, hedging instruments such as exchange-traded futures and options and over-the-counter swaps have become available to manage these kinds of exposures. In an effort to formulate a comprehensive risk management strategy, BP is extending the analytical framework described here to weigh the benefits of managing such financial risks against the costs associated with these other forms of insurance.

BANK OF AMERICA
ROUNDTABLE ON

DERIVATIVES AND CORPORATE RISK MANAGEMENT

Kiawah Island
South Carolina
May 13, 1995

PHOTOS BY DJ JOHNSON

ROBERT McKNEW: Good morning, and welcome to this discussion of derivatives and corporate risk management. My name is Bob McKnew, and I am an executive vice president at Bank of America. As head of the bank's U.S. Capital Markets Group, I am responsible for foreign exchange, securities, and risk management products.

Given the current controversy over derivatives, our subject could not be more timely. And, as often happens when the popular press sets its sights on financial markets, there is a good deal of misinformation in this area. Derivatives, of course, have been blamed for large losses at municipalities, college pension funds, and even a number of large, highly respected corporations. Critics of corporate and market behavior, true to form, are viewing such losses as the tip of the iceberg, the first signs of some expected revelation about the extent of derivatives speculation in corporate America.

But, as most of you in this room are well aware, derivatives, when used properly, are highly effective tools for managing corporate exposures to financial variables such as interest rates, foreign exchange rates, and commodity prices. And if we want to understand why the corporate use of derivatives has exploded in the last 15 years or so, we need only look at the dramatic changes in the volatility of financial markets during the past two decades. Today's extraordinary levels of interest rate volatility, for example, got their start at the end of the 1970s, when Fed chairman Paul Volcker first attempted to target monetary aggregates rather than interest rates—and that is when financial futures, forward rate agreements, and, a couple years later, interest rate swaps began to emerge. And beginning with the oil spike in the early 1970s, commodity prices of all kinds—particularly of petroleum-related products and metals—have continued to experience periodic surges in volatility over the past 20 years. And foreign exchange markets, of course, have not been immune to the financial markets roller coaster. In the past year alone, the dollar has lost 20% of its value against the yen and DM.

But let me stop here and make a confession. I like volatility, I like chaos, I like markets that move. Volatility—whether it's volatility in $/DM, in $/yen, in Mexican pesos, or in Brady bonds—creates demand for derivative products both by corporates and by large investors. It makes all of you here need to do something to manage your exposures—and that, frankly, is how I make my living.

As a kind of nighttime job, I have had the honor of speaking for the securities industry several times this year. I have testified before Congress three times since January on the fallout from derivatives episodes like Credit Lyonnais, Orange County, bank portfolios and money market mutual funds, Gibson Greeting, P&G, and so forth. Let me comment briefly on the lessons to be drawn from that experience before we plunge into our subject of corporate risk management.

In recent years, our financial markets have become quite adept at creating derivative instruments with very specific payoffs. When used properly, these instruments can be used to provide highly efficient, cost-effective hedges of financial risks associated with either an investor's portfolio or a corporation's businesses. In addition, if an investor wants to structure a portfolio that performs well under certain interest rate environments, financial instruments can be tailored to carry out the desired strategy. If interest rates behave the way the investor anticipated, those instruments will perform well. Nevertheless, the investor—and this goes for corporate risk managers, too—should understand that if interest rates do not behave as anticipated, the instruments will produce losses. It should also be understood that if the investor or corporation loses money on a financial instrument, the instruments themselves are not the culprits; they will behave as expected.

Take the much-publicized case of Orange County. The losses suffered by Orange County's cash management fund can be attributed to three principal factors.

First, Orange County invested in medium-term notes which, like all fixed-income securities, are subject to market risk as interest rates change. Throughout much of 1994, such securities fell substantially in price because of sharp increases in interest rates.

Second, Orange County used short-term borrowings to leverage its investment portfolio to several times its original holdings. By borrowing against its portfolio, the County was able to raise additional funds to buy even more securities, thus amplifying the effects of the price fluctuations just described.

Third, the County invested in certain interest-rate-sensitive structured securities, instruments that typically combine an "embedded" derivative such as an interest rate option within an ordinary straight-debt instrument. Because such structured securities are so highly customized—often for a single investor that purchases the entire issue—such securities are hard to value and therefore less liquid, a factor that almost certainly contributed to problems suffered by the County.

In sum, the County appears to have structured a portfolio that would perform very well if rates either fell or stayed the same, but that would sustain large losses if rates increased significantly. And, of course, interest rates went up dramatically. Yields on five-year notes rose over 200 basis points in 1994, producing an overall return of negative 5.01%, the worst one-year performance of that security ever. Twenty-year Treasuries had their second worst year ever. And Orange County's portfolio, with its use of leverage and special structured securities, produced losses on the order of 20%.

The lesson from Orange County, then, is the importance of distinguishing between the County's investment strategy and the instruments used to execute the strategy. The instruments behaved pretty much as expected; the strategy was radically flawed. Instead of protecting the value of its fixed-income portfolio against rate increases, Orange County doubled up, indeed probably *quadrupled*, its exposure to interest rates.

*W*hen abused, derivatives can enlarge existing exposures and create new financial risks. But, when used properly (and this part of the story seems to have eluded the popular press), derivatives have enabled corporations to isolate and manage financial exposures far more efficiently and cheaply than ever before.

Robert McKnew
Bank of America

have enabled corporations to isolate and manage financial exposures far more efficiently and cheaply than ever before. (And this part of the story, as I suggested, seems to have eluded the popular press.) But when abused, as we have seen in cases

And the same lesson, of course, applies to the current controversy over derivatives and corporate risk management. Used properly, derivatives like P&G and Gibson Greeting Cards, they can actually enlarge existing exposures and create new financial risks.

So, with these ramblings as prelude, let me introduce the panelists in this discussion of corporate risk management. In alphabetical order, they are:

TOM JONES, who is Vice President and Treasurer of Union Carbide Corporation. Tom, as you will hear, is a veteran in the practice of corporate risk management and a long-time user of derivatives.

LYNN LANE is Vice President and Treasurer of R.J. Reynolds Tobacco Company. As head of the company's worldwide Tobacco Treasury function, Lynn is responsible for RJR's extensive program for managing its foreign exchange risk.

JONELLE ST. JOHN is Vice President and Treasurer of MCI Communications Corp.. Under Jonelle's supervision, the treasury group at MCI recently developed a proposal for an expanded derivatives program designed to manage the currency and other cross-border risks associated with the firm's overseas expansion plans.

JOHN VAN RODEN is Vice President and Treasurer of Lukens, Inc. Among his many other responsibilities, John is chairman of Lukens' newly-formed risk management team.

And I will now ask John to start things off by telling us about the new risk management program at Lukens.

The Case of Lukens

JOHN VAN RODEN: Let me begin by giving you a brief overview of the history of risk management at Lukens—and this should be very brief, since we really didn't begin to take a systematic approach to managing risk until 1993. Lukens is a producer of carbon, alloy, and stainless steel. Our operating earnings are affected by fluctuations in the prices of nickel and natural gas (among other commodities), and we attempt to limit these price exposures through our risk management process. Prior to 1993,

we did some hedging of nickel and natural gas prices—and, occasionally, of interest rates as well—but this was all done on an ad hoc, unstructured basis. Each business entity made its hedging decisions independently, there were no established limits on trading positions or counterparty credit exposures, and there was no reporting of derivatives positions and the associated risks to management and the board.

Then, in 1993, we developed a more formal approach to risk management, and we put together a team to develop and carry out our risk management policy and strategies. In December of '93, our original risk management team executed its first trade—a purchase of nickel futures on the London Metals Exchange. In 1994, we drafted a formal Risk Management Policy, which was approved by the Finance Committee of our Board near the end of that year. And, in early 1995, we had our risk management process and policies reviewed by an outside consultant, Arthur Andersen. The consultant's most important recommendation—one which we acted upon and which I will discuss later in more detail—was that we strengthen the reporting and communications that take place between the risk management function and top management and the board.

One of the distinctive—and, in my view, most valuable—features of our risk management program is that it takes a *team* approach; it involves participation by people from several disciplines within the company. The team includes the VP-Purchasing of our Carbon & Alloy Group, the Director of Materials Management–Stainless Steel, our Manager of Corporate Accounting, our Corporate Risk Manager, and the VP & Treasurer (that is, me). This risk management team meets regularly to discuss our markets, exposures, and hedging strategies.

We have drafted a mission statement that reads as follows:
"*The team will identify noncontrollable costs and risks that affect Lukens' operations. Alternative strategies will be analyzed, including existing and innovative financial products, in order to determine the most effective way to address these costs and risks. The team will be responsible for executing the optimal risk management strategy that will add value to the business.*"

Our risk management *policy* addresses issues of implementation, such as: Who is to be on the risk management team? Who is responsible for executing trading activities? What are the limits of their decision-making authority, expressed in terms both of hedge size and duration? What approvals are required for decision-making that goes beyond these limits? And how are positions to be reported to management and the board?

In formulating our risk management *strategy*, we began by examining in a more systematic way the various financial exposures of our businesses. Besides fluctuations in nickel and natural gas prices, we also looked at other potential sources of financial risk—for example, changes in foreign currencies and interest rates, and in the price of aluminum and carbon scrap. We collected data on the historical volatility of each of these financial variables; and then, with the help of outside advisers and feedback from our suppliers, we attempted to determine how such volatility affected our bottom line and overall competitive position.

Having identified our major exposures, we then looked at the array of financial vehicles that could be used to hedge these exposures. In reviewing hedging vehicles, we had two major requirements: (1) the instrument must trade in a well-established, highly liquid market; and (2) there must be a strong correlation between the price of the traded instrument and the price exposure being hedged. For each of the different hedging vehicles we considered, moreover, we attempted to evaluate the associated costs and risks—including the counterparty credit risk in OTC derivatives and the basis risk from lack of a perfect correlation between the financial hedge and the underlying exposure.

The conclusion we came to was basically this: We will hedge only significant exposures, principally nickel and natural gas. Moreover, we will pursue a strategy of *active* risk management—that is, we will hedge only a fraction of our exposures and the percentage we choose to hedge will be subject to continuous review. We decided on "active" management for two reasons. First, the cyclical swings in the steel products business mean that there is a lot of uncertainty about the actual size of our exposures; that is, because we don't know at the beginning of any year how much steel we will end up selling that year, we don't know how much to hedge. The second reason for our active management approach is our belief that, by operating with a cross-functional team approach, we can add some value by changing our hedging position when we have a view about future developments in our markets. We will act on our views only in "familiar" markets like nickel and natural—not in interest rates or foreign exchange—and we will act only with the unanimous consent of the team.

After developing the outlines of a hedging strategy for each exposure, we then considered issues of decision-making authority, execution, and control. The result of this process was a risk management policy containing explicit limits, controls, and provisions for centralized recordkeeping and settlements. Finally, there are

extensive regular reporting requirements, along with the stipulation that the entire policy be subjected to further review at the end of each year.

As I mentioned earlier, after formulating our entire risk management policy, we then had our policy and procedures audited by Arthur Andersen. Andersen gave us their "AA" rating, citing as strengths our cross-functional approach in developing

hedging strategies and our record-keeping & settlements and other controls. Our policy audit did suggest, however, that we had not done such a good job in communicating to management and the board our strategy for managing each of our various risks. And we're trying to do better there. In fact, we have designed a new format for reporting on our derivatives positions to our board.

> *O*ur risk management policy is to hedge only our significant exposures, principally nickel and natural gas. Moreover, we pursue a strategy of active *risk management.... We obviously have views on certain markets, and we sometimes take financial risks in the sense that we choose to leave part of our exposures unhedged. But we make such decisions through a team, one that includes operating people with bottom-line responsibility.*
>
> *John van Roden*
> *Lukens, Inc.*

John van Roden

John van Rode

To give you an idea of the kind of information we now report to our board, take the case of nickel. As I mentioned earlier, half of Lukens' business is stainless steel, and 50% of the cost of stainless steel is in nickel. And so we often hedge against nickel price increases.

Here is a chart that shows the path of nickel prices between January of 1985 and October of 1994. There's a good deal of volatility in this picture. As you can see, there was a big spike up to over $8 a pound in '88 and '89. But, by the beginning of 1993, nickel prices had fallen to $2.80 a pound; and, at that price, the cost to Lukens for buying nickel based at then current levels of steel production was $110 million. Today, our nickel costs are running about $230 million, reflecting both a sharp increase in nickel prices since the end of '92 and the increase in the volume of our business.

How has our hedging helped us? Between December of 1992 through August of 1994, there was a 33% increase in the price of nickel. But, by buying nickel futures on the LME representing about half of the nickel we used in our business during that period, we were able to hold the increase in our overall cost of nickel to 19%.

Now, there is one potential source of basis risk in our hedging program. We buy our nickel in scrap most of the time, which does not trade completely in sync with nickel prices on the LME. But the correlation is very strong; when we back-tested the relationship, we found out that the correlation coefficient was about 95% between the scrap and futures prices.

So, this is the kind of information that we provide both our board and the operating people who are concerned about managing their own costs. We share with them the data used in our decision-making process, and our operating people provide

us with valuable added perspective on market conditions—perspective that we draw on in making our hedging decisions.

The Case of MCI

McKNEW: Thanks, John. Now, we will hear from Jonelle St. John, who is Vice President and Treasurer of MCI. JONELLE ST. JOHN: Let me start off by saying a little bit about MCI's risk management policy. Our management is fairly conservative, and our corporate policy has for the most part been to avoid use of derivatives. Our treasury group has made some use of derivatives on a highly selective, case-by-case basis. But these require prior approval by the CFO, and, depending on the size of the transactions, by the board.

Nevertheless, the continued growth of our business—particularly, in the form of overseas investments contemplated in the next few years—is forcing us to rethink this policy. We have developed and submitted to our board a proposal that would allow us to make greater use of derivatives in managing financial exposures. The guidelines that have been proposed reflect the recommendations of the "Group of 30" report on derivatives as well as input from a variety of functional areas within MCI—accounting, internal audit, tax, and so forth. Without getting into specifics, let me just say here that our proposal has counterparty credit limits, exposure limits stated in mark-to-market terms, and a list of permitted and prohibited transactions.

As with all our other financial management policies, our proposed risk management and derivatives policy would be monitored at the top management level, but decision-making would rest with treasury people operating within explicit guidelines and risk tolerance

limits set by management. The policy is designed to keep executive management and the board well-informed about treasury activities, but at the same time to give us enough flexibility to do the things we need to do without going to management for approval.

Now, why do we want to make greater use of derivatives at MCI? The answer, as I've already suggested, is that our exposure to foreign exchange risks is expected to grow significantly in the next few years.

We are already managing some very specific, transaction-based foreign exchange risks. For example, we have annual settlements with foreign "PTTs" that require us to make payments in dollars based on the SDR exchange rate. Because the exchange rate of the SDR is a combination of the U.S. dollar (about 40%) and foreign currencies such as the pound sterling, German mark, French francs, and Japanese yen, a weakening of the dollar relative to these currencies would increase the dollar value of these payments.

To manage this currency exposure, we use FX forwards, options, and collars on the individual currencies comprising the SDR that allow us to hedge against fluctuations in the SDR. At the beginning of each year, we hedge 100% of the plan of our expected foreign settlements based on the contracts we have in place with our customers. Now, because we tend to bring in new business during the year and beat our plan, we generally end up hedging less than 100% of our payments to the PTTs at the end of the year. But that's basically a conservative hedging policy; that is, we can't justify hedging more than our expected outflows without effectively speculating on the SDR.

In the future, we will be making direct equity investments in various foreign countries. Mexico is the one that we're going to be moving on fairly quickly. We've announced a joint venture in Mexico with Banamex. We're going to construct a long-distance network in Mexico that has a number of risks associated with it that we have not encountered in the past. In addition to standard transaction and translation types of foreign exchange risk, we've also got to consider the sovereign and political risks associated with our investments. We also have to think about dealing with restrictions on repatriating and converting our overseas funds back into dollars. Our current plan calls for reinvesting earnings from Mexico for a long period of time; but, at some point, we need an effective means of converting the investment back into dollars.

Fortunately, we did not commit any of our funds to Mexico *before* the recent devaluation of the peso. So that's the good news. But there have also been negative consequences from the current uncertainty in Mexico. Given our intention to invest in Mexico, we now face a very limited market for both financing and hedging facilities. If such facilities were available, financing in pesos would have provided a natural hedge for our investment, since our net revenue stream will be primarily in pesos. But combining revenues in pesos with financing costs in dollars means considerable currency risk for our Mexican P&L, and we need to take that into consideration in the business plan.

Besides Mexico, we are also considering the possibility of expanding into several other countries in Latin America. Indeed, Latin America is one of our strategic expansion areas. For this reason, we are looking at the extent of the correlation among the various Latin American currencies— and, in particular, for the existence of domino effects. We are also exploring the possibility of moving currencies around within the various countries

instead of pulling them all back into U.S. dollars.

In sum, our plans to invest in Mexico and Latin America mean that we're going to have to plan for a host of risks that we would typically not face in more mature markets. The way we

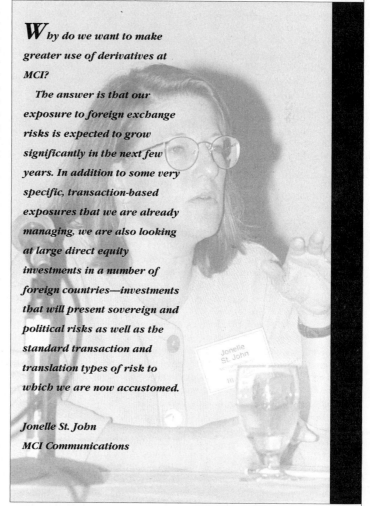

__W__by do we want to make greater use of derivatives at MCI?

The answer is that our exposure to foreign exchange risks is expected to grow significantly in the next few years. In addition to some very specific, transaction-based exposures that we are already managing, we are also looking at large direct equity investments in a number of foreign countries—investments that will present sovereign and political risks as well as the standard transaction and translation types of risk to which we are now accustomed.

__Jonelle St. John__
__MCI Communications__

are going to approach these risks is by developing cross-functional teams within MCI. The tax function will have to be involved in the planning

process. And so will accounting, especially since the FASB is moving forward on changes in how you report hedging facilities—that is, whether changes in the value of derivatives are going to be on the balance sheet or the P&L. Tax and accounting consid-

erations, along with the company's general conservatism, may force us to restrict our hedging products to those that do not affect the P&L.

The Case of Union Carbide

McKNEW: Thanks, Jonelle. Now let's turn to Tom Jones, Vice President and Treasurer of Union Carbide

TOM JONES: Risk management at Union Carbide is nothing new. All corporations face business, physical, and financial risks. But we have been actively managing these risks for many years. The risk management part of the Treasurer's Group works with business management to identify physical and financial risks, to assess the potential impact on the business of these risks, and to determine what needs to be done to control the risks.

Managing physical risk typically involves the purchase of insurance products. But in the financial risk area—interest rates, foreign exchange, commodity price movements, and equity price movements—risk management sometimes means the use of derivative products. Although derivatives are not the only tool for managing financial risks, they have become increasingly popular because they are typically more available, more flexible, and less costly than the alternatives. My focus will be on the use of derivatives in managing these financial risks.

One of the most difficult tasks in financial risk management is to determine your exposure. It's fairly easy to determine interest rate exposure, but foreign exchange is more challenging. We spend a good deal of time trying to determine our exposure on the foreign exchange side. We sell a lot of products in many different currencies. We talk to our business people about their gross margin risk. In cases where they are able to adjust their selling price when a currency moves, they don't have currency risk. But, in many of our businesses, the managers can't adjust their selling price, and so they have currency risk.

But let me start by taking a brief look at interest rate risk. Our debt over the past years has been as much as $3 billion, but today it is running at about $1.2 billion. Our annual interest expense over that period has ranged from about $270 million to $70 million in 1993. Our interest cost for 1994 was about $80 million.

Now, these numbers are a little misleading because we are involved in quite a few joint ventures, and there will be more in the future. We are a partner in a $2 billion joint venture in Kuwait that will start in 1997 and will have $1.2 billion of debt in it. We are also in a $1 billion Italian joint venture with $500 or $600 million of debt. In all of our joint ventures, we will probably have $3 to $4 billion in debt, and thus the interest cost that we try to manage is significantly more than what we have in our corporation.

In the early 1990s, we did a study to try to determine the optimal duration for our debt. After looking at how the performance of our businesses and their competitors were affected by changes in inflation and interest rates, we concluded that a target rate of four years was right for us. And let me explain briefly how we arrived at this target.

Some of our businesses are commodity businesses that do very well when inflation and interest rates are high; but when interest rates and inflation are low, these businesses tend to be at the bottom of their cycle. Because such businesses have no interest rate exposure—or perhaps even a slightly negative exposure to increases in rates—they should be funded with short-term, or floating-rate, money. But we have other businesses that are adversely affected by inflation and high interest rates. And so, by taking a weighted average of the interest rate exposures of all our different businesses, we arrived at a targeted duration of four years.

Now, the target doesn't necessarily mean that the duration of our debt is always going to be precisely at four years. When interest rates are going up, we will generally aim to be somewhat longer than the target to give us partial protection against further rate increases. Conversely, when rates are coming down, we want to be somewhat shorter than the target to benefit from further declines. Given the recent downward trend in rates, the duration of our debt today is probably about three and a half years.

Let me also point out that our duration target would not stop us from going out longer than four years if we thought we saw a financing bargain. We believe interest rates are very attractive today; and, if there was a need for funds, we would do a 30-year bond issue at 8% or lower without any hesitation. But, at the same time, we could swap the issue right back to maintain our three- or four-year duration. And, as this example is meant to illustrate, the use of derivatives is key to our management of interest rate risk. We use interest rate derivatives—mainly swaps—to manage the duration of our debt, to adjust the fixed vs. floating mix of our debt, and to control interest costs.

Now let's talk about foreign exchange, which is where much of our risk management efforts are centered. We have a natural net inflow of European currencies and Japanese yen—about $10 to $15 million a month—that comes from export sales, sales of technology, and dividends from affiliates. But we do not always hedge these currency exposures. We will hedge as much 100% in some cases or we will hedge zero or somewhere in between, depending upon what we feel is the trend in the U.S. dollar. If the U.S. dollar is weakening relative to the DM and yen and we expect that trend to continue, then we will just let the foreign currency come in and convert it when we receive it. But if the dollar is strengthening, then we will hedge up to 100% of the expected inflows by selling all or part of our receivables in advance. Although we generally look out over the next 12 months at our expected inflow of currencies, our hedges typically don't go beyond about six months.

We have the opposite situation in Canadian dollars, in that we pay Canadian dollars rather than receiving a net inflow. And so we use the reverse strategy—that is, the more we expect the Canadian dollar to strengthen, the larger the percentage of our payments we hedge.

We operate in a lot of developing countries where there are not many hedging alternatives. We use natural hedges any place we can—for example, funding in currencies where we produce and sell; or, when possible, locating manufacturing or sourcing in countries where we sell. But there is still considerable room for financial solutions to risk management after the natural hedges are in place. Our primary role in such cases is to act as financial advisers to the subsidiaries and operating units.

In our joint ventures, we strongly recommend the establishment of finance committees to develop and oversee risk management for the joint venture. Such committees will typically have someone from the partner's financial organization, someone from Carbide, and, of course, some financial managers from the joint venture itself. If we are aware of any practice that is contrary to our risk management philosophy, we will see that it is reported to our senior management.

Now, the fact that there are partners in joint ventures and that they may have different views of risk management adds a degree of difficulty in carrying out our policy. It can be especially challenging when you're working with partners who have never

used hedges or derivatives. But there are normally some major currency risks that must be addressed in managing overseas ventures. Take our Kuwait joint venture. It will sell in all different currencies, while funding itself primarily with dollar debt. Our

currencies. Financial management of these overseas ventures requires that you really take a good look at your currency cash flow and understand your exposures. And, as I mentioned, management of these exposures is supervised by finance committees that

> *We all have friends in the financial community that say they wouldn't hedge because derivatives are bad things to use. The irony, of course, is that by making that statement, they've effectively made a decision that they're going to accept the risk. But this hypocrisy, or at least confusion, persists in part because the two kinds of losses don't get accounted for in the same way. Unhedged losses don't show up anywhere. But hedging losses are reported separately— typically independently of the position they're being used to hedge—and they are now being held up for very strong scrutiny.*
>
> *Thomas Jones*
> *Union Carbide*

Italian joint venture is another good example. It's about a $1 billion venture. Fifty percent of it is in lira, but the other 50% is in all the other European

meet at least three or four times each year—and with a very full agenda.

Let me just quickly mention two other areas: commodity risk and equity price risk. We have very strong management in our business areas—people who feel very comfortable living with commodity risk and managing it primarily with non-financial means. They feel comfortable with the cycles in the commodity business, and with their own ability to increase prices to offset increases in their own cost of raw materials.

In the equity market, we have a stock buy-back program that has now been increased to 30 million shares. We sell puts from time to time to help with these stock purchases. Because of the fairly steady appreciation of our stock in the past few years, we have had an almost unblemished record in selling these puts. That is, in most cases, after we have sold the put our stock has continued to move up, and so the put has gone unexercised. And the net effect of these put sales has been a reduction in the cost of our share-repurchase program.

Let me just say something about the management of corporate derivatives programs, which of course has gotten a tremendous amount of attention in the past year or so. At Union Carbide, we have clear and firm rules governing the use of derivatives:

1. We do not allow leveraged derivatives, the kind that have caused problems at other companies. Our derivatives have to move in direct proportional relationship to the exposure that they are covering; they cannot move twice as fast or three times as fast as the underlying exposure being hedged.

2. When we are hedging a financial exposure faced by a specific business, we have to get the manager running that operation to approve the hedge. Even if we think something should be done, if he doesn't approve it, we don't do it.

3. We have a risk management committee that meets weekly, and that includes the principal financial officer,

the treasurer, and assistant treasurer. We have clear exposure and loss limits for all of our derivatives positions, and we report these positions on a regular basis to senior management.

4. One of our most important risk management rules is that we can hedge only specific transactions that have been clearly identified. Now, there is some flexibility in defining "transactions." Export and import transactions in a foreign currency qualify, of course; and so do net inflows and outflows of various currencies expected over the next 12 months—at least in those cases where gross margins are at risk because of pricing constraints. We will also hedge non-dollar dividends or royalties expected over the next 12 months, and non-dollar acquisitions or divestitures with a signed letter of intent. This past January, for example, we signed a letter of intent on our Italian joint venture. Our capital contribution was to be 320 million denominated in DMs, or roughly $200 million. Because the dollar was weakening at this time, we chose to buy the DMs then. By the time the deal closed two months later, we ended up saving about $15 million.

Now, did this decision to hedge involve some risks? Yes, it did; in fact, it was almost controversial. If this joint venture had fallen apart after the letter of intent, we would have had a $200 million uncovered position in DM. And if the dollar had instead strengthened by the same amount that it depreciated, we could have had up to $20 million in losses to explain.

Let me just close with a brief list of the kinds of controls that we have found valuable at Carbide.

Derivatives should be easily priced; you have to know the value of the instrument at any time and be able to unwind the position. We had an expe-

rience years ago in which we had a number of swaps that we wanted to get out of. And when the market turned out to be less liquid than we thought, we lost some money. So market liquidity is essential for us.

In response to the Group of 30 study, we are also doing sensitivity studies designed to show us the range of likely and possible losses on our derivatives positions. We look at what a couple of standard deviations in these positions would do to our profitability and financial condition. And, based in part on these sensitivity studies, Carbide's Board of Directors has set limits on the company's derivatives market risk by setting a cap on losses from the uses of derivatives in managing interest rate, foreign exchange, and commodity price risks.

We are also very sensitive to counterparty credit risks. Counter-parties must have a credit rating not lower than A by Standard & Poor's and BAA by Moody's. And we not only do careful credit analysis when entering into a transaction, but we really work to monitor our credit exposures on an ongoing basis.

We do extensive reporting of our positions; in fact, we mark our derivatives positions to market on a daily basis within the Treasurer's group. Reports to management are weekly. And, if any of our contracts has a loss of 5% or more, continuation of the position has to be approved by senior management. Carbide's risk management activities are also reviewed annually by both the internal audit department and our external auditors.

Well, let me conclude by just telling you that we all have a tough job today. While we all know that derivative products are essential to managing financial risks in today's volatile markets, it has also become clear that derivatives can be abused in ways that end up imposing risk on the corporation. Our job is both to demonstrate to our management and our boards the benefits of derivatives in managing risks, and to reassure them that our risk management program isn't *creating more risk.* I believe that such a comprehensive review of risk management procedures and controls is now going on in every major corporation in America.

The Case of RJR Nabisco

McKNEW: Thank you, Tom. Now, we'll hear from Lynn Lane, Vice President and Treasurer of R.J. Reynolds Tobacco.

LYNN LANE: I want to talk to you today about how we manage our foreign exchange risk at RJR. As a multinational company, our international entities produce significant net revenues, which creates foreign exchange exposure for us. Complicating matters, these overseas entities do business not only in their country of domicile, but often in several other countries as well, thus creating significant cross-border flows.

We address foreign exchange risk management through a multi-stage process. The stages can be summarized as follows: (1) formulation and statement of hedging objective; (2) senior management planning and policy formulation; (3) identification of significant exposures; (4) development of hedging strategy (including decisions whether to hedge various risks); (5) policy implementation; and (6) safeguards and controls. I should also point out that this process does not proceed in just a one-way, linear fashion; it should rather be viewed as one with lots of feedback, and subject to continous monitoring and revision. For example, the evaluations and audits at the back end of the process can in turn provide the basis for adjustments to our policy and even of the objective itself. I will now spend a few

minutes discussing each of these aspects of the process.

First, let's talk about the objective of our foreign exchange program. Our objective is to maintain strong and predictable cash flow and earnings through the management of the company's consolidated foreign exchange exposures, including those arising from specific transactions. Treasury is not a profit center; we aim to minimize risk, not to create risk. And, as I suggested, we also constantly review our objective to ensure that it is providing the proper guidance for our risk management activities.

The second step is to develop a policy. Our policy is best described as one of "selective" hedging. In managing our various currency exposures, we can be hedged anywhere from zero to 100%. Normally, it's not on either end of this spectrum but somewhere in the middle. In our view, hedging either 0% or 100% of an exposure amounts to taking a very strong view on the market. Making a decision to do nothing—that is, hedging 0%—is a decision to take the currency risk. But hedging 100% could mean forgoing a positive movement in prices that one of your competitors may choose not to hedge.

At RJR, both the identification of exposures and the decisions to hedge involve the operating units working together with the treasury department. Treasury provides the expertise in the foreign exchange markets and hedging tools, but the operating managers are the people with direct responsibility for foreign exchange since it hits their bottom line. So, it's very much a team effort, a partnership. We work with the operating units to identify currency exposures and, based on their input, we suggest hedging strategies. But the operating people, as I said, make the final decisions about whether and how much of the exposure to hedge on the local entities' books.

Treasury does, however, have veto power if we feel strongly one way or the other.

The operating units report their exposures to us every two months on a rolling 12-month basis. And although we have the tools to manage our exposures as far out as 24 months, our hedging focus tends to be confined to just the current year.

As I also mentioned earlier, we consider hedging all transaction exposures. As most of you know, transaction exposures result from specific business decisions—say, a large payable or receivable, or a royalty payment or dividend to the parent—involving an actual exchange of funds in two or more currencies.

But we take a somewhat different approach with translation exposures. Translation exposures result from the translation of the earnings of foreign operating units into U.S. dollars for reporting purposes. At present, we do not actively hedge translation in the foreign exchange market, but we may use other mechanisms for so doing.

Before describing our policy, let me give you a couple of examples that affect us on the *transaction* side. We have a company that manufactures product and sells within Germany. But it sources product in dollars, and it also sells in France, Italy, and the U.K. So the company has significant $/DM transaction exposures, as well as several transactional cross-currency exposures. We evaluate each of these exposures as candidates for hedging.

Another example of a transactional exposure is our finance company that was set up in the early '80's in Geneva, Switzerland. The company is used primarily for liquidity netting; that is, our European and Far East entities both borrow from and lend to this center. And because this finance company is a dollar-based company, it has very large transactional exposures that we manage using the swap market.

A good example of *translation* exposure is our subsidiary in Mexico. Before the devaluation of the peso, we spent a lot of time thinking about what we should do to control the currency risk facing the net earnings of that subsidiary. And we decided to make adjustments to the capital structure—specifically, injecting equity and paying off U.S. debt—to reduce the translation exposure of our Mexican earnings. And, as I said, we were fortunate enough to make this adjustment before the devaluation, thus protecting our consolidated P&L.

Our approach to transaction and translation exposures has varied somewhat over time, depending on management's objectives and on how the performance of our operating units are measured. At times we have hedged only transaction exposures and ignored translation effects. At other times, we have hedged both transactions and translation. Today, as I mentioned, we actively hedge transaction exposures but not translation effects.

Having identified our exposures, we next develop a strategy—again, in partnership with our operating units—for dealing with them. In some cases, we decide to hedge such exposures, and in others we choose to do nothing.

But, again, our foreign exchange strategy is dynamic and subject to continuous review. And, before even considering financial hedges, we try to use natural hedges whenever possible, either within specific subsidiaries or even across subsidiaries. Setting up cross-subsidiary natural hedges can be a challenge because what's good for one unit is not necessarily good for another. But while the operating units are focused on their own results, it's our job at treasury to evaluate the entire hedging program on a consolidated economic basis to ensure the hedging activities of the units are not working at cross purposes.

Once we have developed the strategy, we're ready for implementation. All of the execution of financial hedging is done by treasury. We use a variety of products: spot swaps, forwards, and over-the-counter options—all pretty much plain vanilla. We also try to manage the balance sheets of our foreign entities—say, by borrowing in the local currency instead of dollars—to offset their asset or revenue exposures.

And, last, let me briefly mention some of our safeguards and controls, because these are an essential part of any well-run risk management program. First and foremost, senior management must be involved not only in setting up the program and policies, but in continuous monitoring. This is the only way to ensure that there will

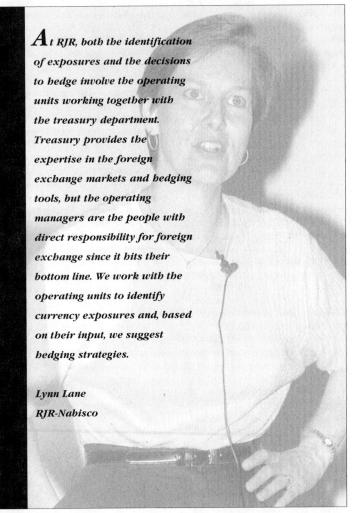

At RJR, both the identification of exposures and the decisions to hedge involve the operating units working together with the treasury department. Treasury provides the expertise in the foreign exchange markets and hedging tools, but the operating managers are the people with direct responsibility for foreign exchange since it hits their bottom line. We work with the operating units to identify currency exposures and, based on their input, we suggest hedging strategies.

Lynn Lane
RJR-Nabisco

be no surprises. Top management must understand both the policy and the basic strategy, and they must be informed on a regular basis as to how it is being carried out.

As part of our formal policy, we have also established operational controls similar to those used by commercial banks. We set limits for our counterparties, and we review the credit ratings of our counterparties on an ongoing basis. We also ensure there is separation of duties between the front-office traders and the back-office operation personnel. We feel this is extremely important, and we've had our internal auditors examine the process to make sure they're comfortable with it. And we have continuous reporting to top management to make sure everyone is on board and knows where we stand.

Risk Management: Hedging or Speculation?

McKNEW: Thanks, Lynn. Now, I'd like to open up the discussion to the panelists and to everyone in the room. But let me start things off by asking each of the panelists a very basic question.

Tom, when you're hedging, do you trade? Do you make money hedging?
JONES: We do not trade, but we may report gains or losses on a derivative position from time to time. We are not a profit center. Our use of derivatives is consistent with Carbide's overall risk management program—a strategy that reduces, but never increases, the financial risk of the company.
McKNEW: Lynn, I assume you would say that RJR doesn't trade either.
LANE: That's essentially right.
McKNEW: But you earlier said that you typically hedged less than 100% of your currency exposures. Why would hedging anything less than 100% hedge of an exposure not be a trade, a kind of speculation?

LANE: It is our philosophy that if you're 50% hedged, that's kind of the neutral position. You have no view. What we try to do is to analyze the market and determine, based in part on our judgment about the likely size and direction of future price movements, what's the best position for our company. We don't say we *know* where the market or rates are going. But based on the particular conditions, and based on what our competitors are doing and what we're trying to accomplish, we end up hedging somewhere between zero and 100% of each individual exposure.
McKNEW: So, you're *managing* risk as opposed to eliminating it totally. John, what do you think about this? Are you always hedged?
VAN RODEN: No, we aren't always hedged. The steel business is a very cyclical business. And we will not hedge more than 50% of our nickel supplies precisely for that reason. That is, we could plan one year that we're going to sell X tons of steel, but sales may well end up being only half of X. And if in that case we hedged the entire amount that we planned to sell, then we would be significantly overhedging—we would end up with a very large uncovered long position in nickel futures.

So, in this sense, yes, we do trade. In fact, our team will get together every week to evaluate our position. And if we were 50% hedged at a given time, but we felt there was going to be a big move up or down in the price of nickel, then we might increase or decrease our hedge to reflect our view.
McKNEW: Okay, so it sounds as if all of you sometimes trade, at least in the sense that you allow your view of the market to influence your hedging position. But, do any of you ever consciously *create* risk? That is, do you ever hedge less than 0%—say, like Orange County, by doubling up an

already existing exposure—or more than 100% of your exposure?
LANE: We do not. Our stated mission, as I mentioned earlier, is to minimize risk. So, even if we felt interest rates or currencies were about to move in a given direction, we would never use foreign exchange products or interest rate products to create a new risk, or to add to an already existing exposure.
McKNEW: How about the rest of you? Does risk management mean totally eliminating risk as best you can do it, taking into consideration operating variables and, therefore, measured exposures? Or does it mean sometimes managing risk down and then managing it back up based on some view of a market rate or price?
VAN RODEN: We try to manage risk, but not to eliminate it.
McKNEW: So you would increase risk if you felt that a certain currency or commodity price was going to move in a certain way?
VAN RODEN: That's right. For example, if we had a strong conviction that nickel prices were not going to rise and might even fall sharply, we might well choose to increase our exposure to nickel by reducing our hedge.
McKNEW: Okay. So, does anyone think there is anything particularly wrong with that?
JONES: Well, it sort of depends on what you mean by increasing risk. If you say, "I've got 5 million DMs coming in, but because I think the dollar is going to strengthen, I'm going to hedge 10 million," I would say, "No, we don't do that." We manage only the risk associated with our operating cash flows. We don't volunteer to take trading risks independent of those cash flows. And we don't double up existing exposures or get into leveraged derivatives.

But, having said that, there are financial risks associated with almost any hedging position you choose to take. We don't choose to create risk, but you have risk one way or the other. If we do a derivative, we've taken a risk. If the position produces losses—even if it's a well-designed hedge—you may have difficulty explaining them to management. Life is full of risk. But we don't try to create any additional risk.

You Can Hedge, But Don't Lose Any Money Doing It

McKNEW: In identifying your financial exposures, do any of you take into account the expected effect of price changes on your competitors? That is, in setting your own hedging policies, do you consider your competitors' exposures and how they will react to the price changes?

LANE: I think this kind of analysis is potentially very useful. In setting a risk management strategy, you ought to know how your competitors are positioning themselves to handle their exposures. In fact, that is one of the reasons we think that a 100% hedge amounts to taking a very strong view of the market. If you hedge 100% of your exposure in the forward market, but prices end up moving against your hedge and in favor of your natural position, you are giving up the upside. And if your competitors are not hedging in this case, then your competitive position could suffer.

JONES: I agree, at least in theory, but I am not sure that this kind of analysis ends up producing any basis for hedging policy. We have done some studies as to where our competitors source their raw materials and what currencies they're paying in. But such studies have never really caused us to change our strategy.

McKNEW: Well, the problem I've always had with trying to sell that approach to corporations is that if you're right, nobody ever knows about it.

Even if a hedging strategy ends up improving your competitive position relative to other companies, nobody will ever credit risk management for that—the credit will go instead to marketing or strategic planning. But, if you're wrong—say, the hedge loses money and your competitors react differently than expected—then everybody will know about it. Explaining to people that you made a fundamentally sound decision that didn't work out is a very difficult message to get across.

LANE: That's right. Unfortunately, in today's market, people focus on the tools instead of the underlying exposure. People in risk management are often judged according to how the tools perform, and independently of what happens to the underlying exposure.

ANIRUDDHA ROY: Yes, that's very true. Even when companies are supposed to be hedging, in practice the success of the risk management function often seems to be judged by how much money they make on their derivatives positions. But, in a properly run corporate risk management operation, the treasury cannot operate as a profit center. If you are really hedging, and not just taking positions, you ought to be expected to show losses from time to time. And that ought to be clearly understood by management and the board from the outset.

JONES: I agree with you that that's how things should work, but it's also clear why companies don't want to report derivative losses of any kind, legitimate or otherwise. Take the case of Carbide. As a company, we're doing very, very well today. And nobody wants something to sidetrack us by having a derivative loss that gets a lot of publicity in the current environment. And I don't think Carbide is unusual in this. Managements and boards everywhere are very concerned about derivative losses, even those

that are incurred in legitimate hedging operations.

ROY: What you're saying, then, Tom, is that losses on derivatives are subjected to much closer scrutiny than losses resulting from leaving an exposure unhedged. For example, let's say you were receiving an inflow of DMs, and that because you expected the dollar to weaken, you chose not to hedge the exposure. In such circumstances, you would receive much less criticism if you turned out to be wrong by failing to hedge than if you had instead hedged the DM with, say, futures, and those futures ended up producing a loss—even when those futures were hedging an expected cash inflow.

So unhedged, or "natural," losses that increase volatility are preferred to "artificial" or derivatives losses that actually serve to reduce overall volatility. Do I have this right?

JONES: Yes, that's right. We all have friends in the financial community that say they wouldn't hedge because derivatives are bad things to use. The irony, of course, is that by making that statement, they've effectively made a decision that they're going to accept the risk.

But this hypocrisy, or at least confusion, persists in part because the two kinds of losses don't get accounted for in the same way. Unhedged losses don't show up anywhere, they aren't broken out into a separate account; and so the board never sees it, and the media never report it. But hedging losses are reported separately—typically independently of the position they're being used to hedge—and they are now being held up for very strong scrutiny.

LANE: You're both absolutely right. This kind of double standard goes on all the time, and I have yet to see much attention—certainly not in the popular accounts of derivatives—being devoted to this problem.

Can You Hedge Without Speculating?

STEPHEN PAGE: I'm a little confused about what I've heard so far in this discussion. Everyone says they are trying to avoid speculation. But, at the same time, everyone also seems to say that they are willing to let their hedging decisions be influenced by their views on interest rates or currencies. In my view, if you have a DM transaction exposure and you leave it up to a local treasurer to decide whether to hedge or not to hedge the exposure, then you are effectively encouraging a form of speculation.

Now, if we surveyed the people in this room today, we would probably hear ten different views of the dollar/DM. So, this tells me that it depends only on who your treasurer is at the time as to whether or not you can speculate. It seems to me that if you hedge anything less than 100% of your exposure, you are choosing to take an open position, you are taking a speculative position.

McKNEW: I understand your point. I've always had problems with the imprecision, or even confusion, that surrounds the terms in this business of risk management. "Hedging," "speculation," "trading," "risk-taking," risk avoidance"—we all seem to be using these words somewhat differently.

So, when someone begins by saying that their treasury is not a profit center, but they add value by taking views on a selective basis, that statement raises questions about the objective of the risk management program. And, because this kind of confusion is so widespread, I would argue that unquestionably the most important step in risk management is figuring out exactly what you're trying to accomplish. And your corporate objective should be expressed in very specific terms, if possible even with quantitative indicators of suc-

cess. For example, you might say that your policy is always to hedge at least 30% but never more than 100% of a certain kind of exposure (and the kind of exposure ought to be identified as clearly as possible). Or, using Tom's policy at Carbide as a model, you might say that you will never deviate more than, say, one year from your targeted interest rate duration of four years.

JONES: Well, Bob, I'm not sure you can ever formulate policy with that degree of precision. When you get into project financing or a joint venture, it may be easier to provide very clear objectives. For example, let's say the success of a project is based on obtaining an all-in financing cost of no more than 9%. In that case, if the project financing was based upon a 9% interest rate and you succeed in locking it in at 8-1/2%, then even if rates end up going to 5%, you've done the right thing. Now, it's true your venture partner may say to you after the fact, "Well, why didn't we get the advantage of the downside, why didn't we get 5%?" But, as long as your objective of beating 9% was clearly stated from the outset, and your partner was part of that understanding, then this is an effective risk management program.

But things are different in a large corporation, with multiple exposures and where everything is changing daily. It is much tougher in such cases to formulate objectives that are not subject to change.

And, by the way, I agree completely with Steve's distinction between hedging and speculation, and we have lots of discussions of these terms at Carbide. If we believe the dollar is strengthening or weakening, then we should either be zero or 100%. If you're in the middle, it's not clear what you are doing: Are you hedging or speculating?

VAN RODEN: I'd just like to add to that. We at Lukens obviously do

have views on certain markets and we do take financial risks. But we do it through a team and so you get the opinion of a lot of people. And you get the opinion of the operating people, as opposed to those of us who don't have responsibility for bottom line.

I would also mention the importance of regular communication and reporting. As of next week, we will begin sending monthly updates to management outlining our positions and strategies for all the various commodities we consider hedging. Now, this won't prevent us from making bad decisions. But, if we turn out to be wrong, at least we will all know why it happened.

LANE: I earlier mentioned the importance of considering your competitors' exposures in developing your own risk management strategy. But let me elaborate on this point a little, because I think this point bears on how you distinguish between hedging and speculation. If you hedge 100% of a currency exposure and the dollar goes against you, but your competitor has chosen to leave the same exposure unhedged, then your ability to maintain market share—that is, your competitive position—could end up being reduced by your hedging decision. So that's why I say that hedging either zero or 100% of an exposure may involve taking a strong view.

ST. JOHN: I tend to agree that the distinction between hedging and trading is not clearcut. I too am not sure that you can hedge without taking a view. That is, whether you choose to hedge 0% or 100% of an exposure, your position will never be completely insulated from changes in financial markets. And so I think the objectives of corporate risk management programs will inevitably have to leave some room for taking speculative positions or trading, if you will.

PAGE: Well, I would like to disagree. I think corporaations can practice risk management without taking a view. For example, you can say that you are going to cover 100% of all transaction exposures. And, at the same time, you can say that you will attempt to hedge all your expected cross-border translation exposures based on current forecasts—for example, much as MCI hedges its expected overseas payment to its PTTs.

Now, although this approach doesn't completely eliminate currency exposure (because your actual exposure may turn out to be somewhat different from what you projected), it neutralizes the effect of currency changes on your *expected* operating performance. And that may be the best you can do. In this kind of risk management system, you will have effectively eliminated any role for subjective judgments about future currency moves; you will not be taking a view.

Moreover, if you do lock in a given currency value by hedging 100% of expected exposure, then the resulting increase in your level of certainty about translated year-end results can help you in setting your pricing structure and in establishing targets for managers of foreign operating units at the beginning of the year.

Mark-to-Market Reporting of Derivatives

McKNEW: As a market-maker and trader in derivative instruments, I actually *can* be in a position of taking no risk simply by choosing to do nothing. In overseeing trading accounts, I can say—at least in theory—that I will take no risk; I will just not write any tickets myself, and completely offset everything that my customers bring to me. In that sense, my job's a lot more straightforward than all of yours, because virtually all of the risks that we take in

trading accounts are explicitly quantifiable and usually explicitly offsettable, more or less simultaneously.

JONES: Bob, why do you want to be paid for it if you don't take any risk?

McKNEW: I fully realize that the Lord don't owe me a living, and if I don't take any risk I won't get paid. But, in fact, we get paid in part for making markets for our customers, and in part based on the outcome of those positions we choose to take in the process of serving our customers.

But that brings me to another point. I live in a mark-to-market world. Everything I do is marked to market on almost a real-time basis. I know when I go home every night how much all of the activities in my department have made or lost, plus or minus a few thousand dollars. And this is real, hit-the-income-statement-of-the-bank kind of money.

But these obvious differences notwithstanding, I'm essentially in the same business that all of you are in. And, for this reason, I'm curious as to how many of you mark to market, in any sense, the risk management activities you engage in. Put another way, if you are not always 100% hedged, how are your decisions not to hedge 100% being reported to management? And when I say "reported," I mean expressed in such a way that somebody in senior management can look at your decisions and evaluate them against an explicit, unambiguous standard. I'm talking about meaningful internal or management accounting systems, not just adhering to external reporting conventions.

JONES: We mark to market daily all of our derivatives positions, but we don't do the same for the underlying exposures. Is that the direction you're going in?

McKNEW: Yes, but that only serves to support my point. My question is: How does marking to market the

hedges but not the positions being hedged give you a reliable guide to the performance of the risk management function?

VAN RODEN: We actually do something like what you're suggesting, Bob. For instance, in the case of nickel, we mark our hedges to market every day. At the same time, on a weekly basis, we update our forecast of total nickel costs for the rest of the year based on current nickel prices. And combining these two measures—that is, actual costs based on current prices plus hedging gains or losses—allows us to project our total nickel costs and their effect on bottom-line earnings.

McKNEW: So, using current price levels, you would estimate both your expected nickel costs and your expected hedging results? And this would in turn give you some basis for judging the effectiveness of your hedging program relative to either doing nothing or, say, hedging 100%?

VAN RODEN: Yes, that's basically right.

McKNEW: That's interesting. Does anybody else do anything similar to that? . . . No response. I wonder why. Is it because the accountants don't require you to do it? Or is it because you cannot develop the systems capable of doing it?

ROBERT BUTLER: We do something like this on a once-a-year basis. But I think the main problem here is that setting up such systems is a costly undertaking. It's not something that goes into the financial statements. It involves calculating all the various exposures, and, perhaps even more difficult and time-consuming, getting agreement on the calculations. If performance evaluations and treasury group bonuses are going to be affected by how you estimate the exposures, then reaching agreement could be difficult.

McKNEW: Yes, I see.

Derivatives and Pension Fund Management

BUTLER: I'd like to bring up one other area in the use of derivatives that has come up in our company—one that is particularly sensitive today. What kind of restrictions or policies do you impose on your investment managers in your pension fund? I think this question is particularly important because you've got to use derivatives in a pension fund, you've got to allow the managers to use them.

McKNEW: Do you need derivatives to manage duration?

BUTLER: Well, yes, duration is one concern. But we're also worried about the currency risk faced by our equity managers. Derivatives have made these financial markets ten times more efficient, no 100 times more efficient, than they were in the past. And by preventing our managers from using derivatives, we are really tying their hands—forcing them to accept exposures that could easily be hedged with derivatives.

Derivatives have gotten a bad name primarily because of people who were trying to make a profit center out of the treasury function. They were trying, for example, to report zero interest cost for the year when they should have taken $200 million of interest cost; and, when rates turned against them, they ended up getting $800 million worth of interest cost. And that's the problem in a nutshell.

For this reason, I think the current crackdown on derivatives is going to end up imposing large and costly constraints on our pension funds. And, I'm interested in hearing what others in this room are experiencing in this regard.

McKNEW: Well, at Bank of America, it is my area—trading—that now gets the most attention in terms of compliance and risk management controls.

And we have lots of infrastructure built up to ensure that we're doing what we're supposed to be doing. As I said, we mark our positions to market every day and our results hit the bottom line directly.

The next most closely scrutinized

part of the bank is corporate treasury, which, in our institution, is very similar to yours. Some of their activity is mark-to-market, some of it isn't. Their decision-making is not as immediate as ours, but its still quite current—and they get a lot of attention. And the third area of derivatives concern is the activities in which we act as a fiduciary—activities such as mutual fund and trust departments in which we manage other people's money.

Now, although the money management area doesn't get as much attention at B of A, I agree with your statement. More and more of the investment that's going to take place in this country, if only because we baby-boomers are getting older, is going to take place in pensions—that is, in fiduciaries, investment companies, investment managers, trust departments, pension funds, all of that stuff. And this means that the potential benefits of using derivatives—and the costs of not using them—are also going to grow.

But, at the same time, it's seems clear to me that the money management industry is going to have to become a lot more transparent in terms of what it's doing. It's going to have to do a much better job explaining to us what they're doing with our money, and what the associated risks are.

JONES: As you know, Bob, there's a lot of education about derivatives that needs to be done in this country. I sit on a committee that looks after employee savings plans and things of that nature. And everyone on that committee was scared to death that any of the funds we were overseeing might be using derivatives. The best answer for a fund manager facing boards like ours was a firm, "No, sir, we do not use derivatives." That was the only response our committee was comfortable with. And, I'm afraid we're not going to make much progress on this issue as long as we keep having episodes like Orange County and Baring Brothers.

McKNEW: Well, let me offer the following suggestion in closing. I wonder if, in a perverse way, the Orange Counties and Barings and P&Gs might not actually be serving to strengthen the long-term outlook for the risk management and deriva-

tives industry. At Bank of America, we currently have somewhere between $250 billion and $750 billion (if you include futures, foreign exchange forwards and options, and all of the other stuff) of derivatives on the books. Yet, I believe it was only a little more than a year ago that our department made its first explicit presentation in an educational sort of way to our board on this activity. And I suggest that this is probably also the case with most of the corporations represented in this room.

And, as a participant in the marketplace, I am frankly grateful for Orange County—not that Orange County happened, but that something like Orange County is causing us to have conferences like this one. Orange County is causing everybody from Congressmen and regulators to accountants to learn more about derivatives and risk management. At the same time, people inside corporations are starting to take documentation seriously. And they're worrying about credit risk, which they maybe never did before.

Over the longer term, these developments are all positive in that they are going to allow us to use these instruments—which I think we would all say are pretty basic tools to our trade—a lot more freely and in a much more transparent way going forward.

One last point I'd like to make in closing: We're all more or less front-office people; we worry about measuring risk and taking care of it. An awful lot of what affects our market, however, takes place in the back office—documentation, operations, accounting, and so on. And we don't talk enough about these back-office functions. I know that we at B of A are spending an awful lot of time making sure that we operate and account for our derivatives activities appropriately. And I'd encourage all of you to do the same thing with your back offices—again, just for the betterment of our markets going forward.

I would like to thank our panelists for taking some time to prepare and share their thoughts with all of us. I think it's been a great discussion.

VI. CORPORATE RESTRUCTURING AND CORPORATE GOVERNANCE

The past decade has given rise to a growing debate over the relative efficiency of different national economic systems. At the risk of oversimplifying, there are two basic corporate finance and governance systems that predominate in developed economies today. One is the Anglo-American "market-based" model, with widely dispersed shareholders and a fairly vigorous corporate control (or takeover) market. The other can be represented by the Japanese and German "relationship-based" systems, with their large bank and intercorporate holdings—and conspicuous absence of takeovers. Given the increasing globalization of business, which of these two systems can be expected to prevail over time? Or will both systems continue to coexist, while seeking to adopt some aspects of the other?

Throughout the 1980s and well into the '90s, the popular business press was telling us that U.S. companies were falling farther behind their global competitors—even as U.S. stock prices were climbing ever higher. We were also told that the corporate restructuring movement was adding to the American competitiveness problem by reducing investment and otherwise reinforcing the "short termism" of U.S. managers. At the same time, Japanese companies were pronounced the victors in the competitive wars, and U.S. managers and investors were urged to cultivate the "patience" of their Japanese counterparts.

Over the same period, however, academic research in corporate finance was telling a quite different story. The average stock price reactions to announcements of all variety of U.S. corporate restructurings—takeovers, LBOs, spinoffs, and large stock buybacks—were consistently positive. And a follow-up set of studies examining the operating performance of restructured companies has by and large vindicated the market's initial endorsement of such restructurings. Researchers have also reported comparable shareholder gains and operating improvements for similar restructuring transactions in the U.K. Perhaps even more striking, a 1993 study published by Morgan Stanley showed U.S. companies accounting for an impressive 48% of worldwide

total profits and 37% of total sales in 19 major global industries over the period 1986-1992 (as compared to only 15% of profits and 32% of sales for Japanese companies over the same period, and 37% of profit and 31% of sales for European firms).

At the same time research in corporate finance was furnishing evidence in support of the Anglo-American market for corporate control, some financial economists were also beginning to question at least aspects of the Japanese relationship-based system. At the end of 1990, my *Journal of Applied Corporate Finance* published an article by Harvard's Japanese corporate finance specialist Carl Kester entitled "The Hidden Costs of Japanese Success." That article identified a fundamental problem with the Japanese corporate governance system that was being masked by Japanese companies' gains in market share and the growing Japanese trade surplus. The problem, which has been called "the agency costs of free cash flow" by Harvard professor Michael Jensen, comes down to this: The Japanese system's ineffectiveness in forcing its large, mature companies to return excess capital to investors (dividends are minimal and stock repurchases were prohibited until quite recently) was leading to widespread, value-reducing corporate diversification as well as massive overcapacity in many industries.

In our lead article in this section, "The Modern Industrial Revolution, Exit, and the Failure of Internal Control Systems," Jensen goes so far as to suggest that squeezing out excess capital and capacity is the most formidable challenge now facing the U.S. economy—and, indeed, the economies of all industrialized nations. In making this argument, Jensen draws striking parallels between the 19th-century industrial revolution and worldwide economic developments in the last two decades. In both periods, technological advances led not only to sharp increases in productivity and dramatic reductions in prices, but also to massive obsolescence and overcapacity. And much as the great M & A wave of the 1890s reduced capacity (by consolidating some 1800 firms into roughly 150), the leveraged takeovers, LBOs, and other leveraged recapitalizations of the 1980s provided "healthy adjustments" to overcapacity that was building in many sectors of the U.S. economy: for example, oil and gas, tires, tobacco, commodity chemicals, food processing, paper and forest products, financial services, publishing, and broadcasting.

Jensen interprets the shareholder gains from corporate restructuring transactions (which he estimates at $750 billion) as evidence of the failure of U.S. internal corporate control systems—that is, managements as supervised by boards of directors—to deal voluntarily with the problem of excess capacity. And, given the restrictions on the takeover market, together with intensifying global competition, worldwide protectionism, and other causes of future overcapacity, Jensen views reform of the U.S. corporate governance system as an urgent matter. Notable among his proposals is that large public companies should seek to replicate certain governance features of venture capital and LBO firms like Kleiner Perkins and KKR—specifically, significant equity ownership by managers and directors, greater participation by outside "active" investors, and smaller and better informed boards.

In "The Methods and Motives of Corporate Restructuring," Bennett Stewart and David Glassman show how current methods of restructuring—especially ESOPs, LBOs, and leveraged "cashouts"—increase corporate values by strengthening management incentives to serve stockholders.

In "Purchase vs. Pooling: Does It Matter?," Eric Lindenberg and Michael Ross of Salomon Smith Barney present evidence that, during the 1990s, the stock market strongly favored purchase acquisitions over poolings, despite the negative (but non-cash) effect of amortized goodwill on earnings. Also worth noting, for companies using purchase accounting, the market appears to raise their P/E ratios just enough to offset the effect of having to amortizing goodwill. Besides providing more testimony to the market's ability to see through accounting cosmetics, this article also provides evidence of managers' tendency to overpay when allowed to use pooling accounting—that is, more evidence of a corporate free cash flow problem.

In "Lessons from a Middle Market LBO," Professors George Baker and Karen Wruck tell the story of the O.M. Scott Company, a $200 million lawn and gardening firm purchased by Clayton & Dubilier in a leveraged buyout from ITT in 1986. According to the authors, the combination of financial leverage (91% debt to capital), concentrated equity ownership (Clayton & Dubilier owned over 60% and Scott

management 17.5%), and an active and financially interested board of directors led to a "fundamental change" in "both organizational structure and the management decision-making process." The details of the transformation of Scott under Clayton & Dubilier also speak volumes about what went wrong at U.S. conglomerates like ITT.

In "Leveraged Recaps and the Curbing of Corporate Overinvestment," David and Diane Denis provide additional evidence of shareholder gains from highly leveraged transactions. In summarizing the findings of their study of 29 large leveraged recapitalizations (also known as "public LBOs," those in which companies borrow to pay out a large dividend or buy back a large percentage of their stock), the Denises offer striking evidence that the companies were systematically overinvesting prior to their leveraged recaps. The massive substitution of debt for equity in such recaps, typically undertaken in response to hostile takeover pressure, forced managements to pay out excess capital rather than continue seeking to pursue corporate growth at the expense of their shareholders. For example, in the case of Goodyear Tire, the company's leveraged of payout of $2.2 billion to Goldsmith and other shareholders effectively brought about a reversal of the company's disastrous diversification strategy (into oil, natural gas, and aerospace), forcing it to return its focus on the tire industry, where it now appears to be prospering.

In "Some New Evidence That Corporate Spinoffs Create Value," Patrick Cusatis, James Miles, and Randy Woolridge present evidence of rapid growth in capital expenditures and operating income by spun-off businesses, as well as significant stock price gains by parent and spun-off companies. They also note a striking tendency of spun-off firms in businesses unrelated to their parents' to be subsequently acquired by companies in related businesses.

The popular explanation for the positive market reaction to spin-offs is that such transactions allow investors to evaluate exceptional growth opportunities on a stand-alone basis. Such an argument appears, at least at first glance, to be premised on an exploitable inefficiency in stock market pricing. While the authors concede that providing investors with more extensive financial disclosure on an involuntary, periodic basis may affect the market's assessment of a subsidiary's value, and while such securities in some cases may even have scarcity value to investors unable to find "pure plays," they also offer other suggestions. The fact that spun-off businesses tend to be parts of large, diversified conglomerates suggests that one of the motives for spin-offs may be expected improvements in operating efficiency. Spin-offs, as the authors point out, are often accompanied by major changes in the responsibilities and incentives of subsidiary management; for example, stock options in the newly-trading subsidiary's shares are almost always provided the top managers.

In "The Evolution of Buyout Pricing and Financial Structure (or What Went Wrong) in the 1980s," Steven Kaplan and Jeremy Stein present the findings of their study of 124 large management buyouts completed between 1981-1989. Of the 41 deals in their sample transacted between 1980 and 1984, only one has defaulted on its debt. Of the 83 deals done between 1985 and 1989, 26 have defaulted and 18 filed for Chapter 11.

So what went wrong with the later deals? The answer supplied by Kaplan and Stein is that the buyout market "overheated." More specifically,

(1) Buyout prices as multiples of cash flow rose sharply, and multiples were especially high in deals financed with junk bonds;

(2) Banks took smaller positions in later deals and, at the same time, accelerated required principal repayments, leading to sharply lower ratios of cash flow to total debt obligations;

(3) Public junk debt displaced both private subordinated debt and the associated practice of "strip" financing (in which subordinated debtholders also receive equity stakes), thereby raising the expected costs of financial reorganization;

(4) Finally, management and other interested parties such as investment bankers and deal promoters took out more money up front in the later deals.

How do we avoid such "overleveraging" in the future? By returning to the principles of the early '80s: (1) more closely-held subordinated debt and strip financing in place of junk bonds, and (2) more equity put up, and less front-loaded compensation taken out, by management, dealmakers, lenders, and other interested parties.

And the markets appear to have taken the advice. For, in "LBOs—Financial Structures and Strategies," Bank of America's Jay Allen notes that LBOs are back, and with a new financial structure. Allen observes, for example, that LBOs have begun to migrate toward higher-growth, "technology-driven" industries like information processing and healthcare—and that such growth LBOs tend to be financed with considerably higher percentages of equity (as much as 35%) and shorter debt maturities (3-4 years as opposed to the customary 6-7-year senior bank debt in slow-growth LBOs). Along with larger equity commitments, Allen also notes "a pronounced shift away from the use of public subordinated debt . . . toward capital structures composed entirely of senior bank debt and sponsor equity capital (and, in a few cases, sponsor-controlled subordinated debt)."

In addition to these changes in financial structure, Allen also describes some fairly recent shifts in the buyout strategies of unaffiliated or "financial" buyers. One approach, known as a leveraged build-up, involves a moderately leveraged acquisition by a financial buyer of a company in a consolidating industry, which becomes the "platform" for further leveraged acquisitions of firms in the same industry. Another involves partnerships between private financial buyers and corporate strategic buyers, who team up to buy companies on a leveraged basis. Allen sees such partnerships as accomplishing "a valuable, if not indeed inevitable, marriage of operating knowhow and financial expertise."

In the "Roundtable on the Role of Corporate Boards in the 1990s" with which the book closes, Michael Jensen discusses the state of U.S. corporate governance with a number of corporate CEOs and directors and two general partners of LBO investment firms. To the extent anything like a consensus emerges, it is that many if not most corporate managements are dedicated to increasing shareholder value, and that many corporate boards conscientiously perform their oversight function. But even the most vigorous defenders of the status quo suggest that boards are clearly failing in something like 20% of all U.S. public companies. And, in the absence of takeovers, no one professed to have a solution to the problem of management entrenchment at persistently underperforming companies.

Nonetheless, one hint at a possible solution was contained in the discussion's clear suggestion of profound differences in the governance systems of public companies and those taken private in LBOs. As James Birle of the Blackstone Group commented, the two necessary conditions for effective board oversight are "adequate information and accountability—neither of which is likely to hold for many public companies." In sharp contrast to the boards of public companies, LBO boards are comprised principally of the company's largest stockholders. And, as Birle suggests, the oversight of a financially interested board makes for significantly tighter financial controls and more demanding performance standards than those typically imposed in public companies. Besides greater accountability, the directors of LBO companies also have far greater knowledge about the companies as a result of participating in the intensive due diligence performed when first investing in the company.

DHC

THE MODERN INDUSTRIAL REVOLUTION, EXIT, AND THE FAILURE OF INTERNAL CONTROL SYSTEMS

by Michael C. Jensen,
Harvard Business School*

Fundamental technological, political, regulatory, and economic forces are radically changing the worldwide competitive environment. We have not seen such a metamorphosis of the economic landscape since the industrial revolution of the 19th century. The scope and pace of the changes over the past two decades qualify this period as a modern industrial revolution, and I predict it will take decades more for these forces to be worked out fully in the worldwide economy.

Although the current and 19th-century transformations of the U.S. economy are separated by almost 100 years, there are striking parallels between them—most notably, rapid technological and organizational change leading to declining production costs and increasing average (but decreasing marginal) productivity of labor. During both periods, moreover, these developments resulted in widespread excess capacity, reduced rates of growth in labor income, and, ultimately, downsizing and exit.

The capital markets played a major role in eliminating excess capacity both in the late 19th century and in the 1980s. The merger boom of the 1890s brought about a massive consolidation of independent firms and closure of marginal facilities. In the 1980s the capital markets helped eliminate excess capacity through leveraged acquisitions, stock buybacks, hostile takeovers, leveraged buyouts, and divisional sales.

And much as the takeover specialists of the 1980s were disparaged by managers, policymakers, and the press, their 19th-century counterparts were vilified as "robber barons." In both cases, the popular reaction against "financiers" was followed by public policy changes that restricted the capital markets. The turn of the century saw the passage of antitrust laws that restricted business combinations; the late 1980s gave rise to re-regulation of the credit markets, antitakeover legislation, and court decisions that all but shut down the market for corporate control.

*This is a shortened version of a paper by the same title that was originally published in the *Journal of Finance* (July 1993), which was based in turn on my Presidential Address to the American Finance Association in January 1993. It is reprinted here by permission of the American Finance Association. I wish to express my appreciation for the research assistance of Chris Allen, Brian Barry, Susan Brumfield, Karin Monsler, and particularly Donna Feinberg, the support of the Division of Research of the Harvard Business School, and the comments of and discussions with George Baker, Carliss Baldwin, Joe Bower, Alfred Chandler, Harry and Linda DeAngelo, Ben Esty, Takashi Hikino, Steve Kaplan, Nancy Koehn, Claudio Loderer, George Lodge, John Long, Kevin Murphy, Malcolm Salter, Rene Stulz, Richard Tedlow, and, especially, Robert Hall, Richard Hackman, and Karen Wruck.

Although the vast increases in productivity associated with the 19th-century industrial revolution increased aggregate welfare, the resulting obsolescence of human and physical capital caused great hardship, misunderstanding, and bitterness. As noted in 1873 by Henry Ward Beecher, a well-known commentator and influential clergyman of the time,

The present period will always be memorable in the dark days of commerce in America. We have had commercial darkness at other times. There have been these depressions, but none so obstinate and none so universal... Great Britain has felt it; France has felt it; all Austria and her neighborhood has experienced it. It is cosmopolitan. It is distinguished by its obstinacy from former like periods of commercial depression. Remedies have no effect. Party confidence, all stimulating persuasion, have not lifted the pall, and practical men have waited, feeling that if they could tide over a year they could get along; but they could not tide over the year. If only one or two years could elapse they could save themselves. The years have lapsed, and they were worse off than they were before. What is the matter? What has happened? Why, from the very height of prosperity without any visible warning, without even a cloud the size of a man's hand visible on the horizon, has the cloud gathered, as it were, from the center first, spreading all over the sky?[1]

Almost 20 years later, on July 4, 1892, the Populist Party platform adopted at the party's first convention in Omaha reflected continuing unrest while pointing to financiers as the cause of the current problems:

We meet in the midst of a nation brought to the verge of moral, political, and material ruin... The fruits of the toil of millions are boldly stolen to build up colossal fortunes for the few, unprecedented in the history of mankind; and the possessors of these in turn despise the republic and endanger liberty. From the same prolific womb of government injustice are bred two great classes of tramps and millionaires.[2]

Technological and other developments that began in the mid-20th century have culminated in the past two decades in a similar situation: rapidly improving productivity, the creation of overcapacity, and, consequently, the requirement for exit. Although efficient exit has profound import for productivity and social wealth, research on the topic[3] has been relatively sparse since the 1942 publication of Joseph Schumpeter's famous description of capitalism as a process of "creative destruction." In Schumpeter's words,

Every piece of business strategy...must be seen in its role in the perennial gale of creative destruction... The usual theorist's paper and the usual government commission's report practically never try to see that behavior... as an attempt by those firms to keep on their feet, on ground that is slipping away from under them. In other words, the problem that is usually being visualized is how capitalism administers existing structures, whereas the relevant problem is how it creates and destroys them.[4]

Current technological and political changes are bringing the question of efficient exit to the forefront, and the adjustments necessary to cope with such changes will receive renewed attention from managers, policymakers, and researchers in the coming decade.

In this paper, I begin by reviewing the industrial revolution of the 19th century to shed light on current economic trends. Drawing parallels with the 1800s, I discuss in some detail worldwide changes driving the demand for exit in today's economy. I also describe the barriers to efficient exit in the U.S. economy, and the role of the market for corporate control—takeovers, LBOs, and other leveraged restructurings—in surmounting those barriers during the 1980s.

1. Walter W. Price, *We Have Recovered Before!* (Harper & Brothers: New York, 1933), p. 6.

2. Donald L. McMurray, *Coxey's Army: A Study of the Industrial Army Movement of 1894* (Little, Brown: Boston, 1929), p. 7.

3. For a rare study of exit in the finance literature, see the analysis of the retrenchment of the U.S. steel industry in Harry DeAngelo and Linda DeAngelo, "Union Negotiations and Corporate Policy: A Study of Labor Concessions in the Domestic Steel Industry During the 1980s," *Journal of Financial Economics* 30 (1991), 3-43. See also Pankaj Ghemawat and Barry Nalebuff, "Exit," *Rand Journal of Economics* 16 (Summer, 1985), 184-194. For a detailed comparison of U.S. and Japanese retrenchment in the 1970s and early 1980s, see Douglas Anderson,

"Managing Retreat: Disinvestment Policy," in Thomas K. McCraw, ed., *America versus Japan* (Harvard Business School Press: Boston, 1986), 337-372. Joseph L. Bower analyzes the private and political responses to decline in the petrochemical industry in *When Markets Quake* (Harvard Business School Press: Boston, 1986). Kathryn Harrigan presents detailed firm and industry studies in two of her books: *Managing Maturing Businesses: Restructuring Declining Industries and Revitalizing Troubled Operations* (Lexington Books, 1988) and *Strategies for Declining Businesses* (Lexington Books, 1980).

4. Joseph A. Schumpeter, *Capitalism, Socialism, and Democracy* (Harper Torchbook Edition: New York, 1976), p. 83.

With the shutdown of the capital markets in the 1990s, the challenge of accomplishing efficient exit has been transferred to corporate internal control systems. With few exceptions, however, U.S. managements and boards have failed to bring about timely exit and downsizing without external pressure. Although product market competition will eventually eliminate overcapacity, this solution generates huge unnecessary costs. (The costs of this solution have now become especially apparent in Japan, where a virtual breakdown of the internal control systems, coupled with a complete absence of capital market influence, has resulted in enormous overcapacity—a problem that Japanese companies are only beginning to address.)

At the close of the paper, I offer suggestions for reforming U.S. internal corporate control mechanisms. In particular, I hold up several features of venture capital and LBO firms such as Kleiner Perkins and KKR for emulation by large, public companies—notably (1) smaller, more active, and better informed boards; and (2) significant equity ownership by board members as well as managers. I also urge boards and managers to encourage larger holdings and greater participation by people I call "active" investors.

THE SECOND INDUSTRIAL REVOLUTION[5]

The Industrial Revolution was distinguished by a shift to capital-intensive production, rapid growth in productivity and living standards, the formation of large corporate hierarchies, overcapacity, and, eventually, closure of facilities. Originating in Britain in the late 18th century, the First Industrial Revolution witnessed the application of new energy sources to methods of production. The mid-19th century saw another wave of massive change with the birth of modern transportation and communication facilities, including the railroad, telegraph, steamship, and cable systems. Coupled with the invention of high-speed consumer packaging technology, these innovations gave rise to the mass production and distribution systems of the late 19th

and early 20th centuries—the Second Industrial Revolution.

The dramatic changes that occurred from the middle to the end of the century clearly warrant the term "revolution." Inventions such as the McCormick reaper in the 1830s, the sewing machine in 1844, and high-volume canning and packaging devices in the 1880s exemplified a worldwide surge in productivity that "substituted machine tools for human craftsmen, interchangeable parts for hand-tooled components, and the energy of coal for that of wood, water, and animals."[6] New technology in the paper industry allowed wood pulp to replace rags as the primary input material. Continuous rod rolling transformed the wire industry: within a decade, wire nails replaced cut nails as the main source of supply. Worsted textiles resulting from advances in combing technology changed the woolen textile industry. Between 1869 and 1899, the capital invested per American manufacturer grew from about $700 to $2,000; and, in the period 1889-1919, the annual growth of total factor productivity was almost six times higher than that which had occurred for most of the 19th century.[7]

As productivity climbed steadily, production costs and prices fell dramatically. The 1882 formation of the Standard Oil Trust, which concentrated nearly 25% of the world's kerosene production into three refineries, reduced the average cost of a gallon of kerosene by 70% between 1882 and 1885. In tobacco, the invention of the Bonsack machine in the early 1880s reduced the labor costs of cigarette production by 98%. The Bessemer process reduced the cost of steel rails by 88% from the early 1870s to the late 1890s, and the electrolytic refining process invented in the 1880s reduced the price of aluminum by 96% between 1888 and 1895. In chemicals, the mass production of synthetic dyes, alkalis, nitrates, fibers, plastics, and film occurred rapidly after 1880. Production costs of synthetic blue dye, for example, fell by 95% from the 1870s to 1886.[8]

Such sharp declines in production costs and prices led to widespread excess capacity—a problem that was exacerbated by the fall in demand that

---

5. This section draws extensively on excellent discussions of the period by Alfred Chandler, Thomas McCraw, and Naomi Lamoreux. See the following works by Chandler: "The Emergence of Managerial Capitalism," Harvard Business School #9-384-081, revised by Thomas J. McCraw, July 1, 1992; *Scale and Scope, The Dynamics of Industrial Capitalism* (Harvard University Press, 1990); and *The Visible Hand: The Managerial Revolution in American Business* (Harvard University Press, 1977). See also Naomi R. Lamoreaux, *The Great Merger Movement in American Business, 1895-1904* (Cambridge University Press: Cambridge, England,

1985); and Thomas K. McCraw, "Antitrust: The Perceptions and Reality in Coping with Big Business," Harvard Business School #N9-391-292 (1992), and "Rethinking the Trust Question," in T. McCraw, ed., *Regulation in Perspective* (Harvard University Press, 1981).

6. McCraw (1981), p. 3.
7. McCraw (1981), p. 3.
8. For most of the examples of cost reduction cited in this paragraph, see Chandler (1992), pp. 4-6.

What has generally been referred to as the "decade of the 80s" in the United States actually began in the early 1970s, with the 10-fold increase in energy prices from 1973 to 1979, and the emergence of the modern market for corporate control and high-yield, non-investment-grade ("junk") bonds in the mid-1970s.

accompanied the recession and panic of 1893. Although attempts were made to eliminate excess capacity through pools, associations, and cartels, the problem was not substantially resolved until the capital markets facilitated exit by means of the 1890s' wave of mergers and acquisitions. Capacity was reduced through consolidation and the closing of marginal facilities in the merged entities. From 1895 to 1904, over 1,800 firms were bought or combined by merger into 157 firms.[9]

THE MODERN INDUSTRIAL REVOLUTION

The major restructuring of the American business community that began in the 1970s and continues in the 1990s is being driven by a variety of factors, including changes in physical and management technology, global competition, new regulation and taxes, and the conversion of formerly closed, centrally planned socialist and communist economies to capitalism, along with open participation in international trade. These changes are significant in scope and effect; indeed, they are bringing about the Third Industrial Revolution. To appreciate the challenge facing current control systems in light of this change, we must understand more about these general forces sweeping the world economy, and why they are generating excess capacity and thus the requirement for exit.

What has generally been referred to as the "decade of the '80s" in the United States actually began in the early 1970s, with the 10-fold increase in energy prices from 1973 to 1979, and the emergence

of the modern market for corporate control and high-yield, non-investment-grade ("junk") bonds in the mid-1970s. These events were associated with the beginnings of the Third Industrial Revolution which—if I were to pick a particular date—would be the time of the oil price increases beginning in 1973.

The Decade of the '80s: Capital Markets Provide an Early Response to the Modern Industrial Revolution

The macroeconomic data for the 1980s show major productivity gains. In fact, 1981 was a watershed year. Total factor productivity growth in the manufacturing sector more than doubled after 1981, from 1.4% per year in the period 1950-1981 (including a period of zero growth from 1973-1980) to 3.3% in the period 1981-1990.[10] Over the same period, nominal unit labor costs stopped their 17-year rise, and real unit labor costs declined by 25%. These lower labor costs came not from reduced wages or employment, but from increased productivity: nominal and real hourly compensation increased by a total of 4.2% and 0.3% per year, respectively, over the 1981-1989 period.[11] Manufacturing employment reached a low in 1983, but by 1989 had experienced a small cumulative increase of 5.5%.[12] Meanwhile, the annual growth in labor productivity increased from 2.3% between 1950-1981 to 3.8% between 1981-1990, while a 30-year decline in capital productivity was reversed when the annual change in the productivity of capital increased from -1.0% between 1950-1981 to 2.0% between 1981-1990.[13]

9. Lamoreux (1985), p. i.
10. Measured by multifactor productivity, as reported in Table 3 of U.S. Department of Labor, Bureau of Labor Statistics, 1990, *Multifactor Productivity Measures*, Report #USDL 91-412. Manufacturing labor productivity also grew at an annual rate of 3.8% in 1981-1990, as compared to 2.3% in the period 1950-1981 (U.S. Department of Labor, 1990, Table 3). By contrast, productivity growth in the overall (or "non-farm") business sector actually fell from 1.9% in the 1950-1981 period to 1.1% in the 1981-1990 period (U. S. Department of Labor, 1990, Table 2). The reason for the fall apparently lies in the relatively large growth in the service sector relative to the manufacturing sector and the low measured productivity growth in services. But there is considerable controversy over the adequacy of the measurement of productivity in the service sector. For example, the U.S. Department of Labor has no productivity measures for services employing nearly 70% of service workers, including, among others, health care, real estate, and securities brokerage. In addition, many believe that service sector productivity growth measures are downward biased. Service sector price measurements, for example, take no account of the improved productivity and lower prices of discount outlet clubs such as Sam's Club. As another example, the Commerce Department measures the output of financial services as the value of labor used to produce it. Because labor productivity is defined as the value of total output divided by total labor inputs, it is impossible for measured productivity to grow. Between 1973 and 1987, however, total equity shares traded daily grew from 5.7 million to 63.8 million, while employment only doubled, thus implying considerably more productivity growth than the zero growth reflected in the statistics.

11. Nominal and real hourly compensation, *Economic Report of the President*, Table B42 (1993).
12. U.S. Department of Labor, Bureau of Labor Statistics, 1991, *International Comparisons of Manufacturing Productivity and Unit Labor Cost Trends*, Report #USDL 92-752.
13. U.S. Department of Labor (1990). Trends in U.S. productivity have been controversial issues in academic and policy circles in the last decade. One reason, I believe, is that it takes time for these complicated changes to show up in the aggregate statistics. For example, in their recent book Baumol, Blackman, and Wolff changed their formerly pessimistic position. In their words: "This book is perhaps most easily summed up as a compendium of evidence demonstrating the error of our previous ways... The main change that was forced upon our views by careful examination of the long-run data was abandonment of our earlier gloomy assessment of American productivity performance. It has been replaced by the guarded optimism that pervades this book. This does *not* mean that we believe retention of American leadership will be automatic or easy. Yet the statistical evidence did drive us to conclude that the many writers who have suggested that the demise of America's traditional position has already occurred or was close at hand were, like the author of Mark Twain's obituary, a bit premature... It should, incidentally, be acknowledged that a number of distinguished economists have also been driven to a similar evaluation..." William Baumol, Sue Anne Beattey Blackman, and Edward Wolff, *Productivity and American Leadership* (MIT Press, Boston, 1989), pp. ix-x.

Reflecting these increases in the productivity of U.S. industry, the real value of public corporations' equity more than doubled during the 1980s from $1.4 to $3 trillion.[14] In addition, real median income increased at the rate of 1.8% per year between 1982 and 1989, reversing the 1.0% per year decline that occurred from 1973 to 1982.[15] Contrary to generally held beliefs, real R&D expenditures set record levels every year from 1975 to 1990, growing at an average annual rate of 5.8%.[16] In one of the media's few accurate portrayals of this period, a 1990 issue of *The Economist* noted that from 1980 to 1985, "American industry went on an R&D spending spree, with few big successes to show for it."[17]

Regardless of the gains in productivity, efficiency, and welfare, the 1980s are generally portrayed by politicians, the media, and others as a "decade of greed and excess." The media attack focused with special intensity on M&A transactions, 35,000 of which occurred from 1976 to 1990, with a total value of $2.6 trillion (in 1992 dollars). Contrary to common belief, only 364 of these offers were contested, and of those only 172 resulted in successful hostile takeovers.[18]

The popular verdict on takeovers was pronounced by prominent takeover defense lawyer Martin Lipton, when he said,

The takeover activity in the U.S. has imposed short-term profit maximization strategies on American Business at the expense of research, development, and capital investment. This is minimizing our ability to compete in world markets and still maintain a growing standard of living at home.[19]

But the evidence provided by financial economists, which I summarize briefly below, is starkly inconsistent with this view.

The most careful academic research strongly suggests that takeovers—along with leveraged restructurings prompted (in many, if not most cases) by the threat of takeover—have produced large gains for shareholders and for the economy as a whole. Based on this research,[20] my estimates indicate that over the 14-year period from 1976 to 1990, the $1.8 trillion volume of corporate control transactions—that is, mergers, tender offers, divestitures, and LBOs—generated over $750 billion in market value "premiums"[21] for selling investors. Given a reasonably efficient market, such premiums (the amounts buyers are willing to pay sellers over current market values) represent, in effect, the minimum increases in value forecast by the buyers. This $750 billion estimate of total shareholder gains thus neither includes the gains (or the losses)[22] to the buyers in such transactions, nor does it account for the value of efficiency improvements by companies pressured by control market activity into reforming without a visible control transaction.

Important sources of the expected gains from takeovers and leveraged restructurings include synergies from combining the assets of two or more organizations in the same or related industries (especially those with excess capacity) and the replacement of inefficient managers or governance systems.[23] Another possible source of the premiums, however, are transfers of wealth from other corporate stakeholders such as employees, bondholders, and the IRS. To the extent the value gains are merely wealth transfers, they do not represent efficiency improvements. But little evidence has been found to date to support substantial wealth transfers from any group,[24] and thus most of the reported gains appear to represent increases in efficiency.

Part of the attack on M&A and LBO transactions has been directed at the high-yield (or "junk") bond

14. As measured by the Wilshire 5,000 index of all publicly held equities.

15. Bureau of the Census, Housing and Household Economic Statistics Division (1991).

16. *Business Week* Annual R&D Scoreboard, 1991.

17. "Out of the Ivory Tower," *The Economist*, February 3, 1990

18. *Mergerstat Review*, 1991, Merrill Lynch, Schaumburg, Illinois.

19. Martin Lipton, "Corporate Governance: Major Issues for the 1990's," Address to the Third Annual Corporate Finance Forum at the J. Ira Harris Center for the Study of Corporate Finance, University of Michigan School of Business, April 6, 1989, p. 2.

20. For a list of such studies, see the Appendix at the end of this article.

21. Measured in 1992 dollars. On average, selling-firm shareholders in all M&A transactions in the period 1976-1990 were paid premiums over market value of 41%. Annual premiums reported by *Mergerstat Review* (1991, Fig. 5) were weighted by value of transactions in the year for this estimate.

In arriving at my estimate of $750 billion of shareholder gains, I also assumed that all transactions without publicly disclosed prices had a value equal to 20% of the value of the average publicly disclosed transaction in the same year, and that they had average premiums equal to those for publicly disclosed transactions.

22. In cases where buyers overpay, such overpayment does not represent an efficiency gain, but rather only a wealth transfer from the buying firm's claimants to those of the selling firm. My method of calculating *total* shareholder gains effectively assumes that the losses to buyers are large enough to offset all gains (including those of the "raiders" whose allegedly massive "paper profits" became a favorite target of the media).

23. A 1992 study by Healy, Palepu, and Ruback estimates the total gains to buying- and selling-firm shareholders in the 50 largest mergers in the period 1979-1984 at 9.1% of the total equity value of both companies. Because buyers in such cases were typically much larger than sellers, such gains are roughly consistent with 40% acquisition premiums. They also find a strong positive cross-sectional relation between the value change and the operating cash flow changes resulting from the merger. See Paul Healy, Krishna Palepu, and Richard Ruback, "Does Corporate Performance Improve After Mergers?," *Journal of Financial Economics* 31, vol. 2 (1992), 135-175.

Takeover activities were addressing an important set of problems in corporate America, and doing it before the companies faced serious trouble in the product markets. They were providing, in effect, an early warning system that motivated healthy adjustments to the excess capacity that was building in many sectors of the worldwide economy.

market. Besides helping to provide capital for corporate newcomers to compete with existing firms in the product markets, junk bonds also eliminated mere size as an effective takeover deterrent. This opened America's largest companies to monitoring and discipline from the capital markets. The following statement by Richard Munro, while Chairman and CEO of Time Inc., is representative of top management's hostile response to junk bonds and takeovers:

Notwithstanding television ads to the contrary, junk bonds are designed as the currency of 'casino economics'... they've been used not to create new plants or jobs or products but to do the opposite: to dismantle existing companies so the players can make their profit... This isn't the Seventh Cavalry coming to the rescue. It's a scalping party.[25]

As critics of leveraged restructuring have suggested, the high leverage incurred in the 1980s did contribute to a sharp increase in the bankruptcy rate of large firms in the early 1990s. Not widely recognized, however, is the major role played by other, external factors in these bankruptcies. First, the recession that helped put many highly leveraged firms into financial distress can be attributed at least in part to new regulatory restrictions on credit markets such as FIRREA—restrictions that were implemented in late 1989 and 1990 to offset the trend toward higher leverage.[26] And when companies did get into financial trouble, revisions in bankruptcy procedures and the tax code made it much more difficult to reorganize outside the courts, thereby *encouraging* many firms to file Chapter 11 and increasing the "costs of financial distress."[27]

But, even with such interference by public policy and the courts with the normal process of private adjustment to financial distress, the general economic consequences of financial distress in the high-yield markets have been greatly exaggerated. While precise numbers are difficult to come by, I estimate that the total bankruptcy losses to junk bond and bank HLT loans from inception of the market in the mid-1970s through 1990 amounted to less than $50 billion. (In comparison, IBM alone lost $51 billion—almost 65% of the total market value of its equity—from its 1991 high to its 1992 close.[28]) Perhaps the most telling evidence that losses have been exaggerated, however, is the current condition of the high-yield market, which is now financing record levels of new issues.

Of course, mistakes were made in the takeover activity of the 1980s. Indeed, given the far-reaching nature of the restructuring, it would have been surprising if there were none. But the popular negative assessment of leveraged restructuring is dramatically inconsistent with both the empirical evidence and the near-universal view of finance scholars who have studied the phenomenon. In fact, takeover activities were addressing an important set of problems in corporate America, and doing it before the companies faced serious trouble in the product markets. They were providing, in effect, an early warning system that motivated healthy adjustments to the excess capacity that was building in many sectors of the worldwide economy.

Causes of Excess Capacity

Excess capacity can arise in at least four ways, the most obvious of which occurs when market demand falls below the level required to yield returns that will support the currently installed production capacity. This *demand-reduction* scenario is most familiarly associated with recession episodes in the business cycle.

24. A 1989 study by Laura Stiglin, Steven Kaplan, and myself demonstrates that, contrary to popular assertions, LBO transactions resulted in increased tax revenues to the U. S. Treasury—increases that average about 60% per annum on a permanent basis under the 1986 IRS code. (Michael C. Jensen, Steven Kaplan, Laura Stiglin, "Effects of LBOs on Tax Revenues of the U.S. Treasury," *Tax Notes*, Vol. 42, No. 6 (February 6, 1989), pp. 727-733.)

The data presented by a study of pension fund reversions reveal that only about 1% of the premiums paid in all takeovers can be explained by reversions of pension plans in the target firms (although the authors of the study do not present this calculation themselves). (Jeffrey Pontiff, Andrei Shleifer, and Michael S. Weisbach, "Reversions of Excess Pension Assets after Takeovers," *Rand Journal of Economics*, Vol. 21, No. 4 (Winter 1990), pp. 600-613.)

Joshua Rosett, in analyzing over 5,000 union contracts in over 1,000 listed companies in the period 1973 to 1987, shows that less than 2% of the takeover premiums can be explained by reductions in union wages in the first six years after the change in control. Pushing the estimation period out to 18 years after the change

in control increases the percentage to only 5.4% of the premium. For hostile takeovers only, union wages *increase* by 3% and 6% for the two time intervals. (Joshua G. Rosett, "Do Union Wealth Concessions Explain Takeover Premiums? The Evidence on Contract Wages," *Journal of Financial Economics*, Vol. 27, No. 1 (September 1990), pp. 263-282.)

25. J. Richard Munro, "Takeovers: The Myths Behind the Mystique," May 15, 1989, published in *Vital Speeches*, p. 472.

26. See the collection of articles on the "credit crunch" in Vol. 4 No. 1 (Spring 1991) of the *Journal of Applied Corporate Finance*.

27. I make this case in "Corporate Control and the Politics of Finance," *Journal of Applied Corporate Finance* (Summer, 1991), 13-33. See also Karen Wruck, "Financial Distress, Reorganization, and Organizational Efficiency," *Journal of Financial Economics* 27 (1990), 420-444.

28. Its high of $139.50 occurred on 2/19/91 and it closed at $50.38 at the end of 1992.

Excess capacity can also arise from two types of technological change. The first type, *capacity-expanding* technological change, increases the output of a given capital stock and organization. An example of the capacity-expanding type of change is the Reduced Instruction Set CPU (RISC) processor innovation in the computer workstation market. RISC processors have brought about a ten-fold increase in power, but can be produced by adapting the current production technology. With no increase in the quantity demanded, this change implies that production capacity must fall by 90%. Of course, such price declines increase the quantity demanded in these situations, thereby reducing the extent of the capacity adjustment that would otherwise be required. Nevertheless, the new workstation technology has dramatically increased the effective output of existing production facilities, thereby generating excess capacity.

The second type is *obsolescence-creating* change—change that makes obsolete the current capital stock and organization. For example, Wal-Mart and the wholesale clubs that are revolutionizing retailing are dominating old-line department stores, thereby eliminating the need for much current retail capacity. When Wal-Mart enters a new market, total retail capacity expands, and some of the existing high-cost retail operations must go out of business. More intensive use of information and other technologies, direct dealing with manufacturers, and the replacement of high-cost, restrictive work-rule union labor are several sources of the competitive advantage of these new organizations.

Finally, excess capacity also results when many competitors simultaneously rush to implement new, highly productive technologies without considering whether the aggregate effects of all such investment will be greater capacity than can be supported by demand in the final product market. The winchester disk drive industry provides an example. Between 1977 and 1984, venture capitalists invested over $400 million in 43 different manufacturers of winchester disk drives; initial public offerings of common stock infused additional capital in excess of $800 million. In mid-1983, the capital markets assigned a value of $5.4 billion to twelve publicly-traded, venture-capital-backed hard disk drive manufacturers. Yet, by the end of 1984, overcapacity had caused the value assigned to those companies to plummet to $1.4 billion. My Harvard colleagues William Sahlman and Howard Stevenson have attributed this overcapacity to an "investment mania" based on implicit assumptions about long-run growth and profitability *"for each individual company* [that,]...had they been stated explicitly, would not have been acceptable to the rational investor."[29]

Such "overshooting" has by no means been confined to the winchester disk drive industry.[30] Indeed, the 1980s saw boom-and-bust cycles in the venture capital market generally, and also in commercial real estate and LBO markets. As Sahlman and Stevenson have also suggested, something more than "investment mania" and excessive "animal spirits" was at work here. Stated as simply as possible, my own analysis traces such overshooting to a gross misalignment of incentives between the "dealmakers" who promoted the transactions and the lenders, limited partners, and other investors who funded them.[31] During the mid to late '80s, venture capitalists, LBO promoters, and real estate developers were all effectively being rewarded simply for doing deals rather than for putting together successful deals. Reforming the "contracts" between dealmaker and investor—most directly, by reducing front-end-loaded fees and requiring the dealmakers to put up significant equity—would go far toward solving the problem of too many deals. (As I argue later, public corporations in mature industries face an analogous, though potentially far more costly (in terms of shareholder value destroyed and social resources wasted), distortion of investment priorities and incentives when their managers and directors do not have significant stock ownership.)

Current Forces Leading to Excess Capacity and Exit

The ten-fold increase in crude oil prices between 1973-1979 had ubiquitous effects, forcing contraction in oil, chemicals, steel, aluminum, and

---

29. See William A. Sahlman and Howard H. Stevenson, "Capital Market Myopia," *Journal of Business Venturing* 1 (1985), p. 7.

30. Or to the 1980s. There is evidence of such behavior in the 19th century, and in other periods of U.S. history.

31. Stated more precisely, my argument attributes overshooting to "incentive, information, and contracting" problems. For more on this, see Jensen (1991), cited in note 27, pp. 26-27. For some supporting evidence, see Steven N. Kaplan and Jeremy Stein, 1993, "The Evolution of Buyout Pricing and Financial Structure in the 1980s," *Quarterly Journal of Economics* 108, no. 2, 313-358. For a shorter, less technical version of the same article, see Vol. 6 No. 1 (Spring 1993) of the *Journal of Applied Corporate Finance*.

> During the mid to late '80s, venture capitalists, LBO promoters, and real estate
> developers were all effectively being rewarded simply for doing deals... Reforming
> the "contracts" between dealmaker and investor—most directly, by requiring the
> dealmakers to put up significant equity—would go far toward solving the problem
> of too many deals.

international shipping, among other industries. In addition, the sharp crude oil price increases that motivated major changes to economize on energy had other, longer-lasting consequences. The general corporate re-evaluation of organizational processes stimulated by the oil shock led to dramatic increases in efficiency above and beyond the original energy-saving projects. (In fact, I view the oil shock as the initial impetus for the corporate "process re-engineering" movement that still continues to accelerate throughout the world.)

Since the oil price increases of the 1970s, we have again seen systematic overcapacity problems in many industries similar to those of the 19th century. While the reasons for this overcapacity appear to differ somewhat among industries, there are a few common underlying causes.

Macro Policies. Major deregulation of the American economy (including trucking, rail, airlines, telecommunications, banking, and financial services industries) under President Carter contributed to the requirement for exit in these industries, as did important changes in the U.S. tax laws that reduced tax advantages to real estate development, construction, and other activities. The end of the Cold War has had obvious consequences for the defense industry and its suppliers. In addition, I suspect that two generations of managerial focus on growth as a recipe for success has caused many firms to overshoot their optimal capacity, thus setting the stage for cutbacks. In the decade from 1979 to 1989, Fortune 100 firms lost 1.5 million employees, or 14% of their workforce.[32]

Technology. Massive changes in technology are clearly part of the cause of the current industrial revolution and its associated excess capacity. Both within and across industries, technological developments have had far-reaching impact. To give some examples, the widespread acceptance of radial tires (which last three to five times longer than the older bias ply technology and provide better gas mileage) caused excess capacity in the tire industry; the personal computer revolution forced contraction of the market for mainframes; the advent of aluminum and plastic alternatives reduced demand for steel and glass containers; and fiberoptic, satellite, digital (ISDN), and new compression technolo-

gies dramatically increased capacity in telecommunication. Wireless personal communication such as cellular phones and their replacements promise further to extend this dramatic change.

The changes in computer technology, including miniaturization, have not only revamped the computer industry, but also redefined the capabilities of countless other industries. Some estimates indicate the price of computing capacity fell by a factor of 1,000 over the last decade. This means that computer production lines now produce boxes with 1,000 times the capacity for a given price. Consequently, computers are becoming commonplace— in cars, toasters, cameras, stereos, ovens, and so on. Nevertheless, the increase in quantity demanded has not been sufficient to avoid overcapacity, and we are therefore witnessing a dramatic shutdown of production lines in the industry—a force that has wracked IBM as a high-cost producer. A change of similar magnitude in auto production technology would have reduced the price of a $20,000 auto in 1980 to under $20 today. Such increases in capacity and productivity in a basic technology have unavoidably massive implications for the organization of work and society.

Fiberoptic and other telecommunications technologies such as compression algorithms are bringing about similarly vast increases in worldwide capacity and functionality. A Bell Laboratories study of excess capacity indicates, for example, that, given three years and an additional expenditure of $3.1 billion, three of AT&T's new competitors (MCI, Sprint, and National Telecommunications Network) would be able to absorb the entire long-distance switch service that was supplied by AT&T in 1990.[33]

Organizational Innovation. Overcapacity can be caused not only by changes in physical technology, but also by changes in organizational practices and management technology. The vast improvements in telecommunications, including computer networks, electronic mail, teleconferencing, and facsimile transmission are changing the workplace in major ways that affect the manner in which people work and interact. It is far less valuable for people to be in the same geographical location to work together effectively, and this is encouraging smaller,

---

32. Source: Compustat.
33. Federal Communications Commission, *Competition in the Interstate Interexchange Marketplace*, FCC 91-251 (Sept. 16, 1991), p. 1140.

more efficient, entrepreneurial organizing units that cooperate through technology.[34] This in turn leads to even more fundamental changes. Through competition, "virtual organizations"—networked or transitory organizations in which people come together temporarily to complete a task, then separate to pursue their individual specialties—are changing the structure of the standard large bureaucratic organization and contributing to its shrinkage. Virtual organizations tap talented specialists, avoid many of the regulatory costs imposed on permanent structures, and bypass the inefficient work rules and high wages imposed by unions. In so doing, they increase efficiency and thereby further contribute to excess capacity.

In addition, Japanese management techniques such as total quality management, just-in-time production, and flexible manufacturing have significantly increased the efficiency of organizations where they have been successfully implemented throughout the world. Some experts argue that such new management techniques can reduce defects and spoilage by an order of magnitude. These changes in managing and organizing principles have contributed significantly to the productivity of the world's capital stock and economized on the use of labor and raw materials, thus also contributing to excess capacity.

Globalization of Trade. Over the last several decades, the entry of Japan and other Pacific Rim countries such as Hong Kong, Taiwan, Singapore, Thailand, Korea, Malaysia, and China into worldwide product markets has contributed to the required adjustments in Western economies. And, competition from new entrants to the world product markets promises only to intensify.

With the globalization of markets, excess capacity tends to occur worldwide. The Japanese economy, for example, is currently suffering from enormous overcapacity caused in large part by what I view as the "breakdown" of its corporate control system.[35] As a consequence, Japan now faces a massive and long-overdue restructuring—one that includes the prospect of unprecedented (for Japanese companies) layoffs, a pronounced shift of corporate focus from market share to profitability, and even the adoption of pay-for-performance executive compensation contracts (something heretofore believed to be profoundly "un-Japanese").

Yet even if the requirement for exit were isolated in just Japan and the U.S., the interdependency of today's world economy would ensure that such overcapacity would have global implications. For example, the rise of efficient high-quality producers of steel and autos in Japan and Korea has contributed to excess capacity in those industries worldwide. Between 1973 and 1990, total capacity in the U.S. steel industry fell by 38% from 157 to 97 million tons, and total employment fell over 50% from 509,000 to 252,000 (and had fallen further to 160,000 by 1993). From 1985 to 1989 multifactor productivity in the industry increased at an annual rate of 5.3%, as compared to 1.3% for the period 1958 to 1989.[36]

Revolution in Political Economy. The rapid pace of development of capitalism, the opening of closed economies, and the dismantling of central control in communist and socialist states is occurring in various degrees in Eastern Europe, China, India, Indonesia, other Asian economies, and Africa. In Asia and Africa alone, this development will place a potential labor force of almost a billion people—

34. The *Journal of Financial Economics*, which I have been editing with several others since 1973, is an example. The *JFE* is now edited by seven faculty members with offices at three universities in different states, and the main editorial administrative office is located in yet another state. The publisher, North Holland, is located in Amsterdam, the printing is done in India, and mailing and billing is executed in Switzerland. This "networked organization" would have been extremely inefficient two decades ago without fax machines, high-speed modems, electronic mail, and overnight delivery services.

35. A collapse I predicted in print as early as 1989. (See Michael C. Jensen, "Eclipse of the Public Corporation," *Harvard Business Review*, Vol. 89, No. 5 (September-October, 1989), pp. 61-74.)

In a 1991 article published in this journal, I wrote the following: "As our system has begun to look more like the Japanese, the Japanese economy is undergoing changes that are reducing the role of large active investors and thus making their system resemble ours. With the progressive development of U.S.-like capital markets, Japanese managers have been able to loosen the controls once exercised by the banks. So successful have they been in bypassing banks that the top third of Japanese companies are no longer net bank borrowers. As a result of their past success in product market competition, Japanese companies are now 'flooded'

with free cash flow. Their competitive position today reminds me of the position of American companies in the late 1960s. And, like their U.S. counterparts in the 60s, Japanese companies today appear to be in the process of creating conglomerates.

My prediction is that, unless unmonitored Japanese managers prove to be much more capable than American executives of managing large, sprawling organizations, the Japanese economy is likely to produce large numbers of those conglomerates that U.S. capital markets have spent the last 10 years trying to pull apart. And if I am right, then Japan is likely to experience its own leveraged restructuring movement." ("Corporate Control and the Politics of Finance," *Journal of Applied Corporate Finance*, Vol. 4 No. 2, p. 24, fn. 47.)

For some interesting observations attesting to the severity of the Japanese overinvestment or "free cash flow" problem, see Carl Kester, "The Hidden Costs of Japanese Success," *Journal of Applied Corporate Finance* (Volume 3 Number 4, Winter 1990).

36. See James D. Burnham, *Changes and Challenges: The Transformation of the U.S. Steel Industry*, Policy Study No. 115 (Center for the Study of American Business, Washington University: St. Louis, 1993), Table 1 and p. 15.

When left to the product markets, the adjustment process [to excess capacity] is greatly protracted and ends up generating enormous additional costs. This is the clear lesson held out by the most recent restructuring of the U.S. auto industry—and it's one that many sectors of the Japanese economy are now experiencing firsthand.

whose current average income is less than $2 per day—on world markets. The opening of Mexico and other Latin American countries and the transition of some socialist Eastern European economies to open capitalist systems could add almost 200 million more laborers with average incomes of less than $10 per day to the world market.

To put these numbers into perspective, the average daily U.S. income per worker is slightly over $90, and the total labor force numbers about 117 million, and the European Economic Community average wage is about $80 per day with a total labor force of about 130 million. The labor forces that have affected world trade extensively in the last several decades (those in Hong Kong, Japan, Korea, Malaysia, Singapore, and Taiwan) total about 90 million.

While the changes associated with bringing a potential 1.2 billion low-cost laborers onto world markets will significantly increase average living standards throughout the world, they will also bring massive obsolescence of capital (manifested in the form of excess capacity) in Western economies as the adjustments sweep through the system. Such adjustments will include a major redirection of Western labor and capital away from low-skilled, labor-intensive industries and toward activities where they have a comparative advantage. While the opposition to such adjustments will be strong, the forces driving them will prove irresistible in this day of rapid and inexpensive communication, transportation, miniaturization, and migration.

One can also confidently forecast that the transition to open capitalist economies will generate great conflict over international trade as special interests in individual countries try to insulate themselves from competition and the required exit. And the U.S., despite its long-professed commitment to "free trade," will prove no exception. Just as U.S. managers and employees demanded protection from the capital markets in the 1980s, some are now demanding protection from international competition in the product markets, generally under the guise of protecting jobs. The dispute over NAFTA is but one general example of conflicts that are also occurring in the steel, automobile, computer chip, computer screen, and

textile industries. It would not even surprise me to see a return to demands for protection from *domestic* competition. This is currently happening in the deregulated airline industry, an industry faced with significant excess capacity.

We should not underestimate the strains this continuing change will place on worldwide social and political systems. In both the first and second industrial revolutions, the demands for protection from competition and for redistribution of income became intense. It is conceivable that Western nations could face the modern equivalent of the English Luddites, who destroyed industrial machinery (primarily knitting frames) in the period 1811-1816, and were eventually subdued by the militia. In the U.S. during the early 1890s, large groups of unemployed men (along with some vagrants and criminals), banded together in a cross-country march on Congress. The aim of "Coxey's industrial army," as the group became known, was to demand relief from "the evils of murderous competition; the supplanting of manual labor by machinery; the excessive Mongolian and pauper immigration; the curse of alien landlordism."[37]

Although Coxey's army disbanded peacefully after arriving in Washington and submitting a petition to Congress, some democratic systems may not survive the strain of adjustment, and may revert under pressure to a more totalitarian system. We need look no farther than current developments in Mexico or Russia to see such threats to democracy in effect.

The bottom line, then, is that with worldwide excess capacity and thus greater requirement for exit, the strains put on the internal control mechanisms of Western corporations are likely to worsen for decades to come. The experience of the U.S. in the 1980s demonstrated that the capital markets can play an important role in forcing managers to address this problem. In the absence of capital market pressures, competition in product markets will eventually bring about exit. But when left to the product markets, the adjustment process is greatly protracted and ends up generating enormous additional costs. This is the clear lesson held out by the most recent restructuring of the U.S. auto industry—and it's one that many sectors of the Japanese economy are now experiencing firsthand.

---

37. McMurray (1929), pp. 253-262, cited in note 2.

THE DIFFICULTY OF EXIT

The Asymmetry between Growth and Decline

Exit problems appear to be particularly severe in companies that for long periods enjoyed rapid growth, commanding market positions, and high cash flow and profits. In these situations, the culture of the organization and the mindset of managers seem to make it extremely difficult for adjustment to take place until long after the problems have become severe and, in some cases, even unsolvable. In a fundamental sense, there is an "asymmetry" between the growth stage and the contraction stage in the corporate life cycle. Financial economists have spent little time thinking about how to manage the contracting stage efficiently or, more important, how to manage the growth stage to avoid sowing the seeds of decline.

In industry after industry with excess capacity, managers fail to recognize that they themselves must downsize; instead they leave the exit to others while they continue to invest. When all managers behave this way, exit is significantly delayed at substantial cost of real resources to society. The tire industry is an example. Widespread consumer acceptance of radial tires meant that worldwide tire capacity had to shrink by two thirds (because radials last 3 to 5 times longer than bias ply tires). Nonetheless, the response by the managers of individual companies was often equivalent to: "This business is going through some rough times. We must invest so that we will have a chair when the music stops."

The Case of GenCorp. William Reynolds, Chairman and CEO of GenCorp, the maker of General Tires, illustrates this reaction in his 1988 testimony before the U.S. House Committee on Energy and Commerce:

The tire business was the largest piece of GenCorp, both in terms of annual revenues and its asset base. Yet General Tire was not GenCorp's strongest performer. Its relatively poor earnings performance was due in part to conditions affecting all of the tire industry... In 1985 worldwide tire manufacturing capacity substantially exceeded demand. At the same time, due to a series of technological improve-ments in the design of tires and the materials used to make them, the product life of tires had lengthened significantly... The economic pressure on our tire business was substantial. Because our unit volume was far below others in the industry, we had less competitive flexibility... We made several moves to improve our competitive position: We increased our investment in research and development. We increased our involvement in the high performance and light truck tire categories, two market segments which offered faster growth opportunities. We developed new tire products for those segments and invested heavily in an aggressive marketing program designed to enhance our presence in both markets. We made the difficult decision to reduce our overall manufacturing capacity by closing one of our older, less modern plants... I believe that the General Tire example illustrates that we were taking a rational, long-term approach to improving GenCorp's overall performance and shareholder value...

Like so many U.S. CEOs, Reynolds then goes on to blame the capital markets for bringing about what he fails to recognize is a solution to the industry's problem of excess capacity:

As a result of the takeover attempt... [and] to meet the principal and interest payments on our vastly increased corporate debt, GenCorp had to quickly sell off valuable assets and abruptly lay off approximately 550 important employees.[38]

Without questioning the genuineness of Reynolds' concerns about his company and employees, it nevertheless now seems clear that GenCorp's increased investment was neither going to maximize the value of the firm nor to be a socially optimal response in a declining industry with excess capacity. In 1987, GenCorp ended up selling its General Tire subsidiary to Continental AG of Hannover, thus furthering the process of consolidation necessary to reduce overcapacity.

Information Problems

Information problems hinder exit because the high-cost capacity in the industry must be eliminated

---

38. A. William Reynolds, in testimony before the Subcommittee on Oversight and Investigations, U.S. House Committee on Energy and Commerce, February 8, 1988.

> *In industry after industry with excess capacity, managers fail to recognize that they themselves must downsize; instead they leave the exit to others while they continue to invest. When all managers behave this way, exit is significantly delayed at substantial cost of real resources to society.*

if resources are to be used efficiently. Firms often do not have good information about their own costs, much less the costs of their competitors. Thus, it is sometimes unclear to managers that they are the high-cost firm that should exit the industry.[39]

But even when managers do acknowledge the requirement for exit, it is often difficult for them to accept and initiate the shutdown. For the managers who must implement these decisions, shutting plants or liquidating the firm causes personal pain, creates uncertainty, and interrupts or sidetracks careers. Rather than confronting this pain, managers generally resist such actions as long as they have the cash flow to subsidize the losing operations. Indeed, firms with large positive cash flow will often invest in even more money-losing capacity—situations that illustrate vividly what I call the "agency costs of free cash flow."[40]

Contracting Problems

Explicit and implicit contracts in the organization can become major obstacles to efficient exit. Unionization, restrictive work rules, and lucrative employee compensation and benefits are other ways in which the agency costs of free cash flow can manifest themselves in a growing, cash-rich organization. Formerly dominant firms became unionized in their heyday (or effectively unionized in organizations like IBM and Kodak) when managers spent some of the organization's free cash flow to buy labor peace. Faced with technical innovation and worldwide competition—often from new, more flexible, and non-union organizations—these dominant firms have not adjusted quickly enough to maintain their market dominance. Part of the problem is managerial and organizational defensiveness that inhibits learning and prevents managers from changing their model of the business.

Implicit contracts with unions, other employees, suppliers, and communities add to formal union

barriers to change by reinforcing organizational defensiveness and delaying change long beyond the optimal time—often even beyond the survival point for the organization. While casual breach of implicit contracts will destroy trust in an organization and seriously reduce efficiency, all organizations must retain the flexibility to modify contracts that are no longer optimal.[41] In the current environment, it takes nothing less than a major shock to bring about necessary change.

THE ROLE OF THE MARKET FOR CORPORATE CONTROL

The Four Control Forces Operating on the Corporation

There are four basic control forces bearing on the corporation that act to bring about a convergence of managers' decisions with those that are optimal from society's standpoint. They are (1) the capital markets, (2) the legal, political, and regulatory system, (3) the product and factor markets, and (4) the internal control system headed by the board of directors.

The capital markets were relatively constrained by law and regulatory practice from about 1940 until their resurrection through hostile tender offers in the 1970s. Prior to the 1970s, capital market discipline took place primarily through the proxy process.

The legal/political/regulatory system is far too blunt an instrument to handle the problems of wasteful managerial behavior effectively. (Nevertheless, the break-up and deregulation of AT&T is one of the court system's outstanding successes; I estimate that it has helped create over $125 billion of increased value between AT&T and the Baby Bells.[42])

While the product and factor markets are slow to act as a control force, their discipline is inevitable; firms that do not supply the product that customers desire at a competitive price will not survive. Unfor-

---

39. Total quality management programs strongly encourage managers to benchmark their firm's operations against the most successful worldwide competitors, and good cost systems and competitive benchmarking are becoming more common in well-managed firms.

40. Briefly stated, the "agency costs of free cash flow" means the loss in value caused by the tendency of managements of large public companies in slow-growth industries to reinvest corporate cash flow in projects with expected returns below the cost of capital. See Michael Jensen, "The Agency Costs of Free Cash Flow: Corporate Finance and Takeovers," *American Economic Review* 76, no. 2 (May 1986), 323-329.

41. Much press coverage and official policy seems to be based on the notion that *all* implicit contracts should be immutable and rigidly enforced. But while I

agree that the security of property rights and the enforceability of contracts are essential to the growth of real output and efficiency, it is also clear that, given unexpected and unforeseeable events, *not all* contracts, whether explicit or implicit, can (or even should) be fulfilled. (For example, bankruptcy is essentially a state-supervised system for breaking (or, more politely, rewriting) explicit contracts that have become unenforceable. All developed economies devise such a system.) Implicit contracts, besides avoiding the costs incurred in the writing process, provide the opportunity to revise the obligation if circumstances change; presumably, this is a major reason for their existence.

42. For this calculation, see the original version of this article in the *Journal of Finance* (Jensen (1993)).

tunately, by the time product and factor market disciplines take effect, large amounts of investor capital and other social resources have been wasted, and it can often be too late to save much of the enterprise.

Which brings us to the role of corporate internal control systems and the need to reform them. As stated earlier, there is a large and growing body of studies documenting the shareholder gains from corporate restructurings of the '80s.[43] The size and consistency of such gains provide strong support for the proposition that the internal control systems of publicly held corporations have generally failed to cause managers to maximize efficiency and value in slow-growth or declining industries.

Perhaps more persuasive than the formal statistical evidence, however, is the scarcity of large, public firms that have voluntarily restructured or engaged in a major strategic redirection without either a challenge from the capital markets or a crisis in product markets. By contrast, partnerships and private or closely held firms such as investment banking, law, and consulting firms have generally responded far more quickly to changing market conditions.

Capital Markets and the Market for Corporate Control

Until they were shut down in 1989, the capital markets were providing one mechanism for accomplishing change before losses in the product markets generated a crisis. While the corporate control activity of the 1980s has been widely criticized as counterproductive to American industry, few have recognized that many of these transactions were necessary to accomplish exit over the objections of current managers and other corporate constituencies such as employees and communities.

For example, the solution to excess capacity in the tire industry came about through the market for corporate control. Every major U.S. tire firm was either taken over or restructured in the 1980s.[44] In total, 37 tire plants were shut down in the period 1977-1987, and total employment in the industry fell by over 40%.

Capital market and corporate control transactions such as the repurchase of stock (or the purchase of another company) for cash or debt accomplished exit of resources in a very direct way. When Chevron acquired Gulf for $13.2 billion in cash and debt in 1984, the net assets devoted to the oil industry fell by $13.2 billion as soon as the checks were mailed out. In the 1980s the oil industry had to shrink to accommodate the reduction in the quantity of oil demanded and the reduced rate of growth of demand. This meant paying out to shareholders its huge cash inflows, reducing exploration and development expenditures to bring reserves in line with reduced demands, and closing refining and distribution facilities. Leveraged acquisitions and equity repurchases helped accomplish this end for virtually all major U.S. oil firms.

Exit also resulted when KKR acquired RJR-Nabisco for $25 billion in cash and debt in its 1986 leveraged buyout. The tobacco industry must shrink, given the change in smoking habits in response to consumer awareness of cancer threats, and the payout of RJR's cash accomplished this to some extent. RJR's LBO debt also prevented the company from continuing to squander its cash flows on wasteful projects it had planned to undertake prior to the buyout. Thus, the buyout laid the groundwork for the efficient reduction of capacity and resources by one of the major firms in the industry. The recent sharp declines in the stock prices of RJR and Philip Morris are signs that there is much more downsizing to come.

The era of the control market came to an end, however, in late 1989 and 1990. Intense controversy and opposition from corporate managers—assisted by charges of fraud, the increase in default and bankruptcy rates, and insider trading prosecutions—led to the shutdown of the control market through court decisions, state antitakeover amendments, and regulatory restrictions on the availability of financ-

---

43. For a partial list of such studies, see the Appendix at the end of this article.
44. In May 1985, Uniroyal approved an LBO proposal to block hostile advances by Carl Icahn. About the same time, BF Goodrich began diversifying out of the tire business. In January 1986, Goodrich and Uniroyal independently spun off their tire divisions and together, in a 50-50 joint venture, formed the Uniroyal-Goodrich Tire Company. By December 1987, Goodrich had sold its interest in the venture to Clayton and Dubilier; Uniroyal followed soon after. Similarly, General Tire moved away from tires: the company, renamed GenCorp in 1984, sold its tire division to Continental in 1987. Other takeovers in the industry during this period include the sale of Firestone to Bridgestone and Pirelli's purchase of the Armstrong Tire Company. By 1991, Goodyear was the only remaining major American tire manufacturer. Yet it too faced challenges in the control market: in 1986, following three years of unprofitable diversifying investments, Goodyear initiated a major leveraged stock repurchase and restructuring to defend itself from a hostile takeover from Sir James Goldsmith. Uniroyal/Goodrich was purchased by Michelin in 1990. See Richard Tedlow, "Hitting the Skids: Tires and Time Horizons," unpublished manuscript, Harvard Business School, 1991.

Capital market and corporate control transactions such as the repurchase of stock (or the purchase of another company) for cash or debt accomplished exit of resources in a very direct way. When Chevron acquired Gulf for $13.2 billion in cash and debt in 1984, the net assets devoted to the oil industry fell by $13.2 billion as soon as the checks were mailed out.

ing.[45] In 1991, the total value of transactions fell to $96 billion from $340 billion in 1988.[46] Leveraged buyouts and management buyouts fell to slightly over $1 billion in 1991 from $80 billion in 1988.[47]

The demise of the control market as an effective influence on American corporations has not ended the restructuring. But it has allowed many organizations to postpone addressing major problems until forced to do by financial difficulties generated by the product markets. Unfortunately, the delay means that some of these organizations will not survive—or will survive as mere shadows of their former selves.

THE FAILURE OF CORPORATE INTERNAL CONTROL SYSTEMS

With the shutdown of the capital markets as an effective mechanism for motivating change, exit, and renewal, we are left to depend on the internal control system to act to preserve organizational assets, both human and otherwise. Throughout corporate America, the problems that motivated much of the control activity of the 1980s are now reflected in lackluster performance, financial distress, and pressures for restructuring. General Motors, Kodak, IBM, Xerox, Westinghouse, ITT, and many others have faced or are now facing severe challenges in the product markets. We therefore must understand why these internal control systems have failed and learn how to make them work.

By nature, organizations abhor control systems. Ineffective governance is a major part of the problem with internal control mechanisms; they seldom respond in the absence of a crisis. The recent GM board "revolt," which resulted in the firing of CEO Robert Stempel, exemplifies the failure, not the success, of GM's governance system. Though clearly one of the world's high-cost producers in a market with substantial excess capacity, GM avoided making major changes in its strategy for over a decade. The revolt came too late; the board acted to remove the CEO only in 1992, after the company had reported losses of $6.5 billion in 1990 and 1991.

Unfortunately, GM is not an isolated example. IBM is another testimony to the failure of internal control systems. The company failed to adjust to the substitution away from its mainframe business following the revolution in the workstation and personal computer market—ironically enough, a revolution that it helped launch with the invention of the RISC technology in 1974. Like GM, IBM is a high-cost producer in a market with substantial excess capacity. It too began to change its strategy significantly and removed its CEO only after reporting huge losses—$2.8 billion in 1991 and further losses in 1992—while losing almost 65% of its equity value.

Eastman Kodak, another major U.S. company formerly dominant in its market, also failed to adjust to competition and has performed poorly. Largely as a result of a disastrous diversification program designed to offset the maturing of its core film business, its $37 share price in 1992 was roughly unchanged from 1981. After several reorganizations attempting relatively modest changes in its incentives and strategy, the board finally replaced the CEO in October 1993.

General Electric is a notable exception to my proposition about the failure of corporate internal control systems. Under CEO Jack Welch since 1981, GE has accomplished a major strategic re-direction, eliminating 104,000 of its 402,000 person workforce (through layoffs or sales of divisions) in the period 1980-1990 without a threat from capital or product markets. But there is little evidence to indicate this is due to the influence of GE's governance system; it appears attributable almost entirely to the vision and leadership of Jack Welch.

General Dynamics provides another exceptional case. The appointment of William Anders as CEO in September 1991 resulted in a rapid adjustment to excess capacity in the defense industry—again, with no apparent threat from any outside force. The company generated $3.4 billion of increased value on a $1 billion company in just over two years. One of the key elements in this success story, however, was a major change in the company's management compensation system[48] that tied bonuses directly to increases in stock value (a subject I return to later).

My colleague Gordon Donaldson's account of General Mills' strategic redirection is yet another

---

45. For a more detailed account, see my article "Corporate Control and the Politics of Finance," in the *Journal of Applied Corporate Finance*, Summer 1991.
46. In 1992 dollars, calculated from *Mergerstat Review*, 1991, p. 100f.
47. In 1992 dollars, *Mergerstat Review*, 1991, Figs. 29 and 38.

48. See Kevin J. Murphy and Jay Dial, "Compensation and Strategy at General Dynamics (A) and (B)," Harvard Business School #N9-493-032 and N9-493-033, 1992.

case of a largely voluntary restructuring.[49] But the fact that it took more than ten years to accomplish raises serious questions about the social costs of continuing the waste caused by ineffective control. It appears that internal control systems have two faults: they react too late, and they take too long to effect major change. Changes motivated by the capital market are generally accomplished quickly—typically, within one to three years. No one has yet demonstrated social benefits from relying on internally motivated change that would offset the costs of the decade-long delay in the restructuring of General Mills.

In summary, it appears that the infrequency with which large corporate organizations restructure or redirect themselves solely on the basis of the internal control mechanisms—that is, in the absence of intervention by capital markets or a crisis in the product markets—is strong testimony to the inadequacy of these control mechanisms.

[At this point, the original Journal of Finance *paper contains a section, omitted here because of space constraints, called "Direct Evidence of the Failure of Internal Control Systems." It presents estimates of the productivity of corporate capital expenditure and R & D spending programs of 432 firms that suggest "major inefficiencies in a substantial number of firms."]*

REVIVING INTERNAL CORPORATE CONTROL SYSTEMS

Remaking the Board as an Effective Control Mechanism

The problems with corporate internal control systems start with the board of directors. The board, at the apex of the internal control system, has the final responsibility for the functioning of the firm. Most important, it sets the rules of the game for the CEO. The job of the board is to hire, fire, and compensate the CEO, and to provide high-level counsel. Few boards in the past decades have done this job well in the absence of external crises. This is particularly unfortunate, given that the very purpose of the internal control mechanism is to provide an early warning system to put the organization back on track before difficulties reach a crisis stage.

The reasons for the failure of the board are not completely understood, but we are making progress toward understanding these complex issues. The available evidence does suggest that CEOs are removed after poor performance;[50] but this effect, while statistically significant, seems too late and too small to meet the obligations of the board. I believe bad systems or rules, not bad people, are at the root of the general failings of boards of directors.

Board Culture. Board culture is an important component of board failure. The great emphasis on politeness and courtesy at the expense of truth and frankness in boardrooms is both a symptom and cause of failure in the control system. CEOs have the same insecurities and defense mechanisms as other human beings; few will accept, much less seek, the monitoring and criticism of an active and attentive board.

The following example illustrates the general problem. John Hanley, retired Monsanto CEO, accepted an invitation from a CEO

... to join his board—subject, Hanley wrote, to meeting with the company's general counsel and outside accountants as a kind of directorial due diligence. Says Hanley: "At the first board dinner the CEO got up and said, 'I think Jack was a little bit confused whether we wanted him to be a director or the chief executive officer.' I should have known right there that he wasn't going to pay a goddamn bit of attention to anything I said." So it turned out, and after a year Hanley quit the board in disgust.[51]

The result is a continuing cycle of ineffectiveness. By rewarding consent and discouraging conflicts, CEOs have the power to control the board, which in turn ultimately reduces the CEO's and the company's performance. This downward spiral makes corporate difficulties likely to culminate in a crisis

---

49. See Gordon Donaldson, "Voluntary Restructuring: The Case of General Mills," *Journal of Financial Economics* 27, no. 1 (1990), 117-141. For a shorter, less technical version of the same article, see Vol. 4 No. 3 (Fall 1991) of the *Journal of Applied Corporate Finance.*

50. CEO turnover approximately doubles from 3% to 6% after two years of poor performance (stock returns less than 50% below equivalent-risk market returns, Weisbach (1988)), or increases from 8.3% to 13.9% from the highest to the lowest performing decile of firms, Warner, Watts, and Wruck (1988). See Michael Weisbach, "Outside Directors and CEO Turnovers," *Journal of Financial Economics* 20 (January-March, 1988), 431-460, and Jerold Warner, Ross Watts, and Karen Wruck, "Stock Prices and Top Management Changes," *Journal of Financial Economics* 20 (1989), 461-492.

51. Myron Magnet, "Directors, Wake Up!," *Fortune* (June 15, 1992), p. 86.

Much of corporate America's governance problem arises from the fact that neither managers nor board members typically own substantial fractions of their firm's equity. While the average CEO of the 1,000 largest firms owned 2.7% of his or her firm's equity in 1991, the median holding was only 0.2%—and 75% owned less than 1.2%.

requiring drastic steps, as opposed to a series of small problems met by a continuously self-correcting mechanism.

Information Problems. Serious information problems limit the effectiveness of board members in the typical large corporation. For example, the CEO almost always determines the agenda and the information given to the board. This limitation on information severely restricts the ability of even highly talented board members to contribute effectively to the monitoring and evaluation of the CEO and the company's strategy.

Moreover, board members should have the financial expertise necessary to provide useful input into the corporate planning process—especially, in forming the corporate objective and determining the factors which affect corporate value. Yet such financial expertise is generally lacking on today's boards. And it is not only the inability of most board members to evaluate a company's current business and financial strategy that is troubling. In many cases, boards (and managements) fail to understand that their basic mission is to maximize the (long-run) market value of the enterprise.

Legal Liability. The incentives facing modern boards are generally not consistent with shareholder interests. Boards are motivated to serve shareholders primarily by substantial legal liabilities through class action suits initiated by shareholders, the plaintiff's bar, and others—lawsuits that are often triggered by unexpected declines in stock price. These legal incentives are more often consistent with minimizing downside risk than maximizing value. Boards are also concerned about threats of adverse publicity from the media or from the political or regulatory authorities. Again, while these incentives often provide motivation for board members to reduce potential liabilities, they do not necessarily provide strong incentives to take actions that create efficiency and value for the company.

Lack of Management and Board-Member Equity Holdings. Much of corporate America's governance problem arises from the fact that neither managers nor board members typically own substantial fractions of their firm's equity. While the average CEO of the 1,000 largest firms (measured by market value of equity) owned 2.7% of his or her firm's equity in 1991, the median holding was only 0.2%—and 75% of CEOs owned less than 1.2%.[52] Encouraging outside board members to hold substantial equity interests would provide better incentives.

Of course, achieving significant direct stock ownership in large firms would require huge dollar outlays by managers or board members. To get around this problem, Bennett Stewart has proposed an interesting approach called the "leveraged equity purchase plan" (LEPP) that amounts to the sale of slightly (say, 10%) in-the-money stock options.[53] By requiring significant out-of-pocket contributions by managers and directors, and by having the exercise price of the options rise every year at the firm's cost of capital, Stewart's plan helps overcome the "free-option" aspect (or lack of downside risk) that limits the effectiveness of standard corporate option plans. It also removes the problem with standard options that allows management to reap gains on their options while shareholders are losing.[54]

Boards should have an implicit understanding or explicit requirement that new members must invest in the stock of the company. While the initial investment could vary, it should seldom be less than $100,000 from the new board member's personal funds; this investment would force new board members to recognize from the outset that their decisions affect their own wealth as well as that of remote shareholders. Over the long term, the investment can be made much larger by options or other stock-based compensation. The recent trend to pay some board-member fees in stock or options is a move in the right direction. Discouraging board members from selling this equity is also important so that holdings will accumulate to a significant size over time.

Oversized Boards. Keeping boards small can help improve their performance. When boards exceed seven or eight people, they are less likely to function effectively and are easier for the CEO to

---

52. See Kevin Murphy, *Executive Compensation in Corporate America, 1992*, United Shareholders Association, Washington, DC, 1992. For similar estimates based on earlier data, see also Michael Jensen and Kevin Murphy, "Performance Pay and Top-Management Incentives," *Journal of Political Economy* 98, no. 2 (1990), 225-264; and Michael Jensen and Kevin Murphy, "CEO Incentives—It's Not How Much You Pay, But How," *Harvard Business Review* 68, no. 3 (May-June, 1990).

53. See G. Bennett Stewart III, "Remaking the Public Corporation From Within," *Harvard Business Review* 68, no. 4 (July-August, 1990), 126-137.

54. This happens when the stock price rises but shareholder returns (including both dividends and capital gains) are less than the opportunity cost of capital.

control.[55] Since the possibility for animosity and retribution from the CEO is too great, it is almost impossible for direct reports to the CEO to participate openly and critically in effective evaluation and monitoring of the CEO. Therefore, the only inside board member should be the CEO; insiders other than the CEO can be regularly invited to attend board meetings in an unofficial capacity. Indeed, board members should be given regular opportunities to meet with and observe executives below the CEO—both to expand their knowledge of the company and CEO succession candidates, and to increase other top-level executives' exposure to the thinking of the board and the board process.

The CEO as Chairman of the Board. It is common in U.S. corporations for the CEO also to hold the position of Chairman of the Board. The function of the Chairman is to run board meetings and oversee the process of hiring, firing, evaluating, and compensating the CEO. Clearly, the CEO cannot perform this function apart from his or her personal interest. Without the direction of an independent leader, it is much more difficult for the board to perform its critical function. Therefore, for the board to be effective, it is important to separate the CEO and Chairman positions.[56] The independent Chairman should, at a minimum, be given the rights to initiate board appointments, board committee assignments, and (jointly with the CEO) the setting of the board's agenda. All these recommendations, of course, should be made conditional on the ratification of the board.

An effective board will often experience tension among its members as well as with the CEO. But I hasten to add that I am not advocating continuous war in the boardroom. In fact, in well-functioning organizations the board will generally be relatively inactive and will exhibit little conflict. It becomes important primarily when the rest of the internal control system is failing, and this should be a relatively rare event. The challenge is to create a system that will not fall into complacency during periods of prosperity and good management, and therefore be unable to rise early to the challenge of correcting a failing management system. This is a difficult task because there are strong tendencies for boards to develop a culture and social norms that reflect optimal behavior under prosperity, and these norms make it extremely difficult for the board to respond early to failure in its top management team.

Attempts to Model the Process on Political Democracy. There have been a number of proposals to model the board process after a democratic political model in which various constituencies are represented. Such a process, however, is likely to make the internal control system even less accountable to shareholders than it is now. To see why, we need look no farther than the inefficiency of representative political democracies (whether at the local, state or federal level) and their attempts to manage quasi-business organizations such as the Post Office, schools, or power-generation entities such as the TVA.

Nevertheless, there would likely be significant benefits to opening up the corporate governance process to the firm's largest shareholders. Proxy regulations by the SEC severely restrict communications between management and shareholders, and among shareholders themselves. Until recently, for example, it was illegal for any shareholder to discuss company matters with more than ten other shareholders without previously filing with and receiving the approval of the SEC. The November 1992 relaxation of this restriction now allows an investor to communicate with an unlimited number of other stockholders provided the investor owns less than 5% of the shares, has no special interest in the issue being discussed, and is not seeking proxy authority. But these remaining restrictions still have the obvious drawback of limiting effective institutional action by those investors most likely to pursue it.

As I discuss below, when equity holdings become concentrated in institutional hands, it is easier to resolve some of the free-rider problems that limit the ability of thousands of individual shareholders to engage in effective collective action. In principle, such institutions can therefore begin to exercise corporate control rights more effectively.

55. In their excellent analysis of boards, Martin Lipton and Jay Lorsch also criticize the functioning of traditionally configured boards, recommend limiting membership to 7 or 8 people, and encourage equity ownership by board members. (See Lipton and Lorsch, "A Modest Proposal for Improved Corporate Governance," *The Business Lawyer* 48, no. 1 (November, 1992), 59-77.) Research supports the proposition that, as groups increase in size, they become less effective because the coordination and process problems overwhelm the advantages gained from having more people to draw on. See, for example, I. D. Steiner, *Group Process and Productivity* (Academic Press: New York, 1972) and Richard Hackman, ed., *Groups That Work* (Jossey-Bass: San Francisco, 1990).

56. Lipton and Lorsch (1992) stop short of recommending appointment of an independent chairman, recommending instead the appointment of a "lead director" whose function would be to coordinate board activities.

Wise CEOs can recruit large block investors to serve on the board. Active investors are important to a well-functioning governance system because they have the financial interest and independence to view firm management and policies in an unbiased way. They have the incentives to buck the system to correct problems early rather than late when the problems are obvious but difficult to correct.

Legal and regulatory restrictions, however, have prevented financial institutions from playing a major corporate monitoring role. Therefore, if institutions are to aid in effective governance, we must continue to dismantle the rules and regulations that have prevented them and other large investors from accomplishing this coordination.

Resurrecting Active Investors

A major set of problems with internal control systems are associated with the curbing of what I call "active investors."[57] Active investors are individuals or institutions that hold large debt and/or equity positions in a company and actively participate in its strategic direction. Active investors are important to a well-functioning governance system because they have the financial interest and independence to view firm management and policies in an unbiased way. They have the incentives to buck the system to correct problems early rather than late when the problems are obvious but difficult to correct. Financial institutions such as banks, pension funds, insurance companies, mutual funds, and money managers are natural active investors, but they have been shut out of boardrooms and firm strategy by the legal structure, by custom, and by their own practices.

Active investors are important to a well-functioning governance system, and there is much we can do to dismantle the web of legal, tax, and regulatory apparatus that severely limits the scope of active investors in this country.[58] But even without such regulatory changes, CEOs and boards can take actions to encourage investors to hold large positions in their debt and equity and to play an active role in the strategic direction of the firm and in monitoring the CEO.

Wise CEOs can recruit large block investors to serve on the board, even selling new equity or debt to them to encourage their commitment to the firm. Lazard Freres Corporate Partners Fund is an example of an institution set up specifically to perform this function, making new funds available to the firm and

taking a board seat to advise and monitor management performance. Warren Buffet's activity through Berkshire Hathaway provides another example of a well-known active investor. He played an important role in helping Salomon Brothers through its recent legal and organizational difficulties following the government bond bidding scandal.

Learning from LBOs and Venture Capital Firms

Organizational Experimentation in the 1980s. The evidence from LBOs, leveraged restructurings, takeovers, and venture capital firms has demonstrated dramatically that leverage, payout policy, and ownership structure (that is, who owns the firm's securities) affect organizational efficiency, cash flow, and hence value.[59] Such organizational changes show that these effects are especially important in low-growth or declining firms where the agency costs of free cash flow are large.

Evidence from LBOs. LBOs provide a good source of estimates of the value increases resulting from changing leverage, payout policies, and the control and governance system. After the transaction, the company has a different financial policy and control system, but essentially the same managers and the same assets. Leverage increases from about 18% of value to 90%, there are large payouts to prior shareholders, and equity becomes concentrated in the hands of managers and the board (who own about 20% and 60%, on average, respectively). At the same time, boards shrink to about seven or eight people, the sensitivity of managerial pay to performance rises, and the companies' equity usually becomes private (although debt is often publicly traded).

Studies of LBOs indicate that premiums to selling-firm shareholders are roughly 40% to 50% of the pre-buyout market value, cash flows increase by 96% from the year before the buyout to three years after the buyout, and value increases by 235% (96% adjusted for general market movements) from two months prior to the buyout offer to the time of going-

57. See my article, "LBOs, Active Investors, and the Privatization of Bankruptcy," in the *Journal of Applied Corporate Finance* (Spring 1989).

58. For discussions of such legal, tax, and regulatory barriers to active investors (and proposals for reducing them), see Mark Roe, "A Political Theory of American Corporate Finance," *Columbia Law Review* 91 (1991), 10-67; Mark Roe, "Political and Legal Restraints on Ownership and Control of Public Companies," *Journal of Financial Economics* 27, No. 1 (September, 1990); Bernard Black,

"Shareholder Passivity Reexamined," *Michigan Law Review* 89 (December, 1990), 520-608; and John Pound, "Proxy Voting and the SEC: Investor Protection versus Market Efficiency," *Journal of Financial Economics* 29, No. 2, 241-285.

59. See the Appendix at the end of this article for a listing of broad-based statistical studies of these transactions, as well as detailed clinical and case studies that document the effects of the changes on incentives and organizational effectiveness.

public, sale, or recapitalization (about three years later, on average).[60] Large value increases have also been documented in voluntary recapitalizations—those in which the company stays public but buys back a significant fraction of its equity or pays out a significant dividend.[61]

A Proven Model of Governance Structure. LBO associations and venture capital funds provide a blueprint for managers and boards who wish to revamp their top-level control systems to make them more efficient. LBO firms like KKR and venture capital funds such as Kleiner Perkins are among the pre-eminent examples of active investors in recent U.S. history, and they serve as models that can be emulated in part or in total by most public corporations. The two have similar governance structures, and have been successful in resolving the governance problems of both slow-growth or declining firms (LBO associations) and high-growth entrepreneurial firms (venture capital funds).

Both LBO associations and venture capital funds tend to be organized as limited partnerships. In effect, the institutions that contribute the funds to these organizations are delegating the task of being active investors to the general partners of the organizations. Both governance systems are characterized by the following:

- limited partnership agreements at the top level that prohibit headquarters from cross-subsidizing one division with the cash from another;
- high equity ownership by managers and board members;
- board members (mostly the LBO association partners or the venture capitalists) who in their funds directly represent a large fraction of the equity owners of each subsidiary company;
- small boards (in the operating companies) typically consisting of no more than eight people;
- CEOs who are typically the only insider on the board; and
- CEOs who are seldom the chairman of the board.

LBO associations and venture funds also solve many of the information problems facing typical boards of directors. First, as a result of the due diligence process at the time the deal is done, both the managers and the LBO and venture partners have extensive and detailed knowledge of virtually all aspects of the business. In addition, these boards have frequent contact with management, often weekly or even daily during times of difficult challenges. This contact and information flow is facilitated by the fact that LBO associations and venture funds both have their own staffs. They also often perform the corporate finance function for the operating companies, providing the major interface with the capital markets and investment banking communities. Finally, the close relationship between the LBO partners or venture fund partners and the operating companies encourages the board to contribute its expertise during times of crisis. It is not unusual for a partner to join the management team, even as CEO, to help an organization through such emergencies.

CONCLUSION

Beginning with the oil price shock of the 1970s, technological, political, regulatory, and economic forces have been transforming the worldwide economy in a fashion comparable to the changes experienced during the 19th-century Industrial Revolution. As in the 19th century, technological advances in many industries have led to sharply declining costs, increased average (but declining marginal) productivity of labor, reduced growth rates of labor income, excess capacity, and the requirement for downsizing and exit.

Events of the last two decades indicate that corporate internal control systems have failed to deal effectively with these changes, especially excess capacity and the requirement for exit. The corporate control transactions of the 1980s—mergers and acquisitions, LBOs, and other leveraged recapitalizations—represented a capital market solution to this problem of widespread overcapacity. But because of the regulatory shutdown of the corporate control markets beginning in 1989, finding a solution to the problem now rests once more with the internal control systems, with corporate boards, and, to a lesser degree, with the large institutional shareholders who bear the consequences of corporate losses in value. Making corporate internal control systems work is the major challenge facing us in the 1990s.

60. For a review of research on LBOs, their governance changes, and their productivity effects, see Krishna Palepu, "Consequences of Leveraged Buyouts," *Journal of Financial Economics* 27, no. 1 (1990), 247-262.

61. See David and Diane Denis, "Managerial Discretion, Organizational Structure, and Corporate Performance: A Study of Leveraged Recapitalizations," *Journal of Accounting and Economics* (January 1993); and Karen Wruck and Krishna Palepu, "Consequences of Leveraged Shareholder Payouts: Defensive versus Voluntary Recapitalizations," Working paper, Harvard Business School, 1992.

■ **Baker, George and Karen Wruck**, 1989, "Organizational Changes and Value Creation in Leveraged Buyouts: The Case of O.M. Scott and Sons Company," *Journal of Financial Economics* 25, no. 2, 163-190. For a shorter, less technical version of the same article, see Vol. 4 No. 1 (Spring 1991) of the *Journal of Applied Corporate Finance*.

■ **Brickley, James A., Gregg A. Jarrell, and Jeffrey M. Netter**, 1988, "The Market for Corporate Control: The Empirical Evidence Since 1980," *Journal of Economic Perspectives* 2, no. 1, 49-68, Winter.

■ **Dann, Larry Y. and Harry DeAngelo**, 1988, "Corporate Financial Policy and Corporate Control: A Study of Defensive Adjustments in Asset and Ownership Structure," *Journal of Financial Economics* 20, 87-127.

■ **DeAngelo, Harry, Linda DeAngelo, and Edward Rice**, 1984, "Going Private: Minority Freezeouts and Stockholder Wealth," *Journal of Law and Economics* 27, 367-401.

■ **David and Diane Denis**, 1993, "Managerial Discretion, Organizational Structure, and Corporate Performance: A Study of Leveraged Recapitalizations," *Journal of Accounting and Economics* (January). For a shorter, less technical version of the same article, see Vol. 6 No. 1 (Spring 1993) of the *Journal of Applied Corporate Finance*.

■ **Denis, David J.**, 1994, "Organizational Form and the Consequences of Highly Leveraged Transactions: Kroger's Recapitalization and Safeway's LBO," *Journal of Financial Economics*, forthcoming.

■ **Donaldson, Gordon**, 1990, "Voluntary Restructuring: The Case of General Mills," *Journal of Financial Economics* 27, no. 1, 117-141. For a shorter, less technical version of the same article, see Vol. 4 No. 3 (Fall 1991) of the *Journal of Applied Corporate Finance*.

■ **Healy, Paul M., Krishna G. Palepu, and Richard S. Ruback**, 1992, "Does Corporate Performance Improve After Mergers?," *Journal of Financial Economics* 31, vol. 2, 135-175.

■ **Holderness, Clifford G. and Dennis P. Sheehan**, 1991, "Monitoring an Owner: The Case of Turner Broadcasting," *Journal of Financial Economics* 30, no. 2, 325-346.

■ **Jensen, Michael C. and Brian Barry**, 1992, "Gordon Cain and the Sterling Group (A) and (B)," Harvard Business School, #9-942-021 and #9-942-022, 10/15.

■ **Jensen, Michael C., Willy Burkhardt, and Brian K. Barry**, 1992, "Wisconsin Central Ltd. Railroad and Berkshire Partners (A): Leverage Buyouts and Financial Distress," Harvard Business School #9-190-062, 11/13.

■ **Jensen, Michael C., Jay Dial, and Brian K. Barry**, 1992, "Wisconsin Central Ltd. Railroad and Berkshire Partners (B): LBO Associations and Corporate Governance," Harvard Business School #9-190-070, 11/13.

■ **Jensen, Michael C.**, 1986, "The Agency Costs of Free Cash Flow: Corporate Finance and Takeovers," *American Economic Review* 76, no. 2, 323-329, May.

■ **Jensen, Michael C.**, 1986, "The Takeover Controversy: Analysis and Evidence," *The Midland Corporate Finance Journal*, 4, no. 2, 6-32, Summer.

■ **Kaplan, Steven N.**, 1993, "Campeau's Acquisition of Federated: Post-bankruptcy Results," *Journal of Financial Economics* 35, 123-136.

■ **Kaplan, Steven N.**, 1989, "The Effects of Management Buyouts on Operating Performance and Value," *Journal of Financial Economics* 24, 581-618.

■ **Kaplan, Steven N.**, 1989, "Campeau's Acquisition of Federated: Value Added or Destroyed," *Journal of Financial Economics* 25, 191-212.

■ **Kaplan, Steven**, 1989, "Management Buyouts: Evidence on Taxes as a Source of Value," *Journal of Finance* 44, 611-632.

■ **Kaplan, Steven N. and Jeremy Stein**, 1993, "The Evolution of Buyout Pricing and Financial Structure in the 1980s," *Quarterly Journal of Economics* 108, no. 2, 313-358. For a shorter, less technical version of the same article, see Vol. 6 No. 1 (Spring 1993) of the *Journal of Applied Corporate Finance*.

■ **Kaplan, Steven N. and Jeremy Stein**, 1990, "How Risky Is the Debt in Highly Leveraged Transactions?," *Journal of Financial Economics* 27, no. 1, 215-245.

■ **Lang, Larry H.P., Annette Poulsen, and Rene M. Stulz**, 1994, "Asset Sales, Leverage, and the Agency Costs of Managerial Discretion," *Journal of Financial Economics*, forthcoming.

■ **Lichtenberg, Frank R.**, 1992, *Corporate Takeovers and Productivity*, (MIT Press: Cambridge, MA). For a shorter, less technical summary of the findings, see Vol. 2 No. 2 (Summer 1989) of the *Journal of Applied Corporate Finance*.

■ **Lichtenberg, Frank R. and Donald Siegel**, 1990, "The Effects of Leveraged Buyouts on Productivity and Related Aspects of Firm Behavior," *Journal of Financial Economics* 27, volume 1, 165-194, September.

■ **Mann, Steven V. and Neil W. Sicherman**, 1991, "The Agency Costs of Free Cash Flow: Acquisition Activity, and Equity Issues," *Journal of Business* 64, no. 2, 213-227.

■ **Murphy, Kevin J. and Jay Dial**, 1992, "Compensation and Strategy at General Dynamics (A) and (B)," Harvard Business School #N9-493-032 and N9-493-033, Boston, MA, 11/19.

■ **Palepu, Krishna G.**, 1990, "Consequences of Leveraged Buyouts," *Journal of Financial Economics* 27, no. 1, 247-262.

■ **Rosett, Joshua G.**, 1990, "Do Union Wealth Concessions Explain Takeover Premiums? The Evidence on Contract Wages," *Journal of Financial Economics* 27, no. 1, 263-282.

■ **Smith, Abbie J.**, 1990, "Corporate Ownership Structure and Performance: The Case of Management Buyouts," *Journal of Financial Economics* 27, 143-164.

■ **Tedlow, Richard**, 1991, "Hitting the Skids: Tires and Time Horizons," Unpublished manuscript, Harvard Business School, Cambridge, MA.

■ **Tiemann, Jonathan**, 1990, "The Economics of Exit and Restructuring: The Pabst Brewing Company," Unpublished manuscript, Harvard Business School.

■ **Wruck, Karen H.**, 1991, "What Really Went Wrong at Revco?," *Journal of Applied Corporate Finance* 4, 79-92, Summer.

■ **Wruck, Karen H.**, 1990, "Financial Distress, Reorganization, and Organizational Efficiency," *Journal of Financial Economics* 27, 420-444.

■ **Wruck, Karen H.**, 1994, "Financial Policy, Internal Control, and Performance: Sealed Air Corporation's Leveraged Special Dividend," *Journal of Financial Economics*, forthcoming.

■ **Wruck, Karen H. and Krishna Palepu**, 1992, "Consequences of Leveraged Shareholder Payouts: Defensive versus Voluntary Recapitalizations," Working paper, Harvard Business School, August.

■ **Wruck, Karen H. and Steve-Anna Stephens**, 1992, "Leveraged Buyouts and Restructuring: The Case of Safeway, Inc.," Harvard Business School Case #192-095.

■ **Wruck, Karen H. and Steve-Anna Stephens**, 1992, "Leveraged Buyouts and Restructuring: The Case of Safeway, Inc.: Media Response," Harvard Business School Case #192-094.

THE MOTIVES AND METHODS OF CORPORATE RESTRUCTURING

by G. Bennett Stewart III and David M. Glassman, Stern Stewart & Co.

T here can be no doubt that the restructuring boom has richly rewarded the dealmakers. But, just as many investors rightly ask their stockbrokers—"but where are our yachts?"—you may be wondering whether the restructurings of the past decade have benefited our economy, shareholders, management, and employees.

Do corporate "raiders," as the label suggests, pillage companies for their personal enrichment, leaving a weakened economy in their wake? Or do they instead promote improvements in corporate performance and increases in market values for all to share? If raiders are a force for good, can we learn from them any lessons about how to structure your company more effectively? You may be concerned, for example, that your company s "break-up" value exceeds its current stock price. If so, you may ask why does the discount exist, and could you do anything to close this worrisome gap?

These and other questions prompted us to undertake a review of some 300 financial restructuring transactions completed in the past decade. Our single most important discovery was that, in the vast majority of cases, corporate restructurings have led to sustained increases in both market values and operating performance.

While initially skeptical of such financial alchemy, and even more reluctant to embrace the explanations proffered by most investment bankers, we eventually became convinced that there were "real" economic explanations for the impressive increases in value and performance accompanying restructurings. Among the most important restructuring "motives" are these:

- Strengthening incentives;
- Achieving a better business fit;
- Sharpening management focus;
- Creating pure plays that have unique investment appeal;
- Curtailing an unproductive reinvestment of cash flow;
- Eliminating subsidies for underperforming businesses;
- Achieving a higher-valued use for assets;
- Increasing debt capacity; and
- Saving taxes.

Our explanations are fundamentally different from those of most investment bankers, who seem to think that restructurings lift stock prices merely by raising the market's *awareness* of the intrinsic value of a company, without any fundamental change in operating efficiency. In view of the strong evidence of market sophistication, and based upon our own evaluations of restructuring transactions, we are convinced that restructuring does indeed change the way corporations are run.

Our research has uncovered some 20 or so recurring methods of restructuring. For convenience, we divide the restructuring methods into three categories:

(1) *Asset restructurings* are techniques that change the ownership of the assets that support a business. These methods include the use of partnerships or trusts to save taxes, discharge surplus cash flow, and split companies into more productive business units.

(2) *Business unit restructurings* can increase value in three ways: (a) by promoting growth through acquisitions, joint ventures, or offering a subsidiary's shares to the public; (b) by separating a business unit from the firm through a sale, spin-off, split-off or partial liquidation; and (c) by undertaking an internal leveraged recapitalization (a transaction which we will describe later).

(3) *Corporate restructurings* change the ownership structure of the parent company through (1) issues of a new form of debt, preferred stock, or common stock; (2) share repurchases; (3) leveraged ESOPs; (4) leveraged cash-outs or leveraged buyouts; or, most radically, (5) complete sales, liquidations or split-ups of the firm.

To introduce our restructuring framework, let's start with what is perhaps the most controversial method of restructuring: increasing leverage.

WHY LEVERAGE MATTERS

The leverage ratios of many American companies have increased dramatically over the past decade, as the result of leveraged buyouts, share repurchases, recapitalizations,

debt-financed acquisitions, and the proliferation of junk bonds. Has this leveraging strengthened or sapped the competitiveness of American companies? Felix Rohatyn, senior partner at Lazard Frères, articulates the naysayers' viewpoint:

This [the high degree of leverage in LBOs] has two consequences, both highly speculative. First, it bets the company on a combination of continued growth and lower interest rates, with no margin for error. Second, it substitutes debt for permanent capital, which is exactly the opposite of what our national investment objectives ought to be.[1]

While increased leverage has probably raised the level of expected corporate bankruptcies, we also believe that there are three reasons why the aggressive use of debt has been a positive force for the economy as a whole, a catalyst for many American companies to increase their productivity and value:

- Debt is cheaper than equity because interest payments are tax-deductible;
- A debt-financed recapitalization, by concentrating the ownership of equity, can strengthen incentives for investors to monitor their investment, and for management and employees to perform; and
- To retire debt, a company may be forced to forgo unprofitable investment and to sell underperforming or unrelated assets or businesses to more productive owners; in general, the need to repay debt creates a compulsion to improve efficiency.

TAX BENEFITS

First of all, debt is a less expensive form of financing than equity because interest expense is tax-deductible while dividend payments are not. Start with the notion that all capital has a cost—if nothing else, an opportunity cost— equal to the rate of return investors would expect to earn by owning other securities of similar risk.

By substituting debt for equity, you will not change the overall amount of capital used in a business, nor the total rate of return needed to compensate investors for bearing business risk. But the implicit cost of equity has been replaced, at least partially, by the explicit tax-deductible cash cost of debt. Substituting debt for equity within prudent limits increases a company's intrinsic market value because debt shelters operating profits from being fully taxed.

This can be true even when the interest rate rises that must be paid on the debt. However high the rate on debt may be, the implied interest rate on the equity it replaces

---

1. "On a Buyout Binge and a Takeover Tear," *The Wall Street Journal* (May 18, 1984).

must be higher still because equity is riskier to own, and its cost is not subsidized by corporate tax savings. Junk bonds, in other words, should not be thought of as expensive debt financing. Junk bonds are rather an inexpensive, because tax-deductible, form of equity.

Corporate raiders know well debt's value as a tax shelter. By highly leveraging their targets, they are able to capitalize the value of pre-tax instead of after-tax profits:

> *"Accountants just assume taxes have to be paid," says Mario J. Gabelli, a money manager, buyout specialist, and aficionado of cash flow analysis long before it was fashionable. "But you don't have to pay taxes... Remember you're an owner-investor, not a passive shareholder, and you have control of the cash. You don't care about profit. So you take on a bundle of debt and devote the cashflow more towards servicing the debt than to producing taxable profits. And as you pay down the debt, your equity in the company automatically grows."* [2]

We frequently encounter chief financial officers who, though they acknowledge the tax advantage of debt, argue against its use because they do not "need" to borrow money. They point out that their companies already generate more cash than they can productively invest; so, for them, borrowing money is unnecessary. We think this view is mistaken. In order to take full advantage of the tax benefit of debt, a company should borrow if it is able to, not because it needs to. In fact, *the less a company needs to raise capital to finance expansion, the more money it should borrow.*

Instead, it is those companies that need to raise new capital that should shun debt, preferring equity to preserve financing flexibility. For Apple Computer, for example, the need to fund technological innovation and market expansion is so much more important than saving taxes that the company quite rightly borrows no money whatsoever: equity supports Apple's growth. It is ironic but true that the more a company needs money to finance a wealth of attractive new investment opportunities, the less money it should borrow.

But when a company has surplus cash flow, making it easy to service debt, new debt should be raised to take advantage of the tax shelter it provides. Raising debt is advisable in these circumstances even if the proceeds are used just to retire common shares.

A leveraged buyout carries this premise to its logical extreme. The classic LBO candidate is eminently bankable precisely because it generates a steady stream of cash to repay debt. Will Rogers apparently was right in observing

that "bankers lend money to their friends, and to those who don't need it." Our recommendation, then, is to borrow money if you can, not because you must. Neglecting debt's tax benefit is one sure way for a strong cash generator to attract the attention of the raiders.

But while we are on the subject of saving taxes, why not convert to a partnership to avoid paying corporate income taxes entirely? As a flow-through vehicle, a partnership incurs no tax liability. Instead, the investors in a partnership are taxed as individuals on their share of partnership income. With the personal tax rate now beneath the corporate tax rate for the first time in memory, the logic of housing income-producing assets in a partnership is compelling. Why put assets in a corporation where earnings are taxed once at 34 percent and twice if distributed, when the same assets put in a partnership would have their earnings taxed just once at 28 percent?

There is a problem, however. Moving assets already housed in a corporation into a partnership triggers a corporate tax on the difference between the current value of the assets and their tax basis. Depending on how the conversion is accomplished, it may require shareholders to pay a tax. A decision to convert an existing corporation to a partnership thus becomes a straightforward capital budgeting exercise, weighing the up-front tax costs against an ongoing tax savings.

Unfortunately, the tax code may be revised to tax certain limited partnerships as corporations, thereby subjecting them to double taxation. The value of the on-going tax benefit must he discounted for this uncertainty, further tipping the present value calculation against conversion. But help is on its way. We can dress up a corporation and make it behave like a partnership. Here's how. What two essential economic attributes distinguish a partnership from a corporation? Partnerships are not taxed and generally distribute all cash flow to investors. The answer, then, is to lever up a corporation and use the proceeds to retire equity. The corporation is thereby effectively converted into a partnership while avoiding any up-front corporate tax! Interest expense now largely shelters the company's operating profits from corporate income tax. The operating profits, instead, mostly flow through as interest income to be taxed to the holders of the company's bonds.

Moreover, paying interest and principal on the debt raised causes the company's cash flow to be discharged, again much as it would be in a partnership. The equity investors that survive the recapitalization, like the general partners in a partnership, still have control of the firm. And yet, unlike general partners, the liability of these shareholders is limited.

---

2. "The Savviest Investors Are Going with the (Cash) Flow," *Business Week* (September 7, 1987).

In short, a highly-leveraged corporation can match the desirable tax and cash flow attributes of a partnership, while retaining the corporate advantages of limited liability and trading liquidity—truly the best of both worlds.

But, however important taxes are in making debt more attractive than equity, the tax benefit alone cannot account for the great increase in leverage in recent years. If anything, the reduction in the corporate tax rate would reduce the incentive to use debt as a tax shelter. The raiders have taught us that there are at least four more reasons to use debt aggressively.

CASH DISGORGEMENT

A good reason to borrow money is to repay it! When a company incurs debt, the obligation to pay it back it removes from management the temptation to reinvest surplus cash in substandard projects or overpriced acquisitions. Like Ulysses lashed to the mast, management's hands are tied by its debts. Then, though the siren calls of investment opportunities may beckon, the company ship rows assuredly onward, avoiding the fate of the failed projects that litter the shore. Repaying debt need not entirely preclude growth, but with the cash flow that a company internally generates dedicated to retiring debt, expansion must be financed with new capital, subjecting management's investment plans to the discipline of a market test.

The Standard Oil Company of Ohio ("SOHIO") provides a good example of the "reinvestment risk" that corporations impose on their stockholders. SOHIO for many years was a sleepy regional refiner and marketer of oil. After finding extensive oil reserves on the Alaskan north slope, it became an enormously profitable cash cow. Curiously, SOHIO sold for a depressed price-to-earnings ratio, even though it earned a very high return on equity and sold for the highest price-to-book ratio of any of the major oil companies.

How do we account for that? The high return on equity and price-to-book ratio resulted from SOHIO's successful investments. Value had unquestionably been added to the capital that SOHIO had invested in Alaska. The low price-to-earnings ratio signaled the market's lack of confidence in SOHIO's future profitability. In fact, it resulted from a downright fear that the flood of cash from the North Slope would be wasted in SOHIO's basic businesses or in unjustifiable premiums for acquisitions.

SOHIO justified investors' fears by choosing both downhill paths. Management splurged on costly oil forays (of which the dry-as-a-prune Mukluk well is but one prominent example), bought extensive mining reserves at inflated prices, and made the exceedingly expensive ($1.77 billion) and highly suspect acquisition of Kennecott, the copper company. The results of SOHIO's capital investments were so bad that British Petroleum, SOHIO's part owner, let go SOHIO's chairman and brought in a new team to reverse the company's misfortunes.

But why single out SOHIO when almost all the major oil companies have made similar blunders (Exxon with its office systems venture and Reliance Electric acquisition, Mobil with Montgomery Ward, ARCO with Anaconda, and so on)? It's just human nature to spend money when you get your hands on it.

Nevertheless, it is a fundamental tenet of corporate finance that the wisdom of making an investment does *not* depend on whether funding comes from inside or outside the company. Even if internal cash flow finances growth, those funds could just as well have been repatriated to investors and then explicitly raised. Internalizing the cost of capital does not avoid it. In practice, however, the inclination to invest is more highly related to the availability of cash than to the presence of attractive uses.

Why is this textbook lesson so widely ignored? The answer lies in reasons of great importance to senior management and of grave concern to investors. A large and growing company is more powerful and prestigious (and, in the past, was less vulnerable to takeover before junk bond financing became available) than a small, contracting one. Moreover, a diversified company is more stable than one reliant on a single business, and can justify a corporate bureaucracy with no direct operating responsibility or accountability. And, as Professor Michael Jensen has observed, middle level managers also are inclined to root for expansion if it creates new senior management positions to be filled.[3] For all these reasons, most companies prefer to reinvest cash flow rather than to pay it out.

Consider the case of Ford, which [at the time of this writing], after two years of record profits, now sits on top of over $9 billion in cash and securities.

Where will Ford pounce? The stock markets buzz almost daily with rumors about takeover plays by Ford, which openly says it wants to buy companies to offset the auto industry's cyclical swings. In recent months, Boeing, Lockheed, and Singer have been rumored targets.[4]

While it is easy to see the benefits diversification may bring to Ford's senior managers and employees (to say nothing of its investment bankers), is diversification in

---

3. "How to Detect a Prime Takeover Target," *The New York Times* (March 9, 1986).

4. "Can Ford Stay on Top?," *Business Week* (September 28, 1987).

the best interest of its shareholders and our economy? Was it not the company's dependence upon the auto market that forced management to streamline production and to innovate in order to survive—and that is thus the cause of their present success?

By making survival less dependent on Ford's ability to compete in the auto industry, diversification will dampen the company's drive to make painful, necessary adjustments should hard times come again. Perhaps Ford can justify buying an electronics or aerospace company to obtain technology. But would it not be more efficient to license the technology, or form a joint venture, if that is the motivation? Most fundamentally, would an acquisition be made if Ford had to raise the cash, or is the mere availability of cash prompting its use?

Warren Buffett, Chairman of Berkshire Hathaway, states the problem in typically eloquent and witty style in his 1984 Annual Report:

Many corporations that show consistently good returns have, indeed, employed a large portion of their retained earnings on an economically unattractive, even disastrous, basis. Their marvelous core businesses camouflage repeated failures in capital allocation elsewhere (usually involving high-priced acquisitions). The managers at fault periodically report on the lessons they have learned from the latest disappointment. They then usually seek out future lessons. (Failure seems to go to their heads.)

In such cases, shareholders would be far better off if the earnings were retained to expand only the high-return business, with the balance paid in dividends or used to repurchase stock (an action that increases the owner's interest in the exceptional business while sparing them participation in the sub-par businesses). Managers of high-return businesses who consistently employ much of the cash thrown off by those businesses in other ventures with low returns should be held to account for those allocation decisions, regardless of how profitable the overall enterprise is.

Are we suggesting, then, that senior managers are tempted by self-interest to sometimes make decisions contrary to their shareholders' welfare? Yes, we are. Reinvesting cash flow without shareholder approval is the corporate equivalent of taxation without representation. Just as our founding fathers understood that no single body of men could be entrusted to serve the public interest and created a system of checks and balances, so do many financial restructurings take away from management the power to reinvest a company's cash flow and restore that power to the shareholders. Management, in such cases, is then forced to appeal to investors to vote for its investment plans by contributing new capital.

Are we also saying that the market is more astute than management in making investment decisions? Yes, again. How, for example, can executives of oil companies know that drilling for more oil is the most productive present use of society's scarce resources? Impossible, obviously. The resources freed up by not drilling for oil would be invested in activities where oil company executives have no relevant experience—for example, developing the next generation of supercomputer, or in biotechnology. Yet such resource allocation tradeoffs are decided by portfolio managers every day when they choose which companies' shares to buy and which to sell. Moreover, the advent of powerful microcomputers, extensive financial databases, and a growing body of business school graduates, well-versed in powerful analytical methods, has enhanced the market's ability to make accurate and rapid-fire evaluations.

Corporate managements, on the other hand, labor under an inflated sense of the importance of their products or industry relative to competing alternatives. They maintain a dogmatic optimism in the face of justifiable market skepticism and, perhaps most important, persist in ignoring the strong evidence showing that stock prices tend to be an accurate barometer of a company's intrinsic value (meaning that the upside potential is offset by an honest assessment of the downside risk).

For all these reasons, we are convinced that *the current wave of restructurings has much to do with the increasing sophistication of capital markets worldwide, and not the alleged lack of it.*

There are five ways that responsible management—or, failing that, a corporate raider—can return control of discretionary cash flow to the market and eliminate the discount on value caused by the market's perception of reinvestment risk. All five can be illustrated with examples drawn from the oil industry.

Repurchase Shares

The most flexible method is to discharge surplus cash voluntarily by repurchasing common shares in the open market over time. Exxon did this. Responding aggressively to overcapacity in the oil industry, Exxon cut its employment, refinery capacity, and service stations by a third from 1980 to 1986. It then used the cash generated by this move to buy back common stock on the open market, over $7 billion worth from June, 1983, earning it the following accolades from *Business Week:*

In effect, Exxon has sent a message to its stockholders and the public: "Our industry is shrinking, at least for the present, and we think we should shrink a bit along with it. So we are returning some capital to our shareholders. They, not Exxon management, will decide how this money should be reinvested in the U.S. economy." That is good for the economy.[5]

Exxon's share return (dividend and price appreciation) since the buyback plan was first announced has bettered the share return produced by both Unocal and Phillips, where restructuring was forced upon management by a raider. Both of those companies had announced aggressive expansion plans despite declining fundamentals in the oil business, an approach guaranteed to put them directly "in harm's way."

Leveraged Share Repurchases

The second way to cure reinvestment risk, then, is to buy back stock aggressively and finance the purchase with debt. In such cases, the retirement of stock that may have taken place voluntarily over time is forcefully discounted to the present. Boone Pickens' threats prodded Unocal and Phillips to use corporate debt and leveraged ESOPs to finance a wholesale stock buyback, thus forcing recalcitrant management to discharge cash they otherwise would have used for unrewarding drilling projects or costly diversification.

Such leverage admittedly leaves Unocal and Phillips less able to withstand or capitalize on changing fortunes in the oil industry—one reason why companies that voluntarily restructure almost always outperform those forced to give in to a raider. *Business Week* concurs:

Exxon's program of stock buyback makes a lot more sense than scrambling around to buy new properties. If the oil business comes back, Exxon, tighter and richer, will be in far better shape to benefit than many oil companies now overloaded with debt.[6]

Partnerships

The third means to give investors control over the reinvestment of cash flow is to house assets in a partnership. We previously noted that a partnership can benefit investors by avoiding double taxation of earnings. Partnerships can cure reinvestment risk as well. By law, the investors in a partnership must include in taxable income their share of the partnership's earnings, whether distributed or not. Because there is no additional tax liability, investors usually insist that partnerships distribute all available cash flow.

On August 25, 1985, the board of Mesa Petroleum announced a plan to convert the corporation to a partnership, explaining the rationale for this move in a shareholders' prospectus:

Historically, the Company has paid out little of its cash flow as dividends and has been committed to a policy of replacing its annual production of oil and gas reserves through exploration and development and through acquisitions. The Company has paid relatively low amounts of Federal income taxes because of deductions resulting from its expenditures. In recent years, however, the Company has significantly reduced its exploration and development expenditures in response to industry conditions, which will result in the Company's paying substantial Federal income taxes if it continues its business as presently conducted.

In view of the limited reinvestment opportunities available to the Company, the Board of Directors believes that the interests of stockholders will be better served if a substantial portion of its available cash flow is distributed directly to its owners. To distribute substantially greater cash flow more efficiently, the Board of Directors believes that the partnership form is preferable to the corporate form.

Mesa's stock price soared from $14 to $18 over the period surrounding the announcement. Although the voice of the market is all that really matters, analysts also saw the wisdom of the change and applauded it. A DLJ research bulletin responded as follows:

Properties appear to be worth full value in partnership form because the owners have control of the reinvestment as the partnership pays out most of its cash flow. Avoidance of the corporate tax and a higher basis for cost depletion add to the appeal of newly formed partnerships.[7]

Or, as an L.F. Rothschild analysis put it,

We anticipate that future capital expenditures, while rather limited, will have a relatively high rate of return because of the selectivity available to management.[8]

Although partnerships normally pay out all available cash flow, this does not preclude them from expanding. Indeed, since becoming a partnership, Mesa has aggressively sought acquisitions, starting with Diamond Sham-

---

5. *Business Week* (August 19, 1985).
6. Ibid.

7. Donaldson, Lufkin & Jenrette, *Securities Corporation Research Bulletin* (September 30, 1985).
8. L. F. Rothschild, Underberg, Towbin, Company Research (September 25, 1985).

rock, usually by offering to swap new partnership units for a target's outstanding shares. Such expansion is not precluded, therefore, but must pass a market test.

Leveraged Acquisitions

Michael Jensen, cited earlier, has noted that debt-financed mergers also can assure investors that future cash flow will not be wasted. After a highly-leveraged acquisition is completed, the consolidated entity must dedicate the cash flows of both companies to repay debt. The result is much the same as if both firms independently had borrowed to buy back their own stock and then agreed to merge through a stock-for-stock swap.[9] A highly-leveraged merger milks two cash cows with one stroke.

SOCAL's acquisition of Gulf provides a good example, with Boone Pickens again playing the protagonist. Mr. Pickens' threats to acquire Gulf and convert it to a royalty trust prompted management to seek out a white knight. SOCAL answered their plea, paying $13.2 billion, all financed with debt, to acquire Gulf. Before the merger, SOCAL's leverage ratio (total debt-to-total debt and equity capital) was 10 percent and Gulf's was 20 percent. Afterwards, SOCAL and Gulf emerged with a consolidated leverage ratio of 40 percent, a debt burden still being paid off.

Our calculations show that in the period surrounding the takeover, the combined market value of SOCAL and Gulf rose over $5 billion, compared to a portfolio of oil stocks. This remarkable increase in value is attributable to three things:

■ first, the value of operating synergies—the textbook benefits derived from consolidation, rationalization, economies of scale, etc.;
■ second, the tax benefit of the new debt; and
■ third, the elimination of a discount for reinvestment risk that had been placed on the value of both companies. Investors would be more inclined to fully value the future cash generated by both companies knowing it would be used to retire debt.

Dividends

The last method that commits a company to disgorge cash is to pay or increase dividends. Because most companies' boards are reluctant to cut dividends once they have been raised, an increase in dividends usually is interpreted by the market as a lasting commitment to pay out future cash flows to shareholders.

Arco, for example, increased dividends as part of an overall restructuring announced in May, 1985. Capital spending was cut 25 percent, annual operating expenses were reduced $500 million, and refining and marketing operations east of the Mississippi were put up for sale, freeing up cash for Arco to buy back 25 percent of its stock for $4 billion and to increase the dividend by 33 percent. Although Arco also took a $1.3 billion writedown of its eastern assets, investors reacted favorably, sending Arco's stock price rocketing from about $50 to $62.50, a gain in market value of $2.8 billion.

Although we have just demonstrated how increasing dividends increased market value as part of an overall restructuring, increasing dividends is usually a less desirable method for distributing cash. For one thing, it is not tax effective. From the company's viewpoint, dividends are less attractive than interest payments because they are not tax deductible. Investors also generally prefer a share repurchase program to receiving dividends for the following reasons: receiving dividends is compulsory but selling shares is voluntary; a capital gain from a stock sale can be offset by capital losses; and while dividends are taxed entirely, the gain to be taxed on repurchased shares is reduced by the investor's tax basis. Perhaps most important, though, the obligation a company incurs to pay dividends is not as compelling as servicing debt with its threat of bankruptcy (a topic we return to later).

Partial Public Offerings

Offering the public stock of a subsidiary unit stands in contrast to the methods that force the disgorgement of cash. A partial public offering binds the *use* of cash. Investors know that the cash raised from such a public sale will be used by the unit they have chosen to invest in, unlike an offering by the parent, where the funds raised must flow through a pachinko machine of competing internal uses with no assurance they will ever reach the most promising ventures.

Consider the case of McKesson Corporation, a $6 billion distributor of drugs, beverages, and chemicals that last year sold to the public a 16.7 percent stake in its Armor All subsidiary. Although Armor All accounted for only $90 million in sales (less than 2 percent of total revenues), McKesson's stock increased by 10 percent (from $60 to $66 a share) upon the announcement of the intended offering.

Armour All, however, is a rapidly growing (20% annually, compared to 10% for McKesson), highly profitable unit that McKesson could use to launch an expansion

---

9. "The Takeover Controversy: Analysis and Evidence," *Midland Corporate Finance Journal*, Vol. 4 No. 2 (Summer, 1986), pp. 6-31.

By making a company self-funding and self-perpetuating, the BCG approach
appealed to corporate managers because it circumvented the monitoring processes
of the capital markets.

into consumer products. Able now to access capital directly, Armour All is more likely to reach its full growth. A public market for Armor All stock also helps establish a separate identity and sense of autonomy for employees, and enables the unit to attract and retain key executives through stock options, an important consideration in a heavily marketing-oriented and entrepreneurially-driven business.

Goodbye, Boston Consulting

These restructuring examples refute a planning paradigm popularized many years ago by The Boston Consulting Group wherein a company's mature "cash cows" were supposed to fund the growth of promising businesses ("question marks") into highly-performing "stars." By making a company self-funding and self-perpetuating, the BCG approach appealed to corporate managers because it circumvented the monitoring processes of the capital markets. In reality, the poorly-performing "dogs" ate the cash, while the "question marks" either were starved, overmanaged, or were acquired for obscene premiums.

Our analysis of stock prices has demonstrated that severing the link between mature cash cows and promising growth opportunities creates value. Let the "cows" pass their cash directly to investors. And let the "question marks" depend directly on the markets. Such a roundabout route is the most direct way to assure that value is created.

INCENTIVES

A debt-financed recapitalization can dramatically strengthen incentives. Raising debt to retire equity concentrates the remaining common shares in fewer hands. This increases the incentive for shareholders to monitor their investment closely and for management and employees, if they are given equity or an equity-like stake, to perform well.

Investor Incentives

The reason why concentrating equity benefits investors is first cousin to the theory that won James Buchanan the Nobel Prize in economics. Mr. Buchanan wanted to understand why Congress passed laws that did not meet with general approval. The reason, he speculated, was that special interest groups successfully lobbied legislators to pass laws to benefit them at the expense of all taxpayers. When benefits are concentrated and costs are diffused, he believed, our democratic system of government lacks a safeguard to stop a minority from exploiting the majority.

A similar conflict exists in large, broadly-capitalized firms, this time between management and shareholders. Suppose that in an understandable search for job security, prestige, stability, and so forth, management made decisions that failed to maximize shareholders' wealth. While all shareholders would benefit from better management, the costs of waging a proxy fight or otherwise rallying investors would be borne selectively. Given the uneven distribution of costs and benefits, it may not make sense for an investor or small group of investors to shoulder the costs of opposing management.

But if debt were raised to retire shares, the equity of the firm would be concentrated in fewer investors' hands. With the cost of the value lost through mismanagement now more forcefully registered on each share, shareholders have a greater motive to monitor the company's performance, giving management a greater incentive to perform.

To illustrate, suppose that a company starts with 10 million common shares selling at $10 each for a total market value of $100 million, and no debt. Assume that misguided management reduces value by $20 million, or $2 a share, so that the shares would trade for $12 if the company were properly managed.

Even this 20 percent discount might not lead shareholders to rebel. But if management could be induced, for example, to borrow $50 million to retire 5 million common shares in the open market, the $20 million of lost value would be spread over only 5 million remaining shares. The result— a $4 a share discount—would now be a full 40 percent of value, a gap which might indeed incite a shareholder revolt. Management, alert to the greater incentive that investors have to monitor their performance, would have to be more attentive to creating value for shareholders and less preoccupied with pursuing their own agenda.

For example, shortly after Sir James Goldsmith prompted Goodyear to buy back 48 percent of its stock, Robert E. Mercer, chairman and chief executive officer, said that Goodyear "will be more attuned to the stock price than before."[10] Goodyear reversed its wasteful diversification program, selling its aerospace unit to Loral and its oil reserves to Exxon for hefty premiums. Goodyear now concentrates on improving the value of its core tire and rubber operations.

A leveraged buyout carries even further the benefit of investor concentration. In these transactions, a broad herd of equity investors is replaced by a small group of "lead steers"—sophisticated debt and equity players—who act quickly and surely to restructure liabilities or replace management if such action is warranted. An LBO realigns management's interests with those of investors.

---

10. "Goodyear Tire and Rubber Sees Proceeds from Asset Sales Exceeding $3 Billion," *Wall Street Journal* (January 19,1987).

In these transactions [LBOs], a broad herd of equity investors is replaced by a small group of "lead steers"—sophisticated debt and equity players—who act quickly and surely to restructure liabilities or replace management if such action is warranted.

FIGURE 1
COMPENSATION RISK MAP

Debt-like					Equity-like
Wage	Lower Wage	Lower Wage	Lower Wage	Lower Wage	X
Defined Benefit Pension	X	X		X	X	X
Interest Expense (Creditors)					
Profit Sharing	Profit Sharing	Profit Sharing	Profit Sharing		X
	ESOP	ESOP	ESOP		X
		Leveraged Equity Purchase Plan	Leveraged Equity Purchase Plan	Leveraged Equity Purchase Plan	
			Leveraged Cash-Out		

Incentives for Management and Employees

If, in the process of recapitalizing the company, management and employees receive an equity stake, the motivational benefits of equity concentration are further amplified. The accompanying "Compensation Risk Map" (Figure 1) shows how restructuring incentives—moving left to right, from low risk to high risk—can create value.

No Guts—No Glory

The most secure, debt-like approach to compensation (on the far left of the chart) would be to pay a wage and provide a defined-benefit pension, a "no guts and no glory" scheme that clearly separates compensation from the success of the business. Employees are treated as bondholders and naturally they adopt the risk-averse mentality of creditors as they go about their appointed tasks. Worse yet, employees effectively become senior creditors because wages and pension payments are paid even before debt is serviced and, in the event of a bankruptcy, are senior to unsecured creditors. Such a compensation scheme robs a company of its capacity to raise debt.

Profit-Sharing

Let's move one notch to the right on the risk map and reduce wages (if not immediately, then over time), eliminate the defined-benefit pension, and introduce a very special sort of profit-sharing plan. This sort of compensation mix works more like a convertible security; one part provides the employee with the fixed return of a bond, while the other, like equity, is tied to the success of the firm.

Restructuring compensation this way accomplishes two things in one fell swoop:
- Incentives for employees are created for the first time; and
- Debt capacity is augmented.

What should concern lenders is where they stand in line for payout on a company's income statement (or, to be more precise, on the cash flow statement), not their alleged priority on the balance sheet. Conventional accounting statements mistakenly show profit-sharing distributions as an expense that is senior to the payment of interest when, in fact, profits are shared only after interest expense has been covered. Because lenders are in line for payout before profits are shared, but after wages are paid, introducing a profit-sharing plan in lieu of wages increases debt capacity. It is unfortunate that most widely-followed leverage statistics fail to capture the substitution of income statement equity for balance sheet leverage that takes place as many companies restructure compensation.

To the greatest extent possible, bonuses should be based on the profits earned at a decentralized level—activity-by-activity, plant-by-plant, business unit-by-business unit—and not according to the results achieved by the company overall. Only that will forge a direct link between performance and compensation. If bonuses are based on general corporate profits, the link between pay and performance is so weak that profit-sharing has little value as an incentive.

Worthington Industries is one of a handful of large American companies that use profit-sharing to account for a major portion of employee compensation—at least 25 percent and in some cases as high as 50 percent. Management insists that its profit-sharing arrangement provides strong productivity incentives to workers. Moreover, by substituting variable for fixed costs, it virtually eliminates the need for layoffs and stabilizes profits in economic downturns.

Most performance measures...capture the results of a single period, while stock prices capitalize the value of good management decisions over the life of the business.

ESOPs

Let's turn the compensation amplifier up another notch by introducing an Employee Stock Ownership Plan ("ESOP"), possibly in exchange for an even further reduction in wages. Providing employees with common stock in the firm through an ESOP accomplishes four things beyond sharing profits.

First, common stock represents a share in current and *future* profits. Employees are given the incentive to consider the long-term consequences of their actions.

Second, ESOP incentives accumulate: the number of shares an employee owns increases with each year's allocation, making his monetary and emotional stake in the firm grow over time. Profit-sharing incentives are unchanging. Nothing carries over from one year to the next.

Third, an ESOP can build up a company's debt capacity more effectively than can a profit-sharing plan because it is self-financing. By law, the cash a company contributes to an ESOP must be applied to purchase common shares in the sponsoring corporation (even if a company chooses to contribute common shares directly to the ESOP, the result is the same as if cash first was contributed to the ESOP and then used to buy company stock). An ESOP makes cash boomerang, carrying it out the front door as compensation and returning with it through the back door as new equity.

With profit-sharing, what goes out, stays out. Profit-sharing distributions, though calculated after interest expense is paid, need to be financed and may not necessarily be financed with company equity. Such financing risks are of concern to lenders and may limit a company from attaining its full debt capacity. ESOP contributions, however, are automatically equity-financed, a distinctive benefit that expands a company's debt capacity in a way that most conventional leverage ratios fail to acknowledge.

Fourth, Congress has granted ESOPs a number of special tax breaks that are not applicable to profit-sharing plans. For example, a commercial bank may exclude from its taxable income one-half of the interest received on a loan made to an ESOP. Because of this, ESOPs can borrow at favorable rates (usually less than 85% of prime) to pre-purchase shares in the sponsoring corporation (a "leveraged ESOP"). The ESOP trustee applies subsequent cash contributions from the company to pay down the ESOP loan and allocates inventoried shares of equivalent value to the employees (with vesting over a three-to-seven year period of plan participation). Even with such a leveraged ESOP, it still is true that contributions to the ESOP are equity financed. The equity financing simply takes place in advance.

Accounting for the formation of a leveraged ESOP is identical to a share repurchase: the company's debt goes up (by the amount of the ESOP loan) and its equity goes down (by the cost of the shares the ESOP purchases). The ESOP loan is considered a company liability because the company guarantees the loan and the loan must be repaid with cash contributed from the company. It is what happens afterwards that makes a leveraged ESOP different from a share repurchase.

As the company makes future cash contributions to the ESOP, its debt goes down and its equity goes up, a double-barreled reduction in leverage that is unique to ESOPs. Company debt declines as the ESOP loan is repaid. Equity is written up by the value of the common shares allocated to employees—a value that matches the debt retired. A share repurchase, by contrast, is followed by just a single-barreled blast at leverage: debt goes down as it is repaid, but equity does not automatically accrue. The two-fisted unleveraging of a leveraged ESOP is perhaps its greatest advantage as a tool of corporate finance: a company's ability to recover quickly from a debt-financed share repurchase dramatically increases with its use.

Having just sung the praises of leveraged ESOPs, we hasten to add that their benefits often are exaggerated by overzealous proponents. For example, much has been made of the fact that, whereas corporate debt must be amortized from a company's after-tax cash flow, ESOP debt is repaid from cash contributions that are tax-deductible. The alleged benefit arises from confusing an operating expense and a financing flow. (See the Appendix for a more detailed account, and qualification, of the tax benefits of ESOP financing.)

The bottom line on ESOPs is that incentive, debt capacity, and tax benefits team up to make them an attractive compensation restructuring device for many companies. A careful evaluation of an ESOP's real advantages is advisable, however, before taking action.

Leveraged Equity Purchase Plans

Now, let's turn the heat up yet several more degrees and make management sweat. While there are many ways to provide key managers with incentives to create value, one of the most exciting new concepts is the "leveraged equity purchase plan," a method popularized by the Henley Group.

Henley was formed in early 1986 as the spinoff of 35 poorly performing units from Allied-Signal. It floated to an initial market value of $1.2 billion, a remarkably lofty value considering that the businesses comprising Henley collectively lost $27 million the year before. To what can we attribute this impressive market value placed upon Henley? To Chairman Michael Dingman, his management team, and the expectation of very strong incentives for management to create value.

Besides providing a powerful incentive to management, the Henley scheme also is an effective form of financial communication. Just by announcing their participation in such a plan, management issues a strong statement about their confidence in and commitment to the value of the company.

Henley unveiled an incentive scheme so powerful that we expect it to be widely imitated. On October 10, 1986, twenty of Henley's top executives bought, at a slight premium to market value, freshly issued shares in Henley amounting to about 5 percent of the company's common equity capitalization. The executive team financed the $108 million price tag for the 5.1 million with (1) a $97 million nonrecourse loan from Henley that was secured by the shares and (2) with $11 million of their own capital. Not only is this a boon for management, it also benefits the company's investors. Here's why.

Should Henley's share value fall after the plan is initiated, the executives may tender their shares to Henley in satisfaction of the loan and without recourse to their personal assets. Granted, management can lose *only* their $11 million investment. But are the other shareholders hurt because the loan is non-recourse? Not in our opinion. An additional $11 million will be in the corporate coffers and no additional shares will be outstanding.

Should Henley perform well, it is true shareholders face a 5 percent dilution in upside value. But remember two things. First, Henley executives fully paid for the *initial* market value of the shares by incurring debt (which must be repaid before the shares could be sold) and by contributing capital. Shareholders are diluted only on the *increase* in value.

And second, management now has a dramatically heightened incentive to create value. Does it not make sense to offer the baker a piece of the pie if, as a result, he is apt to bake a much larger one for all to share?

Some may ask what separates the Henley incentive plan from ones where management simply is paid to increase value or proxies for value. In theory, nothing; in practice, everything.

First, no matter how good the measures used to determine cash bonuses are, there is no substitute for a traded stock price as an indicator of value. Most performance measures, for example, capture the results of a single period, while stock prices capitalize the value of good management decisions over the life of the business.

To illustrate this crucial difference, suppose that sound management leads to a competitive advantage, one improving operating profits after taxes by $20 million a year. If management is awarded a 5% share of the profits, the bonus pool would rise $1 million.

The share value of the company, however, is apt to capitalize the value of the annual profit improvement. If, for example, the cost of capital is 10 percent for our hypothetical company, value would rise $200 million ($20 million/.10). If management had obtained 5% of the shares through a leveraged

equity purchase plan, the value of their stake would increase $10 million, or 10 times what they might expect from a profit-sharing plan. Owning equity amplifies the reward for good management decisions—and the penalties for poor ones.

There is, in addition, a crucial accounting difference between a cash bonus payment and a share ownership scheme. Cash bonus payments are recorded as an expense; an appreciation in the value of shares held by management is not. This remarkable inconsistency in accounting treatment is one reason, we believe, why many boards of directors feel uncomfortable about providing unlimited cash bonuses even in circumstances where management clearly deserves them. The preoccupation with maximizing reported earnings stands in the way of paying people what they are worth.

Another reason cash bonus payments often are limited is that they must be financed by the company whereas share appreciation is financed by the market. Though either selling shares or borrowing against them can compensate the manager who owns stock, neither drains financial resources directly from the firm. So, much like an ESOP, the compensation managers receive by participating in a leveraged equity purchase plan is automatically equity financed. This augments debt capacity, while cash compensation payments use it up.

Besides providing a powerful incentive to management, the Henley scheme also is an effective form of financial communication. Just by announcing their participation in such a plan, management issues a strong statement about their confidence in and commitment to the value of the company. When we encounter senior management groups who claim that their company is undervalued, we suggest it would be an opportune time to introduce a leveraged equity purchase plan. "Well, we are not *that* undervalued," they say.

The Henley plan assures more than just equity investors of management's commitment to creating value. It provides important safeguards for creditors as well. Lender's know that there is no surer way to guarantee the value of their debt than to provide management with an incentive to increase the value of the equity that stands beneath it. And, in a downturn, creditors must be comforted knowing of management's desire to recoup the $11 million of equity they contributed to the business. Again, published statistics on leverage fail to account for the crucial distinction between equity provided by management and equity provided by the market.

Chairman Michael Dingman explains his intentions: *"We believe that substantial borrowing and equity risk taking by key executives will create the entrepreneurial conditions that are critical to Henley's success."* [11]

---

11. "Henley Group Says 20 Officials to Buy 5.1 Million Shares in Unusual Program," *Wall Street Journal* (October 10, 1986).

> By voluntarily taking on a leveraged equity stake, management is expressing its commitment to, and confidence in, creating at least $85 worth of share value out of a company that was selling for just $70 a share at the time of recapitalization.

FIGURE 2
FMC EXCHANGE OFFERS

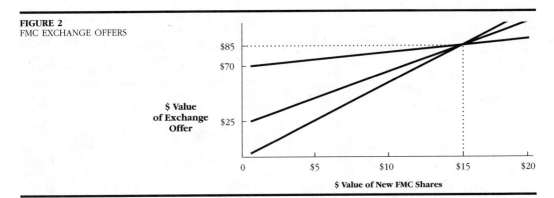

Dingman also commented that the leveraged equity purchase program was modeled on the way executives participate in a leveraged buyout and was better than a stock option plan because executives make an up-front investment and can watch the value of that investment fluctuate with the stock price.

Henley is so pleased with the plan that it is making the same offer to key executives of its subsidiary business units. For example, after a stake in Fischer Scientific, a medical products subsidiary, was distributed to shareholders and began to trade, top executives there were able to purchase stock in the unit under a similar leveraged purchase plan. Henley's restructuring suggests that decentralized, pay-for-performance compensation schemes are coming into vogue for management as well as for the rank and file.

Where does corporate leverage fit into a leveraged equity purchase plan? Corporate leverage can make it easier for management to acquire a significant stake in the assets underlying the equity, an important consideration because managers really manage assets, not equity.

To illustrate, suppose that senior management was willing to invest $1 million to purchase equity in a company that had $100 million of assets. If the company were financed entirely with equity, management could acquire a mere 1% interest. If, however, the company borrowed $80 million to retire common shares, management could obtain a full 5% stake in the remaining $20 million of equity.

Such a recapitalization makes it possible for management to invest an amount equal to just 1% of the assets and to reap 5% of the payoff from improved asset management. Corporate leverage, by amplifying the benefit derived from a more productive use of resources, will multiply management's incentive to perform. This suggests that combining corporate leverage with a leveraged equity stake for management may be an extremely potent formula for creating value. The next step forward along our compensation risk path does just that.

The Empire Strikes Back: Leveraged Cash-Outs

The next step out, actually something of a great leap, takes us to the "leveraged cash-out," a powerful financial restructuring method that uses corporate leverage to amplify the incentive that owning equity provides to management and employees. Leveraged cash-outs have promoted such dramatic increases in market values that they have proven very effective in warding off hostile takeover bids.

With the value generated by the recapitalization as an ace up its sleeve, management can up the ante to the point where raiders usually decide to fold their cards or not enter the bidding at all. Then, instead of a raider, a company's own stakeholders—its management, employees, customers and shareholders—walk away with a pot of added value.

The management of FMC Corporation, for example, sensing the company's vulnerability to an unsolicited offer, initiated a leveraged cash-out. As a preemptive strike to deter a raider, their restructuring followed the masochist's creed: be the first to do unto yourself as others would do unto you. No competing offer was forthcoming, and today FMC operates very successfully as an independent, publicly-traded entity. Let's see why.

On February 20, 1986, FMC proposed to exchange a package of cash and new shares for each common share held. At that time, FMC's shares were selling for about $70. There were three parties to the transaction, and three exchange offers:
■ the "public" received $70 and 1 new share;
■ the thrift plan received $25 and 4 new shares; and
■ management and PAYSOP received no cash and 5 2/3 new shares.

By accepting less cash but more new shares than the public, insiders increased their ownership in FMC from 14% to 41%. The recapitalization thus served to concentrate equity in the hands of management and employees,

TABLE 1 SUMMARY OF FMC'S PERFORMANCE ($ MILLIONS)		Before Recap	After Recap	
		1981-1985*	1986	1987 (6 mo.)
	Revenue Growth	(1)%	(8)%	3%
	EBIT/Capital	13%	18%	23%
	EBIT/Sales	7%	10%	12%
	Working Capital/Sales	13%	3%	5%
	Free Cash Flow**	$250	$320	$500
	Total Debt/Total Capital	20%	100%	90%
	EBIT/Interest	6.6 ×	2.2 ×	1.5 ×
	Stock Price Appreciation	17%	62%	35%

* Average over 5-year period
** Cash flow from operations, after taxes but before financing charges, net of new investment in working capital and fixed assets.

dramatically strengthening their incentive to perform (and to sell the company, should an attractive offer be made). The heightened incentives may be illustrated by plotting the exchange offers (Figure 2).

The horizontal axis represents the value of the new FMC shares, and the vertical axis is the corresponding value of the proposed exchange offer to the three parties. The points of intersection on the vertical axis are the cash portions of the offers: $70 for the public, to fully cash out the current market value of their shares, $25 for the thrift, and nothing for the management. The slope of the lines drawn from those points simply adds the value of the new shares on top of the cash portion (1 share for the public, 4 for the thrift, and 5 2/3 for management).

All three intersect at a common point reflecting the "intrinsic" value of the transaction. Note that, should the new shares sell for $15, all three parties would hold $85 of value. The public, at one extreme, has $70 of cash and one new share worth $15. Management, at the other end, holds 5 2/3 shares also worth $85.

Should the new shares sell for more than $15 each, management (and the PAYSOP) would be the greatest beneficiary. For example, if the new shares sold for $20, management's 5 2/3 new shares would be worth $113.33, while the public's combination of $70 plus 1 new share would sum to a value of just $90. Should the new shares sell for less than $15 each, management would be the greatest loser. This aggressive payoff schedule indicated that, after the recapitalization, management would hold a Henley-like leveraged equity stake in FMC. FMC's message to investors sounds a lot like Henley's, too. By voluntarily taking on a leveraged equity stake, management is expressing its commitment to, and confidence in, creating at least $85 worth of share value out of a company that was selling for just $70 a share at the time of recapitalization.

The message was heeded by the market: FMC's shares rose from a price of $70 to just over $85 as the recapitalization was first announced. Before the deal was sealed, however, FMC's shares nearly touched $100. Apparently Ivan Boesky, as a result of sound financial analysis (and some inside information), was buying FMC shares. To mollify the public and turn back Boesky's threat, management subsequently had to increase the public's cash portion to $80.

With nearly 25 million shares outstanding, the recapitalization increased FMC's total market value by $750 million ($30 price increase × 25 million shares), an increase in value that is net of $60 million in costs incurred and fees paid to professional advisors.

This remarkable appreciation in value (Table 1) can be attributed largely to the benefits of debt financing:
■ Operating profits for the foreseeable future will be sheltered almost entirely from corporate taxation;
■ With discretionary cash flow dedicated to debt service the risk of an unproductive reinvestment has been eliminated; and
■ Management and employees have greater incentives to perform, and more obvious penalties for failure.

Just how much debt financing was used? Gulp!! To finance the cash payments, FMC became *very* highly leveraged. In fact, debt initially increased from 25 percent to over 125 percent of combined debt and equity capital. Because the cash paid to investors handily exceeded the book value of FMC's common shares, the company emerged from the recapitalization with a negative accounting net worth. (Not to worry, however, because market capitalization exceeded $700 million.) How is it possible that such astounding leverage could be serviced?

First, FMC announced that the new shares would not pay dividends. By conserving cash that otherwise would flow to its shareholders, FMC augmented its ability to retire debt. Nontax-deductible dividends were converted to fully-deductible interest payments. But far more important than dividend retention is the fact that every important measure of corporate health, except growth, improved after the recapitalization.

The carrot of incentives and the stick of potential bankruptcy spurred FMC's management and employees to exceptional performances. Widening profit margins and a more efficient management of working capital improved profitability. Free cash flow, the single best indicator of ability to service debt, exploded. The combination of slower growth and improved profitability opened the floodgates on the discretionary cash generated to pay down debt. The money that FMC disgorged will pour back into our economy as investment in promising ventures.

An additional appeal of leveraged cash-outs is that they avoid many of the ethical complications of LBOs. In a leveraged buyout, management benefits richly if the value of the company can be increased beyond the price offered to buy out the public shareholders. This creates a conflict between management's responsibility to shareholders and its self-interest. There is no way to get around the suspicion that management steals the company from the public shareholders in an LBO that subsequently performs well.

With a leveraged cash-out, however, investors participate in the value created after the recapitalization because they retain shares in the sponsoring company. Moreover, a shareholder could, if he wished, duplicate management's stake. In the FMC transaction, for example, the $70 of cash that a public shareholder received could be used to purchase 4 2/3 new shares (at the intrinsic share price of $15). When those new shares are added to the one new share issued in the exchange, the public shareholder, like the insiders, would hold 5 2/3 new shares.

A public shareholder also could reverse the recapitalization. By using the cash received from the exchange offer to buy a representative slice of the debt issued by FMC to finance the exchange offer, a shareholder could restore the claim that shareholders held on FMC's earnings before the recapitalization. Now, however, FMC's original common equity is divided into a lower risk-for-lower expected reward, interest-earning claim (the junk debt) and a higher risk-for-higher expected reward, nondividend-paying claim (the new FMC shares). Such a financial restructuring cannot change the risk in the underlying assets, nor can it force a shareholder, or society at large, to bear more risk.

The benefit of hindsight indicates that joining management, and thus maximizing one's equity stake in FMC, would have been a wise decision. Since the recapitalization, the new FMC shares have sold for as much as $60, giving the 5 2/3 new shares a peak value of $340, certainly not a bad return for a stock that sold for $70 before the recapitalization was announced.

FMC did not escape the October, 1987 market meltdown, however. FMC's common shares by late 1987 were selling for approximately $30 each, at roughly half their $60 peak. The S&P 500 had dropped a mere 30% during that interval. Does this disparity challenge the wisdom of FMC's leveraged cash-out? Not at all.

FMC's shares fell further in value than the S&P 500 because of their greater financial risk, making the comparison grossly unfair. Investment risk must be the same in order to meaningfully compare return outcomes. To properly compare how well FMC's public shareholders would have done with and without the leveraged cash-out, we must assume that the cash proceeds received in the exchange offer were used to purchase FMC's junk debt. Comparing the return on $70 worth of FMC junk debt (actually $80 worth with the revised offer) and one new FMC share with the S&P 500 is a fair measure of the wisdom of the leveraged cash-out. Because FMC's debt declined in value only modestly after the market crash, the risk-adjusted performance of FMC actually was better than the S&P 500—an endorsement of the leveraged cash-out.

That is all well and good for the fortunate public shareholders. But what about management who, by design of the exchange offer, were forced to hold just new shares in FMC? Of course the crash hurt them more than shareholders who could place the cash proceeds from the exchange offer into lower risk investments. But do not weep for management. Even the marked-down $30 value for the new shares they hold is 50% more than their initial $20 value. Moreover, the 5 2/3 shares given to management in the recapitalization are still worth nearly $170, a 140 percent gain over the original $70 share value.

The Ultimate Incentive

The most equity-like compensation on the risk map provides no wage, pension, profit sharing or ESOP. Indeed, the last step is the Lee Iaccoca plan: a $1 salary combined with a load of stock options. Terrific incentive, Lee. How one eats before your ship comes in, we can only surmise.

APPENDIX: QUALIFYING THE TAX BENEFITS OF ESOPs

An ESOP is much the same as compensating employees with cash and then requiring them to purchase an equivalent value of company common shares (all without imposing a current tax on the employee, a benefit common to all qualified retirement plans). A company's contributions to an ESOP are tax-deductible because they are a real compensation expense of the firm. The fact that the compensation is converted into company stock does not diminish its cost, nor does the fact that the company's liability to repurchase those shares may be deferred until the distant future. The expected present value cost to repurchase shares allocated to employees, no matter how far off, is, by definition, the current value of those shares.

A leveraged ESOP is just an ordinary ESOP coupled with an up-front, debt-financed share repurchase. A leveraged ESOP entails much the same thing as:
- first, compensating employees with cash (a tax-deductible expense);
- next, requiring them to use the cash to buy company common shares of an equivalent value from the ESOP; and
- lastly, making the ESOP apply the proceeds from the stock sale to pay down its debt (a nontax-deductible financial event).

By sleight of hand, many ESOP peddlers would have their clients erroneously associate the benefit of deducting the ESOP contribution with the repayment of the debt when in fact, the tax-deduction arises from incurring a compensation expense—the granting of shares to employees. Despite appearances, it simply is not cheaper to amortize debt through an ESOP than it is through the company itself.

In truth, the benefits of a leveraged ESOP over an ordinary one are that money can be borrowed at a lower interest rate (but not that principal can be serviced more cheaply). It permits the company to contribute to the ESOP each year up to $60,000 per employee instead of $30,000, and maybe one more thing.

In the Tax Reform Act of 1986, Congress enacted a change in the treatment of dividends that many leveraged ESOP boosters claim is a sure-fire benefit. In fact, it may or may not be helpful, depending upon the circumstances.

A company can now deduct from its taxable income dividends that it pays on common shares held by an ESOP, but only if the ESOP trustee uses those dividends to repay an ESOP loan, an action that frees up additional shares to be allocated to employees.

If the dividends used to repay the ESOP loan come from shares that the ESOP already had allocated to employees, there is a real benefit. In such a case, the company gets a tax-deduction without incurring an additional expense and without harm to the plan participants. The cash dividends that would have been credited to the participants' accounts are simply transformed into company common shares of equivalent value. No harm done, but the company gets a tax-deduction merely for effecting this bit of financial alchemy.

If, however, the dividends used to repay the ESOP loan come from shares held in escrow—that is, not yet allocated by the ESOP to plan participants—there is an offsetting cost. In such a case, the shares allocated to employees represent additional compensation. The tax deduction the company receives on the dividend is only consistent with the expense incurred in granting employees new shares to which they would not otherwise be entitled. Unless the added expense is offset by the benefits arising from improved employee incentive, or from reductions in other forms of compensation, using such dividends to repay the ESOP loan may turn out to be an expensive way for a company to amortize debt.

Another problem many ESOP aficionados gloss over is that, no matter which of the preceding cases applies, tax-deductible dividends can lead to one of life's most unpleasant experiences—a minimum tax liability. By law, one-half of the difference between taxable income (after certain adjustments) and reported income is a tax preference item subject to a minimum tax of 20%. Deductible for tax but not book purposes, ESOP dividend payments give rise to just such a tax preference, and a potential minimum tax assessment. The Lord giveth and the Lord taketh away.

The IRS reserves one of the most generous of an ESOP's tax benefits for the owners of private companies. They are entitled to sell shares to an ESOP and to defer paying a tax on any gain (provided that the proceeds are reinvested in domestic companies and the ESOP owns at least 30% of the company stock after the sale). This tax code provision enables the owners of private corporations to cash out and diversify their accumulated wealth without incurring a current tax, while providing for the eventual transfer of the shares to company employees—a nifty benefit to be sure.

In addition, private companies can establish ESOPs for employees of individual business units within the overall company, a benefit that generally is denied to public firms. Under such a plan, the ESOP trustee uses cash contributed by a subsidiary to acquire the subsidiary's shares (either existing shares held by the parent or new shares issued by the sub) and allocates those shares to the plan participants, giving them an incentive to improve the performance and value of the particular business unit that they directly influence.

A public company can establish an ESOP for a subsidiary unit only if the unit is taken public through an offering of a partial interest. In the absence of such a partial public offering, a public company is required to use parent company stock in an ESOP, a restriction that makes it difficult for a public company to forge a link between pay and performance as strong as that available to employees of private firms.

HOW STOCK-SWAP MERGERS AFFECT SHAREHOLDER (AND BONDHOLDER) WEALTH: MORE EVIDENCE OF THE VALUE OF CORPORATE "FOCUS"

by Lance A. Nail,
University of Alabama-Birmingham,
William L. Megginson,
University of Oklahoma, and
Carlos Maquieira,
University of Chile

R esearch on mergers and acquisitions (M&A) has long been one of the most intriguing fields of study in corporate finance. Mergers or acquisitions represent major corporate investment decisions—for many companies the largest investments of capital they are likely to consider. Thus, managers who aim to grow their companies in ways that increase shareholder value should be interested in research that aims to distinguish value-increasing from value-reducing transactions.

As in most events, there are three possible outcomes in a corporate merger—win, lose, or draw. A win results if a merger yields a net increase in investor wealth, a loss if there are net wealth losses, and a draw if there are no significant wealth changes.

However, the wealth effects of a merger are not the same across all securityholders. And, in many cases, there are likely to be redistributions *among* security classes. For example, both observation and considerable evidence suggest that the acquired firm's shareholders are the largest (immediate) beneficiaries of corporate mergers. This raises the possibility that although common stockholders as a group may experience net wealth gains as a result of merger, the gains may all accrue to the stockholders of the acquired company while the stockholders of the acquirer suffer losses. Another possibility is that, particularly in conglomerate merg-

ers, bondholders could experience wealth gains at the expense of stockholders.

In order to learn more about these wealth effects on corporate stockholders and bondholders, we conducted a study of 260 "pure" stock-swap mergers over the period 1963-1996 that was published in a recent issue of the *Journal of Financial Economics.*[1] Besides testing the existing theories of merger-related wealth changes and redistributions, the empirical tests described in that study also allowed us to examine a number of other factors that we found to have a significant impact on these wealth changes and their distributions among securityholders.

In this article, we summarize the results of our published study. Stated in brief, our findings suggest that the key to explaining the distribution of net wealth gains or losses generated in mergers is the degree of similarity or "relatedness" between the merging companies' businesses. Mergers and acquisitions of "related" companies tend to produce significant wealth increases—not only for all securityholders as a group, but for the acquiring firm's stockholders, and *even* for the bondholders as well. By contrast, conglomerate mergers tend to add little value to securityholders as a group, and appear to be a fairly reliable way of reducing the value of the acquiring company's shares.

1. See our article, "Wealth Creation versus Wealth Redistributions in Pure Stock-for-Stock Mergers," *Journal of Financial Economics*, Vol. 48 (April 1998), pp. 3-33. Interested readers are referred to this article for results that go beyond those presented in the current article. Included in these results are a more detailed analysis of stockholder-bondholder wealth redistributions, preferred stockholder wealth effects, convertible securityholder wealth effects, and the value of the conversion options on convertible securities.

THEORIES OF MERGER-RELATED WEALTH CHANGES AND DISTRIBUTIONS

In the late 1960s and early 1970s, academic theories on how mergers affected security values were an extension of portfolio theory from the area of investments. Viewing corporations as portfolios of business units, academics posited that combining businesses with less-than-perfectly correlated cash flows would create conglomerate corporations with less volatile cash flows than single-business corporations.[2] The lower risk associated with this corporate diversification was theorized to create value through "financial synergies"—that is, reductions in borrowing costs derived from diversifying conglomerate mergers. These lower borrowing costs were supposed to reduce a firm's cost of capital and make capital investments more profitable. Sources of financial synergies include lower required returns on debt due to the diversified firm's less risky cash flows and the presence of "internal capital markets"—the ability of a conglomerate to finance cash-poor business units with capital from cash-rich units without having to pay underwriting fees to financial intermediaries for raising capital. Because the volatility of cash flows decreases with greater diversification, financial synergies were expected to be greatest in conglomerate mergers.[3]

In the late 1970s and early '80s, however, academic economists began to question whether value was actually being created by financial synergies and conglomerate mergers. The new thinking suggested that the only type of synergy that could create net wealth was an "operational synergy"—an increase in operating efficiency due, say, to economies of scale or scope, or to the elimination of redundant resources. In contrast to financial synergies, operational synergies are expected to be a *positive*, not negative, function of the degree of similarity between the merging firms' businesses. Thus, operational synergies were expected to be greatest in mergers of corporations in the same or similar line of business.

This theory also suggested that if no operational synergies were expected from the combination, then there would be no net increase in wealth and hence any gains experienced by one group of securityholders must be the result of losses suffered by another group. In such cases, there would be no creation of wealth, just a *redistribution* of it. In the case of conglomerate mergers, for example, bondholders are expected to experience gains as the value of their bonds increases with a decrease in the required rate of return. But since there are no net wealth gains expected in conglomerate mergers, the gains of bondholders must be redistributed wealth from stockholders.[4]

The wealth redistribution theory was further expounded with an analysis of the differing effect of changes in risk on the fixed and residual claims on the cash flows of a corporation. In companies with material amounts of debt financing, fixed claims (bondholders) benefit from reductions in risk while the value of residual claims (common stockholders) falls.[5] Viewed in this way, financial synergies that reduce risk and benefit fixed claims are merely wealth redistributions from stockholders to bondholders.

More recent empirical evidence on the financial performance of conglomerates has cast further doubt on the benefits of corporate diversification. A series of academic studies has revealed that diversified companies trade at a significant discount in value relative to single-business (or "focused") firms and that many of the hostile takeovers of the 1980s were motivated by the value that could be created by breaking up inefficient conglomerates into more efficient, focused companies.[6]

---

2. For development of this argument, see Haim Levy and Marshal Sarnat, "Diversification, Portfolio Analysis and the Uneasy Case for Conglomerate Mergers," *Journal of Finance* 25 (1970), pp. 795-802.

3. For further elaboration on the concept of financial synergies, see Wilbur Lewellen, "A Pure Financial Rationale for the Conglomerate Merger," *Journal of Finance* 26 (1971), pp. 521-537. See also J.F. Weston and S.K. Mansinghka, "Tests of the Efficiency Performance in Conglomerate Firms," *Journal of Finance* 26 (1971), pp. 919-936.

4. See Robert Higgins and Lawrence Schall, "Corporate Bankruptcy and Conglomerate Merger," *Journal of Finance* 30 (1975), pp. 93-113.

5. Bondholders, with a fixed priority claim on the firm's cash flows, realize wealth gains when the probability of receiving their claim increases with a reduction in volatility. Stockholders, as residual claimants, receive the cash flows remaining after fixed claims have been paid. Since the residual claim receives no cash flows until the fixed claims are paid, common stockholders actually benefit from an increase in volatility. Risk reduction should lower the probability of a downturn in cash flows, but it limits the upside potential as well. Because stockholders can

benefit only from the receipt of greater cash flows beyond the fixed claims, risk reduction that limits upside potential can only reduce stockholder wealth.

This extension of the wealth redistribution theory may be found in Dan Galai and Ronald Masulis, "The Option Pricing Model and the Risk Factor of Stock," *Journal of Financial Economics* 3 (1976), pp. 53-81. Galai and Masulis actually use option pricing theory to demonstrate how the residual claim of a firm resembles a call option on the firm which benefits from an increase in volatility.

6. These studies include Paul Healy, Krishna Palepu, and Richard Ruback, "Does Corporate Performance Improve After Mergers?" *Journal of Financial Economics* 31 (1992), pp. 135-176; Larry Lang and Rene Stulz, "Tobin's Q, Corporate Diversification, and Firm Performance," *Journal of Political Economy,* 102 (1994), pp. 1248-1280; Philip Berger and Eli Ofek, "Diversification's Effect on Firm Value," *Journal of Financial Economics* 37 (1995), pp. 39-65; Robert Comment and Gregg Jarrell, "Corporate Focus and Stock Returns," *Journal of Financial Economics* 37 (1995), pp. 67-87 ; and Sanjai Bhagat, Andre Shleifer, and Robert Vishny, "Hostile Takeovers in the 1980s: The Return to Corporate Specialization," *Brookings Papers on Economic Activity,* 1990, pp. 1-72.

In light of these more recent findings, we devised a number of statistical tests of the existing theories of merger-related wealth changes to determine whether financial synergies exist, and, if so, the extent to which they really represent redistributions from stockholders to bondholders. Additionally, we tested the wealth effects of other factors such as changes in leverage, stock variance, and regulatory forces on all securityholders. In the sections that follow, we describe the research design and results of our study.

SAMPLE SELECTION AND DATA SOURCES

Stock-swap mergers offer an ideal opportunity to test for wealth creation and wealth redistributions because, unlike other kinds of mergers, there are no cash outflows or asset changes. For this reason, if the merger itself has no effect on the market's assessments, the sum of the market values of the securities of the newly merged company should equal the sum of the market values of the two merged firms' securities (adjusted for overall market movements in financial asset values) just prior to the announcement of the merger. This in turn implies that, if net wealth is created by the market's expectation of either operating or financial synergies, that wealth increase can be measured directly as the increase in the summed market values of the combined firm's securities.

We began our study by compiling a sample of all 100% stock-for-stock mergers initiated between January 1963 and December 1995 and completed by March 1996 between companies listed on either the New York or American Stock Exchanges. (By 100% stock, we meant that only common or preferred stock could have been used as payment to the target firm's shareholders.) We excluded all "partial" mergers from our sample—those in which less than 100% of the target was owned by the acquiring firm after the merger. Also, we eliminated all mergers from our sample for which there was a major "contaminating" event—such as announcement of another merger, a major asset sale or purchase, or a large security issue—during the period from two months before the merger announcement date through two months after the effective date.

Data for this research came from several sources. Merger transactions and their announced and effective dates were obtained from the Securities Data Corporation (SDC) database as well as from delistings

from the Center for Research in Security Prices (CRSP) tapes. Capital structure, security issue, and line of business data were gathered from the appropriate *Moody's Manuals*. Common stock information was obtained from CRSP and bond data was collected from either the *Moody's Bond Record* or *Standard & Poor's Bond Guides*.

The final sample contained 260 mergers, involving the common stocks of the 520 firms included in the sample. We classified all 260 mergers as either "conglomerate" or "related" based on the primary line of business listed for each company in the last annual edition of the *Moody's Manual* preceding the announcement date of the merger. If the merging firms had the same primary line of business, then the merger was classified as "related." But if the two firms had different primary lines, then the merger was classified as conglomerate.

Using this method of classification, our final merger sample was almost evenly divided between conglomerate and "related" mergers. Of the 260 mergers, 135 were classified as conglomerate and 125 as "related." As shown in Table 1, the fraction of conglomerate mergers declines steadily over time. And this finding is, of course, consistent with the more recent empirical evidence on the trend away from corporate diversification.

METHOD OF MEASURING CHANGES IN SECURITY VALUES

The aims of our study required us to devise a means of calculating the net wealth effect of mergers on the publicly traded securities of the merging companies. One difficulty in calculating these wealth effects is that the length of time it takes to complete a merger ranged from 11 to 31 months for the mergers in our sample. We thus had to develop a method of computing valuation changes that allowed adjustments both for overall market movements and for changes in the number of securities outstanding over the appropriate holding period.

Our principal method for determining merger-related value changes was to generate "predicted" post-merger valuations for all of the securities of the merged firm. These calculations required us to consider and track the following:

(1) the pre-merger valuations of each outstanding security issue of the merging firms;

(2) overall market movements in matching asset prices during the "event period" (two months before

Mergers and acquisitions of "related" companies tend to produce significant wealth increases—not only for all securityholders as a group, but for the acquiring firm's stockholders, and *even* for the bondholders as well.

	Year	Total mergers	Conglomerate mergers	Nonconglomerate mergers
TABLE 1 DISTRIBUTION OF SAMPLE MERGERS BY TYPE AND BY YEAR OF ANNOUNCEMENT[a]	1963	9	6	3
	1964	10	7	3
	1965	14	6	8
	1966	18	13	5
	1967	23	14	9
	1968	21	10	11
	1969	11	7	4
	1970	16	9	7
	1971	2	1	1
	1972	9	7	2
	1973	10	3	7
	1974	5	3	2
	1975	4	2	2
	1976	6	2	4
	1977	14	8	6
	1978	3	1	2
	1979	5	4	1
	1980	6	5	1
	1981	8	5	3
	1982	8	5	3
	1983	5	3	2
	1984	5	3	2
	1985	4	1	3
	1986	8	2	6
	1987	4	1	3
	1988	1	0	1
	1989	5	1	4
	1990	4	1	3
	1991	2	0	2
	1992	3	1	2
	1993	5	1	4
	1994	6	3	3
	1995	6	0	6
	Total	260	135	125

a. Distribution of pure stock-swap mergers in the sample, by year of initial announcement and classification as either conglomerate or nonconglomerate.

the merger announcement to two months after the effective date of completion);

(3) any cash distributions made to securityholders during the event period; and

(4) any changes in the number of outstanding securities in a class due to conversions, calls, sinking fund payments, or open-market repurchases.

These predicted values, once again, were the values of each security that one would expect if the merger were expected by the market to have no wealth effects.

Once predicted values were computed for each security issue, the next step was to compute the *valuation prediction errors* (or "VPE") for that security by subtracting the predicted post-merger value from the actual post-merger value. The VPE, which can be interpreted as the cumulative change in the security's value attributable to the merger, is computed in essentially the same manner for all security classes, and can thus easily be aggregated by class, firm, or merger. The prediction method used for calculating the changes in the value of each security is described below.

Generating Predicted Values for Merged-Firm Common Stock

Merged-firm common stock is a unique security in that at least one (and sometimes both) of the pre-merger common stocks outstanding ceases to exist after the merger effective date—either the acquiring firm's common stock continues to trade after the merger, or a new class of common stock of the merged firm begins trading. In either case, the single common stock class resulting from the merger should be equal to the market-adjusted summed value of the merging firms' common stocks, plus any wealth transfers from other securityholders or net wealth gains.

Because we were unable to find reliable exchange ratios for all of our sample mergers transacted before 1977, we calculated VPEs only for the common stock of the merged firm. But for mergers completed from 1977 through 1996, we were able to compute separate VPEs for the common stock of *both* the acquiring and target firms prior to the merger, as well as for the merged firm's equity. In measuring these VPEs, we adjusted the "raw" equity returns (including dividends and other distributions) both for the risk of each security and for market movements over the event period (which, again, runs from two months prior to the merger announcement until two months after the deal closes).[7]

Generating Predicted Values for Corporate Bonds

In addition to the merging companies' stock prices, we also collected prices and issue terms for 535 publicly traded bond issues by the 520 firms involved in these 260 mergers. For each individual bond issue in the sample, we found the U.S. Treasury bond outstanding at that time that most closely matched that bond in maturity and coupon rate. We then subtracted the matched T-bond's yield to maturity (YTM) from the corporate bond's YTM to compute *a pre-merger yield spread* for that bond. We assumed that, unless the merger itself has had an effect on the value of the bond, the pre-merger yield spread should remain unchanged over time, even

though the level and shape of the yield curve can change. This assumption allowed us to compute an expected YTM value for each corporate bond after the effective merger date based on the observed value of its matching Treasury bond at that time. The expected YTM in turn enabled us to compute the expected post-merger price of the bond using the terms of the issue (remaining maturity, coupon rate) and a standard internal rate of return bond pricing formula. The VPE for each bond—again, the change in value that can be attributed solely to the merger—was then computed after adjusting for bond redemptions, conversions, and sinking fund payments.

EMPIRICAL RESULTS

Table 2 presents our VPE results for the securities in our sample categorized by acquirer and target and, more important, by whether the merger was classified as conglomerate or related. Panel A presents common stock results, Panel B presents the effects on corporate bonds, and Panel C shows our measure of net total wealth gains for all securityholders.

The first notable result is that, in related mergers, common stockholders as a group (that is, acquiring firm and target shareholders) experienced average VPEs that were significantly higher (8.58% versus 3.28%) than shareholders in conglomerate mergers. The median difference (8.55% versus 1.98%) was even larger. Further, a statistically significant 66.4% of the related mergers resulted in positive overall VPEs, while an insignificant 56.3% of the conglomerate mergers yielded positive results. These findings are consistent with theoretical models predicting that new wealth will be created only in related mergers through the creation of operating synergies.

As noted above, for the 102 mergers occurring after 1976, we were able to compute VPEs for common stockholders of acquiring and target firms individually. These results strongly suggest that acquiring firm stockholders benefit in related mergers, while acquiring firm stockholders in conglomerate mergers suffer losses. The differences in mean (6.14% versus –4.79%) and median (4.64% versus

---

7. To adjust for market movements over our event period, we computed an index value of the CRSP value-weighted return (including all distributions) over the period beginning two months before the merger announcement through two months after the merger effective date. We then calculated the predicted merged-firm equity value as the sum of the risk-adjusted product of this index number and the equity value of each of the merging firms. The returns of the merged firm were adjusted for risk using a weighted-average beta of the acquirer and the target.

TABLE 2
VALUATION PREDICTION
ERRORS FOR SAMPLE
MERGERS[a]

SECURITY DESCRIPTION Sample or subsample	Number of Observations	Mean VPE	Median VPE	Percent Positive
PANEL A: COMMON STOCKS				
Conglomerate mergers	135	3.28%	1.98%	56.3%
	(1.45)	(1.01)	(1.48)	
Acquiring firms	47[b]	−4.79	−7.36	36.2
	(−1.79)	(−1.78)	(−1.97**)	
Target firms	47[b]	41.65	38.79	83.0
	(6.55*)	(5.04*)	(6.02*)	
Related mergers	125	8.58%	8.55%	66.4%
	(3.75*)	(3.79*)	(3.88*)	
Acquiring firms	55	6.14	4.64	61.8
	(2.27*)	(2.48*)	(1.80)	
Target firms	55	38.08	24.33	80.0
	(4.94*)	(4.67*)	(5.56*)	
PANEL B: CORPORATE BONDS				
Conglomerate mergers	253	0.44%	0.28%	53.0%
	(1.45)	(1.37)	(0.96)	
Acquiring firms	222	0.33	0.24	52.3
	(0.73)	(1.31)	(0.90)	
Target firms	31	1.22	3.89	51.6
	(1.44)	(1.55)	(0.18)	
Related mergers	282	1.44%	0.82%	59.6%
	(3.00*)	(3.65*)	(3.28*)	
Acquiring firms	189	1.90	1.39	64.0
	(3.18*)	(3.55*)	(4.02*)	
Target firms	93	0.50	0.24	50.5
	(0.63)	(0.58)	(0.10)	
PANEL C: NET WEALTH GAINS (COMBINED FIRM, ALL SECURITIES)				
Conglomerate mergers	135	3.08%	1.14%	48.2%
	(1.61)	(0.94)	(0.28)	
Related mergers	125	6.82	6.79	64.0
	(3.69*)	(3.65*)	(3.26*)	

a. Valuation prediction errors (VPEs) are computed as the percentage difference from predicted market value for equity and debt securities from two months before the merger announcement date through two months after the effective date of merger for individual securities. Predicted market values are computed based on overall market movements in the same classes of securities over the measurement period (t-2 months to t+2 months), and t-statistics (mean and percent positive) and Wilcoxon statistics (median) are presented in parentheses. This table presents mean and median VPEs, and percent positive statistics for 260 pure stock-swap mergers, classified according to whether the combination is a conglomerate or a nonconglomerate merger.
b. Acquirer and target stockholder VPEs based on merger exchange ratio. Data available only after 1976.
*Indicates significance at the 1% level.

−7.36%) VPEs, and in the fraction of positive VPEs (61.8% versus 36.2%), between the 55 related acquiring firms and the 47 conglomerate acquiring firms are highly significant.

We also found that the difference between combined stockholder VPEs became much more pronounced after 1977. Stockholders in the 55 related mergers in this subsample experienced significantly positive mean (6.14%), median (4.64%), and percent positive (61.8%) VPEs, while stockholders in the 47 conglomerate mergers from this period earned insignificant −4.79% and −7.36% mean and median VPEs, and only 36.2% of these mergers are value-increasing. These results are consistent with the findings of more recent empirical studies that show that corporate diversification generally reduces value.

As suggested above, then, in the vast majority of cases, related mergers create significant net wealth for the combined firm's stockholders. Although most of this new wealth accrues to target firm stockholders—whose median return is about 25%—acquiring firm stockholders also experience net wealth increases—of about 6%, on average. And, because the acquirers are about 2.5 times as large as the acquired firms, on average, their smaller percentage returns represent large gains in (absolute) dollar terms.

Also consistent with a gains-sharing explanation for related mergers, such mergers appeared to add value for acquiring firms' bondholders as well. As reported in Panel B, we found that acquiring firm *bondholders* in related mergers experienced net wealth increases (of about 2%, on average)—increases that were not only statistically significant in their own right but are also generally greater than for their counterparts in conglomerate mergers.

What is more surprising about the results reported in Panel B, however, is the scarcity of any evidence of wealth transfers between stockholders and bondholders. In particular, the bond VPEs in conglomerate mergers were not reliably different from zero. Thus, the only kind of wealth redistribution for which this part of our study found evidence were transfers from acquiring firm *stockholders* to target firm stockholders in conglomerate mergers.

Panel C of Table 2 presents the summed VPEs for all of the securities (debt and equity) of the merged firms, which is our measure of the net wealth gains created by stock-swap mergers. Given the individual security results, it was not surprising that we found mean (6.82%) and median (6.79%) net wealth gains for related mergers that were significantly larger than the mean (3.08%) and median (1.14%) gains for conglomerate mergers. Furthermore, fewer than half (48.2%) of the conglomerate mergers created net wealth gains for securityholders, while almost two-thirds (64.0%) of related mergers were wealth-creating.[8]

Regression Analysis of VPE Results

In the tests described thus far, we found far less evidence of wealth redistributions than financial theory might have led us to expect. To examine the possibility of wealth transfers more carefully, we performed a series of four regression analyses—one for each security class. One set of regressions examined the combined sample of all common stocks, the next two analyzed the acquirer and target stocks separately, and a fourth regression examined the full sample of corporate bonds.

There were three factors that were explored in each of the four regressions. The first was represented by a dummy variable (*Related*) used to proxy for the type of merger, where one stands for related and zero stands for conglomerate merger. The second (*Pre-Williams*) and third (*Post-1980*) variables were time-related dummy variables intended to determine if there were differing wealth effects due to regulatory changes implemented after passage of the Williams Act in 1968 and also after the beginning of the Reagan administration in 1981. These two events marked important regulatory shifts in M&A history. The Williams Act was implemented as an attempt to protect takeover targets in tender offers and is believed by many academics to have limited the aggregate net wealth gains experienced by all securityholders. The Reagan administration ushered in a more lenient antitrust policy, which increased the probability that related mergers would receive antitrust clearance.

Variables four through six were used in the regression analyses of individual common stock and bond issues. Variable four (*Target*) is a dummy variable taking a value of one if the security in question is issued by a target firm and zero if it is an acquiring firm security issue. As before, we also performed separate regressions on acquiring and target firm common stock (but not bond) VPEs, since there is overwhelming evidence that target firm stockholders earn significantly higher merger-related returns than do acquiring firm stockholders.

The fifth variable, change in leverage (*Leverage*), measures the absolute percentage point change in market value leverage that the securityholders of

---

8. We also examine the correlation coefficients between stockholder and bondholder returns in the two types of mergers, and find generally higher correlations in "related" transactions. The correlation between stockholder and bondholder returns in related mergers is a highly significant 0.24 (z = 2.10), while in conglomerate mergers it is an insignificant 0.13 (t = 1.20).

A CASE OF RELATED MERGER

On June 23, 1986 retailer May Department Stores announced its intent to acquire fellow retailer Associated Dry Goods in a deal valued in excess of $2 billion. Two months prior to this announcement, May had a common stock capitalization of roughly $3.4 billion and that of Associated was around $1.7 billion. At the same time, May's public debt had a market value of $442 million and Associated's was valued at $312 million.

Two months after the 69.7 million share exchange occurred in October of that year, the market capitalization of common stock of the merged firm was $6.13 billion, an amount that exceeded its risk-adjusted expected market value of $5.37 billion by over $750 million (or 14%). The summed market value of debt also exceeded the expected value of $750 million by nearly $10 million (or 1.3%). Viewed as the sum of all debt and equity securities, the market value of the merged firm was $770 million (or 12.6%) greater than the expected value. Viewed separately, May stockholders received an excess return of nearly 4%, while Associated stockholders earned 35%. May bondholders experienced a 2.78% excess gain, as compared to a loss of less than 1% for Associated bondholders.

VPE CALCULATIONS

	Acquirer	Target	Merged Firm
Name	May Department Stores	Associated Dry Goods	May Department Stores
Primary business SIC code	53	53	
COMMON STOCK INFORMATION			
Pre-merger market value	$3,359.38	$1,676.75	
Expected market value[a]	$3,582.10	$1,787.92	$5,370.02
Post-merger market value[a]	$3,716.11[b]	$2,412.61[b]	$6,128.72
Common stock $ VPE	$134.01[b]	$624.69[b]	$758.70
Common stock % VPE	3.74%	34.94%	14.13%
PUBLIC DEBT INFORMATION[c]			
Pre-merger market value	$441.81	$312.00	$753.81
Expected market value	$435.90	$314.16	$750.06
Post-merger market value	$448.00	$311.64	$759.64
Public debt $ VPE	$12.10	($2.52)	$9.58
Public debt % VPE	2.78%	−0.80%	1.27%
NET WEALTH CHANGES			
Expected market value[a]			$6,120.08
Post-merger market value[a]			$6,888.36
Total market value $ VPE			$768.28
Total market value % VPE			12.55%

a. Including any dividends paid
b. Calculated as proportional market value on the basis of the exchange ratio
c. Includes only public debt for which market data was available

a given company are expected to experience. Since no rational investor would willingly trade a less-heavily-indebted financial claim for a more-indebted claim on an asset of identical value, a merger-induced increase in leverage should decrease VPEs for all security classes. To illustrate how this lever-age change was computed, consider an acquiring firm with a 50% debt-to-total capital ratio (with all values in market value terms) and total capital of $1 billion, that acquires a firm with total capital of $500 million and a debt-to-capital ratio of 20%. The resulting combined firm will have a leverage ratio

A CASE OF CONGLOMERATE MERGER

Electric utility Pacific Lighting first announced its acquisition of drugstore chain Thrifty on March 27, 1986 and completed the acquisition on August 1, 1986. Pre-merger market values for Pacific common stocks and public bonds were $1.93 billion and $578 million, respectively. Thrifty had a pre-merger common stock capitalization of $480 million with no publicly-traded debt.

The post-merger common stock value of the merged firm was $2.9 billion—an excess of $190 million (or 7%) over the expected value of $2.71

billion. Bondholders suffered a yield-adjusted loss of $44 million (or –7%) as the actual market value of $588 million was less than the expected value of $632 million. Combining stock and bond values, the net wealth gain from this merger was $147 million (or 4.4%). However, this net-wealth-creating merger exhibits the wealth-redistributive effect of conglomerate mergers. All of the common stock gains accrued to Thrifty shareholders ($307 million or 57%) and were partly the result of losses suffered by Pacific stockholders (–$116 million or –5%).

VPE CALCULATIONS

	Acquirer	Target	Merged Firm
Name	Pacific Lighting	Thrifty Corp	Pacific Lighting
Primary business SIC code	49	59	
Common Stock Information			
Pre-merger market value	$1,934.63	$480.00	
Expected market value[a]	$2,173.55	$539.28	$2,712.83
Post-merger market value[a]	$2,057.08[b]	$846.72[b]	$2,903.80
Common stock $ VPE	($116.47)[b]	$307.44[b]	$190.97
Common stock % VPE	–5.36%	57.01%	7.04%
Public Debt Information[c]			
Pre-merger market value	$578.25	—	$578.25
Expected market value	$631.69	—	$631.69
Post-merger market value	$587.75	—	$587.75
Public debt $ VPE	($43.94)	—	($43.94)
Public debt % VPE	–6.96%	—	–6.96%
Net Wealth Changes			
Expected market value[a]			$3,344.52
Post-merger market value[a]			$3,491.55
Total market value $ VPE			$147.03
Total market value % VPE			4.40%

a. Including any dividends paid
b. Calculated as proportional market value on the basis of the exchange ratio
c. Includes only public debt for which market data was available

of 40%, so the securities of the bidding firm will experience a ten percentage point decrease (from 50% to 40%) in leverage, while the target firm's securities will experience a 20 percentage point increase.

Variable six, change in variance (*Variance*), was the absolute percentage point change in stock

variance resulting from a merger and the key test variable for the financial synergy argument. If net-wealth-creating financial synergies do exist, then greater decreases in stock variance should lead to wealth gains for both stockholders and bondholders. Therefore, theories favoring the wealth-creation potential of financial synergies predict a significantly

Fewer than half of the conglomerate mergers created net wealth gains for all securityholders as a group, while almost two-thirds of related mergers were wealth-creating.

TABLE 3 ■ REGRESSION ANALYSES OF VALUATION PREDICTION ERRORS FOR INDIVIDUAL SECURITY CLASSES AND FOR NET WEALTH GAINS OF THE MERGED FIRM SECURITIES FOR SAMPLE FIRMS[a]

Security Grouping	Number of Obs.	Intercept	Related Merger Dummy	Pre-Williams Dummy	Post-1980 Dummy	Target Dummy	Leverage	Variance	Adj. R^2	Overall F
PANEL A: COMMON STOCKS										
Full Sample	260	0.031 (1.35)	0.062 (2.41)**	−0.007 (−0.24)	−0.019 (−0.62)	—	—	—	0.011	1.96
Subsample of Mergers with Exchange Ratios	204	0.037 (0.55)	0.080 (1.02)	—	−0.083 (−1.34)	0.381 (4.26)*	−0.231 (−1.06)	3.289 (0.72)	0.207	11.58*
■ Acquiring Firm	102	0.032 (0.80)	0.080 (2.01)**	—	−0.065 (−1.49)	—	−0.510 (−1.74)***	5.099 (0.58)	0.034	1.88
■ Target Firm	102	0.436 (3.42)*	−0.021 (−0.19)	—	−0.091 (−0.74)	—	−0.201 (−0.63)	3.247 (0.51)	−0.025	0.39
PANEL B: CORPORATE BONDS										
Full Sample	535	0.012 (1.59)	0.020 (2.80)*	−0.136 (−1.43)	−0.019 (−2.08)**	0.002 (0.17)	−0.135 (−2.34)**	−0.635 (−0.77)	0.019	2.65*
PANEL C: NET WEALTH GAINS										
Full Sample	260	0.028 (1.38)	0.069 (2.68)*	−0.012 (−0.31)	−0.026 (−0.81)	—	—	—	0.017	2.51*

a. Ordinary least squares regressions in which the dependent variable is the valuation prediction error computed for each security of the merging firms and the dependent variables are a measure of the expected change in variance of the merged firm's stock return (Variance); the expected change in firm leverage (Leverage), and a series of dummy variables proxying for whether the merger is a related combination (Related), whether the merger occurred prior to the implementation date of the Williams Act in July 1968 (Pre-Williams), whether the merger occurred after the Reagan Administration took power in January 1981 (Post-1980), and whether the security being examined is from a target firm (Target). Coefficient t-statistics from the regressions are presented in parentheses.
*Indicates significance at the 1% level.
**Indicates significance at the 5% level.
***Indicates significance at the 10% level.

negative relationship between changes in asset variance and net wealth changes.[9]

Common Stock Regression Results

Table 3 presents the results of these regression analyses. The first line of Table 3 shows the VPEs for the combined acquirer and target common stocks for the entire sample of 260 mergers. The only significant variable was the related merger dummy (t = 2.41), and the coefficient value implies that, on average, common stockholders earn an average of over 6 percentage points of extra return if they are involved in a related rather than a conglomerate merger. In the second set of common stock results, which analyzed individual VPEs for acquirer and target firm stocks for 102 mergers

9. Our security class regression equations were defined as follows: common stock issue *j*, in merger *i*: $VPE_{ij} = B1 \, Nonconglom + B2 \, Pre\text{-}Williams + B3 \, Post\text{-}1980 + B4 \, Target + B5 \, Leverage + B6 \, Variance$. The same equation is employed for corporate bond issue *j*, in merger *i*. The regression equation for net wealth gains (summed values of all merged firm securities) for merger *i* is defined as: $VPE_i = B1 \, Nonconglom + B2 \, Pre\text{-}Williams + B3 \, Post\text{-}1980$. The supplemental regressions were performed separately for acquiring and target firm common stocks and for bonds, and were identical to the first equation above except that the appropriate dummy variables are not included. Note that bond issues are examined using the first equation above and that the dummy variables in these equations are designed so that the base case, where all the dummy variables have zero values, corresponds to a conglomerate merger from the period July 1968 through December 1980 involving a security issued by an acquiring firm.

occurring after 1976, the only significant variable in the combined sample was the target dummy variable. Recipients of takeover bids received an average VPE of over 38%.

When acquirer and target stockholder VPEs were examined separately, the explanatory power and overall significance of each regression equation was much reduced (and the only significant coefficient in the target firm regression was the intercept). However, the acquiring firm regression revealed both a significant negative relationship between the change in leverage and acquiring firm stock VPE and a significant positive relationship between acquirer VPE and merger type. On average, a one percentage point increase in leverage for the acquiring firm's stockholders (in the merged firm) was associated with a 0.51 percentage point reduction in VPE. Being involved in a related merger yielded a VPE for acquiring firm shareholders that was nearly 8 percentage points higher than that earned by acquiring firm stockholders in conglomerate mergers. There was no significant relationship between changes in stock variance and common stock VPEs.

On balance, then, our regression results confirmed our earlier finding that related mergers create valuable operating synergies and that conglomerate mergers result in no value-creating synergies (operating or financial). They also suggested that increasing leverage decreases financial asset values. Moreover, the fact that the post-1980 variable was insignificant for both acquirers and targets suggests that the regulatory environment within which the merger occurs had no material effect on common stock returns.

Corporate Bond Regression Results

Our regression analysis of corporate bonds confirmed that increasing leverage reduced bondholder VPEs, but also provided the intriguing result that bond returns were two percentage points *higher* in related than in conglomerate mergers. It also showed that bondholder VPEs declined by 1.90 percentage points after 1980. Overall, conglomerate bondholders experienced insignificant wealth changes. These results strengthen the conclusion

that related mergers create more value than do conglomerate combinations and that merger-induced leverage increases harm all classes of securityholders.

The significant negative coefficient (–0.019, t = –2.08) on the post-1980 dummy variable suggests that the takeover market changed during the 1980s in a way that harmed bondholders. It is unclear why bondholders in stock-swap mergers experienced a post-1980 reduction in merger-related returns— particularly since we cannot identify who might have benefitted at bondholders' expense during this period (all of the other post-1980 coefficients in our security return regressions are insignificant).

As a sensitivity check, we also examined whether some of these bondholder returns could be explained by differences in bond covenants, and found some evidence that this is occurring. In a randomly selected subsample of 100 bonds,[10] we found that only three types of bond covenants were observed in at least 20% of the subsample of bonds: dividend restrictions (in 51% of the issues), minimum asset coverage ratios (24%), and restrictions on asset sale and leaseback agreements (23%).

Our regression analysis suggested that two types of covenants—asset coverage and merger restrictions—had significant effects on bondholder values. On average, the presence of a minimum asset coverage ratio covenant was associated with a nearly 5 percentage point increase in bondholder VPEs, and the presence of a covenant restricting mergers and other corporate control events increased bondholder VPEs by over 7 percentage points. These results are not surprising, since these two covenants appear to offer the best protection against merger-induced wealth redistributions from bondholders to stockholders.

Net Wealth Gains Regression Results

The final line of Table 3 shows regression results for the combined change in value for all of the securities of the 520 firms involved in the full sample of 260 stock-swap mergers over the period 1963-1996. Two key findings emerged from this analysis. First, the time period dummy variables were neither

---

10. The 100 bonds were selected from the full sample using a random number generator, and the appropriate *Moody's Manual* was consulted to determine which covenants were present at the time of the merger offer announcement. In the regression analysis of the impact of covenants described in our *JFE* paper, we also explored the frequency of call provisions, sinking funds, and specific pledges of security on bondholder VPEs. Our analysis revealed that the presence of call features, sinking funds, or specific collateral pledges did not significantly affect bondholder returns in stock-swap mergers.

statistically nor economically significant, thus suggesting that the total gains from mergers did not vary according to whether a merger occurred prior to the Williams Act of 1968, after the Reagan administration came to power in January 1981, or during the 1969 to 1980 period. Second, the significant coefficient on the related merger dummy variable indicates that these mergers typically yield a return to all investors as a group that is 7 percentage points higher than do conglomerate mergers.

SUMMARY AND CONCLUSIONS

In a study recently published in the *Journal of Financial Economics*, we examined wealth changes for all of the publicly traded debt and common equity securities of companies involved in 260 pure swap mergers completed between 1963 and 1996. In that study, we found no evidence that conglomerate stock-swap mergers created financial synergies of the kind suggested by some financial theorists and practitioners. Nor did we find that these mergers benefited bondholders more than stockholders.

Instead, we found economically and statistically significant net wealth gains for the securityholders of firms involved in same-industry, or "related," mergers, but generally insignificant net gains for securityholders in conglomerate mergers. Target firm shareholders almost always experienced net wealth gains—no surprise there—but so did the acquiring firm stockholders in related mergers. In fact, the only major class of debt and equity securityholders in corporate mergers that were systematically hurt by the transactions were the acquiring firm stockholders in conglomerate mergers—all other security holders either broke even or experienced significant wealth gains.

Taken together, then, our findings provide new (and impressive) evidence suggesting that acquiring firm managers who execute related mergers are, on average, acting in their shareholders' best interests. Our results also serve to confirm what considerable evidence, as well as casual observation, has long been telling us—namely, that conglomerate mergers systematically reduce the value of acquiring company shareholders. Perhaps the biggest surprise in our findings, however, is that the *bondholders* in related mergers appear to benefit more than bondholders in conglomerate deals. And the fact that the bondholders in related mergers experience significant wealth increases, while those in conglomerate mergers remain largely unaffected, is simply one more indicator of the dramatic differences in total value created by the two different kinds of mergers.

TO PURCHASE OR
TO POOL: DOES IT
MATTER?

*by Eric Lindenberg and
Michael P. Ross,
Salomon Smith Barney**

T he choice of accounting method in mergers and acquisitions stimulates considerable debate, which has been rekindled by the recent FASB decision to eliminate the pooling-of-interests method of accounting for acquisitions. When accounted for using the purchase method, an acquisition brings goodwill onto the acquiring firm's balance sheet, resulting in amortization of goodwill and a reduction of reported earnings—usually without the benefit of tax savings.

It is widely believed that the market values firms based on fairly rigid price/earnings (P/E) multiples, a phenomenon that would push cash flow multiples and firm value downward after a purchase accounting acquisition, even when a fair price is paid. This perception has created a preference for pooling mergers rather than purchase acquisitions.

Finance theory, however, says that amortization of goodwill should have no impact on a firm's valuation because it is merely an accounting artifact with no impact on cash flow. Thus, the nominal and relative P/E ratios of companies that have completed purchase transactions should expand to maintain appropriate firm value-to-cash flow ratios.

Because pooling puts restrictions on real corporate decisions, such as limiting stock repurchases and corporate restructuring including asset sales, it is critical to test the validity of these perceptions. Pooling will remain available for at least another year and a half—and long after that many firms contemplating acquisitions may continue to think of amortization of goodwill as imposing a real cost. The purpose of this report is to provide guidance on the impact of goodwill and amortization on P/E multiples, firm value (FV)-to-EBITDA[1] ratios, and stock prices by answering the following questions:

■ *Does the choice of "purchase" or "pooling" affect firm valuations?* The evidence from stock market valuations and from stock market reactions to transaction announcements strongly demonstrates that purchase accounting does not adversely affect firm valuations.

■ *How do differences in goodwill and its amortization affect cash flow and P/E multiples?* Balance sheet goodwill has no adverse impact on cash flow multiples. P/E multiples expand sufficiently to offset income statement amortization, leaving stock prices unaffected.

■ *Does the rate of amortization affect valuations?* The evidence suggests that differences in the rate of goodwill amortization have no adverse impact on stock prices. This point is particularly relevant in light of the possibility that the maximum life of goodwill may be reduced from 40 years to ten or 20 years.

■ *How has the market reacted to purchase and pooling acquisition announcements?* The market reacts more favorably to the announcement of purchase acquisitions than to the announcement of pooled mergers. Half of this difference is attributable to the form of consideration.

■ *Will a curtailing of pooling treatment curb M&A activity?* The market's ability to "see through" goodwill amortization suggests that when pooling ends, interest may increase in transactions that are cash accretive, yet EPS dilutive.

*The authors would like to acknowledge the valuable input, advice, and assistance of Niso Abuaf, Stephen Loebs, Bob Cotter, Wilder Fulford, John Chirico, Phil Connell, Amit Solomon, Guy Seebohm, Richard Wenzel, Aaron Cohen, Tim Kane, Colin Campbell, Carolyn Moehling, Arthur Small, and John Turney. Editorial assistance from Peg Pisani, Melissa Wohlgemuth, Kyle Webb, Celia Gong, Kim Grigas, and Maddy McKnight is also appreciated. Any remaining errors are, of course, our own.

1. Earnings before interest, taxes, depreciation, and amortization.

In light of our findings, we make the following recommendations:

■ *Equity analysts and portfolio managers* ought to base their view of a firm's fair valuation on cash earnings, not GAAP earnings. Those who do not are likely to find the market proving them wrong.

■ *Corporate development executives* should ignore goodwill and its amortization in evaluating the expected effect of an acquisition on the firm's profitability and value. Companies with no unfounded bias against purchase transactions will have a strategic advantage over their competition. This will be particularly true in the coming 18 months, as many firms focus exclusively on poolable transactions. After any elimination of the pooling-of-interests method, firms with a bias against goodwill will find themselves at a strategic disadvantage.

■ *Chief financial officers* should capitalize on the market's willingness to see past goodwill amortization by consistently breaking out amortization from depreciation on the income statement. Separate disclosure of cash EPS in press releases or, beginning in 2001, on financial statements could only be beneficial, as well. Stock buybacks and divestitures should be pursued without concern over the tainting of stock.

WHY THIS TOPIC IS MORE TIMELY THAN EVER

On April 21, the Financial Accounting Standards Board (FASB) announced, as expected, its intent to eliminate the pooling-of-interests accounting method for acquisitions, leaving the purchase method as the only accounting treatment for mergers and acquisitions. After FASB issues a final statement and solicits comments, these changes, if implemented, should take effect around January 1, 2001. The rule changes are not expected to be retroactive; pooling transactions already in progress before the deadline will likely be grandfathered.

The approaching world of purchase accounting only will not be so bad. The FASB points out that it will bring U.S. merger accounting in line with standards in the rest of the world, where pooling exists, if at all, under very stringent merger-of-equals conditions. Moreover, the board has apparently decided to reconsider its initial plan to reduce to ten years the time period over which goodwill could be amortized. In a possible concession, the FASB will likely allow for a 20-year maximum writeoff period. In addition, firms that have previously avoided stock buybacks, asset sales, and spin-offs to maintain their pooling eligibility will find themselves less constrained.

In an environment devoid of pooling, investment bankers and stock analysts will begin to appraise transactions and firm valuations overtly on the basis of cash earnings. Recently, for example, First Call announced that it would report cash earnings per share—that is, GAAP earnings per share plus goodwill amortization per share—for a group of Internet stocks. This small step is part of the growing awareness that a firm's ability to generate cash flow is what ultimately determines its value.

In fact, if the FASB does end up shortening the writeoff period for goodwill, the earnings impact of purchase acquisitions will increase at the same time as market participants are forced to focus more directly on cash earnings. Earnings per share will become an increasingly poor metric for making inter-firm comparisons, and cash earnings will become increasingly prevalent as a measure of firm performance.

Our study suggests that the market *already* looks through the impact of amortization on earnings by appropriately differentiating P/E multiples among otherwise identical firms. In addition, our research shows that, on average, the market does not react more favorably to the announcement of pooled transactions than to purchase transactions.

These results appear to contradict conventional wisdom, but after some thought they are not surprising. The notion that investors are too naive to recognize the noneconomic impact of amortization charges would imply an arbitrage opportunity for investors who purchase stocks that are near the end of their amortization periods. No such evidence has been shown to exist.

OVERVIEW OF OUR STUDIES

We have taken a two-pronged approach to investigate whether the method of accounting for M&A transactions affects valuations. First, we performed a study of the stock market reaction to transactions using pooling versus transactions using purchase accounting. Second, we analyzed the market's valuation of companies with different amounts of goodwill. The first study is aimed at identifying any short-term preferences by the market for one method of accounting over the other. The second is aimed at seeing whether the market can "see through" the method of accounting even years after the transactions creating goodwill were completed (see Table 1).

TABLE 1 ■ SNAPSHOT OF STUDIES

	Study of Transactions	Study of Companies
Firms Studied	Purchase and pooling acquirers	Purchase acquirers
Statistics Measured	Stock price reactions to transaction announcements	P/E and CF multiples
Time Frame	Around the transaction's announcement date	Between one and 40 years after a purchase transaction
Data Set	1,442 transactions	3,633 companies
Sample	Target at least 20% of acquirer's market capitalization and at least $100 million in value	Public companies with a market capitalization of at least $100 million
Conventional Wisdom	Stock prices react better to pooled transactions.	Goodwill and amortization hurt cash flow multiples; P/E multiples are sticky.
Theory	Stock prices react similarly to purchase and pooling	No effect on cash flow multiples; P/E multiples increase
Results	Purchase deals earn 3% on average for acquirer. Pooled deals lose 3%-4% on average for acquirer.	Theory is correct. Conventional wisdom is incorrect.

Source: Salomon Smith Barney.

More specifically, the first study examines the stock market's reaction to announcements of 1,442 purchase and pooling transactions to see whether the market prefers either method at the time of the transaction announcement. The conventional wisdom suggests that pooled transactions should receive a more favorable market response because of the lack of a penalty to earnings. On the other hand, theory would lead us to expect either roughly the same price effects, owing to the noncash impact of amortization, or perhaps even a more favorable reaction to purchase announcements, partly resulting from the restrictiveness of pooling and a possible willingness by companies to overpay for poolable transactions.

Our second study examines 3,633 companies and tests whether appropriately higher P/E multiples accompany higher levels of goodwill amortization to offset the accounting dilution to earnings, even many years after a purchase transaction may have taken place. In addition, the study tests whether cash flow multiples are sensitive to increases in balance sheet goodwill. Theory suggests that the amount of balance sheet goodwill should not affect cash flow multiples because goodwill does not affect cash flow. However, if the market penalizes amortization charges, then cash flow multiples should be lower because balance sheet goodwill is a measure of future amortization charges.

HOW HAS THE MARKET REACTED TO PURCHASE AND POOLING ANNOUNCEMENTS?

In a study designed to measure the stock market reaction to the announcement of pooled mergers and purchase acquisitions, we examined 1,442 merger and acquisition (M&A) transactions completed from 1991 to early 1999. For each transaction, we measured the excess return on the acquirer's stock price after removing market movements on a risk-adjusted basis. This involved calculating the cumulative return of the acquirer in excess of the T-bill return from two days before to 20 trading days after the transaction announcement, subtracting the cumulative return of the S&P 500 over the T-bill return, and multiplying by the beta of the acquirer.[2]

Our assumption is that, on average and under normal conditions, a company's performance in excess of the riskless rate should equal the market's performance in excess of the riskless rate times the company's beta, to account for its market-correlated risk. If the average cumulative excess return[3] of several hundred companies is positive (that is, if a large sample of companies beats the market average) and these firms have in common only that they have conducted large purchase acquisitions, then this should indicate the

---

2. Defining α as cumulative excess return, β as the acquirer's beta and r(t) as the day-t return of the asset defined in the subscript, we have:

$\alpha_{acquirer} = \Sigma_{t=-1}^{20}[r_{acquirer}(t) - r_{T\text{-}bills}(t)] - \beta_{acquirer}[r_{S\&P500}(t) - r_{T\text{-}bills}(t)].$

3. Cumulative excess return is also known as abnormal return. By cumulative we mean that excess returns are accumulated from two days before until 20 days after the announcement.

In the first month after a pooled transaction, the acquirer's stock fell by an average of almost 4%, with most of the decline coming within two days of the announcement. In contrast, the market reaction to purchase acquisitions was extremely favorable, with a 3% positive cumulative abnormal return coming in the first month after the announcement, most of it within the first few days.

TABLE 2 COMPLETED M&A TRANSACTIONS BY PUBLIC US FIRMS, 1990—1999[a]	Pooling	Purchase	Stock-for-Stock Purchase	Cash Only	Total
Number of Transactions	387	1,055	120	357	1,442

a. For transactions announced after January 1, 1990. Transaction size greater than $100 million and greater than 20% of acquirer's market capitalization.
Sources: Securities Data Corporation and Salomon Smith Barney.

market's favorable inclination toward the average purchase acquisition.

Furthermore, if the market is efficient, then it will incorporate all relevant information about a company into the stock price as soon as it becomes known. So, in theory, an event study needs to look only a couple of days after an event's announcement for the full market reaction to be measured. Indeed, our results show that the full response to purchase and pooling transactions shows up *within the first two or three days after the announcement*; after that, the average acquirer's performance merely matches the market's performance for at least the rest of the month.

The study was conducted separately for purchase and pooling transactions. The source of the data was the SDC database. The data included all completed and unconditional M&A transactions for majority or remaining interest by U.S.-based, publicly listed companies for which the amount paid for the target was at least 20% of the acquirer's market capitalization and for which the transaction value exceeded $100 million. To examine whether the market's reaction was based on the form of consideration, rather than the form of accounting, we separately examined all-stock and all-cash purchase acquisitions (see Table 2).[4]

The Results

Purchase acquisitions had a positive, statistically significant, announcement effect on the stock price of the acquiring firm (see Figure 1). In contrast, pooling-of-interests mergers as a whole had a negative, and statistically significant, announcement effect on the stock price of the acquiring firm.

The negative returns associated with pooled transactions may reflect the following:
■ The market's view that pooling acquirers have less purchase price discipline than do purchase acquirers.

■ The market's realization that the pooling acquirer will be unable to implement value-creating activities, such as spinoffs or asset sales, or to conduct nonroutine stock buybacks in the near future.
■ The revelation that the management of the acquirer cares more about accounting cosmetics than financial flexibility.

The possibility remains, however, that the superior performance of purchase acquisitions relative to pooling mergers was owing solely to the form of consideration. Most purchase acquisitions are at least partly cash transactions, whereas all pooling mergers are stock transactions.[5] There is reason to believe that the market might be more receptive to cash transactions than to stock transactions.

There are three possible explanations for this favoritism:
■ A company's willingness to use its stock as a currency in a transaction may be a signal to the market that it believes its equity is overvalued.
■ A cash transaction frequently requires outside lenders and, therefore, greater due diligence.
■ In stock transactions, risk arbitrageurs short the acquirer's stock; in all-cash transactions they do not.

Therefore, to place purchase acquisitions and pooling mergers on an equal footing, we decided to look at stock-for-stock purchase acquisitions as well.

In the first month after a pooled transaction, as shown in Figure 1, the acquirer's stock fell by an average of almost 4%, with most of the decline coming within two days of the announcement. In contrast, the market reaction to the announcement of purchase acquisitions was extremely favorable, with a 3% positive cumulative abnormal return coming in the first month after the transaction's announcement, most of it within the first few days. The reaction was also highly statistically significant.

---

4. To qualify as all-stock or all-cash, the number of forms of consideration reported by Securities Data Corporation must not exceed one. This eliminates deals with floors, collars, and any other form of consideration.

5. To qualify for pooling treatment, the consideration must be at least 90% composed of acquirer stock.

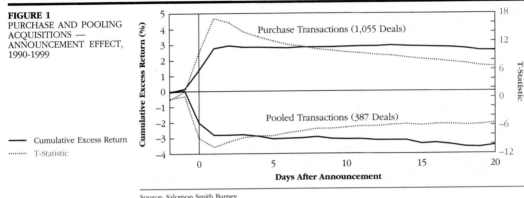

FIGURE 1
PURCHASE AND POOLING
ACQUISITIONS —
ANNOUNCEMENT EFFECT,
1990-1999

Cumulative Excess Return

T-Statistic

Source: Salomon Smith Barney.

In the case of only stock-for-stock purchase transactions, as shown in Figure 2, the announcement effect was between those of purchased and pooled transactions as a whole; the market was, on average, indifferent to the announcement of stock-only purchase transactions. Such indifference is still measurably more favorable than the clearly negative reaction to pooled transactions.

One might hypothesize that the favorable reaction to purchase acquisitions could result from the managerial bias *against* purchase acquisitions. Such a bias would lead to only the most economically attractive purchase acquisitions being done. However, since the market did not reward stock-only purchase transactions, the results for stock-for-stock purchase transactions work against this hypothesis.

DOES PURCHASE ACCOUNTING ADVERSELY AFFECT FIRM VALUATIONS?

The goal of this part of our study is to explain the impact of income statement amortization and balance sheet goodwill on P/E and firm value-to-EBITDA multiples for a large population of public companies. We examined 3,633 public companies with market capitalization exceeding $100 million. Companies with negative or negligible EBITDA or

earnings per share were excluded from the sample,[6] as were firms with pertinent data missing from Compustat's One Source.[7] In one set of regressions, we investigated the effect of amortization on P/E multiples. In another set of regressions we explored the impact of goodwill on firm value-to-EBITDA multiples.

For both sets of regressions, we controlled for industry effects,[8] effectively subtracting the corresponding industry averages from each data item to compare firm multiples fairly with those of industry peers. In both studies, we performed the regressions four different ways:

- *Aggregate sample*. The whole sample was examined together.[9]
- *Targeted sample*. Only firms with goodwill on their balance sheet (for FV-to-EBITDA regressions) or amortization on their income statement (for P/E regressions) were studied.
- *Industry-classified regressions*. The targeted sample was broken up into two subsets, one containing industries in which firms supposedly are priced by earnings ("P/E industries," in which P/E multiples hover around an industry average) and the other containing industries in which firms supposedly are priced by cash flow ("cash flow industries," in which FV-to-EBITDA ratios hover around an industry aver-

---

6. We have included firms with P/E multiples between six and 50 for the P/E regressions and firms with EBITDA multiples between four and 40 for the FV-to-EBITDA regressions.

7. All data were downloaded from the U.S. Equities CD-ROM product of One Source, Compustat, November 6, 1998. Data through October 30, 1998. All market values taken as of October 30, 1998.

8. Using the One Source industry classification, which divides the universe into 51 industries.

9. Because many firms with goodwill do not report amortization separately from depreciation, the aggregate study could not be performed for the P/E study without resulting in a large bias. The aggregate study can be performed for the FV-to-EBITDA multiple study, however, because this regression requires data only on balance sheet goodwill or intangibles and not on income statement amortization.

> **We find that P/E multiples increase significantly in response to goodwill amortization. Furthermore, the increase is sufficient to offset the impact of goodwill amortization.**

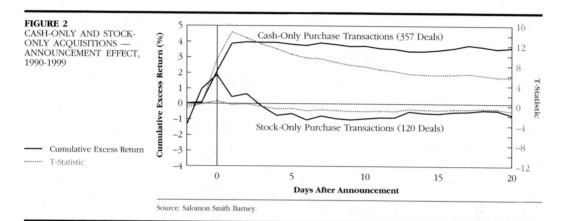

FIGURE 2
CASH-ONLY AND STOCK-ONLY ACQUISITIONS — ANNOUNCEMENT EFFECT, 1990-1999

Cumulative Excess Return (%)

Cash-Only Purchase Transactions (357 Deals)

Stock-Only Purchase Transactions (120 Deals)

——— Cumulative Excess Return
········· T-Statistic

T-Statistic

Days After Announcement

Source: Salomon Smith Barney.

age). We performed separate regressions on each of the two groups. This segmentation was made to address the concern that, in P/E industries, perhaps the market mechanically applies industry P/E multiples and fails to see through amortization, even if investors do see through amortization in cash flow industries.

■ *Amortization and goodwill-stratified regressions.* The targeted sample was broken up into two subsets containing firms with above-average amortization or goodwill for their industries and below-average amortization or goodwill, with separate regressions performed on each of the two groups. This segmentation was made to address the concern that perhaps the market only sees through amortization when there is a lot of it.

Regression Analysis

The Allure of This Approach

Valuation multiples are a measure of both the market's expectations of a firm's future earnings and its over- or undervaluation of that firm. Any such misvaluation may be a function of certain biases, such as a preference for reported earnings over cash flow. Our analysis measures whether such a bias actually exists.

Because most firms with goodwill on their balance sheets completed their purchase acquisi-

tions years ago, this study measures whether a bias against purchase accounting exists even a number of years after transactions have taken place. In contrast, our study of transactions, while providing a direct test of whether the market prefers pooled or purchased transactions, measures whether a bias exists only in the month after a transaction's announcement, as evidenced by above- or below-average stock returns for the acquirer. We believe that our analysis is the first to explore whether purchase accounting has any long-lasting effect on firm values.

A study of multiples can remove sources of noise related to changes in a firm's profitability, expected growth rate, and other value-affecting statistics, enhancing statistical significance and sharpening the study's focus. In short, our regression study can pick up any market bias against purchase acquisitions regardless of when a transaction may have occurred.[10,11]

Which Explanatory Variables to Use?

Income statement amortization measures the effect of prior purchase acquisitions on net income in a given year. Balance sheet goodwill measures the total remaining effect of prior purchase acquisitions on net income for all future years.[12] Therefore, amortization, not goodwill, is the key statistic in explaining the effect of purchase acquisitions on P/E

10. Provided that the firm is continuing to amortize its goodwill.
11. Of course, in this, as in any regression, there is a danger of omitted variables. We believe it plausible that any omitted variables that might explain market multiples are not highly correlated with goodwill amortization, and therefore, the bias is limited.

12. In the rare circumstances in which goodwill is tax-deductible, the effect is on pretax rather than net income.

multiples. This is because the P/E multiple is being applied to earnings that have been expensed for amortization—not for the full balance of goodwill. More simply, to make shareholders indifferent to amortization, P/E multiples need to increase by the ratio of pre- to post-amortization income. Balance sheet goodwill does not enter the equation.

However, in explaining the effect of purchase acquisitions on FV-to-EBITDA multiples, balance sheet goodwill, not income statement amortization, is the key statistic. This is because EBITDA is unaffected by a single year's amortization. If a company were to trade at a discount because of the accounting effects of a purchase acquisition, the discount would be a function of the impact of all future amortization charges, as summarized by goodwill.

HOW DOES INCOME STATEMENT AMORTIZATION AFFECT P/E MULTIPLES?

In our amortization-related regressions, the dependent variable was the P/E multiple and the primary explanatory variable of interest was goodwill amortization in the income statement. In addition, as an alternative, we ran the regressions with the natural logarithm of the P/E multiple (Ln(P/E)) as the dependent variable.

The full set of explanatory variables were:
- *Amortization.* The ratio of amortization per share to earnings per share plus amortization per share.[13]
- *Earnings change.* The percentage change in the firm's earnings per share during the most recent four quarters.[14]
- *Leverage.* The ratio of the firm's book value of debt to book value of equity.[15]
- *Size.* The natural logarithm of the book value of equity.
- *Growth.* Five-year annualized sales per share growth.
- *Industry.* For each variable, the industry average was effectively subtracted from the company data through the use of an industry dummy variable. This adjustment allowed us to remove the industry-specific impact on market multiples.

The latter five variables allowed us to control for other factors that affect the P/E multiple and so isolate the effect of goodwill amortization. Together, these variables serve as a proxy for risk.

The Results

We find that P/E multiples increase significantly in response to goodwill amortization (see Table 3). Furthermore, the increase is sufficient to offset the impact of goodwill amortization. The expansion of P/E multiples in response to goodwill amortization is of comparable magnitude and significance in all five regressions. This result indicates that there is no qualitative distinction between the impact of amortization on P/E industries and that on cash flow industries, but rather that all industries are priced based on cash earnings.[16]

So, how did the perception arise that certain industries focus on earnings and not on cash flow? The perception likely derives from two phenomena. First, earnings changes and surprises are usually highly correlated with changes in cash flow. Second, in some industries, earnings announcements are occasions to draw inferences about a firm's growth prospects and management's credibility. Neither of these phenomena implies that the market is incapable of seeing through goodwill amortization or that the market discounts expected future earnings per share rather than expected future cash flow. They merely suggest that earnings announcements convey useful information.

Is Income Statement Amortization Irrelevant for Valuations?

A Simple Example

Consider our results for the targeted sample of firms with amortization. Assume a representative company, having leverage, growth, and size equal to its industry average. On average, such a company would have a P/E ratio of 18.0, based on our statistical model.

---

13. Amortization/pre-amortization income, most recent fiscal year.

14. Primary EPS (trailing 12 months)/primary EPS (year-ago trailing 12 months) - 1, most recent fiscal quarter.

15. Debt service due within one year plus long-term debt plus preferred stock less cash and marketable securities, all divided by book value of equity, most recent fiscal year. This statistic is then capped between 0 and 1 to limit the effect of outliers.

16. These results also indicate that equity analysts who fail to see through goodwill amortization may find themselves undervaluing firms with relatively large amounts of goodwill.

Regardless of which regression we used, we were unable to find evidence of a
market bias against balance sheet goodwill or against known future
amortization charges.

TABLE 3 ■ P/E MULTIPLES EXPAND WITH INCOME STATEMENT AMORTIZATION*

Sample	Sample Size	Base P/E	Pct. Increase in P/E Mult. for 10-Pct.-Pt. Increase in Proportion of Amort. in Pre-Amort. Earnings[a,b]	Absolute Effect on P/E Mult. of 10-Pct.-Pt. Increase in Proportion of Amort. in Pre-Amort. Earnings[c]	Statistically Significant?[d]
Targeted (Positive-Amortization Companies)	369	18.0×	11.8%	+2.40×	Very
INDUSTRY-STRATIFIED					
P/E Industries[e]	169	18.8×	12.2%	+2.58×	Very
Cash Flow Industries[f]	200	17.0	10.5	+2.31	Very
AMORTIZATION-STRATIFIED[g]					
Low Amortization[h]	193	17.0×	37.3%	+6.45×	Yes
High Amortization	176	18.2	12.1	+2.61	Very
Conclusions			Perfectly offsets earnings hit from amortization	Large average impact	Very significant

*For full results, see Table 7. We also performed the regression using Instrumental Variables; see Table 7 footnote.
a. Derived from the Ln (P/E) regression.
b. For example, an increase from 5% to 15%.
c. From the P/E regression.
d. "Yes" indicates statistical significance at the 95% confidence level. "Very" indicates statistical significance at the 99% confidence level.
e. A P/E industry is an industry in which there is a small variation of P/E multiples across firms.
f. A cash flow industry is an industry in which there is a small variation of FV-to-EBITDA multiples across firms.
g. The cutoff between these two groups is at 1/16 ratio of amortization to pre-amortization earnings, because this breaks up the data set into equal-sized groups, and did so perfectly for an earlier data set.
h. The unexpectedly high coefficient in this regression coincided with the lowest t-statistic and the greatest standard error. This coefficient is not significantly different from the others. The standard error is highest for this group precisely because amortization plays a small role in determining multiples for firms that have very little.
Source: Salomon Smith Barney.

Suppose the firm has earnings per share of $1.00. Then we would expect its stock price to be $18.00. We have found that, on average, the percentage by which amortization reduces net income (the "amortization ratio") for this sample of companies is 10%. If the representative firm were typical, its amortization per share would be $0.11 [i.e, $0.11/ ($1.00 + $0.11) = 10%].

Suppose our representative firm makes a new purchase acquisition, generating no change in pre-amortization EPS but resulting in goodwill of $4.00 per share. This would add $0.10 of amortization charges each year ($4.00 annually by 40 years of amortization), and the firm's EPS would be $0.90. If no P/E expansion results from this amortization, the firm's stock price would drop by 10% to $16.20 (i.e., 18.0 × $0.90) as a result of this added amortization.

The firm's ratio of amortization to pre-amortization income is now $0.21/$1.11 = 19%, exceeding the pre-acquisition ratio by 9%. Our regression model predicts that a 10% increase in the amortization ratio increases the P/E multiple by 2.40. Therefore, the P/E multiple for this company expands from 18.0 to 20.16 [i.e., 18.0 + (2.40 × 9/10)]. Its stock price will therefore be $18.14 (i.e., 20.16 × $0.90), approxi-mately equal to its pre-acquisition stock price of $18.00. Thus, the higher multiple is just enough to offset the dilution to earnings from amortization.

Does the Rate of Amortization Affect Firm Valuations?

We performed a separate set of regressions with an additional explanatory variable, the "burn rate." Burn rate is defined as the rate at which goodwill is amortized. It is calculated by dividing the most recent year's amortization by balance sheet goodwill. The coefficient on burn rate was insignificant when amortization or goodwill was included in the regression. This indicates that the enhancement of P/E multiples in response to goodwill amortization is sufficient to make shareholders indifferent to accounting method, regardless of the speed at which goodwill is amortized. Further, our regressions on high- and low-amortization firms both demonstrate that the market fully sees through amortization, whether there is a lot of amortization or a little. We infer that a shortening of amortization periods should not affect the market's ability to see through amortization.

TABLE 4 ■ FV/EBITDA MULTIPLES ARE UNAFFECTED BY BALANCE SHEET GOODWILL

Sample	Sample Size	Base FV/EBITDA	Effect on FV/EBITDA of 10-Pct.-Pt. Increase in Proportion of Goodwill as Pct. of Book Value[a]	Statistically Significant?
Aggregate Sample	2,318	12.4×	+0.026	No
Targeted (Positive-Goodwill Companies)	1,578	12.5×	+0.043	No
INDUSTRY-STRATIFIED				
P/E Industries	849	14.2×	-0.099	No
Cash Flow Industries	729	10.4	+0.202	Yes
GOODWILL-STRATIFIED[b]				
Low Goodwill	789	12.8×	+0.153	No
High Goodwill	789	12.3	+0.018	No
Conclusions			No noticeable impact	Not significant

a. For example, an increase from 5% to 15%.
b. The cutoff between these two groups is at a ratio of goodwill or intangibles to book value of 11.765%.
Source: Salomon Smith Barney.

HOW DOES BALANCE SHEET GOODWILL AFFECT CASH FLOW MULTIPLES?

In our regressions related to balance sheet goodwill, the dependent variable used was the FV-to-EBITDA multiple. As before, we also ran these regressions with the natural logarithm of FV to EBITDA as the dependent variable. The explanatory variables were:
■ *Goodwill*. The ratio of goodwill to book value.
■ *Leverage*. The ratio of the firm's book value of debt to book value of equity.[17]
■ *Size*. The natural logarithm of firm value.
■ *Growth*. Five-year annualized sales-per-share growth.
■ *Industry*. As before, for each variable, the industry average was effectively subtracted from the company data through the use of industry dummies, allowing us to eliminate the industry-specific impact on market multiples.

These specifications allowed us to control for factors that differentiate FV-to-EBITDA multiples and to isolate the impact of goodwill.

The Results

Regardless of which regression we used, we were unable to find evidence of a market bias against

balance sheet goodwill or against known future amortization charges (see Table 4). In one of the six regressions, we found a statistically significant *positive* impact of balance sheet goodwill on FV-to-EBITDA multiples.[18] Our conclusion is that the amount of goodwill on a firm's balance sheet does not affect its FV-to-EBITDA multiple.

CAVEATS

Our studies do not show that earnings dilution, in general, does not matter. They merely reflect the fact that the earnings dilution resulting from amortization of intangibles does not adversely affect stock prices. In addition, they do not demonstrate that goodwill amortization never matters, only that it does not matter on average.

As an example, in the oil industry it is common to allocate excess purchase price to PP&E. It may be difficult for market participants to make the appropriate adjustments to reverse the impact of purchase acquisitions on earnings in such nontransparent circumstances.

Similarly, in the electric utility industry, very few utilities that have balance sheet goodwill bother to report goodwill amortization separately on their income statement, instead lumping it in with depre-

---

17. Although EBITDA may seem to be a measure that makes leverage irrelevant, tax benefits of leverage may cause FV to EBITDA to increase with leverage.
18. We would not place too much weight on this statistically significant result. If one performs 20 regressions, then even if no effect exists, one of the regressions

should, statistically, produce a statistically significant result. We did six cash flow regressions, so we have about a one-in-three chance of obtaining a statistically significant result where none exists. Conversely, in our amortization-related regressions, all five regressions produced statistically significant results, providing much greater assurance of the presence of a true effect.

ciation. Seeing through the amortization in such cases requires an analyst either to rely on state utility regulatory disclosures (which make SEC disclosures look like light reading), or keep track of how many years ago each utility did each purchase acquisition.

One would not necessarily expect the market to "see through" the noncash charge of depreciation as it does with amortization. Depreciation can be thought of as a smoothed proxy for ongoing capital expenditures. Firms that are more efficient with their physical capital should have lower depreciation and deserve to be rewarded for it.

Therefore, firms with balance sheet goodwill would benefit from making their amortization trans-parent in their financial statements, breaking out amortization from depreciation on their income statements. Likewise, firms in the oil industry may wish to report any difference in depletion charges had pur-chase transactions been accounted for as poolings.

The banking sector offers another example. In this sector, balance sheet goodwill reduces regula-tory capital,[19] impairing a bank's ability to lend as much as it otherwise could. This is a case in which goodwill can have a real economic impact.

These examples are the exceptions to the rule. Our studies show that across large numbers of companies and transactions, the market can make the necessary adjustments.

DOES GOODWILL AMORTIZATION PROVIDE ANY USEFUL INFORMATION?

It is often claimed that the pooling method is unjustifiable and should have been eliminated long ago. Adherents to this school point to the scarcity of pooling outside of the U.S. and, equally, to the benefits of placing U.S. acquirers on an equal footing with each other, regardless of whether they have tainted stock. These arguments fail to address a more fundamental question—what does amortization measure and where is its application appropriate?

Accounting is virtuous only in its ability to advance the following objectives: performance measurement, inter-firm comparison, financial transparency, and mana-gerial honesty. Here we consider only the relationship between amortization and performance measurement.

There are two aspects of performance measure-ment: measuring firm performance and measuring per share performance. When an acquirer buys a target, the target will presumably generate cash flows for the acquirer. However, the cost of acquiring this stream of target cash flows needs to be charged against the cash flows themselves to derive a measure of value added. These charges can take the form of either depreciation or amortization and, apart from tax issues, it hardly matters which; the same end is achieved.

When attempting to measure an acquisition's ex-pected effect on shareholder value (as opposed to its contribution to total firm value/market cap of the firm), the issue is different. For simplicity, we will abstract from capital structure issues and assume an all-stock purchase acquisition. If the acquisition is neither accretive nor dilutive on a cash basis and the target has the same expected growth rate, risk, and leverage as the acquirer, then there should be no impact on shareholder value. The shareholder has already been appropriately diluted by the transaction through an increase in outstanding shares. Translated into economic terms, the expected NPV of the investment represented by the stock granted in the acquisition is zero. In such a case, any amortization charges would have the effect of overpenalizing the acquisition in terms of measuring its impact on the shareholder. Depreciation charges, by contrast, were already being borne by the target, and continuing to expense them accounts for ongoing capital expenditure and keeps the acquirer and target on an equal footing.

When the objective is to measure the value of a firm's assets, rather than to measure value added or per share performance, different issues are involved. An argument can be made that goodwill should never be placed on a balance sheet unless balance sheets are going to be marked-to-market in their entirety. Other-wise, goodwill represents a one-time and arbitrary marking-to-market of part of a firm's balance sheet. Conversely, if one believes that goodwill belongs on a balance sheet, then amortizing it may or may not be appropriate because some goodwill does not deteriorate.

In sum, regardless of which standards are used for balance sheets, the SEC and FASB should consider requiring firms to report EPS on a pre-amortization basis even as net income is reported on a post-amortization basis.

---

19. It is worth noting that stock-for-stock purchase acquisitions do not adversely affect the amount of a bank's regulatory capital, regardless of the amount of goodwill acquired in the transaction.

CONCLUSIONS

- Pooling mergers should not be viewed as preferable to purchase acquisitions.
- P/E multiples expand by a sufficient amount in response to amortization to make amortization irrelevant to a firm's stock price.
- FV-to-EBITDA multiples are unaffected by the amount of goodwill on a firm's balance sheet.
- The stock market responds to purchase transactions more favorably than to pooled mergers, for which the reaction is decidedly negative. The reaction to stock-for-stock purchase acquisitions is much more muted than for cash or mixed cash/stock transactions.

- If and when the pooling-of-interests method disappears, acquisitive firms accustomed to receiving pooling treatment should continue to pursue their strategic objectives, ignoring the accounting effects of purchase treatment.

In light of these results, the prospective elimination of the pooling-of-interests method by FASB should be thought of as a liberation from the pressure to enter into poolings and bear the burden of their restrictions, rather than as a loss of an accounting loophole. The results of this study move the center of gravity of the purchase-pooling debate. With the average firm in the average industry being completely unaffected by amortization charges, the onus is now on those with a bias against purchase accounting to demonstrate why their firm or industry differs from the norm.

LESSONS FROM A MIDDLE MARKET LBO: THE CASE OF O.M. SCOTT

by George P. Baker and Karen H. Wruck, Harvard Business School*

I n 1986 The O.M. Scott & Sons Company, the largest producer of lawn care products in the U.S., was sold by the ITT Corporation in a divisional leveraged buyout The company was founded in Marysville, Ohio, in 1870 by Orlando McLean Scott to sell farm crop seed. In 1900, the company began to sell weed-free lawn seed through the mail. In the 1920s, the company introduced the first home lawn fertilizer, the first lawn spreader, and the first patented blue-grass seed. Today, Scott is the acknowledged leader in the "do-it-yourself" lawn care market, with sales of over $300 million and over 1500 employees.

Scott remained closely held until 1971, when it was purchased by ITT. The company then became a part of the consumer products division of the huge conglomerate, and operated as a wholly-owned subsidiary for 14 years. In 1984, prompted by a decline in financial performance and rumors of takeover and liquidation, ITT began a series of divestitures. Over the next two years, total divestitures exceeded $2 billion and, after years of substandard performance, ITT's stock price significantly outperformed the market.

On November 26, 1986, in the midst of this divestiture activity, ITT announced that the managers of Scott, along with Clayton & Dubilier (C & D), a private firm specializing in leveraged buyouts, had agreed to purchase the stock of Scott and another ITT subsidiary, the W. Atlee Burpee Company. The deal closed on December 30.

Clayton & Dubilier raised roughly $211 million to finance the purchase of the two companies. Of that $211 million, almost $191 million, or 91% of the total, was debt: bank loans, subordinated notes, and subordinated debentures. The $20 million of new equity was distributed as follows: roughly 62% of the shares were held by a C & D partnership, 21% by Scott's new subordinated debtholders, and 17.5% by Scott management and employees.

After this radical change in financial structure and concentration of equity ownership, Scott's operating performance improved dramatically. Between the end of December 1986 and the end of September 1988, sales were up 25% and earnings before interest and taxes (EBIT) increased by 56%. As shown in Table 1, this increase in operating earnings was not achieved by cutting back on marketing and distribution or R & D. In fact, spending on marketing and distribution increased by 21% and R & D spending went up by 7%. Capital spending also increased by 23%.

* This is a shorter less technical version of "Organizational Changes and Value in Leveraged Buyouts: The Case of The O.M. Scott Company," *Journal of Financial Economics* 25 (1989).

We would like to thank everyone at The O.M. Scott & Sons Company and Clayton & Dubilier who gave generously of their time and so made this study possible: Lorel Au, Martin Dubilier, Richard Dresdale, Rich Martinez, Larry McCartney, Tadd Seitz, John Smith, Bob Stern, Homer Stewart, Hank Timnick, Ken Tossey, John Wall, Craig Walley, and Paul Yeager. In addition, we would like to thank Ken French, Robin Cooper, Bob Eccles, Leo Herzel Mike Jensen, Steve Kaplan, Ken Merchant, Krishna Palepu, Bill Schwert, Eric Wruck, and the participants of the Financial Decisions and Control Workshop at Harvard Business School and of the Conference on the Structure and Governance of Enterprise sponsored by the JFE for their helpful comments and suggestions. Support from the Division of Research, Harvard Business School is gratefully acknowledged.

TABLE 1 FINANCIAL AND OPERATING DATA FOR O.M. SCOTT & SONS CO. ($ in millions)	Pre-buyout: Year ended 12/30/86	Post-buyout Year ended 9/30/88	Percent Change
INCOME STATEMENT			
EBIT	$18.1	$28.2	55.8%
Sales	158.1	197.1	24.7
Research & Development	4.1	4.4	7.3
Marketing & Distribution	58.4	70.7	21.1
BALANCE SHEET*			
Average working capital	59.3	36.2	-39.0
Total assets	243.6	162.0	-33.5
Long-term debt	191.0	125.8	34.1
Adjusted net worth	20.0	38.3	91.5
OTHER			
Capital expenditures	$3.0	$3.7	23.3
Employment	868	792	-8.9

* Balance sheet figures are reported at the close of the buyout transaction. Adjusted net worth is GAAP net worth adjusted for associating effects of the buyout under APB no. 16. In Scott's case the bulk of the adjustment is adding back the effects of an inventory write-down of $24.7 million taken immediately after the buyout.

In terms of its capital structure, managerial equity ownership, and improvement in operating performance, Scott is a highly representative LBO. Three major academic studies of LBOs have collectively concluded that following an LBO:

- the average debt-to-capital ratio is roughly 90%;
- managerial equity ownership stakes are typically around 17-20%;
- operating income increases by about 40%, on average, over a period ranging from two to four years after a buyout.[1]

Such findings raise major questions about the effects of changes in organizational and financial structure on management decision-making. For example, does the combination of significant equity ownership and high debt provide management with stronger incentives to maximize value than those facing managers of public companies with broadly dispersed stockholders? Are the decentralized management systems with pay-for-performance plans that typically accompany LBOs likely to produce greater operating efficiencies than centralized structures relying largely on financial controls? Are LBO boards, characterized by controlling equity ownership, an improvement over the standard governance of public companies where directors have "fiduciary duty," but little or no equity ownership?

Although the broad evidence cited above suggests that the answer to all these questions is yes, little academic research to date has examined the changes in organizational structure and managerial decision-making that actually take place after LBOs. In 1989, we were given the opportunity to examine confidential data on the Scott buyout and to conduct extensive interviews with C & D partners and managers at all levels of the Scott organization. We found that both organizational structure and the management decision-making process changed fundamentally as a consequence of the buyout.

In the pages that follow, we attempt to explain the role of high leverage, concentrated equity ownership, and strong governance by an active board in bringing about specific operating changes within Scott. Critics of LBOs will doubtless continue to object that highly leveraged capital structures lead to an unhealthy emphasis on "short-term" results. But the changes we witnessed at Scott lend no support to this view. These changes ranged from sharply increased attention to working capital management, vendor relations, and an innovative approach to production to a much greater willingness to entertain long-range opportunities presented by new markets and strategic acquisitions. Especially in light of Scott's post-LBO performance and spending patterns, it would

1. The studies areas follows: Steven Kaplan, "Management Buyouts: Evidence on Post-buyout Operating Changes," *Journal of Financial Economics*, 1991; Abbie Smith, "Corporate Ownership Structure and Performance: The Case of Management Buyouts," *Journal of Financial Economics*, 1991; and Chris Muscarella and Michael Vetsuypens. "Efficiency and Organizational Structure: A Study of Reverse LBOs," Southern Methodist University working paper, 1988.

TABLE 2
OWNERS OF COMMON
STOCK OF O.M. SCOTT &
SONS CO. AFTER THE LBO
(AS OF 9/30/88)

	Number of Shares	Percent of Shares
Clayton & Dubilier private limited partnership	14,900	61.4%
Subordinated debtholders	5,000	20.6
Mr. Tadd Seitz, CEO	1,063	4.4
Seven other top managers (250,000 shares each)	1,750	7.2
Scott profit sharing plan	750	3.1
Twenty-two other employees	687	2.8
Mr. Joseph P. Flannery, Board Member	100	0.4
Total	24, 250	100.0%

All shares were purchased by owners at $1 per share. Percentages don't foot due to rounding error.

be difficult to argue that any of these initiatives sacrificed long-term value for short-run cash flow.

CHANGES IN INCENTIVES AND COMPENSATION

Management Equity Ownership

The final distribution of equity in the post-buyout Scott organization was the product of negotiations between C & D and Scott's management—negotiations in which ITT took no part. ITT sold its entire equity interest in Scott through a sealed bid auction. Fight firms bid for Scott; although bidding was open to all types of buyers, seven bidders were buyout firms. ITT was interested primarily in obtaining the highest price for the division.

Scott managers did not participate in the buyout negotiations and thus had no opportunity to extract promises or make deals with potential purchasers prior to the sale. Scott managers had approached ITT several years earlier to discuss the possibility of a management buyout at $125 million; but at that time ITT had a no-buyout policy. The stated reason for this policy was that a management buyout posed a conflict of interest.

Each of the bidders spent about one day in Marysville and received information about the performance of the unit directly from ITT. Prior to Martin Dubilier's visit Scott managers felt that they preferred C & D to the other potential buyers because of its reputation for working well with operating managers. The day did not go well, however, and C & D fell to the bottom of the managers list. According to Tadd Seitz president of Scott:

To be candid, they weren't our first choice. It wasn't a question of their acumen, we just didn't think we had the chemistry. But as we went through

the controlled bid process, it was C & D that saw the greatest value in Scott.

There is no evidence that ITT deviated from its objective of obtaining the highest value for the division, or that it negotiated in any way on behalf of Scott managers during the buyout process. C & D put in the highest bid. ITT did not consider management's preferences and accepted this bid even though managers were left to work with one of their less favored buyers. Nor did ITT concern itself with the distribution of common stock after the sale.

Immediately following the closing, C & D controlled 79.4% of Scott's common stock. The remaining shares were packaged and sold with the subordinated debt. C & D was under no obligation to offer managers equity participation in Scott, and the deal clearly could be funded without any contribution by managers. But, on the basis of their experience, the C & D partners viewed management equity ownership as a way to provide managers with strong incentives to maximize firm value. Therefore. after C & D purchased Scott, it began to negotiate with managers over the amount of equity they would be given the opportunity to purchase. C & D did not sell shares to managers reluctantly; in fact, it insisted that managers buy equity and that they do so with their own, not the company's, money.

The ownership structure that resulted from the negotiations between C & D and Scott management is presented in Table 2. There are 24,250,000 shares outstanding, each of which was purchased for $1.00. As the general partner of the private limited partnership that invested $14.9 million in the Scott buyout, C & D controlled 61.4% of the common stock. The individual C & D partners responsible for overseeing Scott operations carried an ownership interest through their substantial investment in the C & D limited partnership. Subordinated debtholders owned 20.6%.

The remaining 17.5% of the equity was distributed among Scott's employees. Fight of the firm's top managers contributed a total of $2,812,500 to the buyout and so hold as many shares, representing 12% of the shares outstanding. Tadd Seitz, president of Scott, held the largest number of these shares (1,062,500, or 4.4% of the shares outstanding). Seven other managers purchased 250,000 shares apiece (1% each of the shares outstanding). As a group, managers borrowed $2,531,250 to finance the purchase of shares. Though the money was not borrowed from Scott, these loans were guaranteed by the company.

The purchase of equity by Scott managers represented a substantial increase in their personal risk. For example, Bob Stern, vice-president of Associate Relations,[2] recalled that his spouse sold her interest in a small catering business at the time of the buyout they felt that the leverage associated with the purchase of Scott shares was all the risk they could afford.

Top management had some discretion over how their allotment of common shares was further distributed. Without encouragement from C & D, they chose to issue a portion of their own shares to Scott's employee profit-sharing plan and other employees of the firm. Although they allowed managers to distribute the stock more widely, C & D partners felt that the shares would have stronger incentive effects if they were held only by top managers. Craig Walley, general counsel for Scott, described the thinking behind management's decision to extend equity to additional managers and employees as follows:

We [the managers] used to get together on Saturdays during this period when we were thinking about the buyout to talk about why we wanted to do this. What was the purpose? What did we want to make Scott? One of our aims was to try to keep it independent. Another was to try to spread the ownership widely. One of the things we did was to take 3% of the common stock out of our allocation and put it into the profit-sharing plan. That took some doing and we had some legal complications, but we did it. There are now 56 people in the company who own some stock,

and that number is increasing. Compared to most LBOs that is really a lot, and Dubilier has not encouraged us in this.

A group of 11 lower-level managers bought an additional 687,500 shares (2.8% of the total) and the profit-sharing plan bought 750,000 shares (3.1%). These managers were selected not by their rank in the organization, but because they were employees who would be making decisions considered crucial to the success of the company.

The substantial equity holdings of the top management team, along with their personal liability for the debts incurred to finance their equity stakes, led them to focus on two distinct aspects of running Scott: (1) preserving their fractional equity stake by avoiding default (including technical default) on the firm's debt; and (2) increasing the value of that stake by making decisions that increased the long-run value of the firm.

If the company failed to make a payment of interest or principal, or if it violated a debt covenant, it would be "in default" and lenders would have the option to renegotiate the terms of the debt contract. If no agreement could be reached, the company could be forced to seek protection from creditors under Chapter 11. Because both private reorganizations and Chapter 11 generally involve the replacement of debt with equity claims, one likely consequence of default is a substantial dilution of the existing equity; and to the extent managers are also equityholders, such dilution reduces their wealth. But managers face other costs of default that are potentially large: they may end up surrendering control of the company to a bankruptcy court, and they could even lose their jobs.[3] In this sense, equity ownership bonds managers against taking actions that lead to a violation of the covenants.

We examined Scott's debt covenants in detail to determine what managerial actions lenders encouraged and prohibited (see Table 3 for a summary). The overall effect of these covenants is to restrict both the source of funds for scheduled interest and principal repayments and the use of funds in excess of this amount. Cash to pay debt obligations must come primarily from operations or the issuance of common

---

2. Scott refers to all of its employees as "associates." Stern's position, therefore. is equivalent to vice-president of human resources or personnel.

3. Stuart Gilson provides evidence that the managers of firms in financial distress are quite likely to lose their jobs as a part of the recovery process. See "Management Turnover and Financial Distress," *Journal of Financial Economics*, 25 (1989), pp. 241-262.

TABLE 3
SUMMARY OF DEBT COVENANTS OF SCOTT BORROWINGS TO FINANCE THE BUYOUT

	Bank Debt Restrictions	**Subordinated Debt Restrictions**
ECONOMIC ACTIVITIES RESTRICTED		
Sale of assets	Only worn-out or obsolete assets with value less than $500,000 can be sold	75% of proceeds must be used to repay debt in order of priority
Capital expenditures	Restricted to specific $ amount each year debt is outstanding	None
Changes in corporate structure	Prohibited	Mandatory redemption if change in control No acquisition if in default Must acquire 100% equity of target Must be able to issue $1 more debt without covenant violation after acquisition
FINANCING ACTIVITIES RESTRICTED		
Issuance of additional debt	Capitalized leases: max = $3,000,000 Unsecured credit: max = $1,000,000	Additional senior debt: max = $15,000,000 For employee stock purchases: max = $4,250,000
	Commercial paper: max = amount available under revolving credit agreement	Pre-tax cash flow interest expense: min = 1.0 for four quarters preceding issuance
Payment of cash dividends	Prohibited	Prohibited if in default Prohibited if adjusted net worth < $50,000,000
ACCOUNTING-BASED RESTRICTIONS		
Adjusted net worth*	Specific min at all times, min increases from $20.5 million in 1986 to $43.0 million after 1992	If adjusted net worth falls below $12.0 million then must redeem $17.0 million notes and $5.0 million debentures at 103
Interest coverage	Min 1.0 at end of each fiscal quarter	None
Current ratio	Min at end of each fiscal quarter	None
Adjusted operating profit	Min at end of each fiscal quarter, min fiscal quarter, min increases from $22.0 million in 1987 to $31.0 million after 1990	None

*Adjusted net worth and adjusted operating profit are the GAAP numbers adjusted for accounting effects of the buyout under APB no. 16. In Scott's case the bulk of the adjustment is adding back the effects of an inventory write-down of $24.7 million taken immediately after the buyout.

stock. It cannot come from asset liquidation, stock acquisition of another firm with substantial cash, or the issuance of additional debt of any kind. Excess funds can be used for capital expenditures only within prescribed limits, and cannot be used to finance acquisitions or be paid out as dividends to shareholders. Thus, once the capital expenditure limit has been reached, excess cash must be either held, spent in the course of normal operations, or used to pay down debt ahead of schedule.

A second important effect of equity ownership was to encourage managers to make decisions that increased the long-run value of the company. Because managers owned a capital value claim on the firm, they had strong incentives to meet debt obligations and avoid default in a way that increased the long-term value of the company. That is, managers had strong incentives to resist cutbacks in brand name advertising and plant maintenance that would increase short-run cash flow at the expense of long run value.

As mentioned earlier, there were no cutbacks in productive capital spending at Scott. In fact, as shown in Table 1 earlier, capital spending, R&D, and marketing and promotion expenditures all increased significantly over the first two years after the buyout. Thus, in Scott's case, high leverage combined with equity ownership provided managers with the incentive to generate the cash required to meet the debt payments without bleeding the company.

The increase in capital expenditures following Scott's LBO is one way in which Scott differs from the average LBO. The large-sample studies cited earlier find that capital spending falls on average following

The large stockholder gains from the leveraged restructuring movement of the 80s
are suggestive evidence that much prior corporate "long-term" investment was little
more than a waste of stockholder funds in the name of preserving growth.

an LBO. Whether this average reduction in capital expenditures creates or destroys value is difficult to determine, because not all corporate spending cutbacks are short-sighted. To make that determination one has to know whether LBO companies were spending too much or too little on capital expenditure prior to their LBOs. The large stockholder gains from the leveraged restructuring movement of the 1980s suggest that much prior corporate "long-term" investment was little more than a waste of stockholder funds in the name of preserving growth.

High leverage combined with leveraged equity ownership provides strong incentives for managers to evaluate long-term investments more critically, to undertake only value-increasing projects, and to return any "free cash flow"—that is, cash in excess of that required to fund all positive-NPV investments—to investors.[4] Leverage will cause managers to cut back on productive expenditures only if such cutbacks are the only way to avoid default *and* the cost to managers of default is greater than the loss in equity value from myopic decisions.

The LBO sponsor—in this case C & D—also plays an important role in guiding such investment decisions and preventing short-sighted cutbacks. Indeed, the experience and competence of the sponsor in valuing the company, evaluating the strengths of operating management, and arranging the financial structure is critical to an LBO's success.[5]

Changes in Incentive Compensation

Among the first things C & D did after the buyout was to increase salaries selectively and begin to develop a new management compensation plan. A number of managers who were not participants in the ITT bonus plan became participants under the C & D plan. The new plan substantially changed the way managers were evaluated, and increased the fraction of salary that a manager could earn as an annual bonus. While some of these data are confidential. we are able to describe many of the features of C & D's incentive compensation plan and compare it with the ITT compensation system.

Salaries. Almost immediately after the close of the sale, the base salaries of some top managers were increased. The president's salary increased by 42%, and the salaries of other top managers increased as well. Henry Timnick, a C & D partner who works closely with Scott, explains the decision to raise salaries as follows:

We increased management salaries because divisional vice presidents are not compensated at a level comparable to the CBO of a free-standing company with the same characteristics. Divisional VPs don't have all the responsibilities. In addition, the pay raise is a shot-in-the-arm psychologically for the managers. It makes them feel they will be dealt with fairly and encourages them to deal fairly with their people.

In conversations with managers and C & D partners, it became clear that C & D set higher standards for management performance than ITT. Increasing the minimum level of acceptable performance forces managers to work harder after the buyout or risk losing their jobs. Indeed, there was general agreement that the management team was putting in longer hours at the office. Several managers used the term more "focused" to described how their work habits had changed after the buyout.

The increase in compensation also served as the reward for bearing greater risk. As stated earlier, Scott managers undertook substantial borrowings to purchase the equity. Requiring managers to borrow to buy equity and adopting an aggressive incentive compensation plan greatly increases managers exposure to Scott's fortunes. Because managers cannot diversify away this "firm-specific" risk in the same way passive investors can, they require an increase in the expected *level* of their pay to remain equally well-off.

Finally, C & D may have increased salaries because Scott managers are more valuable to C & D than they were to ITT. Consistent with this argument, managers at Scott felt ITT depended on them much less than did C & D. One Scott manager reported:

4. See Michael C. Jensen, "Agency Costs of Free Cash Flow, Corporate Finance, and Takeovers," *American Economic Review*, 76 (1986), pp. 323-329.

5. For examples of poorly structured LBOs consider the cases of Revco D.S. and Campeau's acquisition of Federated, both of which have been held up as representative of the problems with LBOs. A case study (by one of the present authors) reveals clearly that top management problems coupled with an inexperienced (and distracted) LBO sponsor contributed greatly to Revco's poor performance (see Karen Wruck and Michael Jensen with Adam Berman and Mark Wolsey-Paige, "Revco D.S., Incorporated," Harvard Business School Case 9-190-202 [1991]). In the case of Campeau's acquisition of Federated, a study by Steve Kaplan has shown that overpayment financed by leverage led to the company's default and subsequent Chapter 11 filing (see Steven Kaplan, "Campeau's Acquisition of Federated: Value Destroyed or Value Added," *Journal of Financial Economics*, 25 (1989), pp. 191-212.

"When ITT comes in and buys a company, the entire management team could quit and they wouldn't blink." As we will discuss later, ITT created a control system that allowed headquarters to manage a vast number of businesses, but did not give divisional managers the flexibility or incentives to use their specialized knowledge of the business to maximize its value.

Because C & D relied much more heavily on managers' operating knowledge, it was presumably willing to pay them more to reduce the risk of the managers quitting. At the same time, C & D was not completely dependent on incumbent managers to run Scott. Several C & D partners had extensive experience as operating managers. These partners had on several occasions stepped in to run C & D buyout firms, and they were available to run Scott if necessary. But, they clearly lacked specific knowledge of the Scott organization and were thus willing to provide financial incentives to incumbent managers to secure their participation.

Bonus. Scott's bonus plan was completely redesigned after its buyout. The number of managers who participated in the plan increased, and the factors that determined the level of bonus were changed to reflect the post-buyout objectives of the firm. In addition, both the maximum bonus allowed by the plan and the actual realizations of bonus as a percentage of salary increased by a factor of two to three.

After the buyout 21 managers were covered by the bonus plan. Only ten were eligible for bonuses under ITT. The maximum payoff under the new plan ranged from 33.5% to 100% of base salary, increasing with the manager's rank in the company. For each manager, the amount of the payoff was based on the achievement of corporate, divisional, and individual performance goals. The weights applied to corporate, divisional, and individual performance in calculating the bonus varied across managers. For division managers, bonus payoff was based 35% on overall company performance, 40% on divisional performance, and 25% on individual performance. Bonuses for corporate managers weighted corporate performance 50% and personal goals 50%.

At the beginning of each fiscal year performance targets (or goals) were set, and differences between actual and targeted performance entered directly into the computation of the bonus plan payoffs. All corporate and divisional performance measures were quantitative measures of cash generation and utiliza-

tion and were scaled from 80 to 125, with 100 representing the attainment of target. For example, corporate performance was evaluated by dividing actual EBIT by budgeted EBIT, and dividing actual average working capital (AWC) by budgeted AWC; the EBIT ratio was weighted more heavily, at 75% as compared to a 25% weight assigned the AWC ratio. The resulting number, expressed as a percentage attainment of budget, was used as a part of the bonus calculation for all managers in the bonus plan.

Thus, the bonus plan was designed such that the payoff was highly sensitive to changes in performance. This represented a significant change from the ITT bonus plan. As Bob Stern, vice-president of Associate Relations, commented:

I worked in human resources with ITT for a number of years. When I was manager of staffing of ITT Europe we evaluated the ITT bonus plan. Our conclusion was that the ITT bonus plan was viewed as nothing more than a deferred compensation arrangement: all it did was defer income from one year to the next. Bonuses varied very, very little. If you had an average year you might get a bonus of $10,000. If you had a terrible year you might get a bonus of $8,000, and if you had a terrific year you might go all the way to $12,500. On a base salary of $70,000, that's not a lot of variation.

The following table presents actual bonus payouts for the top ten managers as a percent of salary for two years before and two years after the buyout.

Rank	Before the Buyout		After the Buyout	
	1985	1986	1987	1988
1	18.3%	26.6%	93.8%	57.7%
2	14.0	23.4	81.2	46.8
3	12.8	18.8	79.5	46.0
4	13.3	20.6	81.2	48.5
5	11.2	19.4	80.7	46.8
6	10.5	17.1	76.5	46.0
7	7.1	10.8	29.6	16.6
8	6.1	22.9	78.0	46.7
9	4.6	6.3	28.7	16.8
10	5.1	6.6	28.4	16.4
Mean	10.3%	17.3%	65.8%	38.8%

The new bonus plan gives larger payouts and appears to generate significantly more variation in bonuses than occurred under ITT. Average bonuses

The experience and competence of the [LBO] sponsor in valuing the company,
evaluating the strengths of operating management, and arranging the financial
structure is critical to the success of an LBO.

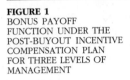

FIGURE 1
BONUS PAYOFF
FUNCTION UNDER THE
POST-BUYOUT INCENTIVE
COMPENSATION PLAN
FOR THREE LEVELS OF
MANAGEMENT

■ Payoff for CEO

■ Payoff for Vice
  Presidents and General
  Manager

■ Payoff for Other
  Participating Managers

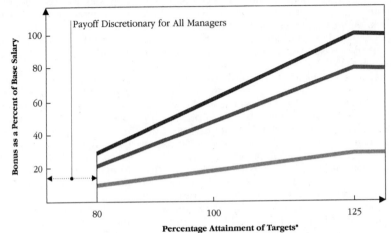

*Based on a weighted average of corporate divisional, and individual performance.

as a percent of salary for the top ten managers increased from 10% and 17% in the two years before the buyout to 66% and 39% in the two years after, a period during which operating income increased by 42%. There also appears to be much greater variation in bonus payout across managers within a given year. In the two years prior to the buyout, bonus payout ranged from 5% to 27% of base salary, whereas over the two years following the buyout, it ranged from 16% to 94% of base salary.

In addition to measures that evaluated management performance against quantitative targets, each manager had a set of personal objectives that were tied into the bonus plan. These objectives were set by the manager and his or her superior, and their achievement was monitored by the superior. Personal objectives were generally measurable and verifiable. For instance, one objective for a personnel manager was to integrate the benefits package of a newly acquired company with that of Scott within a given period. An objective for the president of the company was to spend a fixed amount of time outside of Marysville talking to retailers and sales-people. At the end of the year, the superior evaluated whether the manager had achieved these objectives, and quantified the achievement along the same 80-125 point range. This rating was then combined with the quantitative measures to come up with a total performance measure.

The weighted average of corporate, divisional, and personal target achievements was then used to determine total bonus payoffs. Figure 1 shows how payoffs were varied with rank and performance. If a manager achieved an 80% weighted average attainment of target goals, the payoff varied from about 30% of salary for the CFO to about 10% for lower-level managers.[6] At 125% attainment, bonuses varied from about 100% to about 30%. Between 80% and 125%, bonus payouts as a percentage of salary varied linearly with target attainment. Below 80%, payments were at the discretion of the president and the board.

The combination of equity ownership by eight top managers with a more "highly leveraged" bonus plan for thirteen others substantially changed the incentives of the managers at Scott. For those managers who held equity, the bonus plan, with its emphasis on FBIT and working capital management, served to reinforce the importance of cash generation. Those managers who were not offered equity were nevertheless provided financial incentives to make the generation of cash a primary concern.

---

6. For confidentiality, these numbers have been left intentionally vague.

THE MONITORING OF TOP MANAGERS

Purpose and Composition of the Board

The purpose of Scott's board of directors was to monitor, advise, and evaluate the CEO. As Henry Timnick describes it:

The purpose of the board is to make sure the company has a good strategy and to monitor the CEO. The CEO cannot be evaluated by his management staff so we do not put the CEO's people on the board. Scott's CFO and the corporate secretary attend the meetings, but they have no vote. The outside directors are to be picked by the CEO. We will not put anyone on the board that the CEO doesn't want, but we [C & D] have to approve them. We do not view board members as extensions of ourselves, but they are not to be cronies or local friends of the CEO. We want people with expertise that the CEO doesn't have. The CEO should choose outside directors who are strong in areas in which he is weak.

At the close of the buyout Scott's board had five members. Only one, Tadd Seitz, was a manager of the firm. Of the remaining four, three were C & D partners: Martin Dubdier was the chairman of the board and voted the stock of the limited partnership, Henry Timnick was the C & D partner who worked most closely with Scott management, and Alberto Cribiore was a financing specialist. The outside director was Joe Flannery, then CEO of Uniroyal, which had been taken private by C & D in 1985. Later, Flannery left Uniroyal and became a C & D partner. He stayed on the Scott board, becoming an inside, rather than outside, director.

Over the next few years three new directors were added. One was an academic one was a consumer products expert, and one, Don Sherman, was the president of Hyponex, a company acquired by Scott after its buyout. The academic, Jim Beard, was one of the country's leading turf researchers. Henry Timnick described the process of putting him on the board as follows:

Our objective was to find the best turf specialist and researcher in the country. We wanted someone to keep us up with the latest developments and to scrutinize the technical aspects of our product line. We found Jim Beard at Texas A&M. It took Jim a while to be enthusiastic about being on the board, and it

took Tadd a while to figure out how to get the most out of Jim. After Jim was appointed to the board, we encouraged Tadd to have Jim out on a consulting basis for a couple of days. Now Tadd is making good use of Jim.

Seitz and Timnick wanted an individual with extensive experience in consumer products businesses to be the second outside director. They chose Jack Chamberlain, who had run GE's Consumer Electronics Division as well as Lenox China and Avon Products. All board members were stockholders; upon joining the board they were each given the opportunity to purchase 50,000 shares at adjusted book value. All the directors chose to own stock.

This board structure was typical for a C & D buyout. Martin Dubilier explains:

We have tried a number of board compositions and we found this to be the most effective. If you have too many insiders the board becomes an operating committee. Outsiders fortify the growth opportunities of the firm.

The board of directors met quarterly. A subset of the board, the executive committee, met monthly. The executive committee was made up of Martin Dubilier, Tadd Seitz, and Henry Timnick. In their meetings they determined policy, discussed personnel matters, and tested Seitz's thinking on major issues facing the firm. The board meetings were more formal, usually consisting of presentations by members of the management team other than Seitz.

The Operating Partner

In each of C & D's buyouts, a partner with extensive operating experience serves as "liaison" between the firm's managers and C & D. The operating partner functions as an advisor and consultant to the CEO, not a decision maker. Henry Timnick was Scott's liaison partner. He had been CEO of a division of Mead that was purchased through a leveraged buyout, and had since worked with several of C & D's other buyout firms. Timnick spent several weeks in Marysville after the buyout closed. Following that period, he was in touch with Seitz daily by telephone and continued to visit regularly.

Timnick would advise Seitz, but felt it was important that Seitz make the decisions. When he

"The ITT bonus plan was viewed as nothing more than a deferred compensation
arrangement: all it did was defer income
from one year to the next."

and Seitz disagreed, Timnick told him, "If you don't believe me, go hire a consultant, then make your own decision." Initially, Seitz continued to check with Timnick, looking for an authorization for his decisions. Henry Timnick explains:

Tadd kept asking me "Can I do this? Can I do that?" I told him, "You can do whatever you want so long as it is consistent with Scott's over-all strategy."

This consultative approach to working with Scott managers was quite different from ITT's approach. Martin Dubilier explains:

ITT challenges managers not to rock the boat to make budget. We challenge managers to improve the business. Every company takes on the personality of its CEO. Our main contribution is to improve his performance. All the rest is secondary.

Scott managers confirmed Dubilier's assessment. Meetings between ITT managers and Scott managers were large and quite formal, with as many as 40 members of ITT's staff present. Scott managers found the meetings antagonistic, with the ITT people working to find faults and problems with the operating units' reported performances. By meeting the formal goals set by ITT, Scott could largely avoid interference from headquarters. Avoiding such interference was an important objective. As Paul Yeager, CFO, describes it:

Geneen [then CEO of ITT] said in his book that the units would ask for help from headquarters; that the units came to look at headquarters staff as outside consultants who could be relied upon to help when needed. I have worked in many ITT units, and if he really thought that, then he was misled. If a division vice president went to headquarters for help, in effect he was saying, "I can't handle it." He wouldn't be a vice president for very long.

ORGANIZATIONAL CHANGES AND CHANGES IN DECISION MAKING

The changes in organizational structure and decision making that took place at Scott after the buyout fall broadly into two categories: improved working capital management and a new approach to product markets. These changes were not forced on managers by C & D. The buyout firm made some

suggestions, but the specific plans and their implementation were the responsibility of Scott managers. Few of the changes represent keenly innovative or fundamentally new insights into management problems. As one observer noted, "It ain't rocket science." These changes, however, led to dramatic improvements in Scott's operating performance.

Management's ability and talents did not change after the buyout, nor did the market or the assets they were managing. The only changes were those in the incentive structure described earlier and in the management control system. According to Scott managers, the biggest difference between working at Scott before and after the buyout was an increase in the extent to which they could make and implement decisions without approval from superiors.

ITT, by contrast, maintained control over its divisions through an inflexible formal planning and reporting structure. Changing a plan required approval at a number of levels from ITT headquarters, and a request for a change was likely to be denied. In addition, because ITT was shedding its consumer businesses, Scott managers found their requests for capital funds routinely denied. After the buyout, Seitz could pick up the phone and propose changes in the operating plan to Timnick. This, of course, improved the company's ability to respond quickly to changes in the marketplace.

The Working Capital Task Force

Shortly after the buyout, a task force was established to coordinate the management of working capital throughout the company. The members of the task force were drawn from every functional area. The group was charged with reducing working capital requirements by 42%, or $25 million, in two years. They exceeded this goal, reducing average working capital by $37 million. The task force helped Scott managers learn to manage cash balances, production, inventories, receivables, payables, and employment levels more effectively.

Cash Management. Before the buyout, Scott's managers never had to manage cash balances. John Wall, chairman of the working capital task force, describes how cash was controlled under ITT:

Under the ITT system, we needed virtually no cash management. The ITT lock box system swept our lock boxes into Citibank of New York. Our disbursement bank would contact ITT's bank and say we need

$2 million today and it automatically went into our disbursement account.

To control cash flow in its numerous businesses, ITT established a cash control system that separated the collection of cash from cash disbursements. Receipts went into one account and were collected regularly by ITT's bank. Once deposited, these funds were not available to divisional managers. Cash to fund operations came from a different source, and through a different bank account. This system allowed ITT to centrally manage cash and control divisional spending.

When Scott was a division of ITT, cash coming into Scott bore little relation to the cash Scott was allowed to spend. After the LBO, all of Scott's cash was available to managers. They needed to establish a system to control cash so that operations were properly funded, and to meet debt service requirements. Wall describes the process as follows:

In the first six months after the LBO we had to bring in a state-of-the-art cash management system for a business of this size. We shopped a lot of treasury management systems and had almost given up on finding a system that would simply let us manage our cash. We didn't need a system that would keep track of our investment portfolios because we had $200 million borrowed. Finally, we found a product we could use. Under the LBO cash forecasting has become critical. I mean cash forecasting in the intermediate and long range. I don't mean forecasting what is going to hit the banks in the next two or three days. We could always do that, but now we track our cash flows on a weekly basis and we do modeling on balance sheets, which allows us to do cash forecasting a year out.

Production and Inventories. Between 1986 and 1988, the efforts of the task force increased the frequency with which Scott turned over its inventory from 2.08 to 3.20 times per year, or by 54%. During this period both sales and production increased. Because Scott's business is highly seasonal, inventory control had always been a management problem. Large inventories were required to meet the spring rush of orders; however, financing these inventories was a cash drain. Scott's production strategy under ITT exacerbated the inventory problem. Before the buyout, Scott produced each product once a year. Slow-moving products were produced during the slow season so that long runs of fast-moving products could be produced during the busy season. Before the spring buying began, almost an entire year's worth of sales were in inventory.

The old production strategy took advantage of the cost savings of long production runs. But, under ITT, managers did not consider the trade-off between these cost savings and the opportunity cost of funds tied up in inventory. The cash requirements of servicing a large debt burden, the working capital-based restrictions in the debt agreements, and the inclusion of working capital objectives in the compensation system gave managers a strong incentive to consider this opportunity cost. As Wall explained,

What the plant managers had to do was to figure out how they could move the production of the slow-moving items six months forward. That way the products we used to make in May or early June would be made in November or December. Now [instead of producing long runs of a few products] production managers have to deal with setups and changeovers during the high-production period. It requires a lot more of their attention.

Managing inventories more effectively required that products be produced closer to the time of shipment. Because more setups and changeovers were necessary, the production manager's job became more complicated. Instead of producing a year's supply of one product, inventorying it, and then producing another product, managers had to produce smaller amounts of a variety of products repeatedly throughout the year.

Inventories were also reduced by changing purchasing practices and inventory management. Raw material suppliers agreed to deliver small quantities more often, reducing the levels of raw materials and finished goods inventories. By closely tracking inventory, Scott managed to reduce these levels without increasing the frequency of stock-outs of either raw materials or finished goods.

Receivables and Payables. Receivables were an important competitive factor and retailers expected generous payment terms from Scott. After the buyout, however, the timing of rebate and selling programs was carefully planned, allowing Scott to conserve working capital. Scott also negotiated with suppliers to obtain more favorable terms on prices, payment schedules, and delivery. Lorel Au, Manager of Contract Operations stated,

Within two months of the LBO, the director of manufacturing and I went out to every one of our contract suppliers and went through what a leveraged buyout is, and what that means. We explained how we were going to have to manage our business. We explained our new goals and objectives. We talked about things like just-in-time inventory, talked terms, talked about scheduling. Some suppliers were more ready to work with us than others. Some said, "OK, what can we do to help?" In some cases, a vendor said, "I can't help you on price, I can't help you on terms, I can't help you on scheduling." We said: "Fine. Good-bye." We were very serious about it. In some cases we didn't have options, but usually we did.

The company succeeded in getting suppliers to agree to extended terms of payment, and was also able to negotiate some substantial price cuts from major suppliers in return for giving the supplier a larger fraction of Scott's business.

Scott managers felt that the buyout put them in a stronger bargaining position vis-a-vis their suppliers. Wall states:

One reason we were able to convince our suppliers to give us concessions is that we no longer had the cornucopia of ITT behind us. We no longer had unlimited cash.

The suppliers understood that if they did not capitulate on terms, Scott would have to take its business elsewhere or face default.[7]

Employment. Scott had a tradition of being very paternalistic toward its employees and was a major employer and corporate citizen in the town of Marysville. Some have argued that an important source of cash and increasing equity value in buyouts is the severing of such relationships.[8] There is no evidence of this at Scott. Scott's traditional employee relations policies were maintained, and neither wages nor benefits were cut after the buyout. Scott continues to maintain a large park with swimming pool, tennis courts, playground, and other recreational facilities for the enjoyment of employees and their families. The company also continues to make its auditorium, the largest in Marysville, available for community use at no charge.

Scott did begin a program of hiring part-time employees during the busy season rather than bringing on full-time employees. This allowed the company to maintain a core of full-time, year-round employees who enjoyed the complete benefits plan of the company, while still having enough people to staff the factory during busy season. As a consequence, average annual full-time employment has dropped by about 9%, entirely through attrition, over the first two years after the buyout.

New Approaches to the Product Markets

Scott is the major brand name in the do-it-yourself lawn care market and has a reputation for high-quality products. Ed Wandtke, a lawn industry analyst, says of the company:

O.M. Scott is ultra high price, ultra high quality. They absolutely are the market leader. They have been for some time. No one else has the retail market recognition. Through its promotions, Scott has gotten its name so entrenched that the name and everything associated with it—quality, consistency, reliability—supersede the expensive price of the product.

In 1987, Scott had a 34% share of the $350 million do-it-yourself market. Industry experts report, however, that the market had been undergoing major changes since the early 1980s. Indeed, Scott's revenue fell by 23% between 1981 (the historical high at that time) and 1985. The buyout allowed Scott managers the flexibility to adapt to the changing marketplace, assuring a future for the company.

The do-it-yourself market was shrinking because an increasing number of consumers were contracting with firms to have their lawns chemically treated. Seitz had proposed that Scott enter this segment of the professional lawn-care market for years, but ITT continually vetoed this initiative. Among the first actions taken after the buyout was the creation of a group within the professional division whose focus was to sell to the commercial

---

7. Schelling supports the potential for an increase in bargaining power to occur as the result of a precarious financial situation. He states: "The power to constrain an adversary may depend on the power to bind oneself.... In bargaining, weakness is often strength, freedom may be freedom to capitulate, and to burn bridges behind one may suffice to undo an opponent. ...[M]ore financial resources, more physical strength, more military potency, or more ability to withstand losses...are by no means universal advantages in bargaining situations: they often have a contrary value." T. Schelling, *The Strategy of Conflict*, (Cambridge. Mass: Harvard University Press, 1960).

8. See A. Shleifer and L. Summers, "Breach of Trust in Hostile Takeovers," in A. Auerbach, ed., *Corporate Takeovers: Causes and Consequences* (University of Chicago Press, 1988).

turf maintenance market. Within two years, the segment comprised 10% of the sales of the professional division and was growing at a rate of almost 40% per year.

In response to major changes in Scott's product markets, the company also made a major acquisition less than two years after the buyout. At the time, Scott's position in the do-it yourself market was being challenged by the growth of private label brands sold at lower prices, and by a shift in volume away from Scott's traditional retailers—hardware and specialty stores—to mass merchandisers. Under ITT Scott managers did not try to develop new channels of distribution. Timnick described it as too "risky" an experiment for ITT. The acquisition of Hyponex gave Scott access to the private label market. Says Wandtke,

With Hyponex, Scott will capture a greater percentage of the home consumer market. Hyponex is a much lower-priced product line. It gives them [Scott] access to private labeling, where they can produce product under another label for a lesser price....This will improve their hold on the retail market.

Hyponex was a company virtually the same size as Scott, with $125 million in sales and 700 employees, yet the acquisition was financed completely with bank debt. The successful renegotiation of virtually all of Scott's existing debt agreements was required to consummate the transaction. Because the new debt was senior to the existing notes and debentures, a consent payment of $887,500 was required to persuade bondholders to waive restrictive covenants. That such a large acquisition was possible so soon after the buyout demonstrates the potential flexibility of the LBO organizational form. It also demonstrates the ability of contracting parties to respond to a valuable investment opportunity in the face of restrictions that appear to forbid such action.

CONCLUSIONS

This study documents the organizational changes that took place at The O.M. Scott & Sons Company in response to its leveraged buyout. In so doing, it lends support to the findings of large-sample studies of leveraged buyouts that suggest the pressure of servicing a heavy debt load combined with management equity ownership leads to improved operating performance.

Such improvements were not the result of financial sleight of hand, but of important changes in operating strategy and management decision-making. These organizational changes came about not only because of Scott's new financial structure and equity ownership, but also as a consequence of other factors that have been largely overlooked:
- debt covenants that restrict how the cash required for debt payments can be generated;
- the adoption of a strong incentive compensation plan;
- a reorganization and decentralization of decision making; and
- the close relationship between Scott managers, the partners of C & D, and the board of directors.

We attribute the improvements in operating performance after Scott's leveraged buyout to changes in the incentive, monitoring, and governance structure of the firm. Managers were given strong incentives to generate cash and greater decision-making authority, but checks were established to guard against behavior that would be damaging to firm value. In the Scott organization, high leverage was effective in forcing managers to generate cash flow in a productive way largely because debt covenants and equity ownership countered short-sighted behavior. Value was created by decentralizing decision making largely because managers were monitored and supported by an expert board of directors who were also the controlling equityholders.

We view this study as a first step toward understanding how radical changes in financial structure, equity ownership, and compensation systems can be used as tools to improve managerial incentives and corporate performance. For companies in mature industries, the combination of high leverage and management equity ownership can provide an organizational discipline that adds value.

LEVERAGED RECAPS AND THE CURBING OF CORPORATE OVERINVESTMENT

by David J. Denis and Diane K. Denis, Virginia Tech

During the 1980s the number and size of leveraged buyouts and leveraged recapitalizations increased dramatically. Proponents of such highly leveraged transactions (HLTs) argued that the combination of high leverage and increased management stock ownership would strengthen management incentives to increase operating efficiency and resist the temptation to "overinvest," thereby increasing share values and corporate competitiveness.[1] Critics of HLTs claimed that the heavy debt loads would force cutbacks in productive investment and impose a short-term orientation, thus reducing competitiveness.

In this article, we offer further insights into the economic consequences of HLTs by presenting the findings of our recently published study of 29 leveraged recapitalizations completed between 1984 and 1988.[2] Unlike LBOs, companies undergoing leveraged recaps remain publicly traded after the transaction, thus affording us greater opportunity to observe changes in internal operating and investment decisions *after* the transactions. Our study was designed to answer two questions: Did HLTs in fact reduce the amount of internally-generated funds available for investment—and thus the actual level of investment? And if so, did these constraints on investment serve to increase or decrease shareholder value?

By way of a brief preview, we reached the following conclusions about companies undergoing leveraged recaps:

- their stock prices outperformed the market by 26%, on average, in the period surrounding the recap;
- in the first year after the recap, their ratio of operating (pre-interest) income to assets increased by over 20%;
- even with such an increase in operating cash flow, a 250% increase in interest payments led to a 30% reduction in their undistributed cash flow, and a 35% reduction in capital expenditures;
- over the five-year period *prior* to the recap, the stock market reaction to their announcements of major corporate investments (including acquisitions) was systematically negative;
- after the recap, the market reaction to their (much less frequent) announcements of investments was statistically indistinguishable from zero.

In short, our study provides striking evidence that HLTs added value by forcing management to pay out excess capital rather than diversify through acquisitions or continue to make unprofitable investments in mature businesses.

---

1. Major substitutions of debt for equity—as argued notably by Michael Jensen—would compel managements accustomed to reinvesting in low-return projects to pay out their "free cash flow" to investors. See Michael C. Jensen, "Agency Costs of Free Cash Flow, Corporate Finance, and Takeovers," *American Economic Review* (May 1986), pp. 323-329, and René M. Stulz, "Managerial Discretion and Optimal Financing Policies," *Journal of Financial Economics* (July 1990), pp. 3-28.

2. See David J. Denis and Diane K. Denis, "Managerial Discretion, Organizational Structure, and Corporate Performance: A Study of Leveraged Recapitalizations," *Journal of Accounting and Economics* (January, 1993).

TABLE 1
MEAN AND MEDIAN*
CHANGES IN OWNERSHIP
AND CAPITAL STRUCTURE

Variable	Pre-Recap	Post-Recap	P-Value[a]
Beneficial Ownership of Officers and Directors[b]	5.2%	7.7%	0.003
	(1.7%)	(3.6%)	0.001
Ownership of Officers, Directors, and Employees	9.4%	18.6%	0.000
	(5.9%)	(14.7%)	0.000
Total Debt/Total Assets[c]	41.3%	102.9%	0.000
	(44.6%)	(86.1%)	0.000
Long-term Debt/Total Assets	18.1%	69.2%	0.000
	(15.1%)	(49.9%)	0.000

*Medians in parentheses.
a. P-values measure the statistical significance of pairwise changes in the variables and are computed using a standard *t*-test for differences in means and the Wilcoxon signed-ranks test for differences in medians.
b. Beneficial ownership of officers, directors, and employees is obtained primarily from corporate proxy statements. Where proxy statements are unavailable, ownership information is obtained from *Value Line* and *Spectrum 6*. Changes in ownership structure are measured from the last reported ownership prior to the recapitalization to the first report of ownership following the recapitalization.
c. The change in total and long-term debt to total assets is computed from Compustat data and is measured from the last fiscal year prior to the recapitalization to the first full year following the recapitalization.

WHAT ARE LEVERAGED RECAPS?

Leveraged recapitalizations, also sometimes referred to as "leveraged cash-outs," typically involve significant payouts to common shareholders financed by new borrowings. Although most recaps are set up as large one-time dividend payments, they can also be structured as share repurchases or exchange offers in which some combination of cash, debt securities, and new common shares is exchanged for existing shares. In many recaps, share-owning managers and directors choose not to participate in the cash portion of the distribution, thereby increasing their proportional share ownership. Thus, as in the case of LBOs, leveraged recaps result in significant increases not only in leverage, but also in management's percentage share ownership.

Take the case of Kroger Co. In 1988, responding to takeover pressure from the Haft family and then a formal bid by KKR, Kroger gave its shareholders, in exchange for each share of stock, a $40 dividend, a junior subordinated debenture valued at $8.69, and a new "stub" share of common stock (that initially traded at $8.875). Two months before the Haft family came into the picture, Kroger's stock had been trading at just below $40. The total value of the recap package, estimated at roughly $57.50 per share, thus represented an over 40% gain for Kroger's shareholders (although it was still more than 10% lower than KKR's bid, valued at $64 per share).

Because Kroger's senior management and directors chose to forgo the cash and debt part of the distribution for a portion of their shares, their percentage equity stake more than doubled, from 1.4% to 3.0%. In this respect, the Kroger deal was fairly representative of our entire sample of 29 recaps; as shown in Table 1, the median percentage stock ownership of management and directors increased from 1.7 to 3.6%.[3]

The financing for Kroger's recap, which consisted of almost $3 billion in net new bank borrowings, $1 billion of increasing rate notes, and $704 million of subordinated debt held by selling shareholders, raised the company's debt-to-total capital ratio from just under 30% to over 90%. As shown in Table 1, the median debt-to-capital ratio for the 29 recaps in our sample increased from 45% to 86%.

---

3. For the changes in managerial ownership following large management buyouts in the 1980s, see Steven N. Kaplan and Jeremy C. Stein, "The Evolution of Buyout Pricing and Financial Structure in the 1980s," in this issue. For a sample of 124 large management buyouts between 1980 and 1989, they find that managers own 5.0% of the firm's equity prior to the buyout and 22.3% after the buyout.

THE DATA

We began our study by defining leveraged recaps as any payout to common shareholders financed by new borrowings. In searching the *Dow Jones News Retrieval Service* over the period 1984-1988, we found 39 cases in which companies *proposed* such transactions. The 39 companies consisted mainly of fairly large, well-established firms. At the time of the transactions, the companies had median total assets of over $2.2 billion and had been incorporated a median of 66 years.

Of these 39 companies, 35 had experienced some takeover threat (either explicit or rumored) before making the recap proposal. In 24 of these cases, management received a formal offer for the company. Thus, although leveraged recaps are technically "voluntary" actions taken by management, they were seldom made without outside pressure. This may explain why managers would propose a transaction that would severely limit their discretion over corporate operating and investment policies.

The proposed recapitalizations were completed in 29 of the 39 cases. The remaining ten proposals were not completed; in fact, nine of these companies were acquired. Our study focused on the 29 completed recaps. (For a listing of such companies, see the Appendix.)

The Stock Market Response

We attempted to measure the stock market's reaction to our sample of leveraged recaps by calculating cumulative daily stock price changes—adjusted for broad market movements and differences in risk—for each company over the period surrounding the recap and any associated takeover activity. In the 25 cases of recaps preceded by a takeover threat, we measured the stock price movements over a period extending from 40 trading days prior to the first public mention of outside takeover interest until the day we determined all uncertainty about whether the recap would go through was resolved. In the four cases where there was no

indication of a takeover threat, we started our calculation of daily stock price movements 40 days before the initial announcement of the recap.[4]

The process of summing these daily market-adjusted stock price changes across the recapitalized companies produced a measure of corporate stock market performance known as a "cumulative abnormal return," or CAR. For example, in the case of Colt Industries, on July 21, 1986, management proposed a recapitalization that gave shareholders $85 cash and one new share for each share currently owned. Adding the daily market-adjusted stock price changes from May 22, 1986, through this date, we calculated a CAR of +38%.

For the entire sample of 29 recaps, we found that the shareholders of companies that proposed leveraged recaps experienced substantial increases in value—increases very similar in size and consistency to those observed in LBOs. The median CAR for our sample of completed recaps was +26.2%, and almost 90% of the completed recaps had positive CARs.

THE EFFECT OF LEVERAGED RECAPS ON INVESTMENT POLICY

As stated earlier, one of the two principal aims of our study was to determine the extent to which leveraged recaps limited management's ability to reinvest corporate cash flow. To answer this question, we examined percentage changes in selected operating variables for the 29 completed recaps extending from the last fiscal year prior to the recap (year –1) to the first two full years after the recapitalization was completed (years +1 and +2).

We started by analyzing changes in operating income and undistributed cash flow, each scaled by the corresponding level of total assets. Operating income was measured before depreciation and thus provided an estimate of the cash generated from current operations. Undistributed cash flow was defined as operating income minus the sum of taxes paid, interest payments, and preferred and common stock dividends.[5] (Following leveraged recaps, common dividends and, to a lesser extent, preferred dividends are sharply reduced if not eliminated

---

4. It is possible that recapitalized companies are viewed by the market as still "in play," even after completion of the transaction. If so, the positive CARs would reflect the expected value of a forthcoming bid for the company rather than the value added by the recap itself. But the fact that only one of the 29 firms completing recaps was acquired over the subsequent three-year period would seem to contradict this argument.

5. For the use of this variable as a measure of free cash flow, see Kenneth Lehn and Annette Poulsen, "Free Cash Flow and Stockholder Gains in Going Private Transactions," *Journal of Finance*, (July 1989), pp. 771-788.

Although leveraged recaps are technically "voluntary" actions taken by management, they were seldom made without outside pressure. This may explain why managers would propose a transaction that would severely limit their discretion over their companies' operating and investment policies.

altogether.) By measuring after-tax cash flows not distributed to security holders, we aimed to produce a direct estimate of the extent to which discretionary (or "reinvestable") cash flows were reduced in the post-recapitalization period.

We also reported percentage changes in the above variables relative to a sample of 29 comparable control firms to account for possible industry- or economy-wide factors. In constructing the control group, each of the 29 recap companies was matched with the company in the same industry that was closest in size. For each of the 29 recaps, we then calculated the "control-adjusted" change in each of the operating variables—that is, the percentage change in the operating variable for the recapitalized company minus the percentage change for the comparable control firm over the same period.

Changes in Operating Variables

Increases in Operating Efficiency. As summarized in Table 2, our sample companies achieved substantial improvements in operating performance after the recap.[6] For example, the median increase in the ratio of operating income to total assets from year −1 to year +1 was 21.5%. The control-adjusted change was 21.8% over the same time period, suggesting that the operating performance of the control companies remained essentially unchanged over the same time period. In almost 80% of the cases, moreover, the ratio of operating income to total assets increased for the sample company relative to its control firm.

Reductions in Discretionary Cash Flow. Despite the significant increases in operating cash flow accompanying recaps, the large-scale substitution of debt for equity in these transactions led to significant reductions in the ratio of undistributed cash flow to assets, at least in the first year after the transaction. Relative to the control firms, however, the reductions in these ratios were considerably smaller (and statistically insignificant).

Reductions in Investment. Although the above measure suggests that undistributed cash flow was reduced following the recaps, it did not address the possibility that cash could have been generated by

selling assets of the firm, thereby increasing cash available to management for investment. We accordingly addressed the question of whether recaps limited new investment more directly by examining changes in capital expenditures.

For the sample firms, the median percentage reduction in the level of capital expenditures was 35.5% over the −1 to +1 period, and 41.5% over the −1 to +2 period (although only the second measure was statistically significant). These results were even more suggestive when we compared these changes in capital expenditures for the recapitalized companies to those of the control firms. The median control-adjusted reduction in capital expenditures was 46% over the −1 to +1 period and 65% over the −1 to +2 period. These findings show that the recap companies sharply reduced new investment relative to their industry peers following the transactions.

Reductions in Size. Changes in total assets provide a measure of the firm's *net* investment. The reductions in total assets reported in Table 2 indicate the sample companies actually disinvested on net— that is, they paid out to security holders more than their (pre-interest) operating earnings—in the years following the recaps. The median percentage reduction in total assets over the −1 to +1 period was 6.1%, and the median reduction in the level of total assets was just under $70 million. Much more strikingly, relative to their industry counterparts the recapitalized firms reduced their total assets by 42% through the first year, and by 57% through the second.

More Tests of Effects on Investment

In order to conclude that leveraged recaps reduced managerial discretion over cash flow, we felt we had to establish a more direct link between the reductions in internally generated cash flow and the reductions in capital expenditures. For example, if the reduced year +1 cash flow would still cover the year +1 capital expenditures expected in the absence of the recap, then the link was weak at best.

Accordingly, we calculated the ratio of year +1 undistributed cash flow to three alternative estimates of what year +1 capital expenditures *would have been* if the recaps had not occurred. The first

---

6. These findings are consistent with research demonstrating significant operating improvements by companies undergoing LBOs. See, for example, Steven N. Kaplan, "The Effects of Management Buyouts on Operating Performance and Value," *Journal of Financial Economics* (October 1989), pp. 217-254, Chris J. Muscarella and Michael R. Vetsuypens, "Efficiency and Organizational Structure:

A Study of Reverse LBOs," *Journal of Finance* (December 1990), pp.1389-1413, and Abbie Smith, "Corporate Ownership Structure and Performance: The Case of Management Buyouts," *Journal of Financial Economics* (October 1990), pp. 143-164 for LBO results.

TABLE 2

CHANGES IN OPERATING
INCOME, UNDISTRIBUTED
CASH FLOW, CAPITAL
EXPENDITURES, AND
TOTAL ASSETS[a]

Operating Variable[b]	Year –1 Level	Change Between Years	
		–1 and +1 (N = 29)	–1 and +2 (N = 17)
Percentage Change			
▪ Operating Income/ Total Assets	0.152	21.5%** (62.1)	14.9% (58.8)
▪ Undistributed Cash Flow/ Total Assets	0.076	–31.1%** (37.9)	–14.5% (37.5)
▪ Capital Expenditures	$153.1m	–35.5% (27.6)	–41.5%** (23.5)
▪ Total Assets	$2,234.8m	–6.1%** (31.0)	–5.7% (41.2)
Control-Firm-Adjusted Percentage Change[c]			
▪ Operating Income/ Total Assets		21.8%*** (79.3)	17.7%* (64.7)
▪ Undistributed Cash Flow/ Total Assets		–17.6% (41.3)	–8.4% (47.1)
▪ Capital Expenditures		–45.6%** (32.1)	–65.3%*** (18.8)
▪ Total Assets		–42.3%*** (24.1)	–56.6%*** (17.6)

a. Medians are listed with percentage positive changes listed in parentheses below.
b. Operating income is measured before depreciation and is scaled by the book value of total assets. Undistributed cash flow is defined as operating income minus the sum of interest expenses, tax expense, preferred stock dividends, and common stock dividends and is also scaled by total assets.
c. Control-firm-adjusted change is defined as the percentage change of the sample firm minus the percentage change of the control firm over the same interval. A control firm is defined as that firm with the same 4-digit SIC code that is nearest in market value of equity to the sample firm.
***, **, and * denote significance at the 0.01, 0.05, and 0.10 levels, respectively.

measure assumed that year +1 capital expenditures would have been the same as year –1 capital expenditures. The second assumed that a firm's capital expenditure growth rate between years –1 and +1 would have been the same as the rate over the previous two-year period. The third assumed that the sample firms' capital expenditures would have grown at the same rate as the control firms' between year –1 and +1.

The results of this exercise, as shown in Panel A of Table 3, clearly indicated that management's ability to invest was sharply curbed by the recaps. Assuming the same level of investment in year +1 as year –1, undistributed cash flow would have covered only 63% of capital spending. Assuming growth rates in investment equal to those of the past and to

the control firms', undistributed cash flow would have covered only 46% and 34%, respectively.

As shown in Panel B, moreover, the reductions in discretionary cash flow described above were almost entirely attributable to the sharp increases (257% in the median case) in interest payments. The increased debt-servicing costs far outweighed the positive effects on distributable cash flow of increases in operating income, tax savings from interest shields, and the reductions in dividends on common and preferred stock.

Overall, then, the changes in operating variables documented by our study suggest that the increased debt served to increase operating efficiency, reduce managerial discretion over cash flow, and reduce excess investment.

Over the five-year period *prior* to the recap, the stock market reaction to
announcements of major corporate investments (including acquisitions) by
recapitalized companies was systematically negative.

TABLE 3
MEDIAN RATIOS OF YEAR
+1 UNDISTRIBUTED CASH
FLOWS TO THREE
ALTERNATIVE MEASURES
OF PREDICTED YEAR +1
CAPITAL EXPENDITURES

A. Undistributed Cash Flow/Predicted Capital Expenditure

	Capital Expenditure Measure		
	Year -1[b]	Two-Year Growth-Adjusted[c]	Control Firm Growth-Adjusted[d]
Median Ratio	.634	.464	.343
Percentage < 1.0	75.9	75.9	72.4
Percentage < 0.8	72.4	69.0	69.0

MEDIAN PERCENTAGE
CHANGES IN THE
INDIVIDUAL COMPONENTS
OF THE FIRMS'
UNDISTRIBUTED CASH
FLOW RATIOS BETWEEN
YEAR −1 AND YEAR +1[a]

B. Percentage Changes in Individual Components of Undistributed Cash Flow

Variable	Median Percentage Change Year −1 to Year +1
Operating Income	12.7
Tax	−73.4***
Interest	256.6***
Dividends on Preferred	−57.8
Dividends on Common	−75.2***

a. Year 0 is defined as the fiscal year during which the recap is completed.
b. Predicted year +1 capital expenditure equals year −1 capital expenditure.
c. Predicted year +1 capital expenditure equals year −1 capital expenditure times one plus the sample firm's percentage growth in capital expenditure between year −3 and year −1.
d. Predicted year +1 capital expenditure equals year −1 capital expenditure times one plus the control firm's percentage growth in capital expenditure between year −1 and year +1.
***, **, and * denote significance at the 0.01, 0.05, and 0.10 levels, respectively.

The Case of Holiday Corp. To illustrate our general findings in a specific context, consider the recapitalization of Holiday Corp. in 1986. Following its $2.8 billion payout to shareholders in the form of a special dividend of $65 per share, Holiday's operating income increased from 18.6% of total assets to 24.7%, a gain of nearly 33%, representing an increase of $105 million in operating cash flow. Because of the increased debt payments accompanying the recap, the firm's cash flow available for investment was still approximately $50 million less than the level of capital expenditures ($245 million) in the year prior to the recap. And, indeed, Holiday's management actually reduced capital expenditures by over $70 million (to $173 million) in the first year after the transaction.

IS REDUCED INVESTMENT REALLY GOOD FOR SHAREHOLDERS?

As stated earlier, reductions in managerial discretion over a company's investment policy will increase its value only if the company is "overinvesting"—that is, investing in negative-NPV projects to pursue goals like growth or market share. The alternative possibility, however, is that the debt load from recaps compels management to forgo valuable investments with longer-run payoffs. The second major aim of our study was to attempt to distinguish between these two hypotheses.

The Stock Price Response to Investment Decisions

We do not know what future investments would have been made by the recapitalized firms in the absence of the recap. We simply assumed that companies that had systematically made value-increasing or value-reducing investments in the past would, unless acted upon by an outside force, continue to do so.

We identified 79 announcements of acquisitions and 88 announcements of other major investments by our 29 sample firms over the five years preceding their completed recaps. The number of announcements made by each company ranged from 0 (in five cases) to 29, with a median of 5. We also examined announcements of 63 acquisitions

TABLE 4
THE STOCK MARKET
RESPONSE TO
ANNOUNCEMENTS OF
INVESTMENT DECISIONS

A. Abnormal Returns[a]

Type of Investment	Sample Firms		Control Firms	
	[–1, 1]	[–5, 1]	[–1, 1]	[–5, 1]
All Investments	–0.90%	–0.88%	–0.17%	–0.46%
	(–4.09)***	(–2.84)***	(–0.63)	(–1.21)
	[n = 167]	[n = 167]	[n = 107]	[n=107]
Acquisitions	–0.89%	–0.82%	–0.41%	–0.81%
	(–2.62)***	(–1.71)*	(–1.11)	(–1.53)
	[n = 79]	[n = 79]	[n = 63]	[n = 63]
Non-Acquisitions	–0.91%	–0.92%	0.17%	0.02%
	(–3.14)***	(–2.24)**	(0.38)	(0.03)
	[n = 88]	[n = 88]	[n = 44]	[n = 44]

B. Pairwise Differences in Average Abnormal Returns[b]

	Sample	Control	Difference
Mean	–0.56%	0.05%	–0.61%
t-stat	–2.95***	0.16	–1.64*
Fraction Negative	0.71**	0.56	0.64*
Number of Firms	28	28	28

a. In Panel A, mean CARs are reported with t-statistics in parentheses and sample size in brackets below for all announced investment decisions and for acquisition and non-acquisition subsamples.
b. In Panel B, average abnormal returns for each firm are defined as the average of the three-day [–1,1] CARs associated with the firm's announced investment decisions.
***, **, * denote significance at the 0.01, 0.05, and 0.10 levels, respectively.

and 44 other investments reported by the control firms over the same five-year period.

As shown in Panel A of Table 4, the average stock price reaction to announcements of these investment decisions by recapitalized companies was negative (about 1%), and significantly different from zero (at the 99% confidence level). This is evidence that the recap companies were systematically making value-reducing investments in the years preceding their recaps.

As also shown in the top of Table 4, the market reacted uniformly negatively to announcements of normal capital investment plans as well as to announcements of acquisitions. The negative, non-acquisition CARs are especially notable in light of previous evidence showing that announcements of increased capital spending and increased R & D programs are generally greeted positively by the stock market (with average stock price increases of about 1%).[7] These results support the hypothesis that the correction of value-reducing investment strategies was both a motive for the attempted takeovers of the sample firms and a benefit of reducing managerial discretion over investment decisions.[8]

7. See John J. McConnell and Chris J. Muscarella, "Corporate Capital Expenditure Decisions and the Market Value of the Firm," *Journal of Financial Economics* (September 1985), pp. 399-422 and John J. McConnell and Timothy J. Nantell, "Corporate Combinations and Common Stock Returns: The Case of Joint Ventures," *Journal of Finance* (June 1985), pp. 519-536.

8. Studies of past corporate investment behavior have come to similar conclusions in examining LBO companies for which there is publicly available information. LBOs are associated with significant reductions in capital expenditures and are characterized by poor investment decisions in the years prior to the buyout. See Steven Kaplan, Chris Muscarella and Michael Vetsuypens, and Abbie Smith cited in note 6. For the wealth effects of pre-LBO investment decisions, see David J. Denis, "Corporate Investment Decisions and Corporate Control: Evidence from Going Private Transactions," *Financial Management* (Autumn 1992).

> **Goodyear's leveraged recapitalization limited its ability to continue making value-destroying, diversifying investments. In so doing, it effectively redirected the company's focus back upon the tire business, where it now appears to be having considerable success.**

TABLE 5
THE SHAREHOLDER
WEALTH EFFECTS OF PRE-
AND POST-RECAP
INVESTMENT DECISIONS

A. Abnormal Returns[a]

	Pre-Recap	Post-Recap	Difference
Mean	−0.90%	−0.26%	−0.64%
t-stat	−4.09***	−0.47	−1.16
Frac. Neg.	0.66***	0.56	
Number	167	36	

B. Pairwise Differences in Average Announcement Effects Per Firm[b]

	Pre-Recap	Post-Recap	Difference
Mean	−0.56%	−0.28%	−0.28%
t-stat	−2.95***	−0.70	−0.82
Frac. Neg.	0.71*	0.53	0.57

a. Abnormal returns are three-day [−1,1] CARs associated with announced investment decisions.
b. Panel B presents a pairwise comparison of the average pre- and post-recap average announcement effects for each firm.
***, **, * denote significance at the 0.01, 0.05, and 0.10 levels, respectively.

The Case of Goodyear. A clear example of this pattern of past overinvestment leading to hostile pressure and a defensive recapitalization is contained in the recent history of Goodyear Tire and Rubber Co. When Goodyear announced its diversifying acquisition of Celeron Oil for $800 million in 1983, the stock value fell by over 10%, representing a shareholder loss of almost $250 million.[9] In response to hostile threats from Sir James Goldsmith, whose announced intent was to reverse the company's disastrous diversification, Goodyear paid out $2.2 billion to buy back all of Goldsmith's holdings and an additional 36.5% of the outstanding stock. Following its leveraged repurchase of shares, Goodyear reduced investment from $1.7 billion to under $670 million. Between the period 40 days prior to Goldsmith's first threat through the execution of the share repurchase, shareholders experienced a market-adjusted return of 22.5%, representing an increase of nearly $760 million. As suggested, this is a clear case of a leveraged recapitalization that limited Goodyear's ability to continue making value-destroying, diversifying investments. In so doing, it effectively redirected the company's focus back upon the tire business, where it now appears to be having considerable success.

Interestingly, our sample of control firms did not exhibit the same tendency to "overinvest" as the recapitalized companies. Stock price reactions to control firm announcements of investments, whether acquisitions or otherwise, were not significantly different from zero.

Better Investment Decisions?

We also examined the stock market reaction to announcements of major investment decisions *after* the recaps. The 29 sample firms announced only 36 such investments in the three years following their recaps. This, needless to say, was a dramatic reduction relative to the number of investments made in the years prior to the recap, from a median of 1.2 investments per firm per year to 0.3 investments.

As shown in Panel A of Table 5, there was some difference between the market reactions to announcements of major pre- and post-recap investment decisions. Post-recap investment decisions were associated with an average CAR of −0.28%—statistically indistinguishable from zero. Moreover, only 56% of the post-recap announcements were associated with negative CARs. (Nevertheless, the difference in average announcement effects between the

---

9. See Mark Mitchell and Ken Lehn, "Do Bad Bidders Become Good Targets?," *Journal of Applied Corporate Finance* (Summer 1990), pp. 60-69.

pre-recap and post-recap samples was not statistically distinguishable from zero, as is confirmed by the pairwise comparisons presented in Panel B.)

This last finding led us to conclude that high leverage is beneficial primarily because it constrains investment; there is little evidence of improvements in those investments that companies do make following the recapitalizations.

The Case of Unocal. That curbs on investment can reverse the shareholder losses of recapitalized firms is well illustrated by the case of Unocal. In the five years leading up to its leveraged recapitalization, the company announced five major investments that collectively reduced shareholder value by $640 million. In the three years following its recap, Unocal did not announce any major new investments.

The experience of Unocal appears to have been fairly typical. We computed a measure of the aggregate dollar change in shareholder wealth associated with announced investment decisions in the pre-recap years, and then computed the same measure for the post-recap years. Specifically, we multiplied the percentage two-day stock price reaction for each investment decision by the market value of the firm at the time of the investment, and then summed these wealth effects across all investments. As a group, the sample firms' investment decisions reduced aggregate shareholder wealth by $477.3 million *annually* over the five years prior to their recaps. In contrast, after the recaps, the same companies' investment decisions reduced aggregate shareholder wealth by only $16.0 million annually.

Do Operating Changes Explain Recap Increases in Shareholder Value?

To the extent that curbing overinvestment was the principal source of expected value added in leveraged recaps, we might expect to find a significant positive correlation between the stock market reactions to individual recaps and the extent of the investment reductions that later actually took place. And, indeed, using a statistical measure called Spearman rank correlation, we found that reductions in the levels of capital expenditures and total assets were positively correlated with the size of the initial stock market reaction.

When these investment reductions were measured relative to control firm capital expenditures, however, the correlations were still evident, but statistically insignificant. We found no significant correlations between the size of the market reaction and the changes in operating income or in undistributed cash flow.

CONCLUSIONS AND POLICY IMPORT

The findings of our recent study of 29 leveraged recapitalizations are broadly consistent with the argument that increased debt plays a valuable role in restricting management's discretion over "free cash flow" in companies with limited growth opportunities. Leveraged recaps sharply reduced the amount of corporate reinvestment by the recapitalized companies, and the curbs on investment appear to have significantly increased the market value of such companies. The size of the initial shareholder gains, moreover, were directly correlated with the percentage reductions in investment we observed after the recap. Also telling, our study suggests that the recapitalized companies systematically misallocated resources through poor investment decisions in the years leading up to the recaps.

These results have important implications for the public policy debate surrounding highly leveraged transactions. Failures in the financial sector and by certain well-publicized HLTs created a political climate that led to increased regulation of such transactions, leading to a dramatic reduction in both their size and numbers.[10] Moreover, strengthened state antitakeover laws and more sophisticated takeover defenses have reduced the possibility of a successful hostile takeover. This in turn has greatly reduced the pressure on managers to engage in HLTs to preserve their independence.

To this day, the popular view of HLTs is that they forced cutbacks in productive investment, thereby damaging the long-run competitiveness of the levered firms. Our evidence, however, suggests that the primary consequence of HLTs was to prevent managements in low-growth industries from either "overinvesting" in their core businesses or diversifying away from them. By forcing management to return excess capital to investors and focus on increasing operating efficiency, they appear to have achieved significant increases in competitiveness as well as shareholder value.

---

10. See Michael C. Jensen, "Corporate Control and the Politics of Finance," *Journal of Applied Corporate Finance* (Summer 1991), pp. 13-33.

This appendix contains a brief description of the 29 completed recapitalizations in the sample. Each description contains a synopsis of the relevant events surrounding the recapitalization transaction, and, when available, the dates of the relevant events. We also include the cumulative abnormal return (CAR) and the abnormal dollar change in the market value of the firm's equity (Value) associated with each recapitalization.

■ **CBS Inc.**   CAR = 24.7%, Value = $531.5 million

CBS offered to repurchase 21% of its common stock (7/5/85). The move was in response to a takeover bid by Ted Turner. The contest began with a proposed proxy contest by a politically conservative group (2/8/85) and ended with management retaining control after executing the repurchase (8/2/85).

■ **Caesars World Inc.**   CAR = 26.8%, Value = $153.1 million

Caesars World announced plans to pay a $26.25 special dividend and add $1 billion of new debt (4/6/87). The move was designed to defeat a hostile takeover bid. Caesars World later dropped its recapitalization plan and instead launched a plan to repurchase 31% of its shares (9/8/87). The contest began with a hostile bid by Martin Sosnoff (3/9/87) and ended with Sosnoff dropping its bid (6/16/87) and managers retaining control.

■ **Carter Hawley Hale**   CAR = 28.0%, Value = $156.8 million

Carter Hawley Hale announced plans to spin off a division to shareholders and make a special payout of $325 million (12/9/86). The contest began with a hostile bid from The Limited (11/26/86) and ended with the announced restructuring.

■ **Colt Industries Inc.**   CAR = 37.8%, Value = $457.1 million

Colt proposed a recapitalization that would give shareholders a special dividend of $85 and 1 new share in exchange for each share (7/21/86). The move was financed through $1 billion in bank borrowing and $500 million in new debentures.

■ **FMC**   CAR = 25.7%, Value = $432.1 million

FMC announced plans for a recapitalization that would give shareholders a special dividend of $80 per share and 1 share in the recapitalized firm in exchange for each share (2/24/86). The plan would increase insider ownership from 19% to 41%. The board acknowledged concern about the possible emergence of an unfriendly suitor.

■ **GenCorp**   CAR = 34.9%, Value = $577.4 million

GenCorp announced plans to buy back 54% of its stock for $1.6 billion (4/7/87). The move was designed to fight a hostile takeover bid by a partnership consisting of AFG Industries and Wagner & Brown. The contest began with the hostile bid (3/18/87) and ended when W&B dropped its bid in the face of the repurchase tender offer (4/8/87).

■ **Gillette Co.**   CAR = 18.9%, Value = $405.8 million

Gillette blocked a takeover attempt by Revlon by agreeing to buy Revlon's 13.9% interest. The firm also announced plans to buy as many as seven million of its shares in the open market or through private transactions (11/25/86). The contest began with a hostile bid by Revlon (11/14/86) and ended with the targeted repurchase and announcement of the open market repurchases.

■ **Goodyear Tire and Rubber Co.**   CAR = 22.5%, Value = $759.0 million

Goodyear announced a plan to repurchase as many as 20 million of its shares and sell as many as three major units (11/7/86). The contest began with the disclosure of a large stake held by Sir James Goldsmith (10/29/86) and ended with the firm buying back Goldsmith's stake and announcing a tender offer for a further 36.5% of the firm's shares (11/21/86).

■ **HBO & Co.**   CAR = 135%, Value = $0.2 million

HBO proposed a recapitalization, citing the need to maintain shareholder value and defend against a possible hostile takeover (5/29/86). The firm later withdrew the recapitalization plan and proposed to purchase as much as 26% of its shares in the open market (8/7/87).

■ **Harcourt Brace Jovanovich**   CAR = 63.1%, Value = $674.5 million

Harcourt announced plans to recapitalize by increasing debt and paying a large special dividend (5/27/87). The move was designed to defeat a hostile bid by British Printing & Communications. The contest began with the hostile bid (5/19/87) and ended with the implementation of the recapitalization plan (7/27/87).

■ **Holiday Corp.**   CAR = 30.8%, Value = $471.6 million

Holiday proposed a special dividend of $65 per share (11/13/86). The contest began with a rumored hostile takeover by Donald Trump (9/29/86) and ended with the approval of the recapitalization plan (3/2/87).

■ **Inco Ltd.**　　　　　　　　　CAR = –6.3%, Value = $–145.7 million

Inco announced plans to distribute more than $1 billion to shareholders in a special dividend intended to thwart any takeover attempts (10/4/88).

■ **Interco**　　　　　　　　　CAR = 40.8%, Value = $475.9 million

Interco's board approved a $2.8 billion restructuring program consisting of a special dividend of $14 cash and $11 in senior subordinated debentures per share (9/21/88). The move was aimed at thwarting a hostile takeover bid from a group led by the Rales brothers (7/29/88). The firm retained control after amending its recapitalization plan to consist of cash and securities valued at $71 a share (11/23/88).

■ **Kroger**　　　　　　　　　CAR = 50.4%, Value = $979.9 million

Kroger announced a restructuring proposal which would possibly include a special dividend (9/14/88). The move was in response to the Haft family's receipt of federal clearance to accumulate an unspecified stake in Kroger (9/13/88). Kohlberg, Kravis, Roberts and Co. (KKR) made a subsequent unsolicited bid. The contest ended when KKR ended its bid and left Kroger to pursue its special dividend and restructuring plan (10/12/88).

■ **Multimedia**　　　　　　　　　No stock returns data available

Multimedia's board approved a cash-and-debt recapitalization plan which included an option to take a reduced amount of cash and retain some equity interest (4/9/88). The contest began with an LBO proposal by a management-led group of investors (2/4/85) and became a recapitalization proposal when the option to retain equity was added. The contest ended when shareholders approved the recapitalization (9/27/85) after purchasing the 10% stake of a competing bidder.

■ **Newmont Mining Corp.**　　　　　　　　　CAR = –9.9%, Value = $–185.7 million

Newmont announced plans for a major restructuring that included a $33 per share dividend (9/22/87). The move was designed to defeat a bid from Ivanhoe Partners. The restructuring would grant minority owner Consolidated Gold Fields a bigger stake in the firm. The contest began with the disclosure of a 9.1% stake held by Ivanhoe (8/14/87) and ended with Ivanhoe withdrawing its bid (11/19/87).

■ **Optical Coating Laboratories**　　　　　　　　　CAR = 11.4%, Value = $9.8 million

Optical Coating's board approved a recapitalization plan which involved a $13 per share cash payout (1/6/88).

■ **Owens Corning**　　　　　　　　　CAR = 40.7%, Value = $454.8 million

Owens Corning announced a recap plan, which would give shareholders $52 plus $35 face amount of new junior debt in exchange for each share (8/29/86). The contest began with a hostile bid from Wickes (8/6/86) that was later dropped (9/2/86).

■ **Phillips Petroleum Co.**　　　　　　　　　CAR = 10.3%, Value = $545.1 million

Phillips announced plans to recapitalize the company by more than doubling the firm's debt while reducing public ownership of the firm (12/24/84). The contest began with a takeover bid from T. Boone Pickens (11/8/84) and ended with Pickens dropping his bid and accepting the recapitalization (12/24/84).

■ **Phillips-Van Heusen**　　　　　　　　　CAR = 10.8%, Value = $26.5 million

Phillips-Van Heusen announced an acquisition program and a stock buyback of 5.2 million shares at $28 each (7/31/87). The move may have been designed to make the company less attractive as a takeover target. The contest began with a hostile bid by Rosewood Financial (7/13/87) and ended with Rosewood dropping its bid in light of the repurchase tender offer (8/4/87).

■ **Quantum Chemical**　　　　　　　　　CAR = 0.4%, Value = $9.1 million

Quantum announced a recapitalization plan involving a $50 per share special dividend (12/29/88).

■ **Santa Fe Southern Pacific**　　　　　　　　　CAR = 96.6%, Value = $4,491 million

Santa Fe announced that it would pay shareholders at least $4 billion in a restructuring of the firm (12/14/87). The contest began with the announcement that Henley Group held a 5.03% stake in Santa Fe (3/31/87) and ended with the announced restructuring.

■ **Shoney's**　　　　　　　　　CAR = 0.7%, Value = $5.4 million

Shoney's board approved a recapitalization plan involving a cash-and-debt special dividend (3/8/88).

■ **Standard Brands Paint Co.**　　　　　　　　　CAR = –12.5%, Value = $–29.3 million

Standard Brands offered to buy as much as 53% of its common stock in a recapitalization plan (11/11/87). The contest began with a hostile offer from Entregrowth (7/22/87) and ended with the successful repurchase tender offer (1/5/88).

Appendix (Concluded)

■ Swank Inc.
CAR = 19.2%, Value = $11.2 million

Swank announced a recapitalization plan that included a share repurchase in which most shareholders received $17 in cash and a share of new common stock (9/30/87). The firm also declared a distribution of a preferred stock purchase right. The measures were designed to fend off a hostile takeover.

■ UAL Corp. (Allegis)
CAR = 63.9%, Value = $1,675.7 million

Allegis announced a plan to pay a dividend of $60 per share that would be financed primarily through additional borrowing (5/29/87). The action came after the disclosure that Coniston Partners held a large stake in the firm. The contest began with an offer from the pilots union to buy Allegis (4/6/87) and ended with the resignation of the chairman (6/11/87) and a repurchase tender offer for 63% of its shares (2/1/88).

■ USG Corp.
CAR = 81.3%, Value = $1,609.7 million

USG announced a recapitalization and restructuring plan that offered holders $37 a share in cash, debt and stock (5/3/88). The contest began with the acquisition of a 9.8% stake by Desert Partners (10/6/87) and ended with shareholders approving the recapitalization plan (7/11/88).

■ Union Carbide Corp.
CAR = 56.6%, Value = $1,464.3 million

Union Carbide announced an offer to exchange cash and debt securities for 35% of its shares (12/16/85). The firm was seeking to fend off a hostile takeover attempt by GAF Corp. The contest began with rumors of a GAF bid (8/30/85) and ended with GAF abandoning its bid in the face of the buyback offer (1/9/86).

■ Unocal Corp.
CAR = 3.3%, Value = $209.4 million

Unocal announced a plan to repurchase 49% of its shares using $6.28 billion face value of notes (4/17/85). The $72 per share offer would be made only if a T. Boone Pickens group succeeded in acquiring a majority of Unocal shares in its $54-per-share bid. The contest began when the Pickens group acquired a 7.9% stake (2/15/85) and ended with management retaining control by defeating a Pickens-led proxy bid and completing the repurchase (5/30/85).

SOME NEW EVIDENCE THAT SPINOFFS CREATE VALUE

by Patrick Cusatis, Lehman Brothers, and James A. Miles and J. Randall Woolridge, Penn State University

T ax-free corporate spinoffs—that is, distributions of 80% or more of the shares in subsidiaries to the parent firm's stockholders—have become a very popular means of corporate downsizing in the 1990s. In 1993 alone, spinoff activity amounted to a record $26 billion, up from $4.25 billion in 1992, the previous record. Some recent notable examples include Quaker Oats' spinoff of Fisher Price, Union Carbide's spinoff of Praxair, Ball Corp. of Alltrista Corp., American Express of Lehman Brothers, Adolph Coors Co. of ACX Technologies, and General Motors of EDS.[1]

Several studies in the academic finance literature have documented significantly positive stock price reactions to announcements of corporate spinoffs.[2] From the market's systematically positive response, we can infer that such transactions are expected by investors to bring about significant increases in corporate operating performance.

In this article, we summarize the results of our own recent study of 161 tax-free spinoffs over the period 1965-1990. Our work supports the findings of earlier research on spinoffs by providing evidence of significant operating improvements in spun-off firms as well as stock market gains by both the parent companies and their spinoffs.[3] We also find that the size of the stock price gains achieved by spun-off companies is strongly correlated with changes in operating variables such as growth in sales, operating income, capital expenditures, and total assets. In this sense, our study can be viewed as furnishing yet another testimony to the stock market's efficiency—to its ability to capture future increases in operating profitability in current prices.

WHAT IS A CORPORATE SPINOFF?

Spinoffs represent one of three basic methods of divesting a subsidiary. The other two are sell-offs (in which the subsidiary is sold outright to another corporation or to the sub's managers in an LBO) and equity "carve-outs" (also known as partial public offerings, in which some or all of the subsidiary's stock is offered not to the firm's shareholders, but directly to the public).

Spinoffs differ from the other two options in several ways. First, spinoffs that meet IRS Section 355 guidelines are the only way to divest assets on a tax-free basis. Second, unlike the other two forms of divestiture, spinoffs provide no inflow of capital either to the parent or spun-off firm. Third, and perhaps most important, spinoffs grant complete operational decision-making authority to the subsidiary's management team.

We restricted our study to only those spinoffs meeting IRS Section 355 guidelines as tax-free spinoffs. Distributions of other firms' stock are generally considered by U.S. tax authorities to be dividends, and hence taxable. For a distribution to be tax-exempt under the criteria set forth in Internal Revenue Code Section 355, it must represent at least 80% of the outstanding shares of the subsidiary, and any shares retained by the parent must not constitute "practical control" of the subsidiary. As such, tax-free spinoffs represent restructurings in which a parent firm effectively removes itself from the management and ownership of the subsidiary.

A typical spinoff begins with a public announcement of the parent's intention to divest itself

---

1. We define a pure spinoff as a tax-free, pro-rata distribution of shares of a wholly-owned subsidiary to shareholders. Partial spinoffs, where the parent retains a proportion of the shares of the subsidiary, are actually more common than pure spinoffs.

2. See James Miles and James Rosenfeld, "An Empirical Analysis of the Effects of Spin-off Announcements on Shareholder Wealth," *Journal of Finance* 38 (1983); Gailen Hite and James Owers, "Security Price Reactions around Corporate Spin-

off Announcements," *Journal of Financial Economics*, 12 (1983); and Katherine Schipper and Abbie Smith, "Effects of Recontracting on Shareholder Wealth: The Case of Voluntary Spin-offs," *Journal of Financial Economics* 12 (1983).

3. The stock performance of spinoffs and parents is evaluated in Patrick Cusatis, James Miles, and J. Randall Woolridge, "Restructuring Through Spinoffs: The Stock Market Evidence," *Journal of Financial Economics*, June 1993, Vol. 33, No. 3, pp. 293-312.

of a subsidiary or division through a pro-rata distribution of new shares to shareholders of record in the parent. The transaction normally ends about six months later with the distribution of the new shares.

....

AN EXAMPLE.

The 1981 stock distribution by Standex International of its wholly-owned subsidiary Bingo King Co. provides an example of a tax-free spinoff. Standex, primarily a refrigeration concern, announced its intention to spin off 100% of its ownership interest in Bingo King, the leading manufacturer of bingo equipment in the U.S., on September 9th. The stated reason for the spinoff was to create value for shareholders by enabling investors to participate more directly in the growth of Bingo King and by providing greater visibility and investor interest for Standex. The tax-free distribution was made on December 8th, with shareholders of Standex receiving one share of Bingo King for every five shares owned.

The initial prices of spinoffs are determined in and by the market, and Bingo King began trading on a when-issued basis at $3.00 per share on November 23rd on the OTC market. The stock price of Standex declined $.375 on the ex-date to reflect the distribution, giving Standex and Bingo King total market values of $92.7 million and $4.1 million, respectively.

....

SOURCES OF VALUE: INEFFICIENT MARKETS OR MANAGERS?

Managers provide a variety of reasons for spinning off subsidiaries. Among the most popular, as the Standex case illustrates, is the market's alleged inability to evaluate conglomerate structures with unrelated businesses. Spinning them off to shareholders and thus allowing their shares to trade separately is claimed to enable investors to value them more accurately.

As another example of this argument, consider the following statement by General Mills when spinning off two wholly-owned divisions—Kenner Parker Toys and Crystal Brands—to its stockholders in 1985:

As historically demonstrated, the toy and fashion industries are substantially more volatile than

the company's other businesses. Because of this volatility, the appropriate market value of the toy and fashion operations is not fully realized with these businesses as part of General Mills.[6]

But, as described in Gordon Donaldson's classic study of the restructuring of General Mills,[7] what may have appeared to be market undervaluation to top management was clearly justified by downward trends in the company's profitability (although EPS was growing modestly, ROEs were substandard). As Donaldson argues, the company's drive for diversification in the late '60s and '70s (expressed in the corporate mission of becoming an "All-Weather Growth Company") ended up creating a conglomerate structure with major inefficiencies, including misallocation of resources and dissension among operating managers. In this sense, it was not market undervaluation but the promise of breaking up an inefficient organizational structure that prompted the stock market's strongly positive reaction to the company's decisions to spin off businesses unrelated to its core food processing business. And, in the wake of the spinoffs, the operating performance of both General Mills and its spun-off subsidiaries improved dramatically, thus vindicating the market's judgment.

A more plausible statement of managerial intent was that issued in 1986 by Univar Corporation, a distributor of industrial chemicals, when spinning off VWR Corporation, a distributor of industrial equipment. In that case, management attributed the spinoff to differences in strategies required for success in the two businesses and the benefits of decentralized decision-making in such cases:

A principal purpose of the Distribution Plan is to create independent entities designed to pursue the strategies best suited to their individual markets and goals.[8]

Improved Management Incentives. Besides providing the subsidiary's management with greater decision-making authority and thus gaining the benefits of decentralization, the separation of unrelated business units also offers expected improve-

---

6. *Wall Street Journal*, October 30, 1985, p. 40 and General Mills Inc., *1984 Annual Report*, p. 16.

7. Gordon Donaldson, "The Voluntary Restructuring of General Mills," *Journal of Applied Corporate Finance* (Fall 1991).

8. VWR Corporation, *Prospectus*, January 31, 1986, p. 1.

ments in managerial accountability and incentives. Having a separate stock price for the spun-off entity provides a more visible and objective criterion for evaluating managerial performance, thereby allowing for a more direct linking of managerial rewards with performance (in part, through significant direct stock ownership by managers).

For a more explicit mention of decentralization and the resulting improvement in management incentives, consider the explanation offered by Tandycrafts, a hobby and handicrafts producer, for its 1976 spinoff of Stafford-Lowden, Inc., a printing business:

...the separation will result in more intensive and specialized management leadership in each of the two corporations, the basis for more clearly-defined executive assignments and a stimulus to their executives to maintain management excellence. In addition, following the separation, each of the corporations will have a better framework for management decisions regarding operations and the employment of capital.[9]

In sum, the expected benefits from spinoffs appear to come from improvements in corporate fit and focus. That is, by separating unrelated businesses, spinoffs promise to eliminate operating and managerial inefficiencies stemming from a lack of strategic fit or synergy between the subsidiary and the parent. They can also improve the subsidiary's access to capital, allowing it to appeal directly to the market instead of the parent's senior management. Finally, spinoffs lead to greater decentralization of decision-making, as well as improvements in managerial accountability and incentives.

RETURNING TO THE COORS BUSINESS.

In 1992 Adolph Coors Co., the Colorado brewer founded over 100 years ago, spun off its businesses into a new entity called ACX Technologies. Over the years Coors had invested over $800 million in various pursuits unrelated to the beer business, including computer circuit boards, packaging for soaps and dog food, vitamins for animal feed, and an aluminum can producer. ACX Technologies includes Coors ceramics company, the largest U.S. manufacturer of advanced ceramics for industrial applications; Golden Aluminum Company, which has a pat-

ented technology to manufacture aluminum for packaging; Graphic Packaging Corporation, a producer of folding carton and flexible packaging for manufacturing; and various high-tech embryonic companies involved in biotechnology, advanced electronic modules, and other emerging technologies. Given the growth potential of the spun-off divisions, ACX Technologies was expected to be better able to raise (and allocate properly) the capital required for the growth and development of its businesses.

ACX began trading near $10 when spun off on December 12, 1992 and within 18 months (roughly the date of this writing) was trading near $36. ACX has not yet produced any earnings. Much of this gain has been associated with the potential for ACX's new process to produce aluminum sheet for cans directly from recycled aluminum cans rather than from newly forged ingots.

Meanwhile, the parent Coors has developed a niche strategy in the beverage industry focusing on specialty and light beers while pursuing opportunities abroad. Earnings projections are in the 15% range as compared to the earnings declines experienced over the past several years. Coors' stock price has also moved up, by about 25%, since the announcement of the spinoff 18 months ago.

THE EFFECTS OF SPINOFFS ON OPERATING PERFORMANCE

The evidence from our recent study strongly suggests that spinoffs are accompanied by substantial improvements in operating performance and profitability.

For each of the 161 spinoffs (and 154 parent companies) in our sample, we calculated growth rates for each of the following four accounting variables: net sales, operating income before depreciation, capital expenditures, and total assets. In a second step, we then adjusted each of these growth rates by subtracting from it the corresponding median growth rate for all 12,000 firms listed on *Compustat® II* over the same period of time. For example, if a company reported a 10% growth rate in net sales for the period 1986-1988, and the median growth rate for all Compustat® firms was 7% over the same period, we would report the company's "adjusted growth rate" in sales as a positive 3%. Using this method, we interpreted a positive adjusted growth rate as evidence of superior operating performance.

---

9. Stafford-Lowden, Inc., *Prospectus*, March 26, 1976, p. 3.

Poor Performance Before Spinoffs. Before the spinoffs, our sample of parent companies exhibited substandard operating performance. As shown in Table 1, for example, the capital expenditures of the median firm actually declined over the two-year period from three years before the spinoff through one year before; and when compared to the median growth rate of all other firms over the same periods, the adjusted growth rate was −17%. For operating income, the corresponding figures were an 11% median growth rate for the two-year period and an adjusted growth rate of −3%, again indicating inferior performance for the parent firms prior to their spinoffs. In fact, by all four adjusted growth measures, the parent firms were performing poorly prior to spinoffs.

TABLE 1
ACCOUNTING GROWTH RATES FOR PARENTS (FROM 3 YEARS BEFORE TO 1 YEAR BEFORE THE SPINOFF)

Accounting Measure	Growth Rate[a]	Adjusted Growth Rate[b]
Net Sales	11%	−10%
Operating Income	11%	−3%
Capital Expenditures	−2%	−17%
Total Assets	8%	−7%

a. The Growth Rate is reported as the median of the parent growth rates.
b. To calculate the Adjusted Growth Rate we do the following:
  1. Calculate the median growth rate for all firms listed on COMPUSTAT® for all possible 2-year periods.
  2. For each parent, we calculate the growth rate for the period from 3 years prior to the spinoff through one year prior to the spinoff.
  3. We adjust each parent's growth rate by subtracting the corresponding median for all COMPUSTAT® firms.
  4. We then report above the median of all parent-adjusted growth rates.

Post-Spinoff Consolidated Results Are Better. To assess improvements for *the entire organization* (that is, parent and spinoffs) after the spinoffs took place, we measured growth rates from one year before the spinoffs through two years after the spinoffs for the same accounting variables mentioned above. In calculating the post-spinoff numbers, we added reported figures for the parent company and its subsidiary.

As reported in Table 2, only capital expenditures exhibited a negative median adjusted growth rate. While the other adjusted growth rates reported in Table 2 were not large, they were not negative. Perhaps most important, however, combined operating income was a positive 7%. Thus, while parent firms exhibited poor performance prior to the spinoffs, the spinoffs appear to have enabled the separated organizations to improve their performance to at least the level of average performance across all firms.

TABLE 2
ACCOUNTING GROWTH RATES FOR PARENTS (FROM 1 YEAR AFTER TO 3 YEARS AFTER THE SPINOFF)

Accounting Measure	Growth Rate	Adjusted Growth Rate
Net Sales	17%	0%
Operating Income	17%	7%
Capital Expenditures	0%	−13%
Total Assets	14%	2%

Spun-off Subsidiaries Are Greatly Improved. The first annual reports issued by the spun-off companies provide a break-out of accounting figures for two or three years *prior* to the spinoff. We used these figures when the annual reports were available plus those reported by *Compustat® II* to calculate growth rates from one year before the spinoff through three years afterwards. (Because these figures covered a four-year period, they should be correspondingly larger than figures in the other tables.)

As shown in Table 3, spinoffs experienced very rapid growth in all our key accounting variables. The adjusted growth rates were significant for all categories, but especially large in the cases of operating income and capital expenditures. This growth in capital expenditures is consistent with the notion that capital allocation within a large bureaucratic organization (e.g., a conglomerate) can differ significantly from allocations made by decentralized management teams responding to market-based incentives. Once free of the parent organization, these spinoffs exhibited huge increases in capital expenditures. We also adjusted the growth rates for each spinoff by the median rates for other firms in the same industry and obtained similar results. Thus, these results are not created by spinning off subsidiaries in industries with high growth rates.

TABLE 3
ACCOUNTING GROWTH RATES FOR SPINOFFS (FROM 1 YEAR BEFORE TO 3 YEARS AFTER THE SPINOFF)

Accounting Measure	Growth Rate	Adjusted Growth Rate
Net Sales	55%	15%
Operating Income	72%	24%
Capital Expenditures	61%	39%
Total Assets	53%	20%

TABLE 4 COMMON STOCK RETURNS FOR 142 PARENTS OF SPINOFFS FOR THE 1965-1990 PERIOD*	HOLDING PERIOD (−24-X)	(X-6)	(X-12)	(X-24)	(X-36)	(12-24)	(24-36)
PANEL A: RAW RETURNS							
Mean	.618	0.12	0.23	0.52	0.67	0.21	0.13
Std. Dev.		0.41	0.55	1.10	1.09	0.54	0.49
T-stat[a]		3.54**	4.86**	5.62**	7.29**	4.69**	3.10**
N	154	142	142	142	142	142	142
PANEL B: MATCH-FIRM-ADJUSTED RETURNS							
Mean	.308	0.07	0.12	0.25	0.19	0.08	0.07
Std. Dev.	.872	0.43	0.55	1.16	1.29	0.62	0.65
T-stat[a]	4.64**	2.02*	2.67**	2.58**	1.73	1.53	1.27
N	142	142	142	142	142	142	142

*Returns are reported from 24 months prior to the spinoff ex-date (X) to 6, 12, 24, and 36 months after it.
a. The t-statistics test the hypothesis that the mean holding-period returns equal zero: * denotes significance at the 5% level, and ** denotes significance at the 1% level; two-tailed tests.

IMPROVED CAPITAL ALLOCATION.

One prominent example in this regard was Morton International, which was spun off from Morton Thiokol and experienced growth in capital spending of 67% from one year before through two years after the spinoff. Likewise, InterTAN and ShowBiz Pizza Time both exhibited huge increases in their number of retail locations after being spun off. In fact, an employee of ShowBiz informed us that, prior to the spinoff, the company's management had wanted to increase the number of retail locations for years but could not receive the capital allocation to do so.

THE EFFECT OF SPINOFFS ON STOCK MARKET PERFORMANCE

Although operating performance was poor in the years prior to a spinoff, the stock market performance of the parent companies during the two years leading up to the spinoffs was quite good. Corporate spinoffs are often part of a sequence of transactions in a larger, ongoing restructuring program. It is largely for this reason, we suspect, that by the time many spinoffs are announced, the stock market has already anticipated the eventual improvements in operating performance that come out of this restructuring activity.

For the 154 parent firms in our sample of spinoffs, we calculated both "raw" (or unadjusted) stock returns and "matched-firm-adjusted stock returns (MFARs) over various time intervals from 24 months before the spinoff ex-date (X)—the day that the parent firm's stock starts trading without ownership rights to the subsidiary—through 36 months after the ex-date. In calculating MFARs, we took the parent firm's "raw" return and subtracted the return of another company matched on the basis of industry and size over the same time period.

As shown in Table 4, the parent firms experienced an average return of about 31% in excess of the market for the two years *before* the ex-date, which is consistent with investor expectations that the restructuring will improve performance. For the periods one, two, and three years *after* the spinoffs (months "X-12," "X-24," and "X-36"), the mean raw returns were 23.1%, 54.0%, and 67.2%, respectively, and the mean MFARs were 12.5%, 26.7%, and 18.1%.

Market Returns to Spun-Off Firms. We also calculated longer-term stock returns for spinoffs over subperiods corresponding to buying at the closing price on the initial day of trading (day I) and holding for periods of 6, 12, 24, and 36 months after the spinoff (see Table 5).[10] The mean raw returns (MRRs) for months I-12, I-24, and I-36 were 19.9%, 52.0%, and 76.0%. The mean matched-firm adjusted

10. Short-term spinoff performance was measured for intervals of up to 40 trading days. Although the short-term mean adjusted returns are predominantly negative, none are significantly different from zero at conventional levels.

Spun-off companies experienced large increases in capital expenditures. This is consistent with the notion that capital allocation within a large bureaucratic organization (especially a conglomerate) can differ significantly from allocations made by decentralized management teams responding to market-based incentives.

| TABLE 5 COMMON STOCK RETURNS FOR 161 SPINOFFS FOR THE 1965-1990 PERIOD* | HOLDING PERIOD | | | | | |
	(I-6)	(I-12)	(I-24)	(I-36)	(12-24)	(24-36)
PANEL A: RAW RETURNS						
Mean	0.08	0.18	0.51	0.76	0.29	0.17
Std. Dev.	0.42	0.65	1.03	1.45	0.66	0.56
T-stat[a]	2.39**	3.48***	6.22***	6.67***	5.48***	3.95***
N	161	161	161	161	161	161
PANEL B: MATCHED-FIRM-ADJUSTED RETURNS						
Mean	−0.01	0.04	0.24	0.33	0.19	0.08
Std. Dev.	0.66	0.90	1.21	1.72	0.68	0.83
T-stat[a]	−0.26	0.50	2.48**	2.48**	3.65***	1.18
N	161	161	161	161	161	161

*Returns are reported from the initial trade (I) to 6, 12, 24, and 36 months.
a. The t-statistics test the hypothesis that the mean holding-period returns equal zero: * denotes significance at the 10% level, ** denotes significance at the 5% level, and *** denotes significance at the 1% level; two-tailed tests.

returns (MFARs) for months I-12, I-24, and I-36 were 4.5%, 25.0%, and 33.6%. As both these sets of numbers might suggest, one consistent finding is exceptionally good performance during the second year (months 12-24).

The best performer over three years was Show Biz Pizza Time with a return of over 1000% (a "tenbagger," in Peter Lynch's terms). Other top performers were Kirstrip Communications (a "seven-bagger") and Pennwest, InterTAN, Rollins Environmental, and United Gas (all at least "five-baggers").

....

A BONANZA FOR STOCKHOLDERS (THOUGH AT SOME EXPENSE TO BONDHOLDERS).

In October of 1993, the Marriott Corporation separated into Host Marriott and Marriott International. Host Marriott retains the real estate holdings of the venerable hotel chain while Marriott International focuses on the management of hotels, cafeterias, and other service activities. The proposal to divide Marriott into separate firms was made public in the fall of 1992 when Marriott shares were selling at $17. Immediately after the one-for-one distribution, Host Marriott shares traded at $5.50 while shares of Marriott International traded at $25 for a total of $30.50 (and implying total shareholder gains of $1.4 billion). Moreover, by June of 1994, Host Marriott was at $11 and Marriott International was at $28, thus representing a substantial run-up in shareholder value surrounding the decision to create two separate entities.

Host Marriott retained almost all of the old Marriott's debt and this arrangement created a year-long battle with the bondholders who argued that their security was eroded by the spinoff. In fact, Marriott's unsecured straight debt decreased in value by

16.5%, or $333 million, immediately after the spinoff announcement, which in turn contributed to (but by no means explained all) the shareholder gains. Management justified its decision to concentrate the debt burden on the real estate division, Host Marriott, by saying that this would free the high-growth management services operation to pursue its aggressive strategy unencumbered by the existence of large amounts of debt. Management also cited the benefits of decentralization, arguing that the management services operation requires a different set of executive skills and outlook than those required by the real estate operations, and that executives in the new Marriott International were stifled by the requirements of working within the old Marriott. As one executive was quoted, "This lets the tiger out of the bag."

....

Takeovers of Spun-Off Firms

In evaluating post-spinoff investment performance, we observed an unusually large number of takeovers of both spinoffs and parents. Eighteen of the 154 parent firms, and 21 of the 161 spinoffs in our sample, were taken over in a three-year period after the spinoff. Based on analysis of a control group, we concluded that both our parent firms and their spinoffs were five times more likely to be taken over than other companies.

To evaluate the impact of these takeovers on the stock performance for our sample of spinoffs and parents, we divided our samples into those taken over and those that were not. The 21 spinoffs taken over yielded a mean MFAR of 61.3% for months I-24 and 99.3% for months I-36; by comparison, the other 125 spinoffs provided mean MFARs of 18.9% and 22.5% for the same time periods. Among the parents, the 18 firms taken over after the spinoffs yielded mean MFARs for months X-12, X-24, and X-36 of 42.8%, 56.9%, and 69.6%. For the 113 parent firms not taken over, the mean MFARs were 7.7%, 21.8%, and 9.9% for the same time periods (and although these post-spinoff parent returns may not sound impressive, it should be kept in mind that such parent returns have come on top of 30% returns during the prior two years).

Thus, it is clear that much of the post-spinoff abnormal stock performance of spinoffs and parents is closely associated with post-spinoff takeover activity. For spinoffs, moreover, 19 of the 21 takeovers occurred in years two and three, the years showing the largest abnormal returns. The best parent performance occurred in the first two years after the spinoff, when 13 of the 18 takeovers took place.

Improving Corporate Focus. The fact that spinoffs were involved in a large number of subsequent takeovers suggests they may have created value largely just by facilitating the transfer of the assets of either the parent or the subsidiary to higher-valued bidders.[11] But it's not merely the change in ownership *per se* that was likely to add value in such cases, but rather the kinds of new owners. As our research clearly demonstrates, *the spinoffs in our sample that were taken over tended to be engaged in businesses unrelated to the parent's but closely related to that of the firm later acquiring them.* More specifically, two-thirds of the spun-off subsidiaries subsequently taken over had primary four-digit SIC codes that *did not match* the codes of their parent and *did match* the codes of their eventual partner. Some well-known examples of this refocusing activity included Kenner Parker's spinoff by General Mills and later acquisition by Tonka, and Fisher Price's spinoff by Quaker Oats and subsequent takeover by Mattel.

....

A BETTER HOME FOR FISHER PRICE.
Quaker Oats announced that in the summer of 1991 it would spin off Fisher Price, a wholly-owned subsidiary. In the 1990 Annual Report, Quaker Oats CEO William D. Smithburg cited the potential benefits from the spinoff of Fisher Price as follows:

The spinoff is good for our shareholders in several ways. It lets them decide whether they want to have a toy business in their portfolios. And, in the long term, the spinoff should allow Fisher-Price to operate more efficiently with faster decision-making and better flexibility. That should help it be more competitive and improve its ability to attract, retain and motivate employees. Fisher-Price remains one of the world's strongest and most trusted brand names. We fully expect Fisher-Price to have significantly improved performance over a two- to three-year recovery period. In addition, the spinoff lets Quaker concentrate on our core grocery business, where our future really lies.

As part of Quaker Oats over the period from 1989 to 1991, Fisher Price experienced significant deterioration in net revenues, net income, and capital expenditures. For the last two years as a wholly-owned subsidiary, the company reported *negative* net income figures of $37.3 million and $33.6 million. In its first two years as an independent corporation, Fisher Price showed positive net income of $17.3 million and $41.3 million, respectively. As a partial explanation for such operating improvements, the company provided strong financial incentives for its top people. For example, 14 insiders (officers and/or directors) held 6.2% of the outstanding shares as of March 23, 1993.

On August 19, 1993, roughly two years after the spinoff by Quaker Oats, Fisher Price announced it was being acquired by Mattel, another toy company. The Fisher Price shares had initially been issued at $23, and the (split-adjusted) price of $66 for the same shares after the merger announcement meant that investors almost tripled the value of their investment in less than two years.

....

Correlation between Stock Returns and Operating Improvements. In examining the operating performance of spun-off subsidiaries, we also found a strong relationship between changes in key accounting variables over their first three years of existence as independent firms and the size of their market-adjusted stock returns. Our findings suggest, for example, that for each one per cent rate of growth in sales above the industry median, the spun-off firm provided its shareholders with a stock return 0.68 percent above the return achieved by the overall market. For one percent increases in operating income, capital expenditures, and total assets, the corresponding figures were .40%, .69%, and .14% (and all of these estimates were highly statistically significant).

---

11. These results are consistent with recent theoretical work by Debra Aron in "Using the Capital Market as a Monitor: Corporate Spinoffs in an Agency Framework," *Rand Journal of Economics* 22 (1991), 505-18. She develops a model for a subsidiary in which the benefits of scale economies associated with being part of a larger firm are weighed against the costs of reduced managerial accountability and incentives.

> **At least two-thirds of those spinoffs subsequently acquired were operating in businesses unrelated to their parents... and were acquired by firms in related businesses. This is strong evidence that spin-offs help facilitate asset transfers designed to improve corporate focus.**

SUMMARY

Previous research documents significant shareholder gains from corporate spinoffs. Such work focuses primarily on changes in parent firm share prices at the time of spinoff announcements. The positive abnormal announcement-date stock returns reported for the parent firms presumably reflect investors' expectations of operating improvements by spinoffs and their parents.

Our recent research on 161 tax-free spinoffs over the period 1965-1990 both confirms and extends this body of work by producing the following findings:

■ Parent firms exhibit substandard operating performance prior to spinoffs, but after their spinoffs their performance improves to about average levels.

■ As newly independent and separately trading businesses, spinoffs experience significantly faster growth in sales, operating income before depreciation, return on sales, total assets, and capital expenditures than other comparable firms over the same time period.

■ Over the two-year period prior to the spinoff, the stock price of the average parent company outperforms the stock market by 35%, on average—a finding we attribute to already ongoing restructuring activity at such companies.

■ After the spinoffs, stock returns of both the parent and the spinoff outperform the market, on average.

■ Because both the parent firms and their spinoffs experience a higher rate of takeover activity after the spinoffs than do control groups of similar firms, part of these abnormal returns can be attributed to takeover activity. Nevertheless, even those samples of parents and spinoffs not taken over achieved significant shareholder returns.

■ At least two-thirds of those spinoffs subsequently acquired were operating in businesses unrelated to their parents' to begin with, and were acquired by firms in related businesses. This is strong evidence that spinoffs help facilitate asset transfers designed to improve corporate focus.

The question remains as to the reason for the exceptional operating performance by spun-off firms. Our best guess is that spinning off unrelated businesses has two major benefits:

■ a more decentralized, market-based capital allocation process, which in turn often leads to increased investment opportunities for spinoffs; and

■ a more accountable, focused top management team, often motivated by significant stock holdings.

Also, in those cases where the spun-off business ends up being acquired by a company in the same line of business, the sequence of transactions leads to better strategic fit.

Compustat® is a registered trademark of Standard & Poor's Compustat Services, Inc.

THE EVOLUTION OF BUYOUT PRICING AND FINANCIAL STRUCTURE (OR, WHAT WENT WRONG) IN THE 1980s

by Steven N. Kaplan,
University of Chicago, and
Jeremy C. Stein,
Massachusetts Institute of Technology*

T he leveraged buyout boom of the late 1980s has given way to the buyout bust of the early 1990s. After rising from less than $1 billion in 1980 to a peak of more than $60 billion in 1988, buyout volume fell dramatically, to less than $4 billion in 1990 and to under $1 billion in 1991.

How does one make sense of this enormous rise and abrupt fall? According to a wide range of observers, from financiers to journalists, the story is a straightforward one, albeit one that does not fit comfortably with traditional notions of efficient markets. Simply put, the buyout market overheated—the success of early deals attracted a large inflow of new money and, by the late 1980s, too much financing was chasing too few good deals. The end result was that many transactions were overpriced, recklessly structured, or both. In this view, the decline in buyout volume since 1989 represents a warranted market correction.

Many statements of the "overheated buyout market hypothesis" point directly to the widespread use in later deals of publicly issued, subordinated debt—that is, "junk bonds"—as an important factor. *Forbes* quoted one buyout specialist as saying: "It was so much easier to go to the public markets. It was cheaper, and there were very few covenants... It was fantasy." The *Forbes* article went on to say, "As long as the junk bond market existed, smart money was able to raise dumb money from passive investors—money that would accept high risks for skimpy rewards."[1]

---

*This is a shorter, less technical version of an article originally published in *Quarterly Journal of Economics* (May, 1993).

1. R. Smith, "The Takeover Game Isn't Dead, It's Just Gone Private," *Forbes*, October 1, 1990, 63.

With the benefit of hindsight, there appears to be some support for this "overheating" hypothesis. We recently completed a study of 124 large management buyouts (MBOs) executed between 1980 and 1989. Of the 41 deals in our sample put together between 1980 and 1984, only one defaulted on its debt—a default rate of just over two percent. In stark contrast, 22 of 83 deals completed between 1985 and 1989 had defaulted as of August 1991—a rate of almost 27%. Nine of these defaulted transactions had landed in bankruptcy court by that time. (Since August 1991, four more of the later buyouts have defaulted and nine more have filed for bankruptcy.)

Of course, hindsight is always 20/20, and the poor outcomes in the later deals may have been at least partly the product of subsequent developments, rather than poor deal pricing or structuring. Such developments could have included adverse macroeconomic conditions as well as regulatory actions that made it more difficult and costly to restructure troubled buyouts.[2] The primary aim of our study of MBOs was to determine whether there were indeed important differences *ex ante* between the deals done in the latter part of the decade and those done earlier. In other words, are there reasons to believe the later deals were the product of an overheated market and, thus, more likely to run into difficulties, or should any such difficulties instead be attributed largely to bad luck?

Our study focused on three broad categories of data that bear on the overheating hypothesis. The first relates to the overall prices paid to take companies private. Regardless of the details of the capital structure, or the extent to which there are costs of financial distress, it is clear that investors will earn lower returns as the prices paid increase relative to the fundamental value of company assets.

The second category of data we examined pertains to buyout capital structure. Even if the price paid to take a company private is a reasonable multiple of cash flow, a poorly designed capital structure raises the probability and costs of financial distress, thereby lowering the prospective returns to some classes of investors. In evaluating this possibility, we went beyond relying just on aggregate measures of leverage such as interest coverage and debt-to-capital ratios. While these measures can

provide useful information about the likelihood that a company will fail to meet its contractual obligations, they have less to say about the attendant costs of default. In principle, very low coverage need not impose large costs as long as the debt is structured in such a way as to lead to speedy, low-cost renegotiation. For this reason, we focus not just on the absolute magnitude of the debt burden, but also on the contractual features of the debt—seniority, maturity, and the division between public and private lenders.

The third and final category of data we looked at concerns the incentives of buyout investors. One of the supposed spurs to improved performance in buyouts is the increased equity stake of management; managers who own a large percentage of post-buyout equity might be expected to do a better job. On the other hand, managers who "cash out" a large fraction of their pre-buyout equity holdings at the time of the deal may have more of an incentive to take part in an overpriced or poorly structured transaction. A similar argument can be made when large upfront fees are paid to other interested parties. We examined whether these types of incentives changed over time.

Our study documented a large number of changes in the buyouts of the late 1980s relative to those done earlier:

- Buyout price to cashflow ratios rose, though not more sharply than market- or industry-wide ratios;
- Prices were particularly high in deals financed with junk bonds;
- As prices rose, buyouts were undertaken in riskier industries, and with somewhat higher leverage ratios;
- Banks took smaller positions in later deals and, at the same time, accelerated required principal repayments, leading to sharply lower ratios of cash flow to total debt obligations;
- Public junk debt displaced both private subordinated debt and the associated practice of "strip" financing (in which subordinated debtholders also receive equity stakes), thereby raising the expected costs of financial reorganization;
- Finally, management and other interested parties such as investment bankers and deal promoters took out more money up front in the later deals.

---

2. See Michael Jensen, "Corporate Control and the Politics of Finance," *Journal of Applied Corporate Finance*, Vol. 4 No. 2 (Summer 1991). Jensen subscribes to the view of an overheated buyout market, but then goes to argue that the costs of such overheating were greatly exacerbated by regulatory obstacles to financial reorganization.

TABLE 1
PRICING

Year	(1) Number of MBOs	(2) Capital ($ Millions)	(3) Net Cash Flow to Capital (as %)	(4) EBITDA to Capital (as %)	(5) Market E/P ratio (as %)	(6) Premium (as %)
1980-81	6	397.3	8.85	16.30	11.25	51.1
1982	8	164.2	13.27	17.18	13.24	64.8
1983	10	392.3	7.10	13.54	8.07	34.4
1984	17	383.4	7.85	14.34	9.86	40.8
1985	12	923.3	8.39	12.98	8.53	25.7
1986	15	371.1	7.54	13.48	6.01	38.7
1987	20	439.0	4.48	10.81	5.03	41.2
1988	31	476.7	7.27	11.48	6.93	48.1
1989	5	315.5	9.16	13.32	7.86	56.7
Total	124	395.4	7.56	12.75	7.65	43.0
N Obs.	124		120	124	124	122
Time Trend		(+)	(−)**	(−)***	(−)***	(+)
1980-82 vs. 1983-85		(+)*	(−)**	(−)***	(−)***	(−)***
1983-85 vs. 1986-89		(+)	(−)**	(−)***	(−)***	(+)**

*** Medians significantly different over time or in comparison periods at 1 percent level; ** at 5 percent level; and * at 10 percent level.

THE SAMPLE

Our sample of buyouts was taken from companies listed either as leveraged buyouts or as acquisitions by private companies in Securities Data Corporation's merger database, Morgan Stanley's merger database, and W.T. Grimm's Mergerstat Review from 1980 to 1989. We restricted this sample to large management buyouts (those with transaction value greater than $100 million) in which at least one member of the incumbent management team obtained an equity interest in the new private firm. We focused on MBOs because pre-transaction data for these transactions are generally more readily available and more complete.

We found 124 buyouts completed between 1980 and 1989 that satisfied these criteria. As shown in Column 1 of Table 1, the number of such large MBOs increased steadily (with the exception of 1985) throughout the '80s, and then fell off sharply after 1988. The median buyout in our sample had total capital of $395 million; and although there is a trend toward increasing size over time (see Column 2), that trend was not statistically significant over the entire period.

For each MBO in our sample, we gathered information describing the transactions from proxy, 10-K, 13-E and 14-D statements, and the *Wall Street Journal*, and collected post-transaction data from the COMPUSTAT Tapes. We also attempted to determine the extent of post-buyout financial distress by searching the NEXIS database for the buyout companies and by reading post-buyout financial statements. Post-buyout financial statements and other data were available for 89 of the 124 MBOs.

BUYOUT PRICING

The first question we asked was, How did buyout prices vary over time relative to fundamentals? We measured the buyout price (which we also refer to as "total capital") as the sum of (1) the market value paid for the firm's equity; (2) the value of the firm's outstanding debt; and (3) the fees paid in the transaction; *minus* (4) any cash removed from the firm to finance the buyout.

Of the 41 deals in our sample put together between 1980 and 1984, only one defaulted on its debt—a default rate of just over two percent. In stark contrast, 22 of 83 deals completed between 1985 and 1989 had defaulted as of August 1991—a rate of almost 27%.

Cash Flow to Price Ratios Over Time

We considered buyout prices in relation to two primary measures of operating cash flow. The first was earnings before interest, depreciation, amortization, and taxes (EBITDA). EBITDA is a measure of gross cash generated from operations, and thus represents an upper bound on the cash available to pay investors. The second measure, net cash flow, equals EBITDA less capital expenditures.

The ratios of both net cash flow and EBITDA to capital declined significantly over time, exhibiting a pattern (see Columns 3 and 4) broadly consistent with the popular notion that buyout prices rose relative to fundamentals in the 1980s. Furthermore, both ratios were significantly lower for late-1980s buyouts than for mid-1980s buyouts, and significantly lower for mid-1980s buyouts than for early 1980s buyouts.[3]

The decline in buyout cash flow to price ratios over time was not, however, a phenomenon that distinguished the LBO market from other U.S. capital markets. As shown in Column 5, the earnings to price ratio of the entire S&P 500 also fell during the 1980s, as the general level of the stock market rose.[4]

The fact that buyout prices seemed to move largely in line with the rest of the stock market can be interpreted in two ways. On the one hand, if we maintain the assumption that the stock market as a whole is efficient, then the absence of a buyout-market-specific pattern in prices casts a measure of doubt on the overheating hypothesis. On the other hand, it could be argued that if we are going to entertain the possibility of overheating at all, it may be unnatural to expect it to be completely confined to just the buyout market.

Another way to gauge the extent of a buyout-specific trend in prices is to examine the "premiums" paid in buyout transactions. We measured such premiums as the percentage difference between the price paid for a firm's equity and the price two months before the first announcement of buyout or takeover activity. Here again, as shown in Column 6, the data provided little support for a buyout-specific

pricing phenomenon. Premiums showed no significant trend during the 1980s.

In sum, the time series data presented in this section provide somewhat mixed support for the overheating hypothesis. Although buyout prices increased over the decade, this increase was not specific to the buyout market; it was evident in the broader stock market as well. This is not, however, our final word on buyout pricing. We later discuss how such pricing was affected by other variables in the buyouts, especially the use of junk bond financing.

AGGREGATE DEBT BURDENS AND THE RISKINESS OF BUYOUT COMPANIES

Pricing is only one of several factors that can affect the ultimate success of a buyout. Even if a buyout is completed at the "right" price, it may be structured in a way that leads to higher expected costs of financial distress. We now examine whether capital structures in later deals changed in a way that might have increased the *ex ante* likelihood and costs of financial distress.

Changes in Buyout Company Risk

One cannot, of course, look at debt and coverage ratios in a vacuum. The extent to which a company's debt ratio is deemed "high" or its coverage is deemed "tight" should depend in part on the underlying riskiness of its assets. Thus, we started by analyzing changes in company risk over time.

Our findings are summarized in Table 2, which presents two measures of total risk. Column 1 presents a measure of total risk calculated using financial data for the individual buyout companies—specifically, the standard deviation of the growth rate of operating margins (where operating margin equals the ratio of EBITDA to sales) over the ten-year period leading up the the buyout. This measure trends upward throughout the 1980s (though not significantly). The late 1980s buyouts,

---

3. In much of the analysis in this study, we used two different methods to quantify the statistical significance of the temporal patterns in the data. First, we measured the non-parametric or rank correlation between (all individual observations of) our variables and a simple annual time trend over the entire period 1980 to 1989. Second, as in the results just cited, we also used non-parametric rank tests to compare the values of the variables in three distinct periods: 1980 to 1982 (or the "early 1980s"); 1983 to 1985 (or the "mid-1980s"); and 1986 to 1989 (or the "late 1980s").

4. In our original study, we also provided crude market-adjusted measures of buyout pricing by subtracting the earnings to price ratio of the S&P 500 (for the quarter in which the deal was priced) from the buyout ratios of net cash flow and EBITDA to capital. These market-adjusted measures did not exhibit a significant downward trend; in fact, the trend for the net cash flow to capital ratio was even slightly positive.

TABLE 2
RISK[a]

Year	Risk Measures			
	(1) Std. Deviation Fractional Change in Operating Margin		(2) Brookings Study Estimated Std. Deviation Industry Earnings	
1980-81	0.18	[6]	0.213	[6]
1982	0.19	[8]	0.249	[7]
1983	0.17	[10]	0.074	[9]
1984	0.13	[16]	0.249	[16]
1985	0.13	[11]	0.249	[12]
1986	0.19	[12]	0.348	[13]
1987	0.20	[17]	0.249	[18]
1988	0.18	[24]	0.249	[28]
1989	0.18	[3]	0.262	[5]
Total	0.17	[108]	0.249	[114]
Time Trend	(+)		(+)**	
1980-82 vs. 1983-85	(−)		(−)	
1983-85 vs. 1986-89	(+)**		(+)*	

a. The two columns under each risk factor are the median and number of observations, respectively.
*** Medians significantly different over time or in comparison periods at 1 percent level; ** at 5 percent level; and * at 10 percent level.

however, have significantly more risk than those in the mid-1980s.

Column 2 presents a measure of *industry* total risk used by a 1990 Brookings Institute Study (hereafter referred to as "the Brookings Study")[5]— namely, the standard deviation of the growth rate of industry real earnings. The pattern of changes in this industry measure throughout the '80s was similar to that of our firm-specific measure. The risk was significantly higher for buyouts of the late 1980s than for those of the mid-1980s.

In sum, our measures of total risk suggest that buyout companies in the late 1980s were somewhat riskier than those in earlier years. Other things equal, this would seem to dictate a more conservative capital structure. With this observation in mind, we now turn to the aggregate capital structure data.

Aggregate Debt Burdens

For each of the 124 companies in our sample, we calculated the ratio of total post-buyout debt to total capital, where total post-buyout debt equals the sum of (the market value of) new debt issued to finance the buyout and (the book value of) pre-buyout debt retained. As shown in Column 1 of Table 3, the median debt to total capital ratios increased over time. The time trend was positive and significant, and the ratios in 1986 to 1989 (with a median of 90.3%) were significantly larger than those in 1983 to 1985 (median 86.5%).

Moreover, our measure of total debt may have understated the amount of debt in the capital structure because it excluded preferred stock with fixed commitments. In several cases, such preferred stock was exchangeable into subordinated debt. Accordingly, we calculated yearly medians of post-buyout common stock to total capital, where post-buyout common stock included preferred stock convertible into common stock (but not straight preferred stock or preferred stock convertible into debt). As shown in Column 2, these common stock ratios fell significantly over the '80s, with the lowest ratios (median of 5.56%) from 1986 to 1989.[6]

5. See B. Bernanke, J. Campbell, and T. Whited, "U.S. Corporate Leverage: Developments in 1987 and 1988," *Brookings Papers on Economic Activity,* I (1990), 255-286.
6. As was true of buyout pricing multiples, and will be shown to be true of coverage ratios later, the equity ratios became more conservative in 1989, thus suggesting a turning point. Arguably, the 1989 deals do not belong in our classification of the late 1980s. These buyouts took place as the public junk bond market began to falter and, thus, do not necessarily fit with the overheating hypothesis. Indeed, the few observations we have suggest that the 1989 buyouts were different from those of the preceding three years. Nevertheless, eliminating 1989 buyouts from the late 1980s sample has no effect on our statistical results.

Consistent with the lower cash flow to price ratios and rising leverage ratios, we found a negative time trend for both interest coverage measures, with both net cash flow and EBITDA to interest reaching a minimum in 1987 and 1988.

TABLE 3
AGGREGATE DEBT AND COVERAGE RATIOS[a]

Year	(1) Post-Buyout Debt to Capital (as %)	(2) Common Stock to Capital (as %)	(3) Net Cash Flow to Interest	(4) EBITDA to Interest	(5) Net Cash Flow to Cash Interest	(6) EBITDA to Cash Interest	(7) Req'd Debt Repay in 2 Years to EBITDA (as %)	(8) Net Cash Flow to [Cash Interest + (Repay in 2 Yrs)/2]	(9) EBITDA to [Cash Interest + (Repay in 2 Yrs)/2]
1980-81	88.3	10.53	0.56	1.15	0.56	1.15	0.0	0.56	1.15
	6	6	6	6	6	6	6	5	6
1982	87.3	6.67	0.90	1.28	0.90	1.28	0.0	0.75	1.16
	8	8	8	8	8	8	6	5	6
1983	87.2	11.54	0.67	1.26	0.67	1.2	22.3	0.69	1.18
	10	10	10	10	10	10	7	7	7
1984	88.7	7.91	0.74	1.29	0.74	1.29	32.3	0.66	1.12
	17	17	17	17	17	17	11	11	11
1985	86.0	7.03	0.75	1.22	0.82	1.30	59.2	0.59	1.09
	12	12	12	12	12	12	11	11	11
1986	90.7	5.60	0.73	1.50	0.73	1.75	160.0	0.36	0.72
	15	15	13	15	13	15	10	8	10
1987	88.9	4.04	0.43	1.12	0.52	1.27	103.5	0.21	0.76
	20	20	19	20	19	20	14	14	14
1988	90.5	6.13	0.60	1.11	0.70	1.16	103.5	0.41	0.66
	31	31	30	31	30	31	21	20	21
1989	83.2	13.20	0.83	1.27	0.83	1.27	43.3	0.62	0.89
	5	5	5	5	5	5	4	4	4
Total	89.1	6.52	0.68	1.20	0.74	1.27	60.0	0.46	0.89
	124	124	120	124	120	124	90	85	90

Time Trend

	(+)**	(−)*	(−)	(−)*	(−)	(−)	(+)***	(−)**	(−)***
1980-82 v. 1983-85									
	(−)	(+)	(−)	(−)	(+)	(+)	(+)***	(−)	(−)
1983-85 v. 1986-89									
	(+)***	(−)***	(−)	(−)	(−)	(−)	(+)***	(−)***	(−)***

a. The two rows in each cell are the median and number of observations, respectively.
*** Medians significantly different over time or in comparison periods at 1 percent level; ** at 5 percent level; and * at 10 percent level.

The increase in debt ratios and the decline in equity ratios are interesting and somewhat puzzling aspects of buyout financial structures. The higher prices paid relative to cash flows in late 1980s buyouts, even if perfectly rational, would appear to suggest that these buyouts were associated with more optimistic growth expectations than earlier ones. But if the later deals were associated with expected cash flows that were more "back-loaded" in time (as well as somewhat riskier), one might have expected them to be structured with less debt relative to total value.

To explore this issue further, the remaining columns of Table 3 present several measures of the adequacy of current cash flows relative to contractual obligations. These measures use net cash flow and EBITDA in the last full year before the buyout. We calculated expected interest payments based on the interest rates and debt amounts projected in the proxy or 14D statements describing the buyouts.

Columns 3 and 4 compare net cash flow and EBITDA to expected total interest payments in the first post-buyout year. Consistent with the lower cash flow to price ratios and rising leverage ratios, we found a negative time trend for both interest coverage measures, with both net cash flow and EBITDA to interest reaching a minimum in 1987 and 1988.

The ratios in Columns 3 and 4 use total interest obligations, which include both cash and non-cash interest. Non-cash interest is associated with deferred interest debt, which includes zero-coupon and pay-in-kind (PIK) bonds. Including non-cash interest payments may present a misleading picture because the use of such payments (as we point out later) increased significantly in the second half of the 1980s. In fact, they may have been introduced precisely to allow firms with more "back-loaded" cash flows to support high levels of debt.

To test for this possibility we repeated our coverage calculations using cash interest payments that excluded interest payments on deferred interest debt. As expected, this adjustment improved the relative standing of the coverage ratios of the later deals (see Columns 5 and 6).

Although interest coverage is an often-used measure of financial soundness, it does not fully capture a firm's ability to meet all its debt-related obligations. Cash flow must also be devoted to making principal repayments. Ninety of the 124 transactions in our sample reported a principal repayment schedule for their bank debt. As shown in Column 7, the ratio of required debt payments (including principal repayments) for these 90 buyouts rose sharply over time, with an pronounced break between 1985 and 1986, when principal repayments increased by a factor of more than 2.7.

We next repeated our coverage calculations, this time considering how net cash flow and EBITDA compared to total cash debt obligations (including principal). As shown in Columns 8 and 9, these coverages were substantially lower for 1986-1989 buyouts than for earlier deals. For example, the median ratio of EBITDA to cash obligations was always above one before 1986, but fell to between 0.76 and 0.66 for the 1986-88 period before recovering somewhat to 0.89 in 1989. Similarly, the median ratio of net cash flow to cash obligations, which was always above 0.56 before 1986, did not exceed 0.41 from 1986 to 1988. Again, the ratio recovered in 1989, rising to 0.62.

This change in the coverage ratios after 1985 implies a sharp deterioration in the ability of buyout firms to meet their total debt-related obligations out of operating cash flows. For example, a buyout with the 1988 median ratio of 0.41—the highest median of the 1986 to 1988 period—would have needed to increase net cash flow by 144% (0.59/0.41) in its first year to meet its debt obligations.[7]

These coverage numbers, however, present only part of the overall picture on financial soundness. In many of the later buyouts, asset sales may have represented an alternative means of generating the cash to make debt-related payments.[8] And even if planned asset sales failed to materialize, and required payments could not be met, this would not necessarily have meant disaster. The costs at this point would have depended critically on the ability of creditors to restructure their claims efficiently.

In sum, then, the data in this section strongly suggest that the buyouts of the late 1980s had a higher *ex ante* probability of winding up in a restructuring situation, particularly if planned asset sales were subject to some uncertainty. The data have thus far had less to say about the possible costs of such restructurings.

SENIOR BANK DEBT AND THE ROLE OF ASSET SALES

We now focus our attention on specific components of buyout capital structures. The most senior part of the capital structure for most of our MBOs was a term loan (and, often, an accompanying revolving credit loan) arranged by one or more commercial banks. As we already have seen, banks accelerated required principal payments over time.

As shown in the Column 1 of Table 4, the ratio of bank debt to total debt declined significantly over time, with a distinct break in 1985. Bank debt represented over 70% of total debt in the period 1982 to 1984. In 1985, it dropped to 42% of all debt. After that, the ratio stabilized, ranging between 52% and 57% from 1986 to 1989. As we discuss in more detail later, this decline in bank debt ratios coincided with increasing use of public bonds in the subordinated debt tier of the capital structure.

We next examined the interest rate terms of the bank loans, in part to provide a measure of banks' assessments of the riskiness of buyouts. In most of

---

7. Given that Kaplan's study found a roughly 40% increase in net cash flow for a sample of management buyouts announced between 1979 and 1985, it is hard to see how operating cash flows could be expected to meet required debt service payments. See S. Kaplan, "The Effects of Management Buyouts on Operations and Value," *Journal of Financial Economics*, XXIV (1989), 217-254.

8. See A. Shleifer and R. Vishny, "Asset Sales and Debt Capacity," *Journal of Finance*, XLVII (1992).

The ratio of bank debt to total debt declined significantly over time, with a distinct break in 1985. Bank debt represented over 70% of total debt in the period 1982 to 1984, but dropped to 42% in 1985. This decline in bank debt ratios coincided with increasing use of public bonds in the subordinated debt tier of the capital structure.

TABLE 4
BANK DEBT[a]

Year	(1) Bank Debt to Total Debt	(2) Bank Interest Rate versus Prime	(3) Bank Fees to Bank Debt	(4) Fee-adjusted Bank Interest Rate versus Prime	(5) Asset Sales (% of Deals)	(6) Asset Sale Amount as % of Capital (if Asset Sale)
1980-81	39.0	0.75	0.21	N/A	50.0	15.5
	6	5	1	0	6	3
1982	72.9	1.25	1.28	1.31	0.0	N/A
	8	7	5	5	8	0
1983	75.7	1.38	0.40	1.44	33.3	21.1
	10	8	8	8	9	3
1984	72.0	1.44	0.79	1.59	18.8	23.2
	17	16	14	13	16	3
1985	42.0	1.50	1.94	2.13	33.3	14.2
	12	11	7	7	12	4
1986	52.0	1.50	2.06	2.21	60.0	19.3
	15	13	13	12	15	8
1987	54.3	1.50	2.06	2.13	40.0	22.4
	19	17	15	15	20	8
1988	55.3	1.50	2.49	2.24	32.3	14.8
	29	27	22	22	31	10
1989	57.1	1.50	2.38	1.98	20.0	11.4
	5	5	4	3	5	1
Total	56.4	1.50	1.93	2.12	33.6	18.1
	121	109	89	85	122	40
Time Trend						
1980-82 vs. 1983-85	(−)**	(+)***	(+)***	(+)***	(+)	(−)
1983-85 vs. 1986-89	(−)	(+)	(−)	(+)	(+)	(−)
	(−)*	(+)***	(+)***	(+)***	(+)	(−)

a. The two rows in each cell are the median and number of observations, respectively.
*** Medians significantly different over time or in comparison periods at 1 percent level; ** at 5 percent level; and * at 10 percent level.

the deals, the interest rate on the bank debt was set as the minimum of a spread over the prime rate or a spread over LIBOR. As shown in Column 2, although the spreads over prime trended slightly upward over time (the median values of the prime-based spreads were 1.125%, 1.50%, and 1.50% in the early, middle, and late 1980s), they nevertheless seem to have been remarkably stable.

The relative lack of variation in spreads showed up in other tests we ran as well. For example, when we pooled all deals between 1984 and 1989, we found that 58 of 89 buyouts had prime-based spreads of 1.50%. The highest spread was 2%, the lowest 1%. This uniformity in loan pricing seems puzzling. If we take a heterogeneous group of companies and impose a similar highly leveraged capital structure on all of them, one might expect a great deal of variation in the riskiness of the debt and, hence, a good deal of variation in its pricing.

One explanation for the lack of variation in loan pricing is that banks adjusted their fees over time. As shown in Column 3, the median fee was 0.78% through 1984, and rose thereafter to a peak of 2.49% in 1988. Since the increased fee income may have been viewed as the economic equivalent of higher interest rates, we calculated a fee-adjusted interest rate and a corresponding fee-adjusted spread to the reference rate. As reported in Column 4, the fee-adjusted spreads over prime rate jumped from 1.59% in 1984 to 2.13% in 1985, and remained between 1.98% and 2.24% from 1985 to 1989. This finding is consistent with banks' expectations that later buyouts were more likely to get into financial trouble.[9]

Focusing on interest rate spreads also ignores a potentially important set of "non-price terms of credit," such as collateral and covenants, that bankers can use to adjust their risk-return tradeoff. Non-price credit terms are particularly relevant because banks are the senior lenders in the buyout transactions. Given that bank debt typically equals only 50% of total capital, it may have been possible for banks to structure their loans to largely eliminate default losses. If so, it would have made sense to lend at the same interest rate in all deals.

We were not able to get comprehensive data on collateral or covenants for the bank loans in our sample. As we reported earlier, however, banks both reduced the amount they loaned and required more rapid principal repayments in later deals. Both of these reactions are consistent with banks protecting themselves in reaction to lower overall buyout quality.

As noted earlier, the acceleration of repayment schedules may have reflected an increased reliance on asset sales. In fact, these schedules (and the correspondingly tighter coverages) might have been a mechanism for forcing buyout companies to sell assets in order to raise cash. We attempted to determine the expected role of asset sales by examining statements of the intent to sell assets that appeared in the buyout proxy and 14D statements.

As shown in Column 5, asset sales were expected in 21% of the pre-1983 MBOs, 27% of the 1983-1985 MBOs, and 39% of the 1986-1989 MBOs. For those companies that planned to make major asset sales, the assets to be sold represented a roughly constant fraction of total capital (see Column 6)—at medians of 15.5, 19.8, and 18.5%—during the three different periods.

"Cross-Sectional" Tests. Although we do not report the results here, we also analyzed the strength of the *correlation* between low coverage ratios, high buyout prices, and asset sales by running a series of regressions. The results of the first two regressions suggested, in effect, that buyouts with expected asset sales were associated with ratios of net cash flow and EBITDA to debt obligations that were roughly 0.25 lower than buyouts without expected asset sales (that is, coverages were substantially tighter in buyouts with expected asset sales). A third regression suggested that buyouts with asset sales had net cash flow to buyout price ratios that were a full 2% lower than buyouts without asset sales. For example, a typical 1987 buyout without asset sales had a net cash flow to price ratio of 5.7%, whereas one with expected asset sales had a ratio of only 3.7%.

This last finding seems especially interesting because it is not obvious why plans to sell assets should make companies more valuable in the aggregate. The first-order effect of asset sales would seem to be to transfer value from junior to senior creditors, not to create new value. To see this, consider the extreme case where an asset sale would generate enough cash to repay *all* the senior debt. In this case, the use of asset sales would make the senior debt riskless, thereby increasing its value while shifting more risk onto the junior debt. Given this possibility, it is understandable why senior bank lenders would be willing to lend to more aggressively priced deals only if they could force asset sales. It is not at all clear, however, why junior lenders would be willing to participate in such deals.

To summarize the results of this section: senior bank lenders appear to have placed a relatively small emphasis on interest rate spreads in their structuring of buyout loans. Rather it seems that, over time, they (1) increased fees, (2) reduced the fraction of the total debt they provided; and (3) imposed more rapid repayment schedules. Such repayment schedules likely could be met only by firms selling assets and repaying banks with the proceeds. Asset sales look to have played a somewhat more prominent role in the more aggressively priced deals.

The overall picture that emerges is one of the banks making "defensive" structuring adjustments in the later, higher priced buyouts. While these adjustments may have made sense from the banks' senior perspective, they raise several questions: Who and why were the junior lenders agreeing to these

---

9. There are, however, two reasons it may be misleading to treat fees and interest income as economically equivalent. First, the fees bank lenders receive are not always proportional to the size of their loans. Conversations with bankers indicate that the originating bank retains some fee income even when it sells most of the loan. If so, the fee-adjusted spreads reported in Table 4 overstate the returns to banks that actually fund the loan and bear the risk. Second, banks also might plausibly prefer fee income because of capital regulations and compensation

practices. Fee income shows up in earnings in the first year of the buyout. Because this increases both book net worth and any compensation based on earnings, it can have a higher shadow value to banks and bankers than an economically equivalent interest rate. The greater fee income in the late 1980s buyouts may thus have tempted bankers to make buyout loans that offered a less favorable risk-return tradeoff.

TABLE 5
SUBORDINATED DEBT

Year	(1) Number of MBOs	(2) % of Deals with Public Junk Debt	(3) % of Deals with Cram Down Debt	(4) Average Junk and Cram Down to Capital (%)	(5) % of Deals with PIK or Discount Debt	(6) Average PIK or Discount Debt to Capital (%)	(7) Strips (% of Deals)	(8) Average Strip Debt to Capital (%)
1980-81	6	0.0	0.0	0.0	0.0	0.0	83.3	36.6
1982	8	0.0	12.5	1.2	25.0	3.0	75.0	24.5
1983	10	0.0	10.0	1.1	10.0	1.1	70.0	27.5
1984	17	5.9	23.5	5.7	11.8	2.1	47.1	17.3
1985	12	58.3	58.3	25.9	50.0	7.6	50.0	19.7
1986	15	40.0	26.7	17.5	26.7	5.6	33.3	7.4
1987	20	50.0	45.0	24.9	50.0	9.7	10.0	4.4
1988	31	61.3	38.7	22.5	61.3	8.5	29.0	12.0
1989	5	60.0	40.0	21.5	60.0	10.6	20.0	9.4
Total	124	37.1	32.3	16.1	37.9	6.1	39.5	14.8
Time Trend								
		(+)***	(+)**	(+)***	(+)***	(+)***	(−)**	(−)***
1980-82 vs. 1983-85								
		(+)*	(+)*	(+)**	(+)	(+)	(−)	(−)
1983-85 vs. 1986-89								
		(+)***	(+)	(+)***	(+)***	(+)***	(−)***	(−)***

*** Medians significantly different over time or in comparison periods at 1 percent level; ** at 5 percent level; and * at 10 percent level.

structuring changes? And what are the implications of these changes for the likelihood and costs of financial distress?

SUBORDINATED DEBT

We now turn to an examination of the subordinated debt in our sample transactions. In what follows, we focus on non-price attributes of this debt—private placement versus public issuance, the use of deferred interest securities, and the use of "strip" financing techniques.

As shown in Column 2 of Table 5, the financing of buyouts with publicly issued low-grade, or junk, bonds effectively began in 1985. Only one buyout prior to 1985 used public junk bonds. In contrast, over 54% of the subsequent buyouts used them.

Many buyouts also issued a second type of widely-held debt as part of the buyout financing—commonly called "cram down" debt. Cram down is debt issued by the new buyout firm as part of the payment to the pre-buyout shareholders to take the company private. Because the pre-buyout shares are widely-held, so is the cram down debt. Column 3 also shows an increased reliance on the use of "cram down" debt, particularly after 1984.

Moreover, the ratio of new public buyout debt—that is, combined junk and cram down debt—to total capital also rises sharply over time starting in 1985. Before 1985, new public debt was a small fraction of total capital; from 1985 and beyond, it always exceeded 17% of total capital (see Column 4).[10]

As we noted earlier, the trend toward increased use of public subordinated debt coincided with the adjustment by banks to reduce the size of their loans. To provide a more direct test of the argument that public debt effectively displaced bank debt in later buyouts, we ran several regressions. Although not reported here, the results of these tests suggest that

---

10. Note that these are unconditional averages, including buyouts both with and without widely-held debt. These averages, therefore, understate the importance of public debt in those transactions which actually use it.

the ratio of bank debt to total debt was from 11% to 15% lower in buyouts that relied on junk bonds than in buyouts that did not. This pronounced "crowding out" of the bank debt by junk bonds is consistent with the notion that overheated junk-bond investors were willing to bid more aggressively for buyout loans than were the relatively defensive bankers.

We also found strong evidence of two additional trends in subordinated debt financing. First, the use of deferred interest debt increased sharply after 1984. As shown in Column 5, such debt was used in only 12% of pre-1985 buyouts, but in more than 50% of the buyouts after 1984. Similarly, deferred interest debt as a percentage of total capital increased as well (see Column 6), exceeding 8.5% in all years after 1986.

The increase in deferred interest on the subordinated debt likely had an effect similar to that of accelerating senior debt repayment. That is, it further "juniorized" the subordinated debt, potentially transferring value to the senior bank lenders. In buyouts that used deferred interest debt, much of the bank debt was scheduled to be paid off before the buyout firm began cash payments on the deferred interest debt. Interestingly, the deferred interest debt was disproportionately public subordinated debt—either junk or cram down. Of the 59 buyouts that did not use junk or cram down debt, only three issued deferred interest debt. In contrast, deferred interest securities were present in 44 of 65 buyouts that used public debt.

The use of public subordinated debt also appeared to be related to the overall pricing of transactions. We ran a series of regressions (the detailed results of which, again, are not reported here) that showed the use of junk debt was associated with a decline in both net cash flow and EBITDA to total capital ratios of 1.6%. To illustrate the import of this finding, our regression coefficients imply that 1988 buyouts financed without junk bonds had an EBITDA to total capital ratio of 12.4%, thus representing a multiple of roughly 8X operating cash flow. By contrast, for those buyouts financed with junk bonds, the implied ratio was 10.8%, or about 9.25X. This finding also fits with the notion that junk bond investors were particularly aggressive bidders for buyout loans.

Finally, at the same time that the use of deferred interest and public subordinated debt increased, the use of strip financing declined. Strip financing is present when lenders invest in post-buyout equity.

In most cases of strip financing, it is the subordinated debtholders who hold the equity. However, we also found several cases in which the senior lender or lenders purchased equity.

As shown in Columns 7 and 8, both the percentage of transactions using some form of strip financing and strip debt as a fraction of total capital declined over the '80s. Over 70% of the buyouts before 1984 used some form of strip financing. Also, the debt owned by stripholders amounted to roughly 25% of the total capital in these buyouts. In contrast, fewer than 25% of the post-1985 buyouts used strip financing, with strip debt worth at most 12% of total capital in those deals.

As in the case of deferred interest debt, the use of strip financing was related to the use of public debt, although in this case the relation went the opposite way. Over 59% (35 out of 59) of the buyouts that did not use public debt used strip financing, compared to fewer than 22% (14 of 65) of the buyouts that did use public debt.

In sum, the results in this section indicate that beginning in 1985, financing from the public junk bond market displaced not only private subordinated debt, but also to some degree senior bank debt. Junk bond financing was more likely to involve deferred interest securities, less likely to involve strips, and was associated with higher buyout prices.

INCENTIVES

The third and final category of data we examined concerns the incentives of buyout investors. Conventional economic wisdom holds that significant increases in managers' percentage equity stakes should lead to improvements in operating performance and more successful buyouts generally. But, as we shall show, the conventional wisdom failed to take into account another important change in incentives also taking place during the 1980s.

Columns 1 and 2 of Table 6 report the median percentages of pre-buyout and post-buyout equity (fully diluted to account for stock options) owned by the post-buyout management team. Before the buyout, the new management team owned a median 5% of the equity. This percentage increased significantly during the '80s, peaking at more than 8% in both 1987 and 1988. After the buyout, the median management equity ownership of the post-buyout company was 22.3%, a figure that also increased significantly over time.

The larger the capital gain they are able to "cash out" relative to their new investment, the more managers may be tempted to go along with (or even encourage) a buyout they know to be overpriced or poorly structured.

TABLE 6
INCENTIVES[a]

Year	(1) Old Mgmt. Equity (%)	(2) New Mgmt. Equity (%)	(3) New % / Old % Mgmt. Equity	(4) New $ / Old $ Mgmt. Equity	(5) Total Fees to Capital
1980-81	1.5	10.1	7.58	0.707	2.05
	6	6	6	6	6
1982	2.0	23.1	6.79	0.958	2.66
	8	8	8	8	8
1983	5.2	15.5	3.42	0.524	2.58
	10	9	9	9	9
1984	4.4	27.5	3.81	0.670	2.21
	17	17	17	17	17
1985	3.5	22.5	4.51	0.334	3.69
	12	11	11	11	12
1986	5.1	20.8	6.28	0.314	5.06
	12	13	11	11	15
1987	8.1	19.0	3.54	0.410	4.32
	17	14	14	14	20
1988	8.4	28.5	2.86	0.349	5.97
	25	24	22	22	31
1989	6.2	15.3	2.93	0.542	5.73
	4	4	4	4	5
Total	5.0	22.3	4.14	0.460	3.81
	111	106	102	102	123
Time Trend					
	(+)**	(+)*	(−)	(−)*	(+)***
1980-82 vs. 1983-85					
	(+)**	(+)**	(−)	(−)	(+)
1983-85 vs. 1986-88					
	(+)	(+)	(−)	(−)*	(+)***

a. The two rows in each cell are the median and number of observations, respectively.
*** Medians significantly different over time or in comparison periods at 1 percent level; ** at 5 percent level; and * at 10 percent level.

Column 3 combines the information in Columns 1 and 2 by calculating the ratio of the percentage of post- to pre-buyout equity owned by the management team. This ratio provides a measure of the change in the intensity of the relationship between managerial effort and compensation. The median ratio for the 102 buyouts with both pre- and post-buyout information was 4.14. (The ratio trended downward over time, but not significantly.)

While their large percentage stakes in post-buyout equity suggest that managers will work hard to maximize shareholder value once the buyout has been completed, the large post-buyout stakes alone do not ensure they will enter only into well-priced and -structured transactions. It is important to recognize that managers typically "cash out" in dollar terms at the time of a buyout. Although their percentage ownership of the now-levered equity increases sharply, *the dollar amount* invested tends to fall.

This cashing out could have important and potentially adverse incentive effects on the choice, pricing, and structuring of deals. In particular, the larger the capital gain they are able to realize at the time of the deal, the more managers may be tempted to go along with (or even encourage) a buyout that they know to be overpriced or poorly structured. At the extreme, a manager offered a significant ownership stake in post-buyout equity at no cost may find it hard to turn down what is, in effect, a free option, even if the buyout has only a small chance of success.

As shown in Column 4, the median ratio of the dollar value of post- to pre-buyout equity owned by the management team was 0.46. This means that the management team typically invested less than half as much in post-buyout equity as in pre-buyout equity. Even more telling, however, the time trend of this variable over the 1980s was significantly negative, with a particularly sharp drop between 1984 and

1985. Before 1984, the median ratio was 0.57. From 1985 to 1989, the median ratio was 0.35. Thus, the temptation for management to cash out appears to have been far greater in the buyouts of the later 1980s than in earlier ones.

Management investors are not the only parties driven by incentives. So are buyout promoters, investment banks, and lenders. Most buyout participants were compensated with both long-term security interests and upfront fees. As we noted earlier, banks required higher upfront fees in the later 1980s than they did before. And, as shown in Column 5, the same pattern was true of total buyout-related fees. The largest portion of these fees was paid to buyout promoters, investment banks, and commercial banks. The ratio of total fees to total capital made its biggest jump in the late 1980s. It ranged from 2.05% to 2.66% before 1985, rose to 3.69% in 1985, and peaked at 5.97% in 1988.

INTERPRETING THE EVIDENCE

The evidence we have presented thus far can be used to tell a detailed story of overheating in the buyout market, one which centers largely on the role of publicly issued junk bonds.

Junk Bonds and the Overheated Buyout Market

The story goes as follows: Beginning in 1985, junk bond investors, attracted by the success of earlier deals, poured large amounts of money into the buyout market. This pushed up prices in general, and especially prices in those deals in which junk bonds were actually used. Other, less aggressive classes of lenders such as banks and private subordinated lenders reacted defensively to the "demand push" from the junk bond market. They reduced their participation in deals, and the banks in particular took steps such as accelerating principal repayments and forcing asset sales that would effectively enhance their senior status. The junk bond investors did not prevent themselves from being "juniorized" in this way. Indeed, by accepting large quantities of deferred interest securities, they further encouraged the process.

Even more so than the bankers, other interested parties were also successful in extracting upfront money from the deals. Ostensibly well-informed players such as management, buyout promoters and investment bankers were increasingly able to earn compensation simply for completing a transaction, rather than having their fortunes ride on its eventual success or failure. Thus, instead of providing a system of checks and balances, these "smart money" participants may have been quite eager to participate, even in deals they viewed as overpriced or poorly structured.

If this junk bond/"demand push" story is correct, it implies two channels through which investor returns in later deals could have been reduced. The first, and more obvious, channel was pricing; all else equal, higher prices relative to fundamentals would mean lower returns for some categories of investors. The second channel related to costs of financial distress. Although expected costs of financial distress are hard to assess, many of the capital structure changes that accompanied the inflow of junk bond financing could be viewed as increasing such costs.

First was the dramatic shift from privately-placed to widely-held subordinated debt that began in 1985. With widely dispersed creditors, free-rider problems were more likely to interfere with efficient financial reorganizations. By "free-rider," we mean that even though it can be in the collective interest of subordinated debtholders to contribute new funds for investment, any single holder may find it individually rational not to do so. Adding further to this "free rider" problem was the growing bank practice of selling off senior bank buyout loans.

A second change that may have increased the potential for costly financial distress was the decline of the strip financing technique common in earlier buyouts. When a firm is highly leveraged, conflicts of interest between lenders and equityholders can lead to distorted corporate behavior such as "risk-shifting" and underinvestment that reduces overall firm value. By reducing such conflicts, strip financing arguably limits these distortions.[11] If this logic is correct, the decline of strip financing in the late 1980s is puzzling, to say the least.

In addition to the movement towards public debt and away from strip financing, other changes in

---

11. See M. Jensen, "The Eclipse of the Public Corporation," *Harvard Business Review*, No. 5 (1989), 61-74.

A rapidly growing asset sales market could help explain rising buyout prices in general, to the extent some buyouts created significant portions of their value added by relocating assets to different owners. To the extent this was so, we would expect to see a strong correlation between buyouts premised on large asset sales and the use of junk bonds.

buyout debt structure may also have increased the expected costs of financial distress. One such change was the "juniorizing" of the public subordinated debt that resulted from both faster principal repayments on the senior bank debt and the trend toward deferred interest junk bonds.

How did these changes raise the costs of reorganizing troubled companies? First of all, as with conflicts between lenders and stockholders, conflicts between senior bank creditors and junior public debtholders can also reduce the ability of distressed companies to secure new funds. The logic is as follows: Suppose a firm is in financial difficulty and needs an infusion of funds to make a positive net present value investment. On the one hand, bank lenders would seem to be the best hope for putting up the new money, since they do not face as severe a free-rider problem as the widely-dispersed junior lenders. On the other hand, the banks' senior status probably reduces their incentive to invest; the banks may already be well-protected, and may not have much upside to gain from further investment.[12]

Now consider what happens if the bank's principal repayments are moved forward in time. This has two negative effects. First, the higher debt service burden raises the probability that the firm will be unable to meet its contractual obligations. Second, the fact that the banks extract value more rapidly effectively enhances their senior status relative to the subordinated debt. This further protects the banks, and may correspondingly further reduce their incentives to contribute new money. For this reason, accelerated repayment schedules may well increase the expected costs of financial distress.

An Alternative Interpretation

A different reading of our evidence—one more consistent with investor rationality—might focus on external changes in regulation, capital markets, and the general economy. One likely candidate—though by no means the only one—may have been fluctuations in the liquidity of the asset sales market. A rapidly growing asset sales market could help explain rising buyout prices in general, to the extent some buyouts created significant portions of their value added by relocating assets to different owners.

To the extent this was so, we would expect to see a strong correlation between buyouts premised on large asset sales and the use of junk bonds. Although junk bonds would clearly have made it more difficult for a distressed firm to recast its capital structure, the possibility of asset sales could have been viewed by the planners of the buyout as a potential, low-cost alternative to financial reorganization.[13]

Such a correlation between asset sales and junk bonds would help explain the more aggressive pricing of buyouts involving junk bonds. That is, the use of junk bonds may simply be an indicator that the firm in question had a lot of easily detachable and marketable assets. If the potential for asset sales was in itself value-increasing, this "detachability" of assets may have legitimately commanded a higher buyout price. Also, to the extent junk bonds were a reliable indicator of detachable assets, it would be wrong to conclude that deals with junk bonds had higher expected costs of financial distress.

It should be noted that this alternative story does not explain *all* of our empirical findings. For example, increased liquidity in the asset sales market would not appear to offer much insight into the trend toward more front-loaded compensation for managers and other interested parties.

EX POST EVIDENCE

While it may be impossible to resolve fully the ambiguities raised above, we made an effort in this direction by examining post-buyout data. The overheating hypothesis holds that buyouts in the later 1980s were less soundly structured than earlier deals. This suggests that later deals, even with significant operating improvements, would run into difficulty more often. The alternative interpretation—that the deals were rationally priced and structured, but simply ran into unforeseeable external problems—would suggest that expected operating improvements failed to materialize.

Furthermore, the overheating hypothesis would seem to imply that "poorly structured" deals—in

---

12. See R. Gertner and D. Scharfstein, "A Theory of Workouts and the Effects of Reorganization Law," *Journal of Finance*, XLVI (1991), 1189-1222.

13. Shleifer and Vishny [1992], cited earlier in note 9, argue that it was precisely this increase in asset liquidity in the early and mid-1980s that made the large growth of the public junk bond market possible.

terms of pricing, capital structure, or incentives—should become financially distressed more often. This should be especially true of deals financed with junk bonds because these deals tended to have both higher prices as well as capital structures that were less easily renegotiated.

The alternative interpretation does not make the same predictions about ex-post outcomes. Because variations in price, capital structure, and incentives may reflect legitimate differences in unobserved fundamentals, they should not necessarily be correlated with ex-post difficulties. For example, if junk bonds were (sensibly) used only in deals where asset sales provide an alternative means of averting distress, we should not see a disproportionate number of junk-bond financed deals become distressed.

We now present evidence on (1) the extent to which management buyouts experienced financial distress; (2) post-buyout operating performance; and (3) the degree of correlation between financial distress and various measures of pricing, capital structure, and incentives. Such evidence is inevitably preliminary, especially for those buyouts completed in the last years of the '80s.

Frequency of Distress

We used three different indicators of financial distress. We considered a buyout to have encountered distress if, by August 1991, the firm had (1) attempted to restructure its debt because of difficulty in making debt payments, (2) defaulted on a debt payment, or (3) filed for Chapter 11. Before reporting our evidence on these three kinds of distress, we should emphasize that they do not necessarily have the same import. For example, encountering distress probably means that some class of investors has lost money (and, hence, may suggest a deal was overpriced), but may well have little to say about the deadweight costs of financial distress. In other words, a buyout that encounters distress may be able to restructure at low cost.

As shown in Column 1 of Table 7, over 25% of the 124 buyouts in our sample firms had experienced at least one of these three forms of financial distress by August 1991. The incidence of financial

distress increased significantly over time, with 1985 as the apparent breakpoint. Before 1985, only 1 of 41 buyouts experienced distress; from 1985 and onward, 30 of 83 did. As shown in Column 2, the percentage of defaults among buyouts also increased significantly, again with 1985 appearing to be the year of change.

The time trend for Chapter 11 filings, however, although positive (see Column 3), was not significant. Fewer than one-half of the companies that have defaulted on debt payments have also filed for Chapter 11. However, because defaults usually precede a Chapter 11 filing, this trend could (and has) become more pronounced with the passage of time.

Post-buyout Operating Performance

The increase in defaults may have been caused, of course, by a *combination* of *ex ante* changes in pricing and structuring as well as *ex post* surprises in performance. Columns 4 and 5 present the annual medians of changes in EBITDA and net cash flow to sales in the first post-buyout year relative to the last pre-buyout year. For the entire sample, the ratios increased by 9% and 43%, respectively, in the first year of operations. Over a two-year period following the buyouts, the operating improvements are roughly the same; as shown in Columns 6 and 7, EBITDA operating margins increased by 12% and net cash flow margins by almost 42%.[14]

These patterns of operating changes, therefore, do not offer much support for the view that economic conditions and performance surprises led to the increase in financial distress over time. Many of the buyouts of 1985, 1987, and 1988 experienced financial distress despite improvements in operating performance.[15] Thus, the results overall seem consistent with changes in buyout pricing and financial structure having played an important role in increased financial distress.

Correlation Between Distress and Ex Ante Variables

Our final test was to determine the extent to which the three varieties of financial distress were

---

14. Only the changes in net cash flow margin in the second year trend downward significantly over time. And this is driven by the poor performance of only the 1986 buyouts.

15. In a study of 40 large leveraged buyouts completed between 1985-1989, for example, Tim Opler finds that nominal and industry-adjusted increases in

operating margins and cash flow margins were, if anything, larger for later buyouts than for earlier ones. See "Operating Performance in Leveraged Buyouts: Evidence from 1985-1989," *Financial Management*, XXI, No. 1 (1992), 27-34.

Many of the later buyouts experienced financial distress despite significant improvements in operating performance. Thus, the results overall seem consistent with changes in buyout pricing and financial structure having played the major a role in increased financial distress.

TABLE 7
POST-BUYOUT
PERFORMANCE[a]

Year	(1) Experience Financial Distress	(2) Default on Debt Payment	(3) Chapter 11	(4) Actual Growth Operating Margins t-1 to t+1	(5) Actual Growth Cash Flow Margins t-1 to t+1	(6) Actual Growth Operating Margins t-1 to t+2	(7) Actual Growth Cash Flow Margins t-1 to t+2
1980-81	0.0	0.0	0.0	2.5	22.7	8.9	132.6
	6	6	6	3	2	3	3
1982	0.0	0.0	0.0	1.6	29.4	26.6	48.5
	8	8	8	5	4	5	4
1983	0.0	0.0	0.0	9.2	55.7	26.3	60.1
	10	10	10	8	7	7	7
1984	5.9	5.9	5.9	−1.3	28.4	−1.5	40.0
	17	17	17	12	12	11	11
1985	33.3	25.0	16.7	14.3	30.2	21.9	31.4
	12	12	12	11	11	9	9
1986	46.7	46.7	26.7	−7.9	17.7	−32.6	−45.5
	15	15	15	9	8	9	8
1987	45.0	30.0	15.0	15.6	67.0	22.5	30.8
	20	20	20	17	16	15	14
1988	29.0	16.1	0.0	14.2	48.4	12.3	22.8
	31	31	31	20	19	7	7
1989	20.0	20.0	0.0	25.2	40.7	N/A	N/A
	5	5	5	2	2		
Total	25.0	18.5	8.1	9.1	43.0	12.1	41.8
	124	124	124	87	81	66	63
Time Trend							
	(+)***	(+)*	(+)	(+)	(+)	(−)	(−)*
1980-82 vs. 1983-85							
	(+)	(+)	(+)	(+)	(+)	(−)	(−)
1983-85 vs. 1986-89							
	(+)***	(+)**	(+)	(+)	(+)	(−)	(−)**

a. Number of observations on second line.
*** Medians significantly different over time or in comparison periods at 1 percent level; ** at 5 percent level; and * at 10 percent level.

correlated with measures of pricing, capital structure, and incentives that we found to have changed significantly during the '80s. To measure the strength of such correlations, we ran several series of (multivariate as well as univariate) regressions. Although detailed results are presented in the original study, we simply summarize our findings below:

- The lower the ratio of EBITDA to capital (or, alternatively, the higher the price paid as a multiple of cash flow), the greater the probability that a buyout encountered financial distress in any of its three forms.
- High industry risk had a positive relation to the likelihood of distress and default. (Indeed, buyouts in the highest industry risk quartile—for example, MBOs in retailing—were 19% more likely to encounter distress and 14% more likely to default than the average buyout.)
- A high degree of cashing-out on the part of management was associated with a significant increase—roughly 15%—in the probability of default.
- The use of junk bonds was associated with statistically and economically significant increases in the probability of distress, default, and Chapter 11 of, respectively, 21%, 10%, and 11%.

Because we viewed this last correlation to be the most interesting, we investigated its "robustness" to several multivariate specifications. When the four other independent variables cited above were added both individually and as a group to the junk bond variable in a series of regressions, the estimated coefficients on the junk bond variable were significant in all cases (as well as statistically similar to their values in the univariate regressions summarized above).

We interpret this relatively strong and robust ability of junk bonds to predict future distress as supportive of the overheating hypothesis. According to the story sketched above, one would expect the presence of junk bonds to be an especially useful summary statistic, as it captures a tendency towards both higher prices and more fragile capital structures.

CONCLUSIONS

We now come back to the question we asked at the outset: Were there differences in the pricing and capital structure of buyouts in the late 1980s that might have led one to expect disappointing investor returns relative to those in earlier deals? In brief, our analysis of 124 large MBOs completed between 1980 and 1989 yields the following conclusions:

- Buyout price to cashflow ratios rose (although not more sharply than market- or industry-wide P/E ratios).
- Prices were particularly high in deals financed with junk bonds.
- As prices rose, buyouts were undertaken in riskier industries, and with somewhat higher leverage ratios.
- Banks took smaller positions in later deals, and at the same time accelerated required principal repayments, leading to sharply lower ratios of cash flow to total debt obligations.
- The public junk bond financing that largely replaced private subordinated debt beginning in 1985 was much more likely to include deferred interest securities, and less likely to involve equity "strips."
- Finally, management and other interested parties such as investment bankers and deal promoters were able to take more money upfront out of the later deals.

On balance, our evidence, while not unambiguous, fits well with a version of the overheated buyout market hypothesis. According to this version of the story, the demand push from the junk bond market that began around 1985 fundamentally altered both the pricing and capital structure of later buyouts. We view the changes in capital structure as particularly important. In an apparently defensive reaction, senior bank lenders participated less in the later, junk-bond financed deals and tried to extract their money more rapidly. While this reaction may have made good sense from the narrow perspective of the senior lenders, it arguably increased the expected costs of financial distress by exacerbating conflicts of interest between junior and senior claimants.

Further support for this junk bond/demand push interpretation comes from our analysis of the *ex post* data, which finds the presence of junk bonds in a buyout to be a good predictor of various types of financial distress. Presumably, this is because the presence of junk bonds captures a tendency toward both higher prices and more fragile capital structures.

If this interpretation is correct, the question arises as to *how* the junk bond investors made the mistakes they did. Although such a question is inevitably difficult to answer satisfactorily, our data do provide some hints. To the extent that junk bond investors miscalculated, they probably did so by focusing too much on stated coupon yields and past buyout successes, and too little on the subtle capital structure details of the deals they were investing in. Holding everything else constant, there is a big difference between owning a debenture that does not begin to receive any cash payout until after the senior debt has been largely repaid, and one that gets repaid along roughly the same schedule as the senior debt.

Whether or not one accepts the overheating interpretation, our data provide a useful post-mortem of the buyout boom. At least with the benefit of hindsight, it seems clear that some of the changes in capital structure and incentives seen in the deals of the later 1980s were bad ideas. Thus, one might expect future buyouts to look more like those of the earlier 1980s: with less stringent principal repayment schedules, more closely-held subordinated debt and strip financing, and less front-loaded compensation for management and other interested parties.

LBOs–THE EVOLUTION OF FINANCIAL STRUCTURES AND STRATEGIES

by Jay R. Allen,
Bank of America

ontrary to most reports in the popular business press, leveraged buyouts are one of the remarkable success stories of the 1980s. Between the beginning of 1981 and the end of 1989, there were over 1,400 "going private" transactions. The annual volume of LBOs increased from under $2 billion in 1979 to a record high $88 billion in 1988. The steady increase in the size of the deals throughout the decade culminated in 1989 with the highly-publicized $25 billion buyout of RJR Nabisco by Kohlberg Kravis & Roberts (KKR).

Throughout the 1980s and well into the '90s, skeptics argued that LBOs simply provided a means for Wall Street financiers to earn paper profits by arbitraging differences between public and private markets. In the popular account, corporate raiders borrowed huge sums to acquire companies that were undervalued by a shortsighted stock market, gutted those companies by slashing expenses and cutting employment and productive investment, and then foisted them back on an ever-gullible IPO market.

The research of financial economists, however, has told a very different story. Beginning in the last few years of the late 1980s on through the present, study after study has furnished consistent evidence of major improvements in corporate operating efficiency and increases in value. Take the case of one recent study that was able to look inside 90 LBOs that returned to public ownership through IPOs between 1983 and 1988.[1] In the year before going public again, the study reported, the LBO companies had become almost twice as profitable (on a pre-interest, but after-tax basis) as their industry competitors; were using only about half as much working capital; maintained similar levels of employment; and actually had

---

1. Robert W. Holthausen and David F. Larcker, "The Financial Performance of Reverse Leveraged Buyouts," *Journal of Financial Economics* (forthcoming). For pioneering studies of LBOs, see Steven N. Kaplan, "The Effects of Management Buyouts on Operating Performance and Value," *Journal of Financial Economics* 24 (1989), 581-618; and Abbie J. Smith, "Corporate Ownership Structure and Performance: The Case of Management Buyouts," *Journal of Financial Economics* 27 (1990), 143-164.

larger advertising budgets. Total corporate investment was lower, it's true, but this is what one might expect in industries with excess capacity, which is where most of the deals took place (paper products, tobacco, oil and gas, publishing, retailing, basic manufacturing). Moreover, such trends continued for at least four years *after* the IPOs (the term of the study), with the 90 firms continuing to outperform their competitors both in terms of operating and stock-market returns—a finding that seems all the more impressive, given that the average IPO significantly underperforms market averages over a three-year period after going public.[2]

Even as early as 1989, the academic evidence in support of LBOs was so compelling that Harvard professor Michael Jensen wrote an article in the *Harvard Business Review* entitled "The Eclipse of the Public Corporation." In that article, Jensen argued that for companies in mature industries without productive uses for new capital, LBOs represent a "new" and inherently more efficient form of corporate organization. According to Jensen, the combination of high debt service payments and significant managerial equity ownership in LBOs was providing management with far stronger incentives to increase efficiency and pay out excess capital than those normally present in large, predominantly equity-financed, public corporations. And reinforcing these stronger incentives in many LBOs was the participation and monitoring of LBO sponsors like KKR, Forstmann Little, Clayton Dubilier & Rice (CD&R), and The Blackstone Group—"active investors" who structure the transaction, own the majority of the company's equity, and control the boards of directors.

By the time Jensen's article appeared, however, things had begun to go wrong in the LBO market. Starting with problems with the Campeau-Federated deal in 1989, there was a sharp increase in defaults and bankruptcies that was to continue into the first years of the 1990s. Partly as a consequence of some poorly structured deals, and in part as a result of the regulatory overreaction to perceived "overleveraging," the LBO market (and leveraged lending in general) went into a steep and extended decline. Indeed, the drop was so sharp that it led pundits to predict the death of the LBO and junk bond markets.

But reports of the demise of leveraged transactions proved to be greatly exaggerated. Smaller LBOs—those in the $50 to $150 million range—continued in large numbers, even throughout the 1990-1991 recession. Provided their future financing requirements were modest, such buyouts could be funded with senior debt only (that is, with no reliance on the then nearly defunct high yield market) or with senior debt and a slice of mezzanine capital. In most such cases, the senior debt financing was managed by one of a handful of banks in the deal; and the lead bank in senior-debt-only deals sometimes received equity warrants for its efforts.

Then, beginning in late 1991 and early 1992, larger LBOs began to make a comeback. The new wave of LBOs, however, displayed financial structures that were significantly more conservative than those employed in deals at the end of the '80s. Where some of the LBOs of the late '80s reported leverage ratios as high as 20 to 1 (and dealmakers' fees were reported to exceed total equity in many instances), the debt in the deals of the '90s tended to be supported by at least 20% equity, and in some cases considerably more. And there was a pronounced shift away from the use of public subordinated debt ("junk bonds") as a source of LBO funds and toward capital structures composed entirely of senior bank debt and sponsor equity capital (and, in a few cases, sponsor-controlled subordinated debt).

In this article, I attempt to provide a brief overview of the LBO and leveraged lending markets, discussing the reasons for their effectiveness in the '80s, the causes of their undoing in the early '90s, and the changes in their structure that have allowed them to re-emerge. In commenting on these changes in financial structure, I also attempt to shed some light on certain aspects of the current academic capital structure debate—to offer the "real world" perspective, if you will, of a banker who has participated in the structuring of a good number of leveraged acquisition financings. While acknowledging that public subordinated debt still has its place, I argue that private debt—particularly, senior bank debt and private, sponsor-controlled subordinated debt—is likely to have significant advantages in terms of operating and financing flexibility over public subordinated debt.[3]

---

2. See Roger Ibbotson, Jay Ritter, and Jody Sindelar, "The Market's Problems with the Pricing of Initial Public Offerings," *Journal of Applied Corporate Finance*, Vol. 7 No. 1 (Spring 1994).

3. See Eugene Fama, "What's Different About Banks?," *Journal of Monetary Economics* 15 (1985); and Christopher James and Peggy Wier, "Are Bank Loans Different?," *Journal of Applied Corporate Finance*, Vol. 1 No. 2 (Summer 1988).

In the closing section of the article, I offer a brief description of current trends in the LBO and leveraged lending markets. With stock prices reaching record levels, corporate or "strategic" buyers using their own stock as currency have displaced unaffiliated "financial" buyers as the dominant players in the M & A and buyout markets. In response to such competition, however, financial buyers have found a number of interesting new ways to participate. One technique, known as a *leveraged build-up*, involves a moderately leveraged acquisition by a financial buyer of a relatively small company in a consolidating industry, which in turn becomes the "platform" for further leveraged acquisitions of firms in the same industry. Another approach involves partnerships between private financial buyers and corporate strategic buyers, who team up to buy companies on a leveraged basis. In an age of specialization based on comparative advantage, this last development suggests a valuable, if not indeed inevitable, marriage of operating knowhow and financial expertise.

WHY CAPITAL (AND OWNERSHIP) STRUCTURE MATTERS

One of the major tenets of modern finance theory, as formulated by "Chicago school" economists during the 1960s, was that capital structure "does not matter." That is, whether a company is financed with 10% or 90% debt was not supposed to affect the value of its shares in any predictable way. But, perhaps more than any other single development, the success of the LBO and high yield markets in the early 1980s has focused attention on one critical assumption underlying the argument: namely, that corporate investment decisions and operating efficiency are not influenced by capital structure—and by ownership structure (who holds the shares).[4]

The LBO amounted to a fundamental change in the way companies were run, especially in the 1970s and early 1980s. In those days, companies were run largely to increase size and diversity. The shareholder interest, while certainly not ignored, took a back seat in many public companies to the managerial priority of uninterrupted growth. Given the insistence on growth, moreover, debt capital was used sparingly. After all, the prospect of tripping a covenant and dealing with recalcitrant creditors

could force management to put its expansion plans on hold—or even cost them their jobs.

The major effects of LBOs were two. First, it replaced a dispersed and fragmented set of owners with a highly concentrated, and clearly value-driven, ownership structure. The buyout firms typically owned or represented 80-90% of the stock, and operating managements generally owned about 10%, resulting in a clear alignment of the interests of management and owners. Second, it brought about a major substitution of debt for equity in corporate capital structures (in the average '80s LBO, the debt-to-assets ratio increased from 20% to almost 90%).

Besides providing the means for financial buyers to leverage their relatively small amounts of equity capital in order to make significantly larger asset purchases, such heavy debt financing changed the basic operating goal of the company. Since the managers of LBOs no longer had to concern themselves with reporting higher, accounting-driven earnings per share to an outside shareholder base, they could instead follow the economist's prescription of maximizing cash flow. The primary focus thus became the generation of operating cash flow, not only to pay down debt but to invest in opportunities for growth. In response to this new operating goal, managements were now also much more likely to choose accounting methods designed to minimize taxable income—choices which, together with the large interest tax shields provided by 90% debt financing, served to increase *after-tax* cash flow. And such changes in focus, not surprisingly, led in a large majority of LBOs to significant increases in operating value and attractive returns to owners (and, therefore, to management).

In addition to this shift in operating goals, there was another important way in which debt changed corporate behavior. Until the wave of hostile takeovers in the 1980s, the executives of many large U.S. companies tended to view equity capital as a "free" good (or, if not entirely free, then with a cost no greater than the current dividend yield). By contrast, the cost of debt financing, with its stated schedule of interest and principal payments, was explicit and contractually binding. A missed dividend payment, to be sure, would be a source of some embarrassment to management; but a missed interest payment, or violation of a debt covenant, could eventually mean loss of oper-

---

4. See Merton Miller's Nobel Prize speech, "Leverage," *Journal of Applied Corporate Finance*, Vol. 4 No. 2 (Summer 1991).

> In the LBOs of the '90s, there was a pronounced shift away from the use of public subordinated debt ("junk bonds") as a source of LBO funds and toward capital structures composed entirely of senior bank debt and sponsor equity capital (and, in a few cases, sponsor-controlled subordinated debt).

ating managers' jobs. In the case of an LBO, default could also mean loss of the managers' and the LBO firm's equity investment, as well as a tarnishing of the LBO partnership's reputation.

As Carl Kester and Tim Luehrman put it in a recent *Harvard Business Review* article on LBOs, "Debt and equity are not merely different types of financial claims. They are alternative approaches to monitoring corporate performance and directing management—in other words, to governance."[5] In practice, the heavy use of debt financing functions as a kind of automatic early warning system. If problems are developing, top management will be forced by the pressure of debt service to intervene quickly and decisively. By contrast, in a largely equity-financed firm, management can allow much of the equity cushion to be eaten away before taking the necessary corrective action.

High leverage is also, of course, a double-edged sword. It is clearly not a prescription for all companies. As pointed out in several other articles in this issue, companies with promising growth opportunities and large future capital requirements will be better served by equity than debt—and the same applies to firms with highly specialized assets that are not likely to hold their value in secondary markets. In such businesses, the financial and operating flexibility provided by equity are likely to be more valuable than the discipline exerted by debt. But, for companies in mature businesses with few growth opportunities that will require major capital investment, replacing equity with debt (and concentrating the equity in fewer hands) is likely to be a value-adding approach to corporate governance.

THE EARLY 1990s: THE "CORRECTION"

Despite their accomplishments in the form of large shareholder gains and increases in corporate efficiency, the LBO and leveraged lending movements began to derail at the end of the '80s. As noted earlier, there was a sharp increase in the number of defaults and bankruptcies beginning in 1989 and continuing into the first years of the 1990s. Most of the problems, it turns out, came in the deals trans-

acted in the latter half of the 1980s. In an article published in this journal called "The Evolution of Buyout Pricing and Financial Structure in the 1980s," Steven Kaplan and Jeremy Stein reported that of 41 LBOs with purchase prices of $100 million or more transacted between 1980 and 1984, only one had defaulted on its debt by the end of 1991. By contrast, at least 26 of 83 large deals done between 1985 and 1989 had defaulted—and 18 had gone into bankruptcy—by the end of '91.[6]

The Kaplan and Stein study offered the following analysis of what went wrong with the later deals:

(1) Buyout prices as multiples of cash flow rose sharply, and multiples were especially high in deals financed with junk bonds (since the increase in acquisition prices was funded almost entirely with increased debt).

(2) Banks took smaller positions and accelerated required principal repayments, while at the same time permitting higher total leverage in the capital structure. This meant sharply lower ratios of cash flow to total debt obligations, which in turn increased the probability that companies would get into financial trouble.

(3) Public junk debt displaced both private subordinated debt and the associated practice of "strip" financing (in which subordinated debtholders also receive equity stakes), thus raising the costs of reorganizing companies that did get into trouble.

(4) Finally, management and other interested parties such as investment bankers and deal promoters ended up with smaller net investments in the later transactions for two reasons: (1) a smaller percentage of funds invested as equity in the initial capital structure; and (2) the payment of substantial upfront fees in the form of investment banking, management, and advisory fees. Such changes had the potential to reduce the commitment of all these parties to the long-run success of the deals.

As Michael Jensen described the situation, there was a "contracting failure," "a gross misalignment of incentives" between some dealmakers who promoted the transactions and the lenders and other investors who funded them.[7] Without a significant equity commitment, dealmakers and advisers less

---

5. Carl W. Kester and Timothy Luehrman, "Rehabilitating the Leveraged Buyout," *Harvard Business Review* (May-June 1995).

6. Steven Kaplan and Jeremy Stein, "The Evolution of Buyout Pricing and Financial Structure in the 1980s," *Journal of Applied Corporate Finance*, Vol. 6 No. 1 (Spring 1993).

7. See the comments by Michael Jensen in "The Economic Consequences of High Leverage and Stock Market Pressures on Corporate Management: A Roundtable Discussion," *Journal of Applied Corporate Finance*, Vol. 3 No. 2 (Summer 1990), pp. 8-9. For a more formal elaboration of this argument, see Michael Jensen, "Corporate Control and the Politics of Finance," *Journal of Applied Corporate Finance*, Vol. 4 No. 2 (Summer 1991), pp. 25-27.

concerned about reputation had incentives to promote deals where the purchase prices were too high and the financial structures were less stable. According to Kaplan and Stein, bankers saw the trends developing, and they acted to protect their interest by reducing their commitments and shortening maturities (and the fact that bank losses on LBOs turned out to be minor confirms this impression). While allowing greater leverage in the capital structure, banks continued to require debt service through cash payments of interest and principal. By contrast, the larger proportions of public high yield bonds were increasingly made up of PIK (payment-in-kind) and zero coupon securities that required no cash debt service payments for many years into the life of the LBO.

As noted above, however, such higher debt levels combined with faster amortization of bank debt meant sharply lower ratios of cash flow to debt service. Indeed, the coverages went so low (in some cases below 1:1) as to make the first interest payments of many buyouts dependent on asset sales as well as the realization of major operating synergies and cost reductions. Needless to say, such a financial structure greatly increased the probability that the companies would get into trouble. And the fact that the high yield securities were distributed by underwriters to an increasingly fragmented group of institutional investors virtually ensured that there would be sharp creditor conflicts, and thus large losses, if the companies did get into financial difficulty.

But unsound financial structure was not the only cause of the problems. The Kaplan and Stein study provides some evidence that a private market "correction" was already under way in leveraged lending markets when regulators intervened heavily in the summer of 1989. As I can confirm from my own experience, there was already a general movement toward lower transaction prices, larger equity commitments, lower debt ratios, and lower upfront fees when S&L legislation (FIRREA) contributed to a downward spiral in high yield bond prices (and, as some would argue, in business activity in general). In addition, the new HLT rules,[8] combined with tightened oversight by bank regulators, had a significantly negative impact on banks' appetite for financing new leveraged transactions. Likewise, the fact that banks were being forced by regulators, rating

agencies, and the stock market to reduce their HLT exposures greatly reduced both their tolerance for and flexibility in working with highly leveraged companies that could not meet lending covenants or current debt service payments. As a consequence, it became increasingly difficult to reorganize troubled companies outside of Chapter 11.[9]

Coming on top of all these factors (and caused, in part, by them), the recession of 1990-1991 led to a sharp decline in the number—and, especially, the size—of new LBOs. Indeed, in the first two years of the 1990s, large leveraged restructuring transactions virtually disappeared. Whereas the number of LBOs fell from over 300 in each of 1988 and 1989 to about 200 in 1990 and 1991, the dollar volume of deals dropped much more precipitously—from a high of $88 billion in 1988 to only $7.5 billion in 1991.

THE RETURN (AND RESTRUCTURING) OF THE LBO: 1992-1995

The beginning of a recovery of the market for large LBOs was signalled by the announcement of transactions such as Clayton Dubilier's $1.6 billion purchase of Lexmark in 1991 and KKR's $1.4 billion purchase of American Reinsurance in 1992.

The financial structure of the 1990s deals, however, was notably different from that of most of the LBOs done during the period 1986-1988. The purchase prices were lower (5-6 times EBITDA, down from 7-8 and even 10 times in some cases), equity as a percentage of the initial capital structure increased from 5-10% to 20-30%, and coverage ratios increased substantially (a minimum of 2X interest coverage by trailing EBITDA became the standard, whereas interest coverage ratios in most late-'80s deals started well below that level as discussed earlier).

Another important change was the increased emphasis on the reputation of the sponsors. The troubled deals of the late '80s and early '90s led to a shakeout in the LBO industry, and those buyout firms that produced consistently bad deals disappeared. To raise new equity from limited partners and attract lenders to help fund new investments, LBO sponsors in the '90s had to be able to point to a track record that was strong on both a financial and an operating basis. On top of that, lenders also insisted that the

---

8. "HLT" is an acronym for Highly Leveraged Transactions, a definition developed by the Comptroller of the Currency, the FDIC, and the Federal Reserve Board to classify certain leveraged loans by banks as being in a high-risk category.

9. See Michael Jensen, "Corporate Control and the Politics of Finance," *Journal of Applied Corporate Finance*, Vol. 4 No. 2, pp. 27-29.

*Without a significant equity commitment, dealmakers and advisers less concerned
about reputation had incentives to promote deals where the purchase prices were
too high and the financial structures were less stable.*

LBO firms demonstrate their commitment to a buyout transaction by contributing substantial amounts of the partnership's capital as equity.

> **High-tech vs. Low-tech LBOs.** In contrast to the '80s, moreover, there has been considerably more focus on the appropriate debt-to-equity ratio for specific deals. For example, in financing an LBO of a standard manufacturing company in a slow-growth and relatively mature industry, Bank of America will typically structure a 6-7 year senior bank term loan and revolving credit facility. The amount of the senior debt will typically be 3-4 times EBITDA, with sponsor-controlled capital composing 20-25% of the capital structure.
>
> By contrast, in financing recent LBOs of high-growth, technology-driven investments by Welsh, Carson, Anderson, & Stowe and DLJ Merchant Banking, we provided senior bank facilities with 3-4 year maturities and senior debt-to-EBITDA multiples under 2.5; and sponsor-controlled capital represented more than 35% of the capital structure. This reduction in leverage and shortening of maturities reflects the higher level of cash flow required for capital investment, and hence the lower level available for debt service, in higher-growth businesses. Such adjustments also reflect the generally lower stability and predictability of cash flows in companies with prospects tied to technological developments. A less leveraged capital structure gives issuers (and the owners) greater operating flexibility, while also positioning them to benefit from major improvements in the company's prospects.

In addition to larger equity commitments and thus lower debt-to-equity ratios, there were also important changes in the *kind* of debt used. In general, there was a pronounced shift away from the use of public high yield debt (particularly PIK and zero coupon securities), and toward the use of private debt, mainly senior debt provided by banks. Those deals that were done with subordinated debt were typically either smaller deals using private mezzanine capital, or larger buyouts using subordinated debt through funds raised and controlled by the LBO firm itself for that purpose.

Private (Bank) Debt vs. Public Debt

There are a number of reasons why bank debt, or other forms of private debt, are proving more attractive than public debt in LBOs in general. For starters, there is considerably more flexibility in structuring a loan than a bond issue. Where bond issues tend to be standardized to facilitate distribution to a variety of institutional investors, the terms of loan agreements can be tailored to the specific strategic and financial issues and opportunities faced by the borrower. By tapping a generally relationship-oriented and more consistently liquid bank market—one that is not as subject to the vagaries of public "market conditions"—borrowers can avail themselves of committed credit facilities with various draw-down, maturity, and pricing options to manage the timing, amount, and cost of the loan. In public bond issues, by contrast, there is less control over the timing of the offerings as well as a minimum amount that can be raised in a single offering.

And, if a company's circumstances should change, whether due to improvements in performance, new investment opportunities, or an acquisition, refinancing a bank loan is far less costly than renegotiating the terms of a public bond. There are typically no prepayment penalties associated with bank debt, whereas public bonds generally have no-call periods ranging from three to five years, as well as required prepayment premiums that can run from 3% to 10% of face value.

> **The Value of Financing Flexibility.** When The Blackstone Group acquired a majority interest in UCAR International for $1.2 billion in January 1995, the LBO was leveraged 5 to 1 with $685 million of bank debt priced at LIB+250-300. Less than a year later, UCAR raised new equity through a public offering, thereby reducing its leverage to 3 to 1. The original bank debt was refinanced with a new loan priced at LIB+150-200.

Of course, public high yield debt also has advantages over bank debt. The maturities are longer (generally eight to ten years, as compared to five to seven years for senior bank debt), and there is typically no amortization of principal before maturity. And, whereas LBO bank debt is almost always secured (by all or nearly all of the borrower's assets) and contains a number of financial and operating covenants, public debt is generally unsecured and less restrictive in terms of covenants. In this sense, public debt is often viewed as "more patient" capital. But, of course, the borrower pays for this patience in terms of higher interest rates, fees, and prepayment penalties (and, as I argue below, a less relationship-oriented investor group).

Public debt also trades in highly liquid markets, thus allowing investors to trade in and out of positions more readily. And, in part due to this greater liquidity and the investor market served, and in part due to the willingness of these high yield investors (for a price) to assume a junior position in the capital structure, the use of public subordinated debt allows issuers to maximize leverage and relieve some pressure from the cash flow requirements for debt service in the early years of the LBO. For example, even in today's more conservative financing environment, large buyouts employing high yield subordinated debt are leveraged as high as 6-7 times EBITDA, whereas senior bank debt has generally held at a 4-4.5 multiple of EBITDA.

Although the practice of syndicating loans is causing some banks to behave more like public debtholders in this respect, bank financing is still premised on a long-term relationship between the LBO sponsor, the borrower, and (at least) the "agent" or "lead" banks in a leveraged deal. Unlike the past, the most sophisticated banks that lead LBO financings today are providing their corporate and equity sponsor clients with more than just conventional bank credit. And having a broadly-based relationship with a lender may well turn out to be important for borrowers if only for the following reason: A strong relationship with a bank premised on a continuous series of past and future dealings, together with the bank's typical preferred position in the capital structure, should ensure an easier renegotiation of credit terms in troubled situations—much easier at least than might be expected with an often faceless group of bondholders.

> **The Client-Focused Relationship Approach.** Bank of America, for example, offers a variety of corporate finance products and services designed to help our clients meet their operating and financial objectives. These services run the gamut from capital structure analysis, idea generation, mergers and acquisition advisory, and a variety of capital underwriting and placement activities, to cash management, foreign exchange, and other risk management services. Our professed aim at B of A is to expand our "share of mind" with our clients. To the extent we succeed in helping a client meet its objectives and so contribute to an increase in the value of the company, we will end up creating a partnership, a mutually beneficial relationship that transcends any single financing or transaction.

Junk Bonds Were Once Quasi-Private Debt

But this begs the question: If bank loans do indeed provide significantly greater flexibility than public bonds, then why was the high yield market so successful in displacing bank loans during the 1980s? The answer appears to turn on changes in the public "junk bond" market over the past decade. While Milken and Drexel served as principal market makers during the 1980s, the high yield market was able to combine much of the flexibility of private debt with the liquidity and structural advantages (and less restrictive covenants) of public debt.

Although this seems to have been largely forgotten, junk bonds experienced their first true test not in 1990, but rather in the early 1980s. When the recession of 1981-1982 caused problems for many of its high yield issuers, Drexel responded by transforming the 3(a)9 exchange offering into a low-cost, expeditious alternative to Chapter 11. Because its high yield investors were in those days a small, well-organized group, Drexel could quickly reach a deal to reduce interest payments (by using PIK and zero coupon securities), stretch out maturities, substitute equity for debt, or whatever it took to keep the company afloat. In this sense, the junk bond market as orchestrated by Milken was a "quasi-private" debt market; it effectively combined the liquidity of a publicly traded market with much of the flexibility of bank debt.

But, with the downfall of Milken and Drexel at the end of the '80s, the liquidity of the junk bond vanished—and, along with it, the flexibility it once provided issuers in working out their difficulties. When deals got into trouble, there was no overarching marketmaker to smooth over conflicts among creditors. And, although secured bankers and subordinated debtholders may never feel completely comfortable with each other in the best of circumstances, intercreditor conflicts of interest during the 1989-1991 period escalated into intercreditor warfare. Under pressure from the new HLT regulations, banks were much less likely to cooperate with other creditors. In many cases, banks demonstrated their willingness to push a company into Chapter 11 rather than weaken their security and, hence, their preferred collateral position and prospects for repayment. (And the result, in almost all such cases of the banks' refusal to make concessions, was full repayment of all senior claims outstanding.)

At the same time, vulture investors routinely purchased the distressed subordinated debt at bargain basement prices, and then attempted to use charges of "fraudulent conveyance" as a lever to pry banks loose from their security. This approach met with little success, however; and many junk bond investors experienced significant writedowns in the value of their securities and became equity holders in still highly leveraged companies. In so doing, they provided fodder for what became a popular buyout strategy in the late '80s and early '90s—the leveraged recapitalization of "good companies with bad balance sheets."

Maintaining Control of the Capital Structure

For buyout funds re-emerging in the '90s, the lesson from the highly leveraged, high-yield-driven deals of the late '80s was fairly clear: Transactions that seek to *maximize* leverage using capital sources over which buyout sponsors have little influence can lead to substantial loss of control and value in distressed situations.

In recognition of this problem, one response by a handful of buyout firms has been to develop private sources of subordinated debt. Long before the '90s, Forstmann Little was supplying junior debt for its deals out of capital raised from its own limited partners through subordinated debt funds raised expressly for that purpose (Teddy Forstmann's pride in never having used "junk bonds" in a Forstmann Little deal has been widely publicized). Other firms, including Welsh, Carson, Anderson & Stowe and Bain Capital, have followed a similar funding approach.

By leveraging the capital structure with subordinated debt over which the equity provider/owner has control, the firm preserves operating and financing flexibility that can prove valuable in improving as well as deteriorating situations. Should a company's performance improve substantially, the firm will be in a good position to refinance the subordinated debt with lower-cost debt; that is, it will not have to deal with no-call provisions, prepayment penalties, or identification of the bondholders. In troubled situations, interest rate payments on sponsor-controlled subordinated debt can be suspended, thereby freeing cash flow for capital investment and senior debt service. In the extreme, the subordinated debt can be converted to equity, thereby

providing further comfort to other creditors and eliminating any repayment requirements.

Other buyout firms have responded by relying almost exclusively on larger equity commitments combined with somewhat greater proportions of senior bank debt. One interesting development that has enabled the bank market to bite off a larger portion of the total debt is the relatively recent rise and expansion of "prime rate" funds. Prime rate funds, in brief, are vehicles created by money managers, primarily in the form of mutual funds or similar arrangements, that are specifically designed to invest in higher-yielding bank loans. Investors in these funds are yield-driven, passive investors. The role of the fund managers (in almost all cases, former commercial bankers) is to act much like bank lenders, building relationships with both the banks that underwrite and agent leveraged loans, and the borrowers themselves.

In order to take advantage of this somewhat unique source of debt capital, the so-called alphabet loan market has developed, wherein senior term loans are structured in tranches, with the A tranche funded primarily by senior bank lenders, and the B, C, and even D tranches funded in large part by the prime rate funds. The A tranche is typically a term loan with a 6-7 year maturity, priced at the "standard" LIBOR+200-250, and held by the originating and other participating commercial banks. The B, C, and D tranches, although of equal priority with and having the same security as the A claims, typically have longer maturities (up to nine years) and are priced at 275-375 basis points over LIBOR to compensate for the additional maturity risk. Further, these loans require only nominal amortization prior to full repayment of the A loan, thus relieving some debt service pressure on the cash flows and so increasing the borrower's senior debt capacity. While senior debt lenders will still go only so far in allowing a borrower to stretch its senior debt as a multiple of cash flow, the alphabet loan market has in many cases enabled LBO sponsors to avoid the added cost—and loss of flexibility—that comes with using subordinated debt.

Implications of Widely Syndicated Leveraged Bank Financings

Another important development in leveraged lending, and in the broader bank market in general, is the widespread syndication of bank loans. In response to loan portfolio problems in the 1980s (in part from HLTs, but also from real estate, developing country, and cyclical industry exposures), originating banks began to parcel out pieces of larger bank loan financings to other banks. And that trend has, if anything, accelerated in the '90s. Even the largest money-center banks today hold only relatively small amounts of any one loan—generally, $20-$50 million—in contrast to the $100-$250 million hold levels during the heyday of the '80s LBOs.

The syndication of bank loans has potential implications for the ability of borrowers to maintain some measure of control over their debt capital and the providers of that capital. While syndication clearly benefits the originating bank by allowing it to diversify its credit portfolio, might not the distribution of HLT loans among a large group of participating banks and prime rate funds—sometimes referred to in the business as merely "paper buyers"—be leading to a reduction in borrowers' control over the senior lenders? And doesn't this dispersion of claims have the potential to offset completely the desirable effects of bank relationship financing I described earlier?

Although problems will certainly arise in some distressed situations, they are likely to be exceptions to the rule. Even with widespread syndication of leveraged loans to a growing variety of investors, borrowers will continue to maintain substantial control over their providers of capital—and for a number of reasons. First, as noted earlier, less leveraged capital structures and higher coverage ratios should significantly reduce the frequency with which HLTs get into trouble. And, because of the senior lenders' preferred position in the capital structure, their cooperation in working through difficulties can be expected to be greater than that of subordinated bondholders.

A second factor that is likely to help preserve the benefits of bank financing is the development in the '90s of a highly liquid secondary loan trading market. When faced with troubled situations, whether anticipated or realized, many dissatisfied "paper buyers" are more likely to sell their claims (now trading at prices much closer to their fair value) than subject themselves to protracted negotiations, or resort to obstructive holdout tactics. In addition, only in the worst of credit scenarios should there be a threat of "bondmail"—the practice, noted earlier, in which third-party ("vulture") investors buy up claims in the secondary market with the aim of enriching themselves at the expense of other creditors.

Third, equity sponsors today are taking a very active role in determining which banks will play lead roles in LBO financings—in almost all cases, down to at least the level of the "co-agent" banks. In response to the growing fragmentation of the senior lending market, the sponsors are acting to maintain control over the debt group by insisting on a "core" bank group. Depending on the size of the financing, the core group can contain as few as one or two to as many as ten banks. The shared expectation in such deals is that the lead banks will "do the right thing" for both the borrower and the sponsor if the need for changes in the senior debt arises.

In sum, the relationship approach to financing by Bank of America and other large, sophisticated lead banks is still valuable to borrowers even with a more liquid, fragmented market for senior bank debt. While relationship banks cannot be expected to sacrifice their rights and protections as creditors, their commitment to a "partnership" with a borrower and its owners provides strong incentives to manage difficult situations in a way that maximizes value for the lenders and the client.

CURRENT DEVELOPMENTS: NEW STRATEGIES FOR FINANCIAL BUYERS

Although the current dollar volume of LBOs remains far below that of the '80s, both the number and average size of the deals rose significantly during the past year. The total dollar value of all LBOs reportedly increased almost 60%, from $13.0 billion in 1994 to $20.6 billion in 1995. And, after a very successful year of fundraising, LBO funds are now said to be sitting on an estimated $40 billion in new capital which, if leveraged 4 to 1, could support $200 billion in new deals.

As mentioned earlier, however, financial buyers are facing stiff competition in the buyout market from corporate, or so-called strategic, buyers. With the strength of the stock market, record share prices, and a growing disparity between the valuations of public versus private companies, many publicly-held strategic buyers are using their appreciated stock as currency for acquisitions, bidding aggressively for companies in their own or closely related industries. Driving much of this merger activity is a trend toward consolidation in a number of industries, notably financial services, media and entertainment, telecommunications, and health care. In all of these industries (and a good number of others), strategic buyers are paying up for the chance to capitalize on synergies and scale economies—and, in some instances, to squeeze out excess capacity by rationalizing manufacturing while consolidating administrative functions. Also motivating some strategic buyers is the prospect of access to new distribution channels, or the opportunity to put newly acquired products through existing channels—opportunities not available, of course, to stand-alone financial buyers.

The Leveraged Build-Up: How Financial Buyers Participate in Consolidating Industries

In response to this stepped-up competition from strategic buyers, financial buyers have been forced to develop alternative acquisition strategies. Competitive pressures brought to bear on American companies in the past decade—by hostile takeovers and increased shareholder activism, as well as strong international competition—have seen to it that there are few opportunities today for the classic, financially-engineered LBOs of the '80s.

One strategy used by a number of buyout firms today is the "leveraged build-up," also known as the "buy-and-build" approach. A leveraged build-up typically begins with the identification of a fragmented industry with a number of small to medium-sized players, none of which are dominant. Working with one or more experienced operating managers with industry expertise, buyout firms purchase a company in the targeted industry that serves as a "platform" for further leveraged acquisitions of firms in the same industry. By taking such an approach, buyout firms effectively position themselves as "financial strategic" buyers, thus allowing them to benefit from the opportunities for adding value (discussed earlier) that are available to the corporate strategic buyers. Such a buy-and-build strategy also enables the buyout firm to build top-line growth through acquisitions while reducing the overall cost base, thereby realizing improved margins, increased cash flow, and enhanced value.

A number of firms, notably Golder, Thoma, Cressey, Rauner (GTCR) and Brentwood Associates, have pursued leveraged build-ups as a core buyout strategy for many years. Others have used it selectively, though with more frequency in recent years. Examples

include K-III, KKR's build-up in the trade, media, and educational publications industry; ABRY Broadcasting, Bain Capital's foray in television stations; Dollar Financial Group, Weiss, Peck & Greer's consolidation play in the retail check-cashing industry; Prime Succession, GTCR's funeral home build-up; and Cobblestone Golf, Brentwood Associates' consolidation play in golf courses in the Southwestern U.S.

When acquiring the platform company, it is important to design the capital structure in such a way that it will accommodate a series of future acquisitions. For this reason, the initial transaction is likely to have lower leverage ratios than standard LBOs, and may be funded with as much as 75% equity. Senior debt usually makes up the rest, often in the form of a revolving credit facility, a term loan, and an acquisition facility available for drawdown to finance future add-on acquisitions. This structure is designed to preserve the operating and financing flexibility necessary to make further acquisitions. In future add-ons, moreover, the leveraged build-up can take on progressively higher leverage ratios, as the consolidation proves successful and the borrower grows and establishes a track record of consistent cash flows.

> **A Recent Leveraged Build-Up in the Making.** On November 29, 1995, The Blackstone Group and the management of Volume Services agreed to purchase the concession stand supplier from its parent company, Flagstar Cos., a restaurant conglomerate owned 47% by KKR. The purchase price was approximately $100 million, reportedly representing a multiple of 4 to 5 times EBITDA. According to Howard Lipson, a partner of Blackstone, the equity and debt split of the transaction was 30%/70%, and no subordinated debt was used. The aim of the deal structure, said Lipson, was "overfunding and providing enough equity firepower to double the size of the company without having to go back to the equity market."[10]

In a variation of this strategy—and as another means of competitive differentiation—some financial buyers have developed industry-specific expertise and are applying the leveraged build-up strategy to companies in rapidly changing, higher-growth, technology-driven industries. As one notable example, the buyout firm of Welsh, Carson, Anderson,

---

10. "Blackstone 'Overfunds' Volume Services Deal," *Buyouts* (Securities Data Publishing, January 15, 1996), p. 12.

& Stowe (which raised over $1.4 billion in new funds in 1995) has built a reputation by specializing in health care and information services, two industries more often associated with old-fashioned venture capital than with LBOs. Along with its industry expertise, the key to Welsh Carson's success has been a highly flexible capital structure—one that consists of large proportions of Welsh Carson-controlled subordinated debt and equity, sometimes supplemented, when possible, with senior bank debt. Welsh Carson's ability and willingness to make acquisitions entirely (in many cases) with its own capital, combined with its industry expertise, has enabled the firm to realize significant returns and compete effectively as a financial strategic buyer.

Corporate Partnerships with Financial Buyers

In another, related development in corporate M&A, financial buyers with an industry focus are teaming up with corporate strategic buyers to purchase companies on a leveraged basis. As one recent example, in December 1995 The Carlyle Group, a buyout firm specializing in defense and aerospace transactions, joined strategic buyer Thiokol Corp. in buying Howmet Corp. and certain affiliates for $800 million. Howmet manufactures precision castings of superalloys and titanium used primarily for jet aircraft and industrial gas turbine engine components, and is thus a logical complement to Thiokol's own aerospace business. In a similar deal in 1992, Carlyle joined Northrop in purchasing Vought Aircraft.

The Blackstone Group has also completed a number of successful LBOs by teaming up with corporate partners. Among them are the firm's 1988 acquisition of Transtar with USX (Transtar provides transport services to USX and other companies), the 1991 acquisition of Six Flags with Time Warner, and the 1995 acquisition of UCAR International through a unique arrangement with Union Carbide.

As one would expect, such partnerships hold out benefits to both the financial and strategic buyer. The financial buyer brings to the table significant equity capital along with considerable financial expertise in a leveraged environment—both in the initial capitalization of the transaction, and in the ongoing monitoring of financial and operating performance. In some cases, like those of The Carlyle Group and Welsh Carson, the financial buyer also contributes valuable industry expertise. The corpo-

rate or strategic buyer, on the other hand, supplies significant industry knowhow as well as an experienced operating management team. The corporate partner also presents opportunities for exploiting synergies with the target and, in many cases, even provides a pre-arranged exit strategy for the financial buyer. For example, in the Carlyle/Thiokol purchase of Howmet cited above, Thiokol reportedly has an option to purchase Carlyle's stake in the combined company at a future date—one that will presumably be exercised when Howmet has the financial wherewithal to undergo such a recapitalization.

Financial Buyer Niche Strategies

Many financial buyers are using other strategies to differentiate themselves from their competition and to develop a source of comparative advantage. Clayton Dubilier & Rice, for example, has compiled a track record of success in buying "undermanaged" divisions or subsidiaries of large companies, and many other firms have pursued a similar strategy. Other firms have focused on out-of-favor industries, while still others look for turnaround situations. In another interesting variation, The Cypress Group has demonstrated a keen interest in taking significant minority or shared ownership positions in already established companies; their contribution in such cases is typically to provide additional equity capital for growth and/or to assist private companies in making a transition of ownership. Finally, a number of firms have begun to look outside the U.S. for investment opportunities, though generally with the intent of pairing up with a local partner.

THE EXPANDING ROLE OF BANKS IN THE LBO ARENA

As the buyout market has continued to evolve, so has the role that commercial banks play in the LBO process. Having once been providers of just the senior bank debt, a handful of large, sophisticated banks now offer access to a variety of capital sources at all levels of the capital structure. Besides the traditional senior bank piece, such banks today can provide additional senior debt capital sourced from prime rate funds, private senior and mezzanine capital from institutional investors and banks, high yield financing raised through their own trading and distribution forces, and equity capital contributed by the banks' own private equity investment groups.

*Partnerships between financial and strategic buyers hold out benefits to both groups.
The financial buyer brings to the table significant equity capital along with
considerable financial expertise in a leveraged environment—both in the initial
capitalization of the transaction, and in the ongoing monitoring of financial and
operating performance.*

Several large banks have also developed bridge financing capabilities. Together with an expanded ability to underwrite senior and subordinated loans, such a capability now allows a handful of top-tier banks to offer "one-stop" financing for LBO and other leveraged transactions. As an example, Bank of America has teamed up with Lehman Brothers to form Strategic Resource Partners, a $675 million fund available to provide interim financing for leveraged acquisitions, recapitalizations, and management buyouts. Such financing is intended to be refinanced, at least in part, with high yield or similar securities placed in the public or private markets as timing permits. By means of this joint venture—which effectively unites Lehman Brothers' well-established high yield underwriting capability with Bank of America's senior debt financing expertise and our own high yield underwriting operation (through BA Securities, Inc.)—the two firms have created the ability to step up for the entire debt-financed portion of the capital structure, *on a fully committed basis*, prior to the actual closing and funding of the transaction. In today's competitive leveraged acquisition environment, providing financial or strategic buyers with the assurance that acquisition financing will be available at the time of closing can be critical to our clients' ability to compete successfully for acquisitions.

Besides providing more of the capital, banks are also playing an increasingly important role in originating and facilitating LBO transactions. Bank of America, for example, is using its combination of an established M&A practice, a large U.S. corporate client base, and strong relationships with financial buyers to perform a number of buyout functions traditionally associated with investment banks—namely, (1) bringing together buyers and sellers, (2) lining up potential sources of equity capital for buyers, (3) identifying investment opportunities for both our corporate and financial buyer clients, and (4) introducing management teams to LBO sponsors.

When combined with strong capitalization and an increasingly global presence, this expansion of capital-raising and corporate finance capabilities is positioning a few large commercial banks to become dominant players in the LBO business—a business that, for all but the commodity-like senior bank financing, was until recently assumed to be the near-exclusive domain of investment banks. As the LBO market continues to grow and evolve, banks like Bank of America can be expected to play an increasingly valuable role in the LBO process.

BENNETT STEWART: Yesterday, we heard Michael Jensen talk about the role of the board of directors in creating shareholder value (though after listening to Michael, I suppose we should really think of it as the board of "accommodators"). Professor Jensen identified four main roles our boards *ought* to play in public companies, but in many cases do not. Stated as briefly as possible, they are the hiring, firing, counseling, and compensating of top management. In today's discussion, we will further explore the role of the board with a distinguished panel of senior executives and directors brought together by the Continental Bank.

Current compensation practices are clearly one area where boards seem to be failing—and we will likely talk a little about that today. But there are also more fundamental issues about the relationship between professional management and corporate boards, such as:

- Who really should nominate the board of directors?
- Is it appropriate for management to sit on the board?
- Should the CEO of the company also fulfill the role of the chairman of the company?
- How can we improve the dialogue and decision-making that takes place as a result of the board process?

It would also be interesting to hear the panel's assessment of the import of some current trends. For example, there are a number of public companies that are beginning to feel more pressure from institutional investors to reform the role and function of the board. It can't have escaped anyone's attention that various shareholder interest groups have risen up in recent years to express their dissatisfaction with managements and boards.

Robert Monks, for example, has formed a firm called Institutional Shareholder Partners whose aim is to act with major shareholders to help—or, in some cases, prod—companies into creating shareholder value. You may recall that Monks waged a well-publicized proxy contest with Sears a while back that was designed to serve as a catalyst for change. The United Shareholders Association (USA), a group started by Boone Pickens and now run by Ralph Whitworth, has achieved some modest successes in influencing the corporate governance process. For instance, after a vigorous campaign, USA managed to change the compensation plan of the chairman of ITT; and there are intimations that perhaps more dramatic changes in the overall structure of the company may be forthcoming. So it would be interesting to speculate here about the expected impact of the increasing activism of institutional investors on corporate managements and boards.

To discuss these issues this morning, the Continental Bank has assembled a really first-rate panel. Let me now introduce the panel (and I will do so in alphabetical order).

JAMES BIRLE is a General Partner with The Blackstone Group, the well-known New York investment firm. One of his principal responsibilities at Blackstone is to serve as the co-chairman and CEO of Collins & Aikman Group, Inc., formerly the Wickes Companies, an organization I would describe as a $3 billion conglomerate. Jim also serves on a variety of boards, including that of Transtar, a railroad business acquired by Blackstone in a leveraged buyout from USX. Given that Jim also spent 30 years with General Electric, I expect him to give us some insights as to how internal corporate governance mechanisms differ between public companies and private companies run by so-called financial investors like Blackstone.

WADE CABLE is CEO and a director of The Presley Companies, a prominent California homebuilder. The company went through an initial public offering of stock this past October, largely because of the difficulty most real estate developers have today in convincing their banks to lend to them. So Wade is living proof of the credit crunch.

MICHAEL JENSEN, whose name I've already mentioned several times, is the Edsel Bryant Professor of Business Administration at the Harvard Business School, and among the most vocal and controversial critics of corporate governance in the U.S.

trial installation. Like John's former employer, Johns Manville, the Fibreboard Corporation faces a massive potential liability from asbestos litigation—which, I'm sure, has made John's current job most challenging.

WILLIAM ROPER is Senior Vice President and CFO of Science Applications International Corporation, which claims to be the largest em-

and governance structure—one that may have valuable lessons for our public companies.

JOHN TEETS is Chairman, President, and CEO of The Dial Corp. John presided over a radical restructuring of the company in the 1980s—one which included the sale of the Armour meat-packing business in 1983, the sale of the Greyhound bus lines in 1987, and the recently

ROGER LEE is Senior Vice President-Finance and Administration, as well as a director, of Caesars World, a company which fought off a hostile suitor by undergoing a leveraged recap about five years ago. Roger will thus provide the perspective of—and presumably defend—the management and directors of our public companies.

JOHN ROACH is the Chairman, President, and CEO of Fibreboard Corporation, also a publicly traded company. The company has approximately $300 million in sales and focuses on wood products and indus-

ployee-owned company in America. The company certainly represents an interesting paradigm for us to consider this morning. The firm has approximately $1.2 billion in revenues, and is involved primarily in systems development work.

FRED SIMMONS is a General Partner of Freeman Spogli, an investment company that has been very successful in executing LBOs of 15 companies in a variety of industries, including seven supermarket chains. As I suggested earlier in introducing Jim Birle of Blackstone, Fred also represents an alternative ownership

announced spin-off of Greyhound Financial Corporation, or GFC, to its stockholders. It should be interesting to hear from John about this process, and about the role of the board in overseeing this restructuring.

I am BENNETT STEWART, Senior Partner of Stern Stewart & Co., a corporate finance advisory firm that specializes in valuation, restructuring, and management incentive compensation. I'm not a director of any major company, which is probably the surest sign of the failure of our corporate governance system.

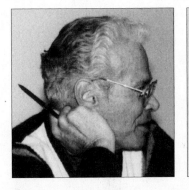

The Case of Dial Corp

STEWART: Let me begin this discussion with John Teets. John, as I just mentioned, last October your company announced its decision to spin off Greyhound Financial Corporation to its shareholders, which caused the firm's stock price to increase from $35 to about $41 a share. And your share price now trades in the vicinity of $50, if I'm not mistaken. The company must be doing something right.

Would you share with us the dynamics of that decision to spin off GFC? And what role did the board play in that process?

TEETS: Well, the decision to sell Greyhound Financial was really made several years ago. At that time we decided The Dial Corp would pursue a strategy focused on consumer products and services. So we knew then that GFC was not part of our long-range plan.

But it turned out to be very difficult to get out of the finance business. We let Salomon Brothers try to sell it for over a year. Then we gave the job to Merrill Lynch, which also had it for over a year without success. GFC has a good record, five years of 15-20% growth in earnings, and a $2 billion portfolio with only 3% non-earning assets. But no one was interested in paying 100 cents on the dollar for a $2-billion portfolio.

Some time later, we realized when we wanted to divest Verex, our mortgage insurance business, we were not going to be able to sell that operation either. In this case, we also faced a tax problem. The business was carrying a $100 million investment tax credit going forward that would have been triggered by a sale of the business. Our solution, which we devised with the help of Gleacher and Company, was to package GFC together with Verex and spin them off to our shareholders. In fact, the new securities will begin to trade on March 4 this year.

What was the board's role in this decision? For the past nine years, we have apprised our board that we want to keep moving into the consumer products and services area. That is our long-term strategy, and our board has been kept informed throughout the process. In the course of this nine-year program, we have sold close to 20 businesses for about $3.2 billion, and have bought others worth about $1.4 billion.

So we have been moving slowly in the direction we want to go. It's been like moving a giant, but we're finally reaching a point where it's starting to pay off.

STEWART: Well, John, your stock has gone up quite dramatically. Is that something that the board is pleased about? Or do they just not care?

TEETS: Our stock has gone from $13 when I took over to almost $50 today. Our board does not sit around looking at the stock on a daily basis, if that's your point. But they have played, and continued to play, an important role in the company's success in adding value for stockholders.

Let me also add here that I think statements like Professor Jensen's that boards are incapable of bringing about necessary change are greatly exaggerated. For one thing, boards often exercise their power to fire CEOs. And most boards understand their responsibility to monitor management and represent stockholders' interest. Now, there are clearly some cases where the board doesn't function and the system doesn't work. We all know the companies that are not performing. But that is probably true in no more than, say, 20% of American companies today. So, the system *is* working.

In my own case, *all* my board members are outsiders and they are all CEOs of other companies. And they are very thorough in their examination of proposals. For example, when we proposed the spin-off of GFC and Verex to our board last August, what was scheduled to be a one-hour meeting turned into a four-hour meeting. And the proposal was not approved at that meeting, but only after further research and discussion.

So, in our case, the governance process works quite well. And the board has been pleased with what we've succeeded in accomplishing for our stockholders. Some of our board members have also participated directly them-

selves in our shareholder gains. We give our board members the option to take their fees in stock or cash. And one of our directors recently reminded me that he has now accumulated a million-dollar's worth of our stock through this program. So he is, I think, quite aware of the fact our stock price is significantly higher today than it was six months ago.

STEWART: John, you mentioned a one-hour meeting that turned into a four-hour meeting. I'm just interested in the kinds of questions and concerns that surfaced during that dialogue.

TEETS: Professor Jensen yesterday objected that the code of politeness that prevails in board meetings prevents serious disagreements from being aired. But that's misleading. It's true that directors don't go to meetings with the idea of antagonizing the CEO, but nor are they the rubber stamp that Jensen suggests. They ask tough questions. They debate important issues.

As I mentioned, our plan to spin off some of our businesses clearly raised questions and concerns among the board. In fact, our original proposal called for combining our bus manufacturing operation along with the finance companies. One important issue the board was especially concerned about was the funding of the spun-off company: They asked questions such as: How could this new entity be financed so as to satisfy the banks and stand up to the scrutiny of S&P and Moody's. How could the banks and

rating agencies be made to accept what amounts to a mini-conglomerate? Wouldn't it be too complicated to understand? (You can't be too careful, I'm told, in explaining these matters to bankers.)

So, it was only after a lot of thought and a long debate that we ultimately decided to spin off GFC and Verex together, and then either sell or spin off the bus manufacturing company as a stand-alone operation. And our board members played an important role in helping us reach this decision.

The Case of Caesars World

STEWART: John mentioned that all of his company's board members are outsiders except himself. Now let me turn to Roger Lee. Roger, you are the Senior Vice President and CFO of Caesars World, as well as a director. Is the composition of your board like that of John's company?

LEE: No. We have a nine-person board that consists of four insiders and five outsiders. We are probably tilting too much to the inside. I personally think there should probably be at least two outsiders for every insider on the board, maybe more. Other companies I've served on have had at most two insiders on the board.

STEWART: Do you think that difference affects the quality of the dialogue that takes place between the board and top management?

LEE: I think it can reduce the amount of dialogue and may tend to create some passivity on the part of the board members. It makes the outsiders more reluctant to take on such a solid nucleus of people in one room at one time.

STEWART: Roger, Caesars World went through a defensive, and fairly dramatic, leveraged restructuring a number of years ago. Can you tell us a little about how what happened, why the company recapitalized itself the way it did, and what the role of the board was during this difficult process?

LEE: We were the target of a hostile takeover bid. The board responded by introducing an in-depth review of values and alternative courses of action, using both management input and several consultants. Based on the specifics of our situation, it was determined that the bid price was considerably lower than the company's value. Further it was believed that an alternate approach—a corporate restructuring using additional leverage to fund a large one-time cash dividend—could deliver more value to shareholders while preserving their proportional ownership in the company.

We aggressively pursued this alternative, eventually gaining shareholder approval and forcing withdrawal of the opposing bid. But one of the casino control commissions that regulate our industry unexpectedly refused to permit the restructuring. The board then investigated alternative courses of action, and decided to use substantially less leverage and repurchase approximately one-third of the outstanding common shares in a Dutch auction—the kind of auction that calls for each shareholder to name his own price within a range of values specified by the company.

Throughout this entire sequence of events, the board was the focal point for initiating, evaluating, and taking actions. It was a difficult task accomplished under enormous pressure.

The Case of the Presley Companies

STEWART: Wade, your company has recently gone public. Could you give us a little background on your company, and tell us how it got to be where it is now? And do you think the corporate governance process and the role of the board will change much as a result of your transition from a private to a public company?

CABLE: Our company was in fact a public company from 1971 through 1984. In 1984 it was acquired by what was then Pacific Lighting. They have since changed their name to Pacific Enterprises. So I've seen a public board of directors at work in a very large, diverse company.

Michael Jensen would probably have some fun looking at how the board of Pacific Lighting performed. As as example, consider the decision the board made in voting to sell the Presley Companies, along with its other real estate companies. At about the same time, Pacific Lighting decided to buy Thrifty Drug Stores for something in the neighborhood of $870 million. To give you a rough sense of how these two transactions affected the shareholder value of Pacific Lighting, Thrifty Drug Stores made approximately $35 million the first year they owned it. The Presley Companies would have made approximately $100 million in the first year we owned it, had it still been owned by Pacific Lighting. Recently, Pacific Enterprises completely elimi-

nated its dividend to shareholders and announced very large losses as a result of its decision to divest their retail businesses. This is a board that, at least in this instance, did not do well by its shareholders.

When we completed our LBO of the Presley Companies from Pacific Lighting in 1987, the deal was reported to be leveraged with a debt-to-equity ratio of 57 to 1. Actually, the entire deal was leveraged, with the equity piece being subordinated debt. We were able to pay down the debt very quickly; and in just two years following the close of the deal, we had a company with a debt-to-equity ratio of less than 4 to 1. We thought this was terrific, feeling that we had hit the home run of all times.

The problem we ran into was that the world changed and suddenly FIRREA-regulated commercial banks changed their view of what constituted an acceptable amount of leverage for a real estate developer. As a consequence, we chose to take our company public in October 1991 in an effort to access other capital markets.

STEWART: What was the role of the board in this decision to go public?

CABLE: Extensive. As a private company, we had a board that was composed entirely of insiders and manager-owners who were very active in the decision to take the company public. On the subject of the role of the board, I was never once asked by potential investors, "Who's on your board?" I don't think institutions that invested in this company really gave a damn. I think they looked at the management and said, "What can you do and what can't you do?" Their decision to buy stock was based on the company's track record and the perceived ability of the management to perform.

Now consider our current board, which is made up of a broad spectrum of people that includes insider owner-managers, our largest shareholder, a university president, other business executives, and an investment banker. I am

confident this board would have taken equally as active a role as our former board in vital decisions such as going public. Our current board is a very astute group of people with a wide variety of backgrounds and expertise; and I am confident that we, as a company, will benefit from their involvement. For example, we currently have an investment banker on our board. This is significant because in our industry the major problem today is capital and how to access sources that we have traditionally not had relationships with.

STEWART: Are you assuming that unless you have an investment banker on your board, you would not be able to get access to capital?

CABLE: No, but we've been forced to educate ourselves very quickly about raising capital from sources that we have had no experience in dealing with. Two years ago, financing in the residential real estate business was pretty simple. We simply asked ourselves, "To which commercial banker were we going to give the honor of making us this loan?" They were lined up outside the door. The only question was, "Who was going to provide the most credit at the lowest rate?" There was little negotiation required, and frankly, our biggest problem was that we could not satisfy all the lenders we had three years ago.

But credit availability has now changed drastically. In the past, profits from our business accrued almost totally to the developer. Now the capital providers are demanding a much larger share.

So, in answer to your question, we could obviously hire an investment banker. But because we had so little experience in this area, we felt it would be advantageous to have someone on our board who could provide us with the benefit of his experience and ideas. Our strategy was not simply go public, pay the banks down, and go on with business as usual. Instead, we viewed going public as a major first step in a long-range

strategy to make our balance sheet match the future capital requirements of our business. To do that effectively, we thought it would be helpful to have an investment banker on the board.

STEWART: But don't you think this investment banker might have an agenda with you as far as maximizing his bank's wealth, possibly at your expense. Doesn't that give you cause for concern, Wade?

CABLE: No. On the contrary, I always like to have somebody whom I know is motivated by profit. This way his motivation is the same as our company's. And if we do another offering, which is something we undoubtedly will explore in the future, his company may or may not be part of that offering.

FRED SIMMONS: So, Bennett, you're suggesting that perhaps Wade should hire a firm like Stern Stewart as his financial adviser, one that couldn't

take him public—so this way there couldn't be any conflict of interest?

STEWART: Well, I must confess the thought did flit through my mind, but only for an instant.

CABLE: Gee, Bennett, I didn't realize that's what you were driving at. I think I'll stick with my investment banker.

The Case of Fibreboard

STEWART: Well, let's change the subject. Let me turn now to John Roach, CEO of Fibreboard. What makes John's company especially interesting, as I mentioned earlier, is that the company is dealing with a major asbestos litigation problem. The stock price, as a consequence, is down to $3 a share. There are four million shares outstanding, so the company has a total market equity capitalization of $12 million.

John, I'm just wondering how the board of your company responds to an obviously very challenging situation—one where you have what appears to be a viable operating business on the one side of the balance sheet, with this terrific liability on the other. All of this would seem to increase the threat of legal liability for the board.

ROACH: At Fibreboard the majority of the board has turned over in less than a year. Four out of seven of our current directors are brand-new, including myself. I am the only insider,

and I believe very strongly that all board members should be outsiders unless there are special circumstances—say, heavy ownership by an individual in the company or by a family. Another likely exception is when a company makes a major acquisition. It then may want to have the CEO of the acquired company on the board. But, aside from these special circumstances, I find it difficult to believe that insiders who spend every day dealing with management and management issues could have an independent perspective on things like executive compensation and the hiring or firing of the CEO.

But, in the case of Fibreboard, as I said, four board members are new. The reason I'm there now is that the prior board finally pulled the plug on the prior CEO. That was an action brought about rather dramatically by some angry shareholders. They were able to put one person on the board. And I have put two new representatives on the board, both CEOs of other firms. Like John Teets, I think the value of having other CEOs on the board is enormous. They understand the issues, they're rarely shy individuals, and they understand the pressures the company is facing. And in this case we needed that kind of experience.

STEWART: John, you mentioned that there was a group of shareholders who were instrumental in tossing your predecessor out of the company. How did that happen?

ROACH: Most of them were from New York, like you, and were very vocal.

STEWART: That's shocking—and how unlike my fellow New Yorkers!

ROACH: So, it wasn't really through the normal process of governance, it was just by being vocal.

STEWART: How much stock did the group own? Was it a formal group of shareholders?

ROACH: It wasn't a formal group. At least they didn't file anything formal. But their combined holdings were on the order of about 30 percent. They had a sizable ownership stake, and they forcefully expressed their view that there was a need for change at the top. So they triggered the change. And when they brought me on, I then had to rebuild the board.

A somewhat similar experience occurred at Manville Corp., a company that also had an asbestos exposure problem. When Manville finally came out of its Chapter 11 proceedings in November of 1988, 11 out of the 13 board members were replaced during the next two-year period. In both these situations, there were unusual opportunities to transform boards into effective agents for necessary change.

But, in both of these cases, it was a crisis, the great sense of urgency, that allowed the changes to take place. Short of a crisis, however, it seems to me very difficult to get boards to assume the role of initiators of dramatic change. But, in these two cases, the new boards were not constrained by the old rules, by the old ways of doing things. It was clear the board was there to enact change. In these two cases, both the board and management had a strong common interest in getting out of a difficult situation and doing what was best for the company.

Now, there are cases where what may be best for the shareholders—or, at least certain shareholders—may not be what's best for the long-term value of the company. I firmly believe that the job of management and the board is to increase the total value of the firm, or the value of the enterprise. There is, however, a secondary issue of how you get that value into the hands of the shareholders; and this is one area where conflict can arise between even conscientious managements and shareholders, and between long-term owners and short-term speculators. This conflict I have in mind really comes down to a matter of financing. Whereas shareholders might prefer a large increase in the firm's debt-equity ratio, perhaps

combined with a major share repurchase program, management may want to capitalize the firm more conservatively—perhaps to protect the value of the firm's human and organizational "capital" from the costs of financial trouble. So, the issue of value maximization gets more complicated when you consider the corporate obligations to creditors, employees, and other constituencies.

But, with that qualification, I do believe the boards of public companies can and should be integrally involved in increasing that shareholder value. This is not to say that the board should initiate or implement policy; they should not attempt to manage the company. But they should have a voice in questions of long-term strategy, in matters like major divestitures, acquisitions, and capital expenditure programs.

At the same time, I think top managements, particularly the CEOs and the CFOs, could do a far better job in educating and informing their boards. I wrote an article a couple of years ago arguing that the CFO, the comptroller, and the financing staff should not view themselves as simply bean counters and opportunistic fund-raisers, but rather as strategic architects who help the CEO do his job better. That same process is an opportunity to provide the board with the kind of information that would enable the board to help evaluate strategic direction and

major decisions to allocate corporate resources. In many companies, top management simply does not provide enough information to the board to allow the board to do its job.

STEWART: As we discussed earlier, John Teets's company spun off Greyhound Financial. John, you have a destination resort that doesn't seem to fit in your kind of company. Now, if you were to consider divesting or spinning off this resort, would you expect the board to *initiate* a discussion about such an opportunity to restructure the company? Or is the board's role simply one of responding to management's proposals?

> *At least once a year management ought to share with the board its long-term view of the company's strategic plan. And there ought to be periodic updates detailing the company's progress in executing the plan. Such meetings should serve to define the corporate goals and performance parameters that Mike Jensen was insisting on yesterday.*
>
> *—John Roach*

ROACH: First of all, let me say that we currently have no intention of divesting or spinning off any of our businesses. Our objective is to enhance the strategic value of each of our businesses and, in so doing, maximize the value of the company.

In response to your question, I think the board should feel free to initiate any idea that management is not smart enough to initiate on their own. It's the management's responsibility, but if management's dragging its feet and doesn't bring that idea forward, any board member should feel completely free to do so.

STEWART: Is that what typically goes on, in your experience? Let me give you an example. Suppose management brings to the board's attention a major capital project for approval. At that point, it's almost too late, it seems to me, for the board to understand all of the factors that could affect the economics of that project. So, given the process, the board is almost put in a position of rubber-stamping a decision that management has initiated. So I'm just wondering whether the board *can* really play an effective role.

ROACH: If that's the way the board is run, they don't have an opportunity to add value. But there is another way—one that I recommended when I was a strategy consultant, and one that we now use at Fibreboard. And that is to have the

company review once a year with its full board the long-term strategy of the company and its individual businesses.

Now, that doesn't have to be more than a quick update if it's been done in great depth before. But, at least once a year management ought to share with the board its long-term view of the company's strategic plan. And there ought to be periodic updates detailing the company's progress in executing the plan. Such updates should tell the board what management expects to accomplish during the year, given the state of the economy and the current competitive environment. Such meetings should shape the board's expectations, it should serve to define the corporate goals and performance parameters that Mike Jensen was insisting on yesterday.

And all this has got to be done within a broad strategic context. So, for example, if management is contemplating a major acquisition in consumer products, the acquisition should not come as a surprise to the board. The same holds if management decides it wants to sell a major line of business. The board should be prepared for such decisions, and should be prepared to understand them as part of a larger strategic plan.

Managements often make the mistake of presenting their boards with acquisitions and then asking them for approval—all during the same meeting. I believe very strongly in putting major projects in front of the board well before a decision is required. Boards ought to be given the opportunity to be educated about such decisions. They should be given the chance to consider and discuss such issues without the pressure that comes from an impending vote.

Governing Private Companies

STEWART: Let me turn now to Fred Simmons. Fred, as a general partner of an LBO firm like Freeman Spogli, you have a very strong ownership interest in the companies on whose boards you serve. To a far greater extent than in the case of public companies, you and your fellow partners have the power to shape the board and to make it what you want it to be. So, given this power, do the boards of your companies end up working differently from what you've heard John Teets and John Roach describe?

SIMMONS: It was very interesting for me to listen to Mike Jensen's comments yesterday about corporate governance by LBO firms—I believe "LBO associations" was the term he used for firms like KKR, Forstmann Little, and our own—because the model of governance Jensen sets forth really does a nice job of describing how Freeman Spogli functions as a firm.

I was struck especially by his discussion of the intensity of the due diligence process that takes place when we first consider investing in companies. As Jensen suggests, the process generates a tremendous amount of research and information about questions that corporate managers are supposed to be asking themselves all the time: Are assets being used correctly? Is management focused in the right problem areas in the business? Is the company spending too much or too little on capital expenditures? Are we financing our assets in the best way possible? Are we in the right businesses? Are we dealing with the competition successfully? Such issues are all looked at in great detail initially upon doing the transaction.

Once our investment is made, the role of the board then becomes one of continually monitoring the company's progress. You continually revisit all those kinds of issues to make sure that the original design is being carried out as was originally planned. And you also re-examine the original plan: Is it still the proper course, or do you need to modify the plan in light of new information?

In putting together our LBO deals, we follow the industry standard of projecting cash flows five or six years into the future. Those estimates determine both the price we are willing to pay and the capital structure we will use in funding our investment in the company.

Another critical determinant of the price we pay for companies—indeed, of our willingness to invest at all—is the extent of the management team's willingness to invest in the deal (and you have to keep in mind that, because of the amount of leverage involved, management's investment is very highly charged equity). If management doesn't want to invest, we get very worried. But if they do want to invest we get very excited. That is a real bellwether for us, an important signal of management's confidence in its ability to achieve projected levels of performance.

STEWART: Fred, do you often see sharp conflicts between the board and the management? Or is it better described as a collaborative interface?

SIMMONS: We try, and generally succeed, in keeping things as collaborative as possible. Of course, there are always issues where there's a natural conflict of interest between management and the board—for example, when it comes to management's compensation. But our philosophy as a firm is that when management invests side by side with us in the equity of the company, then those conflicts are minimized; the goals and interests of the investors and managers are pretty well aligned.

STEWART: How do you combine management ownership with the issue of setting goals and rewarding performance in the company? And what role does the board play in the goal-setting process?

SIMMONS: As majority owners, we clearly call the shots and set the goals in our companies. But before describing our governance process, let me try to explain our investment philosophy. First of all, we try to buy premium companies, well-run companies. We're not in the business of breaking up conglomerates that have problems coordinating all their businesses, nor are we in the business of engineering turnarounds. Our aim is to buy premium companies and then put a lot of capital into them and make them even better.

In the process of investing, we initiate a dialogue with management in which we attempt to come up with a mutually agreeable five-year plan. And, as I mentioned, in our average deal, management typically is asked to buy 5 to 10 percent of the equity of the company up front. They typically buy half of it for cash and half on a full recourse loan. And the company lends them the money at the prime rate of interest, payable quarterly.

So the management has highly charged equity. If the company is

leveraged, say, 3 to 1, and management borrows to fund half its equity purchase, then management has highly leveraged equity. And this equity is also supplemented by performance options that vest over a five-year period. So we feel that management is in there with us with both feet. They're committed to making good on their projections.

STEWART: But because the projected payoffs are highly illiquid—the payoff on their options is at least five years down the road—it also forces management to take a somewhat longer view of the firm's performance. It's forces them to consider longer-run investment as well as near-term efficiency.

SIMMONS: That's right. If the company were sold in less than five years at a premium, the performance options might well vest in part or in full.

STEWART: And this effect is actually quite different from that of the standard stock options given to the managements of most public companies. In most of our public companies, management has an incentive to exercise their options and sell the stock as soon as the options have significant trading value. And this, needless to say, only reinforces whatever pressures management may feel to increase short-run value at the expense of the long term.

Fred, do you ever consider having just regular options as part of your compensation program?

SIMMONS: No, I don't see any purpose to having straight options. The way they're often granted by public companies causes them to be much less efficient than options tied to performance. Let's face it, management can increase earnings, and thus the value of vested options, on a short-term basis. But this may well be to the detriment of medium- or longer-term shareholder value.

ROACH: As long as we're on the subject, let me say a word on behalf of stock options. We have just adopted an unusal option program for senior

management. As I mentioned earlier, our longer-term mission at Fibreboard is to deal effectively with our asbestos litigation problem. But if we can find a solution to the problem, and increase the profitability of our basic operations at the same time, then there's a tremendous potential upside. Our stock price, as mentioned before, is down to $3.

In order to avoid diluting shareholder value, and yet provide manage-

ment strong incentives at the same time, we have decided to set up our option plan so that the prices at which the options can be exercised are considerably higher than today's price of $3. Specifically, one third of management's options will be exercisable if the price hits $10, a second third if the price hits $15, and the final third if the price hits $20. So, our option program will not really pay off unless until our shareholders experience a significant—for example, a five-fold—increase in their wealth. I think that's a good plan, given our current situation. Although I agree that stock options may be abused by some public companies, this is a good use of stock options.

SIMMONS: I agree, John. Although we have not used escalating option prices, that arrangement would seem to create much the same effect as options tied to medium-term or longer-term performance.

The Case of the Blackstone Group

STEWART: Let me ask Jim Birle, who comes from a similar organization, The Blackstone Group, to comment on his views of the governance process. Jim, as both a general partner of The Blackstone Group and co-chairman and CEO of the Collins & Aikman Group of Companies (or what used to be called the Wickes Companies), what do you view as the principal function of the board of directors?

BIRLE: I'm a great believer in the principle that accountability is what makes delegated authority legitimate. In the case of LBO boards, the board delegates to the management of the company the responsibility for managing the enterprise. The board's job is to set the goals for the company and then keep track of whether those goals are being met. If they are not, then it is the board's responsibility to intervene and get things right.

One of the differences between our LBO boards and those of public companies is that if one of our companies fails to meet goals, the consequences to the board members are very significant. We are in the business of investing money on behalf of insurance companies and pension funds. The contractual duration of our fund is 10 years, which means there is a specified time frame within which we have to provide our investors with a competitive return on their invested capital. If we fail to provide adequate returns within the time frame, then we are going to have a hard time raising capital to fund our next set of investments.

And the fact that time is really working against us in terms of providing returns creates a tension between management and the board. The pressure to ensure that the goals are being met is just far greater than that which exists in most public companies. At the same time, this sense of urgency does not prevent us from setting and pursuing long-range goals and encouraging long-term thinking. We spend considerable time and effort analyzing how to strategically reposition some of the Collins & Aikman businesses and we undertake major reinvestment programs—programs that, in some cases, will not pay off for several years. Our goal is maximizing shareholder value, and you can't command a high price for a business if all you've been doing is liquidating its assets and failing to invest in its future earning power.

But to return to my original point, if the management of one of our companies fails to meet its goals, there's a degree of tension at our board meetings that I think is very healthy—and quite different from some of my prior experiences with public companies. Unlike LBO groups, public companies have the staying power that may permit them to accommodate a standard of performance that is significantly below what would be considered satisfactory by The Blackstone Group or other similar merchant bankers.

STEWART: Jim, can you tell us a little about your role as CEO of the Collins & Aikman Companies, and what you have done to turn things around there?

BIRLE: In the case of Wickes, I am in the unique position of being co-chairman of a board in which the partners are a combination of Blackstone General Partners and Wasserstein Perella General Partners, all of which are major stockholders and thus directly affected by the performance of the company. I'm CEO of the Holdings Company to which the individual operating units report.

When we acquired Wickes in December of 1988, it was an overleveraged and underperforming conglomerate comprised of a diverse group of retail, distribution, and manufacturing components. We immediately set up a holding company structure and reassigned to operating managers the functions necessary for them to operate these businesses as self-standing enterprises. Through the divestiture of 25 units, we paid down $1.5 billion in debt during the first two years of ownership. At the same time we also brought in stronger operating executives who put in place new investment and growth strategies for the strongest units. Having a knowledgeable and involved board made it possible to effect tremendous changes in a troubled company in a short period of time.

STEWART: What kind of periodic performance measures do you use in evaluating operating management's performance?

BIRLE: We have much a tighter performance measurement system, by necessity, than most public companies I'm familiar with. In collaboration with management, the board sets both

> *One critical determinant of the price we pay for companies—indeed, of our willingness to invest at all—is the extent of the management team's willingness to invest in the deal. If management doesn't want to invest, we get very worried. But if they do want to invest we get very excited. That is a real bellwether for us, an important signal of management's confidence in its ability to achieve projected levels of performance.*
>
> —*Fred Simmons*

yearly targets as well as longer-term growth goals.

STEWART: What is the nature of the goals?

BIRLE: There are basically two: growth in operating income and return on capital employed. Both of these measures are formulated in terms of cash flow rather than earnings and both are used in evaluating long-term as well as short-term performance. Since management are major equity holders in the company, we are confident that they are constantly attempting to balance short-term versus long-term goals in creating value.

STEWART: Does the board set the goals, or does it instead just ratify goals that have been set by the management in a negotiation throughout the company?

BIRLE: I would say it's more of a negotiation. But, unlike the boards of many public companies, our board members come to the table already knowing a great deal about the operations and the expected behavior of the businesses in various economic and competitive situations. This knowledge comes from the extensive due diligence process we have conducted just prior to the acquisition. So we are able to determine when management has really gotten off the track far more quickly and confidently than most public company directors.

Although we do allow the CEOs to present their own budgets to be ratified by us, there has already been a vigorous dialogue between the CEO and the board when the CEO's plan is presented for ratification. We try and work together with operating management in framing the boundary conditions for performance. For example, what should we expect if the economy turns down? And if the CEO and his management team exceed their targeted goal, they're handsomely rewarded.

STEWART: Is there a cap on the bonus?

BIRLE: For the top guys, yes, there's generally a cap on annual awards. It's roughly twice their base salary. But if

they miss on the downside, then their bonus will be zero. So it's very much a pay-for-performance system. Our system is designed such that the people who really perform can make themselves a lot of money in the short term. And the ones who don't perform are really made to feel the pain of failure. To supplement these short-term programs, we put in place long-term capital

accumulation programs where clearly superior performance really translates into significant wealth accumulation.

Employee Ownership and the Case of SAIC

STEWART: Let me just finish my tour of duty here by asking Bill Roper to describe what is probably the unique ownership structure of his company. It may even have considerable value as a model for the future.

ROPER: I am the CFO of a company called Science Applications International Corporation, or SAIC for short. The company was founded in 1969 by four scientists who wanted to do some interesting work with the government. One of their aims was to generate enough revenues to be able to pay themselves a reasonable salary and live in La Jolla, California.

We just completed a year in which our revenues were about $1.3 billion. We

have about 14,000 employees. We've grown at an average compound rate in the high teens; and although the rate of growth is slowing a little bit, it still is in double digits. The company has had revenue and earnings increases in every year of its existence. We are primarily a government contractor; we do almost two thirds of our work for the government.

The company was founded as an employee-owned company, and it has

> *We are in the business of investing money on behalf of insurance companies and pension funds. The contractual duration of our fund is 10 years, which means there is a specified time frame within which we have to provide our investors with a competitive return on their invested capital. And the fact that time is really working against us creates a tension between management and the board. The pressure to ensure that the goals are being met is just far greater than that which exists in most public companies.*
>
> —*James Birle*

remained that way since 1969. Some 10,000 of the 14,000 employees directly own stock in the company. By that, I mean they have either written a check or have had money withheld from their paychecks to purchase stock or exercise options. Virtually all full-time employees own stock through our retirement programs as well.

STEWART: What price do the employees pay for the stock? As a private company, SAIC doesn't have a stock price. So is the purchase price based on some kind of periodic appraisal?

ROPER: The shares are sold for a price based on a formula. There's a quarterly setting of value of the company that is determined by a formula that relates to earnings, book value, and market comparables.

I think an important component of our company has been from the beginning that most employees, and every member of the management team from middle management on up, make a significant financial commitment to own stock in the company. Our stock programs—which, again, consist of options, direct purchases, and voluntary contributions to retirement programs—encourage key managers and employees toward greater ownership as they rise through the organization. The higher paid you are, and the faster that you move through the orga-

nization, the more the system forces you to forgo current cash for future earnings from your ownership.

STEWART: Are you saying that as people move up through the company they're *obligated* to buy stock?

ROPER: Not obligated technically, but the system drives you to do that. For example, we have a bonus system that covers about 40% of all employees. Bonuses are typically paid out half in stock and half in cash. The stock is vested immediately, so it's taxable. So if you get 50 percent of your bonus in cash and 50 percent of it in stock, you don't have a lot of cash left over after you pay the tax liability.

But it's a great wealth accumulator. I wish I had brought a chart showing the rise of our stock value; it's the most beautiful parabolic curve you've ever seen. Our stock has probably grown about 20 percent a year compounded over 20 years.

STEWART: So the higher you go in the organization, the more stock you're *allowed* to buy?

ROPER: That's right. It's not an obligation, it's a privilege. But it would be very unusual to have any senior management members who didn't have a substantial ownership stake in our firm.

STEWART: But isn't this somewhat of a Ponzi scheme—something that works as long as it works?

ROPER: We joke a little bit about that around the shop. The system recycles a lot of money. When people leave the company and the company repurchases their stock, it recycles a lot of money. So, if there is a sharp downturn, then there will have been a transfer of value from the people still in the system to those who have left. But, as long as the company remains profitable and growing, it pays for people to forgo current cash for future earnings, and the system works. It's all driven on the fact that the company is profitable and growing.

STEWART: To what extent do you think the company's success is due to employee ownership—or is the combination of ownership structure and success just a coincidence?

ROPER: It's very easy to see that widespread employee ownership and significant senior management ownership of the company drive an awful lot of things that we do. It is clearly responsible for a good amount of the success of the company.

STEWART: Can you give us an example where people inside the company sit down and have an informal, "mini-shareholder" meeting to make an important decision? By the way, is that an accurate description of the process?

ROPER: That's essentially correct. The management philosophy is very decentralized; it is slightly to the right of anarchy. Many meetings are very contentious. People at all levels feel free to tell you what they think about how you are spending *their money!* Perhaps the most forceful objection to a proposed management

decision is the statement, "Well, as a major shareholder, I disagree with your proposal to spend my money this way."

So it's an interesting environment. There's an awful lot of challenge and an awful lot of accountability. It ranges from issues as trivial as how much you spend on your office furniture to major expenditures and acquisitions.

MICHAEL JENSEN: Bill, let me ask a question about your plan. Take a middle manager who's been in the company for, say, 10 years. What kind of money would he or she have invested in the stock, and what would the value of that stock be worth today?

ROPER: Well, let me change your question a little, and let's take the case of a hypothetical senior scientist in our company—because scientists, along with engineers and computer programmers, are really the guts of our company. We don't have a lot of management types.

Let's say a typical scientist has been with the company for 15 years, and is making a base salary of $80,000 along with a cash bonus of $10,000. Over the years, that person has likely put into the company in one form or another—exercising options, payroll deductions, or just direct cash purchases, as well as some retirement contributions—that person is probably out of pocket about $100,000. And the stock purchased by that cash is today probably worth half a million. That seems to me to be a representative case at our firm.

STEWART: Are there any openings at your company?

Well, Bill, your company seems to function as a largely self-regulating, self-governing company. In your case, the role of the board of directors has got to be much less important—because the internal control mechanism is literally woven into the share ownership of the key people throughout the company. Would you agree with that statement, especially in view of the other public companies you've been associated with?

The management philosophy [of SAIC] is very decentralized; it is slightly to the right of anarchy. Many meetings are very contentious. People at all levels feel free to tell you what they think about how you are spending their money! Perhaps the most forceful objection to a proposed management decision is the statement, "Well, as a major shareholder, I disagree with your proposal to spend my money this way."

—William Roper

ROPER: That's clearly the case. I think that's a very wise observation. In thinking about the subject of this panel, and especially Mike Jensen's comments yesterday, it became clear to me that our board does not really fit the model Jensen was holding out for public companies. We have a large board. It's composed of 23 members, six of whom are insiders. They meet quarterly for a few hours. I think it's virtually impossible on a quarterly basis to communicate a lot of detailed information about a very complex company. Now, there are other forums where the board members learn about the company. There's a lot of informal contact with them. But our board clearly does not exercise the kind of oversight that, say, the principals of LBOs or venture capital firms do. And yet we have a company that for 23 years running has been phenomenally successful.

So there seem to be two possible answers here: Either we were just lucky for 23 years in a row, or you guys are all full of hot air and we need to have more unwieldy boards packed with insiders. More seriously, I think we are successful largely because of the internal mechanisms and the management ownership structure that the company has maintained throughout its existence. This makes the board's job fairly easy.

STEWART: Bill, I was struck by the similarity of your company to one that I have some familiarity with, Arthur

Andersen. I would also describe that company as a self-governing, self-regulating organization. There are 2500 key partners who own the company. The company is extremely successful; it has been quite profitable even in the face of a shrinking market for public accounting services. It's also extremely entrepreneurial. For example, they built the immensely successful Andersen Consulting from nothing. And they're now a competitor of yours.

ROPER: Yes, and I wish they weren't.

STEWART: And that company too is controlled chaos. In the early 1980s, we made a presentation to a group of top partners in the company; and they were extremely enthusiastic about the possibility of adopting our corporate finance program throughout the organization. So I said to one of the top partners, "We have to find a way to get others in Arthur Andersen to hear this message; so why don't you just send out an edict throughout the organization?"

And the partner said to me, "Bennett, you don't understand the way it works around here. We have offices throughout the world, and they are each run by the partners in charge of those offices. There's nothing that comes from the top down. It's kind of a neural network in which proposals within the organization are transmitted from the outlying areas to the center. And when they reach the center, there are ad hoc

committees and structures put in place to evaluate them."

What's also interesting about Arthur Andersen—and most of the other accounting firms, too—is that without the pressure of external capital markets, the public accounting industry has gone through a major restructuring and rationalization over the past 10 years. It is no longer the Big 8, it's now the Big 6. And maybe it will be the big five at some point. So this partnership model can work in mature, no-growth industries as well as growth industries like Bill's.

So, Bill, perhaps we can view SAIC as pointing the way towards a new kind of organization—one that reduces the importance of the board in the monitoring process and replaces it with widespread ownership.

JENSEN: Well, Bennett, I'm not sure how far you can extend the application of this model. Both of these companies, Arthur Andersen and SAIC, seem to me classic examples of companies that can't be run any other way than by diffusing ownership throughout the company. In the case of the typical law firm or professional consulting organization, you can't have a complicated control mechanism in which decision initiatives are bucked up a hierarchy—because by the time they get there, the chance to exploit the opportunity has already passed. The specific knowledge that is required for many impor-

tant corporate decisions often lies deep in the organization in small teams. The decisions often have to be made there, and they have to be made quickly.

So, if you tried to take either of these companies and turn them into public companies, it just wouldn't work. You could try and substitute the complicated control mechanisms used by public companies, but they wouldn't work very well in that kind of situation. The substitute for those complicated mechanisms is, as Bennett suggested, to push the equity ownership or partnership shares down and throughout the organization. (Besides the two companies you've mentioned, Gore Associates is another good example of this employee ownership model; and it's an industrial company rather than a consulting operation.)

And let me explain why I asked Bill how much money the typical manager has at stake. If people have a significant investment in the firm, you can be much more comfortable turning them loose to make their own decisions because they are going to be motivated not only by their own financial interests, but by their colleagues' financial interests as well. And it's not just money. It's the fact that they've got the right orientation; they have got the interest of the organization at heart. This is really the only way you can run people-intensive as opposed to capital-intensive organizations.

STEWART: Bill, do you think the kind of employee ownership structure that you've put in place would work for, say, a diversified consumer products company?

ROPER: It's really hard to say. Our main asset is our people. While we do make some products, our principal business is technological consulting, systems development and integration, and other things like that. For this reason, our main asset is the brains and experience of our people. Our company is organized around, and driven by, the need to find and retain good people— getting them on board, motivating them, and rewarding them.

JENSEN: I don't know your company, but I would also predict that this kind of employee ownership works best when you have a technology that's not very capital intensive.

ROPER: That's correct. Over the years, we have had lots of debates about going into capital-intensive businesses. But there's only so much capital that you can aggregate among the body of people that work for you. And so it does work better for those businesses that don't require a lot of capital.

JENSEN: I'm not talking about just your ability to raise large amounts of capital. I'm thinking more about what happens to management incentives after you succeed in raising the capital. If you have a lot of capital assets lying around, partnerships and organizations like yours

with lots of owners run into big problems. Companies with highly decentralized ownership structures will likely start to have major internal conflicts when making decisions about what to do with large capital assets. When do you sell such assets, if ever, and distribute their value to partners? Even owning buildings causes partnerships big problems over issues like this. Having lots of owners with different time horizons makes the decision-making a lot harder.

For this reason, partnerships and 100% employee ownership are well suited for companies that don't invest in major capital assets, but that have a sort of constant flow of capital in and out of the business.

Shareholder Activism and Corporate Accountability

STEWART: Let me ask our representatives of public companies whether they are feeling more pressure to be accountable to their shareholders as a result of some of the increasing shareholder activism that is taking place? John, what about The Dial Corp?

TEETS: The only instance of shareholder pressure I can think of has come from Boone Pickens's group—I think they call themselves the United Shareholders Association. My sense is that Boone got burned pretty badly by the Unocal decision; and after he ran with his tail between his legs, he decided to start this shareholder voting project. So, because Boone has decided he doesn't like poison pills, we now have a vote every year on whether or not to rescind our poison pill. And that's okay. Members of Boone's group own a small amount of our stock, and they are entitled to propose measures like this and to vote on them. That's the way the system works.

But we have not had any pressure from any of the major funds that own our stock. We have excellent relationships with all of them, and we invite them every year to meet our management team. They are allowed to voice their concerns, and we attempt to respond to them as best we can.

STEWART: But my sense is that the role of most institutional investors is really to try to figure out how much the company is worth and not to make recommendations for change. We have this peculiar state of affairs in this country where institutional investors are looked upon as short-term investors on the one hand, and yet are expected to behave like owners. Or, at least, when they behave more like speculators than owners, people profess to be disappointed by their "short termism."

So my question is the following: How do we turn investors—people who are inclined to short the stock if the company does poorly—into owners interested in participating in the effort to maximize long-run value? It seems to me that our current system does not allow, much less encourage, institutional investors to become owners in that classical sense. For one thing, they don't have board representation.

So, John, would you encourage institutional investors to nominate and elect a minority of independent directors to your board? This way they might be more inclined to become long-term holders.

TEETS: Any shareholder has the right to nominate a director and vote for him or her. So it's not whether I agree or disagree, that's the way the system is set up.

Would I want to have an institutional investor on my board? Our board is picked by consensus, and I doubt very much that any of the ten outside board members would even consider having someone who is in the business of managing funds sit on our board and tell us how we are supposed to run the business to increase shareholder wealth. But, then again, I can't really speak for my board on this. We've never had the issue on the agenda and we've never discussed it.

STEWART: John, you took a proactive role in restructuring your company several years ago. Do you feel that boards are going to become much more active in the future in terms of initiating restructurings to increase shareholder value? For example, do you think they'll be more aggressive in recommending the increased use of leverage for underleveraged companies? I personally think that boards today are much less likely to view a triple-A rating as a unambiguous sign of corporate success. What are your views in terms of the initiatives that corporate boards will most likely be taking in the future?

TEETS: I can't speak for other boards. But our board often challenges our direction. We go into great detail on both the targeted and the realized return on assets of each of our subsidiaries. Our board members also participate in regular on-site visits in which they meet and question the managers that run those businesses.

In fact, I am skeptical about the idea that boards are becoming *more* challenging today. I think they have always been challenging. The average tenure of a CEO is about six years in the United States. CEOs are fired by their boards all the time. It's not like being a tenured professor in a university—a system that guarantees a job for life. (Let me also say

that I think the colleges and universities in the United States are among the most poorly run group of organizations in the country, particularly in how they nominate their board and how they function. It's almost impossible to function within their own system.)

I think some boards are becoming more proactive today. There are clearly companies that have not performed well, and where boards have failed to act. And we all know which

companies they are; they are in the newspaper every day. At the same time, of course, we never read about the vast majority of companies in which the boards do a good job.

STEWART: John, what is it that makes a board function well and what makes a board function poorly? What are the key ingredients for success in creating a board that will add value?

TEETS: Well, I think it's important for the CEO to make the best use of the board. He should regularly seek the counsel of the board and listen to their suggestions. Board members have exceptional talent and experience, and the CEO ought to make the best possible use of them. They really do bring different kinds of expertise to the table. They see things I don't see, and I think it's important to have advisers like that.

So I think it's up to the CEO to draw out the expertise of the board. At the same time, though, the board members are the bosses. They have the power to hire and fire top management. If the board does not exercise this power when the company is doing poorly, then there can be a problem. As our professor friend suggested yesterday, this is a very complex issue because each company and board operates differently. Let me also say I just don't think consultants and college professors—that is,

But there are a couple of things running through my mind that maybe you can help me understand. I'm sure there are many CEOs who behave exactly the way you say they do; they make a conscientious effort to use their boards properly and to do the right thing by their shareholders. But even in these cases, there's a potential problem. CEOs get older, they may tend to get set in their ways, but meanwhile the world moves on. We

problem we face in these organizations is how to put in place a control mechanism that creates a healthy tension between management and the board—one that ensures that when management does begin to go off-course, the correction happens sooner rather than later.

Let me tell you about a conversation I had when returning from a board meeting with a fellow member on an airplane. There had been some frank discussion during the meeting, some disagreements with the CEO. This board member is also a very senior executive on the board of his own company, and he was one of those who voiced sharp disagreement with the CEO during our meeting. And this board member explained to me that such frank discussion and disagreements would never happen on his own board. His own CEO would simply take the person aside who asked the hard questions, and then make it very clear that either he was going to get on the same track, or one of them was going to leave. And it was also clear which one of them was going to leave.

We've all seen boards operate this way, John. So what can be done about it?

> *With the threat of raiders largely gone, many companies now seem to be looking seriously for new models of corporate governance. In many cases, they are looking for ways of bringing about voluntarily some of the productive changes that were forced upon them during the '80s. One solution is to make the managers and the employees in the company into significant owners. By adopting this self-governing, self-regulating model of governance, we wouldn't have to rely on the capital markets or on the board to bring about change.*
>
> —Bennett Stewart

people who are not active in running businesses themselves—are likely to make good board members. They are not fighting in the war, and they thus have a tendency to be less proactive in many cases than people who are out there facing the competition every day.

JENSEN: John, can I push you a little on that?

TEETS: You're *asking* me?

JENSEN: It's only rhetorical.

STEWART: He's gonna get back at you, John.

JENSEN: By the way, John, I completely agree with your comments about the governance of universities and the way they function—and also about the value of the university tenure system. In fact, I should tell you that I have resigned my tenure at both of the institutions that have granted it to me by submitting unconditional letters of resignation.

all see the world through our own eyes, and it's a very natural and understandable human tendency for people to fail to see the need for radical change.

Now, the problem that troubles me arises when the CEO or the management team begins to get off track—and organizations do this all the time. If the burden is on the CEO and top management to seek out the flagellation from others that will force them to face up to the truth, then we have a serious problem with our system. That is just not going to happen—or not until the deterioration has gotten so bad that it's almost too late to save the organization. (This, incidentally, is my feeling about what has happened recently at General Motors—and maybe even IBM, too, although the organizational changes they just made give me hope for them.) The

TEETS: Let me remind you that, although the board can fire the CEO, the CEO cannot fire a board member—or not at least without the approval of the other board members.

JENSEN: But how will you make this organization work so that the CEO will get a message he doesn't want to hear? Because that's when it counts. It's not when the CEO understands that the world is changing and that the corporation has to change with it. It's the opposite situation; the one when the company is off on the wrong track, and the CEO wants to persist with the old strategy. That is precisely when the unpleasantness has to occur, and that is where our current system breaks down. Under the current governance system, the company has to confront a crisis before the board will intervene. GM had to lose several billion dollars in a single year before management was forced to recognize the need for radical change. And Digital Equipment had to lose about 80% of its market value before its CEO was finally removed by the board.

TEETS: I've sat on a number of boards. And although some disagreements are brought up at board meetings, I generally think it's better practice to take up major issues privately with the CEO first. Then, if they come out at the board meeting later, some of the defensiveness of the CEO will have been removed.

But let me say that I don't have the answer to the problem you're talking about. This issue of the board and the CEO is very complex. Obviously, some boards work and some don't. You can see well-publicized cases in the *Wall Street Journal* where boards are not working. On the other hand, you see many cases where they're working very well. I would also insist that there are a lot more CEOs who are canned than we know about because they generally resign. It looks better that way. **JENSEN:** But the research on total CEO turnover suggests that, even when companies perform poorly, the likelihood of a CEO being fired is less than one in ten. And these numbers attempt to include all those cases where the CEO seems to resign. In fact, a couple of years ago former SEC Commissioner Joseph Grundfest used to say that it was more likely for a Congressman to be indicted for cheating than for a CEO to be fired by a board. But, with the recent cases at GM and DEC, things seem to be changing somewhat.

Information and Accountability

BIRLE: Michael, my opinion is that the current governance system of public companies is based on two important premises—adequate information and accountability—neither of which is likely to hold for the boards of many public companies. If the board is not properly informed, they are really operating in the dark. If they don't understand there is a problem in the first place, then they are not going to be able to take the appropriate action with the CEO.

One of the advantages that Fred Simmons and I have, as controlling owners of private companies, is that we do the due diligence on the companies we buy. We understand the quality of management, the corporate strategy, the operational plan, the competitive environment, the balance sheet issues— we have a good working knowledge of all those factors that differentiate between success and failure. And then after we make our investment, performance factors are very closely monitored by the board as we go forward.

In public companies, by contrast, board members are brought in with little, if any, knowledge of the company. It's really a ceremonial invitation. And, as I said, if that board member does not really understand what is going on inside the company, his ability to add value is limited. So I think it's up to the CEO to make sure that he gives the board members opportunities to add value at both the committee and full board levels.

As John Roach suggested earlier, issues should be presented to the committees as possible steps under consideration, not as final decisions to be ratified. And as the board becomes more informed about what's going on at the committee level, the discussion at the general board meetings becomes much more constructive and proactive. Armed with greater knowledge, board members will not be as reluctant to ask penetrating questions. Asking such questions may in turn stimulate a lot of dialogue in the full board meeting. And, as a consequence, even more information comes to light, and the board can then begin to do its job of holding management to something like accountability. As a party to the decisions, the board members are also likely to feel a greater sense of responsibility to shareholders about the outcome of corporate decisions.

So, again, in my way of looking at it, it's just really a combination of information and accountability. I think you have to build that accountability within your board. It's not something that happens automatically.

STEWART: Besides information and accountability, couldn't financial incentives also serve as an important contributor to board effectiveness? Incentives are likely to make the board work harder to get the necessary information from management; and, once having the information, then to act on it.

Bob Kidder, the CEO of Duracell, said something very similar to your point, Jim. He said that just the process of going through the LBO gave him and his management team a great deal of new insight into their business; it completely changed how they ran the company after the LBO. There were also tighter financial controls put on management; but he also stressed the importance of financial incentives, the carrot as well as the stick, in motivating improvements in performance.

When I was later working with a very large, extremely diversified company, I suggested that they go through a kind of "practice" LBO in order to discover where the value was coming from in their own businesses, and how things might be improved. I even suggested that management put together a mock prospectus saying that a tender offer had been made for the company, and that each one of the units of the company would be challenged to come up with its own plan to maximize value under the new corporate structure.

Initially, top management was extremely enthusiastic about the whole idea. But then the general counsel of the company stepped in and killed the idea. This was several years ago, before the deal market fell apart; and uncovering break-up values was likely getting too close to reality.

There has, however, been one important benefit from the eclipse of the junk bond and takeover markets. With the threat of raiders largely gone, many companies now seem to be looking seriously for new models of corporate governance. In many cases, they are looking for ways of bringing about voluntarily some of the productive changes that were forced upon them during the '80s.

ROACH: Bennett, I'm not so sure the issue is governance. I think there are two structural problems that don't have ready-made solutions. I think the majority of companies are run by CEOs who are genuinely interested in their shareholders and clearly want the board to play the role of active counselors. They solicit board members who are very talented and directed individuals.

But what if you have a company where the CEO is neglecting shareholders and doesn't really want counsel from his board? He's perfectly happy flying around in his Gulfstream, and the directors are perfectly happy collecting their directors' fees, and not getting involved in conflicts. The issue then becomes: Who is going to intervene on behalf of the shareholders to correct such a situation?

The other problem I don't have a solution for has to do with the time horizon of shareholders. Many managements are skeptical about the ability or willingness of shareholders to give them credit for their long-term investment strategies. Now, if management were confident they had a set of classical owners interested in maximizing the long-term value of the firm, then they might be much more enthusiastic about entering into a more collaborative relationship with institutional investors. But what happens if most of your shareholders are speculators? Do you man-

age the company to maximimize the next quarter's EPS, or do look to strengthen the company's competitive position for the long haul? I don't see any obvious way out of this dilemma.

STEWART: Well, one solution, John, is to make the managers and the employees in the company into significant owners. By adopting such a self-governing, self-regulating model of governance, we wouldn't have to rely on the capital markets or on the board as forces for bringing about change.

For example, in the case of CSX, some 160 of the company's top managers came together as a group to purchase a large number of shares. The typical person invested $35,000 to buy stock leveraged 20 to 1. This meant that a typical CSX manager virtually overnight became the owner of $700,000 worth of stock. To avoid diluting the public stockholders, moreover, the exercise price was indexed to the company's borrowing rate. Since this plan was put in place in 1990, the stock's gone up 50 percent. The other perceptible consequence is that you have to look both ways before you cross the railroad tracks because they only run express trains now.

The Search for
More Permanent Owners

JENSEN: I would like to go back to John Roach's comment about the effect of speculators' stock holdings on management's investment decision-making. If John had raised this issue ten years ago, I would have said, "You don't understand financial economics. Short-term prices reflect long-term values." But I think that some financial economists are now coming to understand that the point you're making may be an important one.

Michael Porter, for example, is now arguing in his Council on Competitiveness project that there's a good chance that we have gotten the wrong corpo-

rate ownership and governance system in the United States. Another Harvard colleague of mine, Amar Bhide, has partly convinced me that we as a nation have put too much emphasis as a matter of public policy on having highly liquid securities market with lots of disclosure and constraints on insider trading. This emphasis on liquidity and disclosure requirements has combined with a whole set of laws enacted since the Great Depression to make it very costly for either individuals or institutions to both hold large amounts of stock in single companies and to become involved in the strategic direction of the firm.

Such legislation and public policy have led to a progressive widening of the rift between ownership and control over the past 50 years—a period, incidentally, in which CEOs' percentage ownership of their companies' stock fell by a factor of 10. This separation of ownership from control has in turn created enormous information and agency costs for investors, who have basically been shut out of the governance process. With imperfect information, and little ability to intervene and change the corporate direction if things go wrong, our institutional investors have been forced to keep management on a short tether, selling shares when earnings turn down.

And this of course creates a problem for management: How can management really make long-term value-maximizing decisions when all they've got is a bunch of transitory shareholders that the law prevents them from communicating effectively with?

By contrast, the Japanese and the Germans have legal and regulatory structure systems that encourage strong relationships and information-sharing among management, the company's major banks (which often hold large equity stakes in the companies they lend to), and other major shareholders. It's difficult for management to build trust and informal agreements with a constantly churning group of outside investors who really don't know (or care) very much about what's going on inside the company.

At the same time, there are institutions that have said to me, "Look, we know we're making long-term investments, but we have no way to talk to management or to enter into a contract, and we're certainly not getting an adequate return for placing long-term money." So this is a real problem. It lies at the heart of the problems that show up with large organizations like General Motors where our governance system seems to be failing us.

As I have also argued, the LBO association model that firms like KKR and Forstmann Little have borrowed from the venture capital industry—one in which a principal equity investor controls the board and represents the interests of the major debtholders as well—is at bottom an attempt to deal with these information and agency problems that now bedevil our public companies. As another example, institutional investors delegate to the Blackstone Group, to people like Jim Birle, the job of being their representative, their active investor. Warren Buffett does something quite similar through the vehicle of Berkshire Hathaway (of which he is the 45% owner). And so does Lazard Freres' Corporate Partners.

So, given the demonstrated effectiveness of these kinds of investors, it may be time for major changes in our legal system and in the structure of regulations of our capital markets. Let me also say, however, that the proposed changes to the current system being put forward by Porter and others are not ones that most CEOs are likely to welcome. They call for larger stakes and greater involvement by investors in return for less emphasis on diversification and liquidity.

LEE: Mike, I think our system may already be evolving somewhat in this direction, even under the current legal and regulatory structure. In the past few years, I have seen a pronounced change in the way institutional investors are exerting their influence over corporate management. Caesars World is a publicly held company. Management does not have a major stake collectively; it's only a 4% position in the company. We also have about 75% institutional ownership.

Five years ago, when financial engineering and leveraged restructuring was reaching its peak of activity, we found out that the time horizons of our institutional owners were very, very short. In one 10-day period, we discovered that our stock had moved almost entirely into the hands of the arbitrage community, whose time horizon was between 15 and 20 seconds. That was a real learning experience for us. As I mentioned earlier, we managed to exit from that predicament only by restructuring the company and making a healthy offer to let the arbitrageurs sell their shares. All this happened 21 days before the market crash. And, although our shareholders ended up very happy with the consequences, we took on considerable leverage in order to deliver that value to shareholders.

We now are back up to 75% institutional ownership, but we have noticed a profound change in their behavior. We now appear to have a solid base of fairly long-term institutional investors. They spend the time to come out and talk with us at length about the long-term strategy of the company. And a number of them seem to understand it fairly well and to have done a lot of homework. We were pleasantly surprised at the amount of time they spend studying us. They often have contrary ideas on what we should be doing in order to maximize value; so we have nice, lively discussions. These institutions, I should also point out, are not for

the most part the ones you read about in the newspapers, the ones who have the strong vocal positions on the top 25 corporations in the country.

So our institutional investors are proving to be a very constructive force. My only objection is that, despite their lip service to saying management should have larger shareholdings, several of them have refused to vote for authorization for issuing more stock. So it's not clear to me the how theory and practice of maximizing shareholder value are going to come together—at least on this issue. But I do really detect a much deeper involvement and sense of purpose among institutional shareholders than I did five and ten years ago. It's been a major change.

TEETS: We have had a very similar experience with our institutional investors. For example, representatives of the Delaware Fund, which own almost 10% of our stock, come out to visit us regularly. They've held the stock now for eight years. They've been long-term holders. Fidelity is another. In fact, I could list ten institutional shareholders who have held our stock for a long time, who regularly come out to confer with us, and whom we also visit on a regular basis.

We are very much open to having such investors. They can talk to whomever they want in the company, we open our books to them. They spend time with us, and we have an excellent relationship with all of our institutional shareholders. They have made a lot of money from investing in our stock, and we have made believers out of them. So, by demonstrating good performance and an openness to your institutional investors, I think it's possible—and indeed quite valuable—to build strong relationships between management and investors.

STEWART: Well, let me end our discussion on that positive note, and add my own wish that such a trend continues. Thank you all for participating.

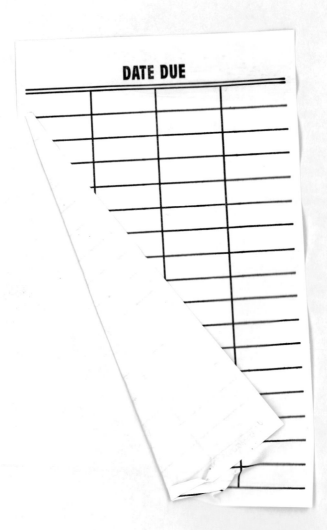